RITUA

Richard J. Evans was ╎   d
modern history at Jesus   ss
honours in 1969, and he went on to take a D.Phil. at St Antony's
College, Oxford, in 1972. After teaching in the history department at
the University of Stirling, he moved in 1976 to the University of East
Anglia, Norwich, where he was Professor of European History from
1983 to 1989. He is currently Professor of History and Vice-Master at
Birkbeck College, University of London. His books include *The
Feminists* (1977), *Rethinking German History* (1987) and *In Hitler's Shadow*
(1989). *Death in Hamburg: Society and Politics in the Cholera Years,
1830–1910* is also published by Penguin and won the Wolfson Literary
Award for History in 1988 and the William H. Welch Medal of the
American Association for the History of Medicine in 1989. Professor
Evans is also a Fellow of the British Academy and of the Royal
Historical Society.

Rituals of Retribution

CAPITAL PUNISHMENT IN GERMANY
1600–1987

Richard J. Evans

PENGUIN BOOKS

PENGUIN BOOKS

Published by the Penguin Group
Penguin Books Ltd, 27 Wrights Lane, London W8 5TZ, England
Penguin Books USA Inc., 375 Hudson Street, New York, New York 10014, USA
Penguin Books Australia Ltd, Ringwood, Victoria, Australia
Penguin Books Canada Ltd, 10 Alcorn Avenue, Toronto, Ontario, Canada M4V 3B2
Penguin Books (NZ) Ltd, 182–190 Wairau Road, Auckland 10, New Zealand

Penguin Books Ltd, Registered Offices: Harmondsworth, Middlesex, England

First published by Oxford University Press 1996
Published in Penguin Books 1997
1 3 5 7 9 10 8 6 4 2

Printed in England by Clays Ltd, St Ives plc

*This book is dedicated to the memory
of all those who have been unjustly executed
in Germany and elsewhere over the ages.*

PREFACE

This is a book about capital punishment. It is called *Rituals of Retribution* because capital punishment has been and continues to be distinguished from other forms of state-sponsored killing, whether on the battlefield, in concentration camps, or through 'death squads' and 'disappearances', by two factors. First, it always involves some form of legally prescribed ritual, however perfunctory; usually the ceremonial attached to its implementation has been quite elaborate, in order to lend an emphatic air of legitimacy to the proceedings. The ritual of execution, as we shall see in the course of this book, has almost always been public in one sense or another, even if only through the fact that it has been written down in published procedural codes or announced through the medium of the press. It follows, therefore, that on the whole this book is not concerned with assassinations ordered by the state, nor with summary executions in time of civil strife or military conflict. Its focus is on the role of the criminal law in civil society. Obviously, the boundaries have sometimes been hard to draw, and in the 1940s in particular, as we shall see, they began to disappear altogether. Nevertheless, they were at most times real enough, and this book does its best to respect them. The second common feature of capital punishment is its retributive character. People have advanced many arguments in favour of the death penalty, among which deterrence and the protection of the community have been prominent. Such reasons have often been contested or cast into doubt, however, even by proponents of capital punishment. Fundamentally, the most powerful and persistent motive for execution has always been retribution, the belief that death can be the only adequate expiation for certain crimes, the feeling that lesser punishments are insufficient, the conviction that those who commit the most serious offences must pay for them by suffering the ultimate penalty, death. Such a feeling has been present in popular culture throughout most of the period covered by this book. It was widely shared by the élites at various times. It informed the writings of lawyers, penal theorists, and philosophers. It continues to be used as a reason for demanding capital punishment today.[1]

The state has no greater power over its own citizens than that of killing them. This book tells the story of the use of that supreme power by the state in Germany from the seventeenth century to the present. It is organized in six

[1] e.g. in the Kantian approach of Tom Sorell, *Moral Theory and Capital Punishment* (Oxford, 1987), esp. 122, 147.

roughly equal parts, subdivided into a total of eighteen chapters. Part I sets the scene with a study of 'traditional' public capital punishments and the rituals and cultural readings associated with them in the early modern period. While taking due account of change over time, especially in its account of the reforms of the 'Enlightened' eighteenth century, it is primarily thematic in approach. Part II deals with the nineteenth century up to the unification of Germany in 1870, and tells the story of how these public punishments were reformed, then gradually brought to an end, attempting in the process an explanation of why this happened. As the death penalty entered a period of crisis, a series of great debates took place, above all in 1848 and 1870, on the principle of capital punishment. The book focuses on the changing ideas and theories which informed these debates, recounts the personal experiences and motives of the men who administered the death penalty, and attempts to account for the fact that more people were executed at some times and in some parts of Germany than at others. Part III takes all these themes on into the period of the German Empire, from 1871 to 1918, in a mixture of narrative and analysis. Part IV covers the Weimar Republic, and follows the varied fortunes of capital punishment and the campaign to abolish it through the politics and culture of the time. Hitler's 'Third Reich' instituted a vast extension of the principle and practice of capital punishment: Part V describes how this came about, and takes a close look at its implementation. Finally, Part VI examines the legacy of capital punishment in the Third Reich for the post-war history of West Germany, and the ways in which the murderous praxis of Nazism resembled, or differed from, that of a more recent dictatorship, the Communist regime in the East which collapsed with the fall of the Berlin Wall in 1989. At the end of the twentieth century, after the collapse of Communism and the end of the Cold War, the politics of the body have gained a new prominence, and one way of dividing the world's states into different groups is to distinguish between those which abuse the bodily integrity of the citizen and those which do not. It may help us to understand how and why such divisions emerge if we examine the experience of a single country over a lengthy period of time and look at the conditions there which favoured the state's violation of bodily boundaries at some times, and worked against it at others. The book's eighteen chapters are framed by a lengthy Introduction and Conclusion which attempt to place its subject in a wider theoretical framework and draw some lessons from it, both for present practice and for the way in which we can try to understand crime and punishment in the past.

Capital punishment is a very specific subject, but at the same time it touches on many different areas of human history and experience. The intention in the present book is to follow it like a red thread through the last four centuries of

German history. This way of approaching the past has become increasingly common in the late 1980s and 1990s. Historians have begun to move away from large structures and grand theories and have concentrated increasingly on small-scale investigations, often selecting the marginal, the irrational, or the seemingly trivial as their topic of research. Rather than seeking underlying patterns, they have focused on the surface textures of history: on language, on gesture, on brief dramatic events. In doing so, they have shown a strong fascination for the violent, the irrational, and the extraordinary: for massacres and conflicts, popular disturbances, apparitions, superstitions, and delusions.[2] It has seemed to many historians that the study of a small community, a single riot, a discrete event, a particular text, a historical family, a personal relationship, or an ordinary individual can often tell us more about the past than the wide-ranging teleologies of the 1960s and 1970s, from Marxism to modernization theory, ever managed to do. Conan Doyle's great detective Sherlock Holmes used to say that 'the observation of trifles' gave him the clues with which to solve the mysteries of detection.[3] The generalizing, social-science approach to the past so common in the 1970s and early 1980s, and in many ways still dominant in German historical writing today, has many virtues; but one of its very great drawbacks is the way in which it wipes out the cultural distance between the past and the present, losing the strangeness and individuality of the past in the process. The past, as the famous opening to L. P. Hartley's novel *The Go-Between* says, is a foreign country; they do things differently there. By visiting this foreign country, we can enlarge our conception of what it means to be human, and perhaps gain a better understanding of the limits and possibilities of the human condition. One of the aims of this book, therefore, is to restore a sense of strangeness to the past. We have to make an imaginative leap of understanding by which to comprehend mentalities which present-day Europeans may find at first encounter repulsive and bizarre. In undertaking this task, the historian can be assisted by the work of structural anthropologists, who have devoted a great deal of intellectual energy to comparable work on non-European societies. And there are major social theorists and philosophers, notably Michel Foucault, Norbert Elias, and Philippe Ariès, who have provided interpretative schema and conceptual tools which can also be of use, and which this book discusses at length in the Introduction and Conclusion. If grand social theory is now in disarray and disrepute, this does not mean that theory as such has to be discarded altogether. The spotlight turned by the historian on small areas of everyday life in the past needs to be augmented by

---

[2] For an outstanding example of this genre in the context of modern German history, see David Blackbourn, *Marpingen: Apparitions of the Virgin Mary in Bismarckian Germany* (Oxford, 1994).

[3] Carlo Ginzburg, *Clues, Myths and the Historical Method* (Baltimore, 1989). See also Edward Muir and Guido Ruggiero (eds.), *Microhistory and the Lost Peoples of Europe* (Baltimore, 1991).

the general illumination of the broader historical landscape if their contours are to be mapped out with any persuasiveness.

Yet the historian is also limited by the texts and documents which the past has bequeathed; if we trespass beyond these limits, the past itself becomes little more than a weapon in present-day political and intellectual debates. This book has not been written as a polemic against capital punishment, nor with the principal intention of demonstrating that the death penalty is barbarous, outmoded, cruel, or ineffective. Readers must make their own moral and political judgements on these issues. I do not wish to conceal the fact that I am opposed to the death penalty: in recent years, writers such as Hayden White have made it easier for us historians to express our own subjectivity, and to acknowledge the literary devices which we use to organize our imaginative appropriation of the past,[4] and I have made no attempt to hide my personal attitude towards the events and opinions with which this book deals. Readers are not so unsophisticated that they are unable to recognize the subjective elements and the literary artifice in historical writing, and to discount them if so desired. Historical writing is far more than merely subjective: good history comes from the tension between commitment and objectivity, between the desire to argue a case and the ability to recognize the constraints placed on the fulfilment of this desire by the intractabilities of the evidence. If we historians wish people to believe that what we are saying is true, we cannot simply gather material to support a thesis; we have to consider honestly the material which counts against it, to discard arguments that turn out to be untenable, and to do justice to every aspect of that area of the past with which we have chosen to deal. Beyond this immediate problem, too, a subject such as the death penalty has multiple historical resonances outside itself. This book tries among other things to show what capital punishment can tell us about German élite and popular mentalities in the past. It uses the subject to examine some larger themes in modern German history: above all, attitudes to, and experiences of, suffering, violence, cruelty, and death, the origins of the human destructiveness and exterminism of the Third Reich, and the perversion of justice in the Nazi dictatorship and in the Stalinist tyranny of the German Democratic Republic. These are not trivial subjects; but then, despite its specificity and its apparent tangentiality to what historians have customarily seen as the central concerns and developmental lines of modern German history, neither is capital punishment. On the contrary, it is of vital concern in our own day, when it is still practised in many countries across the world. In a number of them, above all in the United States of America, it has for some time been on the

---

[4] Hayden White, *The Content of the Form* (Baltimore, 1987).

increase. A study of the death penalty over a long period in the past can thus illuminate some of the questions about its legitimacy and its operation that concern us in the present.

As well as throwing light on many aspects of modern German history, it is hoped that this book will have a wider appeal, to readers whose main interest is not in Germany, but rather in the broader aspects of crime and punishment, both in the past and in our own time. I have tried to write it accordingly, to avoid technical terminology, specialized allusions, and uncommon abbreviations, to explain the historical context fully, and to provide English translations for German terms wherever possible, while remaining conscious that in English the most one can often do is to offer a functional equivalent. Capital punishment has always been regarded as a subject of exceptional social and political importance, and as a result the documentary record it has bequeathed to us is exceptionally rich. The archival material on which this book rests comes principally from state papers in the Justice Ministries of Prussia, Bavaria, and Baden from the eighteenth century onwards, the Weimar Republic, Nazi Germany, the occupying powers from 1945 to 1949, and the Federal and Democratic Republics after 1949. Other ministries and political institutions and other states also have relevant material, and this has been used where appropriate. Often, these central files contain details of individual cases which threw up important points of principle. Smaller local and regional archives have furnished additional information. Except in a few very important individual cases, mainly from the Weimar Republic, when they played an unprecedented role in the history of capital punishment on a general level, it has not been practicable to examine police, prosecution, or trial records. Nor, given the broad perspective from which this book has been researched and written, would it have added significantly to our knowledge of the subject. The interest of this book begins when trials end. While unpublished manuscript material forms the basis for the research presented here, it has at various points been enriched by printed sources, notably in the analysis of popular literature and in the narration of the public debates which took place on capital punishment. Many archival sources also contain large quantities of newspaper clippings; these have been cited by their archival reference, in case the original newspaper should prove difficult to locate.

There is a well-developed secondary literature on the history of penal policy, justice, and punishment for both the early modern period, where the recent researches of Richard van Dülmen and his associates, as well as of other historians, have added enormously to what was already a substantial basis of knowledge created by German folklorists and legal historians in the first half of the twentieth century, and for the 'Third Reich', where there has been a mass of important research published in the last few years, from Lothar Gruchmann's massive study of the judicial system to some extremely useful analyses and printed documentation of cases brought before the Special Courts in various parts of Germany. Yet capital punishment has also been oddly neglected as a specific subject in the Third Reich, while apart from a handful of detailed studies, it remains largely unexplored in the post-war period. For the nineteenth and early twentieth centuries, there is, despite the pioneering work of scholars like Dirk Blasius on the system of criminal justice in the larger sense, very little to go on when it comes to the topic of the death penalty, and it has been necessary to reconstruct its history from the primary sources. An excellent legal dissertation by Bernhard Düsing, published in 1952, has for over four decades been the standard work on the history of the death penalty in nineteenth- and twentieth-century Germany.[5] Düsing's accurate and well-researched book provides a thorough coverage of the great parliamentary debates on the topic from 1848 onwards, but it does not go far beyond them, except (usefully) to provide some detailed statistics of capital punishment's operation, and it does not really set them fully in their social and political context; based entirely on printed sources, it is all that we have on this topic in the way of secondary work. The need to present new material on a neglected subject goes some way to explaining this book's very considerable length, along with the fact that it covers four centuries of German history, and in so doing lets the people of the past speak for themselves as well as being interrogated and commented on by the historian.

After what has already been said, it should be more than apparent that this is not a legal history in the narrow sense, but a study that consciously tries to cut across conventional boundaries and reunite some of the sub-disciplines into which history has become fragmented in recent years. By juxtaposing and linking the well-established genres of social and intellectual history, anthropological and legal history, high political and low cultural history, national and local history, collective history and individual biography, this book hopes to show what each of these approaches has to gain by coming out of its isolation and mingling promiscuously with the others. It also deliberately crosses what is perhaps the most intractable of temporal boundaries, between the 'early modern' and 'modern' periods of history, or roughly speaking before and after 1800, in an attempt to chart far-reaching changes over a very long period of time. Specialists in particular periods or fields with which it deals will have to forgive the intrusion of a non-specialist into their chosen area; I hope that they will also be able to benefit from seeing it treated in a much broader context than is usual. This

---

[5] Bernhard Düsing, *Die Geschichte der Abschaffung der Todesstrafe in der Bundesrepublik Deutschland unter besonderer Berücksichtigung ihres parlamentarischen Zustandekommens* (Schwenningen/Neckar, 1952).

applies in more ways than one, for the book is theoretically as well as methodologically eclectic. We live in a period where some historians at least are experiencing doubts as to the possibility of attaining any certainty about what happened in the past; as a result, there has been a growing tendency to write not about what happened, but about what people thought happened. The turn of historians in recent years to linguistic and cultural analysis has not been uncontroversial; in some of the discussions of the cultural meanings of capital punishment, and in some of the analyses of the discourse of punishment, I hope to show what can be gained from taking this turn. But while this development has brought its benefits, it can also be problematical if carried too far. In the end, it is still not only possible but also necessary to distinguish between history and historiography, between primary and secondary sources, between discourse and extra-textual reality. In the end, there is no escaping the fact that real human beings in Germany were being killed by the state in considerable numbers over the four centuries covered by this book. It is important to remember that what we are dealing with here is real bodily violation, real suffering, real violence, real death. Rather than lose contact with this fundamental fact—with the basic realities which underlay all the fine talk about deterrence, all the political manœuvring, all the administrative punctiliousness, all the literary transfigurations, which characterized the discourse and culture of the death penalty in Germany—this book reminds the reader at various points of what it actually meant: living human beings, executioners, about whom the book has a good deal to say, were torturing, mutilating, and killing other living human beings, offenders, at the behest of the state.[6] It is the duty of such a book as this to say how this was done. 'Where the imagination sleeps,' as Albert Camus remarked in his 'Reflections on the Guillotine', 'words are emptied of their meaning.'[7]

This procedure is not without its risks. Not a few histories of capital punishment have been written with sensational or titillating intent. Many authors have traded in the pornography of suffering and death by producing books which appeal mainly to the reader with sadistic inclinations. This kind of exploitative approach was characteristic, for example, of the turn-of-the-century German author Rudolf Quanter. His two 'histories' of capital and corporal punishment, published in 1901, were adorned with specially drawn illustrations of half-naked men and women undergoing violent acts of humiliation and torture. On the cover of one of them, a screaming human head announced to the bookshop

---

[6] I have been influenced here by the similar approach adopted by V. A. C. Gatrell's superb study of capital punishment in late 18th- and early 19th-c. England, *The Hanging Tree: Executions and the English People 1770–1868* (Oxford, 1994). For another plea for the reinstatement of corporeality in history, see Lyndal Roper, *Oedipus and the Devil* (London, 1994).

[7] Albert Camus, 'Reflections on the Guillotine', in idem, *Resistance, Rebellion and Death* (London, 1961), 127–65, here 127–9.

browser what could be expected inside, while at the back, advertisements for other publications on sado-masochism, torture, and flagellation indicated the audience to which Quanter and his publishers were seeking to appeal.[8] Even where such literature is not deliberately exploitative, it is often hard for the author to avoid a hint of titillation, as he goes through the details of one gory punishment after another. Surrounding elaborate descriptions of acts of cruelty with severe expressions of moral disapproval can merely serve to heighten the sadistic impulse in the reader by accentuating the aura of the forbidden. A number of journalistic publications in this area do not entirely manage to escape this trap.[9] There is no way that an author can exercise complete control over how his work is read, or the purposes for which it is used. The length, and the academic apparatus, of the present work, should be enough to deter anyone hoping to read it for a cheap thrill. But there is no way of being sure. Readers should examine their own reactions and feelings as they go through this book. In reliving through words an act of public execution, we become in some sense witnesses to it. If we reflect on these processes, understanding the violence and cruelty of the past can be a way of comprehending, and perhaps therefore mastering, these impulses in ourselves. At the same time as making these points, however, it is important to resist the suggestion that there is no distinction at all to be made between reading about an execution and being present at it, or between real acts of killing and fictional representations of murder, as some American writers have recently attempted to argue.[10] To concentrate one's fire on words rather than deeds is to avoid the real issues at stake and to confine onself to the imaginative world of the reader and writer instead of grappling with the real world of people in history and society. In the same way, it is important to remember that those who were executed in Germany over the period covered by this book were not simply victims. For the most part, as we shall see, they had committed murders of one kind and another themselves. The real victims were the people they killed, the only people in this story whose voices cannot be recovered. It would be all too easy to arouse sympathy for the executed, and hence for the abolition of capital punishment, by ignoring this fact. Despite the primacy of victimhood in the formation of contemporary American culture and identity,[11] it is a temptation this book does its best to resist. Nowhere in this book

    [8] Rudolf Quanter, *Die Leibes- und Lebensstrafen bei allen Völkern und zu allen Zeiten* (Dresden, 1901); idem, *Die Schand- und Ehrenstrafen in der deutschen Rechtspflege* (Dresden, 1901).

    [9] e.g. Karl Bruno Leder, *Todesstrafe. Ursprung, Geschichte, Opfer* (Munich, 1986); Kurt Rossa, *Todesstrafen. Ihre Wirklichkeit in drei Jahrtausenden* (Bergisch Gladbach, 1979); E. A. Rauter, *Folter in Geschichte und Gegenwart von Nero bis Pinochet*, 2nd edn. (Frankfurt am Main, 1988); Ingo Wirth, *Exekution: Das Buch vom Hinrichten* (Berlin, 1993).

    [10] Wendy Lesser, *Pictures at an Execution: An Inquiry into the Subject of Murder* (Cambridge, Mass., 1994).

    [11] See the brilliant polemic by Robert Hughes, *Culture of Complaint: The Fraying of America* (New York, 1993).

is any individual subjected to the formal process of capital punishment referred to as a victim. In recovering such people's stories, we have constantly to temper the inevitable sense of identification through a realization that—with some exceptions—they were people who had already subjected others to a similar fate themselves. In this, as in other areas of history, human behaviour is too complex, too compromised, to admit of one-dimensional acts of empathy.

Obviously, anyone tackling a subject such as this has to question not only the purposes for which it might be read, but also his own motives for undertaking it. I first became interested in questions of crime and punishment as long ago as the early 1960s, when as a schoolboy I followed with excitement the final, successful campaign for the abolition of capital punishment in Britain led by the veteran Labour MP Sydney Silverman, and experienced a perhaps rather naïve degree of outrage and dismay at the opposition which his campaign aroused before its final success in December 1965. Later, I began to read the new critical criminologists whose work began to appear towards the end of the decade, and applauded as a student the liberal penal reforms of British Home Secretary Roy Jenkins in the Labour government of the time. The question of authority and obedience which all this raised seemed particularly acute in modern German history, and the field of crime and punishment seemed especially worth tilling if one wanted to obtain some fruitful insights into this problem. Reading the work of Philippe Ariès, Norbert Elias, and Michel Foucault in the 1970s focused my attention more sharply onto this area. Towards the end of the 1970s, I started working through the rich archives of the Prussian Ministry of Justice in Berlin, with a view to writing a book on the subject. Coming across a lengthy series of files on capital punishment alerted me to the possibilities of concentrating the research project on this particular area, and in 1984 I published a preliminary study based on this early research.[12] Other projects intervened, but I continued to collect material in a growing number of archives and libraries steadily through the 1980s and into the 1990s. During the research, other points of view and purposes, outlined earlier in this Preface, were added to the original one, and the whole undertaking inevitably grew more complex. I hope, however, that I have not lost sight of the initial impulse behind the project, and that, while this is no longer its primary focus, the book will still have something of interest to say about the history of authority and obedience in Germany along with all the other subjects on which it touches. Nor, I hope, has Prussia, originally the central focus of the research, moved too far away from the middle of the picture. Prussian specificities should not simply be equated with German peculiarities, as has happened too often in

[12] Richard J. Evans, 'Öffentlichkeit und Autorität. Zur Geschichte der Hinrichtungen in Deutschland vom Allgemeinen Landrecht bis zum Dritten Reich', in Heinz Reif (ed.), *Räuber, Volk und Obrigkeit. Studien zur Geschichte der Kriminalität in Deutschland seit dem 18. Jahrhundert* (Frankfurt am Main, 1984), 185–258.

the past; but they had an enormous influence on the course of German history all the same, and by studying them in the context of the practices adopted in other states, expecially Catholic Bavaria and liberal Baden, we can gain a better understanding of what they were, and how and to what extent their influence was exercised over the centuries.

The scholarly apparatus of a book such as this is inevitably rather unwieldy, but every effort has been made to keep it to a minimum. Footnotes are used for guiding the interested reader to the sources on which statements and quotations in the text are based, and providing the means necessary to verify them. They are not designed to provide bibliographical guides to the many subjects on which the book touches, nor are they (with very few exceptions) intended to provide space for the discussion of matters of secondary interest. References to archival sources give the folio number on the file, or the sheet number ('Blatt') if the numeration is on one side of the page only. Where files are unnumbered, this is obviously not possible, but most files in practice are in chronological order, so sources should not be difficult to locate if desired. The Bibliography lists only sources found useful in the preparation of this book and cited in the footnotes; many more were consulted, but discarded as useless or irrelevant and so not listed. The archival files are listed in full, so that the interested reader can check the nature and provenance of the sources cited in the footnotes. Archives in the former German Democratic Republic have been reorganized since reunification, and this has also involved some redistribution of files from West German archives as well. Files are cited in the archive where they were originally consulted, since the process of reorganization is by no means complete at the time of writing. Those who wish to consult the book for specific topics, periods, or individuals are advised to turn to the Index. German law requires the identity of private individuals to be concealed for seventy years after their death; in the few cases in which the name of such an individual is known only through unpublished sources, it has been replaced in the text and notes with an initial rather than with a pseudonym. Nazi terminology, always a problem, is quoted without the cumbersome inverted commas so often used as a distancing device by modern German historians; it should be clear from the context that this does not imply any endorsement of the concepts in question.

Over the years, the researches carried out for this book have received financial and logistic support from many organizations, institutions, and individuals, so many that it is impossible to list them all here. Most important has been the Alexander von Humboldt-Stiftung, which granted me a Research Fellowship at the Free University of Berlin in 1981 and allowed me to renew it on two occasions thereafter. I hope it finds that the results of its rather long-term investment have been worth waiting for. The University of East Anglia, where I taught from 1976 to 1989, granted me several periods of leave and awarded a number of research grants, and Birkbeck College, University of London, has provided a helpful and supportive environment for my research and writing since then. The British Council supported a month-long research trip to the then German Democratic Republic in 1987, while the British Academy and the German Academic Exchange Service have also funded research in Germany on more than one occasion during the preparation of this project. The International Association for the History of Crime and Criminal Justice has helped keep me abreast of current and ongoing work in the field through its circulars and conferences. The Research Seminar in Modern German Social History at the University of East Anglia formed a stimulating intellectual environment for the discussion of many of the broader ideas underlying this study.

The Free University of Berlin and the Institute for European History in Mainz provided me with a base in Germany at various times. Librarians at both these institutions, and at the University of East Anglia, Birkbeck College and Senate House at the University of London, the British Library, the German Historical Institute London, the former Deutsche Bücherei Leipzig, the Institute for Advanced Legal Studies in London, and the University of East Anglia, have been most helpful, as have the staff of the former Zentrales Staatsarchiv in Potsdam and its successor the Bundesarchiv Abteilungen Potsdam, the Bundesarchiv in Koblenz, the National Archives in Washington, the Public Record Office in London, the Geheimes Staatsarchiv Preussischer Kulturbesitz, the Berlin Document Center, and the Stiftung Archiv der Parteien und Massenorganisationen der DDR in Berlin, the Bayerisches Hauptstaatsarchiv and the Staatsarchiv Munich in Munich, the Niedersächsisches Hauptstaatsarchiv and the Stadtarchiv in Hanover, the Nordrhein-westfälisches Hauptstaatsarchiv in Schloss Kalkum, Düsseldorf, the Badisches Generallandesarchiv in Karlsruhe, the Mecklenburgisches Landeshauptarchiv in Schwerin, the Württembergisches Hauptstaatsarchiv in Stuttgart, the Staatsarchive in Bremen, Hamburg, Lübeck, and Weimar, the Stadtarchive in Brunswick, Erfurt, and Lepzig, the Deutsches Volkslied-Archiv in Freiburg, the Universitätsbibliothek Heidelberg, and the Institute for German, Austrian and Swiss Affairs in Nottingham. I am particularly grateful to the staff of the Bundesbeauftragte für die Unterlagen des Staatssicherheitsdienstes der ehemaligen Deutschen Demokratischen Republik, better known as the Gauck-Behörde, in Berlin, for searching out and making available important source material for me in 1994. Several of these archives and libraries, as well as the Historisches Archiv der Stadt Köln, the Archiv der Sozialen Demokratie der Friedrich Ebert-Stiftung, the Ullstein Bilderdienst, the Bilderdienst Süddeutscher Verlag, the Bildarchiv Gerstenberg, the Germanisches Nationalmuseum in Nuremberg, the Mittelalterliches Kriminalmuseum in

Rothenburg ob der Tauber, the Zentralbibliothek Zürich, the Kunstbibliothek Preussischer Kulturbesitz of the Staatlichen Museen zu Berlin, the Staats- und Universitätsbibliothek Göttingen, the Springer-Verlag, the Bibliothek der Hansestadt Lübeck, and the Library of the Royal Society of Medicine, London, have kindly supplied me with illustrations and granted me the permission to print them. Without the help of all these institutions, and the people who work in them, this book could never have been written.

Many people have listened patiently in lectures and seminars at universities in a number of countries to papers presented from work in progress on this book; they are far too numerous to be listed here, but I am extremely grateful to them all for their criticisms and suggestions, many of which have found their way into the text. I would also like to express my gratitude to the many individual friends and colleagues who have helped me in the preparation of this book. There is only space to name a few of them in person. Hartmut Kaelble was generous with his time and support during my Humboldt Fellowship at the Free University of Berlin. Michael Burleigh, Tom Cheesman, Florike Egmond, Robert Frost, Mary Fulbrook, Jeremy Noakes, Lyndal Roper, and Richard Wetzell were kind enough to read all or part of the manuscript and suggested many improvements. Joanna Bourke's detailed and incisive comments on the penultimate draft improved it immeasurably. Many friends and colleagues kindly supplied me with references which I might otherwise have overlooked; I am particularly grateful to Mario Braescu, Hendrik van den Bussche, Richard Gordon, Astrid Irmer, Alf Lüdtke, Rudolf Muhs, Heinz Reif, Ulinka Rublack, and once again Robert Frost, who introduced me to John Taylor, whose observations form the starting-point for the account of capital punishment around 1600 that opens Chapter 1.

Eric Johnson and his colleagues at the University of Cologne have been generous with their time in helping me obtain vital material at short notice. Moral and practical support was provided over the years by Lynn Abrams, Logie Barrow, and Barbara Dabrowski, Volker Berghahn, Liz Harvey, Elín Hjaltadóttir, Eric and Mary Johnson, Ulrike Jordan, Tony and Willy McElligott, Tony Nicholls, Martyn Phillips, and Ilona Wolter. Helga Stachow inspired me with her enthusiasm and support for the project for nearly a decade and kept me supplied with a constant stream of useful references and suggestions. My colleagues and students at Birkbeck have sustained me over the last phase of the long haul through the interest they have taken in the progress of research and writing. At Oxford University Press, Tony Morris was full of encouragement, and waited patiently for a typescript that eventually arrived on his desk nearly a decade after the promised date; Mick Belson and Anna Illingworth oversaw the process of turning it into a book; Veronica Ions was an exemplary copy-editor; and Andrew Garner put the book through production. I am grateful to them all.

Christine Corton revived my flagging energies, kept me going over the final stretch, pushed me over the finishing line, turned a professional eye on the proofs and saved me from many errors. Without her love and support over the past three years, I would never have been able to complete the task of writing up my research into a book. Our cats Mick and Peg helped me at the word-processor; and the arrival in the world of our son Matthew in June 1995 provided a welcome distraction from the tedium of copy-editing, proof-reading and indexing.

After much thought, I decided that it was inappropriate to attach a personal dedication to this book. In view of its subject, it seemed right to dedicate it to the memory of all those who have been unjustly executed in Germany and elsewhere over the ages.

R.J.E.

London
October 1995

CONTENTS

LIST OF ILLUSTRATIONS

LIST OF TABLES

ABBREVIATIONS

AA	Auswärtiges Amt
ADN	Allgemeiner Deutscher Nachrichtendienst
BA	Bundesarchiv
BAOR	British Army on the Rhine
Bl.	Blatt/Blätter
BStU	Der Bundesbeauftragte für die Unterlagen des Staatssicherheitsdienstes der ehemaligen Deutschen Demokratischen Republik
DEFA	Deutsche Film-Aktiengesellschaft
DDR	Deutsche Demokratische Republik
DP	Displaced Person
DVA	Deutsches Volkslied-Archiv
FO	Foreign Office
GLA	Generallandesarchiv
GDR	German Democratic Republic
GStA	Geheimes Staatsarchiv
HStA	Hauptstaatsarchiv
INGASA	Institute for German, Swiss and Austrian Affairs
LHA	Landeshauptarchiv
MInn	Ministerium der Innern
MJu	Ministerium der Justiz
NA	National Archives
NATO	North Atlantic Treaty Organization
NL	Nachlass
OMGUS	Office of the Military Government of Germany, US Zone.
PJM	Preussisches Justizministerium
PRO	Public Record Office
RIAS	Radio in the American Sector (of Berlin)
RKA	Reichskanzleramt
RJA	Reichsjustizamt
RJM	Reichsjustizministerium
SAPM	Stiftung Archiv der Parteien und Massenorganisationen der DDR im Bundesarchiv
SED	Sozialistische Einheitspartei Deutschlands (Socialist Unity Party of Germany)

SS	Schutzstaffel
StA	Staatsarchiv
Sta	Stadtarchiv
Stasi	Staatssicherheitsdienst
ZA	Zentralarchiv
ZAIG	Zentrale Auswertungs- und Informationsgruppe

Introduction

a. Explaining the Transformation of Punishment

The starting-point for this book is the obvious change that has come about in the way society has dealt with deviance over the last four centuries. In medieval and early modern Europe, crime and transgression were punished by measures which appeared to later ages to be cruel, barbarous, and sadistic: physical mutilation, whipping, and branding, and everywhere executions on a scale, and by means, from hanging, drawing, and quartering to breaking on the wheel, that we now regard with incredulity and revulsion. Criminal investigation was accompanied by the bodily torture of the accused; capital and corporal punishments were carried out in public, before crowds that sometimes took an active part in the proceedings themselves. Such practices were an everyday part of European life for many hundreds of years, and were still commonplace in the eighteenth century. Yet a mere hundred years later most of them had vanished, and had been replaced by the almost universal use of monetary fines and imprisonment. Custodial sentences had consigned the branding-iron, the pillory, and the scaffold to a past seemingly gone for ever. For the few crimes remaining that were deemed heinous enough to warrant the death penalty, society now reserved a quick execution, administered by the axe, the rope, or the guillotine, within the relative privacy of prison walls. Trials were no longer dependent on confessions obtained through the thumbscrew and the rack: they were now held in open court, with the verdict resting on the evidence presented. A major change in human social organization and sensibility had taken place in Western Europe. And it had taken place in a remarkably short space of time.

The task of explaining this transformation has long provided a challenge to philosophers, sociologists, and historians. In the nineteenth century writers such as Henry Charles Lea regarded the penal practices of medieval and early modern Europe simply as evidence of the irrationality and superstition of the past. They saw their disappearance in their own time as evidence of the progress which they had made towards a juster and more humane society.[1] In this, they were echoing

---

[1] Henry Charles Lea, *Superstition and Force* (Philadelphia, 1866).

the views of the critics of early modern penal policy whose voices had been so influential in the Enlightenment. Such views are still present in the writings of at least some legal historians on the subject of medieval and early modern punishment.[2] The German legal historian Wolfgang Schild, for instance, who published two major general surveys of the subject in the course of the 1980s, regarded the nature of punishment in the medieval and early modern periods as an indication of the naïve, 'childish' nature of the people at that time. The physical cruelty which such punishments involved demonstrated in his view the orgiastic directness and spontaneity of the life-experience in pre-industrial society.[3] Other writers, too, have portrayed the history of penal policy since the early modern period as part of the history of progress. In this version of the story, courageous thinkers and reformers from the Enlightenment onwards persuaded the legislators of Europe to guarantee the fair treatment of offenders, banish the baying mob from the scene of punishment, replace the arbitrary cruelty of retribution with the rational humanitarianism of rehabilitation, and rid the administration of justice of the barbarous practice of physical mutilation. The result was a major step forward in the direction of a modern society.[4]

But the unhistorical, complacent, and self-congratulatory aspects of this view have long been obvious. In the twentieth century, the rulers of one country after another, beginning with revolutionary Russia and Nazi Germany and going on to numerous regimes in all parts of the world, from Cambodia and Iraq to Chile and Serbia, have perpetrated physical violence and destruction on their own people and often on others too, on a scale, and with refinements of cruelty, far exceeding anything one can encounter in the law codes of early modern Europe.[5] It is scarcely adequate to portray this as a temporary relapse into medieval barbarism, inspired by secularized religions such as fascism or communism; the

[2] For critiques of legal history in this context, see Martin Dinges, 'Frühneuzeitliche Justiz', in Heinz Mohnhaupt and Dieter Simon (eds.), *Vorträge zur Justizforschung*, i. *Geschichte und Theorie* (Frankfurt am Main, 1992), 269–92; and Gerd Schwerhoff, *Köln im Kreuzverhör. Kriminalität, Herrschaft und Gesellschaft in einer frühneuzeitlichen Stadt* (Bonn, 1991), 17–48.

[3] Wolfgang Schild, *Alte Gerichtsbarkeit. Vom Gottesurteil bis zum Beginn der modernen Rechtsprechung* (Munich, 1980), 94–100. These views echo those of the great Dutch historian Johan Huizinga, in *The Waning of the Middle Ages: A Study of the Forms of Life, Thought, and Art in France and the Netherlands in the Fourteenth and Fifteenth Centuries* (London, 1924), ch. 1.

[4] S. McCloy, *The Humanitarian Movement in Eighteenth-Century France* (Lexington, Ky., 1957); M. Maestro, *Voltaire and Beccaria as Reformers of Criminal Law* (New York, 1942); Gordon Wright, *Between the Guillotine and Liberty: Two Centuries of the Crime Problem in France* (New York, 1982); David Cooper, *The Lesson of the Scaffold: The Public Execution Controversy in Victorian England* (London, 1974); Sidney and Beatrice Webb, *English Prisons under Local Government* (London, 1922); J. R. S. Whiting, *Prison Reform in Gloucestershire 1775–1820* (London, 1975); Eric Stockdale, *A Study of Bedford Prison 1660–1877* (London, 1977); Leon Radzinowicz, *A History of English Criminal Law and its Administration* (4 vols.; London, 1948–68); Negley D. Teeters, *The Cradle of the Penitentiary: The Walnut Street Jail at Philadephia* (Philadelphia, 1935); W. David Lewis, *From Newgate to Dannemora: The Rise of the Penitentiary in New York, 1796–1848* (Ithaca, NY, 1965).

[5] Edward Peters, *Torture* (Oxford, 1985), 1–10, 103–40.

practice of official violence against the person embraces states untouched by totalizing ideologies of this kind. Far from exhibiting a thoughtful, adult mentality that contrasts favourably with the unreflective spontaneity of our forebears, the penal policy of advanced industrial societies in the late twentieth century is mainly characterized by helplessness and confusion: in the United States of America, any pretence of one has largely been abandoned, and capital punishment is being implemented on an ever increasing, ever more arbitrary scale.[6] Where ideology has been used to justify state violence in the twentieth century, it has often had little in common with religion, especially if religion is defined, as it should be, in terms of a belief in the afterlife and the supernatural.[7] On the other hand, the significance imparted by religion in this sense to punishment in the early modern period was entirely different from the meanings given to punishment and state violence by German and other European regimes after 1900. Comparisons, therefore, are difficult to make, and often spurious or polemical when they are encountered.

Punishment in sixteenth- or seventeenth-century Europe was far from emotionally spontaneous, orgiastic, or direct; on the contrary, as we shall see, it was highly ritualized and formalized—a feature that has long been apparent to the scholars who have worked in the area. This fact in turn has inspired a tradition of writing and research which has dominated the study of German penal history until very recently: a tradition far removed from the Christian humanism of historians such as Henry Charles Lea. For rather than condemning past penal practices as barbarous, many German writers on the subject have sought to rescue them from the condescension of nineteenth- and early twentieth-century liberals and present them in a sense as examples for the present. This is in part because the field has been dominated not by historians but by folklorists and anthropologists, working in the German discipline known as *Volkskunde*, which developed during the nineteenth century as a way of recovering and understanding popular culture and popular mores in the German past. The links between *Volkskunde* and German nationalism were close, and by the first few decades of the twentieth century, when the discipline was at the height of its power, its studies of peasant customs and artefacts were taking on a distinctly racist tinge.[8] Thus while scholars working within this discipline undoubtedly

[6] See the regular reports of Amnesty International on *The Death Penalty* for details.

[7] For a discussion of this point in the German context, see Richard J. Evans, *Rethinking German History: Nineteenth-century Germany and the Origins of the Third Reich* (London, 1987), ch. 4, pp. 125–55.

[8] For recent discussions of this discipline and the attempts it has made to free itself from these origins, see Wolfgang Jacobeit, *Bäuerliche Arbeit und Wirtschaft. Ein Beitrag zur Wissenschaftsgeschichte der deutschen Volkskunde* (Berlin, 1965); and 'Vom Aufbruch der Volkskunde: Ein Gespräch', in Utz Jeggle *et al.* (eds.), *Volkskultur in der Moderne: Probleme und Perspektiven empirischer Kulturforschung* (Reinbek, 1986), 9–20.

extended our knowledge of penal practice, punishment, and execution in the past, they did so increasingly in order to bolster a view of the German racial soul that linked it directly to the beliefs and customs of the pagan Germanic tribes of the Dark Ages. This line of thinking reached its culmination in Himmler's SS, which attempted in the later stages of the Third Reich to institute sun-worship and other allegedly Germanic cults in the place of what it considered to be the alien, Jewish religion of Christianity.[9]

No writer has ever tackled the penal policy of the past without being aware of its implications for the penal policy of the present; and much of the German literature on the history of punishment has had a direct or indirect function in consciously or unconsciously justifying the human destructiveness that was to reach its culmination in the exterminatory policies of the Third Reich. Thus one of the most influential scholars in the field of legal folklore and the history of punishment, Karl von Amira, claimed in 1915 that capital punishment was principally a means by which the ancient Germanic tribes had maintained their racial purity. Racially impure individuals, he said, were sacrificed in order to serve the interests of the majority. They were, in effect, being killed for the good of the tribe. This function was clothed in the ritual garb of pagan sacrifice. Such ritual practices had become embedded in Germanic law and could still be seen in the early modern period despite the encroachment of Roman law. Thus Amira thought that burning alive, a punishment still in use in the eighteenth century, signified a sacrifice to the god of fire, that dragging to the scaffold wrapped in a wet oxhide, an extra sanction employed against malefactors whose crimes were deemed to be particularly heinous, reflected the sacred status of the cow in 'Indo-Germanic' religion, and that the sentence of burial alive, laid down for some offences in early modern law codes, was a form of sacrifice to the *genius loci*.[10] Another leading figure in this field, the criminologist Hans von Hentig, had similar views. In the Weimar Republic he published an influential survey of the history of punishment, which he rewrote after the Second World War in a greatly enlarged, two-volume edition.[11] A pupil of Amira, he argued that the execution of criminals was a form of Germanic ritual sacrifice. He claimed, for example, that breaking with the wheel was a sacrifice to the sun-god, because the wheel

---

[9] See Jeremy Noakes and Geoffrey Pridham (eds.), *Nazism: A History in Documents and Eyewitness Accounts 1919–1945* (New York, 1989), 490–8.

[10] Karl von Amira, *Die germanischen Todesstrafen. Untersuchungen zur Rechts- und Religionsgeschichte* (Abhandlungen der Bayerischen Akademie der Wissenschaften, Philosophisch-philologisch und historische Klasse, xxxvi. Bd., 3. Abtlg., vorgelegt in der Sitzung am 6. November 1915; Munich, 1922), 67, 213–15, 226–30. Amira was a member of the far-right 'Fatherland Party' in 1917–1918.

[11] Hans von Hentig, *Die Strafe. Ursprung, Zweck, Psychologie* (Berlin, 1932; 2nd edn., 2 vols., Berlin, 1954–5).

constituted a symbolic representation of the sun.[12] Hentig had many pupils who shared this approach, such as Helmut Schuhmann, whose carefully researched account of the German executioner in the medieval and early modern period, published in 1964, remains the standard work, and repeats many of the interpretations advanced by his master.[13] And Hentig's influence can still be seen in studies published during the 1980s, such as Wolfgang Schild's already-mentioned history of punishment and the law in medieval and early modern Germany, which—for example—interpreted the stakes on which the heads of decapitated criminals were displayed as Germanic totem-poles, allegedly perpetuating an ancient form of ancestor-worship.[14]

Like Amira before him, Hentig was principally concerned to relate the nature of the punishments he surveyed to what he saw as eternal and unchanging folk-beliefs which could be found as far back as the barbarian migrations of the Dark Ages. Indeed the whole notion of capital punishment as practised in Germany was interpreted by these writers in terms of the ritual propitiation of pre-Christian gods. The implication of the widespread use of these punishments in medieval and early modern Germany was thus that the Germanic soul had continued to adhere to its deepest pagan instincts despite the influence of centuries of Christian evangelization.[15] Scholars writing during the Third Reich took a favourable view of all this. Bernhard Rehfeldt, in a study of capital punishment among the ancient Germanic tribes published in 1942, suggested that it was 'an instinctive defence action on the part of the racial organism'. Although sceptical of Amira's emphasis on ritual sacrifice, he underlined the conclusion of the older scholar that the principal aim of capital punishment in the Germanic tribes had been 'the eradication of the degenerate and thus the maintenance of the purity of the race'.[16] Thus the negative eugenics of the Third

[12] Ibid. (2nd edn.), i. 293–6. A more prosaic explanation is that it was a relic of a simple medieval punishment in which the condemned was fastened over ruts in a roadway and his body run over by a heavy cart. See Pieter Spierenburg, *The Spectacle of Suffering. Executions and the Evolution of Repression: From a Preindustrial Metropolis to the European Experience* (Cambridge, 1984), 71.

[13] Helmut Schuhmann, *Der Scharfrichter. Seine Gestalt—Seine Funktion* (Kempten/Allgäu, 1964).

[14] Schild, *Alte Gerichtsbarkeit*, 24. For Schild's reliance on Hentig, see e.g. p. 178. Schild's book has a magnificently reproduced collection of illustrations, many of them taken from Amira's personal archive in Munich, but the text relies heavily on work produced in the Third Reich and is full of inaccuracies and imprecisions in matters of detail (e.g. in its account of torture, pp. 161–2, or breaking with the wheel, pp. 202–4).

[15] This line of interpretation is shared by most of the inter-war work in the field, including Else Angstmann, *Der Henker in der Volksmeinung. Seine Namen und sein Vorkommen in der mündlichen Volksüberlieferung* (Bonn, 1928). For the continuing influence of this school, see e.g. Franz Irsigler and Arnold Lassotta, *Bettler und Gaukler, Dirnen und Henker. Aussenseiter in einer mittelalterlichen Stadt. Köln 1300–1600* (Frankfurt am Main, 1989), 228–82.

[16] Bernhard Rehfeldt, *Todesstrafen und Bekehrungsgeschichte. Zur Rechts- und Religionsgeschichte der germanischen Hinrichtungsbräuche* (Berlin, 1942), 165–6.

Reich, its policies of murdering the inmates of mental hospitals, Jews, and other 'racially undesirable' people, could be portrayed by such writers as a natural expression of the Germanic racial character, as revealed in the medieval practice of capital punishment.[17]

Not all of these writers drew the same conclusions from their work. Hans von Hentig, for example, was actually an opponent of the death penalty, both in the early 1930s and subsequently. He devoted much of his career to arguing that punishment should be based on rational, scientific criteria, rather than traditional, historical ones, and he did not agree that the death penalty had any scientific basis or rational utility. Nevertheless, Hentig was a self-confessed 'sociobiologist', whose career was devoted to demonstrating that the roots of criminality were biological. Perhaps, therefore, his notion of criminological rationality was not far removed in the end from that of the National Socialists. His opposition to capital punishment, for example, was based not least on the view that deterrence was ineffective in the face of genetically determined behaviour. Hentig was a bitter opponent of the Treaty of Versailles, and sought to mobilize the working class in a revolutionary movement known as 'National Bolshevism' to regain Germany's lost territories by force. Although he was no socialist, he collaborated with the Communists because they too repudiated the Treaty of Versailles, and in 1925 he raised troops with them for an abortive joint march on Munich. Accused of treason, he was forced to spend the years 1925–1927 in the Soviet Union. One of his early publications put forward the argument that revolutionary behaviour was biologically determined and that revolutions were caused by a confusion of gender roles rooted in the degeneration of the sexes into 'men-women' and 'women-men'.[18] It is in the light of such beliefs that Hentig's lifelong interest in the history of punishment has to be interpreted. Although more recent legal historians may be intellectually far removed from the ideological context surrounding writers such as Hentig and Amira, many of them still depend heavily on their work for the interpretation of the non-legal evidence that comes before them: as late as 1976, for example, Wolfgang Oppelt could attempt to explain popular hostility to executioners by suggesting, following Rehfeldt, that the desire to execute retribution against malefactors was permanently present in the German race and that people resented the right of revenge being appropriated by a particular individual. He even tried to interpret the characteristic late eighteenth-century security measure of surrounding the scaf-

---

[17] Michael Burleigh and Wolfgang Wippermann, *The Racial State: Germany 1933–1945* (Cambridge, 1991), 136–98.

[18] Hans von Hentig, *Ueber den Zusammenhang von kosmischen, biologischen und sozialen Krisen* (Tübingen, 1920), 64–73. See also idem, *The Criminal and his Victim: Studies in the Sociobiology of Crime* (New Haven, 1948) and Otto-Ernst Schüddekopf, *Linke Leute von Rechts* (Stuttgart, 1960).

fold with a line of troops as a survival of an old Germanic custom of inscribing a circle around a cult-object.[19]

Such approaches to medieval and early modern punishments led authors like these to advance interpretations that had very little basis in the historical evidence. As Rehfeldt already pointed out in 1942, in a book which, when it dealt with matters of detail, was more persuasive than its overall ideological thrust would initially lead one to expect, Amira was unable to produce any actual examples of the ritual sacrifice of criminals to particular gods among the Germanic tribes, and virtually all of his readings of the symbolic meanings of executions were purely inferential.[20] Even more problematical is the fact that Amira and, to an even greater extent, Hentig, because they believed in racial or biological determinants of crime and therefore considered that society's responses were racially or biologically determined, drew their evidence indiscriminately from a wide range of sources, mixing up time and place without any attention to historical context.[21] Of course, historians of punishment must necessarily rely to a great extent on official material which provides little direct evidence about its meaning for the broad mass of the population, so it is often impossible to avoid using inferential procedures altogether. But it is important to apply them with careful reference to the precise historical context, and with due attention to the evidence, and this is precisely what the folkloric school of legal historians, in their eagerness to prove racial and cultural continuities with the pre-Christian Germanic past, failed to do. Moreover, they also skipped silently over the centuries when such punishments were not used;[22] but if these were so deeply rooted in the German racial soul and folk traditions, why did they vanish? To this question, such writers provided no satisfactory answer. Finally, because of the failure of this school to take account of historical change, the problem of actually explaining the major shifts in the nature of punishment which took place in the eighteenth and nineteenth centuries remained unaddressed. Valuable though its research has been in empirical terms, therefore, the time has long since come for other approaches to be adopted.

b. Radical Interpretations

For obvious reasons, the German school of penal history has had little influence elsewhere. In Britain, France, and the USA, the teleological paradigm remained

[19] Wolfgang Oppelt, *Über die Unehrlichkeit des Scharfrichters* (Lengfeld, 1976), 56, 135–6.
[20] Rehfeldt, *Todesstrafen*, 110–12.
[21] See Richard van Dülmen, *Theater des Schreckens. Gerichtspraxis und Strafrituale in der Frühen Neuzeit* (Munich, 1985), 195, for some of these points; also Friedrich Sturm, *Symbolische Todesstrafen* (Hamburg, 1962) (largely following Rehfeldt).
[22] Spierenburg, *Spectacle*, 20–3.

dominant, and the history of punishment was still mainly seen as an aspect of the history of a progress from barbarism to enlightenment. The attempt by the German Marxist scholars Otto Kirchheimer and Georg Rusche, writing in American exile in 1939, to explain the changing nature of penal sanctions by relating them to the rising social value of labour was largely ignored, and with good reason, for its economic reductionism was crude and implausible. Why, for example, were labourers transported overseas, sentenced to solitary confinement, or given useless work to do on the treadmill, if the basic reason for governments ceasing to mutilate and execute them in large numbers was, as Kirchheimer and Rusche argued, to use them for productive labour in the emerging capitalist social order? Rusche and Kirchheimer's work did not make much of a dent in the liberal-progressive paradigm of penal history, for all its learning and ingenuity, and despite its origins in the work of the influential 'Frankfurt School' of Marxist philosophers and sociologists, of which, in truth, it has in the end to be regarded as one of the less distinguished products.[23]

The liberal view of the history of punishment thus remained largely intact outside Germany. But in the 1960s the emergence of a new school of 'critical criminology' or 'radical deviancy studies' in Britain, Europe, and the USA began to change this situation. Because the history of imprisonment had so far been studied in Britain mainly as a branch of the history of the welfare state, it began to come under critical scrutiny there as the institutions of the welfare state itself, from medicine and psychiatry to juvenile care and the benefit system, began to encounter criticism for their disciplining, regimenting aspects. The libertarianism of the 1960s, expressed politically in campaigns—some of them successful—for the rights of prisoners, the mentally ill, homosexuals, welfare claimants, and other groups, thus found its way into the historiography of crime and punishment.[24] In Germany, the new emphasis on the repressive aspects of nineteenth-century prison reform also inspired path-breaking historical work in this area, notably by Thomas Berger and Dirk Blasius;[25] in the United States it

[23] Otto Kirchheimer and Georg Rusche, *Punishment and Social Structure* (New York, 1939).

[24] Among many surveys of this subject, see especially Michael Ignatieff, 'Recent Social Histories of Punishment', in Michael Tonry and Norval Morris (eds.), *Crime and Justice: An Annual Review of Research* (Chicago, 1981), 153–91; also Dirk Blasius, 'Kriminalität als Gegenstand historischer Forschung', *Kriminalsoziologische Bibliographie*, 25 (1979), 1–15; idem, 'Gesellschaftsgeschichte und Kriminalität', *Beiträge zur Historischen Sozialkunde*, 1 (1981), 13–19; idem, 'Kriminalität und Geschichtswissenschaft. Perspektiven der neueren Forschung', *Historische Zeitschrift*, 233 (1981), 615–27; idem, 'Kriminologie und Geschichtswissenschaft, Bilanz und Perspektiven interdisziplinärer Forschung', *Geschichte und Gesellschaft*, 14 (1988), 136–49.

[25] Thomas Berger, *Die konstante Repression. Zur Geschichte des Strafvollzugs in Preussen nach 1850* (Frankfurt am Main, 1974); Dirk Blasius, *Bürgerliche Gesellschaft und Kriminalität. Zur Sozialgeschichte Preussens im Vormärz* (Göttingen, 1976); idem, 'Recht und Gerechtigkeit im Umbruch von Verfassungs- und Gesellschaftsordnung. Zur Situation der Strafrechtspflege in Preussen im 19. Jahrhundert', *Der Staat*, 21 (1982), 365–90. See the important critiques of Blasius's approach by John Breuilly, in *Social History*, 3

was eloquently expressed in David Rothman's studies of incarceration;[26] while in Britain it was most powerfully argued in Michael Ignatieff's pioneering study of the penitentiary at Pentonville.[27] But it was in France that it found its most influential statement, in the great work of the French philosopher Michel Foucault, *Discipline and Punish*, originally published in 1975 under the rather different French title of *Surveiller et punir*, 'to *observe* and to punish';[28] a work that has since exerted such a pervasive effect on this field of study that a critical engagement with it must have a central place in any attempt to grapple with the history of punishment on any level above the merely empirical.

Foucault's book begins, famously, with an extended description of the execution of the would-be regicide Damiens in 1757, which he takes as emblematic of the physical punishments inflicted by the *ancien régime* on those who sought to flout its laws. Sentenced to be dismembered alive after having pieces of his flesh torn out with red-hot pincers, Damiens proved inconveniently resistant to the muscle-power of the horses pulling at each of his limbs, and he eventually had to be cut to pieces by the executioner. Foucault contrasts this grisly scene with the description of an ideal prison regime written by a penal reformer just over eighty years later, portraying a world of total regimentation, discipline, order, silence, and industry. The intervening years had seen the disappearance of punishment as a public spectacle. This was not a particularly original observation. But Foucault differed from the liberal historians of penal policy in denying that this was an advance. In the *ancien régime*, he argued, punishment had constituted a symbolic reassertion of the sovereign's power, achieved by inscribing it on the body of the condemned. The lengthy ceremony of execution was a public demonstration of the sovereign's might, not merely branding it on the offender's body but destroying that body altogether, burning it to ashes, dismembering it, crushing it entirely. Punishments had to be spectacles because law enforcement was ineffective. Every group in society had its area of tolerated illegalities, deviant, transgressive activities which the state was powerless to repress. Indeed, public punishments themselves were far from effective as demonstrations of state power; the crowd could just as easily applaud as assail the malefactor at the pillory, while in public executions 'there was a whole aspect of

(1978), 99–102, and Karl-Georg Faber, 'Historische Kriminologie und kritische Sozialgeschichte: das preussische Beispiel', *Historische Zeitschrift*, 227 (1978), 112–22.

[26] David Rothman, *The Discovery of the Asylum* (Boston, 1971); idem, *Conscience and Convenience: The Asylum and its Alternatives in Progressive America* (Boston, 1980).

[27] Michael Ignatieff, *A Just Measure of Pain: The Penitentiary in the Industrial Revolution 1750–1850* (New York, 1978).

[28] Michel Foucault, *Surveiller et punir: Naissance de la prison* (Paris, 1975); idem, *Discipline and Punish: The Birth of the Prison* (London, 1977).

the carnival, in which rules were inverted, authority mocked and criminals turned into heroes'.[29] The crowd, sometimes aided and abetted by the malefactor on the scaffold, frequently ridiculed the authorities, attacked the executioner, and celebrated the transgressions of everyday life in a saturnalian orgy of bloodlust, riot, and revelry. No wonder, therefore, that the authorities eventually concluded that such a system of punishment was no real deterrent to crime.[30]

The penal reform movement of the eighteenth century, in this view, aimed not to punish people less, but to punish them better. Policing became dramatically more effective; crimes of violence declined; and the state began to regulate and control the behaviour of its citizens with an efficacy undreamed of in the past. The principle of equality before the law reduced everyone to a position where they could become the objects of the new classificatory sciences such as psychiatry and criminology. The tolerated illegalities of the various social groups under the *ancien régime* could no longer be allowed in the same form, or to the same extent, in an emerging capitalist society which required order, consistency, and dependency for its effective functioning. Calculability and continuity became the desiderata of the new economy of punishment, in place of the old economy of expenditure and excess.[31] And it was no longer the body that was symbolically assailed in an exemplary restitution of sovereignty, but the mind and soul of offenders that were to be disciplined by the regimentation of their physical existence, by penal labour, solitary confinement, secrecy and silence within the walls of a prison, and total isolation from the outside world. Effective policing would circumscribe the margins of popular illegalities; disciplinary routinization would inure the mass of the popular classes to the new world of industrial capitalism; judicial intervention would divide the majority of the emerging proletariat from a deliberately created substratum of the marginal and the deviant, whose lives were now to be lived within an archipelago of total institutions, from the orphanage and the workhouse to the asylum and the prison. Most important of all, the personalized sovereignty of the monarch, which had been so dramatically expressed in the old system of punishment, gave way to a new, diffuse economy of power and knowledge, in which the prison itself became a model for the whole of society, and everybody supervised everybody else, disciplining and observing each other all the time, and therefore, also, ultimately disciplining themselves.[32] By internalizing the new, scientific discourse of conformity and deviance, people became part of the endless, anonymous carceral network which Foucault considered constituted the fundamental pattern of modern society.[33]

---

[29] Foucault, *Discipline and Punish*, 61.   [30] Ibid. 3–69.   [31] Ibid. 73–131.
[32] Ibid. 135–292.   [33] Ibid. 293–308.

Foucault linked his work to a complex epistemology which he described using the metaphor of the 'archaeology of knowledge'. Rejecting concepts such as individual authorship, intellectual influence, and historical causation, he advanced instead a theory of discursive formations: linguistic and conceptual structures which framed, limited, and moulded the way that people thought; which defined, indeed, the possibilities of conceptualization itself. Individuals were located within discursive fields rather than shaping ideas and influencing each other.[34] Thus the shift of penal practice which Foucault described in *Discipline and Punish* essentially consisted of the replacement of one discourse by another. In taking this line, Foucault owed something to new developments in the history of science, which in the work of scholars such as Thomas Kuhn and Georges Canguilhem was dethroning the influence of the individual scientific genius in favour of what Kuhn called the 'paradigm' of assumptions in which 'normal science' operated until its contradictions became so manifest that it was forced to give way to a successor. Foucault was also influenced by the *Annales* school of French historians, with its emphasis on the continuities of the *longue durée* of structures and mentalities beneath the superficial appearances of political change.[35] Yet in the end, as the philosopher Jean-Paul Sartre commented, Foucault was less an archaeologist than a geologist of knowledge. What he offered was a

series of successive layers that make up our 'ground'. Each of these layers defines the conditions of possibility of a certain type of thought prevailing throughout a certain period. But Foucault does not tell us the thing that would be the most interesting, that is, how each thought is constructed on the basis of these conditions, or how mankind passes from one thought to another. To do so he would have to bring in praxis, and therefore history, which is precisely what he refuses to do. Of course his perspective remains historical. He distinguishes between periods, a before and an after. But he replaces cinema with the magic lantern, motion with a succession of motionless moments.[36]

That Sartre was thereby identifying Foucault as a 'bourgeois' philosopher, whose ideological target was above all the Marxism that he himself espoused at this period, does nothing to invalidate his acute criticism of the younger man. Foucault might fairly be described as a post-Marxist thinker, in his political as well as his academic moments, but in attempting to escape from simplistic Marxist notions of class agency, his work virtually dissolved the concept of agency altogether. Despite its occasional allusions to 'capitalism' and the 'bourgeoisie', and despite its apparent underlying assumption of the pivotal role played

[34] Michel Foucault, *The Archaeology of Knowledge*, tr. A. M. Sheridan Smith (New York, 1972).
[35] See David Macey, *The Lives of Michel Foucault* (London, 1993), 200–3.
[36] Quoted in Didier Eribon, *Michel Foucault* (London, 1992), 163.

by the French and Industrial Revolutions in the discursive shift which is its subject, it remained effectively silent about the origins of discursive shifts and the mechanisms of historical change.

In describing the transition from one mode of punishment to another, Foucault frequently used the passive voice. Disciplining power, he argued, from being located in the symbolic body of the sovereign, became diffused throughout the whole of society, from the bourgeois family to the prison and the factory, by an all-permeating discourse which came to inform the actions and assumptions of everyone. Yet he attempted neither to find out how and why this discursive transition took place, nor to identify who was responsible, nor to determine who benefited from it, nor to trace its relations to the broader social, economic, and political realities which he recognized, if only by allusion, in his work. He did not consider the ways in which the disciplinary discourse itself was the site of contradiction and dispute. And he failed to address the possibility that the discursive shift was resisted from below. For the historian, therefore, *Discipline and Punish* cannot be the last word on the subject of the changes that took place in penal discourse between the eighteenth and nineteenth centuries. It is full of illuminating and provocative insights, and its overarching theory is a powerful and suggestive one; a dialogue with Foucault's book runs right through the present work, and we shall come back to it at some length at the very end. But it still leaves much to be said, and its applicability to Germany, a country which it does not mention at all, is particularly problematical, as we shall see.[37]

c. *Cruelty and the 'Civilizing Process'*

Foucault was by no means the only major thinker of the twentieth century to address the problem of the changing nature of the penal sanctions imposed by European society in the eighteenth and the nineteenth. Less widely known, but in terms of his influence on the historical profession just as important, was the German sociologist Norbert Elias. Born in Breslau in 1897, Elias trained as a sociologist in the Weimar Republic under Karl Mannheim. He taught at Frankfurt University, although he was not a member of the celebrated 'Frankfurt

---

[37] Michael Weisser, *Crime and Punishment in Early Modern Europe* (Hassocks, 1979), is a rather unspecific and unsatisfactory attempt to apply some of Foucault's ideas; see the critique in Blasius, 'Kriminalität und Geschichtswissenschaft'. For Foucault's reception in, and applicability to Germany, see idem, 'Michel Foucaults "denkende" Betrachtung der Geschichte', *Kriminalsoziologische Bibliographie*, 41 (1983), 69–83; Martin Dinges, 'The Reception of Michel Foucault's Ideas on Social Discipline, Mental Asylums, Hospitals and the Medical Profession in German Historiography', in Colin Jones and Roy Porter (eds.), *Reassessing Foucault: Power, Medicine and the Body* (London, 1993), 181–212; Detlev J. K. Peukert, 'Die Unordnung der Dinge. Michel Foucault und die deutsche Geschichtswissenschaft', in Franz Ewald and Bernhard Waldenfels (eds.), *Spiele der Wahrheit. Michel Foucaults Denken* (Frankfurt am Main, 1991), 320–33.

School' of Marxist sociology situated at the Institute for Social Research in the same city. A liberal rather than a Marxist by political inclination, but more to the point in the context of Germany in 1933, a Jew by parenthood and family, he was forced out by the Nazis and spent the rest of his career abroad, mainly in England and the Netherlands. He devoted it to a sociological and historical enquiry, vast in scope and ambition, into 'the great collapse of civilized behaviour, the process of barbarization, which took place in Germany, as something completely unexpected, simply unimaginable, before my very own eyes'.[38] This investigation took the form of a two-volume work, pubished in 1939, entitled *The Civilizing Process*. Largely ignored on its appearance, when the world had more urgent matters on its hands, it was republished thirty years later, in 1969, and quickly attained the status of a classic.[39]

One could not, Elias argued, 'understand the collapse of civilized behaviour and sensibility unless one managed to understand how the construction and development of civilized behaviour originated in European society in the first place'.[40] In his book, therefore, he returned to the medieval period, when, he argued, the state barely existed and power was exercised in a direct, personal way. Life was uncertain and dangerous, and people lived in a manner that was both physically and emotionally unrestrained. Using etiquette books as a source, Elias showed how, as states began to form, so ruling élites began to formalize their feelings and behaviour, using knives and forks instead of their hands while eating at table, for example, behaving with courtly politeness towards one another in public, substituting the code of duelling for the habit of immediate, individual violence, and concealing their grosser bodily functions—and their sex lives—from the public gaze in a way that they had not done before. With the Absolutist state of the late seventeenth and eighteenth centuries, 'civilized' manners became internalized by the élite; with the liberal and democratic nation-state of the nineteenth and twentieth centuries, they spread down the social scale to the rest of society. In order for power to be exercised in an impersonal, rule-bound way, people had to develop a fellow-feeling for their fellow citizens as well as learn to restrain the expression of their own emotions. Self-control became so natural that people had no hesitation in allowing their personal quarrels to be decided by the impersonal operation of the law and the state. Indeed, emotion itself, as well as

[38] Norbert Elias, *Studien über die Deutschen. Machtkämpfe und Habitusentwicklung im 19. und 20. Jahrhundert* (Frankfurt am Main, 1992), 45–6 n. 8.

[39] Norbert Elias, *Über den Prozess der Zivilisation. Soziogenetische und psychogenetische Untersuchungen,* i. *Wandlungen des Verhaltens in den weltlichen Oberschichten des Abendlandes*; ii. *Wandlungen des Gesellschaft. Entwurf zu einer Theorie der Zivilisation* (Berne, 1969). See also Johan Goudsblom, 'Aufnahme und Kritik der Arbeiten von Norbert Elias in England, Deutschland, den Niederlanden und Frankreich', in Peter Gleichmann, Johan Goudsblom, and Hermann Korte (eds.), *Materialien zu Norbert Elias' Zivilisationstheorie* (Frankfurt am Main, 1979), 17–100.

[40] Elias, *Studien*, 45–6 n. 8.

the operation of bodily functions, became something that could only operate in private.

Thus in the course of the rise of the modern state in Europe, people who were unable to restrain the display of their emotions or curb their physical urges in public were gradually labelled as insane and confined to the privacy of asylums. Decorum, formality, and that most civilized of emotions, embarrassment, became the governing factors in social intercourse and public life. And as the private sphere emerged, so it became the framework for the development of the nuclear family, where intimacy and emotionality concentrated themselves, away from the interference of the wider community which had played such a central role in courtship, marriage, birth, and other major life-events in European society up to the late eighteenth century. Death and illness ceased to be matters of public display, mourning ceased to be an open outpouring of grief.[41] Similarly, punishment ceased to be the public stamping of the sovereign's personal authority on the body of the offender. All these changes both helped and were facilitated by the growing stability and continuity of the modern state. As life became more calculable, emotion became more restrained. Nazism therefore, in Elias's view, was a reversion to a state of barbarism in which people's destructive and violent urges were once again given full rein. In analysing the 'civilizing process' over such a lengthy period of the European past, and in advancing the theory that it was, in the end, a universal process driven by historical principles that were valid for every society in the long run, Elias offered the hope that Nazism's rule would only be a temporary phenomenon which could not hold out against the swelling tide of history in the long run.[42]

Elias's argument has been applied to the history of punishment by one of his disciples in the Netherlands, the Dutch historian Pieter Spierenburg. The reason why the early modern state subjected people to judicial torture and punished them before the community as an example to all, Spierenburg has argued, was because the early modern state was chronically insecure. Constantly threatened by warfare, pestilence, natural disaster, noble rebellion, civil and religious strife, and peasant revolts, the state in early modern Europe simply lacked the ability to enforce permanent social order, to prevent crime, or to deter unrest in any really effective manner. In this situation, few people were in a position to exercise emotional self-control, to abandon the satisfaction of their personal feuds, quarrels, and battles to the state, or to sublimate their aggressions and hatreds in the impersonal mechanisms of the law. The punishment of offenders was a vicarious revenge carried out by the sovereign on the malefactor. Criminal acts were taken

---

[41] Pieter Spierenburg, *The Broken Spell: A Cultural and Anthropological History of Preindustrial Europe* (London, 1991), 1–13, applying Elias's theory to recent work on early modern European social history.

[42] Elias, *Über den Prozess der Zivilisation*; idem, *Studien*.

as personal insults to the sovereign. With the growth of the stable state in the age of Absolutism came a process of 'conscience formation'. The 'relative pacification' achieved by the early modern state allowed domesticated élites to establish themselves. It required the self-imposition of emotional restraint and decorum on the members of the élites when they dealt with one another, though 'emotions and aggressive impulses', Spierenburg comments, 'were hardly restrained with regard to inferior classes'. But the more stable the state became, the more these psychic controls began to link the different groups in society with one another. People were more deeply affected than before by witnessing the suffering of others, above all from the late eighteenth century onwards. 'Increasingly, people recognized others as "somebody like me" and were capable of sharing their experiences. One of the results was that they treated fellow human beings more mercifully to a certain extent.'[43] They identified with the offender instead of with the state, as part of a process in which they were experiencing 'increasing inter-human identification'. The growth of such sensibility was also behind the gradual abolition of torture, the display of malefactors' corpses, and other, similar changes.[44]

The culmination of this development came with the emergence of the nation-state during the nineteenth century, and it is no coincidence that it was accompanied everywhere by the ending of violent physical punishments and public executions. Bureaucratization meant that the liberal state was more impersonal than the sovereign monarchies of the *ancien régime*, and so punishment became more impersonal and less visible too. And 'the nation-state,' argued Spierenburg, 'because of closer integration of geographic areas and wider participation of social groups, was much more stable than the early modern state.' State stability and impersonal rule, giving rise to a process of 'conscience formation', were thus the two major factors in the 'privatization of repression'. These were long-term developments; there was no sudden transition from public mutilation to the penitentiary; imprisonment, indeed, had already begun to emerge with the beginnings of the modern state in the seventeenth century. Solitary confinement and the penitentiary, though made into central metaphors for the modern condition by a thinker such as Foucault, were in this view only transitional experiments, which flourished briefly during the period when public punishment was on the wane. The key elements in the process were the concealment of emotionality and the conquest of violent impulses in the individual, not the formation of a 'carceral society'.[45]

While the historical changes which it identified were recognizably the same as those pinpointed by Foucault, the approach pioneered by Elias and applied to

[43] Spierenburg, *Broken Spell*, 5.   [44] Spierenburg, *Spectacle*, 183–91.   [45] Ibid. 200–7.

the history of penal practice by Spierenburg located them in a much longer and above all much earlier period—the late Middle Ages to the nineteenth century—and signified them as broadly positive in character rather than negative. Where Foucault saw 'the great confinement', Elias saw 'the civilizing process'. Where Foucault regretted the advent of the disciplinary society, Elias welcomed the growth of self-restraint. Clearly, any attempt to survey the historical development of punishment over the four centuries since 1600 cannot leave these theoretical contradictions unresolved, nor neglect the task of subjecting them to a rigorous process of empirical testing. Yet Elias's work also confronts anyone concerned with German history with a more particular set of problems. For it was his view that Germany had escaped the civilizing process in a number of crucial respects. This was, indeed, how Elias explained the triumph of Nazism. The Germans, he thought, had not experienced the smooth growth of stable state power over the centuries that had enabled, say, the English and the French to internalize self-restraint and obey the dictates of mutual self-respect. On the contrary, the late development of nationhood and the violent fluctuations of state form, culminating in 1918 in the revolutionary change from authoritarianism to democracy, had left the Germans with a fatal lack of emotional self-control. They had a persistent tendency to obey the external dictates of power in the absence of a strong internal development of conscience and to look for a strong leader as a substitute. Moreover, the principal vehicle of conscience formation in modern societies, the bourgeoisie, had failed for historical reasons in Germany and had instead taken on the mode of behaviour and ideology of the military aristocracy without appropriating its rigorous code of moral values at the same time. The result of all these processes was the human destructiveness of the Third Reich.[46]

Elias was too good a historian to argue that every aspect of the civilizing process had gone wrong in Germany. Clearly, the development of table manners, for example, took place in Central Europe just as it did everywhere else. Nevertheless, in its central features, the formation of conscience, the development of a fellow-feeling for others, the internalization of self-restraint in the exercise of power and violence, it is clear that, for Elias's theory to be applicable in the way he intended it, the 'civilizing process' in Germany has to exhibit, at the very least, features not found elsewhere in Europe. Yet Spierenburg, in seeking to apply Elias's theory to European history between the Middle Ages and the middle of the nineteenth century, does not make any distinctions between Germany and the other countries he studies, even though these are precisely the same ones as Elias himself used as the basis for his theory—England, France, and the Nether-

[46] Elias, *Studien*, 23, 412–32, 488–9.

lands. Indeed, he relies heavily upon German evidence for many of his general arguments. Moreover, Elias's theory, when taken in its proper historical context, is linked to another argument, grounded at least in part in the same tradition of post-Weberian German sociology, which has been the subject of impassioned debate in recent years: the well-known thesis of the German *Sonderweg*, the argument that Germany deviated from the normal evolution of European societies in the nineteenth century and took a 'special path' to modernity, characterized by a failed bourgeois revolution, a hierarchical society, a pre-industrial, authoritarian value-system, and a rejection of democratic politics. Whilst the literature on these aspects of the debate has by now reached almost epic proportions,[47] what Elias does is to focus the argument on the area where, arguably, it most needs to be focused: on power and violence, on authority and obedience, on the willingness to inflict death and suffering on deviants, transgressors, and outsiders, on the human cruelty and murderous intolerance of the Third Reich.

The question of German peculiarity in these respects has not gone unaddressed in recent years. Dirk Blasius, who has pioneered the social history of crime and the law in Germany, has argued that the humanitarian impulse in German penal reform ran into the sands of opposition from the conservative Prussian aristocracy in the course of the nineteenth century. Instead of a humane, liberal penal order, as elsewhere in Europe, Germany consigned its malefactors to a harsh and brutal regime of punishment that boded ill for the future of humanitarian ideals in the country.[48] Yet writers such as Foucault and Ignatieff have demonstrated that the prison regime advocated and installed by penal reformers in nineteenth-century England and France was no less rigorous and inhumane than the one documented by Blasius in Germany, despite the very different contours of politics in those two countries at the time. Far from resulting from a blockage of liberal reform by aristocratic conservatives, the treadmill, the penitentiary, the rule of silence, solitary confinement, and all the other devices used to break the malefactor's will were actually the consciously desired results of bourgeois liberal reformism in this area.[49] A similar attempt to argue the case for German peculiarities has been put in another pioneering study, this time of policing, by the historian Alf Lüdtke, who has argued that the transition to industrial society in Prussia was made by a uniquely potent combi-

[47] For an introduction to the issues, see David Blackbourn and Geoff Eley, *The Peculiarities of German History: Bourgeois Society and Politics in Nineteenth-Century Germany* (Oxford, 1984), and Evans, *Rethinking*, ch. 3.

[48] Blasius, *Bürgerliche Gesellschaft und Kriminalität*.

[49] Breuilly, review of Blasius (see n. 25 above). See also Richard J. Evans (ed.), *The German Underworld: Essays in the Social History of Crime in Germany from the Sixteenth Century to the Present* (London, 1988).

nation of different types of state violence, open and concealed.[50] Lüdtke, however, leaves penal practice almost entirely out of consideration, and concentrates on a relatively narrow area of the history of civil and military policing, so his argument still remains to be validated on a broad historical basis.

The question of the 'civilizing process' and its deficits in Germany runs through this book. Here is another historically based theory that, in its broad sweep and bold conceptualization, has helped to pose the questions that lie at the heart of the present study. Yet at the same time neither Elias himself, nor his follower Pieter Spierenburg, has attempted to explain in concrete historical terms precisely how and why the changes they describe came about. Like Foucault, they too tend to portray a major historical transition without going too deeply into the mechanisms by which it was wrought. And the crucial question of the extent to which Germany deviated from the pattern of penal reform observable in other countries has scarcely been addressed by historians at all. Throughout this book, therefore, we will see how the empirical evidence reflects upon the theory of the 'civilizing process' and the concept of the *Sonderweg*, and we shall come back to a more general consideration of these questions in the Conclusion to this book.

d. Capital Punishment and the History of Death

Both Foucault and Elias linked the history of punishment firmly to the history of the state. But it is possible to see it in the rather different context of the history of mentalities: of the broad sets of attitudes to life and death, sanity and madness, interest and emotion, society and the natural world, religion and the supernatural, to which historians, particularly in France, have devoted so much attention over the past few decades.[51] Attitudes to suffering, cruelty, and death are rooted above all in social experience; they are built on the fabric of everyday life, and there is no doubt that in medieval and early modern Europe, everyday life was full of uncertainty and danger. Food supplies were utterly dependent on the harvest, and a bad summer could spell famine and starvation. The natural world was threatening and uncontrollable. Epidemic diseases such as typhus, smallpox, and bubonic plague swept regularly across the Continent, killing millions as they

[50] Alf Lüdtke, *'Gemeinwohl', Polizei und 'Festungspraxis'. Staatliche Gewaltsamkeit und innere Verwaltung in Preussen, 1815–1850* (Göttingen, 1982). See also idem, 'The Role of State Violence in the Period of Transition to Industrial Capitalism: The Example of Prussia from 1815 to 1848', *Social History*, 4 (1979), 175–221.

[51] Jacques Le Goff, 'Les Mentalités: Une histoire ambiguë', in Jacques Le Goff and Pierre Nora (eds.), *Faire l'histoire*, iii (Paris, 1974), 76–94; Patrick Hutton, 'The History of Mentalities: The New Map of Cultural History', *History and Theory*, 20 (1981), 237–59; Michael A. Gismondi, 'The Gift of Theory: A Critique of the *histoire des mentalités*', *Social History*, 10 (1985), 211–30.

went; more still died every year of endemic diseases such as tuberculosis. There was no antisepsis; a small wound could easily fester, turn gangrenous, and lead to death from septicaemia. Anaesthetics were unknown, except in the rather ineffective form of hard liquor and toxic herbs. Between a third and a half of all children born died before reaching their first birthday; life expectancy at birth, accordingly, was not much over forty years. Human relationships, between husband and wife, parent and child, brother and sister, were repeatedly broken off by sudden or premature death.[52]

In such a society, it seems obvious that attitudes to death and suffering must have been different from our own, living as we do in a world where, in Western Europe at least, real hunger and starvation are virtually unknown, medical science has triumphed over many aspects of suffering and disease, and life expectancy at birth is now nearly twice what it was two or three hundred years ago. Some historians have argued that the prevalence of suffering and death in Europe before the nineteenth century made people indifferent to these things and hardened their souls against too much emotional involvement with others. Far from being creatures of uncontrolled feeling, the people of early modern Europe, in this view, were scarcely capable of feeling for their fellow humans at all; the emotional costs of doing so were simply too high.[53] While this hypothesis might help explain the prevalence of cruel and violent forms of punishment, however, it has in practice received little assent from the majority of historians. There is a mass of evidence to show that parental and conjugal love was widespread before 1750, that people felt for those who suffered, and that grief and mourning for the dead were commonplace, and often expressed more intensely and more keenly than is the case today.[54] Society in this situation had evolved methods of coming to terms with suffering and death, preparing for it mentally and emotionally, and dealing with it when it came. Death, in all its forms, was much more a part of everyday life in the seventeenth century than it is today, and so too, therefore, were social rituals and practices designed to cope with it and bring about its ultimate acceptance by those whom it affected. But this did not mean that people were indifferent to suffering and loss.

[52] For useful general overviews, see Henry Kamen, *The Iron Century: Social Change in Europe 1550–1660* (London, 1976); and Geoffrey Parker, *Europe in Crisis 1598–1648* (London, 1979), ch. 1.
[53] See esp. Lawrence Stone, *The Family, Sex and Marriage in England, 1500–1800* (London, 1975); Michael Mitterauer and Reinhard Sieder, *The European Family: Patriarchy to Partnership from the Middle Ages to the Present* (Oxford, 1982); Michael Anderson, *Approaches to the History of the Western Family 1500–1914* (London, 1980); Edward Shorter, *The Making of the Modern Family* (London, 1975).
[54] Stephen Wilson, 'The Myth of Motherhood a Myth: The Historical View of European Child-Rearing', *Social History*, 9 (1984), 181–98; idem, 'Death and the Social Historians: Some Recent Books in French and English,' *Social History*, 5 (1980), 435–51; Anne Laurence, 'Godly Grief: Individual Responses to Death in Seventeenth-Century Britain', in Ralph Houlbrooke (ed.), *Death, Ritual, and Bereavement* (London, 1989), 62–76.

The scholar who did most to assist our understanding of these practices was the French writer Philippe Ariès. In his books on the subject, he developed a typology of attitudes to death stretching over more than a thousand years of European history. In the early Middle Ages, he argued, death was 'tamed'; people 'did not just die anyhow'; death always gave advance warning of its arrival, and people had time to prepare for it, invoking a familiar ritual described in numerous literary sources of the period. They gathered their friends and relatives around them, and went through their life-history, thanking, forgiving, or begging people for pardon as they felt appropriate; they confessed to a priest and accepted absolution; they died a 'good death', openly and in public, reconciled to their fate. The ritual continued with weeping and lamentation succeeded by eulogy and praise for the departed, the exposure of the body for people to pay their respects, the funeral procession and service, the burial, and erection of a monument, and a prescribed period of mourning. Death was accepted as a stage of existence: the transition, if all went well, to a higher form of being in the life hereafter. For centuries, therefore, cultural practices relating to death were marked by a mixture of 'indifference, resignation, familiarity, and lack of privacy'. Death had been domesticated.[55] This set of attitudes, Ariès suggested, disappeared gradually.[56] As nature began to be brought under control, belief in hell, and then the afterlife in general, declined. And above all, as the sense of destiny began to shift from the collective to the individual, death began to be removed from the public domain. In the Victorian era, death-bed scenes were essentially enacted within the confines of the family home. By the second half of the twentieth century death had become concealed, privatized, and deritualized. As death and suffering became less frequent, so they were removed to the anonymous invisibility of the hospital, becoming sources of embarrassment and shame. Most people now died alone, unprepared for the event, and unwilling to accept it. Funerals became hasty affairs, a brief, formal service followed by a swift, unseen cremation of the corpse. Death had now become wild and untamed, something people feared or ignored as much as they could.[57]

Ariès's great work *The Hour of our Death* illustrates these arguments with a vast collection of stories, beautifully told, about attitudes to death over an immense span of time, drawn from an astonishing array of sources, from medieval legend and Victorian literature to wills and testaments, diaries, and the iconography of funerary monuments. It has been echoed by other major contributions to the

[55] Philippe Ariès, *The Hour of our Death* (London, 1981), 5–139, quotations on pp. 6, 27.
[56] Ibid. 29.
[57] Ibid. 559–614. See also Geoffrey Gorer, *Death, Grief and Mourning in Contemporary Britain* (London, 1965); Norbert Elias, *Über die Einsamkeit der Sterbenden in unseren Tagen* (Frankfurt am Main, 1982); and Spierenburg, *The Broken Spell*, 126–46.

field, which have filled in many of the missing details by careful empirical research.[58] Its relevance to the history of punishment, and especially capital punishment, is obvious. The insights generated by the work of Ariès and others working in this field are crucial to the present work. Yet unresolved questions remain. Ariès is notoriously vague about chronology and causation. At times he seems to argue, in a fashion characteristic of the *Annales* school, that attitudes to death remained essentially unchanged over the *longue durée* from the Middle Ages to the nineteenth century. At others he seems to suggest that they were changing constantly from the twelfth century onwards. His examples, perhaps inevitably for a book covering such an enormous timespan, are often chosen rather arbitrarily. The geographical scope of his work is largely restricted to France, with some material from England, although it claims to have validity for the whole of Western Europe. His emphasis on the rise of individualism and self-awareness as the cultural motor of changes in attitudes to death is problematical. The various categories he developed to denote different attitudes to death— tamed death, the death of the self, remote and imminent death, the beautiful death, invisible death, and so on—are often rather obscure, and the relationships between them are not properly explained.

Quite apart from these general problems, there is the question, central to the present work, of how the changes that undoubtedly did take place in Western European attitudes to death over the last four hundred years related to the mass murder perpetrated by the Nazis. The rise of individualism, even if such a hypothesis can be proven, is of little explanatory value in this context. But the relevance to Auschwitz of a long-term historical process in which death has become depersonalized and anonymous over the last few centuries, separated out from the community, stripped of its sacral and supernatural connotations, and reduced to a mere biological process, is much more apparent. Did this process reach a turning-point at the end of the eighteenth century, as Ariès thought, and if so, does this have anything to do with the French Revolution? Did the desacralization of death in the Enlightenment and its reduction to an anony-mous, mechanical process of mass murder with the advent of the guillotine and the Terror of 1793–4 lead directly to the gas chambers of Treblinka, as the historian Dorinda Outram has argued?[59] No one has yet investigated these

---

[58] See e.g. Clare Gittings, *Death, Burial and the Individual in Early Modern England* (London, 1984); also François Lebrun, *Les hommes et la mort en Anjou aux XVIIe et XVIIIe siècles* (Paris, 1975), and Michel Vovelle, *Mourir autrefois. Attitudes collectives devant la mort aux XVIIe et XVIIIe siècles* (Paris, 1974).

[59] Dorinda Outram, *The Body and the French Revolution: Sex, Class and Political Culture* (New Haven, 1989). See also Wolfgang Schild's remark: 'In this connection Nazism appears as the culmination of the Enlightenment. It attempted the final solution of all human problems and wanted to achieve this by breeding the pure, exclusively good, spotless human being of the Aryan race, while at the same time exterminating all human beings labelled as degenerate', 'Das Strafrecht als Phänomen der

arguments in relation to Germany. The extent to which they are borne out by the history of capital punishment and its execution, by the changing discursive practices and cultural meanings of the death penalty over the last four centuries of German history, is one of the central themes of this book.

e. Discourse, Culture, Experience

These three overarching theories, of Foucault, Elias, and Ariès, provide the general interpretative framework of the present study. They correspond roughly to the three levels at which it deals with the history of capital punishment in Germany over the four centuries under review. The first of these is the level of discourse. In simple terms, this means what people said and wrote about the death penalty, the arguments they used to defend or criticize it, and the ways in which they related it to the wider social and political purposes with which they were concerned. The penal discourse of the last four centuries in Germany, above all when it came to the subject of capital punishment, has been a pre-eminently political discourse. At the beginning of our period it took place largely within the confines of bureaucracies and judicial administrations, but already in the eighteenth century it was entering into the newly emerging public domain, and from the middle of the nineteenth century it was a hotly debated topic that aroused violent passions not only in the deliberations of legislative assemblies but also in political parties, public meetings, pressure groups, and the press. Throughout the period the subject of capital punishment was also repeatedly dealt with in novels, stories, poems, and plays, and during the twentieth century in films as well. All the participants in the penal discourse revealed their attitudes not only to capital punishment itself, but also to crime and criminality, the state, obedience, suffering, compassion, and death. Many of them, especially political figures, also revealed a good deal about themselves.

But it is not enough to remain at the level of discourse if we are to understand the history of the death penalty in all its aspects. As Norbert Elias saw, we also have to study the level of culture. Definitions of culture are notoriously slippery and variable, and many writers on the subject, from many different theoretical standpoints, have applied the concept in a rather narrow way, and concentrated on the objects and artefacts—paintings, poems, songs, buildings, furniture, and so on—which a given society produces. However, for the purposes of a study such as the present one, it is more useful to think of culture as a process, as the way in which people—all the people—in a society construct their relations with one another in everyday life, and attempt to understand and come to terms with

Geistesgeschichte', in Christoph Hinckeldey (ed.), *Justiz in alter Zeit* (Rothenburg ob der Tauber, 1984), 7–38, here 36.

the way in which they relate to the world around them.[60] Particularly in a pre-literate or semi-literate society, people established and renegotiated the contours of their daily lives in a whole series of real and symbolic actions, from singing folk-songs and joining in festivals and processions to engaging in ritual and magical practices of one kind and another. Popular culture in particular never remained static; even before the massive transformations wrought by literacy and the mass media, it was in a constant state of flux. Treating culture in these terms allows us to unravel the meanings of capital punishment for the wider populace and to learn about the ways in which it informed and was informed by popular attitudes to power and authority, deviance and transgression, suffering and cruelty, and the other central concerns of this book.

But an examination of the discourse and culture of capital punishment in German history is still insufficient if we are to see the whole picture. For this we need to involve a third level, that of experience.[61] Death of course is a biological fact as well as a social event. It was, and is, a reality. In recent years, historians have perhaps become too wary of using the tools of their trade to recapture past reality, preferring instead to concentrate on how people have interpreted it. But the problems of reaching an accurate and persuasive account of how people have interpreted the past are no less than those the historian encounters in reaching an accurate and persuasive account of the past itself. Through careful analysis of the original documentation which the past has left us, we can at least approach important truths about what actually happened. The past, of course, never entirely speaks for itself; but that in turn is no reason for silencing it altogether, so that all we hear is the voice of the historian. In dealing with a subject such as capital punishment, we have to remind ourselves that this is more than a mere debate, more than a simple set of cultural interpretations. People, in the end, were being killed by the state, bloodily, messily and often in quite large numbers. We owe it to them to take their predicament, and their fate, seriously. This book, therefore, tries to give the past a voice, by allowing those who lived through it to talk about their experience: not only the executed, but also and particularly those who prescribed and administered the death penalty: politicians, bureaucrats, judges, lawyers, state prosecutors, judicial officials, executioners. All of them were perpetrators in one way or another, and what they felt about the act of execution which they ordered or carried out can tell us a great deal. How they dealt with the everyday details of executions, and how their experience changed over time,

---

[60] See esp. the work of Gerald Sider, 'The Ties that Bind: Culture and Agriculture, Property and Propriety in Village Newfoundland', *Social History*, 5 (1980), 1–39, for this approach to culture.

[61] For some preliminary, though not very coherent, thoughts on this concept, see Konrad H. Jarausch, 'Toward a Social History of Experience: Postmodern Predicaments in Theory and Interdisciplinarity', *Central European History*, 22 (1989), 427–43.

not only gives us clues to the wider questions with which this book is concerned, it also reminds us, as we must be reminded, that capital punishment is not just some abstract principle, to be argued about by jurists and politicians, or celebrated, for good or ill, in popular culture: it is also something real, that happened to real people in the past, and is still happening to them in many parts of the world today.

Part I

1

Theatres of Cruelty

a. The Death Penalty in Early Modern Germany

In August 1616 the Englishman John Taylor—poet, wit, traveller, and eccentric—embarked at Gravesend on a brief trip to the north German seaport of Hamburg. Not long after his arrival, he 'saw at the common jail of the town, a great number of people were clustered together. I asked', he wrote, 'the cause of their concourse, and I was certified that there was a prisoner to be broken upon the wheel the next day, and that these idle gazers did press to gape upon him for want of better employments.' Being 'as inquisitive after novelties, as a traveller of my small experience might be', Taylor made some further enquiries. He discovered that the prisoner had been found guilty of murdering his small daughter with an axe in a fit of rage. He determined to attend the execution, which was scheduled for the next day.

Monday the 19. of August, about the hour of 12. at noon, the people of the town in great multitudes flocked to the place of execution, which is half a mile English without the gates built more like a sconce than a gallows, for it is walled and ditched about with a drawbridge and the prisoner came on foot with a Divine with him, all the way exhorting him to repentance, and because death should not terrify him, they had given him many rouses and carouses of wine and beer: for it is the custom there to make such poor wretches drunk, whereby they may be senseless either of God's mercy or their own misery; but being prayed for by others, they themselves may die resolutely, or (to be feared) desperately.

On arrival at the gallows, the prisoner and his executioners crossed the drawbridge and went inside, leaving the crowd to gaze on the ensuing events from a respectful distance. A good view was easily to be had, as Taylor explained, because once the drawbridge had been drawn up,

the prisoner mounted on a mount of earth, built high on purpose that the people without may see the execution a quarter of a mile round about: four of the hangman's men takes each of them a small halter, and by the hands and the feet they hold the prisoners extended all abroad lying on his back: then the Arch-hangman, or the great Master of this mighty business took up a wheel, much about the bigness of one of the fore wheels of a coach: and first, having put off his doublet, his hat, and being in his shirt, as if he meant to play at tennis, he took the wheel, and set it on the edge, and turned it with one hand like a top or a whirligig, then he took it by the spokes, and lifting it up with a mighty stroke he beat one of the poor wretch's legs in pieces, (the bones I mean) at which he roared grievously; then after a little pause he breaks the other leg in the same manner, and consequently breaks his arms, and then he stroke four or five main blows on his breast, and burst all his bulk and chest in shivers, lastly he smote his neck, and missing, burst his chin and jaws to mammocks; then he took the broken mangled corpse, and spread it on the wheel, and thrust a great post or pile into the nave or hole of the wheel, and then fixed the post into the earth some six foot deep, being in height above the ground, some ten or twelve foot, and there the carcass must lie till it be consumed by all-consuming time, or ravening fowls.

'This', noted Taylor in conclusion, 'was the terrible manner of this horrid execution'; and, looking around at where it had taken place, he noted 'twenty posts with those wheels or pieces of wheels, with heads of men nailed on the top of the posts, with a great spike driven through the skull', displayed for the edification of the city's inhabitants.

Such was breaking upon the wheel, or, more accurately, breaking with the wheel (*Rädern*).[1] It was one of the commonest methods of capital punishment to be employed in Germany at this time. But it was by no means the most fearsome. 'The several kinds of torments which they inflict upon offenders in those parts', Taylor observed, 'makes me to imagine our English hanging to be but a flea-biting.' Adultery was punishable by decapitation, and arson by burning alive; while

he that counterfeits any Princes coin, and is proved a coiner, his judgment is to be boiled to death in oil, not thrown into the vessel all at once, but with a pulley or a rope to be hanged under the arm pit, and let down into the oil by degrees: first the feet, and next the legs, and so to boil his flesh from his bones alive.

The hanged were left on the gibbet until their bodies rotted away or were consumed by carrion birds. For those who were beheaded, Taylor went on,

the fashion is, that the prisoner kneels down, and being blinded with a napkin, one takes hold of the hair of the crown of the head, holding the party upright, whilst the hangman with a backward blow with a sword will take the head from a mans shoulders so nimbly, and with such dexterity, that the owner of the head shall never want the miss of it.[2]

    [1] The commoner term 'breaking upon the wheel' derives from the equivalent punishment in France, where the wheel was placed horizontally on the scaffold, and the malefactor fastened to it with ropes. The executioner then broke the malefactor's limbs with an iron bar. In Germany this method only seems to have been used in Hanover. See Thomas Krause, *Die Strafrechtspflege im Kurfürstentum und Königreich Hannover vom Ende des 17. Jahrhunderts bis zum ersten Drittel des 19. Jahrhunderts* (Untersuchungen zur deutschen Staats- und Rechtsgeschichte, NS 28; Aalen, 1991), 184.
    [2] John Taylor, *Three Weekes, three daies, and three houres Observations and travel, from London to Hamburgh* (London, 1617), repr. in C. Hindley (ed.), *The Old Book Collector's Miscellany*, iii (London,

Nor were these punishments enumerated by Taylor the only ones provided for by the law. In the great legal codification known as the *Constitutio Criminalis Carolina*, promulgated by the Holy Roman Emperor Charles V in 1532, the death penalty was prescribed not only for murder, arson, and counterfeiting, but also for treason, blasphemy, conjuring, witchcraft, rape, abortion, unnatural sex, forgery, highway robbery, robbery with violence (actual or threatened), and theft at the third conviction.[3] Although the code allowed a wide variety of local and regional variations based on custom and tradition to continue, in practice these provisions held good, with varying degrees of emphasis, for most parts of the Holy Roman Empire in the sixteenth and seventeenth centuries.[4]

The punishment of breaking with the wheel, which had so impressed John Taylor on his visit to Hamburg, was reserved almost exclusively for male offenders, and was·applied only to those convicted of aggravated murder—committed either while carrying out a robbery (*Raubmord*) or against a member of the offender's own family, as in the case observed by Taylor. The method applied on that occasion—'from the bottom up'—was regarded as the most severe, because it caused greater suffering to the condemned by being carried out mostly while they were still conscious. A less extreme grade was 'from the top down', in which the first blow of the wheel landed on the neck, causing instantaneous death. The number and sequence of the blows was usually laid down precisely in the sentence, and where the offence was judged particularly severe, the condemned person was wrapped in a raw, wet oxhide and dragged on a hurdle to the scaffold by a horse beforehand; on the way pieces of the offender's flesh might also be torn out with red-hot tongs; and after execution, the head was usually severed and put on top of a pole, as observed by Taylor, and the body tied to a cartwheel, placed horizontally on top of another pole, and similarly left to rot; in some cases the offender's remains would be burned and the ashes scattered or thrown into the nearest river. Equally severe was the punishment of burning at

---

1873). For a brief study of Taylor's life and works, see Wallace Notestein, *Four Worthies* (London, 1956), 169–210. Taylor (1580–1653) financed his trips by advertising in advance for subscriptions to the written account of the voyage, which he promised to write if he returned successfully.

[3] Friedrich Malblank (ed.), *Geschichte der Peinlichen Gerichtsordnung Kaiser Karls V.* (Nuremberg, 1763), 237–8, and Gustav Radbruch (ed.), *Die Peinliche Gerichtsordnung Kaiser Karls V. von 1532 (Carolina)*, 4th edn. (Stuttgart, 1975), Clauses cvi–clxvi. See also J. Kohler and W. Scheel (eds.), *Die Carolina und ihre Vorgängerinnen. Text, Erläuterungen, Geschichte* (4 vols.; Halle, 1900–15; repr. Aalen, 1970), and F. C. Schroeder, *Die Carolina. Die Peinliche Gerichtsordnung Kaiser Karls* (Darmstadt, 1986). For an important collection of legal-historical studies, see Peter Landau and Friedrich Schröter (eds.), *Strafrecht, Strafprozess und Rezeption: Grundlagen, Entwicklungen und Wirkung der Constitutio Criminalis Carolina* (Frankfurt am Main, 1984).

[4] Schild, 'Das Strafrecht', 16–18. For local variations, see Bernd Roeck, 'Criminal Procedure in the Holy Roman Empire in Early Modern Times', *Bulletin of the International Association for the History of Crime and Criminal Justice*, 18 (spring 1993), 21–40. For a case-study of the implementation and amendment of the *Carolina*, see Krause, *Strafrechtspflege*, 21–38.

FIG. 1. *Execution according to the* Carolina. Following the prescriptions laid down in the Emperor Charles V's Law Code of 1532, a woman convicted of infanticide is buried alive and her heart is impaled, and a man convicted of aggravated murder is broken with the wheel. A late sixteenth-century illustration from Freiburg (Switzerland).

the stake, applied to blasphemers, heretics, witches, coiners, poisoners, and sodomites. The intention was to destroy the offender's body so completely that nothing remained; not only were straw and dry wood used to construct the massive bonfire to which the malefactor was bound, but coal, pitch, tar, and sulphur as well.[5] After the fire had burnt out, any remaining bones were ground to dust and buried under the gallows or thrown into a nearby river with the ashes. Whilst both men and women were subjected to this punishment, drowning was mainly though not exclusively reserved for female offenders, and again applied above all to crimes against morality and religion, such as adultery and heresy. Water, like fire, had a purifying function; the offender was lowered into it, usually from a bridge, and kept under by the hangman's assistant until she was dead. In particularly severe cases the condemned person could be put into a sack, together with a cat, a hen, and a snake (the last-named usually only in picture form, since snakes were hard to come by in Germany) before being let down into the water.[6]

[5] StA Bremen 2.-D. 18. i: Specification, Derer geräthschaften so zu einem Malificanten lebendig zu verbrennen, erforderlich sind (Brandt, Scharfrichterey-Pächter, Berlin, 8 Aug. 1786).
[6] See more generally E. P. Evans, *The Criminal Prosecution and Capital Punishment of Animals* (London, 1906).

More severe still—the female equivalent of breaking with the wheel—was the punishment laid down in the *Carolina* for infanticide:

Item whatsoever woman shall privily, maliciously and with intent, kill a child of hers that hath life and limb, shall customarily be buried alive and impaled. But in order that this shall not cause despondency, the said malefactresses may be drowned, in court districts where the convenience of water is available for this purpose. Yet where such wickedness oft occurs, we also wish to permit the said custom of burial and impalement for such malevolent women, in order that their fear may be the greater.[7]

Here the offender would be tied up and laid in a shallow grave below the gallows, covered in thorns, and then buried alive from the feet up; during or immediately after this process, a stake would be driven through her heart, perhaps to prevent the body from returning from the dead, in a reflection of folk beliefs about vampirism.[8] Burial alive was still practised in the sixteenth century, although it was relatively unusual. Boiling in oil, as described by Taylor, was extremely rare, though one case was apparently recorded in Venlo as late as 1728.[9] Another rarity was the punishment of quartering, reserved in the *Carolina* for high treason, above all for cases of the assassination or the attempted murder of a sovereign. This was not carried out, as it was in France, by getting four horses to pull the offender's limbs apart—a method whose spectacular impracticality was illustrated by the notorious case of the would-be regicide Damiens, condemned in Paris in 1757. In Germany, the law laid down that the offender's body should be tied down horizontally, slit down the middle with a specially made large knife, and disembowelled. The hangman had to strike the offender across the mouth with the heart or innards, then cut the body into four quarters and display each at a separate place on the common highway.[10]

Such punishments were only the most severe among a whole range of bodily sanctions applied to offenders of all grades and varieties in sixteenth- and seventeenth-century Germany. The *Carolina* provided for minor blasphemers to have their tongue slit or cut out, unwanted and disorderly vagrants to be branded

---

[7] Radbruch (ed.), *Die peinliche Gerichtsordnung*, 84 (§ 131).

[8] See Paul Barber, *Vampires, Burial, and Death: Folklore and Reality* (New Haven, 1988) for a sensible survey of these beliefs.

[9] Johann Glenzdorf and Fritz Treichel, *Henker, Schinder und Arme Sünder* (Bad Münder am Deister, 1970), 60. Glenzdorf and Treichel's compilation is full of useful material, but unreferenced, and not always reliable.

[10] Dülmen, *Theater*, 127–9; Schuhmann, *Scharfrichter*, 49–78; Radbruch (ed.), *Die Peinliche Gerichtsordnung*, Clause 192. For the local operation of such punishments, see e.g. Hermann Knapp, *Das alte Nürnberger Kriminalrecht, nach Rats-Urkunden erläutert* (Berlin, 1896), 52–60; Georg Schindler, *Verbrechen und Strafen im Recht der Stadt Freiburg im Breisgau von der Einführung des Neuen Stadtrechts bis zum Übergang an Baden (1520–1806)* (Freiburg, 1937), 46–59; H. Nordhoff-Behne, *Gerichtsbarkeit und Strafrechtspflege in der Reichsstadt Schwäbisch-Hall seit dem 15. Jahrhundert* (Schwäbisch-Hall, 1971); and E. Lindgen, *Die Breslauer Strafrechtspflege unter der Carolina und der Gemeinen Strafrechtswissenschaft bis zum Inkrafttreten der Josephine von 1708* (Breslau, 1939).

(often on the cheek or forehead), immoral women to lose an ear, and persistent thieves to have their fingers chopped off, or even one or both hands. Offenders were brought to the pillory (*Pranger*) to receive such punishments in public. Attached to it by an iron collar, sometimes with a picture or object denoting the nature of their offence, they were exposed to the scorn and violence of the populace as well as to the attentions of the hangman. Most commonly of all, they were publicly whipped, either at the pillory, or along the streets to the town gate. Many of these corporal punishments were accompanied by the malefactor's expulsion from the town or the territory where the offence was committed (*Landesverweisung*); some of them, like branding, were designed among other things to make sure that offenders would be instantly recognized if they were ever foolish enough to return. Frequently a number of them were used in combination, such as display at the pillory and whipping, followed by expulsion from the land. Capital punishment, too, was sometimes preceded or accompanied by forms of corporal mutilation designed to draw attention to the particular nature of the offence.

Sometimes this could go well beyond what was prescribed by the *Carolina*, above all in cases involving witchcraft or sorcery.[11] But the rules were flexible even in more concrete criminal cases where the offence was considered to have been especially reprehensible. In 1597 a murderer who confessed to having done away with no fewer than fifty-five victims was quartered in Eschwein,[12] while in 1654 a robber who had taken advantage of the chaotic circumstances of the Thirty Years War to kill and plunder, it was alleged, the astonishing number of 251 innocent victims over the course of fifteen years, was executed in Breslau in the following manner:

To begin with, he is put onto a cart on the public square before the town hall by the executioner ordered for this purpose, and there the top joints of all his ten fingers are torn off one by one with red-hot tongs. Thereafter his body is torn four times by red-hot tongs at the four corners of the square. Then he is dragged out of the city to the gallows on an oxhide placed on a hurdle pulled by two horses. There, on a specially erected stage, in the presence of some thousands of both native and foreign persons who have made their way from near and far, his arms and legs are crushed for a very long time with the wheel.[13]

[11] See e.g. Karen Lambrecht, '"Jagdhunde des Teufels". Die Verfolgung von Totengräbern im Gefolge frühneuzeitliche Pestwellen', in Andreas Blauert and Gerd Schwerhoff (eds.), *Mit den Waffen der Justiz. Zur Kriminalitätsgeschichte des späten Mittelalters und der Frühen Neuzeit* (Frankfurt am Main, 1993), 137–57.

[12] Anon., *Eine wahrhafftige newe Zeyttung, so sich begeben hat zu Eschwein, wie allda ein Mörder ist eingebracht worden, welcher 55. Mord mit seiner eygen Hand verbracht hat, biss er endlich von Gott gestrafft vnnd gericht ist worden den 1. tag May in diesem 97. Jahr/Im Thon Kompt her zu mir spricht Gottes Sohn &c* (Coburg, 1597).

[13] Anon., *Melcher Hedloffs sonst Schutze-Melcher genannt, von Kautinchen auss Medziborischer Herrschaft bürtig verübete und begangene Mord-Thaten, welche er innerhalb 15. Jahren mehrerentheils mit seinen zwey Röhren verrichtet. Auch wie er den 19. Januarii dieses 1654 Jahrs seiner Arbeit nach, den Lohn empfangen*

It was not only for crimes of violence that such additional punishments were reserved. In 1686, when Dirk Surbick, a financial official in the north German town of Bremen, was executed for embezzling funds by applying forged seals to official documents, two fingers were chopped off his right hand before he was beheaded.[14] And in 1741 a woman in Nuremberg who had killed her child by throttling it with her left hand was condemned to have the hand cut off on the scaffold before she was decapitated.[15]

Punishments like these could be found even in the age of the Enlightenment. In the mid-eighteenth century, for example, a band of Polish and German travelling entertainers and bear-keepers were sentenced to death for having robbed and killed some twenty people in eastern Germany by setting their bears on them until they were torn to pieces.

First, after the judgment, the three Polacks were dragged out on a cowhide, torn with red-hot tongs, and fitted with pitch-gloves, which were set alight, and all three were torn apart by horses and their quarters hanged on the open road. After these, the other two German murderers got their reward. Carl Grau was laid out on the scaffold, glowing sulphur was poured on his breast, and he was broken with the wheel from the bottom up and his body placed on the wheel. Hartmann, however, who had been among this gang for no more than a year, had both hands cut off, and was broken with the wheel from the top down.[16]

In cases of witchcraft or multiple murder, it was not uncommon in the fifteenth and sixteenth centuries for female offenders to have their breasts torn out with glowing tongs.[17] What was laid down in the lawbooks was thus in many cases varied and exceeded by the ingenuity of the judge and the hangman. For especially heinous crimes, the authorities required especially severe physical punishments. Alternatives to corporal and capital punishment in early modern Germany were limited to mostly brief and seldom precisely specified periods of imprisonment and modest fines, or banishment from the territory where the offence was committed. Confinement to the galleys, or to military service or forced labour on public works, was not common as a punishment in Germany as

(Breslau, 1654). For a sceptical discussion of this case, see Robert Ergang, *The Myth of the All-Destructive Fury of the Thirty Years War* (Pocono Pines, Pa., 1956), 17. The point at issue here, however, is the punishment not the crime.

[14] StA Bremen 2.-D. 16. g. 1: Das sogenannte Schwartze-Buch des Bremischen Criminal-Gerichts von 1238 bis 1813, entry for 1686.

[15] Richard van Dülmen, *Frauen vor Gericht. Kindsmord in der frühen Neuzeit* (Frankfurt am Main, 1991), 50–1.

[16] Anon., *Traurige Nachricht von einer erschröcklichen Mordthat, welche sich bey Prenzlau von fünf Bärenführern zugetragen; dabey die grosse Hinrichtung, welche den 10. Weinmonat 1751. gehalten worden, mit mehreren ausführlich zu ersehen seyn wird. Gedruckt nach dem Berlinischen Exemplar* (1751).

[17] See e.g. Michael Kunze, *Highroad to the Stake: A Tale of Witchcraft* (Chicago, 1987), esp. 406–15; and Tom Cheesman, *The Shocking Ballad Picture Show: German Popular Literature and Cultural History* (Oxford, 1994), ch. 5 nn. 17–18.

FIG. 2. *An 'aggravated death sentence'.* Franz Seuboldt is executed in Nuremberg on 22 September 1589. The top left-hand corner shows him shooting his father from behind as the old man is setting up bird-traps in the woods. For this particularly heinous crime—a parricide, premeditated and carried out with stealth and deceit—Seuboldt was condemned to death, with the additional punishment of having his flesh torn out with red-hot tongs on the way to the scaffold, as shown bottom-left. Note the servant heating the fire with a pair of bellows, and the two priests speaking 'consoling words' to Seuboldt on the tumbril. The right-hand side of the picture shows him being broken with the wheel on a square ravenstone. Clearly visible are the wooden blocks used to raise his limbs in order to make it easier for the executioner to break the bones with the wheel. Note also the presence of women and children in the rather small crowd, and the heads and bodies exposed behind. The caption reads: 'Dreadful news and terrible, murderous deeds of Franz Seuboldt'.

it was in France.[18] There were, of course, gaols but they were small, they made no attempt at reforming the offender, and they frequently confined other categories of people such as lunatics as well.[19] The wilful infringement of the criminal law, above all if it was regarded as serious, called forth in a large number of cases a sentence prescribing the public violation of the offender's body. And in about a third of all sentences, that meant death.[20]

b. Crime and the Law around 1600

The punishments observed by John Taylor on his visit to Hamburg in 1616 had emerged during the Middle Ages in a haphazard fashion, as the blood feud and its substitutes had gradually given way to more impersonal forms of penal sanction. Medieval law had frequently attempted to control feuding by ordering the perpetrator to pay monetary compensation to the victim in relation to the severity of the injury caused. But as justice ceased to be a mere arrangement between individuals and their families or communities, and came to represent a central aspect of the sovereign power of princes and cities, so fines and compensations yielded to whippings and hangings, and judicial executions replaced the feud and the fight. Such arrogation and display of power by the state may well have met a common need for security and stability in a violent age. And it was particularly important in the sixteenth century. This was not only the century in which the territorial state established itself in Germany, it was also the century of the Reformation, a period of unprecedented upheaval in religious and community life. And it was an age marked by widespread social and political insecurity. The massive Peasants' Revolt of 1525 was followed by repeated bouts of rural disorder, and helped provide the peasantry with a language of disobedience which their lords found highly alarming. Organized bands of robbers up to fifty strong were reported to be attacking villages, castles, and isolated farmhouses on a regular basis in Baden, Hesse, and Bavaria during the 1570s and 1580s. In Württemberg during the same period there were widespread fears of gangs of arsonists, who were said to put whole villages to the torch after plundering them of their valuables. The anxiety spread by such disorder was aggravated by the depredations of large numbers of beggars, vagrants, and heavily armed mercenary soldiers or *Landsknechte* who roamed the countryside in search of food and money, and were none too particular about how they found them.[21]

---

[18] Dülmen, *Theater*, 62–9. For some exceptions to this generalization, see P. Frauenstädt, 'Zur Geschichte der Galeerenstrafe in Deutschland', *Zeitschrift für die gesamte Strafrechtswissenschaft*, 16 (1896), 518–46.

[19] Schwerhoff, *Köln*, 123–58.   [20] Ibid. 60, 154–5.

[21] Bob Scribner, 'The *Mordbrenner* Fear in Sixteenth-Century Germany: Political Paranoia or the Revenge of the Outcast?', in Evans (ed.), *The German Underworld*, 29–56; idem, 'Politics and the

At the same time, the instruments of control available in the sixteenth and early sevententh centuries were pathetically ineffective. Policing arrangements did exist, but this was an overwhelmingly rural society, in which more than eight out of every ten people lived on and from the land. Vast tracts of the countryside were uncultivated; from the plains of the north to the hills of central Germany and the mountainous areas of the south, much of the land was covered in forest, the haunt of wolves, bears, and wild boar. Roads were unmade, frequently little more than tracks that became impassable after heavy rains. In winter, thick snow cut off settlements in the Alps, the Harz, and other mountain ranges, for months on end. The small towns and cities that dotted the land-scape—most of them numbering only a few thousand inhabitants—thought of themselves as oases of civilization and order in a wild, untamed and dangerous world. The thick stone walls that protected them from marauding armies also enabled them to keep control over comers and goers; the town gates were closed at dusk, and a suspicious eye was kept on strangers. The possibility of successfully pursuing robbers and criminals into the wild was very limited and fraught with terrible dangers.[22]

Moreover, there was no central authority in Germany which could take responsibility for law enforcement in the sixteenth century. The Holy Roman Empire of the German Nation was the nearest approximation, but it could hardly be considered a state in the modern sense of the word. It had no civil service, no standing army, and no regular income from taxation. It was not, of course, entirely impotent. It undoubtedly had prestige and influence enough to ensure that the *Carolina*, the great law code of 1532, was generally used as the basis of the criminal law throughout its lands and even beyond. But it had few real powers, and seldom intervened to any great or lasting effect in the affairs of the two thousand or so separate states which belonged to it. These ranged from large, relatively well-organized principalities and dukedoms such as Saxony and Bavaria, through a hundred or more ecclesiastical jurisdictions, on to over eighty Free or Imperial Cities, scores of small or medium-sized secular lordships, and over a thousand, mostly minuscule patches of territory belonging to the Imperial Knights. Each of these was responsible for enforcing the law within its own boundaries, so the patchwork quilt of authorities in the Holy Roman Empire offered ample opportunity for wrongdoers to decamp from the scene of their

Territorial State in Sixteenth-Century Württemberg', in E. I. Kouri and Tom Scott (eds.), *Politics and Society in Reformation Europe: Essays for Sir Geoffrey Elton on his Sixty-Fifth Birthday* (London, 1987), 103–20; Kunze, *Highroad*, 133–8. For a recent, wide-ranging introduction to early modern criminality, see Gerd Schwerhoff, 'Devianz in der alteuropäischen Gesellschaft. Umrisse einer historischen Kriminalitätsforschung', *Zeitschrift für historische Forschung*, 19 (1992), 385–414.

[22] See generally Richard van Dülmen, *Kultur und Alltag in der Frühen Neuzeit*, ii. *Dorf und Stadt, 16.– 18. Jahrhundert* (Munich, 1992), esp. 62–84; and Schwerhoff, *Köln*, 49–70.

crime into other jurisdictions, where they could not be pursued. And the lumbering procedures of the emerging judicial bureaucracies were seldom able to track down offenders unless their identity was already known. Punishments were not, however, savage and exemplary merely because the state had no other means of enforcing its will. On the contrary, because the police and judicial apparatus of the state was so weak, the apprehension and punishment of offenders depended to a considerable degree on the co-operation of the community. When someone was brought to the scaffold, it was therefore more often than not as the result of a series of social transactions in which the community as well as the state expressed its disapproval of the offence in question. Correspondingly, where the authorities felt that the imposition of a punishment would offend the community, they held back. Moreover, if they failed to restrain themselves in this way, community feeling on behalf of the offender could express itself through petitions for clemency or even pardon, which it did with a good deal of success in a high proportion of cases.[23]

What the punishments commonly used in sixteenth-century Germany attempted to do was therefore to stamp the authority not just of the prince or city-state, and, through the implementation of the *Carolina*, the Holy Roman Empire, but also that of the community onto the physical body of the offender. It was a very public demonstration of sovereign and collective power at a number of different levels. And it was public not least because all other aspects of the judicial procedure were carried out in conditions of considerable secrecy. The codification of 1532 and its adoption in many parts of the Empire signified not only the intention of these states to monopolize punishment but also their determination to control justice. The Germanic customary law prevalent in the Middle Ages had pursued and tried offences in the open. Trial by ordeal had been a very public kind of event. But by the sixteenth century Roman law was in the ascendant. It brought with it the introduction of the inquisitorial system. Cases were now investigated and tried by judges appointed by the prince or the town council, without any recourse to popular participation. Oaths and purgations were no longer accepted as proof of innocence. Once delivered to the authorities, the offender was completely at their mercy. There was no question of any courtroom battle between prosecutor and defender, no possibility of cross-examining witnesses, no presence of any jury. Instead, the determination of guilt or innocence depended almost entirely upon the interrogation of the accused. And the aim of the interrogation was to produce a confession. Of course, the testimony of witnesses was important, but it was presented only in written form, and there was no chance for the accused to question the individuals concerned in

[23] Schwerhoff, *Köln*, 168–73, 442–3.

person. And if the accused denied the validity of the evidence, the investigating judge could order the use of torture.[24]

This had been introduced gradually in the later Middle Ages, and had become widely used by the sixteenth century.[25] The law code of 1532 included an attempt, one of a series made in Europe at this time, to lay down systematic rules for its use. The rules were considerably elaborated over the next two hundred years. Torture was not supposed to be applied arbitrarily, and the investigating judge had to seek the permission of higher authority before ordering it to begin. It could only commence if the accused had refused to confess voluntarily during the initial interrogation. The first step as laid down in the rules was simply to show the instruments of torture to the accused. Only if no confession was forthcoming under these circumstances were the thumbscrews put on, but even at this stage of the process no force was applied until the accused had denied the charges once again. Finally the hangman proceeded on orders to inflict actual bodily pain. Here again there were strict rules, and commonly accepted limits to what could be done. Beginning with the thumbscrews, the process escalated to the tightening of legsplints, laying the accused over a wooden horse (the *Spanischer Bock*) and administering a whipping, and finally hanging the offender from the ceiling by the hands (tied behind the back) with (as a last stage) heavy weights attached to the legs in a procedure known to jurists as the strappado. At each juncture the inquisitor repeated his demand for a confession, and if it was given, it had to be freely repeated when the accused had been released from the torture, otherwise it was not acceptable in law. The allowable degree of torture varied with the offence, but in general the whole process was not supposed to be repeated more than three times. And for women it usually went no further than the thumbscrews; the dubious privilege of the strappado was mainly reserved for men.[26] While there were instances recorded of accused individuals being released after having withstood even prolonged torture,[27] and as many as 22 per cent of accused

[24] Roeck, 'Criminal Procedure', 25–7.

[25] Peters, *Torture*, esp. chs. 1–2, for an introduction to the history of this subject. For an older but still useful local study, see Hermann Knapp, *Das Lochgefängnis. Tortur und Richtung in Alt-Nürnberg* (Nuremberg, 1907).

[26] Wolfgang Behringer, 'Mörder, Diebe, Ehebrecher: Verbrechen und Strafen in Kurbayern vom 16. bis 18. Jahrhundert', in Richard van Dülmen (ed.), *Verbrechen, Strafen und soziale Kontrolle* (Frankfurt am Main, 1990), 85–132, here 92–3; Van Dülmen, *Theater*, 22–34; and Schuhmann, *Scharfrichter*, 188–92. See also John H. Langbein, *Torture and the Law of Proof* (Chicago, 1972); A. Esmein, *A History of Continental Criminal Procedure* (Boston, 1913); and Eberhard Schmidt, *Einführung in die Geschichte der deutschen Strafrechtspflege*, 3rd edn. (Göttingen, 1965). For two excellent examples of torture instructions from the eighteenth century, see Sta Hanover A 1117, Bl. 79–96: Osnabruckische modus torquendi, and ibid. Bl. 110–23: Generale Instruction behufs des Tortural-Verfahrens.

[27] For one such, see Sta Hanover A 1117, Bl. 125–6: Urphede eines Juden nach ausgestandenen Tortur (1754). More generally, see Otto Ulbricht, 'Kindsmörderinnen vor Gericht: Verteidigungsstrategien von Frauen in Norddeutschland 1680–1810', in Blauert and Schwerhoff (eds.), *Mit den Waffen*, 54–85; Gisela Wilbertz, *Scharfrichter und Abdecker im Hochstift Osnabrück. Untersuchungen zur Sozialgeschichte zweier*

persons tortured by the courts in sixteenth-century Cologne managed to secure an acquittal, it is not surprising that the overwhelming majority of serious cases tried under this system ended by producing a confession.[28]

Such a confession was not the end of the matter. Central to the whole procedure was the separation of the investigation from the actual trial. On completion of the interrogation, the investigating judge's report, with other papers such as the deposition of witnesses and the accused's confession, were sent to the sovereign authority—either the prince or the town council—who then, in person or through delegated representatives, acted as the trial judge, armed with the sole authority to reach a final verdict and pass sentence. By the eighteenth century, it was normal for officials to stick fairly closely to the rules of inquisitorial justice. But in the sixteenth and early seventeenth centuries they were often broken by over-zealous inquisitors. Moreover, like other artisans, all torturers had their own particular style and pride in their work, which could frequently lead them to ignore the rules; in Augsburg, for example, one executioner actually boasted of his ability to make witches confess.[29] The process of torture could be repeated on occasion up to ten times a day for days on end, with a final total of over sixty sessions documented in a number of cases, instead of the legally prescribed limit of three; and investigating judges frequently had recourse to forms of torture not laid down in the regulations.[30] This was particularly likely in witchcraft trials, which occurred with increasing frequency through the sixteenth century and reached their peak between 1580 and 1640. It was the inquisitorial procedure, with its use of torture, which more than anything else allowed the elaborate myths of the demonologists to find confirmation in the confessions of the accused. The number of people executed for witchcraft or sorcery in Germany in these years was considerable. In Würzburg, for example, 157 persons were burned at the stake in twenty-nine separate executions between 1627 and 1629, while in a mere seven years, from 1587 to 1593, 368 people from twenty-seven villages in the diocese of Trier were burned alive for sorcery.[31] These were

'unehrlicher' Berufe im nordwestdeutschen Raum vom 16. bis zum 19. Jahrhundert (Münster, 1979), 82; eadem, 'Das Notizbuch des Scharfrichters Johann Christoph Zippel in Stade (1766–82)', Stader Jahrbuch, 25 (1975), 62–3.

[28] Schwerhoff, *Köln*, 114–15.   [29] Schuhmann, *Scharfrichter*, 188–92.

[30] Behringer, 'Mörder, Diebe', 94.

[31] Kamen, *The Iron Century*, 270–1. See also H. C. Erik Midelfort, *Witch-Hunting in Southwestern Germany 1562–1684: The Social and Intellectual Foundations* (Berkeley, 1972); and E. W. Monter, 'La Sodomie à l'époque moderne en Suisse romande', *Annales ESC* 29/4 (1974), 1023–33. There have been numerous excellent studies of witchcraft in Central Europe in recent years. For some outstanding examples, see Susanna Burghartz, 'The Equation of Women and Witches: A Case Study of Witchcraft Trials in Lucern and Lausanne in the Fifteenth and Sixteenth Centuries', in Evans (ed.), *The German Underworld*, 57–74; Gerhard Schormann, *Hexenprozesse in Deutschland* (Göttingen, 1981); idem, *Der Krieg gegen die Hexen. Das Ausrottungsprogramm des Kurfürsten von Köln* (Göttingen, 1991); Eva Labouvie, *Zauberei und Hexenwerk. Ländlicher Hexenglaube in der frühen Neuzeit* (Frankfurt am Main, 1991); and

unusual outbursts of persecution, of course. More common was a fairly low level of witchcraft prosecution, with isolated cases occurring every few years.[32] Social historians have shown how witchcraft accusations frequently emerged from tensions within the village community, and arrests were often made as a result of local denunciations and with at least tacit popular consent. Once in the hands of the law, however, a person accused of witchcraft was as likely as not to be exposed to inquisitorial procedures which went a good way beyond what was normally permissible.[33]

Witchcraft trials have to be seen in the context of other aspects of law enforcement at this time. The state was turning its attention towards the behaviour and conduct of ordinary people and during the sixteenth century increasingly sought to enforce what it saw as basic standards of Christian morality. Secular jurisdiction was taking in a growing number of cases of moral and social deviance, both in Protestant states, where the old ecclesiastical courts which had previously dealt with such matters ceased to function, and in their Catholic counterparts, where the new spirit of the Catholic Reformation (or Counter-Reformation) extended the role of the secular courts in the same directions. So witchcraft trials were accompanied by a simultaneous growth of prosecutions for offences such as homosexuality, sodomy, incest, adultery, prostitution, and infanticide. Little distinction was made in practice between moral and religious offences, including blasphemy and heresy, and secular offences such as murder or theft: all were seen in the first instance as violations of the godly order which the secular authorities were divinely appointed to enforce. Sexual deviance was not regarded as any less open to community and state control than was theft or violence. Religious extremists like the Anabaptists, whose revolutionary reign in the town of Münster in 1534 sent shivers of fear throughout the Holy Roman Empire, confirmed the authorities, Protestant and Catholic alike, in their evident belief that idleness, heresy, deviance, and sexual immorality could lead to disorder and homicide if they went unchecked.[34] An offence against the law was thus an offence against God. Secular authority wielded the sword of justice by

Helmut Pohl, *Hexenglaube und Hexenverfolgung im Kurfürstentum Mainz. Ein Beitrag zur Hexenfrage im 16. und beginnenden 17. Jahrhundert* (Wiesbaden, 1988).

[32] Wolfgang Behringer, *Hexenverfolgung in Bayern. Volksmagie, Glaubenseifer und Staatsräson in der Frühen Neuzeit* (Munich, 1987); Richard van Dülmen (ed.), *Hexenwelten. Magie und Imagination vom 16.–20. Jahrhundert* (Frankfurt am Main, 1987); Walter Rummel, 'Soziale Dynamik und herrschaftliche Problematik der kurtrierschen Hexenverfolgung. Das Beispiel der Stadt Cochem (1593–1595)', *Geschichte und Gesellschaft*, 16 (1990), 26–55; idem, *Bauern, Herren und Hexen. Studien zur Sozialgeschichte sponheimischer und kurtrierischer Hexenprozesse 1574–1664* (Göttingen, 1991).

[33] However, for discussion of witchcraft cases not involving torture, and of the voluntary element in confessions, see Roper, *Oedipus*.

[34] See Ronald Po-chia Hsia, *Social Discipline in the Reformation: Central Europe 1550–1750* (London, 1989).

divine ordinance. Wicked acts were a result of temptation by the Devil; whether it was witchcraft, murder, or theft, and no matter what the malefactor's motives were for yielding to temptation, the ultimate cause was the same. Punishment was thus directed at the criminal's body, to restore the injured sovereignty of the body politic, to purify God's order on earth by annihilating the incorporation of the Devil's purposes, to redress the balance of the divine creation by cancelling out the offence which had upset it. Punishment in early modern Germany was couched in the language of religious ritual; punishment was a Christian ceremony that signified the unity of the godly and the secular order.

It would be wrong to see these developments simply in terms of a one-way, downward imposition of authority by the state on society. Both Foucault and Elias, in their very different ways, have taught us to see the operation of power in more complex terms: Foucault by emphasizing its structural aspects, Elias by stressing its dependence on the consent of the governed. Applying a less direct, more diffuse model of political and judicial power to German society in the sixteenth and seventeenth centuries enables us to recognize that the state's drive against moral deviance reflected aspects of the moral order within the village community. Popular culture had its own sanctions against minor forms of what it regarded as immorality, from ritual cursing to 'rough music' and the *Haberfeldtreiben*, the German charivari. By targeting deviants such as unpopular wisewomen and witches, pregnant women who killed their babies without the sanction of the village community, religious deviants, open homosexuals, adulterers who went beyond what family and neighbours regarded as permissible, or incestuous partners who disturbed the sexual economy of kinship relations in a small-scale society, the state, backed by the churches, gained legitimacy for its role as an agent of moral policing. Given the general weakness of law enforcement in this period, state agencies were very dependent on popular denunciation in moral offences, as indeed in all types of crime. The intervention of the state in the prosecution and exemplary punishment of representatives of all these types of offender against communal values was a means by which it sought to gain popular legitimacy for its gradual monopolization of the function of law enforcement and control. We shall see in the following chapters a considerable amount of evidence to support the view that the emergence of early modern judicial and penal practice rested at least in part on a basis of implicit popular consent.

c. *The Decline of Capital Punishment*

With few other sanctions available apart from various forms of corporal punishment, and with so many offences, from sodomy to theft, classified as capital crimes, it was not surprising that executions in early modern Germany were a frequent occurrence. Given the fact that there were nearly two thousand different state authorities in the Holy Roman Empire, all of them enjoying full legal powers to punish offenders according to the law, aggregate figures are impossible to compile. However, a good deal of research has been carried out on individual towns, which indicates the broad dimensions of capital punishment in the era of the Reformation and the period following. This research has confirmed historians' previous general impression that, up to 1600 or thereabouts, executions were carried out on a relatively large scale in most German towns for which statistics have been compiled.[35] But during the seventeenth century the situation began to change. In Frankfurt am Main, for example, the number of people executed fell from 248 in the sixteenth century to 140 in the seventeenth, with the biggest drop coming early on, from 106 executions in the two decades 1581 to 1600, to 78 in the years 1601–20, 28 in 1621–40, and 12 in 1641–60. Similarly in Nuremberg executions fell from a peak of 180 in the period 1561 to 1580, to 167 in 1581–1600, and then much more rapidly to 113 in 1601–20, 66 in 1621–40, and 28 in 1641–60. In Augsburg there were 167 executions in the period 1545–96, 81 in the period 1596–1653, and 34 in the years 1654–99. The small town of Mecheln saw a similar decline, from 203 in the fifteenth century and 255 in the sixteenth, to 66 in the seventeenth century and a mere 23 in the eighteenth.[36] Other towns such as Hanover and Celle also saw a long-term fall in the number of executions setting in from the last quarter of the seventeenth century.[37] By the 1700s, therefore, it is unlikely that capital punishment in Germany, across the domains of the Holy Roman Empire, was being carried out at a significantly higher level than in other countries such as France, where it has been estimated, for example, that executions were running at about 300 a year at this time.[38]

A large part of this decline reflected the impact of the Thirty Years War. As plundering and marauding armies repeatedly laid waste whole tracts of the countryside between 1618 and 1648, leaving massive devastation in their wake, the ability of state authorities to detect and prosecute normal criminal offences was sharply reduced. Occasionally they responded to crises of subsistence or natural disasters by unleashing waves of persecution against deviants of various kinds. But these were generally short-lived and did little to restore order.[39] Summary justice by armies frequently replaced the regular operations of the courts. When

[35] Schwerhoff, *Köln*, 155, for 16th-c. statistics.

[36] Dülmen, *Theater*, 113–14; Schuhmann, *Scharfrichter*, 142–4; Karl-Ernst Meinhardt, *Das peinliche Strafrecht der Freien Reichsstadt Frankfurt am Main im Spiegel der Strafpraxis des 16. und 17. Jahrhunderts* (Frankfurt am Main, 1957).

[37] Krause, *Strafrechtspflege*, 196.

[38] John McManners, *Death and the Enlightenment: Changing Attitudes to Death among Christians and Unbelievers in Eighteenth-Century France* (Oxford, 1981), 369.

[39] Andreas Blauert, 'Kriminaljustiz und Sittenreform als Krisenmanagement? Das Hochstift Speyer im 16. und 17. Jahrhundert', in Blauert and Schwerhoff (eds.), *Mit den Waffen*, 115–36.

FIG. 3. *The execution of Melchior Hedloff.* To the right of Hedloff, scenes of his crimes; to the left, the procession from the town to the scaffold, breaking with the wheel, quartering and display of the remains. Note the severed limb on the gallows, bottom left. The title reads: 'Melchior Hedloff, poacher, has committed 251 known murders, and receives therefore his just deserts, in Oels in Silesia, on 19 January 1654, in the 48th year of his life.' The legend points to: 'A. The town hall, where his forefingers are pulled off with red-hot tongs. 1, 2, 3, 4. At 4 places in the town his body is torn with red-hot pincers. 5. Here he is dragged to the scaffold on a hurdle. B. Placard on which his name and murderous deeds are inscribed.'

the war was over, princely authorities were able to generate increased community support for their judicial role by restoring order. At the same time, however, the greater security which they felt after 1648 enabled them to resist popular pressures for a continuation of witchcraft prosecutions. By the second half of the century, the witch-crazes were effectively over, though isolated cases continued to be brought for many decades afterwards. Morality offences also began to decline in number. In Munich, they fell from 30 per cent of all offences in the first half of the seventeenth century to 14 per cent in the first half of the eighteenth, while convictions for crimes against property rose from 25 per cent to 52 per cent. The savage and exemplary penal sanctions of the sixteenth century were gradually giving way to a close mesh of disciplining institutions, including Church courts, regular visitations, and a whole range of other control measures, which were largely in place by the end of the seventeenth. These seem to have succeeded in imposing a much tighter moral order on the community. The price paid was often high. In the Calvinist canton of Zurich, for example, homicide cases declined sharply from a sixteenth-century peak of 35 to 40 a year down to a mere two or three annually well before 1800, but at the same time, the mental and emotional stress which the new regime of godly discipline imposed on the people was indicated by a massive rise in suicide, which by the later eighteenth century reached the levels attained by homicide two centuries before.[40] The devastation caused by the war, the broadly peaceful period of reconstruction that followed, and a new concern with the successful regulation of social and political conflict, all played their part in bringing about major changes in the landscape of crime and law enforcement in Central Europe by about 1700.

With the long-term decline in crimes of violence that began in the seventeenth century, the proportion of men and women among people condemned to death and executed began to alter. In the half-century from 1558 to 1608, for example, women formed 13 per cent of all offenders executed in Danzig. But then the percentage increased dramatically. From 1608 to 1657 they made up 34 per cent, and from 1657 to 1707, 38 per cent of malefactors executed in the city. The figures from Nuremberg tell the same story: the proportion of women among the total of executed offenders rose from 10 per cent in 1533–82, to 12 per cent in 1583–1632, then 38 per cent in 1633–72, and 34 per cent in 1673–1722. In some periods, indeed, as in 1653–62 or 1683–1702, more women than men were executed in Nuremberg. In general, by the middle decades of the eighteenth century, women formed between a third and a half of all those offenders brought to the scaffold in German towns for which figures are available.[41] And this was despite the drastic fall in witchcraft prosecutions that took place in this period. Obviously these proportional changes arose to some extent out of the long-term downward trend in capital offences committed by men in these decades. But this was only part of the story. For the change also reflected an increase in capital offences committed by women, in particular, in convictions for infanticide.

---

[40] Markus Schär, *Seelennöte der Untertanen. Selbstmord, Melancholie und Religion im Alten Zürich 1500–1800* (Zurich, 1985); Hsia, *Social Discipline*; Lyndal Roper, *The Holy Household: Women and Morals in Reformation Augsburg* (Oxford, 1989), 56; Heinz Schilling, 'Sündenzucht und frühneuzeitliche Sozialdisziplinierung. Die calvinistische, presbyteriale Kirchenzucht in Emden vom 16. bis 19. Jahrhundert', in Georg Schmidt (ed.), *Stände und Gesellschaft im Alten Reich* (Wiesbaden, 1989), 265–302.

[41] Dülmen, *Frauen*, 67–71.

Until the middle of the sixteenth century, prosecutions for infanticide seem to have been relatively rare in Germany. Whether this was because infanticide itself was not commonly practised must be doubted; it is more likely that infanticide enjoyed a degree of toleration in community and state which prevented most cases from coming to court. By the middle of the seventeenth century, however, such cases had grown in number to such an extent that infanticide ranked with witchcraft in frequency as a female offence. In Danzig, in the half-century from 1558 to 1608, seven women were executed for infanticide; in the next half-century, twenty-one; and in the following half-century, twenty-two. Moreover, in the first of these three periods, infanticides formed only 17 per cent of all women executed in the city, while in the second it was 43 per cent and in the third, 58 per cent. In 1708–17, nine women were executed in the city for infanticide and only three for other offences (all murder). This development was paralleled in other cities. In Nuremberg, twenty-eight women were executed for infanticide from 1543 to 1633, making 41 per cent of all women executed in the town during this period. In the following ninety years, up to 1722, thirty women were executed for infanticide out of forty-eight in total, or 63 per cent. In Leipzig there was one execution in each of the years 1750, 1751, 1757, and 1762, four in 1763, two in 1764, and one each in 1769, 1774, 1776, and 1790. Half of the fourteen people executed were women, all of them for infanticide.[42] And this absolute increase went far beyond any increase in the overall female population of the towns in question. With the decline in witchcraft prosecutions that had set in by the middle of the seventeenth century, infanticide had become the major female capital offence.

The increase in executions for both crimes during the sixteenth and seventeenth centuries reflected the emergence, once more, of a moral offensive directed by the authorities, both in the Free Cities and in the territorial states, towards strengthening marriage and the household as the basis of the social order. Many witchcraft prosecutions were aimed at women who did not have family ties or were sexually or socially deviant in some way. Whether or not any real increase in infanticide took place from the sixteenth to the eighteenth century, as worried contemporaries maintained it did, has been hotly disputed by historians.[43] Whatever the case may be, the growing number of executions for this offence certainly reflected a determination on the part of both secular and ecclesiastical authorities in Reformation and post-Reformation Germany to stamp it out. It may also have signified a declining tolerance for infanticide in

---

[42] StA Leipzig L XII G 23b vol. ii Bl. 4: Executiones seit Ao. 1750; also Dülmen, *Theater*, 62.

[43] Ulbricht, 'Kindsmörderinnen', in Blauert and Schwerhoff (eds.), *Mit den Waffen*; and idem, 'Infanticide in Eighteenth-Century Germany', in Evans (ed.), *The German Underworld*, 108–40.

urban and rural communities at the same time. The moralization of society during this period, the difficulty of an unmarried mother retaining her honour, her prospects, and her position in such a society, and the tendency of the organs of social and moral control to stigmatize allegedly promiscuous females as social outcasts, with all the hardships this implied—all these developments encouraged any woman who gave birth outside wedlock to conceal her pregnancy as far as she could and kill her baby as soon as possible after birth: a combination of actions observable in the vast majority of cases which came before the courts. Most of these women were poor serving-girls with no means of obtaining employment or supporting their child once its father—almost always a man of the same social standing, such as a farmhand or rural labourer—had refused marriage and decamped from the scene.

Infanticide was held to be a particularly heinous crime by the authorities in the early modern period. Like parricide or matricide, it was killing one's own flesh and blood. Like robbery with murder, it was committed against a defenceless victim. Both these other offences were treated especially harshly for these very reasons. Official proclamations against infanticide repeatedly declared it to be 'bestial' and 'against nature': a decree issued in Nuremberg in 1702 declared that 'such Godforsaken infanticides and depraved women surpass the nature even of the cruelest wild beasts, which are still accustomed to feed and protect with all due care the young they have brought into the world'.[44] Above and beyond this, infanticide was a crime committed against a guiltless, spotless, innocent human being; it was not only inhuman, it was also unchristian. Murdering an infant affected its soul as well as its body, by depriving it of baptism and thus of eternal as well as earthly life. It was not by chance that infanticide formed a central part of the demonological mythology of the witches' sabbath, where babies were supposed to be ritually killed in order to provide magical potions and ointments for the witches; and it is not surprising that many women convicted of the crime attributed their actions to the blandishments of the Devil when the time came to confess.[45] Finally, by killing their new-born infants, women denied the primacy of their role as mothers, and rejected the function for which they were intended by society, the reproduction of the Christian community and the state. Even in the first few decades of the eighteenth century, infanticide prosecutions continued unabated.[46] Authorities reacted to what they perceived as the increased incidence of infanticide by making punishments more severe. In Prussia, drowning, effectively abandoned a few years earlier, was reintroduced for infanticide under Friedrich Wilhelm I. In Danzig, infanticides were now dragged to the

---

[44] Dülmen, *Frauen*, 21–2.   [45] Ibid. 23.
[46] Burghartz, 'Equation', 57–74. See also Dülmen, *Frauen*, 109–12.

scaffold bound in an oxhide; unusually for women, they were then broken with the wheel; and their remains were displayed on the scaffold after death.[47]

By the late seventeenth century, Germany was becoming a more ordered society, with falling levels of violent crime, the decline of the witchcraft hysteria, the end of religious wars, and a much lower level of capital offences than before. All over Europe, levels of interpersonal violence were falling drastically in the late seventeenth and early eighteenth centuries.[48] Executions in Germany were now taking place far less frequently than they had been a hundred or so years before, and the variety of punishments laid down by the *Carolina* was gradually becoming less extravagant.[49] In particular, breaking with the wheel, common in Taylor's day, was on the decline in most parts of Germany. In Augsburg, for example, there was only one case recorded in the whole of the seventeenth century, and only one in the eighteenth (up to 1806), while there were only six cases in Nuremberg in the seventeenth century and one in the eighteenth. In Frankfurt no one was broken with the wheel at all after 1640.[50] Elsewhere, particularly in Prussia, the practice continued, but there can be no doubt of its decline on a more general scale. In the course of the sixteenth century, too, hanging gradually became a less frequently used method of execution. The normal punishment for theft at this time, it was, like breaking with the wheel, mainly carried out on male offenders. Here too the body was left to rot on the gallows, for a period that corresponded roughly to the severity of the offence as determined by the court. Up to about 1600 it was one of the most frequent means of execution used in Germany. In Cologne between 1568 and 1617, forty offenders were hanged, compared to 112 beheaded with the sword, but in other cities the proportions were reversed.[51] In Frankfurt am Main, for example, twice as many executions were carried out by hanging in the period 1562–80 as by all other methods combined. But by the period 1621–40 hangings were in a clear minority among capital punishments in the city. In Augsburg hangings outnumbered all other types of execution in the years 1545–96, but here too they declined, and by the years 1654–99 they made up less than 10 per cent of the executions held in the city.[52]

What replaced them was above all decapitation by the sword, which applied to people convicted of manslaughter, robbery, incest, infanticide, or major fraud.

[47] Dülmen, *Frauen*, 50–1.

[48] Eric A. Johnson and Eric H. Monkkonen (eds.), *Violent Crime in Town and Country since the Middle Ages* (forthcoming), present a series of statistical and historical studies in support of this contention.

[49] Schwerhoff, *Köln*, 158–9.

[50] Dülmen, *Theater*, 117; Schuhmann, *Scharfrichter*, 142; Schindler, *Verbrechen*, 51–3.

[51] Schwerhoff, *Köln*, 158–9.

[52] Dülmen, *Theater*, 117; Schuhmann, *Scharfrichter*, 142; Schindler, *Verbrechen*, 48–51. For the continued dominance of hanging in Hanover, see Krause, *Strafrechtspflege*, 181–2.

Once the traditional privilege of the nobility, it was used by the later seventeenth century for all classes of offenders. With the establishment of more settled political circumstances and the growing stability of the state, armed revolts and conspiracies led by the nobility became rare in Germany, and condemnations and executions of members of the aristocracy virtually disappeared. The need to preserve a special means of dispatch for overmighty subjects thus disappeared as well. Execution with the sword was carried out by a horizontal, backhanded blow, much in the manner described by Taylor. As late as 1856, instructions issued to executioners in the Kingdom of Hanover laid down precise details of the size of the sword—four feet long, including the grip, and 4 inches wide—and the way in which the blow was to be dealt: 'The executioner must grasp the lower side of the hilt with the left hand and the upper with the right. . . . He must put his left foot forward and his right back. . . . He must strike the blow from left to right. . . . He must look, not at the blade, but at the middle part of the neck.'[53] Despite the difficulty of executing such a manœuvre, it was undoubtedly quicker and less painful than hanging or breaking with the wheel, provided it was carried out correctly. Of the various other forms of capital punishment enumerated in the *Carolina*, many were in practice already falling into disuse by the time of the Englishman John Taylor's visit to Hamburg in 1616. Burial alive, the equivalent for women of breaking with the wheel for men, was no longer practised after the early seventeenth century. Drowning, which was also applied to women, especially for offences against religion or morality, such as infanticide, adultery, and heresy, did continue to be used into the early eighteenth century, but with rapidly diminishing frequency. In many towns, such as Speyer, it had already fallen into desuetude well before Taylor's time.[54] Burning at the stake, used above all against witches and heretics, but also against sodomites and arsonists, was also declining in incidence. In Nuremberg, for example, six cases of burning alive were recorded in the sixteenth century, only two in the seventeenth, and none at all thereafter.[55] There was a burning in the Tyrol in 1778, and isolated instances elsewhere until shortly after 1800, and burning at the stake remained a punishment in law a good deal longer than this, but it had become extremely rare in practice by the end of the eighteenth century. Capital punishment not only

---

[53] HStA Hanover Hann. 173a Nr. 436, Bl. 18–19: Anweisung für Scharfrichter über das Verfahren bei Enthauptungen (15 Dec. 1856). It follows that the numerous drawings and paintings depicting a forehand blow are either imagined, or wrongly remembered, by the artist, or have been reversed in reproduction. The Hanover instructions carefully noted that the positions described should be reversed in the case of a left-handed executioner.

[54] Theodor Harster, *Das Strafrecht der Freien Reichsstadt Speyer in Theorie und Praxis* (Breslau, 1900), 72.

[55] Dülmen, *Theater*, 122–6; Schindler, *Verbrechen*, 57.

Fɪɢ. 4. *Burning at the stake*. Public execution of a gang of convicted arsonists in Frankfurt an der Oder on 5 October 1725. Note the priests attending the malefactors, the ravenstone, the gallows and wheel on the right, and the gentry and women among the spectators. The legend reads: 'No. 1: Johann Friedrich Gottlieb is burned alive. No. 2: Maria Elisabeth Neumann is beheaded and then burned. No. 3: Andreas Sottmeyer on the skinner's wagon is burned next. No. 4: The old Frau Neumann is beheaded, her head nailed to a post, and the rump burned. No. 5: The old Sottmeyer woman looks on, is then burned alive. No. 6: Johann Chrystoph Neumann, his hands bound, looks at Gottlieb being burned.'

declined in overall incidence during this period, therefore, it also lost much of its former complexity and variety.[56]

As they became less frequent, executions became occasions for ever more emphatic demonstrations of state and community power. As the forms of punishment which had not been tied to a specific place, such as burial alive or drowning, declined, the spatial structure of executions became more determinate, allowing tradition and custom to form a fixed basis on which they could be elaborated.[57] The ritual and ceremonial aspects of capital punishment grew steadily more complicated and formalized as the occasions themselves became less of an everyday occurrence. This process was reinforced by the emergence of Absolutism under the influence of the French model of kingship epitomized by the figure of Louis XIV towards the end of the seventeenth century. As the state arrogated to itself more and more of the right to punish, so it dispensed with modes of execution the utility of which it no longer recognized. Chief among these were forms of capital punishment that could be seen as invoking the power of the natural elements—fire (as in burning at the stake), earth (as in burial alive), and water (as in drowning). In the world of Absolutism, punishment had to be seen as coming directly from the state itself, through concrete physical actions undertaken by the state's servant, the executioner, on the body of the offender.[58] The full execution ritual, with its elaborate procession and ceremonial procedures at the scaffold, was a phenomenon of the late seventeenth and eighteenth centuries, and crowds attending it were a consequence of the state's increasing tendency to orchestrate such occasions, as well as of the increasing rarity of capital punishment itself. Illustrations of executions in the fourteenth and fifteenth centuries show them as casual and unceremonial affairs, with a handful of people standing informally around while the hangman does his work; but the iconography of execution becomes more elaborate from the late seventeenth century onwards, until by the late eighteenth century execution prints are vast and complicated representations with numbers and legends to indicate what is going on in various parts of the picture. Absolutism, from the great patrimonies of Austria and Prussia, Saxony and Bavaria, down to the petty principalities and city-states that littered Central Europe in this period, demanded that sovereignty be asserted with pomp and circumstance, and executions, as embodiments of the ultimate power of the state over its subjects, clearly translated this demand into practice, inscribing the sovereign's and the community's will on the subject's body and displaying it for all to see.

---

[56] Heinz Moser, *Die Scharfrichter von Tirol. Ein Beitrag zur Geschichte des Strafvollzuges in Tirol von 1497–1787* (Innsbruck, 1982), 108.

[57] Spierenburg, *Spectacle*, 44–5.   [58] Dülmen, *Theater*, 121.

FIG. 5. *The informality of the sixteenth-century execution.* A crowd at an execution in Chur, Graubünden (Switzerland), in 1575, stones a drunken executioner who has taken several blows to dispatch three condemned men and is sawing off the head of the last one. Stoning was the traditional reaction of crowds to executioners who bungled their job and thereby disrupted the execution ritual. Note the informality of the circumstances: no ravenstone, no troops, and a crowd numbering just twenty, including several children.

FIG. 6. *The elaboration of the eighteenth-century execution.* This print shows Matthias Klostermaier, a famous poacher known as the 'Bavarian Hiesl', being dragged to the scaffold wrapped in a raw, wet, oxhide (top right), and broken with the wheel (centre). Note the military presence, the numerous priests on the scaffold, and the large crowd, including women and children (especially the woman holding up her daughter to get a better view, bottom right).

d. Honour and Dishonour

In medieval and early modern Germany, as in other parts of Europe at this time, the body was not simply the integral possession of the individual human being, but rather a socially defined entity, signifying status and standing in a corporate, highly stratified social system. Class divisions based on income and property were less meaningful in this pre-industrial world than were status distinctions based on rank and degree. Such distinctions were so important that they were publicly advertised, for example, by codes of dress, with sumptuary laws enforcing the wearing of clothes and appurtenances (such as swords) appropriate to one's given station in life. And they were cemented by the pervasive notion of honour (*Ehre*), an almost tangible yet abstract set of socially defined qualities that marked people as belonging to a particular station in life through the attitudes and behaviour patterns they manifested.[59] Honour in this society was apportioned according to status; it was *Standesehre*. Courtly or princely honour differed from knightly honour; both could be augmented by an individual through princely or knightly deeds, or maintained by following the appropriate rules of behaviour laid down in the handbooks and guides that proliferated during this period; but however great the deeds, an honourable reputation was inevitably confined to the station within which it had been inherited or acquired.[60] Moreover, the position in society held by princes, nobles, and knights was signified not only by their titles but also by a mass of legally binding rights and privileges. These included special treatment under the law, such as the right not to be subjected to corporal punishment or the right, in other words, to be punished in accordance with their dignity and station in society should they commit an offence. The nobility were also allowed to defend their honour, as others could not, in a duel, should it be impugned. And they were expected to avoid demeaning activities such as trade, which were thought inappropriate to their noble status.

Every station in life was apportioned its appropriate form of honour. Substantial peasant farmers were 'honourable', a fact which allowed them to defend their position in lawsuits brought against grasping feudal lords who attempted to force on them labour dues and services not laid down in custom or law.[61] The

[59] Ute Frevert, 'Bourgeois Honour: Middle-Class Duellists in Germany from the Late Eighteenth to the Early Twentieth Century', in David Blackbourn and Richard J. Evans (eds.), *The German Bourgeoisie: Essays in the Social History of the German Middle Class from the Late Eighteenth to the Early Twentieth Century* (London, 1991), 255–92, here 255–7.

[60] Friedriche Zunkel, 'Ehre', in Otto Brunner, Werner Conze, and Reinhart Koselleck (eds.), *Geschichtliche Grundbegriffe. Historisches Lexikon zur politisch-sozialen Sprache in Deutschland*, ii (Stuttgart, 1975), 1–63, here 14–16.

[61] William W. Hagen, 'The Junkers' Faithless Servants: Peasant Insubordination and the Breakdown of Serfdom in Brandenburg-Prussia, 1763–1811', in Richard J. Evans and W. R. Lee (eds.), *The German Peasantry: Conflict and Community in Rural Society from the Eighteenth to the Twentieth Century* (London, 1986), 71–101.

merchants, lawyers, patricians, and notables who provided the ruling caste in most of Germany's towns and cities at this period, especially among the eighty or more Free or Imperial Cities that were not beholden to any territorial lord or prince, had their own honour too, signified by their common description as *Honoratioren*. Even those townsfolk who worked with their hands had an appropriate degree of honour. Artisans such as silversmiths, carpenters, tailors, shoemakers, and the like, were organized in fixed corporations which exercised a tight control over the provision of the relevant goods or services. The possession of honourable status was crucial to the members of guilds, especially the guild masters. Their honour was the guarantee that they could be relied upon to produce genuine, well-made, and unadulterated goods, to charge a just price for them, and to take their proper share of responsibility in running the affairs of the town they lived in. Should they lose it, they also lost their membership of their guild, their right to trade, and their livelihood.[62] Honour was the glue that held this society together; only the honourable could play a part in exercising power; and the loss of honour was a serious business that could spell ruin. For women, much more than for men, honour was a product of sexual propriety and conformity; and here too, infamy could mean the end of marriageability and the threat of poverty and destitution.[63]

Thus many of the punishments meted out by German justice in the medieval and early modern period involved an implicit or explicit branding of the offender as dishonourable, using the language of the body to reassign him or her to a new place in the social hierarchy.[64] In some cases this meant little more than a public recognition of an infamy that had already been conferred by the nature of the crime. In others, it conferred an additional burden, for example in the form of a 'mask of shame' (*Schandmaske*) which the offender was obliged to wear at the pillory, or the more common wooden yoke or collar known as the 'fiddle' (*Geige* or *Fidel*). Such minor punishments as these often had no lasting effect on the status of the offender, especially where, as in the overwhelming majority of cases, this was already low or dishonourable, or where they were meted out to people with whose offences—poaching, perhaps, or resistance to an unpopular land-

[62] Zunkel, 'Ehre', 40–4; Jutta Nowosadtko, 'Die Ehre, die Unehre und das Staatsinteresse. Konzepte und Funktionen von "Unehrlichkeit" im historischen Wandel am Beispiel des Kurfürstentums Bayern', *Geschichte in Wissenschaft und Unterricht*, 44 (1993), 362–81; Dülmen, *Kultur und Alltag*, ii. 194–214. More generally, see Martin Dinges, 'Die Ehre als Thema der Stadtgeschichte. Eine Semantik am Übergang vom Ancien Régime zur Moderne', *Zeitschrift für historische Forschung*, 16 (1989), 409–40.

[63] For women, see Roper, *Holy Household*; Susanna Burghartz, 'Weibliche Ehre', in Gisela Bock, Heide Wunder, and Karin Hausen (eds.), *Frauengeschichte—Geschlechtergeschichte* (Frankfurt am Main, 1992), 173–83; and Gerd Schwerhoff, ' "Mach, dass wir nicht in eine Schande geraten!" Frauen in Kölner Kriminalfällen des 16. Jahrhunderts', *Geschichte in Wissenschaft und Unterricht*, 43 (1993), 451–73.

[64] Kai-Detlev Sievers, 'Prügelstrafe als Zeichen ständischer Ungleichheit', in Karl Köstlin and Kai-Detlev Sievers (eds.), *Das Recht der kleinen Leute. Festschrift für Karl-Sigismund Kramer* (Berlin, 1976), 195–206.

lord—the local community sympathized.[65] But punishments such as branding or mutilation cast a permanent stigma of dishonour upon the offender from which it was extremely difficult to escape. And more serious crimes often brought with them a higher degree of infamy. Modes of execution which denied the condemned any freedom of bodily movement, such as hanging or breaking with the wheel, when they went to their death bound and helpless, were dishonourable, while decapitation with the sword was not, because the condemned remained free and unbound, received the fatal stroke kneeling and therefore upright, and had to show enough 'honourable' self-control to remain still so that the executioner could deliver an accurate blow.[66] A description of the execution of a nobleman in 1720 emphasized, for instance, that he 'disrobed himself, kneeled down, and as the priest cried out to him the words "Lord Jesus, I live", etc. etc., endured the swordstroke quite bravely and with unbound eyes.'[67] Thus were noblemen supposed to die. Even as late as 1854, a report on methods of execution drawn up in the Bavarian Ministry of Justice noted the widespread belief

that beheading with the sword is the worthiest and at the same time the least agonizing and the quickest of all forms of death. In particular, the merit of this form of death is derived from the fact that the criminal apparently mounts the scaffold freely and receives the deathstroke in an upright position. Thus the impression is given that the criminal freely submits to the law and the punishment meted out to him. Moreover, through the upright posture, the human being is accorded respect even in the person of the malefactor.[68]

The relative absence of infamy conferred by execution with the sword could be judged from the fact that the body was usually not displayed after death, but was often removed by the family and given a Christian burial. Only in more severe cases would the authorities rule that the body had to be buried underneath the gallows or bound to a wheel and left to rot.[69] The stipulation that a capital offender should be dragged to the scaffold wrapped in an oxhide was extremely degrading, on the other hand, because it rendered the condemned helpless from the very outset, not permitting them to walk upright through the streets on the way to the scaffold. Zedler's *Universal-Lexicon* of 1745, one of the earliest of the

[65] Gerd Schwerhoff, 'Verordnete Schande? Spätmittelalterliche und frühneuzeitliche Ehrenstrafen zwischen Rechtsakt und sozialer Sanktion', in Blauert and Schwerhoff (eds.), *Mit den Waffen*, 158–88.

[66] Dülmen, *Theater*, 65–6; Karl-S. Kramer, *Bauern und Bürger im Nachmittelalterlichen Unterfranken. Eine Volkskunde auf Grund archivalischer Quellen* (Veröffentlichungen der Gesellschaft für fränkische Geschichte, IX. 12, Würzburg, 1957), 94–5; Hinckeldey (ed.), *Justiz*, 335–48.

[67] Anon., *Umständliche Nachricht von der am 1sten Martii Anno 1720 geschehenen Enthauptung des auf der Festung Königstein gefangen gewesenen und zu zweyen Mahlen auf der Flucht aus den Arrest ergriffenen bekannten Barons von Kettenberg, welcher desselben letzte Klage und Trost-Worte, auch darauf erfolgte Antwort beygefüget sind* (1720).

[68] HStA Munich MJu 13066: Alleruntertänigster Bericht des Staats-Ministeriums der Justiz an seine Majestät den König, dem Vollzug der Todesstrafe betreffend, 30 May 1854.

[69] Dülmen, *Theater*, 138–40; Schindler, *Verbrechen*, 46–8.

new encyclopaedias that heralded the arrival of the German Enlightenment, considered that the degradation of this punishment came from the fact that the offender 'is dragged to the scaffold by a brute beast'. But the dishonour also derived from the fact that the oxhide was fresh, or in other words still untanned, and therefore dirty, bloody, smelly, and polluting.[70] The exposure of the corpse on the scaffold after execution added to the infamy of the offender: 'For, though no more bodily pain is inflicted hereby, yet the shame done to the body by the denial of burial is accounted an increase in the punishment.'[71]

e. The German Executioner

The most dishonouring element of all in a German execution was the touch of the executioner. Zedler's encyclopaedia explained that this functionary— variously known as 'hangman, executioner, after-judge, bogeyman, freeman, malletmaster'—was the man

who carries out criminal judgments and executes bodily and capital punishments. . . . Those who let themselves thus be used are separated from the rest of human society in several respects. Nay more, they are accounted dishonourable, and accordingly their children are excluded from crafts and guilds on roughly the following grounds: because they kill their fellow humans and co-religionists, people by whom they have not been injured or insulted, for wages, and not straightforwardly, but by all manner of torment, people who are bound, and cannot defend themselves, and who have also been branded dishonourable by their misdeeds.[72]

But this was far too simple and rationalistic an account of the stigma under which the executioner had to suffer. Dishonourable he was: the mere touch of his hand could rob people of their honour, defiling them and rendering them unfit for intercourse with society.[73] In the prison at Glückstadt as late as 1839, it was declared: 'All those criminals who have been in the hands of the hangman are called dishonourable and will be kept separate from the others, while they are working, eating, and sleeping, in chapel, or when they are sick.'[74] If an executioner bungled his work and aroused the wrath of the crowd, their invariable response was not to lay hands upon him but to stone him from a safe distance.[75]

[70] J. R. Nöggeler, *Der Bayerische Hiesel. Wahre unentstellte Geschichte des Matthäus Klostermeier* (Reutlingen, 1807), 198–9.

[71] *Zedlers Grosses Vollständiges Universal Lexicon aller Wissenschaften und Künste* (Leipzig and Halle, 1745), xl. 585: 'Straffe (peinliche)'.

[72] Ibid., xii. 1,359: 'Hencker'.

[73] Zunkel, 'Ehre', 16. See also Richard van Dülmen, 'Der infame Mensch. Unehrliche Arbeit und soziale Ausgrenzung in der Frühen Neuzeit', in idem (ed.), *Arbeit, Frömmigkeit und Eigensinn* (Frankfurt am Main, 1990), 106–40.

[74] Oppelt, *Unehrlichkeit*, 523.

[75] For stoning in France, see G. Lenôtre, *The Guillotine and its Servants* (London, 1929), 211–12.

When the cadavers of executed criminals were taken for dissection, as a later account testified, 'even the learned physicians at the Anatomical Institute forbore to dissect a cadaver that had been touched by the hands of the executioner's servants until it had been rendered honourable once more by pressing the seal of office against the left side of the head'.[76] Hanging and breaking with the wheel were considered infamous not least because they involved the executioner and his assistants manhandling the offender, while decapitation with the sword was honourable because it did not, apart (in some instances) from the holding of the head, which by the eighteenth century was in practice usually done with a leather sling, thus involving no direct physical contact between the executioner, or his servants, and the criminal. The shift from the rope and the wheel to the sword in the seventeenth century was not least the result of constant petitioning from the relatives of the condemned for the commutation of the sentence from one that would degrade them to one that would not.[77] A public whipping at the pillory (*Staupenschlag*) dishonoured offenders because it involved the executioner or his servants handling them while making them fast.[78]

Infamy of this kind also left its mark on the offender's closest relatives. Status, in this society, was above all linked to family and lineage. Executioners were considered so infamous that it was difficult for any of them to get married except to another executioner's daughter, a fact which helped create large and ramified dynasties of hangmen and further cut them off from the rest of society. The extent to which an executioner could be isolated from honourable society was suggested by a case that came up in 1796 in the Bavarian town of Kaufbeuren, where the guilds punished three journeymen weavers because they had danced with an executioner's daughter. The town council forced the guilds to withdraw the punishment and declare the journeymen to be 'honest and honourable lads', on the grounds that the Holy Roman Empire had passed a law in 1731 declaring all trades except skinners to be honourable. This was indeed the case, the result not least of frequent disputes between various infamous trades and the guild masters during the seventeenth century. But the guilds had never accepted the decision, and they continued to stigmatize executioners in various ways for decades thereafter.[79] Their children could still find it difficult to get employment even in the late eighteenth century.[80] In Frankfurt am Main, it took a lawsuit of three and a half years and an appeal to the Holy Roman Emperor himself before Johann Michael Hofmann, son of the local executioner, was admitted to the

---

[76] Max Roderich, *Verbrechen und Strafe. Eine Sammlung interessanter Polizei- und Criminal-Rechtsfälle, nach den Acten bearbeitet* (Jena, 1850), 326–30.

[77] Dülmen, *Theater*, 44–8.

[78] Wilhelm Breithaupt, *Die Strafe des Staupenschlags und ihre Abschaffung im Gemeinen Recht* (Jena, 1938), 9.

[79] Schuhmann, *Scharfrichter*, 160–8, 209–10.   [80] Moser, *Scharfrichter von Tirol*, 39.

college of physicians in the town, even though he had studied medicine at three universities and had a doctorate from Strasbourg.[81] In many towns, the executioner was barred from entering the local inn, or, if he did, had a special mug to drink from, which no one else was allowed to touch. Sometimes a special small room would be reserved for him in a particular inn, to remove him from the rest of the company. In Augsburg, the executioners even had their own special brewer, who had no other customers. They obtained their meat from a particular butcher, who was enjoined to serve no one else. Complaints were recorded in Burgau in 1771 and Tangstedt in 1772 about the executioner sitting in the same pew as the other citizens in church; normally a special seat was reserved for him.[82] Even burial was a problem, for no one wanted to touch the executioner's corpse.[83] Sometimes, as in 1779, in the principality of Ansbach, the executioner's coffin was borne by his relatives and colleagues on a bier specially constructed for the purpose. Another solution was for representatives of all the guilds to participate in the funeral, so as to neutralize the ill-fame by spreading it across the whole of the urban social structure.[84]

Of course, the dishonorable status of the executioner varied in degree from place to place, partly according to local law and custom, partly in response to varying social structures and the relative strength of the artisan guilds in different cities. It was also possible for executioners to hire others to perform the most dishonourable of their functions—hanging as opposed to beheading, for example—and so to improve their own personal status, a practice which seems to have been particularly widespread in north Germany.[85] The boundaries of honour and dishonour were always uncertain and contested. Different guilds could interpret them in different ways. When tensions between artisans and others in the urban community ran high, contact with a dishonourable person could be a far more serious matter than at other times. Executioners were ostracized neither completely nor universally in early modern Germany. The strong support lent by both the Catholic and the Protestant churches to capital punishment throughout the early modern period meant, for example, that they regarded executioners not as sinful and murderous individuals, but as executors of God's will, and so admitted them to Holy Communion. In many parts of Germany, however, the boundaries between the executioner and honourable society began to harden from the late seventeenth century. The decline in capital punishment reduced executioners' income and forced their children to seek honourable employment,

---

[81] Meinhardt, *Strafrecht*, 54.   [82] Oppelt, *Unehrlichkeit*, 479–80.

[83] Otto Beneke, *Von unehrlichen Leuten. Cultur-historische Studien und Geschichten aus vergangenen Tagen deutscher Gewerbe und Dienste, mit besonderer Rücksicht auf Hamburg* (Hamburg, 1865), 156–7, 161–2.

[84] Oppelt, *Unehrlichkeit*, 413.   [85] Wilbertz, *Scharfrichter*, provides numerous examples.

which led to a massive growth in disputes as artisan guilds insisted ever more strongly on their ineligibility for membership. Even before this time, whatever the variations from town to town, there can be no doubt about the centrality of executioners and their assistants to the social economy of dishonour; and indeed artisans frequently deduced the dishonourable status of other marginal groups in society from their contact with the executioner or one or other of his numerous official functions.[86]

The role of dishonour in punishment and its execution can also be clearly read from the taboos surrounding the gallows in many parts of Germany. When the scaffold belonging to a town was repaired or rebuilt, a special 'gallows festival', the *Galgenfest*, was usually held by all the guilds acting together, to make sure that those who carried out the task would not be defiled by it. Such ceremonies were often extremely elaborate and expensive, and sometimes went on for several days.[87] In 1681, when the gallows were repaired in Hallstadt, the mayor and town council led all the guilds apart from the butchers in a procession which paced ritually round the scaffold three times both before and after the repairs had been carried out. Large amounts of food and drink were consumed on such occasions. At a gallows festival held in Bamberg in 1601, 924 loaves and 363 pounds of beef were eaten, washed down with 54 measures of wine and 16 pitchers of beer.[88] In 1794, the restoration of the scaffold in the north German Hanseatic city of Lübeck required elaborate arrangements to ensure that none of the guildsmen who took part was dishonoured. The artisans went in solemn procession and accompanied by music, to a formal meeting with the city's Master of Buildings, who appeared before them 'in a red coat decorated with gold, a yellow waistcoat and yellow breeches, also carrying a sword with a gold scabbard and accoutered with boots and spurs.' A military band, the guildsmen and senior journeymen, sixty grenadiers and fifty other troops, all in festive clothing, marched through the town and gathered before the scaffold, where the Master of Buildings gave a formal justification of the need for repairing them, and struck the first three blows on the structure with each kind of tool to be used. After the renovation was completed, the tools were ceremonially thrown away by the youngest apprentice; they were too dishonoured to be employed for any other task.[89] All this testified to the potency of the gallows as an object of ill-fame. In the same year, the master

---

[86] Kathleen Stuart, 'The Boundaries of Honor: Dishonorable People in Augsburg, 1510–1800' (Ph.D. diss., Yale University, 1993).

[87] Kramer, *Verbrechen*, 90.

[88] Ibid. 245–7. See also Uwe Danker, *Räuberbanden im Alten Reich um 1700. Ein Beitrag zur Geschichte von Herrschaft und Kriminalität um 1700* (Frankfurt am Main, 1988), 188. For another example, see Oppelt, *Unehrlichkeit*, 569.

[89] Johannes Warncke, 'Die Reparatur des Prangers und des Hochgerichts zu Lübeck im Jahre 1794. Ein Beitrag zur Verrufserklärung seitens der Handwerker', *Die Heimat*, 21 (1911), 278–83.

tailor Johannes Graser was declared infamous and fined five schillings by his fellow guild masters in the town of Gengenbach because he 'wilfully leaned on the gallows during the execution of the glazier Peter Heim'. Graser retorted that 'the gallows were built by honourable people, and he could not therefore be punished for this imagined infamy'. The authorities eventually told the guilds to reinstate him.[90] But the incident, like others of its kind,[91] demonstrated how that which honourable men had built could quickly be dishonoured by the use to which it was put.

Gallows were rendered infamous by the mere touch of malefactors and executioners. Thus it seemed natural for the latter to carry out other duties in society which involved contact with physically or socially polluting bodies. This also proved a useful way of providing them with an adequate income, so it became increasingly common from the sixteenth century onwards to link the executioner's job with other duties.[92] John Taylor, on his visit to Hamburg in 1616, confessed himself deeply impressed with the wide variety of functions fulfilled by the local hangman. These made him, in Taylor's view, a wealthy and important figure, 'compared to whom our Tyburn tatterdemalion, or our Wapping wind-pipe stretcher, is but a ragamuffin, not worth the hanging'. 'The privileges of this grand halter-master', he wrote, 'are many.' To the hangman, for example, belonged the privilege of collecting the annual dog tax and attaching a label to all dogs already paid for:

Once a year in the dog-days he sends out his men with baits instead of Bulls, with full power from his greatness, to knock down all the curs without contradiction, whose masters or owners will not be at the charge to buy a pardon for them of his mightiness, which pardon is more durable than the Popes of wax or parchment, for his is made of a piece of the hide of an ox, a horse, or such lasting stuff, which with his stigmatical stamp or seal is hanged about every dog's neck who is freed from his fury by the purchase of his pardon.

Moreover, reported Taylor, 'all oxen, kine, horses, hogs, dogs, or any such beasts, if they die themselves, or if they be not like to live, the hangman must knock them on the heads, and have their skins'; anyone else who dared to do this would be 'abhorred and accounted a villain without redemption'. All this, said Taylor, made the hangman a good deal of money, and 'with hangings, headings, breakings, pardoning and killing of dogs, flaying of beasts, emptying of vaults, and such privy commodities, his whole revenue sometimes amounts to 4. or 5. hundred pounds a year'.[93]

[90] Oppelt, *Unehrlichkeit*, 547.
[91] For a comparable case from 1769, see Uwe Puschner, *Handwerk zwischen Tradition und Wandel. Das Münchener Handwerk an der Wende vom 18. zum 19. Jahrhundert* (Göttingen, 1988), 208–9.
[92] Wilbertz, *Scharfrichter*, 27–8.   [93] Taylor, *Three Weekes*.

The 'vaults' to which Taylor referred were the town drains and cesspits, which executioners were still charged with clearing in many towns during the eighteenth century. They had to clean out people's toilets and take excrement out of the city on a cart.[94] It also fell to them to drive out lepers from the town, and to capture and kill rabid dogs. This was the purpose of the annual round-up of stray curs; for all of those which were not reclaimed by their owners or kept indoors during the round-up would be put down by the executioner as dangers to public health. In Hanover, for instance, the executioner's contract required of him: 'When he is commanded at certain times to strike the dogs dead, he is to make not the slightest pecuniary demand relating to this duty, under no pretext whatsoever, but is to carry out the said killing and also the immediate disposal of the carcasses without payment.'[95] Similarly, it was the hangman's job to dispose of the bodies of suicides, who of course could not be given a Christian burial. Even as late as 1794, the Prussian legislators reaffirmed the principle that suicides who had shown no evidence of having repented before their death should be buried by the executioner.[96] This was usually done by interring them beneath the gallows or, as in a case in Schongau in Bavaria in 1732, burning the body and scattering the ashes in the river. In Hanover the executioner had to provide four large hunting dogs, 'and if wolf-hunts are held in the above-named districts, to obtain the bait to lure the quarry wherever it is asked for'.[97]

Most common of all was for the office of executioner, especially in smaller communities, to be combined with that of the local skinner or knacker (*Abdecker* or *Wasenmeister*). The leases signed for knacker's yards often made virtually no distinction between the two offices. The contract signed by the Bremen town Senate and the executioner Johann Christian Göppel on 27 June 1738, for instance, required the latter to officiate not only 'whenever a person is beheaded, hanged, broken with the wheel, or executed by any other means, or tortured, flogged, or expelled here for his misdeeds' but also when any of the citizens 'has a dead horse, cow, bullock or ox fetched from his house or stall and taken away'. It laid down fees for the burial of suicides and the removal of excrement from the city's 'closets' (paid by the cubic foot), and prescribed maximum rates 'for castrating a dog or tomcat'. These formulas had remained virtually unaltered since the sixteenth century and continued unamended for another eighty-five years.[98] A similar contract agreed to by the hereditary lessee of the knacker's yard

---

[94] Klaus Gimpel, 'Nachrichten über die Henker (Büttel, Scharfrichter) in Münster', *Westfälische Zeitschrift*, 141 (1991), 151–68, here 156–8.

[95] Sta Hanover A 1209, Bl. 58: contract of city government with executioner Voss, 1831.

[96] Albrecht Keller, *Der Scharfrichter in der deutschen Kulturgeschichte* (Bonn and Leipzig, 1921), 193.

[97] Sta Hanover A 1209, Bl. 58: contract of city government with executioner Voss, 1831.

[98] StA Bremen 2.-D. 19. k. 3. b.: Scharfrichter: Bestallung derselben, Instruktion und Eid, 1598–1822; ibid., Nr. 10, Scharfrichter-Vertrag, 27 June 1738.

in the Prussian town of Thorn in 1802 obliged Gotthardt Bockenhäuser to require his servants to clear dead animals 'and rubbish' off the streets of the town and its suburbs as a regular part of his duties. 'During the dog-days' he had to collect unlicensed dogs before seven o'clock in the morning and put them down, though in his yard rather than on the streets, except when 'rabid dogs or other animals are reported, he is to beat them to death straightway and without any prevarication'. He had the right to claim a fee for removing 'horses or cattle that have dropped dead' or other dead animals, and could also skin them and keep the hides. Then, after enumerating all the other various rights and duties attaching to the property, the contract went on:

Concerning the execution fees, the hereditary lessee shall be paid five thalers when he executes someone with the sword, one thaler for putting a poor sinner's head on a stake, one thaler for burying his body in the earth, but two thalers in addition if the head is put on a stake and the body on the wheel, two thalers for execution with a rope, five thalers for dispatching with the wheel, five thalers if he burns someone to death with fire, however if an animal is burned along with him an extra thaler, for tying to the pillory one thaler and for tying and tearing at the same time, if a rope is placed around the malefactor's neck, one thaler thirty groschen.[99]

As late as 1820, the official list of instructions for the executioner issued in the Hanseatic city of Lübeck ordered him to carry out the same mixture of functions: it was his duty 'to carry out executions with the sword by his own hand' as well as to collect 'carcasses or fallen animals' from the city streets and to bury 'the corpses of suicides and criminals'.[100]

In most towns, as these contracts suggest, there were fixed rates of payment for the diverse tasks carried out by executioners, ranging in Augsburg in 1748 from one thaler 'for cutting off a person's nose and ears' to seven thalers 'for tying the executed corpse to the wheel and placing the head on a pole'. The more elaborate the execution, the more the hangman earned, with an extra thaler 'for every pull of the tongs', for example, and another three thalers 'for taking someone out on the hurdle'. Breaking with the wheel was especially lucrative, since the executioner was paid four thalers 'for every blow with the wheel', the number, however, usually being precisely laid down in the sentence.[101] They could also earn money by performing small surgical operations on people, or by supplying them with magical cures for illnesses, provided that this could be done without dishonouring the patient.[102] So manifold and various were their sources of

---

[99] GStA Berlin Rep. 181/4152, Bl. 9–12.
[100] StA Lübeck Rep. 49/1,2816: Instruktion für die Scharfrichter, 1820.
[101] Schuhmann, *Scharfrichter*, 137. See also Moser, *Scharfrichter von Tirol*, 29–33; and StA Bremen 2.-D. 19. k. 3. b.: 'Notizen' (Nr. 11). Spierenburg, *Spectacle*, 33–8, confirms this impression with figures from Holland.
[102] See e.g. Sta Hanover A 1212, 'Die Kurpfuscherei der Nachrichter 1730–1785', *passim*; Schuhmann, *Scharfrichter*, 148, 216, 277–9; and Horst Matthias, *Die Entwicklung des Medizinalwesens im Lande Lippe*

income, indeed, and so grasping their demands, that one prince, the Duke of Brunswick, was moved to complain in 1712 that

It is not without displeasure that Our attention has been drawn to the fact that the executioners who have been employed and paid by Us and engaged by Our towns and courts stop at nothing to increase their wages and fees for executions, thereby mutiplying the activities apertaining to such acts for the sake of their unauthorized emoluments and profts, and demanding a threefold or even fourfold hangman's wages in advance if several malefactors are brought to the place of execution, though not all of them are to be executed, if they are handed over to them, and demand to be paid before the same, and irrespective of whether the execution takes place in the town or near the gate demand travelling costs, and whatever other similar unauthorized demands there may be in addition.

He promised 'at last to set an end and a limit to this' by laying down what he regarded as a reasonable level of fees in future and ensuring that the executioners stuck to it.[103]

The reasons for combining some of the various jobs which executioners undertook were fairly obvious, so obvious indeed that they were combined in other parts of Europe as well.[104] Both killing and skinning animals and executing humans required similar abilities, including a knowledge of physiology and anatomy, a familiarity with blood and guts, a steady hand, a keen eye, and a certain degree of physical strength. But there was clearly more to it than this. The executioner, especially when he combined his office with that of town knacker, was the man charged with keeping all kinds of dirt, disorder, and disease out of the community. He was dishonourable because he was constantly handling sources of pollution, such as dead cows, mad dogs, and human excrement. Making him dishonourable was a way of sanctioning and at the same time containing behaviour which would normally be forbidden.[105] The same stigma attached to other outsiders to the community, including tanners, charcoal-burners, molecatchers, shepherds, Jews, Turks, gypsies, bastards, lepers, criminals, and prostitutes. All of these belonged to the wild, either geographically, by living much of the year far from centres of human habitation, or socially, by living outside the prescribed moral boundaries of Christian society, or physically, by living in an obvious state of infection and disease. The executioner stood between the settled and honourable society of the towns, the guilds, and the princely order, and the threatening and uncontrolled world of the sick, the rabid, the violent and the deviant. He patrolled the border between culture and nature. He was responsible for dealing with all the dirt that accumulated in the

---

unter besonderer Berücksichtigung des Scharfrichterwesens und seiner Stellung in der Heilbehandlung (Münster, 1947). For the medical activities of French executioners, see Lenôtre, *Guillotine*, 223 and 247.

[103] Sta Hanover A 1215, Bl. 2–3. Ordinance of 16 Jan. 1712.
[104] For France, see Lenôtre, *Guillotine*, 255 n. 3.   [105] Nowosadtko, 'Ehre', 366.

community. He acted as a conduit through which the excrement of the social body flowed into the world beyond.[106]

It was no wonder, therefore, that his touch was considered polluting; that even where offenders were already infamous or had been further dishonoured by the crime committed, society regarded the act of physical contact with the public hangman as dishonouring them yet more. In almost every society, those whose task it is to deal with dirt of various kinds, from sewermen to mortuary attendants, are regarded at the very least with distaste. It is not necessary to adduce elaborate psychological theories of transference, guilt, resentment against the executioner's appropriation of the right of vengeance, or shame at his subversion of the knightly ethos of the tourney, for which there is in any case no historical evidence of any kind, in order to explain his status in the social order.[107] Punishment in sixteenth- and seventeenth-century Germany was a symbolic discourse in which ritual acts demonstrated to a largely illiterate population the cohesiveness of an ordered society faced with physical and moral pollution. It was carefully scripted, and the players in the drama, such as the executioner, were carefully chosen for the symbolic resonances they aroused in the audience. It was based on a set of shared assumptions between the corporations that governed society, from the princely authorities and rulers of the territorial state to the guild masters and councils of Germany's myriad small towns and cities, and the masses of subjects and citizens for whom it was drafted. And it was based on a shared culture betweeen the élites and the populace. It spoke to all a language that was understood by all: the language of the martyred and suffering body. As the French historian Arlette Farge has remarked in her study of executions and the common people in Paris,

Because society at that time was so visual and mannered, it was customary to interpret much on the basis of the body's signs and signals; for, before it is anything else, and least of all a public spectacle, the body is a language. Naked and dying, it was both language and spectacle. Its appearance and constitution afforded the spectators a vast amount of information and nothing was considered unworthy of comment or lengthy interpretation.[108]

Decoding the language of the violated, destroyed, and dismembered body, a language expressed not merely in words, but also in movement, space, colour, and gesture, is indeed the key to understanding the meanings of punishment in this period, as we shall now see.

---

[106] Zunkel, 'Ehre', 16–17; Beneke, *Unehrliche Leute*. For the theoretical basis of these observations, see Mary Douglas, *Purity and Danger: An Analysis of Concepts of Pollution and Taboo* (London, 1966).

[107] See Spierenburg, *Spectacle*, 24–8, for speculations of this kind.

[108] Arlette Farge, *Fragile Lives: Violence, Power and Solidarity in Eighteenth-Century Paris* (Oxford, 1993), 199.

2

Rites of Blood

a. Pronouncing Sentence

A German execution in the early modern period usually began with a formal meeting of the court, held in the town hall or the representative building of the sovereign authority, to announce the verdict to the offender. In the south German town of Dillingen, for example, the rules for this occasion, drawn up in 1716, laid down that the offender had to be brought in chains to the town hall and released to stand before the two judges and five 'honest citizens'. Here a summary of the confession would be read out. All present had to sign it, including the prisoner, who could of course append a cross or mark if unable to write. At this point the prisoner was formally handed over from the representative of the princely authority under which Dillingen fell, to the town council, whose duty it was to make the necessary arrangements for the execution. The presiding official then told the offender:

The day after tomorrow, that is, next Friday, you shall die, and you must be brought by judgment from life to death. Therefore you are hereby admonished that you turn with your whole heart to God, that you take your sin to heart and repent it, and that you humbly beg forgiveness of God, the high authorities, and also your fellow men who have suffered because of you, so that you prepare yourself for a pious and happy death. God have mercy upon your poor soul.

The language by which condemned people were described emphasized above all the moral and religious aspects of their status. They were known as 'poor sinners' (*arme Sünder*), and the cell to which they were now conducted by the town bailiff to await execution was customarily referred to as the 'poor sinner's parlour' (*Armensünderstube*). Here every offender was allowed a priest or pastor, and could consult with and be visited by him as often as desired during the days between the verdict and the execution. As the instructions laid down in Dillingen indicated, a major purpose of this gap in time between the two events was to give the condemned a period of religious contemplation and reconciliation with God.

Indeed, priests were instructed not only to tell the condemned of the 'glory of the life eternal' but also to threaten them with eternal damnation should they fail to repent;[1] in some places, the clergy were told precisely which psalms and prayers to read or sing with the malefactor at various points of the three days they spent in the condemned cell together.[2]

If, as the Brandenburg lawyer Johann Brunnemann wrote, an offender

prove himself so Godless and stubborn that he refuses to be moved either by the preachers or by the authorities to admit his sins and repent of them, so it is beyond doubt that Christian authorities are obliged to see to it that his soul is redeemed and that he is brought by any means possible, through a succession of different preachers, to repentance. Should all this have no effect upon him, and should he be brought to mend his ways neither by the depiction of the cruel torments of hell nor by the threat of harsh bodily punishments, the execution is to proceed none the less, and he shall be regarded the more severely, as a public scoffer against God and His Holy Sacraments.[3]

Assuming that all went well, however, the rules allowed the prisoner to take communion the day before the execution.[4] In the Bavarian town of Illerbeuren, the members of the court also took communion early in the morning before attending the formal sentencing.[5] Brunnemann portrayed the conversion of the 'poor sinner' as a collective task for the whole community:

One or more priests shall be officially seconded to the poor sinner, to attend upon him daily before the execution, to instruct him in God's Word, to admonish him to penitence and contrition, to hear his confession, to strengthen him in true belief and trust in God and the merit of Jesus Christ, to caution him to be patient, and to pray diligently with him, and it shall be arranged that in various places there shall be prayers said for the poor sinner and for his conversion, his faith and his patience, in public church meetings, after the sermon.[6]

About the centrality of religious repentance, conversion, and absolution to the whole ceremony from the very beginning there could therefore be little doubt.

The condemned usually remained in the 'poor sinner's parlour' for three days, a period that recalled the three days spent by Christ in the tomb between the Crucifixion and the Resurrection. This allowed the prisoner to be visited for the last time by friends and relatives, and ministered to by the clergy. It was striking how the condemned were fed during this time quantities of rich food which, since they were usually poor, they had probably never seen before in their life. In eighteenth-century Nuremberg it was normal for the offender to be given a

---

[1] Danker, *Räuberanden*, 176.
[2] StA Hamburg Senat Cl. VII. Lit. Mb. No. 3, Vol. 4b: Ordnung bey Ausführung eines Delinquenten.
[3] Johann Brunnemann, *Anleitung zu vorsichtiger Anstellung des Inquisition-Processes* (Halle, 1697), 53.
[4] Schuhmann, *Scharfrichter*, 171–2, quoting regulations listed in the *Peinliche Executionsordnung des Hochstiftes Augsburg 1716.*
[5] Ibid. 175.   [6] Quoted in Danker, *Räuberbanden*, 175–6.

whole roast goose for the last meal in prison.[7] And in Augsburg in 1772 one condemned malefactor spent his last days on earth eating his way through a roast chicken, game birds, capon, fish, veal, beef, lamb, soup, pâté, salad, rice, sausages, noodles, bread, and various sweets, washed down every day by beer and finished off with a good quantity of 'Neckar wine', doubled to three measures on the last day.[8] This helped reconcile offenders with those who were about to execute them, and was thought to reduce the danger of nervousness and melancholia. The theme of reconciliation was particularly prominent in Bavaria, where the executioner visited the condemned cell early on the morning of the execution and formally asked the condemned for forgiveness for the actions he would perform later in the day. The two would share a ritual drink, in a ceremony known as the *Johannessegen* (St John's Blessing) or *Johannistrunk*, to recall the blessing given by John the Baptist to those who were about to kill him.[9]

The malefactor was then brought up from the dungeon to take part in the so-called Hangman's Meal (*Henkersmahlzeit*). This was attended by officials, judges, condemned and (sometimes) executioner, all seated at the same table. The Hangman's Meal powerfully suggested that all were willingly collaborating in the event, and was supposed to give the offender the strength to get through the day's ordeal. It was, if anything, even more extravagant than the series of repasts which had preceded it. In Frankfurt am Main in 1772, at the Hangman's Meal for Susanna Margarethe Brandt, the infanticidal mother who was the inspiration for the character of Gretchen in Goethe's *Faust*, seven people were served with a repast consisting of three pounds of fried sausages, ten pounds of beef, six pounds of baked carp, twelve pounds of larded roast veal, soup, cabbage, bread, a sweet, and eight and a half measures of 1748 wine. Neither the condemned woman, who consumed nothing except a glass of water, nor the others, had the stomach for much of this.[10] But the richness and quantity of the food on this occasion were far from untypical. Indulging in an orgy of consumption emphasized the physicality of life and underlined the state of being which the offender was about to leave. The meal constituted a structural point of departure for the ritual that was to follow. The clerics who had attended the prisoner in the 'poor sinner's parlour' were also present at the Hangman's Meal. To mark clearly the contrast between their function of administering God's mercy to the prisoner's soul, and the judicial authorities' function of denying the state's mercy to the prisoner's body, clerical and lay officials at the meal were sometimes served different kinds

[7] Willi Heim, *Das Henkersmahl* (Erlangen, 1941), 18.   [8] Schuhmann, *Scharfrichter*, 127–30.
[9] Otto Freiherr von Völderndorff und Waradein, *Harmlose Plaudereien* (2 vols.; Munich, 1892–8), i. 104–5; Heim, *Henkersmahl*, 18.
[10] Siegfried Birkner (ed.), *Leben und Sterben der Kindsmörderin Susanna Margarethe Brandt* (Frankfurt, 1973), 115–16.

of food. Thus in eighteenth-century Leipzig the judges, officers of the court, local notary, and town scribe consumed savoury food—'fried sausages, scrambled eggs, four jugs of hock'—while the officiating clergy were given sweet items—'coffee, a bottle of dessert wine with sweets and biscuits'.[11] The contrast was underlined by the formula used by the official in charge of the execution when ritually asked, by the hangman, for 'mercy for my malefactor': 'There is no mercy here; mercy lies with God alone!'[12] An added subtlety was sometimes provided by the custom of serving lemons at this meal, as happened in Leipzig.[13] And when Susanna Margarethe Brandt heard the formal reading of her sentence in Frankfurt in 1772, she was given a 'large lemon' to hold while she did so.[14] Lemons, the bitterest of fruit, symbolized death and were frequently used to this effect in many still-life paintings of the period. They may have helped slow down putrefaction in corpses while they were lying-in. The use of lemons at the Hangman's Meal thus signified life-in-death; the beginning of a ritual transition of the condemned from a living being to a corpse.

A further indication of the transitional nature of the occasion was the fact that the malefactor usually appeared at the Hangman's Meal already dressed in a burial shroud. Susanna Margarethe Brandt, for example, appeared in a 'shroud' consisting of a white bonnet, a white linen jacket with a black bow, a white dress, and white gloves.[15] At public executions in the Bavarian town of Straubing, 'a special dress was to be provided for the person to be executed, namely: 1 grey jacket with collar, 1 pair of white stockings, 1 pair of leather breeches, 1 white sackcloth. This also constituted the shroud for the corpse.'[16] In Walddürn, as late as 1818, the farmer Justin Baumann, the last person to be executed in the town, stepped forward to hear the sentence dressed 'in a shroud'.[17] In Hesse, too, the condemned in the early nineteenth century were 'provided with the usual shrouds'.[18] In Osnabrück the prisoner's clothing was unbleached and had black

[11] Sta Leipzig L XII G 23b vol. ii: Nachricht, was bey einer Execution zu besorgen, §§ 11–12 (18 Aug. 1769). For the 'hangman's meal' in France, see Lenôtre, *Guillotine*, 52.

[12] Friedrich Hartl, *Das Wiener Kriminalgericht. Strafrechtspflege vom Zeitalter der Aufklärung bis zur österreichischen Revolution* (Vienna, 1973), 421.

[13] Sta Leipzig L XII G 23b vol. ii: Nachricht, was bey einer Execution zu besorgen, § 10 (18 Aug. 1769). Lemons were also placed over the tips of the ceremonial swords carried by the sons of small masters at the 'gallows festival' held to inaugurate the rebuilding of the scaffold in Frankfurt in 1720 (Dülmen, *Theater*, 100).

[14] Birkner, *Leben und Sterben*, 117.   [15] Ibid.

[16] HStA Munich MJu 13067: Direktorium des Bezirksgerichts Straubing to King Ludwig II, 4 May 1866 (reporting earlier customs).

[17] Wilhelm Eggler, *Der Waldstetter Mord und die letzte Hinrichtung in Walddürn (1818)* (offprint from *Alemmania, Zeitschrift für alemannische und fränkische Geschichte, Volkskunde, Kunst und Sprache*, Freiburg im Breisgau, 1916), 24.

[18] Karl Krämer, *Mord und Todesstrafe in Hessen 1817–1929* (Jur. Diss, Giessen, 1932; offprint from *Monatsschrift für Kriminalpsychologie und Strafrechtsreform*, 3 (1932)), 136.

buttons.[19] Only high-status malefactors retained their own clothing, and even here they dressed appropriately for the occasion, in mourning costume, as in the case of Dirk Surbick, a financial official executed for embezzlement in Bremen in 1686, who went to his death 'dressed in black, with a black cloak, black cuffs and a black shirt with a black gauze ruff'.[20] More usually, the prisoner's clothing signified repentance and the state of purity which it conferred. Susanna Margarethe Brandt, for example, carried a folded sackcloth in the procession to her execution in 1772, and the white shroud in which she was dressed marked not only her transitional state between life and death but also the way in which she was being purged of the stain of sin through confession, repentance, and absolution.[21] In Osnabrück a witness to the execution of two women convicted of infanticide reported in 1789 that they 'were led to the scaffold as brides to the altar, in white dresses decorated with black ribbons'.[22] The marriage was to be with Christ, through a sanctifying death, for the pure in heart—an image that would have been understood by everyone versed in the Pietistic imagery of Christian hymns and prayers in the eighteenth century and before.

The clothes worn by the secular officials at the formal sentencing were, in contrast to those of the offender, predominantly red and black. Red signified the power of the state over the body of the subject; it advertised the fact that this was a 'blood court' (*Blutgericht*) at which the process of shedding blood was formally inaugurated. Black, the colour of mourning, was an added signifier of the transitional state of the condemned between life and death. This colour scheme was echoed in the various accessories used at the ceremony. Black was the predominant colour in Walddürn, where the officials' table on the scaffold was draped with black cloth.[23] In Osnabrück both the scaffold itself and the officials' table nearby were covered in 'black material', as was the table at which the public condemnation was held.[24] In Munich the sentence was usually announced to the crowd by an official standing in the city court 'from an upper window from which a red cloth was hanging out', and the scaffold itself was draped in red cloth.[25] At the execution of Susanna Margarethe Brandt in 1772, the judges

[19] HStA Hanover Hann. 173a Nr. 438, Bl. 24: Geschehen zu Osnabrück (etc.), 31 July 1857 (official account of an execution by Dr Brüggemann).

[20] StA Bremen 2.-D. 16. g. 1.: Das sogenannte Schwartze Buch des Bremischen Criminal-Gerichts 1238 bis 1813, entry for 1686.

[21] Birkner, *Leben und Sterben*, 116.

[22] Wilbertz, *Scharfrichter*. See also Richard Oertel, *Die letzte Hinrichtung in unserer Heimat* (Oelsnitz in Estel, 1939), 37 (including a white cap).

[23] Eggler, *Waldstetter Mord*, 24.

[24] HStA Hanover Hann. 173a Nr. 438, Bl. 23–6: Geschehen zu Osnabrück (etc.).

[25] Anon., *Die kgl. Bayer. Staatsminister der Justiz in der Zeit von 1818 bis 1918. Ihre Herkunft und Werdegang und ihr Wirken* (Munich, 1931), 56, citing the *Augsburger Allgemeine Zeitung*, 18 May 1850.

appeared wearing a special 'execution dress', mainly black, over which they had draped large red cloaks emblazoned with the Frankfurt coat of arms.[26] In Heidelberg, when members of the Hölzerlips band of robbers were executed in 1812, 'blood banners' were hung from the balcony of the town hall while the formal sentence was being pronounced, and at the scaffold, the court sat on a black-covered table on black-covered chairs.[27] In the Swiss city of Berne the executioner wore a black and red cloak.[28] At executions in the Bavarian town of Ansbach in the eighteenth century, the officials wore black, while the blood-judge, whose task it was to conduct the ceremony, was dressed in red.[29] When the notorious bandit Schinderhannes was beheaded in Mainz in 1803, the guillotine was painted red and the scaffold coloured black.[30] And forthcoming executions in the seventeenth and eighteenth centuries were announced in some cities by the hanging of a red sheet from the town hall window,[31] a practice echoed well into the twentieth century by the bright red paper and thick black print of the official notices of executions which were posted up on advertising columns in the town where they had taken place.

Executions were announced well in advance, by word of mouth and in print, and were frequently held on market days, to ensure the maximum number of spectators. In the early modern German town, the market-place or town hall square was the centre of communal life. The market square was the central civic space, used for displays of community solidarity and civic power.[32] Here offenders were placed in the stocks or the pillory; but here also the town held its great affirmatory civic festivals and began the processions with which it advertised its honour and pride. The square was therefore the obvious place for the populace to gather to witness the public sentencing of capital offenders in the ceremony generally known as the *Hochnotpeinliches Halsgericht*. In most places the condemned person was again obliged to make a formal confirmation of identity and assent to the verdict. The town clerk or responsible official then read out the judgment of the court, a description of the condemned person's crimes, and the full sentence to the crowd, either from a window or balcony of the town hall or on the market-place itself. In Dillingen the offender was taken out and fixed to the pillory with an iron collar while the sentence was being proclaimed.[33]

[26] Birkner, *Leben und Sterben*, 116.   [27] Keller, *Scharfrichter*, 280–5.
[28] Peter Sommer, *Scharfrichter von Bern* (Berne, 1969), 120–5.   [29] Oppelt, *Unehrlichkeit*, 130–5.
[30] Curt Elwenspoek, *Schinderhannes. Der rheinische Rebell* (Stuttgart, 1925), 230.
[31] Dülmen, *Theater*, 102. For the red and black robes worn by the confraternities at French executions in the 18th c., see McManners, *Death*, 382–3.
[32] Roper, *Holy Household*, 8.
[33] Schuhmann, *Scharfrichter*, 170–2, citing the 'Peinliche Executionsordnung des Hochstiftes Augsburg' issued in the year 1716. See also Dülmen, *Theater*, 81–5. For more descriptions, see Erich Wettstein, *Die Geschichte der Todesstrafe im Kanton Zürich* (Winterthur, 1958), and Nordhoff-Behne, *Gerichtsbarkeit*.

This was the first moment in the whole process of the trial where there was any popular participation, and it was invested with an appropriate degree of ritual solemnity. In the town of Oelsnitz in Estel, in the territory of the Count of Schönburg, according to a report of 1767, it involved the repetition of numerous formulas three times. Once the session was opened in this way, the bailiff (*Amtsfrohn*) cried: 'Hear ye people gathered here! The high criminal court of the high-born count and lord N.N. is now declared open—with judgment and sentence. It is declared open for the first time! It is declared open for the second time! It is declared open for the third time with criminal jurisdiction!' This kind of thing went on for some time, with the threefold repetition of numerous other ritual phrases, before the ceremony was concluded.[34] In some places it was accompanied by a ritual exchange with the crowd known as the 'murder-cry' or 'hue-and-cry' (*Mord-Geschrey* or *Zeter-Geschrey*),[35] in which the attendant populace gave its assent to this procedure by shouting loudly at the appropriate moments. In Bavaria, the assembled spectators shouted 'Io!' three times at the officiating judge's bidding. As late as the 1850s, this custom continued in a more general form, though it had long since been abolished in law, and the handing-over of the condemned to the executioner was accompanied by a 'fierce shout' from the crowd.[36] Pious critics complained that all this disturbed the 'Christian devotion' of the condemned and the preachers, and alleged that the 'the hue-and-cry or proclamation customary in many places often causes more suffering and pain to the poor sinner's body and soul than the *executio* itself might'.[37] But the elements of popular justice and participation introduced at this stage were crucial, as we shall see, so the practice generally remained in place.

It was at this point that the officiating judge or town clerk proceeded formally to release the condemned person from his power into the hands of the executioner. This was done, as laid down in the *Carolina*, by breaking a wand of office, coloured red, white, or black according to local tradition, and often filed to a thin point in the middle so as to make it easy to snap in two. In Leipzig, the wand of office was placed next to the sword of execution on the judges' table. The judge picked it up and held it aloft, while he read out a description of the crime and the

[34] Oertel, *Hinrichtung*, 32–3. See also the description in Danker, *Räuberbanden*, 173–7.

[35] Gottfried Schütze, *Register über die sämmtlichen zwölf Theile der Sammlung Hamburgischer Gesetze und Verfassungen mit historischer Einleitung*, Part V (Hamburg, 1774), 566. For a further description of this procedure, see Schild, *Alte Gerichtsbarkeit*, 167–8. See also StA Bremen 2.-D. 16. g. 1: Das sogenannte Schwartze-Buch des Bremischen Criminal-Gerichts von 1238 bis 1813, entry for 1705.

[36] Völderndorff und Waradein, *Plaudereien*, i. 102.

[37] Anon., *In dem königlichen preussischen Amte Ermsleben bey verschiedenen Executionen bislang gehaltene und auch kunftig bey denen daselbst inhaffiirten und bereits zum Rade und andern abscheulichen Todes-Straffen verurtheilten 3. Mördern und Räubern, nemlich: Hans Jürgen Jeckeln, Annen Catharinen Kahnen und Eleonoren Julianen Behtgen, wiederum den ( ) Martii 1715 öffentlich zuhegende Hochnoth-peinliche Hals-Gerichte, welches von denen überflüssigen und unnöthigen Solenniteten gesäubert und in eine kurze Ordnung gebracht ist* (1715), 4.

verdict of the court. 'Do you confess to this crime once again?' he was supposed to ask the condemned offender. 'Yes!' Pronoucing the sentence of death, the judge, as the instructions said, 'breaks the wand and casts the shards to the ground before his feet and says: the wand is broken. Court bailiff, summon the executioner! Executioner, I commit the condemned to you, carry out the sentence!'[38] This act had a number of symbolic meanings. Besides marking the end of the secular authorities' power over the offender, it also signified a further moment in the condemned person's transition from one state of being into another, and indeed was frequently accompanied by a form of words to this effect. In Walddürn the town actuary told the prisoner:

'Whosoever sheddeth man's blood, by man shall his blood to be shed.' These are your own words, whereby you yourself have declared to me that you are worthy of death. Thus you have long since confessed the justice of your sentence, you have recognized that your life is at an end. So receive then the well-merited punishment for your misdeed. You are doomed to die, and in hereby [with the following words the wand is broken and cast down before the malefactor's feet] sundering the tie which has bound you to civil society, I ask God to have mercy upon your soul.

The account added that the prisoner picked up the broken wand of office, kissed it, and put it back on the table, thanking the judges for his sentence as he did so.[39] At the execution of Hölzerlips and his band of robbers in Heidelberg in 1812, the presiding official said:

Your life is over, there is no place on this earth for you any more, and in breaking this wand (it is broken and cast down before the poor sinner's feet) I also break the tie between you and the human race. Only with God may you still find mercy. Woe upon you here! Woe! Woe!!!
OFFICIALS. Woe! Woe!! Woe!!!
BAILIFFS. Woe! Woe!! Woe!!![40]

Once more, the threefold repetition of the phrase followed a common ritual practice at these ceremonies. It signified finality and irrevocability, and gave added emphasis to the moment of transition from civil society into the hands of the executioner. It marked the moment of civil death for the prisoner. In Hamburg, indeed, when a citizen—one of a small, privileged minority of the politically enfranchised—was to be executed, it was at this moment that the

---

[38] Sta Leipzig L XII G 23b vol. ii, Bl. 269: Hegung des peinlichen Halsgerichts des vereinigten Criminal Amts der Stadt Leipzig, 27. viii. 1824; also ibid., Bl. 271–3.

[39] Eggler, *Waldstetter Mord*, 27.

[40] Keller, *Scharfrichter*, 283. See also Paul Sauer, *Im Namen des Königs. Strafgesetzgebung und Strafvollzug im Königreich Württemberg von 1806 bis 1871* (Stuttgart, 1984), 24, for the same basic formula ('Your life is over'). Wilhelm Renger, 'Hinrichtungen als Volksfeste,' *Süddeutsche Monatshefte*, 10/2 (1913), 8–21, also describes the breaking of the wand of office. See also Dülmen, *Theater*, 60–1.

black cloak signifying his status was removed from his shoulders and the executioner formally rendered him dishonourable by touching him on the arm.[41]

b. The March to the Scaffold

From the moment the sentence was formally announced, a bell began to toll, and it continued until the actual moment of execution.[42] It had the function of marking off the ceremony in time from the normal course of the daily round before and after, as a special period in which everyday activities and behaviour were suspended. It also summoned the community to witness and participate in the day's events. Most people, however, had probably long since gathered round the scaffold or in the market-place or town hall square. People also came from miles around. Although contemporary estimates must be taken with a pinch of salt, it is clear that the crowds at these events were frequently very large. It was said that 20,000 people attended an execution in the Thuringian town of Clingen in 1788, for example,[43] and the same number the last public burning, held in Eisenach in 1804,[44] while in 1771, the night before the execution of Matthias Klostermaier, the town of Munich was

already so filled with outsiders that they could barely be accommodated any more in private houses; thus the next day's dawn had scarcely broken when a wave of people came flooding through all the streets and alleyways, and while one part of the crowd pressed on to the town hall, the other hastened over the Danube bridge to the place of execution, where the masses multiplied more and more.[45]

In the Saxon capital of Dresden, at the execution of the bandit Lips Tullian and four of his companions in crime on 8 March 1715, 'more than 20,000 people, 144 carriages, and some 300 horses looked on', according to a contemporary report.[46] On 19 February 1807, 'thousands of spectators surrounded the high market' in Vienna, 'where the condemned man got onto the wagon with the two preachers. . . . Thousands of people filled the streets', and 'many thousands of spectators stood around in a circle' at the place of execution.[47] In a small town like Sweenemünde, on the Baltic coast, where the novelist Theodor Fontane

---

[41] Beneke, *Von Unehrlichen Leuten*, 180; StA Hamburg Senat Cl. VII Lit. Mb, no. 3, vol. 8: Gehorsamster Bericht of 22 Nov. 1841. For parallels to and variations on these procedures in the Netherlands, including the clothing, the meal, the sequence of events, the wand of office, and so on, see Spierenburg, *Spectacle*, 45–7.

[42] Elwenspoek, *Schinderhannes*, 233; Hartl, *Wiener Kriminalgericht*, 420; Sommer, *Scharfrichter von Bern*, 60–1, for examples. For the use of the bell in the Netherlands, see Spierenburg, *Spectacle*, 47–51.

[43] Oppelt, *Unehrlichkeit*, 122.   [44] Keller, *Scharfrichter*, 265.

[45] Nöggeler, *Bayerischer Hiesel*, 197.   [46] Danker, *Räuberbanden*, 196.

[47] Anon., *Anreden, gehalten bey der Hinrichtung des unglücklichen Johann Nicolaus G**, nebst einigen Nachrichten über sein Betragen in den drey letzten Tagen seines Lebens und im Tode. Zum Besten der armen Familie des Hingerichteten* (Vienna, 1807), 14–15.

remembered an execution having taken place in his childhood, in 1828, practically the entire population turned out, and the streets and houses away from the square were completely devoid of life.[48]

After the breaking of the wand of office, a procession formed and began to make its way from the market or town hall square to the scaffold. Usually the procession made its way on foot, with the most important personages riding on horseback. The condemned generally walked, only riding in a cart if they needed to, like one malefactor executed in Bremen in 1757, who 'was not able to walk because of his thickly swollen legs'.[49] In specially severe cases of murder or armed robbery with violence and homicide, as we saw in Chapter 1, the court could order the offender to be bound in an oxhide and dragged to the scaffold on a hurdle by a horse. The most severe additional punishment that could be meted out was for pieces of the offender's flesh to be pulled out with red-hot tongs on the way as well. Frequently the prisoner was plied with drink.[50] This too was ritualized and pre-ordained. In 1718, for example, the innkeeper Marcus Lüder in Bremen petitioned the city Senate to be released from the duty 'incumbent and obligatory since time immemorial upon my house, called the Green Huntsman, situated next to St Ansch. Gate . . . that when a malefactor is led out, every malefactor shall be handed a glass of wine for his refreshment from the said house'.[51] Providing the prisoner with alcohol was another gesture of goodwill and reconciliation. It was well known as a means of calming the nerves and dulling the sensibilities and was also commonly used at this time and long afterwards in armies and navies before battle commenced.

There was usually a precise order laid down for the procession to the scaffold. In Leipzig, for example, the regulations of 1769 prescribed the following sequence:

1. A non-commissioned officer. 2. Two files of city soldiers. 3. The Senior Steward. 4. The 3 outriders on horseback. 5. The lamplighters, whitesmocks, beer-drawers, before and beside the schoolboys. 6. The schoolboys. 7. One of the two market-masters. 8. Two files of city servants in armour. 9. The armoured city servants, so 10. Accompanying the poor sinner, the clergymen walking next to him. 11. The executioner's servants. 12. The two sextons. 13. The city-master. 14. Three city servants and 15. The other market-master in armour. 16. The carriages in which the noble members of the city courts are seated. By their side, the court bailiff rides with the execution sword belted on. 17. The senior forester. 18. Eight hunters. 19. The administrator of the city farms, on horseback.[52]

[48] Theodor Fontane, *Meine Kinderjahre. Autobiographischer Roman*, ed. C. Cole (Leipzig, 1955), 112.

[49] StA Bremen 2.-D. 16. g. 1: Das sogenannte Schwartze-Buch des Bremischen Criminal-Gerichts 1238 bis 1813, entry for 1757.

[50] Dülmen, *Theater*, 86; Schuhmann, *Scharfrichter*, 129; Sommer, *Scharfrichter von Bern*, 16–19.

[51] StA Bremen 2.-D. 18. k.: Lüder to Senat, n.d. [1718].

[52] Sta Leipzig L XII G 23b vol. ii Bl. 18: Ordnung im Hinauszuge bey Ausführung eines armen Sünders (ca. 1769). For an illustration, see Karl Spengler, *Münchener Historien und Histörchen* (Munich, 1967), 195.

In Hamburg the procession was acompanied by the mounted retainers and the domestic retainers of the Senate.[53] In Eisenach in 1804 the procession was scarcely less elaborate.[54] In Bremen, the two members of the city council nominated as 'bloodlords' waited in the town hall until informed that the procession had passed through the city gates, then rode in the 'city council carriage, which is drawn by four horses' to the place of execution, to supervise the proceedings, followed by 'the mounted retainers in pairs, holding their drawn swords aloft'.[55] Whatever the arrangement, it is clear that this was no disorderly mob; on the contrary, here were the many members of the urban community arranged by rank and degree, with the guilds in their separate groupings often following behind.[56] And the presence of troops on such occasions was all-pervasive. But they were not there merely in order to prevent disturbances. They were there as a symbol of state authority; and official documents on their disposition were concerned not so much with their deployment in defence of public order, as with the arrangements made for them to present arms at appropriate moments such as the appearance of the judges or the opening of proceedings at the scaffold. They were, in other words, ceremonial troops, wearing the dress uniform of the day (including, as the Leipzig regulations made clear, breastplates and horse-armour, scarcely necessary to deal with minor civil disturbances). Their presence, however, guaranteed the orderliness that had often been missing from executions in the sixteenth and early seventeenth centuries.[57]

A striking feature of these processions was the presence of schoolboys. Their principal function was to sing hymns, sometimes—as at one execution in 1683—at the request of the malefactor himself.[58] It was normal right through the eighteenth century for schools to be closed in a town when there was an execution, and the pupils brought along either to take part in the procession or to witness the execution itself, or both. In Leipzig in the 1680s the famous St Thomas's School, where the composer Johann Sebastian Bach subsequently trained choristers for the church to which it was attached, was closed on execution days,

---

[53] Beneke, *Von Unehrlichen Leuten*, 181–2.   [54] Keller, *Scharfrichter*, 264.

[55] StA Bremen 2.-D. 16. g. 1: Das sogenannte Schwartze-Buch des Bremischen Criminal-Gerichts 1238 bis 1813, entry for 1787.

[56] For the involvement of the guilds, see below, Ch. 6.

[57] StA Hamburg Senat Cl. VII. Lit. Mb. no. 3, vol. 4a: Nachricht, wie es bey der Ausführung eines zum Tode verurtheilten Delinquenten gehalten, und was für Mannschaft von der Garnison dabey commandirt wird 1780, and Pro Memoria of 24 Nov. 1780.

[58] C.D., *Eigentlicher | Wahrhafftiger und Acten-Mässiger Bericht, | Welcher Gestalt | Der Bösewicht | Augustin Pauli | Von 19. Jahren seines Alters | An Zwoen Personen Mord-Thaten verübet, Darauff offenbar worden, und in Hafft gebracht, peinlich gefraget, und gebührend abgestrafft worden* (no place of publication, 1683), 16.

for today a poor sinner is to be beheaded on the market-place; on which occasion, therefore, no one from the junior classes, comprising only small boys and day-boys, is accustomed to attend school, for the parents themselves are wont to keep their children away from school so that they can go with them to watch the execution.

The school also provided a choir to sing hymns for the prisoners and the crowd.[59] Whether or not Bach officiated at any of these occasions does not seem to have been recorded. But they were far from unusual in the eighteenth century. At the execution of the infanticide Anna Elisabeth Blume in 1767, for instance, the officiating preacher recorded that 'she joined in the hymns which were sung by the school'.[60] Schoolboys were also reported standing near the gallows at a hanging in Hanover in 1771.[61] Often their function was to sing 'dirges' on the way to the scaffold.[62] In Mainz in 1802 the schools were closed for the whole day, so that the pupils could attend the execution of Schinderhannes and his band of nineteen robbers, due to begin at 1 p.m.[63] In 1818, the town council in Walddürn announced: 'The schoolboys must also attend the execution, led by their teachers; the town council has to ensure that the teachers betake themselves immediately after 9 o'clock to the place of execution, where a fitting place shall be assigned to them.'[64] As late as 1843, schoolboys in Göttingen, in the ultra-conservative Kingdom of Hanover, were commandeered to sing hymns alongside a condemned man on his way to the scaffold, though the custom had by this time become unusual.[65] And after the singing, the children would stay to watch the execution itself. Parents also frequently brought their offspring along, as contemporary illustrations attest. The dramatist Karl von Holtei, writing his precocious memoirs at the age of 40, towards the middle of the nineteenth century, remembered as a child being sat on the shoulders of an adult to get a better view of a woman being broken with the wheel in Breslau during the Napoleonic Wars.[66]

Noteworthy too was the presence of the clergy, walking beside the condemned. In Vienna, indeed, it was usual for a priest to hold a crucifix up steadily before the condemned's eyes all the way to the scaffold; in Bavaria prisoners held a crucifix themselves.[67] In Catholic areas such as these, the prisoner was encour-

[59] Danker, *Räuberbanden*, 197.

[60] Johann Samuel Patzke, *Aufrichtige Nachricht von der Bekehrung und den letzten Stunden einer Kindermörderin, Nahmens Anna Elisabeth Blumin, welche den 1. des Maymonaths 1767. den Rothensee mit dem Schwerdte den Lohn ihrer That empfing; aufgesetzt von den beyden Predigern an den Heiligen Geist Wache. Nebst der Rede, die an der Gerichtsstädte gehalten worden* (Magdeburg, 1767), 21.

[61] Sta Hanover A 1173: Hinrichtungsprotokoll 1771, Bl. 70 (S. 16).   [62] Renger, 'Hinrichtungen'.

[63] Elwenspoek, *Schinderhannes*, 232.   [64] Eggler, *Waldstetter Mord*, 25.

[65] *Göttinger Monatsblätter*, June 1980, 5.

[66] Karl von Holtei, *Vierzig Jahre*, i (Berlin, 1843), 132–3.

[67] Hartl, *Wiener Kriminalgericht*, 32–3; *Augsburger Allgemeine Zeitung*, 18 May 1850, cited in Anon., *Die kgl. Bayer. Staatsminister der Justiz*, 556; Anon., *Anreden, gehalten bey der Hinrichtung des unglücklichen Johann Nicolaus G***, 15.

aged to pray *en route* to the scaffold and to make confession to the priest, even if this meant holding up the progress of events. In the small Bavarian town of Illerbeuren in 1772, one prisoner took advantage of this custom to such an extent that the procession on foot to the place of execution 'dragged on for four hours, right up to almost 1 o'clock, because of the repeated prayers of the poor sinner, and also her frequent confessions'.[68] In Frankfurt am Main the same year, the procession of the infanticide Susanna Margarethe Brandt went to the scaffold 'with continual singing and praying'.[69] The religious emphasis was undiminished even in cases of the most severe and dishonouring forms of execution, such as that of Matthias Klostermaier, the poacher and bandit known as the *Bayerische Hiesl*, on 6 September 1771:

After the wand had been broken over him, he was placed on a hurdle and wrapped in a fresh cowhide in such a manner that only his head and his hands with the crucifix were still visible, whereupon the procession set off for the place of execution under strong military escort. On the way there, Hiesl's gaze was fixed unwaveringly on the Saviour's picture, and he seemed to listen zealously and with truly Christian devotion to the consoling word of the four clerical companions who surrounded the hurdle. On arrival at the scaffold, Klostermaier was straightway freed from his cowhide, and after he had confessed in the so-called poor sinner's parlour, and thereupon drunk a glass of wine, he climbed the steps to the judgment platform bravely and spiritedly, and completely unaided.

Here too he remained 'under the continual ministrations of the priests' until he was tied down by the executioner in preparation for breaking with the wheel.[70]

c. The Scene at the Ravenstone

Although some executions were held on the town or market square itself, especially in very large towns, most took place at a permanent scaffold, of the kind described by John Taylor in 1616 on his visit to Hamburg, situated just outside the town walls.[71] This was known as the 'ravenstone' (*Rabenstein*), from the fact that it was surrounded by carrion birds which picked at the corpses displayed there. Its construction was generally of stone, and it was hollow, with a wooden platform reached from inside by a ladder. Sometimes it could consist of a mound, surrounded by a retaining wall. During the fifteenth and sixteenth centuries, more and more of these edifices were built, and the number of

---

[68] Quoted in Schuhmann, *Scharfrichter*, 175.   [69] Birkner (ed.), *Leben und Sterben*, 119.

[70] Nöggeler, *Bayerischer Hiesel*, 198–9; see also Paul Ernst Rattelmüller, *Matthäus Klostermaier, vulgo der Bayrische Hiasl* (Munich, 1971), 84–7.

[71] For one example of an execution on a market-place, see Anon., *Ausführliche und wahrhaffte Relation von dem de 21. Maji dieses 1726. Jahres in Dresden von einem GOtt-vergessenen Bösewicht an dem wohlseligen Herrn M. Hahnen grausam verübten Priester-Mord. Nebst unterschiedenen gewissen Particularien, so denen bisherigen unwahren Erzehlungen entgegen gesetzet werden* (Dresden, 1726), 19, 21.

executions held within town boundaries decreased.[72] In small towns, where executions were infrequent, the ravenstone would be little more than a rough, low wooden platform, specially erected for the occasion.[73] There were obvious practical as well as symbolic reasons why the rotting heads and bodies of executed criminals could not be displayed on the market square, despite the relative lack of squeamishness of people in early modern Europe: the square, which was generally quite a small space, would be needed not only for the weekly market but also for other ceremonies and events, where the presence of dishonourable cadavers would be regarded as polluting. So executions inside the town walls were generally confined to the 'honourable' sort, where the display of the corpse was not involved. In eighteenth-century Vienna, for example, beheadings were still carried out on the New Market, while other, more severe forms of execution involving the public display of the corpse were held outside the city, at the ravenstone, just beyond the Schattentor, or at the 'wheel-crossing' on the Vienna hills.[74] In the Westphalian town of Münster, too, executions were generally held outside the walls.[75] The ravenstone's location, just outside the town gates, was pregnant with symbolic meaning. A traveller coming towards a city would see the scaffold as the first indication of its sovereign power, a warning not to transgress its rules. A traveller leaving it would be reminded of the worst that could befall an offender, of the power of the urban community to expel those who did not conform to its rules, of the danger and dishonour threatened by the wilderness. By passing outside the city walls into the world beyond, the execution procession crossed a number of symbolic boundaries once more, between civilization and the wild, between the community and the outer world, between life and death. This symbolism was maintained in rural areas by the erection of scaffolds and gallows at crossroads or on the boundaries of districts or parishes. On reaching the scaffold, the prisoner had already passed the point of no return.[76]

On arrival at the place of execution, where large crowds had also gathered, some of them camping out overnight to get the best places,[77] the condemned was usually given further opportunity to pray and confess. Here the religious element in the ritual became central, and the devotions of the 'poor sinner' and the accompanying clerics rose in a crescendo of pious fervour. In Austria and southern Germany the authorities sometimes provided a 'confession hut' or 'poor sinner's parlour' near the scaffold, where the condemned could make their last confession in private.[78] Occasionally communion was held in prison before

[72] Schuhmann, *Scharfrichter*, 50–3.   [73] Fontane, *Kinderjahre*, 113.
[74] Hartl, *Wiener Kriminalgericht*, 133.   [75] Gimpel, 'Nachrichten', 165.
[76] See e.g. Ludwig Böer, *Der Scharfrichter von Bruchsal* (Bruchsal, 1972), 3–4.
[77] Holtei, *Vierzig Jahre*, i. 130.
[78] Herbert Klein, 'Zum Antoni-Honeder Lied von 1790: Wirklichkeitsgestalt einer salzburgisch-bayerischen Moritat', *Sänger- und Musikantenzeitung. Zweimonatsschrift für Volksmusikpflege*, 11/1 (1968),

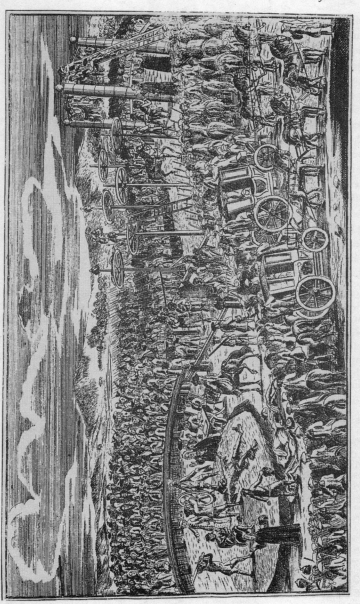

FIG. 7. *A mass execution in 1726.* A band of gypsies convicted of murder and robbery is executed in an elaborate ceremony held in Giessen on 15 November 1726. On the left, breaking with the wheel and decapitation (note the backhanded swordstroke); in the middle, display of the remains; on the right, hanging from a gibbet. Note the presence of two priests at each execution, raising their hands in benediction, and the coaches of fashionable and well-to-do spectators, bottom right.

the public ceremony.[79] But normally the confession was conducted in the open, in front of the scaffold. Often, indeed, prisoners received communion and absolution on the scaffold.[80] More time was taken up with prayers and pious speeches than with the actual execution itself. In one account, published in 1745, the prayers of the malefactor and the priests and the biblical quotations shouted out by the preachers on the scaffold took up more than ten pages of the text.[81] Such pious activities continued throughout the entire execution. In 1683, for instance, one malefactor's flesh was torn with red-hot tongs 'amidst the continual singing and admonishing' of the preachers and the choir.[82] The robber Nickel List, broken with the wheel in Celle on 23 May 1699, 'still called upon the Lord Jesus's name after he had already received the blows on both legs and arms'.[83] On 6 December 1713, at the execution of seven robbers in Brunswick-Lüneburg, no fewer than five pastors were present to ensure that the malefactors died a godly death even though the men had committed the heinous crime of murdering a young preacher for his money. After the condemned men had all prayed and received the Holy Communion, the preachers granted them absolution and stood by them as they were executed. As one of them, detailed to accompany Kahle, the last of the malefactors, reported:

I approached him and began to pray loudly before him. This last execution, however, was the most terrible, for Kahle was not only broken with the wheel from the bottom up but also before this, as he lay stretched out on the ground, had the flesh pulled from his arms twice with red-hot tongs; but I did not allow myself to be deterred by such a cruel sight and, standing right by him, called to him in a strong voice: Ah JESUS thou Son of David, have mercy on me! Father, I commend my spirit into Thy hands! LOrd JEsus help me! LORD JESUS receive my soul &c. Until I finally saw that he had lost all his senses, and then I commended him into the faithful embrace of God's compassion.[84]

3–11. In France, the procession stopped at a church on the way to the scaffold, for the condemned to perform the *amende honorable*. See François Lebrun, *Les Hommes et la mort en Anjou aux 17e et 18e siècles: Essai de démographie et de psychologie historique* (Paris, 1971), 420, and McManners, *Death*, 380–3.

79   C.D., *Eigentlicher | Wahrhafftiger und Acten-Mässiger Bericht*, 16.

80   Danker, *Räuberbanden*, 197–8.

81   Friedrich Leopold Harte, *Die Hirten-Treue Christi, welche er an einem seiner verlorenen Schafe, nemlich an Gertrud Magdalene Bremmelin, einer vorsetzlichen Kindermörderin, erwiesen zum Preise desselben unendlicher Menschenliebe, wie aus zur Warnung und Besserung, beschrieben, nebst seiner auf dem Rabenstein gehaltene Rede* (2nd edn. Wernigeroda, 1745), 71–81. The preacher's address took up a further thirty-two pages (pp. 82–113).

82   C.D., *Eigentlicher | Wahrhafftiger und Acten-Mässiger Bericht*, 16.

83   Quoted in Danker, *Räuberbanden*, 194.

84   Anon., *Nachricht von denen Prediger-Mördern, Raubern und Spitzbuben | Welche den 28. Januar. 1713. Nachts zwischen 12. und 1. Uhr Ihren allerseits Beicht-Vater und 22. jährigen Prediger, Herrn Johann Heinrich Meiern | Zu Rehburg (im Ambte Stolzenau) jämmerlich ermordet | Und der Auf Chur-Fürstl. Durchl. zu Braunschweig Lüneburg Gnädigsten Befehl ergangenen Inquisition und darauf den 6. Dec. 1713 erfolgten Inquisition und darauf den 6. Dec. 1713 erfolgten Execution* (Frankfurt am Main, 1715), 67–8.

The bandit Lips Tullian, beheaded in Dresden on 8 March 1715, spent the night before his execution praying and singing hymns, and on the scaffold 'assured everyone that he wished to go to his death willingly and resignedly, because he was sufficiently assured of God's grace in his spirit, and knew for certain that God's angels awaited his soul'.[85] In 1804 another most edifying scene took place at a burning in Protestant Eisenach: 'The criminal kneeled down before the pyre and prayed. As he recited the prayer "Christ's Blood and Justice", he was bound to the stake at the centre of the pyre.'[86] The next year, the robber and murderer Anton Lueger paused at the foot of the gallows in Catholic Vienna for the same purpose. 'Lueger', reported one of the officials present, 'uttered his prayer in a loud, unwavering voice, with his eyes raised towards heaven. Then he kneeled, confessed, and gave himself up resolutely to the executioner.'[87]

As all this suggests, the purpose of the execution was not to cause pain or suffering for its own sake, but rather to ease the criminal's passage into the afterlife, however severe or dishonouring the mode of execution. The lawyer Johann Brunnemann advised officials on such occasions

earnestly to admonish the executioner to discharge his office faithfully according to the sentence, and to shorten the poor sinner's suffering as much as possible. Thereby also to require him not to approach him and afright him with harsh words, but to urge him in a kindly manner to have patience and to think upon his Saviour, and tell him that he will easily endure this pain and enjoy eternal delight thereafter.[88]

Such was the emphasis placed on the repentance, confession, and absolution of the condemned criminal that Johann Jakob Moser even compiled a whole book describing, with the true fervour of Lutheran Pietism, the *Blessed Last Hours of Executed Persons*, published in 1761 for the edification of the pious reader. Typical was his account of the infanticide Marie Hausmann, executed in Nördlingen on 16 August 1715. On the morning of the execution, her pastor greeted her with the words: 'Verily I say unto thee, today thou shalt be with me in Paradise'—the words, of course, addressed by Jesus on the cross to one of the two malefactors crucified with him, and therefore singularly appropriate to the occasion. The two of them prayed continually on the way to the scaffold, and her last words were 'Lord Jesus, receive my spirit!' The last words of Anna Tüpler, an arsonist executed in Spiller, in Silesia, on 6 November 1744, were very similar: 'Lord Jesus,' she cried, 'I'm here! Lord Jesus, I'm coming now! Lord Jesus, take my soul up to Heaven!' Moser's compilation described numerous obstinate sinners reconciling themselves to God after a long struggle with their pastor, and yielding their

[85] Quoted ibid. 197.   [86] Keller, *Scharfrichter*, 265.
[87] Hartl, *Wiener Kriminalgericht*, 422.   [88] Brunnemann, *Anleitung*, 55.

'pardoned soul' to 'Christ their Redeemer'.[89] Many other accounts, by less distinguished authors, repeated this theme with more or less minor variations. 'Yea,' said a malefactor in Vienna in 1807 as he went to his death, 'I die trusting God and my Jesus. Into Thy hands, O Lord, I commend my spirit!'[90]

The parallel between the execution of a repentant malefactor and the martyrdom of Christ was drawn explicitly by 'Mahne-Friedrich', a member of the Hölzerlips band of robbers much given to writing poetry, in verses addressed to his mistress 'Kathrinchen' shortly before his execution in 1812. They concluded:

> At last let us now think on
> Lord Jesus' martyr's death
> That makes our soul to sink down
> Into His Wounds so red;
> So oft have I thus dwelt on
> His suffering and woe.
> Good night, my little woman!
> Now I from life must go.
> The words you must remember
> He spake upon the cross:
> I hasten off to Heaven,
> It's done, all praise to God!![91]

Sometimes the criminal addressed the crowd with a short pious speech from the scaffold. In 1683, one malefactor

held a Christian speech at the place of execution, addressed to the numerous assembled people, who had come from many, even far-off, places, and were standing by in a numberless crowd. Therein he beseeched God's Will not only that he should be forgiven everything, but also that his parents should not be blamed for anything. Whereby it was noteworthy that at the moment of this speech, the Heavens clouded over and cast down such a thick snowstorm that people could scarcely see one another. But as soon as he had finished, the storm ended, the Heavens cleared, and the sun shone pleasantly. Perhaps the hellish murder-spirit had been angered because God's assistance had ensured that a soul had been snatched from its grasp.[92]

On 7 March 1708, Barthel Stix, hanged in Augsburg for robbery and other offences, 'even as he was on the ladder, issued a warning to parents to bring up

[89] Johann Jakob Moser, *Selige letzte Stunden hingerichteter Personen* (Munich, 1761).
[90] Anon., *Anreden, gehalten bey der Hinrichtung des unglücklichen Johann Nicolaus G***, 23.
[91] DVA Freiburg, Gr. I: 'Nun hör' mein Lieb Kathrinchen'. 'Mahne-Friedrich' wrote a number of verses during his lifetime. See e.g. Karl Riha (ed.), *Das Moritatenbuch* (Frankfurt am Main, 1981), 423–4. For other probable writings by the condemned, see also ibid. 425–6. More generally, however, the authorship was spurious, as seems likely with ibid. 421–2. See Ch. 4, below, for further discussion of this literature.
[92] C.D., *Eigentlicher | Wahrhafftiger und Acten-Mässiger Bericht*, 16.

their children in a Christian manner and admonish them to do good, and begged children not to get into bad company and not to let themselves be led astray'.[93] More often than not, however, the offenders simply contented themselves with praying, while the pastors or priests standing on the scaffold shouted encouraging biblical quotations to them. If they were beheaded, kneeling for the fatal swordstroke allowed the condemned to die in an attitude of prayer; and many illustrations indicate them with their hands not bound behind their back, but clasped in front of them as they commended their soul to God.[94]

An officiating pastor described an almost ideal example of such terminal religiosity in writing about the execution of Friedrich Christian Lorenzen near Hanover in 1825. Lorenzen had thrown his mistress and their two children off a bridge, in despair at the poverty in which they lived, but had failed to kill himself as agreed. He had been condemned to death for murder and was to be beheaded with a sword.

With a firm step he climbed onto the bloody scaffold, and as the accompanying clergy-men asked him here whether, in the face of imminent death, he admitted the magnitude of his crime and the just nature of his death sentence, he answered with a definite, firm 'yes'. Thereupon his pastors bade him kneel down, and as he himself raised his hands and his gaze to Heaven with burning fervour, they prayed . . . that the All-Compassionate should not reject him completely, but should have mercy upon him, for Christ's sake. . . . As the blindfolds were tied on him, the clergymen called out to him the words: 'Lord, hear, Lord, hear me, do not forsake me in this last struggle, for Christ's sake! Let all who are witnesses of my death, let them all feel the horror of sin! Mercy, mercy, all-compassionate God! Lord Jesus, receive my spirit!' and other brief, pithy words of encouragement from the Bible, so that he should not feel completely abandoned in these moments, until a swift death ended his earthly life and brought him before the mercy-seat of the All-Pitying.[95]

Such scenes constituted a kind of exemplary death. They underlined the ele-ments of expiation and reconciliation in the execution ritual.[96] Their prospect constituted a powerful inducement to the condemned person to comply with the ceremony all the way through. It took exceptional boldness to rebel. And indeed,

[93] Schuhmann, *Scharfrichter*, 125.

[94] See e.g. Hartl, *Wiener Kriminalgericht*, 32–3. It was precisely this aspect of executions which attracted artists. See Lionello Puppi, *Torment in Art: Pain, Violence and Martyrdom* (New York, 1991). There is no evidence to support the contention of Spierenburg, *Spectacle*, 53, that the religious elements were more pronounced in Catholic areas.

[95] Anon., *Erzählung von dem Leben, dem Verbrechen und der Bekehrung des Friedrich Christian Lorenzen, welcher am 19. April 1825 in der Nähe von Hannover enthauptet wurde. Entworfen von den, mit der Todes-Vorbereitung desselben, beauftragt gewesenen Geistlichen* (Hanover, 1825), 41–2.

[96] For another example of such pious scenes, see Anon., *Beschreibung des Johann Friedrich Starke, aus Weiler, bey Kreuznach gebürtig, welcher wegen vieler begangenen Diebstähle 34 Monate im Amte Callenberg in Arrest gesessen, und am 15ten November 1808 im 29sten Jahre seines Alters, den wohlverdienten Lohn seiner Taten, am Galgen erhielt* (no place of publication, 1808).

ribald or rebellious actions or utterances by the condemned were rare.[97] In almost every instance they complied willingly with the whole procedure.[98]

The only real sign of dissent, itself remarkably rare, was the occasional ritual cursing of the judges at the passing of the verdict, when offenders who considered that they had been unjustly treated issued a formal invitation to those who had condemned them to join them at the Last Judgment in the Valley of Jehosaphat, where God would judge those who had judged unjustly. Such ritual cursing, however, was severely punished. If combined with an outright affirmation of innocence, it was liable to lead to the postponement of execution while the prisoner was subjected to another round of torture.[99] And this, of course, was a principal reason why condemned prisoners generally acquiesced willingly in their own execution. The pain of torture was such that death often came as a relief; and the prospect of further suffering in the eventuality of a formal denial of guilt was enough to keep most prisoners quiet on the scaffold. Moreover, the effects of religious faith and the massive psychological pressure to which the condemned were subjected by the clergy immediately before and during the execution ceremony should not be underestimated. The robber Andreas Schwartze, for example, executed in Celle in March 1699, complained bitterly at the reading of the sentence in the town hall that the punishment to which he was being condemned was excessively severe. As the officiating priest later reported:

> The man was filled with hatred and violent dissatisfaction with his sentence, and would not be moved to acceptance of it by any depiction (of heaven or hell). His spirit burned incandescent with the heat of vengeance, and in the presence of all the onlookers every now and then spat out monstrous horrible clods like Vesuvius.

On the scaffold, however, Schwartze relented, delivered a moving speech to the crowd, and met his fate 'with steadfast courage'.[100] The rule, indeed, was for malefactors to thank the authorities for their 'leniency' after having been rewarded for their repentance by the reduction of their sentence from hanging or breaking with the wheel to simple decapitation. The psychological effect of the linked choices between heaven or hell for the soul, and a quick, painless end or a slow and terrible death for the body, was always powerful.[101]

---

[97] For a few examples from the Netherlands, see Spierenburg, *Spectacle*, 56–66. For one example from Germany, see Georg Philipp Harsdörffer, *Der grosse Schau-Platz jämmerlicher Mord-Geschichte* (Hamburg, 1606; repr. Hildesheim, 1985), 722–3.

[98] For a similar conclusion in relation to French executions, see Ariès, *The Hour of our Death*, 27. See also the descriptions of the death of the Earl of Essex on the scaffold in Lucinda McCray Beier, 'The Good Death in Seventeenth-Century England', in Houlbrooke (ed.), *Death*, 43–61. For the role of religion and the clergy in English executions during the 18th c., see Harry Potter, *Hanging in Judgment: Religion and the Death Penalty in England from the Bloody Code to Abolition* (London, 1993), 17–29.

[99] Dülmen, *Theater*, 58–61.   [100] Danker, *Räuberbanden*, 190–1.   [101] Ibid. 196.

The drama of capital punishment in early modern Germany was thus not least a religious drama. And there was an epilogue delivered in the form of a sermon from the scaffold by the officiating clergyman.[102] In Vienna on 19 February 1807 the execution of a forger was even preceded by a lengthy sermon from one of the officiating priests, followed by prayers, and then a blessing on the malefactor's soul, with a second sermon by another priest delivered after the execution.[103] The sentiments uttered by the preacher Andreas Schmid in his sermon after an execution in Berlin were characteristic. He told the crowd:

Were I to name but one more thing through which these people became so unfortunate and many more after them can yet become so unfortunate, it is wretched idleness and laziness. The devil finds work for idle hands. Stay here where you can earn an honest living, keep your poor children at school and at work, and give them through your Christian way of life a better example than those executed here today have given.[104]

Such sermons were usually prefaced by and concluded with intercessions for the soul of the executed malefactor. The preacher commonly described the criminal's soul as heavenward-bound.[105] Frequently, too, the inscription on the executioner's sword underlined this belief. '*Soli deo gloria*', to the glory of God alone, was a common dedication. Many swords were inscribed at the top of the blade with the words: 'When I raise the sword, I wish the poor sinner eternal life.'[106] Eternal life was indeed what the malefactor sought and what the ritual was designed to provide. Almost without exception, the condemned gave the impression of being penitent Christians who went straight to heaven after making a 'good death'.[107] It was a sacred ritual that depended on the acceptance of all concerned of the possibility of an afterlife. The 'good death' of the malefactor purged the community of its blood-guilt and cancelled out the 'bad death'—sudden, unprepared, and bereft of the opportunity to make peace with God and the world—of the malefactor's murdered victim.[108] It assured the community

---

[102] There were often two clerics present on the scaffold. See e.g. Sta Hanover A 1173: Hinrichtungsprotokoll 1771, Bl. 70 (S. 16).

[103] Anon., *Anreden, gehalten bey der Hinrichtung des unglücklichen Johann Nicolaus G***, 20–9.

[104] Quoted in Danker, *Räuberbanden*, 198.

[105] Gottlieb Graef, 'Hochgericht', *Fränkische Blätter. Monatsschrift für Heimatkunde des badischen Frankenlandes*, 3 (1920), unpaginated. See also Siegmund Bärensprung, *Anrede bey der Execution Maria Charlotta Sanels. Die wegen an der verwittweten Teleni zuvor Mischlets den 7. Februarii dieses Jahrs in Neu Angermünde begangenen Mordthat, den 7. Augustii von oben gerädert und aufs Rad geleget worden* (Berlin, 1733), and Johann Helung Engerer, *Treue Warnung von GOttes wegen vor Blut-Schulden, und dem dazu verleitenden Ehe-Bruch, bey vollstreckter Execution einer Kindes-Mörderin zu Schwabach* (Schwabach, 1737). For further examples of sermons, from the mid-19th c., see Oppelt, *Unehrlichkeit*, 140–50.

[106] StA Bremen 2.-D. 19. k. 3. b.: Richtschwert des Johann Georg Göpel, 1755 (Nr. 9a); Schuhmann, *Scharfrichter*, 55 (Memmingen sword, dated 1712); Theodor Hoch, 'Über ehemalige Folter- und Strafwerkzeuge im Museum und ihre ehemalige Anwendung in Lübeck', *Die Heimat*, 14 (1904), 179–85, 202–8.

[107] Dülmen, *Theater*, 161–3.

[108] For the 'bad death' and its variants, see Beier, 'Good Death', 59–61.

that the spirit of the executed would not return to haunt the survivors, as was so often believed to be the case with the restless souls of the suddenly departed.[109] It guaranteed the peace of society by ensuring a 'grateful corpse'. And it reassured those who witnessed it that they had done a good deed. They had paved the way to eternal life for a soul seemingly beyond redemption. If it was possible for an evil criminal to go to heaven in this way, then it was surely possible for the ordinary people who witnessed the execution to do the same. The need for such reassurance accounts to a considerable extent for the fascination with which the crowd looked upon the malefactor's final moments. An idealized description of this attitude was provided by an officiating priest in 1825. Executions, he wrote, made a deep impression on the people who watched them.

A numberless crowd accompanies the malefactor on his last journey, observes every glance and every expression of the same, wishes to hear every word he yet speaks, and when he climbs the bloody scaffold, awaits, in complete stillness and with fast-beating heart, the decisive moment which completes the execution of earthly justice and places him before the judgment seat of the Everlasting. A melancholy sympathy overcomes those present as soon as they are convinced that true repentance has suffused the spirit of one who has sunk so low, and a doubtless honest prayer rises involuntarily from the hearts of the assembled thousands to the throne of the All-Merciful, that He should not completely reject the unfortunate before them.[110]

The concentration on the 'decisive moment' was central to the whole ritual. Everything built up to this instant of transition, everything revolved around it. It was the focal point of the entire ceremony.

d. Languages of the Dismembered Body

The execution did not end with the fatal blow. In Bavaria at least, the regulations required that 'the executioner's assistant, as soon as the head has been separated from the rump, grasps it by the hair and displays it to the people on all four sides of the stage'.[111] An additional element of obloquy was provided by the fact that, at least up to the end of the eighteenth century, this executioner's assistant was traditionally known as *Spitzwürfel*, perhaps because he 'threw the top' or head of the malefactor around, or at least brandished it at the crowd. He was dressed in a colourful coat, wore a pointed grey felt hat, and acted as a kind of comic character. Enlightenment reformers considered his caperings inappropriate to the seriousness of the occasion and, with the new Bavarian Criminal Code of 1813, his colourful clothing was outlawed, he was expressly forbidden to make any

---

[109] Claude Lévi-Strauss, *Tristes Tropiques* (London, 1973), 301–6.
[110] *Erzählung* (n. 95 above), 1–2.
[111] StA Munich, App. Ger. 5704, 'Was bey der Verkündung des Todes-Urtheils zu beobachten ist', 22 Feb. 1812, § 14.

comical gestures or movements, and his functions were restricted to holding the head in the leather sling and showing it to the crowd after decapitation. But he continued to be known by his old name in popular parlance, and as late as 1850 the raising of the severed head was inevitably accompanied at Bavarian executions by cries from the crowd of 'Hold it tight, *Spitzwürfel*; *Spitzwürfel*, don't let go!'[112] Treating the head in this way once more emphasized the power of state and community over the body of the malefactor. The irreverence of *Spitzwürfel*'s actions added to the dishonour brought upon the offender's remains. The soul was departed; what was left was mere dust.

Sometimes the punishments inflicted after death included the treatment of the offender's corpse in a manner that echoed the sanctions laid down in the *Carolina* for application to living bodies. In 1773, following the decapitation of the infanticide Maria Egger, the Tyrolean hangman was ordered to drive a stake through the corpse, in a simulation of part of the punishment of burial alive which was the measure ordained for this crime by the code of 1532.[113] And after Matthias Klostermaier had been broken with the wheel on 6 September 1771, a form of quartering took place:

the dead body was taken below the scaffold, which was covered in beneath the stage on all four sides with planks, and eviscerated and quartered there. The innards were immediately buried beneath the scaffold and the head placed above it. Next to it the upper right quarter was hanged on a so-called 'express gallows'. The other parts of the body, however, were taken further away, the upper left quarter to Schwabmünchen, the lower right to Oberdorf, and the lower left to Füssen.[114]

Similarly, when Melchior Hedloff was executed in Breslau in 1654, it was reported that 'lastly his body was divided into four pieces, said pieces (to one of which, namely the right quarter, the head was left attached) were hanged on four public highways each with a copper placard put up beside it'.[115]

More generally, a number of the more severe variants of capital punishment required the display of the head and body of the offender after death, not so much as a simple means of advertising the majesty of the law,[116] as an additional, final form of degradation and dishonouring of the malefactor. This was normal, as we have seen, in the case of breaking with the wheel, and often occurred with hanging too. The length of time for which a body was displayed on the gallows or the wheel varied widely. In Walddürn in 1818, the head of an executed criminal was left on the pole for twenty-four hours only,[117] while just over a century before, one corpse had been left to rot on the gallows outside Munich for no less than five years, from 1697 to 1702, and there were reports that another stayed on

---

[112] Völderndorff und Waradein, *Plaudereien*, i. 104.   [113] Moser, *Scharfrichter von Tirol*, 105.
[114] Nöggeler, *Bayerischer Hiesel*, 199.   [115] *Melcher Hedloffs Mord-Thaten*.
[116] As Spierenburg, *Spectacle*, 56–8, maintains.   [117] Eggler, *Waldstetter Mord*, 27.

FIG. 8. *Disposal of the remains.* Quartering of the robber Matthias, commonly known as 'Windbag', in eighteenth-century Bavaria. Note the limb attached to the gallows on the right, and the executioner's servant sorting through the condemned man's clothes below it; the garments, after biblical precedent, became the executioner's property. The wheel, and the block and cord used for tying the offender down, can be seen at the back of the ravenstone. The caption reads: 'Behold, you robbers, look, you thieves | Behold the bloody sight today | In just this manner, you will see | You all shall die, in just this way.'

the scaffold in Stadtroda from 1776 all the way up to 1784.[118] The doctor Louis Stromeyer even remembered seeing 'the blackish remains' of an executed malefactor on the gallows near Hanover over a period of at least ten years during his youth at the beginning of the nineteenth century.[119] More normal was some length of time in between these extremes, such as the fourteen days common in Berne in the mid-eighteenth century.[120] Sometimes the executioners took down the corpses on their own initiative, to make room for new ones and save on materials.[121] Popular belief does not seem to have considered that such practices

---

[118] Behringer, 'Mörder', 112; Glenzdorf and Treichel, *Henker*, 61.

[119] Georg Friedrich Louis Stromeyer, *Erinnerungen eines deutschen Arztes*, 2nd edn. (Hanover, 1875; repr. Berlin, 1877), i. 74.

[120] Sommer, *Scharfrichter von Bern*, 108.

[121] Sta Hanover A 1200, *passim*, recording complaints by the authorities at this unauthorized practice.

impeded the condemned person's chances of salvation.[122] Nor were there objections when, as sometimes happened, the body, instead of being displayed, was taken off to the anatomists for dissection,[123] or when, for a brief period at the end of the eighteenth century and the beginning of the nineteenth, experiments were made on the spot to see if the brain was still working inside the severed head.[124] Nevertheless, whether it was undertaken by the executioner or by the medical men, such treatment of the corpse was still dishonouring, because it involved display and interment outside the city walls, once more symbolizing the malefactor's status as an outcast even in death.[125]

The friends and family of the condemned seem to have had few, if any, claims on the body, unlike in England, where it was customarily given to them for burial. Until the nineteenth century, at least, the disposal of the malefactor's corpse in Germany was almost always a matter for the authorities. Often it was just buried without ceremony in an unmarked grave beneath the scaffold or close by. In this highly status-conscious society, the punishment dishonoured the condemned's family and deprived it of rights, and it would have increased their dishonour still further had they handled the infamous remains. A respectable burial was in any case not possible. In a curious imaginary dialogue between two men executed in Hamburg in 1733, one of them, a Jew who has died without converting to Christianity, meets the other, a cobbler who had refused to confess and repent, in hell, and asks him whether he has any regrets now:

COBBLER. I was, to be sure, content to have my head cut off, but I wanted to be buried in the churchyard and to be borne there by the shoemakers' guild.
JEW. Didn't they want to permit that for you?
COBBLER. No! I had the masters asked on my behalf, but I got the answer that it couldn't be done, because an honourable guild wouldn't carry someone to his grave who had died such a violent death.[126]

---

[122] Hartl, *Wiener Kriminalgericht*, 422.

[123] Danker, *Räuberbanden*, 200. For popular and family opposition to the anatomization of criminal corpses in England, see Peter Linebaugh, 'The Tyburn Riot against the Surgeons', in Douglas Hay *et al.* (eds.), *Albion's Fatal Tree: Crime and Society in Eighteenth-Century England* (London, 1975), 65–118; and in America, Steven Robert Wilf, 'Anatomy and Punishment in late Eighteenth-Century New York', *Journal of Social History*, 23 (1989), 507–30. See also S. Edgerton, *Pictures and Punishment: Art and Criminal Prosecution during the Florentine Renaissance* (London, 1985).

[124] Manfred Franke, *Schinderhannes. Das kurze, wilde Leben des Johannes Bückler, Nach alten Documenten neu erzählt* (Düsseldorf, 1984), 318–19. On this occasion, two medical students shouted into the ears of the severed heads, 'Can you hear me?' For the record, the heads showed no reaction. For another, similar experiment, see Holtei, *Vierzig Jahre*, i. 123–4.

[125] Spierenburg, *Spectacle*, 90.

[126] Anon., *Curieuses Gespräch im Reiche der Todten, zwischen dem am 21ten Julii dieses 1733ten Jahres, in Hamburg, wegen verübten Diebstahls, gehängten Juden: Susmann Moses, und dem am 10. Augusti H.A. in Altona, wegen begangenen Mords an seiner leiblichen Frauen, hingerichteten Schusters: Samuel Rattge, worinnen beyde einander ihren bösen Lebens-Wandel erzehlen, und bedauern, dass sie in dem Unglauben und Unbussfertigkeit gestorben sind* (Hamburg, 1733).

In Vienna a special cemetery was reserved for executed criminals, and their burial was carried out by a religious confraternity whose foundation had been explicitly approved by Pope Urban VII.[127] The family could not even claim the clothes worn by the offender before he had put on the burial shroud. These traditionally went to the executioners and their assistants.[128] In 1750 the town council of Augsburg formally gave the executioner the right to claim the clothes put aside by the condemned person when the poor sinner's shroud was donned.[129] Sometimes the informal claim to this presumed perquisite was a cause of trouble. In 1837, the executioner Otto filed a lawsuit in Königsee to gain possession of the clothes of an offender whom he had beheaded,[130] while two years later, in 1839, it was reported that

> at an execution that recently took place in the Frankfurt Department, one executioner's servant inflicted such a head injury on his fellow servant with a spade, in a quarrel over a piece of clothing from the criminal whom they had just dispatched, that it was only by a lucky chance that a homicide was not committed at the place of execution itself.[131]

But the clothes of the condemned were not the only prerogative of the executioner. Perhaps the most extraordinary feature of executions in early modern Germany, and indeed well into the nineteenth century, was the sale of the condemned person's blood to members of the watching crowd after decapitation had taken place.

There are numerous reports of this practice dating from the seventeenth century onwards. In 1674 it was noted in Nuremberg that the blood of executed criminals was caught in a cup as it spurted from the severed neck, in order 'to give it variously to poor and afflicted people who were burdened with the heavy disease or falling sickness, whereby they were cured and healthy and healed'.[132] There was another report of a blood-sale at a beheading in Dresden in 1731. In the same city in 1755, as a murderer was due to be decapitated, two journeymen tailors asked the authorities in charge of the proceedings for permission to let a fellow journeyman suffering from epilepsy to drink the blood of the condemned after decapitation. The request was granted.[133] At the guillotining of the notorious bandit Schinderhannes in Mainz in 1802, eyewitnesses reported that the executioner's servants caught the blood in a beaker and that some of the onlookers drank it as a cure for epilepsy.[134] Ten years later, the 8-year-old Louis

---

[127] Hartl, *Wiener Kriminalgericht*, 133. For the role of religious confraternities at French executions, see McManners, *Death*, 382–3, and in Italy, Puppi, *Torment*, 40–50.

[128] Schuhmann, *Scharfrichter*, 134.

[129] Oppelt, *Unehrlichkeit*, 724. In 1756 this was restricted to criminals whose bodies were subsequently sent to the anatomists for dissection.

[130] Glenzdorf and Treichel, *Henker*, i. 113.   [131] GStA Berlin Rep. 84a/7782, Bl. 105.

[132] Nürnberg Amts- und Standbücher, 1674, quoted in Dülmen, *Theater*, 163.

[133] Keller, *Scharfrichter*, 232.

[134] Elwenspoek, *Schinderhannes*, 233; Franke, *Schinderhannes*, 318.

Der Reburgischen Prediger Mörder Straffe

| 1 | 2 | 3 | 4 | 5 | 6 | 7 |

| Christoph Koch *Ein Schneider* | Dietrich Kahle *Ein Schlächter* | Hans Heinrich *Voigt Kellerwirth* | Fridrich Wilhem *Flehpeg Guarde Reuter* | Michel Most *Braumeister* | Levin Voigt *Hoppenführer* | Johan Herman *Meier Ein Schuster* |

FIG. 9. *Bodies displayed on the wheel.* This etching shows the bodies of a gang of seven robbers and murderers, each entwined on a wheel, with his head impaled on the pole. In the background, the various punishments meted out to the men beforehand are indicated: beheading, breaking with the wheel, and pulling-out of the flesh with red-hot tongs. The illustration is not intended as a literal representation of the punishment, merely as a kind of visual shorthand provided to show the fate of each of the offenders. In fact, the head would have been clearly separated from the body in each case, and the body displayed horizontally rather than vertically. The name and trade of each offender is indicated below the appropriate portrait.

Stromeyer, son of a well-off professional family in Hanover, was taken by the family servant to see a beheading, and observed how women dipped handkerchiefs in the decapitated malefactor's blood to use as a cure for epilepsy. The epileptics then ran off through the crowd, accompanied by those administering the cure, and were supposed to keep running until they dropped.[135] Other instances of blood-drinking at executions were noted in Neustadt (Hesse) in 1812 and Schneeberg, near Zwickau, the following year. At a beheading in Stralsund in 1814 an observer wrote that:

The most remarkable phenomenon at this execution was that of two riders, apparently outsiders. They led a poor sick man, probably an epileptic, and filled a moderately large jug to the brim with the executed person's blood. After the invalid had drained the ghastly contents right to the bottom, he was bound fast between the horses with strong reins and pulled away at a breakneck gallop.[136]

Similarly, in 1820, at the execution of Karl Ludwig Sand, the nationalist revolutionary student who had assassinated the conservative writer August von

---

[135] Stromeyer, *Erinnerungen*, i. 75.
[136] Ernst Bargheer, *Eingeweide. Lebens- und Seelenkräfte der Leibesinneren* (Berlin, 1931), 266–7.

Kotzebue and thereby provoked the notorious Karlsbad Decrees in 1819, on-lookers were reported to have stormed the scaffold, soaked up his blood with kerchiefs, broken up the stool on which he had sat, and distributed the pieces.[137] This event may for some of those concerned have represented a political adaptation of the tradition, but for others it may have had no more than the usual medicinal significance. So widespread indeed was the belief in the healing powers of a malefactor's blood that, on one occasion at least, a sick person even committed murder in order to obtain it. In 1824, a young, mentally ill rural labourer, Johann Georg Sörgel, arrested for the murder of an elderly peasant, confessed: 'I've killed him, so that I can get a poor sinner's blood to drink; the man has horns on.'[138] He heard voices in his head and was liable to bouts of violence, and evidently thought that he could cure himself in this way.

Incidences of spectators at executions drinking the malefactor's blood continued throughout the 1820s, including for example one reported from Reutlingen in 1829. But in 1843, an incident in Stockhausen, in the Kingdom of Hanover, illustrated the increased difficulty that such requests were encountering by the mid-nineteenth century. Six epileptics, equipped with drinking-mugs, had gathered round the scaffold, but the officials refused them access to the blood on the advice of a medical specialist, who told them it had no effect on the disease. The local court assessor, however, took pity on them and secured a certification from two professors at the nearby University of Göttingen that drinking the blood could have a beneficial psychological effect. After this, the officials at the execution relented and allowed the epileptics onto the scaffold.[139] The following year, at a beheading in Oldenburg, no such difficulties were encountered when members of the crowd came up to drink the dead man's blood. In 1854, at an execution in the small Franconian town of Adelsheim, it was noted that

after the execution was completed, a number of people, mainly women, hurried eagerly to the scaffold to dip their aprons, handkerchiefs and whips in the poor sinner's blood. For thanks to its expiatory healing effect, this 'very special juice' keeps sickness and witches from house and stable and protects them against the danger of lightning.[140]

In 1858 an eyewitness at an execution in Göttingen gave a particularly detailed and graphic account of this practice. After the officers of the law had formally handed the condemned man over to the executioner on the scaffold,

The assisstants led him to the execution chair, and he sat down on it. They pulled a white cap over his head and eyes and bound his arms and legs securely to the chair. Under his

137 Oppelt, *Unehrlichkeit*, 754.
138 Paul Anselm Ritter von Feuerbach, *Aktenmässige Darstellung merkwürdiger Verbrechen* (2 vols.; Giessen, 1828–9), i. 267.
139 *Göttinger Monatsblätter*, June 1980, p. 8 (suppl. to *Göttinger Tageblatt*).
140 Graef, 'Hochgericht'.

chin they placed a leather sling, by means of which one of the assistants pulled his head back tightly, and held it there. . . . The executioner drew the great, broad, sharp, highly polished execution sword from under his cloak, stepped to the left side of the condemned, drew back his arms, and in a trice severed the head from the rump, cutting through the neck more with a smooth stroke than with a blow. The head remained in the leather sling, and two columns of blood spurted up from the surface of the neck-wound, to fall back and rise, and fall again a few more times, ever lower and weaker, with the succeeding heartbeats. . . . Close by the scaffold a few sufferers from epileptic fits had posted themselves. They had handed the assistants glass vessels in which the assistants caught the blood as it bubbled over and gave it to the epileptics, who drank it immediately. . . . A peasant woman, who also took some blood away with her in a little bottle, (said), 'I'm going to paint the front door with it, it's good against the danger of fire.'[141]

The practice of blood-drinking was still being recorded in the 1860s, for example in Hanau in 1861. In 1862, the governors of the workhouse in Appenzell gave an epileptic inmate permission to attend a nearby execution to seek a cure, advising her to drink three mouthfuls of warm blood from the dead malefactor's corpse.[142] In Berlin as late as 1864, executioners' assistants were reported to have sold for two thalers a piece a considerable quantity of white handkerchiefs which had been dipped in the blood of two executed criminals. The last recorded instance of blood-drinking at an execution took place in Marburg in 1865.[143]

If they were unwilling to pay for the blood, people could always try to raid the gallows or the wheel after everyone had gone home, to secure a part of the criminal's body displayed there. In 1770 the fingers were cut off and removed from the body of a criminal hanged in Memmingen.[144] In the Swiss town of Saanen, 'between 11 and 12 p.m. on Christmas Eve 1795, the dyer Christian St. carried out superstitious acts and ceremonies near the gallows and dug around for the body of a man who had been executed and buried here a year before'. He was obliged to 'ask pardon for this nuisance caused to the whole community . . . in front of the entire assembled corps of honorable citizens'.[145] In Hamburg in 1801, a doctor complained that the corpses of executed criminals were 'completely ransacked in a moment for the purposes of anti-epileptic pharmacology'. In 1811, the Pomeranian High Court reported the display of the dead bodies of executed criminals at the place of execution in the following terms: 'The general superstition of the common mob, that the possession of a limb of an executed malefactor or a piece of his clothing brings good luck, has led to frequent misappropriations of such items from those places; two such cases have recently

[141] GStA Berlin Rep. 84a/7785, Bl. 316 ff.: Auszug aus den Lebenserinnerungen von Wilhelm Waldeyer-Hartz. See also Stromeyer, *Erinnerungen*, 283.

[142] H. Bächthold-Stäubli (ed.), *Handwörterbuch des deutschen Aberglaubens* (10 vols.; Berlin, 1927–42): 'Blut'.

[143] Ibid.: 'Hinrichtung'; Oppelt, *Unehrlichkeit*, 749–51.   [144] Schuhmann, *Scharfrichter*, 220.

[145] Sommer, *Scharfrichter von Bern*, 87.

come to our judicial notice.' Two journeymen cobblers, continued the report, had taken a bone from a criminal's body from the wheel in Pollnow, while a postman had removed the chain with which it was secured.[146] In 1823 the thumbs were cut off a criminal's corpse in Schneeberg, Saxony, the day after execution, and within a week all the fingers, toes, and clothing had disappeared;[147] and in Rochlitz in 1837 the head of a decapitated murderer disappeared without trace the night after the execution.[148]

These relics were used for a variety of purposes. The finger of an executed person was said to be a cure for warts or a defence against witchcraft; buried under one's house, it brought general good luck to the inhabitants; carried in the pocket or on the person, it warded off lice and vermin; kept in one's purse, it brought money. Innkeepers could suspend it in their beer-barrels to attract customers (presumably only if they were unaware of its presence!); cattle would become fat if scratched with it. Pieces of skin from executed criminals were used in amulets to ward off various kinds of evil, while the pubic hair of an offender's corpse would increase the likelihood of conception if carried in a bag wrapped around the genitals.[149] Lightning and fire could also be warded off by the use of the blood. But the most common use of such relics, and above all the blood, was, as we have already seen, as a cure for epilepsy. The disease had been regarded as a sign of demoniacal possession in ancient times. A Hippocratic text of the fourth century BC, after describing the symptoms of epilepsy, noted that 'they purify the sufferers from the disease with blood and such like, as though they were polluted, blood-guilty, bewitched by men, or had committed some unholy act'.[150] In the New Testament, the associations of bewitchment, guilt, or 'unholiness' had become concentrated into the notion of demoniacal possession. In the Gospel of St Mark 9: 17–29, a man is reported saying to Jesus:

Master, I have brought unto thee my son, which hath a dumb spirit; And wheresoever he taketh him, he teareth him: and he foameth, and gnasheth with his teeth, and pineth away . . . and when he [Jesus] saw him, straightway the spirit tare him; and he fell on the ground, and wallowed foaming. . . . Jesus . . . rebuked the foul spirit, saying unto him, Thou dumb and deaf spirit, I charge thee, come out of him, and enter no more into him. And the spirit cried, and rent him sore, and came out of him, and he was as one dead . . . But Jesus took him by the hand, and lifted him up; and he arose.[151]

In the first century AD, the Roman writer Pliny noted that 'the blood of gladiators is drunk by epileptics as though it were the draught of life.'[152] In the Byzantine

[146] GStA Berlin Rep. 84a/7781, Bl. 214.   [147] Keller, *Scharfrichter*, 232.

[148] Bächthold-Stäubli, *Handwörterbuch*, 'Hinrichtung'.

[149] Ibid.; also Keller, *Scharfrichter*, 228–9.

[150] *Hippocrates*, ii, ed. and tr. W. H. S. Jones (Cambridge, Mass., 1923): 'The Sacred Disease', 127–8 (word order amended).

[151] For parallel accounts of this episode, see Matthew 17: 14–20, and Luke 9: 37–43.

[152] Pliny, *Natural History*, Book 28, I. 3 to II. 5.

Empire, the blood of executed criminals was used as a substitute.[153] By the Middle Ages, writers were combining these two ideas of possession and 'quasi-death' by arguing that in an epileptic fit the soul was driven out of the body by a demon.[154] Thus St Hildegard of Bingen, writing in the twelfth century, argued that epilepsy was a symptom of the withdrawal of the soul from the body, which then fell down and remained still until the soul returned. St Thomas Aquinas agreed that the disease rendered its victims 'quasi-dead'.[155] Ostensibly because of the presumed liability to periodic bouts of demoniacal possession, epileptics were regarded as dishonourable; even their breath, as the thirteenth-century preacher Berthold of Regensburg, warned, was contaminating.[156] In the guild regulations of 1510 in Nuremberg, epileptics were specifically listed among those considered unworthy of membership, while a century or so earlier, the city council in Basel had urged their expulsion from the urban community altogether.[157]

The practice of using the blood and body parts of executed criminals to treat epilepsy thus reflected a popular belief that the life-force which resided in them could be transferred to the sufferers from the disease in order to prevent them succumbing to these bouts of temporary 'quasi-death'. Sudden death cut off people before their time, and lent potency to those parts of their body—the fingernails and toenails and hair—that appeared to carry on growing after death, as well as to the blood itself, the life-force which continued to flow for some time after the execution had taken place.[158] Moreover, these relics were especially holy, since they belonged to people who had died a good death, left the world in a state of repentance and grace, and, it was generally assumed, had gone straight to heaven. They could not dishonour people who were already outcasts from honourable society, as epileptics were, but the status of both offenders and epileptics was in any case highly ambivalent, the former both polluting and healing, and the latter rendered not only infamous but also in some sense sacred by the symptoms of their affliction, which had been known since antiquity as 'the sacred disease' (*Die heilige Krankheit*). Their symptoms, including trembling, convulsions, frothing at the mouth, and a trance-like state, were virtually identical to those exhibited by holy prophets and religious enthusiasts such as the Quakers. Whether the possession which they were thought to indicate was satanic or divine depended very much on the context. In their different ways, executed criminals and epileptics were both special, sacred people, different in the very nature of their being from ordinary mortals. Through physical contact with another sacred being, the epileptic could be healed, just as,

[153] Leo Kanner, 'The Folklore and Cultural History of Epilepsy', *Medical Life*, 37 (1930), 159–215, here 199.

[154] Owsei Temkin, *The Falling Sickness: A History of Epilepsy from the Greeks to the Beginnings of Modern Neurology*, 2nd edn. (Baltimore, 1971), 97–157.

[155] Ibid. 105, 110–17.   [156] Ibid. 115.   [157] Ibid. 110–17.   [158] See Barber, *Vampires*.

in the manner described by the great French historian Marc Bloch, the victims of scrofula were treated up to the eighteenth century in England and France by 'the royal touch' administered by the monarch.[159] Epileptics and the condemned were both 'contaminated by holiness', marked off from society and the community by their transitional status, on the boundaries of life and death. Attitudes to epilepsy, including the drinking of human blood as a cure, may well have been part of the 'underlying Eurasian mythological unity' which the Italian historian Carlo Ginzburg believes he has discovered in relation to witchcraft beliefs.[160] Yet the evidence for their transmission across the centuries is too unsatisfactory to be wholly convincing. In the end, beliefs surrounding the mutual relationship of epilepsy and executions would not need to have been passed down from generation to generation; they emerged functionally from the structurally liminal position of both in the context of popular attitudes to death and disease.[161]

The practice of blood-drinking was confined from the seventeenth century, when it first appears in the records, to Protestant areas of Germany.[162] It is possible, indeed, that its absence from the record before this time is not coincidental. For the same moralizing offensive that swept across Germany in the wake of the Thirty Years War was also directed in Protestant areas against the cult of saints, holy relics, and other aspects of what the Reformation historian Bob Scribner has called popular 'crypto-materialism', still prevalent in Catholic parts.[163] Gradually deprived of recourse to such sources of blessing and good luck by the actions of the Protestant Church and its network of lay and ecclesiastical courts, the common people in these areas, when faced with the desperate and in many ways unusual problem of dealing with an epileptic child, relative, friend, or colleague, fell back onto the collection of blood and body parts from executed criminals. The criminal on the scaffold took over in Protestant folk culture the role which continued to be played by the statue of Christ on the cross, the figure of the Virgin carried in procession, or the relic of the saint preserved in the church, in its Catholic counterpart. The blood and body of the executed criminal constituted a lesser but still symbolically potent version of the Communion service, a service which Protestant theology had robbed of many of the aspects

---

[159] Marc Bloch, *Les Rois thaumaturges. Essai sur le caractère surnaturel attribué à la puissance royale particulièrement en France et an Angleterre* (Paris, 1961).

[160] Carlo Ginzburg, *Ecstasies: Deciphering the Witches' Sabbath* (London, 1990), 267. For a penetrating critique of this work, see Perry Anderson, *A Zone of Engagement* (London, 1992), 207–29.

[161] Edmund Leach, *Culture and Communication: The Logic by which Symbols Are Connected* (Cambridge, 1976), esp. 78.

[162] The practice of blood-drinking at executions was also recorded in Denmark. See the report by Hans Christian Andersen quoted in Kanner, 'Folklore', 199–200.

[163] Discussion and references in Richard J. Evans, 'Religion and Society in Modern Germany', *European Studies Quarterly*, 12 (1982), 249–88, esp. 258–60.

Hier ist Koſmophilus mit Feſſeln angethan,
Fängt ſeine Gottesfurcht, mit Reü und Thränen an.
Iuſtitia tritt auff, hat Galgen Radt und Stahl,
Gott ſpricht, Theophile komm in des Himmels Saal!

FIG. 10. *The criminal's redemption through death*. This title-page of a biography of the robber Lips Tullian, executed in Dresden in 1715, shows Justice, sword in hand, beckoning Tullian's body to the wheel and gallows behind, while God (bearded ancient in cloud, top left) beckons his soul to Heaven in a parallel gesture, and the rays of divine mercy shine on Tullian's spirit (which is apparently located in his head) from top right. The caption reads: 'Here the worldling now all bound in fetters lies | starts to fear his God, his tears flow from his eyes | Justice comes along, with gallows, wheel and sword: | God tells the pious man to enter Heaven's door.'

and connotations for which popular, magico-religious culture still found a use. In Catholic areas, by contrast, the doctrine of purgatory made it difficult to regard the holiness of executed criminals as untainted. Even if it was certain that they would go to heaven, the route was by no means direct or instantaneous for them. Only in very exceptional cases, such as the execution of Louis XVI during the French Revolution, is the use of the blood of the beheaded for medico-magical purposes recorded in Catholic societies.[164]

The prevalence of such practices in Protestant areas added another dimension to the structures of opposites and inversions discernible in the rituals of execution everywhere. These structures corresponded closely to the borderline or liminal character of the rituals to which they belonged, just as the location of the execution on the edge of the town, between civilization and the wild, symbolized its location on the threshold of death. As a 'rite of passage' from life to death, the execution ceremony, from the formal condemnation to the display of the corpse after death, contained reversals and paradoxes which symbolized the transitional nature of the state of being which they signified.[165] These were contained within a formal structure of ritual which played out for ordinary mortals the religious drama of a 'good death'. The participation of the community by rank and order underlined the social character of the ritual: for dying in early modern Europe, as the French historian Pierre Chaunu has remarked, was 'a great social rite, in which the dying person is the principal actor, and a pedagogic rite: pedagogic because progressively taken over . . . by the clergy'.[166] As 'one of the purest forms of death as a "social rite"',[167] public executions contained a mixture of sacred and secular images of authority, and reflected broader patterns of attitudes towards death and dying.

---

[164] For Louis XVI's blood, into which spectators dipped handkerchiefs, paper, linen, and even a couple of dice, see Lenôtre, *Guillotine*, 105–6. For Italy, see A. Prosperi, 'Il sangue e l'animà. Richerche sulle compagnie di giustizia in Italia', *Quaderni Storici*, 51/17 (1982), 959–99.

[165] Victor Turner, *Dramas, Fields and Metaphors: Symbolic Actions in Human Society* (Ithaca, NY, 1975).

[166] Pierre Chaunu, 'Mourir à Paris (XVIe–XVIIe–XVIIIe siècles)', *Annales ESC*, 31 (1976), 39, quoted in J. A. Sharpe, '"Last Dying Speeches": Religion, Ideology and Public Executions in Seventeenth-Century England', *Past and Present*, 107 (1983), 144–67, here 160–1. For further evidence of parallels between English and German executions in this period, see Douglas Hay, 'Property, Authority and the Criminal Law', in Hay *et al.* (eds.), *Albion's Fatal Tree*, 17–64; Randall McGowen, 'The Body and Punishment', *Journal of Modern History*, 59/4 (1987), 651–79; idem, '"He Beareth Not the Sword in Vain": Religion and the Criminal Law in Eighteenth-Century England', *Eighteenth-Century Studies*, 2 (1987/8), 192–211; John Delaney, 'Bourgeois morals/public punishment. England c.1750s–1860s' (Ph.D. thesis, Australian National University, 1989), 21–2, 32–3, 35–6, 39–40, 45; Thomas W. Laqueur, 'Crowds, Carnival and the State in English Executions, 1604–1868', in A. L. Beier, D. Cannadine, and J. M. Rosenheim (eds.), *The First Modern Society: Essays in English History in Honour of Lawrence Stone* (Cambridge, 1989), 305–55, here 306–9.

[167] Sharpe, '"Last Dying Speeches"', 161.

e. Reversing the Signs

In the early modern town, processions and ceremonies of all kinds marked almost every formal occasion and took place all through the year. Carnivals, guild festivals, weddings, official visits and progresses by the sovereign, coronations, the installation of a new burgomaster or bishop, the opening of a court session, holy days, saints' days—all these and many more such events provided welcome occasions for public festivals and processions. People of all degrees and stations in life were used to these events, and regularly watched or took part in them. So familiar was the unwritten language of the urban procession that the smallest variations in route and ritual, in order and composition, in personnel and practice, bore a heavy burden of meaning. Historians have often compared executions to carnivals,[168] but in fact both were examples of a much more basic, pre-literate popular cultural practice, in which the urban community took to the streets in order to mark occasions of varying import to itself. The ritual of execution thus has to be understood as a variation on ritual processions and ceremonies that took place in other contexts and with other purposes. All of them were a normal part of the fabric of life on the streets of the early modern German town.[169]

The ceremony of execution would have been popularly understood, among other things, as a variant of the normal ceremony of death and burial. Both were rites of passage from life to death, from one state of being—the physical and temporal—into another—the eternal life of the soul.[170] The various stages of the ritual, and the symbolic acts, objects, and words associated with them, recalled to all who witnessed or participated in them the similar but contrasting stages of a normal funeral. As the historian Joachim Whaley has remarked, funerals in seventeenth- and eighteenth-century Germany were public, communal events. 'Mourners of differing grades wore clothes corresponding not only to their own status, but also to their relationship with the departed. . . . The legal and social differences which divided men in life were mirrored in death.'[171] Such rituals were, like the closely related execution rites, essentially created in the sixteenth century, as the Reformation brought about a greater involvement of the state and the secular community in a ceremony that had previously been the exclusive

---

[168] See Laqueur, 'Crowds', for examples.

[169] Farge, *Fragile Lives*, 184. See also R. Weismann, *Ritual Brotherhood in Renaissance Florence* (New York, 1982), and Edward Muir, *Civic Ritual in Renaissance Venice* (New York, 1983).

[170] See Nigel Llewellyn, *The Art of Death: Visual Culture in the English Death Ritual c.1500–c.1800* (London, 1991), 18.

[171] Joachim Whaley, 'Symbolism for the Survivors: The Disposal of the Dead in Hamburg in the Late Seventeenth and Eighteenth Centuries', in Joachim Whaley (ed.), *Mirrors of Mortality: Studies in the Social History of Death* (London, 1981), 80–105, here 83–4.

province of the Church. But it was only in the seventeenth century that funerals in Hamburg, as elsewhere, became really elaborate. Announced in advance by a placard posted outside the Exchange, the city's main meeting-place, the ritual was accompanied by the tolling of bells and commenced with a communal meal held in the deceased's house, where the funeral orations were delivered. Then a procession formed, headed usually by a school choir, with the music master, after which came the corpse, followed by the chief mourners and four principal guests wearing long cloaks. The clergy would usually come next, together with doctors of law and medicine. Then came a series of other guests in order of precedence; it was even possible to hire the burgomasters and the entire Senate, the ruling body of the city, for such an occasion, if the money was available to pay the very substantial fees which they demanded. The procession was also attended by professional mourners (*Leichenbitter*) and—if the deceased's family was especially prominent or wealthy—fully caparisoned Senate servants riding on horseback (*Reitendiener*). Finally anyone else from the urban community was invited to join the procession in the appropriate place should they so wish. At the funerals of leading officers of state, such as the burgomasters, anything up to four thousand people were recorded as participating. They made their way through the streets to the church, often circling around if the direct way was too short. 'The ensuing service', as Whaley remarks, 'was short. Funeral orations were rare and sermons brief. . . . The interment itself was an anti-climax, a hurried end to a remarkably elaborate and lengthy ritual.'[172]

As this description suggests, many aspects of seventeenth- and eighteenth-century funerals and executions were remarkably similar. They shared a common culture of death and dying. In both cases, the dying person was expected to make a speech, to comfort and admonish those left behind. The repast in the deceased's home before the funeral paralleled the Hangman's Meal in the town hall before the execution. The size and composition of the funeral and execution processions were broadly comparable, with state officials, children (sometimes from found-ling hospitals), clergy, outriders, and members of the public taking part in both. The brevity of the church service and burial was matched by the short duration of the execution and disposal of the body. The major difference, of course, was that the person at the centre of the execution ritual was physically alive for most of the proceedings, unlike the person at the focus of the funeral ceremony. The dying person's last edifying speech and confession, made on the death-bed before assembled friends and relatives just before the ritual mourning and funeral ceremonies began, was made in the case of executions before the assembled

---

[172] Joachim Whaley, 'Symbolism for the Survivors: The Disposal of the Dead in Hamburg in the Late Seventeenth and Eighteenth Centuries', in Joachim Whaley (ed.), 87–95. For the importance of funeral processions in late medieval and early modern France, see Ariès, *The Hour of our Death*, 165–8.

crowd on the scaffold, just before these procedures ended. Indeed, many of the signs inscribed in the normal rituals of death and dying were reversed in the execution ceremony. The death-bed and the 'poor sinner's parlour' were both public places, and the death itself was played out before an audience in both instances, but while the normal dying person was surrounded by friends and well-wishers, concerned to keep his or her social body alive within the community through acts of remembrance and reconciliation, the malefactor's end was witnessed by a community whose main purpose was rejection, expulsion, and the erasure of memory and belonging. Funeral orations for the naturally deceased were echoed by verdict and sentence read over the condemned malefactor, with each containing an elaborate description of the subject's life and works; but the former were held after death, towards the end of the ritual process, the latter before death, and at the beginning. A bell was tolled during both ceremonies, but at executions, instead of a funeral bell, it was usual for the tocsin (*Sturmglocke* or 'storm bell') to be sounded, in a symbolic reversal of the normal funeral rite. It was not an honoured citizen who was being laid to rest, but a danger to the community who was being disposed of. The same bell was also commonly rung when a sentence of banishment (*Verbannung*) was being carried out, and continued to toll until the offender concerned had been taken out through the city gate. In 1747, too, it was sounded in Augsburg as the executioner burned some libellous publications banned by the town council.[173] The direction of the procession in normal funerals, circling round the streets from the house to church and cemetery, emphasized the fact that the deceased was being interred as an honoured member of both the religious and secular communities of the town, while the direction of the execution procession, passing through the streets out of the main gate into the world beyond, emphasized by contrast the fact that the malefactor was being expelled from the community and would only survive in its collective memory as an outcast. The period of exposure of the malefactor's corpse constituted an infamous obverse to the period of mourning for the righteous dead.[174]

As the great ethnologist Arnold van Gennep observed, funerals, like other rites of passage, such as those, for example, marking the transition from adolescence to adulthood, can be divided into rites of separation, where the previous state of being is left behind; rites of transition, where the change actually takes place; and rites of incorporation, where the individual concerned is assimilated to the new state of being. In funerals, rites of separation are usually very minimal, while rites of transition and incorporation are often extremely elaborate. The visit to the death-bed or condemned cell, the respects paid to the laid-out body of the

[173] Schuhmann, *Scharfrichter*, 177.   [174] See Whaley, 'Symbolism', and also Beier, 'Good Death'.

deceased, and the subsequent funeral feast or Hangman's Meal may be taken as a rite of separation, where a formal farewell is taken of the deceased or condemned person. Already with the clothing of the condemned in the burial shroud and the breaking of the wand of office, the rites of transition had begun. The act of walking or processing through the town was a bodily signification of transition, and on arrival at the graveyard or the place of execution, the rites of separation began: the interment, with its formulaic intonements, the ritual phrases, speeches, and actions on the scaffold, integrating the departed into the new state of being in the world hereafter. In all this, the rites of transition were by far the lengthiest and the most powerful. Not only were they important in order to ensure that the dead did not return, they also lent the condemned an unusual ritual potency which formed another source of their healing power;[175] for executions were above all collective rituals, where authority and community joined together in a ceremony of retribution, expiation, and purification, expressed in the symbolic language of religion, and where everybody, including the malefactor, played a foreordained part. They were given meaning by both their similarities with, and their deviations from, other ceremonies of a similar kind. Public executions took place in a society where social interaction of all kinds was highly formalized and ritualized, from modes of address to styles of clothing; where rights and duties were prescribed according to social standing; and where honour, status, and a place in the social order were not only largely inherited by birth but were also signified in death by funerary monuments in churches and graveyards.

Public executions also took place in a society where death was omnipresent. The violence visited by the state upon the body of the malefactor exceeded in degree rather than in kind the violence visited by the hardships of everyday life upon the body of the ordinary citizen. Familiarity with death did not imply indifference to it, otherwise nobody would have bothered to attend an execution at all.[176] But it did mean that the methods people had developed to cope with it had to be powerful ones. In the harsh world of early modern Europe, they had evolved a variety of social and psychological strategies to come to terms with the fragility of their bodies, with the physical pain and suffering which all of them had to undergo. The ritual drama of the scaffold can be seen as one such strategy. The sequence of judgment, retribution, repentance, and redemption acted out for all the hope of a future life for those who were eventually cast out from the human community by death. Religion, the attribution of earthly events to divine disposition, and the belief that they could be influenced by appeals to the

[175] Arnold van Gennep, *The Rites of Passage* (1908; repr. Chicago, 1960). See also Anton Blok, 'Openbare strafvolstrekkingen als rites de passage', *Tijdschrift voor Geschiedenis*, 97 (1984), 347–69.
[176] Farge, *Fragile Lives*, 185–6.

supernatural, was another, even if it was, of course, much more than that too. To the authorities and the people alike, the execution of a malefactor appeared, therefore, as the expression of a divine justice of which the prince or the city-state was merely the earthly arm.

Executions in seventeenth- and eighteenth-century Germany bore very little resemblance to carnivals, except to the extent that they involved people processing through the streets. As David Kunzle has remarked, they were a kind of 'tragic drama . . . The public lacked the light-hearted spirit which they brought to the fairground farce or the carnival play.'[177] A public execution was no insensate eruption of an instinctual delight in suffering and cruelty. The festive and transgressive element in the execution ritual was minimal. Michel Foucault, followed by the American historian Thomas Laqueur, as we have seen, described public executions in England and France as carnivalesque events, with the condemned prisoner frequently behaving like a kind of jester, joining with the crowd in subverting the state's intention of mounting a tragic drama of official deterrence and retribution. Before the scaffold, according to Laqueur, the people 'gathered in a carnivalesque moment of political generativity':

The crowd at British executions was specifically a carnival crowd. It was so generically because executions bore a quite specific structural resemblance to carnival as the Lenten feast in which Christ's triumph over death is prefigured by the election: feasting accompanied with much ribaldry, trial and sacrifice of a carnival king in whose disorderly demise the ultimate chaos of death is contained.[178]

Invoking the work of the Russian literary critic Mikhail Bakhtin, Laqueur argued that executions, like carnivals, celebrated a temporary liberation from rank and hierarchy, signified by the ribald self-assertion of the criminal and the crowd. But Bakhtin, unlike some of his modern followers, did not mean to extend the concept of the carnivalesque until it embraced the whole of early modern social life.[179] He was careful to delimit it by remarking that carnivals 'were sharply distinct from the serious official, ecclesiastical, feudal and political cult forms and ceremonials'. They offered a subversive commentary on the formal rituals which accompanied so many aspects of everyday life in the early modern community. There was not one single or unified 'carnivalesque' culture in this world, but, Bakhtin argued, two cultures, the serious and the humorous. In serious, official feasts and festivals, the existing pattern of things was celebrated and reaffirmed; in carnivals, it was overturned. 'Rank was especially evident during official feasts;

[177] David Kunzle, *The Early Comic Strip; Narrative Strips and Picture Stories in the European Broadsheet from c.1450 to 1815* (Berkeley, 1973), 163.

[178] Laqueur, 'Crowds', 332, 339.

[179] See Peter Stallybrass and Allon White, *The Politics and Poetics of Transgression* (London, 1986), for conceptual inflation of this kind.

everyone was expected to appear in the full regalia of his calling, rank and merits and to take the place corresponding to his position. It was a consecration of inequality.' In carnival, by contrast, rank and hierarchy were suspended. All were considered equal during carnival. People were liberated from normal forms of speech and etiquette and developed 'special forms of marketplace speech and gesture, frank and free'.[180]

None of these aspects of the Bakhtinian carnivalesque could be observed in early modern German executions. As we have seen, the rituals which took place at these events were celebrations rather than subversions of hierarchy and order, serious rather than humorous, sacred as much as secular. The language, written, spoken, gestural, symbolic, in which they were conducted was not frank or free, but carefully prepared, stereotypical, formulaic, and pre-ordained, from the colours in which people and objects were presented to the phrases which they exchanged on the town square and at the scaffold. The executed criminal was not seen as a carnival king but as an avatar of Christ himself, physically humiliated but spiritually triumphant. Of course, it is much too simple in practice to divide early modern culture merely into the official and the carnivalesque; early modern society was never rigidly compartmentalized, and a certain amount of cultural interpenetration was inevitable. Executions, as we have seen, were not merely 'official', they also involved the active participation of the community as well. In Bavaria, at least, the caperings of *Spitzwürfel* injected an obvious element of the carnivalesque, though only after the fatal blow had been struck. But this did not detract from the popular understanding of the event as a religious ceremony, any more than did the secular accompaniments of pilgrimages, church services, and other sacred rituals at this time. In popular religion, the sacred and the secular, the spiritual and the material, were inextricably mixed. Executions were neither orgiastic celebrations of cruelty, nor carnivalesque outbursts of subversive popular ribaldry, nor one-way demonstrations of state power. They were representations of communal solidarity in the face of transgression, rites of passage from life to death, ceremonies of expulsion and reintegration, rituals of retribution, expiation, and redemption. Even where there was popular sympathy for the executed malefactor, execution was still seen as a fate pre-ordained by God, and it continued to be treated by the crowd as a rite of atonement and redemption in which the state was merely the instrument of a higher power. Nobody attacked the executioner because they thought his victim was being unjustly executed. The crowd's sympathy was expressed instead through participation in a collective ritual of absolution.

[180] Mikhail Bakhtin, *Rabelais and his World*, tr. Hélène Iswolsky (Cambridge, Mass., 1968), 4–10.

Although the emphasis placed by Foucault and Laqueur on the carnivalesque elements in executions thus seems exaggerated and based on a highly selective reading of the evidence,[181] it is none the less likely that the German ritual of capital punishment differed from its counterparts in England and France in a number of significant respects, particularly during the eighteenth century. In England, in contrast to Germany, the centrality of religious ritual to executions began to decline after about 1700. Efforts by the clergy to bring the offender to repentance became less marked, and a process of secularization began to set in. As James Sharpe has pointed out, 'by the early eighteenth century public execution, despite the continued presence of clergymen at the scaffold, was becoming more of an embodiment of secular power. Concern for the defence of property had replaced concern that the world would be overwhelmed by a deluge of sinfulness.'[182] Although most felons executed even in Tudor and Stuart England had been condemned for crimes against property,[183] the quantity and range of offences of this sort liable to capital punishment increased vastly in the course of the eighteenth century. In 1688, for example, there were only about fifty capital statutes in England; by 1820 the number had grown to more than 200.[184] Correspondingly, the acceptance of the execution process by felon and crowd alike began to decline. In England, capital punishment was applied to a large extent to thieves and others with whom the poor who formed the majority of the crowd at executions could, as the historian Peter Linebaugh in a recent study of executions in London has remarked, be expected to sympathize.[185] Similarly in *ancien régime* France during the eighteenth century, the death penalty was applied to over a hundred offences, including not only petty theft but also forgery, armed smuggling, fraudulent bankruptcy, breaches of the press censorship, and the abduction of an heiress. It was not surprising, therefore, that there was a relatively large number of instances of popular unrest at executions, above all where petty theft had been the crime. Here too there was evidence of a decline in general acceptance of the malefactor's fate, and a significant number of prisoners who repudiated the ministrations of religion.[186] In Germany, however, the state did not outrage its citizens by executing people for stealing a sixpence. Even in the seventeenth century, the vast majority of executions met with popular approval or acquiescence.

[181] See Gatrell, *Hanging Tree*, for an elaboration of these points.
[182] Sharpe, '"Last Dying Speeches"', 165–6; see also McGowen, 'The Body', 654–5.
[183] J. A. Sharpe, *Crime in Seventeenth-Century England: A County Study* (Cambridge, 1983), 143.
[184] Radzinowicz, *History*, i. 4.
[185] Peter Linebaugh, *The London Hanged: Crime and Civil Society in the Eighteenth Century* (London, 1991).
[186] McManners, *Death*, 368, 386.

In England, the crowd not only had a stronger motive for resisting, but also greater opportunities. According to Laqueur, closely following the arguments of Foucault, the state in England did not appear in public executions as 'the writer and director of a drama in which it appropriates to itself the active, authorial role while the people and the condemned are assigned subsidiary parts as compliant actors and appreciative viewers who understand the semiotics of state power to which they are being treated'.[187] Far from being solemn, well-orchestrated rituals, public hangings in England were squalid, hasty, often chaotic affairs. Tyburn itself was a shabby, semi-rural location, and, like execution sites in other cities, far removed from architectural embodiments of state power. Relatively few representatives of the state were present, and security measures were lax. The condemned were given licence to behave virtually as they liked, and did so. Many subverted the role assigned to them by playing the fool, wearing outrageous clothes, or making contrary speeches from the scaffold. By contrast, Peter Linebaugh has interpreted the behaviour of the crowd in terms of resistance to authority rather than consumerist demand for entertainment. The drama of execution was supposed to proceed according to a script prepared by the authorities, but the crowd, outraged by the hanging of poor people for acts of petty theft, resented the imposition of this scenario of ruling-class power and held the law and its operation in contempt. So frequent were riots and disturbances at executions, and so deep were the class antagonisms they expressed, that in 1773 the procession to the scaffold at Tyburn was abolished and hangings held in more secure surroundings, outside the prison at Newgate,[188] although it is probable that objections raised by aristocratic landowners around Tyburn, who feared for the value of their property, also played a role. Victor Gatrell has recently underlined this argument with a richly detailed account of the numerous acts of resistance by crowd and malefactor alike which took place during executions in England and Wales between 1770 and 1868, despite the presence of obvious ritual elements in the proceedings.[189] All this contrasted strongly with the characteristics we have observed in German executions in the seventeenth and eighteenth centuries. The lengthy ceremonial, from the announcement of the verdict and the procession to the scaffold to the execution of the malefactor, and the display of his or her body in Germany, was very elaborate, and often accompanied by a

[187] Laqueur, 'Crowds', 306–9. A major problem with Laqueur's analysis is its failure to examine change over time in the history of public executions from 1604 to 1868.

[188] Linebaugh, *The London Hanged*, 74, 150, 216–17. See also idem, 'The Ordinary of Newgate and His "Account"', in J. S. Cockburn (ed.), *Crime in England 1550–1800* (Princeton, 1971), 246–69. For the relative absence of crowd disturbances in American executions at this time, see Louis P. Masur, *Rites of Execution: Capital Punishment and the Transformation of American Culture, 1776–1865* (New York, 1989), 46.

[189] Gatrell, *Hanging Tree*, esp. 80–9 and 99–105.

massive turn-out of troops, officials, clergy, guildsmen, schoolboys, and other representatives of the community. The site of execution, whether on the town square or at the 'ravenstone' outside the town gates, was pregnant with the symbolism of princely, urban, and community authority. The crowd was much more structured in Germany than in England. The presence of several distinct categories of spectators and participants, from court officials and troops to schoolboys and priests, was required by custom, ordinance, or law, while other groups, such as epileptics, traditionally attended for specific reasons of their own. German society was rigidly divided into a hierarchy of orders, with the rights, duties, dress, and behaviour of each carefully prescribed. While the condemned in England could choose what clothes to wear, for example, German malefactors had to don a burial shroud while their own clothing was appropriated by the executioner. The ritual and ceremonial aspects in the German execution were more elaborate, less open to variations, and less secularized than in England. Popular consent, similarly, was also anchored in secular acclamation and religious participation by the crowd.[190]

The traditional execution in Germany was no outburst of unbridled mob violence, no carnivalesque celebration of popular power, but an elaborate ritual in which elements of élite and popular justice, formal church piety, and informal folk religion were combined. It constituted a series of symbolic acts, an individual and collective rite of passage from life to death, in which a person who had transgressed the moral and social norms of the day, as well as offended against its capital laws, was formally expelled from the community of the living in a manner that assuaged the collective conscience by offering the offender redemption and forgiveness through a final act of expiation. The attitude of the community to the offender was marked, therefore, not by hatred, still less by sadistic pleasure in witnessing physical suffering, but by a kind of compassion. Of course, the bodily language of punishment in this largely illiterate or semi-literate society was graphic, explicit, and physically violent. But in an age where medicine, even folk medicine, was largely ineffective, death rates were extremely high, and sickness and injury affected almost everyone with a frequency impossible to imagine today, physical suffering was accepted as an act of fate. Religious faith, virtually universal in German society in the early modern period, helped people come to terms with their hard lot and promised them that it would be transcended in the bliss of eternal life in the world hereafter. Towards the end of the eighteenth

[190] The elements of ritual and crowd consent were also strong in other European countries. For the infrequency of crowd disturbances at Dutch executions, see Spierenburg, *Spectacle*, 91–4. For studies of the ritual aspects of executions in late medieval France, see Esther Cohen, *The Crossroads of Justice: Law and Culture in Late Medieval France* (Leiden, 1993), and eadem, 'Symbols of Culpability and the Universal Language of Justice: The Ritual of Public Executions in Late Medieval Europe', *History of European Ideas*, 11 (1989), 407–16.

century, however, this situation was beginning to change. The unity of élite and popular culture had broken down, and the authorities and the crowds were becoming increasingly unwilling to collaborate in the rituals of execution as they had previously done. As we shall now see, the consequences of this breakdown were momentous.

3

A Rational Degree of Pain

a. The Decline of Torture

On 16 July 1734 Johann Schmid, accused of theft, was brought to the town hall in Brunswick to be interrogated by the investigating judges. Despite being confronted with the evidence of his crime, he denied all the charges brought against him. On the advice of the Law Faculty at Wittenberg University, the judges therefore decided to put Schmid to the torture. He was

admonished most earnestly not to withhold his confession any longer, in order that it should not have to be extracted from him by the torment that had been ordered to be carried out on him; but since he persisted in protesting his innocence, with the additional point that it would be enough if he had to let himself be tormented, he was . . . interrogated once more in a kindly manner.

To a series of questions drawn up by the Wittenberg jurists, Schmid consistently replied that he knew nothing about the crimes he was supposed to have committed; if he had been guilty, he said, they would surely have found the stolen goods in his possession; but, he added triumphantly, they had not. Unwilling to volunteer a confession, he was now handed over to the executioner, and, as the attendant scribe noted,

brought to the place of torture, where he is yet again earnestly admonished to admit the truth, so as not to submit himself to torment through his obstinacy; but since he continues to persist in protesting his innocence, adding that he can't do anything about it if they want to have him tormented, he is handed over to the executioner, who lays out before him the instruments assigned for the torture, and gives him to understand that if he won't confess, he will be tortured with them, and thereupon undresses him, allowing the interrogatee to help, whereupon he is fastened to the ladder, and the *thumbscrews* are put on, and the same screwed tight. Whereby he cries: 'Ah Lord Jesus, for God's sake! God have mercy on me, ah that hurts! Ah Lord Jesus! My thumbs, they'll never heal; ah I'm going to die!' Thereupon the *cords* are tied on him, whereby, when the chains are fastened tight, he cries with a loud voice: 'Ah strike my head off, ah my God, ah Lord Jesus, I have sinned, my head's bursting in my body, ah my arms, I'm a poor sinner, ah

FIG. 11. *The rack.* Illustration from the Austrian Code of 1768, showing how this torture is to be carried out. On the left: 'Sketch of the interrogatee's torso, seen from the front'. Centre: 'Sketch of the complete extension of the interrogatee on the ladder, seen somewhat from the side'. Right: 'Sketch of the extended interrogatee, seen from the side'. The descriptions A, B, C, etc., mostly refer to the same things. B denotes the executioner holding down the body of the interrogatee; F his servant turning the rack. Note the unashamedly graphic representation of pain on the interrogatee's face.

Lord God my arms, I'll confess everything; what shall I say afterwards, I'm being forced to do it, have mercy on me/ ah! Lord Jesus, that hurts so much, ah my Lord, my God have mercy on me, I did it all, I'll confess everything, I've offended my father and mother, ah I don't know what I can say for this terrible pain, ah thou Lord have pity on me, ah! Stop, for God's sake, ah I'm dying, my soul is departing', whereby he thrashes about with his head and legs and cries out the above-mentioned lamentations. After this he is pulled up the ladder, whereby he cries 'ah, that hurts! God will desert me if I don't confess, I did it all'. Since he now swears that he will tell the unadulterated truth, the instruments of torture are removed from him and he is thereupon interrogated on the charges, after he has withstood the torment for nearly an hour.

Questioned once more by the investigating judge, Schmid now readily confessed to the theft of which he stood accused.[1]

Torture was still a normal part of criminal proceedings in early eighteenth-century Germany, as this dramatic verbatim report indicates. Some historians have suggested that physical violence of this kind was more bearable in medieval and early modern times because people were more inured to pain and hardship.[2] But the record of Schmid's interrogation leaves little room for doubt that the thumbscrew and the strappado were just as painful in the eighteenth century as they might be for a late twentieth-century European. Human physiology has not changed substantially in the intervening period. As Edward Peters has noted,

The techniques of torture used chiefly in early European history principally assaulted the musculoskeletal system, heat sensory receptors, and highly innervated tissue. The strappado—suspension by ropes—and the rack greatly distended and often dislocated muscles and joints. In the case of strappado, by traumatically extending the muscles of the arms and the brachial plexus and by depriving the muscles of an adequate blood supply (muscle ischaemia) through constriction of the arteries, and by dislocating joints at hand and shoulder, intense pain was generated. In the case of the pressure-type legsplints and thumbscrews, the pain thresholds of innervating fibres were lowered by mechanical pressure . . . Thus, the torture techniques of early Europe produced substantial amounts of pain.[3]

The effects of such pain, so graphically recorded in the protocol of Schmid's interrogation, were well known to jurists. Even in the late medieval period, many commentators were concerned to regulate these procedures and structure the interrogation which they accompanied, so as to avoid the danger of false confessions. From the authors of the *Carolina* of 1532 to the influential jurist

[1] Sta Hanover A 1117, Bl. 22–30. The same file contains other, similar verbatim accounts of interrogations under torture. It was also far from uncommon to publish them: see e.g. Anon., *Gründliche Nachricht | Von denen | von Einigen | Räubern und Spitzbuben | An dem Pfarrer zu Edderitz | Herrn Alrico Plesken | Und einem Schneider Hansen Lingen und dessen Ehe-Weibe | In Februariu und Martio 1713. | Ausgeübten Diebstahl | gebrauchten entsetzlichen Marter und respective begangenen Mord* (Cöthen, 1714).

[2] Gustav Radbruch, 'Zur Einführung in die Carolina', in Radbruch (ed.), *Die Peinliche Gerichtsordnung*, 9.

[3] Peters, *Torture*, 166–7.

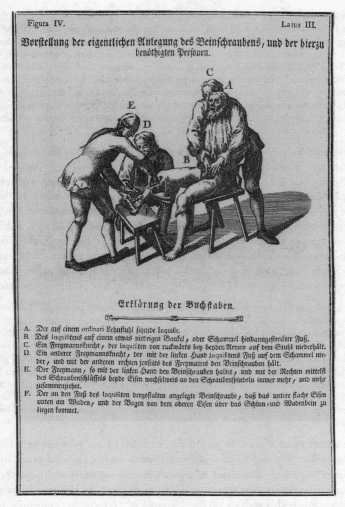

Figura IV.   Latus III.

Vorstellung der eigentlichen Anlegung des Beinschraubens, und der hierzu benöthigten Personen.

Erklärung der Buchstaben.

A. Der auf einem ordinari Lehnstuhl sitzende Inquisit.
B. Des Inquisitens auf einem etwas niedrigen Bankel, oder Schammel hindanngestreckter Fuß.
C. Ein Freymannsknecht, der Inquisiten von rückwärts bey beyden Armen auf dem Stuhl niederhält.
D. Ein anderer Freymannsknecht, der mit der linken Hand Inquisitens Fuß auf dem Schammel nieder, und mit der anderen rechten jenseits des Freymanns den Beinschrauben hält.
E. Der Freymann, so mit der linken Hand den Beinschrauben haltet, und mit der Rechten mittelst des Schraubenschlüssels beyde Eisen wechselweis an den Schraubenspindeln immer mehr, und mehr zusammenziehet.
F. Der an den Fuß des Inquisiten dergestalten angelegte Beinschraube, daß das untere flache Eisen unten am Waden, und der Bogen von dem oberen Eisen über das Schinn- und Wadenbein zu liegen kommet.

FIG. 12. *The legsplint.* Instructions on how to carry out this form of torture, from the Austrian Code of 1768. The caption reads: 'Presentation of the actual fitting of the leg-screw, and of the persons required for this'. The 'persons' in the depiction are: A: the interrogatee with B: the interrogatee's leg, placed on a bench; C: an executioner's servant, pinning back the interrogatee's torso; D: another servant, holding the interrogatee's leg with his left hand and keeping the legsplint steady with his right; E: the executioner, holding the legsplint with his left hand and tightening the screw (F) by turning it clockwise with his right. Note the precision and detail of the instructions, and the role of the executioner as the man who actually performs the torture.

Benedikt Carpzov in 1636, the lawyers of the early modern period refined and elaborated the inquisitorial procedures of the day in a concerted effort to ensure a just outcome for such investigations.

Provided it was surrounded by safeguards, commentators did not raise any really fundamental objections to the employment of torture in criminal investigations. The Austrian jurist Johann Christoph Fröhlich von Fröhlichsburg (1657–1729), for example, who conceded that 'torture' was 'a dangerous matter . . . through which an innocent person can just as easily be condemned and executed because of the pain he has suffered as a guilty person can get off without the prescribed punishment on account of the toughness of his spirit', none the less argued that it was 'almost impossible for a completely innocent person to be burdened with torture if all the circumstances that might cause the legal application of torture have been taken into account'. 'So torture', he concluded,

is still a matter very useful, indeed necessary, for the general good; for if villains knew that they were not to be put to the torture, their resistance would generally be hard to overcome; if they were not tortured in order to discover the truth, they would have to be released as innocent; and then the world would be completely filled with villains and criminals to the detriment of the common weal.[4]

One of the first important encyclopaedias of the German Enlightenment, Zedler's *Universallexicon* of 1745, continued to defend the infliction of physical pain on suspected criminals under investigation, and even as late as 1768, the great Austrian law code known as the *Theresiana* laid down comprehensive provisions for torture and accompanied them with a series of elaborate drawings showing how it was to be carried out.[5]

Yet by this time the practice was already coming under heavy attack. The fact that torture, often applied far beyond the limits of the law, had been the essential factor in producing the mass confessions of bewitchment, sorcery, and consorting with the Devil, that had driven on the great witch-crazes of the sixteenth and seventeenth centuries, inevitably meant that its effects in more ordinary criminal cases were going to be called into question once the confidence of jurists, churchmen, and state officials in the confessions of alleged witches began to decline. The mistrust with which ordinary officials had come to regard the results of torture were typified by the comments of one investigating judge during a case in Weimar in 1752. Accused of infanticide, Gertraud Catharina Schmidt claimed persistently that her baby had died because it fell 'from her onto the ground'. This was a common excuse given by infanticidal mothers, and met with predict-

---

[4] Quoted in Franz Helbing and Max Bauer, *Die Tortur. Geschichte der Folter im Kriminalverfahren aller Zeiten und Völker* (Berlin, 1925), 327 (punctuation modernized).

[5] F. Merzbacher, 'Folter', in Hinckeldey (ed.), *Justiz*, 241–8. See also Jan Philipp Reemtsma (ed.), *Folter. Zur Analyse eines Herrschaftsmittels* (Hamburg, 1992), 239–63.

able official scepticism.[6] So Schmidt was taken into the torture chamber and 'through torture, or at least through the apparent threat of the same and the fear induced by the presence of the executioner and his instruments of torment' she was induced to confess that she had indeed killed the infant, contrary to her original claim. But the judicial officials responsible for the investigation now began to have serious doubts about the reliability of her admission of guilt. It was clear, as one of them remarked,

from the experience of many indisputable cases, how deceptive is this means of obtaining the truth, and it is well known at the same time how strong are the terms in which men who are not evil individuals but thorough, reasonable, and learned, have written against the use of this irrational, cruel, and deceptive method of obtaining the truth, even though others have still praised it most highly.

So the law faculty of Helmstedt University was consulted. Notwithstanding these objections, the professors considered the confession to be sound, and Schmidt was duly executed in July 1753.[7]

But the problem did not go away. In 1760 another case arose in Weimar, in which a prisoner, Rudolph Börner, retracted a confession which had been elicited from him under torture. The authorities ignored the retraction, clearly convinced of his guilt. But they feared he might repeat his retraction in public on the day of his execution and thereby pose a threat to law and order. A mass of damning evidence was assembled to present before the public should he do so, in order that the execution could go ahead smoothly.

Even if Börner revokes his confession after the public sentencing ceremony, the punishment ordained for him shall none the less be carried out, all the more so since in the whole business the main point is that the interrogatee has been brought to confess by mere torture, and he has otherwise been sufficiently incriminated by the evidence, so that if he withdraws his confession, it will not be because he is convinced of his own innocence, but rather because of his own wickedness, or because of his fear that the death sentence will be carried out if he does not.[8]

In the end, it does not seem that Börner retracted. But the case demonstrated once more the considerable uncertainties which the use of torture to elicit confessions was now creating. Officials were admitting that a confession produced by 'mere torture' was less sound than indicative and circumstantial evidence produced by other people.

The eighteenth century saw the phasing-out, then the abandonment of torture in virtually every German state. Already in the second half of the seventeenth century, torture began to be less widely applied, with its incidence in Munich

[6] Ulbricht, 'Kindsmörderinnen', in Blauert and Schwerhoff (eds.), *Mit den Waffen*, 54–85.
[7] StA Weimar B 2693 Bl. 1–5, 21, 28.   [8] Ibid. B 2693 Bl. 12–13 (22. 10. 1760) and Bl. 30.

falling from 44 per cent of criminal cases in 1650 to merely 16 per cent forty years later.[9] In Prussia King Friedrich I already required all cases where torture was proposed to be referred to him for advance approval.[10] It was limited to cases of murder and treason by order of Friedrich II in 1740, then abolished formally by him on 4 August 1754.[11] Other German states followed suit in the second half of the eighteenth century, dropping torture in practice even before it was abandoned in law. Torture was last used in Württemberg in 1778, and it was formally abolished there in 1809. A similar step-by-step process of abolition took place in Baden between 1767 and 1831 and in Austria between 1769 and 1776. In Brunswick and Saxony torture ceased to be applied after 1770; it ceased to be employed in Mecklenburg in 1769 and Saxe-Weimar in 1783; in Hamburg it was last used in 1786.[12] In Bavaria, torture was restricted in 1767 to cases where a member of a group of accused prisoners refused to name others involved in the crime or persisted in concealing the whereabouts of relevant evidence.[13] It was eventually formally banned from 17 July 1806.[14] In Hanover torture was last applied as late as 1818, but only four years later, in 1822, it was made completely illegal. By 1819 the laws providing for the employment of torture had been abrogated in Saxe-Weimar as well, by a decree which ordered that 'no authority may consider itself entitled to force a confession from an accused person, or to have a confession so forced, by beating, whipping, imprisonment, punishment cells, irons, heavy fetters, hunger, thirst, or other similar means of compulsion.'[15] In Saxe-Coburg-Gotha torture remained a theoretical possibility at least until 1828, but long before this, it was described as 'silently regarded as having been abolished' in the whole of Thuringia. By and large, torture was phased out in all the German states between the 1740s and the 1820s, with the major turning-point coming around the 1770s.[16]

The abolition of torture was a result in part of wider changes in the law, in which confession was gradually being dethroned from its overwhelmingly dominant place in the hierarchy of criminal proofs. This was a very long-drawn-out process. The confession was always, under the inquisitorial procedure, to remain the queen of proofs. Already in the eighteenth century, however, judges were beginning to sentence offenders on suspicion, where the evidence was sufficient

---

[9] Behringer, 'Mörder', 92–3, 99; Labouvie, *Zauberei*, 251–9.   [10] Peters, *Torture*, 90–1.

[11] Merzbacher, 'Folter', 241–8.

[12] Friedrich Wilhelm Lucht, *Die Strafrechtspflege in Sachsen-Weimar-Eisenach unter Carl August* (Berlin and Leipzig, 1929), 49; Richard Wosnik, *Beiträge zur Hamburgischen Kriminalgeschichte* (Hamburg, 1926), i. 58.

[13] GStA Berlin Rep. 84a/7781, Bl. 290–1: Prussian Ambassador in Munich to PJM, 21 Mar. 1828.

[14] HStA Munich GR Fasc. 324, Nr. 24.

[15] StA Weimar B 2387a, Bl. 101–6, decree of 7 May 1819.

[16] Ibid. Oberappellationsgericht Jena 267, Bl. 9 and 11: reports from Heinrich Fürst Reuss and from Sachsen-Coburg-Gotha, Jan. 1824.

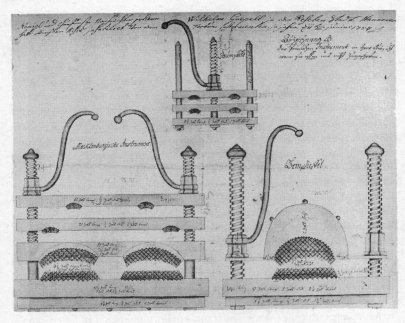

FIG. 13. *The 'Mecklenburg instrument'.* Sketch of thumbscrews used in Hanover, by executioner Johann Wilhelm Göppel, dated 1754. Torture was only gradually phased out as a method of obtaining confessions from the accused in Germany during the second half of the eighteenth century.

to establish the likelihood of guilt, but insufficient to justify the application of torture. In due course, sentencing on suspicion (*Verdachtstrafe*) was extended to cover even cases where the crime might in earlier times have been thought to have required more serious levels of proof. Judges were enabled to do this not least because capital punishment was no longer so inevitable as it had been before. Lesser sentences were beginning to be imposed, even before the drastic restriction of capital punishment from the 1740s onwards.[17] Imprisonment was beginning to provide an alternative to the pillory and the scaffold. For some time, institutions such as the *Rasphuis* in Amsterdam, founded in 1596, had allowed judges to sentence offenders to a period of forced labour in a house of correction as well as, or sometimes even instead of, the pillory and the lash. Established especially though not exclusively in Protestant areas, particularly in towns ruled by commercial élites, these houses of correction implemented the Protestant work-ethic

---

[17] Langbein, *Torture*.

against beggars and vagrants, but could also accommodate other types of offenders if so desired.[18] They were founded in Bremen in 1609, Lübeck in 1613, Hamburg in 1618, and Danzig in 1630, mainly to deal with beggars and the 'idle poor'. Prisoners were expected to work, and if they were physically incapable of doing so, they were expelled from the institution. The notion of a fixed term of imprisonment had not yet emerged. All this was clearly still a long way from the prison as it came to be understood later on.

A second wave of prison foundations followed in the later seventeenth century, beginning with Breslau in 1668 and Vienna in 1671 and continuing into the 1700s. By the early eighteenth century, it was becoming common to incarcerate the insane as well as vagrants and beggars in such institutions, as in the house of correction established in Celle in 1731. Crucially, they now began to function as prisons as well. The original houses of correction had been designed to inculcate the habit of industriousness and return the inmates to society equipped to carry out a trade so that they would not be a burden on the state or private charity. They were thus 'honourable houses' and resisted any attempt to admit individuals tainted by contact with the executioner. By the early eighteenth century, however, they were beginning to relent. As long as 'dishonourable' prisoners could be kept apart from the others, they could be admitted. In Danzig they were put into a separate building constructed next door to the house of correction in 1690. It was this development that led judges to regard imprisonment as an addition to the existing forms of corporal punishment or, increasingly, an alternative to execution, and thus to start sentencing in the absence of a confession forced through torture.[19] The decline of public corporal and capital punishments in Weimar, for example, began with the construction of the penitentiary (*Zuchthaus*) in 1719.[20]

It was some time before this development really took hold. Ironically, the wave of prison foundations that swept the German states in the late seventeenth and

---

[18] Gustav Radbruch, *Elegantiae juris criminalis. Vierzehn Studien zur Geschichte des Strafrechts* (Basle, 1950), 116–29; see also Hellmuth von Weber, 'Calvinismus und Strafrecht', in Paul Bockelmann and Wilhelm Gallas (eds.), *Festschrift für Eberhard Schmidt zum 70. Geburtstag* (Göttingen, 1961), 39–53.

[19] Albert Ebeling, 'Beiträge zur Geschichte der Freiheitsstrafe', *Zeitschrift für die gesamte Strafrechtswissenschaft*, 18 (1898), 419–94, 608–66; R. von Hippel, *Die Entstehung der modernen Freiheitsstrafe und des Erziehungs-Strafvollzugs* (Jena, 1932); Herbert Lieberknecht, *Das Altpreussische Zuchthauswesen bis zum Ausgang des 18. Jahrhunderts* (Charlottenburg, 1921); Albrecht Meyer, *Das Strafrecht der Stadt Danzig von der Carolina bis zur Vereinigung Danzigs mit der preussischen Monarchie* (Danzig, 1935); Ernst Rosenfeld, 'Zur Geschichte der ältesten Zuchthäuser', *Zeitschrift für die gesamte Strafrechtswissenschaft*, 26 (1906), 1–18; Günther Seggelke, *Die Entstehung der Freiheitsstrafe* (Breslau, 1928); Hannes Stekl, *Österreichs Zucht- und Arbeitshäuser, 1671–1920. Institutionen zwischen Fürsorge und Strafvollzug* (Vienna, 1978); Adolf Streng, *Geschichte der Gefängnisverwaltung in Hamburg von 1622 bis 1872* (Hamburg, 1878); Pieter Spierenburg, 'The Sociogenesis of Confinement and its Development in Early Modern Europe', in idem (ed.), *The Emergence of Carceral Institutions: Prisons, Galleys and Lunatic Asylums 1550–1900* (Rotterdam, 1984), 9–77.

[20] Lucht, *Strafrechtspflege*, 32–3.

early eighteenth centuries was part of a general crackdown on crime and deviance that also included a number of draconian extensions of the death penalty. In 1725, King Friedrich Wilhelm I of Prussia issued an edict declaring that all gypsies found within the boundaries of his kingdom were to be strangled, while sodomites would be burned alive. In 1736 the same monarch threatened to hang thieves in Berlin from gallows erected in front of the houses which they had burgled.[21] The next year, Duke Ernst August of Saxe-Weimar proclaimed that anyone caught stealing money to the value of more than two thalers 'without regard to person and without pardon together with their accomplices, no matter how much money they offer for their lives, shall be hanged'. The same applied to anyone convicted of theft for the third time, irrespective of the sum involved.[22] Punishments against infanticide were sharpened at the same time, as we saw in Chapter 1.[23] Nor did the early eighteenth-century crackdown stop at crimes against property or the person. It also included moral offences such as blasphemy. On 25 October 1751, for example, a soldier was executed in Freiburg for this crime. After taking Holy Communion, he had 'taken the Sacred Host from his mouth and melted it down into a bullet, and went with it to a shooting competition in the hope of winning the first prize'. He was 'first mercifully beheaded for blasphemy in front of the Prädiger Gate and then his body and head were burned on the adjacent pyre and the ashes were thrown into the stream that flowed close by'.[24] This was rather late for an execution for such an offence in Germany. Yet in 1768 the new Austrian Law Code retained the full range of death penalties and tortures, and the same was the case with the Bavarian Code which came into force in 1751.[25]

However, this development was relatively short-lived. Not only was it being gradually undermined by the increasing availability of imprisonment as an alternative to these draconian physical sanctions, it was also threatened by the growth of order and stability in German society in the eighteenth century. Recent studies have shown that a long-term decline in crimes of violence began in the late seventeenth century, and continued well into the twentieth. Far from representing a shift from crimes against the person to crimes against property, as used to be thought, this was part of a long-term reduction in overall crime rates which went hand in hand with the growing control of the state over its citizens. In his pioneering work on eighteenth-century crime, Carsten Küther concluded

[21] *Stenographische Berichte über die Verhandlungen des Reichstages des Norddeutschen Bundes, 1. Legislatur-Periode, Session 1870, Anlagen zu den Verhandlungen des Reichstages von Nr. 1–72*, vol. 3, 2: *Anlage zu Nr. 5 (Motive des Strafgesetz-Entwurfs für den Norddeutschen Bund): Ueber die Todesstrafe*, iii.
[22] StA Weimar B 2218, Bl. 6: Proclamation of 24 Oct. 1737.   [23] Dülmen, *Frauen*, 50–1.
[24] Schindler, *Verbrechen*, 57.
[25] *Stenographische Berichte* (as n. 21), iii; and Albert Berner, *Die Strafgesetzgebung in Deutschland vom Jahre 1751 bis zur Gegenwart* (Leipzig, 1867), 7.

that the state 'was unsuccessful in combating bands of robbers, and not very successful in controlling and integrating lower-class itinerants. All its comprehensive attempts to assert its authority were regarded with deep suspicion by large parts of the population.'[26] The police were few in number and slow to act. Bands of robbers found it easy to escape their clutches. The state's oft-repeated proclamations that bandits and vagrants would be hunted down and dealt with were mere empty words. There is no doubt that this judgement holds good for troubled times such as the Revolutionary and Napoleonic Wars, when disputed border zones like the Rhineland were constantly subject to pillage and destruction by rampaging armies, orderly policing was impossible, and bandits such as Schinderhannes managed to sustain a career of robbery, murder, and intimidation for a number of years.[27] Earlier times of continuous warfare in Central Europe had also seen the emergence of robber bands.[28] But in a more normal situation, things were becoming less easy for the criminal. The eighteenth-century German state was quite capable, for instance, of launching periodic round-ups of vagrants and of apprehending individuals who lacked proper legitimation. It could use torture and other forms of pressure to get arrested offenders to incriminate others. It ran an elaborate system of official correspondence, the so-called *Steckbriefe*, in which details of crimes and criminals were widely circulated across the country. In a small-scale, settled society, unusual occurrences and suspicious strangers easily attracted attention. The situation, in other words, was very different from the disorder and crisis which had characterized so much of the sixteenth and seventeenth centuries. The careers of most robbers, of the majority of capital offenders, if one is to judge from the way they were described in ballads and broadsides, included long periods under investigation in prison, frequent punishments, little profit, and fewer prospects. Historians such as Uwe Danker have argued persuasively that the late seventeenth- and eighteenth-century state was normally a good deal more effective in apprehending and controlling crime than previous writers have given it credit for.[29]

[26] Carsten Küther, 'Räuber, Volk und Obrigkeit. Zur Wirkungsweise und Funktion staatlicher Strafverfolgung im 18. Jahrhundert', in Reif (ed.), *Räuber*, 17–42, here 37. See also idem, *Räuber und Gauner in Deutschland. Das organisierte Bandenwesen im 18. und 19. Jahrhundert* (Göttingen, 1976), and Hermann Arnold, 'Ländliche Grundschicht und Gaunertum. Zur Kritik von Küthers Buch: Räuber und Gauner in Deutschland', *Zeitschrift für Agrargeschichte und Agrarsoziologie*, 25 (1977), 67–76.

[27] B. Becker, *Actenmässige Geschichte der Räuberbanden an den beyden Ufern des Rheins* (2 vols.; Cologne, 1804); for the background, see T. C. W. Blanning, *The French Revolutionary Wars in Germany: Occupation and Resistance in the Rhineland, 1792–1802* (Oxford, 1983).

[28] Hermann Bettenhäuser, 'Räuber und Gaunerbanden in Hessen. Ein Beitrag zum Versuch einer historischen Kriminologie Hessens', *Zeitschrift des Vereins für hessische Geschichte und Landeskunde*, 75–6 (1964–5), 275–348, for some local examples.

[29] Uwe Danker, 'Bandits and the State: Robbers and the Authorities in the Holy Roman Empire in the Late Seventeenth and Early Eighteenth Centuries', in Evans (ed.), *The German Underworld*, 75–107, esp. 100–3.

Norbert Elias's thesis of the 'pacification' of society in a 'civilizing process', in which the growing certitude of state sanctions forced people to restrain their own violent impulses for fear of retribution, may thus have some explanatory value here, even if one does not accept the terminology in which it is put.[30] But Elias and his disciple Spierenburg are wrong to see the high levels of violence in medieval and early modern society as reflecting a culture of immediate emotionality, where physical assault originated in 'suddenly infuriated passion rather than in long pent-up tensions'.[31] Sources such as the Icelandic sagas indicate clearly that violence was often well prepared, ritualized, and built into the social structure in the Middle Ages. It could even in some circumstances be increased by the disruptive incursions of the disciplining state.[32] Medieval and early modern violence was no more insensate or spontaneous than was medieval or early modern punishment. Recent research has shown that violence in early modern German villages was driven above all by the need to use the language of the body in reasserting an honourable status diminished by the actions of another. Even murder could be tolerated if it was committed for 'honourable' motives and posed no wider threat to the local community. Such acts of violence were no more spontaneous or 'uncivilized' (in the sense of expressing emotions that people had not learned to control) than were the ritual killings of the Corsican vendetta.[33] A situation where the organs of official justice were poorly equipped to deal with theft, burglary, and other individual crimes against property often left people with little alternative but to use violence against those they believed to be the culprits if they wished to have any means of redress.[34] Moreover, the growing power of the state is only one possible explanation for the decline in violence that set in from the late seventeenth century onwards. The ending of the great wars of religion that devastated Europe for a century and a half after the Reformation left European society searching for peace and order in an altered world. In a depopulated Germany, in particular, the competition for land and resources had become markedly less severe in the wake of the Thirty Years War. And the end of the 'seventeenth-century crisis', the improvement in climatic conditions with the gradual ending of the 'little ice age', and the start of a

---

[30] Johnson and Monkkonen (eds.), *Violent Crime in Town and Country*; for the older view, see Howard Zehr, *Crime and the Development of Modern Society: Patterns of Criminality in Nineteenth-Century Germany and France* (London, 1976).

[31] Spierenburg, *Broken Spell*, 195.

[32] See Stephen Wilson, 'Conflict and its Causes in Southern Corsica 1800–35', *Social History*, 6 (1982), 33–69.

[33] Walter Rummel, 'Verletzung von Körper, Ehre und Eigentum. Varianten im Umgang mit Gewalt in Dörfern des 17. Jahrhunderts', in Blauert and Schwerhoff (eds.), *Mit den Waffen*, 86–114; and Wilson, 'Conflict'.

[34] Ibid., see also Robert Muchembled, *La Violence en village. Sociabilité et comportements populaires en Artois du XVIe et XVIIe siècle* (Paris, 1989).

prolonged period of growth and prosperity in agriculture, meant a slow improvement in living standards which also played its part in the transformation of social attitudes. The eighteenth century was an era of relative social peace after the upheavals of the previous two hundred years. In the long run, this was bound to have an effect on the way that penal sanctions operated.

b. Penal Reform in the Enlightenment

While long-term developments in the history of the law, the state, and society all undoubtedly underlay the trend towards milder punishments that began in Germany towards the middle of the eighteenth century, it remains the case that the power over penal policy lay in the hands of the princes, and that legislation to restrict and abolish torture and to do away with the more baroque forms of public punishment was enacted by individual monarchs. Here the crucial figure was Friedrich II (known to his English admirers as Frederick the Great), who succeeded to the Prussian throne in 1740. Like many eighteenth-century monarchs, he was on extremely bad terms with his father, and determined to reverse many of his policies when he became king. Friedrich was not only an able soldier, he was also a notable intellectual. He grew up under the emerging influence of the European Enlightenment, a current of thought that was spreading outwards from France by the middle of the eighteenth century, questioning the religious and traditional foundations of state and society, seeking to reorganize human life on a rational, logical basis, and attacking what it saw as the barbarous and uncivilized superstitions and abuses of previous ages. Friedrich II shared these views to the full. He corresponded with Voltaire and other leading thinkers of his day, and he wrote a number of important political tracts himself, such as the *Antimachiavell* and the *Political Testament*, in which he laid down the rational principles on which he thought state and society in Prussia should be governed in future.[35]

Friedrich II paid particular attention to the legal system. 'Princes are born to be judges of the people,' he wrote; 'everything that makes them great has its origin in the administration of justice.'[36] He found the confusion of Germanic and Roman law, the variety of local practice and custom, the prevalence of

[35] Reinhold Koser, *Geschichte Friedrichs des Grossen*, 5th edn. (4 vols.; Berlin, 1912–14); Ingrid Mittenzwei, *Friedrich II. von Preussen: eine Biographie* (Berlin, 1979); Theodor Schieder, *Friedrich der Grosse: ein Königtum der Widersprüche* (Frankfurt am Main, 1986); Detlev Marten, 'Friedrich der Grosse und Montesquieu. Zu den Anfängen des Rechtsstaats im 18. Jahrhundert', in Willi Blümel *et al.* (eds.), *Verwaltung im Rechtsstaat. Festschrift für Carl Hermann Ule zum 80. Geburtstag am 24. Februar 1978* (Cologne, 1987), 187–208; Jürgen Regge, 'Strafrecht und Strafrechtspflege', in Jürgen Ziechmann (ed.), *Panorama der friederizianischen Zeit. Friedrich der Grosse und seine Epoche* (Bremen, 1985), 365–75.

[36] Quoted in Peter Brandt, *Preussen. Zur Sozialgeschichte eines Staates. Eine Darstellung in Quellen* (Reinbek, 1981), 13.

corruption and delay, and the revival and extension in the eighteenth century of what he regarded as medieval punishments both irrational and counter-productive. He appointed a series of leading jurists to advise him, especially Samuel Cocceji (1679–1755), Johann Heinrich von Carmer (1721–1801), and Carl Gottlieb Svarez (1746–98). Their ideas on the civil and criminal law were shaped by the doctrines of the French *philosophes*. In 1740 they undertook a comprehensive programme of judicial reforms, including the effective abolition of torture, as well as the replacement of drowning in a sack with beheading as the punishment for infanticide.[37] A characteristic example of the Prussian monarch's attitude towards penal sanctions and their purpose can be seen in his attitude to the punishment laid down by his father for the crime of unnatural sexual intercourse. Ten years before Friedrich II came to the throne, in 1730, Andreas Lepsch had been burned at the stake in Potsdam for sodomy.[38] In 1746 Friedrich II criticized this procedure on the grounds of its effects on the public, remarking:

It is undeniable that through frightful public capital punishments, many young and innocent spirits, who naturally want to know the reason for such a terrible execution, especially if they are also unaware of the finer sentiments (just as the criminal is), will be scandalized rather than improved, and it is even possible that evil tendencies may be awakened in them, tendencies of which they previously had no inkling.[39]

He ordered therefore that the practice should stop. Nor was this the only example of the new attitude to penal policy. The Prussian monarch issued a similar decree in 1749 concerning the punishment of breaking with the wheel. The objective was 'not to torment the criminal but rather to make a frightful example of him in order to arouse repugnance in others'. Friedrich commanded therefore that, providing the offender's crime was not of 'such enormity' that 'a completely abhorrent example' was necessary, 'the criminal should be strangled by the hangman before being broken with the wheel, but secretly, and without it coming to the special attention of the assembled spectators, and then his execution with the wheel can proceed'.[40] Nothing could express more clearly the monarch's understanding of the purpose of punishment. It did not matter in the least that the malefactor was actually dead when the sentence was carried out, or that a deliberate deception was being played on the public. For the rationalistic Friedrich II, the execution was a kind of pedagogical theatre, drawing its purposes and its methods from the model of baroque tragedy. Its purpose was not to inflict suffering, but to deter by making an example of the offender. And it had to awaken feelings of revulsion in the onlooker. Anything that seemed likely to

[37] *Stenographische Berichte* (as n. 21 above), p. iii.   [38] Moser, *Selige letzte Stunden*, 182–4.
[39] Eberhard Schmidt, *Die Kriminalpolitik Preussens unter Friedrich Wilhelm I und Friedrich II* (Berlin, 1914), 33–4.
[40] GStA Berlin Rep. 84a/7781, Bl. 4: decree of 11 Dec. 1749.

frustrate this purpose was to be avoided. This included the infliction of pain to such a degree that the sympathy of the crowd might be evoked. Apart from this obvious political purpose, it is also important to note that Friedrich did in the end consider that excessive suffering was if possible to be avoided. The degree of pain was to be calculated precisely, in rational terms.[41]

Along with these measures, Friedrich II and his advisers also issued new procedures to speed up the administration of justice and remove abuses. The King thought that if there were fewer executions, each one would constitute a more impressive spectacle.[42] The point was not to kill offenders but to educate the public. A crucial step was taken in 1743, when Friedrich II removed the death penalty for theft.[43] Where he considered that education would be effective with offenders as well as with the public, he encouraged a switch from capital and corporal punishment to imprisonment. The prison, as a Berlin judge wrote in 1770, should 'be a place not only of punishment but also of improvement'.[44] The prisons and workhouses which were now constructed reflected the widespread eighteenth-century belief that poverty, crime, and vagrancy were chiefly the result of an idle and disorderly lifestyle. Hard work and submission to the prison rules were intended to encourage a change of attitude on the part of prisoners and make them useful members of society once more.[45] The new, rationalistic concentration on public punishment as a theatrical demonstration designed to make the public abhor the criminal was part, in other words, of a broader concentration on the educative and deterrent function of punishment. It is easy to see that this concept of penal policy ran counter to the religious and crypto-materialist rituals which played such a major part in capital punishment in the early modern period, and which before the eighteenth century were accepted in élite as well as popular culture. An Absolutist monarch such as Friedrich II of Prussia did not see an execution as a means by which a community, a town, or a village expelled a malefactor from its ranks. By the mid-eighteenth century, the kind of courtly society which the King was establishing in Potsdam had lost all understanding of popular culture. It regarded the common people as a brute, untutored, and insensate plebeian mass, the object of policy, to be educated and disciplined by the state.[46] Executions therefore had to be removed from the hand

---

[41] For the same measure enacted in *ancien régime* France, see McManners, *Death*, 372. On occasion, the strangulation failed to work, as in an execution remembered by Karl von Holtei in Breslau during the Napoleonic Wars, when a woman being broken on the wheel cried out when the executioner's servant slackened the cord round her neck (Holtei, *Vierzig Jahre*, i. 133).

[42] Schmidt, *Kriminalpolitik*, 34.   [43] Ibid. iii.   [44] Quoted ibid. 190.

[45] Eberhard Schmidt, *Entwicklung und Vollzug der Freiheitsstrafe in Brandenburg-Preussen bis zum Ausgang des 18. Jahrhunderts* (Berlin, 1915). See also Hermann Weill, *Frederick the Great and Samuel von Cocceji* (Madison, Wis., 1961).

[46] For the educating drive of 18th-c. states, see Hamish Scott (ed.), *Enlightened Absolutism: Reforms and Reformers in Later Eighteenth-Century Europe* (London, 1990).

of the community and transformed into a rational instrument of law enforcement and popular education. Given this attitude, it is not surprising that the
Prussian government began to criticize the religious elements in executions.
'Many souls among the poorly informed rabble', it considered in 1768, would
believe that 'the executed criminal has assuredly died in a state of grace, and that
this is the surest way to die a similarly blessed death'. By contrast, the real
purpose of capital punishment, as the city court at Königsberg put it, was to
ensure that 'the malefactor's death is as terrifying as possible in the public eye'.
Friedrich II agreed.[47] Soon a debate began about the role of the clergy in the
execution ritual, and spread well beyond the borders of Prussia.

Critics focused in particular on what they saw as the inadvisability of allowing
clerics to accompany the malefactor to the scaffold. An official in the Hanseatic
city of Hamburg, in an internal memorandum, considered that this custom
frustrated the purposes of punishment:

> Most of the common herd, which is only accustomed to look for superficialities, and to
> abandon itself to the impressions arising from them, regard this public accompaniment
> and the preachers' speeches to the criminal, the admonitions and consolations they
> address to him, and the final blessing of the same at the place of execution as nothing
> other than an infallible *licence*, which leaves no further doubt as to the state of grace of the
> individual who is about to be executed.

The fact that the ministrations of the clergy made it clear that 'the malefactor's
soul must go directly to heaven' even prompted some people to commit murders
simply in order to 'die in a state of grace'.[48] Another commentator, bringing the
debate into the public realm, agreed that the practice was harmful and should be
stopped. He saw in it a sinister attempt by the clergy 'to render visible their
predominance over the social order of the secular authorities and to strengthen
them in the regard they have attained through the superstition of the mob'. The
clergy might depend on superstition, but the secular authorities should obey
the dictates of reason. The current practice was contradictory: 'The malefactor
passed from the hands of justice into the bosom of Mother Church. The world
had rejected him as a useless and dangerous member of society. But the priest
now opened to him the portals of Heaven!'

The purpose of the public execution, thundered the rationalist pamphleteer,
was being completely undermined by this contradiction. It was unfortunately
true, he declared,

> that the rabble is not motivated by the desire to hear something good and thus be moved
> and uplifted, but merely by the wish to see something new, and to satisfy its curiosity,

[47] Schmidt, *Kriminalpolitik*, 31–2.
[48] StA Hamburg Senat Cl. VII. Lit. Mb. no. 3, vol. 4b: draft memo of 14 June 1784 and preceding notes.

even, on many occasions, at the cost of human feelings. . . . The ultimate purpose of public punishment is largely frustrated if the malefactor dies in circumstances that arouse a kind of admiration and respect. . . . An infanticidal woman clothed and adorned purely in white, going joyfully to her spiritual wedding accompanied by the preacher, is a very dangerous sight for other people in the conduct of their daily life. And a murderer going to his death accompanied by the sighs, prayers, and admonitions of the preacher, and by the singing of inspiring funeral hymns, often has the deleterious effect of causing weak and melancholy natures to desire for themselves a form of extinction which, as they think, allows them to meet their end more peacefully, indeed, more joyfully, than on their death-bed after a lengthy illness.

Of course, the malefactor should not be denied the ministrations of religion altogether. But these should take place in the privacy of the condemned cell. The inevitable nervousness, weakness, and physical decrepitude of offenders on the scaffold, after weeks or even months in the unhealthy atmosphere of the prison, and in the face of unavoidable death, meant that they were in no condition to pay attention to the preachers. The presence of the clergy at the execution was not only useless, it was also dangerous: 'When the malefactor is laid out, the preacher, in the eyes of the rabble, is like the bailiff or the executioner: no more than a necessary character in the tragic drama, to be stared at and briefly assessed as to whether he plays his role badly or well.' It was time for this abuse to be brought to an end.[49] Even those who pleaded in the ensuing controversy for the practice to be continued admitted that the clergy should appear on the scaffold without any form of 'ceremoniousness', and that their humanitarian duty to comfort the condemned in their last moments should not get in the way of the main purpose of capital punishment. For, as one defender of the clergy affirmed, 'terror and repugnance, in accordance with the purposes of criminal justice, are the only emotions which the sight of a malefactor being led to the bloody scaffold should arouse in the spectator's heart'.[50]

The debate over the role of the clergy was particularly revealing of the assumptions of Enlightenment thinkers and officials about the purpose of punishment. For the moment, it appears not to have had any concrete effect. Nor were Enlightened principles of penal policy immediately implemented in the rest of Germany, outside Prussia. The harsh practices of the early eighteenth century continued in Bavaria, for instance, well into the 1770s. It was only in the last quarter of the eighteenth century that a real fall in the number of executions took place. In Munich, for example, 126 people were executed from 1749 to 1758, largely as a product of the massive drive launched by the Elector Maximilian III

---

[49] Ibid.: Anon., *Über die Gewohnheit, Missethäter durch Prediger zur Hinrichtung begleiten zu lassen* (Hamburg, 1784), 1–15.

[50] Ibid.: Anon., *Auch etwas über die Gewohnheit, Missethäter durch Prediger zur Hinrichtung begleiten zu lassen* (Hamburg, 1784), 5, 33.

Joseph against robbery in the early 1750s: over half of the executions were for this offence. This was a very high number, already unusual in the German context. In the late eighteenth century thieves and robbers continued to be executed in Bavaria, including a substantial number in the 1770s, and torture continued to be employed in the extraction of confessions. But complaints from Bavarian jurists about the 'severe and purposeless laws' of the Bavarian Code multiplied from the 1770s onwards, and led to a determination from the turn of the century to introduce at last a set of criminal laws appropriate to the Age of the Enlightenment: it finally came into effect in 1813.[51]

Here, as in other respects, Friedrich II of Prussia was ahead of his time. In considering the purposes of punishment, the Prussian King did not allow sentiment to obfuscate a rational critique. If traditional practices stood in the way of the fundamental aim of deterrence by example, then they had to be abolished. Justice, regularity, order were the watchwords of the new policy. And humanity too. A civilized society meant for an Enlightened monarch such as the Prussian King a society in which people were not routinely subjected to barbarous and painful tortures either on the scaffold or in the inquisitorial chamber. Penal policy was to be measured by human standards, not divine; it was to be based on human psychology rather than religious precept. The Enlightenment concept of 'humanity' was based on a rational calculus of reason and emotion, where capital and corporal punishments were to be restricted to what was regarded as effective in terms of deterrence. They were not to be eliminated altogether. Indeed, the severest sanctions, such as breaking with the wheel, were now explicitly reserved for a small number of aggravated, major offences, so as to increase the impact they made upon the populace. Excessive exposure to such cruelties would, it was thought, harden the people and reduce their impressionability; but no one thought of eliminating them altogether. And effective though it might have been in comparison to its predecessors, the Absolutist state was still subject to extensive limitations on its power. Beneath the neat, logical sets of rules and regulations it devised for itself lay a complex mess of local and regional traditions which it was ill-equipped to eradicate. The ideal of the educative execution remained in many ways just an ideal, and popular participation, as we saw in Chapter 2, was in most respects as vigorous at the end of the eighteenth century as it had been at the beginning. Finally, by converting penal sanctions into an instrument of moral education, the Prussian government inaugurated a process whereby capital punishment began to appear as an anomaly in the overall context of penal policy. While other punishments were intended to educate those who received them, execution could only, by definition, educate others. Legislators were to spend

---

[51] Behringer, 'Mörder, Diebe, Ehebrecher', in Dülmen (ed.), *Verbrechen*, 111–17.

many decades grappling with this contradiction as it grew steadily more apparent. Already in the middle of the century, indeed, one Enlightenment author took the obvious step, and, as we shall now see, put forward a powerful case for the abolition of capital punishment altogether.

c. Beccaria and the Abolition of the Death Penalty

What Enlightenment thought lacked in its early decades was a systematic treatment of penal policy. Despite the importance which the critique of *ancien régime* justice assumed in their thought, none of the *philosophes* had devoted a systematic treatise to the subject. Montesquieu and other French writers had dealt with it but all of them, even Voltaire, had only treated it as part of a wider disquisition or approached it with reference to particular, individual cases. It was not until 1764 that a writer finally gathered together and reformulated the scattered ideas and proposals which Enlightenment thinkers had developed about penal policy into a systematic argument grounded on first principles, in a tract specifically devoted to this subject and to no other. This was the achievement of Cesare Beccaria (1738–94), a member of the Lombard aristocracy and thus a citizen of the Holy Roman Empire ruled from Vienna. Beccaria had received a doctorate in law from the University of Pavia and read widely among the French *philosophes* before settling down to write his treatise on crime and punishment, *Dei delitti e delle pene*, which appeared in 1764.[52] It was immediately recognized as a central, defining document of Enlightened thought on the subject, and remained the most influential tract on penal policy well into the second half of the nineteenth century. For this reason, it is important to subject it to particularly close examination.

In his treatise, Beccaria took his stand on two general principles which were common to a great deal of political thinking in the Enlightenment. In the first place, he declared that secular punishment had to be sharply distinguished from divine justice and retribution, which applied only to the afterlife. Penal sanctions had to be grounded on reason, not on religion, faith, custom, or arbitrary power. Beccaria thought that legislation in general should aim at 'the greatest happiness of the greatest number'.[53] It was the duty of the legislator to ensure that penal policy conformed to this general principle. Beccaria's second general principle

---

[52] Wilhelm Alff, 'Zur Einführung in Beccarias Leben und Denken', in Cesare Beccaria, *Über Verbrechen und Strafen*, tr. from 1766 edn. and ed. Wilhelm Alff (Frankfurt am Main, 1966), 7–46, here 7–19. On the various editions, see ibid. 183–8. See Bettina Strub, *Der Einfluss der Aufklärung auf die Todesstrafe* (Zurich, 1973) for a brief general survey. Kirchheimer and Rusche, *Punishment*, 72–83, analyse Beccaria from a Marxist perspective. The quotations here are from the English edn. of 1770: Cesare Beccaria, *An Essay on Crimes and Punishments, translated from the Italian*, 3rd edn. (London, 1770), 2.

[53] Beccaria, *An Essay*, 2.

was that the logic of penal sanctions should be grounded on a contract theory of the state. Human beings, he argued, implicitly contracted away a portion of their individual autonomy to the state in order to protect themselves through the establishment of a reasonable degree of law and order:

Thus it was necessity that forced men to give up a part of their liberty; it is certain then, that every individual would chuse to put into the public stock the smallest portion possible, as much only as was sufficient to engage others to defend it. The aggregate of these, the smallest possible, forms the right of punishing: all that extends beyond this is abuse, not justice.[54]

Building on these general principles, Beccaria argued that penal sanctions were only justifiable in so far as they served to hold society together and prevent its dissolution into a state of nature. 'It is not only the common interest of mankind, that crimes should not be committed, but that crimes of every kind should be less frequent, in proportion to the evil they produce'.

Thus punishments should, he thought, be precisely graded according to the severity of the crime. 'If an equal punishment be ordained for two crimes that injure society in different degrees, there is nothing to deter men from committing the greater, as often as it is attended with greater advantage.'[55] It followed from these principles that the motive or status of the offender was irrelevant to the nature or degree of the punishment handed down. The damage done to society was the only relevant criterion for assessing the sanction applied to the criminal, and the aim of punishment was 'no other, than to prevent the criminal from doing further injury to society, and to prevent others from committing the like offence'. Punishment should not be applied to the innocent. This in itself in Beccaria's view was sufficient justification for the abolition of torture. The innocent either had to make a false confession and so suffer for a crime they had not committed, or undergo pain of steadily increasing severity until the torturers relented and admitted their innocence. The guilty, on the other hand, escaped such suffering by admitting their crimes before any torture could be applied. Thus torture was a form of punishment weighing more heavily upon the innocent than upon the guilty. Psychological torture should also be avoided, he argued, by applying penal sanctions as soon as possible after the crime to which they related. This would spare 'the criminal the cruel and superfluous torment of uncertainty', while also creating an association in the popular mind between crime and punishment that would be all the stronger for being the more immediate.[56]

The most important point that he wished to stress was that criminals should not be allowed to get away with their offences:

[54] Beccaria, *An Essay*, 9.   [55] Ibid. 2.   [56] Ibid. 25–6, 43, 74.

The certainty of a small punishment will make a stronger impression, than the fear of one more severe if attended with the hopes of escaping; for it is the nature of mankind to be terrified at the approach of the smallest inevitable evil, whilst hope, the best gift of heaven, hath the power of dispelling the apprehension of a greater; especially if supported by examples of impunity, which weakness or avarice too frequently afford. If punishments be very severe, men are naturally led to the perpetration of other crimes, to avoid the punishment due to the first. The countries and times most notorious for severity of punishments, were always those in which the most bloody and inhuman actions and the most atrocious crimes were committed.[57]

Thus Beccaria found the European society of his day to be suffering from a 'useless frequency of punishments'.[58] It was the task of enlightened government, he believed, to reduce them to a condition where their rational construction both conformed to the contractual basis of state and society and also achieved the maximum benefit in terms of the operation of the principles of deterrence and improvement on the human psyche.

Judged by these criteria, the death penalty, so widely applied in eighteenth-century Europe, had no place in a rational structure of penal sanctions. It was certainly not justifiable in terms of the social contract, the conditions of which Beccaria had enunciated at the outset of his work: the state's right to punish relied after all on the surrender to it by each citizen of the minimum quantity of freedom necessary for the citizenry's own protection. 'Is it possible', he asked, 'that in the smallest portions of the liberty of each, sacrificed to the good of the public, can be contained the greatest of all good, life?' Of course not. The death penalty could only possibly be supported because it was necessary for the protection of society against offenders, or because it would deter others from committing crimes. History, Beccaria judged, had demonstrated that capital punishment had failed to achieve the latter goal. The situation with the former objective, however, was less clear-cut. Execution of an offender might, Beccaria conceded, be justifiable

when, though deprived of his liberty, he has such power and connexions as may endanger the security of the nation; when his existence may produce a dangerous revolution in the established form of government. But even in this case, it can only be necessary when a nation is on the verge of recovering or losing its liberty; or in times of absolute anarchy, when the disorders themselves hold the place of law.[59]

But in normal times, under a lawful form of government that enjoyed the approbation of the multitude of citizens, there was no reason why the death penalty should be applied. The concession which Beccaria made in admitting the legitimacy of capital punishment in times of emergency was to return to haunt abolitionists on many subsequent occasions over the next century and beyond.

---

[57] Ibid. 98–100.   [58] Ibid. 103–4.   [59] Ibid.

Carefully delimited and cautiously circumscribed by Beccaria himself, it never-theless compromised the principle of abolition by admitting that the death penalty could be used in circumstances the exceptionality of which was open in practice to a multiplicity of definitions. For the moment, however, and not surprisingly in view of the prevalent ethos of European penal policy in the eighteenth century, it was Beccaria's general condemnation of capital punish-ment in normal circumstances that caught the eye.

Beccaria combined his attack on the principle of the death penalty with a critique of its application in practice. Executions were held in public, he noted, not least with the aim of deterring the spectators from committing a crime similar to the one for which the punishment was being meted out. But, he declared,

It is not the intenseness of the pain that has the greatest effect on the mind but its continuance. . . . The death of a criminal is a terrible but momentary spectacle, and therefore a less efficacious method of deterring others, than the continued example of a man deprived of his liberty, condemned, as a beast of burthen, to repair, by his labours, the injury he has done to society.[60]

Public executions in Beccaria's view were soon forgotten by the spectators; the emotions they induced soon faded away: 'The execution of a criminal is, to the multitude, a spectacle, which in some excited compassion mixed with indig-nation. These sentiments occupy the mind much more than that salutary terror which the laws endeavour to inspire.'[61] In the end, he thought, an execution constituted no more than the cold-blooded repetition of the crime, murder, which it was supposed to deter. As far as the potential offender was concerned, he added, public execution was far from being the infallible deterrent which its supporters imagined.

There are many who can look upon death with intrepidity and firmness; some through fanaticism, and others through vanity, which attends us even to the grave; others from a desperate resolution, either to get rid of their misery, or cease to live; but fanaticism and vanity forsake the criminal in slavery, in chains and fetters, in an iron cage, and despair seems rather the beginning than the end of their misery.[62]

The greatest deterrent in Beccaria's view was thus the prospect of lifelong forced labour; and since he evidently had in mind forced labour on street and canal constuction and maintenance and other public works, it was clear that this punishment was to be carried out just as much before the eyes of the law-abiding citizenry as public executions had been.

What was interesting about Beccaria was not merely the clarity with which he argued for a more rational and humane form of penal policy, but also the

[60] Beccaria, *An Essay*, 105–6.   [61] Ibid. 106–7, 113–14.   [62] Ibid. 107–8.

boundaries which he set to his arguments. Beccaria saw human nature in pessi-
mistic terms. The passions were dangerous and had to be kept in check by the
threat of punishment. Indeed, punishment was more important than justice or
human rights or the dignity of the individual human being. It should gain its
deterrent effect through terror, and correspondingly, offenders were to be punished not because they had done wrong, or to reform them, but in order to stop
others following their example. The humanitarian principles enunciated by
Beccaria were strictly utilitarian. Cruelty was condemned not as immoral but as
'useless'. It was on strictly limited grounds that Beccaria advocated the abolition
of capital punishment, namely, its violation of the social contract and its inefficacy as a deterrent. It was to a strictly limited extent that he urged the introduction of more humane alternatives, for, as he himself pointed out, lifelong
imprisonment in an iron cage, with chains, blows, and perpetual hard labour,
was possibly a more frightful punishment even than death. And it was in a strictly
limited fashion that he envisaged his new penal philosophy as fulfilling the
dictates of the greatest good of the greatest number or representing the will of the
citizenry as expressed through a rational fulfilment of the social contract. Beccaria
was no democrat; he was not even a liberal. On the contrary, he directed his
appeal above all to the Enlightened rulers of his own time. The power of custom
and habit, which he saw as the main forces behind the continuation of capital
punishment, could only be swept away, he thought, by decisive action from
above, and he saw this as coming solely from the autocratic state:

How happy were mankind, if laws were now to be first formed; now that we see on the
thrones of Europe, benevolent monarchs, friends to the virtues of peace, to the arts and
sciences, fathers of their people, though crowned yet citizens; the increase of whose
authority augments the happiness of their subjects, by destroying that intermediate
despotism, which intercepts the prayers of the people to the throne.

The voice of the people, he said, was articulated through 'a small number of
sages, scattered on the face of the earth', and these were the men, such as himself,
on whose advice the modern monarch would become an eighteenth-century
version of the enlightened Roman emperors of old, a latterday Antoninus or
Trajan. Because of the difficulty of reforming the law, he concluded, 'every wise
citizen will wish for the increase of their authority'.[63]

Beccaria was right to address himself to Europe's princes. In the eighteenth
century, there was in practice no other way for his ideas to be realized. Following
the publication of his book in 1764, the *philosophe* d'Alembert commissioned a
French translation, which appeared in 1766 and was read by Diderot and
Rousseau; Voltaire published a commentary on the book; and the Russian

---

[63] Ibid. 116–17.

Empress Catherine II asked Beccaria to undertake the reform of the legal system in Russia, an invitation which he was, however, sensible enough to refuse; the unpredictable Catherine had in fact already abolished the death penalty in her empire twelve years before. A Polish translation of Beccaria's treatise appeared in 1772, and in 1775 the book was published in Spanish. The American statesman and author of the Declaration of Independence Thomas Jefferson copied extensive extracts from the English translation of 1773 into his notebook. In 1768, Beccaria was appointed professor of cameral science in Milan, on the instructions of the Imperial Chancellor Kaunitz in Vienna. Within a very short space of time, therefore, he was indeed reaching some of the leading princes and politicians of his day, through the enthusiasm with which his ideas had been received by many of Europe's leading intellectuals. And in his own state he exercised a direct influence on the shaping of penal policy, not least through the various offices he subsequently occupied in the higher civil service in the Habsburg Empire. His influence was evident in the decision of the Austrian Empress Maria Theresia in 1776 to restrict the death penalty to '*delicta atrocissima*', explicitly proposing imprisonment as an alternative:

> with the proviso that in all Our lands, the necessary public works will be selected, prisons built (or existing ones enlarged) for the appropriate disciplining and punishment, and that the authorities in the same will proceed with such rigour and severity against criminals and administer punishment to such a full extent, that the oft-repeated sight of such prisoners will mirror the repugnance aroused in the populace by the death penalty, and to this extent society will also gain its own benefit from the labour of such criminals.[64]

In 1788, the Emperor Joseph II, most thoroughgoing and dogmatic of the Enlightened Despots, introduced a new general law code which dispensed with the death penalty altogether.[65] Two years previously, in 1786, the death penalty had also been abolished in the Grand Duchy of Tuscany, and when the Duke succeeded his brother Joseph II as Holy Roman Emperor in 1790, he appointed Beccaria to help draft a new Criminal Code for Lombardy as well.[66] Beccaria, therefore, was more than a mere theorist: his ideas had a material effect on the law. Yet their 'humanitarianism' was strictly limited. Thus although Joseph II abolished capital punishment, he replaced it with the punishment of pulling barges along the Danube, the kind of public forced labour Beccaria recommended. The criminals were to be chained at night, had to work without pause,

---

[64] Quoted in Michael Schewardnadse, *Die Todesstrafe in Europa. Eine rechtsvergleichende Darstellung mit einer rechtsgeschichtlichen Einleitung* (Munich, 1914), 16–17.

[65] Hartl, *Wiener Kriminalgericht*, 20–1.

[66] Alff, 'Zur Einführung', 20–36. H. Hetzel, *Die Todesstrafe in ihrer kulturgeschichtlichen Entwicklung* (Berlin, 1870) is a rather confused and inconclusive survey of the opinion of the time. See also Marcel Normand, *La Peine de mort* (Paris, 1980), 20, and Horst H. Lewandowski, *Die Todesstrafe in der Aufklärung* (Bonn, 1961).

were fed only a minimal diet, and were often immersed in mosquito- and malaria-infested water for hours on end. Of the first hundred felons sent to haul barges in Hungary in 1784, seventy-five were dead within a year. When the operation of royal clemency on capital cases is taken into account, it is probable that more offenders died from this punishment than from the death penalty itself.[67]

d. The Prussian General Law Code of 1794

Beccaria's work was known not only in the Habsburg Empire, but also in many parts of Germany, where three translations had already appeared by the end of 1767.[68] Ludwig Eugen of Württemberg, brother and heir-apparent of the reigning Duke, wrote to Beccaria early in 1766 assuring him that he would do all in his power to ensure the adoption of his ideas in his realm. Friedrich II of Prussia read Beccaria's work and wrote to Voltaire that he considered it the last word on penal policy.[69] His influence can also be discerned in the Prussian monarch's decision to draft a systematic General Law Code (*Allgemeines Landrecht*) for his domains, incorporating all the latest penal doctrines of the Enlightenment. Initially, at least, his intention was to unify Prussia on the basis of a systematic, rational, legal underpinning of the social order. The legal experts charged with drawing up the code aimed to impose a single structure of law under the direct control of the monarch, in place of the myriad local and regional customs and practices that had existed previously, despite the influence of Imperial codifications such as the *Carolina* and the various edicts promulgated by Friedrich himself since the 1740s. The first draft was based squarely on the assumption that the individual was a rational being, and that penal sanctions would only be effective if they appealed to rational interests. Emotions, predominating among the common people, were a kind of perversion of rationality. Revulsion at the criminal displayed on the scaffold, for example, was an emotional version of a principle of self-interest which was at bottom strictly rational in content.[70] The earlier drafts of the General Law Code incorporated notions of natural law that were not dissimilar to those enunciated as the guiding principles of the French Revolution: 'General human rights are based on the natural freedom of the

---

[67] T. C. W. Blanning, *Joseph II* (London, 1994), 81–2.

[68] Beccaria, *An Essay*, 183–4. For a good discussion of Beccaria's influence in America, see Masur, *Rites*, 50–70.

[69] Maestro, *Voltaire and Beccaria*, 117. See also B. Kreutziger, 'Argumente für und wider die Todesstrafe(n). Ein Beitrag zu Beccaria-Rezeption im deutschsprachigen Raum des 18. Jahrhunderts', in G. Deimling (ed.), *Cesare Beccaria. Die Anfänge moderner Strafrechtspflege in Europa* (Heidelberg, 1989), 99–125.

[70] Reinhart Koselleck, *Preussen zwischen Reform und Revolution. Allgemeines Landrecht, Verwaltung und soziale Bewegung von 1791 bis 1848*, 2nd edn. (Munich, 1989), 22–8.

individual to be able to seek and further his own welfare without infringing the rights of others.'[71] But these ran into fierce criticism from Prussian traditionalists. The final version, which came into effect in 1794, made a number of crucial compromises with existing social structure and traditional penal practice. It did not introduce full equality before the law, but retained different provisions for offenders of different social standing. The natural law element did remain in this rather contradictory document, and found its way into the clauses listing the penal sanctions applied to various kinds of offence. But a thoroughgoing Beccarian system of penal sanctions was not implemented, and in particular, capital punishment was in the end retained.[72]

The Prussian General Law Code of 1794, which was to govern civil and penal policy in Prussia for many decades, consolidated the reduction in the varieties of capital punishment which had been taking place during the eighteenth century. It linked punishment as systematically as possible to the nature and degree of the offence committed. While Beccaria's suggestion of abolishing the death penalty altogether was not accepted, his principle of grading the severity of punishments to correspond to the heinousness of the crime certainly was. For the most part, the symbolic links and resonances of public punishments were superseded by a scheme dominated by steadily increasing degrees of elaboration. Decapitation with the sword was the punishment laid down for infanticide, manslaughter, and lesser forms of treason (*Landesverrat*, third class, and aiding and abetting second-class *Landesverrat*). The next gradation of punishment, breaking with the wheel from the top down, was to be applied to simple murder. If the victim was a brother or sister of the offender, then this was to be preceded by a period of standing at the pillory. A conspiracy to murder was considered more severe than murder by a single individual, so the leader of such a conspiracy was to be broken with the wheel from the bottom up, while his followers suffered the fate of normal murderers and were broken from the top down. The framers of the Code seem to have considered poisoning a particularly underhand and deceitful form of murder, so they prescribed that those found guilty of it should be dragged to the scaffold wrapped in an oxhide as well as broken with the wheel from the bottom up. First-class treason (*Landesverrat*) was to receive the same punishment, with the additional disgrace of exhibiting the corpse on the wheel afterwards, which meant that the corpses of offenders found guilty of lesser types of treason or murder were no longer to suffer this fate. Parricides and matricides were to get the same treatment with the addition of a public whipping before-

[71] Quoted in Brandt, *Preussen*, 192.

[72] J.-U. Heuer, *Allgemeines Landrecht und Klassenkampf. Die Auseinandersetzungen um die Prinzipien des Allgemeinen Landrechts Ende des 18. Jahrhunderts als Ausdruck der Krise des Feudalsystems in Preussen* (Berlin, 1960).

hand. Finally, high treason (*Hochverrat*), formerly punishable by quartering, was now made punishable by 'the severest bodily and capital punishments', a phrase that left the precise method to the imagination. Similar gradations of punishment were observable in other areas, for example in highway robbery, where the severest punishment was reserved for robbers who killed victims who had put up no resistance, while lesser punishments applied to less violent forms of the crime.[73] Despite all this, however, the Code did not establish the 'rule of law' in Prussia. The King and his judges retained the right, explicitly written into the Code, to set prison terms as they wished, taking into account not just the degree of the offender's crime but also the degree of the threat they thought he posed to society. The doctrine of 'special prevention' which this reflected allowed the judiciary to pass indefinite prison sentences merely on suspicion that the offender would repeat his crime if released. In this way too, therefore, the Code fell some way short of the ideals prescribed by Beccaria.

The General Law Code of 1794 was in many ways the summation of Enlightenment thinking on criminal law. It attempted to mould society and establish a set of rules for people's conduct to such a degree that it included prescriptive as well as preventive provisions. It was intended not just to prevent evil but actively to promote good. It was a classic document of the Absolutist police state. Its most important step as far as penal policy was concerned was the replacement of numerous corporal punishments by carefully graded terms of imprisonment. Of course, corporal punishment continued, as a means of disciplining the lower classes in particular, and was also carefully graded according to the severity of the offence. The problem for the legislators was that the right to administer chastisement belonged not only to the state, but also to parents (over their children), masters (over their servants and apprentices), husbands (over their wives), teachers (over their pupils), and landlords (over their serfs). Authority, indeed, sometimes seemed to rest to a large extent on violence or the threat of it. Disentangling all these various legal rights took many decades, especially where they were bound up with the general rights of patrimonial justice.[74] But the Prussian General Law Code inaugurated a process by which this system was gradually dismantled. In 1794, one senior judicial official declared:

In the spirits of the lower classes of the people, the sense of honour and self-respect which in better organized natures is such a potent influence in preventing many kinds of crime, is already weak, and it is completely and utterly smothered and killed off by corporal punishments, especially by those which also dishonour the offender.[75]

[73] *Allgemeines Landrecht für die Preussischen Staaten von 1794*, text with intro. by Hans Hattenhauer, 2nd edn. (Frankfurt am Main, 1994), II, 20: §§ 965, 806, 826, 881, 839, 841, 870, 103, 873, 93, also §§ 1197–1202. Hattenhauer's introduction to this edition is the best overall account of the Code, its origins, and its influence.

[74] Koselleck, *Preussen*, 643.   [75] Ibid. 642.

Dishonouring punishments such as the 'fiddle' and the 'Spanish cloak', halters placed around the neck of offenders, especially women, were still being used, alongside the pillory and the iron collar, in a number of provinces ten years later.[76] In 1810 their use, still common in the patrimonial jurisdictions of the Junker estates in cases of 'unruliness on the part of His Majesty's subjects', was officially banned as contrary to 'the spirit of the age'. The real point was that they were considered as part of the system of serfdom, which was now being run down, and were therefore deemed inappropriate to the newly free status of the East Elbian peasants. However, Junker landowners continued to object to the substitution of imprisonment for punishments such as these: 'For when a farm labourer or servant is forced to sit in gaol . . . it is not he who is punished, so much as his lord, by being forced to do without his services.' Not surprisingly, therefore, reports continued to come in to the Prussian Ministry of Justice about the use of corporal punishments such as the 'goat' (a wooden apparatus to which offenders were tied in an uncomfortable position and whipped) as late as 1832.[77]

By this time, however, imprisonment had become overwhelmingly the major medium for punishing offenders. Already before the promulgation of the General Law Code, the connection between the spread of imprisonment and the decline of corporal punishment had been made explicit by a directive of the Prussian state allowing dishonouring punishments such as the 'fiddle' only in areas where there was an absence of 'regular prisons'.[78] The shift from corporal punishment to imprisonment in the 1790s was accompanied by a serious interest in prison reform. Influenced by the ideas of the English prison reformer John Howard, men such as Heinrich Wagnitz condemned the carceral system of Prussia in radical terms. Thousands of offenders, he complained in 1791, were locked up 'in musty dungeons, on filthy straw, half eaten by vermin'.[79] Yet these people too, he said, were human beings, God's creatures, with souls, Wagnitz said that the German prisons of the future 'must be sacred to the state as places which in some instances prevent society's fallen from sinking any lower, in others secure people and render them innocuous, and in yet others cater for the sick'.[80]

[76] GStA Berlin Rep. 84a/8912, Bl. 1: Friedrich Wilhelm III note, 24 Nov. 1804.

[77] Ibid., Bl: 6: notes of Neumärkischer Regierungs- und Kriegs- und Domänen-Kammer allergehorsamster Gericht, 23 Sept. 1806; ibid., Bl. 13: notes of Oberandesgericht Neumark, 23 Mar. 1810; ibid., Bl. 18: Friedrich Wilhelm III to Oberlandesgericht Neumark, 28 Apr. 1810; ibid,. Bl. 29–30: Regierung Breslau to PJM, 24 Apr. 1818; ibid., Bl. 44–5: Oberlandesgericht Naumburg to PJM, 26 Nov. 1824.; ibid., Bl. 47: notes to the Minister of Justice, 28 Oct. 1832.

[78] Koselleck, *Preussen*, 642.

[79] Heinrich Wagnitz, *Historische Nachrichten und Bemerkungen über die merkwürdigsten Zuchthäuser in Deutschland. Nebst einem Anhange über die zweckmässigste Einrichtung der Gefängnisse und Irrenanstalten* (2 vol., Halle, 1791), here i. p. xi.

[80] Heinrich Wagnitz, *Ideen und Pläne zur Verbesserung der Policey- u. Criminalanstalten. Dem 19. Jahrhundert zur Vollendung übergeben* (Halle, 1801).

His plea set the tone for numerous critiques of the prison system in subsequent decades. Most of them were utterly ineffective. At the beginning of the nineteenth century, Prussian prisons were already so overcrowded that the central judicial administration in Berlin, invoking the arbitrary doctrine of 'special prevention', began to consider transportation as an alternative, and did indeed manage to ship off a substantial number of supposedly incorrigible prisoners to Siberia at this time.[81] Cost-cutting and economy were the rocks on which the grandiose schemes of the prison reformers were to founder time after time in the coming century. Prussian prisons proved highly resistant to ideas of moral reform, education, and character formation. They remained in general dumping-grounds for society's unwanted.[82]

Underlying this transformation of punishment was a decline in the social importance of honour, as reformers moved to break down the barriers of status in the wake of the French Revolution. Already the writers of the German Enlightenment were redefining honour as attaching less to outward station than to inner character. Part of the new bourgeois ideology of the late eighteenth century, the values and beliefs of the emerging educated public in Germany rested on the claim that honour transcended status; that civil honour, the honour of the citizen (*bürgerliche* or *staatsbürgerliche Ehre*) was what above all else justified the claim of the non-noble educated élite to equal rights. The Prussian General Law Code of 1794 still upheld the status-bound definition of honour, prescribing different penalties for offenders of different stations in life, and even banning nobles from engaging in trade on pain of losing their title. But after the defeat of Prussia by Napoleon in 1806 the reformers got the upper hand, and set in motion a radical transformation of the Prussian state. The far-reaching steps taken in 1807 and 1811 towards the abolition of serfdom were accompanied by the revocation in the former year of the laws of derogation, allowing nobles to engage in trade and other formerly demeaning occupations. At the same time, education and ability became the essential qualifications for offices of state. And lower down the social scale, the privileges of the guilds were removed in Prussia and the legal underpinnings of infamy gradually done away with, so that by 1820 only knackers and executioners were still subject to the formal, legal definition of 'dishonourable people'.[83] These changes, part and parcel of the gradual transition that was beginning in these years from a status-based to a class-based society in Germany, inevitably had an effect on the nature of penal sanctions, as specific penalties of dishonour began to lose their social meaning, a development already foreshadowed, and also to a large extent advocated, in the pages of Beccaria.

---

[81] See Richard J. Evans, *Szenen aus der deutschen Unterwelt* (Reinbek, 1997).
[82] See Blasius, *Bürgerliche Gesellschaft, passim.*   [83] Zunkel, 'Ehre', 26–9, 34–7, 47.

The trend towards imprisonment was strengthened by major changes in sensibility that complemented the new emphasis on a rational policy of deterrence by developing a new, gender-specific theory of the emotions. This mixture of rationalism and sensibility was observable above all in the dramatic changes that took place in the treatment of infanticide during this period. Already in the mid-eighteenth century, the religious and moralistic foundations of the seventeenth-century horror of infanticide had begun to weaken under the impact of Enlightenment thought. Concerned to encourage population growth irrespective of moral considerations, the Enlightened monarchs of the period began to decriminalize extramarital sex. These changing attitudes were also reflected in the growth of more lenient practices among the judiciary. Already beginning to fall in the 1740s under the impact of such ideas, the number of executions for infanticide really began to plummet in most parts of Germany in the 1770s and 1780s.[84] In rural Württemberg, for instance, there were only three executions for infanticide in the period 1748–87, compared with fifteen in the previous thirty years. In courts all over Germany, death sentences for the offence grew less common. In Bremen, infanticide still carried the death penalty in the 1750s, but by the end of the 1780s, imprisonment had become the norm.[85]

This shift in sensibility was signalled by a widespread public debate on the subject of infanticide in the 1770s and 1780s. The crime became a central topic of the *Sturm und Drang* movement in German literature, and featured in works such as Goethe's *Faust* (1774–5), Lenz's *Zerbin* (1776), Heinrich Leopold Wagner's drama *Die Kindermörderin* (1776), and Friedrich Schiller's poem *Die Kindsmörderin* (1781). These works portrayed unmarried mothers not as the servant girls seduced by peasant and labouring men which in reality they mostly were, but as decent young women seduced by cynical and world-weary aristocrats. They formed part of an emerging bourgeois discourse in which the aristocracy was portrayed as immoral and corrupt. Such views were reflected in the massive response to a public invitation issued in 1780 by an anonymous donor—subsequently revealed to be an official at the court in Mannheim, Adrian von Lamezan—for essays to be submitted to him on the best way of dealing with infanticide. Lamezan's prize of a hundred ducats for the best essay attracted over 400 responses. This in turn sparked an even more widespread debate in the journals, clubs, and meetings which were such an important part of the emerging bourgeois public sphere in Germany at this time. Opinion in the debate was overwhelmingly on the side of the unmarried mother, who was no longer portrayed as wicked, bestial, or driven by the Devil, but as good-natured,

[84] Dülmen, *Frauen*, 111–12.
[85] StA Bremen 2.-D. 17. c. 2. vol. 1: cases of Christiana Tockhausen (1753), Beke Becker (1773), Elizabet Schierbrink (1786), Lucke Helmers (1789).

trusting, weak, or desperate. Correspondingly, the general view seemed to be that the solution to the problem lay in the establishment of confidential nursing homes where the women could be taken care of from the early days of pregnancy without losing their reputation, and foundling hospitals where the infants could be looked after by the state after the mothers had returned to their former life. If anyone should be punished, it was in this view the father, inevitably portrayed as a wicked and heartless seducer. Almost every entrant in the competition agreed that penal sanctions against sexual immorality should be abolished.[86] A religious understanding of crime and punishment had given way in this discourse to a secular, moral understanding based on individual psychology. Guilt was measured not externally, by actions, but internally, by motive, intention, and character.

The consequence for penal policy was drawn by a legal official in Weimar, who argued in 1783, adapting an argument first made popular by Beccaria, that infanticide should no longer be punishable by death because

Women who murder their babies belong to the lowest of the plebeian classes, and the impression which the example of an execution makes on the spirit of this kind of people, who are not accustomed to reflection, only lasts as long as the frightful scene is present before their senses, or at least not much longer, no matter how great the terror which initially accompanies it. Such an impression very quickly either disappears completely or becomes so weak that when the unfortunate moment comes when they are tempted to commit a similar crime, it is no longer able to overcome the full force of the fear of the obloquy and of the other problems that they hope to avoid by carrying out the terrible act of killing their baby, and they have almost always done the deed before the more remote vision of the equal or greater fear of the death penalty has swum into their stream of consciousness.[87]

In applying it specifically to infanticidal women, however, the official was adumbrating a shift towards a gender-based definition of the emotions that was coming into fashion at this time: men as goal-oriented and serious, women as flighty, impressionable, and subject to swift changes of the emotions.

In the early eighteenth century, as Karin Hausen has pointed out, common definitions of the nature or character of men and women, as provided by the dictionaries and encyclopaedias of the day, concentrated on their role and status within the household. Men and women were defined by their social position, and it was this from which the corresponding virtues and characteristics were derived. Between about 1780 and 1810, however, this mode of definition came under increasing criticism. A new code of values and a new definition of the family was

[86] Dülmen, *Frauen*, 104; Ulbricht, 'Infanticide'; Beate Weber, *Die Kindsmörderin im deutschen Schrifttum von 1770–1795* (Bonn, 1984); Christine Wittrock, *Abtreibung und Kindesmord in der neueren deutschen Literatur* (Frankfurt am Main, 1978).
[87] Lucht, *Strafrechtspflege*, 39.

beginning to emerge. Instead of being defined as the union of a man and a woman for the purpose of producing children and running a household, marriage came to be regarded as the free union of two individuals based on romantic love. The social and political role of the family came under fire, and it was redefined on a contractual basis. The status-bound household gave way gradually to the bourgeois family. Bourgeois individualism defined men and women in terms of their character rather than their station in life. By 1815, Brockhaus's encyclopaedia was defining the male and female character in the following terms:

The male spirit is more creative, having greater effect on the outside world, more inclined to strive, to process abstract subjects, to form wide-ranging plans. . . . The man must acquire, the woman seeks to preserve, the male with force, the female with her virtue or her wiles. The former belongs to bustling public life, the latter to the quiet domestic circle.

The prevalence of infanticide as the pre-eminent female crime could only be reconciled with this new image of women by portraying the perpetrators not as bestial but as weak, driven to actions they knew to be wrong by the actions of unscrupulous male seducers.[88] Indeed, their crimes were now increasingly presented as emerging from a noble emotion—modesty—and the desire not to lose their reputation. Well before the middle of the nineteenth century, these 'unfortunates' were being sentenced to terms of imprisonment as short as five years.[89] Here was another influence, therefore, in the transformation of penal practice which began in the period of the Enlightenment.

e. The Legacy of the Guillotine

In recent years, some historians have come to see the penal reform movement of the Enlightenment in largely negative terms. Whereas it was once portrayed in simple terms as a contribution to liberalism, progress, and humanitarianism, it is now commonly regarded as authoritarian or even proto-totalitarian in inspiration and effect. When Enlightenment thinkers and legislators vented their spleen on the barbarities and cruelties of the penal regimes of the past, they were, in this view, objecting principally to what they saw as their ineffectiveness. When they spoke, as they often did, of the need for a milder and more humane system of punishment, their aim, as Foucault declared, was 'not to punish less, but to

---

[88] Karin Hausen, 'Family and Role-Division: The Polarisation of Sexual Stereotypes in the Nineteenth Century—An Aspect of the Dissociation of Work and Family Life', in Richard J. Evans and W. R. Lee (eds.), *The German Family: Essays on the Social History of the Family in Nineteenth- and Twentieth-Century Germany* (London, 1981), 51–83, here 54.

[89] StA Bremen 2-D. 17. c. 2. vol. 2: esp. case of Helene Raschen (1846).

punish better'.[90] A 'humane' system of penal sanctions was simply one which based itself on the recognition that humans were rational beings. It therefore appealed, as in Beccaria's theory, to rational self-interest by a carefully graded set of punishments that were predictable, consistent, and proportional to the crime. This would be a far more effective deterrent, it was thought, than the arbitrary and capricious justice of the age of religion, when punishment was not 'humane' but based on notions of the Divine which Enlightenment thinkers repudiated. Indeed, some historians have gone so far as to argue that the Enlightenment's concern for open trials, equality before the law, and the legal rights of the individual to a fair hearing was motivated principally by the desire to legitimate the new system of punishment and control, while the attacks of Enlightenment thinkers on lengthy and over-elaborate trial procedures have been portrayed as deriving from a desire to secure the rapid conviction and punishment of offenders rather than from a concern for their civil rights.[91]

In emphasizing the primary thrust of the Enlightenment movement for penal reform towards a totalizing system of social control, recent historians have contributed to a wider argument which locates the origins of the French Revolutionary Terror of 1793–4 not just in the preceding years but in the preceding decades.[92] And in doing so, they have taken up once more a much older thesis that links the Revolution and Terror to the rise of totalitarianism in the twentieth century.[93] The classic symbol of this continuity is the guillotine. On 3 May 1791 the revolutionary regime in France replaced the panoply of methods used under the *ancien régime* with a single form of execution that would apply to all: decapitation. On 20 March 1792 the machine perfected by the leading medical authority of the Revolution, Dr Ignace-Joseph Guillotin, was declared as the sole method of decapitation to be used. The idea of a mechanical form of execution was not new. It had been used in Renaissance Italy and early modern Germany, where it was known as the *Fallbeil* or *Fallschwerdt*, the falling axe or the falling sword. All that Dr Guillotin did was to introduce a few minor modifications. The *modus operandi* of the new machine was accurately described by the poet Heinrich Heine in the following terms:

> Here you'll be tied onto a board
> Which sinks down—then they quickly shove

[90] Foucault, *Discipline and Punish*, 82.

[91] Richard Andrews, 'The Cunning of Imagery: Rhetoric and Ideology in Cesare Beccaria's Treatise "On Crimes and Punishments"', in M. Campbell and M. Rollins (eds.), *Begetting Images: Studies in the Art and Science of Symbol Production* (New York, 1989), 121–2; Joanne Kaufmann, 'In Search of Obedience: The Critique of Criminal Justice in Late-Eighteenth-Century France', *Proceedings of the Sixth Annual Meeting of the Western Society for French History* (1979), 188.

[92] Classically, Simon Schama, *Citizens: A Chronicle of the French Revolution* (New York, 1989).

[93] J. L. Talmon, *The Origins of Totalitarian Democracy* (London, 1952).

You 'twixt two posts; triangular
The blade which hangs far up above;
They pull a cord, and then the blade's
Quite happy down the posts to go.
When this occurs, your head falls off
And drops into a sack below.[94]

What caused Guillotin's name to be associated so indelibly with the machine was not his role in its perfection, but rather the universality of the machine's application. From the Revolution's point of view, establishing the guillotine as the sole means of execution had a number of crucial advantages. First, it substituted what was widely regarded as a quick, painless, and humane form of execution for the slow, painful, and often cruel forms that prevailed under the *ancien régime*, from burning at the stake to breaking on the wheel. It thus satisfied a demand for a more humane penal practice that had already been widespread before the Revolution. Secondly, it removed the status inequalities attached to the variety of pre-Revolutionary capital punishments, in which the nobility were executed with honour and the commonalty dispatched with infamy. The victims of the guillotine, equal citizens in life, retained this equality in the manner of their death. Decapitation had once been reserved, as the only honourable mode of execution, for the nobility; now it was applied to all.[95]

But there was a practical as well as a symbolic reason for the French adoption of the guillotine by the revolutionary regime in France. The Criminal Code of 1791 replaced the vast range of offences, ranging from sodomy and murder through to minor theft and the cutting down of trees, punishable by death under the *ancien régime*, with a much more limited number, mainly various forms of theft and murder. But it also opened the way to the Terror of 1793–4 by including a variety of crimes against the state. Even in 1792 the official executioner, Henri Sanson, was complaining that if the hand-held axe continued to be used, the result would be nothing more than a 'massacre' when a number of offenders had to be executed on the same occasion. The 'immensity of blood which it produces', he said, would reduce the offenders waiting for their turn to quivering heaps of abject terror. Under the guillotine, which immobilized the victims and required no particular fortitude on their part, such scenes would not be possible. Bound to a board and held mechanically in place, the offender no longer had to exercise any bodily self-control in order to offer a steady target for the fatal blow. Yet at the same time, Dorinda Outram has argued, the new machine replaced the elaborate drama of the execution ritual under the *ancien*

---

[94] Heinrich Heine, *Deutschland—ein Wintermährchen* (Hamburg, 1844), Kaput xvi.
[95] Outram, *Body*, 107–9. See also Daniel Gerould, *Guillotine: Its Legend and Lore* (New York, 1992).

régime with 'a brief, virtually invisible passage into death, which, devoid of drama, was perilously close to losing significance altogether'.[96]

Under the *ancien régime*, executions were relatively infrequent in occurence, ceremonial and prolonged in nature, and participatory in spirit and intent; under the Revolution, they were quick, unceremonious, and mechanical. The scaffold was sealed off from the crowd by ranks of mounted troops obstructing any possibility of popular involvement. It was only on their journey to the scaffold that the condemned were directly exposed to the crowd.[97] Around the guillotine itself, the crowds were passive, and deprived of any possibility of a relationship with the victim. Mechanized death was desacralized death: there was no priest on the scaffold, and the victims had no public opportunity of making their peace with God. Deprived of the religious connotations so central to executions under the *ancien régime*, decapitation by machine became a merely physical act, reflecting the rationalism of Revolutionary ideology. Between March 1793 and August 1794 14,000 death sentences were passed in Paris. They could only possibly be carried out mechanically. Mass executions such as those of Robespierre and over a hundred of his followers, carried out in a mere two days, presaged the mechanized mass slaughter of the Nazi regime one and a half centuries later. They also contained some of the ambiguities and contradictions of subsequent acts of mass extermination; between, for example, the regime's desire to advertise its exterminatory purpose, and its determination to conceal that purpose's implementation from the public view. Such contradictions were to reappear in many of the nineteenth century's attempts to deal with capital punishment. They reflected in turn the manifold uncertainties that attended the redefinition of the public and private body by the Revolution.[98]

It is easy to see why such arguments have been put forward, at a time when the collapse of Communism in Eastern and, some time before, in Western Europe, has invited a negative reassessment of the revolutionary tradition. But it is less easy to accept them as they stand. In the first place, Outram's depiction of the process of revolutionary execution is far from convincing. Other historians, basing their views on a close examination of revolutionary iconography, have emphasized by contrast the very public nature of the guillotine and its operation: the machine, standing on a platform and rising out of the crowd, the public display of the severed head after the fall of the fatal blade.[99] The public knew who

---

[96] Outram, *Body*, 109–10, 114. The voluminous 'diaries' or 'memoirs' of the Sanson family, published in German as Henri Sanson, *Tagebücher der Henker von Paris 1685–1847* (2 vols.; Potsdam, 1923) are a 19th-c. fabrication (see G. Lenôtre, *Guillotine*, 74–6).

[97] Outram, *Body*, 116–17.   [98] Ibid. 110, 163.

[99] Ronald Paulson, *Representations of Revolution (1789–1820)* (New Haven, 1983), 23.

the executed people were, and the offender's fate was neither secret nor anonymous. The execution itself was only the culmination of a lengthy ceremony, which began with a slow procession along a pre-ordained route through the streets, with frequent verbal and symbolic exchanges between the onlookers and the prisoner in the tumbril. The whole, as the French writer Daniel Arasse has observed, constituted a kind of theatre in which the people was no mere passive spectator, 'no mere audience; it was an actor in the procession, and determined to make a success of the spectacle'. It was not until 1832 that the procession was decisively shortened; not until 1851 that the scaffold was abandoned and the guillotine placed on the ground.[100] During the Revolution itself, the ceremony remained open to the public and observable by all.

Moreover, like other historians who have sought to link the essence of the Revolution to Terror and totalitarianism, Outram elides crucial stages of the historical process in order to balance her historical equation. Before we can place the guillotine in the broad framework of historical comparison, we have to situate it carefully in the context of its own time. The law which introduced it also provided for abolishing differences in the method of punishment according to rank, forbidding the stigmatization of the condemned person's family and securing their rights over the corpse, and abolishing the confiscation of the offender's goods. It was voted, in other words, as an act of justice and humanity; and the later events of the Terror should not blind us to the importance of the principles it introduced.[101] Before the Revolution, such principles had been advocated by Robespierre and Marat, among many others; and Guillotin himself, in advocating them, spoke of the punishments customary in the *ancien régime* as 'tortures in which man shows himself more ferocious than wild beasts'.[102] The machine's designer was sincere enough in 1792 when he described 'the guillotine as an act of humanity', just as Robespierre had been sincere enough the previous year when he had advocated the abolition of capital punishment altogether.[103] Humane justice, in the eyes of the thinkers and politicians of the Enlightenment and early Revolutionary period, meant the implementation of a rational and consistent structure of penal sanctions. And it meant the recognition of the rights of the rational human being to a fair trial in which every side would have the opportunity to advance the cause of truth by reasoned argument.

The punishments of the *ancien régime* were regarded as barbarous because they belonged to an irrational age. They were thought to be ineffective as deterrents because they were arbitrary in their application. They offended the sensibilities of the Age of Reason. 'How sickened one becomes,' exclaimed the Girondin leader

[100] Daniel Arasse, *The Guillotine and the Terror* (London, 1989), 95, 109. See also Olivier Blanc (ed.), *Last Letters: Prisons and Prisoners of the French Revolution 1793–1794* (London, 1987).
[101] Arasse, *Guillotine*, 11–12, 19.   [102] Quoted ibid. 14.   [103] Ibid. 19–20, 24.

Brissot de Warville in 1781, 'when one sees the bloody penalties faced everywhere by the guilty . . . when one sees justice arming itself blindly with a dangerous severity against disorders which arise out of the defects of society . . . trying to make up for the shedding of blood by shedding blood and to repair losses by causing losses.'[104] Even in their treatment of political crimes, the judicial tribunals of the early Revolutionary years followed the maxims of the Enlightenment critique of the wide and often arbitrary definitions of treason current under the *ancien régime* and treated political offenders with a fairness and leniency entirely consonant with their belief that they were living, as Robespierrre put it, in an age 'in which the voice of reason and humanity resounds'.[105] Even before the Revolution, in fact, the practice of the courts in such cases had grown steadily more lenient.[106] What changed the situation was not the logic of Revolutionary judicial doctrine but the escalating interventions of the judicial practice of the crowd. 'Will future generations believe', asked one shocked observer after the massacres of July 1789, 'that in such an enlightened century, the entrails of a man were torn open and his heart carried on the end of a lance, that his head was passed from hand to hand in triumph through the streets and his cadaver dragged all through the capital?'[107] Such tones of distaste at the popular familiarity with the blood and guts of the dismembered body counted for little as the popular movement gained in power with the leftward drift of the Revolution under the impact of war, and men like Robespierre sought to keep pace with it by advocating increasing judicial severity towards political offenders, while continuing to defend a lenient stance towards the poverty-stricken common criminals whose sufferings from the arbitrary justice of the *ancien régime* had aroused so much bitterness in previous years. All this, and above all the guillotining of King Louis XVI, was to make the use of the guillotine highly problematical in Germany during the nineteenth and twentieth centuries. Yet the truth is that while the French Revolution rehearsed in the space of a few short years the history of many of the ideologies and movements that were to dominate Europe in the next two centuries, it was in no way inevitable that any one of them should triumph in the end. The judicial maxims of the Enlightenment did not lead directly or inevitably to the mechanized mass executions of the Terror. There was no straight line from Robespierre to Hitler, from the guillotine to Auschwitz and Treblinka.

Nevertheless, changes of some significance were taking place in penal policy in Europe at this time. In the course of the eighteenth century, the élites withdrew

---

[104] Quoted in Barry M. Shapiro, *Revolutionary Justice in Paris 1789–1790* (Cambridge, 1993), 4.

[105] Ibid. 8 for the quotation, and *passim* for the argument. See also Antoinette Wills, *Crime and Punishment in Revolutionary Paris* (London, 1981), 36–9, 57–64.

[106] Wright, *Between the Guillotine and Liberty*, 5–22; McCloy, *Humanitarian Movement*.

[107] Shapiro, *Revolutionary Justice*, 9.

from participation in popular culture, and began to view such communal rituals as executions with increasing disapproval. With the rise of Enlightened Absolutism, monarchs and their officials came to see the religious elements in executions as contrary to the purposes of deterring potential offenders. Instead of arousing the spectator's revulsion, executions won their sympathy by dramatizing the offender as a penitent sinner on the way to heaven through dying a 'good death'. The portrayal of physical suffering was all too close to the heroic stories of the sufferings recounted in the Protestant martyrologies, which had edified their readers by recounting in gruesome detail the sufferings of the saints in the face of persecution. Especially in Protestant states like Prussia, therefore, the range, scope, and variety of capital punishment was reduced in the eighteenth century with the explicit justification that it was wrong for excessive suffering to be inflicted upon the offender. Later, as the influence of Beccarian precepts of graded punishments began to spread, these measures were taken further. Penal policy was rationalized, and if Enlightenment monarchs and bureaucrats spoke, as they sometimes did, of the need for a more humane system of punishment, they meant in the first place one that was more attuned to what they conceived of as human nature and human needs. They rejected the divine aspect of punishment as irrelevant, even counter-productive. Punishment was to be based on a rational degree of pain, a calculus of terror, a system of punishment graded according to the degree of deterrence required. The guillotine in France, at the apex of this system, belonged essentially to the humanistic armoury of Enlightenment penal policy, and its later role as an instrument of rapid mass execution should not be allowed to obscure this point. There can be no doubt that the Enlightenment, taken in Germany at least as extending into the early years of the nineteenth century, was the crucial intellectual influence in bringing about the transition from a system of physical punishments for virtually all offences to one in which imprisonment was the norm, but capital punishment was retained, on retributive principles, for homicide. Like all historical processes, of course, this transformation was partial and incomplete. It also took place against the background of major social changes, including a long-term decline in crimes of violence, the pacification of society after the turmoil of the previous centuries, the ending of serfdom and the dissolution of urban hierarchies based on ascribed status and honour, which made it seem to its authors both necessary and inevitable. But by 1800 it had been largely achieved in the majority of the German states.

How plausible is the view that it resulted from a process of conscience formation, increasing inter-human identification, and the spread of compassion and sympathy for fellow citizens across and down the social scale as a consequence of the rise of poltical stability under Absolutism and the formation of the nation-state, as Norbert Elias and his disciple Pieter Spierenburg have maintained? The evidence we have examined does little to support this position. To begin with, as we saw in Chapters 1 and 2, their starting-point appears to be wrong. The public who witnessed executions in the early modern period were neither openly emotional nor lacking in sympathy and compassion for the malefactor on the gallows. On the contrary, Enlightenment authorities were inclined to think they showed rather too much sympathy, and they reduced the severity of bodily punishments not least in an attempt to remedy this situation. But the sympathy the crowd displayed was not for the bodily suffering of offenders, but for the fate of their spirit or soul. There is no real evidence from the history of crowd behaviour at executions for a process of 'conscience formation' in the eighteenth and nineteenth centuries. Ordinary people did not turn in revulsion and horror from the spectacle of one of their fellow humans being broken with the wheel, nor did they desert these occasions through indifference; on the contrary, there is plenty of evidence that crowds grew steadily larger in the course of the nineteenth century, and attendance at public executions reached a peak in the period immediately preceding their abolition. If anything, as the ritual and religious elements faded or were removed, the crowd's sympathy for and identification with the offender probably decreased rather than grew. In any case, there is no evidence that it was direct popular pressure for a more humanitarian penal policy that impelled the authorities to restrict, reform, and, as we shall see, finally abolish the public execution, certainly not in Germany, where popular opinion had very little possibility of asserting itself in the absence of parliamentary representation. This was one of many areas of German history where, in formal, legal terms at least, the initiative for change came from above.

Among the justifications used by judicial officials for changing the nature of capital punishment and then for bringing public executions to an end, 'humanity' was certainly one. Humane punishments were not least those which were most closely fitted to the human constitution, to producing the desired effects in terms of the human reactions of the spectator. Like torture, punishments such as drowning, burial alive, or burning at the stake were abandoned not only because enlightened opinion thought they were cruel, but also because the framers of judicial policy thought they were ineffective. Throughout the period covered by this book up to this point, legislators' primary concern was with the maintenance of law and order, not with the avoidance of cruelty. The search for a satisfactory method of execution was above all a search for one that would be effective as a deterrent, efficient as an instrument of penal policy, and meaningful in terms of the human psychology of the masses as it was understood by the judicial and administrative élite. If public executions were abolished in the name of a more effective law-and-order policy, therefore, rather than solely, or even primarily, in the name of humanity, does this mean that Foucault's explanation is the more plausible one? Here too, as we have seen, the empirical evidence does not really support the overarching theory. Early modern executions did not conform to Foucault's model of the carnivalesque confrontation of state power and popular resistance. And Foucault exaggerated the uniformity and consistency of the disciplining institutions which replaced them. Certainly, early nineteenth-century Germany, as the historian Alf Lüdtke has shown, was covered—especially in Prussia—with a dense network of surveillance institutions. But early modern society was closely policed as well. From church courts and visitations in the villages to guilds and councils in the towns and cities, an extensive apparatus of moral and social control emerged in the wake of the Thirty Years War, and surely played its part in bringing about the long-term reduction in violent crime that characterized the late seventeenth and eighteenth centuries in Germany. It is important, of course, not to overestimate the effectiveness of this system. But it is doubtful whether the policing arrangements of the late Enlightenment were any more effective. Moreover, imprisonment in the late eighteenth and nineteenth centuries was not, on the whole, designed along the lines of the totalizing, disciplining panopticon of Bentham's imagination: this would simply have been too expensive. Prison reforms urged by those who wished to see Germany's gaols becoming educational and character-forming institutions rather than mere dumping-grounds for society's unwanted were frustrated by the continual penny-pinching attitude of governments and penal authorities.

Public corporal and capital punishments were replaced by imprisonment as part of a long series of initiatives taken by Enlightened monarchs and reforming bureaucrats which aimed to break down the barriers of honour and status which had ossified German society and made it vulnerable to outside attack. Public punishments, as we saw in Chapters 1 and 2, made sense only in a society to which honour and dishonour were central, because a major function of capital and corporal punishments was to heap obloquy and infamy on the offender. As German society began the slow, complex transformation away from divisions based on status to stratification based on class, honour began to lose its importance and public punishments their meaning; a development compounded by the separation of élite and popular culture and the growing secularization of the former. This did not involve a process of privatization in penal policy so much as a redefinition of the public sphere, inaugurating a series of increasingly desperate attempts by the élites to control it and wrest it to their own purposes in an age of rapid change from a feudal, corporatist society to a capitalist, free-market social system. What both Foucault and Elias neglect is the extent to which shifts in penal policy in the late eighteenth and early nineteenth centuries were brought about in the end, despite everything, from below, both by broad social changes, to which governments had to react, and by the resistance of popular culture to the interpretations of crime and punishment forced on it from above. The turn to imprisonment as the standard penal sanction was not merely imposed unilaterally from above, whether by a discursive shift among the élites or by a process of state formation and the downward seepage of élite values into the masses. In order to underline these points, and take them further, we have to examine the role of capital punishment in popular culture, as illustrated by the broadsheets, ballads, and songs about executions which circulated among the masses from the seventeenth to the nineteenth century. Here too, as we shall now see, there was no timeless, unchanging 'traditional' situation, but a series of transformations that in many ways paralleled those which we have observed in the execution ritual itself.

4

Farewell Songs and Moral Speeches

a. Execution Verses 1680–1760

On his visit to Munich in 1781, the writer Friedrich Nicolai was horrified to find that 'death sentences are printed in numbered editions alongside the *Urgicht* or confession of every condemned criminal' and were sold on the streets 'in their thousands'. The 'moral speeches' which accompanied them were, he complained, 'miserable doggerel':

People believe in a simplistic way that they ought to deter robbers and improve the morals of the common people. They contain idiotic reflections and disgusting, horrible descriptions, which are repeated in a different manner for each death sentence and are necessarily bound in the end to render the people insensitive to feeling.

Nicolai thought that lengthy descriptions of torture and punishment were ill-calculated to encourage proper contemplation of the roots of criminality. 'Instead of reflecting in a mature way on the origins of the horrible crimes that are the occasion for such terrible executions, people read reports on both the crime and its punishment, and even the wretched moral speeches attached to them, with interest.' These verses appeared to educated men such as Nicolai as tasteless, crude, and embarrassing. Worse still were the pictures that were sold to the crowds at executions, portraying punishments meted out to offenders 'in the most horrible manner':

The physiognomies of the hangmen and executioners are far more repulsive than those of the malefactors; these latter, which should surely arouse the real abhorrence, look like those of martyrs by comparison. The common people gawk at these pictures in a thoughtless way and with complete indifference; children even make jokes about them.[1]

Nicolai's strictures betrayed some characteristic anxieties of educated Germans about the nature and purpose of punishment in the late eighteenth century. Like

---

[1] Friedrich Nicolai, *Beschreibung einer Reise durch Deutschland und die Schweiz im Jahre 1781*, vi (Berlin and Stettin, 1785), 758–63.

many other commentators of the time, he thought that capital punishment in particular should not aim to cause suffering to the offender, but should seek principally to arouse feelings of fear and revulsion in the populace. Excessive cruelty on the scaffold was more likely in his view to elicit the onlookers' sympathies for the condemned criminal. To be sure, Bavarian practice, on which Nicolai was commenting, was less enlightened than its counterparts in Austria and Prussia in this respect. In their own way, however, the Bavarian authorities too were trying to implement a new, rationalistic understanding of punishment as deterrence. It was only the means by which they sought to do it that seemed to writers like Nicolai to be rather old-fashioned.

The propaganda which so aroused his wrath in 1781 had a long and venerable tradition going back at least as far as the early seventeenth century. It was common in funerals in early modern Germany to print the sermon, with its account of the deceased's life and an appreciation of the moral career and good deeds of the person interred. These *Leichenpredigte* were echoed in the execution ceremony by similar printed documents, with a list of crimes and prison sentences replacing the enumeration of good deeds and contributions to the community, dated acts of deviance and immorality replacing the chronology of marriages and the births of children, and the moral career described in terms of a road to the gallows marked by crimes and misfortunes rather than an ascent to social worth and a happy death marked by beneficence, hard work, and stoicism in the face of suffering. The commemoration of executions, and the crimes and misdeeds that led to them, was undertaken not by the clergy, nor by the friends and relatives of the deceased, but by state-approveed printers and by street balladeers, or *Bänkelsänger*. These itinerants, often husband-and-wife teams, set up a small stage or bench in each town they visited, and, unfurling a series of large canvases, sang and mimed the 'true stories' which the canvases depicted, pointing to the relevant part with a long white stick as they did so. After the performance, they sold printed broadsheets of the ballads to the crowd, an activity which formed their main source of income. Known by 1900 as *Moritaten* (probably a corruption of the word *Mordtat*, ('murderous deed'), which the singers were forbidden by the police to use in order to advertise their wares),[2] these street ballads served from the end of the nineteenth century as one of the models for the emerging German cabaret, receiving perhaps their most famous incarnation in Brecht's 'Ballad of Mack the Knife'. Although the genuine article was far removed by this time from its increasing number of imitators in high

---

[2] Jacob and Wilhelm Grimm, *Deutsches Wörterbuch* (Leipzig, 1885), 2554. Another euphemism, which soon became obsolete, was *Morgendat* (see Otto Freiherr von Reinsberg-Düringsfeld, *Das festliche Jahr* (Leipzig, 1863), 302). The alternative reading of *Moralität* (Gerhard Wahrig, *Das Grosse Deutsche Wörterbuch* (Gütersloh, 1966), 2476 and 2479) is less likely.

F I G. 14. *Street balladeers.* Satirical print of 'Hans Pumsack, officially appointed market- and news-sheet-singer | with his musical wife', *c.* 1721. The singer is pointing to a picture of the execution of the French robber Cartouche (1692–1721) and his band. The bilingualism of the print suggests that itinerant balladeers and their wares could often cross linguistic boundaries.

literature, it did not represent an uncorrupted expression of popular consciousness. Street singers required licences to perform. So they were obliged to adhere reasonably closely to official attitudes as far as crime and criminals were concerned, otherwise they fell foul of the censorship which was virtually universal in Germany until the middle of the nineteenth century.[3] Provided they followed this rule, they were considered 'harmless' by the authorities.[4] At the same time, they had to appeal to a popular audience as well. These two needs were sometimes congruent, sometimes in conflict; and the varying and changing forms of

[3] For the censorship of popular reading in the 18th and 19th c., see Rudolf Schenda, *Volk ohne Buch. Studien zur Geschichte der populären Lesestoffe 1770–1910* (Frankfurt am Main, 1970), 91–141. For examples of censorship, see P. Thiel, 'Vom Schiffsunglück zur Moritat. Entstehungsweise, Verbreitung und Zensur anonymer Literatur', in Anon., *Schilder, Bilder, Moritaten. Sonderschau des Museums für Volkskunde im Pergamonmuseum 25. 9. 1987–3. 1. 1988* (exhibition catalogue, Staatliche Museen zu Berlin, 1987), 58–62, and Leander Petzoldt, *Bänkelsang. Vom historischen Bänkelsang zum literarischen Chanson* (Stuttgart, 1974).

[4] Schenda, *Volk,* 364, for this comment, on an execution broadsheet of 1812.

the street ballad, as it dealt with crime and punishment, reflected among other things the varying and changing relationships between authority and populace over time.[5]

In the sixteenth and seventeenth centuries, the street balladeers' main product was the '*Zeitung*' or 'news-sheet'. This bore little relation to the newspapers of a later age. It used a very small page size, and usually consisted of two or three versified 'stories', with subjects varying from natural catastrophes to miracles and 'wonders' involving human beings. News-sheets were hawked on the streets and purchased by rich and poor alike. By the seventeenth century, they were frequently carrying the 'farewell songs' (*Abschiedslieder*) of executed criminals, as of other notable individuals. These were not, of course, the words uttered by the malefactors themselves on the scaffold. They were made up by the street balladeers in their entirety. Indeed, the texts often changed little from one execution to another. They were cast in formulaic, stereotypical, and above all pious language, much of it taken from sermons, hymns, psalms, prayers, or phrases from the Bible. They bore a close resemblance to the literary renditions of the last speeches of ordinary people who died in their beds.[6] The original models for these 'farewell speeches' of executed malefactors appear to have been the 'last dying prayers' of Anabaptist heretics executed in the sixteenth century for their religious nonconformity. They were only lightly adapted to the particularities of the crime in question.

One such 'farewell song', published in 1683, and purporting to come from the mouth of a student condemned to death for murder, began, for example, as follows:

1. This day I shall die | Heaven shall be mine | This day I'll see God | Ere the hour shall strike | of me they shall speak: Ah! he is now gone! He is no more | so bury him | on his corpse the cool earth cast | ashes to ashes, dust to dust.
2. Look into thy tomb | rest from every woe | thou extinguished flesh; soul fly up to Heaven | from the body's cavern | for with Christ to rest. Rest, o soul, in Heav'n | rest awhile my limbs | until the soul returns.
3. O thou troubled hearts | why do you lament | over my demise? I've gone to where I should | to where I long since would | so wipe thy tearful eyes: For I've been sent before | to where you all must go | every one of you.

[5] See Wolfgang Braungart, *Bänkelsang. Texte—Bilder—Kommentare* (Stuttgart, 1985), 389–425; Christopher Thomas Cheesman, 'Studies in the History of German Street Balladry in the 18th and 19th Centuries, with a Select Annotated Catalogue of Printed and Manuscript Sources, 1580–1950' (D.Phil. diss., Oxford, 1988), 1–17; idem, *Shocking Ballad Picture Show*; Leander Petzoldt, *Die freudlose Muse. Texte, Lieder und Bilder zum historischen Bänkelsang* (Stuttgart, 1978); idem, *Bänkellieder und Moritaten aus drei Jahrhunderten* (Frankfurt am Main, 1982); Gunnar Müller-Waldeck (ed.), *Die tote Braut und andere Moritaten von dem jetzigen Übelstand in der Welt* (Reinbek, 1984).

[6] For this genre in the English context, see Beier, 'Good Death'.

4. If someone should enquire | where I am, reply: In a higher school | where GOD Himself instructs | and His praise accepts | on His exalted stool | I study there always | What I never learned | and things I never read.

After more verses in the same vein, the song ends with the student saying 'Ade | Ade' to his family and friends: 'Good night! I'm passing away!' There is no mention of the malefactor's crime; indeed, the student's 'farewell song' is preceded in this particular news-sheet by a description of a different crime altogether. And there is no attempt to use the occasion in order to admonish the audience to tread the straight and narrow.[7] The occasion of an execution is in effect little more than a pretext for a set of elevating images of the good Christian death and the joys of the life to come.[8]

Such verses underlined the seventeenth-century concept, widely shared by state and community, élites and people, of the execution ceremony as a religious act; the penitent sinner going to the life everlasting. Their generalized, stereotypical character suggested the generalized, stereotypical character of the ceremony itself. The malefactor processing to the scaffold stood for every Christian soul. Both the judicial, state, and city authorities, and the mass of people, from notables and guildsmen to common folk of every sort, who attended these ceremonies and read these verses, or heard them read out loud, seem to have shared this set of assumptions about the nature of the ritual in progress. The verses helped them to grasp the religious, expiratory, and redemptorial aspects of the execution ritual. Certainly, the publishers of such 'farewell speeches' seem to have had no difficulty in obtaining the necessary licence to print. But by the beginning of the eighteenth century, this situation was changing. The educated and properted classes, nobles, and notables, had begun to withdraw from sharing in these and other manifestations of popular culture, and to retreat into an exclusive courtly world of their own. They were already looking upon the rituals, festivals, and street processions in which they had once participated as vulgar or superstitious manifestations of the ignorant plebs, requiring either reformation and improvement, or suppression and abolition. The news-sheet became a purely popular institution, distinguished with increasing sharpness from the 'learned' or 'state' newspapers which now served the educated.[9] The street hawkers and balladeers who sold such 'farewell speeches' had to pay ever

---

[7] DVA Freiburg Gr. I: 'Kommt her zu mir wohl Frau und Mann' (*Bericht von einer erschrecklichen und grausamen Mordthat zweyer gottlosen Kinder oder Bauernsöhne*, Hamburg, 1683).

[8] For another example, see ibid. Bl. 1327: *Zwey Schöne Newe Geistliche Lieder. Das Erste. Ein schöne Bekantnuss | oder Klaglied, | Welches ein Malefiz Person | Namens Simon Debel selbsten auffgesetzt, | wie in jedem Gesetz der erste Buchstaben andeutet, | auff seinen Namen gemacht worden. Ist hingerichtet worden durch das Schwerd | zu Peggstall in unter Oesterreich | Anno 1657* (Augsburg, 1657).

[9] Kaspar Stieler, *Zeitungs Lust und Nutz. Vollständiger Neudruck der Originalausgabe von 1695*, ed. Gert Hahelweide (Bremen, 1969).

more heed to the censors, who insisted on the portrayal of the malefactor in terms that were increasingly negative and specific. And official concern for the maintenance of order at executions ensured that preventive censorship was even more attentive and more severe towards such 'farewell songs' than to other products of the balladeers.

By the early eighteenth century, as the news-sheet went into decline, it had become customary to preface the 'farewell song' with a prose account that went into specific detail on the life and crimes of the malefactor and put them together into a single broadsheet, folded in two, rather than a more substantial publication. It was clear that there was considerable co-operation in this between the authorities and the authors of these broadsheets, with the former making details of the case available to the latter, on condition that they downplayed the theme of martyrdom so apparent in the seventeenth-century model, and emphasized instead the moral lessons to be learned from the malefactor's life of crime. Early eighteenth-century 'farewell songs' generally carried the message home in their very title, which usually began with the 'well-deserved sentence' or 'well-deserved final sentence'. The recounting of the malefactor's crimes was precise. In 1735, for instance, one such document was issued on the execution of 'Andre N.', a 33-year-old waiter, born near Regensburg, who had

On the 14th of November 1730 cut the cloths from three billiard-tables, and thus caused 149 florins worth of loss, then on the 24th of the same he helped to misappropriate 69 florins and 6 crowns worth of pewter, clothing, bed-linen, etc. by means of highway robbery with violence, moreover on the 14th day after that he helped misappropriate money and objects to the value of 235 florins 21 crowns from a certain dealer in game by the same sort of robbery; then once again two days before Christmas of the above year he misappropriated various pieces of poultry and 60 Zeller sausages.

The verses that followed still contained some of the religious rhetoric and phraseology of the seventeenth century, but this was now heavily mingled with the specificities of the execution. Thus out of thirteen verses devoted to 'Andre N.' in 1735, the first five and the last three consist entirely of generalities, still following the model of the 'farewell song' handed down from the previous century, but with the addition of repeated warnings to the reader or listener to follow the paths of righteousness. The verses begin in familiar pious style:

> O farewell day! O stringent day! At last thou now art present,
> To free me from my misery, from heavy chains and fetters,
> O day, thou dawned this morn for me to mine own joy and sorrow,
> So thus I wish to be prepared to enter Heav'n this morrow.

By verse 3, the malefactor is telling his audience that he has come to this pass by ignoring God's commands. 'Had I obeyed | the priest's good word,' he tells them in verse 5, 'The court's verdict | I'd ne'er have heard.' In the five central verses, he repeats the catalogue of crimes already given in the prose introduction, reminding the readers and listeners that this has brought him to a shameful end on the gallows. Finally, 'Andre N.' adds a general warning not to follow suit, and then concludes with a traditional expression of hope for redemption:

> Now JESUS in Thy holy wounds myself I will right soon enfold,
> Receive me into them today, have mercy on my sinner's soul,
> Admit my soul to Heav'n above by virtue of Thy Cross's tree,
> To praise Thy Highest Name and Thee for ever in eternity.
>
> O dearest Mother, o Mary, Thou must not leave me now, today,
> Command me up to Thee above because I rush along death's way,
> And Mary Magdalena too, stand by me with Thy tears of rue,
> That I may be today with Thee, myself to call right blessed too.[10]

By the 1730s, therefore, additional elements were entering the execution broadsheet. Not only did malefactors' crimes feature much more prominently than before, but there was also a new concentration on the moral and educational failings which set them on the road to the scaffold.[11] The courts were seen as rewarding sinfulness and ungodliness with shame and death. Seventeenth-century 'news-sheets' had ascribed murder and theft directly to 'the Devil's word and deed'.[12] The notion of susceptibility to satanic temptation, still observable in some of the documents of the 1730s,[13] was being replaced by the supposition of a lifelong career of moral deviance, of which murder or highway robbery formed the culmination.[14] There was still very little mention of the punishments which

---

[10] Repr. in Braungart, *Bänkelsang*, 15–19. See also ibid. 329–30.

[11] See e.g. DVA Freiburg Bl. 4012: Anon., *Eine erschreckliche und fast unerhörte Mordthat, Welche ein Vater, Christian Langer, an seinem eigenen und einzigen Zehnjährigen Sohne, begangen, Indem er ihn wegen entwendeter zwey Grüschel, mit einem Messer, mit zwey langsam nach einander geschehenen Schnitten, bey grossem Geschrey, den Kopf abgeschnitten, auch wie er hernach in Grunau, eine Viertel-Meile von Schweidnitz, den 30. Apr. 1739. Nach Urthel und Recht In eine Ochsen-Haut eingenehet, mit Pferden zur Gerichtstädte ist geschleiffet wordem, Auch allda Mit dem Rade, vom Leben zum Tode gebracht worden* ([Schweidnitz?], 1739).

[12] Ibid. Gr. I: 'Hört zu ihr Christen ins gemein' (*Wahrhafftige Zeitung und traurige Geschicht . . .*, Regensburg, 1618, verse 15).

[13] Anon., *Letzter Zuruff der Armen Sünder als Dieselbe den 3. Januarii 1736. den wohl verdienten und gerechten Lohn ihrer greulichen Mord-That, so sie den 23. Dec. 1735 in Berlin an drey Personen verübet, empfiengen* (Berlin, 1735).

[14] See e.g. DVA Freiburg Bl. 2139: Anon., *Eine erschröckliche Mord-Geschichte, So sich zugetragen Anno 1741, den 14ten Tag May zu Ramsen im Legau, Stockacher-Herrschaft, Welcher Bösswicht, Jacob Sigerist, seinen Vetter, Ulrich Graf, und seiner Frau, Anna Sigristin, und die dritte Anna Maria Titelreichin, eines Musicanten Frau, mit Gifft vergeben, und was sich dabey ferner zu getragen, wie der günstige Leser alles ausführlich in diesem Lied sehen wird* (1714). Moral lessons were drawn even in sensational literature: see e.g. Miletus Hedrusius, *Neu eröffnete Mord- und Trauer-Bühne | Darauf sich unterschiedliche | Theils gar sehr traurige und Mord-Exempel, als auch der verschlagenen so genannten Spitz-Buben oder Beutelschneider arglistige Räncke und Tücke | und verschiedene Erscheinungen der Geister repraesentiren. Aus denen beglaubtesten und neuesten Scribenten treulich herausgezogen | und männiglichen zur nothwendigen Warnung, als auch Gemüths- Schaff und Ergötzung herausgegeben* (Schwabach, 1708).

FIG. 15. *The inevitability of punishment.* The story of a band of arsonists executed in Frankfurt an der Oder on 19 and 20 May, 1723, told for popular edification in three scenes. The top scene shows them planning their campaign of arson, the middle shows them carrying it out, and the bottom shows them being burned at the stake—virtually the last of the 'mirror punishments' to survive the penal reforms of the eighteenth century. The caption reads: 'Like the plan, thus the deed. Like the deed, so the quittance'. The names of the offenders are given under the graphic representation of their punishment. This picture is not intended to give an accurate representation of the punishment, merely a graphic indication; it is taken from the same source as Fig. 4.

they had to suffer, however, and the narrative still ended in a lengthy account of the offender's repentence and redemption.[15]

By the middle of the eighteenth century, the hand of the authorities in writing such documents was even more evident. The stock religious phrases and prayers had virtually disappeared and had been replaced by extensive and largely secular moral narratives. The religious aspects of the verses now concentrated on the offender's repentance and linked this firmly to the final redemption. There was increasing emphasis on the physical suffering which the condemned person underwent, included as an expression of the authorities' growing tendency to treat executions and other punishments as deterrent acts rather than religious rituals. A characteristic example from the middle of the century, distributed at the execution in Erlangen in 1756 of Johann Leonhard Freymann, a 20-year-old huntsman who had stabbed a former Franciscan to death, included a lengthy prose account, giving details of the condemned man's confession, followed by the full verdict and sentence in formal legal language, then a nine-verse 'farewell song' remarkable for its secular tone. The traditional opening verse announcing the speaker's forthcoming death scarcely made any reference to religion:

> O must I in the flower of youth,
> In my most lovely time and age,
> When life's young bud has scarcely bloomed,
> When its appeal has yet to fade,
> Be taken into death's sharp grip,
> O pain, predicament so deep!

The description of the offender's crime is followed by an account of the verdict and sentence ('the judges speak a verdict fair') and then a lengthy narrative of repentence ('With God I'm reconciled') and redemption, ending with a warning to the audience not to follow his example.[16]

A similar note was struck in the 'last dying speeches' of three notorious robbers 'Josse Hinrich Low, Hans Jürgen Schrage, and Johan Tobia Reichart, dispatched from life to death with the sword on 16 December 1754 at Münster in Westphalia'. Low says:

> Bring irons, fetters, cords and chains
> For Low, who was so cruel,

[15] For a good example, see the 'Klage-Lied' attached to Anon., *Die betrübte Mord-Notification, der grausamen und unmenschlichen Mordthaten, so der Tausend-Künstler der Teufel, durch den Mann Hanss Nicolaus Künstler, zeithero gewesener Bauer und Einwohner in Grossen-Rudolstadt, verübet* (Erfurt, 1733).

[16] Anon., *Lebens Abschieds Lied des Missethäters Johann Leonhard Freymann, der ein gelernter Jäger, bey 20, Jahr alt aus Deutenheim in Franken gebürtig ist, Welcher den ehem. hl. Franciscaner aus dem Kloster Rastadt bey Strassburg Franz Hortig aus Sulzbach in der Pfalz gebürtig im 30sten Jahr seines Alters den 1ten May 1756, früh vor 1. Uhr zu Erlangen auf eine jämmerliche Art ermordet und daselbst den 6ten Julii dieses Jahres mit dem Rad von unten auf von Leben zum Tod gebracht wurde* (1756; repr. in Braungart, *Bänkelsang*, 36–43).

And bind him by the feet and hands;
And yet he stays so cool,
For all the peril and the pain
He brought upon the world.
To suffer also sword and shame
His heart is now resolved.

My deeds were bad, as was my faith,
A weight on God and men.
Wickedness, thieving, sin, and theft
My actions, joy and gain.
But at the ending of my life
You'll see with your own eye
That black is changèd into white;
A good death Low shall die.

Schrage, for his part, emphasizes how 'his soul he doth redeem | Freely gives up his life', for if he was once the greatest of robbers, he tells the crowd, 'Now witness also in my being | The greatest penitent.' All three end by admonishing the onlookers 'keep your soul pure | shun wickedness.' Here again, the precision of the date indicates that the broadsheet was distributed among the crowd at the execution itself, while the emphasis is on the crimes and their punishment, the wickedness and repentence of the malefactors, rather than on Christian death and expectation of the life eternal.[17] All this underlined once more the religious understanding of executions in both popular and élite culture which persisted well into the eighteenth century, as we saw in Chapters 2 and 3. It was precisely this interpretation that commentators during the Enlightenment, however, were beginning to challenge.

b. Gender and the Representation of Punishment

By the 1770s, the authorities not only viewed the religious elements in these verses as entirely inappropriate, but the very notion of inviting the onlookers to identify with the malefactor through the device of a 'farewell song' was itself coming under official suspicion. Although it continued to be used as a narrative device in popular descriptions of individuals who had died an honourable death,[18] the 'farewell song' began to be replaced by the 'moral speech' (*Moralrede*) when an executed malefactor was the subject. The 'moral speech' was cast in the

---

[17] DVA Freiburg Gr. I: Mörder, Räuber: Anon., *Abschiedslied deren berüchtigten dreyen Rauberen Josse Hinrich Low, Hans Jürgen Schrage and Johan Tobia Reichart, am 16ten Decembris 1754 zu Münster in Westphalen durchs Schwerdt vom Leben zum Todt geschieckt* (Munich, 1754).

[18] See e.g. Anon., *Abschieds-Lied des Johann Ehrenfried Weishaupts, welcher, nachdem er bey seinen Eltern noch 4. Wochen gelebt, und 8. Tage bettlägerig war, endlich den 11. Fbr. 1789 im Heerrn selig verschieden, und den 15. darauf auf den Gottesacker zu St. Peter und Paul christlich beerdiget worden ist, nachdem er sein Alter auf 31. Jahr, 10. Monath und 12. Tage gebracht hat* (prefaced by the story of the person concerned, a

third person rather than the first, and the only time the criminal was allowed to speak in person was at the end, in a brief admonition to the audience not to follow the path of crime that led to the gallows. The use of the third person distanced the malefactor from the audience, and increased this effect by the extremely negative terms in which the executed person's life of crime was recounted and the considerable detail which these speeches sometimes contained about the tortures and punishments to which such a life invariably led in the end. Rather than describing the crime or the criminal, which was now done in the initial prose statement, these verses provided stereotypical accounts of the inevitability of execution once a career of social deviance and moral turpitude had been embarked upon, and underlined the incorrigibility of such an offender: 'Though he be washed an hundred times | The moor remains a moor.'[19] By this time, in other words, the religious element in such broadsheets had been reduced to a minimum.

A characteristic example of the 'moral speech' as it had developed in Bavaria by the second half of the eighteenth century was contained in the broadsheet issued in Munich on 30 June 1774, the day of execution of the 38-year-old 'Barbara N., *vulgo* Gerner-Waberl'. As with all such accounts by this time, it was prefaced by the *Urgicht*, a formal statement, in prose, of the crimes of the person to be executed, based on the confession and read out from the scaffold to the crowd after the condemned person had arrived, and immediately before the execution commenced. The inclusion of this document, which must have been given to the printer at least a day before the execution took place, indicated once more the close involvement of the authorities in the compilation of the broadsheet as a whole. Printed in an edition of 2,600, the broadsheet was undoubtedly on sale on the city streets from early in the morning of 30 June, if not before. Its depiction of Gerner-Waberl's life was highly gender-specific. Her inner disregard for morality was shown as soon as she reached adulthood:

> A mother she became, gave birth to several children;
> But husband had she none; in sinfulness she bore them.

After numerous convictions, as the printed confession put it, 'partly for theft and purse-cutting, partly for other aspects of her extremely dissolute way of life', and a period in the penitentiary, she joined a band of criminals and helped them carry out '4 aggravated robberies . . . in which the victims were so cruelly maltreated that two persons indeed lost their lives'.

chimney-sweep from Liegnitz captured by the Turks, sold into slavery, and bought free in 1788; printed in Braungart, *Bänkelsang*, 60–7).

[19] Anon., *Wohlverdientes Todes-Urtheil nebst einer Moral-Rede des Antoni Pittersohn, welcher auf gnädigste Anbefehlung eines churfürstl. hochlöbl. Hof-Raths allhier in München wegen ausgeübten diebischen Verbrechen halber heut den 20. October 1764 durch das Schwerd vom Leben zum Tod hingerichtet worden* (Munich, 1764).

Gerner-Waberl's example threatened the social order and turned men, young and old, to a life of crime:

> A woman, then, from whom respect and self-dominion
> Have really been smoked out, will hear no admonition,
> Will follow no advice, takes no consideration,
> And presses on with force to feed off rotten carrion.
> She is an untamed stream, that leads to foul morasses,
> A stinking, reeking swamp, untouched by any breezes,
> A proper child of Hell, a sister of the Gorgon,
> The key, the open gate, to that sulphurous ocean:
> A path well-trodden too, that to the pit doth plummet,
> A worm that poison spreads, in body and in spirit,
> A net filled with deceit, that many youths doth capture,
> And aged hearts also, in artful toils enrapture:
> A dreadful gaping chasm, that swallows all like Scylla,
> An omnivore that still cannot be free from hunger.

'Discipline' had been unable to achieve a return to the paths of convention and morality. 'For habit cannot just with simple ease be vanquished.' What began with 'idleness' and 'whoring' ended with 'murder and robbing'.[20] The language used in this document to describe Gerner-Waberl's life reflected the new definitions of gender identity that were coming into fashion in the 1770s. It was full of images of dangerous femininity: of foul and ungovernable liquids ('an untamed stream . . . morasses . . . swamp . . . ocean'), of voracious and untamable, gaping sexual organs ('pit . . . gaping chasm, that swallows all') that left no doubt about either the fundamental passivity of the female sex nor the dangers it posed if it remained 'untouched by any breeze'.[21] The tone here could hardly be more different from that of such documents a century before. It is secular not only in its language, but also in its account of the moral career of the malefactor. The only religious element is the inevitable reference to repentance and grace at the end: 'Let Heaven now admit, that she through sword and wheel | Has made atonement here, above His grace may feel.'[22] Social deviance rather than irreligion is portrayed as the origin of the criminal life.

The characterization of male offenders in such verses placed a similar emphasis on the pre-ordained nature of their continuous moral decline from cradle to gallows. Here too, idleness and immorality were seen as the first steps on the road

---

[20] HStA Munich GR 324: 32, Nr. 6: Anon., *Wohlverdientes Todesurtheil nebst einer Moral-Rede der Barbara N., welche auf gnädigste Anbefehlung eines churfürstl. hochlöbl. Hofraths allhier wegen ihren ausgeübten Diebstahl heut den 30ten Junii 1774 auf der inneren Richtstätt mit dem Schwerd vom Leben zum Tode hingerichtet worden* (Munich, 1774).

[21] For the *locus classicus* of linguistic analysis of such imagery, see Klaus Theweleit, *Male Fantasies* (2 vols.; Oxford, 1989 and 1991).

[22] HStA Munich GR 324: 32 Nr. 6 (as n. 20 above).

to the scaffold. Here too, however, there is hope of redemption through remorse and penitence: 'He dies alone, and dies, well-armoured and full ready | Makes good now through his death, his chief iniquity.'[23] The imagery of wildness and bestiality in such doggerel, when it applied to male offenders, was striking. A robber of this kind was no more than a 'wild tiger wrapped in a human skin',[24] a 'bear' or 'tiger' suffering from 'raving frenzy',[25] a 'fox' indulging continually in 'mad frenzy',[26] or 'A beast of prey, that'll always plot and think | On how its claws in strangers' blood can sink'.[27] In another such broadsheet, issued on the occasion of the hanging of the robber 'Windfliegl Sepp' in Munich on 17 October 1771, the offender was compared to a wolf or a tiger. Images of hard, active masculinity predominated throughout:

> The robber in the wood endures both frost and rainstorm
> And gives by treachery the traveller his death-blow,
> He creeps into the town, breaks every lock and doorway,
> Gives free rein to his rage, attacks all in his frenzy.
> Spares neither age nor sex, and oft enough he even
> Rewards philanthropy with bloody retribution:
> A hardened robber's heart will never lead to weeping,
> And on his coat of arms there's only blows and fighting:
> All this did farmer Mayr in Riedsberg now discover.
> The band of robbers came and pulled him by his own hair
> Into a cellar down, where he was bound and beaten.
> They plundered everything that any of them could hit on.
> The man was just about to eat his evening's bread,
> And therefore not prepared to escape from the raid.
> Another knavish trick they did not let him know,
> For one of them was dressed in serving-women's clothes.[28]

---

[23] HStA Munich GR 324: 32 Nr. 4: Anon., *Wohlverdientes Todesurtheil nebst einer Moral-Rede des Jakob N., vulgo kleine Hansel, welche auf gnädigste Anbefehlung eines churfürstl. hochlöbl. Hofraths allhier wegen ihren ausgeübten Diebstahl heut den 30ten Junii 1774 auf der inneren Richtstätt mit dem Schwerd vom Leben zum Tode hingerichtet worden* (Munich, 1774).

[24] Quoted in Nicolai, *Beschreibung*, 765.

[25] Anon., *Wohlverdientes Todesurtheil, nebst einer Moral-Rede des Joseph N., vulgo Kramerseppel, welcher auf gnädigste Anbefehlung eines churfürstl hochlöbl. Hofraths allhier in München wegen seinen ausgeübt dieb- und räuberischen Verbrechen heut den 9. Dec. 1774 mit dem Strange vom Leben zum Tode hingerichtet worden* (Munich, 1774).

[26] Anon., *Wohlverdientes Todesurtheil, nebst einer Moral-Rede des Johann N., welcher auf gnädigste Anbefehlung eines churfürstl hochlöbl. Hofraths allhier in München wegen seinen ausgeübt dieb- und räuberischen Verbrechen heut den 5. Jan. 1775 mit dem Strange vom Leben zum Tode hingerichtet worden* (Munich, 1775).

[27] Anon., *Wohlverdientes Todesurtheil, nebst einer Moral-Rede des Johann Heinrich N., welcher auf gnädigste Anbefehlung eines churfürstl hochlöbl. Hofraths allhier in München wegen seinen ausgeübt dieb- und räuberischen Verbrechen heut den 13. Oct. 1774 mit dem Strange vom Leben zum Tode hingerichtet worden* (Munich, 1774).

[28] Ludwig Hollweck, '. . . *Vom Leben zum Tode hingerichtet*'. *Todesurteile vor 200 Jahren* (Munich, 1980), reprinting the *Wohlverdientes Todesurteil, nebst einer Moralrede* for 'Windfliegl Sepp' (Munich, 1771).

The fact that one of the robbers, who was known to the victim, had dressed as a woman to avoid detection was singled out for special disapprobation. It confirmed the comprehensive nature of the offender's deviance and underlined the centrality of gender-role definitions to these documents. The 'moral speeches' on his accomplices once more emphasized their animal nature, comparing them to wolves, tigers, lions, and harpies:

> A nasty garden-worm, that's full of awful filth . . .
> This servant base and vile, who lives off theft alone,
> Lives like the dumbest beast.[29]

Male criminals, therefore, were raging, active, bursting the bounds of law and propriety, and preying on the law-abiding like carnivores on a flock of ruminants.[30] Like their female counterparts, they belonged to wild nature, from which civilization had to be protected.

The inevitable end to such a career was torture and the scaffold, described in such writings in terms so graphic and detailed that the reader would be left in no doubt as to the inadvisability of following such a course. Impudence, contempt for morality and refusal to confess and repent could only lead to the horrors of the torture-chamber:

> . . . the torment now begins.
> Now in the Falcon Tower the prosecution scheme
> Is drawn up point by point. He must confess his deed,
> His co-conspirators, accomplices, reveal.
> He will deny it all, so torture now is used
> Up to the set degree, to bring the liar to truth,
> Yet wooden goat and birch are often powerless
> To loosen up the tongue of hard unfeeling men.[31]

As the verse emphasized, the physical torment to which the offender was subjected was orderly, lawful, and limited in its extent. Nevertheless, once a confession had been obtained and sentence passed, the male offender could expect a violent death upon the scaffold:

> O dreadful sight! That heart, and all the senses moves,
> For this poor sinner now out to the gallows goes.
> They stretch his body out, to hollow stakes attached,
> The hangman grasps the wheel: and soon his limbs are cracked
> By oft-repeated blows, his heart has burst asunder,
> So now the robber's dead, his punishment is over.[32]

---

[29] Ibid., on Hanns Georg Rhein and Caspar Rhain. Four members of this band, including two brothers, were executed on four successive days in Oct. 1771.

[30] For parallels in the prose literature on bandits in the 18th c., see Danker, *Räuberbanden*, i. 452–3.

[31] Nicolai, *Beschreibung*, 765.   [32] Hollweck, *Vom Leben*, on Johann Michael Schwaiger.

In some examples the descriptions of the condemned's sufferings could reach a quite extraordinary level of detail, in the attempt to rob them of any remaining honour and dignity and prevent the readers from showing sympathy or admiration:

> Whose heart would not be moved, although of stone 'twere made,
> To see a poor sinner there, out on the cowhide laid,
> With face all deathly pale, covered in dust and shit,
> O how he sighs and groans under the hot tongs' bite,
> O God what fear he feels, how terror o'ercomes him,
> Who can describe to me the fright that courses through him,
> To see the place of skulls before his eyes appearing?
> O now he is exposed! O now his limbs are trembling,
> O now he's lying down upon his hard death-bed.
> O now the strangler's there, the wheel above his head,
> O now blow follows blow; the countless crowd's sharp ear
> The cracking of his limbs resoundingly doth hear.
> And now his pulverized heart his life brings to an end.[33]

Despite appearances, this was not so much an example of literary sadism, as an attempt by the authorities who sanctioned such broadsheets to underline their concept of public executions as moral dramas in which death, suffering, and dishonour formed the inevitable outcome of a downward moral career that began with laziness and immorality.

The lesson was stated explicitly on innumerable such occasions. Morality was the responsibility of the individual, to be inculcated by secular means of education:

> You parents! Witness here just what you can expect
> When children's discipline you sleepily neglect!
> When you would rather see your son under the wheel
> Than make him from the start your punishments to feel.[34]

The punishment of the body was thus the measure recommended for application not just by the state, but also by the family, to restrain the wild and unbridled instincts of the disobedient. Execution was merely the last act in a drama punctuated by bodily sanctions at every stage:

> You loafers! From the world you steal, and from your God
> The days, and from yourselves the fruits of hope do rob,
> Look here upon this blood, its lessons now imbue,
> And learn to fear the law, and honour justice too.[35]

---

[33] Nicolai, *Beschreibung*, 764.   [34] Hollweck, *Vom Leben*, on Johann Michael Schwaiger.
[35] Quoted in Dülmen, *Theater*, 169.

Morality was to be instilled by physical terror throughout life, beginning virtually in infancy and continuing if necessary into adulthood: 'His body stretched upon the wheel | a warning children all should feel.'[36] Yet such verses commonly stressed the failure of such sanctions and betrayed a measure of despair at their effectiveness:

> O penal justice! Stern enough the way that you proceed,
> O terrible is your intent, revealed in word and deed,
> Black torture chambers you construct, the domiciles of pain,
> By rope, wheel, fire, sword and the like your temple wins its name. . . .
> And yet this pack will carry on with its accursed trade,
> E'en though the whole Black Forest were now into gallows made.
> We hang them, break them with the wheel, they just keep going on,
> For still they say, the thieves, the gallows are our home.[37]

In the face of irrational bestiality, such sanctions were of dubious effectiveness. That is why criminals of this kind had to be removed from human society:

> We cut their heads off, hang them, burn and break:
> A robber's rabid nature will not change,
> Not one converts out of an hundred thieves,
> The wolf alone on stolen booty feeds,
> The cat for mice in corners waiting lies,
> The fox eats chicken, but he never buys.[38]

Creatures that hunted others deserved no better than to be hunted down themselves: an image which would have been widely understood in a society where virtually everybody hunted and killed some kind of animal for food or pleasure on a fairly regular basis.

This linguistic representation of punishment, and its celebration in the officially approved doggerel of the 'moral speeches', drew heavily on the language and form of German baroque tragedy, as it had developed in the second half of the seventeenth century, as a 'theatre of cruelty', portraying executions, torture, rape, arson, madness, seduction, incest, parricide, and other acts of violence on stage in a graphic, immediate, and explicit manner. In the tragedy *Cleopatra*

---

[36] Anon., *Zwey erschreckliche Mord-Geschichten. Die erste handelt von einem Sohne, aus dem Coburger Lande, welcher seinen Vater und seine Mutter auf die erbärmlichste Art ermordet hat. Die zweyte handelt von einem Hauptmann, welcher seine Frau und Kinder auf eine grausame Weise ermordet hat* (Frankfurt am Main, 1798), no. 1, verse 14.

[37] Anon., *Wohlverdientes Todesurtheil, nebst einer Moral-Rede des Mathias N., welcher auf gnädigste Anbefehlung eines churfürstl hochlöbl. Hofraths allhier in München wegen seinen ausgeübt dieb- und räuberischen Verbrechen heut den 12. Dec. 1774 auf dem Hochgericht mit dem Strange vom Leben zum Tode hingerichtet worden* (Munich, 1774).

[38] Anon., *Wohlverdientes Todesurtheil, nebst einer Moral-Rede des Michael N., vulgo Berndl, welcher auf gnädigste Anbefehlung eines churfürstl hochlöbl. Hofraths allhier in München wegen seinen ausgeübt dieb- und räuberischen Verbrechen heut den 15. Oct. 1774 auf dem Hochgericht mit dem Strange vom Leben zum Tode hingerichtet worden* (Munich, 1774).

(1661) by the lawyer and later city official in Breslau, Daniel Casper von Lohenstein, for instance, the ghost of the murdered Ptolemy conjures up the nightmares of torture with which his assassin Mark Antony will be plagued before his actual death:

> The brute must surely feel his death draw nigh.
> A quick death's merciful, no punishment of course.
> For twelve days long may he the hangman's sport provide;
> His twisted body limp upon the wooden horse,
> And feel the whip and molten lead upon his back:
> An iron comb shall scratch his skin to shreds,
> His arms and legs to pieces screws shall hack,
> The seesaw press him down upon a naily bed.
> O let them cut his tongue out, break his teeth,
> And give him bastinados numberless,
> And tie his nails tight with a thong until they bleed,
> O let them tear his hairs out, one by one,
> Drip sulphur, molten ore, and boiling oil upon his breast,
> And cover him with honey, so by wasps he's stung.
> His body now a meal for mice shall make,
> And let the wheel his shinbones cruelly break.[39]

In another play of the same period, the heart is torn out of the body of one character, while another is anatomized while still alive. Such actions were not merely reported in speech, though this was in itself violent enough; in some plays, it was actually simulated on stage, and models and dolls were used to show corpses and parts of bodies. In the tragedy *Catharina von Georgien* by Andreas Gryphius (1615–64), for example, the central character's severed head appears on the stage in one scene, while in another drama, a doll representing the villainess is filled with chunks of raw meat, blood, and bones, and torn to pieces on stage by a pack of dogs.[40]

Tragedies of this kind were exercises in moral pedagogy. They aimed to bring home to the audience the bestial nature of unbridled passion, lust, and tyranny, so that they would learn the reasoned self-control necessary for living in an ordered society, a self-control that appeared vital for the establishment of normality after the end of the destructive Thirty Years War in 1648. The pedagogical function of such plays was underlined by the fact that they were frequently performed by schoolboys, as for example Lohenstein's drama of incest and revenge, *Agrippina*, was in 1666. As the author wrote in the notes to his play, 'the present tragedy portrays a scene of the most horrible depravity and a picture of

---

[39] Quoted in Reinhart Meyer-Kalkus, *Wollust und Grausamkeit. Affektenlehre und Affektdarstellung in Lohensteins Dramatik am Beispiel von 'Agrippina'* (Göttingen, 1986), 223.
[40] Ibid. 234, 183, 187–9, 214–16, 221.

frightful punishments'. That the latter inevitably followed the former in retributive sequence was the point of the drama. The explicit and bloody presentation
of violence and torture reflected the baroque theory of the passions, according to
which 'a frightened spectator is more willing and prepared to take the lesson from
a sermon than is one who is calm and collected'.[41] It drew for its language and
emplotment on the model of suffering presented by the martyrologies of the
sixteenth and seventeenth centuries, turning them to secular use as illustrations
of the fate that awaited those who let their passions get the better of them. This
theory of the passions, and the language it used to get its message across, bear
obvious similarities to the narrative and linguistic structures of the officially
sponsored execution broadsheet in the eighteenth century. Both genres built on
the familiarity of death and suffering in everyday life to achieve their desired
effect on the emotions of the onlooker. For these scenes continued, as we have
seen, even if in a more restricted compass and a partially diluted form, through
the eighteenth century, while German baroque tragedy did not. By the 1730s,
Lohenstein was no longer regarded in fashionable literary circles as a classic; and
the violent language and action of his plays, and those of his fellow tragedians,
were beginning to appear to the theatre-going public as embarrassingly crude.
Educated taste demanded something far more refined, classical, and cool. Moral
pedagogy could continue to be directed at the common people; but as élite and
popular culture drew ever further apart, aristocratic and bourgeois theatre-goers
began to seek celebrations of their own rationality rather than lessons in what
would happen if they abandoned it. So the forms of representation in baroque
tragedy were transferred to the scaffold at a time when they were already beginning to disappear from the fashionable stage. In theatrical forms which still
sought to appeal to the common people, however, many traces still remained. In
the popular Hamburg opera of the first half of the eighteenth century, for
example, it was still true that 'sadistic . . . scenes (e.g. the sabering-down of
prisoners' heads or suicides in which blood spurts vigorously out of a pig's
bladder hidden beneath the jacket) met with the greatest acclaim from the
public'.[42] For some decades, the linguistic shell of baroque drama continued to
exist, wrapped anachronistically around the real drama of the axe and the wheel.
Yet although they were highly unfashionable in literary terms, execution verses
had become so elaborate by the second half of the eighteenth century that they
can scarcely have appealed any more to the common people. In their efforts to
ensure that officially sanctioned execution broadsheets reflected the official point
of view, the authorities had gone too far.

[41] Ibid. 281–2, 101, 183–4.
[42] Richard Petzold, *Die Kirchenkompositionen und weltlichen Kantaten Reinhard Keisers (1674–1739)*
(Düsseldorf, 1935), 1.

c. *The Silence of the Malefactor*

Both in style and in content, the 'moral speeches' were now far removed from
the understanding of those whose minds they were primarily intended to reach.
The ever-widening gap between élite culture and popular culture ensured that
even popular documents which the élite had a hand in composing had taken
on an élite character, full of literary imagery and ornament and ill-suited to make
an impact on the semi-literate masses. Verses such as these were not meant to be
sung, and could not easily be memorized, so they had only a very short life.
They were increasingly composed and printed by permanent concessionaries,
resident in the place of execution, who enjoyed a state monopoly of their
production. It was not easy to sell them after the execution itself had taken place
and the malefactor had been forgotten. Their usefulness as a source of income for
street balladeers thus diminished. The balladeers therefore began to compose
their own narratives for such occasions, in a style more suited for popular
consumption, memorization, and subsequent performance. These ballads spoke
a language very different to that of the officially approved 'moral speech'. While
execution broadsheets were intended for use on the day, street ballads were
designed for a longer life. They were not usually tied to a specific date, did not
contain official documents such as the judgment or the confession, and avoided
complex literary imagery and ingenious figures of speech. Often they were
accompanied by illustrations.[43] Generally, too, the reader or listener was given
written instructions on the tune to which the verses were to be sung. The
intention was for the public to buy the ballads and sing them for entertainment
at home, at work, or in the inn. The emphasis was on the crime rather than on
the execution. The ballads offered secular narrative rather than moral contemplation. But they still did not represent popular attitudes in an unmediated form.
The balladeers always had to be wary of the censor, and so they were careful to
reflect official attitudes towards crime in case their texts were confiscated or they
were refused permission to print.[44] Thus it was only rarely, for example, that
street ballads dealing with crime and punishment were narrated in the first
person, for this kind of identification between the singer and the malefactor
would most likely have invited immediate intervention on the part of the
authorities.

---

[43] Kunzle, *Comic Strip*, 157–96, provides a useful thematic survey of the illustrated German crime-and-
punishment broadsheet of this period.
[44] For an example of the censors effecting the deletion of a number of verses describing the details of
a murder from one of these texts, see 'Abschied eines reuevollen Sünders im Kerker (1786)', in Riha (ed.),
Moritatenbuch, 418–20.

The contrast with the officially sponsored execution broadsheets can be illustrated by a street ballad which was bound together with the confession, verdict, and 'farewell song' of Johann Freymann, executed in Erlangen on 6 July 1756, which have already been mentioned. The ballad title does not give the date of execution, and it is accompanied by illustrations, including a specific portrayal of the crime, and pictures of the malefactor in prison and being broken with the wheel. All this suggests it was not sold at the execution itself but afterwards; and the appended verses, too, are much simpler than those attached to the confession. They are in the third person, and begin without ceremony by portraying the murder itself:

> A murder cry! O deed so grave!
> In Erlangen there's trouble!
> A soldier who's a wicked knave
> Has hacked a man to rubble.

This particular ballad takes another ten verses to describe the murder in extensive detail ('The left hand it was split in two | A finger had flown off . . .' etc.), before we reach the murderer's discovery and judgment and end with a brief warning against 'Satan's wicked ways'. There is no indication of any repentance on the malefactor's part, nor any suggestion of his eventual redemption; but there is no description of the punishment either: this is left to the crude woodcuts with which the ballad is illustrated.[45]

In another street ballad of this kind, a girl kills a rich young lieutenant to whom she has been betrothed against her will. The woman's mother protests, and the girl kills her too, before the lieutenant's servant apprehends her and takes her to the authorities. The offender is portrayed as wilful, not least because of the eminent suitability of the match which she has spurned. Her basic wickedness is then compounded not only by the initial murder but above all by the matricide. The story is told entirely in the third person, and to complete the distancing

---

[45] Anon., *Natürliche Vorstellung u. accurater Abriss des ermordeten Franciscus Hortig, ehemal. Franciskaners aus dem Kloster Rastadt, welchen im 30. Jahr seines Alters den 1. May d. J. früh um 1 Uhr ein Soldat zu Erlangen Namens Freymann, der ein gelernter Jäger, aus dem Fränkischen gebürtig, u. bey 20. Jahr alt ist, auf eine erstaunliche und unerhörte Art erbärmlich um das Leben gebracht, nebst einer Ode von der ganzen Begebenheit dieser grausamen Mordthat* (1756), repr. in Braungart, *Bänkelsang*, 28–36. For further examples see DVA Freiburg Bl. 4365: Anon., *Zwey neue merkwürdige Beschreibungen . . . zum zweyten eine erschröckliche Frevel-That eines verruchten Meuchelmörders, Nahmens Sebastian Krug, gebürtig von Rappolsweiler, wohnhaft zu Hunneweyer, ohnweit Colmar im obern Elsass, welcher seine Mordthat an einer Dienstmagd verübet hat, indem er sie in einen tieffen Brunnen gestürzet, allwo er vor seine Bosheit zu Colmar den 13. Oct. 1758. durch das Rad die Straffe empfangen* ([Colmar ?], 1759); and DVA Freiburg Bl. 3904: Anon., *Drey Schöne Lieder, Das erste: Ich wär nie dahin gegangen, so wär, &c. Welches ein Übelthäter in der Gefangenschafft selbsten aufgesetzt . . .* (1756).

effect the woman's punishment is described here in some detail, as a warning to
others:

> And on a hurdle she was borne
> By horses to the judgment stand,
> Her breasts with pincers they were torn:
> 'Ah God', she spake, 'Thine own right hand
> Doth touch me so, o shame, o woe,
> That I was led to Satan's land.'
>
> The wheel broke her up from below,
> Her corpse displayed atop.
> Thus God doth punish all the host
> Of those who Him forgot.

Here was a figure who could be expected to earn popular as well as official
disapproval for her crime.[46] The verses make no mention of any remorse on the
part of the murderess, and there is no indication that she is destined for Heaven;
rather, indeed, the reverse. The woman only speaks at the end of the story, and
then only to express her pain and her regret at the 'shame' of having been seduced
by the Devil.[47]

Where popular opprobrium for a criminal could not be counted on as safely
as official disapproval, the street balladeers temporized, and tried to satisfy both
points of view. In 1779, for example, another ballad recounted, again in the third
person, the life and death of the infanticide Margaritha Härdin, describing her as
a 'nameless criminal—murderess of the fruit of her womb', who wickedly persisted in protesting her innocence despite prolonged torture. If she had felt
remorse at her deed, it was out of 'love of life, and in the erroneous belief that
she could find God's mercy without dying by the sword'. Only the prospect of
lifelong imprisonment had brought her to confession. At the same time, both
prose and verse texts emphasize that Margaritha had been an innocent and
honest woman until seduced by her employer, who had refused to take any
responsibility for the infant. And the gushing prose narrative goes into enthusiastic detail on the happiness which repentance and reconciliation with God
brought her:

How she was uncommonly thankful to her pastors and her prison warders for this—
spoke with Christian beauty, and undismayed by all the circumstances of the nearness of

---

[46] Anon., Gr. I: 'Ihr lieben Christen seid getrost.' From Anon., *Eine grausame Mordthat / welche
geschehen Zu unser frauen Hall / drey studen von brüssel / wie sich ein amt mannss sohn mit einer Reichen
Jungfer versprochen / und von der selben mit gifft ver geben / ihm und ihre mutter jämmerlich umss leben
gebracht* (1736). The typescript betrays some uncertainties in the reading from the manuscript copy.
Capitalization and spacing as in original.

[47] For other, similar examples, see Braungart, *Bänkelsang*, 116–23, and Gimpel, 'Nachrichten', 165
(verses from 1754).

her death: Yea, o beautiful morn of her execution—thou shouldst never fall from my remembrance!—How she—near to death—for the funeral bell was already sounding—how she asked each of the five pastors present for a final blessing, one after the other, with tears of appreciation—of zeal for her salvation and of joyful hope in her eyes—listened to the same with the deepest expressions of gratitude, and so saying farewell, she turned to the judgment-seat, never taking her eyes off the pastors who were comforting her—and finally in the 26th year of her life died—o God! we may, we should hope—died the death of a pardoned sinner.[48]

Such sentiments would not have been possible in the officially sponsored broadsheet handed out at the execution itself, but could still be expressed in independent productions such as this.

The great bulk of the verse section of this street ballad is devoted to a narrative of the infanticide and the malefactor's attempts to conceal it; it is here, rather than in the religious message, that the audience's interest is engaged. The language is simple and straightforward:

> They put her to the test,
> But she denied the deed,
> And so they locked her in,
> For life there to remain.
>
> At length she did confess,
> All freely and precise,
> And showed repentance there,
> For death she did prepare.

Here, as in all these street ballads, the authorities rightly triumph in the end, and female deviance is properly punished, after the malefactor has repented.

These themes occurred again and again in street ballads of the late eighteenth and early nineteenth centuries. Typical, for example, was the *Remarkable Account of a Triple Murder, which was Committed in a Hunting Lodge in the Thuringian Forest—Everything Described in Detail—With a Song* of 1801. Here there was a detailed prose description of the crime, followed by a brief account of the sentence and execution, and a simply written 'song' in nine verses, of which the first seven narrated the crime and only the last two recounted the malefactor's repentence and death and admonished the readers and listeners not to follow suit.[49] A similar account of a 'sevenfold murderer' in Celle, printed in 1804, had a comparable structure, though here the first three of the eight verses were

[48] Anon., *Mit Belehrungen vermischte Geschichte der Kinds-Mörderin M.H. von T. Welche zu Arau den 2. Merz 1779, mit dem Schwerd ist hingerichtet worden* (repr. in Braungart, *Bänkelsang*, 44–50 and 333–5).

[49] Anon., *Merckwürdige Beschreibung einer dreifach verübten Mordthat, welche sich in einem Jägerhause, im Thüringer Walde zugetragen hat. Alles ausführlich beschrieben. Nebst einem Liede* (1801; repr. in Braungart, *Bänkelsang*, 76–81). For another example, see 'Schaurige Mordthat, wie zwey Brüder, Müller geheissen, am 20sten July 1736 ihre Tante in Berlin ermordet', in Riha (ed.), *Moritatenbuch*, 354–7.

devoted to a generalized statement of how immorality leads to crime. When it was reprinted a few months later in Hanover, the date of the execution was altered from January to May, to make it seem more up-to-date; the street balladeers could reckon on few people outside Celle itself being familiar with the details of the case, or its chronology.[50] In all these cases, and others, the main interest is in the crime; little is said about the criminal's early life, and the notion of a downward moral career, so central to the officially sponsored execution broadsheets, is barely present. The malefactor is duly apprehended by the authorities and brought to justice; repentance and contrition are followed by execution; and the audience is warned not to follow suit. In almost every case, the narration is in the third person, and there is little or no hint of a 'farewell speech'.[51] The popular audience is wooed by the juicy story; the censor is appeased by the triumph of the authorities at the end.

Where street ballads dared to put words into the mouth of a prisoner on the scaffold, the balladeers took particular care to distance the audience from the malefactor in other ways; for example, by stressing the offender's fear of death, as in a number of officially approved street ballads dealing with the notorious bandit Johannes Bückler, known as Schinderhannes. One ballad, probably distributed at Schinderhannes' execution, emphasizes his fear of the guillotine ('Now I'm worried and afraid'), and his criminality ('my depraved heart'). Another, narrated in the third person, portrays him as lacking in physical courage, except when inflamed by 'rage and greed', and has him breaking down in terror when the court finds him guilty:

> He's moved and asks the president:
> 'Herr President,' he says, 'can you
> Say if the wheel my life will end,
> It would be terrible if true!'
>
> 'O no!' they say, and reassure:
> 'That punishment takes place no more.
> The guillotine we now reserve
> For criminals who death deserve.'[52]

All the 'last dying speeches' which the street balladeers put into Schinderhannes' mouth stress his repentance. 'Schinderhannes's Farewell Song', for example,

---

[50] Anon., *Sieben Mordthaten, welche der Schneidermeister Hammelmann zu Celle im Hannoverschen ausgeübt, welcher den Lohn für seine Greuelthaten durchs Rad empfangen hat* (Hanover, 3 January 1804), repr. in Braungart, *Bänkelsang*, 87–92.

[51] For further examples, see Braungart, *Bänkelsang*, 76–81, 93–7, 108–15; Riha (ed.), *Moritatenbuch*, 365–7; and Roland W. Pinson (ed.), *Liebe, Mord und Schicksalsschlag. Moritaten, Bänkel-, Gassen- und Küchenlieder aus drei Jahrhunderten* (Bayreuth, 1982), 376–7, 380, 382, 385.

[52] Otto Stückrath, 'Unedierte Schinderhanneslieder', *Rheinisch-westfälische Zeitschrift für Volkskunde*, 7/3–4 (1961), 149–55. See also DVA Freiburg Gr. I: Schinderhannes.

takes the form of a confession, in which the robber ascribes his moral downfall in classic terms to his 'idleness' as a youth, and warns his young listeners not to follow suit. Very little is said in this particular ballad about his deeds; well over half of the fifteen verses are devoted to generalized statements of repentance and moral admonition. After asking for forgiveness, Schinderhannes concludes with the following elevating sentiments:

> Oh joyful, happy and consoled
> I go into eternity,
> The tumbril acts as my springboard,
> I'm swift and willing and ready
> To go into that death machine
> And not feel terror, hurt, or pain,
> And die under the guillotine
> Then God will lead me into Heav'n!![53]

'Bückler's Remorseful Farewell' was another street ballad about Schinderhannes, in which the stress on repentance was already adumbrated in the title.[54] At the same time, the balladeers were bound to make concessions to the widespread popular sympathy which Bückler enjoyed. In many instances, as in the 'Remorseful Farewell', the verses were in the first person, indicating a greater degree of identification on the part of the audience. But to compensate for this they generally avoided romanticizing him, said relatively little about his adventures, and portrayed him in terms that on the whole were acceptable to the authorities.[55]

d. The Ambiguities of Folk-Song

If street balladeers tried to mediate between the demands of popular culture on the one hand and official ideology on the other, folk-songs provided a more immediate indication of the attitudes of the common people to murder and execution, crime and punishment. Of course, in practice, there was often no hard-and-fast dividing line between these various categories; street ballads sometimes drew on folk-songs for their inspiration, while folk-songs sometimes originated as street ballads, or even as poems written by literary figures such as

[53] 'Schinderhannes Abschiedslied', in Otto Stückrath, 'Der Schinderhannes im deutschen Volksliede', *Mitteilungen des Vereins für Nassauische Altertumskunde und Geschichtsforschung*, 15/1 (1911), 94–8.

[54] Stückrath, 'Unedierte Schinderhanneslieder'.

[55] For another, similarly ambivalent street ballad on a bandit, where the religious element is missing because the man concerned was Jewish, see Braungart, *Bänkelsang*, 142–51. For an example of the general point about the fear and repentance shown in first-person narratives at this time, see DVA Freiburg Bl. 4417: Anon., *Lied eines armen Sünders, Namens: Kaspar Sailer, von Langenau, evangelischer Religion, 36 Jahr alt, verheuratheten Standes. Welcher wegen vielen verübten Diebstählen von einer hohen Obrigkeit in Ulm den 5 September 1788 zu dem Schwert verurtheilt wurde* (Ulm, 1788).

Friedrich Schiller in imitation of street ballads.[56] What is important about folk-songs, however, is not their origins but their meaning for those who sang them. They may not have been a pure or unadulterated expression of the popular soul, as was sometimes believed by those who collected them; and the message they carried may not have been entirely unaffected by the dictates of authority; but they none the less give important clues to the way capital punishment and the crimes for which it was ordained were regarded by the mass of ordinary people. This is particularly obvious in the case of infanticide, which is portrayed in folk-song in a far more prosaic, instrumental, and morally ambivalent manner than in street ballads or official 'moral speeches'.[57] Thus, for example, in the song 'The Infanticide,' which probably derives from the eighteenth century, although official censorship prevented it appearing in print until the nineteenth, the infanticidal woman mainly tells her own story, and is seen primarily as a victim:

> 'Ah Joseph, dear Joseph, ah what did you mean
> By causing fair Bertha misfortune and ruin?'
>
> Ah brought to her downfall so fair and so young,
> Because she has murdered her own only son.
>
> 'Ah Joseph, dear Joseph, it's over for me,
> The gate of disgrace I'll soon pass beneath.
>
> The gate of disgrace, before the green sward
> Ah soon you will witness what loving has brought.'
>
> The judge he came by, the wand he did hold,
> And to the fair Bertha her sentence he told.
>
> 'Your Lordship, dear Lordship, ah punish me soon,
> I want to die quickly, to go to my son!
>
> My brothers and sisters and parents, don't cry!
> A lifetime in prison? I'd much rather die.
>
> Ah Joseph, dear Joseph, come give me your hand,
> I want to forgive you, God knows where I stand.'
>
> The ensign came riding, his flag he did wave:
> 'Now stop the proceedings, I bring a reprieve!'
>
> 'Ah ensign, dear ensign, she's already dead!'
> Good night, my fair Bertha! Your soul is in Heav'n!'[58]

Here, the literary historian Tom Cheesman has argued, the loss of the woman's life is seen as much more serious than the loss of her child's. Her calmness in going to her death represents, he argues, a popular appropriation of the state's

---

[56] Friedrich Schiller, 'Die Kindsmörderin,' in Riha (ed.), *Moritatenbuch*, 336–9.

[57] For songs giving this alternative view, see Elsbeth Janda and Fritz Nötzoldt (eds.), *Die Moritat vom Bänkelsang oder das Lied der Strasse* (Munich, 1959), esp. 50, 114.

[58] Ludwig Erk and Franz W. Böhme (eds.), *Deutscher Liederhort*, i (Leipzig, 1925), 186.

ritual of retribution, as a religious act of penitence by the 'poor sinner'. Nothing is said about her character, and there is no mention of any other crimes or failings on her part. The late arrival of a state pardon underlines the popular view of the essential arbitrariness of state justice and of executions for such crimes. Here, he argues, is folk-song as counter-cultural text, articulating the popular view of infanticide in contrast to the official one. Yet this perhaps makes too much of the gap in understanding between the élites and the masses even at this late stage. The acceptance of death for the crime of infanticide, and the inevitability of retribution of some kind, is scarcely counter-cultural; while at the same time, if the song dates from the later part of the eighteenth century, it may also reflect the growing ambivalence of the élites towards infanticide which could be observed, as we have seen, in the period of the *Sturm und Drang* from the 1770s onwards.[59] In this case at least, élite and popuar sensibilities had some congruence.

Nevertheless, popular belief in the possibility, even likelihood, of unjust executions for infanticide was perhaps expressed more clearly in another very widespread song, dating probably from the sixteenth century, and recorded in the nineteenth. It is worth quoting in full, both to give a flavour of the repetitive and formulaic character of these folk-songs, and to get across the full import of the complex set of messages which it seeks to convey:

> In Frankfurt by the bridge
> They drank much wine and beer;
> A maiden they betrayed,
> Her honour they did steal.
>
> Her father tramped the streets
> The midwife he did see.
> 'My daughter you must aid,
> A virgin she must seem.'
>
> 'A virgin she'll appear—
> Of course I'll give my aid.
> We'll kill the baby child
> And blame it on the maid.'
>
> The maid was washing clothes,
> She came home late at night.
> She went up to her bed.
> And what now did she find?
>
> Oh what now did she find?
> A tiny, murdered corpse;
> The maid was terrified
> The daughter she did call.

[59] Cheesman, 'Studies', 381–2. For other versions of this theme, see Erk and Böhme (eds.), *Deutscher Liederhort*, 187–8.

The cunning daughter came,
Her mother she did tell:
'The maid has borne a babe,
And murdered it as well!'

If she has borne a child,
And also murdered it,
We'll have her strung up high
In Frankfurt, by the gate.

The maid she had a lover,
On Saturdays they met.
'Oh where's my darling, then,
Why doesn't she me greet?'

'We've left her hanging high
In Frankfurt by the gate:
For she has borne a child
And also murdered it.'

He gave his horse the spur
And to the gallows flew:
'How high you hang up there,
You're almost out of view!'

'But I'm not hanging high,
I'm resting in God's care:
His angels from the sky,
Are feeding me up here.'

He gave his horse the spur,
Rode to Authority:
'Oh what have you done here!
For innocence, pity!'

'If we have wrongly judg'd,
And harm to her have done,
Well then we'll cut her down
And hang the other ones!'

The father lost his head,
The daughter shared his fate,
The midwife got the wheel
In Frankfurt by the gate.[60]

Here, as Cheesman suggests, the infant is treated with a remarkable lack of sentimentality, reflecting a popular belief that the life of a baby, exposed as it was to the manifold dangers of disease, debility, malnutrition, and death, was worth less than that of an adult. The crime is not linked with sexual promiscuity, the influence of the Devil, nor a downward career of immorality and deviance, but

---

[60] Erk and Böhme (eds.), *Deutscher Liederhort*, 638–9. See also 'Die Rabenmutter' (ibid. 632–6), which portrays retribution against multiple infanticides as a matter of divine and popular justice.

with male lust and ruthlessness and female weakness and emotionality. There is also an element of social criticism against the employers of the innocent serving-maid; and indeed other versions portray the maid's seducer as a rich merchant. Secular justice is once again convicted of a serious error, and divine justice steps in to right the wrong. Here too, the popular understanding of justice as a divine act, as in popular attitudes to the execution ceremony, comes to the fore. Secular justice appears as human and fallible and not, as in official broadsheets and censored street ballads, the inevitable expression of God's will.[61] Once again, however, these arguments should not be pushed too far; secular justice, after all, does have its way in the end, and is still ultimately guided by the divine hand.

In another folk-song, recorded in the Sudetenland in 1840, a young woman asks her listeners rhetorically:

> Oh what am I carrying in my heart?
> Oh woe how I'm weighed down.
> Hangman, oh hangman, hangman mine,
> Write me a letter, a letter fine,
> To tell my parents they should come
> To see me wed to my bridegroom!

The parents arrive at the town gates full of joy, only to find that an execution is about to take place. Her mother asks:

> Oh daughter, my daughter, oh where is he,
> Your bridegroom all so fine,
> You're running from to me?
> Mother, oh mother, mother mine
> The hangman, it is he.

The phrase is a metaphorical one; the woman is referring not to the custom by which an executioner could rescue a condemned woman's life with an offer of marriage, but to the double meaning of an execution as a wedding with Christ. A young man from the crowd offers to marry her, and the authorities indicate that they will spare her if she accepts. But she turns the offer down:

> Oh no, that cannot be,
> The world is not for me.
> If longer I should stay,
> Myself I'll only blame.
>
> Oh hangman, draw your sword
> Before mine eyes to see,
> When I am lying in blood
> A-fainting you'll all be.

[61] See Cheesman, *Shocking Ballad Picture Show*, ch. 5, for a discussion of this song.

> You parents turn you round,
> That you too will not see
> Spurt out your flesh and blood.
> Receive in God's own Name
> Blessedness and Amen.[62]

Here once more the story is told from the point of view of the infanticidal woman herself. She is depicted as overcome by guilt for what she has done. The punishment prescribed by the law is viewed as arbitrary and uncertain, revocable up to the last minute. The decision to die is her own, and it is taken in a spirit of morality, honour, and Christian love. The crowd, like those who would have sung the song, is sympathetic to the victim and shocked by the punishment, as indeed crowds at the execution of infanticidal mothers sometimes were in the seventeenth century.[63] Folk-song frequently portrays infanticides as more unfortunate than wicked. In one song, recorded around the turn of the century in Styria, the girl sings of her deed ('I've killed my own child | Ah God, how grave is my sin') and begs her judges for mercy. Refusing to grant it, they are depicted, metaphorically speaking, as cannibals:

> At half-past sev'n in the morning dawn,
> Give me breakfast to take and eat.
> The finest lords they have come to town,
> I'm the breakfast they're wolfing down.

But she is confident that she will go to heaven ('My angels will accompany me') and that the Virgin Mary will protect her. Once again, putting the song in the first person assured an element of identification with the girl on the part of whoever sang it.[64] Perhaps this accounts for the fact that treatments of infanticide were rarely to be found in commercially available street ballads: caught between fear of the authorities' disapproval and knowledge of the public's sympathy, street balladeers more often than not preferred to remain silent.[65]

It was not only infanticidal women who received sympathetic treatment in folk-songs. Bandits too, especially the legendary Schinderhannes, were widely celebrated in terms that said more about the popular need for mythical vehicles of social justice than about the violent and squalid reality of his life of robbery, murder, and extortion.[66] In one of the best-known folk-songs, 'Up, up, you comrades', Schinderhannes tells his band:

---

[62] DVA Freiburg Gr. I: 'Ach weh in meinem Herzen'. Noted in Krummendorf bei Strehlen, 1840. The metre and rhyming of the original are irregular.
[63] Dülmen, *Frauen*, 158, for some examples.
[64] DVA Freiburg Gr. I: 'Ich bin ein Mädchen von jungen Jahren'.
[65] Cheesman, *Shocking Ballad Picture Show*, ch. 5.   [66] Franke, *Schinderhannes*, 327–97.

> But hear the poor folk's pleading,
> And aid them in their need.
> Their cries you must be heeding,
> With them you'll share your bread.
>
> The wand'rer on the highway
> You must in peace let go.
> And watch out on the byway
> For those who spurn the poor.[67]

In another, 'My Young Life is Over', Schinderhannes, in a 'farewell song' from the scaffold, describes his career in terms reminiscent of Robin Hood, though with a characteristically anti-Semitic twist:

> I wandered through the land, and in the wood lay low,
> And plundered all the rich, and also many a Jew
>
> In pitiless fashion! To set my conscience free,
> I'd give some to the poor, perhaps one time in three.

The robber ends by warning the young not to follow his example, but it is clear that he is a figure to be admired as well as pitied, and the song emphasizes repeatedly how his behaviour on the scaffold is 'worthy', 'without any horror or fear | steadfastly and in right good cheer'.[68] The contrast with his portrayal in officially sanctioned street ballads could not have been more striking. Another song, also sung in the first person, has Schinderhannes and his comrades defying the scaffold and making a nonsense of the theory of capital punishment as a deterrent, as they sing:

> Give us a place to dwell
> Out on the gallows field,
> Where the old ravens call;
> What could be half as sweet?
> There the blue skies are clear.
> In the fair summertime
> Every herb and flower
> Grows for our own delight.[69]

Certainly, such songs would not have won the approval of the authorities for printing and distributing at Schinderhannes' execution, or indeed at any time thereafter. If bandits were the subjects of a growing number of Romantic novels and stories from the beginning of the nineteenth century onwards, then they were more often than not entirely fictional bandits, whose activities were set in far-off countries a long way from Germany.[70]

---

[67] DVA Freiburg Gr. I: 'Auf, auf ihr Kameraden'.
[68] Ibid.: 'Aus ist mein junges Leben', recorded in the mid-19th c.
[69] Stückrath, 'Der Schinderhannes'.   [70] Danker, *Räuberbanden*, 471–7.

Apart from infanticides and bandits, offenders who killed for love or revenge were also treated more leniently in popular song than in officially approved broadsheets. A favourite motif here was the soldier betrayed while away from home. In one such song, recorded in 1909, but certainly dating from much earlier, the hero, a young hussar, becomes concerned when his parents stop sending him money and his fiancée stops writing him letters. A friend tells him a wicked suitor has reduced them to penury in his vain attempts to force the girl to marry him. Returning home, the hussar kills the man, and is arrested and condemned to death by firing-squad: 'His comrades take aim, | Ten shots at his breast. | But none doth strike home | God shows him His grace.' While the hussar, his parents, and his faithful girlfriend are congratulating themselves, a messenger arrives with the royal pardon, and the young man is saved.[71] Folk-songs, indeed, often showed sympathy for a young man whose anger and jealousy at being betrayed or rejected by his betrothed led him to murder her, as in some versions of the popular song 'I am a lad of one-and-twenty years'.[72] Often, the murderer does not receive any punishment, indeed the law and the authorities are not mentioned at all.[73] In some folk-songs in this genre, the murderer commits suicide immediately after the deed.[74]

In a variation on this theme, the jealous lover is deceived by another woman into thinking his mistress unfaithful, and kills her in a fit of anger. Brought to a realization of his mistake by the appearance of his mistress's ghost in the purest white, he confesses his deed in a spirit of remorse, and is led to the scaffold:

> He spoke: 'Turn unto God your friend,
> With Him you can find grace,
> And go with patience to your end,
> And penitence embrace,
> That you avoid what I have done.'
> He turned his eyes to Heav'n,
> And then he was beheaded.
>
> The head was placed upon a pole,
> The corpse was ta'en away
> And bound right fast onto the wheel.
> Now hear ye what I say:
> The hangman's serf took out his cane

---

[71] DVA Freiburg Gr. I: 'Nimm, Florian, des Vaters Segen'.

[72] Ibid.: 'Ich bin ein Bursch von einundzwanzig Jahren'. This song existed in many versions, including several in which the narrator was the student Karl Ludwig Sand, and the subject-matter the murder of the playwright and Russian agent August von Kotzebue.

[73] See ibid.: 'Einst ein Mädchen voller Tugent', for a similar story.

[74] See ibid.: 'Es war einmal ein Bauernbub'; and ibid. Bl. 4673: Anon., *Der Mord aus Eifersucht und Liebeswuth, ausgeübt von dem Maurergesellen und Landwehrmann Carl Gottfried Mecke aus Mühlhausen an seiner ehemaligen Geliebten Louise Hagemann zu Erfurt* (Hamburg, n.d.).

> And beat that lying maid.
> And that's where false tongues lead![75]

Here the punishment is strongly featured at the end of the song, and the narration is in the third person, both creating a distancing effect. Nevertheless, the audience is invited to sympathize with the offender, both through the words he addresses to them directly, and through the knowledge that he is going to heaven. Once again, human justice has failed, and it is the malefactor's own remorse, brought about by the supernatural, that has led to his death.

e. Popular Culture and Capital Punishment

There were some kinds of capital offences which met with little popular understanding. Multiple murder, for example, was almost always the cause of popular outrage. An infanticidal woman might get some sympathy if she had been deceived by a man with a promise of marriage into a sexual relationship, then abandoned, poor, and without prospects of employment, when she became pregnant. But if this happened more than once, then she was likely to be thought of in the same terms as the authorities thought of so many infanticidal women— as persistently promiscuous and thoroughly deserving of her fate. Here there was considerable congruence between official and popular attitudes, and folk-songs made no bones about the justice of such women's execution:

> She was beheaded with the sword,
> Her right hand cut away,
> To be a warning and a word
> To people there that day,
> So learn ye from that frightful scene
> That ye be not as she has been.[76]

Whether or not a woman was tried for infanticide, indeed, often depended on the attitude of the local community, and this could vary according to the circumstances and the standing of the woman and her family in local life. Little went unnoticed in the tight-knit world of the German village, and if one infant murder might be tolerated, then several by the same woman were not, any more than was the murder of a child that had reached even a few months of age.[77]

It was normal in songs where there was only minimal sympathy with the offender for a distancing effect to be achieved through the medium of third-

[75] Ibid. Gr. I: 'Es möcht ja wohl ein hartes Herz (Kutscher)'.

[76] Ibid.: 'Es möcht ja wohl ein hartes Herz (Kindsmörderin)'. For a hostile street ballad about a multiple infanticide, see Braungart, *Bänkelsang*, 168–73.

[77] Ulbricht, 'Infanticide', and Regina Schulte, 'Infanticide in Rural Bavaria in the Nineteenth Century', in Hans Medick and David Warren Sabean (eds.), *Interest and Emotion: Essays on the Study of Family and Kinship* (Cambridge, 1984), 77–102.

person narration. If the malefactor was quoted at all, it was often only to heighten the effect of shock, as in the following folk-song:

> A youth of twenty years
> Did grasp his mother's hair
> He pulled her out of doors
> Pathetic to behold.
>
> 'Oh you're no mother to me
> I tell you frank and free
> If you'd brought me up good
> You wouldn't get this reward.'
> And then an axe he took
> And cut her head in two.
>
> Arrested then was he,
> Before the judgment-seat.
> With red-hot tongs was pinched
> And they tore off his skin.
> Upon the wheel he came,
> A richly merited fate.

Here the malefactor was not allowed to show penitence, and was not portrayed as receiving divine absolution; it was only the audience who were told that they could die 'a blessed death' if they abhorred the malefactor's example and honoured and obeyed their parents.[78]

Adulterous motives for murder almost always earned popular disapproval. In one folk-song, recorded in Lower Austria, the first-person narrator, speaking from the scaffold, is a young woman who has 'a good marriage' and a kind husband. She is 'bedazzled' by 'the rage of love' for another, is 'unfaithful to my husband', and poisons him in order to be with her lover. Popular, community justice is emphasized through the stress in the song on the woman's remorse, a stronger force than the punishment meted out by the state:

> The rope is so frightful
> Through which I now atone,
> But yet more terrible
> My conscience pangs alone.

The woman, sensing the hostility of the community, begs her audience: 'Do not curse me after I am gone.' Remorse will bring redemption, and after a lengthy admonition to her listeners ('do not become sinners'), she concludes:

> And now I mount the ravenstone
> A last time round I gaze,

[78] DVA Freiburg Gr. I: 'Ihr Christen stehet still'.

> And then I turn my face to Heav'n,
> Where new life doth await.[79]

Another stock figure in folk-song was the man whose wife worked hard and looked after the children while he spent the days carousing at the inn and the nights sleeping with other women. In a song in this genre from Saxony, one such man returns home at midnight and murders his wife in order to marry another woman:

> The natural eye of God
> Has seen his dreadful crime.
> He's brought before the judge
> Next day at morning time.
> And now before the court
> To death he is condemned.
> Upon the ravenstone
> He'll meet a rascal's end.[80]

There is no identification with the malefactor here; indeed the song is as full of moral disapproval as any officially sanctioned broadsheet; the contrast is in the matter-of-factness of the narrative, and in the ascription of the offender's arrest to divine rather than human intervention. Similarly, in another folk-song, when a young man murders his pregnant mistress rather than take responsibility for his child, it is his own pangs of conscience, rather than the operation of the law, that reveal the deed and seal his fate.[81] Popular disapproval of common murder was shown in a mass of songs and ballads recounting crimes and acts of violence, in many cases without mentioning the sanction of the law or the punishment of the offender at all. It is noticeable in these songs that little detail is given of the malefactor's punishment, in contrast to the elaborate descriptions provided in the official and semi-official broadsheets handed out to execution crowds. This is true not only of the songs which the offender narrates from the scaffold, but also of third-person narratives. Justice is mainly seen as the operation of God's purposes, the individual conscience, or the community's will. Human justice, the justice of the authorities, is seen as fallible, or not seen at all.

Nor did the depiction of crime and punishment in German folk-song stop at domestic crimes or crimes of passion. Multiple murder, whether or not in connection with robbery, attracted much hostile attention, and ballads describing them were particularly widespread. Punishment was always portrayed as

---

[79] Ibid.: 'Ihr lieben Landsleut, lebet wohl'.   [80] Ibid.: 'Die heisse Sonne strahlet'.
[81] Ibid.: 'Eine traurige G'schicht von einem Mordtatgericht'.

deserved in such cases.[82] Sometimes such street ballads caught the popular imagination and were transmogrified into folk-songs. One such was the ballad 'What's knocking dreadfully at the door?':

What's knocking dreadfully at the door?
Go, wife, and find out: who is there?
A poor old man, perhaps it might
Be, seeking shelter for the night.

The poor wife hurried to the door
As on it fell a blow, and more.
The first one through, he stabbed her dead
And twenty more rushed in ahead.

They murdered master, serf, and maid
And plundered till the break of day.
A single child escaped this hell
And hid inside the dog kennel.

As soon as dawn was in the sky,
Off to the judge the child did fly.
With trembling and with tears did he
Say: 'Dearest man, please come with me!
Today I heard a cry of fear!
The village smith, he too was there.'

The judge, and several soldiers with
Him went straightway up to the smith.
'He's not at home, he's gone away,'
The people in his house did say.
A small child stood there by the door,
So free and gay, as children are.

The judge spoke to the little lad:
'Oh quickly, tell me, where's your dad?'
'He's in the cellar,' said the child,
'And with him many men so wild!'
And listen, how the coins do roll!
They're counting money, weighing gold.

The judge arrested all the men
And put upon them many a chain.
They are too wicked for this world!
A hangman's death these men have earned.
And for the ugly bloody deed
Each murderer pays upon the wheel.[83]

---

[82] See e.g. DVA Freiburg Gr. I: 'Kommt und hört, was jetzt geschehen'; Anon., *Siebenfacher Mord, welcher sich am 22sten October 1838 zu Bebering zugetragen und von einem Manne Namens Wilhelm, Heinrich Schmidt verübt worden ist* (1840).

[83] Ibid.: 'Was pocht so grässlich an der Tür?' (recorded in Hasselbach v. d. Rhön, near Halle, in 1933). The second verse, missing in this version, was supplied from the version given on pp. 66–7 of Hoffmann

Here it is the innocence and honesty of children, first the victim's child, then the smith's, which betrays the robbers to the authorities. The robbers' dishonesty is contrasted with the charitable motives of the victims in opening the door to them. It is the victims who give to the poor, and the robbers who, therefore, at second hand, as it were, steal from them. Justice is seen as the expression of the community's will, articulated through the two children, and the judge as the community's servant. Few robbers became the stuff of legend as Schinderhannes did; indeed, his example was probably enough to satisfy the popular need for a mythical social champion of the poor against the rich; other songs about robbers, like 'What's knocking dreadfully at the door?', put them in a much more realistic perspective, and portrayed the robber in grimmer terms, from the point of view of the victim, as another burden which the common people had to bear, along with war, famine, death, and disease.

Popular culture, as expressed, however imperfectly, in folk-song, could thus range from the compensatory fantasy of bandits who robbed the rich to feed the poor and lived a life of romanticism, bravery, and excitement, to the sober narrative of brutal and violent gangs that terrorized village communities and isolated farmhouses for money and valuables which they undoubtedly intended to keep for themselves. It was not entirely separate from élite culture, or necessarily opposed to it. But it did have a different agenda, based on the realities of life on the margins of existence. The role of women in popular culture, for example, was very different from the rigidly prescribed norms that emerged in élite culture during the period in which a male-dominated 'public sphere' was being formed in the late eighteenth and early nineteenth centuries. Folk-songs, more often than not sung and listened to by women, were aware of the real, painful life-choices the female sex often had to make, in a way that street ballads and official documents, always composed, written, and printed by men, seldom were. Only in cases of witchcraft, especially where, as so often, old, single or widowed females, midwives, and 'wisewomen' were the object of community fear and hostility, leading to rumour, ostracism, and still in the seventeenth and eighteenth centuries to prosecution, was there no popular sympathy. The 'people' was not an undifferentiated mass, sunk in a timeless folk culture and standing in the way of the social, economic, and cultural modernization pursued by the élites. It was both structured, as we have seen in the formation of the execution procession, and divided, by class, occupation, age, and gender.

and Richter, *Schlesische Volkslieder*, also in DVA Freiburg Gr. I under the same first-line title. The word 'Männer' in verse 6, line 4, common to most other versions, was substituted for the original 'Kinder' in the Hasselbach song, to make the sense clearer. The original street ballad was printed in Anon., *Wahrhafte Beschreibung und Abbildung eines 32fachen Raubmordes, welcher sich bei Paris den 25 July 1825 zugetragen hat.* In the folk-song, however, the location and date were entirely lost.

Execution ballads and songs always represented a specific set of attitudes, which varied according to the categories to which the singers and their subjects the malefactors belonged. And popular attitudes, for example towards illegitimacy and premarital sex, could be more 'modern' than those of the authorities and the state, just as the primacy accorded to community sanctions in popular culture could be more democratic.[84]

To point this out is not, however, to bathe the popular culture of the eighteenth and early nineteenth centuries in the warm afterglow of postmodern nostalgia. The social and physical realities with which the common people, and especially perhaps the women of the poorer classes, had to deal in the period were harsh, the choices that faced them often stark. In recognizing this, popular culture often took a matter-of-fact, instrumental view of aspects of life such as child-bearing and child-rearing that the emerging bourgeoisie already found shocking at the beginning of the nineteenth century. This sense of shock should not lead us to suppose, as some historians have done, that the poor did not experience love or affection for their children, or for each other.[85] But in a world in which infant mortality ran at 30 to 50 per cent, where pain, malnutrition, disease, and disability were commonplace, where epidemics and famines still, though to a decreasing extent, threatened the existence of all, popular culture provided a discourse of accommodation, reconciliation, and sometimes resistance, because at bottom it constituted, as the historical anthropologist David Sabean has written, 'a series of arguments among people about the common things of their everyday lives'.[86] And popular culture was not just presented on the printed page, it was also expressed through the spoken and sung word, through formal and informal ceremonies and actions, and through real and symbolic behaviour, such as took place in public executions.

Justice in eighteenth-century Germany, as the ballad and folk-song record suggests, and the execution rituals which were the focus of Chapter 2 confirm, was not simply a matter of the mature Absolutist state imposing its will upon a supine and downtrodden people. Power did not simply operate in one direction, from above to below; it was multi-layered, reciprocal, negotiated, and fragmented.[87] The execution ceremony was the result of a many-faceted set of implicit negotiations between different groups and institutions within the com-

---

[84] Wolfgang Kaschuba, 'Ritual und Fest. Das Volk auf der Strasse. Figurationen und Funktionen populärer Öffentlichkeit zwischen Frühneuzeit und Moderne', in Richard van Dülmen (ed.), *Dynamik der Tradition* (Frankfurt am Main, 1992), 240–67. See also idem, 'Mythos oder Eigen-Sinn. "Volkskultur" zwischen Volkskunde und Sozialgeschichte', in Jeggle *et al.* (eds.), *Volkskultur*, 469–507.

[85] e.g. Shorter, *Making of the Modern Family*.

[86] David Sabean, *Power in the Blood: Popular Culture and Village Discourse in Early Modern Germany* (New York, 1984), 95.

[87] Ibid. 25–6.

munity and between the community and the sovereign power. And on a more general level, the relations between the judicial apparatus and the common people were complex and shifting. Peasants could, and did, use the courts as means of redress against overbearing feudal lords in eighteenth-century East Elbian Brandenburg,[88] just as women of lowly status could, and did, bring charges against men who they felt had wronged them in eighteenth-century Frankfurt am Main.[89] Of course, the law did not necessarily give them what they wanted; and sometimes it could give them a good deal more than they bargained for; domestic complaints brought before the courts could well lead to punishments imposed by the authorities that were far more severe than those intended by the complainants.[90] The power of the local community, in this small-scale, and by modern standards very thinly populated society, was enough to take offenders to court if that was the consensus view, or to conceal their crimes if the ordained punishment was thought to be too severe. The machinery of law enforcement at the state's disposal was simply too weak to impose itself on society without at least some degree of popular consent; even witchcraft persecutions depended heavily upon popular participation and often grew out of accusations first articulated in the village community.[91] That is why most German executions were not merely displays of state authority, but expressions of various kinds of popular justice as well; and that is why folk-songs dealing with crime and punishment were no mere endorsements of princely or magisterial power, but celebrations of community solidarity and purpose that sometimes stood obliquely to the vertical imposition of authority from above.

What mattered in the popular view was God's infallible judgment of the soul, not the law's highly fallible judgment of the body. When death was inevitable, therefore, as the malefactor, whether rightly or wrongly judged, began the march to the scaffold, the issues of the crime itself were forgotten as the community began a collective act of piety and penitence in the hope that the malefactor would be saved for eternal life, as they themselves hoped to be saved. It was for this reason that the suicide of murderers aroused such pity and horror, for by depriving themselves of the saving grace and the cleansing ritual of trial and execution, they had deprived themselves of eternal life. When the master-joiner Moog killed himself after murdering his wife and five children in Frankfurt am Main in 1817, the authorities decided to execute his dead body anyway:

---

[88] Hagen, 'Junkers' Faithless Servants'.

[89] Rebekka Habermas, 'Frauen und Männer im Kampf um Leib, Ökonomie und Recht. Zur Beziehung der Geschlechter im Frankfurt der Frühen Neuzeit', in Dülmen (ed.), *Dynamik der Tradition*, 109–36.

[90] Ibid. 128–35.   [91] Labouvie, *Zauberei*.

Some several thousand from our town
Did go behind the biers.
As to the graveyard they came down
Oh God! So many tears,
And deepest pain and sorrow too
The hearts of all did now imbue
During this funeral.

And on the execution road
The body on a wheel,
The head they put upon a pole
For everyone to see,
And so that all will bear in mind
Until the very end of time
The deed and punishment.

So always think upon the crime
That joiner Moog committed,
For which until the end of time
His body now is spitted;
Yet no one should depart this scene
Until the unhappy man has been
Bewailed with all his tears.[92]

In normal cases, the onlookers did not weep for the malefactor; instead, the ceremony of execution was almost an act of celebration, with the sanctified soul of the condemned rising to heaven at the end.

The malefactor's contrition was essential to this ritual, and it is no accident that it forms the element most common to all three forms of popular commentary on capital punishment, the news-sheet or execution broadsheet, the street ballad, and the folk-song. At the same time, however, urban and feudal élites were becoming manifestly more uneasy with the religious essence of executions as the eighteenth century progressed, and as they distanced themselves increasingly from the popular culture of which it was a part.[93] As far as the Absolutist police state was able, it secularized the language in which the ceremony of punishment was celebrated, and it distanced the audience of the printed texts which it was empowered to approve from the malefactor whom it was engaged in destroying. Images of demoniacal possession were replaced by images of bestiality. The malefactor was individualized and provided with a moral curriculum vitae. The majesty and power of the state were emphasized by elaborate

[92] 'Beschreibung der 7fachen Mordthat, welche am 21. August 1817 der Schreinermeister Johann Gottlieb Moog zu Frankfurt am Main an seiner Ehegattin, fünf Kindern und an sich selbst verübt', in Riha (ed.), *Moritatenbuch*, 294-7.

[93] Peter Burke, *Popular Culture in Early Modern Europe* (London, 1978), 270-81. For an analysis of the rather different tradition of 'flash ballads' and execution broadsheets in England, see Gatrell, *Hanging Tree*, 109-96.

descriptions of its impact on the malefactor's body. All this was part of an effort, undertaken by the Absolutist state from the middle of the century onwards, to reform the penal system and bring it into line with new, rationalistic concepts of punishment as deterrence by example. Judicial reformers like Friedrich II of Prussia cut down the number and variety of capital punishments and later systematized the application of the law to offenders along lines laid down by Beccaria. And state authorities intervened in the production of execution ballads to try and popularize the new concept of execution as a one-way assertion of state power, designed to arouse feelings of fear and revulsion in the populace. The last three chapters have shown in various ways the limited effectiveness of this policy. The popular understanding of capital punishment remained obstinately impervious to official attempts to steer it in the desired direction. Whether through the continuation of magico-religious practices or through the medium of folk-song, popular culture persisted in treating executions as manifestations of divine as well as, or rather than, secular justice, as rituals of expiation and reconciliation, rather than demonstrations of the majesty of the state, as participatory events involving the whole Christian community rather than theatrical displays of the power of the authorities over the people. As the nineteenth century dawned, the unease of the authorities at this state of affairs began to be translated into action.

Part II

5

The Wheel, the Sword, and the Axe

a. An Execution in Berlin

On 16 September 1800 the city of Berlin was treated to the unusual spectacle of a woman being broken with the wheel. As was normal in such cases, members of the public were allowed into the 'poor sinner's parlour' during the period between the delivery of the verdict and the day of execution. 'The crowds', it was reported, 'were so great that military assistance was already required the day before the execution to prevent disorder.' The report continued:

The execution was to have taken place early in the morning, but was improperly delayed because the numerous staff required to hold the public condemnation ceremony only gathered in front of the city hall at 8 o'clock, and the offender, who was taken to the gallows on foot, could only walk slowly, had to stop for a rest, and used this time to take her leave of the accompanying rabble. . . . The mob had already gathered around the place of execution at the crack of dawn, and, inflamed by brandy and tired of the long wait, was already showing signs of discontent.

While the crowd was waiting, the executioner's servants allowed spectators onto the platform 'for a tip' to get a better view. This in turn elicited a loud 'grumbling' from the crowd, whose sight of the ceremony now seemed likely to be impeded. Nevertheless, as the executioner, the condemned, and the rest of the procession arrived, the crowd grew still and the bloody ceremony took its course. The woman was tied down and quickly strangled, and her limbs and neck were broken by a series of blows with the heavy cartwheel wielded by the executioner. In accordance with standard practice, her body was then untied and fastened to the wheel, which was placed horizontally on a long upright pole fixed into the ground next to the scaffold, to be left as a warning to others. The head was cut off and stuck on the top of the pole. Another public execution had seemingly run its course in the usual fashion.

It was at this point that things began to go wrong. 'As the executioner's servants now cleaned the ravenstone,' the report continued, 'the crush of those who wanted to mount it either out of curiosity or for the purpose of buying some of the bloodied sand for the supposed curing of epileptic fits, or for other superstitious uses, became very heavy.' In particular, a number of journeymen offered the executioner's servants money to be allowed onto the scaffold. But the servants wanted to charge what seemed to the journeymen to be an exorbitant fee. There followed an 'exchange of words' which culminated in the journeymen's attempt to climb onto the scaffold anyway, without paying. One of the journeymen was seized by an executioner's servant and thrown bodily from the platform, 'and a few journeymen artisans were hit with cords which were still bloody from the execution. They considered themselves to have been dishonoured by this, the people agreed with them, and they all now decided to wreak their revenge on the executioner's servants by stoning them.' The small contingent of infantrymen who had been in attendance had long since departed the scene by this point, and the officials still present were too few in number to control the crowd. All they could do was summon the cavalry. But by the time the hussars arrived, the executioner and his servants had all fled, apart from one Matthäus Täubler, the person whose behaviour had started off the riot. He had been caught by the crowd. Already dishonoured by his touch, the journeymen now had no compunction about laying their hands on him. 'Grievously mishandled by blows', Täubler was picked up by the cavalry and rushed off to the guardhouse at the Oranienburg Gate. Led by the journeymen, the crowd followed the cavalry and attempted to storm the building. Fearing for Täubler's safety, the hussars escorted him to the more secure premises of the city governor's house.

Here the crowd, persistent in its anger, gathered once more, shouting for Täubler to be surrendered. The city governor then appeared and tried to calm the rioters, threatening them with stern measures should they fail to disperse. At the same time he promised them that Täubler would be punished for his behaviour. He 'offered to give his hand to those who considered themselves to have been rendered dishonourable by the touch of the executioner's servant, in order thus to make them honourable again according to the customary procedure'. The degree of honour which he possessed was sufficient for this; and dishonour in any case seemed to weaken when passed on through a third party. But those at the back of the crowd could not hear him, and more people were continually arriving to swell the 'mob', so a further contingent of troops was summoned and finally broke up the crowd by force. In the aftermath of these events, some twenty tailors, cobblers, joiners, silk-workers, and other journeymen were arrested and imprisoned or given a whipping. Täubler, the offending executioner's servant, was questioned, and admitted having pushed back the journeymen who had come onto the platform without paying. Witnesses confirmed that it was indeed

Täubler who had hit them with the bloody cords. The city authorities, wishing to avoid any possibility of further disturbances, had him whipped in the presence of the senior masters and journeymen of eleven guilds, who were instructed to inform their fellow guildsmen of what they had witnessed and warn them against taking any further steps towards 'self-help' in the matter.[1] With these steps taken, the affair was over and any danger of further disturbances averted.

The incident was in many ways unusual. Execution riots were relatively uncommon in Germany, as we have seen. The immediate cause of this particular one was the dishonouring of the journeymen by the executioner's servants. More indirectly, the trouble had started over the difficulty which members of the crowd had experienced in exercising their traditional right to obtain the executed criminal's blood for purposes of magical healing. There was no thought here of rescuing the offender, or of offering direct resistance to the authority of the state. As usual, indeed, the crowd had been moved to protest by a disruption of the symbolic economy of honour, magic, and religion that surrounded the execution. Nevertheless, the crowd's behaviour also indicated that this economy was now beginning to break down. On the one hand, the executioner and his servants had taken matters into their own hands by selling places on the scaffold. On the other, the drunkenness of the onlookers, plied, it was reported, by 'a numberless crowd of vendors with brandy and liquor', was also new.[2] Most of the religious aura of the ceremony seemed by now to have disappeared, a tendency that can be observed in a number of other major public executions of about the same time, especially in big cities like Berlin. Yet this was not, as hostile commentators claimed, a mere example of the drunken irresponsibility of the 'mob'. There were broader influences at work which not only increased the frequency of such disturbances in the first decade of the nineteenth century but also made them appear particularly alarming to the authorities. The turn of the eighteenth and nineteenth centuries was a particularly bad time for artisans, not least in Berlin, where economic problems since the mid-1780s had made it increasingly hard for journeymen to find employment. It was not surprising, therefore, that they were more than usually sensitive to incidents of 'dishonouring' that might make it even more difficult for them to get a job than was already the case.[3] Little more than ten years after the outbreak of the French Revolution, the Prussian authorities were for their part more than usually sensitive to the potential danger of serious rioting and unrest among the artisan population of the capital city. The

[1] GStA Berlin Rep. 84a/7781, Bl. 25–8: Bericht vom 16. Sept. 1800.
[2] Cited in Glenzdorf and Treichel, *Henker*, 66–7.
[3] Jürgen Bergmann, *Das Berliner Handwerk in den Frühphasen der Industrialisierung* (Veröffentlichungen der Historischen Kommission zu Berlin; Berlin, 1973), 25, 122, 172, 212, 221, 250. See also more generally Andreas Griesinger, *Das symbolische Kapital der Ehre. Streikbewegungen und kollektives Bewusstsein deutscher Handwerksgesellen im 18. Jahrhundert* (Frankfurt am Main, 1981).

incident showed how easy it was for crowds to get out of hand. The events of 1789–94 in Paris had demonstrated how fatal this could be for the state's authority. And the spread of revolutionary ideas across Europe, not least among artisans, suggested that crowd disturbances of this kind could all too quickly take on a political colouring.

Under the impact of the Revolution, a bureaucratic reform movement was gathering strength in Berlin, aiming to adopt what high officials regarded as the best institutions and ideas of the French Revolution in order to prevent the continuation of old abuses and inefficiencies from alienating the populace and endangering the Prussian state. Judicial officials on a number of levels seized on the opportunity of the execution disturbances of 1800 to push for a radical reform of the whole execution procedure in Prussia. Their arguments were characteristic of the radical and ruthlessly rationalistic programme of the Prussian reform movement, which was to lead in a short number of years, under the leadership of Stein and Hardenberg, to a range of sweeping reforms, from the abolition of guild privileges to the ending of serfdom on the land. The immediately responsible judicial officials at the time of the execution disturbances in Berlin in 1800, the Directors and Counsellors of the Berlin City Courts, were quick to complain that the riot showed the urgency of the need for an 'abolition of the numerous abuses, resting on ingrained prejudices' connected with public executions—abuses which, they said, had been widely recognized at least since the great judicial reforms of the 1740s, but which had continued in existence because of disputes between various authorities over who had the power to deal with them. Nobody, they complained, had managed to reform the way in which executions were carried out, and the results of this failure had been all too easy to see in the events of September 1800. But now there was a new determination to tackle the problem and bring the conduct of executions into line with their purpose:

Problematic though the utility of the death penalty may be, it is none the less certain that it can serve to deter others from committing serious crimes. . . . Yet the milder penal laws and the rarer pronouncements of death sentences by the courts indicate that it will gradually become unnecessary for non-military crimes with the progress of civilization. . . . However, precisely this rarity of executions prompts extra vigilance when one takes place, for now the public focuses its entire attention upon it, and the tiniest circumstance can often have the effect of diverting the impression which punishment should give in the wrong direction, or cancelling it out altogether, whereby the entire purpose of the punishment is frustrated.[4]

The major purpose of executions, in the eyes of the authorities, was to deter people from crime. This was to be achieved not least by getting them to regard

[4] GStA Berlin Rep. 84a/7781, Bl. 14.

the offender with 'revulsion'. Yet, as Friedrich Nicolai had complained in 1785, writing about Bavaria: 'Frequent executions do not help at all, rather, they do a good deal of harm, they have become mere spectacles for the people and make them even more unfeeling than before.'[5] The public, as many other commentators had complained, seemed to admire, or sympathize with the person of the criminal instead of feeling the revulsion and contempt which enlightened opinion considered proper.

Even the great philosopher Immanuel Kant, whose work was widely read within the German bureaucracy in the first half of the nineteenth century, took this view. People went to see executions, he thought, because they took pleasure in seeing someone in a worse situation than their own. Commonly, he said,

the people rush with tremendous enthusiasm to watch a malefactor being led out and executed, just as to a play. For the emotions and feelings which he expresses on his face and in his behaviour have a sympathetic effect on the spectators, and they leave—after these people have been frightened by the execution's power over their imagination (a power increased still further by its ceremoniousness)—a gentle but yet earnest feeling of fatigue, which makes them feel the pleasure in life which follows afterwards all the more strongly.[6]

Kant was no more in favour of abolishing the death penalty than any other German writer at this time. He thought Beccaria had advanced his theories 'from the participatory and enthusiastic sentimentality of an affected humanitarianism'.[7] Like Goethe, who thought that the abolition of capital punishment would lead to people taking the law into their own hands, he supported the idea of full retribution for murder, as for other crimes in proportion.[8] Kant believed that punishment could only be retributory. His philosophy did not permit it to be considered in terms of morality or utility. For Kant, unlike for Beccaria, punishment could only be defended in terms of its justice. 'The criminal law', he declared, 'is a categorical imperative.' While this made him argue on the one hand that capital punishment should only be applied to murder, it caused him on the other to demand that it be carried out every time:

Even if civil society should dissolve itself with the consent of all its members (e.g. if the people living on an island resolve to leave it and go their separate ways), the last remaining criminal in prison must still be executed, so that everyone experiences what his deeds are worth, and that the blood-guilt does not lie upon the people because it has not insisted

[5] Nicolai, *Beschreibung*, 762.

[6] Immanuel Kant, *Anthropologie in pragmatischer Hinsicht abgefasst* (Breslau, 1798).

[7] Idem, *Metaphysische Anfangsgründe der Rechtslehre*, 2nd edn. (Breslau, 1798), 232.

[8] Idem, *Metaphysik der Sitten*, Part II, in *Werke*, iv, ed. Wilhelm Weischedel (Frankfurt am Main, 1968), 455; see also Lucht, *Strafrechtspflege*, 41; and Johann Wolfgang von Goethe, 'Maximen und Reflexionen', nos. 110–11, in *Goethes Werke*, Hamburger Ausgabe, ed. Erich Truntz (Hamburg, 1949–55).

on this punishment, and therefore can be regarded as a participant in this public violation of justice.[9]

Even Kant's closest disciples found this view somewhat extreme. Nevertheless, his fellow philosopher Georg Wilhelm Friedrich Hegel, immensely influential as a teacher at the newly founded Berlin University in the 1820s, agreed that the punishment should fit the crime. Criminals, he thought, would not transgress if they did not, as rational beings, desire to be punished. Thus it was only right that they should be punished in a manner that adequately expiated the crime they had committed. Crime, he insisted in his dialectical fashion, was the negation of the law; punishment therefore could only be seen as the negation of the negation, a retribution that had to be equivalent to the offence in order to restore the integrity of the law that had been contradicted.[10] Many other influential voices also helped ensure that the abolition of capital punishment along Beccarian lines was never seriously considered by the bureaucratic judicial reformers of the early 1800s. The first review of Beccaria's work in Germany, published by the forensic medical scientist Albrecht von Haller in 1766, rejected it so vehemently that it even argued for the death penalty to be used in Germany on the same scale as it was in England, with trivial cases of theft leading to execution. Moses Mendelssohn, though less strong in his views, also argued against Beccaria in 1866. Even those who supported the Italian thinker's views in general, like Karl Ferdinand Hommel (known by some as 'the German Beccaria'), considered his rejection of capital punishment to be unjustified. The judge Viktor Barkhausen, who published a serialized commentary on Beccaria in 1776–7, considered that the death penalty should be replaced by the more useful employment of convicted murderers for medical and surgical experimentation, but since he saw death as the inevitable result, the difference in the end was little more than academic. Johann Gottlieb Fichte defended the death penalty in the same breath as he defended 'the noble Beccaria', arguing that a murderer had broken the social contract by his deed and returned to a state of nature, thus allowing the state to use its superior strength as a merely natural power and kill him in self-defence in order to stop him reoffending. Only a handful of commentators, like Johann Adam Kühn or Karl Häss, were bold enough to point out that since the crime had already been committed, the execution of the perpetrator by the state was not an act of self-defence but of revenge.[11]

[9]   Kant, *Metaphysische Anfangsgründe*, 196–9. See also Wolfgang Nauecke, 'Über den Einfluss Kants auf Theorie und Praxis des Strafrechts im 19. Jahrhundert', in Jürgen Blühdorn and Joachim Richter (eds.), *Philosophie und Rechtswissenschaft. Zum Problem ihrer Beziehung im 19. Jahrhundert* (Frankfurt am Main, 1988), 91–108.

[10]   Georg Wilhelm Friedrich Hegel, *Grundlinien der Philosophie des Rechts* (Berlin, 1821).

[11]   Kreutziger, 'Argumente für und wider die Todesstrafe(n)'.

No one at this stage was prepared to call for an end to punishments administered in public. Not even Beccaria had done so. Given the fact that judicial investigations and trials continued to be carried out behind closed doors, even after the ending of torture, a public affirmation of the authorities' success in apprehending the malefactor, and an open confirmation of the offender's guilt, were considered absolutely essential:

The deterrent element in capital punishment lies not in the frightful sight of a violent form of death, but only in the conviction that the criminal laws will be applied against the offender with unrelenting rigour. Doubt as to whether the legal punishment has actually been carried out is the first thing likely to provoke the ill-disposed to break the law, and this doubt, which the common herd is already inclined to nurture, would really take root if it were decided to carry out death sentences in secret. Contempt for the law and the growth of crime could easily result.[12]

Yet as they were currently being conducted, it was clear that public executions were failing to get this message across in the right way. The fundamental problem with which the bureaucrats were attempting to grapple was that the size of the crowd, the nature of the ritual, and the presence of various popular 'superstitions' all combined to focus an excessive degree of attention on the person of the executed criminal. They criticized

above all the adventurous ritual of the so-called public sentencing ceremony which has its origins in the dark days of violence and lawlessness, and contributed more than anything else to lending the whole business a theatrical air, and thereby encouraging people to gather and to make the day of execution into a popular festival: while it is going on, the numerous mass of spectators has eyes only for the external practices of the execution, and among these principally for the behaviour of the malefactor.[13]

The Prussian bureaucrats had long since lost all understanding of the crowd's concentration on the behaviour of the condemned person. Nor did they display any sympathy with the rituals and customs which accompanied the execution. In the later decades of the eighteenth century, their disapproval had focused on the person of the accompanying clergyman. Taking up these debates, an anonymous complainant wrote to Grand Chancellor Heinrich Julius von Goldbeck, the top legal official of the day, on 21 August 1800, claiming 'that the ceremonial and emotional atmosphere which always prevails now when an offender is led out, particularly his white clothing, his decorations, and finally all the ceremonies hitherto customarily associated with it', had awakened 'in some miserable people who have witnessed such a scene' the desire to kill someone so that they too could die in the same way.[14] In fact, this possibility had already been catered for in the Prussian General Law Code of 1794, which laid down that those committing a

[12] GStA Berlin Rep. 84a/7781, Bl. 15.   [13] Ibid., Bl. 14.   [14] Ibid., Bl. 9.

crime with the express purpose of being executed were to be perpetually imprisoned and given regular whippings for the remainder of their life.[15] But the continued complaints reflected a long-standing concern that the magico-religious and ceremonial aspects of the execution ritual created sympathy and admiration for the malefactor by constituting a process of absolution and sanctification. It was this problem that the zealous and determined Prussian reformers now began to tackle.

Fundamental to their enterprise was the bureaucrats' conviction, instilled into them since the days of Friedrich II, that the desired deterrent effect could only be achieved if the execution awakened 'contempt and revulsion' among the onlookers. It was patently wrong that the criminal's behaviour could arouse admiration 'among the ignorant herd'.[16] In accordance with these considerations, the Directors and Counsellors of the Berlin City Courts made eleven recommendations. First, as soon as the sentence of death was passed, the condemned person was to be isolated in a special prison cell, and all visits except those of 'officials and clergymen' were to be forbidden. Secondly, the 'distribution of popular literature' at executions was to be banned. As we have seen, observers like Nicolai thought this too frustrated the deterrent purpose of executions, and the Prussian authorities evidently agreed. Thirdly, 'the day of execution must not, to be sure, be kept secret, but at the same time it must not be brought unnecessarily to the public attention'. Here the authorities began to betray a fear of the mob which opened up a yawning contradiction in the very idea of public punishment itself. Nevertheless—a fourth point—crowds were to be discouraged by the holding of executions very early in the morning, at 5 a.m. in high summer, or shortly after dawn at other times in the year. Fifthly, the public sentencing ceremony was to be abolished. The objection that this might deprive the condemned of the opportunity of making a public retraction of the confession was countered with the rather complacent assertion that

our laws and judicial procedures protect the criminal sufficiently against forced and hasty verdicts. What damage could possibly be done to the court's dignity if some miserable criminal chooses this opportunity for a baseless retraction of his confession? Public order surely cannot be made to depend on the whims of such a person.

Next, the condemned were no longer to be dressed in white, but were to wear their own clothes—the shabbiest available, if there was a choice, and sackcloth if there was nothing else to hand—a stipulation soon rescinded on the grounds that sackcloth was in its own way just as theatrical as white. No longer was there to be a slow procession on foot to the place of execution; instead, the condemned was to be tied to a bundle of straw and transported in a cart, accompanied by a

---

[15] ALR II, Th. 20, §§ 831, 832.   [16] GStA Berlin Rep. 84a/7781, Bl. 11: Notiz, 23 Aug. 1800.

detachment of cavalry. The transport, it was emphasized, 'must take place quickly'. The scaffold was to be sealed off in advance by infantry, keeping the crowds well back. A ninth point laid down the most important condition necessary for preventing the public from sympathizing with the condemned: 'The executioner must do his duty as quickly as possible and without allowing the criminal time to let the onlookers observe his behaviour in the final moments.' The soldiers were to stay until the crowd had dispersed and all traces of the execution had been removed:

We regard the clearing-away of all traces of the execution as all the more necessary because, as is well known, coarse superstitions are practised with some of them, for example with the blood, and this seemed at least on the surface of it to be one of the principal causes of the disturbances that took place after the recent execution, next to the premature withdrawal of the troops.

Finally, an announcement was to be published, complete with a detailed description of the offender's crimes, certifying to the public that the execution had actually taken place.[17]

These recommendations were immediately put into effect in Berlin, confirmed by edict in 1805, and applied thenceforth to the whole of Prussia.[18] The state seemed to be acting now to impose its own interpretation of the meaning of capital punishment on a populace that had obstinately refused up to this point to accept it. If educated observers such as Nicolai had been horrified by popular attitudes towards executions in Bavaria, the rationalistic bureaucrats of the Prussian reform movement, with their drive to renew and strengthen the state by re-establishing its authority on a rational and secure basis, were equally appalled by the evident indifference of the crowd in the Berlin execution of 1800 to what they considered to be the event's proper meaning. Accordingly, they were determined to force the spectacle of punishment into a mould prepared for it by the state alone. Popular participation had to be reduced to a minimum, and everything possible had to be done to ensure that the state got its message of deterrence and retribution across. Offenders were not to be seen as suffering divine punishment, the playthings of fate and chance, but on the contrary as objects of secular justice, rightly administered by the authorities in the interests of all.[19] Only in this way could the spectacle of capital punishment be rendered effective once more in the fight against crime—a fight which was taken especially seriously by the authorities in view of the marked increase in theft convictions registered at this time.

[17] Ibid., Bl. 15–16; see also ibid. 7784, Bl. 70.
[18] Ibid., Bl. 61: Zusammenstellung der bei Vollstreckung von Todesurtheilen im Bezirk des Königlichen Kammergerichts zu Berlin zu beobachtenden Vorschriften.
[19] For parallel decisions in the Netherlands, see Spierenburg, *Spectacle*, 48.

b. 'Coarseness and Immorality'

These considerations were no more confined to the Prussian bureaucrats than was the general desire to rationalize and reform. Comparable measures were enacted at about the same time in other parts of Germany, often prompted by similar incidents. A fresh wind of judicial reform, led by the great jurist and penal reformer Paul Anselm von Feuerbach, now blew through the institutions of justice in Bavaria. The immediate reasons for reforming the practices customary in public executions at this point were painfully obvious. Fear of the mob was the moving force. By 1810, the authorities in Munich were openly apprehensive of the danger posed to law and order by public executions.

Since the execution of Johann Klobensteiner, currently a prisoner in the Falcon Tower, is to take place in the next few days, and is likely to bring a large crowd of people out from the city to the place of execution, it is necessary, especially in view of the currently prevailing insecurity, to provide special military and policing measures, to maintain order within the city and without, and to provide proper security for the property of the citizens.[20]

The document betrays the state's consciousness of the contingency of public order at a time of war and revolution. So too did an incident which occurred the following year in another Bavarian town, Augsburg, where the directors of the city court were alarmed by a number of 'excesses' that took place before and during the execution of a young Italian, Joseph or Giuseppe Antonini and his German wife Therese. The offenders' story, as it had come to light during the confessions they had eventually made under prolonged and repeated interrogation, might have been calculated to inflame the Romantic imagination and create the maximum sensation among the educated and the fashionable. The 30-year old Joseph Antonini was a Sicilian who had, he said, been captured by Algerian corsairs on a sea voyage to Naples when he was 11 or 12. On the voyage to the slave market at Alexandria, however, he had been rescued by a French ship, and he had subsequently served in the French army. Deported across the border by the French authorities on suspicion of theft, he had made his way from Mainz to Berlin, where in 1806 he had married a German woman four years younger than himself, Therese Marschall, daughter of a poor factory worker and according to popular repute a prostitute. They seem to have moved in the criminal underworld in Berlin, and to have been under suspicion of possessing stolen goods when they left the city for the south, accompanied by Therese's younger brother Karl, in 1809. It was at this point that the events which led to their eventual arrest and execution began.

[20] HStA Munich MJu 13065: Justizministerium to Innenministerium, 18 July 1810.

In Dresden the couple discovered a fashionably dressed young gentlewoman, Dorothea Blankenfeld, travelling to Vienna with a large amount of baggage. Inveigling their way onto her coach, the Antoninis joined her on the journey south, Therese dressed in man's clothing and disguised as a postillion, with the intention of murdering her and stealing her possessions, which included two thousand gold thalers. After several false starts, they finally succeeded in their plan after stopping for the night at a posthouse on the way to Augsburg. Drugging her with brandy laced with opium, they attacked Blankenfeld while she slept, and although she awoke and resisted, beat her head in with a four-pound mangle-pin. The deed was discovered shortly after their departure, and a swift messenger overtook them and alerted the police in Augsburg, where they were arrested on arrival at the city gate. Although the young Karl Marschall, who had been intended by the couple to take the blame, was spared because of his age and his remorse, Joseph and Therese were condemned to death and the verdict was confirmed by the King, on the advice of the jurist Paul Anselm von Feuerbach, who found the Sicilian a 'rascal' full of 'boundless guile, moral turpitude, and dreadful roguery' and his wife 'from childhood onwards, a wild, obstinate, wicked, and slovenly creature'.[21] As this language suggests, there was in his view no way of rescuing or reforming them.

Joseph Antonini fell ill and cheated the gallows by dying in prison. However, his wife survived to climb 'the bloody scaffold, where she died as she had lived, cheeky, and without feeling or regret'.[22] Although the execution itself went off without incident, the same was not true of the events that had preceded it earlier in the day, and between the time the verdict was confirmed and the sentence carried out. As the directors of the Augsburg city court reported on 22 July 1811:

To begin with, the cruelty of a murder carried out on a beautiful young girl was enough to make the murderers the topic of frequent, virtually daily debate; then the supposed handsomeness of the young Sicilian, and the lissomness of a young Berlin good-time girl, rendered him the object of curiosity among the female sex, and her the object of curiosity among the male.

The young and mostly aristocratic Bavarian army officers stationed in the town had managed to overcome the 'feeble resistance' of the gaoler and had paid frequent visits to Joseph Antonini in his cell before he died. Using the excuse that they had to be present to supervise the changing of the guard, they had also gathered in the corridor opposite Therese Antonini's cell and spoken with her on a number of occasions. 'Only after repeated requests on the part of the poor

[21] Paul Anselm Ritter von Feuerbach, *Merkwürdige Verbrechen* (abr. edn.; Frankfurt am Main, 1981), 55–78, quotes on 59–60.
[22] Ibid. 78.

sinner and repeated instructions to the key-master did these visits decline in frequency, on the last morning of her life.' As the verdict was read out in front of the town hall and the wand of office broken, a group of officers forced their way through the cordon of troops guarding her and 'crowded round her, enclosing her on all sides', and accompanied her in this way until she reached the scaffold, conversing with her along the way. There were even unconfirmed rumours that they had examined her body as it lay on the scaffold after the executioner had done his duty with the sword.[23]

The Antonini affair led to a new determination on the part of the Bavarian authorities to maintain order during executions. The Augsburg authorities had been forced to denude the town of police to assist at the event, since the cavalry, as they complained, were unavailable. They considered it necessary to provide proper military protection in future,

for a prisoner who has been condemned cannot be abandoned to arbitrary treatment by a public . . . that can obstruct his path at any moment in order to satisfy its curiosity; or that, according to its mood, either weeps for him, or abuses him and pelts him with dung. How easy it would thus be for society's outcasts to snatch their condemned comrade from the hands of the few accompanying bailiffs![24]

The proposals for better military protection soon became caught up in much more far-reaching reforms, which echoed the measures taken in Prussia a few years earlier. A consolidated set of rules governing the procedures to be followed was issued in 1814, after the promulgation of a new Bavarian Criminal Code the previous year. 'All ceremonial accompaniments to the prisoner, such as the procession, customary here and there, of city dignitaries, schoolboys, and the like, and in addition all singing of funeral hymns, are hereby forbidden.'[25] Similarly, in Walddürn in 1818 the authorities forbade the playing of music and singing during executions.[26] The Munich authorities also ordered the scaffold to be surrounded by troops, and the prisoner to be transported there in a cart instead of on foot. In addition, they tried to speed up the execution process itself by dropping the official warning read out from the scaffold not to harm the executioner, along with the executioner's customary request for approval of his work after the event. In these various ways they followed the Prussian authorities in shortening the ceremony, reducing the ritual aspects, and placing new barriers between the crowd and the condemned. On the other hand, the element of

---

[23] HStA Munich MJu 13065: Directores des Stadtgerichts Augsburg to King, 22 July 1811, and report of 28 June 1811 by the Königl. Bayer. Stadtgerichts-Assessor.

[24] Ibid.: Directores des Stadtgerichts Augsburg to King, 22 July 1811.

[25] StA Munich App. Ger. 5704: 'Was bei der Verkündung des Todes-Urtheils zu beobachten', 22 Feb. 1814.

[26] Eggler, *Waldstetter Mord,* 26.

publicity was unequivocally retained. Executions in Munich continued to be held on market days, and to be announced by a 'ceremonial announcement of the sentence' in public. The regulations still required that 'as soon as the head is severed from the rump, the executioner is to grasp it by the hair and show it to the people on all four sides of the stage'. And the ceremony was to be completed by a previously approved 'speech of religious admonition to the people', after which the head and body were to be placed without delay in a coffin and taken away for burial.[27]

Similar reforms took place in other parts of Germany too. In the Kingdom of Württemberg, the public sentencing ceremony was replaced in 1816 by a much simpler announcement of the verdict and sentence, and it was explicitly ordered that the malefactor should wear 'a fustian costume without any decoration'. The Hangman's Meal was abolished, although executioners were still allowed to claim it on their expenses. The custom of singing hymns on the way to the scaffold was stopped, and new security precautions were brought in, with the cavalry now attending every execution in order to prevent disturbances.[28] All this suggested a new level of concern on the part of the authorities at the danger which public executions were now seen as posing to public order. Measures such as those taken in Prussia, Bavaria, or Württemberg amounted to much more than a mere case of political neuroticism in an age of revolution. Just how sensitive artisans and guilds could be to any infringement of their honour at this period, when their livelihood was being undermined by war, blockade, and economic depression, and indeed their very existence was under threat from the rationalizing imperatives of bureaucratic reformers, was illustrated by an execution riot that took place in Erfurt in 1806. The courts had condemned one Johann Lätsch 'to the punishment of the wheel from the bottom up, and exhibition of his body upon the wheel'. The problem began when he frustrated their intention of punishing him by committing suicide on the eve of the execution. The authorities none the less pointed out that 'the intention of the law is that the sentence shall be carried out on suicides of this kind, as far as is possible, to serve as an example for the deterrence of others, and we are therefore enjoined to have the dead body of this criminal displayed upon the wheel at the place of execution here'. It was already clear that this unusual situation had put the authorities into something of a panic, and that they had decided to carry out the punishment as quickly as possible. Accordingly, they resolved to cut back on some of the more arcane ceremonial aspects of the occasion. It was this decision that led to trouble

---

[27] StA Munich App. Ger. 5704: 'Was bei der Verkündung des Todes-Urtheils zu beobachten', 22 Feb. 1814.

[28] Sauer, *Im Namen*, 23–5.

since it involved a clear infringement of the rights of some of the guilds. The local police chief reported that

At 8 o'clock the procession set off in the best order from the town hall to the place of execution, without the slightest disorder occurring. Upon its arrival there, it encountered a crowd of at least a thousand people, gathered round the wheel, which had already been set up, and after consultations with the commanding captain, I rode up with Herr Graberg [an official], and spoke to the people in order to try and make them give way; but the masons and carpenters, who were assembled there in a crowd, did not follow my instructions, but resisted them to such a degree, with hard, tempestuous words—above all the senior masters Sehling and Gramm saying that they had the right to stand there—that a veritable riot and tumult broke out.

For his part, Gramm claimed that it was an 'ancient custom' that the carpenters should set up the pole on which the body was to be displayed on the wheel:

I was standing with all the craftsmen . . . on the execution place, where we had to set up the pole with the wheel. We weren't ready yet, the masons were still doing the plastering, and the carpenters were holding the pole, and we still had to lead the ladder up against the wheel after the old custom, but we were stopped from doing this by the director of police. For as we were still standing by the wheel, the director of police dashed up to us on horseback with the words 'Get away, get away!'

'Mr Director of Police,' they shouted, 'we're not ready yet!' This was no 'riot', claimed Gramm, but merely a group of guildsmen insisting on their rights. And he pointed out in self-defence that his co-accused, the senior master, Sehling, was 80 years of age, and so could hardly be regarded as dangerous.

But other accounts portrayed their attitude as far less polite. As the police chief came riding up, they were said to have shouted 'We are citizens of Erfurt, what does he want?'; they had raised an 'extraordinary racket', and had 'shouted loudly and made a lot of noise'. So he called the military and cleared the square. Clearly shaken by these events, the police chief concluded:

I do not wish to paint an overdrawn picture of this spectacle, but I must underline the fact that these people would certainly have dared to cut me down from my horse with their picks and spades had military assistance not been at hand. . . . If I am not respected by the people as a police officer, I can predict that disorder and riotous assemblies will be the result.

The leaders of the disturbance were brought to account, and at the next execution in Erfurt, which took place in 1809, troops with fixed bayonets were present and the town hall was sealed off.[29] Here too, therefore, public order

[29] Sta Erfurt 1–1 XVI: Polizei-Sachen i. Nr. 17: notes of 9 and 10 Jan. 1806, 12 Sept. 1806, and 12 Nov. 1809; and the Untersuchung wider die Zimmermeister Christian Sehling, Johann Andreas Sehling, Johann Andreas Gramm, and the Zimmergesellen Andreas Sehrenberg and Georg Ludewig on 23 Jan. 1806. The wheel was not the one used at executions, but specially made, as was the pole, and untouched by criminal

considerations had been the main motor of reform. It was clear that the authorities in Erfurt had in fact panicked unnecessarily, thrown into uncertainty by the unexpected problem of having to punish a dead body. It was only a matter of time before such executions were brought to an end, as they were in Prussia in 1811.[30] Nevertheless, the disturbance had shown once more the difficulties inherent in trying to minimize or ignore the elements of popular participation which the execution ritual demanded. This was another instance of the way in which public disturbances at German executions were mostly triggered not by overt popular resistance to the state's punishment of offenders with whom people sympathized, but by departures from the pre-ordained ritual process, in this case on the part of the police chief and the town council. As the town council in Ansbach noted in 1798, when told by the Prussian authorities to prevent any recurrence of the 'unbelievable coarseness and immorality . . . which was revealed during the renovation of the ravenstone, in that not only was music continually being played throughout the three days of the operation, but people were actually dancing by the place of execution', abolishing traditional guild customs and ceremonies was bound to lead to disturbances. With a touch of weariness and resignation, the council explained 'that we know from experience that it has never been possible to make any headway in such matters in which craftsmen are involved, when any attempt to overcome such prejudices has been contemplated'.[31]

c. *Cultural Change and the Reform of Executions 1800–1835*

The nervousness shown by the authorities in Erfurt, as in Augsburg, Munich, and Berlin, in the early 1800s, reflected the troubled times in which they were living. Napoleonic armies were rampaging across South-Central Europe following their spectacular victories at Ulm and Austerlitz towards the end of 1805. State power in the region was severely shaken, and the role of artisans and sansculottes in the French Revolution was still fresh in everyone's memory. The guilds were in a state of crisis as well, both economically and politically. Up to this point, as the Erfurt disturbances indicated, public executions in Germany had always been far more than simple expressions of state power. They involved the whole community in a ritual process that combined elements of popular justice, communal obsequy, and hierarchical display. For most of the eighteenth

or executioner, so therefore without dishonouring effect at this point. For other aspects of guild rights at executions, in the Netherlands, see Spierenburg, *Spectacle*, 49.

[30] GStA Berlin Rep. 84a/7784, Bl. 63–4: Zusammenstellung der bei Vollstreckung von Todesurtheilen im Bezirke des Königlichen Kammergerichts zu Berlin zu beobachtende Vorschriften.

[31] Quoted in Oppelt, *Unehrlichkeit*, 569–73.

century, the mixture of sacred and secular that characterized the German public execution continued unchanged apart from its growing elaboration, and the potent combination of state power and communal ritual continued to find widespread acceptance on all sides, though with varying degrees of enthusiasm. Despite the penal and judicial reforms promulgated in a number of states under the influence of the Enlightenment, few attempts seem to have been made to alter the nature of the ritual process of public execution in this period. Kings, princes, and urban authorities seem in practice to have accepted the religious and magical aspects of popular participation in the event even if in theory they regarded them as irrational, superstitious, and unbecoming. The official understanding of public executions placed increasing emphasis during the eighteenth century on moral education as the primary purpose; but this concept was gradually becoming more secularized, and underneath the surface the state's confidence in religion as the guarantor of social and moral order was in decline. Other sanctions were coming to the fore, and an attack on the sacred elements in the execution ritual had been under way, as we have seen, since well before the end of the eighteenth century.

The disturbances of the early 1800s indicated that executions in Germany were increasingly causing public order problems for the authorities. A variety of influences was responsible, ranging from the attempts of the authorities themselves to restructure the execution ceremony along secular, Absolutist lines, reducing the religious elements and cutting down community participation, to the political, economic, and social upheavals taking place in Germany in the wake of the French Revolution and under the impact of the British industrial revolution on Continental economies. The behaviour of the guildsmen in particular had become less predictable. In this situation, the authorities were justified in worrying about the possibility that public executions would provide the occasion for hostile demonstrations by one element or another within the community, or even indeed by malefactors themselves. Even where community hostility to the condemned was taken as read, the orderliness of the execution process, now increasingly shorn of its religious connotations, could no longer be taken for granted. When trouble was feared, especially where the crimes of the condemned person were thought to have aroused strong popular disapproval, the authorities now began to distribute leaflets in advance warning people to behave with restraint. In Leipzig the town council printed 2,500 such leaflets on the occasion of the execution of Johann Christian Woyzeck, the unfortunate murderer immortalized in the play by Georg Büchner and the opera by Alban Berg. It banned people from climbing onto the roofs of the houses round the market-place where the execution was due to take place, adding that 'moreover, during the execution it is absolutely forbidden to place carts, barrels, and similar objects anywhere on the market-place or in the adjoining streets and alleys for spectators to stand on'. 'Order and calm' had to be preserved, and 'any impetuous pushing and shoving' strictly avoided.[32]

The authorities in Bremen were similarly worried in 1831 when the time came for the public dispatch of the serial poisoner Gesche Gottfried, because, as the Citizens' Assembly said,

The execution of a criminal whose punishment has aroused the public interest to a rare degree is likely to attract a mass of in part emotional and excited spectators, who would otherwise be far from easy to gather together in one place, and so it turns the maintenance of calm, decorum, and personal safety into a problem the satisfactory solution of which it would be difficult to guarantee by the usual means which the infantry of the line or even the part of the Citizens' Militia which is at the Senate's disposal would provide.

The whole of the Citizens' Militia was therefore ordered to turn out for the occasion, and a special poster was put up round the city in advance of the execution, banning carts and wagons from the streets and warning that it was expected 'that this earnest act of justice shall not be disrupted by outbreaks of coarseness and insensitivity, but will be executed with the proper calmness and orderliness'. Householders were told 'not to allow spectators to take up position on the gables or rooftops or other dangerous places on their buildings'. Furthermore:

3. Any forcible entry into the houses or buildings situated on the execution square or near the same is strictly forbidden, on pain of severe punishment, as is any excessive pushing and shoving on the execution place itself or on the way there.
4. The stations taken up by the armed forces, particularly the circle of troops to be drawn up round the scaffold, are to be strictly kept, and no spectator is permitted to dare to push through the circle. . . .
7. No one is allowed on pain of serious punishment to insult the offender in any way, either *en route* to the execution square or after she has arrived there, and it is also forbidden on pain of severe punishment to obstruct the executioner in the performance of the duty with which he is charged, or to assault him or his assistants should it—against all expectation—be unsuccessful.[33]

It was evidently no solemn ritual of expiation and redemption that was expected here. There were serious fears of crowd disorder.

The authorities were unable to see in the crypto-materialist religiosity of the traditional ceremony anything but a bundle of inappropriate superstitions which evinced a regrettable tendency to treat the malefactor as a martyr. Their imagination reduced the motives of the crowd to a collection of insensate lusts and

---

[32] Sta Leipzig L XII G 23b vol. ii, Bl. 243 (23 Aug. 1824).
[33] StA Bremen 2.-D. 18. k.: Bürger-Konvents-Verhandlungen am Dienstag, den 19. Apr. 1831, 151; and 'Bekanntmachung' of the Polizeidirektion, 18 Apr. 1831.

hatreds. Public execution in their view was designed to stamp a rational appreciation of the consequences of crime and immorality upon an uneducated and
impressionable, and therefore emotional and volatile, 'mob'. This led in turn to
fresh fears of disorder and hastened the process of restructuring the execution
ceremony. And in the early 1800s there was growing evidence that divisions in
the community were beginning to deepen. The reform initiative taken by the
Prussian bureaucracy both recognized the early adumbrations of class formation
that had developed in town and country under the impact of the long price rise
of the eighteenth century, and hastened the process of transition from a status-
bound 'society of orders' to the class-based society of the nineteenth century.
Ironically, by reducing or abolishing guild privileges and by dismantling the
hierarchical structures of the execution procession, the state was reducing the
execution crowd to the chaotic, formless 'mob' which was the source of its
anxieties in the first place. Beyond this, too, the bureaucratic reform movement
ultimately formed part of wider social processes. The gradual emergence of a
middle class, imbued with the bourgeois values of order, decency, and self-
restraint, demanded the discursive construction of the masses as the embodiment
of everything that it was trying not to be: unrestrained, disorderly, indecent,
liable to violent and inexplicable changes of mood. Caught between the desire to
impress popular feelings, and the fear of arousing them, the authorities were
conscious that anything they did to heighten the impression made by the public
execution on the crowd would also run the risk of stirring up its emotions in ways
that might prove dangerous.

The new reforming spirit reflected the influence of significant cultural changes
which had begun in the second half of the eighteenth century, changes of which
the new, rationalistic thought of the Enlightenment was only one aspect. This
was a period of growth and prosperity in European society. The great famines
and crises of mortality that had devastated the populations of Europe in previous
centuries were disappearing. A long-term price rise had begun, which was removing growing numbers of peasant farmers—the vast majority of Europe's population at this time—from the margins of subsistence, while at the same time
creating an underlying crisis in the artisan population of the towns. Professions
such as medicine and the law were becoming better organized, more numerous,
and more prosperous. Above all, life expectancy among the better-off classes,
though still far lower than the average of today, was at last beginning to increase;
a few diseases, such as smallpox, were beginning to be conquered; and standards
of health and hygiene were slowly starting to improve. For the well-off, for the
aristocracy at court and on their estates, and for substantial merchants, financiers,
professionals, and master artisans in the towns and cities, death was beginning to
lose its terror in the late eighteenth century. As studies of wills and similar

documents in France at this time have shown, such people were becoming markedly less pious in their attitude to death, and were dropping the religious clauses from their testamentary provisions.[34] During epidemics, they had already begun to turn from providentialism and religious intercession to medical and administrative prophylactics, while sickness and disease were increasingly seen as natural phenomena rather than as the wages of sin. Suicides were looked upon with more sympathy, as weak and desperate rather than wicked and vicious.

Along with this incipient secularization of death came the beginnings of its retreat into the family. Towards the end of the eighteenth century, family relations were acquiring a new sense of emotional closeness in the upper and middle ranks of society, and this was reflected in the gradual decline of the public death, with friends, neighbours, and clergymen all present to witness the last ceremonies and conduct the last dialogues with the dying person. Instead, death took on a hushed intimacy, in which the doctor was beginning to replace the priest as the principal outsider admitted to the family home.[35] This did not mean, however, that death was becoming an embarrassment. On the contrary, the nineteenth century was to witness an extraordinary flourishing of funerary culture, with commercial enterprise taking advantage of the desire for the display of mourning by providing an ever more elaborate paraphernalia of death, from black-edged stationery and black-coloured crêpe for wrapping door-knobs in, to the massive graveyard monuments which are still such a feature of Victorian cemeteries today. The rise of the professional undertaker, paid to provide a funeral with all the trappings, from black horses to pull the hearse to black ostrich feathers to be carried by the mutes, ministered to this new level of necrolatrous ostentation.[36] All this display was intended to advertise the social standing of the deceased's family, and at every stage, from the death-bed scene in the family home to the final, ceremonious interment in the family mausoleum, it was the family rather than the community which was signified as the social context within which death now took place.

With the growth of the intimate nuclear family also came the emergence of new concepts of gender divisions and new, more elaborate definitions of the masculine and feminine 'character' at this time. As we have seen, these concepts played a material part in the ending of capital punishment for infanticide in the last quarter of the eighteenth century. But they also had a wider importance in the history of executions. To the mind of the educated bureaucrat, the crowd

---

[34] Michel Vovelle, *Piété baroque et déchristianisation en Provence au XVIIIe siècle* (Paris, 1978); Pierre Chaunu, *La Mort à Paris: XVIe, XVIIe et XVIIIe siècles* (Paris, 1978). See also McManners, *Death*.

[35] Roy Porter, 'Death and the Doctors in Georgian England,' in Houlbrooke (ed.), *Death*, 77–94, esp. 84–7.

[36] See Ruth Richardson, 'Why Was Death so Big in Victorian Britain?', in ibid. 105–17, esp. 105–7.

began to appear, in part at least, as 'feminine' in character: normally passive, but emotionally labile, irrational, and superstitious, and easily roused to fits of temper. Arguments, derived ultimately from Beccaria, about the transience of the effect of watching an execution on the spectators, were inserted into the new discourse of gender. Writers began to note with disapproval the presence of women and children at public executions, not just because they thought the spectacle indelicate, but also because they considered it too strong for their nerves, and liable therefore to cause emotional disturbance. The rational effect of deterrence was aimed principally at men. After all, once capital punishment had been deemed inappropriate for infanticide, over 90 per cent of executions were carried out on men, and so the crimes which they were intended to deter were overwhelmingly crimes committed by men. New notions of female delicacy also led in 1833 to the Prussian state banning the corporal punishment of females over 10 years of age.[37] Gradually, the attendance of women and children at public executions was discouraged.[38] In Württemberg and Bavaria, the judicial reforms of the early nineteenth century dropped the requirement for choristers to accompany the malefactor to the scaffold.[39] In Bremen in 1831, a poster put up around the town three days before the execution of the mass poisoner Gesche Gottfried noted, among other things:

Parents and guardians are earnestly admonished to keep their under-age children away from the place of execution and not to expose them thoughtlessly to the dangers which must necessarily threaten them when a great crowd of people comes together. Women and persons of a weak disposition are also reminded not to venture into the crowd.[40]

By the middle of the century, the town council in Ansbach was urging that measures be taken to tell 'the schoolboys who are always strongly represented on such occasions . . . that they must at least keep away from the procession to the execution square and the crush that goes with it.' The Bavarian government ordered that schools should open especially early on the day of an execution, and that any children playing truant should be heavily punished. Pupils were to be kept in class all morning, so that they 'thereby be prevented from attending the coming execution'.[41] Yet while executions continued to be carried out in the open, there was no way that the authorities could wholly prevent women and children from attending. Imposing a greater distance between the execution and the crowd was one step towards greater control; speeding up the ceremony

[37] Koselleck, *Preussen*, 657.
[38] For this development in the Netherlands, see Spierenburg, *Spectacle*, 96–8.
[39] StA Munich App. Ger. 5704: 'Was bei der Verkündung des Todes-Urtheils zu beobachten', 22 Feb. 1814; Sauer, *Im Namen*, 23–5.
[40] StA Bremen 2.-D. 18. k: Bekanntmachung der Polizei-Direction, 18 Apr. 1831,
[41] Oppelt, *Unehrlichkeit*, 139.

and divesting it of some of its ritual aspects was another. All these reforms, however, created as many problems as they solved.

d. *Reducing the Variety of Punishments 1794–1839*

On 13 July 1812 Christoph Horst, born on 22 March 1783, and Friederike Delitz, born on 12 October 1791, were found guilty in Berlin of a series of devastating arson attacks. Altogether they had caused some 300,000 thalers' worth of damage and the death of at least ten people. During their career of crime, they had composed and published songs about their deeds, threatening destruction to the whole city and expressing a contempt for officialdom and morality that could almost be called revolutionary:

> You gentlemen, you heed my word
> And keep Berlin well under guard:
> I'm telling you, it shall be known,
> Berlin is going to be burned down!
>
> So let us now be blithe and gay,
> Let's drink a glass of wine today.
> I'll never leave this place again
> Until the fire's consumed Berlin![42]

The official investigation of the couple's career of crime filled over 300 files. There could be no doubt about their fate. Prussian law laid down that those convicted of such crimes were to be burned alive. Horst and Delitz were accordingly sentenced to be dragged to a pyre on an oxhide and there 'brought from life to death by fire'. As had been common practice since the 1740s, it was also ordered, however, that they should be 'strangled in a manner not visible to the spectators', and to this end the executioner ordered two large cotton nightcaps to be provided for them, under which this operation could be carried out. In effect, they were to be hooded while they were being executed. A large crowd was expected at the event. For this reason, executioner Kraft gave his opinion 'that the square by the judgment-scaffold is unsuitable because the field on one side is sown and the bit on the other side is too small and has unfenced gardens so close to it that they would be totally ruined by the spectators for this year.' The authorities agreed therefore to hold the execution in the north of Berlin, in the large open space on the borders of Wedding known as the Jungfernheide. It took place on 28 May 1813. The two malefactors were transported on a cart to the vicinity of the execution place, then they were laid on an oxhide and dragged the

---

[42] Heinrich Ludwig Hermann, *Kurze Geschichte des Criminal-Prozesses wider die Brandstifter Johann Christoph Peter Horst und dessen Geliebte, die unverehelichte Friedericke Louise Christiane Delitz* (Berlin, 1818), 115.

last 150 metres to the foot of the pyre. Here a large crowd was waiting, with many fathers holding their children up to get a good view.

On being released from the oxhide, Horst was said to have invited his mistress to climb up the steps to the pyre 'with a gallant motion of his hand', and when he himself reached the top, he continued his jaunty behaviour by throwing his cap into the air 'with a satisfied "Halloh!"' to the crowd. Now, the report continued,

Delitz asked the judges if she could say a few more words to the public. She was granted this request. From the top of the pyre, she then gave the following speech: 'I've certainly led a dissolute life and deserve to be punished, but I'm too young a girl to deserve the death penalty!' Hereupon she struck her breast a few times with the flat of her hand, raised her eyes heavenwards, and cried several times: 'God have mercy on my poor soul!' Horst also held a 'speech', in which among other things he admitted that he was a great criminal who had brought poverty and misfortune to many people and doubly deserved his punishment. Delitz was now bound to the chair, but when it was Horst's turn, he tore himself free, dashed over to Delitz and kissed her a last time. Then he went calmly back to his place. After they had been bound tight, the condemned had their heads covered with the aforementioned hoods and the pyre was lit. The strong wind fanned it into flames in a few minutes.

In a short time the pyre, with the bodies, was completely reduced to ashes. Nothing was left of the two malefactors, and the crowd broke up and went home, or off to begin their day's work.[43]

This turned out to be the last occasion on which arsonists were burned at the stake in Berlin. Everywhere else, the punishment had also effectively ceased by this time. The behaviour of the two malefactors, Horst and Delitz, still conformed in large measure to the customary dramaturgy of executions, with religious fervour, at least on her part, and humble acceptance of the sentence, at least on his; but the fact that both of them showed signs of rebelliousness and 'cheekiness' also suggested that this traditional pattern of behaviour was now beginning to be disrupted as well. The condemned could no longer be relied upon to play the game. Incidents of refractory behaviour were beginning to multiply. In 1824, for instance, one offender spent the journey to the scaffold in Weimar insulting the two clergymen travelling with him in the tumbril, causing them, as a report of the incident primly recounted, 'inconveniences which compromised the dignity of their sacred office'. Duke Carl August of Saxe-Weimar was obliged to proclaim on 12 May 1824

[43] Hermann, *Kurze Geschichte*, 115 and BA Potsdam 61 Re 1/1770, pp. 111–12: *Berliner Tageblatt*, 28 May 1913. See also Ernst Rosenfeld, 'Die letzte Vollstreckung der Feuerstrafe in Preussen zu Berlin am 28. Mai 1813. Auf Grund amtlichen Materials zusammengestellt', *Zeitschrift für die gesamte Strafrechtswissenschaft*, 29 (1909), 810–17.

that the person of the accompanying clergyman, whether the offender walks to the execution square or is transported there on a tumbril, must be protected from the importunities and improprieties of the criminal, and in the latter case must never, as recently happened, be driven with him in a *single* tumbril, but separately, in a *decent* carriage, so that he can still give him courage and consolation at the place of execution through the ministrations of religion.[44]

Such behaviour would have been almost unthinkable half a century before. Yet now it was becoming increasingly common.

Not only were the authorities worried about incidents like these, they were also increasingly subject to feelings that a ceremony such as burning at the stake was simply inappropriate for the purposes for which punishment was intended. Punishments that re-enacted the crime, such as had been common in the early modern period, were no longer comprehensible in an age of judicial rationalism. Indeed, burning at the stake for arson seemed to contradict the careful system laid down in the Prussian General Law Code of 1794 of grading the punishment according to the severity of the offence. It rested on a different principle altogether, so it is not surprising that in the process of judicial reform it was phased out not only in Prussia but in other parts of Germany at this time as well.[45] Neither burning at the stake nor any of the other punishments that had survived from older times into the Code of 1794 was in fact put into practice after the early nineteenth century. Burial alive, drowning, quartering, pulling out flesh with red-hot tongs, dragging to the scaffold on an oxhide, and many other variants on and additions to the death penalty listed in the *Carolina* of 1532 were now definitively abandoned. This left the sword, the axe, and the wheel as the only methods of execution in most parts of Germany, together with hanging in Austria after the reintroduction of capital punishment there at the beginning of the century.

During the early nineteenth century the sword too came under attack. The officials who undertook in the early nineteenth century the task of imposing their concepts of rationality on the German execution were aware of the fact that the commonest occasion of crowd disturbances in the past had been a wrongly aimed blow by the executioner. Mistakes seem to have been growing in number at this time, especially after the sharp decline in infanticide condemnations towards the end of the eighteenth century. In the early modern period every town in Germany had had its executioner, and there had been not a few in rural districts as well. So numerous and so frequent had been the tortures and punishments they

[44] StA Weimar B 2402: Oberkonsistorium report, 30 Mar. 1824, and rescript of Duke Carl August, 12 May 1824.
[45] The last public burning in Münster took place in 1798. See Gimpel, 'Nachrichten', 168.

had had to administer that they had never been short of something to do. But in the second half of the eighteenth century this situation began to change. As we have seen, the number of executions decreased and their variety became less marked. Corporal punishment declined. Torture ceased altogether. Moreover, with the beginnings of urban growth after the end of the Napoleonic Wars, additional tasks such as cleaning out the town drains were now increasingly beyond the executioners, and began to be taken over by municipalities. The emerging idea of the paternalistic 'police state' left urban authorities dissatisfied with the previous contractual basis on which such services had rested, and led them to organize them centrally under the aegis of city police departments.[46] All this posed serious problems for executioners.

Up to the eighteenth century, the system where the duties of executioner had been carried out by the local knacker had worked reasonably well. The assumption that the two offices were combined lasted well into the nineteenth century. In France the Revolution had abolished the feudal status of executioners at a stroke and had turned them into salaried officials.[47] In Germany the same process took many decades and was still not complete by the middle of the nineteenth century. Nevertheless, the role played by executions as an important source of income for such men was clearly over by the end of the eighteenth century. At the same time, some of the rights of the knackers themselves were being eroded. Thus in 1788 the executioner in Bruchsal complained 'that the farmers are withholding their dead animals from him and burying them themselves; in this way, an important part of his income is being lost to him'.[48] In 1794 an ordinance allowed Bavarians to sell old and useless horses on the open market instead of, as earlier, having to surrender them free of charge to the knacker. The knacker and executioner Xaver Vollmayr complained as a result that he was finding it hard to make ends meet:

If I were adequately paid as an executioner I would gladly abandon the knackery, but I mainly live off the latter, and on account of this I have to keep a servant with wages and board, and two horses, for the service of the parish, and from time to time stock up with expensive new horses, tubs, and equipment, and run a great risk of sickness and death to my horses and people when cattle diseases are raging. . . . Thus I must resign myself to closing down the knackery and taking the beggar's staff together with my wife and children and going completely to rack and ruin.[49]

On the other hand, as Bavarian financial officials pointed out in 1810, the hereditary nature of the dual office, coupled with the general decline in the functions of both, meant that some executioners, such as Abraham Nacker of

---

[46] StA Bremen 2.-D. 19. f.: Reinigung der heimlichen Gewässer etc.; see also the details of contracts provided in Schuhmann, *Scharfrichter*, 209–10.

[47] Lenôtre, *Guillotine*, 27.   [48] Böer, *Scharfrichter*, 3.   [49] Schuhmann, *Scharfrichter*, 195.

Lindau, were being paid as much as 155 thalers a year by their local authority and provided with a free house and garden for doing practically nothing, and certainly not for carrying out any executions.

In Nacker's case, perhaps, this was just as well. It would hardly have been wise to have called upon him to wield the sword at an execution, since he was 80 years of age by this time.[50] Elderly executioners were by no means uncommon, since they clung to office in the hope of earning a little extra income. Only when they showed distinct signs of 'bodily feebleness', as the Hanoverian executioner Renzhausen, in his thirtieth year of office, did in 1818, were they forcibly retired.[51] In 1816 Bavarian officials noted that most of these unemployed executioners were leading an 'absolutely wretched existence' and would certainly fall as a burden on the parish, with their large families to be supported by the poor relief as well, should they be deprived of their emoluments altogether.[52] The Bavarian Finance Ministry, noting on 28 June 1811 that fewer executioners were now required than in earlier times, suggested that most of them be pensioned off and only a minority retained. Acting on this suggestion, the authorities proceeded to collect all the available information on the Bavarian executioners, a task that was evidently far from easy, since it took over five years to complete. By 1816 they had established that there were some 146 knacker–executioners in Bavaria, many of them with their own official residence.[53] Sorting out the pensions and payments to be made to these men or their widows took the Bavarian authorities almost another decade. They eventually managed to reduce the number of executioners to nine, located in the larger towns and cities. Even this, however, was insufficient to keep pace with the decline in their functions. Only five out of the nine were said by the Finance Ministry in the 1840s to be 'genuinely employed . . . as executioners'.[54]

In the Hanseatic city of Bremen, a commission of enquiry reported to the Senate in 1822 that 'the office of executioner is completely redundant, God be thanked, and will always be redundant, since in emergencies we can always engage executioners from the hinterland'. The petition of the widow of the recently deceased local executioner, a member of the Göppel family, a far-flung and long-established dynasty of north German executioners, for the appointment of her son as the city's executioner, was rejected. The family had already fallen on hard times, since the city fathers had sold off its free accommodation in 1817,

---

[50] HStA Munich MF 21592: Tabellen über die Zahl, Namen, Alter, dann Pensions und Gehalts-Genusse an Geld und Naturalien der im Isarkreis befindlichen Scharfrichter und Wasenmeister, 6 Dec. 1810.

[51] Sta Hanover A 1209, Bl. 3: Anstellung des Nachrichters Joph. Heinr. Christoph Hartmann 1818.

[52] HStA Munich MF 21592, Steuer- und Domänen Sektion, 'Allerunterthänigster Antrag', 28 July 1816.

[53] Ibid., memoranda of 28 June 1811 and 31 July 1816.

[54] See ibid., MF 21593, for the details.

compensating the executioner with no more than 200 thalers a year,[55] and a number of other privileges had also been withdrawn.[56] But the Senate remained adamant. Indeed, it soon sought to dispense with the executioner's services altogether. An execution was now such a rare event, it seemed, that its occurrence was regarded by the authorities as an 'emergency'. 'The duties', they added, 'which were customarily connected with the knackery here, such as skinning, cleaning the closets, etc., can in any case be transferred outside to a so-called half-master, and in this way the salary of an executioner, which has hitherto amounted to 200 T[halers], can be saved.'[57] From 1827 the city engaged an executioner from elsewhere on the rare occasions that it needed to.[58]

In the late eighteenth and early nineteenth centuries, therefore, there were in effect many more executioners around than there were executions to perform. Nevertheless, the beheading of a malefactor was still carried out by the responsible executioner in the town or court district where the trial and condemnation took place. With many fewer jobs than before and the same number of people to do them, it was not surprising that the executioners themselves found it ever more difficult to acquire the necessary experience at their trade to become really proficient at it. Most of them were, in short, woefully out of practice by the beginning of the nineteenth century. Concrete evidence of their inexperience was provided by an investigation carried out in the Grand Duchy of Baden in 1836, which revealed that in this medium-sized and not very heavily populated state, a good deal smaller than Bavaria, in which the executions carried out between 1812 and 1847 numbered a paltry twenty-three, there were no fewer than forty-three official executioners available to perform them. Of these, only sixteen actually had any experience of decapitating offenders at all, while the hereditary nature of the post meant that a good many were also quite elderly by contemporary standards. Joseph Ritter, in Konstanz, was 66 and had not executed anybody since 1802, although on enquiry, reported the investigating official, Ritter 'believes himself still strong enough for such a task'. His relative Georg Ritter, in Überlingen, had not been active as an executioner for thirty-two years. Paul Schönbein, veteran of three executions, was 70 years of age, but even he, anxious for a little extra income, 'claims however still to feel strong enough for such a duty'. A few of them still drew regular pay as executioners even though it was decades since they had executed anybody by this time.[59] None of

[55] StA Bremen 2.-D. 19. k. 3. n.: Der Scharfrichter: dessen Wohnung (*passim*).

[56] Ibid. 2.-D. 19. k. 3. m: Sophie Göppel to Senat (Rath), 23 Dec. 1816.

[57] Ibid. 2.-D. 19. k. 3. a: J. C. Goepel, 1817: Commissionsbericht, genehmigt in der Senatssitzung am 3ten July 1822 (Nr. 3).

[58] GStA Berlin Rep. 84a/9397: Schwarz to Justizministerium Hanover, 24 Feb. 1860.

[59] GLA Karlsruhe 234/6772: Der Vollzug der Todesstrafe –Tabelle über die im Grossherzogthum Baden angestellten Scharfrichter (1836).

Baden's forty-three executioners had wielded the sword more than four times, so it was obviously impossible for any of them to have gained any significant experience of the job.

Thus it is not surprising that there were so many mistakes with the sword in the early nineteenth century; a far higher proportion than had been recorded in previous centuries.[60] What could happen in such circumstances was graphically illustrated by an incident that took place in the Grand Duchy of Hesse in 1820, when the regular executioner Johannes N. was called upon to behead a malefactor with the sword. As the responsible judicial official reported:

Although now the man nominated for the task, J.N., had already carried out several executions of this sort, including just a few years previously that of H. and M. decently and without error, and although furthermore the same had just said on the 23rd of this month, when the judicial official had asked him in the presence of four village mayors whether in view of his advanced age he still trusted himself to undertake executions, that he had not yet noticed even the tiniest diminution of his powers, and if necessary would trust himself to cut off fifteen heads in one session without problems, and that he would be ashamed if an outside executioner was called in to carry out the task, nevertheless this man had the misfortune to strike somewhat too high, and so to cut off the head not with the first stroke, but with the second, which followed after it with lightning speed. However, it is sufficiently comforting to know that it was not merely by appearances, but also according to the assurances of the physician in attendance, that life must already have completely departed after the first stroke, since the head had been cut through from behind as far as the chin. The blame for this accident evidently lay in the fact that after the malefactor had been seated on the judgment stool and his eyes bound, and the executioner had taken up position behind him with drawn and raised sword, the clergy delayed too long with their blessings, and so the otherwise so hale executioner got tired and lost strength.[61]

Here it was age rather than inexperience that seems to have caused the problem. Action was obviously required to put the hiring of executioners onto a more satisfactory footing. While the authorities in various parts of Germany decided in the early nineteenth century to rationalize the execution service and reduce the number of executioners, this task would obviously take years and possibly even decades, given the complicated nature of the tenures and contracts involved. In the mean time, as mistakes grew in number, they decided to blame not the workman, but his tool.

This seemed a particular possibility when the method used was decapitation by the sword. The backhanded horizontal blow had to be aimed from behind at

[60] Spierenburg, *Spectacle*, 14–15, 240, argues that mistakes were committed all the time, but is only able to present fifteen examples from three and a half centuries in Germany and the Netherlands, beginning in 1464. For two more examples of mistakes made when executioner Göppel was drunk, in 1745 and 1756, see Sta Hanover A 1198, *passim*.

[61] Quoted in Krämer, *Mord*, 138.

the side of the neck, at a space of no more than a couple of centimetres, between the shoulders and the chin. It also required a considerable amount of force to sweep the head off at a single stroke. The combination of precision and power was particularly difficult to achieve and needed practice as well as great steadiness, muscularity, and skill. In 1811 an execution in Breslau provided a graphic illustration of this point. On 6 March the senior executioner, from Liegnitz, proved unable to carry out a decapitation properly:

His first stroke went too high and only caused a little blood to flow, his second missed altogether, and at the same time the offender's blindfold fell off, and as the latter tried to look round, the third stroke was struck and once more missed. At this point the Breslau executioner snatched the sword from him and carried out a fourth stroke, which finally separated the head from the rump to the extent that it only needed a fifth stroke to complete the severance.

While this grisly pantomime was proceeding, the crowd 'let out a yell of anger', and it was reported that 'the Liegnitz executioner could only be protected against the rage of the mob with difficulty'. It was clear that mistakes of this kind could 'easily lead to an act of public disorder and affray'. So the Prussian authorities decided to replace the sword with the axe, adding that this was also in consideration of 'the considerable insecurity of the execution of death sentences by means of the sword, whereby it is possible for the criminal to suffer a greater punishment than he is supposed to according to the law and the judgment of the court'.[62] 'The public', noted the Breslau Police President on 17 July 1811, in all probability referring to no more than the opinion of local notables in the town, 'recognizes in the abolition of the punishment of death by the sword renewed evidence of the humanity of our legislation.'[63] The axe was more likely to be accurate because it did not require as much skill as the sword. A massively heavy weapon, weighing eight and a half pounds, with a short, two-foot handle and a huge blade a foot in width,[64] it merely had to be dropped horizontally onto the neck of the offender. No great physical force was required, merely the strength to lift the axe into position; and mistakes do indeed seem to have been much less common than with the sword after its introduction in Prussia in 1811.

Similar developments took place in other parts of Germany. In 1827 it was reported that an execution with the sword had taken place in Heidelberg 'in unfortunate circumstances that were particularly terrifying for the offender, in that it required repeated strokes to sever the head from the rump'.[65] There had, indeed, been at least five executions in recent times in the Grand Duchy of Baden

[62] GStA Berlin Rep. 84a/7784 Bl. 67: rescript of 10 June 1811; ibid. 7781, Bl. 168, 172.

[63] Ibid. 9268 Bl. 12: Extract aus dem Bericht des Polizei Präsidenten zu Breslau vom 17. July 1811.

[64] Ibid. 7784 Bl. 67: Rescript of 12 July 1811.

[65] GLA Karlsruhe 234/6774, 1: Justizministerium memo of 16 Nov. 1827.

at which similar mistakes had occurred. Such errors caused 'scandal and outrage in the face of the people'.[66]

If this mode of execution should cause a criminal to suffer no more than a moment longer than is necessary for carrying out the death sentence, this still constitutes an aggravation of the punishment, by which humanity and justice itself are injured. All the more detrimental is the impression which such tormenting executions make on the people, who are swept away by sympathy for the criminal instead of being deterred.[67]

'The obligations of humanity', it was argued, 'demand that a criminal who has been condemned to die be brought from life to death in the easiest and least painful manner.'[68] But this was not the only reason for considering a replacement for the traditional method. 'A further consideration counting against executions by the sword lies in the fact that they are carried out directly, by the hand of a fellow human, and so the executioner appears in the people's eyes too much as a butcher, which is contrary to his human dignity.'[69] The best way of avoiding this problem was seen by some officials in Baden to lie in the introduction of the guillotine—a striking example of how its reputation as a humane method of execution had managed to survive even the rigours of the Terror of 1793–4. As for the political resonances which the Terror had left, it was argued that the guillotine's misuse in France for acts of injustice would not be confused by people in Baden with its proper use for acts of justice.[70]

A commission was set up to prepare legislation to reduce the suffering of criminals in a number of ways, including the abolition of torture and of corporal punishment.[71] But in the end it could not bring itself to recommend the introduction of the guillotine, because

this guillotine was devised by the French Reign of Terror, in order to sacrifice as many people as possible in a short time to various passions and to the rage of party; and indeed several thousand innocent people were brought like beasts to the slaughter in this manner, and France even had to mourn the disastrous crime of the murder of its King and his relatives, killed in the same way. These scenes of cruelty which occurred in a neighbouring country are still so fresh in our thoughts that the introduction of this murder-machine would reawaken painful and unpleasant memories, and so your commission believes that the introduction of the said machine should be postponed to a time and a generation in which the recollection of these atrocities has faded away.[72]

---

[66] Ibid. 15: Oberhofgericht-Beschluss Nr. 3739.

[67] Ibid. 23: Hofgericht/Gutachten des Medizinalreferenten, 11 Dec. 1827.

[68] GStA Berlin Rep. 84a/7781, Bl. 290–301 (Preussische Gesandtschaft, 21 Mar. 1828, and Kommissionsbericht, here Bl. 295).

[69] GLA Karlsruhe 234/6774, 11: Gutachten betreff der Einführung des Fallbeils, statt der Enthauptung durch das Schwert (copy).

[70] Ibid. 23: Hofgericht/Gutachten des Medizinalreferenten. 11 Dec. 1827.   [71] Ibid.

[72] GStA Berlin Rep. 84a/7781 Bl. 290–310 (Preussische Gesandtschaft, 21 Mar. 1828, and Kommissionsbericht, here Bl. 295.) See also GLA Karlsruhe 234/6774, Bl. 12: Gutachten betreff der

At this sensitive moment, therefore, the plan was dropped, although in the Rhineland, which had been under French revolutionary and Napoleonic law for some years before its incorporation into Prussia after the Congress of Vienna in 1815, the guillotine continued in use, along with the rest of the legal and penal innovations introduced by the French, such as trials in open court. Others objected to the guillotine on different grounds. The Medical Board in Stuttgart brought a number of relevant general points to bear on the debate:

The main reason for preferring the sword and the axe assuredly lies, from the point of view of the dignity of the procedure and the achievement of an impression of seriousness, in the fact that the offender remains more active, and the executioner's business provides a more direct impression of the workings of the arm of the law, than with the guillotine, where the offender remains passive and appears as an object, and the whole process is contrary to human dignity in many respects.

Balanced against this, however, was the greater security of the guillotine. Mistakes were more likely with the sword. And mistakes caused 'sympathy and horror or even indeed outrage' on the part of the crowd. Indeed, the executioner 'is even in danger from the spectators if he makes a mistake'. The major point to bear in mind was the impact of executions on 'the people' and the use of the sword, especially when it went wrong, was bound to remind them of the slaughterhouse.[73] All this outweighed the memories of the French Revolution in the minds of at least some officials.

In the search for more humane methods of execution, enthusiastic inventors filled the files of German Ministries of Justice with their suggestions in the course of the first half of the nineteenth century. As early as 1830, the Bavarian Ministry of Justice had inspected a model 'beheading machine' constructed by a locksmith in Landshut. It seemed less than reliable, however, because it involved decapitating the offender sitting up. This had been precisely the objection that had been raised to the use of the sword earlier in the century. An upright position might be more dignified, but it led to mistakes because it robbed the blade of the guiding power of gravity.[74] But this did not stop the flow of death-dealing inventions coming in to the Justice Ministries of the German states. In 1839, the Prussian Ministry of Justice also gave lengthy and detailed consideration to a similar device, 'Dr Messerschmidt's beheading machine'. The town doctor of Naumburg, Heinrich Messerschmidt, was an enthusiastic supporter of capital punishment, but was critical of the way in which it was carried out:

Einführung des Fallbeils, statt der Enthauptung durch das Schwert. The guillotine, of course, was devised and made the legal means of execution in France well before the Reign of Terror. See Ch. 3*e*, above.

[73] GLA Karlsruhe 234/6774, 65–8: Bericht des Medizinal-Kollegiums Stuttgart, 6 Aug. 1834.

[74] StA Munich App. Ger. 5704, Justizministerium to Apellationsgericht für den Isarkreis, 20 July 1830, Anlage: Protokoll der Appellationsgericht-Commission, 24 Feb. 1831.

The *sword* must be guided by human hand, and so there have often been cases where repeated strokes were needed before the neck was hit in the right place. The *axe* was chosen in order to avoid this. But this also has to be wielded by a human being, and so it is just as uncertain. Then an executioner is not a coarse or unfeeling person, and he cannot be indifferent to the task which he has to carry out, that of killing another human being, and he must, even more so the first time he has to perform this duty, be in a state of nervous excitement, which he may well attempt to overcome and gain some courage by drinking hard liquor, so that in this state, just at the moment when he has to strike the deadly blow with the axe, he may easily *miss his target* because his hand is shaking, or his arm gets cramped and twitches, or he is overcome by giddiness or stumbles.

In these circumstances, the guillotine might seem the logical choice. But Messerschmidt objected to it in the strongest terms, not only because of 'the deterrent memory, that they were once in France the murder-weapon of a bloodthirsty *Robespierre* and *Marat* and their accomplices' but also because by binding the offender to a board it treated him 'like a dumb animal'. His own machine, which he dubbed the *Collumpön* (from the Latin *collum*—neck— and *poena*—punishment) he regarded as humane and appropriate to the seriousness of the act. But in trying to avoid treating the offender with indignity, it allowed him too much freedom of movement. The Prussian Ministry of Justice, after three years' debate, rejected the *Collumpön* as impractical.[75] In the early 1840s the Ministry of Justice in Baden considered and turned down a similar 'execution machine'.[76] Twenty years later another ingenious device was submitted, once more without result, this time to the Hanoverian authorities, with the aim of avoiding, as its originator claimed, both the 'cruelty' of the hand-held German axe and 'the Germans' revulsion at the murder-machine of the French, the guillotine'.[77] Even at this late stage, therefore, almost half a century after the Terror, the political associations of the guillotine still remained remarkably powerful.

In Bavaria, the association of the guillotine with the French Revolution was still too strong for it to be introduced even when it was advocated by so influential a judicial reformer as Paul Anselm Feuerbach. The model Bavarian Criminal Code of 1813, largely drawn up according to Feuerbach's precepts, rationalized capital punishment by abolishing all the previously used means of execution save decapitation. Unfortunately the Code neglected to specify the

[75] GStA Berlin Rep. 84a/7782, for this discussion. See also Heinrich Messerschmidt, *Ueber die Rechtsmässigkeit der Todesstrafe durch Enthauptung und über die bis jetzt gebräuchlichen, aber verwerflichen Verfahrungsarten beim Enthaupten; nebst genauer Beschreibung einer unter dem Namen* Collumpön *neu erfundenen, allen vernünftigen Anforderungen entsprechenden Enthauptungs-Maschine* (Weimar, 1840).

[76] GLA Karlsruhe 234/6774, 131–3, 'Die durch Clemens Wezler von Saulgau erfundene Hinrichtungs-Maschine betr.', 11 Dec. 1840.

[77] GStA Berlin Rep. 84a/9397, submission of 12 Feb. 1859. This file was later incorporated into the files of the Prussian Ministry of Justice when Hanover was annexed by Prussia after the war of 1866.

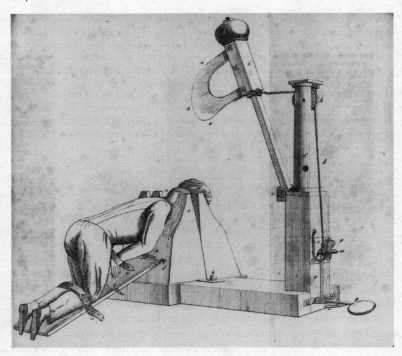

F IG. 16 *Dr Messerschmidt's* 'Collumpön'. A local doctor's plan for a humane beheading-machine which would avoid the unfortunate political associations of the French guillotine. It was one of a number of such inventions submitted to the Prussian Ministry of Justice in the course of the nineteenth century. The Ministry gave it lengthy consideration in 1840 but rejected it because of its obvious impracticality.

means by which the decapitation was to be carried out. Faced with insurmountable objections to the guillotine, Feuerbach prompted King Maximilian I to agree in 1810 'that because of so many unsafe instances of execution by the sword it is now time to abolish it and bring in execution by the axe, as in Denmark'. Surprisingly perhaps, however, the executioners objected to the axe, arguing conservatively, when interviewed by officials on 28 July 1810, 'that in many cases the axe is as unsafe as the sword, and if the offender has a very short neck, completely impossible to use'. So after the introduction of the Criminal Code in 1813 it was simply assumed that the principal method previously employed would continue to operate, and the idea of introducing either the guillotine or the axe was dropped.[78] The executioners' touching faith in the superiority of the traditional method of decapitation proved ill-founded. In the following decade, from 1814 to 1823, Bavarian officials subsequently reported that 'the executioner missed his stroke in *six* executions', and it was suggested 'that these six executions were more or less a torment for the offender and repulsive to the public'. Several of these events were said to have been of 'a truly dreadful character', and it was often unclear whether the first blow had actually succeeded in killing the condemned person. The most notorious of these cases of 'mishandled execution' took place in 1823:

At the execution of Johann Scheid in Aschaffenburg, for example, the first stroke cut the condemned man so deeply in the shoulder, from behind, that he rose up with a loud scream and fell over backwards, whereupon, after he had rolled over on the ground, his head was cut off from behind. Executioner Kaiser, who was responsible for this mishap, has died of a nervous fever as a result, and the investigating judge is seriously ill.

The Bavarian monarch was subsequently moved to protest that it seemed that condemned malefactors were being subjected to an '*aggravated*, tormenting death that fills the people with outrage and revulsion' through such methods, despite such kinds of death sentence having long since been abolished.[79] Nevertheless, such was the conservatism of the Bavarian judicial administration in the Restoration period, and its obstinate refusal to undertake any reforms during the *Vormärz* decades leading up to 1848, that the sword continued to be used as the normal method of decapitation in the south German kingdom, as it did in the most conservative states in other parts of the German Confederation, such as Hanover, further north.[80]

e. Paradoxes of Reform

Meanwhile other reforms were in progress too. In particular, judicial authorities all over Germany moved in the early nineteenth century to end the exposure of criminals' corpses on the gallows. As the police chief in Landshut wrote to his superiors in Munich on 4 May 1808: 'The ill-starred times of terrorism are over, but their misshapen monuments, gallows, and scaffolds still insult the bright eye of the wanderer and carry his mind involuntarily back to the days when the

[78] HStA Munich MJu 13066: Allerunterthänigster Bericht des Staats-Ministeriums der Justiz an Seine Majestät den König, den Vollzug der Todesstrafe betreffend, 20. v. 1854; Anon., *Die kgl. Bayer. Staatsminister der Justiz*, 62–3.

[79] HStA Munich MJu 13067: Justizministerium to King, 13 Nov. 1854.

[80] StA Bremen 2.-D. 18. 3: report of 28 Apr. 1786.

hangman was one of the state's busiest servants.' Why, he asked, did they have to stay there? These 'portraits of terror', he wrote, were hardly necessary to deter people from criminality, unless it was thought that they were naturally so inclined. Education in the schools was far more likely to produce the desired effect. The zealous police chief reminded his superiors that he had already asked them to provide for the removal of the hated monuments two years previously. 'Men of generally accepted knowledgeability', he wrote, 'have criticized them in their writings and argued that it is incompatible with the principles of the present to have the gallows as the first thing one sees on approaching every important place.' It simply did not correspond to 'the humanity which is now in charge': and indeed, following this initiative, orders soon followed for their widespread demolition.[81] Three years later, in 1811, King Friedrich of Württemberg ordered the dismantling of permanent gallows and ravenstones and the ending of the practice of exposing malefactors' corpses. Henceforth, the bodies of the condemned would be taken to the anatomy schools or buried in a special graveyard, while executions—now running at fewer than ten a year in the kingdom—would be carried out on temporary scaffolds erected *ad hoc*.[82]

The Prussian Ministry of Justice also decided in 1811 to cease the practice of exposing the corpses of malefactors. In 1810 the workers hired to repair the scaffold in Berlin had 'made it an explicit condition that the poles and wheels situated in the vicinity be removed, together with the bodies displayed on them, so that the repulsive sight of these objects is no longer before their eyes'.[83] The Police President in Breslau noted that the scaffold in his town, situated as usual outside the gate, was 'on a very busy road, and the houseowners there had to live for several weeks with the terrible stink of the body displayed on the wheel'. It was, he said, unfair to expose them all the time to the 'revolting sight' of rotting corpses. 'So many thousands of the local inhabitants had come for a look', he said, that they were constituting a real disturbance to the peace of the neighbourhood. Indeed, the numbers were so great that the local paper 'suggested, with ghastly wit, that a bar should be opened there to provide refreshments for the visitors'.[84] The King himself declared in 1810 that 'the exposure of bodies on the wheel is part of a time-honoured judicial practice and cannot be regarded as an aggravation of the death penalty'.[85] But the complaints from Breslau convinced the Ministry of Justice officials that the practice should

[81]   HStA Munich MJu 18016: Königl. Polizeidirektion Landshut to Kgl. Landesdirektion von Bayern, 4 May 1808.

[82]   Sauer, *Im Namen*, 23–4.

[83]   GStA Berlin Rep. 84a/9268, Bl. 1: Oberbürgermeister Berlin to PJM, 1 Nov. 1810.

[84]   Ibid. 7781, Bl. 12: Extract from Zeitung des Polizei-Präsidenten Streit zu Breslau, 17 July 1811.

[85]   GStA Berlin Rep. 84a/7781, Ibid., B. 153: Friedrich Wilhelm III to Kammergericht Berlin, 22 Sept. 1810.

be ended on grounds of public health.[86] Quickly implemented in Prussia, this order was followed some time later in most of the other German states, if indeed they had not abandoned the practice already. In any case, in some areas the decline in the incidence of capital punishment meant that the gallows themselves began to fall into serious disrepair. In Leipzig, for instance, it was reported in 1821 that the

> ravenstone situated in front of the Grimmaischer Gate here, together with the said gallows there as well, is in such a poor state of repair that both of them must soon be partly demolished, partly renovated, because there is concern that passers-by, especially children, who often use it as a playground, might be killed by falling masonry.[87]

The fact that children were accustomed to play on the ravenstone suggested not only that bodies had long ceased to be displayed there, but also that the site had by now lost its former terror for the popular mind. The dangers of falling masonry, and the escalating costs of repairing these structures, led to the scaffolds outside many German towns being pulled down in the course of the early nineteenth century.

These developments reflected a wider change in sensibility that was taking place at this time. Already in the later eighteenth century an increasing number of municipalities in Western Europe had begun to abandon the burial of the dead within the urban precincts and to create new cemeteries outside the city walls, reflecting not only the overcrowding that was accompanying the beginnings of urban expansion and population growth, but also a feeling on the part of officialdom and citizenry that the smell of putrefaction that frequently emanated from graveyards was obnoxious, especially in the summer months, and dangerous to health. With the discovery of oxygen and the beginnings of a new bourgeois sensitivity to odour, expressed in the emergence of the perfume industry, people were beginning to experience smells in a new way, and bad smells were increasingly linked to 'miasmas', from which disease and debilitation were thought to emanate. They were associated in the middle-class mind above all with the unwashed masses, from whom the bourgeoisie was now making strenuous efforts to distance itself.[88] It was the sight as well as the smell of the rotting corpses of malefactors to which people were now objecting. The new bourgeois sensibility was founded among other things on a concealment of bodily functions from the public gaze. This was the age when bourgeois fastidiousness reached its greatest heights: the age when sex and excretion, illness and

---

[86] Ibid., Bl. 205, 207, 208: Erlass of 19 Oct. 1811.

[87] StA Leipzig L XII G 23b vol. ii, Bl. 197–200: Bericht vom 29. 10. 1821.

[88] Alain Corbin, *Pesthauch und Blütenduft. Eine Geschichte des Geruchs* (Berlin, 1984). For the removal of cemeteries outside town walls, see Ariès, *The Hour of our Death*, 470–96.

death became not only private as activities but also unmentionable in public except in terms of elaborate euphemisms. The exposure of malefactors' corpses on the public gallows offended these new sensibilities profoundly. The dishonouring function which had been its principal *raison d'être* was now obsolete and evidently quite forgotten by the officials who demanded its cessation. It is scarcely surprising, therefore, that the practice was effectively abandoned by the beginning of the 1820s.

Major changes had taken place in the administration of capital punishment by the beginning of the 1840s. The traditional public execution had largely been robbed of its ceremonial, symbolic, and ritual aspects, and popular participation had been drastically reduced. Yet so far no one in Germany had seriously suggested that capital punishment was wrong in principle. Nor had anybody dared to argue openly that executions should not be held in public. Many of the reforms had been explicitly justified in terms of humanitarianism, but nobody seemed to doubt that those who fell victim to the sword, the axe, or the wheel were richly deserving of their fate. Nevertheless, the number of executions carried out in Germany fell fairly steadily in the first few decades after the Restoration of 1815. At the height of the reactionary regime imposed on the German Confederation by the Austrian chancellor Prince Metternich, in the five-year period 1818 to 1822, the annual average of condemnations in Prussia stood at twenty-one and executions at seven. It remained at a similar level for the next five years, from 1823 to 1827, with an annual average of twenty-one condemnations and eight executions. In the next five-year period, however, from 1828 to 1832, spanning the first European outbreak of liberal and nationalist revolutionary activity, condemnations averaged twenty-three a year, but executions fell to an annual average of only five. The annual average of executions fell in the next five-year period, 1833–7, to four, while the figure for condemnations stayed roughly the same, at twenty-two. In the following period (1838–42), the annual figures stood at twenty-four condemnations and six executions. In the mid-1840s, from 1843 to 1847, the annual condemnation figure rose significantly to thirty-three, while the annual execution figure rose slightly, to seven.

These were relatively low figures by general European standards. In England and Wales, for example, with a population (at around 16 million) roughly comparable to that of Prussia, the number of death sentences passed from 1815 to 1830 was some five hundred times greater. From 1816 to 1820, some 5,853 capital sentences were passed in England and Wales, and 518 of them were carried out: from 1821 to 1825 the figures were 5,220 and 364; from 1826 to 1830, 6,679 and 308; from 1831 to 1835, 4,984 and 207. That makes an annual average of death sentences over the whole period from 1816 to 1835 of 1,137 in England and Wales compared to an annual average of twenty-one in the Kingdom of Prussia.

Even after taking into account the fact that well over 90 per cent of all death sentences passed in England and Wales were never carried out, therefore, it remains the case that sixty times as many people were executed as in the Kingdom of Prussia over this period. In Prussia between 1818 and 1827 one person was executed a year for every 1,200,000 inhabitants of the kingdom, while in England and Wales the comparable figure for the period 1904–11 was one for every 153,000. Two-thirds of those hanged in England and Wales in the 1820s were guilty of property crimes, and only one-fifth of murder. England and Wales adhered to the 'Bloody Code' because of a traditional fear that a regular uniformed police could become an instrument of despotism, and the consequent use of the terrorism of the death penalty as a substitute in a capitalist society where property had an extremely high value; with the creation of Peel's Metropolitan Police and the county police forces in the 1830s, accompanied by the expansion of the prison and penitentiary systems, and the growing security of the social order after the 1832 Reform Act and the expansion of the political nation, came also the repeal of a large number of capital statutes and a sharp decline in the number of executions. Already in 1831–5 the number was less than half of what it had been in 1816–20; by the 1840s it had fallen much closer to the European norm, comparable to the number of executions in France, which was thirty a year in the decade 1831–40 and thirty-four a year in the following decade.[89] In Prussia, Absolutism and a highly organized policing system had allowed the state to reduce the number of capital offences in the Enlightenment, as we have seen; while the slowness of the transition from a neo-feudal, hierarchical, status-based society to a capitalist, class-based society meant that crimes against the person were still regarded as more serious than crimes against property in the early nineteenth century. Thus of the 657 people sentenced to death from 1818 to 1847, some 247, or 38 per cent, were condemned for simple murder, ninety-one, or 14 per cent, for aggravated murder (i.e. committed in the course of a robbery), and eighty-eight, or 13 per cent, for manslaughter. Eighty-one, or 12 per cent, were sentenced to death for arson, where a death had been caused as a result of the fire. Ninety-six, or 15 per cent, were condemned for infanticide. One person was condemned for duelling, again involving a homicide. Altogether, 604 out of the 657 death sentences, or 92 per cent, were for homicide of one kind and another. Only thirty-three, or 5 per cent of the condemnations, were for theft, and these were no trivial acts of stealing, but highway robbery involving serious injury to the victim. Twenty people, or 3 per cent of the total, were condemned for coining, and one for high treason (this was Heinrich Ludwig Tschech, from Brandenburg, who attempted to assassinate the King of Prussia in 1844). All

---

[89] Düsing, *Abschaffung*, 27–8.

this contrasted strongly with the far greater use of the death penalty, and its concentration on property crimes, in England and Wales.[90]

The gap between death sentences and executions in Prussia, though dramatically smaller than in England and Wales, also reflected the role that the royal clemency was now playing in the administration of capital punishment. Once new law codes had effectively restricted the death sentence to murder and treason, imprisonment had become available as an alternative to the scaffold, and capital punishment had become limited enough in scope for every individual case to be reviewed without clogging up the machinery of judicial bureaucracy, princes and other sovereign authorities in Germany, advised by their legal officials, began to apply the right of reprieve, the power over life and death, in a systematic way, as a real and symbolic instrument of sovereignty.[91] Unlike in England and Wales, where aristocratic and gentry patronage operated in a very extensive way to secure the reprieve of the vast majority of the many thousands who were condemned, the decision in Prussia and the other German states was made almost exclusively by the monarch and his advisers in the royal administration. The operation of this right, as the figures show, was quite extensive. The proportion of condemned offenders executed in Prussia fell from 46 per cent in 1818–22, to 35 per cent in 1823–7, 18 per cent in 1828–32 and 14 per cent in 1833–7, before rising once more to 27 per cent in 1838–42 and falling back to 22 per cent in 1843–7.[92] These fluctuations were solely due to the application of the royal right of commuting death sentences into life imprisonment. The slight increase over the 1830s perhaps reflected a heightened fear of social disorder in the period when the Revolution of 1848 was brewing. Overall, therefore, it seems that royal clemency was exercised much more freely in the relatively liberal 1830s and after than it had been in the reactionary aftermath of the French Revolutionary and Napoleonic Wars. The commutation of death sentences may in detail have reflected the moral and legal judgments of judicial officials in Berlin on the individual circumstances of particular cases. But seen in this broader perspective, as the supreme symbol of the power of the sovereign over his subjects, it reflected a development that was essentially political: the determination of the leading

[90] For the execution figures for England and Wales, see Gatrell, *Hanging Tree*, app. 2, pp. 616–19. For Prussia, see GStA Berlin Rep. 84a/8143, Bl. 70–1, 79–80, 96–7, 104–5, 120–3, 126–9, 134–5, 144–5, 152–3, 161–2, 175–6, 195–6, 213–14, 218–19; and ibid. 8144, Bl. 5, 10–11, 22–3, 26–7, 45–6. See also the Statistical Appendix, below.

[91] For the prehistory of this, see. P. Frauenstädt, 'Das Begnadigungsrecht im Mittelalter: Ein Beitrag zur Geschichte des Strafrechts', *Zeitschrift für die gesamte Strafrechtswissenschaft*, 17 (1897), 887–910. See also Karl Schué, 'Das Gnadenbitten in Recht, Sage, Dichtung und Kunst. Ein Beitrag zur Rechts- und Kulturgeschichte', *Zeitschrift des Aachener Geschichtsvereins*, 40 (1918), 143–386, esp. 171–3 and 186.

[92] See below, Statistical Appendix, for the sources and comments on their reliability and variants. In this case, the higher figures for condemnations have been used. See also n. 90 above.

men in the state to assert either the state's authority, as in the 1820s, or its liberalism, as in the 1830s and to a lesser extent the 1840s.

In other parts of Germany rates were roughly comparable. Austria registered an average of ten executions a year from 1803 to 1848 (compared to twenty-eight condemnations), Saxony seven in the period 1815–38, Württemberg two a year from 1816 to 1848, Hanover four a year from 1841 to 1848, and Baden four a year from 1829 to 1848.[93] In the Kingdom of Bavaria the effective restriction of capital punishment to homicide offences by the Criminal Code of 1813 brought about a decrease in the number of condemnations and executions. In the decade 1818 to 1827 there were seventy-two condemnations and thirty-four executions, or 47 per cent. In the following decade, however, out of sixty-three offenders condemned to death, only fourteen were executed, or 22 per cent, less than half the figure for the earlier decade. By the 1830s executions in Bavaria were running at not much more than one a year. In the decade 1838 to 1847, the number of condemnations fell still further, to fifty-five, while executions totalled only six, marking a further dramatic fall in the proportion of death sentences carried out, this time to no more than 11 per cent. In the years 1847 to 1849, as the Bavarian throne tottered under the impact of financial crisis, sexual scandal, political incompetence, and social revolution, the death penalty was quite explicitly used as a means of intimidating the populace and symbolizing the government's determination to maintain order. In these three years alone, no fewer than sixty-five people were condemned to death in the south German kingdom, more than in all the previous ten years put together. The government's relative impotence, however, was signalled by the fact that only three of these condemned offenders, or less than 5 per cent, were actually executed in these years. Here was clear evidence for the use of mercy as an instrument of power.[94] If a government wished to signal its determination to crack down on crime and disorder and to brook no opposition to its policies, what better way of doing so than to consign the majority of capital offenders to the block? On the other hand if, perhaps under liberal pressure, a government wished to signal its humane and benevolent intent, an increase in the number of capital offenders granted the royal clemency was a simple and striking way of doing so. Throughout the nineteenth century and beyond, the number of executions mirrored with astonishing accuracy successive waves of liberalism and authoritarianism in German history. For the individual offender, of course, this fact meant that life or death depended not just on the circumstances of the particular case but on the general political context as well.

[93] Düsing, *Abschaffung,* 26.
[94] HStA Munich MA 93516: Die Anwendung der Todesstrafe in Bayern, mit statistichen Listen, i; see also the relevant lists in the archival *Findbuch* to the Ministry of Justice files.

In a more immediate sense, the operation of clemency reflected not the arbitrary operation of petitioning and patronage, but a fairly systematic application of current views in the governing élite about the threat posed to society by various types of capital offence. Not one of the ninety-six women sentenced to death for infanticide in Prussia between 1818 and 1847 was executed, for example; only two out of eighty-one persons convicted of arson were executed, mainly because intention to kill had been proven. No one who had been sentenced to death for robbery, coining, or duelling went to the scaffold in Prussia in this period. On the other hand, 113 out of the 247 offenders condemned to death for murder did suffer execution, a rate of almost 46 per cent. Of the eighty-eight capital sentences for manslaughter twenty-eight (32 per cent) were carried out. The offenders most likely to lose their heads were those convicted of robbery with murder. Sixty-four of the ninety-one people condemned to death for this offence, or more than 70 per cent, were executed during this period. Clearly, therefore, the death penalty was in no sense a deterrent for the majority of offences to which it applied, since it was clear to all that it was extremely unlikely to be carried out. This policy reflected not only élite attitudes to crime but was also grounded in popular cultural perceptions. Execution for infanticide, as we saw in Chapter 4, had relatively little popular support, and from the 1770s it was increasingly regarded as inappropriate by the élites as well. Beheading for arson and robbery was similarly unlikely to win widespread backing. Murder, on the other hand, especially when carried out in furtherance of a robbery, was widely abhorred, as the folk-song record indicates, and was generally accepted as a crime worthy of death. The exercise of royal clemency could act as a means of maintaining hierarchy and order not least because it reflected popular as well as bureaucratic attitudes in its operation. Hierarchy and order were based on gender as well as status and class. Although death was still the penalty for infanticide in the Prussian General Law Code of 1794, newer notions of gender, largely absent from the Code, dictated that women were weak creatures easily led astray and subject to violent fluctuations of emotion. They were perceived in most cases as posing a minimal threat to the social order. Over the period 1818 to 1847, 26 per cent of death sentences passed in Prussia were meted out to women, but only 10 per cent of those executed were women. 36 per cent of men sentenced to death in Prussia were executed (190 out of 530), while only 12 per cent of women were (21 out of 171). Even if we remove infanticide from the statistics, we still find women being treated more leniently. Only seventeen of the fifty-three women sentenced to death for murder, for example, or 32 per cent, were executed, while 96 out of the 194 men sentenced to death for the same offence, or 49 per cent, took the march to the ravenstone. Other capital offences were also heavily male-dominated, with no women at all sentenced to death for manslaughter, robbery, or coining, and only three women out of a total of ninety-one offenders sentenced to death for robbery with murder.[95]

Some good examples of how clemency decisions were taken in practice were provided by the Bavarian judicial reformer Paul Anselm Ritter von Feuerbach, father of the philosopher Ludwig Feuerbach and great-uncle of the popular painter Anselm Feuerbach. Paul Anselm von Feuerbach made his principal mark on legal history as the author of the Bavarian Criminal Code of 1813. But he became widely known outside legal circles as the author of another work—the *Narrative of Remarkable Crimes, Based on Official Documents*, published in two volumes in 1828–9. These were conceived as literary narratives of capital crimes in early nineteenth-century Bavaria, with character-sketches of the perpetrators, after the example of the famous series published by the Parisian lawyer Pitaval in 1792. Such collections fed the fascination of the Romantics with the violent and the macabre, with the passions that led individuals to transgress moral and social norms. But Feuerbach's stories betrayed their origin in the detailed notes which he had prepared on the cases in question as he had drawn up his recommendation for (or against) reprieve to the Bavarian monarch some years before. His account thus allows us to examine some of the criteria which determined the exercise of clemency in this period.[96]

The first and most obvious of these was social hierarchy. If the victim of the crime was lower down the social scale than the perpetrator, a reprieve was on the cards; the more so if the offender had led a previously blameless life. In the case of Josef Auermann, a 'blameless man and citizen, who did not gamble, was charitable to the poor, friendly, obliging, and ready to be of service to everyone', who killed a former servant who was demanding a substantial sum in unpaid wages, Feuerbach argued that the death sentence was excessive, even if legally correct:

To assist the inadequacies of the law in its application, to redress with wisdom the misproportion between the legal sentence and the culpability of an individual malefactor, between the unbending severity of the unchangeable general law and the changeable mutability of individual blame, and so to reconcile legality with justice—this power rests in the hands of the sovereign, in the form of the right of clemency.

In Auermann's case the misfit between crime and punishment was particularly crass because the murder had been unpremeditated, committed under the influence of drink, and in response to a series of 'insults to his honour' which the

[95] As in n. 90, above.
[96] Gustav Radbruch, *Paul Johann Anselm Feuerbach—Ein Juristenleben* (Vienna, 1957); Ludwig Feuerbach, *Anselm Ritter von Feuerbach's Leben und Wirken, aus seinen ungedruckten Briefen und Tagebüchern. Vorträgen und Denkschriften* (2 vols.; Leipzig, 1832); Feuerbach, *Aktenmässige Darstellung*; see also the selection edited by Rainer Schrage in the Insel Taschenbuch series (no. 512): Feuerbach, *Verbrechen.*

FIG. 17. *Paul Anselm Ritter von Feuerbach (1775–1833)*. Author of the Bavarian Criminal Code of 1813, adviser to the Bavarian monarch on clemency for capital offenders, and writer of a celebrated study of crimes and criminals, Feuerbach was the most influential criminal jurist of the first half of the nineteenth century. A firm supporter of capital punishment, he was instrumental in replacing the arbitrary principle of 'special deterrence' aimed at individual offenders, with a fixed scale of punishments relating to particular crimes and based on the principle of 'general deterrence'.

perpetrator had had to endure from a social inferior. The crime did not reveal inner passions such as 'violent anger . . . desire for revenge . . . greed . . . selfishness . . . frivolity . . . lethargy' which would be a danger to society. 'Auermann', wrote Feuerbach, 'does not belong to the category of those criminals whose

depraved spirit looks to commit crime from an inner drive and internal inclinations and passions.' He had confessed and repented. Accordingly, he was recommended for clemency and spared.[97]

Clemency thus depended not only on the nature of the offence, but also on the
legal adviser's judgment of whether or not the offender was of good character,
upon the status differences between murderer and victim, and upon the motives
with which the deed had been committed. Among the latter, 'avarice' was
especially frowned upon because it implied a challenge to the social order. It was
not least for this reason that robbery with murder was particularly severely
treated by clemency officials such as Feuerbach:

Murder for gain belongs by its very nature to the most dangerous types of murder. For
it derives from a passion which rules over men to a greater degree, and with greater power,
than any other, namely self-interest. Leniency and mild forbearance would be most
dangerous here, and would break through the dam which protects society from this
powerful passion seeking its satisfaction from taking the lives of others even more
frequently than it does already.

Feuerbach consistently recommended execution for such cases.[98] 'Envy and
hatred', two more emotions which he regarded as extremely dangerous to the
social order, could lead to the denial of reprieve even in cases where no one had
been killed, as in that of Lorenz Simmler, convicted of setting fire to his older
brother's farm on his return from the wars as a penniless beggar. Simmler's
previous career of gambling, drinking, and fighting showed him to be, wrote
Feuerbach,

a very malicious person, sunk deep in every vice. The entire history of his life is evidence
for his coarseness and moral decadence. . . . The motives for his last crime are among the
wickedest and most dangerous that can ever appear in degenerate human natures. Merely
in order to cool off his vengefulness and envy in the misfortunes of others, he set light
to his paternal house; and the persons whom he was sacrificing to his passion, who are
they? His own relatives, his own brother.

Not only had Simmler attacked his older brother, he had, as Feuerbach repeatedly emphasized, committed a kind of parricide by destroying his parental home.
Although only property and animals had been destroyed, Simmler was therefore
denied a reprieve and executed.[99]

Feuerbach could also be tough on offenders who had killed in order to evade
their social responsibilities—for example, a man like Johann Hahn, who killed
his pregnant mistress in order to avoid having to marry her.[100] He was angered by

---

[97] Feuerbach, *Aktenmässige Darstellung.* i. 341–57.
[98] Ibid., i. 202, 54–96, 156–70, 171–85, 186–202.
[99] Ibid., i. 203–17. For the prevalence of this crime in Bavaria, see Regina Schulte, 'Feuer im Dorf', in
Reif (ed.), *Räuber*, 100–52.
[100] Feuerbach, *Aktenmässige Darstellung*, i. 228–44.

the light sentence of confinement imposed by the courts upon a priest who had murdered in order to avoid being exposed as a compulsive womanizer and father of several children, even though his female victims were of a lower status than himself.[101] In the case of Andreas Bichel, an otherwise blameless character who killed two young women of similar status from sexual motives, Feuerbach declared that the man's quietness derived from 'a cowardly feminine spirit. . . . Cowardice', he remarked, 'is always combined with guile, and related most intimately to cruelty.' Images of the dangers of uncontrolled femininity were particularly prominent in Feuerbach's account when it came to assessing female capital offenders such as Anna Margarethe Zwanziger, a housekeeper and midwife in her late forties arrested for poisoning a number of victims, initially in order to further her marriage plans, later, it seems, for no obvious reason at all. A social climber, Zwanziger had lived off a series of wealthy men until her growing age and fading looks combined with a reading of Goethe's *Werther* led to an unsuccessful suicide attempt. As she sank to the status of a servant, she turned to the compensatory power of poison: 'Poison punished every real or imagined insult; poison castigated every little piece of teasing; poison stopped unwelcome guests from returning; poison disrupted the social events she so envied.' For all his insight, however, Feuerbach thought that the emotions driving Zwanziger were two of the most dangerous there could be: 'poisonous envy and furious delight in the misfortunes of others'. Instead of being happy with the position life had allotted her, she wanted a higher social status, sexual gratification, money, power. Three of her victims were her own employers. Death could be the only proper punishment, and she was executed on 17 September 1811.[102]

Feuerbach's anxiety about the effects of envy on the social order were characteristic for the early nineteenth century, when the example of the French Revolution was still present in everybody's mind. Bourgeois respectability had to be asserted as an antidote to violent outbreaks of destructive emotion. The bitter search for power and revenge drove a number of women to the use of poison in these decades, and not just in Germany. Chemistry had not yet reached the state of sophistication which enabled it to detect the presence of substances such as arsenic in the body; women's role in the house, in preparing and serving food and drink, gave them the opportunity to administer poison; above all, perhaps, in the first decades of the nineteenth century, women were suffering general reductions of their freedom, independence, and power over their own lives as the new bourgeois society was being constructed. It was not until the revolutionary moment of 1848 and above all the rise of liberal nationalism in the 1860s that they

---

[101] Feuerbach, *Aktenmässige Darstellung*, ii. 48–122.   [102] Ibid., i. 9–54.

began to organize in the cause of their own emancipation.[103] At the beginning of the century, the phenomenon of the female poisoner appeared to jurists such as Feuerbach to be particularly dangerous. The subordination of women to men in the social hierarchy, even more, the need to maintain undisturbed the unequal relationship of servant and master, dictated that clemency should be refused under most circumstances to anyone breaking these patterns of authority by an act of murder or manslaughter.

Early nineteenth-century judicial officials not only considered whether death sentences should actually be carried out, they also made recommendations on the method to be used. When considering the effects of public execution, early nineteenth-century judicial officials generally paid attention to what the Appeal Court in Jena called 'the pretty generally acknowledged truth, that *cruel* death penalties, such as the wheel, burning, quartering, etc., virtually inevitably frustrate the purpose of all punishments for criminal offences by arousing the sympathy of the spectators'.[104] This growing perception probably reflected more the feelings of officialdom than the realities of popular culture. But it gave rise to an increasing practice of moderating the severity of the punishments laid down by the law, by exercising the royal or princely clemency to reduce them in most cases to the next most severe of the punishments laid down by the criminal law. This conflicted with the growing concern for law and order and social stability that was also evident at this time. In Prussia all these factors led in the early decades of the nineteenth century to a gruesome paradox. The system of gradations of execution laid down in the Prussian General Law Code of 1794 only really made sense if all the death sentences passed were actually carried out. Otherwise the principle of tougher punishments for worse forms of murder would be rendered inconsistent. But the more death itself came to be considered by the authorities as the real punishment, the more they felt it necessary to commute from death to life imprisonment the sentences of those criminals about whose guilt there was a possible element of doubt, or whose crime seemed to have been committed under mitigating circumstances, or who showed in their demeanour a suitable degree of contrition and remorse. All of these categories, however, were precisely those for which the law laid down the least severe forms of capital punishment. Neither the King, with whom the prerogative of mercy lay, nor the Ministry of Justice, upon whose advice he frequently acted, was disposed to regard robbery with murder, parricide, or any of the more heinous forms of homicide with the slightest leniency. So while the lower degrees of

---

[103] Mary Hartman, *Victorian Murderesses: A True History of Thirteen Respectable French and English Women Accused of Unspeakable Crimes* (New York, 1977).

[104] StA Weimar Oberappellationsgericht Jena 452, Bl. 4–5: Oberappellationsgericht Jena to Herzog von Hildburghausen, 11 Aug. 1825.

murder were quite likely to result in commutation to life imprisonment by the exercise of the royal mercy, the higher ones were subjected to the full rigours of the law. The most that really serious offenders could be granted was a slight moderation of the death penalty, often no more than from breaking with the wheel from the bottom up to breaking with the wheel from the top down.

This meant that in the early decades of the nineteenth century the most severe forms of capital punishment were also the ones most frequently employed. Thus out of fourteen people executed in Prussia in 1821, the great majority—eleven— were broken with the wheel. Only three of those who had been condemned to simple decapitation were executed. The mitigating circumstances which had led to the commutation of the sentences of the others were not thought to be present in the cases of the eleven sentenced to breaking with the wheel, indeed their absence had been a major factor in bringing about that sentence in the first place. This paradox continued to operate for some years. In 1828, for example, ten malefactors were broken with the wheel in Prussia, and only two beheaded. In 1831 eight out of nine executions were carried out with the wheel. As late as 1836, such executions were still in the majority. It is fair to say, therefore, that breaking with the wheel was the normal method of execution in Prussia from the early years of the nineteenth century up to the middle of the 1830s. Only at this point was the anomaly corrected and the decision taken to commute the sentence of breaking with the wheel to decapitation with the axe unless the heinousness of the crime was particularly unforgivable. In 1838, seven out of nine executions in Prussia were simple beheadings, five of them commuted from the wheel. By the 1840s it had become common in Prussia to find years in which the wheel was not used at all.[105] Breaking with the wheel was from this time effectively a thing of the past; it was finally removed from the law books in Prussia in 1851. Nevertheless, it was extraordinary that the use of the royal clemency in the interests of humane execution had for more than two decades led to the most cruel type of execution in Prussia also being the most common. It was not a system designed to convince Beccarian critics of capital punishment of the error of their ways.

The changes which took place in the administration of the death penalty in Prussia and other parts of Germany in the first few decades of the nineteenth century thus created almost as many problems as they solved. The official attack on the role of popular culture, religion, and ritual in public executions, taking place against the background of the decline of the guilds, serfdom, and other aspects of the old hierarchical order, shattered the synthesis of communal and state purposes which they expressed, and turned these occasions into precisely that kind of confrontation between the forces of order and an inchoate, volatile

[105] GStA Berlin Rep. 84a/8143, Bl. 5–9, 15–19, 54–7, 85–8, 149–51, 158, 200–11.

'mob' which the authorities most feared. There was no evidence that the crowd regarded the malefactor on the scaffold with 'contempt and revulsion' in the 1840s, however, any more than it had done so half a century before. Reducing the number of executions had merely led to more people attending each, while executioners were more prone to make mistakes, with the consequent expressions of protest by the crowd, because they were no longer as practised or as experienced as they used to be. The systematic operation of princely clemency, by linking capital punishment to the state and those who led it, instead of to the impersonal operation of abstract principles of justice, as had been intended by the great law codes of the Enlightenment, politicized the issue of the death penalty and identified it with the principle of monarchical rule. In Restoration Germany, in the period of the 'Holy Alliance', Austria, Russia, and Prussia sought to control the demons liberated by the French Revolution by claiming a legitimacy for the existing order that was grounded in the precepts of the Christian religion. Princely sovereignty was officially portrayed as the expression of Divine Right. The royal prerogative of mercy aptly symbolized this claim. Opposing principles of sovereignty, deriving from the contractual theories of the eighteenth century and spreading across Europe as the ideological legacy of 1789, emphasized the primacy of the nation and the people instead. It was not surprising, therefore, that those who championed them saw the death penalty as a supreme expression of the backward and irrational nature of princely neo-Absolutism; nor that they adhered closely to the doctrines of Beccaria, who had applied the contract theory of sovereignty to penal policy and drawn the consequence that capital punishment should be abolished. By the 1840s, the failure of the bureaucratic, neo-Absolutist state to achieve a satisfactory resolution of the problems surrounding public executions and the death penalty had become obvious. The result, as we shall now see, was that the very legitimacy of capital punishment itself came to be called into question.

6

From Reform to Revolution

a. Reforming the Criminal Law 1813–1848

Over the first few decades of the nineteenth century, as we have seen, imprisonment gradually became the standard penal sanction against non-capital offenders. In the wake of the General Law Code of 1794 in Prussia and the gradual decline of corporal punishment as the institution of serfdom was dismantled, it became normal for prison sentences to be imposed on the vast majority of criminals. New gaols were built to cope with this shift in policy, but the construction programme failed to keep pace with the massive population growth of these decades. The situation was exacerbated by a rising crime rate as pauperism spread under the impact of industrialization, and rural theft reached epidemic proportions following the enclosure of common lands. Huge overcrowding in Prussian prisons was the result. By the 1830s they were so full that there was no way of separating the prisoners from one another, and officials complained that they were little more than schools for crime. The very high rate of recidivism at this period testified to the accuracy of this assessment. The Justice Ministry wanted to reform prisons in order to improve the inmates and reduce reoffending rates, but its proposals were regarded by other ministries as too costly, and gradually the control of prison administration was taken away from it. In 1805 a new set of regulations had laid down rules for post-release care which amounted to a very close supervision of ex-convicts.[1] If criminals were carefully controlled, then perhaps they would not reoffend, and so the overcrowding of the gaols would be reduced. The control of deviance through a network of police surveillance, censorship, and repression was also one of the central planks of the post-1815 political order in Central Europe, under the guiding hand of the Austrian Chancellor Prince Metternich.[2] But none of this

---

[1] Blasius, *Bürgerliche Gesellschaft*, 66–75.

[2] Lüdtke, '*Gemeinwohl*'. See also Wolfram Siemann, '*Deutschlands Ruhe, Sicherheit und Ordnung'. Die Anfänge der politischen Polizei 1806–1866* (Tübingen, 1985).

was deemed sufficient to meet the new challenges of rising criminality and the possibility of public disturbances that might threaten the stability of the state now that capital and corporal punishment had been reduced. Not only in Prussia, but in other German states as well, officials concluded that the only way to deal with the situation was to reform the criminal law itself.

The first half of the nineteenth century saw a whole series of new Criminal Law Codes come into effect in the various states of the German Confederation. The earliest and most influential was the Bavarian Criminal Code, passed in 1813. Written by Paul Anselm von Feuerbach, it was a late product of the German Enlightenment. Its emphasis, following Beccarian principles, was on deterrence. Feuerbach insisted that the Prussian principle of 'special deterrence', which allowed the indefinite detention of offenders until they 'reformed', was arbitrary and unjust. His law code implemented in a much more thoroughgoing way than its Prussian predecessor of 1794 the principles of 'general deterrence' which Beccaria had enunciated. It also abandoned the Absolutist idea of trying to shape people's lives and characters with a liberal Kantian postulate that all the law could do was to prevent people from misbehaving. For Feuerbach, like Kant, punishment was both deterrence and retribution; it could not be used to reform the offender. It was still to be some time, therefore, before the ameliorative principle came to dominate liberal thinking on penal policy. Moreover, Feuerbach was too much a pillar of the social order to go along with Beccaria's hostility to capital punishment in his law code. The code laid down the death penalty for murder of various kinds, for robbery with violence, when the victim was permanently physically damaged or subjected to torture by the offender, for treason and *lèse-majesté*, for the poisoning of wells, and for stirring up riots in which lives were lost. All extra flourishes to the death penalty were removed, apart from a compulsory appearance at the pillory beforehand.[3] The Kingdom of Saxony followed suit with its own new Criminal Code in 1839, the Kingdom of Hanover and the Duchy of Brunswick in 1840, the Grand Duchy of Hesse in 1841, the Principality of Lippe-Detmold in 1843, the Grand Duchy of Baden in 1845, and the Thuringian states in 1850. All of these codes severely restricted the application of the death penalty. Under Napoleon, as we have seen, a new penal code along French lines had been introduced in the Rhineland, and after this territory was allotted to Prussia at the Congress of Vienna in 1815, it was agreed in Berlin that it would remain in force until a full revision of the Prussian General Law Code of 1794 came into effect. Rhenish practice thus perpetuated for the time being many of the legal innovations of the French Revolution, as modified

---

[3] See Eberhard Kipper, *Johann Paul Anselm Feuerbach* (Cologne, 1969), and Richard Hartmann, *P. J. A. Feuerbachs politische und strafrechtliche Grundanschauungen* (Berlin, 1961).

under the Napoleonic Empire, including equality before the law, a proper system of appeal, and a verbal rather than a written trial, held before a twelve-man jury in open court, at which witnesses could be cross-examined. All these were major planks in the platform of liberal legal reformers in the nineteenth century, and none of them existed as yet in the 'old provinces' which had constituted the Kingdom of Prussia before 1815.[4]

Amidst all this legislative activity in other German states, the Prussian authorities, especially after the defeat of the most radical reformers, Stein and Hardenberg, remained hesitant and cautious. The bureaucrats of the early 1800s in Prussia had wanted to take what was best in the French Revolution and adapt it to German circumstances. The bureaucrats of the 1820s were more conservative. They thought that the French Revolution had spread dangerous ideas and habits among the common people. They felt that the defeat of Prussia by the French, and what they thought of as the over-hasty reforms that followed, had broken down the old social system of status-groups or *Stände* too quickly, with a resulting 'absence of barriers', as one of them put it. The lower classes were getting above their station in life, and they could not afford it; theft and crime were the results. Alcoholism and irreligion only made things worse, and the modern tendency for the poor to marry and have children too soon, before they had the means to live, aggravated the situation further. The Silesian Estates (*Landstände*) urged a more summary and expeditious system of justice in 1837, and criticized the softness of the judicial and penal systems.[5] These cries of alarm reflected the fact that both the penal system and the society which it sought to regulate were changing too fast for the liking of many.

Influenced by the ideas of Feuerbach, Prussian judicial officials considered the educational and formative purposes of the 1794 Prussian General Law Code to be rather outmoded. But none of the drafts of a new Criminal Code prepared in Berlin in 1826, 1833, or 1836 met with enough support in the Prussian bureaucracy to enable it to go through the legislative process. They all failed to go significantly beyond what the law already provided. It was only with the fourth draft, begun in the late 1830s and completed in 1843, that radical new ideas began to be introduced, reflecting a renewed and even more acute apprehension of the seriousness of the crime and public order situation. The new proposals emerged above all from a massive inquiry launched by the Prussian King in 1836 into the causes of the increase of crime in his realm.[6] Basing their proposals on the results

---

[4] Blasius, *Bürgerliche Gesellschaft*, 115–18; *Ueber die Todesstrafe* (*Stenographische Berichte über die Verhandlungen des Reichstages des Norddeutschen Bundes. 1. Legislatur-Periode, Session 1870. Anlagen zu den Verhandlungen des Reichstages von Nr. 1–72*), Bd. 3, 2: *Anlage 2 zu Nr. 5 (Motive des Strafgesetz-Entwurfs für den Norddeutschen Bund)*, p. vii.

[5] Blasius, *Bürgerliche Gesellschaft*, 53–62, 99.

[6] Ibid. 99, 93–138.

of the inquiry, the officials thought that far-reaching changes were necessary. Many of them were evidently more than aware of the inadequacies of capital punishment as they had been discussed in the Justice Ministry at various times since the beginning of the century. In the 1826 draft, it had been agreed 'to narrow down the area covered by the death penalty in the (General) Law Code (of 1794) and to remove all aggravated forms of execution'.[7] By the late 1820s more detailed consideration was being given to the death penalty. A debate in a semi-official periodical aimed at judicial officials, judges, and prosecutors testified to the new concerns which the principle and practice of capital punishment were arousing. While some jurists attacked the sword and the rope as inhumane,[8] others advocated the replacement of aggravated death sentences such as the wheel by milder, more symbolic punishments,[9] and a few spoke out in favour of outright opposition[10]—a view which, to be sure, was still very much in the minority in judicial circles at a time when jurists argued that death by the sword or axe was far more humane than a natural end by lingering disease.[11] As the commission on the reform of the criminal law came to debate the clauses on the death penalty in December 1839, some members doubted whether capital punishment had any deterrent effect at all. 'Anyone who carries out a crime in cold blood believes that he has taken such preparations that the punishment laid down for it cannot possibly touch him; punishment has absolutely no deterrent force for such a person.'[12] Another member of the commission argued 'that a being endowed with reason has no right to bring about the moral extermination of another being endowed with reason and thereby to cut off the road to improvement for him, as happens with the death penalty'.[13] By this time, therefore, some officials were regarding character reform as the primary purpose of imprisonment, and taking a wholly negative line in the question of capital punishment as a result.

The majority of the commission, however, took the point of view that deterrence, not improvement, was the principal purpose of punishment.[14] Of course, they agreed, the progress of culture and civilization was eliminating the need for

---

[7] *Ueber die Todesstrafe*, p. iv.

[8] Prof. Dr. Lichtenstädt, 'Ueber Todesstrafe ohne Qual', *Zeitschrift für die Criminal-Rechts-Pflege in den Preussischen Staaten mit Ausschluss der Rheinprovinzen* (ed. Julius Hitzig), 25 (1829), 338–42.

[9] Carl Ernst Jarcke, 'Die Lehre von der Tödtung: Von den durch härtere Bestrafung qualificirten Arten der Tödtung', ibid. 8 (1826), 351–89.

[10] Prof. Eschenmayer, *Ueber die Abschaffung der Todesstrafen* (Tübingen, 1831).

[11] Anon., 'Noch eine bedeutende Stimme für die Todesstrafe', *Zeitschrift für die Criminal-Rechts-Pflege in den Preussischen Staaten mit Ausschluss der Rheinprovinzen* (ed. Julius Hitzig), 24 (1829), 405–23; see also Julius Hitzig, 'Nachwort des Herausgebers', ibid. 45 (1833), 223–8; and Anon., 'Noch etwas über neue Gesetzbücher', ibid. 21 (1828), 223–34.

[12] GStA Berlin Rep. 84a/7782: Staatsraths-Kommisison, 38. Sitzung am 18. xii. 1839; also 39. Sitzung am 21. xii. 1839, pp. 105–13, here 111.

[13] Ibid. 105.   [14] Ibid. 105–6.

the cruel and barbarous punishments which had been so common a century or
so before:

General opinion is more and more against the use of the death penalty, and the moment
for the abolition of the latter may well not be far away. For the moment, to be sure, it still
seems impermissible to abolish this penalty altogether; but in its execution we must avoid
anything which goes against the more lenient manners of our time.[15]

Arguments such as these were to be repeated on many subsequent occasions. Yet
they ran up against the persistence of strongly retributive Kantian ideals of
justice. As another member put it:

By its very nature, punishment is an act of retribution, and originally its vindictive
character could be found everywhere. In earlier times, when manners were more brutal,
this character was expressed in a brutal way; hence the numerous and tormenting forms
of death which are to be found in the older law codes, including the *Carolina*. The
progress of civilizaion has objected to the use of such excessively severe punishments, and
judges have sought to avoid them through the use of even the slightest defect in the
evidence. Such a consequence will always follow when the law is too severe; but nothing
damages the reputation of the law so much as a failure to implement it. Hence it must
only consist of applying a punishment which is appropriate in view of the laws of
humanity and the moral state of civilization of the people. The improvement of the
criminal, or the deterrence of others from committing crimes, cannot serve as the leading
principle here, since it will cause the punishment either to exceed the proper measure of
retribution or to fall behind it; new theories such as the principle of improvement,
prevention, or deterrence have led to many mistakes in legislation and in the practice of
the courts. The legality of the death penalty follows of itself from the principle that
punishment is retributory, since the denial of freedom or property does not constitute an
adequate retribution for murder or other crimes of similar severity.[16]

Others objected that if the principle of retribution were taken too seriously, it
would lead to 'an eye for an eye, a tooth for a tooth' and thus to inhumane
punishment: 'revenge' and 'cruelty' were surely to be avoided.[17] On this point at
least, everyone seemed to be in agreement.

The death penalty could, it was argued on Beccarian lines, be regarded as a
kind of 'emergency self-defence' by the state against open enemies of human
society, who would be a danger to it as long as they lived. Capital punishment
had always been a weapon in the state's armoury. It was sanctioned by the
Christian religion, as the Bible showed. The alternative of life imprisonment,
said one member of the commission, would mean 'lifelong torment for the
criminal'.[18] The real basis for the death penalty, it was agreed, was as a 'manifestation of the sanctity of the law'.[19] It was an act of 'justice'. King Friedrich

[15] GStA Berlin Rep. 84a/7782: Staatsraths-Kommisison, 38. Sitzung am 18. xii. 1839; also 39. Sitzung am
21. xii. 1839, p. 109.
[16] Ibid. 107.   [17] Ibid. 108.   [18] Ibid. 107.   [19] Ibid. 108.

Wilhelm III himself, appearing at one of the commission's key sessions, summed up the arguments in the following terms:

He could only see the principle on which the right to punishment rests as basing itself on the fact that punishment must be carried out *so that justice is done*. This followed on from what was said in another way about punishment as an act of retribution, as a manifestation of the sanctity of the law, and as a necessary expression of justice. The theoretical principles of improvement, deterrence, or prevention in His Opinion ran contrary to this. The right to punish did not derive from empowerment by human society but from the duty of the authorities, based on Divine Right, to maintain the application of the law.[20]

While the conclusion of this argument—that the basic pattern of punishments outlined in the Law Code of 1794 should be retained—was not accepted by the Prussian commission, the members none the less voted unanimously that the death penalty as such should continue to be carried out.[21]

In pursuit of the rational hierarchy of punishment suggested by Beccaria, some of those involved in the discussions then pleaded for the retention of the different degrees of the death penalty. In 1839, in the thirty-ninth sitting of the commission, one official argued as follows:

In popular opinion as well as in the criminal's heart, punishment is an act of retribution; and the legislator must uphold this character of punishment. A single kind of death penalty is not sufficient for this. According to the doctors, strangulation is a milder form of death penalty than beheading; none the less, popular opinion holds the former to be the more severe and humiliating than the latter. The punishments of the wheel and the pyre surely make a more powerful impression upon the people than does that of beheading, even if they are softened by prior strangulation. We must lay great stress on the popular idea of the shamefulness of a punishment and the impression which its execution makes; the removal of any distinction between different kinds of death penalty will thus have a disadvantageous effect.

Nevertheless, this opinion, though strongly held, proved to be in a minority, particularly in view of the prevalent belief that punishment was an act of self-protection by society rather than an attempt at moral education for the populace.

Three objections in particular were especially telling. The first was that additional punishments beyond that of death itself were unnecessarily cruel. The commission held that the death penalty 'should not be accompanied by intensifications which increase or prolong the agony of the person to be executed and which are reprehensible according to the dictates of humanity and civilization'. It emphasized 'the inadmissibility of any intensification which, as in the present aggravated death penalties, increases the sufferings of the person to be executed' and declared that such painful additions to death itself, as breaking

[20] Ibid. 112.   [21] Ibid. 113.

with the wheel, pulling the condemned person's flesh with red-hot tongs, and the like, would 'frustrate the desired effect of the punishment on the people by arousing sympathy for the criminal rather than revulsion'. Yet, as a second argument made clear, there would be no purpose in replacing physical additions to the death penalty, such as breaking with the wheel, by symbolic ones, such as erecting a placard on the gallows in an attempt to expose the criminal to 'contempt and degradation', even though this in itself, all agreed, was a necessary objective of the exercise. A placard would harm the offender's family by remind-ing society of the fact that their relative had been executed. 'Everyone would recoil before such a family, and this could easily give rise to fresh offences.' This was a new point which reflected the bourgeois individualism that was to an ever-increasing extent entering into the discussion of penal policy in Germany towards the middle of the nineteenth century. In a society based on hereditary status-groups, few had questioned the fact that dishonour brought on offenders extended to their families as well. Now, however, it was being argued that only those directly guilty of a crime should be punished for it. The final point was novel too. The commission argued that death was a sufficient deterrent in itself. If the axe was not enough to stop someone from committing murder, then a placard or other dishonouring addition would scarcely be enough either.[22] The point behind these arguments was perhaps best summed up in a judgment of the Appeal Court in Frankfurt an der Oder, which declared in 1853:

Death expiates all guilt here on earth; the human judge's hand should not stretch out beyond it. Anything which is added to the death penalty as an intensification of it hurts and offends not the guilty criminal but his innocent relatives. It is a punishment visited upon them without a verdict. 'As ye have sinned, so shall ye atone.' According to this principle, murder can only be expiated by death, but with death the expiation is com-plete, and thus any intensification of the death penalty is inadmissible.[23]

Such belief in the finality of death as a punishment testified to a wholly secular attitude towards capital punishment, which had been steadily gaining influence among the élites since the eighteenth-century Enlightenment.

Quite apart from these reasons, judicial opinion in the first decades of the nineteenth century was also increasingly worried, as we saw in Chapter 5, by the possibility that the spectacle of suffering would inflame the animal passions of the spectators. As Paul Anselm von Feuerbach put it in 1828:

Reason and long experience have long since struck out really painful forms of death from the list of allowable punishments. This is cruelty without purpose and indeed frustrates the aim of punishment. Death is the most extreme of the ills that can befall a person as a sentient being; to increase or prolong this ill artificially is contrary to humanity, and the

[22] GStA Berlin Rep. 84a/7782, Bl. 105–13.   [23] Ibid. 7783, Bl. 39–40.

state may not deny humanity since it is obliged to present itself as an example to the people. If someone is not deterred by death, they will not be deterred by death by the wheel. The state is sinning against the nation's character by applying real or even merely apparently cruel forms of the death penalty, in that it is putting on barbaric blood-spectacles which contribute to blunt people's feelings, feed their coarseness, and drive their spirits wild.[24]

Thus it was common in Bavaria at least, before they were effectively done away with by the Criminal Code of 1813, to use the royal clemency to dispense with the 'intensifications' of the death penalty which were sometimes imposed by the law.[25] Death was a sufficient penalty in itself. Loss of honour brought about by physical degradation on the scaffold was regarded as dispensable in view of the harmful effects of such degradation on the sentiments of the crowd. Similarly, the Prussian State Council voted in 1839 by twenty-two votes to seventeen against any form of elaboration of the death penalty, which was to be carried out in Prussia exclusively by beheading. In the end, however, there was no comprehensive reform of the law. The draft Code was submitted for general discussion, but came to nothing because of the opposition of representatives of the Rhenish liberal bourgeoisie, who objected to its failure to provide juries and thus its implicit proposal to remove jury trial from the Rhineland, where it had been introduced under Napoleonic law.[26]

These internal debates of the late 1830s give a fascinating glimpse into the views of governing élites in Prussia on the issue of capital punishment at a time when it was beginning to be widely questioned as an instrument of penal policy. They indicated deep divisions on the subject. If capital punishment were to be retained, then majority opinion was clearly in favour of further simplification and rationalization, and desired its uniform application without any special gradations or additions. The death penalty was to mean death and nothing else. In 1842, for example, Prussian Minister of Justice Heinrich von Mühler urged the King to abolish additional capital punishments:

When I say for my part that I affirm the lawfulness and indispensability of the death penalty, nevertheless I am deeply convinced that justice is served if a criminal who is condemned to lose his life is simply executed, and anything which constitutes cruelty towards the (usually penitent) offender, or merely seems so to do, is abolished.[27]

Such considerations led to the draft of 1843, in which, as the Minister for the Revision of Legislation, the legal scholar Friedrich Karl von Savigny (1779–1861), said in defending it four years later, the aim was 'to be sparing with capital punishment, to confine it just to the most serious and significant cases, and thus

---

[24] Feuerbach, *Aktenmässige Darstellung*, i. 244.   [25] Ibid. for numerous specific examples.
[26] Blasius, *Bürgerliche Gesellschaft*, 134.   [27] *Ueber die Todesstrafe*, p. iv.

to *limit* it as far as possible'. Indeed, in future, he added, it might even be possible to abolish capital punishment altogether, when general standards of moral education had improved. To abolish it at present, however, he admitted, would give the impression 'that the legislator has become less grave, the impression of weakness, of giving in to the appearance of humanity'.[28] There was thus no immediate intention to abolish executions. And the draft still included the additional penalty of being dragged to the scaffold in cases of premeditated parricide or matricide, murder committed in the course of a robbery or other crime, murder by poison, or murder under any kind of aggravated circumstances as decided by the judge.[29] From the official point of view, therefore, relatively little seemed to have changed. But Savigny's defensive attitude towards the principle of abolition, and his concession that it might be possible some day, indicated that they were becoming much more influential in the 1840s. In the 1830s, as we have seen, the number of individuals prepared to argue for getting rid of capital punishment altogether was still quite small. In the following decade, their ranks swelled rapidly and began to extend far beyond the confines of officialdom and into the liberal, largely bourgeois public in general.

b. The Attack on the Death Penalty in the 1840s

Worries about the growing crime rate, the need for a new policy of education and improvement towards offenders in order to combat it, and the belief that a spectacle of public cruelty on the scaffold would only inflame the passions of the onlookers, render them insensible to finer emotions, brutalize them and make them more rather than less liable to create crimes of violence themselves, combined in Germany in the 1840s to undermine the principle of capital punishment among a growing number of liberal jurists, writers, and political activists. Not only the great Beccaria but also other judicial reformers since had evinced a high degree of scepticism with regard to the deterrent effect of capital punishment. And, as we have seen, by identifying the operation of the death penalty with princely sovereignty, the growing use of the prerogative of clemency had seemed to link executions indissolubly to the concept of the state as a hereditary patrimony legitimated by Divine Right. Liberals, adhering to notions of popular sovereignty and contractual theories of the state, increasingly followed Beccaria in drawing the conclusion that capital punishment was a symbol of tyranny. To these general concerns were added more specific ones. For by the 1830s jurists were beginning to pay increasing attention to the psychology rather than the

---

[28] *Ueber die Todesstrafe*, pp. iv–v, quoting *Verhandlungen des ständischen Ausschusses*, i. 53, 181, 223–5 and ii. 117, 569–71.

[29] *Entwurf des Strafgesetzbuchs für die Preussischen Staaten* (Berlin, 1843), 4, 38, 81.

morality of offenders, and to argue that the primary purpose of penal sanctions was to change the personality of criminals and make them useful members of society, rather than to punish them as an example for others. This new penal discourse was reflected in the emergence of new definitions of criminal insanity, pioneered by the early French psychiatrists Philippe Pinel (1745–1826) and Jean Esquirol (1772–1840), who argued that insanity was a disturbance not of the intellect but of the will, expressing itself in a 'monomania' (such as pyromania, kleptomania, megalomania, erotomania, or dipsomania, for example) that could coexist with complete intellectual and social normality in every other respect.[30] The plea of insanity could, of course, be entered under the provisions of the *Carolina*, which laid down that an accused person who was obviously insane could not be prosecuted. But it was only in the course of the Enlightenment, with the emergence of the concept of the individual free will, that it became possible to argue on a systematic basis that people whose will was not free because of temporary or permanent insanity could not be held accountable for their own criminal actions.

This implied the confinement of the criminally insane in madhouses, which indeed is what was taking place from the late eighteenth century onwards. But it also handed a growing power to the medical profession whose task it was to provide expert testimony in such cases. In 1835, J. B. Friedrich published the first serious textbook of forensic psychiatry in Germany, and other, similar volumes followed. The growth of the medical profession, and its psychiatric branch, began to fill the gap which had been left by the retreat of the priesthood in the course of the Enlightenment, and psychiatry started to replace moral judgement in the assessment of the accused.[31] Debates began to arise on specific cases as to whether the culprit was sane and responsible. At the trial of the poisoner Gesche Gottfried in Bremen in 1830, for example, the defence used the new theories to argue that she had been in the grip of 'a blind drive which suggests a disturbed state of being'.[32] At the time, the Bremen Senate declared that it could think of 'nothing more fruitless than asking doctors as such to give an opinion in a concrete instance as to whether the person's will was restricted or not, as to whether the subject acted . . . in a legally free sense or at the behest of a blind

---

[30] Klaus Dörner, *Bürger und Irre. Zur Sozialgeschichte und Wissenschaftssoziologie der Psychiatrie* (Frankfurt am Main, 1969), 171–3.

[31] Dirk Blasius, *Der verwaltete Wahnsinn. Eine Sozialgeschichte des Irrenhauses* (Frankfurt am Main, 1980), and for some illuminating examples, see Schulte, 'Feuer im Dorf'.

[32] Friedrich L. Voget, *Lebensgeschichte der Giftmörderin Gesche Margarethe Gottfried, geborene Timm* (2 vols.; Bremen, 1831), ii. 80. See also the play on the subject by Rainer Werner Fassbinder, *Bremer Freiheit. Frau Gesche Gottfried. Ein bürgerliches Trauerspiel* (Frankfurt am Main, 1983), and Christian Marzahn, 'Scheussliche Selbstgefälligkeit oder giftmordsüchtige Monomanie? Die Gesche Gottfried im Streit der Professionen', in Johannes Feest and Christian Marzahn (eds.), *Criminalia: Bremer Strafjustiz 1810–1850* (Beiträge zur Sozialgeschichte Bremens, 11; Bremen, 1988), 195–244.

impulse'.[33] Similarly, the celebrated case of Johann Christian Woyzeck, the 41-year-old hairdresser who stabbed his mistress Johanne Woost in 1824, gave rise to a heated debate as to whether or not he had been mentally fit to stand trial—the first such debate in Germany.[34] By the 1830s, therefore, the idea that mental disturbance could be a mitigation rather than a reinforcement of guilt was becoming widespread, even if it was not yet generally accepted by the authorities. The mentally ill or handicapped were being removed from the community and put into institutions run by the psychiatric profession. In parallel, the sane offender was intended to be subjected to a regime which would break the criminal will and reform it in the spirit of honest citizenhood.

This new emphasis on individual psychology and the ameliorative purposes of imprisonment had serious implications for the future of capital punishment. For execution, obviously, cut off any chance of improvement for the offender. It was thus an anomaly in the new liberal discourse on punishment that was emerging in the 1830s and 1840s. Moreover, while conservative officialdom in this period still considered the threat of execution as a necessary means of maintaining social order, liberals and radicals became increasingly disturbed by the fact that the vast majority of the offenders who went to the scaffold in these decades were powerless and poor. At the beginning of the nineteenth century jurists like Feuerbach paid scant attention to their circumstances. Crime, as far as he was concerned, was the outcome of moral weakness and wickedness. But by the 1830s and 1840s poverty and exploitation were becoming the subjects of a new, radical discourse in sections of the educated élites. The beginnings of industrialization, and the destabilizing effects of British industrial supremacy on Continental economies, were creating widespread immiseration, and the burden of poor relief on urban and rural society was growing all over Germany. Officials were becoming increasingly aware of the relationship between crime and poverty. 'Hunger', a local Prussian official wrote in 1845,

knows no law and no legislation, and no police, judicial, or military power is so strong as the cry of a hungry crowd for bread. Thus not only private crimes such as theft, robbery etc. can result from widespread poverty, but also revolutionary movements, resistance to the existing order of things, even the total disintegration of a polity.[35]

Other writers and thinkers too were beginning to turn to the theme of the relationship between crime and poverty, most famously perhaps Friedrich Engels in *The Condition of the Working Class in England*, published in 1844. Statistical investigations began to link crime rates with bread prices. Among radicals and

[33] Marzahn, 'Scheussliche Selbsgefällgkeit', 124.

[34] Hans Mayer, *Georg Büchner, Woyzeck. Vollständiger Text und Paralipomena. Dokumentation*, 9th edn. (Frankfurt am Main, 1962). This reprints contemporary medical reports on Woyzeck.

[35] Quoted in Blasius, *Bürgerliche Gesellschaft*, 60.

liberals, attention began to regard the moral psychology of the individual criminal as a product of the social inequalities which they now began to see as the root cause of crime in general. Capital punishment thus came more and more to appear as a draconian sanction designed to maintain a social order that was increasingly regarded as outmoded and unjust.

By the 1840s the ameliorative principle had even penetrated the operations of the judicial bureaucracy in Prussia. It was generally accepted by this time that if a capital offender showed signs of a moral conscience, the death sentence should be commuted. Those incorrigibles who had none were destined for the scaffold. Yet liberal officials began to doubt whether any offenders were really completely incapable of improvement, providing of course that they were not insane, in which case they would not be executed anyway, but confined to an asylum. In 1848, an official report written by a liberal jurist threw doubt on the whole procedure of clemency. Surveying a whole range of individual cases, it concluded that it was inconsistent to the point of irrationality, and was certainly grossly unfair to the offender. The report, citing prison records, showed that even the most cold-blooded, premeditated, deliberate murder could be committed by an offender whose character nevertheless proved capable of amelioration in the penitentiary. If it was true of this person, then might it not be true of anybody? And if this were the case, did it not seem only just to do away with capital punishment altogether? Such problems and inconsistencies in the application of the royal prerogative of mercy were compounded in the view of judicial officials in the 1840s by similar variations in the categorization of offences; and they were able to cite a number of cases in which judges had disagreed with each other over whether to convict an offender for murder or manslaughter. Why was it, for example, that Johann Gottfried Blichmann, from Silesia, had been executed in 1837, for causing four fires and the death of one person, although he had shown 'much resignation and repentance' in prison, while Franz Kaiser, also from Silesia, a blind beggar condemned to death in 1826 for burning down a workhouse and causing the death of one of the inmates, had been reprieved? There seemed no obvious reason.[36] Often such judgments depended on hair-splitting attempts to estimate the degree of premeditation involved in the homicide. It was necessary at the very least, liberal officials thought, to draw a much firmer line between murder and manslaughter in the new Prussian Criminal Code which had been almost continuously under consideration since the 1820s, so that 'we can prevent the judgment over life or death of a human being from depending on a variable definition of concepts'.[37]

[36] GStA Berlin Rep. 84a/8144, Bl. 35: *Justiz-Ministerial-Blatt für die Preussische Gesetzgebung und Rechtspflege*, 10/30 (28 July 1848), 276.
[37] Ibid. 253.

But this objection to capital punishment was not the only one raised by inconsistencies in the application of the royal prerogative of mercy. Far more serious in its implications for the place of capital punishment in the planned new Criminal Code was the sharp difference in the exercise of clemency between death sentences meted out in the Rhineland, which had been ceded to Prussia by the Treaty of Vienna in 1815, and death sentences handed down in the other Prussian provinces. In the period 1826 to 1843, six out of 189 death sentences in the Rhine Province were confirmed; ninety-four out of 237 in the other provinces: a difference between 3 per cent and 40 per cent.[38] The contrast was even more striking in the case of murder, the crime which accounted for the great majority of executions in the first half of the nineteenth century. While only five out of forty-eight death sentences handed down in the Rhine Province in this period were actually carried out (10 per cent), no fewer than seventy-one out of 135 persons condemned to death in the rest of Prussia found their way to the scaffold, a proportion of no less than 53 per cent.[39] An even greater contrast could be found between the Rhine Province and the Eastern provinces—Posen, Silesia, West and East Prussia—with their large Polish minorities and their backward rural economies and poverty-stricken small towns. Between 1818 and 1830, for example, while there were 98 condemnations and 11 executions (11 per cent) in the Rhine Province, the comparable figures were 16 and 6 in West Prussia (36 per cent), 27 and 11 in the Kurmark (41 per cent), 20 and 11 for Posen (55 per cent), 21 and 13 in East Prussia (62 per cent), and 39 and 25 for Silesia (64 per cent).[40] These were differences that no-one could ignore.

The explanation for these striking discrepancies lay neither in the undoubtedly more violent character of the Eastern provinces, nor in any possible consequent variation in the categories for which offenders were condemned by region, nor in any particular animus of judges and officials against Prussia's Polish subjects, though this certainly existed. The fundamental reason was that under the Napoleonic law which held sway in the Rhineland, trials were open and depended mainly on the oral presentation of evidence by witnesses, while under the Prussian regulations, which ruled procedure in the other provinces, trials were secret and depended mainly on the evaluation of a confession by the accused. As an official in the Ministry of Justice noted:

In the Rhine Province, indeed, too little weight may be placed upon the importance of the confession, whereas in the other parts of the state . . . we work with all our strength and all the means open to us for months, indeed years on end to obtain a confession from the offender.—When the decision is taken on the confirmation of a death sentence,

---

[38] GStA Berlin Rep. 84a/8144, Bl. 35: *Justiz-Ministerial-Blatt für die Preussische Gesetzgebung und Rechtspflege*, 10/30 (28 July 1848), 247.

[39] Ibid. 251.   [40] Ibid. 8143, Bl. 152–3.

however, the practice hitherto has been to determine the degree of guilt exclusively on the basis of the Prussian regulations and the old Prussian principles which rest on them.

Thus during the entire period from 1826 to 1843 only three out of 186 death sentences passed by Rhineland courts in the absence of a confession had actually been carried out. The other three out of the total of six cases in which an offender in the Rhineland was executed were considered safer because a confession had been obtained from the accused, and so in Prussian law the conviction was regarded as a good deal firmer.[41]

This fact was regarded as the most anomalous of all towards the end of the 1840s. The death penalty had virtually ceased to exist in the Rhineland. Yet it was highly likely that trial by jury in open court with verbal questioning of witnesses and assessment of evidence would shortly be introduced in the whole of Prussia. What would be the result? The Justice Ministry official, writing in the liberal atmosphere of 1848, had no doubt

that the death penalty can and must be abolished for the whole state, if on the one hand jury-courts are introduced and the positive rules of evidence are removed, and on the other hand the confirmation of death sentences continues according to the principles hitherto applied. To be sure, confessions probably will not fade into the background to the extent that they have in the Rhine Province. But the investigating judge will surely no longer use all his strength and all the means open to him to obtain a confession, without considering the length of the investigation. It follows that in many cases in which a confession has to a certain extent been obtained by force, no confession will in future be forthcoming. If therefore the confirmation of death sentences continues to be made according to the principles which have been applied up to now, then the majority of death sentences will not be executed following the introduction of jury-courts.

On the other hand, if legal practice was to be unified across the whole state, then the royal prerogative of mercy could no longer be exercised in cases deriving from the failure of courts in the Rhineland to ground convictions on a confession. Commutation could only be recommended if it was thought that the law had been too harsh in its application, for reasons which the judges had left unconsidered. The reform of the law in the Rhineland would remove the main reason for such commutations, and so many offenders would now be executed for crimes for which in the past they could reasonably have expected to have been granted a reprieve. At the same time, the downgrading of the status of the confession in trial practice in the rest of Prussia would lead to an increase in capital sentences there too, since mere evidence would now count even where a confession had not been obtained. The policy implication was clear: 'This evil, this increase in the severity of the existing criminal law, can only be prevented by the complete abolition of the death penalty.'[42]

[41] Ibid., Bl. 35 (as n. 36), 251.   [42] Ibid. 252.

This concentration on the anomalies of capital punishment reflected the fact that writers on the subject were for the first time beginning to employ statistical arguments in their assessment of the death penalty. A particularly powerful influence was exerted by the Heidelberg professor of law Carl Joseph Anton Mittermaier (1787–1867), whose comparative study of capital punishment in a number of states appeared in 1840.[43] Mittermaier had already published articles on the subject over a number of years, during which he had steadily worked his way round to a whole-hearted opposition to the death penalty. In 1840 he brought his researches together in a powerful indictment of capital punishment.[44] Mittermaier pointed out that the number of executions in Germany was now so small that it was probable that the state could do without them altogether. He rejected religious arguments in favour of the death penalty as irrational. It was not for the state to rescue a malefactor's soul by exterminating his body. Most significantly, Mittermaier demonstrated statistically that the reduction or abolition of capital punishment, wherever it had occurred, had not led to any noticeable increase in capital offences. On the other hand, the threat of the death penalty led to many acquittals by courts whose members had been reluctant to use it. With these arguments, Mittermaier not only moved the argument about capital punishment onto a new intellectual plane, but also placed himself at the head of the growing movement to abolish the death penalty in Germany. His influence can be seen in a number of other abolitionist tracts published in the 1840s, most notably in a book published jointly by Philipp Moriz Carrière and Friedrich Noellner in 1845. The two authors from Giessen cited Mittermaier's work copiously in an essay aimed at influencing the deliberations of the Prussian Provincial Estates on the draft Criminal Code of 1843. Abolition, they argued, was a necessary step in the progress of civilization. Like many social commentators of the period, they were deeply concerned with the poverty that was manifesting itself in Germany, above all in areas affected by industrial competition from Britain. 'It is pauperism,' wrote Noellner, 'the characteristics and causes of which need to be investigated, and which must then be combated not by punishments but by other, quite contrary measures.' Yet this was not happening. 'The death penalty', he observed, 'is applied almost exclusively against the proletariat.' But deterrence was no way to solve the social question: education and civilization were needed. Mittermaier, said Noellner,

[43] Carl Joseph Anton Mittermaier, 'Die Todesstrafe nach dem neuesten Stande der Ansichten in England, Nordamerika, Frankreich, Belgien, Dänemark, Schweden, Russland, Italien und Deutschland über die Abschaffung dieser Strafart', *Archiv des Kriminalrechts*, NS (1840), 442–63 and 583–610, and (1841), 1–23, 311–48.

[44] Martin Fleckenstein, *Die Todesstrafe im Werk Carl Joseph Anton Mittermaiers (1787–1867). Zur Entwicklungsgeschichte eines Werkbereichs und seiner Bedeutung für Theorie- und Methodenbildung* (Frankfurt am Main, 1991), is a useful monographic study.

FIG. 18. *Carl Joseph Anton Mittermaier (1787–1867).* The nineteenth century's most influential critic of the death penalty, Mittermaier was the first person to provide statistically based arguments for the inefficacy of capital punishment as a deterrent.

had shown how little the death penalty was now used. It was time to do away with it completely. Real deterrence would only be achieved by efficient policing and open trials. Public executions only made things worse. They led to a 'demoralization of the people' through their appeal to the lower instincts. Imprisonment according to the 'penitentiary principle' would be far better.[45] These publications, and many more,[46] amounted to a regular literary campaign against the death penalty by the late 1840s. They testified to the centrality of bourgeois concerns with the mounting problems of poverty, crime, and disorder which characterized the decade.

In the 1840s, therefore, as the liberal constituency began to form itself, and voluntary associations sprang up everywhere to demand reforms ranging from parliamentary government to greater rights for the professions, belief in the need to abolish the death penalty became one of the central tenets of liberalism both within the bureaucracy and without. In 1824, when the lower (elected) chamber of the Württemberg legislature had debated the issue of capital punishment, only one deputy had been bold enough to speak out against it. Fourteen years later, however, in 1838, no fewer than twenty-nine deputies voted in favour of abolition. The death penalty, said one, was 'a punishment that outrages human feelings'. Punishment, said another, 'must not nourish the spirit of revenge, but go beyond inadequate popular educational and moral standards'. Liberals such as Ludwig Uhland were now in the forefront of the movement for abolition. They were still in a minority in 1838, of course, and fifty-three deputies still voted against them in the Württemberg Chamber. Indeed, there was even a majority of sixty-two to thirty-three in favour of continuing to execute malefactors in public.[47] In Saxony there was also a controversy over the death penalty as a new Criminal Code was being prepared in the 1830s.[48] Here too, the proponents of capital punishment still held the field. But there was no doubt that, as the 1840s began to draw to a close, the liberals, bolstered by the emergence of similar movements in other countries,[49] began to feel that the future was theirs, and that the death penalty would eventually go the same way as all the other institutions of Absolutism which they intended to remove in the course of constructing

[45] Philipp Moriz Carrière, *Wissenschaft und Leben in Beziehung auf die Todesstrafe. Ein philosophisches Votum von Dr. M. Carrière . . . ein strafrechtliches Gutachten von Dr. F. Noellner* (Darmstadt, 1845), 30–2, 44–6, 64–5, 78–80, 94.

[46] See also e.g. Mauritius Moeller-Jochmus, *Ueber die Todesstrafe. Eine principielle Untersuchung* (Lepizig, 1845), and Wilhelm Neumann, *Ueber die Nothwendigkeit der Abschaffung der Todesstrafe* (Berlin, 1848).

[47] Sauer, *Im Namen*, 122.

[48] Anon., *Ueber Zulässigkeit und Anwendbarkeit der Todesstrafe. Sendschreiben an den Herrn Obersteuerprocurator Eisenstuck, veranlasst durch dessen Separatvotum bei den Verhandlungen der Deputation der Zweiten Ständischen Kammer zur Prüfung und Berathung des Entwurfs des Criminalgesetzbuchs* (Leipzig, 1837).

[49] For the USA, see David Brion Davis, 'The Movement to Abolish Capital Punishment in America 1787–1861', *American Historical Review*, 63 (1957), 23–46, and Philip English Mackey, *Hanging in the Balance: The Anti-Capital Punishment Movement in New York State 1776–1861* (New York, 1982); for England, Cooper, *Lesson*, and Gatrell, *Hanging Tree*.

a new, united Germany based on the principles of popular sovereignty, parliamentarism, and the nation-state.

c. Public Executions and Public Order

Official reactions to these changes were slow. As we have seen, the judicial administration in Prussia rejected abolition during the 1840s. At the same time, it became increasingly concerned by the threat to public order which it believed that public executions posed. Yet the general problems which prevented the reform of the Prussian Criminal Code in the 1820s and 1830s also frustrated the reform of public executions. Nobody was prepared to remove executions from the public eye while criminal trials continued to be held in secret.[50] Public trials could only be introduced with the promulgation of a new Criminal Code. Throughout the early decades of the nineteenth century, judicial reformers had been advocating open trials and coupling this with a demand for the ending of public executions. The great Bavarian jurist Paul Anselm Feuerbach, for instance, had urged the holding of the final stages of the inquisitorial procedure in public. This, he thought, would remove the necessity for the antiquated ritual of the public condemnation ceremony and replace it with a more rational alternative. He summed up his objections to the existing procedure in a sarcastic description penned in 1813:

The accused is investigated in a secret interrogation chamber, on the basis of a secret denunciation; he is judged by a secret court, which is placed under secret supervision—only at the end of the mysterious tragic drama is the mysterious curtain drawn back—the accused mounts the scaffold![51]

Yet neither in Bavaria, nor anywhere else, did governments seriously consider the abolition of public executions before the 1840s.

What made the difference in the end was the growing danger of mob violence which these occasions presented. By the 1840s the decline in the frequency of capital punishment since the beginning of the century, coupled with rapid population growth, was ensuring that execution crowds were very large indeed. At Breslau in July 1841, for instance, between twelve and fifteen thousand people were said by the police to have been present at an execution.[52] In 1831 35,000 people were estimated to have attended the decapitation of the poisoner Gesche

---

[50] Dirk Blasius, 'Der Kampf um die Geschworenengerichte im Vormärz', in Hans-Ulrich Wehler (ed.), *Sozialgeschichte Heute. Festschrift für Hans Rosenberg zum 70. Geburtstag* (Göttingen, 1974), 148–61.

[51] Anon., *Die kgl. Bayer.Staatsminister*, 63–4.

[52] GStA Berlin Rep. 84a/7782, Bl. 70: Wöchentlicher Polizeibericht Breslau, 24 July 1841.

Gottfried in the Hanseatic city of Bremen.[53] Similar figures were reported else-where. Already in 1820 the authorities in Berlin considered moving the place of execution from the Oranienburg Gate to the Jungfernheide, which lay a good deal further away from the city centre and had been used for executions on a few occasions previously. Local house owners had alleged that the presence of the scaffold was reducing the value of their property. Principally, however, it was argued that the gallows had to be moved 'because experience demonstrated what great masses of people are drawn thither and what excesses occur as a result', if they were near the town and easily accessible to the general public. It would, of course, be less of a deterrent: 'To be sure', admitted the Criminal Division of the Royal Supreme Court in Berlin, 'the further the gallows are from the city, the less people will read what is attached to them', but this disadvantage could, it was considered, be overcome by greater publicity 'through the public bulletins'. The court considered gloomily the next year, however, that crowds were in reality unlikely to be deterred from going to an execution by having to walk some way out of town to see it.[54]

By 1836 the complaints had become even more shrill. 'On the morning of the execution thousands of the curious fill the route from the city governor's head-quarters to the execution place at the Oranienburg Gate', it was reported of an execution in Berlin that year, 'and many more thousands fill the area around the gallows'; the anxiety of the authorities about the 'crowd, which is excited by the anticipation of the forthcoming spectacle' was palpable. Gatherings of this sort were inevitably 'inclined to excess', and disorder would quite possibly be the result.[55] An attempt to shift the scaffold further north, to Plötzensee, foundered when it was discovered that the chosen spot was used for 'target practice' by the army. In 1840 it was proposed to move the place of execution to the still more distant suburb of Spandau, which had the additional advantage from a security point of view of being a military base.[56] In 1843 the Royal Supreme Court in Berlin was complaining that the army was failing to send any cavalry to cover executions there. 'Infantry will obviously not offer any adequate protection against the brutal and unrestrained popular masses which Berlin will provide for an execution at a time of year when the weather is good.'[57] It seemed that nothing could prevent the assembly of large numbers of people at public executions, nor stop the riotous and unseemly behaviour of which the authorities were now so obviously afraid.[58]

[53] L. Scholz, *Die Gesche Gottfried. Eine kriminalpsychologische Studie* (Berlin, 1913), 87.
[54] GStA Berlin Rep. 84a/9268, Bl. 32: Brief vom 20. Nov. 1820; ibid., Bl. 41, Brief vom 12. Feb. 1821.
[55] Ibid. 7782, Bl. 5–6: Criminal-Deputation des Königl. Stadtgerichts zu Berlin zu PJM, vom 11. Jan. 1836.
[56] Ibid., Bl. 76 and 89–94.   [57] Ibid., Bl. 156, Brief vom 2. Apr. 1843.
[58] For further reports, see Holtei, *Vierzig Jahre*, i. 130–3.

By this time not only the 'mob' but also the offender on the scaffold was becoming the object of official anxiety. Now that the element of Christian and communal ritual in the execution ceremony had largely vanished, and criminals who misbehaved on the gallows were no longer confronted by the judges and clergy with the prospect of renewed torture and eternal damnation should they misbehave, the freedom of the 'poor sinners' to write their own part in the drama of capital punishment was greatly increased. As a result, it became almost impossible for them to win the approval of officialdom. Already in 1813 malefactors such as the arsonists Horst and Delitz had experienced no qualms about protesting on the scaffold, or mocking the execution ceremony, as we saw in the last chapter, while at about the same time, at another execution, in Breslau, a young female offender insulted the monk who was accompanying her through the streets and could not be silenced.[59] Particularly worrying for the judicial bureaucrats of Germany's Justice Ministries was the evident fact that cool and impenitent behaviour by the condemned in the last moments before execution now gained widespread popular admiration and quickly became the subject of legend. 'That's the way it goes!' said a condemned man on the scaffold in the small Franconian town of Adelsheim, with a shrug of the shoulders; and the saying became a local proverb.[60] Everyone seemed to have heard of the incident that occurred in Vienna when the state prosecutor, Count Lamezan, accompanied a criminal to the scaffold, and at the foot of the steps paused to shake his hand with a 'Farewell!' 'Now', replied the condemned man, returning the handshake, and casting a glance towards the gallows, 'I won't be faring well for much longer!' A similar story was recounted of an execution in Straubing in the mid-nineteenth century, when 'Red Sepp', condemned to death for having committed a murder in the course of a robbery, was made to wait in the company of the state prosecutor, out of sight of the gallows, so that he would not have to witness the execution of the chief accomplice in his crime (a precaution introduced in the early 1800s):

Now an old woman was sitting by the wayside selling fruit to the crowd of spectators. As the condemned man saw her, he said: 'If only I had a few of those plums.' The state prosecutor, surprised by this request, purchased some and put them in his bound hands, whereupon Sepp pushed one after the other into his mouth and ate them with the greatest calmness of spirit, conscientiously spitting out each stone. The sign was then given that his turn was next; the procession started up again, and without letting himself be distracted, Sepp carried on eating and spitting out the stones, but in a faster tempo, until all the plums were consumed just as he reached the foot of the gallows. 'They tasted good, I thank you, Herr State Prosecutor,' he said, as he climbed up.[61]

[59] Ibid. 130.   [60] Graef, 'Hochgericht'.
[61] Völderndorff und Waradein, *Plaudereien*, i. 103.

Stories of this sort were legion by the middle of the nineteenth century. This was a world away from the funeral hymns, prayers, confessions, and religious devotions which had accompanied executions a century earlier.

Such behaviour stood in subtle contrast to the far more deferential demeanour of the 'poor sinner', the repentant criminal acting the pre-ordained part in the quasi-religious ritual of execution which a previous age had regarded as the ideal. But by the mid-nineteenth century, if not earlier, the bureaucrats of the Justice Ministries of the major German states had begun to operate on the assumption that the condemned person's behaviour on the scaffold was an expression, not of ritual role-playing, but of human psychology: precisely that human psychology which they were hoping to break and remould in the prisons that were being erected at this time. Coolness on the scaffold was therefore seen as an expression of defiance. An official in Bavaria complained

that the more fearless and courageous the criminal appears to be, the more unsuited the bloody spectacle of an execution is to procure the effect of terror and revulsion among the crowd of onlookers. In this connection a writer has correctly remarked: 'A guilty person dying cold-bloodedly and demonstrating courage during the proceedings is a fresh encouragement to vanity and crime. There are heroes of all kinds, in all ranks of civil society, but the murderer who holds his head high on the scaffold is also a hero; he will find not only admirers but also all too often imitators.'[62]

Once more, the fear was expressed that public executions would encourage people to commit crimes rather than deter them; the ability of the criminal to remain calm was seen as the reason for the crowd's admiration and the conse-quent temptation to play the hero. The removal of the religious element by the authorities did not, therefore, seem to have achieved its desired effect.

Many criminals, of course, were unable to remain calm and went to their death in a state of abject terror. But this was no better in the eyes of *Vormärz* officials than was defiant sang-froid. The Bavarian legal official Baron Otto von Völderndorff und Waradein, who attended numerous public executions in the first half of the nineteenth century, remarked that

Usually the person to be executed was a real 'poor sinner', which naturally aroused the sympathy and regret of the public, and indeed not infequently to such an extent that one could not speak any longer of a 'deterrence' (which according to theory was the purpose of holding the execution in public). Instead, the criminal was completely forgotten, and the punishment was seen not as the expiation of a violated law but merely as an act of cruelty. It also depended on what the spectators got to see. The pitiful creature was dragged onto the stage supported by the executioner's servants half-conscious, his knees having given way.[63]

[62] HStA Munich, MJu 13066: Alleruntertänigster Bericht des Staats-Ministeriums der Justiz an Seine Majestät den König, den Vollzug der Todesstrafe betreffend, 30 May 1854.

[63] Völderndorff und Waradein, *Plaudereien*, i. 103–4.

By the middle of the nineteenth century, it was not unknown for the condemned person to be too nervous to stand still during the sentencing ceremony and to be offered a chair to sit on.[64] In the seventeenth and eighteenth centuries, the condemned still internalized religous sanctions to a sufficient degree to enable them to play the role of repentant sinner. The authorities' attempts to strip the execution of its religious aspects and reduce it to nothing but a demonstration of state power accelerated the tendency of the condemned to abandon their appointed role, and to behave either with unseemly boldness or with undisguised terror. Thus, as legal officials in Berlin complained as early as 1800,

Whatever the behaviour of the malefactor at the execution . . . may be, it always has the effect of frustrating the purpose of the punishment; for the people usually only show *revulsion* for the hangman and his business, while they *admire steadfast* or *unfeeling* malefactors, and *sympathize* with those who completely *feel* the seriousness of their situation.[65]

For nearly half a century after these comments were penned, judicial and state authorities across Germany had struggled to try and realize the 'purpose of punishment' by attacking the popular culture of executions and wresting the drama of public punishment to their own purposes. In 1847, however, a new set of circumstances, deeply threatening to social and political stability, raised their anxiety levels to such a degree that they abandoned these fruitless attempts and reached for a more radical solution altogether.

For in the second half of the 1840s, general crime rates in Prussia, and indeed the rest of Germany, began to rise sharply as a result of deteriorating economic conditions. Although the rise was concentrated in theft, and scarcely affected capital offences, it gave renewed urgency to the question of a general penal reform, and fuelled official anxieties about public order.[66] At the same time, and for much the same reason—the economic crises brought on by a series of very bad harvests in the second half of the 'hungry forties'—bread riots and other popular disturbances in Germany began to increase to unprecedentedly high levels.[67] Anything that could be done to remove a possible occasion of rioting was now receiving urgent consideration. In Prussia the growing financial difficulties

[64] HStA Hanover Hann. 173a Nr. 438, Bl. 24–5: report of an execution in Osnabrück, 31 July 1857.

[65] GStA Berlin Rep. 84a/7781, Bl. 14–15: Directores und Räthe der Berliner Stadtgerichte, letter to the King, 1 Sept. 1800.

[66] Blasius, *Bürgerliche Gesellschaft*, 115–32; idem, *Kriminalität und Alltag. Zur Konfliktgeschichte des Alltagslebens im 19. Jahrhundert* (Göttingen, 1978), 51.

[67] Charles, Louise, and Richard Tilly, *The Rebellious Century 1830–1930* (London, 1975), 208–14; Rainer Wirtz, *'Widersetzlichkeiten, Excesse, Crawalle, Tumulte und Scandale'. Soziale Bewegung und gewalthafter sozialer Protest in Baden 1815–1848* (Frankfurt am Main, 1981); Arno Herzig, *Unterschichtenprotest in Deutschland 1790–1870* (Göttingen, 1988); Heinrich Volkmann und Jürgen Bergmann (eds.), *Sozialer Protest. Studien zu traditioneller Resistenz und kollecktiver Gewalt in Deutschland vom Vormärz bis zur Reichsgründung* (Opladen, 1984).

of the Crown forced it to give increased representation to the well-off Rhenish bourgeoisie in the long-delayed preparation of the new Criminal Code. The growth of a vocal liberal movement in many German states had for some time made itself felt in a number of aspects of penal policy, for example in reducing the role of the wheel in Prussian executions from the second half of the 1830s onwards, and in the growing criticisms of the inconsistent exercise of the royal prerogative of clemency.[68] Liberals were just as anxious as anybody else about the maintenance of public order, and more critical than most of the 'excesses' and other 'unworthy' aspects of crowd behaviour at public executions. Their increased influence in the 1840s made it feasible for the first time to consider the introduction of public trials in Prussia, which, as we have seen, was the *sine qua non* of the ending of executions in the open air.[69]

Under the impact of these events, a final draft of the Criminal Code which had been under preparation for so long in Prussia was produced in 1847. It limited the death penalty to treason; the manslaughter of close relatives; premeditated murder; infanticide by someone other than the mother, or when it was not committed immediately after the birth; and the deliberate burning down of buildings, wrecking of ships, poisoning of wells, or flooding of land, if this caused someone to lose their life. This removed a number of offences, such as simple arson, aggravated highway robbery, counterfeiting, and infanticide, from the roster of capital crimes. It was calculated that, if the new Code had been in force during the period 1826–43, then the number of offenders condemned to death in Prussia would have been 187 instead of 426, and nineteen out of the 100 criminals executed would have escaped this fate and been sentenced to imprisonment instead.[70] The overall reduction of capital crimes was a major concession to liberal opinion. Just as significant, however, was the fact that the draft Code laid down that executions were no longer to be held in the open. Instead, they were to take place 'in an enclosed space invisible to the public'. This way, there would be no problem about limiting attendance or controlling the behaviour of the spectators. Every effort was to be made, however, to ensure that there would be no suspicion of secrecy. Executions were to be announced by the ringing of a bell, 'while in the mean time preachers will address the people gathered round the execution place'. In other words, it was envisaged that a crowd would still be there, but outside the prison, learning the moral lesson of the event rather than witnessing the execution itself. This, finally, seemed to be the only way possible

---

[68] GStA Berlin Rep. 84a/7782, Bl. 79–81: *Pannonia* (Pressburg), 5. Jg., 13. 8. 1841; ibid., Bl. 87: Friedrich Wilhelm IV to PJM, 16 Apr. 1842.

[69] Blasius, 'Der Kampf'.

[70] GStA Berlin Rep. 84a/8144, Bl. 35: *Justiz-Ministerial-Blatt für die Preussische Gesetzgebung und Rechtspflege*, 10/30 (28 July 1848), 247.

of ensuring that the official understanding of the meaning of capital punishment, and no other, was conveyed to the public. The King himself urged the Justice Ministry to act without delay.[71]

After gathering information from academic authorities in the United States about the method of execution customary in the prison at Philadelphia,[72] Savigny and the Justice Minister, Karl von Uhden (1798–1878), replied to the King in a memorandum of 17 November 1847, which constituted the decisive document in the decision-making process. They began by summing up the many criticisms which had long since been common in the bureaucracy's reporting of public executions in Prussia:

Executions in the open, outside the city limits or on the market-place, are generally regarded by the people as a spectacle in which their curiosity can seek and find satisfaction. The aim of deterrence is mostly lost. The mob often gives itself over at a whim on such occasions to outbreaks of coarse behaviour; instead of making a deep and serious impression on morality, public executions provide the occasion for many an excess. On the other hand, they also fail to achieve the desired effect by encouraging either a brutal pleasure in the melancholy sight, or sympathy with the offender, or a kind of admiration for his courage and steadfastness. The ceremonies with which the execution is connected, and the regard and attention paid to the malefactor, have even, as examples have shown, lured people to wish to die in a similar way, and so have led to serious crimes being committed.

Moreover, they added, all this public attention made the condemned person vain, and thus produced an 'inappropriate spiritual state' in which to die. These problems could all be overcome if the execution took place away from the gaze of the general public. To avoid any impression of secrecy, they labelled the proposed new procedure the 'intramural execution' in contrast to the old 'extramural execution'. Thus it was clearly the intention, they emphasized once more, 'not to replace public with secret executions, but extramural with intramural'. In sum, they claimed: 'Intramural executions remove the above-mentioned abuses, among which can also be counted the superstition which attached certain effects to the blood, the clothing, and other remains of the executed person.' These too they considered inappropriate to the intended solemnity of the occasion.[73]

The Ministers insisted strongly on the need for such a measure to be accompanied by the introduction of public trials in place of the secret inquisitorial procedure that was still in operation in 1847. For, they declared, in a classic passage of bureaucratic thinking—and style—that is worth quoting at considerable length:

---

[71] Ibid. 7782, Bl. 203: Friedrich Wilhelm IV to PJM, 6 Aug. 1847.
[72] Ibid., Bl. 184. For the American system, see Masur, *Rites*, 93–116.
[73] GStA Berlin Rep. 84a/7782, Bl. 213–20.

The introduction of intramural executions can easily be misunderstood, with an unfortunate effect on popular opinion, if inquisitorial trials are still carried out according to the Criminal Regulations. The view that the intention is to execute in secret will gain currency among the uncomprehending, the evil-minded, and the credulous, and will be all the more difficult to refute since their ignorance of the proceedings of the investigation and the papers on which the judicial verdict is based will not leave them any choice but to conclude that there are motives for the abolition of executions in the open other than the removal of the abuses with which they are connected. It would be different if public investigations and trials were introduced, the evidence of the accused's guilt openly displayed, and thus every doubt about the true content of the case banished from the public mind. In this case, intramural executions could not provide the occasion for any reservations or concern in the public mind. After the trial and condemnation of the criminal had taken place under the public eye, no one would lay any great stress on the fact that the sentence should also be carried out under the public eye. On the contrary, people would regard the legal measures taken to ensure that the death penalty was carried out according to the law as sufficient reassurance.

They therefore agreed to the introduction of 'intramural executions' only on the express condition 'that public and verbal inquisitional procedures are introduced beforehand'.[74]

The subsequent deliberations of the Justice Ministry were concerned above all to get two points right. First, the authorities had a strong desire to put an end to the dramatic and ceremonial aspects of executions. And secondly, they insisted as strongly as possible on the fiction that executions were not being *removed* from the public eye; it was merely, they claimed, that public access was being *restricted*. What comes across most clearly in the document of 17 November 1847 and the subsequent discussions is a strong whiff of fear of the mob.[75] For reality it *was* the 'abuses' connected with public executions that were the cause of these reforms, and the attempt to deny this was, as the document suggested, merely propaganda. Gone were the self-confident attempts of the early 1800s to turn the execution into a public act of deterrence. After half a century the authorities were now giving up the struggle and withdrawing the execution from the general public out of fear of popular unrest. In pursuit of these ambitions, indeed, the Justice Ministers rejected some of the more imaginative proposals emanating from the monarch. They decided to avoid using the term 'intramural executions' because (in so far as it was intelligible to the general public at all) it would 'give encouragement to the erroneous opinion that public executions are to be replaced by secret ones, which is in no way intended'.[76] The ringing of the bell and

[74] GStA Berlin Rep. 84a/7782, Bl. 220–1.

[75] For comparable motives for the abolition of public executions in England, see Gatrell, *Hanging Tree*, 589–611, and Michael Jasper, ' "Hats Off!" The Roots of Victorian Public Hangings', in W. B. Thesing (ed.), *Executions and the British Experience* (London, 1990), 139–48.

[76] GStA Berlin Rep. 84a/7782, Bl. 241.

the hiring of preachers were judged to be 'ceremonies' which would attract crowds outside the prison, and these would in practice be impossible to control.[77] The composition of the actual crowd attending the execution was to be carefully regulated. Following the American model, a group of twelve witnesses from the local community was to be invited. This caused some difficulty because the procedures did not exist for empanelling a jury on American lines. 'All the same, the summoning of respected people who, because they do not occupy any office of state, can be expected to possess a greater degree of independence, is to be recommended.' Nobody, however, should be compelled to attend. Thus the local authority and 'other respectable members of the community' were to be requested to send twelve witnesses, 'who are suited for acting as guarantors by their official position, their place in civil society, and their character'. The public attending the event was also to be exclusively male. Not even the women of the condemned person's family were to be allowed in.[78] These reforms were approved in principle by the King on 4 November 1847.[79] No further obstacles seemed to remain, therefore, in the way of their becoming law.

It seemed that public executions were to be abolished in Prussia not because the élites thought they were inhumane, or because popular identification with the offender had led to protest or indifference towards their operation, but because a series of changes in the nature of public executions, brought about largely by official attempts to wrest them to the purpose of deterrence, had combined with social and political change and government nervousness about popular revolts to turn them into a public order problem. As a result, a wholesale change in the nature of the judicial and penal system was being undertaken, above all with the introduction of public trials. These reforms were undoubtedly a concession to liberal pressure. But they were also an attempt, undertaken in an increasingly desperate situation, to recover some legitimacy for a judicial system badly affected by the critical onslaught of the preceding years. In the process, the state showed itself willing to concede significant new rights to those of its citizens who were accused of serious crimes. The decision to remove executions to prison courtyards cannot be reduced, therefore, to a mere desire to 'punish better'. It signified, rather, the fact that penal policy in mid-nineteenth-century Prussia was caught in a web of structural contradictions from which it was difficult to escape without major changes in the direction of liberalization and the rights of the individual. Public order was to be restored, and criminality checked, not least by making the judicial system more acceptable to the ordinary citizen. These were far-reaching reforms indeed, even if they were balanced out by new measures to ensure the maintenance of public order. But the pace of events was moving even

[77] Ibid., Bl. 220, 248–9.   [78] Ibid., Bl. 243.   [79] Ibid., Bl. 263.

faster than the Prussian government. Preparation of the final draft of the new Criminal Code and execution regulations was interrupted by violent public disturbances in Berlin, which forced the withdrawal of the King and his ministers from the city in March 1848. The relevant document, summarized above, appears in the file with an incomplete date ('—th March 1848') and a hastily scribbled note, 'to be resubmitted in 6 months' time, 15/v/48'.[80] It quickly became apparent that this was a wildly over-optimistic estimation of the time it would take for the disturbances to pass. The long-feared, long-hoped-for revolution had finally arrived, and its effects upon the status and operation of capital punishment were to be dramatic.

d. *The Debate in the Frankfurt Parliament*

By April 1848 the whole of Germany was in uproar. In the countryside, peasants were spontaneously throwing off the last shackles of feudalism. In the great cities and state capitals such as Berlin, Munich, and Vienna, crowds of journeymen, students, and workers were forcing the retreat or overthrow of the existing regimes. New, liberal ministries were forced onto the princes, who accepted them in order to try and stem the tide of revolution which, especially in the south-west, was threatening to abolish monarchy altogether. The ministries in turn were forced to yield to massive pressure for the election of a national parliament, drawing its deputies from all over the German Confederation. On 18 May 1848 the National Assembly met in St Paul's church in Frankfurt am Main, elected by a wide though not quite universal manhood suffrage. It was no 'parliament of professors', as it has sometimes been dubbed by hostile commentators, but a mixture of lawyers, civil servants, journalists, merchants, factory-owners, doctors, teachers, landowners, and many others. But it was not representative of the people as a whole. Its members were overwhelmingly bourgeois, propertied, and educated. It soon became clear, indeed, that they were at least as afraid of the 'mob' as they were of the old princes, if not more so.[81] The task of the Frankfurt Parliament was to prepare a constitution for a united Germany. On 24 May 1848 it began debating the first stage of this process, a draft list of 'Basic Rights of the German People' which, it hoped, would set strict limits on the executive power whose establishment would be the next stage in the constituent process. The model, of course, was the Declaration of the Rights of Man and Citizen which had been the fundamental document of the great French Revolution that had

---

[80] GStA Berlin Rep. 84a/7782, Bl. 140.

[81] Among many different accounts of the 1848 Revolution, see the classic narrative by Veit Valentin, *Geschichte der deutschen Revolution von 1848–49* (2 vols.; Berlin, 1930–1), and the recent brief survey by Wolfram Siemann, *Die deutsche Revolution von 1848/49* (Frankfurt am Main, 1985). For an account of the capital punishment debate, see Düsing, *Abschaffung*, 29–53.

broken out nearly sixty years before. A thirty-man Constitutional Committee was set up, charged with drafting the Basic Rights. The idea of including the abolition of the death penalty among these rights was suggested by the fact that it had recently been abolished by the revolutionary National Assembly in France. The motion to include the abolition of capital punishment in the draft list of Basic Rights to be forwarded to the Constitutional Committee quickly ran into opposition, as some deputies wanted to keep the death penalty for high treason. But an amendment to this effect was rejected by the overwhelming margin of 315 votes to 28. A second amendment, proposing to retain capital punishment for murder, was also rejected by a huge majority, 248 votes to 80. However, a third amendment, to retain capital punishment in time of emergency and war, was won by 193 votes to 164.[82]

These votes paved the way for the final decision that would be reached on the issue later on. They were, in other words, no more than preliminary. A majority of the Constitutional Committee wanted the relevant paragraph—number 7—merely to guarantee freedom from arbitrary arrest, and did not think the abolition of the death penalty belonged in it at all. A minority, consisting of Robert Blum and Franz Wigard from the political left-wing grouping known (like the others, from the inn where they met) as the Deutscher Hof, Friedrich Scheller from the broadly right-wing Casino Party, and the independent lawyer from Württemberg, Friedrich von Römer, wanted it to include the abolition of capital punishment. Another group of deputies, mostly lawyers, and including Heinrich Ahrends from the centre-left Westendhall group, Scheller, Friedrich Bassermann, Carl Wippermann, and August Hergenhahn from the Casino Party, Wigard, and the well-known academic jurist Carl Mittermaier from the centre-left Württemberger Hof, put forward a further amendment abolishing the death penalty for political offences. Ernst Moritz Arndt, on the other hand, another member of the right-wing Casino Party, preferred to retain the death penalty for 'traitors, parricides, and matricides', while yet another member of the same party, Major Teichert, urged that military courts should keep their power of condemning soldiers to death. In Frankfurt, as this division of opinion shows, there were no disciplined party groupings in the modern sense. All these options, ranging from the complete abolition of all capital punishment to abolition only for certain categories of offence, were put forward as amendments to Paragraph 7 of the Basic Rights when the Constitutional Committee submitted its final report on 3 July. For it was only now, in fact, that the process of debating the individual clauses of the Basic Rights on the floor of the Chamber began in

[82] Franz Wigard (ed.), *Stenographische Berichte über die Verhandlungen der deutschen constituirenden Nationalversammlung zu Frankfurt am Main*, i (Leipzig, 1848), 622–4.

earnest.[83] On 3 August, towards the end of the day, the deputies once more reached the clause dealing with the right to life.

The debates on Paragraph 7 of the Basic Rights lasted for the rest of the sitting of 3 August and took up the whole of the next day's proceedings. They exhibited a characteristic mixture of procedural pedantry and confusion on the one hand, and lofty declarations of principle on the other. The Parliament did not begin debating the substance of the matter straight away, but started by arguing about whether it was appropriate to discuss it at all. The Constitutional Committee's majority view was that the matter belonged more properly to the proposed debate on a new Criminal Code. It considered that the decision on whether or not to abolish the death penalty 'should be referred to the Criminal Codes of the individual states'. In effect, this meant that any attempt to create a unified German approach to the matter would be postponed to a later date.[84] The Constitutional Committee was extremely influential, and its advice was often followed. But not on this point. For many deputies believed that this was going about the business the wrong way. As Gustav Siemens, a lawyer from Hanover and member of the Casino Party, argued, the abolition of the death penalty for the whole of Germany would undoubtedly force a revision of the criminal codes of the individual states. Yet why should this be an objection? The same was surely true of virtually every clause in the Basic Rights. Stipulations on freedom from arbitrary arrest, equality before the law, liberty of religious practice, and other matters could equally be said to belong more properly to laws on the conduct of trials, on the church, on the police, and so on. If everything were to be left to the individual states or to special legislation, there might as well be no declaration of basic rights at all. The purpose of the Basic Rights was to draw up a list of fundamental principles which by their very nature ought to have an effect on specific areas of the law and its implementation in the individual states. If there was any one such fundamental principle, he argued, it was surely the right to life.[85] Friedrich Scheller, from Frankfurt an der Oder, and a moderate right-wing liberal, underlined the argument that the abolition of capital and corporal punishment belonged in the Basic Rights of the German People:

Everything which is before us in the Basic Rights is merely concerned with property matters and a few petty personal things. But honour and life, which are now the question, are the highest possessions of humanity; therefore something has to be said about them in the Basic Rights, if we do not want to accord them less importance than those property matters and petty personal things.

[83] Franz Wigard (ed.), *Stenographische Berichte über die Verhandlungen der deutschen constituirenden Nationalversammlung zu Frankfurt am Main*, ii, nos. 55–6, pp. 1351–3.

[84] Ibid. 1379.   [85] Ibid. 1381.

The German people, he concluded, had the basic right to have their life and honour guaranteed.[86] Similarly, in a speech that earned cheers from the left and 'laughter on the right', Emil Rossmässler, a professor of zoology from Leipzig and member of the left-wing Deutscher Hof, declared that so far the Basic Rights seemed to leave out the right to live.[87] But despite the laughter, this view was repeated by other speakers,[88] and these arguments eventually won the day. Now that this hurdle had been cleared, the Assembly plunged straight into an impassioned debate on the principle of capital punishment itself.

The lawyer Friedrich Scheller declared in a powerful opening speech in favour of abolition: 'I had already been in the judicial service for almost twenty years when I put the motion to abolish the death penalty before the State Council in Berlin fifteen years ago; and here I can only repeat what I said then.'[89] Even if he was defeated, he said, he was certain that the death penalty would be abolished 'in twenty-five years at the latest'. Torture had been regarded by its defenders in the eighteenth century as a regrettable but indispensable tool for the interrogation of suspects. Now, however, it was clear that its abolition had in no way made interrogation more difficult. The same would doubtless be the case with the abolition of the death penalty. There was simply no evidence that it deterred crime. The removal of the death penalty from many offences in England in the 1820s and 1830s had not led to any marked increase in their incidence. The French still executed people for a number of offences which merited only imprisonment in Germany, yet these crimes did not seem to be any less common to the west of the Rhine than they were to the east. 'No matter how great the punishment you lay on a crime, however trivial that crime may be,' said one speaker, 'it will still be committed, for the person who commits it never reckons on being caught.' The only real way of fighting crime was to improve methods of detection, and the only true deterrent was the certainty of being found out.[90] Carl Beseler, another jurist, Professor of Law at Greifswald University and member of the right-wing Casino Party, disagreed with these views, and played down deterrence in favour of retribution and atonement. But this idea was roundly condemned by other speakers as belonging 'to the days of superstition'.[91] The death penalty, it was argued, placed an intolerable moral burden on the shoulders of those faced with pronouncing or confirming it. This was a parliament full of lawyers, and many of those who spoke had substantial judicial experience. Ernst Moritz Arndt (Bonn), who wanted to retain capital punishment, had been a member of a prisoners' aid society since the 1820s. Remigius

---

[86] Ibid. 1370.   [87] Ibid. 1372.   [88] Ibid. 1381.   [89] Ibid. 1371.
[90] Ibid. 1370.   [91] Ibid. 1387 (Paul von Reisse).

Vogel, a pastor from Dillingen, and like Arndt a member of the Casino Party, told the Assembly that as a priest he had had 'to discharge the melancholy duty . . . of providing consolatory ministrations in prison to a criminal who had been condemned to death, and to accompany him to the scaffold. There, gentlemen,' he added histrionically, 'I learned to feel what is terrible about the death penalty.' Dietrich von Buttel, from Oldenburg, and a member of the Landsberg Party, declared himself to have been a judge for over twenty years, and for many of them he had been a convinced supporter of capital punishment. He had not only pronounced several death sentences himself, 'but also once had to officiate while one was being carried out'.[92] He had done all this, he confessed, with 'an unalloyed earnestness', but had subsequently changed his mind and was now a committed abolitionist. Similarly, Franz Heisterbergk, from Rochlitz, a member of the Deutscher Hof, revealed that he had been 'head of an administrative and judicial authority for twenty years' and also 'on one occasion had to send four people from life to death in a single day'. He too declared that 'severing someone's throat is unhuman, it's brutality'.[93]

According to the zoology professor Emil Rossmässler, judges were only prepared to pass sentences of death because the actual responsibility for deciding whether they should be carried out lay with the monarch, whose right of clemency the speaker criticized in ironical terms as 'the water of guiltlessness with which the humanitarianism of the judge washes its hands'. 'In my eyes', he declared, 'there is no more horrific right than this, which places all the weight of condemnation upon the shoulders of the poor, guiltless monarch.' The Pomeranian law professor Carl Beseler informed the Assembly:

I have lived in a land where the death penalty has in practice not been carried out for six years because the ruler could not bring himself to confirm a death sentence. But a case has now occurred there, a most terrible crime, in which cruelty, lust, and every base passion of the human heart have come together to bring about something terrible. Yet in this case too there has been no death penalty, since the sovereign did not want to make an exception, and this has made a very deep impression upon the people. There was general dissatisfaction at the decision—the people's sense of justice was offended.[94]

Many of those present recognized that there was widespread popular support for capital punishment. On the whole, however, the deputies paid very little attention to the opinions of the mass of the people—a characteristic sign of the mingled apprehension and disdain for the lower classes which characterized the men of 1848 and made it so difficult for them to gain the kind of popular support that had driven the French Revolution of 1789 forward.

---

[92] Franz Wigard (ed.), *Stenographische Berichte über die Verhandlungen der deutschen constituirenden Nationalversammlung zu Frankfurt am Main*, ii, nos. 55–6, p. 1374.

[93] Ibid. 1382.   [94] Ibid. 1390.

The debate was characterized by that concern for principle, that lofty idealism, for which the Frankfurt Parliament was famous, and which Bismarck was subsequently to ridicule as politically ingenuous and unrealistic. A typical point was that made by Friedrich Scheller: 'No person is entitled to take even so much as a minute of another person's existence away by force, a minute in which this other person could prepare himself for the Beyond and thus make himself worthier for it.' Nobody knew whether atonement was possible in the Hereafter; thus no mere human had the right to interfere by condemning a fellow human to enter it. On the contrary, the death penalty would frustrate the purpose of penal policy, namely the moral improvement of the offender. As Sylvester Jordan, another professor and civil servant, from Marburg, and member of the centre-left Württemberger Hof, said, 'the system of improvement is the only correct system of punishment. . . . Who has the right to cut the thread of life, the only precondition of the moral development, improvement, and perfection of the human being?'[95] Other speakers alleged that capital punishment was incompatible with Christianity. 'The death penalty robs a person of his future and thus of his destiny; it wields power over something which no man has a right to control for himself.'[96] Its abolition would usher in a time 'of humanitarianism, a time of true Christian love' in the criminal law. Or, alternatively, it would inaugurate 'the hegemony of reason'.[97] Indeed, as Friedrich Biedermann, yet another professor, from Leipzig, and also a member of the Württemberger Hof, noted, religion could be used to justify capital punishment as well as oppose it. But 'from the standpoint of naturalism you will never be able to justify the right to curtail the capacity of a person to develop and shape himself.'[98] More than one speaker returned to the theme of depriving people of the possibility of self-improvement. 'A person's destiny consists of his perfectibility, and as long as he lives, to devote all his powers to perfecting himself.'[99] This was the chief difference, indeed, between men and brute animals. If the state denied its citizens this possibility, it was contradicting its very purpose, which was to provide them with it. The abolition of capital punishment was thus an essential part of moral as well as social progress, 'and in future times people will look back on the death penalty as a piece of barbarity just as we now look back on torture'.[100] Finally, the abolition of capital punishment was a symbolic act for the Revolution itself. One speaker portrayed 'the abolition of capital punishment as the last element in the fraternization of a state'. 'Let us not bring the death penalty from the times of the police state into the times of the state ruling by law', pleaded another. 'The retention of capital punishment will perpetuate submissiveness and serfdom for all time, for it really turns the condemned man into the bodily property of state and society.'[101] 'The state itself must be human, if it is to do justice to humans.'[102] Abolition would be an act of general moral education; by demonstrating the state's respect for human life, it would encourage others to respect it too. It would thus provide 'the most lasting cornerstone for a higher morality' for the future; an essential part of a new concept of the law and the state. The law assumed that humans were endowed with reason; if criminality constituted a lapse of reason, then the law had to provide the criminal with the possibility of regaining it. Capital punishment was also incompatible with the rationality of the state, because the state existed in order to guarantee the safety of the individual, and to give the citizen the possibility of development and improvement. Murderers were citizens too, and therefore the state was contradicting its own purpose if it cut this possibility off.[103]

The deputies were attempting to establish a new state on the basis of national unity and liberal political institutions. Yet this confronted them with the problem of how to deal with that new state's potential internal and external foes. 'I can't see', said one speaker, perhaps thinking of the confrontation in progress with the Danes over the Schleswig-Holstein question, 'how one can keep an army in order during a war without the fear of the death penalty.'[104] As another speaker, Philipp Wernher, a landowner from Nierstein on the Rhine and a member of the centre-left Württemberger Hof, remarked, the state surely had to retain the right to execute those who sought to overthrow it. The French Revolution of 1789 had begun by abolishing the death penalty, but in due course had found it indispensable. Unfortunately at this point Wernher's argument became somewhat confused, as he went on to note that Robespierre, initially an opponent of capital punishment, had eventually made executions into an everyday instrument of rule. This seemed to be more of an argument against the death penalty in such circumstances than a point in its favour. Other speakers, however, returned to the thesis he had seemed to be developing at the outset of his speech. Ernst Moritz Arndt argued that the state had to be able to make an example of the leaders of treasonable political movements, since if such movements were substantial in size, it would be impossible to incarcerate or otherwise punish everyone who was involved in them. This seemed to be an almost Robespierrist plea for allowing the Revolution to defend itself by cutting off the heads of its leading opponents. It did not meet with much sympathy in the milder climate of 1848, and Arndt's speech was forced to a conclusion by cries of 'Stop! Stop!' from the floor. As Friedrich Scheller pointed out:

[101] Franz Wigard (ed.), *Stenographische Berichte über die Verhandlungen der deutschen constituirenden Nationalversammlung zu Frankfurt am Main*, ii, nos. 55–6, p. 1372.
[102] Ibid. 1384 (Dham).   [103] Ibid. 1385.   [104] Ibid. 1360 (Leve).

None of us is certain that tomorrow the situation won't be different, or that it won't change again the day after next. . . . Yesterday the death penalty for treason was meted out to deeds which are rewarded with civic honours today. . . . We all know how often political viewpoints and political constellations change; let us not make people's lives dependent on this mutability of political viewpoints.[105]

The deputies were indeed aware of the fact that the legal definition of treason was subject to the possibility of rapid change, especially in a fast-developing revolutionary situation. As one speaker recalled: 'Gentlemen, many an upright man speaking here would have counted as a political offender according to the laws and the erroneous views prevailing forty years ago, and if he had been caught, punished with death [*Many voices*: Four months ago!].'[106] No doubt many of those present were aware, some four months after the outbreak of the Revolution, when the initial euphoria had long since dissipated in the face of increasingly obvious political realities, of the grim possibility that what had been treasonable in 1847 might once again become treasonable in 1849. Thus caution was advised before passing a measure which might eventually be turned against its authors. More practical and immediate considerations also spoke against the retention of the death penalty for political offences. Even if the prospect of execution might deter an individual from killing someone for purely personal reasons, or for pecuniary gain, it was unlikely to deter someone whose motives were political. 'It is', said one speaker, 'almost like it was with the Christian martyrs of about 1,700 years ago; they were executed as political offenders, but the martyrs' blood was always the seed from which fresh Christians sprang.'[107]

After all these arguments had been rehearsed, the Assembly finally brought the matter to the vote. An attempt to retain the death penalty for parricides and traitors found too few seconders to qualify for a general vote. The same fate befell a further amendment retaining capital punishment in wartime. Then the motion to reject the inclusion of the whole issue from the Basic Rights and refer the matter to the Legislative Committee was defeated by 265 votes to 175, thus opening the way for the main motion to be put. This was a major victory for the abolitionists. The principle had now been established that the abolition of capital punishment, unlike other matters of penal policy, could legitimately be included in a constitutional document rather than having to wait for the promulgation of a new Criminal Code. At this point, however, the inexperienced and confused management of the Frankfurt Parliament caused an interruption, as the deputies descended into a procedural wrangle about whether to take the remaining amendment before or after the main motion. Astonishingly enough, it was decided to vote on the general issue first—contrary to all normal parliamentary

[105] Ibid. 1371–2.   [106] Ibid. 1373 (Vogel).   [107] Ibid. 1373 (Vogel), 1380 (Mittermaier).

procedure, which dictates of course that motions must be amended before being put to the vote. Nevertheless, the vote on the main motion now went ahead. The abolitionists won by an overwhelming majority, nearly two-to-one, drawn from virtually every grouping in the Parliament, but on the whole reflecting the dominance of the left and centre-left in the Parliament. There were 288 votes in favour of including the abolition of capital punishment in the Basic Rights, and 146 votes against. The voting on the main motion went to a surprising degree along party lines though, given the looseness of the groupings in the Frankfurt Parliament, there was inevitably a good deal of cross-voting. The main groupings inclining towards abolition were the Augsburger Hof (20 for, 14 against), the Donnersberg (36 for, 9 against), the Deutscher Hof (48 for, 6 against), the Landsberg (26 for, 16 against), the Nürnberger Hof (7 for, 3 against) and the Westendhall (32 for, 9 against). The Württemberger Hof was split down the middle, with 28 in favour, and 23 opposed. The groupings inclined towards opposing the motion were the Café Milani (8 for, 37 against), the Casino Party (40 for, 77 against), and the Pariser Hof (6 for, 20 against).[108] Party discipline was not particularly strong in the Frankfurt Parliament. After this vote, the Parliament went on to agree to the amendment providing for the retention of the death penalty in military law. Amid repeated cheers and bravos, the final version of Paragraph 7 of the Basic Rights was then read out to the Assembly in full.[109] The paragraph was confirmed in a second reading on 7 December by 256 votes to 176, and an attempt, led by Mittermaier, to restrict the use of the death penalty in military law to wartime was defeated by 283 votes to 155.[110]

The Frankfurt Parliament finally approved the Basic Rights as law on 27 December 1848. The abolition of the death penalty was widely noted, and a sharp-witted satirist penned a mock-ballad claiming that the decision would put street balladeers out of business since they now had nothing left to sing about: 'The death penalty brought us our bread', the imaginary balladeer told the Parliament, 'you're making us all hungry instead!'[111] Everything, however, still remained to be done before the abolition of the death penalty could actually come into effect. It was entirely characteristic of the Frankfurt Parliament that the debate was couched almost exclusively in terms of grand principle. Very little was said about the details of penal policy. Virtually the only practical point at

---

[108] Of those whose affiliations could not be discovered, 36 voted for abolition and 39 against; of those who did not belong to any grouping, 34 voted in favour and 32 against. A number of members belonged to more than one grouping, which obviously had an effect on the figures; their votes have been counted twice. Biographical information is taken from Max Schwarz, *MdR. Biographisches Handbuch der Reichstage* (Hanover, 1965), 43–112.

[109] Wigard (ed.), *Berichte*, ii. 1393, 1399–1410.   [110] Ibid., v. 3943–6.

[111] Riha (ed.), *Moritatenbuch*, 13–17: 'Bettizion eines brodlosen Künstlers die Zurückgenehmigung eines Gesetzes anbelangent'.

issue was that of deterrence. Neither the retributive theory of justice, nor the traditional religious arguments in defence of the death penalty, featured much in the debate. Perhaps this was appropriate to the context of a discussion on the Basic Rights of the German People. But it also indicated how tenuously the Assembly's deliberations were connected to concrete political and legislative realities. Some of the deputies at least were aware of this fact. As Wilhelm Schaffrath pointed out:

> If we . . . decree the abolition of capital punishment, *this* does not get rid of it *immediately* unless we replace it with another punishment, and that is quite natural. For we would disturb the administration of justice in the individual states if we did this. All we are saying is that these states must promulgate a new law in the near future which no longer includes the death penalty; or that we ourselves replace it with another in a law to this effect.[112]

So it was already clear in December 1848 that individual states which took the Basic Rights seriously would have to prepare legislation abolishing the death penalty.[113] In the Grand Duchy of Baden, a bill to this effect was drafted shortly after Christmas, and went through the legislature in February and March.[114] From 16 March 1849, capital punishment was no longer valid in Baden except in military law.[115] Similarly, in the neighbouring south German Kingdom of Württemberg, capital punishment was abolished on 13 August 1849.[116] It was also removed in Oldenburg, Hesse-Nassau and Saxe-Anhalt.[117] In the Kingdom of Saxony the government decided on 5 January 1849 that all death sentences would be commuted to life imprisonment, with immediate effect, pending the introduction of a new Criminal Code. This decision was endorsed by the decision, by 61 votes to 3, of the lower chamber of the legislative assembly on 30 April 1850 to abolish the death penalty.[118] By the spring of 1849, capital punishment had been outlawed through laws implementing the Basic Rights and the Reich Constitution in the Grand Duchy of Hesse and the Electorate of Hesse, Baden, Saxe-Weimar-Eisenach, Oldenburg, Brunswick, Saxe-Coburg-Gotha, Saxe-Anhalt-Dessau and Cöthen, Schleswig-Holstein, Schwarzburg-Rudolstadt and Schwarzburg-Sondershausen, Waldeck, and the Free Cities of Bremen, Hamburg, and Frankfurt am Main.[119]

---

[112] Wigard (ed.), *Berichte*, ii. 1385.

[113] GLA Karlsruhe 234/6109: Justizministerium, note 12831 of 26 Dec. 1848: 'die Aufhebung der Todesstrafe betr.'

[114] Ibid.: *Verhandlungen der 2. Kammer 1847/49: Beilage Nr. 1 zum Protokoll der 141sten öffentlichen Sitzung vom 1. Februar 1849; Beilage Nr. 438 zum Protokoll der 89. Sitzung vom 1. März 1849.*

[115] Ibid.: *Grossherzoglich Badisches Regierungsblatt* Nr. 15, p. 147 (21 Mar. 1849).

[116] Ibid.: *Regierungs-Blatt für das Königreich Württemberg,* Nr. 17, p. 170.

[117] Ibid. 6609: *Der Beobachter, Ein Volksblatt aus Schwaben* (Stuttgart, 22 Mar. 1864).

[118] *Ueber die Todesstrafe*, p. vi.   [119] Ibid., p. vii.

Well before any of this, another blow had been struck against the death penalty by the Constitutional Assembly which had been elected, on a notably wider franchise than the Frankfurt Parliament, to carry through the liberal revolution in Prussia. A motion to abolish capital punishment was put before the Assembly on 7 July 1848. It demanded a specific law rather than a constitutional provision. The matter became urgent when two executions were reported from Koblenz later in the month. The revolutionary government in Berlin promised to stop executions and the top civil servant in the Justice Ministry, Carl Anton Märcker, delivered a speech in favour of abolition on the final day of the debate. Like many others, he poured scorn on the argument that the death penalty was a deterrent, and suggested that it was up to the legislators to educate the people if the latter were still in favour of it. The Rhenish Catholic lawyer Peter Reichensperger objected that it was wrong to abandon the wisdom of centuries in a moment of enthusiasm, and reminded the deputies that even Beccaria had allowed the death penalty for treason. Recalling the traditional view that the imminence of death prompted the capital offender to repent, Reichensperger declared that Christianity strongly supported capital punishment, 'the highest and final guarantee for the freedom of the citizen'. But the majority of the Assembly rejected these arguments, and voted on 4, 8, and 9 August 1848 to abolish the death penalty by 294 votes to 46, an even greater majority than that obtained in the Frankfurt Parliament. Here too, however, the deputies backed away from abolition across the board. The motion to dispense with capital punishment without exception was lost by 193 votes to 164, thus opening the way to further votes which would water down the general principle. Reichensperger's amendment providing for the death penalty to be retained for high treason was lost overwhelmingly by 315 votes to 28—not surprisingly, since many deputies must have had at the back of their minds the fear that this was precisely the offence they themselves would be accused of if the revolution failed and the old regime was reinstated. A further motion to retain capital punishment for murder was also rejected, by 248 votes to 80. However, a motion to retain the death penalty in time of emergency was lost by a much smaller majority (172 votes to 166); and a more precise formulation of the same principle, according to which it would be retained for offences for which it was already prescribed in time of war or a state of siege, was carried, by 165 votes to 160. Here too, therefore, the principle of abolitionism did not triumph completely.[120]

This wave of abolitionist legislation suggested that the Basic Rights of the German People were not wholly without effect. It seemed as if the death penalty

[120] *Verhandlungen der Versammlung zur Vereinbarung der Preussischen Staatsverfassung* (3 vols.; Berlin, 1848), i. 619–65; ii. 416–20.

would soon be a thing of the past. The move towards ending public executions which had begun in 1847 had been overtaken by a far more radical stroke: one which encapsulated all the lofty principles and idealistic precepts for which the 1848 Revolution in Germany was famous. The crisis of legitimacy which public executions had been suffering for some decades had now spilled over into the very idea of capital punishment itself. The coincidence in time of these two crises strongly suggests that they were related, and indeed we have seen how the ending of public, physical punishments was closely connected with a whole series of other judicial reforms, from the rise to prominence of the ameliorative discourse in penal policy to the introduction of trial in open court with the participation of lay assessors and the jury principle. It would be viewing all these changes far too narrowly to see them simply as the outcome of a discursive shift among political and social élites, as the result of a decision to replace old methods of punishment with new ones because the latter were more effective. Real social and political conflicts were involved, not only between élite and popular understandings of public punishment, or between conservative and liberal recipes for justice and the law, but also between organic and contractual concepts of the state, between authoritarianism and representative democracy in law and politics, between rival precepts for a just and equitable society. On the outcome of these larger conflicts the fate of the Basic Rights, and therefore of capital punishment in Germany, would largely depend.

e. Capital Punishment in the 1848 Revolution

The apparent victory of the Frankfurt Parliament in securing the acceptance of the Basic Rights in a number of German states early in 1849 was deceptive. Already by this time, in fact, real power was slipping out of its hands. It had failed to gain any real hold over the governments and their military forces; indeed, it had increasingly placed itself in their hands by approving the military suppression of nationalist revolts in Poland and Bohemia and lower-class uprisings in Baden and Frankfurt itself. It had been powerless to intervene when the Habsburg army under Windischgrätz had marched into Vienna in October 1848 and put down the revolution in the city amidst considerable bloodshed, including the execution of one of the leading deputies in the Frankfurt Parliament, Robert Blum, by a drumhead court martial. The following month, the Prussian King, who had delayed signing the law abolishing the death penalty and put forward counter-proposals of his own, based on the retention of capital punishment in time of emergency, had also recovered his nerve.[121] He installed a

---

[121] For this counter-proposal, see ibid., ii. 698–9.

reactionary ministry in Berlin, dissolved the revolutionary Prussian Assembly, and imposed a new, illiberal constitution. Too frightened to make common cause with the popular movement, the liberals in Frankfurt had condemned themselves to impotence. Their election of King Friedrich Wilhelm IV of Prussia as sovereign of the new united Germany was a confession that the route towards a 'big Germany', including the parts of the Habsburg Empire that had been included in the German Confederation since 1815, was now closed. And this election was rebuffed in April 1849 by the Prussian monarch, who had no intention of owing his sovereignty to an assembly of revolutionaries. The Parliament's campaign to get the constitution of a united Germany which it had finally voted through on 28 March 1849 adopted by the states was a failure. Divided over how far to go in exerting pressure on the states, the deputies drifted apart. Amid growing confusion, the moderates now agreed on a new plan for a united Germany without Austria, a plan jointly proposed by the governments of Prussia, Saxony, and Hanover.

This was in fact little more than a gesture, since these states had no intention of fulfilling this plan. It was in any case very different in spirit from the constitutional documents produced by the Revolution. It included a sharp rejection of the clause in the Basic Rights which had abolished the death penalty by constitutional law. In a joint memorandum dated 11 June 1849, the three governments of Prussia, Saxony, and Hanover attacked the clause at what they had quickly recognized to be its weakest point:

Paragraph 139 of the constitution voted through at Frankfurt opted for the inadmissibility of capital punishment in principle but allowed exceptions in practice which rendered the general principle superfluous and incapable of implementation. Once the state's right to destroy an individual is admitted, it is no longer in reality possible to understand why it should be confined to martial law—for which neither the actual outbreak of a war nor any other necessity is required—and here moreover without reference to any particular offence. This makes this amendment of the existing criminal law, which is unfounded and incalculable in its effects, all the more remote from reality, so this most serious and important question must be reserved for a more profound legislative exploration at a later date.[122]

The problems caused by the retention of capital punishment in military and emergency law were very real, and would surface dramatically later in German history. The point made was far more than merely logical, for revolutionaries had already been shot, as we have seen, after being condemned under martial law for their part in the events of 1848–9. Nor was this the last time that the argument that abolition did not belong in a constitution would be advanced. But this particular constitution was a dead letter from the start. The other states apart

---

[122] Quoted in *Ueber die Todesstrafe*, p. vii.

from Prussia either opposed it or withdrew from it almost immediately, while the Austrians now resurrected the pre-revolutionary institutions of the German Confederation, winning Prussian support in the Treaty of Olmütz on 29 November 1850. By this time, the rump of the Frankfurt Parliament had long since ceased to meet, broken up by Prussian troops. The Revolution was over.[123]

All along, the Prussian King and his advisers had in fact proved unwilling to abandon the principle of capital punishment. Prussia had not been among those states which had sought to implement the Basic Rights in their legislation. Rather than death sentences passed in 1848 being commuted automatically by the Prussian King pending abolition, no fewer than ten of them had been deferred for a final decision on the issue of the royal clemency until the following year. Already in March 1849, King Friedrich Wilhelm IV and his Justice Minister rejected one plea for clemency because to accede to it would, they said, give the impression 'that the government agrees to the abolition of capital punishment'.[124] Altogether four offenders were executed in Prussia in 1849.[125] By 1850 the government had fully recovered its nerve, the Revolution was broken, and reactionary politicians had been appointed to key posts with the aim of wiping out the legacy of 1848 and clamping down on all forms of disorder and dissent. No fewer than fifty-three offenders were condemned to death in Prussia in this year, including five for high treason; eighteen of them were executed. Offenders were, of course, still being condemned under the provisions of the General Law Code of 1794; thus in January 1850 the Justice Ministry had to consider the case of a woman who had been condemned to be dragged to the scaffold wrapped in an oxhide and broken with the wheel from the bottom up, after her conviction for torturing her husband to death. Justice Minister Louis Simons noted, however, that legal opinion held 'dragging to the scaffold incompatible with current ideas and circumstances'. It constituted, he said, 'an anachronistic extension of the death penalty', and the woman's sentence was commuted to simple decapitation with the axe, as indeed were all other similar sentences passed in Prussia at this time.[126] The last person to be condemned to breaking with the wheel in Prussia, and in fact in Germany as a whole, Ignatz Kusch, from Silesia, who had killed a man in the course of committing a robbery, had his sentence commuted to beheading on 3 January 1852.[127] Even after the revolution, therefore, serious capital offenders were still being sentenced to breaking with the wheel, and had to wait some time to hear whether they had escaped this fate. Thus, long before the Basic Rights were finally abrogated by the reactivated Confederation Diet on 23 August 1851, states such as Prussia had begun to circumvent them as far as capital punishment was concerned.

[123] Siemann, *Revolution*, for these developments.   [124] GStA Berlin Rep. 84a/7787, Bl. 265–8.
[125] Ibid. 8144, Bl. 70–1.   [126] Ibid. 7787, Bl. 273–4.   [127] Ibid. 8144, Bl. 118–19.

In the larger German states, the votes of legislatures such as the Prussian National Assembly in favour of abolition were simply ignored by post-revolutionary governments as they regained confidence.[128] And in 1850 and 1851, the princes rushed to reverse the abolition legislation introduced in the wake of the Basic Rights and the Constitution of 1849. The new Criminal Law Code introduced in the Grand Duchy of Baden on 5 February 1851 reintroduced the death penalty that had been abolished under the influence of the Revolution two years previously.[129] In June 1850, the Kingdom of Saxony reversed the decision it had taken the previous year to commute all death sentences automatically. The government introduced a new Criminal Code in 1853 which justified the retention of capital punishment on the grounds that 'unfortunately, since the year 1838 and right up to the present, there have been cases in which it was not possible to avoid the execution of the death sentence, not even by the exercise of clemency, without offending popular concepts of justice'.[130] Similarly, the government of the Grand Duchy of Hesse reintroduced a bill to restore capital punishment on 15 July 1851, remarking:

The arguments which at all times and among all peoples have spoken for the necessity of capital punishment are still fully valid; and especially times when discipline and order and respect for the law have sunk so low, as in the present, raise an urgent demand for the restoration of a protection for the life and property of the citizen, as well as the maintenance of the state itself, which only the threat of the death sentence can guarantee.

The measure was rushed through a reluctant lower chamber of the legislature by twenty-three votes to twenty-one after a four-hour debate and passed into law at the beginning of 1852.[131]

In Bavaria the reactionary Minister of Justice, Baron Karl von Kleinschrod, justified the reintroduction of the death penalty by referring to the anarchy which he believed had reigned in the Revolution itself:

Even the most determined optimist would not seriously wish to claim that morality and lawfulness have made such progress in popular life in recent times that crimes worthy of death no longer occur and that as a consequence the death sentence can be abolished. On the contrary, the seeds of anarchy, of atheism, and of immorality, sown in speeches and writings, have borne manifold fruit.[132]

In Württemberg, the death penalty was reintroduced on 17 June 1853 for murder, high treason, and premeditated physical assault on the monarch.[133] The preamble to the law declared:

---

[128] GLA Karlsruhe 234/6609: *Der Beobachter. Ein Volksblatt aus Schwaben* (Stuttgart, 22 Mar. 1864).
[129] Ibid.: Auszug aus dem Gesetze 'die Einführung des Strafgesetzbuchs, des neuen Strafverfahrens und der Schwurgerichte betr.' vom 5. Feb. 1851.
[130] *Ueber die Todesstrafe*, p. v.   [131] Krämer, *Mord*, 143.
[132] Anon., *Die Kgl. Bayer. Staatsminister der Justiz*, 555.
[133] GLA Karlsruhe 243/6609: *Regierungs-Blatt für das Königreich Württemberg*, 20 June 1853, 170.

The view that the most serious crimes, especially crimes against the life of others, can only be atoned for by the death of the criminal is deeply rooted in popular consciousness, and penal legislation cannot be permitted to set itself up against this dominant popular view, the less so when, as experience has shown, serious crimes in general and crimes against the life of others in particular have most regrettably increased in comparison with earlier times and are still constantly increasing today.

There had been, it went on, no more than seven death sentences passed in Württemberg in the 1830s, while in the 1840s there had been seventeen, and in the first two full years of abolition, 1850 and 1851, no fewer than six offenders had been imprisoned for offences that would have merited the death penalty according to the Criminal Code of 1839. This showed that the hope of 1849, that the improvement of morality would make the use of the death penalty superfluous, had not been fulfilled. In any case, the preamble went on: 'The abolition of the death penalty in 1848 derived more from the general political run of things at the time than from a genuinely felt need, or from an appreciation of people and things as they were, that was either unprejudiced, or based on popular opinion.' Typically for politicians of the era of reaction, therefore, the government of Württemberg in the 1850s claimed that it was far more closely in touch with the real feelings of the mass of the people than the liberals were.[134] For good measure it reintroduced corporal punishment at this time as well.[135]

In 1851 a new Prussian Criminal Code was quickly rushed through, on the basis of the draft of 1847, as amended by the legislature, in the haste of the bureaucracy and the bourgeoisie alike to provide a more effective and more widely accepted way of dealing with lawbreaking after the widespread disorder, criminality, and unrest of the revolutionary period. High treason, murder, and manslaughter or intentional homicide in connection with a crime were made punishable by death.[136] The draft laid before the legislative assembly in December 1850 declared:

The severity of the criminal law must necessarily correspond to the gravity of the crime committed. The death of the murderer can only be expiated by the loss of life. The existence of the state can only be secured by the execution of the death penalty. The legal consciousness of the people recognizes the necessity of expiating the most serious crimes by death.

The government, not taking any chances with this touchy subject, pushed it through *en bloc* with all the other clauses of the Code, and did not allow a

---

[134] Ibid.: *Bericht der Justizgesetzgebungskommission der (württembergischen) Kammer der Abgeordneten über die Motion des Abgeordneten Becher auf Abschaffung der Todesstrafe*, 28 Jan. 1865.

[135] Sauer, *Im Namen*, 171.

[136] For the definitions of murder and manslaughter as they evolved through the 19th c., see Friedrich Wachenfeld, *Die Begriffe von Mord und Totschlag sowie vorsätzlicher Körperverletzung mit tödlichem Ausgange in der Gesetzgebung seit der Mitte des 18. Jahrhunderts. Ein Beitrag zur vergleichenden Geschichte der Strafgesetzgebung* (Marburg, 1890).

separate debate on it.[137] Thus the death penalty was brought back by virtually all German states as the Revolution subsided. Only the minor states of Oldenburg, Anhalt-Dessau-Cöthen, and Bremen did nothing to reintroduce capital punishment at this time.[138] Once more, capital punishment was serving as a symbol of the determination of reactionary governments to pursue a tough, authoritarian line against crime and disorder.

Nevertheless, despite the failure of the Revolution to achieve its central objectives, and despite the rapid reintroduction of the death penalty all over Germany, penal and judicial policy after 1848 did not go back to what it had been before. In Prussia, for example, the new Criminal Code provided for the introduction of public trials, as foreseen by the pre-revolutionary draft of 1847. Henceforth, too, lay assessors (*Schöffen*) and juries (*Geschworenen*) had a role to play in the courts, though it was by no means as decisive as that of their counterparts in common-law countries such as England and the USA. Aspects of the inquisitorial process, such as the questioning of the accused by the judge instead of, as under common law, by the prosecution, remained central to Prussian, and subsequently German, criminal procedure. Still, the holding of trials in public was a major concession to liberal opinion. As the historian Dirk Blasius has pointed out: 'The bourgeois "achievements" of the Revolution of 1848—verbal and public criminal trial, jury courts, abolition of private jurisdictions and legal privilege—were confirmed by the "revised constitution" passed under conservative auspices in January 1850.'[139] The same mixture of restoration and reform characterized the states' policy towards capital punishment in this period as well. Almost everywhere, for example, the new law codes introduced a higher minimum age at which an offender could be executed—21 in Brunswick and Lippe-Detmold, for example, and 18 everywhere else. Only Prussia failed to raise the age and continued to execute offenders over the age of 16, though in practice most death sentences passed on criminals under the age of 20 were commuted to life imprisonment. More important, the new codes drastically restricted the number and range of capital offences. Murder and treason were the only grounds for a death sentence in most parts of Germany from now on, although in Hesse robbery with grievous bodily harm could earn it as well, at least in theory, and in the Duchy of Lauenburg the law still laid down the death penalty for horse-stealing, the bribery of officials, peculation, duelling, and fraudulent bankruptcy. In practice, of course, these clauses were inoperative. In Prussia a physical attack on the monarch could earn a death sentence according to the Criminal Code of 1851, and so too could aggravated manslaughter, if someone was killed in the course of a robbery being carried out.[140] Nevertheless, while capital punishment was gen-

---

[137] *Ueber die Todesstrafe*, p. v.   [138] Ibid., p. v.   [139] Blasius, *Bürgerliche Gesellschaft*, 133.
[140] *Ueber die Todesstrafe*, pp. iii, viii, ix, xi.

erally reintroduced in Germany after the failure of 1848, its impact was softened by a further narrowing of the range of offences to which it could be applied.

This did not prevent the numbers of death sentences and executions in most German states from rising sharply in the repressive climate of the post-revolutionary years. In Prussia, condemnations, which had been averaging twenty-six a year during the 1840s, rose to an annual average of forty-four during the first five years of the following decade, peaking at sixty in 1851. Similarly, while there had only been six executions a year on average in Prussia during the 1840s, there were no fewer than twenty-six a year on average during the first half of the 1850s. Of all condemned offenders 59 per cent went to the block in the post-revolutionary quinquennium, while only 23 per cent were executed in the 1840s. All this testified to the determination of the reactionary Prussian government to advertise its toughness after the failure of the Revolution. Indeed, during this period there were more people condemned and executed in Prussia than in England and Wales, in sharp contrast to the situation in the early nineteenth century. Across the Channel, there were only seventeen condemnations and ten executions a year in the decade 1851–60, far fewer than in Prussia, and although the campaign against public executions, which were not abolished in Britain until 1868, obviously played some part in producing these low figures, the main responsibility for the contrast clearly lay with the reactionary politics of the time in post-revolutionary Prussia.[141] Similar, though less marked, increases in the incidence of capital punishment can be observed in other German states, such as Hanover, at the same time. In the Grand Duchy of Baden, there were eleven executions in the 1850s, where there had only been one during the whole of the 1840s. Yet this was not permanent. As soon as the immediate aftermath of the Revolution was over, condemnations and executions began to fall. In the second half of the 1850s, the average number of offenders condemned to death in Prussia dropped from forty-four to thirty-eight, and the average number sent to the block from twenty-four to fifteen.[142] Clearly, the post-revolutionary administration of the death penalty in criminal cases—and these were all cases of common murder, without exception—was to a considerable extent politically inspired. Equally clearly, things were beginning to return to a kind of normality once the political situation seemed to Prussia's rulers to be more secure. And, as we have seen, the normalization of capital punishment went hand in hand with major reforms designed to make its operation less of a threat to public order.

All this suggested that, although the Revolution had failed in its principal objectives, it nevertheless ushered in a number of major changes in German society and politics. The fact that the thrones of Austria and Prussia had tottered,

[141] Düsing, *Abschaffung*, 75.
[142] See Statistical Appendix, below, for the full time-series and source notes.

and that other monarchs, most notably the King of Bavaria, had been forced to abdicate by popular pressure, came as a terrible shock to governing élites, and was not soon forgotten. If things simply went back to what they had been before the Revolution occurred, there was an obvious danger that it would be repeated. Princes and governments had started to think seriously about reform during the 1840s, and not always with a view to making timely concessions to the liberals. Often, as with the decision to end public executions, taken in Berlin in 1847 and only prevented from being implemented by the outbreak of revolution the following March, reform was designed to protect public order rather than appease liberal demands. At the same time, the liberals themselves had received a series of unpleasant shocks during the Revolution. Popular unrest, rioting, and the violence of the 'mob' had been a major influence in persuading them to compromise with the existing order. The defence of property and civil society was a major concern of aristocratic and middle-class liberals in the following period, and some of them at least were inclined for the moment to support capital punishment as a regrettable necessity in the light of their experiences.[143] The 1850s have rightly been called a decade of reaction, but they were also far more than that. Parliamentary assemblies had clearly come to stay in Germany, and increasingly provided a platform for liberal politics as they began to resurface during the decade. And in other respects, too, turning the clock back to the days before 1848 was out of the question. In many ways, therefore, the post-revolutionary settlement marked a compromise between the old regime and the liberals, rather than a simple reassertion of the pre-revolutionary order. It is not surprising, therefore, that it proved to be the starting-point for a series of major changes in the administration of capital punishment right across Germany. The crisis of public executions that began in the early nineteenth century had culminated in a widespread if temporary abolition of capital punishment altogether in 1848–9. It was not to be resolved by simple restoration. Throughout the 1850s and 1860s, German governments struggled to square the circle once more, in trying to reconcile the sovereign principle of capital punishment with the penal practice of correction and the political premium on public order. The transition from the old penal regime of public physical punishment to a new one of incarceration had broadly been accomplished, but the place of the death penalty in the new penal economy was by no means settled. As the last echoes of the 1848 Revolution died away, state authorities all over Germany resumed the execution of malefactors in public almost as if nothing had happened. But this situation was not to last for long.

---

[143] J. H. Steinhagen, *Ueber Todesstrafen* (Hamburg, 1855), 8.

7

Restoration and Change

a. The Condemned and the Reprieved

Reactionary governments in Germany after the failure of the 1848 Revolution regarded the axe and the block as vital instruments in the restoration of order. In Prussia the new Criminal Code, introduced in 1851, sought to carry out this restorative function while making a number of concessions to bourgeois opinion. The death penalty in particular was restricted to various kinds of homicide, and to treason. But this did not mean that the letter of the law was necessarily adhered to. For as part of the arsenal of restored, divinely-sanctioned monarchical authority, the Prussian King insisted on the royal prerogative of clemency. This was not new, of course, but had been wielded systematically since the eighteenth century, when the founding of prisons and penitentiaries had first provided a workable alternative to execution in the form of lifelong imprisonment. Every death sentence had to receive the formal approval of the monarch before it could be carried out. The Prussian King was advised on such cases by his judicial officials. In order to guide their recommendations in the light of the new provisions of the Criminal Code, and to maintain some kind of consistency, officials at the Prussian Ministry of Justice began keeping detailed notes and statistics on each capital case after the Criminal Code came into effect at the beginning of 1852. The notes offer a fascinating insight into the workings of the judicial-bureaucratic mind. Clemency was thought of in the nineteenth century as a way of balancing out the law with a measure of justice which the courts were sometimes unable to provide. Not legal, but moral and social reasons lay behind most of the recommendations arrived at. To be sure, reprieves were sometimes granted by the King on the ground that one or another aspect of the court's verdict was uncertain. Moreover, conviction without a confession was still considered relatively unsafe, despite the introduction of trial in open court and the greater weight given to evidence supplied by third parties in the new Criminal Code. This too was reflected in the application of the royal clemency. Of those condemned to death for murder during the period 1854 to 1865, 179 had confessed their crime in court, 122 had not; eighty-one of those who had confessed, or 45 per cent, were executed, while forty-six of those who had refused to admit their guilt, or 38 per cent, went to the gallows.[1] Certainly, the 7 per cent difference in the execution rates suggested that failure to confess was considered, in some instances at least, as sufficient ground for doubt about the soundness of the verdict for the King to grant a reprieve.

But such considerations were generally secondary. More important as a factor influencing the Prussian Ministry of Justice in recommending or refusing to recommend a reprieve was the kind of offence committed. The offender most likely to come under the axe in Prussia in the period of reaction was someone who had committed a murder. From 1848 to 1854 inclusive the commutation rates for both murder and murder with robbery were roughly the same, at 46 per cent and 44 per cent respectively; commutation of a death sentence to one of life imprisonment was much more likely in cases of manslaughter, where only 8 per cent of those sentenced were executed, and arson, where the figure was 7 per cent. In cases of aggravated theft and highway robbery, and treason, indeed, none of the sixteen death sentences passed in these years actually led to an execution. And only two of the thirty-five people condemned for infanticide were brought to the gallows, one of them being a man. These cases, of course, were in large part decided under the provisions of the General Law Code of 1794. But even before the new Criminal Code came into effect on 1 January 1852, removing all offences apart from murder, manslaughter, and treason from the roster of capital crimes, homicides made up the vast majority of capital cases: 137 men and 38 women were sentenced to death for murder from 1848 to 1854 inclusive; 55 men and 1 woman were sentenced to death for robbery with murder; 33 women and 2 men for infanticide; 14 men for fatal arson; and 40 men and 3 women for manslaughter. The small proportion of women is noticeable. Altogether women made up 22 per cent of offenders sentenced to death and 16 per cent of those executed in these years. For the commonest female capital offence, however, namely murder—a reflection of the legal changes introduced in the middle of the period, when infanticide disappeared as a capital crime—the execution rate was very similar to that of men, namely 45 per cent compared to 46 per cent. Clearly, the new Criminal Code was having an effect on the statistics.[2]

These figures already begin to suggest that non-legal criteria were paramount in the recommendations made by Prussian judicial officials on the exercise of the royal clemency—recommendations which were almost invariably followed by

[1] GStA Berlin Rep. 84a/8144, Bl. 118–19, 131–2, 141–2, 170–1, 231–2, 267–78; Ibid. 8145, Bl. 61–2, 144–5.

[2] Ibid., Bl. 70–1, 74–83, 86–7, 106–14, 118–19, 131–2, 141–2.

the monarch. A typical case from this period was that of the 24-year-old farm servant Andreas Bornberg, from Sachsen, convicted of murder on 12 December 1853.

The accused had intended to find accommodation in Schlottheim; on the way there, near Kirchheiligen, he met with the $15\frac{1}{2}$-year-old Goswin Krackrügge, with whom he had not been previously acquainted. Krackrügge, the son of a merchant in Erfurt, was going to Schlottheim to meet his grandmother, who lived there, and walked along with the accused to the edge of a nearby wood on the territory of the Dukedom of Schwarzburg-Rudolstadt. At this point the accused began to consider how poor his shoes were, how he had no money at all, and how this would prevent him from easily finding a job; so he demanded money from his companion, and when the same said that he had none, hit him a sharp blow on the head with his blackthorn stick. Krackrügge fell over, but got up again and called for help. Now the accused hit him several more times on the head and dragged him deeper into the wood, took a knife out of his pocket and stabbed him several times in the chest until he was dead. He stole the dead man's pocket-watch, pulled his boots off and took several pieces of clothing and a drawing instrument out of his vasculum.

Bornberg was refused clemency on 26 January 1855 and beheaded.[3] His crime was typical of murders for gain at this time; an individual act of violence, carried out in the open, for the sake of a few clothes and a handful of valuables. The mid-nineteenth century was not a time of great robber bands such as had roamed the countryside in the disordered circumstances of the revolutionary and Napoleonic Wars. It was much more a period of individual crimes, often committed on the spur of the moment.[4] Unlike earlier figures such as Schinderhannes, few men at this time seem to have made a career for themselves out of robbery with violence.

As often as not, such crimes were perpetrated by one poor man against another. The victims were generally of a similar social status to that of the perpetrator, and were usually known to the murderer. Robbery with violence was seldom a matter of lying in wait for a passing merchant, or breaking into a great house in the city. It usually meant plundering someone in one's own social milieu. Bornberg's assault on the merchant's son Krackrügge was a chance encounter. Frequently, too, murder was casually committed in the course of robbery, in order to silence a witness who would otherwise be able to identify the offender, as in the case of Wilhelm Timm, a non-commissioned officer in the 5th Hussars, convicted of murder on 23 March 1855:

The accused, having a few debts, fell upon the idea of purloining the squadron's wages, which, as he knew, Sergeant Borchard drew on the afternoon before the day when they were due to be paid out, and kept in his home until the next day. Armed with an old axe,

[3] Ibid., Bl. 158–9 (the cases are numbered in the file, and this is case 32).
[4] For another example, see ibid., Bl. 192–3 (case 31).

to break open the desk where Borchard usually kept the money, and thereby to get his hands upon it, he made his way just before 9 o'clock in the evening on 31 December 1854 towards Borchard's home. On his arrival he found Borchard's wife sitting at a table reading. Her husband was out. Behind her chair stood a cradle with her 1-year-old son. Striking up a conversation, the accused found the opportunity to get close to the desk, near which he sat down on a chair. After he had taken a book in his hand for appearance's sake, he prised open the desktop with his axe and grabbed through the opening for the money. But the rasping of the desktop made Frau Borchard aware of what was going on. Noticing this, the accused stood up from the chair, struck Frau Borchard on the head with the back of the axe, took the money from the desk and when Frau Borchard cried out again, killed her with further blows of the axe and made himself scarce, taking with him on a commode the money-bag containing 167Th. 12S. 10Pf. in wages.

This murder for gain (*Raubmord*), as it was exceptionally described in the file, was made worse by having been perpetrated against the domestic scene so carefully described in the document. The presence of the cot was quite immaterial to the crime itself, and therefore did not need to be mentioned except as a means of indicating that this was an assault on the family and the home as well as on an innocent and defenceless woman. Here was an idyll much treasured by the civil servants and politicians of the reaction: the German family as the source of social order. And it was being ruthlessly attacked in search of pecuniary gain. Not surprisingly, Timm was refused clemency on 12 June 1855 and duly beheaded shortly thereafter.[5]

Manslaughter frequently attracted the death penalty and the refusal of the royal clemency if it was committed 'in furtherance of another offence'. The defence of property was paramount. One example from 1854 was the case of Johann Thomiczny, a 27-year-old casual farm labourer from Silesia:

On the afternoon of 23 December 1853 the accused, who had one previous conviction, went into the house of his neighbour, the cottager Schwan, in Mistitz, to buy turnips and barley. The latter's wife was there and did not want to do business. Thereupon Thomiczny pushed her so hard that she sank unconscious to the ground across a wooden tub that was standing in front of her. He struck her three blows on the back of the head with an axe which he had found under the bench around the stove, in order to carry out a theft. This brought her life to an end. In order to give the impression that she had killed herself, the accused tied a cloth around Frau Schwan's neck and hanged a rope over it, fastening it to a wardrobe.

Whether the offender was refused service by Frau Schwan because he had a previous conviction, or because he was Polish, does not emerge from the files. The offence was considered to be manslaughter rather than murder because there was no evidence of premeditation. Nevertheless, the fact that it was carried out

⁵ For another example, see GStA Berlin Rep. 84a/8144, Bl. 182–3 (case 16). For a similar example, see ibid., Bl. 189–90 (case 26).

in connection with an apparently equally unpremeditated theft was quite enough to earn Thomiczny the death sentence on 4 April 1854 and the rejection of clemency on 20 September.[6]

Prussian judicial officials were inclined to recommend the monarch to refuse a reprieve where the defence of what they considered to be key institutions of society, such as property or the family, were concerned. Murder of a social superior, especially of a parent by a son or daughter, or a master by a servant, was also treated with great severity. Parricide and matricide were extremely rare at this time. They were almost certain to lead to execution. In October 1863, for instance, the 19-year old gardener Franz Winkler was sentenced to death for the murder of his 60-year-old father:

The investigation, which was initiated as a result of a rumour, resulted in the discovery that the deceased had been poisoned with arsenic, that the accused had mixed this poison into the breakfast which he had prepared for his father on 6 February, that embitterment at a corporal punishment meted out to him for his irresponsible life had driven him to commit this act, that finally the accused had also attempted to poison his stepmother, who—he believed—had gossiped about him to his father, by putting arsenic into a medicine which she used. The result in the mother's case was not fatal because she had only used a small quantity of the medicine.

Winkler was one of only a handful of malefactors sent to the block in 1864.[7] Parricide was still regarded as the severest form of attack on the social hierarchy outside high treason. Refusing clemency to an offender found guilty of it would advertise to society the heinousness of this offence. Scarcely less serious, and a good deal more common, was the murder or manslaughter of masters by apprentices or servants. The law explicitly regarded masters as standing *in loco parentis* to their servants, even going so far as to give them the legal power of corporal punishment over them. So the two kinds of offence were comparable. One such case, tried on 8 October 1853, was that of the 26-year-old domestic servant Gottfried Holland:

Holland, who was finding it difficult to maintain his illegitimate child and its mother, intended to remove himself from their claims by emigrating to America. In order to obtain the means to do this, he killed the merchant and silk goods dealer Schulke, a 25-year-old man whose manservant he was, and who customarily slept in the room next to his, in his bed in Berlin on 13 March 1853 by blows struck upon his skull with an axehead and by strangulation with a piece of string. He seized the keys, opened the cupboard, and took possession of the money and valuables therein.

After the deed was discovered, suspicion fell on Holland, and he was arrested and sentenced to death. On the advice of his officials, the King refused to grant a reprieve when he came to consider the case on the following 11 April, and

Holland was duly beheaded.[8] Even more likely to lead to execution was the murder or manslaughter of a 'person in authority' such as a landowner.[9] The operation of the clemency procedure in the post-revolutionary period was closely tied in with the defence of social hierarchy.

Patriarchalism was a guiding principle for the judicial bureacracy in the reactionary period when it came to judging capital cases in the light of what they revealed about relations between not only different status groups but also men and women. Women were less likely than men to commit a homicide in one of the categories which generally led to execution. They seldom attempted robbery with violence, and it was very rare indeed for them to attack a social superior such as a master or mistress in the household or on the farm. The great majority of murder cases involving women were domestic. The case of Karoline Schaumann, a 33-year-old woman, described in the file as a 'joiner's wife', was a characteristic example of the rare kind of offence that brought female offenders to the block in this period:

In order to obtain greater freedom to pursue her adulterous relationship with David Abrolat, who was a servant of her husband, the potter Kuhnke in Stablaken, the accused poisoned her husband by giving him a beer soup boiled up with poisonous herbs on 23 December 1849. He passed away as a consequence on 25th of the same month. Later, in March 1851, she married the joiner Schaumann. The rumour which began circulating soon after Kuhnke's death—that the latter had been poisoned—did not reach the ears of the authorities until March 1853.

By murdering her husband, or in other words, a person *in loco parentis* over her— women in German law were formally regarded as minors until the *Personenstandsgesetz* of 1884 removed the parental power of husband or father from females, married or unmarried, over the age of 21—Karoline Schaumann had committed precisely the kind of offence most likely to end in execution in the 1850s. During this period the authorities were particularly concerned to re-establish the paternalistic structure of the body politic that had been so seriously challenged by the revolutionary events of 1848. In addition, the rebellion of a number of women against their social and political disenfranchisement during the revolution had caused serious alarm in the governing circles and led to a complete ban on women's participation in political activities and associations in Prussia from 1851 onwards.[10] Such were the weighty considerations that affected even relatively obscure murders at this time. So, despite the fact that she stead-fastly refused to confess to the crime, Karoline Schaumann was condemned to

[8] For another example, see GStA Berlin Rep. 84a/8144, Bl. 145–6 (case 1).

[9] Ibid. 8145, Bl. 5–6 (cases 3 and 4). See also Bl. 44–5 (case 8), and Bl. 166–7 (case 4).

[10] Ute Frevert, *Frauen-Geschichte. Zwischen bürgerlicher Verbesserung und Neuer Weiblichkeit* (Frankfurt am Main, 1986), 15–62.

death on 20 April 1854, refused the royal mercy on 23 September, and beheaded shortly thereafter.[11]

A tough line was also taken with Charlotte Podbielski, who poisoned her husband with arsenic on 24 April 1855. 'Domestic disharmony, which arose out of the fact that the woman Podbielski committed adultery, and that she was frequently beaten by her husband, who was a heavy drinker, led the accused to consider ridding herself of her husband.' The crucial point in this catalogue of reasons was the assertion that Charlotte Podbielski had been having an extra-marital affair. In the face of this disobedience, the husband's abusive behaviour counted for little, and her death sentence, passed on 3 June 1856, was confirmed on the following 25 April.[12] Even where the murder of an abusive husband by his wife did not involve adultery on her part, the legal administration of the 1850s still regarded the offence as particularly severe. In the case of Karoline Friederike Henseling, for example, it was enough that she was known as

an untidy, quarrelsome, slovenly woman, and was therefore unhappily married to her husband, who was known to be a respectable man. Since the latter sometimes beat her, she developed a grudge against him and made up her mind to kill him. She carried out this plan on 10 October 1851 by placing a meal laced with arsenic before him when he came home from work.[13]

In this case, the character references seem to have been decisive, and there may well have been an assumption on the part of the authorities that the 'respectable' Herr Henseling was within his rights to beat his 'slovenly' wife. Karoline Henseling was therefore duly executed.

Whatever the facts were, indeed, the authorities always took a very dim view of a woman who murdered her husband. One example was that of the 50-year-old Marianna Warszawska, sentenced to death on 24 October 1854. She had been unhappily married since 1836 to a man ten or fifteen years younger than herself, one Joseph Warszawski, and lived outside the village of Omulle, in West Prussia, with her child Eva from her first marriage, and the couple's own three younger offspring, Antonia (born 1836), Marian (born 1839), and Marianne (born about 1841).

Around Shrove Tuesday 1851, Joseph Warszawski disappeared, and his family explained that he had gone to Osterode to buy cattle, but had not come back. In the village there was a widespread rumour that he had died, and that his wife had had a hand in it. This rumour had arisen because the latter had lived in a violent and quarrelsome relationship with Warszawski, who had been inclined to drink, and because she was also held to be not

---

[11] GStA Berlin Rep. 84a/8144, Bl. 147–8 (case 6). For a similar, if more complicated, case, see no. 10/11, Bl. 149–50; another case of a lover and his mistress murdering the latter's husband, can be found in ibid., no. 19/20, Bl. 153–4; both offenders were executed.
[12] Ibid., Bl. 210–22 (case 8).   [13] Ibid., Bl. 212–13 (case 11).

entirely guiltless for the death of her first husband. Warszawski's disappearance, however, remained unknown to the authorities until November 1852, so that the investigation was not started until then. The accused admitted that she and her children had decided to murder Warszawski because of the frequent beatings they had suffered from him. The deed had been done one evening when Warszawski came home drunk. To begin with, they had tried to strangle him by pulling his neckerchief as he lay sleeping in bed; but this had woken him up, although they had then calmed him down. In order to overcome his resistance, they had then bored two holes in the plank wall next to the bed. Through one of them they had pulled a rope tied around his neck, through the other, a rope around his feet, and then from the adjacent room the accused and her daughter Eva had pulled one rope, Antonia and Marian the other, with all their strength, for about a quarter of an hour. By the time they had let go, they had assured themselves that the man was dead. The accused and Eva had thereupon buried the corpse in the potato store under the floorboards, then when the frost had left the ground, she had buried it in a field with the aid of her children.

The authorities found nothing here to justify commuting the sentence, especially—one may imagine—since Warszawska had involved her children, two of whom had not even reached their teens, in the crime. By showing such a degree of organization, persistence, and cool premeditation, she had revealed herself to be unwomanly, going against contemporary views of feminine weakness, irrationality, and emotionality. Despite the repeated physical abuse which Warszawska had received from her husband, she was refused clemency on 9 June 1855 and executed shortly thereafter.[14]

Even in the following case, no mitigating circumstances were found. It concerned Margarethe Hübenthal, from the Prussian province of Saxony, who was found guilty of murder on 5 April 1856. She readily confessed to the crime during the preliminary investigation and again in open court. The Ministry of Justice officials noted:

The accused owned a house in Birkenfeld, which she inhabited with her daughter and son-in-law, called Koch. The son-in-law, Lorenz Koch, 30 years old, was a coarse man who had abandoned himself to drink. He ill-treated his wife and his mother-in-law in the most appalling manner, also repeatedly forcing the latter to have sexual intercourse with him. Not only was the marriage extremely unhappy, but life in the house in general was unbearable. To get themselves some peace and quiet, the two women agreed to do away with Koch. They carried out this plan on the night of 23–24 March, by inflicting on Koch such grievous blows with a meat-cleaver and an axe, as he lay in bed, that he died the following midday.

The daughter was condemned to life imprisonment for manslaughter, but the mother, despite these circumstances, was refused clemency on 11 November 1856 and executed.[15] Here the degree of premeditation and the evident conclusion that Hübenthal, as the older woman, had been the moving force in the murder of a

---

[14] GStA Berlin Rep. 84a/8144, Bl. 17–18 (case 2).   [15] Ibid., Bl. 223–4 (case 29).

man by his wife, clearly outweighed the maltreatment the two women had been suffering—maltreatment so gross that it moved even the bureaucrats of the Prussian Ministry of Justice to use exceptionally strong language ('appalling . . . unbearable') to describe it. Once again, despite extreme provocation, un-womanly behaviour and the murder of a social superior (a man by a woman) posed a threat to the social order that could not be ignored by the Ministry of Justice officials in drawing up their recommendations for the King's decision.

Similar considerations played a role in the case of the 44-year-old Louise Lüdke, whom the Prussian King consigned to the block along with the 29-year old labourer Ferdinand Raschke, on 21 January 1860. The circumstances of the case were as follows:

The widow Lüdke lived with her 55-year-old brother-in-law Gottlieb Lüdke, who was retired, her children, and her sister's daughter on a lonely piece of ground in the woods a quarter of a mile from the village of Santorp. Since Lüdke ill-treated her and her children, in particular beating her (the widow) very badly, she persuaded one Raschke and the day-labourer Girndt to 'do away with' the said Lüdke by promising to reward them. Accordingly, Girndt, after he had got the said Lüdke drunk on spirits, threw him to the ground in the garden of the aforementioned plot of land and on the night of 24 June 1858. Raschke then cut his throat with Girndt's knife and the two immediately threw the corpse into a water-hole in the garden. After this, at the further bidding of the widow Lüdke, Raschke stopped her 17-year-old son Eduard from betraying the first deed by pulling his belt around his neck and, with the said Girndt's aid, dragging him out of the house into the garden, where they also slit his throat with the same knife and threw him into the said water-hole. At the further request of the widow Lüdke they then placed a stolen goat, which Girndt had slaughtered at the scene of the crime, on the said Lüdke's body, to give the appearance of the said Lüdke having been caught red-handed and murdered by the goat's owner. The widow Lüdke gave each of them 2M. for carrying out the deed. Girndt died from the effects of a bullet-wound received as he was being arrested.

The widow Lüdke had not only murdered her brother-in-law but she had also shown an extremely unfeminine degree of calculation, determination, and resolution in going about it. Her conduct and character had been anything other than weak, and, once more, it was precisely the assumption of women's emotional and intellectual weakness that lay behind the regular commutation of death sentences which had been passed on them. Not surprisingly, therefore, she was refused clemency and executed.[16]

Female sexual deviance was also likely to be defined in much broader terms than male. In the 1850s women were most likely to be refused clemency if they had shown themselves to be morally or sexually nonconformist, or even if they failed to correspond to contemporary notions of the normal female character. It

[16] Ibid. 8145, Bl. 33–5 (cases 20, 21). See also Bl. 130–1 (case 6), a woman refused clemency by Wilhelm I in 1864 for similar reasons, Bl. 170–1 (case 15), a woman who poisoned her husband and was refused clemency by the King, and ibid., Bl. 181–3 (case 36), the same.

was striking how, in the brief accounts penned by the officials in the Prussian Ministry of Justice in the commutation files, the language of moral disapproval was mainly reserved for women, whether as victims or perpetrators. Even in a rare case of a murder carried out by three women in consort, against another woman who they feared would betray their involvement in a theft, the authorities could not help noting that the accused 'had all long since given themselves over to an immoral and more or less criminal way of life'. They were all refused clemency and executed at the end of August 1855.[17] But such cases were extremely unusual. Much more common were domestic murders where the accused woman was described as lacking in the feelings appropriate to the female sex, as in the case of the 42-year-old Henriette Grigutsch, who was convicted of murder on 4 January 1854:

Without any sense of shame, the accused, who was married to the landlord Martin Grigutsch in Lampen, a man thirty years older than her, had intercourse with other men, so that there was constant discord over this matter, and the relationship in which the couple lived was for a long time extremely unhappy and antagonistic. This circumstance, and the desire to free herself of her ancient husband, who did not satisfy her sensuality, gave Henriette Grigutsch the idea of poisoning her husband. She proceeded to carry out the deed by preparing scrambled eggs and fatty milk on 17 April 1853, and putting arsenic in it, in consequence of which poisoning Grigutsch died on 20 April 1853.

Here the damning facts were the woman's marital disobedience, her adulterous relationship with another man, and her unfeminine display of lustfulness; this was a period, after all, in which women were widely held by middle-class opinion to be sexually passive. Henriette Grigutsch did not confess to the crime of which she was convicted. Nevertheless, she was refused the royal mercy after the sentence was confirmed in July, and escaped the block only by dying a natural death in prison shortly before the decision was due to be published.[18]

Infanticide, though no longer a separate offence after the introduction of the new Prussian Criminal Code in 1852, still accounted for a substantial proportion of the capital cases involving women. Almost invariably, such cases appeared to the authorities as the expression of female weakness and vulnerability, and hence deserving of mercy. One such was that of Ernestine Leetz, condemned to death on 26 June 1854:

The accused, who had only been married to the labourer Leetz for a short time, became extremely aroused through her fury and anger during a domestic quarrel with her husband, who said to her on this occasion '*she should get out, he never wanted to see her again*', and came to the decision to kill her 11-month-old son Herrmann and herself. While her husband was away, she sharpened a kitchen-knife for this purpose on the doorstep and cut the boy's throat with it while he was lying in bed. The attempt to kill herself with the same knife failed, and so did hanging, as well as drowning by plunging her head in a jug filled with water.

The incompetent would-be suicide confessed to the murder under questioning, but her sentence was commuted by royal rescript to life imprisonment on 4 October. The fact that the case approximated to one of infanticide, although the victim was by no means newly-born, was probably another reason for commutation. Clearly the authorities judged that Ernestine Leetz had acted under a degree of provocation, and in a state of considerable emotional upheaval.[19] Yet social grounds were involved too. For while infanticide had become less common on a number of grounds, including improvements in the rural economy, children could still very often be a burden on the poor and extreme poverty sometimes helped drive men and women to rid themselves of them. In 1854, for instance, Caroline Reichelt, from Silesia, killed her two young children 'in despair at her poverty'; her death sentence, passed in February 1855, was commuted into one of life imprisonment the following May.[20] In such a case the judicial officials were in all probability influenced by the fact that a social superior—a parent—had killed her social inferiors, her children. But poverty and female emotional weakness also clearly played a role.

If a husband murdered his wife, even where premeditation was clearly in evidence, he was unlikely to be executed in the 1850s if it could be shown that he had been provoked by his spouse's disobedience. Such was the case with the 40-year-old butter-seller August Langner, convicted of murder on 14 October 1853:

Langner's wife left her husband after a domestic quarrel and as she stubbornly refused to come back to him, he shot her at 10 o'clock in the morning on 21 January 1853 in public at the butter market in Breslau with a two-barrelled pocket-pistol, and sought to kill himself as well with a second loaded weapon he was also carrying on his person, but was prevented from doing so.

This crime of passion was clearly regarded as having been mitigated by the 'stubborn' and disobedient behaviour of the offender's wife, and on 4 July 1854 his death sentence was commuted into life imprisonment.[21] Similarly, some understanding was shown for the feelings of August Mann, a 24-year-old labourer living in Berlin, condemned to death on 27 May 1857:

On the evening of 21 January 1857 the accused shot his mistress, the 26-year-old unmarried servant Louise Brandt, in her master's house, in the chest with a pistol. She died of the consequences on 25th of the same month. The motive for the deed was jealousy.

---

[19] Ibid., Bl. 146–7 (case 3). For another, similar case, see ibid., Bl. 211–12 (case 10).
[20] Ibid., Bl. 184–5 (case 19).   [21] Ibid. 8144, Bl. 153–4 (case 21).

Brandt had persistently refused to become the said man's wife; and he did not want to allow another to possess her.

Mann's sentence was commuted to life imprisonment on 7 October 1858, evidently in the belief that he had acted from motives that could not be seen as rough or dishonourable. In a sense, the officials evidently thought that he could be said to have been provoked.[22]

Rather different was a case that might almost have come straight out of a romantic ballad, that of the 19-year-old shepherd Joseph Kasparck, from Silesia, who, it was reported,

shot his mistress Franziska Kaurpiela, daughter of a retired farmer . . . on the evening of 16 Oktober 1856 during a walk near her village, with her consent, in the left breast, with the intention of killing her. The shot was fired from a pistol loaded with small pebbles, and led to the death of the wounded girl within a few hours. There had been a love-affair between Kasparck and Kaurpiela for a long time already, but her father did not approve of it and wanted to bring it to an end by betrothing her to another man. The lovers did not want to part from one another, and agreed to die. Kasparck's attempt to kill himself as well after he had done this to Kaurpiela did not succeed because the pistol failed three times to go off. After this, the courage to bring his life to an end also seems to have failed.

The unhappy lover was spared by the monarch, who commuted his sentence to one of life imprisonment on 31 August 1857. Whatever the romantic circumstances of the tragedy, the fact remained that the victim, as a woman, had been the social inferior of the murderer, and the perpetrator's motives had been apparently free from any hint of greed, hatred, or revenge.[23]

Where the emotions guiding the murdering hand were not so pure, where a whiff of greed or adultery could be smelt, where murderer and victim were married, or where the wife had conformed to the role which social convention had marked out for her, the clemency authorities were not so understanding. Karl Hannig, a 31-year-old farm labourer from Silesia, married a woman twenty-two years older than he was—a common source of problems in this society. She was said to have lived with him 'in discord', so that he 'was inclined to marry his employer's young and hard-working maid, who pleased him'. In order to clear the way, he strangled his wife in bed on 31 October 1853. The authorities took the view that she had not provoked him in any way, and he was refused a reprieve on 26 January 1855. The difference in age may also have evened up the social disparity in the eyes of the judicial officials.[24] But a decade or so later, the 28-year-old labourer Franz Figuck, from Prussia, met with an equal lack of understanding

[22] GStA Berlin Rep. 84a/8144, Bl. 241–2 (case 6).

[23] Ibid., Bl. 251–2 (case 25). See also Ibid., Bl. 256–7 (case 33), an unmarried woman convicted of murdering her rival for a man's hand in marriage; her death sentence was commuted to life imprisonment.

[24] Ibid., Bl. 154–5 (case 23).

when he was condemned for drowning his young wife, whom he had married only a few weeks before. The marriage, commented the officials at the Ministry of Justice, was 'an unhappy one, since the accused's wish to improve his disastrous financial situation through what he hoped would be a good dowry had not been fulfilled'. Sentenced to death on 2 July 1864, he was refused clemency on 29 April 1865 and executed shortly thereafter, evidently because his motives had been mercenary. Here again was a case in which a dangerous lust for property and possessions outweighed other factors in the minds of officialdom.[25]

Where a man was found to be sexually or morally deviant, the official attitude was also generally severe. There are no cases recorded in the 1850s and 1860s of murders involving bestiality or homosexuality, but there was at least one case involving incest, and it ended in the execution of the offender, one Ephraim Bilitzki, yet another member of an ethnic minority in the eastern provinces.

After the death of his wife, the accused had lived for a long time with his daughter Marie, who later married the carter Jacob Bogai in Neudorff, in an incestuous relationship, to which he had forced her to submit, and through this sired the boy Friedrich Bilitzki, whom he raised in his house until he was $5\frac{3}{4}$ years old. On 28 May 1854 the boy suddenly disappeared. The accused's daughter, the above-mentioned Marie Bogai, accused her father of the murder of their child Friedrich Bilitzki. The principal accused was strongly suspected of both crimes. On the day after being found guilty, he freely confessed that he had been made desperate by the unfeeling attitude of his legitimate son Carl Bilitzki, to whom he had sold his land on condition that he be allowed to carry on living in the house in his old age, and with whom he had indeed stayed, but who did not want to tolerate Friedrich Bilitzki in the house any longer. Therefore he had come to the decision to kill Friedrich Bilitzki in the churchyard at Gellen, where he had gone with him. He had done the deed by untying the boy's neckerchief, making a sling out of it, and pulling it tight around his throat; the boy had thereupon fallen down and after a while passed away. After this, he buried the corpse first in a field of peas, then in a rye-field, and later sank it in a swampy part of Lake Czaika after weighing it down with stones.

Bilitzki's 'desperation' counted for nothing under these circumstances. He was denied the royal mercy on 10 December and executed forthwith. The officials explicitly noted in his case that his crime was 'incest and murder', although the former did not carry the death penalty, and was strictly speaking irrelevant to the sentence and therefore to the clemency decision.[26]

Murder in connection with a sexual crime, such as rape, was extremely rare at this time. The term 'sex murder' (*Lustmord*) did not come into currency until the 1880s. Sexual motives were usually relevant only in domestic situations, where a husband or wife wanted to be rid of a spouse in order to marry a lover. The 1860s, however, did see the first serial sex killer recorded in the files. Carl Maasch, a 40-year-old labourer, who lived in the forester's house at Brunken, in Brandenburg,

[25] Ibid. 8145, Bl. 156–7 (case 14).   [26] Ibid. 8144, Bl. 180–1 (case 10).

was convicted in October 1862 for a series of crimes that had begun in April 1858 with the murder of a 60-year-old widow, and continued in October 1860 with another. Maasch had demanded sexual intercourse from the women and, when it was refused, strangled them and then 'had intercourse with the corpse'. In August 1858, he was loitering outside the manor house at Albertinenburg, with the intention of breaking in, when he saw a maidservant through a window in the act of undressing; 'excited by the sight of her taking her clothes off, he climbed into her room, killed her by pressing her windpipe, and satisfied his lust on the corpse'. In September 1860 he carried out a double murder at the request of an acquaintance, beating and hacking to death a young married couple in their bed. On the night of 10–11 May 1861 he broke into a mill with his brother Martin, in order to rob it of its contents, and killed the miller and his wife, their three children, and the maidservant. Finally in August 1861 he graduated to highway robbery and, encountering the merchant Pieper on the road from Tiefensee to Heckelberg, shot him and stole his money. A serial sex killer and a necrophiliac as well as a murderer for gain, Maasch was executed in 1864, having confessed everything. In cases of extreme moral deviance such as this, moral considerations applied to men as well as women.[27]

On the other hand, despite the submergence of the liberal discourse on pauperism after the Revolution, poverty as a motive for murder often elicited the sympathy of Prussian judicial officials engaged in preparing clemency recommendations. Who could fail to be moved, for instance, by the story of Michael Kopietz, a 40-year-old man from Silesia, who was condemned to death on 4 October 1854?

The accused, married for nine years to Hedwig, née Leschnitz, had two children from this marriage. The older, called Marianna, 8 years old, worked as a shepherdess. After the death of his wife in 1852, he and his younger, 5-year-old daughter Josepha sought to eke out an existence in service, which ended in November 1853. After this, Kopietz, wandering round from village to village with his child, tried to live from begging. The child, which often cried from hunger, became a burden to him, and at the end of February 1854, tramping towards the village of Kostuchna, he came to a decision to kill it. He carried her into a nearby wood, with the words: I can't feed you any more, and must strike you dead, and took its life with three blows to the head from a foot-and-a-half-long branch of spruce.

Kopietz was himself also evidently ill and weak from hunger and, after confessing to his crime, he died in prison before the sentence could be confirmed or commuted by the King. There can be little doubt, however, that after the Ministry officials had described his crime in such moving terms, Kopietz would have been spared the block had he lived.[28]

[27] GStA Berlin Rep. 84a/8145, Bl. 123–9 (case 2).   [28] Ibid., Bl. 183–4 (case 18).

Sometimes the motive for child murder could be more complex and less direct, as in the case of Carl Biermann, a 35-year old lithographer in Berlin, condemned to death on 3 July 1855.

On the evening of 7 November 1854, the accused, filled with feelings of hatred and revenge against his parents, who had recently kept him fed but had now barred him from their house and thus for the moment deprived him of his bread because of the beatings he had given them, left his home with his four children, aged between $1\frac{1}{4}$ and $6\frac{1}{4}$, and equipped with a washbasket. He went with them to the Silesian bush, not far from the Silesian gate, with the intention of killing them. Here he put the four children in the washbasket, tied them fast, and carried them to the nearby bridge over the so-called link canal, let the basket down into the water, and left the scene. The children's bodies were variously found in the water on the same evening, on 18 November 1854 and on 5 March 1855.

In this case, clearly, although poverty played a role, the authorities convinced themselves that the offender was violent by nature and driven by dangerous emotions such as hatred and revenge. Biermann was refused clemency on 6 May 1856, almost a year after he had been sentenced.[29]

Where the poverty was extreme, and where the offender showed signs of human feeling, above all, signs of remorse, clemency was far more likely to be recommended. The story told by the file on Clemens Urban, a 'day labourer and colporteur', aged 38, from Silesia, was written by the official responsible in such language that it was clear almost from the outset that he would be reprieved, despite the horrific nature of his crime:

Urban, plagued for a long time by poverty and privation, returns home from a day's journey which he has undertaken as a salesman for the weekly 'Farm Labourers' Newspaper' published by the printer Fischer in Neurode. There he not only finds his family hungry and in the greatest wretchedness, but also hears that their request for alms from the neighbourhood has been rejected with hard and hurtful words. In order finally to escape this misery, his wife, née Rosenberger, to whom he has been married for eight years, demands that he put an end to her life, and her children's, and repeats this urgently in the night of 13 June 1854. Finally he resolves upon the terrible deed, and with a mangle-pin lying in the room he bludgeons his wife, his 9-year-old son Clemens and his $1\frac{1}{4}$-year-old little daughter Marie to death. After doing this deed, at about $3\frac{1}{4}$ in the morning, Urban leaves his house, tortured by the pangs of conscience, and follows the path to Nieder Steine, in order to hang or drown himself some way away from Neurode, as he has promised his wife. However, he does not carry out this plan, but, in order to starve himself to death, builds himself a stone hut on the so-called red mountain, by Regensdorf, and remains in it for six days without food until, agitated by a violent thunderstorm, he places himself on 21 June 1854 before the authorities in Glatz to be indicted.[30]

[29] Ibid., Bl. 176–7.   [30] Ibid., Bl. 186–7 (case 22).

Not only had Urban been evidently put up to the murder by his wife, he had also felt remorse almost immediately and ended by giving himself up to the authorities. It was not surprising that they spared his life. Unusually for the documents in these files, this account was written in the dramatic present, with the effect of reducing the distance between the reader and the story, and thereby subliminally generating greater understanding for the actions described. Despite their intentions of reaffirming the social order in the face of revolutionary threat, therefore, Prussian officials in the 1850s were moved to regard poverty and destitution as reasons for commuting death sentences to life imprisonment.

b. Structures of Mercy

These lapidary narratives, written in order to clarify the minds of the Justice Ministry officials about the criteria for recommending clemency under the new Criminal Code, were in a sense multi-authored; the malefactor, the witnesses, the prosecutor, and the bureaucrats all had a hand in their composition, and each of them had a particular purpose in mind. The offenders and their lawyers presented their case for clemency in terms they thought the authorities would understand, emphasizing mitigating circumstances such as age, sex, poverty, or upbringing; the authorities presented their case to the monarch in terms that placed far more stress on character and morality, and drew on court and prison reports in doing so. In their final form, the clemency reports may have reflected the angle from which judicial officials wanted to view the offence and the offender, but they also refracted, in a less obvious way, all these other narratives as well. Through them, therefore, we can glimpse something of the world of the murderer in post-revolutionary Prussia: overwhelmingly poor, ignorant, brutal, and desperate. By the 1860s, however, the quality of the reports was declining. Judicial officials had established a widely understood if unwritten set of conventions, and were increasingly contenting themselves with statistics. These too shed a good deal of light on the nature of the offenders as well as the practice of commutation during the post-revolutionary period. From 1854 to 1865 inclusive, a total of 398 offenders of known occupation were condemned in Prussia, and 140 of them executed. Only a few of them were drawn from non-manual trades and professions such as scribes, teachers, clerks, innkeepers, millers, and merchants (the last-named on almost any scale of buying and selling, but probably mostly very modest on the whole). The one Catholic priest among the condemned in this period, Albert Osowicki, who had killed the illegitimate child borne him by his maidservant, was probably the most educated person to suffer this fate. There were no aristocrats, no doctors of any kind, no lawyers, no professors. Among this broad category of people roughly known as the

Mittelstand, or 'middle estate', consisting of shopkeepers, petty scribes, and tradesmen of various sorts, there were thirty-two individuals sentenced to death in Prussia in 1854–65, or 8 per cent of the total, and five of them were executed, making 16 per cent of the total condemned in this category, or 4 per cent of the total executed in all categories. Since the average ratio of executions to condemnations in this period was 35 per cent, it is clear that offenders of this middling sort were let off especially leniently by the clemency process, thus underlining once more the important role played in the Justice Ministry's recommendations and the monarch's decisions by considerations of social status.[31]

A second broad social category of offenders condemned to death in Prussia in these twelve years was made up of farmers, who varied from peasants living on semi-feudal and almost landless tenured holdings to outright freehold owners of small and self-sufficient farms (the latter, in East Elbian Prussia, very much in the minority). Fifty-seven of these farmers were sentenced to death in this period, or 14 per cent of the total, and twenty-three of them were executed (40 per cent, or 16 per cent of all those executed). Their prominence among the social categories into which the condemned can reasonably be divided reflected the fact that this was still a rural world, in which violence was a good deal more common than it was in the towns. Similarly, virtually all the 49 servants or labourers (*Dienstknechte*) condemned to death in this period are likely to have been rural; some of them had named occupations in the lists, such as shepherd or huntsman, but most of them were simple farm labourers. They made up another 12 per cent of the total condemned, and twenty of them were executed (41 per cent, or 14 per cent of all those executed). The two largest categories among the condemned, however, were predominantly (though not exclusively) urban: artisans (*Handwerker*) and labourers (*Arbeiter*). The artisans were overwhelmingly skilled labourers associated with guild-organized trades, although the category also includes a handful of policemen, watchmen, and soldiers. They numbered ninety-six, or 24 per cent of the condemned, and their chances of obtaining clemency were about the same as those of farmers and farm labourers. Thirty-eight of them, or 40 per cent, were executed, making 27 per cent of the total number of capital offenders refused clemency during this period. The final category, that of manual labourers, was most harshly treated of all. Seventy-seven of them were condemned to death (19 per cent of all those condemned), and thirty-three were executed (43 per cent, or 24 per cent of all those executed). Still, taken overall, there were few really sharp variations between most of these groups with respect to the granting of clemency: the only really striking difference was between the non-manual or *Mittelstand* occupations, where the great majority of the condemned were granted clemency, and all the other occupational groups taken together.

Leniency continued to be shown to women during this period, as it had been since the late eighteenth century. Eighty-nine of the Prussian capital offenders condemned in 1854–65 were women, or 22 per cent. Nineteen of them, or 21 per cent, were executed. This was only roughly half the proportion of men executed in all except non-manual occupational categories. The executed women made up 14 per cent of all Prussian offenders beheaded in this period. Considerable leniency was shown to those who (like all the fifteen maidservants condemned to death) had been found guilty of infanticide. For most women, however, no occupation was given. These figures can be eked out by some rough statistics from Bavaria which indicate a continuity of practice from the first half of the nineteenth century and across the north–south divide: fifty-nine women were condemned to death in Bavaria in the years 1817 to 1850 inclusive, and nine of them were executed, or 15 per cent. Altogether in this period, 333 offenders were condemned to death in Bavaria, and sixty were executed, so women made up 18 per cent of those condemned and 15 per cent of those executed.[32] These figures are broadly comparable to those available for Prussia in the period after 1850, though they suggest that clemency towards women was more marked in Protestant Prussia than it was in Catholic Bavaria, where the proportion of condemned women executed was only just slightly below the overall average of 18 per cent. Figures are also available for the age-distribution of condemned and executed offenders in Prussia in the years 1854–65. Of the 321 condemned offenders of known age, fourteen, or 5 per cent, were aged 16 to 20; 139, or 43 per cent, were aged 21 to 30; ninety-seven, or 30 per cent, 30 to 40; sixty-one, or 19 per cent, 40 to 60; and ten, or 3 per cent, 61 and over. And of the 314 whose marital status could be ascertained, 102, or 32 per cent, were married men; 132, or 43 per cent, were unmarried men; 44, or 14 per cent, were married women; and 36, or 11 per cent, were unmarried women. Of those whose fate was known, 36 per cent of the married men (28 out of 77) were executed; 20 per cent of the unmarried men (19 out of 93); 20 per cent of the married women (5 out of 25); 21 per cent of the unmarried women (3 out of 29). None of these figures suggested any special consideration for a particular group of people, though the high execution rate of married men was noticeable.

The principles and assumptions underlying commutation in the period 1854–65 can be observed in two further sets of statistics. The first, a breakdown of the methods by which the homicides (whether murder or capital manslaughter) were

---

[32] HStA Munich MA 93516: Die Anwendung der Todesstrafe in Bayern, mit statistischen Listen; and MJu *Findbuch* in the archive, with a list of the cases.

committed, showed that strangulation, where 26 out of 68 perpetrators, or 38 per cent, were executed, was the method most strongly disapproved of by clemency officials. Altogether, strangulation cases made up 20 per cent of the 339 cases for which the method used was known. Next most likely to lead to execution was knifing, which accounted for 10 per cent of these homicides; here 11 out of 33 perpetrators, or 33 per cent, were executed. Third came the most common form of homicide during this period, namely beating to death with a blunt instrument such as a hammer or chopping to death with an axe: with 89 cases, this made up 26 per cent of the total, and 27 of these cases, or 30 per cent, went to the block. These three methods were characteristic of lower-class violence, strangulation being used particularly where women and children were the victims. Poisoning, the favoured means of homicide chosen by women, was also relatively harshly treated: out of 49 cases (14 per cent of the total), 15 ended in execution, or 31 per cent. These four categories of homicide were much more severely dealt with than the two remaining methods on the list. The first of these, shooting, despite the expense of such weapons, was still common, with 40 cases, or 12 per cent of the total, but as a more middle-class method it was treated more leniently by the commutation officials and by the King, and only 7 cases, or 18 per cent, led to execution. Drowning, the favoured method above all for killing infants and small children, accounted for 37 cases (11 per cent of the total), but only 4 of the perpetrators were executed, or 11 per cent.

Most revealing of all was the table of motives. Here lay a crucial reason for the exercise or refusal of clemency. It was striking that the discourse of pauperism which had been so widespread and influential among the educated classes since the 1840s left its mark in a distinct tendency to recommend clemency where a homicide appeared to have been committed because of 'poverty'. Only 3 out of the 35 condemned offenders in this category were executed, a rate of 9 per cent. Similarly, homicides committed 'from fear of treachery' were also treated leniently, despite the fact that the perpetrators were likely to have been involved in another crime beforehand. Only 1 out of the 8 offenders condemned in this category was executed, a rate of 13 per cent. Another motivation treated with understanding was more surprising. Out of the 57 offenders condemned for homicides committed out of sexual or adulterous motives, only 9, or 16 per cent, were executed. As we have seen, where the offender was a man, he stood a good chance of escaping the gallows. Moreover, the category was slightly artificial, because it excluded domestic crimes, which fell under a separate heading of their own, so that sexual homicides were in practice committed against victims who were not members of the perpetrator's family and not usually, therefore, in a socially superior position. These two latter factors, on the other hand, especially where the perpetrator was female (a wife killing her husband, for example) ensured that domestic homicides were the most harshly treated of all, with 11 out of 21 offenders, or 52 per cent, going to the gallows.

Sexual motives were perhaps regarded as less dangerous to the social order than others. The two motives which jurists regarded as informing not only homicides but also political crimes, riots, and revolutionary conspiracies—'self-interest' or 'greed' on the one hand, and 'hatred' or 'revenge' on the other—were far more harshly treated in the clemency process. Fully 40 per cent of those condemned for homicides committed out of greed were executed, and the comparable figure for hatred and revenge was even higher, at 43 per cent. Moreover, homicides committed from greed constituted by far the largest category of condemnations, with 131 offences out of a total of 301. When put together with the 49 offences committed out of hatred or revenge (16 per cent), they constituted, indeed, the majority. The fact that homicides committed from greed were also particularly liable to end in execution meant that a majority—53 out of 98, or 54 per cent— of executions in this period were for homicides judged to have been committed for mercenary or pecuniary motives. The 21 offenders in the category 'hatred or revenge' constituted an additional 21 per cent of those executed. Three-quarters of all executions carried out in this period were thus for homicides involving these two types of socially threatening motivation. The numbers involved in the other categories were correspondingly small: 35 condemnations for homicides committed 'from poverty', or 12 per cent of the total, leading to 3, or 3 per cent, of the total executions; 21 condemnations in the 'domestic' category (7 per cent), leading to 11 executions (11 per cent of the total number); 8 condemnations for homicides committed 'from fear of treachery' (3 per cent), leading to 1 execution (1 per cent of the total). The largest number of crimes based on a motivation that did not appear to threaten the social order fell into the category of 'sexual or adulterous', where there were 57 condemnations (19 per cent) and 9 executions (9 per cent).[33]

The granting of the royal clemency to convicted murderers in the middle of the nineteenth century thus served a variety of purposes. Capital punishment, though no longer carried out in public in Prussia after 1851, was public none the less in the sense that it always attracted widespread attention. Murder cases formed the subject of newspaper reports, colportage, and pamphlet literature. Trials were a form of public entertainment. The fate of convicted murderers was widely discussed. The royal power of reprieve was not only an advertisement for the divine prerogatives of the monarchy and its literal power over life and death, it was also a warning to society, and especially to the lower classes, that emotions such as envy and greed had to be kept in check, and that the patriarchal social order would be defended with the guilliotine and the axe. Yet, despite themselves, Prussian judicial officials could not but recognize the problems of poverty and destitution which the social order harboured. If murderers or their defenders could convince them that need rather than greed was the motivating force of the crime, they stood some chance of success in escaping the scaffold. For all their attempts to use the death penalty as a means of shoring up the existing social order, therefore, Prussian officials were compelled to admit that criminals were not simply impelled by evil and immoral hostility to the social hierarchy. In the very language they used to justify their decisions on clemency cases, an involuntary admission of the injustice of the social order which they sought to maintain all too often shone through.

c. *The Abolition of Public Executions 1851–1863*

The novelty of the situation with which Justice Ministers were confronted in the 1850s was underlined by the ending of public executions in every German state within the space of a few short years. The first major step in this direction was taken by the Prussians. As a pendant to its introduction of trials in public, the Prussian Criminal Code of 1851 also contained regulations providing for the exclusive employment from that time of executions inside prison precincts. The authorities' fear of popular disturbances arising from public executions, and their despair at ever being able to impose their own understanding of the execution on the public if they were unable to control the composition of the attending crowd, had in no way diminished since 1847, when the decision to end public executions had been taken in principle. Much the same reasons were behind the inclusion of this provision in the Criminal Code of 1851. In the new procedure, executions were held within prison walls, in the presence of the local chief state prosecutor, the governor of the prison, two members of the court that had passed the sentence, a priest or pastor, a small number of police officers, twelve witnesses, and a limited number of honourable citizens from the locality.

After some debate, it had been decided to announce the event through the ringing of a bell, either in the local church or in the prison chapel, because it was thought

that the leap from the public nature of an execution in the open air to one in a narrow, enclosed space offering access to only a small number of people would be too abrupt, and that, if the law suddenly went over from the form of an absolutely public execution in the open air to a mode of execution which allowed no spectators at all and only a few witnesses to vouch for the solemnity of the occasion, the impression of a *secret* execution procedure would easily be aroused.[34]

Through the ringing of the bell, therefore, a certain publicity continued to be guaranteed. The Ministry of Justice had abandoned the idea, originally mooted in 1847, that crowds should be encouraged to gather outside the prison gates to be addressed by preachers on the significance of the events. But it did substitute something similar:

The ceremonious tones of the bell should not only warn the members of the community in which an execution is being administered that the most serious of penalties is being carried out on a criminal, but should also summon the same to a contemplation whose seriousness matches that of the event in progress.

Indeed, they even suggested that the ringing of the bell 'is well-suited to bring parents to gather their family around them in this hour for religious and moral contemplation'. The date and place of the execution were also to be announced in advance, and a further element of publicity was afforded by the provision that the inhabitants of the area in which the execution took place could apply for entry cards. If they were found to be admissible, they could join the others privileged to witness the event itself.[35] This provision above all others ensured that executions continued to be neither secret nor private events. Nevertheless, a decisive step had been taken. The uncontrollable crowd had been selected, ordered, and confined. No longer was the display of state authority at Prussian executions to run the risk of being undermined by the assertion of popular interpretations of its cultural meaning.

Neither the executioners nor the crowds seem immediately to have accepted this new situation. In 1853 the executioner's assistants in Cottbus, after an execution in the local gaol, took the body out through the prison gates on a horse-drawn cart 'amidst the cheering and hurrahs of the crowd which had gathered in large numbers near the prison'.[36] Followed by the crowd, they proceeded to the site of the former public gallows, where they buried the body in the traditional manner. The police had ordered that the bodies of condemned malefactors should be 'buried in remote and cordoned-off parts of the public graveyard, as far as possible avoiding the arousal of any attention'. But the local magistrates had insisted that there was no room available in the local cemetery. They had refused to organize the transport and burial of the corpse. Left without any instructions as to what to do, the executioner and his servants had therefore

---

[34] GStA Berlin Rep. 84a/7783, Bl. 81: 'Über die Bestimmung im § 8 des StGB, dass die Vollstreckung eines Todesurteils durch Glockengeläut anzukündigen sei'.

[35] Ibid.   [36] Ibid., Bl. 37–9.

reverted to the practice of former times. The case eventually landed before the courts, which found

something really dishonouring in the transport by executioner's assistants, whom the common man still calls knacker's servants. This does not affect the criminal, who had already expiated his crime before the earthly judge, but the innocent surviving relatives. It is against the law, which does not recognize a so-called infamous burial and which does not want a human corpse to be carted away like a hacked-off piece of meat.[37]

Clearly, the new individualism represented by the court's view was only permeating local society and institutions slowly and unevenly. Popular understanding of the execution was a long time in dying. In 1864, after an execution in Berlin, the hangman's servants were caught by the local authorities selling handkerchiefs dipped in the malefactor's blood to members of the waiting crowd outside. The executioner was warned not to let such an incident happen again.[38] Any idea that putting executions inside the prison would bring about an immediate transformation of popular attitudes was evidently misplaced.

Indeed, after public executions had been abolished in Prussia, gallows crowds in the rest of Germany were bigger after 1848 than they had ever been. Popular, crypto-materialist magical and religious rituals continued to take place wherever the opportunity presented itself, as we saw in Chapter 2, and the consequences of the crowd getting out of control now appeared in the light of the events of the Revolution to be more serious than ever before. In 1857, the execution of Ernst Fleischer in Osnabrück took place, according to the official report, 'surrounded by a very large crowd of people'.[39] In 1854, the authorities in Leipzig, faced with having to carry out the public beheading of the robber and murderer Ebert, tried to ensure 'limited publicity' by holding the ceremony so far outside the city limits that the inhabitants of Leipzig would not be obliged to witness 'a spectacle of this sort', while the organization of costly security measures would no longer be necessary. Nevertheless, they still feared the 'attendance of the curious', and noted that 'disturbances of public order' were likely 'in increased measure' at 'such an occasion, when a numberless crowd of people presses together in one place'.[40] In the end, the measure saved neither the city fathers money nor spared them the usual anxiety attendant upon such events. But it was clearly only a matter of time now before such pressures brought about the abolition of public executions in Saxony altogether.

In Bavaria, too, official anxiety about the dangers of public executions made itself felt with the defeat of the Revolution and the inauguration of a period of

---

[37] Ibid., Bl. 45.   [38] Bächthold-Stäubli, *Handwörterbuch*, article on 'Blut'.
[39] HStA Hanover Hann. 173a Nr. 438, Bl. 26 (report by Dr Brüggemann, 31 July 1853).
[40] Sta Leipzig L XII G 23, vol: III, 1854, Bl. 1–4: Hinrichtung des Raubmörders Ebert.

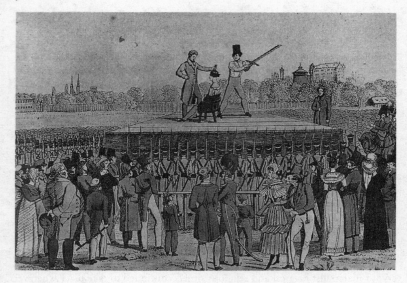

FIG. 19. *A Bavarian execution in 1850.* The double murderer Friedrich Cörper is beheaded in Nuremberg on 21 October 1850. At this time, the sword was still used for executions in Bavaria; after 1854, it was replaced by the guillotine, and from 1861, executions no longer took place in the open. Note the absence of priests on the scaffold, the military precautions, and the presence of women and children in the crowd.

reaction. In 1850, having regained its confidence and committed itself to the reintroduction of capital punishment, the Bavarian Interior Ministry expressed renewed concern about the threat to public order posed by public executions. In a note to the Ministry of Justice, it made clear its worry that 'the planning of such an execution can under certain circumstances rouse and excite a whole province'.[41] Subsequent experience amply confirmed this fear. Given the fact that they continued to carry out executions in public, the Bavarian authorities were still confronted with the attendance of large and thus potentially unruly crowds at executions, despite all they could do to discourage it. In 1850 an official in the Bavarian Palatinate referred disapprovingly to the presence at an execution of 'the press of curious onlookers, mostly consisting of women and children'. His estimation of the age and sex of the participants is more likely to have reflected his shocked perception that the crowd did not constitute the kind of adult, bourgeois male assembly that officialdom had come to expect of the public

[41] HStA Munich MInn 46136: Innenministerium to Justizministerium 27 Apr. 1850.

sphere by this time, than any really accurate perception of its composition. Some 20,000 spectators were counted at an execution in Ansbach in February 1851, and there were said to have been so many people at the decapitation of the murderer Josef Stopfers in Munich on 18 May 1850 that it took the procession fully an hour to get from the prison to the square in front of the City Law Court, where the breaking of the wand of office took place. 'An immeasurable crowd', it was reported, 'mobbed the melancholy procession, in which cuirassiers were in the vanguard and the rear; and the bloody scaffold itself, towards which it was wending its way, was surrounded by numberless masses.'[42] Holding executions early in the morning made no difference; indeed, as the Munich police noted on 31 August 1854, if they took place before 7 a.m., people could stop by for a look on their way to work.[43] Even when, as in Munich in April 1856, the time of the execution was fixed for 5.30 in the morning, there were still 'many spectators' present.[44]

As an official in Amberg noted in 1854, 'If the public wants to see something, it will see it, whether it's at midday or midnight.' How true this could be was indicated by the same official in reporting an execution that took place there on 24 August 1854 at dawn, which was roughly 4.30 in the morning at that particular time of year. 'There was no peace in the town of Amberg or in the surrounding places for the whole of the night from the 23rd to the 24th of this month. Every hour, new crowds of pedestrians came, and new carts heavily laden with spectators from every area.' All the local inns were said to be full, since those who could afford it had long since booked themselves rooms for the night preceding the execution. But, the report continued,

The curious portion of the population here was also on its feet well in time. At 4 o'clock in the morning the whole of the so-called old parade-ground was filled with people . . . As the undersigned came from there to the place of execution at half-past four, the whole place was occupied by thousands of spectators.

The official added that 'all the masons, carpenters, apprentices, day labourers and domestic servants attended the same' before going to work. As far as he was concerned, all this went to show that: 'Such an execution is nothing more than a dramatic spectacle for both educated and uneducated, costs the state a lot of money, and robs many people of the most varied social standing of their precious time.'[45] These objections were characteristic of the work-oriented ethic now

---

[42] *Stenographische Berichte über die Verhandlungen des Bayerischen Landtags, 1866–7*, i. 396–8; Anon., *Die kgl. Bayer. Staatsminister der Justiz*, 555–6.
[43] HStA Munich MInn 46136: Kgl. Polizeidirektion Munich to Kgl. Reg. Oberbayern, 31 Aug. 1854.
[44] Ibid., Unterleutnant Schefmann to Commando Compagnie in Munich, 7 Apr. 1856.
[45] Ibid., Kgl. Stadtkommission Amberg to Kgl. Regierung Oberfranken, Kammer des Innern, 25 Aug. 1854.

spreading through Germany with the onset of industrialization. More traditional in its prioritization of public order and morality was the view of the authorities in Passau, who, reporting an execution in the city in September 1854, noted that 'as usual, a numberless crowd streamed in from near and far, and that on this occasion once more the degeneration of this earnest act into a popular spectacle which does no more than satisfy the coarsest type of curiosity made itself observable in the most repulsive manner.' The 'main purpose' of the occasion, they thought, 'namely deterrence, is certainly not achieved; on the contrary, abuses and harmful consequences of various kinds are inevitably bound up with it.'[46] Such language indicated the offence that the spectacle of executions and the behaviour of the crowd was now causing to bourgeois sensibilities. For the bourgeois imagination, a solemn state act such as an execution demanded silent and deferential crowds watching top-hatted and frock-coated gentlemen going about their duties with a serious mien and a sense of responsibility. Over the previous decades, the execution ritual had become secularized in pursuit of this ideal. The vast numbers of spectators, the ritual shouting of the crowd, the attendance of women and children, all these remnants of the traditional execution, largely cut loose from their traditional anchorage in a collective religious ceremony of retribution and redemption, were now incomprehensible to bourgeois commentators except as aspects of the dangerous and barely controllable emotionality and licentiousness of the mob.

The Bavarian Ministry of Justice also launched an attack on the priest's sermon at the end of the ceremony. Like so many secular officials over the preceding decades, the Bavarian judicial bureaucrats were no longer prepared to tolerate the religious character which had once given the execution ritual its cultural meaning. They were afraid, they wrote in 1854,

that the clergymen often take a different point of view in these admonitory sermons from that which is required in the interests of the state through the execution of the death penalty. The cleric often interprets the criminal from a subjective point of view, and thus it can happen that a man condemned to death for a terrible crime is portrayed as a penitent and remorseful converted sinner, who is sure of God's forgiveness. This is not the way to achieve fear of the death penalty and deterrence from crime; on the contrary, the procession to the scaffold is bound to summon up the impression of the triumphal march of a converted sinner.[47]

From this point onwards, therefore, the sermon was dispensed with. But this was not the only problem public executions were running into in Bavaria at this time. By the 1850s, because of the decrease in capital sentences since the middle of the

---

[46] HStA Munich MInn 46136: Stadtkommissariat Passau to Kgl. Reg. Niederbayern, Kammer des Innern, 2 Sept. 1854.

[47] HStA Munich M Ju 13066: Justizministerium to King, 2 Aug. 1854.

eighteenth century, many of the smaller towns in the Kingdom had gone for decades without witnessing an execution. All the more alarming, then, for the inhabitants of a municipality such as that of Zweibrücken, in the Bavarian Palatinate, when, as the law required, the final rejection of clemency for one Christoph Schneider was followed within twenty-four hours by his public beheading on the market-place on 4 June 1856. The event took place, as traditionally prescribed, on the regular market-day, but by this time the authorities were beginning to find this coincidence unfortunate. Writing to the King on 13 September, the President of the Bavarian Appeals Court declared: 'The feelings of the inhabitants and the people who have come to market are deeply hurt by the death sentences which are executed there.' Indeed, he added, an old woman present for the vegetable market on 4 June had fainted at the sight of the execution and died the following day. He suggested therefore that executions could be held on the Castle Square outside the centre of town.[48] But the General State Prosecutor of the Bavarian Palatinate, writing to the King on 22 December, took the view that 'it would be even more possible for the curious to crowd in than it is on the spatially restricted market-place', if executions were moved to the Castle Square. As for the old woman, nobody had forced her to look, and she could have stayed among the stalls on the other side of the market-place from the scaffold had she wished.[49]

The military, who drilled on the Castle Square, and were evidently accustomed to use the castle for social purposes, also objected. As the Ministry of War noted in a letter to the Justice Ministry:

The removal of executions to the drill square would make just as bad an impression on the NCOs and soldiers of this community, who mostly belong to the older age groups, since the sites of executions in this part of Bavaria are situated outside the towns and are rightly avoided by the people as places of horror.[50]

It did not say much for the quality of Bavaria's soldiers that they were elderly and evidently afraid of the sight of blood. Perhaps it is not surprising that Bavaria was on the losing side in the Austro-Prussian War of 1866. In the mean time, however, the military seem to have won their point. So many years had passed since the last execution in Zweibrücken that the traditional venue outside the town walls was in any case no longer in a suitable condition. The market-square was thus confirmed as the appropriate site. But the local notables were clearly less than happy about this decision. It was pressures such as these that led to the steady erosion of the most public aspects of capital punishment in Bavaria.

[48] Ibid. 13068: President of the Appellationsgericht der Pfalz to the King, 13 Sept. 1856.
[49] Ibid., Generalstaatsprokurator der Pfalz to the King, 22 Dec. 1856.
[50] Ibid., Kriegsministerium to Justizministerium, 15 Jan. 1857.

Already in 1854 a new set of execution regulations issued in Munich called for the sentence to be read out and the wand of office broken in prison and no longer outside, and the condemned to be taken 'to the scaffold as far as possible avoiding the better frequented parts of town'.[51] In 1856 a further innovation was introduced when the Bavarian Ministry of Justice began to worry that popular disturbances might be caused by the requirement to take the corpse of the executed malefactor back through the streets to the university's Anatomical Institute. The problem was that it had to be rushed away in a cart 'on the trot' rather than carried off at a dignified slow walking pace: 'Thus in this way offence may be caused to the many prejudices held by the crowd in respect of executions, and lead to demonstrations and excesses.'[52] These concerns testified more to the neurotic anxiety of the authorities about the public order implications of executions than to the putative irascibility of 'the crowd', which never actually manifested itself in this way. In 1861, finally, public executions in Bavaria were abolished altogether.[53]

The period of reaction after the failed Revolution of 1848 was the occasion for the removal of executions inside prison walls in other parts of Germany as well. In the Grand Duchy of Baden, the Prussian system of 'intramural' executions was introduced, complete with the twelve witnesses, in 1856. The authorities in the Central Rhine District had already urged on 9 June 1854 'that public executions should be given another form better corresponding to the spirit of the age and the moral constitution of our century'. Anyone familiar with public executions knew 'that the general excitement following the execution of the punishment expresses more a pleasure in the unusual and the horrific, more curiosity, than revulsion at the crime, and quite often sympathy with the criminal and disapproval of the type of sentence that has been meted out'. What was needed was the restriction of public executions to 'a sufficient number of persons to record' them.[54] This was necessary in order to avoid the 'troubles' that had attended executions carried out in public:

That the moral effects which could be expected from the public nature of executions are not brought about as much as one would wish has been testified to by numerous witnesses both here and abroad. Only a few people among the numberless crowd which is gathered in the wide open space manage to bring about in themselves the serious and worthy state of mind in which they can receive and store up the moral impressions which the act

[51] StA Munich App. Ger. 5707: Justizministerium to Appellationsgericht Oberbayern, 10 Aug. 1854.

[52] HStA Munich MInn 46136: Justizministerium to Innenministerium, 16 Jan. 1856. See also HStA Munich App. Ger. 5704: Justizministerium to Appellationsgericht Oberbayern, 10 Aug. 1854.

[53] See Stephan Schurr, 'Studien zur Geschichte der Hinrichtung in Bayern im 19. Jahrhundert' (MA diss., Ludwig-Maximilians-University, Munich, 1987), 35–8, 61–75.

[54] GLA Karlsruhe 234/6774, 159–61: Grossherzoglich Badische Regierung des Mittel-Rheinkreises to Justizministerium, 9 May 1854.

taking place in front of their eyes would be suited to evoke; the vast majority only sees a spectacle, the satisfaction of coarse carnal desires in front of them, and instead of feeling revulsion at a crime which has to find its human expiation, and respect for the law and the undeviating path of justice, they feel sympathy for the criminal, and may even experience an even warmer empathy if his behaviour in the last moments seduces them into doing so.

'Such effects', the Baden government decided after disturbances at an execution in Freiburg on 13 April in 1855,[55] 'contradict too much the interests of morality and justice, to be ignored any longer.'[56]

Instead of being applauded by the 'popular crowd', executions in the Grand Duchy were now to be attended only by 'a limited number of persons in authority and of witnesses'. The connection with the introduction of public trials was clear:

In earlier times people thought that the public nature of executions provided a guarantee for the legality of this act. But the public nature of execution does not provide a guarantee for the justice of the verdict and sentence in itself; the legality of the execution procedure can be confirmed much more easily by other means. The general feeling of legality is satisfied by the public court procedure which precedes the verdict and sentence, and in the certainty that this sentence has been carried out. This certainty will be guaranteed by the requirement that persons in authority, whose profession leads them to take part in this most earnest act of human justice, be compelled to attend, and that apart from this a number of respectable citizens will be called to attend as witnesses, and that finally such persons whose relationship to the condemned gives them a close interest in his fate, the relatives of the victim of his crime, or other persons who particularly request admittance, will be admitted in so far as the space is available and there is no other objection to it.[57]

Here too, therefore, no strict limits were set on the numbers attending, and descriptions of executions published in Baden in the late 1850s continued to describe those who attended as 'the public'.[58] All that was demanded was that those present be persons capable of treating the occasion with the necessary seriousness, or in other words members of the educated classes. An exception was made for the relatives of the person who had been the condemned murderer's victim, who, given the patterns of crime prevalent in Germany in the 1850s, were likely to be poor and uneducated. The admission of these people to the execution was a peculiarity of Baden law, and was not to be found elsewhere in Germany. It was not normally intended to include the victim's female relatives, since the rules stipulated that those present would be 'as a rule only adult persons of the male sex'. The public sphere in the nineteenth century was a masculine sphere;

[55] Ibid. 6609: Justizministerium, R. No. 1741, 22. März 1856, den Vollzug der Todesstrafe betr.
[56] Ibid.: Beilage Nr. 40 zum Protokoll der 4. Sitzung vom 15. Jan. 1856, 4.   [57] Ibid. 3.
[58] Anon., *Der Freundesmörder Stephan Werner von Bleichstetten. Seine Lebensbeschreibung, Flucht, Verurtheilung und Hinrichtung. Nach den öffentlichen Verhandlungen vor dem Schwurgerichte in Tübingen vom 28. Juni bis 2. Juli 1858. Mit einer Abbildung der Guillotine*, 2nd edn. (Tübingen, 1858), 13.

women, like the mob, were considered too emotional to be relied upon to behave with the appropriate degree of decorum. Bourgeois belief in the weakness of the female sex, its delicacy, its liability to fainting fits and attacks of the vapours when confronted with the harsh realities of an event such as an execution, were reflected in a stream of comments from observers of these occasions from the end of the eighteenth century onwards. Well before the introduction of 'intramural executions', the authorities had tried to ensure that only men would be present when an offender was dispatched. It was only with the abolition of executions in the open air that the authorities at last had the opportunity to put this policy into effect.[59]

The Baden provisions for the introduction of 'intramural executions' were similar to those introduced in other states. They included the breaking of a black wand of office before the condemned, with the words 'Your life is at an end, God have mercy upon your soul!' and also the tolling of a bell from the beginning of the ceremony to the end.[60] The first of the new 'intramural' executions in the Grand Duchy took place in Freiburg at 7.25 in the morning on 25 April 1856. The novelty of the occasion impressed the officiating state prosecutor; but so too did its orderliness:

The enclosed space and the presence of a relatively small number of people in contrast to the previous procedure may strike some people as uncanny, perhaps embarrassing, but on the other hand the impression of the quiet and orderliness which obtained throughout and followed from the purpose of the meeting without doubt lent the whole proceedings a more serious, more worthy character, and gave all those who had anything to do with it . . . far more confidence in the security of the execution, which is what I most missed in the earlier procedure, as I remarked in my report of 7 July last year.

As in other parts of Germany, officials were concerned that the walls of the prison yards in which the executions took place were not high enough to block the view from the upper storeys of neighbouring houses, and recommended they be raised by several feet before any more executions took place. That this was no idle anxiety was demonstrated by an incident in Darmstadt in 1853, when a local businessman erected a grandstand outside the prison yard and sold seats overlooking the prison wall to local people, thus frustrating the purposes of the Hessian authorities, who had introduced 'intramural' executions earlier that year.[61] In Baden, too, there were also worries about the effect the noise of the hammering together of the scaffold and guillotine might have on the offender in

[59] For the exclusion of women from 'intramural' executions in the USA, see Masur, *Rites*, 111–12.
[60] GLA Karlsruhe 234/6609: *Grossherzoglich Badisches Regierungs-Blatt*, 15 Apr. 1856, 83–6.
[61] Krämer, *Mord*, 137.

the days before the execution was due, and it was recommended that these structures be erected permanently so as to avoid any kind of disturbance.[62]

All over Germany, therefore, the 1850s and early 1860s saw the end of public executions and their removal to the confined and controllable space of prison yards. Only Saxe-Altenburg had already taken this step before the 1848 Revolution, the first German state to do so, in 1841.[63] In the Kingdom of Württemberg the reintroduction of capital punishment in 1853 was used as the opportunity to remove it from the public eye.[64] In Hamburg public executions were abolished in October 1854 on the occasion of the beheading of a notorious robber, Wilhelm Timm, who had become something of a popular hero after his numerous adventures and escapes. The Senate gave as its reason fears that 'the many unacceptable consequences of public executions, especially those taking place in large cities', would occur there too.[65] The Duchy of Brunswick abolished public executions the same year. The Kingdom of Saxony followed suit in 1855, and the Kingdom of Hanover in 1860.[66] 'Intramural' executions were introduced in Upper Hesse and Starkenberg in 1853 and in Rhenish Hesse in 1863.[67] The predominant, immediate motive for this change was official fear of the mob. Public executions attracted huge crowds, and the emotions which they were thought to arouse were now considered dangerously unpredictable. Decades of official attempts to secularize the execution ritual, remove it from the arena of popular culture and 'crypto-materialist' religion, and convert it into a solemn expression of state power had only succeeded in destabilizing it. The transition from a status-bound society to one of growing class antagonism between bourgeoisie and proletariat had broken asunder the synthesis of state and community ritual that had created the early modern public execution. The educated middle classes now found the crowd's behaviour repugnant, while its deliberate desacralization at the hands of the authorities had gradually stripped it of its meanings for the common people. The dismantling of guild privileges and other aspects of the urban hierarchy through the political reforms and social changes of the first half of the nineteenth century had destroyed the structured crowd and replaced it in the eyes of the authorities with a formless, volatile mob. Efforts to

---

[62] GLA Karlsruhe 234/6609: Staatsanwalt am Grossherzoglich Badischen Hofgericht des Ober-Rhein-Kreises an das Grosshezoglich Justiz-Ministerium, 28 Apr. 1856.

[63] *Ueber die Todesstrafe*, p. xiv.

[64] GLA Karlsruhe 234/6609: *Regierungs-Blatt für das Königreich Württemberg*, 17 (20 June 1853), 170.

[65] StA Hamburg Senat Cl. VII. Lit. Mb. no. 3, vol. 9: Verordnung über die Vollziehung der Todesstrafe, Oct. 1854.

[66] Ibid.: *Gesetzes- und Verordnungs-Sammlung Nr. 49, Braunschweig*, 27 Aug. 1853; HStA Hanover Hann. 173a Nr. 436, Bl. 24: *Gesetz-Sammlung für das Königreich Hannover*, Jahrgang 1860, Nr. 20; *Ueber die Todesstrafe*, p. xvi.

[67] Krämer, *Mord*, 137.

restructure the crowd in terms of bourgeois concepts of the public sphere, above all through the removal of women and children and the encouragement of solemnity and self-control among the men who were supposed to remain, had failed. The only solution, as the Prussian government had already recognized before the 1848 Revolution, was to bring the ceremony inside the prison walls, where access could be controlled and the attending 'public' selected from approved constituents.

Public executions were brought to an end above all because authorities and bourgeois liberals alike feared in the aftermath of the 1848 Revolution that they would lead to popular disorder. The experience of popular unrest in 1848–9 had shown how dangerous this could be in the eyes of the liberals as well as of the state authorities. The public that was recreated in the prison yard was the same public that was recreated after the Revolution by the compromise between the old order and the commercial, industrial, educated, and professional middle class on a wider scale, in the voluntary associations and parliamentary assemblies of the 1850s and 1860s: a public of sober, responsible men, a public of local notables and state officials who, whatever their political differences, could all agree that public order had to be maintained and the clash of opinion moderated by the rules of bourgeois decorum. In the ending of public executions, they saw a means of putting this new-found consensus into effect. The post-revolutionary consensus also rested on far-reaching reforms which conceded some of the major demands of the liberals of the *Vormärz* era, from trial in open court to the establishment of juries and the appointment of lay assessors. For the moment, the liberal bourgeoisie had to accept the restoration of the death penalty which they had so enthusiastically abolished in the heady, idealistic days of the Frankfurt Parliament. In the circumstances of the reassertion of state power in the 1850s, those who continued to believe that it should be abolished had to bide their time and wait until the political situation became more relaxed. In the mean time, however, many abolitionists could take comfort in the view that the ending of public executions was a step in the direction of complete abolition and a blow for the humanitarian cause. They were, indeed, swimming with the European tide. Public executions were abolished in a number of other countries at this time, including Austria and Britain in 1868.[68] There were, to be sure, some major exceptions, including Belgium, Holland, Italy, Portugal, Spain, and above all France. In the last-named country, indeed, executions continued to be carried out in public all the way up to 1939, largely because the opponents of capital punishment in the Chamber of Deputies consistently voted for the continuation of this practice on the somewhat paradoxical grounds that the ending of public

---

[68] For Austria, see Hartl, *Wiener Kriminalgericht*, 420.

executions would make the death penalty more acceptable. The guillotine was, however, sited outside prison gates, so that ceremonies, processions, and the like were as far as possible avoided, elaborate security precautions were taken, and the crowds attending them were kept relatively small. So while this practice allowed abolitionists to complain in the time-honoured manner about executions being 'the occasion of scandalous scenes among the crowds of the curious who came to take part in this spectacle as if in an act of pleasure', it was in reality not so very different from what was happening elsewhere by the late nineteenth century.[69]

The abolition of public executions made it clear that neither official nor liberal opinion was satisfied in the aftermath of the 1848 Revolution with a mere return to the status quo ante. In some parts of Germany, traditional methods such as the sword and the hand-held axe continued to offend bourgeois sensibilities with their brutal physicality and to cause official concern with their liability to error. In south Germany attempts to replace the sword with the guillotine earlier in the century had fallen foul of the seemingly indelible association of the latter with the execution of the French King and Queen and a large number of French aristocrats during the Terror of 1793–4. In Bavaria the sword continued to be employed throughout the first half of the nineteenth century as a result. Dependent for its effectiveness on a difficult combination of precision and strength, it was all too liable to miss its target if the executioner for some reason was not up to the job. In 1841 the Grand Duchy of Hesse had already followed Prussia in replacing the sword with the guillotine on the grounds of greater security. The executioner, said the official justification of this measure, 'must live in fear of a wrongly aimed blow', and it was 'a contradiction in terms to punish murder, then ask someone to practise beheading'.[70] Bungled executions were always liable to enrage the crowd. On 11 May 1854, in a public execution in Munich, the executioner Lorenz Scheller took no fewer than seven strokes to sever the head of Christian Hussendorfer of Syburg from his body. He subsequently admitted that he had been so drunk that he had seen two heads instead of one, and 'so didn't know which of the two was the real one'. An eyewitness reported that 'the people would have torn him to bits despite all the gendarmerie', but the day was saved by the presence of mind of one of the officials on the scaffold. Aware that the crowd was overwhelmingly Catholic in composition, he told them that the executioner's sword had been dedicated to the Virgin Mary, and noted that the executed malefactor was a Protestant, the first such ever to be decapitated in Munich, or

[69] BA Potsdam Auswärtiges Amt IIIa Nr. 51, Bd. 7, Bl. 81: *Le Temps*, 8 May 1905; ibid., Bd. 3, Bl. 52–4: *Report of the Commission to Investigate and Report the Most Humane and Practical Method of Carrying into Effect the Sentence of Death in Capital Cases* (New York, 1888), 48; Wright, *Between the Guillotine and Liberty*, 168–70. For the primacy of the public order issue in bringing about the end of public executions in the USA, see Masur, *Rites*, 100–2.

[70] Krämer, *Mord*, 137.

so he claimed. 'So the executioner couldn't prevent the sword from being so unskilled.' This seemed to satisfy people, and the crowd eventually dispersed without further incident.[71]

However, the affair left the Bavarian King 'disturbed', and he wrote to the Ministry of Justice on 17 May 1854, expressing his disquiet. Prompted by this move, the Bavarian government now began to investigate alternative methods. As the Ministry of Justice remarked on 30 May 1854, 'humanity and justice' demanded the prevention of such incidents in future, preferably by the use of a safer means of execution:

> The death penalty is already in itself the greatest of earthly punishments for a crime. It declares the criminal's life, that is, his highest earthly possession, lost, and thus satisfies the demands of the law. Death expiates the crime and fulfils the state's requirements. But if *death itself* rather than *the manner* of death must be regarded as the punishment, it follows that the state is obliged to select the manner of death which brings life to an end in the safest and quickest way.[72]

The responsible officials in the Ministry of Justice thus sought to find convincing reasons for the introduction of the guillotine as the standard method of execution in Bavaria. They laid particular stress on the 'general wrath' of the crowd when the executioner missed the target with his swordstroke, whether it was because his arm was unsteady, his eye blinded by the sun, or his concentration disturbed by a biting insect. The guillotine, it was argued, would effectively eliminate the possibility of popular disturbances. The same principle would apply if public executions were abolished: 'If the hangman's stroke should go awry in any execution held in an enclosed space, rumours would steadily grow, exaggerations would occur and find an audience, and instead of the public being reconciled to the law, it would be exploited for spreading mistrust in it.'[73] In fact, prison executions, as we have seen, were not to be introduced in Bavaria until 1861. The arguments for the guillotine were therefore all the stronger in the minds of judicial officials. As long as frequent checks and repairs were carried out, and the operators were careful and observant, the likelihood of a mistake was small.

The weight of learned and forensic opinion was on the side of the guillotine, which was already being used in France, Belgium, Greece, Saxony, Württemberg, Hesse-Darmstadt, and the Rhineland. The alternative of hanging, as practised in England, was rejected, not because it was dishonourable, but because it was inappropriate to the religious principle of retributive justice: 'The

[71] HStA Munich MInn 46136, Urgicht C.H.; Dülmen, *Theater*, 159–60; Völderndorff and Waradein, *Plaudereien*, i. 101–6.

[72] HStA Munich MJu 13066: Allerunterthänigster Bericht des Staats-Ministeriums der Justiz an Seine Majestät den König, den Vollzug der Todesstrafe betreffend, 20. v. 1854; Anon., *Die kgl. Bayer. Staatsminister der Justiz*, 62–3.

[73] HStA Munich MJu 13067: Justice Minister (Ringelmann) to King, 13 Nov. 1854.

method of death by *beheading* seems without doubt to be the quickest and safest. It is deeply rooted in the popular spirit because of the biblical saying "Whosoever sheddeth man's blood, by man shall his blood be shed."' As long as executions continued to be carried out in public, as was the intention in Bavaria when this report was written, due attention continued to be paid to their effect on popular attitudes, and thus care was taken not to offend those common beliefs which were thought to underline the function of capital punishment as an act of judicial retribution. Hence, argued the 1854 report, there were no practical objections to the introduction of the guillotine, rather the contrary:

There is only one objection which the opponents of the use of the guillotine have some justification in raising, namely its connection with the memory of the evil deeds which were done in France with this instrument, and the fear that the availability of such machines could lead to their being similarly abused in possible future periods of unrest. But against this one should bear in mind the fact that while the period of the Terror in France and the guillotine's role in it will always remain an indelible stain on the honour of the people and the era, no one can ascribe the blame for this to a dead machine. History shows that when nations have erred, the bullet, the sword, and the axe have been the means by which the same cruelties have been carried out. They none the less remained in use until a better and more appropriate method was discovered, and its possible abuse must not deter us from employing it. Otherwise people would never use knives, because they *could* become murder weapons.

Thus, rather than supposing, as the Baden commissioners had predicted thirty years before, that the time had come when the revolutionary associations of the guillotine had finally faded into oblivion, the Bavarian report sought to dispense with these associations altogether by suggesting that they only existed in France.

The reactionary Bavarian Minister of Justice Friedrich von Ringelmann (1803–70) informed the King on 13 November 1854 that, while the French people would always associate the guillotine with 'the darkest page in its history', 'the sight of this machine, or a similar one, will surely make a very different impression on peoples of German origin'. For, he argued, the religious character of the Bavarian people, and their proven loyalty to the Crown 'under the beneficent sceptre of the exalted House of Wittelsbach', had ensured that the French Revolution had never found a parallel in Germany. 'The German people,' declared Ringelmann, in a prediction to which the experiences of the Third Reich some eight decades subsequently lent a savage note of irony, 'as one can deduce with certainty from their character, would always recoil from murder *in legal form*.' Instead, he continued, the introduction of the guillotine in a German state—Bavaria—was likely to arouse altogether different sentiments among the populace.

It would be welcomed as an absolutely sure means of preventing the abuses which often sadly occur after unsuccessful executions with the sword, it would not lead to any diminution of the worthy and earnest character of the execution of death sentences, and finally the memory of the fact that political murders were committed in France with a similar machine will continue to serve as a deterrent and a warning, and will perpetuate a burning desire to preserve the people's own fatherland from such horrors.

In Ringelmann's view, the guillotine's association with the French Revolution thus became positive rather than negative, reflecting the assumption, typical of the reactionary politicians of the post-1848 period, that popular opinion was unshakeably conservative and loyal to the Crown. Such a belief, indeed, was to lead just over a decade later to the reactionary Prussian Minister-President Otto von Bismarck bringing about universal manhood suffrage, first in the North German Confederation, and then in the German Reich founded in 1871. Subsequent experience was to prove it ill-founded. The thought that this might be so, however, did not deter Ringelmann from his enthusiasm for the guillotine: 'Should it be ordained on the dark paths of Providence that the horror of a revolution is visited upon the German people, it must be borne in mind that the *refusal to introduce* one particular type of execution machine does not of itself render bloody deeds impossible.' In this prediction, as the course of German history in the twentieth century was to show, he was surely right.[74]

The new humane method of execution went into action for the first time in Bavaria in Amberg, on 24 August 1854. The experience was not an auspicious one. The local officials were obliged to include in their report on the newfangled instrument that 'when the miller Lobenhofer was tied to the board, he could grasp it with both his hands and thus prevent the board from being propelled into the machine, at least for a time'.[75] On subsequent occasions, the condemned person's hands were bound. But this was not the only problem. The guillotine, said the police in Munich, took over two minutes to prepare while the condemned were in it, and so it prolonged their suffering to a regrettable degree. The undignified position of the victim and the lack of freedom of movement allowed by the guillotine were also regarded as unfortunate by some. 'The fastening of the malefactor's head', as the Munich police noted, made 'a very unpleasant impression on the public.'[76] An official in Amberg agreed. The guillotine, he said, was 'cruel . . . to the malefactor . . . who is manhandled like a beast being slaughtered, and is forced to allow various manipulations to be carried out on him, so that he is left hanging in the fear of death for much longer than he would be during an execution with a sword at the hands of the hangman'.[77] Bavaria was

[74] HStA Munich MJu 13066: Allerunterthänigster Bericht des Staats-Ministeriums der Justiz an Seine Majestät den König, den Vollzug der Todesstrafe betreffend, 20 May 1854.

[75] Ibid. MInn 46136: Kgl. Stadt-Kommissariat Amberg to Kgl. Regierung Oberfranken, Kammer des Innern, 25 Aug. 1854.

[76] Ibid.: Kgl. Polizeidirektion Munich, Bericht to Kgl. Regierung Oberbayern, 31 Aug. 1854.

[77] Ibid.: Kgl. Stadt-Kommissariat Amberg to Kgl. Regierung Oberfranken, Kammer des Innern, 25 Aug. 1854.

not the only German state to drop the sword for the guillotine in the 1850s. In April 1856 the Baden government also nominated the guillotine as the means by which executions were to be carried out.[78] In October 1854 the parsimonious city fathers of Hamburg opted for the guillotine 'because it is the safest method of execution and does not require a trained hangman'.[79] And in 1859 the Kingdom of Hanover followed suit, for much the same reasons of security and decorum.[80] This left only a few small states like Mecklenburg still committed to the use of the sword, and here too in due course it was replaced in practice, if not in law, by the guillotine. By the end of the nineteenth century, the only methods in use for German executions were the hand-held axe, above all in East Elbian Prussia, and the guillotine, in other parts of Germany. The introduction of the guillotine in a number of German states was an ironic postscript to the Revolution of 1848. In France in 1789–94 the guillotine had proved the real and symbolic means by which the old order was finally crushed. In Germany in 1848, the guillotine emerged only when the old order had re-established itself. As Ringelmann so perceptively noted, it had transformed itself from a symbol of disorder into a symbol of order. The embodiment of boundless, bloody destructiveness in 1793–4, it had become the incorporation of decorum and restraint sixty years later. Yet it retained its essentially bourgeois character throughout its transmogrification from the instrument of bourgeois terror against the aristocracy, into the machinery of bourgeois collaboration in the maintenance of law and order. Fear of the common people had been one of the major elements in driving the liberal revolutionaries of 1848 into the arms of the existing order when it looked as if things were getting out of hand. Now it was symbolized in the establishment of the guillotine as a means of capital punishment that would draw the line between the educated and propertied and the masses even more firmly than before; a transformation completed not only in Germany, but also in France, where one of the first acts of the revolutionary Paris Commune of 1871 was to burn the guillotine in public, at the foot of a statue of Voltaire, as an instrument of 'monarchic domination', in a public gesture for 'the consecration of liberty'.[81]

d. The Revival of Abolitionism in the 1860s

By the early 1860s the chastened German liberals had recovered from the shock of defeat in the Revolution of 1848 and were on the march once more. Legislative assemblies had emerged in a number of states as part of the political compromise arrived at in the wake of the Revolution. They provided a useful springboard for

[78] GLA Karlsruhe 234/6774, 235–91 and following pages (unnumbered).
[79] StA Hamburg Senat Cl. VII. Lit. Mb. no. 3, vol. 9: Commission report of 26 July 1854.
[80] GStA Berlin Rep. 84a/9397, Bl. 95: Notiz vom 26 July 1883; HStA Hanover Rep. 173a Nr. 436, Bl. 28: *Gesetz-Sammlung für das Königreich Hannover*, Jahrgang 1859, Nr. 81.
[81] Arasse, *Guillotine*, 131.

liberalism's fresh forward leap. In Prussia the elected lower chamber of the legislature had a liberal majority by 1862. The new liberal party, the Progressives, used their position to bid for control over that bastion of aristocratic reaction, the army, by refusing to agree to a budget. Resisting this attack on his sovereignty, the soldier-king Wilhelm I brought in a well-known ultra-conservative to take the liberals on as the new Minister-President: Otto von Bismarck. For the next four years Bismarck defied the legislature by collecting taxes without its approval. The stand-off seemed insoluble. Yet parliamentarization, the first of the two great objectives of 1848, was firmly back on the agenda none the less. The other great issue of 1848, the unification of Germany, also re-emerged at this time. The Austrians had taken the lead in re-establishing the German Confederation after the Revolution. But by the beginning of the 1860s they were running out of ideas. And the Prussians were gaining rapidly in strength as industrialization gathered pace in Silesia and the Ruhr and provided them with increasing wealth and resources. Liberals recognized these facts of life, and many of them put their faith in Prussia as the political and military force that alone could bring the unification of Germany about. This gave the issue of the army budget added urgency. As the liberals organized, both in the Progressive Party and in the National Association, to put pressure on the Prussian and other governments to start moving towards unification, Bismarck began to realize that it was inevitable. If he was to save what was left of the old order in Prussia, he had to ensure that the unity of Germany was achieved on his terms, not theirs.

While Bismarck contemplated these problems and turned over in his mind the prospects for wresting hegemony from Austria within the German Confederation, the liberals were rapidly gaining the political initiative on a number of fronts. In many ways, to be sure, they were more cautious, more sober, more realistic than they had been in the heady, idealistic days of 1848. But it would be wrong to ignore their continued belief in a number of key liberal principles. One of the most important of these, as in 1848, was the principle of basic civil and human rights. As in 1848, the abolition of capital punishment was a central plank in this platform. So when the liberals began to dominate the representative assemblies of the other German states once more, resolutions demanding the abolition of capital punishment were passed with growing frequency. The legislature of the small Thuringian Dukedom of Saxe-Weimar, for example, voted to abolish the death penalty by nineteen votes to ten in 1862, twenty-three votes to five in 1865, and twenty-five votes to five in 1868.[82] These were impressive majorities, even if the total numbers of votes were small. In the much larger south German state of Württemberg, the elected legislative chamber, convinced by the

[82] BA Potsdam RKA 632 Bl. 47: Staatsministerium Sachsen-Weimar to Reichskanzler, 12 Aug. 1868.

argument that restoration in 1853 had not brought about the desired fall in the number of murders over the following decade, voted to abolish the death penalty by fifty-six votes to twenty-seven in 1865, and repeated the vote in 1869.[83] In the Kingdom of Saxony the Chamber of Deputies resolved to remove capital punishment from the Criminal Code by forty-two votes to twenty-three on 7 April 1868, repeating this by twenty-two votes to fifteen on 19 May and again by twenty votes to sixteen on 4 September, after the upper house had rejected the original resolution the previous May.[84] In Bavaria the Chamber of Deputies voted to abolish the death penalty in 1867, but the motion was rejected by the upper house.[85] In the Grand Duchy of Baden a similar sequence of events took place in 1870.[86] Even where abolitionist motions failed, as in Vienna in 1867, the defeat was usually a narrow one.[87] All these votes testified to a renewed ground swell of liberal opinion in favour of abolition. Moreover, despite the reluctance of many governments and upper legislative chambers to support the principle of abolition in this period, there were none the less increasing numbers of leading politicians in government office who did their best to implement it. Liberally inclined ministers came to power in several German states at this time. One of the most important was Baron Hermann von Mittnacht, Chief Minister of Württemberg from 1870 to 1900, who had spoken in favour of abolition during the debate of 1865 and refused to recommend any executions during his term of office as Justice Minister from 1867 to 1878. After 1866, therefore, executions in the Kingdom effectively ceased.[88] Elsewhere, too, the former men of 1848 were now beginning to achieve government office, and similar developments could confidently be expected; for if they had abandoned some of their principles in the compromise with the post-revolutionary order, they still adhered to others, and the abolition of capital punishment was emphatically one of the latter.

All this demonstrated a rediscovered self-confidence on the part of German liberals after the setbacks of the post-revolutionary 1850s. Even more than it had

---

[83] Ibid. RKA 631, Bl. 29–30: *Verhandlungen der Kammer der Abgeordneten* (Bavaria), 1867, Beilage LI, 332–3: Vortrag des Abgeordneten Behringer. See also GLA Karlsruhe 234/6609: Bericht der Justizgesetzgebungskommission der (württembergischen) Kammer der Abgeordneten über die Motion des Abgeordneten Becher auf Abschaffung der Todesstrafe, 28 Jan. 1865; and ibid.: *Staatsanzeiger für Württemberg*, 54, 5 Mar. 1864 (reporting 66. Sitzung der württ. Kammer der Abgeordneten, 4 Mar. 1864).

[84] BA Potsdam RJA 5664, Bl. 225: *Ueber die Todesstrafe*, 13–14 (extract).

[85] HStA Munich MInn 46136: *Verhandlungen der Kammer der Abgeordneten*, 1867, Beilage Bd. I, 331–5 (22 Mar. and 16 Nov. 1867).

[86] *Stenographische Berichte über die Verhandlungen des Reichstags des Norddeutschen Bundes*, I. Leg. Per., Sess. 1870, 52. Sitzung, 1125, Abg. Lasker; GLA Karlsruhe 234/6609: Beilage zum Protokoll der 59. öffentlichen Sitzung der zweiten Kammer vom 21 Feb. 1870, Kommissionsbericht der Ersten Kammer (Beilage 496 zum Protokoll der 25. Sitzung von 18. März 1870).

[87] Eduard Herbst, *Zur Frage der Aufhebung der Todesstrafe* (Vienna, 1879), 31.

[88] GStA Berlin Rep. 84a/7784, Bl. 163: *Berliner Tageblatt*, 2 Aug. 1895; GLA Karlsruhe 234/6609: *Der Beobachter* (Stuttgart), 38 (25 Feb. 1865), 225, and Anlage A zur III. Sitzung der Kommission zu Ausarbeitung eines neuen Strafgesetzbuchs für Württemberg.

been during the Revolution, however, German liberalism was now rooted in a belief in the superior judgement of educated men elected to representative assemblies on a limited franchise, and strongly conditioned by fear of the mob. As one of the proponents of abolition declared in the Bavarian Chamber of Deputies in 1867, it might be argued that

The voice of the people still demands this punishment; there is still a deep-rooted feeling among the people that justice will be insulted if there is no equivalence between crime and punishment. To everyone the fruits of his own labour, and if this is not generally true, then at least it should be for murder, for which the death penalty provides the only corresponding expiation.

But the *real* 'people's will' was, he said, the *representative* people's will, of elected deputies, whose task it had always been to give a lead to public opinion in such matters. Surely it would be wrong to pay heed to 'cries of rage from the old bloodthirsty, vengeful mob'.[89] Albert Friedrich Berner, Professor of Law at the University of Berlin, agreed: 'Is it all right', he asked rhetorically, 'if the legislator yields to popular outbreaks of rage and allows himself to be governed by such coarse elements?'[90] Similarly, a liberal abolitionist in Württemberg declared in 1864 that he doubted 'whether the people's voice is entitled to demand human sacrifices'. In any case, he said, it was wrong to say that one should wait until the common people were ready for abolition.[91] The fears of popular brutality which had been so powerful in bringing about the end of public executions were now transferred to the very issue of capital punishment itself. Abolition was presented as a means of civilizing the masses and conditioning them to avoid the kind of violent outbursts that had so terrified the liberals in 1848.

The liberals of the 1860s were able to base the argument for abolition on the fact of its congruence with the vast mass of reforms in criminal law and procedure that had been introduced in the period of reaction, expressing the shared determination of the restored state structures and the chastened bourgeoisie to establish a firm and effective bulwark against the tide of crime and disorder that had threatened to overwhelm them both in the revolutionary years of 1848–9. As the Württemberg Chamber of Deputies was told by its commission for judicial legislation in 1865,

Crime exists in the criminal's will, thus the concept of punishment is inherently a compulsion of the criminal's will; the total removal of this will, the extermination of the personality, therefore contradicts this principle completely; it would only be justified if

[89] BA Potsdam RKA 631, Bl. 29–31: *Verhandlungen der Kammer der Abgeordneten* (Bavaria), 1867, Beilage LI, 351–7: Vortrag des Abg. Behringer.

[90] Albert Friedrich Berner, *Abschaffung der Todesstrafe* (Dresden, 1861), 10.

[91] GLA Karlsruhe, 234/6609: *Staatsanzeiger für Württemberg*, 54, 5 Mar. 1864 (reporting 66. Sitzung der württ. Kammer der Abgeordneten, 4 Mar. 1864).

there was a crime in which the individuality of the criminal proved to be irreparably evil; but no such crime exists, for even murder does not qualify, since experience demonstrates that the character of murderers too can be improved.[92]

This principle testified to the optimism which suffused nineteenth-century German liberalism. Future ages would disagree with the argument that irremediable evil did not exist. Yet the abolition of capital punishment was seen by its proponents not as a reversion to the abstract liberalism of 1848, but rather as a fulfilment of the principles of the Criminal Law Codes that had been introduced during the period of reaction afterwards. Capital punishment, liberals now argued, was bad because it was ineffective, not just because it was wrong.

Executions in general, complained a number of respectable citizens of the Bavarian capital in a petition to the King in 1863, tended to 'blunt feelings and barbarize morals'.[93] Looking back on the reintroduction of capital punishment after its temporary abandonment in the 1848 Revolution, liberals also argued that this had not led to any noticeable decline in the number of murders. Where the death penalty had been removed from other crimes, as in Saxony through the reforms of 1838, there had been no increase in the incidence of these offences either. It therefore had no observable deterrent effect.[94] 'Punishment's deterrent effect', argued one liberal spokesman, following Beccaria, 'does not . . . lie . . . in the threat it poses, nor in the absolute degree of the penalty, but principally in the sure expectation that it will happen'.[95] Moreover, judges, witnesses, and juries would feel more confident in dealing with serious murder cases if they were sure 'that a human life was no longer at stake'. As well as pragmatic arguments of this kind, the abolitionists now also borrowed a classic proposition of the conservatives, namely that getting rid of the death penalty was not a matter of asserting the rights of the individual against society, but of asserting society's duty to protect the individual. Such arguments won a number of conservative jurists and bureaucrats over to the abolitionist cause during these years.[96]

Nevertheless, many of the points put forward by liberal abolitionists during the 1860s did look back to the debates of 1848–9 and beyond. The possibility of judicial error (hotly denied by the retentionists, who argued that this had vanished from capital cases since the eighteenth century as verdicts and sentences had grown more cautious), the failure of executions to deter, and the barbarous

---

[92] Ibid.: Bericht der Justizgesetzgebungskommission der (württembergischen) Kammer der Abgeordneten über die Motion des Abgeordneten Becher zur Abschaffung der Todesstrafe, 28 Jan. 1865.

[93] HStA Munich, MJu 13967: Petition to King, 20 Jan. 1863.

[94] BA Potsdam RJA 5664, Bl. 225: *Ueber die Todesstrafe*, quoting *Motive* of Juristen-Eingabe an die Sächsische Abgeordneten-Kammer, 25 Jan. 1868.

[95] Ibid., RKA 631, Bl. 31: *Verhandlungen des Kammer der Abgeordneten* (Bavaria), 1867, Beilage LI, 335: Vortrag des Abg. Behringer.

[96] Ibid. RJA 5664, Bl. 225: *Ueber die Todesstrafe*.

nature of capital punishment all featured centrally in the abolitionist case put before the Württemberg Chamber of Deputies in 1865. So too did the argument that the Old Testament doctrine of 'an eye for an eye' was outdated. A penal system based on the improvement of the offender had no place for capital punishment. As Carl Mayer, a local versifier in Tübingen, put it:

> From lawful paths to err and stray
> For humans is a crime.
> The law must indicate a way
> To get back into line.
>
> By cutting off the murd'rer's head,
> By seeking just to strike him,
> The law is off the track instead
> And has become just like him.[97]

In the numerous debating clubs, public meetings, and parliamentary debates which accompanied the rapidly expanding public sphere of the 1860s, abolitionists honed their arguments against the opposition of conservative, aristocratic, and clerical speakers who feared that abolition would open the floodgates of disorder. Even more than in the Revolution of 1848, abolition now became a classic liberal cause, part of the construction of a liberal, orderly, secular civil society that was the project of the revived bourgeois politics of the period. Carl Mittermaier, the leading intellectual advocate of abolition, put forward his views in a further revised and expanded version, published in 1862, and taking account of developments since 1848. He thought 'that the time is nigh when the death penalty will be abolished as a remnant of the old days', and further attacked 'the outrageous scenes which are observable at public executions'.[98] His arguments were closely followed by other writers who now came forward with tracts demanding abolition.[99] They released a flood of pamphlets and publications comparable to that of the 1840s.[100] All this amounted to another literary campaign against the death penalty, though attempts to form an association specifically devoted to abolition did not get very far.[101]

Although motions such as those passed in the Bavarian Chamber of Deputies could fall at the hurdle of the Upper House and the appointed government, the

[97] GLA Karlsruhe 234/6609: *Der Beobachter* (Stuttgart), 40 (17 Feb. 1865), 233.

[98] Carl Joseph Anton Mittermaier, *Die Todesstrafe nach den Ergebnissen der wissenschaftlichen Forschungen, der Fortschritte der Gesetzgebung und der Erfahrungen* (Heidelberg, 1862), 168, 161.

[99] See e.g. J. A. Berger, *Ueber die Todesstrafe* (Vienna, 1864), esp. 23, 28.

[100] Georg Friedrich Schlatter, *Stimmen gegen die Todesstrafe* (Mannheim, 1862); Richard Edward John, *Ueber die Todesstrafe. Ein populärer Vortrag* (Sammlung gemeinverständlicher Vorträge, ed. Rudolf Virchow and Friedrich von Holtzendorff-Vietmansdorff, 36; Berlin, 1867); Boje Karl Christiansen, *Die Absurdität der sogenannten Todesstrafe* (Kiel, 1867); Anton Beyerle, *Ueber die Todesstrafe* (Stuttgart, 1867).

[101] F.C.D., *'Kein Schaffot mehr!' Ein Votum gegen die Todesstrafe, zugleich als Anregung zur Bildung eines deutschen Vereins zur Abschaffung der Todesstrafe* (Darmstadt, 1865).

growing movement in favour of abolition in the 1860s also had an impact on the thinking of some of the monarchs and princes in whose hands the power to sign death warrants lay. Often men of deep religious conviction, they were frequently concerned that the application of the death penalty should be fair, consistent, and orderly. Monarchical reluctance to apply the death penalty was nothing new. In 1832, for instance, Grand Duke Ludwig II of Hesse had confessed that he found it 'deeply distressing to have to take the *final* decision on a person's life or death' and actively sought grounds for sparing capital offenders if he could.[102] But in the 1860s the number of German monarchs who felt in this way seemed to increase dramatically. King Wilhelm I of Prussia, a military reactionary, but also a pious Protestant, was well known for his reluctance to confirm death sentences, and the numbers of executions declined sharply on his assumption of the throne. In 1857, before his accession, twenty-four out of the fifty-six offenders condemned to death in Prussia had been executed. But the same year, the Prussian King Friedrich Wilhelm IV was declared unfit to rule on account of a stroke, and Wilhelm acted as his deputy. A stickler for propriety, Wilhem did not consider that this entitled him to assume the power of commutation, and he stuck to this position even when he was formally appointed regent in October 1858. So he refused to take any decisions on clemency cases either in 1858 or in the following year, 1859. Thus executions in Prussia suddenly ceased. It was only in 1860, when he was finally persuaded that the regency was likely to last a long time, and that it therefore gave him the divinely appointed right over life and death which rested in the monarchy, that Wilhelm began to sign death warrants and grants of clemency. Fortunately for his conscience, his brother died the following year, and as King from 1861 onwards, Wilhelm had no doubt about the prerogatives to which he was entitled. But the scruples and hesitations which had attended his decision-making on capital sentences did not go away. For the rest of his life, Wilhelm remained extremely reluctant to consign condemned prisoners to the gallows.

The consequences of this pernickety attitude were not all positive. From Wilhelm's assumption of the regency onwards, capital offenders in Prussia often had to wait on death row for well over a year while the monarch wrestled with his conscience. Michael Martin, for example, who had shot a merchant on the open road and stolen his horse and cart, selling them with the goods they contained on the market at Posen, was condemned to death on 6 July 1858 but had to wait until 7 January 1860 to learn that he had been refused the royal clemency. One of only two people to suffer this fate in 1858, he was perhaps unlucky, for all of the offenders condemned to death in Prussia in 1859 had their

[102] Krämer, *Mord,* 140.

sentences commuted the following year.[103] Delays of some months, to be sure, were far from new. For one thing, it had been customary in the 1850s for the Prussian Ministry of Justice to forward capital cases to the King in quite large batches. Ten cases had been dealt with by Friedrich Wilhelm IV on 11 April 1854, the dates of their final sentences ranging from 7 September to 7 December 1853.[104] This procedure had inevitably caused some delay in reaching a decision. The appeals procedure introduced in 1852 had also slowed things down, for the higher courts dealt with cases in batches in the same way as the monarch did (four on 7 September 1853, for example). At the time, however, nobody seems to have thought that there was anything wrong with a delay of several months between a capital verdict and the final decision on whether or not to execute. But the delays of 1858–60 were virtually unprecedented.[105] Nevertheless, the accession of the new Prussian King did lead to a marked decrease in the rate of execution. In the decade from 1848 to 1857, while Friedrich Wilhelm IV was still exercising the power of clemency, some forty-nine offenders were condemned to death each year on average in Prussia, of whom fifteen, or 31 per cent, were executed. In the first decade of Wilhelm I's regency and reign, from 1858 to 1867, the number of condemnations fell, to an average of thirty-four per year, suggesting a greater liberalism and leniency on the part of the courts; but far more striking was the fall in executions, to a third of the previous number, at an average of five per year in this period, or 15 per cent of those condemned. This latter development was almost solely due to the new monarch's exercise of the royal prerogative of mercy, and by far the largest element in his generous application of the prerogative was his own personal reluctance to sanction executions: in this, as we shall see, he was a good deal more merciful than the judicial officials who advised him on such matters.[106]

Other German princes went even further in their reluctance to confirm death sentences. The Grand Duke of Baden refused to sign any death warrants at all after 1861. Not a single capital offender was executed in the Grand Duchy for the remainder of that decade and the whole of the next.[107] Nor were there any executions during the 1860s in Bremen, Oldenburg, or Saxe-Anhalt and Cöthen also. Executions ceased in Anhalt-Bernburg (another of the small Thuringian states) in 1865.[108] Most influential of all was the *de facto* abolition of capital punishment in the Kingdom of Saxony—an event which was also largely the

---

[103] GStA Berlin Rep. 84a/8145, Bl. 61–2.   [104] Ibid. 8144, Bl. 143–7.
[105] Ibid. 8145, Bl. 157–8, for some examples.   [106] See Statistical Appendix, below.
[107] GStA Berlin Rep. 84a/7784, Bl. 49: Preussischer Gesandte Karlsruhe to PJM, 16 Nov. 1880 (copy). The recommendations of the Baden Justice Ministry during this period were, however, almost invariably in favour of commutation. See the cases in GLA Karlsruhe 234/6609 (1867–9).
[108] BA Potsdam Auswärtiges Amt III a Nr. 51 Bd. 3, Bl. 23–4: Uebersicht . . . für die holländische Regierung, 1888.

result of the personal scruples of the reigning monarch. As the Prussian ambassador in Dresden reported on 26 February 1868:

His Majesty King Johann has always found it difficult to confirm death sentences, and has only done so after the most minute perusal of the files. In 1866 one particular individual had been condemned to death on the basis of circumstantial evidence, which had, to be sure, fully convinced the judges of his guilt, but without having confessed. He continued to protest his innocence even at his last communion. The King, who was in Berlin, therefore telegraphed a reprieve to Leipzig in December 1866. The telegram only reached the place of execution minutes before it was due to take place, so that the condemned was only saved from being executed by *a kind of coincidence.* After this incident the King did not allow any more executions to be carried out.

While other governments continued to ignore the votes passed by their legislatures in favour of abolition, therefore, King Johann issued a decree bringing capital punishment to an end on 25 January 1868 and welcomed the resolution of the Chamber of Deputies not to support its inclusion in the Criminal Code of the North German Confederation in his speech closing the parliamentary session the following May:[109]

The decision . . . did not merely arise from theoretical reservations, but from the consideration that since under normal circumstances the character of the Saxon people makes this means of punishment superfluous, the weighty doubts which attach to it in general terms do not seem to justify its further retention. And so I hope that the fortunate experience which Saxony enjoys in this matter will accord it the honour of having taken a step which will soon be followed by others.[110]

The role of the individual monarchs in assisting the decline of capital punishment in the 1860s was therefore crucial in a number of German states.

e. The Debates in the North German Reichstag 1870

Abolitionist liberals in the 1860s were thus building up their campaign in an atmosphere in which a growing number of monarchs and ministers in the German states seemed in practice to be agreeing with them. They could be all the more confident that they were swimming with the tide of humanitarianism because similar developments were taking place in other countries at this time. The death penalty was abolished by law in Greece in 1863, Romania in 1864, and Portugal in 1867.[111] The King of the Belgians, Leopold II, automatically com-

---

[109] Ibid. RKA 631, Bl. 4: Eichmann to PJM, 26 Feb. 1868.

[110] Quoted in *Ueber die Todesstrafe*, p. vi. Also quoted by Abg. von Kirchmann, *Stenographische Berichte über die Verhandlungen des Reichstags des Norddeutschen Bundes*, 1. Leg. Per., Sess. 1870, 11.–12. Sitzung, 28 Feb./1 Mar. 1870, 107.

[111] BA Potsdam Auswärtiges Amt IIIa Nr. 51, Bd. 7, Bl. 97: *Chambre des Députés, No. 388: Neuvième Legislature, Session Extraordinaire de 1906—Annexe au procès-verbal de la séance du 5 Novembre 1906*, 2.

muted all death sentences from the moment of his accession in 1865, and the death penalty was deleted from the Belgian Law Code in 1866.[112] In the Netherlands King Willem III refused to sign death warrants after 1855, and capital punishment was formally abolished in 1870.[113] In 1872 the King of Norway and Sweden began systematically granting requests for clemency and declared himself opposed to the death penalty.[114] The King of the new liberal monarchy in Italy also refused to sign death warrants from 1863, and no executions took place from that moment until the confirmation of the abolition of capital punishment in the Criminal Code of 1888.[115] All this made it seem only a matter of time before a similar formal measure of abolition was enacted in Germany as well.

The opportunity to bring this about arrived unexpectedly soon. In 1866, as a result of Bismarck's diplomatic manœuvrings, the rising tension between Austria and Prussia within the German Confederation broke out into open conflict. In a swift, ruthless military action, the Prussian army defeated the Austrians at Sadowa and forced them, along with their south German allies, to come to terms. Bismarck annexed the Kingdom of Hanover and the Free City of Frankfurt am Main to Prussia and intimidated the other north German states into falling in with his plans. The German Confederation was abolished, and in its place Bismarck established a new North German Confederation, which was intended from the start to provide the basis for a united Germany eventually including south German states such as Baden, Württemberg, and Bavaria, but firmly excluding the Austrians because of their ties with other parts of the Habsburg Empire such as Hungary and Bohemia. These dramatic developments took place amidst an outburst of nationalist fervour. The liberals in particular were ecstatic. A majority of them split from the Progressives and agreed to indemnify Bismarck retrospectively for his illegal collection of taxes in Prussia since 1862. Now known as the National Liberals, they provided the basis of support for Bismarck in the new legislature of the North German Confederation, the Reichstag, while the diehard Progressives continued to demand parliamentary power over the government. Not only did Bismarck disappoint them, however, by establishing a constitution which made the government responsible to the monarch and not to the legislature, he also sought to undermine electoral support for both groups of liberals by the introduction of universal manhood suffrage. A bold, almost revolutionary stroke, this was designed to mobilize the conservative, rural masses behind the government parties and create a counterbalance to the mainly

[112] BA Potsdam Auswärtiges Amt IIIa Nr. 51, Bd. 7, Bl. 8: *Vossische Zeitung*, 5 Jan. 1899.
[113] Ibid., Bd. 4, Bl. 43: *Kreuzzeitung*, 21 Apr. 1892.
[114] HStA Munich MJu 13067: *Augsburger Allgemeine Zeitung*, 25 Mar. 1867.
[115] BA Potsdam Auswärtiges Amt IIIa Nr. 51, Bd. 3, Bl. 800: *Vossische Zeitung*, 1 June 1888; ibid., Bl. 104; *Vossische Zeitung*, 22 Nov. 1888.

middle-class electorate which supported the liberals. In the short run, this move achieved very little, for the masses were slow to learn the habit of voting, and low percentage polls for the next decade and more ensured that the National Liberals and Progressives continued to be strongly represented in the Reichstag because their own supporters were much more likely to go to the polls. In the long run, it was to open the way to a massive growth, not of Conservatism, but of the new, Marxist, Social Democratic Party, as Germany's rapid industrialization created a burgeoning working class in the towns and cities.

In 1867, however, this development still lay some way in the future. Once it had convened after the elections, the Reichstag of the North German Confederation began the task of drafting laws which would unify the different member states and provide the basis for an eventual national set of institutions. The first really major piece of legislation which it considered was a new Criminal Code, based on the Prussian model of 1851. On 28 February 1870 the Reichstag reached the clauses relating to the death penalty. For two days they were subjected to intense scrutiny in the most important set-piece debate on the subject since 1848.[116] From the outset, the retentionists were on the defensive. The effective ending of executions in a number of German states made it easy for abolitionists to claim that it would be grossly unfair to convicted murderers in these states if they were to be beheaded merely because they had had the bad luck to have been convicted after a new Criminal Code including provision for capital punishment came into force.[117] Moreover, the signs of the times pointed to abolition. 'We hear every day', observed a leading liberal abolitionist in 1870, 'that the number of opponents of the death penalty is growing, while ever more important men are abandoning the retentionist camp and going over to the other side.'[118] This was in many ways an accurate perception. Even a Prussian government memorandum urging the retention of capital punishment in 1868 did so on the grounds that the time was not ripe for abolition, conceding in principle that 'the total abolition of the death penalty cannot be avoided in the long run'.[119] Two decades earlier the jurist and Prussian Minister for the Revision of Legislation, Savigny, had also looked forward to the day when capital punishment would be abolished, and warned merely that 'this would require as a prerequisite condition the general extension of a degree of moral education which cannot be seen to exist at the moment'.[120] So strong was the expectation that the death penalty would soon be abolished that even die-hard retentionists made no

[116] For an account of the debate, see Düsing, *Abschaffung*, 80–101.
[117] *Stenographische Berichte über die Verhandlungen des Reichstages des Norddeutschen Bundes*, 1 Leg. Per., Sess. 1870, 11.–12. Sitzung, 28 Feb./1 Mar. 1870, 99 (Geh. Justizrat Klemm).
[118] Ibid. 101.   [119] Ibid., RKA 632, Bl. 145: Denkschrift, 11 Feb. 1868.
[120] BA Potsdam RJA 5664, Bl. 223: *Ueber die Todesstrafe*, 1.

attempt to defend the draft provisions in the Code which prescribed the death penalty for 'serious physical insult' to the sovereign. Nor did they speak in favour of the clause which applied it to 'intentional homicide during the commission of a criminal offence'.[121] Instead, they concentrated on justifying capital punishment in cases of simple murder and high treason.

Opening the debate, one of the leading Catholic deputies, the lawyer Peter Reichensperger, who had already spoken on the topic in the Prussian constituent assembly of 1848, laid heavy stress on the state's right to self-defence in a strong attack on the Beccarian premiss of contractual sovereignty:

The state is the absolute form of human existence, of human society, and whatever is needed to maintain this state and its order is necessary, and so justified in human and moral terms. . . . Today it is no longer necessary to refute the argument that the state merely owes its legal existence to a contract, that it is therefore only permitted to exercise the rights made over to it by this contract, and that human life is an inalienable right and that it cannot therefore be made over to the state and disposed over by it. Gentlemen, the error of this principle is, I believe, recognized on all sides. For the state is something absolute, it exists by virtue of the nature of human society.

It had the right, continued Reichensperger, a right which nobody doubted, to demand that its citizens give up their life in order to defend it against an enemy in wartime. Who could therefore question its right, a right possessed by every individual, to destroy someone's life as an act of self-defence in peacetime?[122] This attempt to portray the contract theory of the state as outmoded met with widespread opposition on the left. The proponents of abolition reiterated in a number of speeches

the principle that according to a certain view that is widely adhered to among the people, and by which such significance is stored, that the state was created by a contract, that nobody is permitted to contract away his own life, and that therefore the state, in so far as it derives all its rights from the social contract, does not have the right to dispose over the lives of its citizens.[123]

Even if one did not accept the contractual theory of sovereignty, it was still possible to disagree with the retentionist argument that the state had the right to defend itself against its internal enemies: for, as the lawyer Eduard Lasker, a leading critic of Bismarck and a prominent figure on the left of the National Liberals, asked rhetorically, would anyone really go so far as to suggest 'the state's existence will be undermined by the abolition of capital punishment?'[124] The

[121] See the speeches by Reichensperger (p. 96), von Brauchitsch (p. 110), and Miquel (p. 1130), on 23 May 1870) in *Stenographische Berichte über die Verhandlungen des Reichstags des Norddeutschen Bundes*, 1. Leg. Per., Sess. 1870, 11.–12. Sitzung, 28 Feb./1 Mar. 1870.

[122] Ibid. 96.

[123] Ibid. 106, deputy von Kirchmann; also deputy von Handjery, pp. 110–11.   [124] Ibid. 113.

threat to the state as a whole from an individual murderer was insufficient to justify killing him in self-defence. Reichensperger argued that there was only one way of protecting society against such monsters as murderers, and that was 'by expunging this person from the book of the living'. And it was surely undeniable that the death penalty had a deterrent effect 'on the great mass of less hardened criminals', he added. Life imprisonment was no substitute, because it always gave the criminal the hope of escape, and because it effectively removed any appropriate means by which the murder of a prison warder by such a person could be punished.[125] Wilhelm Genast, a civil servant from Weimar and member of the National Liberal Party, was neither the first nor the last to put the obvious counter-argument: 'The person who commits such a deed is either swept along by overpowering passions, which do not allow him to be deterred by any prospective punishment, or is so hardened and cold-blooded that he thinks he is clever enough to escape the punishing arms of the law.'[126] The idea of the death penalty as an instrument of the state's self-defence through deterring its enemies from undermining it was therefore untenable.[127]

Retentionists tried to counter this point by arguing that abolition would lead to popular disorder. They claimed 'that the German people of the present day is sticking to the death penalty and to the conviction of its necessity with all its consciousness of what is just'. But they did not use this simply to suggest that liberal opinion was unrepresentative. Abolition, they suggested, would 'summon up the feeling of a kind of lawlessness among a great proportion of the German people'. There would be a rash of revenge killings and vendettas, leading to general disorder; for 'self-help is excused everywhere, where the law does not guarantee the necessary security'.[128] As a consequence of this inevitable spread of 'blood-revenge', one speaker prophesied in apocalyptic mood, it was clear 'that the state, that the authorities, would lose a great deal in moral reputation'.[129] Abolitionists, not unnaturally, strongly disagreed. It was no longer true, said one speaker, that the 'voice of the people' demanded the continuation of the death penalty. The 'voice of the people' in this view was principally articulated through the speech organs of representative parliamentarism.[130] This point was repeated by other liberals during the debate. The views of Lasker were typical of this kind of thinking:

The all-too-democratic implementation of the theory . . . that the people in a sense decides first, that only then we should get to work on drawing up laws backed by the mandates and the previous votes of the people, goes much too far for me. I cannot agree to such an implementation because I think that it would make a representative legislature absolutely impossible.

[125] Ibid. 97.   [126] Ibid. 126.   [127] Ibid. 100–1.   [128] Ibid. 111 (deputy von Aegidi).
[129] Ibid. 127 (deputy von der Schulenburg-Beetzendorf).   [130] Ibid. 100–1.

It was the duty of the people's representatives to lead public opinion, not to follow it. Once the legislature had given a lead by abolishing capital punishment, public opinion, he was sure, ought to follow, because the moment for such a change was now finally ripe.[131] Such reasoning expressed much of the liberal nationalist optimism and self-confidence on which the abolitionist case rested. Rejecting the gloomy view of conservatives that the German people would resort to vendettas and revenge killings if the death penalty were abolished, Lasker asked the deputies:

Are you afraid that concepts of law will be so obscured by the abolition of capital punishment that public security will be generally undermined? Gentlemen, none of us is afraid that murder of any kind will find approval in the way it regrettably does in other states. In the south of Italy, where brigandage is cloaked in the appearance of politics, the populace conceals the robbers, and a certain romantic air clings even to banditry and murder in Greece, where the same thing happens without any political pretext, at times also in Hungary. If it is said of these countries that the death penalty cannot be abolished yet because the state needs to defend itself, then, gentlemen, *that* is all very laudable and correct. But anyone who claims of Germany that the state has to protect its existence, and that this can only be achieved by allowing the death penalty and by destroying the individual by killing him, is not expressing correctly the morality or the spiritual condition of our nation [*loud* Bravo! *on the left*].[132]

'The continued existence of the death penalty', he declared in conclusion, 'however little it is carried out, indicates a certain lower state of culture.' For liberals like Lasker, the connection between the retention of the death penalty, the authoritarian state, and cultural backwardness seemed almost too obvious to mention. Lasker's optimism and belief in progress even led him to suggest that underlining the sanctity of human life by abolishing capital punishment might take the nations of the world a step in the direction of settling international disputes by some means other than killing each other's citizens.[133] This powerful vision of the significance of abolition as a symbol of human progress was echoed by others who spoke in the debate on the abolitionist side.[134] Progress, insisted the abolitionists, meant that penal policy had to be based without exception on 'the principle of amelioration, which contradicts the death penalty directly, since of course with execution, all improvement stops'.[135] Lasker asked:

What then is the difference between life imprisonment and capital punishment? The yawning chasm is that the person *lives* and has the opportunity to improve himself to the

---

[131] *Stenographische Berichte über die Verhandlungen des Reichstags des Norddeutschen Bundes*, 1. Leg. Per., Sess. 1870, 11.–12. Sitzung, 28 Feb./1 Mar. 1870, 112–14.

[132] Ibid. 114.   [133] Ibid. 117.

[134] Ibid. 126; the point was also conceded in a speech delivered during the debate by the Prussian Minister of Justice Leonhardt, ibid. 1133.

[135] Ibid. 18 (deputy von Kirchmann).

highest level of humanity with his moral strength, that he can die as one who is pleasing to God. You must not stretch out your hand against this if the stability of the state does not make it absolutely necessary, if there is no situation of self-defence. [*Animated applause*] Gentlemen, do you not have sufficient examples at your disposal of criminals whose soul has been illuminated in prison, in the tightest corner, do you not have sufficient examples of a total transformation? And you presume to render this transformation impossible?[136]

Lasker was perhaps a little too fond of rhetorical questions. But no one else put this crucial point quite so forcefully as he did. And it went powerfully together with the argument, advanced by other speakers, that the remorse felt by a criminal in the face of imminent execution was hardly likely to be the outcome of deep thought or profound self-examination.[137]

In the end, however, such arguments only played a secondary role. Most conservatives believed fundamentally in the death penalty as divinely ordained retribution. Only death, as Gerhard von Thadden, a Conservative landowner, declared, was an adequate punishment for murder:

For death is the King of Terrors. It has been said of the penitentiary that this punishment is worse than death for many people, that many would prefer death. But that can be conceded only for a very few, isolated cases. Regrettably there are enough people for whom the penitentiary constitutes an improvement of their situation. The prisoner in a penitentiary is clothed, fed, kept warm, kept healthy, like hardly anyone else. He is mostly occupied only with light work. He lives a carefree life, but not without hope, and his hope is all the more justified if he is a political offender with friends outside who are trying, whether openly or secretly, to liberate him.[138]

'Whosoever sheddeth man's blood, by men shall his blood be shed.' This was the Divine Command, whose implementation was the right and the duty of 'the authorities' as part of the 'divine order of things'.[139] This right could not be diminished by a mere legislative assembly. As Gustav von Diest, another Conservative landowner, former Provincial President of the Merseburg District, quoting at length from Portia's 'quality of mercy' speech in Shakespeare's *The Merchant of Venice*, declared, it was clear that 'clemency is an attribute of the sceptre, of the throne, that we must not limit, not even through our vote . . . For the law on the basis of which the death penalty has been passed for many centuries is a *Divine* law.' 'Are we then so much cleverer', asked Hermann Wagener, a Conservative civil servant from Berlin, 'than all those who have lived before us?'[140] Count von der Schulenburg-Beetzendorf, yet another Conservative landowner, thought not. The Ancient Greeks and the Jews of the Old Testament

---

[136] Ibid. 116.   [137] Ibid. 121.   [138] Ibid. 119.

[139] Ibid. (deputy von Thadden). The same phrase was also quoted by deputy von Diest, ibid. 134, and deputy von Brauchitsch, 110.

[140] Ibid. 124.

were just as advanced, he argued. It was, von Diest exclaimed, not for mere humans to set aside Christ's command, 'He who lives by the sword shall die by the sword'. That this command would appear to have applied equally to those who decided upon the use of the sword to execute offenders as to those who had killed people without the sanction to the law was a point von Diest evidently preferred not to contemplate.[141]

Religious arguments in favour of capital punishment had not always been so widely held. In the heady days of 1848, the existence of strong liberal currents within both the Protestant and Catholic Churches had been reflected in the fact that 81 per cent, or thirty-one, of the clergymen in the Prussian Constituent Assembly had voted for abolition, while in the Frankfurt Parliament nine out of the fourteen clergymen had taken the same line, including the founder of the Catholic social movement, the later bishop Baron Wilhelm Emmanuel von Ketteler.[142] But by the end of the 1860s, the tightening of controls by the state over the Protestant Church, especially in Prussia, and the sharp reactionary turn taken after the Revolution by the long-lived Pope Pius IX, had ensured that liberalism in the two churches had undergone a marked decline. The overwhelming weight of religious opinion in Germany was now firmly behind the death penalty; it was to remain so for many more years to come.[143] Correspondingly, abolition was confirmed as a principle of progress and modernity in the eyes of its supporters in the 1860s by the fact that the retentionists drew much of their support not only from the aristocracy but also from the clergy. Among the minority of twenty-seven voting against abolition in the Württemberg Chamber of Deputies in 1865, for example, were nine aristocrats and four clergymen, while among the fifty-six who voted in favour there were only seven aristocrats and two clerics, a far smaller proportion. On 27 May 1869 the Pastoral Conference of the Evangelical Church, the official state Church in Prussia, issued a ringing declaration in favour of retention. It was certain, declared the Church,

that the abolition of capital punishment, which replaces the sovereign's right of clemency with the criminal's demand for justice, damages the moral seriousness of the law, the dignity and the reputation of the Christian authorities as God's servants and as the avengers of his Holy Order and the Christian conscience of the people.

[141] *Stenographische Berichte über die Verhandlungen des Reichstags des Norddeutschen Bundes*, 1. Leg. Per., Sess. 1870, 11.–12. Sitzung, 28 Feb./1 Mar. 1870, 134.

[142] Düsing, *Abschaffung*, 53, 67. The minority of retentionists included the well-known Catholic theologian Ignaz von Döllinger.

[143] See G. von Mehring, *Die Frage von der Todesstrafe* (Stuttgart, 1867); Gottlob Kemmler, *Die Berechtigung der Todesstrafe. Mit besonderer Berücksichtigung der Schrift des Prälaten von Mehring, 'Die Frage von der Todesstrafe'* (Tübingen, 1868); and Leopold Noerdlinger, *Mord und Todesstrafe nach dem alten Testament. In Briefen von Herrn Dr. Oscar Wächter, Rechtskonsulent in Stuttgart, Abgeordneter des Bezirks Herrenberg; Herrn Prälat von Moser in Stuttgart und dem Herausgeber, Leopold Noerdlinger, Rechtskonsulent in Stuttgart* (Stuttgart, 1865).

As one of the supporters of the declaration explained: 'Not everyone has the right of vengeance, for the Lord has said: "vengeance is mine, I will repay", and the authorities appointed by God then carry out this right in God's name.' Clearly this argument—echoing the justifications of capital punishment advanced by some members of the Prussian Commission for the Reform of the Prussian Criminal Code in 1839—were diametrically opposed to the views of the liberals, who believed that punishment had to be justified in terms of secular rationality.[144] It was for this reason that many retentionists in 1870 tended to suggest that irreligion was a force behind the movement for abolition:

One of the most far-reaching and deepest arguments against the current tide of opinion with respect to capital punishment can be found in the increase of doubts about the life eternal and about the quality of this life. We must speak openly to one another on this subject. Gentlemen, if I believed that after death there was a great void with nothing in it, then it would be with a heavy heart that I would decide to take the life even of the greatest of criminals . . . Therefore I say, let us look at this cultural progress a little more exactly on our side. Not all that glitters is gold, not all that purports to be humanitarianism is what it seems to be; it is materialism, it is doubt, which plays the main part in these matters.[145]

Amongst the laity, the predominantly Protestant and secular character of the abolitionist movement underscored an emerging confessional divide over the issue of capital punishment.[146]

Some retentionist speakers were reluctant to enlist God among their ranks. Christianity, thought the Catholic spokesman Reichensperger, for example, neither demanded nor forbade the operation of the death penalty. The religious arguments, he thought, should remain in the background so long as practical considerations predominated: a striking indication of the secularization of the debate on the subject that had taken place since the deliberations of the Prussian Criminal Law Commission in the 1830s.[147] The Bible could not be a guide to penal policy, as one speaker remarked, not least because it was written by human hand.[148] Human beings in any case, as even believers had to admit, did not have the right to intervene in God's mysterious purposes. As Lasker remarked: 'In every individual person a part of God's providence is working itself out from the day he is born until the day he dies . . . And now I ask you, gentlemen, what right have you to stretch forth your hand to cut off the thread which providence is

---

[144] BA Potsdam RKA 631, Bl. 110: *Neue Preussische Zeitung*, 31 May 1869.

[145] *Stenographische Berichte über die Verhandlungen des Reichstags des Norddeutschen Bundes*, 1. Leg. Per., Sess. 1870, 11.–12. Sitzung, 28 Feb./1 Mar. 1870, 124 (deputy Wagener).

[146] GLA Karlsruhe 234/6609.: *Der Beobachter* (Stuttgart), 38 (15 Feb. 1865), 223–5, and 39 (16 Feb. 1865), 229–31. See also Berner, *Abschaffung*, 12–16. For the strong support of the Established Church of England for capital punishment throughout the 19th c., see Potter, *Hanging in Judgment*, passim.

[147] *Stenographische Berichte* (as n. 145 above), 98.   [148] Ibid. 110 (deputy von Handjery).

spinning, by ordering: this man must die now!' The obvious retort to this was that God might have destined the person for the scaffold from the start anyway. How could one possibly know whether or not one was interfering in his purposes, if they were so mysterious? But Lasker won tremendous applause from the deputies by going on to cite the words of the Bible: 'For the Lord does not want the sinner to die, but to live and repent of his ways.'[149] As Count Eduard von Bethusy-Huc, a member of the Free Conservative Party, a rather mixed grouping on the right, said: 'Precisely if one believes in the immortality of the soul, one should recoil before knowingly and deliberately curtailing the time which can be granted him by his highest judge for preparing on earth for the life beyond.'[150]

The religious justification for the death penalty was put most eloquently by Bismarck himself, who took the floor towards the end of the debate to give a powerful speech in favour of retention. The Chancellor was struck by the 'overestimation on the part of the opponents of the value which they attach to life in this world, and the importance which they ascribe to death'. Death, said Bismarck, drawing on the Protestant piety he had cultivated for so many years, was only 'a transition from one life to another'. 'I would not wish on this occasion', he said, 'to refer to Hamlet's tragic soliloquy which lists all the reasons for deciding not to live any longer, if there were no possibility after death to dream, perhaps to experience—who knows what . . . ?' Death, he went on, was only of central importance as a punishment for those for whom 'death is the peace, the sleep which Hamlet longs for, dreamless'. Bismarck therefore rested his case partly on the traditional, religious justification of capital punishment that had already been put forward by previous speakers on the retentionist side in the debate. But he also went onto the counter-attack against some of the specific points raised by the abolitionists. He did not attempt to defend the penal practice of previous ages. Certainly, he admitted, there had been more crime when punishments had been harder. But, he asked the deputies, 'Are you then quite sure that the decline of crime which has undoubtedly occurred isn't also the consequence of the stern administration of justice by the authorities over many centuries?' The abolition of the death penalty, he said, was a risky experiment, which had only been attempted very recently in a few small states, and should not be tried on a larger scale. Turning to the argument from experience put forward by many of the lawyers on the abolitionist side, he launched a full-scale attack on

one of the maladies of our time: shyness of responsibility, reluctance to take the personal responsibility for pronouncing a death sentence, reluctance on the part of jurors to reach a verdict which they know from the law can have as its consequence the killing of the

149 GLA Karlsruhe 234/6609.: *Der Beobachter* (Stuttgart), 38 (15 Feb. 1865), 117; echoed by Künzer, 121.
150 *Stenographische Berichte über die Verhandlungen des Reichstags des Norddeutschen Bundes*, I. Leg. Per., Sess. 1870, 11.–12. Sitzung, 28 Feb./1 Mar. 1870, 133.

offender. This fear of responsibility is a malady which in the whole of our time reaches high up the human hierarchy; even the sovereign finds the responsibility of dealing with the power of execution cumbersome and sensitive to the highest degree.

It was scarcely surprising, he said, that judges were human enough to want to evade such responsibility by removing the death penalty from the Criminal Code altogether. Yet this weakness should be resisted—whether by Wilhelm I as well, he did not say, though the criticism was more than implied.

God, he said, would help them discharge their duties, for 'a human power which does not sense in itself any justification from above is not strong enough to wield the sword of execution!' He urged the deputies not to give way to the 'morbid sentimentality of the times', nor to share in the 'pathological tendency . . . to treat the criminal with more care and consideration and more inclination to protect him from injustice than his victims'. Like other speakers on the retentionist side,[151] Bismarck exploited the contradictions in the abolitionists' case opened up by their concession that capital punishment was necessary in wartime or during a state of siege for members of the armed forces. If, as they argued, the death penalty was necessary to give soldiers more security under these circumstances than the threat of mere imprisonment was able to do, 'then', he told the abolitionists, 'you owe it to the peaceable citizen to provide him with this additional protection which the law can supply against robbers and murderers'. Why, he asked them again, did they favour the use of force by the state to protect property in time of tumult, when they conceded that troops could legitimately fire on rioters, but deny it to protect life against the individual murderer in time of peace and normality? They either had to deny the state the right to kill altogether, he said, or admit it for the protection of life as well as property. The liberals were prepared enough, he insinuated, to risk and even to waste the lives of workers in the factories, mines, railways, and industrial enterprises on which they depended for their wealth. 'Why', he asked, 'do your emotions turn to the protection of the criminal when you have not done what lies in your power in this direction?' Bismarck concluded by reminding the Reichstag that the Federal Council, representing the governments of the member states of the North German Confederation, had already voted to retain the death penalty by a substantial majority, and would do so again if the draft Criminal Code was sent up to it for ratification with the clauses on capital punishment removed. Thus the Code would not become law in the present session, or indeed at all, until the dispute was resolved. He could not speak on behalf of the other states, he said; he could 'only speak with complete certainty of the Prussian votes and Prussian influence, but that will be mobilized to put its whole weight behind the retention

---

[151] Cf. Count von der Schulenburg-Beetzendorf, ibid. 127.

of the death penalty, I can assure you of that'. His listeners were aware, of course, that Prussia could in effect pressure the other states into following the line it laid down. Indeed, only Oldenburg and Saxony, among the North German states, supported abolition in any case. The will of the Federal Council should not be ignored, concluded Bismarck. It was anchored in the constitution, and could not be swept aside.[152]

Despite Bismarck's arguments, the liberals in the Reichstag were confident enough to discount his constitutional warnings and stand their ground even at the cost of a possible conflict with the federated states. It was still their view that the representative assembly, not the meeting of unrepresentative princes, should decide on the law. The motion that the death penalty should be included in the new Criminal Code was put to the vote, and lost by 81 votes to 118.[153] The retentionist camp consisted almost entirely of aristocrats—sixty-seven of them in all[154]—though twenty-five aristocrats were also among those voting with the majority for abolition. The voting split more or less along party lines. Forty-eight Conservatives, mostly East Elbian landowners from Prussia, and eighteen Free Conservatives, who represented a somewhat broader spectrum of right-wing opinion, more reconciled than the Conservatives to the absorption of Prussia into the Confederation, and including industrialists as well as landowners, voted for retention. The abolitionists drew their main strength from the National Liberals—fifty-two—and the Progressives—twenty-seven. The indeterminate position of the Free Conservatives can be gauged from the fact that sixteen of them voted for abolition, thus splitting the party neatly down the middle over the issue. Yet abolition remained, as the speeches in the debate suggested, one of the classic political questions over which conservatives and liberals divided. Only one Conservative—Prince Handjery—voted for abolition, and not one Progressive for retention. Two National Liberals broke ranks and sided with the retentionists—Johannes Miquel, a former 'man of 1848' whose increasing conservatism was to earn him ennoblement and government office by the end of the century, and Carl von Schwendler, a deputy from Weimar who subsequently joined the Free Conservatives. Among the smaller parties, the five members of the Catholic Centre—still in its infancy—supported retention, while the Social Democrats and Polish Nationalists voted for abolition.[155] Liberalism might have

---

[152] *Stenographische*, 129–31.

[153] GStA Berlin Rep. 84a/7784, Bl. 255: *Frankfurter Zeitung*, 2 Oct. 1904, gives different figures. Those quoted were arrived at simply by adding up the names in the list of deputies voting for the two sides. At this relatively early stage in the development of political parties in Germany, party affiliations were still fluid and it has not always been possible to assign individuals precisely to a given group. See also Düsing, *Abschaffung*, 92, for a third set of figures, generally lower because less biographical information was available at the time when he wrote his book (1952).

[154] BA Potsdam, RJM 6097 Bl. 76: Erich Eyck, 'Die Todesstrafe', *Vossische Zeitung*, 25 Oct. 1927.

[155] Data on the deputies from Schwarz, *MdR*.

moved to the right since 1848 but, on this issue at least, it seemed to be as firm in the defence of its principles as ever.

After a suitable pause for thought following the abolitionist triumph in the Reichstag, Wilhelm I and his ministers went over the whole vexed question once again at a meeting held on 18 May 1870. The majority agreed that it was desirable to push the new Criminal Code through as quickly as possible, otherwise the forthcoming election of a new Reichstag would put the entire discussion back to its starting-point once more. Given the stiff opposition aroused by the proposed retention of the death penalty, most members agreed to a compromise 'by sacrificing the death penalty for high treason', provided that the deputies could be persuaded to vote for the reinsertion of capital punishment for murder. After all, they argued, three member states had already abolished the death penalty for both these types of offence. However, a minority of the cabinet held out for the retention of capital punishment for treason, even if this meant delaying the approval of the Criminal Code. Popular opinion demanded it. What was especially important was the fact that this minority was led by King Wilhelm I of Prussia, the dominant state in the Confederation. In a personal note, written on 14 April 1870 and widely circulated among officials, he had declared:

I must be certain that the position which has been vouchsafed to me by God is also secure for my successor, so that as far as is possible by human calculation, nothing must be left undone if it can guarantee this security. But to abandon the death penalty for the offence of high treason would appear in my eyes to abandon this security.

Thus the King regarded the matter as one of sovereignty rather than penal policy. He argued 'out of deepest conviction' that capital punishment should be retained for treason. The only compromise he was prepared to make was to abandon it for murder.[156] Wilhelm's position was thus diametrically opposed to that of the majority in the council. The impasse strengthened Bismarck in his evident determination not to allow the liberals in the Reichstag to have their way. He proposed to write in the abolition of the death penalty for both murder and treason in peacetime to the new Criminal Code, and persuaded the Federal Council, representing the member states of the Confederation, to back this stance.

On 23 May 1870 the clauses of the draft Code from which capital punishment had been removed by the vote of 1 March came before the Reichstag for a third reading. As the Prussian Justice Minister Adolf Leonhardt told the assembled deputies:

Gentlemen, the question of whether a general Criminal Code comes into life on 1 January 1871 depends solely and uniquely upon the question of whether you want to keep the

---

[156] GstA Berlin Rep. 84a/7788: Allerhöchstes Handschreiben Sr. Majestät des Königs Wilhelm I. vom 14. April 1870, betreffend Vollstreckung der Todesstrafe.

death penalty for murder, and for attempted murder against the head of the Confederation, your own sovereign, and the sovereign of the state in which the attempt is made.[157]

The issue as presented by the government was therefore now no longer a matter of penal principle or policy; it was whether or not the Reichstag was prepared to compromise with the Federal Council on the issue of capital punishment in order to get the Code through. This was the point which Bismarck, in a classic appeal to the National Liberals to put their nationalism before their liberalism, now hammered home. The overriding priority, he said, had to be to create a unified system of criminal law and penal practice for the whole of the North German Confederation. In this case, the wish of the majority of member states, which was to retain capital punishment in the Code, had to prevail. The minority of federated governments opposed to the death penalty had agreed to sacrifice their standpoint 'to the higher national cause'. It would be quite wrong if member states such as Saxony and Oldenburg, which had abolished the death penalty, were allowed to continue applying a penal principle so markedly different from those in place in the rest of the Confederation. This would mean, he suggested sarcastically,

that to a certain extent we would be creating two classes of North Germans—a top class, which thanks to its moral standing and its education has progressed so far that even its most evil members no longer require the corrective instrument of the executioner's axe, and then the *profanum vulgus* of 27 million, who have not yet reached this Saxon-Oldenburgian stage of civilization, and who require the executioner's axe on their neck to keep them in order.

Various clauses in the draft Criminal Code, including, he hinted, those relating to the death penalty, could be amended later on, once the Code had come into force. 'But we will never be able to make good a departure from our fundamental principles with reference to the unity that we have to create in Germany.' What they were creating, he declared dramatically, was 'a unified criminal law for the German nation in future'. Playing on the national theme for all it was worth, Bismarck recalled his determination over the past few years 'to crush with an iron tread everything that stood in the way of the establishment of the German nation in its splendour and power', and as the Social Democrats, the sharpest critics of his methods and his purpose, shouted their objections, Bismarck retorted to repeated 'stormy applause' and 'animated applause from every part of the chamber' that he was delighted at 'the testimonial which has been accorded me by the disapproval of the opponents of German unity and German greatness'.[158]

---

[157] *Stenographische Berichte über die Verhandlungen des Reichstags des Norddeutschen Bundes*, 1. Leg. Per., Sess. 1870, 52. Sitzung, 23 May 1870, 1133.
[158] Ibid. 1121.

In the face of such an appeal, a number of abolitionists immediately withdrew the amendments through which they had hoped to devolve the issue onto the member states. Legal unity, after all, had been a liberal dream at least since the 1840s.[159] The general enthusiasm with which Bismarck's speech was greeted showed how easy it was for him to manipulate the Reichstag deputies by appealing to their nationalism during this transitional period between the defeat of Austria in 1866 and the creation of the German Empire in 1870–1. Everyone was aware that the North German Confederation was only a temporary solution to the problem of German unity, and that some further stroke was needed to bring the south German states into the fold and complete the creation of the new German Reich. Since the beginning of the year a dispute had been simmering with France over the prospect of a member of the Prussian royal family being put forward as a candidate for the Spanish throne, a move which the French regarded with great alarm. French objections, if they were accompanied by threats, could be used by Bismarck to rally the south German states behind Prussia in an outburst of nationalist enthusiasm. On 15 May 1870 changes in the French government brought the anti-Prussian party in Paris to the fore, and it was amidst the heightened international tension generated by this new development that the debate on capital punishment was renewed on 23 May. But the abolitionists, however strong their commitment to the completion of German unification, were not going to give up without a fight.

It was once more Eduard Lasker who put their case and asserted the right of the people, represented through the legislature, to have their views taken into consideration by the government. His speech provided a dramatic illustration of the contradictions which Bismarck had been forcing out into the open since the middle of the 1860s between nationalism and liberalism. For most of the nineteenth century, nationalism had been a liberal force. Bismarck's intervention was part of a consistent drive on his part to make it conservative and authoritarian in character. Yet again, the death penalty had become the symbolic issue over which liberal and authoritarian concepts of politics were fought through. As Lasker was forced to confess:

It is the idea of national unity which enthuses us, which drives us on to work with all our strength for the success of the project; but against this stands the great cultural idea which is finally coming into its own after millennia: now at last, society has pulled itself up to a position, things in Germany have got to the point where death by the executioner's sword has become superfluous and cannot be tolerated any more.[160]

[159] Michael John, *Politics and the Law in Late Nineteenth-Century Germany: The Origins of the Civil Code* (Oxford, 1989), esp. 15–72.
[160] *Stenographische Berichte über die Verhandlungen des Reichstags des Norddeutschen Bundes*, 1. Leg. Per., Sess. 1870, 52. Sitzung, 23 May 1870, 1126.

This was the issue at stake. It had hardly played any part at all in the debates of 28 February and 1 March. It was Bismarck's achievement to have placed it at the top of the agenda by 23 May. Lasker tried to cut through the National Liberal dilemma by arguing that the draft Criminal Code was so full of imperfections anyway that it would do no harm for its passage into law to be delayed while further improvements were made. But his opponents rightly pointed to the symbolic blow that a failure to agree on a unified Criminal Code would strike at the cause of national unity.[161] Johannes Miquel, the prominent National Liberal who had already voted for retention in March, pointed out that 'the question of capital punishment is not an isolated question: it is linked to the whole Criminal Code'. To postpone the final vote on the Criminal Code because of failure to reach agreement with the Federal Council on the clauses relating to the death penalty was to give up the chance of establishing legal unity across the North German Confederation. This chance might not occur again. Lasker had claimed that a year's delay in promulgating the Code would do no harm. But, warned Miquel, elections were due within that year, and who was to say how the new Reichstag would deal with the issue? Taken as a whole, the new Criminal Code marked a major step forward in the direction of national unity and humanitarian penal practice, and it was wrong to hold it up and consign it to the vagaries of an uncertain political future over the single issue of the death penalty. Looking back implicitly to the days of the Frankfurt Parliament and the 1848 Revolution, Miquel reminded his listeners that it was mistaken to believe

that politics in Germany is a dispute about absolute truths, the kind of disputation that students undertake in the search for absolute philosophical truths and their proof. No, politics is a struggle from power to power, a struggle which in a monarchical state cannot now and cannot ever be resolved except on the basis of compromise. Gentlemen, accept the compromise!

In the face of such pragmatic appeals, issued in the name of the new *Realpolitik*, the arguments of the abolitionists did not stand a chance.

They might object that a mere vote against the death penalty could not possibly 'endanger the highest and final aims of national unification'; they might claim, with some justification, that a vote to retain capital punishment would still leave the North German Confederation with two classes of people—those fortunate enough to live in member states where princely clemency routinely commuted all death sentences to life imprisonment, and those unlucky enough to live in states where it did not; they might point out that everywhere in Germany, including the south, it was the supporters of the national unification movement

---

[161] *Stenographische Berichte über die Verhandlungen des Reichstags des Norddeutschen Bundes*, 1. Leg. Per., Sess. 1870, 52. Sitzung, 23 May 1870, 1122–6.

who urged the abolition of capital punishment, while the retentionists were to be found among the particularists and 'ultramontanes'; they might advocate a concept of national unity that sought 'to establish humanitarianism as a state principle';[162] but none of this counted against the overwhelming force of the nationalist argument, as Count Bethusy-Huc confessed towards the end of the debate, speaking on behalf of those abolitionists who had decided to change their minds as a result of Bismarck's intervention. Taking up the admission of Lasker and other abolitionists that the death penalty could be applied by the state in self-defence in time of war or serious emergency, Bethusy-Huc pointed out that this concession moved the debate from one of absolute principle to one of relative utility. Seen in the light of the national interest, which was more important than anything else, the issue had to be decided for the moment in favour of retention, he concluded. In any case, it would not be long, he surmised, before another vote would be taken to amend the Criminal Code, once it had come into effect, and bring about the abolition of the death penalty once and for all.[163] Even before he had finished speaking, it was clear that a substantial number of deputies were going to follow his lead and switch their vote to the retentionists.

On this occasion, 246 deputies cast their vote as against only 174 deputies who had done so on 1 March, indicating that the issue had since become more pressing; a major effort had evidently been put in by all sides. Those (apart from the speakers) voting for retention on 23 March included the general Helmuth von Moltke, the industrialist Karl von Stumm, and the future Catholic Centre Party leader Ludwig Windthorst. Abolitionists included the Social Democrats August Bebel and Wilhelm Liebknecht, the National Liberals Rudolf von Bennigsen and Georg von Bunsen, and the Progressives Conrad Haussmann and Eugen Richter. Once more, the Conservatives, this time with 59 votes, provided the backbone of the retentionist side, while the National Liberals, with 48, and the Progressives, with 35—both similar numbers to those voting on 1 March— were the mainstay of the abolitionists. The smaller parties were better represented than on the previous occasion, with 11 Catholic Centre deputies voting for retention, and 10 Poles and 6 Social Democrats voting against. But there was a major difference in the way the Free Conservative vote divided. On 1 March it had been small, and split more or less evenly down the middle. Now, however, the Free Conservative deputies turned out in strength, with 31 voting for retention and only 7 for abolition; 6 had changed sides between the two votes. Even more dramatic was the shift in the National Liberal vote. No fewer than 25 of the party's deputies supported retention on 23 May; 16 of them had changed sides since 1 March, the rest of them having been absent on that occasion. When splinter-groups and isolated individuals were counted in, there were 127 votes for retention and 119 for abolition. The higher turn-out of deputies, and the defection of 22 National Liberals and Free Conservatives from the abolitionist side under the influence of Bismarck's nationalist rhetoric, had succeeded in reversing the earlier decision.[164] The following day the death penalty was approved for the murder or attempted murder of the sovereign under Paragraph 75 of the Criminal Code by 128 votes to 107.[165] The death penalty had been retained, and was written into the Criminal Code as mandatory for murder and high treason. States which had abolished it would be obliged to reintroduce it when the Reich Criminal Code came into effect.

Not for the last time in German history, a substantial group of abolitionist parliamentarians sacrificed their principles on the altar of what the retentionists had persuaded them was the national interest, in the belief that victory would be theirs before long anyway. It soon became clear, however, that what at first sight appeared to be a tactical switch by some members of the National Liberal Party presaged a deeper and more wide-ranging shift of opinion on the capital punishment issue. And whether the abolitionists' continued and seemingly unshakeable belief in the historical inevitability of their cause was justified, was far from clear. For, as Johannes Miquel warned his listeners in the Reichstag on 23 May: 'No one should presume to prophesy the political future.'[166] Within a few weeks of the vote, the simmering row with France that had heated up the nationalist side in the debate boiled over into a full-scale crisis. The south German states proved unable to resist the power of the nationalist enthusiasm that now swept the country, and mobilized their troops for the full-scale war that began in July. By early September the crushing victory of Sedan had brought about the fall of Napoleon III's Second Empire in France and paved the way for the proclamation of the German Empire at the Palace of Versailles the following January. Its institutions were modelled on those of the North German Confederation, with a Federal Council representing the twenty-five member states, dominated by Prussia, the Prussian King Wilhelm I as Emperor, and a Reichstag with limited powers elected by constituencies all over the country. The new Criminal Code had just been voted through before the storm broke; it was implemented in the new Reich immediately after it was founded, in 1871. Capital punishment for murder and high treason remained as one of its provisions, and the deliberations

---

[164] *Stenographische Berichte über die Verhandlungen des Reichstags des Norddeutschen Bundes*, 1. Leg. Per., Sess. 1870, 52. Sitzung, 23 May 1870, 1140; biographical data from Schwarz, *MdR*; see also Düsing, *Abschaffung*, 99 (giving different figures, including a much higher proportion of unknown or questionable allegiance).

[165] *Stenographische Berichte über die Verhandlungen des Reichstags des Norddeutschen Bundes*, 1. Leg. Per., Sess. 1870, 53. Sitzung, 24 May 1870, 1164–5. Murder fell under para. 211.

[166] Ibid., 52. Sitzung, 23 May 1870, 1130.

of 1870 proved to be the last full-scale debate on the subject for nearly half a century. National unification had been grounded on a series of compromises on human rights issues, of which the retention of the death penalty, given its symbolic role in the politics of 1848, was perhaps the most striking.

Part III

8

The People's Executioners

a. Capital Punishment and the Foundation of the German Empire

Bismarck might have secured the inclusion of capital punishment in the Criminal Code for the North German Confederation by his intervention in the Reichstag debate of May 1870, but he had in fact achieved less than a total victory. The constitution of the new German Reich, which was effectively the same as that of its predecessor the North German Confederation, simply extended to include the south German states and Alsace-Lorraine, did not contain any statement of human rights—the only modern German constitution not to do so—and so failed to provide any oppportunity for the debating of such issues of principle as capital punishment. However, neither did it contain any explicit affirmation of the death penalty or indeed have any bearing on such issues as the sovereign power of clemency. Part of the price that he had paid to the old order for securing its acquiescence in the creation of the German nation-state was a constitution that preserved the fiction that the new German Empire was a federation of sovereign powers. The individual states such as Prussia, Bavaria, Saxony, the Hanseatic cities, and so on, retained their own sovereigns and their own legislative assemblies, if they had any. They continued to exercise control over a wide range of domestic matters, from education to law and order. They continued to have their own government ministries, headed, as before, by a Minister-President or his equivalent. The fiction of sovereignty among the federated states was symbolized by their retention of the prerogative of mercy. It remained the case that criminals convicted of capital offences were dependent on the clemency of the King of Württemberg, the Grand Duke of Baden, or whoever the sovereign was in the state where they had been tried, and not the German Emperor. Clemency was exercised on the advice of Ministries of Justice, as before, and not the new Reich Justice Office, whose powers were limited.

Individual monarchs still had a powerful personal influence on the outcome of such recommendations. And a number of them continued to have serious reservations about confirming death sentences and to commute them without exception into life imprisonment. As Bismarck himself had hinted during his speech to the Reichstag, the Prussian monarch Wilhelm I was among them—a fact which he had doubtless hoped would help persuade the waverers to vote for retention in the belief that it would have little practical effect.[1] For while the debate had been in progress between the end of February and late May, Wilhelm had decided that it would be unfair to execute criminals whose life might be spared a few months later, if capital punishment was no longer in force after the promulgation of the new Criminal Code. Although he had fought very hard for its retention, the Prussian monarch was simply unable to reconcile the continuation of executions under these circumstances with the dictates of his Protestant conscience. In practice, he had already begun the systematic exercise of the royal prerogative of mercy in 1869, in anticipation of an abolitionist triumph in the forthcoming debate. The Reichstag's vote on 1 March 1870 to abolish capital punishment prompted the monarch to regularize this policy by putting it into writing. On 14 April 1870 he wrote to the Prussian Minister of Justice:

Although for higher reasons known to you I have declared myself for the retention of the death penalty in the course of the current clash of views and opinions on this subject, nevertheless, while this clash continues, in other words before it has been decided, I am unable to order the execution of death sentences which—it is undeniably possible—may no longer be legally pronounced after a short time.[2]

In 1869–70 the monarch automatically commuted death sentences to life imprisonment even where his Justice Ministry advised him not to.[3] Caught in the logic of his own argument, the King then continued to refuse to sign death warrants throughout the 1870s, on the grounds that it would now be unfair to execute criminals whose life might have been spared had they been condemned a few months earlier, when it looked as if capital punishment was indeed going to be abolished. Wilhelm had now abolished the death penalty *de facto* in Prussia, even if it was retained *de jure* by the vote of 23 May.

Not every German sovereign took this view, of course. The eccentric King Ludwig II of Bavaria, passionate admirer of the composer Richard Wagner, was one such: his enthusiasm for the Middle Ages, which found its most noteworthy expression in the monstrous *kitsch* of the fairy castles he had built at Neuschwanstein and Hohenschwangau, was accompanied by an equal enthusiasm for the death penalty. In 1873 he went so far as to complain to the Bavarian Ministry of Justice that he had lately been receiving too many recommendations for clemency from its now rather liberally-inclined officials. 'I am,' he added, 'to be sure, willing to exercise mercy if there are decisive grounds for moderating the severity of a judicial sentence, but if such grounds are not present in an individual case, it is My desire that the reporting of death sentences to Me also sticks strictly to the principle that the legal sentence is to be carried out.'[4] In taking this line, of course, the Bavarian monarch was continuing to insist on the kind of symbolic assertion of his sovereign rights that had caused Bismarck such trouble when he was drawing up plans for the constitutional structure of the new Reich. Nevertheless, it ensured, at least while Ludwig remained relatively sane and still capable of carrying out his duties, that executions continued in Bavaria, even if they were in abeyance in most other parts of Germany. Even here, however, they were very few in number, with no executions at all in the years 1868–72, and only seven during the rest of the decade. In Hamburg, the exercise of the death penalty was very limited, with no executions in the period 1864–75, and a modest resumption in the three succeeding years, with one execution each in 1876, 1877, and 1878 followed by a further nine years without any executions at all.[5] Two people were executed in Saxe-Weimar between 1873 and 1879, and three in the Duchy of Brunswick-Lüneburg. One offender was executed in Baden in 1876, the first since 1861. But in most of the larger states the death penalty was effectively in abeyance. There were no executions in Württemberg during the 1870s, none in the Kingdom of Saxony, none in Hesse, and none in Oldenburg. Altogether, in the states for which figures are available, there were no executions at all in the years 1869–72, and only isolated cases in the following years. The inclusion of the death penalty in the Reich Criminal Code did not open the floodgates to a wholesale resumption of capital punishment. Few things symbolized the essentially liberal character of the 1870s better than this fact. Yet at the same time, one of the principal obstacles to the reintroduction of capital punishment as a matter of accepted penal routine was the arch-conservative, Protestant conscience of Wilhelm I, German Emperor and King of Prussia. Any stroke of Bismarck's to overcome liberal hesitations about applying the death penalty would also have to be a stroke against the Kaiser, his master. This seemed out of the question; until the whole structure of German politics was suddenly turned upside-down towards the end of the decade.

On 11 May 1878, while Kaiser Wilhelm I was driving along Unter den Linden, a broad boulevard in the centre of Berlin, a 21-year-old apprentice plumber named Max Hödel stepped into the road and fired two shots at him. Both went over his head, and the Kaiser did not notice anything until a footman jumped from the carriage and tackled the would-be assassin. Hödel was quickly arrested

[4] HStA Munich MJu 13067: Ludwig II to Justizministerium, 14 Oct. 1873.
[5] GLA Karlsruhe 234/6609: Erster Bürgermeister Weber to Badischer Justizminister, 13 Nov. 1879.

and put into police custody. The incident created a sensation in Germany. It came at the beginning of a period of European history marked by widespread acts of terrorism and 'propaganda by the deed' committed by the anarchist movement, which was in retreat and disarray after the failure of the Paris Commune in 1871 and the break-up of the First Working Men's International in 1876. Already in February 1878 a bomb had been thrown into the coronation procession of King Umberto of Italy; a few months later another attempt was made on his life. And in January the governor of St Petersburg had been murdered by a young revolutionary, Vera Zasulich, with what proved to be the first shot in a campaign of terrorism and violence that culminated in the assassination of Tsar Alexander II three years later, in 1881. Fear of the growing menace of anarchist violence was haunting the chancelleries of Europe, and they linked it in their minds with the rise of socialism and the legacy of the Paris Commune of 1871.[6] Nevertheless, despite appearances, Hödel was no anarchist; by 1878, he no longer had any political affiliations at all. At one time or another he had belonged to the Social Democratic Party, from which he had, however, been expelled, and the anti-Semitic Christian Social movement led by the Court Preacher Adolf Stöcker. His deed came at an opportune moment for Bismarck. The Chancellor immediately set about exploiting it for his own purposes.[7] Uppermost in Bismarck's mind at this time was the long-standing problem of the National Liberals. For the best part of a decade they had exercised a dominating influence in the Reichstag. By 1878 they were seriously impeding his plans for a reform of the Empire's finances. Together with the Progressives, they had driven on the anti-Catholic legislation of the 1870s, in the so-called *Kulturkampf.* Its main result had been to weld together the Catholic community, above all in south Germany and the Rhineland, in support of the rapidly growing Catholic Centre Party, which by the late 1870s was represented in the Reichstag with more than ninety seats. Now Bismarck wanted to bring the *Kulturkampf* to an end and free himself from his constricting dependence on the National Liberals. Increasingly, he sensed that the Catholic Centre and the Conservatives could provide a more pliant basis of support in the Reichstag. Hödel's shots offered the opportunity, once more, of impaling the liberals on the horns of a dilemma. Bismarck decided to do this, indirectly, by means of an attack on the Social Democratic Party, the small, radical, partly Marxist working-class political grouping that was in the course of gaining new strength through the uniting of the two warring factions into which it had so far been divided. On the very same day as the assassination attempt, Bismarck telegraphed Berlin from his summer retreat at Varzin to order

[6] For the general European background, see James Joll, *The Anarchists* (London, 1964), 117–48.
[7] Ernst Engelberg, *Bismarck. Das Reich in der Mitte Europas* (Berlin, 1990), 228–9.

the preparation of a new bill placing severe restrictions on the civil liberties of the Social Democrats, upon whom he demagogically (and quite unjustifiably) placed the blame for Hödel's act. His purpose was to force the liberals to choose between betraying their principles of freedom of speech, freedom of assembly, and freedom of association, and being accused of condoning violence against the monarch and attempts to overthrow the government by force. But the plan misfired, largely because of the unseemly haste with which the bill was drafted. On 23–4 May, in an impassioned debate, the liberals and their allies in the Reichstag threw it out by a decisive majority.

Not much more than a week later, however, an event took place which breathed fresh wind into Bismarck's sails. Unharmed and seemingly unruffled by Hödel's shots, the Emperor had resumed his habit of driving down Unter den Linden with what a modern head of state would regard as an irresponsible absence of proper security. Down in Dresden, an unhappy economist in the employment of the Saxon Bureau of Statistics, Dr Karl Nobiling, had read of Hödel's deed, and determined to earn a similar notoriety by repeating it. On 2 June 1878, as the Emperor passed by, Nobiling leant out of a window of one of the buildings on Unter den Linden, and blasted off a shotgun at the aged monarch. Thirty pellets were subsequently recovered from the scene. A good number of them lodged in Wilhelm's body. The Kaiser was lucky to escape with his life. Immediately after firing the gun, Nobiling turned it on himself and committed suicide. When Bismarck heard the news, he immediately decided to dissolve the Reichstag. The subsequent election, fought by the government and its allies on a strong law-and-order platform, delivered a crushing blow to the liberals, reducing their combined strength in the Reichstag from 163 to 125. The two conservative parties increased their seats from 78 to 116. The Catholic Centre Party effectively held the balance. So demoralized were the National Liberals that they offered little more than token resistance to the new Anti-Socialist Law that Bismarck now laid before the legislature. It passed by a substantial majority. With the fledgling Social Democratic Party now banned from publishing any newspapers or holding any meetings, and subject to heavy police persecution, the whole political atmosphere became much more repressive. Bismarck followed his move with a further blow to liberal principles by abandoning free trade and introducing import tariffs in 1879. In due course, the liberals' fortunes declined even further.[8] A decisive turn to the right had been achieved.

While these dramatic and far-reaching political events were unfolding, Hödel was still languishing in gaol, his fate undecided. Bismarck resolved to execute

---

[8] For a convenient summary of these events, see Gordon A. Craig, *Germany 1866–1945* (Oxford, 1978), 86–98; also Engelberg, *Bismarck*, 247–54.

him to symbolize the government's new, authoritarian course. It was to be a signal to the nation and the world that it would have no truck with socialists and revolutionaries. Beyond this, too, it would be another blow to the National Liberals, whose adherence to abolitionism in 1870 had led to the *de facto* abandonment of capital punishment by the Prussian King. By attempting to assassinate the monarch, Hödel had clearly committed high treason within the terms of the Criminal Code. He was duly brought before a court, found guilty, and condemned to death as the law required. But Bismarck was now faced with a delicate problem. For in the normal course of events, as they had developed since the end of the previous decade, Hödel would have been granted clemency by the Kaiser (acting in his capacity as King of Prussia) and sent to prison for the rest of his life. No criminal, not even the most violent murderer, had been executed in Prussia since 1868. Reversing this customary pattern would not be easy. On 14 July 1878, the day after the end of the great international Congress of Berlin, held to resolve a series of conflicts in the Balkans and the Near East, Bismarck convened a secret session of the Prussian cabinet to discuss the matter. So concerned was he to keep their deliberations from going any further that he called the meeting in his own Berlin residence rather than in the usual committee room. At Bismarck's prompting, the cabinet agreed to discuss the problem of Hödel under 'any other business'. No formal minutes were taken of the item, in case they got into the wrong hands.

Bismarck began by persuading the cabinet that what was required was not a 'perception of the purely judicial point of view' but 'a political act'. It would be politically undesirable, the cabinet agreed, simply to let the process of clemency take its usual course. Political expediency demanded that Hödel be executed as quickly as possible.[9] But Bismarck and his colleagues were faced with a number of obstacles. Since the Kaiser had been incapacitated by Nobiling's shot-gun, his powers had devolved onto the Crown Prince. There were grave doubts as to whether Friedrich actually had the right to sign a death warrant. Indeed, during Wilhelm I's own exercise of the regency for his mentally incapacitated brother Friedrich Wilhelm IV from October 1858 to January 1861, he had initially refused to confirm any death sentences at all. Wilhelm I had been unable to reconcile the general use of the death penalty with his own religious feeling that the God-given power of the sovereign over life and death still remained with his brother. It was only in 1860, when he had finally been persuaded that there was no chance of the King recovering, that Wilhelm had relented. Similar doubts were obviously warranted in the case of the Crown Prince in 1878; and if Wilhelm recovered, he might not be at all pleased to find that Friedrich had used a prerogative which,

---

[9] GStA Berlin Rep. 84a/7784, Bl. 19–20: Vertrauliche Sitzung des Staatsministeriums am 14. 7. 1878.

he considered, was not properly his. Indeed, Crown Prince Friedrich was never actually appointed Regent. All that happened was that an edict was issued in Wilhelm I's name two days after the Nobiling attempt commanding the Crown Prince to 'deputize' for the Kaiser and King of Prussia while he remained incapacitated, on the precedent of the action taken in 1857, when Wilhelm himself had 'deputized' for his sick brother months before his appointment as Regent the next year. In formal constitutional terms, therefore, the Crown Prince certainly lacked the right to grant or refuse clemency.[10] Moreover, Friedrich was well known for his progressive views. Born in 1831 and married to Queen Victoria's favourite daughter, he was widely regarded as a champion of 'English'-style liberalism. The German liberals held out great hopes of his eventual succession. Like many of them, he made no secret of his opposition to capital punishment. He was determined, he once said, 'if I should ever be called upon to mount the throne, always to choose the fairer right of clemency when I exercised my prerogative over life and death'. Friedrich had no intention of allowing Hödel to be executed. 'I had welcomed with the greatest satisfaction', he wrote later, 'the practice which the Kaiser had followed for a number of years of commuting death sentences to life imprisonment.'[11] Even if he could be persuaded that he had the power to do so, it seemed very unlikely that he would agree to consign Hödel to the block.

Bismarck therefore had to mount a particularly powerful campaign behind the scenes to put pressure on the Crown Prince to fall in with his plans. Following the secret meeting of the Prussian cabinet on 14 July, a memorandum was prepared outlining the case for execution. It was sent to Friedrich, along with a 'Confirmation Rescript' for him to sign, on 2 August. It began by reminding him of the legal and political importance of Hödel's offence. 'An insult and a serious affront to the law has been visited upon every individual member of the German people by the fact that a German has dared to make an attempt on the precious life of a monarch to whom the nation looks up with pride and gratitude.' More important still, the assassination attempt had been directed not just at the person of the monarch, but at the institution of monarchy itself, 'the firmest support of the Reich'. Thus it was also an attack on the state. And it had implications beyond the boundaries of the Reich too. It was 'a fatal fruit of those Social Democratic attempts to bring about a revolution, which are spreading from nation to nation like an epidemic'. It was generally agreed that the law had to be tightened up and applied more strictly against 'the Social Democrats' attempts to

[10] Ernst Rudolf Huber, *Deutsche Verfassungsgeschichte seit 1789*, iii. *Bismarck und das Reich* (Stuttgart, 1963), 811.

[11] 'Kaiser Friedrich zur Todesstrafe. Schwerer Gewissenskampf vor der Hinrichtung Hödels. Eine unveröffentlichte Aufzeichnung', *Berliner Tageblatt*, 1 Aug. 1928, copy in BA Potsdam RJM 6097, Bl. 252.

undermine the existing order of state and society'. Hence it was necessary to ensure that 'public opinion, which has been tremendously upset, is calmed down'. And public opinion demanded Hödel's execution. 'The exercise of clemency in the present case would not be understood', the Prussian cabinet informed the Crown Prince. Thus Bismarck told Friedrich that he would in effect be contributing to the overthrow of the monarchy, the undermining of state and society, the triumph of the socialist revolution, and the alienation of popular opinion from the Crown, were he to refuse to sign the death warrant. The memorandum pointed out that Wilhelm I had insisted, in the teeth of stiff opposition, that the death penalty should be retained in the Criminal Code for acts of treason. There was no written evidence, it added, to support the supposition that Friedrich was unable to exercise any of the powers vested in the monarch on whose behalf he was acting. It went on to suggest 'that a prison sentence is not capable of deterring high treason, since the traitor expects his release from prison, expects even to be rewarded, with the anticipated victory, sooner or later, of his revolutionary ideas'. This was a neat reversal of the argument that was used in 1848 to justify the abolition of capital punishment for political crimes, namely that a crime under one regime might not be a crime under another. Now, fear of revolution was being whipped up to such an extent that the best method of assuring revolutionaries that they would never come to power was reckoned to be to execute them.

The most important argument deployed by Bismarck and the cabinet to browbeat the Crown Prince into executing Hödel was in many ways the simplest. Whatever the reasons for the Kaiser's commutation of death sentences as Regent and King, they said, the fact was that Hödel's crime was so appalling that it fell 'completely outside the category of those cases which are commuted by royal clemency'. Exceptional evil demanded exceptional punishment.[12] It was certainly true that the other cases in which Wilhelm I had, over the years, exercised his royal prerogative of mercy were all of common murder rather than high treason. Nevertheless, Hödel had of course only *attempted* to assassinate the head of state; the injuries which had incapacitated him resulted from the second attempt, by Nobiling, and even that had failed to kill him. The Crown Prince hesitated, hoping that the Kaiser would recover quickly and take the weight of the decision off his shoulders. But it was soon obvious that the old man would not be in a position to resume his duties for several months. So Friedrich was forced to come to a decision. He had already been assured by Bismarck and his ministers that he was entitled to sign the death warrant. He was equally—though quite erro-

[12] GStA Berlin Rep. 84a/7784: Eingabe des Staatsministeriums an den Kronprinzen, 2 Aug. 1878 (Bl. 23–5). See also *Schulthess' Europäischer Geschichtskalender* (1878), 130.

neously—convinced that Hödel's crime had been part of a widespread and extremely dangerous socialist conspiracy. After carrying the 'Confirmation Rescript' around with him for several days, 'looking with real reluctance', as he confessed later, 'at the drawer which held these fateful papers', the Crown Prince finally came to a decision. Describing the thoughts which brought him to this point, Friedrich wrote:

I thought of the many soldiers who had been sent to their death at my command. A similar consciousness of duty now came upon me. On top of this there was the consideration that the death penalty was the only possible expiation, and a deterrent example for those who shared Hödel's views, and that a deed directed not against me but against the incumbent of the throne had to be atoned for. I was convinced that the Kaiser, to whom I had deliberately not let any word come about the matter, would approve of the full rigour of the law being applied and would thank me for not having delayed the decision until he got better. . . . Finally, after a terrible struggle with my conscience, which I overcame before God, I sacrificed my convinced opposition to the death penalty, and exclusively obeyed my duty to punish the crime which had been committed against my Emperor and Father, and signed the death warrant at Homburg, before the hill on 8 August 1878.[13]

Just to make sure that he was not influenced by his forceful wife, who was generally thought to be the dominant partner in the marriage, and whose English origins as the daughter of Queen Victoria gave her an even more liberal reputation than the one he enjoyed himself, Friedrich did not inform her of the business until after Hödel's death, which was fixed for 6 a.m. on 16 August 1878. The day before, he cancelled all engagements and took his family into the country. 'In a deeply emotional state', he spent much of the time praying for Hödel, and continued to do so right up to the moment of his execution.

The night before it, during which I had almost no sleep, and which was made a particular torture for me by the mournful screeching of owls, my thoughts turned again and again to the condemned man, who was said to have behaved in a more cynical way than ever since learning of his fate. I commended his soul in prayer to the Highest Judge, before whom he was brought by the beheading carried out at 6 o'clock in the morning on 16 August in the Moabit prison without having shown any remorse beforehand.[14]

It had been so long since the previous beheading in Berlin that a new axe had to be made, and a new executioner engaged, according to whom Hödel remained 'cheeky' throughout the short ceremony. On hearing the verdict and the denial of clemency read out by the officiating state prosecutor, Hödel was said to have let out an ironic 'Bravo!' and spat on the ground. Walking round to the wrong

[13] GStA Berlin Rep. 84a/7784, Bl. 28: Konfirmations-Reskript, 8 Aug. 1878. For Friedrich's text, see 'Kaiser Friedrich zur Todesstrafe'.
[14] 'Kaiser Friedrich zur Todesstrafe'.

side of the block, he did his best to impart an air of ridicule to the whole proceedings up to the moment when he was beheaded.[15]

In this way, capital punishment was reintroduced into the Kingdom of Prussia after a ten-year gap. Hödel was executed because the Crown Prince was too weak to stand up to the massive pressure exerted on him by Bismarck to sign the death warrant—an indication, perhaps, that had he succeeded to the throne for more than the hundred days of terminal illness which marked his brief reign in 1888, he would not have lived up to all the hopes of a turn to more progressive policies and attitudes placed in him by the increasingly desperate liberals. In justifying his own decision to himself, Friedrich, while mentioning briefly that an example had to be made in order to deter those who he imagined were Hödel's political friends, repeatedly returned to the belief that death was the only adequate punishment, the only proper expiation, for such a crime. Appropriately enough, it was the retributive functions of punishment that were uppermost in his mind as he signed the fatal paper. Contemporaries were clear that Hödel went to his death for political rather than legal reasons. The Reichstag too, wrote Max Kegel the same year in a poem addressed to the legislature, was intended to be a victim of these proceedings:

> The Fed'ral Council grinds the blade
> And lays it clean before you.
> The scaffold on the yard is laid,
> The block stands fast before you.
>
> The sentence now has been pronounced
> The Chanc'lor has decided.
> It's freedom that is now denounced
> And socialism derided.
>
> It's not for evil nor for crime
> The axe is being prepared,
> But for the people, all of them,
> And freedom everywhere.
>
> And as the hangman you've been named,
> To strike the deadly blow.
> And if you strike it, you'll be blamed,
> For History will know.
>
> To heed the warning there's still time:
> Avoid this daring game!
> Or else yourself you soon will find
> Experiencing the same.

---

[15] BA Potsdam, RJM 6098, Bl. 122: *Vorwärts*, 14 Mar. 1930; Maximilian Schmidt, *Julius Krautz, Der Scharfrichter von Berlin. Ein Kulturbild aus dem neunzehnten Jahrhundert* (Berlin, 1893), 21–6.

> But freedom, which you kill today
> Will never meet its end.
> Tomorrow it will rise again
> And victory portend.[16]

In signing away the civil rights of the Social Democrats, the Reichstag was inaugurating a new, more authoritarian chapter in German history after the brief mid-century liberal interlude. The turn to the right in 1878–9, accompanied by a purge of the last remaining liberal ministers from the Prussian cabinet, was so sharp that many historians have seen it as a sort of 'second foundation' of the German Empire, the moment when the Bismarckian Reich was finally set on the illiberal and repressive course which it was to pursue to the end. This view may in some respects have been overstressed in recent years.[17] None the less, the rightward turn in Bismarck's policy was real enough. It was entirely appropriate that it should be symbolically announced by the resumption of capital punishment in Prussia, and by extension, as was soon to become apparent, in the rest of Germany as well. Once more, the death penalty was being used more as a symbol of the state's political intentions than as an instrument of penal policy.

b. The Re-establishment of Capital Punishment in the 1880s

After Hödel's dispatch, there was no reason in theory why other executions should not follow, and Prussian state prosecutors began to arrange for the repair of long-disused guillotines in anticipation.[18] Wilhelm I had originally stopped signing death warrants because he considered that it would be unfair for one criminal to go to the block after it had been decided to keep the death penalty, while others escaped merely because they had been sentenced while the issue was still in the balance. Hödel's death invalidated this principle. Any unfairness there was had already been suffered by him. And it had not really been unfair to execute him anyway, because his crime had been so exceptionally heinous. But now, the same argument could be applied to others. The definition of what constituted an exceptionally heinous crime could be broadened out to cover murder as well as treason. Initially, to be sure, the responsible officials in the Prussian Ministry of Justice hesitated before taking this step. Perhaps, too, the

[16] In Helmut Lamprecht (ed.), *Deutschland, Deutschland. Politische Gedichte vom Vormärz bis zur Gegenwart* (Bremen, 1969), 242–3.

[17] For a critique, see Margaret L. Anderson and Kenneth D. Barkin, 'The Myth of the Puttkamer Purge and the Reality of the *Kaiserreich*: Some Reflections on the Historiography of Imperial Germany', *Journal of Modern History*, 54 (1982), 268–84.

[18] HStA Düsseldorf Rep. 145/324, Bl. 6–7: Königliche Staats-Anwaltschaft zu Coblenz to Erste Staatsanwalt Köln, 17/19 Dec. 1881 and following correspondence, ibid., Bl. 46: 'Verzeichniss der zur Guillotine gehörenden Theile', for one example.

new conservative spirit in the civil service had not yet penetrated to this particular part of the bureaucracy. Although some twenty offenders were condemned to death in Prussia in 1879, all these sentences were commuted because of insufficiently strong evidence either about the case or about the necessary element of premeditation, or because of 'the condemned's youth, hope of improvement', 'genuine remorse', 'penitent confession', 'insufficient spiritual education', 'poverty', 'desperate plight', or even 'reference to clemency granted in earlier cases of similar severity'. But in 1880, possibly as a result of a purge of liberal officials, the jurists in the Prussian Ministry of Justice began to take a tougher line. The first malefactor since Hödel whose crime seemed to the bureaucrats in the Prussian Ministry of Justice to be sufficiently heinous for him to be executed was Franz Krok, condemned to death for robbery with murder at Beuthen on 3 July 1880. In the belief that they could use the precedent of Hödel's execution to persuade Wilhelm I to sign his first death warrant since 1868, the officials pointed to the 'cruelty of the deed, which was committed on the open road against a defenceless old woman' and their belief that the motive had been 'low avarice'. But on 13 August the Kaiser rejected their advice and decided on clemency because of the offender's youth. A second attempt by the Ministry was made in October 1880, in the case of Louis Rammelt, convicted in Magdeburg of murdering his wife. This time the officials changed their language, brought in the element of exceptionality, and claimed that the offender's character was so bad that it could not be reformed. But their plea for Rammelt to be executed on the grounds of the 'unusual coarseness and cold-bloodedness with which the deed was committed, depravity of the culprit', was rejected by the monarch for the same reason as before, namely the offender's youth. So far, therefore, Hödel's deed seemed to have had no special consequences for the ordinary murderer.

However, these arguments were clearly on the right lines, for on 3 February 1881 the Kaiser finally gave in. The dubious privilege of being the first common criminal to be executed in Prussia since the 1860s fell to one Heinrich Gehrke, condemned to death in Köslin on 27 October 1880 for murdering his wife. The Justice Ministry referred to the 'shocking cruelty with which the deed was committed' and the 'complete depravity of the murderer', and recommended execution. These arguments persuaded Wilhelm I, and Gehrke was executed on 19 February 1881.[19] Emboldened by this success, Ministry officials increased the number of recommendations for execution to eight out of fifty-five in 1882. But they still had to overcome considerable reluctance on the Kaiser's part. Without further ado, he turned four of the recommendations down. For the first time since Hödel, the Justice Ministry was citing 'public interest' as a reason for

---

[19] GStA Berlin Rep. 84a/8145, Bl. 227–33.

refusing clemency, alongside what were fast becoming the usual reasons of the 'coarseness', 'wildness', and 'moral depravity of the culprit' and the 'cold calculation', 'great brutality', and 'cruelty' of the deed. But this tactic backfired, for the Kaiser was then able in two of these cases to grant the offenders clemency to mark the occasion of the wedding of his grandson, later to become Kaiser Wilhelm II. There could have been no clearer way of marking the symbolic nature of the monarch's power over life and death than this. It was a quasi-feudal gesture which at the same time made an explicit appeal to monarchical sentiment in the populace. It also seemed to make a nonsense of the Kaiser's earlier scruples about executing offenders unlucky enough to have committed their crime at one particular moment rather than another. Wilhelm I managed to find other reasons for commuting two further sentences. In one case, where the Ministry said roundly that execution was 'demanded in the public interest', he disagreed and granted the offender clemency because of doubts about whether he was responsible for his actions and the extent to which the murder had been premeditated. In another, the offender, whose crime had, as was now usual in such cases, been described by the Ministry as especially cruel, was considered too young by the Kaiser, who also noted his 'later remorse' and 'good conduct'. Wilhelm's authoritarian instincts guided his pen towards signing the death warrant for Johann Hass, a labourer convicted of leading a 'plot' to murder a 'person in authority', namely the landowner Holz in the province of Köslin in March 1881; Hass was executed on 8 July. Similarly, he agreed to the execution of Carl Lippert, who had murdered two women and a 4-year-old child with 'bestial cruelty' and had 'subsequently maltreated the corpse by kicking it'. Lippert was beheaded on 18 June. This did indeed seem an exceptionally unpleasant case. Whether these two men would have been executed had their files landed on Wilhelm's desk at the time of his grandson's wedding is, of course another matter.[20]

After the failure of their initial experiment in claiming that 'the public interest' demanded that certain offenders be brought to the block, Justice Ministry officials tried a new, more elaborate tactic. In two cases which they put before the Prussian monarch in 1881, they noted—alongside the usual references to coarseness, low motives, depravity, and so on—that it was necessary for an example to be made. Thus they considered it necessary to execute Heinrich Potthoff, a cobbler condemned to death for murder for gain in Dortmund in May 1881, because 'it is necessary to make an example in view of the increase in crime in the province of Westphalia'. Similarly, Wilhelm Schiff, a broom-maker condemned in October in Essen for a 'threefold sex murder', was recommended for decapitation to placate 'the popular sense of right and wrong; execution is also recom-

---

[20] Ibid., Bl. 234–9. The relevant cases are underlined in red pencil in the file.

mended in view of the many other similar crimes committed there'. This new argument reflected not only the contemporary panic in the Bochum area over a series of sex crimes,[21] but also the early stages of an increasing feeling in Berlin that the rapidly growing heavy industrial area of the Ruhr, where both these offenders lived, was creating a serious threat to social, political, and moral order of the German Empire. Parts of the district were sometimes referred to as 'Germany's Wild West', and the spread of strikes, unions, and not least of Social Democracy was already beginning to cause unease among Prussia's ruling bureaucrats. Wilhelm I was evidently amenable to these arguments, for he signed both death warrants and the two men were executed on 14 September 1881 and 11 January 1882 respectively.[22]

Up to this point, the Ministry officials had not dared to recommend the execution of a woman. But now that executions had become firmly re-established, the moment seemed right to do so. In April 1882 they forwarded to the Kaiser the case of Albertine Barüske, condemned in Köslin for murdering her husband. The list of reasons for requesting him to refuse her clemency was unusually long: 'cruelty in committing the deed before the eyes of her 14-year-old daughter, subsequently dismemberment of the corpse, moral depravity of the condemned woman, impudent behaviour, without any remorse; motive for the deed—common greed'. But the Kaiser's reply was short and to the point: 'commute the death sentence to life imprisonment. The condemned person *a woman.*'[23] Clearly, while he remained on the throne, execution was a privilege that was going to be reserved for men. The Ministry did not try again. Indeed, for a time it seemed that the Kaiser had gone back to his old ways. He rejected all its recommendations for execution in the first three quarters of 1882, on one occasion actually retracting an initial agreement to sign a death warrant. It was not until November that he finally came round. The case in question was the first in 1882 where the officials took up their previously successful argument for an exemplary punishment in a lawless area, and once more it worked. This time the area was Graudenz and the two men in question were Poles, Karl and Johann Przynski, convicted of robbery with murder. The Ministry pulled out all the stops on the crime itself, informing the monarch that execution was necessary for a whole bundle of reasons, ranging from the 'deceit' with which the crime was planned to the 'cruelty' of the murder, the 'inhuman behaviour' of the offenders after the deed, and the 'complete moral depravity (without any remorse)' which they had shown after their apprehension. But the clinching arguments were 'the

---

[21] See *Zwei neue Mordthaten aus der Gegend von Bochum, verübt I. am 10. April dieses Jahres an der 16jährigen Dienstmagd Ostermann aus Histrop, II. am 21. Mai dieses Jahres an der Dienstmagd Gantenberg aus Dahlhausen* (1882), repr. in Braungart (ed.), *Bänkelsang,* 226–34.

[22] GStA Berlin Rep. 84a/8145, Bl. 234–9.   [23] Ibid., Bl. 240 (case 8). Underlining in original.

grievously offended public sense of justice' and 'the increase of homicidal crime in that region'. Wilhelm signed their death warrants on 24 November 1882 and they were both executed on 2 December. Building on this success the Ministry officials went on to recommend execution for the carter Karl Conrad, condemned on 4 October 1882 in Berlin for the murder of his wife and four children, with 'reference to the public interest shown in it: the deed has aroused outrage everywhere'. The Kaiser signed the death warrant on 4 April 1883 and Conrad was executed five days later.[24]

Wilhelm I thus continued to take his exercise of the royal prerogative of mercy with the utmost seriousness. Sometimes he asked for more information, sometimes he requested longer to make up his mind.[25] While he remained on the throne, it was unlikely that the Ministry would get anything like all its recommendations for execution through. The mere knowledge of how difficult the task was inhibited it from proposing more than a handful of cases in any one year. When the judicial officials did decide that they had a case which he might find persuasive, they used the strongest language they could find, and put their emphasis above all on two points: the incorrigibility of the offender and the necessity of making an example of him in the public interest. Thus in 1883 they lectured the Prussian monarch in the following terms on one Adolf Muntz, sentenced to death in Düsseldorf for 'sex murder in combination with robbery':

The culprit is a totally depraved person, without any remorse; the outrageous cruelty and bestiality with which the deed was committed; execution of the sentence further required with reference to the many similar crimes which have been committed in neighbouring places in Westphalia and are alarming the populace to the highest degree.

The emphasis on 'bestiality', implying that the offender had disqualified himself from membership of the human race, was new to the 1880s; previous clemency papers, as we have seen, emphasized motive rather than method. Muntz was duly beheaded on 19 May, one of four men executed in Prussia that year. A total of five had been proposed by the Ministry, and in all of these cases the public interest was given as a major reason for carrying out the sentence.[26] At any rate, this then set the pattern for the rest of Wilhelm I's reign. A compromise had been reached. Everyone knew where they were. The number of executions stayed constant.

Once under way in Prussia again, capital punishment began to be extended in practice and principle to parts of Germany where it had been in abeyance for even longer. There had been no executions in the Kingdom of Saxony since 1866, for instance. King Johann, whose personal refusal to confirm death sentences had been the immediate cause of the suspension of executions in 1866, had died in 1873 and been succeeded by his eldest son King Albert, who was said to enjoy a

[24] Ibid., Bl. 244–5 (cases 47, 62).   [25] e.g. ibid., Bl. 246 (case 66).   [26] Ibid., Bl. 246–50.

better relationship with Bismarck. Just as important, however, was the fact that the 1880s were a period of Conservative ascendancy in Saxony, when the abolitionist majorities of the previous decades were no longer to be found in the legislature. In 1882, executions began again in Saxony. In Hesse, a twenty-year gap was followed by the resumption of beheadings in 1880, three years after the accession of Grand Duke Ludwig IV, whose attitude to the Bismarckian Reich was also said to be more favourable than that of his predecessor. In Saxe-Weimar, two offenders were beheaded in 1878, the first since 1861. The death penalty in the Kingdom of Württemberg had been in abeyance since 1866; it was applied for the first time again in 1880, despite the continued ascendancy of leading minister von Mittnacht, and soon became a regular practice once again.[27] Even in Bavaria there were no executions between 1867 and 1873, because of the uncertainty over the new Reich Criminal Code. In each case the pretext for the resumption of executions was, in effect, the exceptionally heinous nature of a particular crime. The Grand Duchy of Baden, for instance, had not witnessed a single execution since the year 1861. But in 1879–80 the case of a man who had deliberately murdered his two children, aged 3 and 6, by drowning them in the Rhine, was considered so unusually callous and reprehensible that it could serve as the occasion on which capital punishment could be reintroduced, and the man was duly guillotined.[28] The Baden Ministry of Justice took the opportunity to set up a permanent scaffold in every major gaol, in anticipation of the further executions it now expected in the following years.[29] The fact that the National Liberals were in the ascendancy here pointed once more to a significant shift in the attitude of this previously abolitionist party towards the death penalty.[30]

By 1885, as critics noted, capital punishment had been firmly re-established in most parts of Germany: 'The execution of death sentences has become the rule, reprieves the exception. Views on the morality of capital punishment are hardly likely to change. . . . Bit by bit, we have already regressed so far that scarcely anyone dares to raise his voice for the abolition of the death penalty any more.' This was only too true. The liberal abolitionist majorities of the decades from the 1840s to the 1870s, were now beginning to disappear.[31] Even when taken together

---

[27] HStA Stuttgart E130b Bü 886: Gutachten des Geheimen Raths, 4 Mar. 1880, and list of executions 1895–1905.

[28] BA Potsdam RJA 5664, Bl. 99: Zusammenstellung der eingegangenen und vollstreckten Todesurtheile (1886); GStA Berlin Rep. 84a/7784, Bl. 49: *Karlsruher Zeitung*, 14 Nov. 1881, and Preussischer Gesandte in Karlsruhe to PJM, 16 Nov. 1880 (copy).

[29] GLA Karlsruhe 234/6609: Grossherzogliche Bezirksbauinspektion Karlsruhe (6 Jan. 1881), Offenburg (10 Jan. 1881), Mannheim (15 Jan. 1881), Freiburg (17 Jan. 1881), Bruchsal (21 Mar. 1881), and Konstanz (4 May 1881) to Badisches Justizministerium.

[30] Details of state party affiliations and princely succession from Ernst Rudolf Huber, *Deutsche Verfassungsgeschichte seit 1789*, iv. *Struktur und Krisen des Kaiserreichs* (Stuttgart, 1969), 401–4, 419.

[31] For the last liberal abolitionist tract of this period, dedicated to Lasker, see Franz von Holtzendorff, *Das Verbrechen des Mordes und die Todesstrafe* (Berlin, 1875).

with the Progressives, the National Liberals could not manage to win as many as 100 Reichstag seats in the elections of the 1890s and 1900s. Opposition could certainly be expected from the Social Democrats. But they were gravely hampered by the Anti-Socialist Law, which banned their newspapers and made their meetings illegal. Until the 1890s they had only a handful of deputies in the Reichstag. The largest party in the legislature was now the Catholic Centre, an enthusiastic supporter of capital punishment; and together with the Conservatives, Free Conservatives, and right-wing splinter-groups such as the Anti-Semites, the vast majority of whose deputies were also retentionists, they now provided capital punishment with a strong majority. Thus the Bismarckian turn to the right at the end of the 1870s was also reflected in terms of electoral politics: 1870 did indeed prove to be the last occasion on which a majority could be found in the Reichstag in favour of abolition. Capital punishment had achieved political respectability once more.

The abolitionist convictions of the National Liberals themselves, already seriously compromised by the vote of May 1870, had now begun to give way under pressure.[32] Significant parts of bourgeois opinion swung round in favour of capital punishment during the 1880s, not least under the impact of the growing threat of anarchist violence during this decade. Society, writers began to argue, had to be protected against murderers, and the interests of society had to come before those of the individual.[33] Hödel and Nobiling were only the first two in a long line of assassins and would-be assassins who cast their shadow over European politics in the closing decades of the nineteenth century. It was people such as these, rather than common criminal or domestic murderers, who inspired a diatribe published in October 1880 by an impeccably bourgeois newspaper, the *Berliner Börsen-Curier*, fulminating against the 'humanitarians' who wanted to keep murderers in prison in the hope that they would feel remorse for what they had done. What, the paper asked rhetorically, would be the result of such a policy? It expressed its answer in a new linguistic mode, emphasizing the bestiality of the common murderer:

The beast is put in prison, but it gets fed there. The beast gets used to the cage, and, animal that it is, it does without freedom and enjoys the food. The humanitarians' premiss is that they are dealing with human beings here. They forget that individuals who are human in form but equipped by nature with bestial instincts, without morality, without scruples of conscience, are not to be ranked any higher than the beasts one meets in the tropics or the wastes of the north. If humans come across such a beast, they strike it dead. And that's that.[34]

---

[32] See Düsing, *Abschaffung*, 119–20.

[33] Ambrosius Voelker, *Ist der menschliche Wille frei? Mit besonderer Rücksicht auf die Frage der Zulässigkeit der Todesstrafe* (Stuttgart, 1880), 23–4.

[34] GStA Berlin Rep. 84a/7784, Bl. 47: *Berliner Börsen-Curier*, 510 (8 Oct. 1880).

In making this point, the newspaper betrayed a characteristically nineteenth-century attitude towards wild animals. They were only good for killing or for putting in zoos. For an age that saw big game-hunting as a major participator sport, and hung trophies of slaughtered tigers and polar bears on its living-room walls, the analogy was clear and acceptable to all. But placing people in this category was something new.

c. The Explosive Substances Law of 1884

The new climate of opinion became even more apparent when, in 1884, the government proposed to extend the death penalty to a new offence by means of the Explosive Substances Bill (*Sprengstoffgesetz*). This was prompted by an attempt by a group of anarchists to blow up Bismarck, the Kaiser, and the German princes during the unveiling of the statue of 'Germania' overlooking the Rhine above Rüdesheim. The enterprise itself was a ludicrous failure. Its organizer, the well-known anarchist agitator August Reinsdorf, injured his foot while crossing a railway line, was forced to go to hospital, and had to ask two of his accomplices to let off the bomb instead. They concealed the dynamite in a drain beneath the path along which the dignitaries were to walk to the unveiling, but, being short of money, as anarchist conspirators often were, they ignored Reinsdorf's instructions to buy waterproof fuses, preferring ordinary ones because they were cheaper. Unluckily for them, it rained heavily the night before the unveiling. The fuses were soaked, and on 28 September 1883, as the Kaiser and the princes approached the statue, and the two anarchists Rupsch and Küchler applied a lighted cigar to the fuses, nothing happened. The conspirators managed to retrieve their equipment afterwards and vanish. Then Reinsdorf was released from hospital. On 23 October 1883 he blew up the main police station in Frankfurt am Main, which was known as a centre for police spies active in winkling out radicals wanted under the Anti-Socialist Law. Reinsdorf and the rest of his group were quickly arrested. In attempting to save their skins, Rupsch and Küchler tried to heap the blame on Reinsdorf, and for good measure threw in the details of the 'Germania' attempt as well.

On 15 December they were brought to trial at the Reich Supreme Court in Leipzig, along with four other anarchists with whom they had associated. In typical anarchist fashion, Reinsdorf admitted everything, but maintained he had been right to do it. It was only a question of power, he said. If the anarchists had had a few army corps at their disposal, it would not be he who would be standing in the dock, but his accusers, the enemies of society. Asked by the judge to outline his theory of anarchism, he responded with a lengthy political speech. 'If I had ten heads left', he declared in conclusion, in reference to his inevitable fate,

'I would gladly lay them on the block for the same cause.' He eventually went to his death on 7 February 1885, shouting 'Down with barbarianism! Long live anarchy!' Küchler was also executed, and put up a fight as he was being led away by the executioner's assistants. Both of them refused spiritual assistance; anarchists regarded the Church merely as an instrument of political mystification. A third anarchist, Julius Lieske, who had murdered the Frankfurt police chief on 13 January 1885, in an act of revenge for Reinsdorf's condemnation, was also executed, shouting, 'I die innocent!' Two other conspirators were given ten years' penitentiary, and two were acquitted. The second of the incompetent dynamiters, Rupsch, was also sentenced to death, but was granted the royal clemency on account of his age (he was only 20 at the time of the attempt). Forty years later, in 1924, he was reported still occupying a cell in the main prison in Halle. When taken together with anarchist outrages in other countries at around the same time, the incident proved very alarming to the government. It seemed to demand sharp deterrent measures.[35]

The attempted assassination of the Kaiser and the princes placed abolitionists in the unenviable position of appearing to condone treason if they did not agree to the death penalty being proposed for such crimes in the Explosive Substances Bill. There was far less abolitionist resistance in the Reichstag than there had been during the 1870s. Clause 4 of the bill proposed a mandatory death sentence for anyone convicted of causing an explosion by which 'a person's death has been caused, if the offender could have foreseen such a consequence'. This extended the existing application of the death penalty quite considerably. The offender was not even required to have envisaged the explosion causing someone's death, let alone to have set off a bomb with the deliberate intention of killing someone. All the court had to show was that in its judgment it was *possible* for the offender to have foreseen such an eventuality. Nevertheless, not one of the six deputies who spoke in the very brief debates that took place on the bill in the Reichstag on 13 and 15 May 1884 even so much as mentioned the law's extension of the death penalty. Such debate as there was, concentrated on Clause 8 of the bill, which made possession of explosives punishable by imprisonment, a provision which the Social Democrats evidently feared might leave them open to police chicanery, the planting of evidence, and similar tricks. Even so, the Social Democrats abstained, on the grounds that if they did not wish to help the government in its fight against the 'propaganda of the deed', neither did they wish to lay any obstacles in its path. The measure was passed overwhelmingly on 15 May. Like many laws of this kind, it had more of a symbolic value than a real one. Passed

---

[35] Rudolf Rocker, *Johann Most. Das Leben eines Rebellen* (Berlin, 1924), 202–15; Schmidt, *Krautz,* 55–9.

at the height of a 'moral panic' sparked not only by events in Germany but also by bomb-throwing outrages in France and Spain, and following on an Act of Parliament passed in the United Kingdom to similar effect the previous year, it underlined the determination of all political parties to be seen to reject the violence of the anarchist bomb-thrower.[36] Nevertheless, it was a startling example of the decline of abolitionism in the Reichstag since the defeat of 1870.

Capital punishment was now firmly embedded in German law, and met with the approval of a majority of deputies in the Reichstag. As a respected liberal daily, the *Vossische Zeitung*, declared in 1888:

The times in which the sentimental school of thought in criminal law was the ruling school of thought are truly over, and the dreadful crimes of anarchist murder-gangs over the last few years have at least had the beneficial effect of putting an end to the all too soft-hearted doctrines of penal experts and of spreading the conviction that we cannot dispense with capital punishment as long as these scoundrels continue to make the world unsafe with their misdeeds. In view of the connections that exist between the anarchist destroyers of every country, all states have an interest in ensuring that legislation does not rob themselves of the means by which they can be exterminated.[37]

Such attitudes were strengthened by further anarchist killings during the 1890s, the victims of which included President Sadi Carnot of France, President William McKinley of the United States, King Umberto I of Italy, and the Empress Elizabeth of Austria, as well as by numerous unsuccessful assassination attempts at killing prominent politicians and a string of more general outrages, in which ordinary members of the public were the main victims.

Bourgeois anxiety about big-city crime in the age of urbanization underpinned this shift in attitudes. By 1892, even that paragon of cosy middle-class family values *Die Gartenlaube*, one of Imperial Germany's most popular magazines, was printing reassuring portraits of Berlin's criminal underworld trembling with fear every time the red placards appeared on the advertising columns in the city's streets announcing that one of their number had met his just deserts.[38] Capital punishment provided the insecure middle classes with an outlet for their aggression, a vicarious means of venting their fear and hatred of the looming sociopolitical threat from below. This, after all, was a cultural world in which the promise of violence was held out in popular literature by a figure such as Wilhelm Busch, one of the best-loved versifiers and cartoonists of the age, who portrayed

[36] Joll, *Anarchists*, 130–2, 140–1. For the debate, see *Stenographische Berichte über die Verhandlungen des deutschen Reichstags*, 5. Leg. Per., 4. Sess., 26. Sitzung am 13. Mai 1884, 579–81, and 28. Sitzung am 15. Mai 1884, 630–3. For the text of the *Gesetz gegen den verbrecherischen und gemeingefährlichen Gebrauch von Sprengstoffen*, see *Verhandlungen des deutschen Reichstags: Drucksachen*, vol. 78a, 290–1.

[37] BA Potsdam Auswärtiges Amt IIIa Nr. 51, Bd. 3, Bl. 104: *Vossische Zeitung*, 22 Nov. 1888.

[38] Quoted in Peter Gay, *The Bourgeois Experience: Victoria to Freud*, iii. *The Cultivation of Hatred* (London, 1994), 177.

even the most minor of childish transgressions ending in the decapitation of the offender. A stolid north German nationalist and closet anti-Semite, Busch amused his vast audience with sadistic portrayals of violence and mutilation which paralleled the inevitability of beheading for the real-life murderer.[39] The role that violence played in the bourgeoisie's own lives was closely linked to the suppression of disorder, as beating, caning, and whipping were widely used at home and in schools in Imperial Germany as sanctions against even the most petty forms of disobedience or misbehaviour. In the late nineteenth century, as a hundred years before, capital punishment stood at the apex of a pyramid of physical sanctions which were widely accepted in society. Violence in the pursuit of order had not disappeared; it had merely been taken off the streets and relocated within disciplining institutions such as the home, the school, the prison, and the army camp.[40]

These anxieties sustained a growing acceptance of capital punishment among the middle class's representatives in the political world. By the mid-1890s, indeed, many National Liberals were quite prepared to see the death penalty applied in the interests of what they conceived as liberal, progressive values. In May 1895, another new bill resulted from liberal pressure to use the new German colonies in Africa as a basis for combating the remnants of the slave trade. This committed the Reichstag to the principle of capital punishment by extending it to those who caused a death by the theft of a slave. Here the Social Democrats did indeed object, though purely on the grounds that murder was already punishable by death under existing law. The government spokesman rejected this argument, however, and rammed home the use of the death penalty for an ostensibly liberal cause by reminding the deputies: 'What the current Governor of East Africa, Major von Wissmann, has reported about the cruelties of slave-stealing in his books, on the basis of his own experiences, will not leave you in a moment's doubt that the severest punishment here is also the most just.' As another speaker pointed out, anyone who was against the death penalty altogether would have to vote for the Social Democrats' amendment for it to be removed from the bill. However, capital punishment for murder was part of existing penal law, which also applied to the colonies, so they could not expect those who supported the Criminal Code as it stood to vote with them. This was not a vote on the death penalty *per se*, pointed out the Social Democrats' opponents, but on its extension to homicidal slave-dealers: 'To proceed merely with imprisonment against people who carry out great plundering raids for a living, in order to steal hundreds of slaves and to kill perhaps thousands of people in the process, to speak out against the death penalty in this case, serves no

[39] Ibid. 408–23.   [40] Ibid. 186–90.

practical purpose.' That it would be applied to men of other races than the Germans was understood, though the Social Democrats did use the occasion to point out that German colonial officials had themselves been responsible for numerous gross violations of human rights in the colonies. But this did not stop the bill from becoming law. By this time, indeed, it was clear that the role of leading the fight against capital punishment had passed from the National Liberals to the Social Democrats, despite their equivocation on the Explosive Substances Law in 1884. But the Social Democrats were still relatively thinly represented in the Reichstag, even if they were no longer labouring under the burden of the Anti-Socialist Law, which lapsed in 1890. So the retentionist majority which had emerged at the end of the 1870s remained intact right up to the eve of the First World War.[41]

d. The Professionalization of the German Executioner

For most of the 1870s, there had been no executions in Prussia, so that when it was decided to behead the would-be assassin Max Hödel in 1878, the Ministry of Justice needed to find someone new to do the job. The man they chose, obviously, needed to have had some experience as an executioner. Their choice fell upon Julius Krautz, born in 1843 as the sixteenth child of a knacker, and brought up in a military orphanage after the death of his father. Krautz had been apprenticed to a confectioner but left in 1859 to work in a knacker's yard owned by relatives, and from here he had graduated to serve as assistant to the knacker and executioner August Reindel in Brunswick. After assisting at an execution in Gera in 1862, he had moved to Berlin the next year and had settled down to work for yet another knacker. Krautz had fought at the battle of Königgrätz in 1866 and also in the Franco-Prussian War in 1870. The same year, he had been appointed executioner in Hanover in succession to the prison warder Bormann, but had had no duties to carry out for the rest of the decade, and the execution of Hödel was said to have been the first at which he had actually struck the fatal blow. Two days before it, indeed, he had been made to pass an executioner's examination by the Ministry of Justice in Berlin.[42]

Krautz has a good claim to be regarded as the first truly professional executioner in modern German history. It was he who invented the standard

[41] *Stenographische Berichte über die Verhandlungen des deutschen Reichstags*, 9. Leg. Per., 3. Sess., 96. Sitzung am 20. Mai 1895, 2339–57, and 98. Sitzung am 22. Mai 1895, 2416–19. The death penalty was debated only briefly (pp. 2346–7).

[42] BA Postsdam RJM 6098, Bl. 122: *Vorwärts*, 14 Mar. 1930 (Krautz, *Diensttagebuch*); Paul Kuschbert, *Quellen und Nachrichten über deutsche Scharfrichter-Sippen*, ii (Cologne, 1941), app. 149; Schmidt, *Krautz*. Schmidt's book was based on interviews with Krautz and also made use of the executioner's account-book (ibid. 86, 95).

executioner's dress of top-hat, frock-coat, waistcoat, and white gloves which all subsequent executioners wore when they were performing their official duties. Dissatisfied with the traditional, rather medieval-looking red cloak, Krautz evidently sought to give his trade a kind of bourgeois respectability more in keeping with the culture of the times. Indeed, from now on, as the condemned entered the execution yard, they would scarcely be able to distinguish the executioner and his assistants from all the other top-hatted and frock-coated gentlemen in attendance. It was only after the offender was led away to the block that Krautz, out of his sight, divested himself of the frock-coat, under which he had been concealing the axe, and made ready to wield the fatal blow in his shirt-sleeves and waistcoat. The innovation was striking enough to cause comment from contemporaries. 'In black frock-coat and white waistcoat' wrote one versifier, 'did Krautz young Hödel amputate.'[43] Krautz also made some modifications to the design of the block, and other minor, technical changes which also stood the test of time.[44] In November 1878 he revealed the extent of his professional ambition by sending a mimeographed circular letter to other German states offering his services as an executioner, and enclosing a certificate attesting his skill in the execution of Hödel. It was customary to use the axe in Prussia, he wrote, but 'If the laws of the state of —— prescribe another form of death, whether it be by sword or guillotine, —— can also command my attendance, since I also carry out executions by these methods.' (The circular left the name of the state in question to be filled in by Krautz himself.)[45] The creation of a national railway network in Germany during the 1860s and 1870s allowed Krautz to nurture the ambition of becoming the sole German executioner and earning his living as a true, if by no means full-time professional. But the federated states were too tradition-bound to take up his offer, and particularist sensibilities prevented many of them from putting the necks of their citizens under the axe of a Prussian executioner. Before long, Krautz was largely confining his advertising campaign to the parts of Prussia where he was not yet employed, such as the province of Hanover, where the news that the authorities were looking for a new executioner prompted him to write offering his services in 1881 and drawing attention to the executions, including Hödel's, which he had already carried out successfully elsewhere.[46] Repeating the offer two years later, Krautz assured the state prosecutor in Celle that he was more than capable of operating the guillotine which provided the normal method of execution in the province, 'since I am completely familiar with the construction, as well as with the mechanism of the machine. Up to now', he added, 'I have carried out seventeen executions with the axe in various provinces

[43] Max Kegel, in Lamprecht (ed.), *Deutschland*, 242.   [44] Schmidt, *Krautz*, 56, 85.
[45] GLA Karlsruhe 234/6772: Krautz circular of 4 Nov. 1878.
[46] HStA Hanover Hann. 173a Nr. 436, Bl. 63: Krautz to Oberstaatsanwalt Celle, 7 Aug. 1881.

of Germany. The minimum honorarium was 300 marks including travel expenses for myself and three men, the maximum 600 for double executions.'[47] Even after his expenses had been paid, therefore, Krautz could hope to earn enough to live on after only half a dozen or so executions a year, and if he made double figures, he could count himself quite comfortably off.

Krautz gained considerable notoriety in Germany. Not only did he earn money from making his notebooks available to journalists, he also became the subject of numerous verses and popular broadsheets. He reached the height of his fame in a best-selling, six-volume series of 'penny dreadfuls' by Victor von Falk, called *The Executioner of Berlin*, for which he allegedly supplied material. Published in no fewer than 130 weekly instalments, and extending to well over 3,000 pages, the novel had little to do with Krautz himself or indeed with any kind of real events, but focused on a group of aristocrats (including the villain, Count Waldemar von Marco-Sternenberg, and, oddly, Lord Nelson), criminals, policemen, and executioners. The female figures followed the same social pattern, mixing aristocrats such as the nymphomaniac Lady Nelson with the innocent working-class girls Olga and Sophie, and omitting all reference to the middle classes and petty bourgeoisie who would have formed the bulk of the readership. The actively villainous or heroic male figures (the latter including Krautz) put the passive female figures through a series of trials and torments in a kind of nineteenth-century soap opera, in which the characters remained throughout but the action and scenery were constantly changing, from stately homes to underworld dens and back. Executions were depicted, though one at least ended with the revival and flight of the executed person, and there were attempted poisonings, acts of espionage, kidnappings, railway accidents, adulterous affairs, scenes of hypnosis, duels, exhumations of bodies, drownings, accidents, and chases to enliven the action (and all these occurred within the first ten episodes). The crimes described in the book included arson, parricide, infanticide, assault, attempted rape, and almost anything else the author could think of and, until very near the end, the criminals almost always got away. Small wonder, therefore, that the book attracted criticism from moral entrepreneurs. It offended conservatives by its merciless depiction of poverty, exploitation, and social inequality, and outraged progressives by its portrayal of all these things as inevitable. Yet it was not openly pornographic, it respected religion, and it praised bourgeois institutions and values such as tolerance and humanitarianism. It ended, somewhat implausibly, with Krautz throwing his axe into the river and swearing to give up his trade. Despite its obvious remoteness from the realities of his own life, the novel doubtless helped gain Krautz the notoriety he enjoyed to the end of his

---

[47] HStA Hanover Hann. 173a Nr. 436, Bl. 72–3: Krautz to Oberstaatsanwalt Celle, 15 June 1883.

FIG. 20. *The executioner as hero.* Title-page of *The Executioner of Berlin*, a penny-dreadful published in 130 weekly instalments at the beginning of the 1890s and reputedly the best-selling German novel of the nineteenth century. The portrait in the centre is a reasonably accurate likeness of the official Prussian executioner, but the rest of the title-page refers to purely imaginary events. The representative scenes in the margins give a good idea of the novel's contents: romance, violence, crime, and mystery.

days, since it sold millions of copies and was subsequently reckoned to have achieved the highest sales of any novel published in Germany during the whole of the nineteenth century.[48]

Yet Krautz never succeeeded in making executions his main source of income. He continued to function between executions as a knacker in Charlottenburg.[49] Altogether he claimed to have carried out fifty-five executions by 1889, making an average of between four and five a year. At this point, however, he ran into serious trouble. One of his assistants, Gummich, had turned up drunk at a number of executions, so Krautz had been forced to sack him. Bitterly resentful at his treatment, Gummich went to Krautz's local pub to confront him. The altercation turned into a fight, and Krautz knocked him down, administering a kick to finish him off. As Gummich tried to kick back from his prone position on the pub floor, Krautz kicked him again. The blow was so violent that Gummich died shortly afterwards from internal injuries. Claiming that he had been 'seriously provoked', Krautz was charged with 'grievous bodily harm with fatal consequences'. Rumour had it that his business at the knacker's yard in Charlottenburg had not been doing too well, and he too had taken to heavy drinking as a result. His marriage had broken up in 1881 after nine years, and he was evidently a lonely and somewhat embittered man.[50] Bourgeois respectability had in the end eluded him. His murderous assault on his former assistant could not be ignored. Yet the moderation of the indictment suggested already that the aura which surrounded the executioner was starting to have an effect on those called upon to deal with the case. Certainly the apparent absence of any premeditation, and the fact that the killing had not been carried out in connection with any other crime, ruled out a charge of murder. But manslaughter was still a definite possibility. When all was said and done, however, it would in any case have been difficult for the state prosecutor to have arraigned Krautz on a capital charge. For if he was convicted, who would execute the executioner?

Even stranger events were to follow. For the jurors (*Geschworene*) proceeded to procure Krautz's acquittal on the grounds that he had acted in self-defence. The state prosecutor was moved to protest that this was mistaken, since nobody had actually offered any physical violence to Krautz in the pub at all. The most

---

[48] Victor von Falk, *Der Scharfrichter von Berlin. Roman, nach Acten, Aufzeichnungen u. Mittheilungen des Scharfrichters Jul. Krautz (Berlin)* (6 vols.; Berlin, 1890–1); Schenda, *Volk*, 310–14. 'Victor von Falk' was possibly a pseudonym for Heinrich Sochaczewsky (ibid. 310–11 n. 222). Official disapproval ensured that only one copy could be found in a publicly funded German library by the 1960s (ibid. 324). There is an incomplete copy of the novel in the British Library.

[49] GStA Berlin Rep. 84a/9317, Bl. 95 (notes of 26 July 1883); ibid. 4591: Oberstaatsanwalt Berlin: Bericht über die Verlegung des Wohnsitzes seitens des Scharfrichters Krautz, 11 Oct. 1884.

[50] Ibid., Bl. 26: Erster Staatsanwalt beim Landgericht (Alt-Moabit) to PJM, 9 Apr. 1889; HStA Hanover Hann. 173a Nr. 436, Bl. 119: Oberstaatsanwalt Berlin to Oberstaatsanwalt Celle, 14 Nov. 1889; Schmidt, *Krautz*, 20, 90–2.

that could be said, he added, was that the executioner had been verbally provoked and that therefore the killing was accompanied by mitigating circumstances; but this was already taken care of in the reduced charge. However, the jurors were clearly overawed by the fact that they were trying an executioner. One who had killed so many in cold blood already, they must have felt, could surely not be imprisoned on account of merely one more death. Perhaps they were also unwilling to believe that Krautz, whose job required the steadiest of nerves, was capable of losing his temper even when drunk. But while a career of state-funded violence may well have made it easier for Krautz to kick a man to death in a pub brawl, it certainly did not convince the authorities of their executioner's respectability on the scaffold. After the trial was over, he was summarily retired; he left for Magdeburg, before returning to run another knacking business in the Weberstrasse in Berlin, where he remained until his death in 1921. Not only did he continue to enjoy his celebrity as a former executioner, he cashed in on it by using his early training as a pastry-cook and confectioner to open a restaurant as well.[51] In 1893, his biographer reported: 'Not a week passes, even though he has not been an executioner for four years now . . . without Krautz receiving personal or written requests to "remove curses" from cattle, or to provide pieces of rope and shards from the scaffold or handkerchiefs dipped in the blood of the beheaded.' Old beliefs evidently died hard, at least in the countryside. The former executioner, however, added his biographer primly, 'did not place his work at the service of dim-witted superstition'.[52] Whether or not this was true, in other respects Krautz, who had been denied a pension by the Justice Ministry, seldom missed an opportunity to make money out of his reputation, selling his account book for a substantial sum not long after he retired, and no doubt attracting adventurous members of the bourgeoisie to his restaurant to enjoy the thrill of being served cream cakes by a former state executioner.[53]

Krautz's status in Prussia reflected among other things the fact that, by this time, the number of executioners had long since been reduced to a tiny handful. Indeed, there appears to have been only one other executioner serving in Germany's largest state at this time, Friedrich Reindel, a member of an old family of knackers and executioners, who had begun his career in 1843 at the age of 19 and subsequently assisted at numerous executions in various parts of north Germany.[54] A similar process took place in other parts of Germany. When Martin Hörmann, executioner in Munich since 1813, died in 1841, for example,

[51] GStA Berlin Rep. 84a/4591, Bl. 47: Erster Staatsanwalt beim Landgericht, notes of 25 June 1889. See also BA Potsdam RJM 6098, Bl. 122: *Vorwärts*, 14 Mar. 1930 (Krautz *Diensttagebuch*), and Glenzdorf and Treichel, *Henker*, 145–6.
[52] Schmidt, *Krautz*, 89.   [53] Ibid. 86, 92.   [54] Ibid. 93.

„In die Fluth hinab, Du blutiges Beil, und nie möge Dich ein menschliches Auge mehr sehen!" rief der Scharfrichter.

F I G. 21. *Fictitious remorse*. The official Prussian executioner Julius Krautz throws his axe into the river, crying: 'Down into the stream, you bloody axe, and may no human eye ever see you again!' A purely imaginary scene from the novel *The Executioner of Berlin*, published in 1890. In fact, Krautz was forced to retire from his office in 1889 after killing one of his assistants in a fight.

he was not replaced by the Bavarian government.[55] His functions were carried out instead by the Augsburg executioner, Anton Leisner, who travelled to Munich on the handful of occasions every year when his presence was required.

[55] HStA Munich MInn 72777: Justizministerium to Finanzministerium, 22 June 1841 (copy).

Leisner was not replaced on his retirement in 1852, and, similarly, the executioner for Lower Bavaria had no successor on his death in 1844.[56] By 1852 there were only three executioners left in Bavaria. One functioned for the Bavarian Palatinate, but since for various reasons no executions took place there, Heinrich Graul, the responsible individual, was effectively redundant. This left two functioning executioners, who were able to use improved communications by road, and, from the 1840s, the new railways, to travel to the sites of executions as required.[57] Executioners were now effectively becoming professionals, carefully selected by the authorities for their character and abilities, subjected to an examination before taking up their duties, and provided with regular jobs and a regular income.[58] Nevertheless, the traditional connection between knackers and executioners proved to be remarkably resilient. It remained the case that skinners and knackers, like butchers, were more accustomed to dealing with blood, dead bodies, and so on, than were most other professions. Their willingness to act as executioners seemed to be undiminished. The influential hereditary traditions of handing down the trade from father to son or nephew, and marrying into each others' families, all combined to make the executioner's social circle as restricted as it had ever been.

When the director of the prison in Cologne in 1887 was asked to find someone to assume the responsibility of operating the guillotine, he replied that

there is no possibility of any warder here becoming available for the said service, because in view of the air of disrepute which in the public eye still clings to the activity of a man who carries out the death sentence, they fear with some justification that it will lead to serious if not direct insults to his honour and to other disadvantages for this person himself and for his family in their private life, quite apart from the fact that in my opinion the authority of such a warder over the prisoners could only be maintained with great difficulty.[59]

All these influences helped ensure that the traditional connection between knackers and executioners survived the period when executions were largely in abeyance in Germany and underwent a revival once they resumed in the 1880s.[60] Despite the drastic reduction in the number of executioners in the early to mid-nineteenth century, and the growing professionalization of the trade, the family tradition threfore continued. In 1854, when the Kingdom of Bavaria replaced the

[56] Ibid.: Justizministerium to Innenministerium, 20 Mar. 1844.
[57] Ibid.: Justizministerium to Kgl.. Appellationsgericht, 1 Jan. 1855.
[58] For a survey of the executioners in office during the mid- to late 19th c., see Glenzdorf and Treichel, *Henker*, 139–41.
[59] HStA Düsseldorf Rep. 145/324, Bl. 111: Strafanstalts-Director Cologne to Oberstaatsanwalt Cologne, 11 June 1887.
[60] Ibid., Bl. 184: Zeugnis of the 'executioner and knacker' Louis Hirsch in Gotha, for the continuation of this connection in the person of the Thuringian executioner.

sword with the guillotine, the Ministry of Justice decided that it should be operated by the existing executioner's son. The young man seemed perfectly capable of operating the new machine, said the Ministry officials:

On the other hand, the executioner Lorenz Scheller in Amberg seems no longer capable of carrying out his business in any respect. The said man is at present 60 year old and was already appointed executioner by All-Highest Command on 22 February 1829. . . . Apart from this, it is surely inappropriate to commission a man who is in the twilight of his days with the functions of an executioner by the new method of execution.

In fact, the report added, the older Scheller had not carried out an execution for many years, but had employed an assistant instead. Perhaps for this reason he raised no objection to his retirement, which was made all the more acceptable by the award of a pension of 540 marks a year.[61] He was succeeded by another member of his family, then eventually by an assistant, Franz Reichhart.[62]

In a similar way, having ordered a changeover to the guillotine in 1859, the authorities in the Kingdom of Hanover took the opportunity to order the retirement of the serving executioner. To add insult to injury, they engaged a prison warder, one Bormann by name, to operate the new machine.[63] The existing executioner, Christian Schwarz, objected vehemently that he was quite capable of understanding the novel device.[64] Hanoverian executioner since 1843, he had in fact been carrying out executions for the city of Bremen since 1827 and was 67 years of age at the time of his dismissal. In January 1859 he wrote the first in what proved to be a long series of letters of protests to the Hanoverian Ministry of Justice. Or rather, he had the letters written, since they were signed with a cross, for the 'executioner Schwarz, who is capable neither of reading nor writing'.[65] In his first letter, he reminded the Ministry that since his appointment thirty-two years previously he had carried out thirty-eight executions, 'and a few days ago I delivered proof at an execution in Göttingen of how I am still capable of wielding my sword'. Schwarz's arithmetic seems to have been as shaky as his writing, however, since in another letter,[66] he claimed that the number of executions he had performed was forty-one, and in a third, thirty-four. Like

[61] HStA Munich MJu 13066: notes of 30 Sept. 1854 and letter to Appellationsgericht Oberpfalz, 23 Sept. 1854.

[62] HStA Munich MInn 72777: Justizministerium to Innenministerium, 20 July 1851; Justizministerium to Kgl. Appellationsgericht 1 Jan. 1855; Justizministerium to Finanzministerium 19 Feb. 1864; Justizministerium to Regierung Oberbayern 7 Aug. 1880; Kgl. Bezirksmamt Wunsiedel to Innenministerium 5 Nov. 1880; Will Berthold [i.e. Stefan Amberg], *Vollstreckt. Johann Reichhart, der letzte deutsche Henker* (Munich, 1982), 22.

[63] HStA Hanover Hann. 173a Nr. 436, Bl. 30: notes of 24 Sept. 1870; GStA Berlin Rep. 84a/9397, Bl. 95: notes of 26 July 1883.

[64] GStA Berlin Rep. 84a/9397, Bl. 96: Schwarz to Justizministerium Hannover, 29 Jan. 1859.

[65] Ibid.: Schwarz to Justizministerium Hannover, 24 Feb. 1860.

[66] Ibid.: letters of 31 Oct. 1859 and 24 Feb. 1860.

many executioners at this time, Schwarz was beginning to fall into financial difficulties. He did receive some income from his knacker's yard and horse butchery in Hanover, but he had to give this up early in 1860, and the income of 100 thalers a year which he received for his duties as executioner in Bremen was insufficient for his support. Even before his retirement he had asked for a pay rise, 'so that I am not compelled to live in poverty and destitution'.[67] Although he recognized that the introduction of the new machine spelled the end of his career, the formal announcement that his services were no longer needed came, he protested, as an unexpected blow. He had, he said, been a faithful servant of the state for thirty-three years and deserved at least a decent pension.[68] Whether or not he received one, the Ministry did not record. Meanwhile, prison warder Bormann continued to operate the guillotine until he left the city for another job in 1870. His assistants were also drawn from the ranks of the prison warders in Hanover.[69] Thus by the second half of the nineteenth century executioners were being appointed by the Justice Ministries of the various German states and given responsibility for a wide area, rather than deriving their duties directly from the terms of the tenure of knacker's yards. With the resumption of executions on a regular basis from the 1880s, it was clear that there was a living of sorts to be had from the trade. But only if the number of executioners was kept to a minimum.

This led in the late nineteenth and early twentieth centuries to growing competition between executioners for the available jobs. The problems to which this could give rise became evident in the growing rivalry between the two families from whom the executioners for the Grand Duchy of Baden were drawn, the Burckhardts and the Müllers. The Grand Duchy had traditionally employed two executioners, and it continued this practice after capital punishment was reintroduced in 1880. Michael Müller, executioner since 1854, who resumed his duties after a gap of fifteen years in 1879, was elderly, and the local police were asked to check regularly on his health and notify the authorities should he die at any time.[70] When he did indeed die in 1886, his son Franz Müller, described as 'Protestant, married, propertied, with a good reputation', succeeded him. Although he was officially categorized as a 'farmer', Müller, like his father, was in fact a knacker. Now aged 40, he had assisted his father at executions since their resumption, but he was only allowed to carry them out in Karlsruhe and Mannheim, while the deputy executioner Benjamin Burckhardt was promoted

---

[67] Ibid., Bl. 63: note of 17 June 1859.   [68] Ibid.: letter of 31 Oct. 1859.
[69] HStA Hanover Hann. 173a Nr. 436, Bl. 30 (notes of 24 Sept. 1870), Bl. 35–8 (memo of 26 Oct. 1870).
[70] GLA Karlsruhe 234/6773: Bericht 'die Scharfrichter betr.', Aug. 1884. See also ibid.: report of 25 Oct. 1885. The practice of sending in annual reports on the executioners' health continued from this point until the end of the First World War.

to senior executioner for Offenburg, Freiburg, and Konstanz.[71] Burckhardt was said in 1884 to be 'physically and mentally hale and hearty, fresh and healthy'. 'The said man is in good propertied and family circumstances and enjoys general respect in view of his peace-loving and orderly character.'[72] Both men functioned at every execution, acting as chief or deputy executioner according to where the execution was held, with the deputy receiving a fee of 80 marks and the assistant 30.[73] Even so, the fees and expenses were set at such a low rate that it was hardly surprising that Burckhardt complained.[74] In 1888 it was reported of Müller that

for a long time, and recently as well, he has revealed a periodic tendency to drunkenness. This tendency makes itself observable virtually every four weeks, namely when there is a festival, during long spells of rainy weather, and when he does not have anything urgent to do. On such occasions, he regularly gives himself over to drink for three or four days on end.[75]

Müller was promptly dismissed.[76] The sacked executioner immediately wrote to the Baden Ministry of Justice protesting that he had done nothing wrong. His reputation was good, he said, and he had never made any mistakes at an execution. 'I am the father of twelve children,' he wrote, 'who are all still under age, so that an unexpected contract is a good turn for me.'[77] The Justice Ministry, however, was not inclined to regard according the right to behead people as an act of charity on its part towards those who received it. But the authorities turned to the Müller family again, this time to Jakob Müller, aged 40, another 'farmer', who was described as 'physically fit', living 'in well-ordered propertied circumstances' and leading a 'solid, sober life'. Müller was duly appointed, giving the Burckhardt family another reason to resent their rivals in the trade.[78] When Benjamin Burckhardt died in 1896, and was succeeded by Burckhardt's nephew Karl, aged 25, a tanner,[79] Jakob Müller protested in his turn

The person appointed *leading* first executioner for the state of Baden—a 26-year-old man called Burhard [*sic*] from Endingen, does not possess the necessary tranquillity, solidity, or reliability, and his pecuniary position (he is a 'factory owner') does not afford the guarantee which the high Ministry has the right to expect of the person of a serving executioner.

[71] GLA Karlsruhe 234/6773: Schnitzler, Wachtmeister, to Amtsgericht Mannheim, 28 Sept. 1888; Justizministerium memorandum of 21 Oct. 1886, 'die Scharfrichter betr.'; Müller to Justizministerium, 5 Feb. 1889.

[72] Ibid.: Bericht des Grossherzoglichen Amtsgericghts Kenzingen, die Scharfrichter betr., 1 Oct. 1884.

[73] Ibid.: Scharfrichterdienstordnung, 2 June 1888.

[74] Ibid.: Burckhardt to Staatsanwaltschaft Freiburg, 12 Aug. 1888.

[75] Ibid.: Gendarmerie-Corps Station Ladenburg to Gendarmerie-Bezirk Mannheim, report of 28 Dec. 1888.

[76] Ibid.: Justizministerium draft of 11 Jan. 1889.

[77] Ibid.: Müller to Justizministerium, 5 Feb. 1889.

[78] Ibid.: Gendarmerie Ladenburg, report of 1 July 1889, and memo of Justizministerium, 8 July 1889.

[79] Ibid.: letter of Karl Burckhardt, 5 Mar. 1897.

The younger man was, said Müller, 'not punctual or reliable enough. . . . It is not easy for me, as a 50-year-old man who takes his office seriously . . . to be obliged to render "auxiliary service" to this Mr Burhard.' Müller demanded to be made chief executioner for the whole Grand Duchy.[80] Müller complained that Burckhardt 'was extremely agitated,' and 'trembled' at his first execution in 1899, while the officiating state prosecutor added that Burckhardt

displays an appearance which is really unexpected for an executioner. His thin, weedy build, his pale, narrow, somewhat hectic face, his big eyes, constantly looking out on the world as if astonished and questioning, make the man appear a good deal younger than he is and stamp him with the mark of immaturity and inexperience.[81]

Burckhardt was ordered to act only as Müller's assistant, at least for the time being.[82] The Müllers seemed to have stolen a march on their hated rivals.

In 1903, however, at another execution, the truth about Burckhardt's alleged incompetence finally emerged. For the officiating state prosecutor noted on this occasion, as he had not previously, 'that Müller and his—very useful—assistant Jakob Lösch tried to make Burckhardt unsure of himself.' Herr Ihle, the carpenter whose job it was to oversee the proper funtioning of the guillotine, reported 'that executioner Müller talked a lot to Burckhardt, but I warned him to stop it, so as not to make B. crazy'. But it was too late, for 'he completely lost his head during the execution. The officials could not see this because they were standing some way off.' As a consequence, Burckhardt had failed to put all the safety devices in place on the machine, and it was only with luck that the execution had gone ahead without incident. For his part, Burckhardt renewed the claim that Baden was too small for two executioners, and that the entire Grand Duchy should be given to him alone as a single 'executioner's district'. Nor was Müller necessarily any more efficient as an executioner than his rival, since when acting as assistant to Burckhardt's father on one occasion, he too had failed to set the guillotine properly, with the result that the blade had smashed the offender's head instead of severing his neck. The Ministry of Justice in Karlsruhe did not let itself be swayed by these conflicting claims. It resolved to revive its previous practice of dividing the Grand Duchy into two, with Müller in charge of one, and the younger Burckhardt, who, despite his mistakes, was judged none the less to have shown strong nerves and 'cold-bloodedness', in charge of the other.[83] In 1908 it was ordered that the two executioners had to alternate in the job, irrespective of which part of the Grand Duchy it was carried out in, with each

[80] Ibid.: Müller to Justizministerium, 11 July 1899.
[81] Ibid.: Auszug aus dem Bericht des I. Staatsanwalts Karlsruhe, 22 Sept. 1899.
[82] Ibid.: Amtsgericht Kenzingen, no. 12641, 'den Scharfrichterdienst betr.', 21 Nov. 1899.
[83] Ibid. 234/6610: Vernehmungsprotokoll Ihle, 18 July 1903; Erste Staatsanwalt am Grossh. Bad. Landgericht Freiburg to Badisches Justizministerium, 3 Aug. 1903.

taking turn to act as the other's assistant.[84] This arrangement finally laid the family feud to rest. It continued until the death of Jakob Müller at the age of 59, in 1908.[85] He was then succeeded by his son Karl, born 1882, who had already assisted his father on two occasions.[86] Both executioners served in the army during the First World War, and survived to take up their duties once more in the Weimar Republic.[87]

e. 'Licensed Pieceworkers'

The competition for business between the rival executioners in Baden paled into insignificance in comparison with the war that broke out during the Wilhelmine period between their counterparts in Prussia. In 1889, the long-serving state executioner Julius Krautz, as we have seen, was summarily retired after his trial for killing one of his assistants in a brawl. Ignoring for the moment the flood of applications for employment as state executioner that inevitably flowed in from the lessees of various knackers' yards after this well publicized event,[88] the Ministry of Justice in Berlin turned to the old-established Reindel family. They engaged Friedrich Reindel, brother of the former, and still active, executioner August Reindel, in whose employ Krautz had started his career back in the 1860s. Friedrich was soon carrying out executions in Berlin, as well as in the western provinces of Prussia, with the assistance of his son Wilhelm and the advice of his brother August.[89] Before long the two older men had retired, leaving Wilhelm in charge. But here too the symptoms of stress began to show, as the number of executions began to rise during the 1890s. In 1899 Wilhelm Reindel was reported to have been drunk while carrying out a beheading in Neuwied.[90] His services had been used 'frequently' in the preceding few years, and the strain was obviously telling.[91] The local state prosecutor complained of his 'conspicuous manner' and, later on, once more, of his 'unfortunate . . . manner'.[92] Reindel's habit of cracking jokes about the execution the day before he was due to carry it out also offended the sensibilities of humourless Prussian bureaucrats. On 7 February 1900, on the instructions of the Ministry of Justice, the state prosecutor in Magdeburg, where Reindel now lived, issued the errant executioner with strict

---

[84] GLA Karlsruhe 234/6773: Ministerium der Justiz, des Kultus und Unterrichts, order no. 23807, 11 Aug. 1908.

[85] Sterbeurkunde dated 3 Oct. 1908 in GLA Karlsruhe, 234/6673.

[86] Ibid.: Karl Müller to Justizministerium, 6 Oct. 1908.

[87] See the successive reports from 1914 to 1920, ibid.

[88] GStA Berlin Rep. 84a/7784, Bl. 122: Staatsanwalt beim Königl. Kammergericht, 14 Nov. 1889.

[89] HStA Düsseldorf Rep. 145/324, Bl. 145: Erste Staatsanwalt Düsseldorf to PJM, 19 Apr. 1890.

[90] GStA Berlin Rep. 84a/4592, Bl. 12: Oberstaatsanwalt Frankfurt am Main to PJM, 13 Nov. 1899.

[91] Ibid., Bl. 13: PJM to Oberstaatsanwalt Naumburg.   [92] Ibid., Bl. 12.

instructions to lay off the bottle.[93] Reassuringly, Wilhelm's uncle August was said to be a calming influence.[94] But reports of the chief executioner's drunken behaviour continued to come in, and he was even said to have given the impression of 'feeble-mindedness' on some of his official appearances.[95] On 12 March 1900 he was reported to have been 'in a state of pretty strong insobriety' while carrying out a beheading in Ratibor.[96] In 1901 he was so drunk at an execution in Münster that he needed two blows to cut the victim's head off. Taking advantage of this mistake—a traditional occasion for showing official disapproval of an executioner—the Prussian Ministry of Justice issued a general instruction that Wilhelm Reindel's services were no longer to be used.[97]

In the mean time, the authorities in Prussia had begun the search for a successor. In 1889 the state prosecutor in Breslau had already drawn attention to Lorenz Schwietz, one of Krautz's assistants. Schwietz had been running a knacker's yard in the town since 1886. Further investigation had revealed him to possess a criminal record. This had caused some hesitation in the minds of the Ministry officials. But when it had transpired that the criminal record merely consisted of a conviction for cruelty to animals (*Tierquälerei*), their minds had been set at rest. This was hardly the kind of crime to stand in the way of employment as as executioner.[98] Schwietz had been described as of strong and athletic build, cool and calm in character, and experienced in the job: an ideal candidate. He had even been issued with an official certificate testifying that he 'has passed the executioner's examination which he was set'.[99] In 1889, as we have seen, despite the fact that Schwietz, like Krautz before him, circulated state prosecutors advertising his services, and included a copy of his examination certificate as executioner,[100] the authorities had made do with the Reindels.[101] But the increased number of executions in the 1890s and the declining powers of the Reindel family towards the end of the decade turned their attention to Schwietz once more. In 1898 he gave up his knacker's yard. Two years later he expressed himself willing to take on the job of chief Prussian executioner. Since the 1880s, as the state prosecutor in Breslau reported, Schwietz had kept and maintained the

[93] Ibid., Bl. 16: Erster Staatsanwalt Magdeburg to PJM, 7 Feb. 1900.
[94] Ibid.: Erster Staatsanwalt Hagen to PJM, 19 May 1900.   [95] Ibid.: notes, Bl. 24.
[96] HStA Düsseldorf Rep. 145/325, Bl. 96: PJM to Oberstaatsanwalt Cologne (copy of letter to Oberstaatsanwalt Naumburg), 8 May 1900; see also HStA Hanover Hann. 173a Nr. 436, Bl. 179–80, PJM to Oberstaatsanwalt Celle, 8 May 1900.
[97] GStA Berlin Rep. 84a/4592, Bl. 55: Erster Staatsanwalt Münster to PJM, 16 Aug. 1901; also Bl. 60; HStA Düsseldorf Rep. 145/325, Bl. 197: PJM to Oberstaatsanwalt Cologne, 23 Sept. 1901.
[98] GStA Berlin Rep. 84a/4591, Bl. 55: Oberstaatsanwalt Breslau to PJM, 16 Oct. 1889.
[99] Copy in GLA Karlsruhe 234/6773, dated 16 Oct. 1889.
[100] HStA Hanover Hann. 173a Nr. 436, Bl. 132–3: Schwietz to Oberstaatsanwalt Celle, undated.
[101] Ibid., Bl. 154–60: Vertrag mit Friedrich and Wilhelm Reindel, 1–3 Mar. 1893.

full set of execution equipment he had taken over from Krautz. 'With his athletic personality', added the prosecutor, 'and with his energetic appearance, which at the same time gives the impression of the most complete lack of emotion, Schwietz should be well suited for the office of executioner.'[102]

This time, Schwietz was subjected to a thorough medical examination, was asked some basic questions about human physiology and anatomy, and had to give his examiners a brief account of how he would carry out an execution. He seems to have passed the test, for on 21 June 1900 the Justice Ministry in Berlin approved his appointment, and on 9 and 10 August he carried out his first executions.[103] The state prosecutor's report on his conduct provided some significant pointers to the kind of behaviour and appearance now considered appropriate in an official executioner:

He himself made a very calm, secure impression; he appeared in impeccable posture and in a good frock-coat. His three assistants were in black suits and in their outward appearance clean and proper. None of them betrayed his profession in his appearance; they all looked very solid on the outside and made a modest impression.[104]

The lawyer's language was telling: the executioners were now required not to look like executioners, but to appear in suits, like ordinary citizens. But they were only 'solid on the outside': underneath the surface appearance of normality, they were not solid at all. The word 'dishonourable' was no longer employed; but the language used by the state prosecutor in describing them nevertheless expressed feelings that the executioner was not really a normal member of everyday human society. Such feelings were perhaps a necessary means of creating psychological distance between the command to kill and the responsibility for carrying it out; they represented a continuity of older patterns of behaviour as well.

Reassured by Schwietz's first performance ('everything went off very calmly'[105]), the authorities began employing him all over Prussia, even before Wilhelm Reindel was finally forced out of office. But the Reindels were not going to give up without a struggle. In 1900 Friedrich Reindel's son-in-law Alwin Engelhardt, a barman, who had assisted the family at a number of executions, also passed the examination set for Schwietz and was officially approved as state executioner.[106] Fortified by this success, the Reindels now began to complain that the stories of Wilhelm's drunkenness which had led to his reprimand in June were being spread by Schwietz in an attempt to win all the execution contracts for himself. Rumours also began to circulate that Schwietz did not wield the axe with the skill previously shown by the Reindels. In December 1900 it was

[102] GStA Berlin Rep. 84a/4591: Oberstaatsanwalt Breslau to PJM, 8 June 1900.
[103] Ibid., Bl. 30: PJM to Oberstaatsanwalt Breslau, 21 June 1900.
[104] Ibid. 4592, Bl. 38: Oberstaatsanwalt Breslau to PJM, 14 Aug. 1900.   [105] Ibid.
[106] Ibid., Bl. 54: Oberstaatsanwalt Naumburg to PJM 13 June 1900 and reply 21 June 1900.

reported that Schwietz's assistants were not doing their job properly. Schwietz himself received an official warning after requiring two blows to sever the head of a criminal at an execution in Plötzensee.[107] Within a year, the 'athletic' appearance he was said to have possessed in the 1880s and 1890s had apparently disappeared, and he was described by the state prosecutor in Königsberg as 'extremely corpulent and evidently very short of breath'.[108] None of this, however, stopped Schwietz's continued employment. Once he had been appointed, even an executioner as unsatisfactory as this proved remarkably difficult to dislodge. For if he too was dismissed, then who was there left to take his place?

One man who had a clear answer was his rival Alwin Engelhardt. Unable to prevent the enforced retirement of the by now thoroughly alcoholic Wilhelm Reindel in 1901, or to oust the hated Schwietz from his post, the Reindel family had none the less managed to persuade the Prussian Ministry of Justice to engage Engelhardt to carry out executions on a regular basis once Wilhelm had left the scene.[109] But Engelhardt soon began to get into difficulties. At an execution in Hanau in 1902 the condemned man resisted so strongly that it took the combined efforts of Engelhardt's assistants and a prison warder to bring him to the block. Evidently the struggle unnerved the executioner, so that his hand lost its steadiness, and he required two blows to sever the man's head from his body. The whole scene, it was reported, made 'an extremely embarrassing impression'. Engelhardt was asked by the Ministry as a consequence if he could not find stronger men to assist him. For his part, Engelhardt blamed the prison warders for rejecting his advice to put the prisoner in chains. It was clear that the offender was going to resist, and the job of restraining him properly belonged to the man's gaolers, not his executioners.[110] Once this incident was over, Engelhardt's next few performances seem to have been more satisfactory, and he was confirmed in his post by the Ministry. Bolstered by these signs of official approval, Engelhardt now moved to claim the whole of the Reindels' inheritance for himself. On 5 May 1902 he wrote to the Ministry pointing out that Schwietz was a retired man with a private income, and so did not need the job of executioner to make his living. Engelhardt, on the other hand, was unemployed. So it would only be fair if he were now appointed official state executioner for the whole of Prussia.[111] The Ministry was unwilling to go along with this. Executioners were only hired for specific jobs. 'The fundamental assignment of all executions to one particular

[107] Ibid., Bl. 45a: PJM to Oberstaatsanwalt Breslau, 18 Dec. 1900.
[108] Ibid., Bl. 68: Oberstaatsanwalt Königsberg to Justizministerium, 26 Nov. 1901.
[109] HStA Düsseldorf Rep. 145/325, Bl. 110–12: Oberstaatsanwalt Celle to Oberstaatsanwalt Cologne, 24 Oct. 1901. See also the correspondence between Engelhardt and the Oberstaatsanwalt Celle in HStA Hanover Hann. 173a Nr. 436, Bl. 183–200.
[110] GStA Berlin Rep. 84a/4591, Bl. 79: Erster Staatsanwalt Hanau to PJM, 30 Apr. 1902.
[111] Ibid., Bl. 76–7: Engelhardt to PJM, 5 May 1902.

executioner does not take place.'[112] This did not deter Engelhardt from persisting with his claim. Soon, a macabre competition had broken out between the two executioners, as each tried to win the majority of contracts for himself.

The Ministry of Justice initially sought to resolve the conflict by establishing a rough geographical division of responsibility between the two men. Engelhardt was supposed to carry out executions in the Prussian provinces west of the River Elbe and Schwietz in the remaining provinces east of the the river. But Engelhardt complained that this gave the lion's share to Schwietz. So, in an attempt to appease him, the Ministry officials ordered that he was to be given roughly the same number of executions to carry out as his rival.[113] This meant, however, that Engelhardt started to get contracts for executions east of the River Elbe, which caused Schwietz in turn to complain that Engelhardt was poaching on his territory.[114] Schwietz added, in a dignified rider, that the job could only be treated as a 'matter of honour'; no one could, or should be in it for the money, as he implied Engelhardt was. Nevertheless, the sums the two men earned from their duties were not to be sneezed at. In 1901 Schwietz carried out thirteen executions, for which he was paid 4,018 marks, and in 1902 another thirteen, for which he earned 3,937 marks. This money had to be used to cover his travel and maintenance expenses as well as paying his assistants. But it still put him at least into the earnings bracket of the upper working class, for a living wage for a manual worker around this time is generally reckoned to have stood at between 1,000 and 1,500 marks a year.[115] The arrival of Engelhardt on the scene caused a serious loss of income for the older man. In 1901 the Reindels, and after them Engelhardt, were paid a mere 1,900 marks for the nine executions they carried out. In 1902 Engelhardt managed to increase his earnings to 3,372 marks from the same number. Admittedly, 1902 was a bumper year for executions in Prussia, with no fewer than twenty-six offenders decapitated in a total of twenty-two separate events, so that Engelhardt's employment scarcely cut into Schwietz's earnings at all. But in 1903, a lean year, Schwietz's earnings fell to 2,415 marks from seven executions, while Engelhardt could only get 1,756 marks for the four that he carried out. This was the disparity that prompted Engelhardt to persuade the Ministry to let him carry out executions east as well as west of the Elbe. The result could be seen in a dramatic increase in his earnings for 1904, when fifteen executions brought him no less than 5,660 marks, while Schwietz's earnings fell to 2,066 marks from a mere five executions. No wonder that the older man was moved to complain: within two years his earnings had been cut by half. Employ-

---

[112] GStA Berlin Rep. 84a/4591, Bl. 77: PJM to Engelhardt, 15 May 1902.
[113] Ibid., Bl. 97: note of 28 Apr. 1903.   [114] Ibid., Bl. 116–17: Schwietz to PJM, 30 Sept. 1905.
[115] See Gerhard A. Ritter and Klaus Tenfelde, *Arbeiter im Deutschen Kaiserreich 1871 bis 1914* (Bonn, 1992), 469–90.

ment as a state executioner might have been a matter of honour for him, as he said; but he was still not going to stand idly and let his rival systematically destroy his livelihood.[116]

The year 1904 proved to be Engelhardt's best. In 1905 only nine offenders went under the axe and the guillotine in the whole of Prussia. Schwietz's earnings were halved again, to 1,093 marks from a mere three jobs. But it was Engelhardt who suffered the most serious consequences. Even though he was given five separate contracts, this still only brought him a total of 2,010 marks. For a man who had no other source of income, this was scarcely enough to live off, especially because he had to pay his assistants from this sum, as well as meet all the travelling and maintenance costs accruing from an execution and cover the expenses involved in transporting his equipment and keeping it in working order. The possibilities of augmenting their fees by the sale of blood, clothes, relics, and other appurtenances of the deceased, which had existed for executioners in earlier times, were now as distant a memory as the early modern executioner's additional earnings from providing medical services, cleaning the town drains, collecting the dog tax, or carrying out torture and corporal punishments. Modern times had, to be sure, brought some new opportunities of earning additional income. In 1882 it had been revealed that the ever-enterprising executioner Krautz was being paid by Carstans' *Panoptikum*, an exhibition of the kind popularized in the same period by Madame Tussaud in London, to allow his axe and block to be displayed in the 'Chamber of Horrors' between jobs. At this time, such intervals were fairly lengthy, and no doubt Krautz needed the money. Carstans had also paid Friedrich Reindel for the display of the axe with which a would-be assassin of Friedrich Wilhelm IV had been executed some decades previously. Further investigations brought to light the fact that no fewer than twenty-seven death-masks of murder victims were also exhibited in the same show. They had been taken 'directly after the murder', presumably by police officers who had been well paid by Carstans for their services. Outraged by these revelations, Minister of the Interior von Puttkamer had ordered the police to remove all these objects from the show. Strict orders had been issued to ensure that this kind of thing did not recur.[117] Opportunities such as this were no longer open to executioners, therefore, after the early 1880s.

Almost wholly dependent on execution fees for his livelihood, Engelhardt began to get into serious financial difficulties after the lean year of 1905. By the spring of 1906, he was desperate. On 17 March he wrote to the Senior State Prosecutor in Celle:

[116] Figures of earnings in this and following paragraphs from GStA Berlin Rep. 84a/4593, Bl. 151–2.
[117] Ibid. 4590, Bl. 212–14.

I ask and plead with Your Honour in my great embarrassment that you should not take my most humble entreaty amiss. I have learned from a notice in the newspaper that the murderer Küntner has been executed in Hanover by executioner Schwietz from Breslau. Since I have earned nothing for a good half-year, this is a great loss for me, the more so since I have to cover my living expenses exclusively from executions, and at the moment I do not even have bread for my family, which consists of a wife and three small children.[118]

The Hanoverian authorities refused to employ him, however. Soon Engelhardt was no longer able to meet his obligations. Here too the stress of the job may have been having an effect. For, as one of his assistants reported later, by this time Engelhardt was spending very considerable sums of money on drink.[119] Faced with rapidly mounting debts, he began to appease his creditors by promising them the fees payable for executions for which he had not yet been commissioned. In January 1906, indeed, one of his creditors obtained a court order 'for the distraint of such claims . . . as the said debtor has against the Royal Prussian Treasury represented by the senior state prosecutor at Celle for the payment of an honorarium and the repayment of expenses and the remuneration for the debtor's activity in the execution of the murderer Ruther'.[20] Since the execution in question had not yet taken place, and since no public announcement had yet been made about whether or not the offender had been granted a royal reprieve, the state prosecutor was understandably upset. The court order opened up the possibility of a whole string of future executions being subject to legal proceedings of this kind, in which the judicial authorities would be obliged to hand over Engelhardt's payment straight to his creditors. The idea that the executioner was promising money to people on the basis of the assumption that one or another condemned offender would be denied the royal clemency seemed highly improper to the official mind. It mixed up mere financial considerations with what was supposed to be a high act of state. It pre-empted the royal prerogative of mercy and was thus a kind of *lèse-majesté*. Engelhardt was gambling on future deaths to postpone his own bankruptcy. And the whole affair inevitably got into the papers as well, further embarrassing the state prosecutor's office and the Prussian government.[121]

This proved too much for the authorities in Celle, who handed the matter over to Berlin. In May 1906 the Prussian Ministry of Justice summarily dismissed Engelhardt from office.[122] This sudden turn of events brought the grotesque

---

[118] HStA Hanover Hann. 173a Nr. 437, Bl. 48: Engelhardt to Oberstaatsanwalt Celle, 17 Mar. 1906.
[119] GStA Berlin Rep. 84a/4595, Bl. 99: *Neue Berliner Zeitung-12 Uhr Blatt* (undated clipping, 1930).
[120] HStA Hanover Hann. 173a Nr. 441, Bl. 3: Rechtsanwalt Benfey to Oberstaatsanwalt Celle, 23 Feb. 1906.
[121] Ibid., Bl. 8: *Viertes Blatt des Hannoverschen Couriers,* 2 Mar. 1906.
[122] GStA Berlin Rep. 84a/4592, Bl. 144: PJM notes, 21 May 1906.

rivalry between the two Prussian executioners to an abrupt end. But if the Ministry officials thought they had heard the last of Engelhardt, they were mistaken.[123] On 7 September 1908 the newspaper *Welt am Montag* printed a sensational interview with the former executioner, in which he attributed his dismissal to the appointment of a new Minister of Justice, Maximilian von Beseler, whom he regarded as a partisan of Schwietz.[124] In order to keep him quiet, the Ministry tried to find him a job. These efforts went on for nearly two years and fill well over a hundred pages of the relevant file in the Ministry's papers. In 1909 success seemed close as Engelhardt was found an appointment as caretaker of the court-house in Lauenburg, Pomerania; but the job fell through when he demanded to be given it as a lifetime appointment. Characteristically, he kept the 250 marks with which the Ministry had supplied him to cover his removal expenses, even though he had failed to move.[125] The next year, in 1910, the Ministry finally found him a knacker's yard, thus renewing the traditional connection between the two trades. This satisfied the importunate executioner, and he moved in. Thus Engelhardt finally ceased to trouble the harassed bureaucrats and disappeared from the files. But that was not the last of him. He was to reappear under dramatically different circumstances many years later, to trouble them briefly once again.

Engelhardt's sudden dismissal left Lorenz Schwietz, temporarily at least, as the sole occupant of the office of Prussian state executioner. Indeed he had already substituted for Engelhardt while the latter's case was being decided in Berlin.[126] As his erstwhile rival did not omit to point out, in one of his many vain attempts to get his job back, Schwietz was now more than 60 years of age (while Engelhardt was only 31 at the time of his sacking).[127] The Ministry, not surprisingly, decided that carrying out executions over the whole vast area of the Prussian Kingdom would be too much for him. It therefore continued to engage him for the East Elbian provinces only.[128] Increasingly he was assisted in the task by his son Richard, who ran a bar in the Oranienstrasse in Berlin. In 1913 Richard Schwietz gave up the bar and moved to Breslau to take over the knacker's yard which his father still owned in the town.[129] The older Schwietz, now aged 67, took the opportunity to retire as executioner at the same time. His son successfully passed the usual examination and carried out his first beheading under his father's supervision in 1914. On this occasion, as the state prosecutor reported,

[123] HStA Düsseldorf Rep. 245/325, Bl. 167: Engelhardt to Oberstaatsanwalt Cologne, 1 May 1906.
[124] GStA Berlin Rep. 84a/4592, Bl. 201: *Welt am Montag*, 7 Sept. 1908.
[125] BA Koblenz R22/1323, Bl. 94 (Vermerk, 25 Apr. 1936).
[126] HStA Düsseldorf Rep. 145/325, Bl. 166: Oberstaatsanwalt Celle to Oberstaatsanwalt Cologne, 18 Apr. 1906.
[127] GStA Berlin Rep. 84a/4592: Engelhardt to PJM, 3 June 1906.   [128] Ibid. 4593, Bl. 174.
[129] Ibid. 4594, Bl. 1, Bl. 6: Oberstaatsanwalt Breslau to PJM 11 Nov. 1913 and 20 Dec. 1913.

'Richard Schwietz dealt the fatal blow with the same sureness of touch as his father had once done.'[130] Richard Schwietz was described as a strong, calm individual.[131] The authorities were particularly impressed by the fact that he was a non-commissioned officer in the army reserve. This seemed to the Prussian official mind to be telling evidence of his sobriety and reliability. But it also meant in 1915 that Richard Schwietz was called up and sent to the front. On 12 August 1916 he was killed in action.[132]

Meanwhile, ignoring the inevitable petitions by the owners of various knacker's yards for appointment to the job, the Ministry had taken what was by now the usual course and turned to Engelhardt's chief assistant, Carl Gröpler. Like other executioners, Gröpler had experience in the knacking trade, but by the time of his appointment he had abandoned his career as a horse-butcher and was earning his main living from running the *Edelweiss* laundry in Magdeburg.[133] Gröpler was an altogether tougher customer than his former boss. He had no truck with the older Schwietz's claim that carrying out executions was a matter of honour. From the outset it was clear that he was in it for the money. Indeed, just as Julius Krautz had done, he quickly wrote to state prosecution authorities in other north German states offering them his services, 'after I took and passed the executioner's examination set by the Royal State Prosecution Service in Magdeburg'. He assured them 'that I am precisely acquainted with all the actions of an execution, I employ unimpeachable assistants, and that anything likely to cause offence will be strictly avoided'.[134] Meanwhile, however, Schwietz was attempting to secure contracts west of the Elbe after the dismissal of Engelhardt by writing to individual state prosecutors offering to underbid his new rival.[135] The Ministry, annoyed at this attempt to bypass its authority,[136] and firmly wedded to the idea of two executioners rather than one, rejected this idea out of hand.[137] As the senior state prosecutor in Naumburg, effectively Gröpler's patron, pointed out, his client 'has newly obtained all the necessary equipment and has undoubtedly gone to some expense in doing so. He would certainly be grievously damaged if contracts were concluded with Schwietz in the Western provinces.'[138] But while Carl Gröpler certainly enjoyed a regular income from his

[130] GStA Berlin Rep. 84a/4592, Bl. 24: Oberstaatsanwalt Breslau to PJM, 12 Feb. 1914.

[131] Ibid., Bl. 7.

[132] Ibid., Bl. 94: Obersstaatsanwalt Breslau to PJM, 18 Aug. 1916; HStA Düsseldorf Rep. 145/326, Bl. 27: PJM to Oberstaatsanwalt Cologne, 21 June 1916.

[133] Glenzdorf and Treichel, *Henker*, 148.

[134] StA Bremen 4, 89/1.236: Gröpler to Erster Staatsanwalt Bremen, 5 Nov. 1906. See also HStA Düsseldorf Rep. 145/325, Bl. 172–3: Oberstaatsanwalt Naumburg to Oberstaatsanwalt Celle, 12 Nov. 1906 (copy), and HStA Hanover Hann. 173a Nr. 437, Bl. 77: Gröpler to Oberstaantsanwalt Celle, 27 Nov. 1906.

[135] GStA Berlin Rep. 84a/4592, Bl. 153: Schwietz to PJM, 5 Nov. 1903.

[136] HStA Düsseldorf Rep. 126/81, Bl. 35: PJM to Oberstaatsanwalt Düsseldorf, 30 Nov. 1906 (copy).

[137] Ibid., Bl. 36: Oberstaatsanwalt Naumburg to PJM, 12 Nov. 1906.

[138] Ibid., Rep. 145/325, Bl. 171: Oberstaatsanwalt Naumburg to PJM, 12 Nov. 1906.

laundry, and soon became notorious among state prosecutors for exceeding his expense allowances,[139] he quickly became irritated with the low rate of pay he earned for executions and the fluctuating and unpredictable income he gained from them.[140] In 1906, he earned 1,075 marks, in 1907, 1,800, and in 1908, 2,550. Perhaps as a result of his expressing his dissatisfaction, he began to make more serious money in 1909, earning 5,350 marks for the eleven executions which he carried out that year, and a further 4,950 from another ten the next year. Thus he caught up with and then overhauled the older Schwietz, who made 3,349 marks in 1906, 3,381 in 1907, 1,416 in 1908, 2,670 in 1909, and 4,346 (from twelve executions) in 1910.[141] But the uncertainties of the income still made the two men's position far from satisfactory.

At this point, the situation was dramatically altered by a fresh intervention from an unexpected quarter. As part of his campaign against the Prussian Ministry of Justice, former executioner Alwin Engelhardt had written a number of letters to the young Social Democratic Reichstag deputy Karl Liebknecht, a man generally known as an extreme radical, on the far left of the party. Liebknecht was a lawyer, and never lost an opportunity of embarrassing the government. Armed with the information supplied by Engelhardt, Liebknecht launched a sarcastic attack on the death penalty in the Prussian Chamber of Deputies during the budget debate in 1911. 'Our executioners', he complained, 'are not civil servants but licensed pieceworkers.' He asked for more information on the costs of 'the executions which have taken place, as it seems to me, in greatly increased numbers in Prussia in recent times'.[142] Given the rules of parliamentary procedure, to which even the Prussian government had to pay due respect, the Ministry of Justice had no choice but to supply the information. Clearly concerned to prevent such embarrassing questions arising in future, however, it then decided to put the state executioners on a fixed salary, plus expenses.[143] With characteristic modesty, Lorenz Schwietz asked for a mere 2,700 marks a year, from which he was also willing to pay his assistants.[144] But Carl Gröpler put in an equally characteristic, and far more ambitious bid. His demand for an annual salary of no less than 4,500 marks, noted the Ministry officials in alarm, 'goes . . . much too far'. Gröpler was told that it was unacceptable. After

[139] StA Bremen 4, 89/1.236: Der Erste Staatsanwalt berichtet über die Hinrichtung des am 23. Januar 1908 durch das Schwurgericht zu Bremen wegen Mordes zum Tode verurteilten Gärtners Pohl aus Doberwitz, 17 July 1908, 9.
[140] GStA Berlin Rep. 84a/4595, Bl. 99–108 (*Neue Berliner Zeitung*, Bl. 151–2).
[141] Ibid. 4593, Bl. 151–2.
[142] BA Koblenz R22/1323, Bl. 94: Vermerk, 28 Apr. 1936; GStA Berlin Rep. 84a/4593, Bl. 122: *Stenographische Berichte über die Verhandlungen des Preussischen Abgeordnetenhauses*, 6 Feb. 1911. For Liebknecht, see Helmut Trotnow, *Karl Liebknecht. Eine politische Biographie* (Cologne, 1980).
[143] GStA Berlin Rep. 84a/4593, Bl. 122: PJM to Oberstaatsanwalt Naumburg, 16 Oct. 1911.
[144] Ibid., Bl. 163 (notes).

some negotiation, a compromise was reached by which each of the two executioners would be paid an annual salary of 3,800 marks, from which they had to
pay their assistants, plus travel expenses to individual executions. This was
enough to secure both men a modest but secure livelihood, at least as much as
that of a skilled manual worker; in addition, however, Schwietz had the income
from his knacker's yard and Gröpler the takings from his laundry. This probably
put them well into the ranks of the *Mittelstand*, that amorphous lower-middle-
class grouping to which people such as shopkeepers, master artisans, white-collar
employees, and small businessmen were thought to belong. In the eyes of the
bureaucrats in the Prussian Ministry of Justice, however, the two executioners,
solid though their economic position might now be, continued to count as less
than respectable citizens. To make their status perfectly clear, the Ministry
reminded them that when they travelled by rail to perform their duties, they
would be expected to sit in a third-class carriage.[145]

The executioners' lack of 'solidity' was evident not least in their propensity to
alcoholism. It is remarkable that time and again through the nineteeth century
executioners turned up to perform their duties in a thoroughly inebriated state.
Lorenz Scheller in Bavaria, Franz Müller in Baden, Julius Krautz, Wilhelm
Reindel, and Alwin Engelhardt in Prussia, all either drank on duty or spent so
much money on alcohol in their leisure time that it got them into serious
financial difficulties and even, in Krautz's case, into trouble with the law. Drunkenness was common enough at all levels of German society in the late nineteenth
and early twentieth centuries, but drunkenness among executioners seems far to
have exceeded the average. It is surely not too fanciful to see this as a consequence
of the psychic and emotional strain which their job imposed on them. Studies of
the psychology of professional military and police torturers in twentieth-century
regimes such as the Colonels' Greece in the 1960s indicate that, in order to
perform their jobs, such men have to undergo a process of brutalization in a
training that is so violent and harsh as to blunt many of the normal human
feelings which they may possess. Even so, interviews with such men have
suggested that they still experienced considerable stress as a result of the tasks
they carried out, and seldom stayed—or were seldom kept—in the job very
long.[146] Executioners in Imperial Germany were largely drawn from a milieu
where they were used to the brutal killing of living things. It was not merely
because of family tradition that they were overwhelmingly drawn from the trades
of butchery and knackery, despite the severing of the feudal ties which had
originally bound these trades to provide execution services for the state. It was

---

[145] GStA Berlin Rep. 84a/4593, Bl. 172 (Vertrag—draft).
[146] Mika Haritos-Fatouros, 'Die Ausbildung des Folterers. Trainingsprogramme der Obristendiktatur
in Griechenland', in Reemtsma (ed.), *Folter*, 73–90.

also because the daily familiarity with blood and guts, death and suffering hardened them to the task of progressing from butchering animals to killing humans, and provided that coolness and 'cold-bloodedness' which judicial bureaucrats found so indispensable. Nevertheless, even with this background, the growing frequency of executions in the 1880s and the sharp increase in their number in the early 1890s clearly imposed a severe degree of stress on many executioners. Their new status as professionals, with a qualifying examination, apprenticeships and training schemes, regular employment, and a salary, had been achieved at a price.

Well before the First World War, Prussian and other executioners had in effect joined the civil service as salaried officials. This was yet another indication that capital punishment was firmly embedded in the institutional framework of politics and law in Wilhelmine Germany. The vagaries of legislative fortune which had overcome the death penalty in the thirty-year period from 1848 to 1878 now belonged indisputably to the past. Capital punishment had finally been rescued in principle, as well as being transformed in practice. Yet in their dealings with the executioners, there was some evidence that Prussian officials were becoming increasingly embarrassed, and that a growing desire for secrecy and discretion was replacing the concern for a continued public involvement which had accompanied the introduction of 'intramural' executions in the 1850s and 1860s. The culture of capital punishment was changing once more, and in the next chapter, we turn to an examination of some of the ways in which its meanings and significances altered between its reintroduction at the end of the 1870s and the outbreak of the First World War.

9

The Culture of Embarrassment

a. The Issue of Entry Cards

As we have seen, on the introduction of 'intramural' executions, every effort was made to avoid the impression of secrecy, from the announcement of the event through the red posters put up in advance in the town where it was scheduled to take place, to the issuing of entry cards to citizens who wished to view the proceedings for themselves. Thus the authorities could continue to regard executions as taking place in public; the difference from the previous practice of holding them in the open air was simply that the public attending them was now carefully controlled and selected. The only change, as the Bavarian Ministry of Justice informed the monarch when considering the change in 1854, was that the new system required executions to be carried out before a 'limited public' in an 'enclosed space'.[1] Theoretically, as the Württemberg authorities reported in 1886, entry cards to executions were only issued to 'such persons as offer an adequate guarantee that they do not intend to abuse the privilege'. Thus they only made 'careful and sparing use' of the right to admit unofficial spectators, restricting it, they said, to people with a legitimate scientific interest in the event, as required by the Reich regulations of 1879.[2] In Prussia, spectators did not have to demonstrate a scientific interest, but the local judicial authorities were enjoined to ensure 'that their motive was not mere curiosity'.[3] It was invariably assumed, as in Württemberg, or made explicit, as in Baden, that only men could be trusted to behave with the necessary dignity and restraint, and so only men were admitted. The purpose of controlling attendance through the issue of cards was meant to ensure that the spectators participated in the execution in the spirit in which it was intended by the authorities. Here too, therefore, the new mode of capital punishment after the failure of the 1848 Revolution

---

[1] HStA Munich MJu 13067: Ringelmann to King, 13 Nov. 1854.

[2] BA Potsdam RJA 5664, Bl. 36: Württ. Staatsminister für auswärtige Angelegenheiten to Reichsjustizamt, 8 Apr. 1886.

[3] HStA Hanover Hann. 173a Nr. 439, Bl. 39: PJM to Oberstaatsanwalt Celle, 18 Feb. 1892.

signified the collaboration of the bourgeoisie in the maintenance of law and order and the strengthening of the legitimacy of the penal system.

A copy-book example of how the system worked was provided in the diary of the governor of the women's prison in Bruchsal on the occasion of the execution of one of his charges in January 1857:

Apart from the civil servants, forensic physicians, and witnesses assembled on the designated tribune, about sixty–seventy people (all men) were present in the courtyard, partly behind barriers, partly behind the windows of the prison corridor. The earnest proceedings were held precisely as prescribed by the law, and took place in such quiet and with such dignity, and at the same time such speed and security, that any comparison with public executions, which more resembled popular festivals and were associated with such noise and such scandals, must fall out much to the advantage of the present mode of execution, so that even those who are opposed to it will surely soon change their minds. The only disturbance was created by the condemned woman herself, who made the most repulsive impression with her continual coarse and bestial bellowing. I had picked up my pocket-watch, and found that the whole proceedings—reading-out of the sentence, prayer with the condemned woman (who continued bawling throughout this as well), the execution itself and the concluding prayer—lasted altogether 8 minutes; the execution lasted $1\frac{3}{4}$ minutes and would perhaps have been over in 1 minute if this person had not repeatedly sat herself down on the ground as she was being led across from the court tribune to the scaffold and obstructed the preparations by waving her arms etc. about. In just such a case as this an execution by the sword could be very unsafe, whereas no amount of resistance can prevent the sure and rapid success of an execution by the present method.[4]

Thus did the authorities and the representative assemblies of the German states congratulate themselves on joining forces to ensure that the beheading of a malefactor was a dignified and worthy event.[5]

In so far as the condemned allowed it, executions in Imperial Germany were still rituals which aimed, as one state prosecutor wrote, to make 'an earnest and ceremonious impression' on those who witnessed them.[6] But in comparison to the elaborate ceremonies of the eighteenth century, they were, as this example shows, simple and straightforward affairs, with a minimum of speechifying and no opportunity for the condemned to play an independent role. Their formulaic brevity may well have offered less comfort to the offender than the spectacular, semi-sacral procedures of an earlier day. For by now the emphasis was above all on speed. Normally the entire proceedings lasted not much more than three or

---

[4] GLA Karlsruhe 234/6609: Auszug aus dem Tagebuch des Hr. Vorstehers Szuhany vom Monat Januar 1857 für die Weiberstrafanstalt Bruchsal.

[5] The execution in Bruchsal in 1857 became the focus of criticism by abolitionists in the 1860s. See ibid.: *Staatsanzeiger für Württemberg*, 54, 5 Mar. 1864.

[6] HStA Hanover Hann. 173a Nr. 441, Bl. 128: Der Erste Staatsanwalt Hildesheim, to Oberstaatsanwalt Celle—Betrifft die Vollstreckung des Todesurteils an dem Kuhwärter Jakob Esser, 3 June 1912.

four minutes from the moment the prisoner entered the courtyard to the moment of execution itself.[7] Only in a few states were there ceremonious variations recalling the days of public punishment. In Baden the rules for execution introduced in 1881 still required the official in charge to read out the Grand Duke's rejection of clemency, and then, picking up 'a black wand, breaks the same in pieces and throws it down before the condemned person's feet with the words: "Your life is over; God have mercy on your soul!" '[8] Similarly, in Bavaria, the state prosecutor in charge of an execution was still obliged to read out a version of the traditional *Urgicht*, a 'short, easily comprehensible history of the condemned person's crimes and the tenor of the court's judgment at the place of execution, in the presence of the person to be executed', a procedure which by this time was felt by some officials at least to constitute an unnecessary 'extension' of the sentence because it prolonged the agony for the victim.[9] Such hangovers from the time of public executions were increasingly found to be irrelevant and distasteful by state prosecutors and others present at executions. In 1875, for instance, it was reported in Munich 'that at the execution this morning of Michael Battistella from Tauria, one of the executioner's servants, instead of taking his severed head out of the guillotine and putting it straight into the waiting coffin, lifted it up and showed it to the people who were present at the execution.' This reversion to the practice prescribed by Bavarian law in the days, now two decades since, when executions had taken place on a scaffold in front of a crowd, met with strong disapproval. It was, said a Ministry of Justice official, noting that this was not provided for in the execution instructions, 'in open contradiction of the spirit of these regulations, which is to divest the act of execution of all unnecessary additions which are inappropriate to the serious nature of the same'.[10]

It was not only incidents such as these, however, which embarrassed the authorities. Soon after the introduction of 'intramural' executions, it became apparent that rather more people were attending them than had originally been envisaged. True, they were all respectable, and there was no suggestion of a wild, superstitious, or unruly crowd in the gatherings that now assembled within prison walls to watch executions in Germany. Even a well-behaved and carefully vetted crowd of responsible men, however, appeared before long to pose difficult-

---

[7] The procedure was similar in all the German states after 1879. See e.g. the procedure followed in Württemberg, ibid.: *Regierungs-Blatt für das Königreich Württemberg*, Stuttgart, 7 (16 Mar. 1880), 79–83, and more generally the *Reichsstrafprozessordnung* (1879) § 486, Abs. 17.

[8] GStA Berlin Rep. 84a/7784, Bl. 53: *Gesetzes- und Verordnungs-Blatt für das Grossherzogthum Baden*, 14 Feb. 1881, § 9.

[9] HStA Munich MJu 13067: Erster Staatsanwalt Munich to Oberstaatsanwalt Appellationsgericht Munich, 6 Feb. 1876.

[10] Ibid.: Justice Ministry to Direktorium, Königliches Landgericht Munich, 20 Dec. 1875.

ies. For even if they remained silent and respectful, as they invariably did, how could one tell what was going on in their minds? How could one be sure that they had the right motives for attending an execution? It was all the more difficult to be certain of this point because in many small and medium-sized towns so many people attended that practically the whole adult male population of the local governing class seemed to be there. In 1856 the state prosecutor in the university and garrison town of Freiburg reported that in following the instruction in the Baden execution regulations that entry cards were to be issued to 'as many other persons as the space can comfortably hold', he had granted no fewer than 380 requests for entry cards to an execution held on 25 April. The prison yard, indeed, he noted, could probably hold up to 600. 'The public', he told the Justice Ministry, 'consisted mostly of younger persons, mainly students and soldiers, and behaved very decently.' Nevertheless, 380 was held to be excessive. As a result, future executions were held in a much smaller courtyard within the prison, thus restricting the number of spectators.[11] In the same year the Prussian Ministry of Justice had discovered that some 200 people had been present at an execution in the Moabit prison in Berlin. The courts defended this on the grounds that they were all lawyers and medical men, and thus had a legitimate psychological interest in studying the final moments of a cold-blooded killer, and nothing more was done.[12] Whether anybody really believed this claim was quite a different matter. Even after they were resumed towards the end of the 1870s, executions continued to be attended by larger numbers of spectators than originally envisaged. As Franz von Holtzendorff recalled in 1875: 'I have known men from the best social classes who were very keen to apply for admission to intramural executions, although they did not intend to make any scientific study of them, and who were not accustomed to miss any execution that took place.'[13] In 1877 the state prosecutor in Munich complained to the Bavarian Ministry of Justice: 'As soon as the news spreads among the public that an execution is to take place, the official in charge is overrun in his office and even in his private home with men of all classes asking for entry cards to the prison so that they can attend the execution.' At the last execution in the city, when two offenders had been beheaded in a single session, the number of applications for entry cards had been particularly large. Forty-five had been issued, mostly, it was claimed once more, to doctors and lawyers.[14]

[11] GLA Karlsruhe 234/6609: Staatsanwalt am Grossherzoglich Badischen Hofgericht des Ober-Rhein-Kreises an das Grossherzogliche Justiz-Ministerium, 28 Apr. 1856, 5; and further report, 17 May 1856. For the regulations, see ibid.: *Grossherzoglich Badisches Regiergungs-Blatt*, 15 Apr. 1856, 85, Abs. 9.

[12] GStA Berlin Rep. 84a/7783, Bl. 66: PJM to Kammergericht, 29 May 1856; Kammergericht to PJM, 14 June 1856.

[13] Holtzendorff, *Verbrechen*, 117.

[14] HStA Munich MJu 13067: Erster Staatsanwalt Munich to Justizministerium, 23 Jan. 1877.

It was far from unusual for much larger numbers of entry cards to be issued.[15] Those who obtained them were, like the twelve witnesses required by law, male representatives of the local notability, the professional middle class, and state servants of one kind and another. A typical list of the twelve required witnesses, drawn up in Lübeck in 1913, showed the group to consist of three doctors, two lawyers, an apothecary, a headmaster, three businessmen, and two master artisans.[16] The numbers of additional people of this kind attending as observers, armed with entry cards, was far larger. On 4 June 1898, for instance, some 82 card-holding observers attended an execution in Munich, including 15 law students, 12 doctors or medical students, 10 reporters, 8 clerks, 7 legal officials (apart from those whose presence was already required by law), 6 merchants, 3 army officers, 3 officials from the government finance office, 3 members of the Bavarian Chamber of Deputies, 2 policemen, 2 railway officials, an art painter, a literary historian, an apothecary, a newspaper owner, a printer, a baker, a hotelier, a basketmaker, and a parquet flooring manufacturer. Reporting on the event, an official in the Bavarian Ministry of Justice wondered sarcastically whether all of these people could really be said to have possessed the 'scientific interest' that the law required.[17]

At an execution held the same year in Bayreuth, a small town where the influence of local notables could more easily be brought to bear than in the Bavarian capital, no fewer than 177 people were discovered to have obtained entry permits. They included 35 army officers and NCOs, 30 civil servants, 10 doctors and male nurses, 15 lawyers, 5 newspaper editors, a teacher, a judge, and a secretary. The number of official observers was 21 instead of the usual 12, and the crowd was completed by a substantial contingent of no fewer than 61 artisans, manufacturers, and businessmen of various sorts (*Gewerbetreibende*). The difference between such an event and the public executions of previous centuries was beginning to be hard to define, except that women and children were no longer present. At one execution, in Essen, in the 1880s, it was noted that 'the place of execution was thickly packed with people'.[18] People were now beginning to travel to see executions again, so long as they could get influential friends in the locality to obtain entry cards for them: those present at the execution in Bayreuth in 1898 included, for instance, two gentlemen of private means, one of whom was not from Bayreuth at all, but had journeyed to the execution from Coburg.[19] And local notables seem to have expected to have been issued with cards as an automatic right. In May 1886, a local newspaper in Magdeburg reported that

[15] For similar arrangements at 'intramural' executions in the USA, see Masur, *Rites*, 111–14.
[16] StA Lübeck Rep. 49/1, 45: Erster Staatsanwalt beim Landgericht Lübeck, notes of 7 May 1913.
[17] HStA Munich MJu 13144, no. 16/07 (13 June 1898).   [18] Schmidt, *Krautz*, 35.
[19] HStA Munich MJu 13144, no. 16/07 (13 June 1898).

although an execution had recently taken place in the town, 'to the great distress of every good Magdeburger the number of entry cards issued was very limited. For this reason many people take the view today that executions should be carried out in public, for anyone who pays his taxes and dues regularly has the right to witness them.'[20] 'Very limited' probably meant a figure fairly close to that mentioned in a report of an execution in Graudenz the same year, when 'perhaps forty–fifty people were admitted, all belonging to the educated classes'.[21]

The practice attracted increasing criticism. In 1895 a leading opponent of the death penalty, the pacifist Alfred Fried, complained that sixty entry cards had been issued for an execution held on 16 October that year. 'Various gentlemen, among them many officers, drive to the rare spectacle in their elegant carriages in the early morning. Are these sixty or so persons of standing', he asked sarcastically, 'supposed to form the public that is to be deterred?'[22] The chorus of disapproval reached a height in 1908 over the case of Grete Beier, daughter of the mayor of a small town in Saxony, condemned to death for murdering her fiancé. Because she was young, female, and middle-class, liberal and even conservative opinion recoiled at the idea of execution. Yet not only was the sentence confirmed, despite a public campaign in favour of clemency, but over 1,500 people applied for entry cards to her execution. Despite the fact that the vast majority of them could have had no conceivable 'scientific' interest in the event, the Saxon authorities issued cards to more than two hundred spectators. 'Where so many *aficionados* can be found for such a spectacle', commented the liberal *Berliner Tageblatt*, 'it is clear that the rule of the late-born representatives of the Middle Ages still isn't firm enough!'[23] The newspaper condemned both the 1,500 applicants, and the 200 who had obtained entry, in the strongest possible terms. The thousands who gathered outside the prison in Freiberg on the morning of the execution, on 27 July 1908, were said to have been present mainly as a protest; but they added in effect to the public nature of the event. Even the Conservative Party in Saxony criticized the 'spectacle'. Nevertheless, there is no evidence that the scandal stopped the practice of issuing entry cards, and certainly nobody took any initiative to revise the rules for executions on this point. This execution in 1908 was far from being the last occasion on which the attendance of hundreds of card-holders at an execution was recorded in Germany.[24]

---

[20] GStA Berlin Rep. 84a/7790, Bl. 23: *Gerichts-Zeitung für Magdeburg und die Provinz Sachsen*, 23 May 1886. There was no hint of irony in the report.

[21] Ibid., Bl. 31: Bericht des Oberstaatsanwalts zu Graudenz, 9 Aug. 1886. See also ibid., Bl. 54: *Oberschlesische Grenz-Zeitung* (Beuthen), 15/25 (1 Feb. 1887), for another example; and ibid. 9269, Bl. 63: 'Beschränkung der Ausgabe von Einzelheiten behufs Beiwohnung des Hinrichtungsaktes', 25 Apr. 1891.

[22] Ibid. 7783, Bl. 165: Alfred Fried, 'Hinrichtungen in Preussen', *Ethische Kultur*, 3/45 (9 Nov. 1895), 355.

[23] Ibid. 7787, Bl. 277: *Berliner Tageblatt*, 27 July 1908.

[24] Ibid., Bl. 275: *Die Welt am Montag*, 27 July 1908; Bl. 276: *Kreuzzeitung*, 27 July 1908. For further examples, see below, Ch. 13.

The popularity of these events even after they began to be held behind prison walls, and the continued demand for entry cards on the part of the educated and better-off sectors of the community, suggests that it would be wrong to imagine that the abolition of executions 'in the open', before an unrestricted crowd, reflected any long-term process of 'conscience formation', mutual identification, and reluctance to inflict suffering on fellow humans. Still less did it suggest that such attitudes originated with the élites. Liberal opinion in 1848 and again in 1870, as we have seen, was overwhelmingly opposed to the continuation of capital punishment in any form. But liberal views were never universally held among the notables of Germany's cities and small towns, and after the resumption of executions at the end of the 1870s, as we have seen, bourgeois opinion began to shift in favour of capital punishment once more. The high level of demand for entry cards in the 1880s and through the 1900s may well, at least in part, have reflected this shift in opinion. Support for capital punishment seems to have gone together with a willingness, even a desire, to see it inflicted. But this was not, as some hostile commentators claimed, a residue of medieval blood-lust. What the bourgeois spectators wanted to see was a quick, clean death, not a messy, bloody spectacle. In witnessing the event, they invariably maintained a dignified silence, as all reports agree. It is perfectly possible that a good number of them may have closed their eyes as the blade fell, though the prevalence of militaristic values in Germany in this period must surely also have convinced many of them that watching a killing with an unflinching eye was a test of manliness and strength of character. Whatever their motives, however, and whatever the emotions they experienced, bourgeois men continued to bombard prison authorities with requests for entry cards to executions as long as the custom continued. There was no widespread desire to have the execution of malefactors take place either out of sight or out of mind. It was only in the last decade before the First World War that the breakdown of the local hegemony of old-style 'notables' made it possible for a new culture of capital punishment, with the accent on anonymity and privacy, to emerge, and for the attendance of substantial crowds at German executions to become the focus of increasing criticism. Even then, however, there was little evidence that élite opinion at large considered the idea of execution too horrible for contemplation.

b. *The Printed Public Sphere 1880–1914*

Towards the end of the nineteenth century, the decline of censorship, improvements in educational standards, technological developments in printing, and the emergence of a fast distribution network through the penetration of the railway into the most distant corners of the land, combined to give rise to a new phenomenon in Germany: the popular press. The daily and weekly papers that began to appear in ever-increasing numbers in the 1880s and 1890s sought to attract readers by providing graphic accounts of sensational events, among which, not surprisingly, murder trials and executions were very prominent. By the mid-1880s no execution could be held without elaborate and circumstantial reports appearing immediately afterwards in the local dailies. The form in which such accounts was cast was designed by reporters and editors to appeal not least to traditional expectations of the dramaturgy of executions. Thus they customarily began by describing the condemned person's last meal. By using the term 'hangman's meal' to describe this repast, the press deliberately recalled the grand Hangman's Feasts of the eighteenth century and before. A substitute for the public's traditional right to visit the condemned person's cell was provided by detailed descriptions of the offender's reactions on being told of the denial of the royal prerogative of mercy. Press reporters discussed the feelings of guilt or remorse shown—or not shown—by the offender in question, and gave an hour-by-hour account of the condemned person's last night of sleep. Press accounts of Grete Beier's last night in 1908 included a minute description of her clothing and a long narrative of the last visit paid to her by her mother.[25] The reader was led to feel that the reporter was there in the cell, the whole time, with the prisoner. These stories—probably based on confidential and unattributable interviews with warders—culminated in a narrative of the arrival of the executioner with his assistants and the tools of his trade, and a minutely detailed description of the execution itself, with each action timed to the second. Often, such accounts took up the whole of a 'special issue' of the paper.[26]

This kind of publicity caused a good deal of concern to the authorities, who tried to track down the source of such reports, but without success.[27] They went to some lengths to ensure 'appropriate' reporting of these events. In 1886 fears were expressed in the Saxon legislature that 'such glorification could inspire further crimes'—an echo of the old anxiety, expressed in the Prussian General Law Code of 1794, that the public attention paid to a criminal during an execution might lead to people committing murder with the sole purpose of sharing in a moment of such glory themselves. The 'more decent sections of the press' could still legitimately be admitted to executions, decided the legislature, provided they guaranteed that reporting 'would only be carried out with the

---

[25] GStA Berlin Rep. 84a/7787, Bl. 275: *Die Welt am Montag*, 27 July 1908; Bl. 276: *Kreuzzeitung*, 27 July 1908, recognizing no contradiction with their disapproval of the demand for entry cards.

[26] Ibid. 7790, Bl. 20, 22, 34, 54, 65 for examples of such reports; see also HStA Hanover Hann. 173a Nr. 438, Bl. 112: *Extra-Blatt der Göttinger Zeitung*, 23 Mar. 1889, 'Die Hinrichtung des Raubmörders Haase aus Einbeck (Original-Bericht der "Göttinger Zeitung")'. For parallels in the USA, see Masur, *Rites*, 114–15.

[27] HStA Hanover Hann. 173a Nr. 438, Bl. 231: Staatsanwaltschaft Hannover, Bericht zur Strafsache wider den Arbeiter Hermann Rensch aus Grünthal.

required seriousness'. But in general, no one except the officials and others required by law was to be present. Reporting this debate to his masters in Berlin, the Prussian ambassador in Dresden conceded that such stories in the Saxon press 'have in general become briefer and more factual, and no longer exclusively serve the mania for scandal and as advertisements for the underworld'.[28] Nevertheless, the Saxon authorities agreed

that it is an abuse of the press if the papers exploit the execution of a death sentence in sensational reports, treat the events of such an execution like a topic for entertaining reading, thereby blunt the feeling of revulsion at the crime which the malefactor has committed, and through their depictions cloak the person of the condemned in a nimbus which can exercise a misguiding influence.[29]

This was a familiar litany from the days of public executions. It indicated how far press reporting had gone in providing a substitute kind of publicity, and how little, therefore, the changes of the 1850s had done to solve the dissatisfaction which officials had expressed about the effects of capital punishment expressed in the earlier decades of the century.

These complaints were taken up in 1886 by none other than Reich Chancellor Bismarck himself. Having engineered the reintroduction of executions in Prussia eight years previously, he now believed that their purpose was being frustrated by sensational reporting in the press.[30] 'The depiction of the criminal's last moments', he complained on 19 March 1886, 'has degenerated into a glorification of the same.' It was all very well to say that reporters would only be admitted if they promised not to sensationalize the event, he added in a further note on 13 April; but: 'A journalist will take a different view of what is sensational from that of a state prosecutor, if only in the interests of his trade.'[31] Majority opinion in the federated states was against the Chancellor. Judicial officials in the Baden Ministry of Justice reported that the press had behaved responsibly on the two occasions when executions had taken place in recent years, and that 'after the execution had been carried out, there were none of the descriptive reports which are usually printed and are so fatal and so unfruitful for the education of the public'.[32] The Bavarian authorities remarked that, if reporters were excluded from executions altogether, then things would only get worse:

[28] BA Potsdam RJA 5664, Bl. 8: Königl. Gesandtschaft in Dresden to Bismarck, 11 Feb. 1886.

[29] Ibid., Bl. 34: Sächs. Ministerium für auswärtige Angelegenheiten to Bismarck, 24 Apr. 1886.

[30] See Bismarck's marginalia to GStA Berlin Rep. 84a/7784, Bl. 8–9: Königliche Gesandtschaft in Dresden to Bismarck, 11 Feb. 1886.

[31] Ibid., Bl. 84: Bismarck to PJM, 19 Mar. 1886; ibid., Bl. 100: Votum des Ministeriums für Auswärtige Angelegenheiten, 13 Apr. 1886. Copies of the memorandum of 19 Mar. were sent to the federated state governments (see e.g. GLA Karlsruhe 234/6609 and StA Lübeck Rep. 49/1, 45: Auszug aus dem Senats-Protokoll, 24 Mar. 1886).

[32] GLA Karlsruhe 234/6609: Erste Staatsanwalt Offenburg to Badisches Justizministerium, 1 Apr. 1886, and Staatsanwalt am Landgericht Karlsruhe to Badisches Justizministerium, 3 Apr. 1886.

The press will make an effort to satisfy the interest aroused in the public by the nature of the event, and instead of the reports which up to now have derived from personal observation, we will get descriptions grounded on hearsay, provided—as can never be fully prevented—by third parties, which now as before will pander to the public's need for sensation, and be further removed from the real course of events than ever.[33]

Moreover, the Prussian Ministry of Justice added, press reports of executions continued to play an important part in the administration of justice. As it declared on 5 April 1886:

After no executions had taken place in our state for over a decade, and the idea had taken root in many parts of the public, and particularly in the underworld, that no death sentences would ever be carried out in Prussia again, it was necessary for the general consciousness of right and wrong, as well as for the defence of the law in the country, that the certainty was restored to the people that the legally valid death penalty would not merely be pronounced by the courts but would also actually be carried out. We have not least the press's reporting of executions to thank for the fact that the conviction that this is now happening has been so widespread.[34]

The Prussian cabinet, meeting on 10 November 1886 in Bismarck's absence, agreed with the Prussian Justice Ministry. The Minister himself reported that the press had in general covered executions in a responsible manner, and Bismarck was informed on 28 November 1886, not entirely truthfully, that his wishes in the matter had been met.[35]

So reporters continued to be invited to attend executions, though state prosecutors were now instructed to be more circumspect than before in whom exactly to admit.[36] The press did not take kindly to these measures, despite the fact that they did not go nearly so far as originally proposed, or as Bismarck had wanted. On 1 February 1887, for example, the local newspaper in Upper Silesia, the *Oberschlesische Grenzzeitung*, complained that, although the police in Beuthen had sent invitations to a number of citizens to attend an execution in the town, 'curiously, no invitations were sent to the editor of the *Oberschl. Grenz- Zeitung*—and as we have learned—none was sent to the editors of other papers here either. The reason for this measure', complained the paper huffily, 'is not known to us.'[37] Similarly, at an execution in Dresden on 25 May 1887, there was 'no representative of the press, which has never happened before'.[38] Censorship

[33] GStA Berlin Rep. 84a/7784, Bl. 100: Staatsministerium der Königlichen Hauses und des Äussern, Bavaria, to Bismarck, 17 Apr. 1886.

[34] Ibid., Bl. 95: Votum des Justizministeriums, 5 Apr. 1886.

[35] BA Potsdam Auswärtiges Amt III a Nr. 51, Bd. 3, Bl. 9: Abschrift Staatsministerium 10 Aug., and Reichsjustizamt to Bismarck, 26 Nov. 1886 (Bl. 11).

[36] GStA Berlin Rep. 84a/7784, Bl. 10a: Staatsministerium, Sitzung am 10 Nov. 1886. This measure was strengthened in the 1890s. See ibid. 8313, Bl. 40a, 127 and ibid. 7782, Bl. 219.

[37] Ibid. 7790, Bl. 54: *Oberschlesische Grenzzeitung*, xv. Jahrgang, Nr. 25, 1 Feb 1887.

[38] BA Potsdam Auswärtiges. Amt IIIa Nr. 51, Bd. 3: *Neue Freie Presse*, 27 May 1887 (Bl. 14).

was now being found necessary in the continuing battle to impose the official understanding of capital punishment on a recalcitrant public. In 1847, Savigny and von Uhden had expressed the hope 'that the effect on people's emotions will be purer and none the weaker if they do not observe them in person but are left to imagine the act'.[39] Just short of forty years on, the prospect of leaving events to the imagination was filling the authorities with acute alarm.

Thus Bismarck's wish for 'responsible' reporting, despite his intervention of 1886, was seldom fulfilled. The press went on reporting executions the way they wanted to. In 1900, for example, the *Kölner Tageblatt* reported that the murderer Paul Wiegand, condemned to be executed on 18 August, received the news of the monarch's confirmation of his sentence 'with total calmness'. He promised the priests 'to remain strong to the last breath, on the last walk as well'. 'Completely resigned to his fate', the report went on, Wiegand 'refused the usual last meal, but ate some grapes and pears which the priest gave him, smoked five cigars and drank a cup of tea and a cup of milk'. His last night was spent talking quietly with his warders and with the priest. In the morning, the warders pulled back his shirt to expose his neck, and the senior state prosecutor and the prison director arrived to take him to the prison yard, where executioner Reindel had already been testing out the guillotine.

The prison clock showed precisely 6 a.m. as the poor sinner's bell began to toll and Wiegand appeared, led out by the prison padre, who was fully robed, and the other gentlemen. Wiegand looked very pale, and as he came out of the building, he threw a long glance at the scaffold and then walked with a firm step to the little table, which was covered in black cloth, and on which was placed a crucifix, with one lighted candle on either side of it. Behind the table stood the state prosecutor and two gentlemen from the court; the state prosecutor, Herr Viebig, read out the sentence of the Royal Jury Court to the malefactor, who was carrying a small crucifix in his hand, and then the imperial confirmation. As he showed him His Majesty's signature, Wiegand responded with a short nod of his head; and when he was asked if he had anything to say, Wiegand remained silent.

Each tiny move in the spectacle was carefully narrated, from Wiegand's return of the crucifix to the priest, to the last preparations undertaken by executioner Reindel's assistants before the blade fell. The papers concentrated above all on the offender's behaviour in the face of imminent death. The condemned man remained the protagonist throughout; and the repeated descriptions of his outward appearance during the ritual echoed in print the preoccupation of the spectators at similar ceremonies which had been enacted in the open a century and more before.[40] Clearly, therefore, Bismarck's efforts a few decades earlier to keep sensationalism out of press reports such as these had not succeeded.

---

[39] GStA Berlin Rep. 84a/7782, Bl. 219.
[40] HStA Düsseldorf Rep. 145/327, Bl. 23: *Kölner Tageblatt*, 18 Aug. 1900.

Thus official complaints about press reporting of executions continued unabated. From 1889 at the latest, until the First World War, the standard letter issued by the Prussian Minister of Justice to local authorities when an execution was about to take place included the following warning:

The fact that reports of executions have repeatedly been published in the press in a manner and of a kind that make it clear that they are mainly designed to satisfy the public's desire for sensation, prompts me to accompany my instructions with the following remarks: The publications which I have just described run counter to the general trend of the legal regulations on the execution of death sentences and give rise to the danger that—quite apart from the reports not corresponding to the facts—the earnest nature of the matter will be compromised according to the way the report is coloured, indeed, that the description of the criminal's last moments might even possibly degenerate into a glorification of the same.[41]

Instead of the 'mob' indulging in 'outbreaks of emotion', as the authorities had complained in 1800, the 'public' was now expressing 'a need for sensation'; but the result in the eyes of the authorities was the same: a concentration on the last minutes of the offender, resulting in sympathy, or even admiration, instead of a concentration on the majesty of the law, resulting in deterrence or revulsion. What had happened was a transformation of the public nature of executions rather than their complete removal to the private sphere. As a French commission on capital punishment noted in 1907: 'In our time, the public nature of an act consists not in its taking place in front of a number of spectators, but in its divulgence by the press.'[42]

A press report of the execution of the miner Peter Nowak in 1914 showed that little had changed in this situation by the time the First World War began: 'When executioner Göbel arrived in Duisburg from Magdeburg with his two assistants on Thursday afternoon, the hour was nigh in which Nowak had to be told the last, the most terrible news.' By emphasizing 'the last, the most terrible news', the newspaper sought to draw in the readers to share empathetically in the condemned man's death as means of imaginatively rehearsing their own, however different it might eventually be. After describing in colourful detail the appearance of the prison at night, a solitary lighted window breaking the gloom indicating where the condemned man was spending the night, the report continued:

[41] HStA Hanover Hann. 173a Nr. 438, Bl. 72–3: PJM to Oberstaatsanwalt Celle, 13 Mar. 1889. For subsequent repetitions of this warning, see e.g. HStA Düsseldorf Rep. 145/327, Bl. 211–12: PJM to Oberstaatsanwalt Cologne, 14 Apr. 1906; and ibid., Rep. 145/328, Bl. 84: PJM to Oberstaatsanwalt Cologne, 3 May 1910.

[42] BA Potsdam Auswärtiges Amt IIIa Nr. 51, Bd. 8, Bl. 73–4: *Chambres des Députés, No. 1260: Neuvième Législature. Session Extraordinaire de 1907. Annexe au procès-verbal de la séance du 22 octobre 1907. Repport au nom de la commission de la réforme judiciaire et de la législation civile et criminelle chargée d'examiner le projet de loi et les propositions de loi relatifs à la peine de mort.*

The most dreadful thing which a death sentence brings for the condemned man is this last night, the certainty of a death whose time has been set to the minute. No pen will ever be able to describe what takes place in the soul of a criminal in such hours as these, for those who are compelled to live through them will soon be silent for ever. One thing is certain, however, and that is that these last hours are harder and crueller than the bloody execution itself. Nowak bore his last night quietly and resignedly, in contrast to his previous state, remained calm and willingly accepted the priest's ministrations.[43]

A curious error in the report suggested how, in approaching the subject in this way, the press not only represented the process of public executions but reflected popular memory of them as well; for the executioner's name was in fact not *Göbel* but *Gröpler*; the Göppel family had provided north-west Germany with executioners for centuries, but they had ceased their activities many decades before this report was penned.[44] Here indeed was a newspaper story that, however many interviews with warders it might have drawn upon, clearly represented the kind of conjecture that had so worried officials in 1886. Not only the Prussian bureaucrats but even the Social Democrats were worried by the tendency of the 'yellow press', when 'an execution has taken place, to publish long *biographies* and similar things, so that such a criminal is held up to many people as a kind of hero'. As a deputy in the Prussian Chamber of Deputies uttered this complaint on 6 February 1909, there was, as the stenographic report noted, a 'shout from the Social Democrats: quite right!'[45]

The authorities and the Social Democrats were worried about these developments for very different reasons. For the government and the ruling groups in German society, the threat of riot and public disorder, which had been so important in prompting the establishment of 'intramural' executions in the middle of the nineteenth century, had largely been replaced by the danger of organized subversion by the Social Democratic Party. What caused the working class to flock to the socialists' banner, it was widely believed in the Establishment, was not poverty and the denial of basic civil rights, but immorality and irreligion. The redistributive ideology of the organized labour movement was regarded by the law enforcement agencies and the ruling bureaucracy as little more than a justification for theft, born of envy. It was in practice, therefore, virtually indistinguishable from criminality. Anything that caused an unwholesome fascination with crime and criminals, still more, anything that caused people to admire or sympathize with serious offenders such as murderers, would drive people into the arms of the Social Democrats. Thus 'irresponsible' and 'sensational' reporting of murders and executions would alienate readers from the existing social and

[43] *General-Anzeiger für Oberhausen*, 20 Mar. 1914.

[44] See Wilbertz, *Scharfrichter*, for details of the Göppel family.

[45] GStA Berlin Rep. 84a/7784, Bl. 299: *Stenographische Berichte über die Verhandlungen des Preussischen Abgeordnetenhauses*, 24. Sitzung, 6 Feb. 1909, col. 1738–9, Abg. Strasser (Breslau).

political order and destabilize state and society as a result. For their part, the Social Democrats also distanced themselves from crime, disorder, and violent revolution. With a membership largely drawn from the organized, skilled, and stable parts of the working class, with a sizeable contingent of the petty bourgeoisie as well, they were very concerned to draw a clear line between their own movement and the criminal and marginal elements in the population, whom they disqualified as a *Lumpenproletariat*. Crime, they argued, was the product of poverty, exploitation, and social inequality; but this did not mean that they justified it. On the contrary, the Social Democrats were proud of their moralizing and educative functions, and sought to extend them as far across society as they could. It was for this reason that they too were hostile to the advent of the depoliticized, commercial 'yellow press' and condemned the sensational reporting of executions as morally and socially subversive.[46]

While Bismarck was trying to get the press under control, a much older form of publicity was continuing, apparently unnoticed in the educated and cultured circles of governments and parliamentary assemblies. Street ballads had continued to be published throughout the nineteenth century,[47] but they had become more commercialized by Bismarck's time. Small printers had gone to the wall and the firm of Reiche, based in Berlin, built up what eventually became a monopoly position in their production. As educational standards improved and with them the circulation of the regular press, street ballads became more and more sensational in the effort to retain their readership. Fictional accounts of executions increasingly replaced more or less factual ones. Even so, the balladeers could not ignore the opportunities provided by resumption of executions in the 1880s. So sensational had their mode of expression become by this time that they ignored all the attempts to conceal executions from the public eye that had taken place since the middle of the century and imagined them still taking place in public. One street ballad, published in 1882, for instance, described a murderer's victims crying:

> The gallows call, away, away!—
> What holds back now the murd'rer's feet?
> We light death's candle here today
> And Hell's prepared for you to meet!
> So bow ye down, and fear no hurt,

[46] For these arguments, see Evans, *Rethinking*, ch. 8 ('"Red Wednesday" in Hamburg: Social Democrats, Police and *Lumpenproletariat* in the Suffrage Disturbances of 17 January 1906', 248–90); idem, *Death in Hamburg: Society and Politics in the Cholera Years 1830–1910* (Oxford, 1987), 550–6; and Eric A. Johnson, *Urbanization and Crime: Germany 1871–1914* (New York, 1995), 75–8.

[47] See e.g. 'Hinrichtung des Raub- und Doppelmörders Wilhelm Timm, mit der Guillotine, am 10. April 1856, morgens 6 Uhr', in Hans Adolf Neunzig (ed.), *Das illustrierte Moritaten-Lesebuch* (Munich, 1973), 37–41. Such collections contain many more examples from this period.

> The axe doth flash to fright the crowds,
> A stroke, a blow, the blood doth spurt,
> We are avenged!—Hurrah for Krautz!

Breathing heavily a spirit of revenge, the ballad consigned the murderer without ceremony to the pains of eternal damnation; not, to be sure, in any religious sense, but simply in an outburst of bloodthirstiness that imitated in words what the murderer had already accomplished in deeds.[48] By this time, too, short stories and prose accounts of executions, hawked in the streets by colporteurs, were also widespread. A typical example was *A Fourfold Execution, or: The Expiation of a Marital Murder*, published by Reiche in 1898. As the title suggested, the pamphlet's selling-point was not the crime, but the execution; the life and misdeeds of the four executed offenders, who included a woman, were merely told as a preliminary ('Before we describe the details of the executions, it is necessary to set the context'). The description of the executions took up four of the pamphlet's eight pages and went into minute detail, recounting every word, and every move of the participants.[49] A similar pamphlet, published by Reiche four years later, covered *A Double Execution at Hirschberg in Silesia* without even troubling to mention the crime on the cover-page.[50] The writers narrrated the last hours of the condemned, described their appearance as they entered the prison yard ('Maatz, who had not slept the whole night, looked very wan'), named the executioner, and ended with a formulaic account of the execution ('a dull blow, and the head rolled in the sand').[51] These productions were written without literary flourishes, they were simple in style, and they obviously catered for a popular readership equipped with only the most basic level of literacy; they eschewed character analysis and psychologizing; and to placate the censor, they always included a justification of the death penalty as a 'just expiation'. As the literary historian Rudolf Schenda has remarked: 'These reports are not principally concerned to provide a deterrent warning, they are much more interested in the creation of suspense through the extreme situation of the malefactor.'[52] Once more, the reader was invited to identify with the criminal rather than with the state or the law, not as popular hero or repentant sinner, but as victim, a symbolic representation of the situation of so many working-class people in an age when the

---

[48] *Zwei neue Mordthaten aus der Gegend von Bochum, verübt I. am 10. April dieses Jahres an der 16jährigen Dienstmagd Ostermann aus Hiltrop, II. am 21. Mai dieses Jahres an der Dienstmagd Gantenberg aus Dahlhausen* (Hanover, 1882), repr. in Braungart (ed.), *Bänkelsang*, 226–34.

[49] *Eine vierfache Hinrichtung, oder: Die Sühne des Gattenmordes* (Schwiebus: Druck und Verlag von Hermann Reiche, 1898; DVA Freiburg, Bl. 9443).

[50] *Eine Doppel-Hinrichtung zu Hirschberg in Schlesien zum 17. Februar v. Js.* (Schwiebus: Druck und Verlag von Hermann Reiche, 1904; DVA Freiburg, Bl. 9465).

[51] *Der Doppelmord von Langwasser vor dem Schwurgericht* (Schwiebus: Druck und Verlag von Hermann Reiche, n.d.; DVA Freiburg, Bl. 9496).

[52] Schenda, *Volk*, 365.

Ausführliche

Beschreibung der Verbrechen

des Räuberhauptmanns

Hermann Rohland

und seiner Bande.

Nebst einem dazu verfaßten schönen Liede.

1851.

FIG. 22. *Popular literature and executions.* Title-page of a chapbook, 'Extensive description of the crimes of the bandit-chief Hermann Rohland and his gang, along with a pretty song written about it', 1851. Despite the title's concentration on Rohland's crimes, the illustration only depicts his execution, reflecting the real emphasis of many of these accounts. The executioner's assistant is displaying the head of one of Rohland's accomplices to the crowd (a Bavarian custom formally abolished early in the nineteenth century). The event takes place on an old-fashioned ravenstone. On the right, a depiction of breaking with the wheel. Note the women in the crowd, and the presence of a priest on the scaffold, next to the cloaked executioner. In almost all these respects, the picture deliberately refers back to a number of practices that were long obsolete by the time it was published.

punitive and controlling influence of the state was making itself felt in their lives in a myriad new ways.

Although the authorities tried from time to time to ban such productions, they had little success in controlling either their printing or their distribution.[53] The vast majority of so-called trashy literature (*Schund- und Schmutzliteratur*) of the era was indeed devoted not to sex, but to crime, to robbers and bandits, infanticides, murderers, poisoners, and the like. At the turn of the century, an order was issued by the judicial authorities in Berlin: 'The printing and sale of biographies of the malefactor, of songs and other broadsheets with reference to forthcoming executions must not be permitted, and authors, printers, and distributors who contravene this regulation must be punished by the police.'[54] By leaving it up to the local police to prosecute such publications, at a time when they were being produced by no more than a couple of printers and sold all over the country, the authorities virtually ensured that nothing effective would be done. Moreover, there were now numerous other opportunities for popular involvement with the fate of condemned murderers. The introduction in Prussia in 1851, and generally in Germany in 1879, of trial in open court meant that the public galleries were now filled with eager spectators at major criminal trials. An account of a murder trial, held in Danzig in 1870, described how the 'spectators, who belonged exclusively to the better class of society' had created such a 'crush' that 'not only was the public gallery filled to the brim, but the stairway and corridor were crowded with people and a part of the public stayed on the street outside to hear the verdict'.[55] At a murder trial in Bremen in 1883, it was reported:

Towards 9 o'clock in the morning, before the proceedings began, the detention house and the old exchange were already positively besieged by people, and when the accused was led in a hansom cab into the court-house towards 10 o'clock, the cab could hardly get through the gate of the old exchange by the churchyard. The mob shouted and made a great noise, and tried to stop the cab, and indeed isolated criminal demands could be heard.[56]

Press reporting of trials soon became a regular feature in daily newspapers. Illustrated magazines like *Die Gartenlaube* began to carry crime stories, both true and fictional. The detective novel began to enter German literary culture,

[53] HStA Hanover Hann. 173a Nr. 438, Bl. 101, for comments of the state prosecutor in Göttingen on an execution pamphlet he found for sale on the market-place in 1889.

[54] HStA Düsseldorf Rep. 145/324, Bl. 49: Zusammenstellung der bei Vollstreckung von Todesurtheilen im Bezirk des Königlichen Kammergerichts zu Berlin zu beobachtenden Vorschriften, § 539.

[55] K. Engler, *Der Giftmord-Prozess wider die Frau Hofbesitzer Rosalie Schindler geb. Senkspiel zu Heubude bei Danzig wegen vorsätzlicher und überlegter Tödtung ihres Stiefsohnes George Schindler* (Danzig, 1870), 75–6.

[56] StA Bremen 2.-D. 17. c. 1. Bd. 7: *Bremer Nachrichten*, 9 Feb. 1883.

spurred on by the gradual downgrading of the confession in German criminal law and procedure, as the search for clues to the murderer began to gain an importance as great as that of the drive to achieve an admission of guilt.[57] In real life, this development was paralleled from the 1860s onwards by the emergence of something like a modern, specialized criminal police, and the detective gradually replaced the investigating judge as the central figure in the solution of major crimes. By the turn of the century, modern methods of forensic science, police medicine, fingerprinting, and detection had joined more traditional weapons such as the police circular or *Steckbrief* and the 'wanted' list in the armoury of criminal investigation.[58] All this stimulated public interest in crime and the criminal. In the face of such developments, the hope of keeping the fate of capital offenders secret, controlling the depiction of their life and crimes, and ordering the public discussion of murder and execution to serve the perceived purposes of the state was doomed from the outset. A new kind of mass public was in the process of formation, articulated not least through the medium of print, and official attitudes to executions now began to change once more in response to official fears of what this might mean for the future stability of the political order created under Bismarck.

c. The Search for Secrecy

In the last couple of decades before the outbreak of the First World War, judicial officials became increasingly concerned to keep the news of executions secret and to impose a kind of quarantine on all those who had anything directly to do with them. Those who were granted the right to attend executions had to be told the date and time in advance and, although they were enjoined to maintain the strictest secrecy, not all of them were always able to resist the temptation to talk.[59] And even where local notables might still be trusted to keep the time and date of a forthcoming execution confidential, the populace at large certainly could not. When Prussia's chief executioner Julius Krautz travelled on a train with his axe and block, he was often recognized:

The railwayman who was handling his luggage whispered it unobserved to his neighbour, and this news flashed like an electric spark to the place to which Krautz was travelling. At the various stations to which he came, people were saying nothing but: 'Krautz is on the

[57] Hans-Otto Hügel, *Untersuchungsrichter—Diebsfänger—Detektive. Theorie und Geschichte der deutschen Detektiverzählung im 19. Jahrhundert* (Stuttgart, 1978).

[58] For the development of the police, see Albrecht Funk, *Polizei und Rechtsstaat: Die Entwicklung des staatsrechtlichen Gewaltmonopols in Preussen 1848–1918* (Frankfurt am Main, 1986).

[59] HStA Hannover Hann. 173a Nr. 439, Bl. 49: Bericht des Ersten Staatsanwalts bei den Königlichen Landgericht zu Stade über die Vollstreckung des Todesurtheils gegen den Fabrikarbeiter Heinrich Hagemann aus Harburg, 2 Mar. 1892.

train! Where is he?' The curiosity of the public, which exhibited a great interest in Krautz on every occasion, beggared all description.[60]

In 1886, the year of Bismarck's abortive initiative to control the press reporting of executions, a legal official reported in Magdeburg: 'The sudden appearance of the hangman and his satellites in the midst of a peaceable population is by no means pleasant for the latter'. This showed a poor knowledge of public attitudes, for people in the town could be heard boasting the following day that they had seen the executioner or even drunk a mug of beer with him.[61] It was obviously not difficult to do such a thing if the executioner booked into an hotel, as seemed to be the normal practice before the First World War. In 1914, indeed, a local newspaper in Oberhausen, in the Ruhr, even reported which hotel he was staying in (the Düsseldorfer Hof).[62] Officials were increasingly unhappy with such contacts. A first, significant step in the drive to make executions secret was taken in Prussia in November 1889, when the red 'Warning Notice' posted up on the Littfass advertising columns in Prussian towns to announce that an execution was going to take place was changed to an 'Announcement' issued only after the event.[63] This reform was only the beginning of a series of measures designed to keep forthcoming executions secret from all but officials and local notables, or, in other words, those who could be trusted to have a 'correct' attitude towards them. State prosecutors continued to be worried about possible repetitions of incidents such as that which took place at an execution in Cologne in 1900, when, as a newspaper reported: 'Numerous persons had posted themselves on the roofs of the houses opposite the prison so that they could observe the melancholy event from there.'[64] But by this time, this kind of thing had become extremely rare.

Official attention also turned to the person of the executioner and his assistants. The arrival of these gentlemen in a town, with their conspicuous, strangely-shaped, bulky luggage and their official dress—top hat, black frock-coat, black leggings, and white gloves—was a sure signal that an execution was about to take place. By the early 1900s officials were undertaking increasingly desperate and grotesque measures to try and keep their identity from the general public. Executioners now frequently travelled to their place of work under assumed names. ('As proof of identity,' the state prosecutor in Bremen told the ex-

[60] Schmidt, *Krautz*, 84.

[61] GStA Berlin Rep. 84a/7790, Bl. 23: *Gerichts-Zeitung für Magdeburg und die Provinz Sachsen*, 23 May 1886.

[62] *General-Anzeiger für Oberhausen*, 20 Mar. 1914.

[63] GStA Berlin Rep. 84a/7790, Bl. 122: Memo of the Staatsanwalt bei dem Königlichen Kammergericht, Berlin, 14 Nov. 1889. For copies of these notices, see HStA Hanover Hann. 173a Nr. 439, Bl. 360, 378.

[64] HStA Düsseldorf Rep. 145/327, Bl. 23: *Kölner Tageblatt*, 18 Aug. 1900.

ecutioner travelling from Magdeburg in 1908, 'you will use the name "Lop".'[65])
In 1904 the authorities in Baden reported: 'At the execution which was carried
out last November in Konstanz, the news of the guillotine's arrival got out
beforehand, so that a large number of the curious were gathered on the platform
when it came in.' Prison directors were instructed to make arrangements for the
transport of the machine centrally in future, rather than with the local
stationmaster or the railway goods office. They were told that the prison officers
sent to collect the machine should not be dressed in uniform. The loading and
unloading of the machine had to be done if possible under cover of darkness.[66]
It was also suggested that the equipment might be loaded onto 'a closed furniture
wagon which can be placed on a railway bogey here without being unloaded, and
on arrival at the town where the execution is due to take place can be taken off,
again without being unpacked, and driven directly into the execution yard'. A
containerized guillotine could be transported by day, and it would be unnecessary to inform the railwaymen of what they were transporting.[67]

In 1908 the guillotine in Hanover was sent by goods train to Bremen for an
execution under the description 'machine parts'. Steps were taken to ensure that
it was kept secret, in order, as the state prosecutor reported, to prevent 'gatherings of people' outside the prison. He went on to complain, however,

> that despite the strict entry controls, two apparently drunken persons managed to get into
> the corridor of the prison's entry wing. One of them, whom I encountered with a lighted
> cigar, was rapidly shown out of the prison by one of the warders, the other followed right
> after him of his own free will, at the bidding of the prison director. Outside the prison
> I only saw a few people; so despite the indiscretion of the *Bremer Tageblatt*, which
> distributed a special number about the execution on the evening of 13 July, the confiden-
> tial treatment of the execution prevented it from becoming very widely known.

The paper's evidently rather scruffily dressed reporter, who appeared at the
prison gates and asked to be admitted to the execution, received 'an energetic
reprimand' from the state prosecutor, 'because his appearance was in no way
appropriate to the seriousness of the occasion'. He was let in on condition that
he stood at the back of the assembled witnesses.[68] In 1912 the state prosecutor in
Bromberg, noting that 150 people had gathered outside the gaol during an
execution, commented in terms that made it clear how keeping the event quiet

[65] HStA Bremen 4, 89/1.236: Erster Staatsanwalt to Gröpler, 11 July 1908, copy.
[66] GLA Karlsruhe 234/66109: Badisches Ministerium der Justiz, des Kultus und Unterrichts, to Grossh.
Direktion der Centralstrafanstalten, 12 Feb. 1904, and ibid. 234/10178: Generaldirektion der Badischen
Staatseisenbahnen to Gr. Ministerium der Justiz, des Kultus und des Unterrichts, 23 Dec. 1903.
[67] Ibid. 234/10178: Auszug aus dem Jahresberichte des Direktors des Landesgefängnisses und der
Weiberstrafanstalt Bruchsal für das Jahr 1904.
[68] StA Bremen 4, 89/1.236: Der Erste Staatsanwalt berichtet über die Hinrichtung des am 23. Januar
1908 durch das Schwurgericht zu Bremen wegen Mordes zum Tode verurteilten Gärtners Pohl aus
Doberwitz, 17 July 1908.

was now a priority: 'The imminence of the execution remained completely secret. It was only through the arrival of the executioner and later on the two clergymen that some attention was aroused among a few people living near the prison.'[69] The senior state prosecutor in Frankfurt am Main had even more alarming things to report the same year. He noted 'that we succeeded in keeping the forthcoming execution in the Pöllmann case as far as possible secret from the press'. But railwaymen had noticed the oddly shaped luggage of executioner Gröpler and his assistants on the station, and had tipped off the press about their arrival. He suggested that in future they should transport their equipment in 'an unobtrusive luggage-case, for example, one such as travelling salesmen use to carry their samples in'.[70]

But if it was not the executioners themselves who posed a threat to the secrecy in which executions were increasingly being held, then it was the anatomists who sought to profit from the execution after the event. In 1894 the directors of the anatomical institutes in the Prussian universities asked if they could be given the bodies of executed criminals for experimentation. This would mean they would have to be told in advance about the time and place of execution (since the bodies, they explained, had to be fresh) and to inform their staff beforehand. The Prussian authorities refused:

At the moment, the place and time of executions are kept strictly secret as far as can be managed, in order to avoid exciting the public. In my humble opinion it is not possible to reconcile this policy, which is necessary in the interests of justice, with the notification of certain medical personnel of forthcoming executions and with the equipment which they must set up as close as possible to the execution site every time in order to prepare experiments on the executed person's corpse.[71]

The authorities in other parts of Germany, including the Rhineland, were less fussy.[72] In Baden the request of the Anatomical Institute at Heidelberg University to be allowed to attend the execution itself in order to obtain 'fresh human

---

[69] GStA Berlin Rep. 84a/7785, Bl. 44: Erster Staatsanwalt Bromberg to PJM, 12 July 1912.

[70] Ibid. 4593, Bl. 206b: Oberstaatsanwalt Frankfurt am Main to PJM, 18 Mar. 1912.

[71] Ibid., Bl. 132, 143–6: Kultusministerium to PJM and reply (5 Jan. 1894). For the request of the anatomical institutes to be informed in advance, see BA Potsdam Auswärtiges Amt IIIa Nr. 51, Bd. 4, Bl. 57–8: Weyrauch to Caprivi, 24 Jan. 1893.

[72] The bodies of executed criminals were routinely delivered to the anatomy schools in Baden, Bavaria, the Duchy of Saxony, Alsace-Lorraine, and Mecklenburg; in most cases (except Alsace-Lorraine), however, the relatives had a prior claim. This exception of Alsace-Lorraine was a characteristic example of the kind of petty discrimination to which the inhabitants of this province, annexed from France in 1871 and under direct rule from Berlin, were subjected. See BA Potsdam Auswärtiges Amt IIIa Nr. 51, Bd. 5, Bl. 74–7: Zusammenstellung der amtlichen Mitteilungen aus verschiedenen Bundesstaaten und aus Elsass-Lothringen über das Verfahren mit den Leichen Hingerichteter zu medizinisch-wissenschaftlichen Zwecke (1893). For Baden, see GLA Karlsruhe 234/6610: memo 3672 of the Badisches Justizministerium, 19 Feb. 1893. For the Rhineland, see HStA Düsseldorf Rep. 145/325, Bl. 203–4: Minister des Innern to Regierungspräsidenten Aachen, Düsseldorf, Coblenz and Trier, 21 Feb. 1911.

material' from the offender's corpse 'immediately after the execution' met with a sympathetic response from the Justice Ministry, at least where the offender had no relatives who wanted to claim the body for burial.[73] In Munich, the university's pathologists were allowed to set up a special laboratory in the prison, 'in direct proximity to the site of the execution', so that they could experiment on the bodies of decapitated offenders while they were still warm.[74] The Prussian attitude was once again evidence of the growing uncertainty and embarrassment surrounding the operation of the death penalty in this period. 'We kill modestly and shamefacedly in prison yards', remarked one observer in the early 1890s.[75] The truth of this observation had already been confirmed in 1889 by the Prussian authorities' decision to move the execution site in Berlin from the Moabit prison, near the centre of the city, to Plötzensee, much further out, to escape undue public attention.[76]

All these measures were justified at least in part by the need to control the public reaction to executions. Better education, the development of a new, enlarged public sphere, and the mobilization of new means of communication had enabled the news of forthcoming beheadings to escape the magic circle of local and urban notables and reach the popular press and the wider 'general public' that was in the course of formation at the end of the nineteenth century. The authorities were confronted with substantial gatherings of people outside prisons when executions were about to take place, and the 'sensation' which this denoted was the kind of disturbance of public morality which they obviously wanted to avoid.[77] Yet the increasing official secrecy which now surrounded executions represented something more fundamental than a mere desire on the part of officialdom to avoid public gatherings. A graphic illustration of the processes at work was provided by changing official attitudes to the ringing of the prison bell during executions. In 1847 the idea in Prussia had been that a bell should sound out far beyond the prison walls and summon families to religious and moral contemplation in their sitting-rooms. It signified in the most obvious way that there was nothing secret or private about 'intramural' executions, that they were public events in almost every sense except that the public reaction was to be orderly and controlled. But by 1859 this idea had been abandoned. The

---

[73] GLA Karlsruhe 234/6610: Fürbringer to Gr. Ministerium des Gr. Hauses, der Justiz und des Auswärtigen, 20 Apr. 1912, and reply 22 May 1912.

[74] Ibid.: Bayerisches Aussenministerium to Badisches Aussenministerium, 18 Oct. 1901.

[75] Alfred Fried, 'Hinrichtungen in Preussen', *Ethische Kultur*, 3/45 (9 Nov. 1895), 354 (copy in GStA Berlin Rep. 84a/7784, Bl. 165–7).

[76] GStA Berlin Rep. 84a/7784, Bl. 122: Staatsanwalt beim Königlichen Kammergericht, memo of 14 Nov. 1889.

[77] HStA Hanover Hann. 173a Nr. 438, Bl. 211: report of people gathering outside the prison during an execution in Lüneburg, 29 Jan. 1890; ibid. Nr. 441, Bl. 128, report of people gathering outside the prison in Hildesheim during an execution, having been alerted by the arrival of the guillotine.

Prussian authorities considered it important to prevent the inmates of the prison in which the execution was to be held from looking through their cell windows into the yard, which is where executions usually took place. A great deal of ingenuity was spent on finding a suitably obscure part of the gaol in which to carry out the decapitation. Yet the fact remained that the ringing of the bell would still alert the prisoners to what was going on. So the solution arrived at in 1859 was to avoid as far as possible publicizing the event in advance, and to use, not church bells, nor even the regular prison bell, but a special *soft* bell, of which 'the sound does not carry far enough to frighten the other prisoners detained in the penal institution'.[78] Thus in little more than a decade the bell's purpose had become almost purely ritual. In Stade, for example, a portable 'small bell' was placed inside the courtyard and tolled during the execution. It certainly cannot have been audible far beyond the confines of the yard itself.[79]

In Bavaria the new Criminal Code passed in 1862 ordered a bell to be rung during executions, 'in order to make a deeper impression on the public when death sentences are executed, and at the same time to encourage religious-moral impulses while this most serious of penal acts is being carried out'.[80] As in Prussia, this apparently simple order soon led to unexpected complications. Executions in Munich were now carried out in the yard of the Frohnveste, a prison in the Altstadt. Inhabitants of the district in which the prison was situated quickly began to object to the ringing of the bell during executions. The public attending such executions was supposed to be exclusively male. Yet a convent school, they pointed out, was located nearby. What would happen when the 'shrill tones' of the bell announced that an execution was in progress? 'What nervous excitement will this cause in the quiet halls of a nunnery, in the hearts of the young female novices? How easily can such excitement become the cause of physical and psychological afflictions such as epilepsy, apathy, neurasthenia, etc.'[81] The association of epilepsy with executions was perhaps a faint echo of popular beliefs of old. The complaint reflected once more the notion that the public execution was something best concealed from women. But whether these dire psychological consequences would actually ensue was debatable, even in the view of the Bavarian authorities. Executions in the Fronveste were a very rare occurrence, they pointed out, and each one only lasted a few minutes anyway. The purpose of the bell was to prevent the appearance of executions being carried out in secret, and this still seemed to be the cardinal point to the authorities in 1863.[82] What the

[78] GStA Berlin Rep. 84a/9270, *passim*, for these discussions.

[79] HStA Hanover Hann. 173a Nr. 439, Bl. 229: Bericht des Ersten Staatsanwalts betreffend die Vollstreckung der wider den Dienstknecht Wilhelm Handt aus Stettin erkannte Todesstrafe, 21 June 1893.

[80] HStA Munich MJu 13037: Ministerium des Innern (Kultusministerium) to Justizministerium, 11 June 1862.

[81] Ibid.: petition to King, 30 Jan. 1863.

[82] Ibid.: Justizministerium to King, 5 July 1863, Referat Dr Rosenkrantz.

Prussian authorities feared so much, however, now began to happen in Bavaria. The tolling of the bell led to curious crowds gathering outside the prison, and accounts of the execution were soon being distributed among them by the enterprising local press. The *Bayerische Zeitung*, a Munich daily, recalled that in the Wilhelmine period there were

executions in Straubing to which the whole population of the town and the surrounding district, and even to some extent from further afield, came in order to listen to the tolling of the poor sinner's bell. . . . After the execution the papers quickly issued descriptions of it, which people eagerly purchased and took back to their homes, where they were kept for years.[83]

The speed with which this process took place suggests that the bulk of the story was already written up before the event occurred, and only the final times remained to be added. Not surprisingly, official unease grew. By the time of the First World War, even the *sound* of an execution was causing embarrassment. This emerged as the result of a new complaint about the bell that was customarily rung in the prison during Prussian executions. Even though this was by now so quiet that it could scarcely be heard beyond the execution yard, it still appeared to the director of the state prison in Cologne in 1915 as excessively 'theatrical', and he asked if the practice could be abandoned. The local state prosecutor replied, however, that the peal of the bell was useful because it covered the sound of the blade from the spectators as it rushed down the guillotine, the thump of the head as it hit the sand, and the gushing blood as it spurted from the severed neck, 'as well as any possible screaming from the condemned person'.[84] Thus the primary justification of the bell was now that it concealed what was going on—a telling contrast to the reason given for its introduction in the original proposals of 1847, where the intention had been that it should announce the proceedings as loudly as possible to the local community outside the prison walls. As late as 1924, when the bell was still being used in the traditional manner in Bavaria, the state prosecutor in Aschaffenburg reported that it had made 'an embarrassing and in no sense ceremonious or dignified impression' when he had heard it at an execution in Amberg. He argued that it was time to stop using it. But it continued none the less. More slowly in Bavaria than in Prussia, but just as noticeably all the same, the publicity provided by the bell led to hostile comments from embarrassed officialdom.[85]

[83] Ibid., MJu 13144: *Bayerische Zeitung*, 23 Feb. 1922.

[84] GStA Berlin, Rep. 84a/7785 Bl. 56–8: memorandum of Cologne prison director, 10 Sept. 1915, and reply by Oberstaatsanwalt Cologne, 14 Sept. 1915.

[85] Ibid.: Erster Staatsanwalt to Oberstaatsanwalt Bamberg, 2 July 1924. The bell continued to be rung in Baden, too, from the moment the condemned person was led from the cell up to the moment the execution ended. See GStA Berlin Rep. 84a/7784, Bl. 53: Nr. III: Gesetzes- und Verordnungsblatt für das Grossherzogthum Baden, 14 Feb. 1881: Landesherrliche Verordnung, den Vollzug der Todesstrafe betreffend.

It was in late Bismarckian and above all in Wilhelmine Germany that the concern to make executions into secret, private affairs really became evident. As we have seen in the course of the last few chapters, it is far too simple in the German context to think of the 'privatization' of executions as occurring at a single stroke with their removal from open spaces to prison yards. Both at the time and subsequently, the authorities were adamant that they were not going to be held in secret, and a variety of measures, from the ringing of the bell to the issuing of substantial numbers of entry cards, was taken in order to ensure that they continued to be 'public' events. What changed decisively, however, was the nature of the public involved. In the period of reaction in the 1850s, governments all over Germany tried to mould, form, and restrict the public so that it would not escape control and threaten their legitimacy as it had done in 1848. The introduction of 'intramural' executions falls firmly into this context. The public which was to be allowed to witness executions was male and middle class. It was expected to behave in a sober and responsible manner and to do no more than witness and acquiesce in the act of killing taking place before it. But it proved no more possible for governments to bend the public to their purposes after 1848 than before. In the first place, the new regulations in no way solved the crisis of capital punishment that had begun in the 1840s. Not until the end of the 1870s did the prospect of its being done away with altogether, either on a *de facto* or a *de jure* basis, finally recede into history. When it was decisively reinstated, with the support of a majority of the political representatives of the people, in the 1880s, fresh problems quickly emerged. For in the mean time the public sphere had begun to experience a further transformation, putting it increasingly beyond the ability of governments to control. This time it was the new press, newspapers, magazines, and cheap novels and pamphlets, the reporting of trials, condemnations, and executions in fact and fiction which, despite numerous legal restrictions and police regulations, soon frustrated all the attempts of the authorities, from Bismarck downwards, to supervise. Capital punishment had become a permanent, regular part of the penal arsenal of German justice. The chances of removing it under the political conditions of Imperial Germany were remote. But like so many other aspects of the Bismarckian and above all the Wilhelmine political system, it now became the focus of permanent controversy and debate. This was not merely because, as we shall see, a vocal and changing minority continued to object to the death penalty in principle. It was also because, alongside the structural shift in public discourse, there were also major cultural changes under way which were beginning to have a discernible effect on the way in which the operation of the death penalty was regarded even by those who supported it.

d. The Growth of Squeamishness

However much they tried, judicial authorities in Germany could never make an execution into a straightforward, painless 'elimination' of the condemned. An execution in Imperial Germany was always a violent and sanguinary event. It was not for the faint-hearted. Among those who attended executions, whether out of interest or duty, feelings of embarrassment became increasingly evident in the last years before the outbreak of the First World War. The desire to witness and empathize with the offender's final moments seemed undiminished; but people were growing unwilling to tolerate the bloody mess that so often constituted the execution itself. They wanted to see criminals die; but they wanted them to die cleanly and without emotion. They sought reassurance, perhaps, that death was not a terrifying or painful experience. After executions were resumed on a regular basis in the 1880s, complaints were soon heard as minor errors by executioners, although certainly no more common than earlier, caused increasing feelings of revulsion in the onlookers. In 1882, for example, the executioner's assistants failed to control the 'convulsive movements and spasms' of a terrified offender whom they were trying to pin down on the block at an execution in Gera. The result was 'that the first blow which executioner Krautz aimed . . . at the neck did not manage to sever the head completely from the rump, so that a second blow, aimed precisely through the opening created by the first, was necessary, and this succeeded in severing the head from the rump.' Krautz refused to stay to be told by the state prosecutor in charge of the event of his 'disapproval of the inadequate conduct of the execution', and went straight back to Berlin. The event led directly to the introduction of the guillotine in this part of Thuringia.[86] In 1900 the executioner in Plötzensee failed to strike his first blow with sufficient force, so that 'before the body was lifted off the execution block the assistants had to pull the partially severed head away from the rump. This only took a short moment, but made a repugnant impression'.[87] Here too, the officiating prosecutor commented adversely on the incident. Failure to sever the neck with a clean blow dramatized the physical reality of what was happening in a way that almost nothing else could; and the discomfiture of those who attended and observed an execution of this sort was palpable. The embarrassment was all the greater when news of such an event reached the press. 'What a terrible and upsetting sight!', reported the *Berliner Zeitung* of an execution in 1903: 'the axe had not gone all the way through but only cut through the neck to the extent that the windpipe was certainly cut, but the head was not severed from the rump but hung down from it and wobbled about; a piece of the coat was also stuck between

[86] GStA Berlin Rep. 84a/6447, Bl. 36–41: Staatsanwalt Gera, Bericht, 20 July 1882.
[87] Ibid. 4592, Bl. 45a.

the axe and the block.'[88] The left-liberal, middle-class public by which this particular newspaper was read could not but feel a shudder of horror at such a report; it was amost calculated to bring them around to the paper's editorial line in favour of the abolition of the death penalty. Yet the voyeuristic fascination to which it testified was undeniable too.

It might be thought that the Prussian insistence on sticking to the traditional means of beheading with a hand-held axe was mainly to blame for mistakes such as these, and that the solution therefore lay in the adoption of a more up-to-date means of execution. Certainly criticism of the axe was widespread before the First World War. The hand-held axe had been introduced in some parts of Germany as an improvement earlier in the century, but by the Wilhelmine period critics regarded it as medieval and barbaric. Some lawyers who had to attend executions now complained about 'the terrible coarseness of the act', and declared it had converted them to abolitionism, while others waxed indignant about the barbarity of its 'repulsiveness, dripping with blood', especially when, as happened in Ratibor in 1914, it was a female offender whose head rolled.[89] Even supporters of the death penalty often took the view that the axe should no longer be used. *Geheimer Justizrat* Stelling, who as a state prosecutor in Hanover had attended many executions, remarked some years later that the axe was open to objection 'because the executioner's activity is obviously direct in this case'.[90] He was echoing a Bavarian official who had complained in 1854 that the axe was objectionable because it was 'directly wielded by human hands'. An indirect, mechanical method seemed preferable and expressed the impersonality of the judicial process.[91] Watching one human being kill another at the state's behest and with his own physical strength seemed too much like witnessing and colluding in an individual act of murder. It brought the spectators into a kind of direct complicity which a mechanical method would enable them to avoid. With the state increasingly thought of as representative, not so much of the sovereign, as of the nation, an impersonal means of execution seemed increasingly to be the most appropriate. Thus when people damned the axe as 'medieval', it was not because of the effect it had on the condemned, but because of the impression it made on the onlookers.

But incidents, errors, and mistakes in German executions were by no means merely confined to beheadings by the hand-held axe. Early in 1892, for example, in the small harbour town of Stade on the lower Elbe, during the execution of

[88] GStA Berlin Rep. 84a/7784, Bl. 251: *Berliner Zeitung*, 10 Sept. 1903.
[89] BA Potsdam 62 Re 1/1768, 148: *Berliner Tageblatt*, 26 Sept. 1910; ibid. 1766, 1/1: *Vorwärts*, 2 Feb. 1914.
[90] GStA Berlin Rep. 84a/7792: *Hannoverscher Kurier*, 26 Mar. 1929.
[91] HStA Munich MJu 13066: Allerunterthänigster Bericht des Staats-Ministeriums der Justiz an Seine Majestät den König, den Vollzug der Todesstrafe betreffend, 30 May 1854.

Heinrich Hagemann, a factory worker from Harburg, the blade of the guillotine, according to a report in a local newspaper, stopped half-way down the drop. The Prussian Ministry of Justice ordered an immediate investigation. As so often, it emerged that the press had over-dramatized the affair. What had actually happened was bad enough in the eyes of the officiating state prosecutor, who reported back to the Ministry

that after the executioner had pulled the lever, the blade of the guillotine did not fall down to the bottom but jammed in such a way that the right-hand side of the blade did not quite cover . . . the opening in the neck between the two pieces of wood that were holding it in position. The result was that the right-hand part of the throat and neck of the malefactor Hagemann was not cut through completely but that a small segment of the muscle (prison warder Linde thinks: at most a seventh or eighth part of the neck) remained attached to the rump.

Upon noticing this, the executioner's assistants immediately 'pulled and dragged the rump', while someone else moved the blade back up the frame. A voluminous correspondence followed as the authorities tried—unsuccessfully—to prise from executioner Reindel the details of what exactly had gone wrong. In future, greater care was taken to keep the machine in proper working order. It was concluded that the guillotine was no more 'humane' than the axe when the latter was wielded by a sober and practised hand. The way in which the guillotine robbed offenders of dignity and subjected them to a prolonged period of waiting while it was made ready remained a disadvantage in the eyes of many.[92]

Beheadings of both kinds continued to depend for their smooth execution on the co-operation of those who were subjected to them. From the late nineteenth century onwards, the condemned frequently resisted. In doing so, they provided the onlookers with an unwelcome reminder of the reality of what they were there to witness and approve. A decapitation that took place in Insterburg on 28 January 1911 caused such revulsion among those present that one of them broke the obligatory confidentiality and provided a description to the oppositional, abolitionist Social Democratic press. As the condemned person, a non-German-speaking domestic servant, Auguste Milkoweit, was led into the prison yard for the ceremony, it seemed to the eyewitness, who cited the woman's almost complete lack of even the most basic kind of education, that she did not really understand what was going on:

Two of the assistants gradually approached Milkoweit and then took her by the arms and walked her to the red-painted execution block, while a third followed. The executioner, who was waiting, dressed in frock-coat, top-hat, and gloves between the judges' table and

[92] GStA Berlin Rep. 84a/9397, Bl. 122–4: Bericht 1 Mar. 1892, and subsequent correspondence of Oberstaatsanwalt and PJM 9, 14 and 26 Mar. 1892; also HStA Hanover Hann. 173a Nr. 439, Bl. 50–52: Bericht 2 Mar. 1892, and subsequent correspondence to Bl. 137.

the block in an obvious state of nervous excitement, took off his hat and gloves and as Milkoweit was led past him, went to a nearby table to pick up the axe and deal the deadly blow. At this point, however, the unexpected occurred, ghastly to behold. In the moment in which they got to the block and the assistant who was following behind M. tore the blouse from her shoulder, and in which Milkoweit should have been laid across the block, she threw herself to the ground and clasped the block with all her strength, howling and screeching like a cat. While the executioner stood there, axe in hand, unable to carry out his duty, one of his assistants attempted with a huge effort to turn her head until it rested on the cutting surface of the block, so that the deadly blow might perhaps be dealt in this position, but was unable to do so. Finally after much pulling hither and thither, M.'s strength failed her and she was now placed on the block, as one of the assistants, as described above, pressed her head over it and the other two held her hands behind her back and kept hold of her feet. In this instant the executioner, who had raised his axe with both hands, let it whistle down. The head was severed from the rump and fell roughly a metre to the right of the block onto the sand. The blow was dealt with such force that the axe remained stuck in the block.[93]

Events such as these were now regarded as 'horrors' likely 'above all to contribute to that brutalization' which was supposed to be prevented by the deterrent effect of executions. This was not because they had a bad effect on the spectators, who were by now few in number and all drawn from the very groups who used this language, but because it was recognized that there was no way of preventing reports of them reaching a wider public through the medium of the press.[94] Not surprisingly the Prussian Ministry of Justice eventually took steps to stop this kind of incident recurring. As the Minister himself wrote to the senior state prosecutor of Cologne on 25 March 1912:

According to the report submitted to me, the execution of death sentences has been repeatedly disrupted by unbound offenders offering strong resistance to the executioner and his assistants. Even if this resistance has always been quickly overcome, nevertheless such incidents must if possible be prevented, as a rapid conduct of the execution is desirable in particular with regard to the condemned themselves. It is therefore recommended that the condemned's hands be bound in good time, unless particular circumstances make this appear inappropriate.[95]

Whether his concern was exclusively, or even mainly, for the condemned themselves, however, may be doubted. What really lay behind this measure, it may be surmised, was a twofold anxiety, first for the nerves of those actually present, which should not be unsettled by any departure from the pre-ordained, impersonal ritual in the direction of reminding them of the real human significance of what was in train; and secondly for the legitimacy and acceptability of capital

[93] BA Potsdam RJA/5665, BL. 61: *Frankfurter Zeitung* (repr. from a Social Democratic paper), 23 Mar. 1911.

[94] GStA Berlin Rep. 84a/7784, Bl. 251: *Berliner Zeitung*, 10 Sept. 1903.

[95] HStA Düsseldorf Rep. 145/326, Bl. 4: PJM to Oberstaatsanwalt Cologne, 25 Mar. 1912.

punishment in the populace at large, should news of such incidents reach the oppositional, liberal, or Social Democratic press.

By this time, officiating state prosecutors were beginning to feel embarrassment even about beheadings which went as planned. As the state prosecutor in Bromberg noted in his report of an execution which took place in July that year, 'what struck me and what has struck people during other executions, as I hear, was the fact that the executed person's head fell freely into the sand and rolled about there and even changed places because of its muscular spasms'. The Prussian Ministry of Justice agreed that a box should be provided for the head to fall into. But executioner Gröpler, whom the Ministry consulted on this point, while conceding that 'in exceptional cases it can happen that the chin still makes some chewing motions', denied that the whole head moved. He persuaded the Ministry to drop the idea by pointing out that a box of the necessary size would require 'a conspicuous piece of luggage' of the sort which he was supposed to avoid using. In any case, he added, it was normal practice for an assistant to catch the head as it fell. He agreed, however, to cover the head with a piece of cloth if the onlookers did not want to see it.[96] Such a move would no doubt have been welcome to those who witnessed an execution in Essen in the 1880s, which made an 'embarrassing impression on the numerous onlookers' when the offender's head fell off with the fatal blow and 'the chattering of its teeth made a strange clacking noise'.[97] Not surprisingly, alternative methods to beheading were constantly under discussion. After the resumption of capital punishment, Bismarck and his officials began to look around for a substitute for the axe. They had the advantage of being able to consult a commission set up in New York in 1888 to report on 'the most humane and practical method' of executing criminals. Most methods, it seemed, had serious disadvantages of one kind or another. The main drawback of the guillotine was said to be 'the profuse effusion of blood which it involves. It is, above all others, essentially a bloody method. This feature,' declared the New York commission, 'even if the execution is strictly private, must be needlessly shocking to the necessary witnesses.' The report cited the opinion of *Harper's Magazine* that 'the fatal chop, the raw neck, the spouting blood, are very shocking to the feelings, and demoralizing, as such exhibitions cannot fail to generate a love of bloodshed among those who witness them'. In fact, the reverse was more likely, and a good many people, at least in Germany, seem to have been converted to abolitionism by seeing the guillotine or the axe

---

[96] GStA Berlin Rep. 84a/7785, Bl. 44–55: correspondence of Erster Staatsanwalt zu Bromberg, Scharfrichter Gröpler and Oberstaatsanwalt Breslau, 12 July 1912, 9 Aug. 1912. Muscular spasms in the severed head were a well-attested phenomenon. See Anthony Kershaw, *History of the Guillotine* (London, 1958), for various examples.

[97] Schmidt, *Krautz*, 36.

in action. As for the military method of shooting, the American report considered it 'demoralizing particularly because of its tendency to encourage the untaught populace to think lightly of the use of fire-arms'. But the experience of the Wild West was already demonstrating, as indeed the subsequent course of American history has shown, that it did not require the use of the firing-squad for executions to encourage the American love-affair with the gun. Hanging, previously the favoured method in New York, was dismissed in 1888 as barbarous and inefficient. Electrocution, the report recommended, was the safest and most humane way of doing away with capital offenders.[98]

Electrocution was duly essayed in New York the same year. Such was the interest it generated in Berlin that Bismarck himself wrote to the German Consul-General in New York in 1888 asking for detailed information about the first attempt to use electrocution as a means of administering the death penalty. But the reports were not encouraging. Accounts of the experiment in the American press made it clear that the electric chair failed to kill the offender at the first attempt and was the cause of considerable pain and suffering. So this idea too was dropped.[99] Isolated voices continued to be raised in its favour right up to the First World War, but without any effect.[100] Other methods were canvassed too. Not surprising, perhaps, in an age of classical education, was the suggestion advanced by one writer in 1912 that the condemned criminal should be given a poisoned chalice with which to administer his or her own death. This suggestion was not taken up at the time, but it formed the subject of serious discussion some years later.[101] More ominously, in 1895 the Prussian authorities gave some consideration to the possibility of using the gas chamber, a proposal that emanated from the not entirely disinterested source of the *Zeitschrift für die gesamte Kohlensäureindustrie*, the house magazine of the carbon monoxide industry. This was another device first employed to carry out executions in the United States, though not in this case until 1924, in Nevada. It was also dismissed by the Prussian Ministry of Justice as unreliable. Carbon monoxide was not a deadly enough gas to bring about a quick death, and gassing, as was reported in the

[98] BA Potsdam Auswärtiges Amt IIIa Nr. 51, Bd. 3, Bl. 49–51: *Report of the Commission to Investigate and Report on the Most Humane and Practical Method of Carrying into Effect the Sentence of Death in Capital Cases*, in State of New York, *In Senate*, 17, Jan. 17, 1888 (New York, 1888).

[99] GStA Berlin Rep. 84a/7784, Bl. 125, 129: letter of Harold P. Brown, on behalf of Thomas Edison, and cutting from *Deutsches Tageblatt*, undated (*c.*1890), both reporting the execution of William Kemmler by electrocution in New York on 6 Aug. 1890, in which the current was too weak to cause immediate death. See also BA Potsdam Auswärtiges Amt IIIa Nr. 51, Bd. 3, Bl. 26–7: Bismarck to Consul-General in New York, 23 Mar. 1888; Bl. 82: *Vossische Zeitung*, 9 June 1888, and *Neue Preussische (Kreuz-) Zeitung*, 12 Aug. 1890; ibid., Bd. 5, Bl. 53: *New York World*, 7 June 1853, and numerous other reports in the same file.

[100] B. Freudenthal, 'Eine elektrische Hinrichtung im Staate New-York', *Zeitschrift für die gesamte Strafrechtswissenschaft*, 28 (1908), 61–6.

[101] BA Potsdam 61 Re 1/1770, 43: *Deutsche Tageszeitung*, 18 Oct. 1912; see also pp. 652–5, below.

German press at the time, was rejected by the Pennsylvania legislature in 1896.[102] It would be some decades before it was eventually applied in Germany, and then not to individual offenders, but to thousands of innocent people.

All these techniques were reviewed in Germany shortly before the First World War by a legal commission set up to draft a reform of the Reich Criminal Code. The members of the commission agreed that it was a good idea to have a uniform method of execution across all the states of the Reich. And some of them at least took the view that the axe was by now somewhat out of date. 'When the hand-axe is used, there have, even if only occasionally, been unacceptable incidents, and it is necessary to prevent such repulsive scenes from occurring.' But the majority, while admitting that the guillotine was less liable to error, considered the axe quicker and less fussy. Medical opinion, it was pointed out, had concluded that both methods were admissible. By contrast, electrocution and hanging both seemed too slow and uncertain. By 1893 the guillotine was in use in the Prussian Rhineland and in Hanover, in Baden, Bavaria, Alsace-Lorraine, Hamburg, Bremen, Lübeck, Oldenburg, Hesse, Saxe-Weimar, Saxe-Coburg-Gotha, Saxony, Schwarzburg-Rudolstadt, and Württemberg.[103] There remained the fact that some of the smaller states in the Reich, at least in theory, still appeared to prescribe the use of the sword. But the commission in the end was content to let this situation continue:

Even if a uniform method of execution is desirable with respect to the unity of the law across the Reich, such a uniform method might perhaps clash with the habits and opinions of substantial parts of the population, since the methods used in the individual states are justified by their origin. Beyond this, the legal unity of the Reich is guaranteed in the essential point by the exclusion of all other forms of death apart from beheading.[104]

Thus popular custom and expectation were now being used to justify the continuation of varying methods of execution. Tradition, rather than rational consideration, has often sanctioned the method of execution, and not only in Germany. An ingrained, almost mystical prejudice in favour of one method rather than another did more to inform decisions about the execution of capital sentences in Germany than any weighing-up of the advantages and disadvantages of the various options available. This, together with the conservatism of the executioners themselves—perhaps, too, a certain artisanal pride in their skill—was the main influence behind what might seem, from the perspective of the end

[102] GStA Berlin Rep. 84a/7784, Bl. 168: copy of E. Luhmann, 'Verwendung der Kohlensäure zur Hinrichtung der zum Tode verurteilten Verbrecher', *Zeitschrift für die gesamte Kohlensäureindustrie*, 20 (25 Oct. 1895).

[103] BA Potsdam Auswärtiges Amt IIIa Nr. 51, Bl. 73: Reichsjustizamt to Auswärtiges Amt, 3 Mar. 1893.

[104] Ibid. Reichsamt des Innern 8426, Bl. 55–6, 6. Sitzung am 24 April 1911, 2–3. See also copy in this file of *Vierteljahrschrift für gerichtliche Medizin*, 41/2 Suppl. [1911], 153–5.

of the twentieth century, the surprising decision to continue using the hand-held axe as the major method of execution in most parts of northern and eastern Germany during the Imperial period.

e. New Justifications for the Death Penalty

These decisions were taken at a time when executions had once more become a regular, indeed a frequent occurence in Germany. In Prussia they had averaged under five a year in the period 1881–5. But numbers increased sharply at the end of the decade, with seven executions in 1889 and thirteen in 1890, bringing the annual average for the years 1886–90 to almost eight. In 1892 they jumped again, to twenty-five. The average number of executions per year in Prussia in the quinquennium 1891–5, at just under twenty-three, was almost five times greater than it had been in the 1880s. The first, and most obvious reason for this change was the accession of a new Prussian King who shared none of Wilhelm I's scruples about consigning offenders to the block. When the old King died in 1888, the Crown Prince succeeded as Friedrich III, but he was already fatally ill, and within the year he too had died, to be succeeded in turn by his son, the young Wilhelm II. Bombastic, self-important, authoritarian, illiberal, and determined to make his mark on the world, Wilhelm II often mistook the appearance of power for the substance, and preferred gestures and symbols of authority to the real thing.[105] The exercise of the royal clemency, with its right of decision over life and death, was just the sort of symbolic power Wilhelm II enjoyed most. It enabled him to sign away a life with a stroke of the pen, without having to consult anybody, and without having any pressing political reason to follow the recommendations of his advisers. For a man who quickly became accustomed to urge his troops to mow down strikers and revolutionaries, and to show no mercy to foreign insurgents in colonial wars, such a power posed no problems of conscience such as had assailed the hesitant Wilhelm I. Even before he forced the resignation of Bismarck and became 'his own Chancellor' in 1890, the new monarch was already making his influence felt in the exercise—or, to be more precise, the refusal—of the royal clemency.

The results of this were apparent in the virtual doubling of the number of executions between 1889 and 1890. But it was in 1892 that the most startling increase occurred, setting a pattern that remained fixed for the rest of Wilhelm II's tenure of the throne. At the outset of his reign, partly influenced by the great Ruhr miners' strike of 1889, partly as a means of expressing his opposition to

---

[105] Among numerous biographical studies, the most comprehensive is John Röhl, *Wilhelm II* (Munich, 1993), i: *Die Jugend des Kaisers 1859–1888* (further vols. in preparation); for the argument that Röhl overestimates Wilhelm's grasp on real power, see Evans, *Rethinking*, ch. 2.

Bismarck, who had wanted to renew and indeed drastically sharpen the provisions of the Anti-Socialist Law, Wilhelm had cut a figure as the workers' friend, a benevolent and paternalistic monarch concerned to mitigate the severities of the Iron Chancellor's rule. The Anti-Socialist Law did indeed lapse in 1890, and the Social Democratic Party could henceforth operate legally once more. But in 1892 Wilhelm dropped this somewhat artificial posture. The workers had not become loyal, and the Social Democrats had passed a strongly Marxist programme in their Erfurt Congress the previous year, full of revolutionary phrases and radical ideology. The relatively liberal policies of the new Chancellor, Caprivi, were arousing growing opposition on the political right. The police, the judiciary, and the state authorities, increasingly worried by the Social Democratic threat, desperately sought substitutes for the Anti-Socialist Law in prosecutions of the party's speakers, editors, journalists, and activists for all kinds of offences ranging from *lèse-majesté* to contravention of the law of assembly and association. What better way for Wilhelm to signal his new determination to crack down on opposition than to refuse to grant clemency to capital offenders? In common with most of the Prussian police and judicial apparatus, he believed that Social Democrats were essentially criminal and immoral; lacking all respect for order, religion, and established authority, all they wanted to do was to get their hands in the state's coffers. No doubt the clemency officials in the Ministry of Justice, frustrated in the 1880s by the old Prussian monarch's reluctance to sign death warrants, shared many of these beliefs. From 1892 to 1914 a majority of offenders sentenced to death in Prussia were executed in every year except one. Almost as many people—eighty-three—were executed in Prussia in the first five full years of Wilhelm II's reign as in all three decades of his grandfather's occupancy of the throne. In Wilhelm I's reign, counting from 1859 through 1888, there had been a total of eighty-five executions in Prussia. In Wilhelm II's, from 1889 through 1918, there were 498, more than five times as many in the same number of years. Under Wilhelm I, executions in Prussia averaged just under three a year; under Wilhelm II, the annual average was almost seventeen. These figures were the highest since the 1850s. And there was no sign of any downward trend before 1914. The personal role of the monarch can clearly be observed in the comparison with executions in other German states, which did not undergo any remarkable increase at this time and remained very low in comparison. Moreover, while Wilhelm I refused to sign death warrants for women, no fewer than forty-four were executed in Prussia during his grandson's reign, or 10 per cent of those condemned, and 9 per cent of those executed altogether, a comparable figure to those observable in the early part of the century.[106]

---

[106] See Statistical Appendix, below; and GStA Berlin Rep. 84a/7786: Übersicht, Bl. 1–3.

FIG. 23. *Gallows humour at the turn of the century.* This cartoon by Thomas Theodor Heine, which appeared on the front page of the satirical magazine *Simplicissimus* in 1899, correctly shows the execution being carried out in a prison yard with a hand-held axe, and before an audience, but is wrong in almost every other detail. In a real execution, there would have been no such raised scaffold; the spectators would have stood well back; the executioner would have taken off his top hat and frock-coat and would not have worn any medals; the axe would not have been swung over the shoulder, but held vertically, directly in front of the executioner, and only raised three or four feet high before coming down on the neck; the block would have been much lower, and with no drainage pipe; there would have been no box for the head to fall into, just a sand-pit; the prisoner's head would have been placed further forward and his eyes not blindfolded; his feet would not have been tied but pinioned by the assistants; and the coffin would not have been marked for dispatch to the Royal Anatomical Institute, since the offender's relatives had the right to remove the remains for burial if they wished. The caption reads: 'Just be quiet, my good chap! Just be glad you're not a Social Democrat, otherwise you'd be having a much worse time!' The cartoon reflects the magazine's disquiet, shared by many on the left and centre of German politics in the late 1890s, at the government's attempts to introduce tough penal sanctions against Social Democrats who advocated strikes or engaged in revolutionary activities.

The increase in executions at the beginning of the 1890s also reflected wider trends. Judicial officials had been waiting for the opportunity to bring it about, as their repeated attempts to overcome Wilhelm I's reluctance to endorse the rejection of clemency in the 1880s clearly indicated. An execution rate of roughly twenty a year did not seem unduly disturbing to Prussian officialdom. And, as we have seen, the principle and implementation of the death penalty were widely accepted, even by liberals, in Germany from the early 1880s onwards. But judicial officials found the personal role of Wilhelm II in refusing clemency a source of political embarrassment. In 1902, Ministry of Justice officials took steps to dissociate him personally from the executions which he had instituted with such enthusiasm. They wrote to local state prosecutors in the following terms:

It has come to our attention that announcements of executions contain a statement that His Majesty the Kaiser and King has made no use of his right of reprieve. Such a turn of phrase used in announcements designed to be posted up in public places does not appear appropriate, since it is calculated to arouse erroneous ideas and in connection with these to give rise to unpleasant criticisms of the All-Highest decision. The use of the said phrase, or anything similar, by which the execution of a death sentence is connected to the All-Highest Person, is therefore always to be avoided.[107]

Despite the obvious personal involvement of the Prussian monarch, therefore, the refusal of clemency was now presented as an impersonal, anonymous act of justice. It is not clear whether or not Wilhelm II actually knew about this. It is reasonable to conclude that here, on a small scale, was yet another example of government officials, this time somewhat belatedly, stepping in to rescue the standing of the monarchy from what they perceived in other contexts as tasteless and counter-productive interventions in policy-making by the monarch.

In other parts of Germany also, capital punishment re-established itself as a regular feature of the judicial scene, though without the fluctuations noticeable in Prussia. Between the resumption of executions in the Kingdom of Saxony and the outbreak of the First World War, for example, 93 offenders were condemned to death and 38 executed, an execution rate of 41 per cent. The comparable figures in Hesse were 27 and 19. Altogether in the Reich as a whole, there were on average 76 condemnations and 15 executions a year in the quinquennium 1882–6, and 52 and 55 condemnations a year in each of the following two five-year periods (figures for executions are not available). In the period 1897–1901 the annual averages were 42 and 25, in the period 1902–6 they were 37 and 23, and in the period 1907–11 they were 37 and 21. Wilhelm II's partiality for the axe and the guillotine thus ensured that, while executions in the rest of Germany declined, their number remained roughly constant in Prussia after the sharp

[107] HStA Düsseldorf Rep. 145/325: PJM to Oberstaatsanwälte, 25 Apr. 1902.

increase of the early 1890s, so that Prussian executions made up a far higher proportion of the Reich total by the eve of the First World War than they had done two or—still more—two and a half decades earlier.[108] Yet no major German state entirely abandoned the death penalty before 1914; all of them continued, however sporadically, to execute criminals convicted of murder throughout the Wilhelmine period.

Whatever the embarrassment with which it was attended, it was clear that, after a long period of crisis and debate, the death penalty was now permanently embedded in the principle and practice of Imperial Germany's administration of the law. A new economy of capital punishment had been established. Doubtless its greater frequency from the early 1890s onwards was one reason why it disturbed many of those state prosecutors and officials who were now forced to witness it in person for the first time. But there were also deeper influences at work. The crisis of capital punishment from the 1840s to the 1880s had largely been brought about by its role as a symbol of Absolutist state power. Religious arguments, as we saw in earlier chapters, played a remarkably small part in the assault that was launched on the death penalty in 1848 and 1870. Rather than centring on penal policy, discussion had focused on contractual versus organic or religious views of the state, on the rights of the individual, and on other Enlightenment principles which mid-century German liberals held so dear. If religious arguments were used, they tended to be on the side of the retentionists. The strongest defenders of capital punishment had been those, like the representatives of the Catholic Centre Party or the German Conservatives, whose religious convictions were also the strongest. To some extent, these positions were maintained during the Wilhelmine period. In particular, the Protestant or Evangelical Church in Prussia, formed by the merger of the Lutheran and Calvinist congregations early in the nineteenth century, took an overwhelmingly authoritarian line on issues of law and order. To its traditional role in supplying theological justifications for the maintenance of the social hierarchy, the obedience of the subject, and the authority of the state, it added a growing fear of atheism and revolution that increased the more the fiercely anti-religious Social Democrats gained in strength and support. Murder appeared to many Protestant pastors above all as the fruit of irreligion, and thus as a direct consequence of the spread of socialist doctrine. Writing in 1908, for example, a conservative pastor revealed how closely he associated socialism and crime when he described the murderers of his time as 'these producers of infernal machines, explosive devices, in short these mass murderers, who refuse to recognize any authority, whether human or divine, these devils in human form, these poisoners, who have more than one

---

[108] Düsing, *Abschaffung*, 132; see also Statistical Appendix, below.

person's life on their conscience.' Imprisonment was unlikely in his view to improve the nature of such people: 'Unfortunately most of our murderers are atheistical characters totally without religious faith.'[109] These sociopolitical fantasies were a long way from the truth. Wilhelmine Germany was still a society in which there were more murders in the pious countryside than in the godless town, where domestic killings far outnumbered other categories of homicide, and where political murder, in the absence of a serious anarchist movement, was unknown. Few prisoners rejected the consolations of religion. In 1907 the 19-year-old Wilhelm Schilly, condemned to death for robbery with murder, and refused a reprieve by Wilhelm II despite the view of legal officials that he was too young to be executed, told his prison warder 'I don't believe in religion any more, take the crucifix, book, and rosary out of my cell, I can't look at them any more . . . If the crucifix stays hanging up there any longer today, I'll strike it down off the wall, I'm not here to pray to idols.'[110] But this incident was reported precisely because it was so unusual. Murderers in Wilhelmine Germany were seldom politically active, and the predominance of rural, often backward, and mainly Catholic districts in the statistics of violent crime also meant that the overwhelming majority of capital criminals were people of some religious conviction, even if it was not very deeply held.[111]

Yet what had converted National Liberals and others to the desirability of capital punishment was, as we saw in the debates on the Explosive Substances Law of 1884, precisely the argument that crime and politics were linked. More than anything else, it was the conviction that murder was a product of anarchism and extreme left-wing revolutionism that brought about the reinstatement of the death penalty in the 1880s and early 1890s and ensured that it was retained thereafter. Executions became a way of assuaging the sociopolitical fears of German élites in a time of rapid industrialization and urbanization, as the Social Democratic movement was growing at a seemingly unstoppable rate, and as bourgeois culture seemed increasingly threatened by the organized radicalism of the world's largest labour movement. It was not coincidental that, as we shall see in the next chapter, the Social Democrats were the most prominent and vociferous opponents of the death penalty throughout the Wilhelmine period. Bourgeois opinion was reconciled to the death penalty not least because it seemed a

[109] GStA Berlin Rep. 84a/7784, Bl. 291–2: *Die Reichsbote*, 12 and 13 Aug. 1908.
[110] HStA Düsseldorf Rep. 145/327, Bl. 255: report of prison *Hausvater*, forwarded to Ersten Staatsanwalt Aachen by Strafanstalts-Direktor Aachen, 7 Jan. 1907. For the recommendation for mercy see ibid. Bl. 252: Landgerichtsrat Mayer to Oberlandesgerichtspräsident Cologne, 4 Oct. 1906.
[111] Johnson, *Urbanization and Crime*, 158–71 provides statistics for urban/rural differentials in violent crime. See also idem. 'The Roots of Crime in Imperial Germany', *Central European History*, 15 (1982), 351–76; and idem and Vincent E. McHale, 'Urbanization, Industrialization, and Crime in Imperial Germany', *Social Science History*, 1 (1976/7), 45–78 and 210–47.

means of defending the cultural and political order of the Bismarckian nation-state, achieved in 1870–1 and reformulated in 1878–9. This cultural and political order was primarily secular. So justifications for capital punishment had to be found that were primarily secular and rationalistic in character. At this time, therefore, penal theory and practice in Germany began to move away from defining criminals as morally 'fallen' individuals in need of re-education, and towards a new conception of criminality as determined by heredity.

Once more, as in the eighteenth century, it was an Italian penal theorist whose views proved most influential. Cesare Lombroso, born in 1835, studied medicine in Vienna, among other places, and like many northern Italians reacted to the endemic problem of brigandage and banditry in the backward south of the newly unified state in the 1860s and 1870s by concluding that the southern peasants were lower down the human scale than their more advanced northern compatriots. Indeed, he considered them little better than animals. Lombroso, however, thought it was possible to develop an exact scientific approach to the problem, in which the nature and degree of a people's criminality could be read off from their physical appearance. He was able to take advantage of the growing sophistication of sciences such as physical anthropology, intellectual currents such as Darwinism, which became extremely influential in Italy, and new techniques such as photography, to construct a whole portrait gallery of the physical characteristics which announced to the trained observer the presence of a criminal being. Lombroso argued that criminals were born, not made. They represented a hereditarily determined degeneracy, in which whole families and clans regressed to an atavistic, primitive form of human nature, red in tooth and claw. Punishment was futile against the force of evolutionary regression. Instead, the chain of hereditary degeneracy had to be broken. Craniometry and physiognomy would identify the born criminal and distinguish him from the casual offender driven by temporary need. The purpose of penal policy was to eliminate the atavistic from human society by permanent segregation, incarceration, sterilization, castration, or death.[112]

Lombroso's ideas, propagated in a number of works, several of which were translated into German, had an enormous impact on European thinking about crime and punishment.[113] By the turn of the century, international criminologi-

[112] Cesare Lombroso, *Crime: Its Causes and Remedies* (London, 1911); idem, *L'Homme criminel* (Paris, 1895). The most accessible introduction to Lombroso's ideas, setting them in the context of 19th-c. Italian crime and punishment, is John A. Davis, *Conflict and Control: Law and Order in Nineteenth-Century Italy* (London, 1988), 326–38.

[113] For the German reception of Lombroso, see Cesare Lombroso, *Die Ursachen und Bekämpfung des Verbrechens* (Berlin, 1902); idem, *Der Verbrecher in anthropologischer, ärztlicher und juristischer Beziehung* (3 vols.; Hamburg, 1890–6); idem, 'Über den Ursprung, das Wesen und die Bestrebungen der neuen

cal congresses were discussing practically nothing else. German forensic psychiatrists and criminologists joined in the debate with gusto. For Lombroso's ideas began to be propagated just as German legal theorists such as Otto Mittelstädt and Franz von Liszt were launching a major attack on the ideas of deterrence and retribution as the foundation of penal policy in the country. Imprisonment had failed to achieve its ameliorative purpose, they argued, and society needed instead to return to the old Prussian principle of 'special prevention', imprisoning incorrigible recidivists indefinitely, in order to protect society. Prison doctors and forensic psychiatrists, frustrated by the restrictions placed on them by the narrow definition of criminal insanity contained in the German Criminal Code, saw in these ideas the opportunity to gain influence. By the end of the 1880s some were already arguing that criminality and insanity were closely connected, on a general level, not just in a minority of specific cases, and invoking newly fashionable ideas of degeneracy or 'inferiority' (*Minderwertigkeit*) to lay claim over the mass of habitual criminals whose degree of mental abnormality fell short of insanity as defined by the law. Lombroso's ideas were popularized in the 1890s not only by his most assiduous German disciple, the psychiatrist Hans Kurella, but also by a number of critics such as Abraham Baer, Paul Näcke, Julius Koch, and Robert Sommer, all of whom attempted to use them to bolster their concept of social-psychological degeneracy while rejecting the more dogmatic aspects of the Italian theorist's insistence on the physical signifiers of criminality. By the turn of the century, the debate was moving towards a synthesis. The psychiatrist Gustav Aschaffenburg, author of a standard text on criminology first published in 1902, shared a widespread feeling that some of Lombroso's ideas went too far. Not all criminals were born, and it was not always possible to recognize those who were, just by a cursory perusal of their physical features. Aschaffenburg was equally sceptical about the notion of criminals as atavistic beings regressing to some point further back in the evolutionary chain. Nevertheless, like many of those who discussed Lombroso's theories at this time, he accepted the Italian's basic premiss that criminality could be explained in good measure as the product of biological and hereditary factors. Criminals, he wrote, were made from inherited 'inferior human material':[114]

Life takes its course and crushes those who can't go along with it. Just as the struggle for existence is being played out today and will continue to be until the end of time, just as

anthropologisch-kriminalistischen Schule in Italien', *Zeitschrift für die gesamte Strafrechtswissenschaft*, 1 (1881), 108–29; and Emil Kraepelin, 'Lombrosos Uomo delinquente', ibid. 5 (1885), 669–80. For Lombroso's work in the context of international thinking on these subjects, see Daniel Pick, *Faces of Degeneration: A European Disorder c.1848–c.1918* (Cambridge, 1989), esp. 109–52.

[114] Gustav Aschaffenburg, *Das Verbrechen und seine Bekämpfung*, 3rd edn. (Heidelberg, 1923), 222.

popular custom forces everyone under the yoke of joining in, so must we reach a judgement with an unprejudiced eye on the dangers to which we are all exposed. These dangers are far greater than the powers of all these inferior people to resist them.[115]

Thus criminals were both born and made. Others agreed. On the whole, Aschaffenburg came down on the side of the milieu when it came to deciding what finally pushed a weak individual into breaking the law. Others were not so sure. Another standard textbook, on forensic psychiatry, published in 1901, was more inclined to accept Lombroso's argument that criminality could be recognized by physical signs such as malformations of the ear or the size and shape of the forehead. 'In general,' wrote its editor, Alfred Hoche, who later became an advocate of involuntary euthanasia, 'the morbid reduction of a person's capacity to resist his criminal tendencies can be estimated to be the higher, the more he displays physical and mental signs of degeneration under investigation.'[116]

Paying tribute to Lombroso as the pioneer of hereditarian approaches to criminality, Aschaffenburg drew the consequence that penal policy should direct itself at the criminal, not the crime. 'The task is to fit the punishment to the individuality of the offender, the solution is the abolition of fixed sentences for specific crimes.'[117] It followed from this that punishment could not be a deterrent, and that the amelioration of the hereditarily degenerate offender was an impossibility. Where the criminal concerned had murderous inclinations, the death penalty should be imposed in order to protect society not only in the present but also for future generations as well, by cutting off irrevocably any chance of the murderer reproducing himself. Capital punishment in this view was justified 'in the interests of social selection'.[118] At this stage, many criminologists were wary of taking this view too far. Enrico Ferri, along with Lombroso the main representative of the new Italian school in this period, argued that capital punishment could not become eugenically effective without at least a thousand executions a year in Italy alone. This was surely politically unacceptable. The alternative was therefore to lock up serious criminals for life, or deport them. As a deterrent, capital punishment was completely useless, given the hereditary influences to which seriously degenerate offenders were exposed.[119] Aschaffenburg himself shared Ferri's doubts, and during the Weimar Republic came to support the abolition of the death penalty. Yet the new way of thinking opened up the possibility of greater violations by the state of the bodily boundaries of its citizens than had occurred since the early eighteenth century. Even for less dangerous criminals, for example, German criminologists before the First

---

[115] Gustav Aschaffenburg, *Das Verbrechen und seine Bekämpfung*, 3rd edn. (Heidelberg, 1923), 223.
[116] Alfred Hoche (ed.), *Handbuch der gerichtlichen Psychiatrie* (Berlin, 1901), 414, 419.
[117] Aschaffenburg, *Verbrechen*, 339.   [118] Ibid. 296–7.
[119] Enrico Ferri, *Das Verbrechen als soziale Erscheinung* (Leipzig, 1896), 435–41.

World War came increasingly to believe that compulsory sterilization was the remedy. 'Individuals of an anti-social disposition' and 'moral idiots' had to be stopped from reproducing. They should be removed from society for an indefinite period, irrespective of the nature of their crime, in the interests of an 'improvement of social hygiene'.[120] Monstrous, inhuman specimens like Jack the Ripper should not be kept alive, with the possibility that they might reproduce: they should be eliminated from the chain of heredity.[121] Even if criminologists shied away from advocating capital punishment on a large enough scale to be eugenically effective, some at least were prepared to support it for the most extreme of human 'monsters'.[122] The particular branch of criminology which was most vociferous in advocating such policies—criminal anthropology—was dominated by Germans and Austrians. Some of them advocated the most far-reaching measures of compulsory sterilization. In 1913, for example, Hans Gross, editor of the leading journal in the field, argued that society was under such threat from criminals that humanitarianism would only be a weakness. He wanted the castration not only of sex offenders but of all young men of violent disposition currently confined in corrective institutions, and the sterilization of anyone suffering from alcoholism or exhibiting what he considered to be a strong criminal disposition.[123] But by 1914 such biologistic ways of thinking about crime had become widespread among forensic psychiatrists as well. The increasingly professional nature of policing and detective work in the late nineteenth century also helped spread these ideas and techniques. Policemen saw them as lending added legitimacy and status to their profession, and soon textbooks of policing too were filled with pages of photographs detailing the physiognomical features of various types of criminal, while prison authorities in cities such as Hamburg began to collect the death masks of executed capital offenders in the hope of applying Lombroso's techniques to them, as well, when they had eventually amassed a sufficient number.[124]

The growing influence of Lombroso's ideas was part of a wider set of changes in thinking about society in Germany around the turn of the century. Social Darwinism, previously mainly liberal, emphasizing free competition as the prin-

---

[120] Gustav Aschaffenburg (ed.), *Bericht über den VII. Internationalen Kongress für Kriminalanthropologie* (Heidelberg, 1912). See esp. the articles by Graf Gleispach, 'Die unbestimmte Verurteilung' (pp. 226–43), Prof. Dannemann, 'Die Entmündigung chronisch Krimineller als Mittel zur Verbesserung der sozialen Hygiene' (pp. 313–21), Hans Maier, 'Erfahrungen über die Sterilisation Krimineller in der Schweiz und Nordamerika als Mittel der sozialen Hygiene' (pp. 323–31), and H. Klaatsch, 'Die Morphologie und Psychologie der niederen Menschenrassen in ihrer Bedeutung für die Probleme der Kriminalistik' (pp. 56–73); and Richard F. Wetzell, 'Criminal Law Reform in Imperial Germany' (Ph.D., Stanford, 1991).

[121] See the account of these views, and the controversy they aroused when they were put forward in the *Archiv für Kriminal-Anthropologie und Kriminalistik*, in Gay, *Cultivation*, 165–6.

[122] Paul Näcke, cited ibid. 165.   [123] See the list of delegates in Aschaffenburg (ed.), *Bericht*.

[124] Gustav Roscher, *Grossstadtpolizei* (Hamburg, 1906).

ciple of human endeavour, or socialist, stressing the inevitability of social evolution, took on a new, darker character, with its adherents increasingly underlining the 'struggle for existence' and the threat of decline should nothing be done
to restore the principle of 'natural selection' which society, they believed, had
interfered in by preserving the weak and the degenerate.[125] Ernst Haeckel, one of
the most widely read authors of the Wilhelmine period, famous both for his
popularization of Darwinism in his book *Die Welträtsel* and for his founding of
the Monist League, a small but vocal movement which aimed to propagate his
views in politics and society, used Darwin's name to advocate a vast extension of
capital punishment. Haeckel was nothing if not consistent in his application of
Darwinism and eugenics. He supported capital punishment because, as he said,
'it has a directly beneficial effect as a selection process'. It was a useful means of
eliminating criminal and degenerate elements from the racial stock. Besides
supporting 'rendering incorrigible offenders harmless', Haeckel also thought that
the mentally ill should be killed off by the state, because psychological disturbances were the expression of a physical degeneracy of the brain, and could
therefore hold up human progress unless they too were eliminated from the chain
of inheritance. In keeping with this rationale for capital punishment, Haeckel
wanted the traditional and ceremonial elements eliminated from executions and
modern methods such as electrocution or cyanide poisoning to be introduced
instead.[126] All this sounded suspiciously like a form of proto-fascism, and has
been taken by some historians as such.[127] Yet Haeckel was an idiosyncratic figure,
difficult to pigeon-hole in straightforward political terms. He was, for instance,
a strong supporter of pacifism, because he thought that wars eliminated the best
and bravest of the young men of the fighting generation, and in so doing severely
weakened the human stock.[128] His criticisms of religion made him popular to
some extent among radicals and Social Democrats. In terms of penal policy, his
ideas did, however, represent a point of view that looked forward to that of the
Nazis to the extent that they regarded criminality as inheritable and punishment

[125] Ted Benton, 'Social Darwinism and Socialist Darwinism in Germany: 1860 to 1900', *Rivista di
Filosofia*, 23 (1982), 79–121; Paul Crook, *Darwinism, War and History: The Debate over the Biology of War
from the 'Origin of Species' to the First World War* (Cambridge, 1994), 31; Peter Weingart, Jürgen Kroll, and
Kurt Bayertz, *Rasse, Blut und Gene. Geschichte der Eugenik und Rassenhygiene in Deutschland* (Frankfurt am
Main, 1992), 114–21; Richard J. Evans, 'In Search of German Social Darwinism: History and
Historiography of a Concept', in Manfred Berg and Geoffrey Cocks (eds.), *Medicine and Modernity.
Public Health and Medical Care in Nineteenth- and Twentieth-Century Germany* (New York, 1996).
[126] BA Potsdam Aswartiges Amt IIIa Nr. 51, x. 135–6: *Deutsche Juristen-Zeitung*, 16/1 (1 Nov. 1911).
[127] e.g. Daniel Gasman, *The Scientific Origins of National Socialism: Ernst Haeckel and the Monist League*
(New York, 1971), 11–15.
[128] GStA Berlin Rep. 84a 7784, Bl. 203–5: Alfred Fried, 'Die Todesstrafe im Urtheil der Zeitgenossen',
Die Zeitgeist: Beiheft zum Berliner Tageblatt, 2 Dec. 1901. See more generally Jürgen Sandmann, *Der Bruch
mit der humanitären Tradition. Die Biologisierung der Ethik bei Ernst Haeckel und anderen Darwinisten
seiner Zeit* (Stuttgart, 1990).

as an instrument of eugenic policy. At the same time, Haeckel, along with other scientific writers such as Alfred Ploetz, Alexander Tille, and Eugen Schallmeyer, argued that children's illnesses should be left untreated so that the weak could be weeded out from the chain of heredity by natural causes.[129] From here it was only a short (though crucial) step to arguing that such people should be deliberately exterminated.

Few writers in Wilhelmine Germany went as far as Haeckel in their reduction of capital punishment to a form of biological engineering. Yet a symptomatic reading of the justifications advanced for the death penalty by its most vociferous supporters, the presence in their writings of a new set of biological metaphors and hereditarian assumptions, strongly suggests that the reinstatement of capital punishment on a permanent basis in late nineteenth-century Germany was facilitated by the spread of a vague, only partially articulated belief that it was now justified by the precepts of science. Whatever one might say about lesser forms of criminality, murder, at least in its severest forms, could now be taken as evidence of complete hereditary degeneracy. Capital punishment fitted in very well to the new, hereditarian discourse on penal policy, just as it had been completely anomalous in the old ameliorative one. Growing numbers of writers argued that the health of the nation required the removal by one means or another of its 'less valuable' members.[130] A kind of 'vulgarized Social Darwinism' gained currency in public discourse. With the advent of Wilhemine imperialism and '*Weltpolitik*', it was soon being applied to foreign policy and the relations between nations or 'races', so that the 'elastic and capacious concept of "struggle" was narrowed down to a pitiless fight, indeed to war'.[131] The application of this ideology to capital punishment was obvious. So widespread did it become after the turn of the century that abolitionists now felt obliged to counter it specifically. The numerous offenders who went to the block in Wilhelmine Germany at the age of 18, 19, or 20, argued one abolitionist writer in 1909, were surely capable of moral improvement:

If people want to deny this possibility, if they claim that they are criminals by their *entire disposition* and must remain such, then their bloody elimination really does appear as an unnecessary cruelty, for one surely cannot punish people for an inborn abnormal disposition, even if one has to *protect* society from them![132]

[129] Hans-Walter Schmuhl, *Rassenhygiene, Nationalsozialismus, Euthanasie: Von der Verhütung zur Vernichtung 'lebensunwerten Lebens' 1890–1945* (Göttingen, 1987), 60–1.

[130] Hans-Günter Zmarzlik, 'Der Sozialdarwinismus in Deutschland als geschichtliches Problem', *Vierteljahreshefte für Zeitgeschichte*, 11 (1963), 246–73.

[131] Hans-Ulrich Wehler, 'Sozialdarwinismus im expandierenden Industriestaat', in Imanuel Geiss and Bernd-Jürgen Wendt (eds.), *Deutschland in der Weltpolitik des 19. und 20. Jahrhunderts* (2nd edn.; Düsseldorf, 1974), 122–42, here 139.

[132] GStA Berlin Rep. 84a/7784, Bl. 300: *Die Tribüne*, 1 Sept. 1909.

Time was to prove, however, that this could indeed be done. It was not punishment, but simple, biological elimination that was eventually to be proposed.

In Wilhelmine Germany, this was still some way off. But even relatively liberal writers in this field shared many of the basic premisses of the biological approach to crime. The young Hans von Hentig, for example, made his name as a criminologist with a book, published shortly before the First World War, in which he advocated the indefinite preventive detention of recidivists, and even the refusal of the state to give economic assistance to first-time offenders and their families, on the grounds that the resulting privation would test their mettle, and lead to rapid reoffending if they were not up to it, thus saving society a lot of trouble in the longer term. At the same time he argued against the need for sterilizing or exterminating criminals because, as he said: 'Criminals belong in no small measure to parts of the race that are dying out of their own accord.' Their 'inferiority' was inherited, he conceded, but it also meant they were unlikely to have many children.[133] Others placed their emphasis on positive measures of improvement. The turn towards hereditarian views of criminality and immorality went together with a movement towards the development of a more elaborate social welfare system in Germany, in which a range of institutions emerged to care for individuals who were regarded in some sense as weak, in need of help, disadvantaged, or deviant. From social and medical insurance to ante- and post-natal clinics, asylums for people now defined as mentally ill or retarded, and many other similar institutions, the new welfare system represented to a considerable extent the growing power and prestige of medical and biological science in Germany following on its discovery of the causes of a wide range of diseases in the 1880s and 1890s.[134] Penal policy in other countries besides Germany was also redirected towards the therapeutic management of damaged human material rather than the improvement of the immoral or uneducated individual. For the optimistically-minded, Lombroso's ideas held out the eventual prospect of engineering heredity so as to eliminate criminality altogether.[135] Such a positive view of the benefits of science was characteristic of the later nineteenth century. Criminals could be discouraged from reproducing, while welfare measures could increase the survival chances and quality of life for the honest classes. Such views were widely shared by the professionals—psychologists, psychiatrists, social workers, and others—who were establishing their role in the penal process at this time. But among some writers, as we have seen, Lombroso's biological approach to criminality also lent a darker colour to penal thinking. Against the background of Wilhelmine *Weltpolitik* and fears that

[133] Hans von Hentig, *Strafrecht und Auslese* (Berlin, 1914), 216.   [134] Evans, *Death*, 505–7.
[135] Martin J. Wiener, *Reconstructing the Criminal: Culture, Law, and Policy in England, 1830–1914* (Cambridge, 1990), esp. chs. 6–9.

Germany's declining birth-rate was causing the country to fall behind in the struggle for international supremacy, anxiety began to spread about the faster reproduction of 'inferior' elements in German society. Where Lombroso himself led with the argument that Italian anarchists were the victims of an inherited tendency towards mental derangement, bourgeois Germans afraid of the seemingly inexorable rise of the working-class Social Democrats, with their revolutionary Marxist rhetoric, were not slow to follow. Respectable fears of social disorder presented by poverty, vagrancy, begging, alcoholism, violence, and crime were compounded by a new, materialistic emphasis on the 'negative' cost to German society of maintaining the chronically ill, the disabled, and the 'inferior' in institutions—a view propagated by Haeckel and widely discussed within his Monist League before the First World War.[136]

Well before this point, jurists were beginning to employ the new biological metaphors in their condemnation of the 'sentimentality' which some of them alleged was being displayed towards

obdurate monsters and parasites on life, who have for years made a profession out of pillaging the possessions of humanity and destroying its most noble treasures with a frivolous hand, ruffians of the mafia, who for years have avoided an honest living, live by night, and, fleeing from any kind of occupation that is worthy of humanity, are sapping away at society—such creatures could only be improved if they were given a new childhood and a new adolescence.

Since this was plainly impossible, the only sensible thing to do with such people, argued a legal official in 1912, was to execute them.[137] The biological metaphors in this passage—'parasites', 'creatures'—were striking. It was becoming increasingly common in the years leading up to the First World War. It found its way into the preface to the eighth edition of Karl Binding's standard textbook on German criminal law, which advocated an extension of the death penalty to nonfatal categories of violent crime in order to achieve the 'elimination of this tribe'.[138] A speaker in the Baden legislature in 1904 used it in defending the execution of murderers: 'The state must have the right of self-defence against beasts in human form and the possibility of ridding itself of such elements.'[139] A right-wing newspaper, the *Tägliche Rundschau*, declared in 1907 that murderers were lower down the evolutionary scale and should be put down without delay. Adding to the chorus of biological metaphors, it condemned the abolitionists for

[136] Michael Burleigh, *Death and Deliverance: 'Euthanasia' in Germany c.1900–1945* (Cambridge, 1994), 11–15.

[137] BA Potsdam 61 Re 1/1770, Bl. 44: *Staatsbürger-Zeitung*, 23 Oct. 1912: 'Für die Todesstrafe. Vom Oberlandesgerichtsrat Petrich, Friedenau.'

[138] Karl Binding, *Grundriss des deutschen Strafrechts* (8th edn.; Leipzig, 1913), preface.

[139] GLA Karlsruhe 234/6610: *Stenographische Berichte über die Verhandlungen des Badischen Landtags*, 19. öffentliche Sitzung der Zweiten Kammer, am Dienstag, den 26 Jan. 1904, 255.

indulging in 'a regular sickness, this weak-nerved sentimentality, when it comes to cutting out a disgusting sore cleanly from the body of society'.[140] The death sentence was the only language that subhumans of this kind understood, wrote the journalist Richard Nordhausen in 1908. 'Sensitivity towards tough punishments and the fear of them is strangely enough very strong in so-called inferior people', he declared: 'What is humane is to show the murderous pack an iron fist and never cease to tell them clearly that the state is determined on bloody retribution for every bloody deed.'[141]

The new tone of harshness towards criminality was unmistakable, even though it represented what was in most respects still very much a minority view. Whatever the claims of psychiatry, 'racial hygiene', criminology, and eugenics, penal policy in Wilhelmine Germany remained in the hands of the lawyers. The demands of the criminal anthropologists for punishment to be measured by the criminal, not the crime, failed to elicit a positive response from legal officials engaged in drafting a new Criminal Code at this time. The political thrust of the new ideas, directed against the Marxist view of crime as the product of environmental factors exerted by the social and economic injustices of capitalism and the bourgeois state, was blunted by the continued growth of the Social Democrats, who became the largest party in the Reichstag in 1912. Of course, here too, fears of the '*Lumpenproletariat*' and consciousness of the vulnerability of the working-class respectability, on which the labour movement drew for its active support, made some social welfare experts susceptible to the appeal of eugenics. These too were very much in a minority before 1914.[142] Nevertheless, the new thinking was more than merely marginal or eccentric. Increasingly, those professionally concerned with crime and criminality were using the language of Darwinism, eugenics, and biology in their discussion of issues such as the death penalty. In this way, debates about capital punishment proved to be the testing-ground for a number of ideas which were to become part of the exterminatory discourse and practice of National Socialism within twenty years of the outbreak of the First World War.

The reinstatement of capital punishment in Germany in the 1880s and above all in the 1890s coincided not only with the arrival of the new hereditarian discourse on criminality but also with the final triumph of a new synthesis of bourgeois-nationalist culture and values. Forces which had been critical of

---

[140] GStA Berlin Rep. 84a/7784, Bl. 216: *Tägliche Rundschau*, 9 Oct. 1907.

[141] Ibid., Bl. 273: *Der Tag*, 26 July 1908. For the spread of the concept of the 'inferiority' of criminals among German lawyers, see Wetzel, 'Criminal Law Reform', 267–87.

[142] Evans, *Rethinking*, ch. 8; Karl Heinz Roth, 'Schein-Alternativen im Gesundheitswesen: Alfred Grotjahn (1869–1931)—Integrationsfigur etablierter Sozialmedizin und nationalsozialistischer "Rassenhygiene"', in idem (ed.), *Erfassung zur Vernichtung. Von der Sozialhygiene zum 'Gesetz über Sterbehilfe'* (Berlin, 1984), 31–56.

German nationalism in the 1870s, from particularist Prussian conservatism to south German Catholicism, had largely embraced it by the 1890s. Similarly, the last vestiges of feudalism, such as patrimonial jurisdictions, also disappeared. Despite the existence of a few die-hards in the backwoods, German aristocrats shared most facets of bourgeois culture by the time Wilhelm II came to the throne.[143] At the same time, the industrial, mercantile, and professional middle classes had abandoned a significant part of their liberal heritage. By 1890 they had accepted many aspects of the Bismarckian political synthesis which it had still been the ambition of a large number of them to reform twenty years before. Nothing illustrated this transformation better than their growing acceptance of capital punishment in this period. Yet conflicts and contradictions still remained. The bloody beheadings through which the death penalty was administered in Wilhelmine Germany seemed to make a mockery of the bourgeois proprieties. This was an age of prudery and decorum, in which the Reichstag could spend weeks discussing the censorship of 'immoral' literature, and political parties could put the suppression of 'vice' at the top of their agenda. Many of the values and practices which we think of as 'Victorian' arrived in Germany in the late 1880s. Concealment of the grosser physical aspects of life became a priority, and a whole range of devices, from the water-closet to the bathing-machine, came into use in order to maintain decency. This was the period of the rise of cremation. Bourgeois disgust with the physical processes of putrefaction was paramount among the motives for its introduction.[144] As we have seen, the spirit of prudery was also affecting the practice of execution by the turn of the century. Disgust and disquiet at the physical aspects of executions continued to be expressed by those present at them. The reinstatement of capital punishment on a firm basis thus coincided with the emergence for the first time of a real desire to make it private. A package of attitudes had been assembled which was to grow in importance as time went on. Belief in the death penalty as a means of eliminating the biologically degenerate was now coupled with the feeling that it had to be administered quickly and secretly, with a minimum of ceremony, so that those who ordered it and were responsible for it would not have to witness the bloody killing of an offender in more than minimal numbers, or for a moment longer than was strictly necessary.

Such processes of cultural change did not proceed smoothly. The Wilhelmine political scene also experienced a widespread process of political mobilization. By the 1890s, voter participation in elections was running at over 80 per cent. The Social Democrats became a mass party, with over a million members by 1914.

---

[143] See Blackbourn and Eley, *Peculiarities*.
[144] Jennifer Leaney, 'Ashes to Ashes: Cremation and the Celebration of Death in Nineteenth-Century Britain', in Houlbrooke (ed.), *Death*, 118–35.

FIG. 24. *The normality of capital punishment.* The death penalty was so widely accepted by the mid-1900s that it could be used to advertise a magazine. This imaginary scene by Thomas Theodor Heine was printed in the satirical journal *Simplicissimus.* 'Despite everything,' says the caption, 'the murderer Allramseder could not bring himself to be executed before Tuesday because he wanted to have a look at the new issue of *Simplicissimus.*'

Pressure groups and voluntary associations of all kinds sprang up. A new popular press took the place of older forms of popular literature and provided a vehicle for the articulation of new forms of commercialized popular culture. The departure of Bismarck and the lapsing of the Anti-Socialist Law provided the stimulus for the re-emergence of left-wing liberal and radical projects of reform and renewal. Among the many new social movements, it was almost inevitable that there should be a movement for the abolition of capital punishment. If its prospects for success in the Reichstag were minimal, then the possibilities for mobilizing public opinion by other means were beginning to seem rather brighter, as we shall now see.

10

The Revival of Abolitionism

a. Liberals, Pacifists, and Capital Punishment 1895–1912

As the political climate began to relax a little after the departure of Bismarck and the ending of the Anti-Socialist Law in 1890, opposition to the death penalty began to revive. It was fuelled by the sharp increase in the number of executions that took place in the early years of this decade. The issue of capital punishment had been effectively dormant since the early 1870s. But now the left-liberal opponents of the death penalty began to raise their voices in protest once more. Many of their arguments were familiar ones. They continued to believe in the ameliorative theory of punishment. The left-liberal *Berliner Tageblatt* declared in 1907: 'Capital punishment is reprehensible from a human and a Christian point of view because it prematurely destroys the inner developmental potential of the condemned person.' They continued to believe in progress: 'Torture has been abolished, and corporal punishment restricted to particular exceptional cases. . . . Sensibilities are becoming more humanitarian from generation to generation.'[1] 'The death penalty', proclaimed another left-liberal paper on 18 August 1900, 'is a remnant of a barbaric age, unworthy of a civilized people. The purpose of punishment, namely amelioration, disappears by definition.'[2] In the abolitionist rhetoric of the left-liberals, the 'medieval' and 'barbarous' character of capital punishment still took pride of place in this period. It was 'regrettable', declared a left-liberal newspaper in 1909, 'that capital punishment still exists in the twentieth century.'[3] 'The *Frankfurter Zeitung* sarcastically described the execution of an 18-year-old criminal in 1903 as 'assuredly another testimony to the utility of capital punishment, another sign of the high level of our culture'.[4] Many liberals continued to feel that cruel punishments would encourage such crimes rather than deter them. 'History has demonstrated that an age in which

---

[1] GStA Berlin Rep. 84a/7784, Bl. 267: *Berliner Tageblatt*, 16 Oct. 1907.
[2] HStA Düsseldorf Rep. 145/327, Bl. 24: *Rheinische Zeitung*, 18 Aug. 1900.
[3] Ibid., Bl. 301: *Berliner Tageblatt*, 2 Oct. 1909.
[4] GStA Berlin Rep. 84a/7784, Bl. 250: *Frankfurter Zeitung*, 5 Sept. 1903.

the most terrible varieties of capital punishment existed was also an age in which the most terrible crimes were committed.'[5] 'To hack a person's head off legally is a bestial brutality, a brutality which demeans the state and avenges itself upon the society which it is supposed to protect.'[6] Another writer added that the brutality of the execution blotted out the brutality of the crime.[7] Such arguments were open to the retort that more modern and less brutal methods of execution could be employed instead. Abolitionists remained sceptical. 'In olden times', said one abolitionist mockingly in response to this point, 'people were beheaded, broken with the wheel, immured alive, and quartered. Nowadays university faculties are racking their brains to see how a person's life can be destroyed without hurting him.' But this was absurd. The conclusion, he said, was clear: 'In other words, there is no modern way of carrying out the death penalty.'[8]

As all this indicated, many left-liberal opponents of the death penalty felt themselves by this time to be on the defensive. One abolitionist was forced to admit in 1909 that 'in our day, the prospects for the abolition of capital punishment, a punishment which points back to the most melancholy times of the Middle Ages, are worse than they have ever been'.[9] The criminologist and legal expert Franz von Liszt confessed: 'I lack the courage to demand the abolition of the death penalty in the German Empire, although I am of the opinion that it will very quickly prove to be superfluous and counter-productive in an effective penal system with a rationally ordered custodial policy.'[10] Much of the abolitionists' time was devoted to countering the prevailing arguments of the retentionist majority. To the objection that imprisonment was no deterrence against murder, they responded 'that it is questionable whether a crime that in any case presupposes the absence of all intellectual and ethical restraint could be influenced at all by a deterrent example'.[11] To the accusations of weakness and sentimentality levelled against them by among others, the nationalist historian Heinrich von Treitschke, they retorted: '*He* was the "sentimental" one here, who gave way to atavistic impulses of feeling.'[12] A rational person would not wish to retain capital punishment as Treitschke had. To the argument that only the death penalty provided a sure protection for society against murderers, abolitionists replied that

[5] Ibid., Bl. 257: *Frankfurter Zeitung*, 5 Oct. 1904.
[6] BA Potsdam Auswärtiges Amt IIIa Nr. 51, Bd. 10, Bl. 63: *Frankfurter Zeitung*, 29 Aug. 1911.
[7] Ibid., Bl. 258: *Strassburger Post*, 21 Nov. 1904.
[8] BA Potsdam Auswärtiges Amt IIIa Nr. 5, Bd. 10, Bl. 99: *Vossische Zeitung*, 6 Sept. 1912.
[9] GStA Berlin 84a/7784, Bl. 301: *Berliner Tageblatt*, 2 Oct. 1909.
[10] Franz von Liszt, *Strafrechtliche Aufsätze und Vorträge*, i (Berlin, 1905), 390. Liszt was the founder-editor of the *Zeitschrift für die gesamte Strafrechtswissenschaft*, the most influential academic journal in the field of criminology and criminal law.
[11] GStA Berlin Rep. 84a/7784, Bl. 267: *Berliner Tageblatt*, 16 Oct. 1907.
[12] Ibid., Bl. 272: *Die Tribüne*, 24 July 1908. See also BA Potsdam Auswärtiges Amt IIIa Nr. 51, Bd. 10, Bl. 95: *Vossische Zeitung*, 25 Aug. 1912.

German prisons were secure, and escapes by convicted murderers unknown. To the recruitment of public opinion and popular concepts of justice in defence of the death penalty, they objected that 'nobody pays any attention to the people's feelings for what is right and wrong when large parts of society take offence at someone committing homicide with intent and premeditation, in other words, murder, in a *duel*, and getting away with a brief confinement in a castle'.[13] As another abolitionist writer pointed out, the retentionists' appeal to public opinion was inconsistent and hypocritical: 'Our law contains an infinite number of things which contradict the general sense of right and wrong held by the vast mass of the people. Nevertheless, nobody pays the least attention to it. Only when it comes to capital punishment must we suddenly adhere to the "popular sense of right and wrong"!'[14] True public opinion, radical and left-liberals continued to believe, was representative in character. 'The task of the leading spirits in society consists precisely in fructifying the people with new social and ethical ideas.' The élitism of the Progressives and left-liberals at this time reflected among other things the fact that their strong representation on municipal councils and state legislatures all over the German Reich depended heavily on the continued existence of a restricted franchise in which only the propertied male élite had full voting rights. Wealth gave them a stake in society, they believed, and thus impelled them to behave responsibly; education and upbringing put them on a superior moral and cultural plane to that of the masses. Thus they argued 'that from a certain stage of civilization, capital punishment must be regarded as culturally backward'.[15]

All this had an extremely familiar ring to it. Most of these arguments could be found on the abolitionist side in 1870, and many of them even in 1848. No doubt this helps explain why the left-liberal abolitionists met with such little success. Progress by this time had become associated in the minds of many not with humanitarianism and civilization but with science and planning. From the point of view of someone who believed that scientists such as Lombroso had proved that criminality, or at least susceptibility to it, was hereditary, such arguments seemed old-fashioned and sentimental. And the left-liberals' belief in the ameliorative possibilities of imprisonment was far removed from reality. Although they still considered the aim of imprisonment to be the improvement and rehabilitation of the offender, and regarded capital punishment as a total anomaly in the penal system of their day, in truth, little attention was ever paid in German prisons to the moral improvement or education of inmates. For some retentionists, indeed, prisons were little more than comfortable hotels maintained at the public expense. What, asked one supporter of the death penalty, was

13 GStA Berlin Rep. 84a/7784, Bl. 272: *Die Tribüne*, 24 July 1908.
14 BA Potsdam Auswärtiges Amt IIIa Nr. 51 Bd. 10, Bl. 102: *Vorwärts*, 7 Sept. 1912.
15 GStA Berlin Rep. 84a/7784. Bl. 297: *Berliner Tageblatt*, 9 Jan. 1909.

the fate of the vile anarchist beast who had assassinated the unfortunate Empress Elizabeth of Austria?

Four meals a day, two walks a day, a few hours of comfortable and by no means unpaid work, language lessons, literature lessons, a clean pipe of tobacco, enough time for reading 'favourite authors', and the happy prospect of the 'Memoirs' of the noble assassin, that is the punishment which befell the cowardly beast who some years ago committed that treacherous and villainous murder of the Austrian Empress.[16]

However, another newspaper, the *Reichsbote*—in no way a proponent of abolition—reported in 1908 that the murderer of the Empress Elizabeth of Austria had tried to kill himself in gaol on more than one occasion. This was hardly evidence that imprisonment was a soft option. Surely, it remarked, execution would have been more humane.[17]

Others agreed. Although it seemed that retentionists were trying to have it both ways, many of them supported their arguments for execution by citing the Beccarian argument that life imprisonment could be a harsher sentence than decapitation.[18] Death brought the murderer a kind of peace. But a life in gaol did not. 'Let him drag out his guilt-laden existence, shut out from human society and denied the freedom that makes life worth living. Let him be oppressed by internal and external sufferings for as long as it takes to admit the terrible nature of his deed and to repent of it.' Such an argument was even used in recommending clemency for offenders who showed a degree of remorse towards their crime. Writing of the clemency appeal of one Friedrich Bösche, born in 1867, and condemned to death in 1896 for murder, the state prosecutor in Bremen noted that after the death sentence Bösche's previously defiant attitude had changed, and he now seemed to be capable of improvement:

Remorse alone, once it has been awakened, will not in my firm opinion die away again, if the fear of imminent death can be expunged from his mind, and if life imprisonment in the penitentiary replaces it—a punishment no less hard, if not harder, than a quick death—it will provide no lack of opportunity for remorseful thoughts and thus constitute an even juster expiation than capital punishment.[19]

Bösche was duly granted a reprieve by the Bremen Senate despite the recommendation of the clemency board to the contrary. The changed attitude that the state prosecutor had noted in Bösche seems, however, to have been the first sign of a descent into depression and despair, for the offender was found hanged in his cell three months later.[20]

---

[16] Ibid., Bl. 266: *Tägliche Rundschau*, 9 Oct. 1907.   [17] Ibid., Bl. 291: *Reichsbote*, 12 July 1908.
[18] GLA Karlsruhe 234/6610: *Stenographische Berichte über die Verhandlungen des Badischen Landtags*, 19. öffentliche Sitzung der Zweiten Kammer, am Dienstag, den 26. Januar 1904, 275 (deputy Fehrenbach).
[19] StA Bremen 2.-D. 17. c. 1. Bd. 7: Erster Staatsanwalt to Senat Justiz-Kommission, 7 Feb. 1896, 26–7.
[20] Ibid.: Auszug aus dem Senatsprotokolle, 15 May 1896.

Whether a murderer experienced remorse or not made no difference to the length of the sentence: it remained life.[21] Throughout the nineteenth century the release of convicted murderers on parole was extremely rare except where the offender was regarded as so old that no further danger was posed to society. In the Grand Duchy of Hesse, out of 587 capital offenders granted clemency between 1817 and 1929 whose fate could be traced, twenty-four died in prison, including two after a sentence lasting between forty and fifty years, and one after a total of fifty-four years in gaol. Twelve were released on condition that they emigrated across the Atlantic, and fifteen were paroled, again frequently after periods of up to half a century in gaol.[22] Things were no different in Prussia. The private scribe Eduard Kyms, condemned to death in 1860 at the age of 33, and then consigned by the royal clemency to imprisonment for life, was still in gaol fifty years later, and died in prison aged 84 in September 1911.[23] In 1840, Gottfried Haecker, aged 18, and Augustin Baeck, aged 20, were convicted by a Bavarian court of planning and carrying out a murder in order to steal the clothes worn by their victim. The two men were granted clemency by the King and consigned to a penitentiary for life. Haecker, whose file containing the details of his imprisonment has survived, was exhibited at the pillory beforehand. For the first twelve years of his sentence, until the age of 30, he was forced to wear an iron ball and chain day and night. They were removed in 1852. Ten years later, in 1862, he was still in prison, when the promulgation of a new Bavarian Criminal Code made it arguable that the crime he had committed should not have merited a death sentence, since the circumstances under which it had taken place fell under the new Code's definition of manslaughter. Haecker's petition to be released was refused on the grounds that his condemnation had been legally valid at the time. Fifteen years later, in 1877, he sent in a second petition. But the Ministry of Justice officials pointed out that the Reich Criminal Code, which had superseded the Bavarian legislation, now meant that his crime could be defined as murder again, so his petition for release was rejected once more. The file ends at this point, with Haecker, now aged 55, having been in prison for a total of thirty-seven years and doomed to spend the rest of his life there.[24] A similar instance, also from Bavaria, not only underscored the fact that life imprisonment really meant what it said, but illustrated how the element of public opinion could be used by legal officials to justify their harsh application of the law. The schoolteacher Dominikus Hahn, his brother Egid, and Egid's wife Magdalena had

---

[21] GStA Berlin Rep. 84a/7784, Bl. 258: *Strassburger Post*, 21 Nov. 1904.
[22] Krämer, *Mord*, 166–7.
[23] BA Potsdam 61 Re 1/1769, 20: *Berliner Volkszeitung*, 12 Sept. 1911.
[24] HStA Munich MJu 17962: Justizministerium to King, 12 Dec. 1840; Oberappellationsgericht der Pfalz to King, 7 Nov. 1862, and further notes to 1877.

conspired to murder Dominikus's wife in 1844. All three were condemned to death in 1847. Dominikus's lawyer complained to the Ministry that 'it is public opinion and morality and not the judge that has broken the wand over my client'. The King was not disposed to listen to such liberal contempt for the 'mob', and signed the death warrant. Hahn was executed on 13 August 1847.[25] The 'popular view', said the Ministry, would be satisfied if the sentences passed on the other two were commuted to life imprisonment. And so it was. Egid Hahn was 26 years old when he killed his sister-in-law in 1844. As time went on, he began to appeal for release. His last recorded attempt was made in 1887, when he was in his seventieth year. His wife Magdalena had died in prison four years previously. The Ministry was unrelenting. Egid's character might have improved during his forty years in gaol, conceded the officials; but the cardinal point remained the fact that it had been Egid who had actually committed the murder, and his release would have confounded 'the main aim of punishment, expiatory retribution'. In all these instances, therefore, the retributive aspect of justice remained paramount; deterrence and improvement were barely mentioned at all.[26]

So even if the prison authorities did try to bring about the moral or educational improvement of a 'lifer', it was to no purpose. In any case, commentators noted that the vast majority of inmates in German gaols had previous convictions, a fact which seemed to give the lie to the notion that imprisonment led to moral improvement.[27] Many inmates complained that the long sentences which they were serving robbed them of moral initiative and left them apathetic, while the poor food and conditions encouraged anaemia and tuberculosis.[28] The Catholic padre at the men's penitentiary in Bruchsal reported in 1900 that the spiritual condition of the 'lifers' was particularly wretched. It was, he said,

changeable as the weather, quiet as a lamb today, patient, pious, resigned; full of anger tomorrow, wrathful, raging and foaming like the sea, so tired of life that they cry out: 'Chop off my head today' or, 'It would have been more sensible if my head had been cut off then with an axe, than to have had me tortured so long and so slowly with the *cold guillotine.*'

After fifteen or twenty years, reported the chaplain, the rejection of an application for clemency and release from prison was bound to make such a man 'even more hardened, furious, and embittered against God, religion, the Church,

[25] Johann Baptist Reisinger, *Dominikus Hahn's Lebensbegebnisse, seine Vorbereitung zum Tode und seine Hinrichtung, dargestellt in einer Predigt* (Straubing, 1847).
[26] HStA Munich MJu 17965: Justice Ministry to King, 10 June 1847; Hölzl to Justice Ministry, 31 July 1847; Justice Ministry to King, 10 July 1846, and following documents, up to letter from Justice Ministry to King, 25 Apr. 1887.
[27] BA Potsdam 61 Re 1/1525, Bl. 17: *Dresdener Zeitung*, 6 June 1903.
[28] Ibid., Bl. 37–8: *Münchener Neueste Nachrichten*, 26 Oct. 1903: Hans Leuss, 'Aus dem Zuchthause'.

human society, the "unjust and unforgiving state" and against the prison officers, in whom they only see their "torturers" and "hangmen".' They must, he argued, be granted at least some hope of release, if they were not to be spiritually destroyed altogether.[29] But no one listened to informed opinion of this kind. Even abolitionists fought shy of arguing for a system of remission for lifers, because it would weaken their case for the ending of executions by giving ammunition to the retentionist argument that they were soft on crime.

All this undermined the traditional left-liberal argument that capital punishment was an anomaly and that the amelioration of the offender was the primary purpose of penal policy. In an age where criminology and penal policy was starting to be debated in terms of science instead of religion, it was no longer enough for the abolitionists to continue equating progress with liberal humanitarianism. A minority of radical intellectuals realized this and began to reformulate abolitionist rhetoric in terms more appropriate to the scientific penal discourse of the age. Many of the new abolitionists were associated with radical pressure groups of the liberal left which emerged in the period of political mobilization that followed the ending of the Anti-Socialist Law. Most important of these was the pacifist movement, which found its most significant organizational incorporation in the German Peace Society, founded in 1892. Given their belief that war, violence, and conflict were inimical to human progress and unjustifiable in terms of an ethical culture based on a scientific knowledge and understanding of human nature and human interests, it is not surprising that most of the pacifists were active opponents of capital punishment. The pacifists were overwhelmingly middle-class, professional, and intellectual, and had no mass constituency. But they made up for their lack of widespread support by their tireless energy in propagandizing their cause. By the eve of the First World War, the abolitionists had begun to attract a considerable variety of literary and journalistic talent to their cause. Among those who campaigned for the ending of capital punishment was the young Kurt Tucholsky, who was to become one of the best-known and most controversial radical literati of the Weimar Republic. In one of his earliest published pieces, Tucholsky penned a bitingly sarcastic description of an execution held in Saxony in 1912. Sixty people were waiting in the prison courtyard, he wrote:

A door opens and they drag a person out, who has to die and doesn't want to. (His victim didn't want to either, but why repeat the horror?) The state prosecutor, a civil servant right to the tips of his moustache, reads something out to the half-mad man, who has been reduced to the level of an animal by his fear: '. . . has not made use of his right of reprieve'. . . . He is rendered inaudible by the bellowing and screaming of the madman,

[29] GLA Karlsruhe 234/6610: Auszug aus dem Jahresbericht des kath. Hausgeistlichen am Männerzuchthaus in Bruchsal, 6 Mar. 1900.

who is twisting and struggling in the hands of the executioner's servants. This man (Göhlert is his name) shouted for example that he had been wrongly condemned. . . . Among the spectators are the murdered woman's three sons and a son-in-law!—I am convinced that there was also a Holy Joe there with a bible: Judge not, that ye be not judged!—What were the sons thinking during this horror?—Revenge?— Satisfaction?

Tucholsky concluded ironically that the event was only 'a modest display' in comparison with the 'small popular festival' which had accompanied the execution of Grete Beier. The whole procedure had undoubtedly 'provided valuable material for the cause of abolishing the death penalty'.[30]

Many of the abolitionists were journalists and writers, and they had connections in mainstream left-wing liberalism which opened up the columns of major daily newspapers such as the *Berliner Tageblatt* and the *Frankfurter Zeitung* to their views. They were connected to many other new movements of the radical, non-socialist left, from the feminists to the free-thinkers, and many of them believed in the notion that social and political ethics had to be taken out of the sphere of religion, which had failed humankind, and placed on a truly scientific and rational basis. This brought them into the orbit of other new organizations which emerged in the ferment of political mobilization in the 1890s, such as the Ethical Culture Society and the free-thinkers, and there was a substantial overlap in membership between virtually all of these groups. In 1895, for example, one of the most prominent of the new pacifists, the cantankerous but prolific journalist Alfred Fried, launched a strong attack on the practice of capital punishment in Prussia in the magazine *Ethische Kultur* ('Ethical Culture'). Fried condemned capital punishment in traditional liberal language as a pointless medieval relic. There was no evidence that it deterred anyone from committing any crimes, he said. The months that the condemned had to wait between the sentence and its execution were a mental torture which was unjustifiable in a modern state. The aim of punishment must be rehabilitation.[31] None of these arguments was very new. But their appearance in the journal of the Ethical Culture Society signalled the fact that the fight against the death penalty was now moving outside the parliamentary arena and into the area occupied by the pressure groups. In due course other radical-liberal voices joined the new chorus of opposition to capital punishment. None of them was a major parliamentary politician. They included the leader of the 'ethical culture' group, Moritz von Egidy, the pacifists Wilhelm Förster and Bertha von Suttner, the sociologist Ferdinand Tönnies, the free-thinking Darwinist Ludwig Büchner, and the

---

[30] Kurt Tucholsky, *Gesammelte Werke*, ed. Mary Gerold-Tucholsky and Fritz J. Raddatz (Reinbek, 1960), i. 19.

[31] Alfred Fried, 'Hinrichtungen in Preussen', *Ethische Kultur*, 3/45 (9 Nov. 1895), 355 (copy in GStA Berlin Rep. 84a/7783, Bl. 165). For the history of German pacifism, see Roger Chickering, *Imperial Germany and a World Without War: The Peace Movement and German Society 1892–1914* (Princeton, 1975).

sexologist Richard von Krafft-Ebing. All of these people were active in the world of the radical-liberal pressure groups. Of course, not all pacifists supported abolition. Otto Umfrid, a dissident Protestant pastor who was one of the leaders of the German Peace Society, considered that the time for abolishing the death penalty was not yet ripe. It seems reasonable to suppose, however, that his views on this point were influenced by his religious beliefs, and they were not shared by the vast majority of leading pacifists and adherents of the idea of a scientifically based 'ethical culture'.[32]

Yet the opponents of the death penalty in Wilhelmine Germany, vociferous though they were, never formed a specific pressure group dedicated to the cause of abolition. The major reason for this was most probably their realization that the chances of such a society achieving its only possible aim—persuading the Reichstag to abolish the death penalty—were extremely remote. Not only was the largest party, the Catholic Centre, firmly retentionist, but the majority of the National Liberals, once the major proponents of abolition, had long since come round to the view that the death penalty had to be retained. The Conservatives, who remained the fiercest defenders of the death penalty, were much reduced in number by the turn of the century, but so too were the left-liberals, who had mostly stayed loyal to the abolitionist cause. The parliamentary arithmetic was not likely to work out in the abolitionists' favour. Moreover, neither parliamentary parties nor individual deputies were entitled to bring bills before the Reichstag. This could only be done by the government, acting through the Federal Council, the assembly of princes and sovereigns of the federated states. With Wilhelm II on the throne, there was no chance at all of this happening as far as the abolition of capital punishment was concerned. Finally, the German pacifists themselves were, throughout this period, a tiny, embattled minority, struggling against the predominantly positive attitude to warfare and conflict in the political culture of the age. They sought to influence public opinion on the issues they believed in, and these included capital punishment; but they were too remote from political reality, too intellectual, too far above the hurly-burly of parliamentary business and party politics to have much of an effect.[33] For pacifists, in addition, and for many radical liberals after the turn of the century, the looming threat of global war and killing on a vast scale far outweighed in urgency and importance the execution of a couple of dozen capital offenders every year. Abolition was always a secondary issue for those radical-liberal politicians and journalists who were most committed to it by their ethical stance.

[32] Alfred Fried, 'Die Todesstrafe im Urtheil der Zeitgenossen', *Die Zeitgeist, Beiblatt zum 'Berliner Tageblatt'*, 48, 2 Dec. 1901 (copy in GStA Berlin Rep. 84a/7784, Bl. 203–5).
[33] Chickering, *Imperial Germany*, 384–420.

Moreover, by refusing to submit themselves to party discipline, even though their arguments were directed at a single issue of legislative reform, abolitionists condemned themselves to parliamentary ineffectiveness. Too radical for the mainstream left-liberals, who were increasingly favourably disposed to nationalism and imperialism in the years leading up to the war, and too independent for the Social Democrats, who demanded ideological subservience to a Marxist ideology which they found impossible to accept, the liberal-pacifist abolitionists stood no chance of success before 1914. Nevertheless, in the last years of peace, the gloom which had hung over the abolitionist cause to some extent began to lift. In 1906 the government began to consider drafting a new Criminal Code. Its introduction into the Reichstag as a bill would allow deputies to propose the abolition of capital punishment by means of amendment. Given the sensitivity of the issue, this was bound to spark an impassioned debate both within the Reichstag and without. The Social Democratic Party was also gaining continually in strength throughout this period. In the 1912 elections it overtook the Catholic Centre as the largest party, just as the preparation of the draft Criminal Code was nearing completion. The Social Democrats were from the very beginning firmly committed to the abolition of the death penalty, so the parliamentary arithmetic was at last beginning to swing back in abolitonism's favour. A great deal therefore depended on the seriousness with which the socialists and the labour movement took the issue of capital punishment, and the degree to which they could count on popular support for the stance they took on it.

b. The Social Democrats and the Death Penalty

The Social Democratic Party emerged from the dark days of the Anti-Socialist Law strengthened both in numbers and in ideological commitment. It regarded itself among other things as the true heir of the radical liberals of 1848, and sought to pursue many of the issues of the failed Revolution which it thought the weakened and half-hearted liberals of the Wilhelmine period were no longer willing to take up. Social Democratic thinking on law and order developed only slowly, and it was not until the Reichstag debate of 1870 that any condemnation of the death penalty is recorded as having been made by either of the two leading figures in the party, August Bebel and Wilhelm Liebknecht. Social Democrats shared many of the basic ideas of liberals about punishment. The aim of modern penal policy, wrote one Social Democratic journalist in 1900, was not retribution or deterrence so much as improvement and rehabilitation. 'Chopping the condemned man's head off certainly doesn't improve him'.[34] The party wrote the

---

[34] GStA Berlin Rep. 84a/7784, Bl. 202: *Berliner Volkszeitung*, 13 July 1900.

abolition of the death penalty into its Erfurt Programme of 1891, which remained in force up to the First World War and beyond, and reaffirmed it unanimously at its Congress in Chemnitz in 1912.[35] But it was not only a proponent of liberal and humanitarian causes, it was also an exponent of Marxism, and its attacks on capital punishment were part of a more widespread concentration on what it regarded as 'feudal' relics in German society, from the practice of duelling to the powers of the aristocracy. These could in the end only be removed by a socialist revolution, so the campaign for abolition of the death penalty was pessimistically regarded by many Social Democrats as 'without any prospect of success' until this happened.[36] Such an attitude was characteristic of much of the party's thinking, in which it justified its relative inaction in concrete political terms by placing its faith in a future revolution which would somehow automatically deliver total political power into its hands.

Nevertheless, even if the Social Democrats' Marxist radicalism was at times more verbal than actual, they still kept up a continual barrage of criticism of capital punishment. As the *Berliner Volkszeitung* remarked on 13 December 1900,

To be sure, if one looks at the Golden Age of beatings and hangings in the name of the law, when people beheaded others, hanged them, broke them with the wheel, and burned them at the stake to their heart's content, when towns were as proud of their scaffold as they now are of a good hospital, where was the deterrence there?[37]

The paper added for good measure that decapitation was arguably not the most deterrent of punishments. Many people voluntarily threw away their lives in duels and suicides, but nobody voluntarily committed themselves to a lifetime in prison. The judicial system was to a large extent a means of protecting the existing social and economic order. In their daily newspapers and periodical publications, the Social Democrats concentrated on scandals and offences involving the rich and the titled, of which there were indeed not a few in Germany in the decades leading up to the First World War.[38] Should an upper- or middle-class citizen carry out a murder, the likelihood, complained the Social Democrats, was commital to a lunatic asylum. For the proletarian offender, the matter stood very differently:

The propertied class requires a cruel and barbaric penal system crowned by capital punishment . . . And since poverty and destitution often enough lead to murders for gain, and a poor upbringing, schnapps, and lack of education frequently bring forth capital crimes, the propertied are trembling with fear for their lives and are demanding the death penalty to rescue them from murderers.

[35] Düsing, *Abschaffung*, 130.
[36] *Stenographische Berichte über die Verhandlungen des Deutschen Reichstags*, 274. Sitzung, 5 Apr. 1903, 8395–6.
[37] GStA Berlin Rep. 84a/7784, Bl. 202: *Berliner Volkszeitung*, 13 Dec. 1900.
[38] See Johnson, *Urbanization and Crime*, 61–78, for examples.

Capital punishment, concluded the paper, was a tool of the ruling classes. 'It is the task of the working class to protect even their degenerate offspring from the revenge of the capitalist society as whose victims they have become "guilty".'[39] The writer was certainly not arguing that murder was excusable when the offender was working-class. Rather, the intention was to suggest that the capitalist system comprehensively denied the working class the means of self-improvement, from beginning to end. Penal policy first enforced this denial and then attempted to ward off its worst consequences. The Social Democrats were strongly committed to the improvement of living standards, to education, to sobriety, to obedience to the law, and to self-control. These things, they thought, could only be achieved through the organization of the masses into the labour movement and its implementation of a new social order through the socialist revolution. In 1912 the Social Democratic daily paper *Vorwärts* argued that what was needed was not a harsher penal code but a policy to deal with the 'causes of crime, social misery, and the physical, spiritual, and moral degeneration to which it gives rise'.[40] In 1910, to underline this, the Congress of the Second Socialist International, meeting in Copenhagen, and dominated by the Germans, resolved that a world-wide demonstration should be mounted against the death penalty. The bourgeoisie, it declared, had now abandoned its former hostility to capital punishment as a 'barbaric legacy of the darkest Middle Ages' and was using it with increasing ruthlessness 'not only to rid itself of the products of the decomposition of its own capitalist society, but also to repress the fighting proletariat'.[41] In fact the demonstration never seems to have taken place.

The public opinion to which the Social Democratic Party addressed itself was overwhelmingly working-class and petty-bourgeois. Despite its size, the degree of its social and political ostracism by the Establishment was such that no judge, state prosecutor, or judicial official would ever dare to think of becoming a Social Democrat. Indeed, even university professors who did so were summarily dismissed, while state employees in industries such as the railways had to conceal their membership of the party for fear of getting the sack.[42] Here, however, there is evidence that the Social Democrats' efforts on behalf of the abolitionist cause did indeed meet with some success. Both as a political party and as a wider cultural movement, the Social Democrats prided themselves on their educational activities among the German working class. Working through an impressive array of daily newspapers, weekly and fortnightly magazines, cheap book and pamphlet series, libraries, educational courses, lecture series, and so on, the Social

[39] Ibid., Bl. 302: *Tribüne* (Erfurt), 24 Oct. 1909 (suppl.).
[40] BA Potsdam Auswärtiges Amt IIIa Nr. 51, Bd. 10, Bl. 97: *Vorwärts*, 5 Sept. 1912.
[41] Ibid., Bl. 33: *Vorwärts*, 1 Sept. 1910.
[42] Alex Hall, 'By Other Means: The Legal Struggle against the SPD in Wilhelmine Germany, 1890–1914', *Historical Journal*, 17 (1974), 365–80.

Democrats sought to uplift and improve the ordinary working man and, increasingly after the turn of the century, woman whose cause they represented.[43] These efforts were not without their effect. But at the same time, rank-and-file party members, sympathizers, and voters were also exposed to many other influences, ranging from their family upbringing to their education at primary school—a strongly monarchist and conservative institution in Imperial Germany—and their socialization in the army (for men), in the church congregation (for women), or in the neighbourhood and at the workplace (for both). Nor were workers restricted to Social Democratic newspapers and magazines for their information; this period saw the rise of a new cheap mass-market press, dependent on advertising, which was beginning to make serious inroads into the party-political media by the outbreak of the First World War.[44] Most important of all, the manual labourers who provided the backbone of the Social Democratic movement and ensured that despite a heavily biased electoral system the SPD became the largest party in the Reichstag in 1912, were influenced by the experience of their own daily lives: by poverty, by hard, grinding work, and by constant clashes with authority.[45]

The attitudes of ordinary Social Democrats to capital punishment were thus shaped not just by party policy and propaganda, but by an amalgam of influences, not all of them operating in the same direction. For this reason, some middle-class commentators seriously doubted whether the official Social Democratic party line on capital punishment really found much support among ordinary working men.[46] The truth of this allegation is hard to gauge; but some evidence of their views can be found in a series of secret reports compiled by the political police in Hamburg—the only German city where this practice is known to have existed—before the First World War. For nearly twenty years, a changing team of policemen, dressed up as workers, toured the pubs and bars of the port, especially those known to be the haunts of Social Democrats, and listened to what was being said. Back at the police station, they wrote down anything that had been of interest; and they seem to have been remarkably honest in the way they did so. Ultimately, their superiors were not interested in scare stories about working-class susceptibilities to revolutionary appeals, or proletarian disrespect for law and order; they wanted as far as possible to hear the truth, so that they

---

[43] Vernon L. Lidtke, *The Alternative Culture: Socialist Labor in Imperial Germany* (New York, 1985).

[44] Guenther Roth, *The Social Democrats in Imperial Germany: A Study in Working-Class Isolation and Negative Integration* (Totowa, NJ, 1963); Alex Hall, *Scandal, Sensation and Social Democracy: The SPD Press and Wilhelmine Germany 1890–1914* (Cambridge, 1977). See also Lynn Abrams, *Workers' Culture in Imperial Germany: Leisure and Recreation in the Rhineland and Westphalia* (London, 1992).

[45] See Richard J. Evans (ed.), *The German Working Class: The Politics of Everyday Life* (London, 1982).

[46] BA Potsdam, 61 Re 1/1770, 45: *Kölnische Zeitung*, 25 Oct. 1912.

could judge correctly how far the party activists' message was getting across to the mass of the people.[47]

When the conversation in Hamburg's working-men's pubs turned to the question of the death penalty, there was plenty of evidence that the party was indeed having an influence on rank-and-file views. A constant diet of stories about miscarriages of justice in the Social Democratic press convinced many of its supporters that a good number of criminals must have been wrongly executed, although no such case was explicitly mentioned either by the press or in their conversations. 'Above all', one worker was overheard saying in a pub in 1901, 'capital punishment is really cruel in the present day, and yet it is often used.' Another was reported two years earlier as being of the view that

Corporal and capital punishment doesn't belong in our time any more. It's been proven that when someone gets used to being beaten, he soon gets hardened to being beaten black and blue. Nor has the death penalty deterred people from committing crimes either. In any case, a lifetime behind bars is a much tougher punishment for a well-brought-up person than the death sentence.[48]

These views were very much the party line. But in discussing individual cases the workers often forgot their principles as they became fascinated by the prospect of a criminal going to the block. Ordinary Social Democrats not only discussed the cases of 'class justice' that so frequently featured in the party press; they also devoured every detail of the sensational murder trials that provided such an important source of popular entertainment at this time, before the advent of public radio, and in the infancy of the cinema. Early in 1895, for instance, a number of pub conversations were reported on the trial of the local sex murderer Breitrück, speculating on whether Breitrück 'goes to the King with a plea for mercy' or whether he would 'soon be made shorter by a head'. They went over every detail of the case as it had been reported, argued about whether the witnesses—who included a prostitute—were reliable, and disagreed as to the correct punishment. While one said 'that if Breitrück is executed, in my view a judicial murder will have been committed', another took the view that it was 'a scandal that the Altona District Court is delaying Breitrück's execution'. Typically, they compared his case, where—most of them seemed to agree—endless delays were being caused by clever defence tactics and appeals, with those of fellow Social Democrats accused of *lèse-majesté*, which landed the accused in gaol almost as soon as they had started.[49] Rank-and-file Social Democrats had a strong respect for justice in the abstract, and this made them object all the more strongly

---

[47] Richard J. Evans (ed.), *Kneipengespräche im Kaiserreich. Die Stimmungsberichte der Hamburger Politischen Polizei 1892–1914* (Reinbek, 1989); see pp. 7–39 for an extended discussion of the reliability and limitations of this source.

[48] Ibid. 207–8, 221–2.   [49] Ibid. 189–93.

when they read in the party press that the law was being applied unfairly or without due process in practice. But individual criminal cases were not used as a basis on which to argue that the death penalty was wrong. Realistically enough, the conversation partners assumed that it would continue to operate for the forseeable future; and it was this fact as much as anything that gave murder cases such as that of Breitrück their popular fascination. That there was a ready audience for newspaper reports of murders, capital trials, and executions did not necessarily mean, therefore, that there was the kind of overwhelming popular support for the death penalty that conservative politicians and commentators liked to think there was.

The declared aim of the Social Democrats to abolish capital punishment when they achieved power thus in all probability enjoyed a fair degree of support among the rank and file. Yet the problem remained that the means by which they proposed to achieve power was that of the overthrow of the Wilhelmine political system in a proletarian revolution along Marxist lines. Their opponents were able to point out that revolutions were seldom peaceful events, and suggested that the Social Democrats were insincere in their advocacy of abolition. All they wanted to do in reality was to undermine the legitimacy of the existing legal system. History showed the left to have been more than reluctant to abolish capital punishment when it had been in power itself. The spectre of 1789—or rather, 1793–4—was raised again, and for the right, it could only be laid to rest by a strict application of the Criminal Code:

When certain social or other revolutionaries get the idea of laying their hands on goods which they claim they alone can distribute in an equitable manner, when the heirs of the great French Revolution get ready to abolish everything they consider reactionary, then the last thing they think of is the abolition of the death penalty.[50]

In fact, the German Social Democrats thought that the coming revolution would be a peaceful one, in which they would achieve power by parliamentary means. What they would do if, as was more than likely, Wilhelm II responded to the election of a socialist majority in the Reichstag by staging a military coup, was not something to which they ever gave much thought. Once the revolution became violent, however, their commitment to the abolition of the death penalty was bound to be put to the severest of tests. The Social Democrats' tendency to renege on their ideological principles was already apparent in a number of areas before 1914. By voting for war credits in the Reichstag in August that year, they made it clear that their opposition to war had been little more than skin-deep. Only time would tell if the same could be said of their opposition to the principle and practice of capital punishment.

[50] GStA Berlin Rep. 84a/7784, Bl. 228: *Die Reichsbote*, 21 Jan. 1909.

FIG. 25. *Karl Liebknecht accused of treason.* The Social Democrats fear the worst. The cartoon reflects the Social Democrats' perception that justice in Wilhelmine Germany was 'class justice' directed above all against themselves and the people they represented, the working class. Karl Liebknecht (1871–1919), a leading left-wing radical in the party, was tried for high treason, for which the penalty was death, in Leipzig on 9–12 December 1907, as a result of the publication of his book *Militarism*, which the prosecution held to be prone to undermine the Kaiser's prerogative of command over the Army. The caption beneath it read: 'We've got him!' Liebknecht was sentenced to eighteen months' detention in a fortress, but the case fuelled Social Democratic suspicions of the widened treason provisions in the new Criminal Code being drafted at the time. There are the usual inaccuracies in the representation of the execution, from the preponderance of judges around the scaffold (an allusion to the conservative bias of the judiciary) and the exaggerated closeness of the spectators to the events, to the medals on the chest of the executioner and the blindfold over the eyes of the offender, neither of which would have been present in a real event of this kind.

c. *Reforming the Criminal Code 1906–1914*

Just as the Social Democrats were achieving the position of being the largest party in the Reichstag, a four-man criminal law commission established by the Reich Justice Office in May 1906 to draft a new Criminal Code was nearing the completion of its task. Three of the civil servants who sat on it were from the Prussian Ministry of Justice, the fourth was provided by the Reich Justice Office. In 1908 the original representative of the Office left the commission and was replaced by Curt Joël, whose lengthy bureaucratic career was to culminate in his appointment as Reich Justice Minister in a 'cabinet of experts' under Heinrich Brüning in the early 1930s. By 1909 the commission had met over a hundred times and was making good progress.[51] It decided therefore to issue a preliminary draft for public discussion, which laid down the death penalty for murder, high treason, and the attempted assassination of the Kaiser or the head of one of the federated states. The authors of the draft commented:

All four cases concern offences which are considered so serious and such a danger to society, not only by the law but also by the predominant popular view of right and wrong, that only the destruction of the offender, the highest penalty the state can impose, appears to offer a just retribution and an adequate means of protecting society.

Thus the argument that public opinion demanded the death penalty had now found its way into official policy. Life imprisonment, in this view, offered no equivalent deterrent or protection for society.[52] Contrary to the expectations of abolitionists, instead of restricting capital punishment still further, the commission recommended what one legal expert called a 'greatly expanded application of the death penalty in the case of high treason'. For a normal conviction of attempted manslaughter, a sentence as low as one year's imprisonment was theoretically possible. But for an attack on the life of the Kaiser or the princely head of one of the federated states, the death penalty was mandatory.[53] As the Social Democrats pointed out, this proposed new clause replaced one in which only attempted *murder* was liable to the death sentence:

The words 'attack on the life of' offer very considerable room for the exercise of the arts of interpretation from the judges' bench. That deeds which are committed without premeditation are included in this category is explicitly underlined in the Preamble. If one recalls that press libels have recently been treated by the courts as cases of physical assault because the victim of the libel has been sick with anger at them, one cannot

[51] BA Potsdam 61 Re 1/1768, 1: *Freisinnige Zeitung*, 26 Oct. 1909. For the origins of the decision to undertake a reform of the Criminal Code, and a detailed account of the debates about penal policy which took place during the drafting, see Wetzell, 'Criminal Law Reform', 213–24.

[52] Ibid., Reichsamt des Inneren 8422: Vorentwurf zu einem neuen Deutschen Strafgesetzbuch nebst Begründung, Bl. 44–6, § 13, pp. 16–20. See also Düsing, *Abschaffung*, 102–3.

[53] BA Potsdam 61 Re 1/1768, 10a: *Freisinnige Zeitung*, 26 Oct. 1909.

exclude the possibility that an ingenious state prosecutor might sometime see in such an article an attack on the life of the people protected by the above-mentioned paragraph and demand the death penalty.[54]

Nor was this mere hyperbole, for the ingenuity of state prosecutors in finding grounds on which to send the editors of Social Democratic newspapers to gaol was indeed legendary, and grew rather than diminished after the lapsing of the Anti-Socialist Law.[55] Moreover, the Social Democrats did not fail to point out that the Explosive Substances Law and the Slave Robbery Law remained unaffected by the new draft, and that the death penalty was also provided for 'offences constituting a common danger' under martial law, which, as Wilhelm II and numerous generals were wont to point out, could be declared by the army at any time.[56] All these measures, of course, the Social Democrats thought, with good reason, would be directed principally against themselves; and their conviction that the new Criminal Code would make 'class justice' worse than ever was reinforced by the provision of relatively light sentences for duelling, sentences which, as their daily newspaper, *Vorwärts*, noted, were more lenient than those laid down for street begging and vagabondage.[57]

The proposal to retain and indeed extend the death penalty in the new draft attracted criticism from left-wing liberals as well. The *Freisinnige Zeitung*, for example, was astonished that rather than provide an elaborate justification for the decision to retain capital punishment, the commission simply referred back to the preamble to the Criminal Code of 1871. This in turn did little more in the newspaper's view than perpetuate the provisions of the Prussian Criminal Code of 1851. Yet on both occasions it had been widely thought that capital punishment could be dispensed with in the fullness of time. The newspaper commented:

Since 1851 the level of civilization of our people has made massive progress, the intellectual and moral standard of the population has risen substantially, culture has spread widely and allowed every class of the people to participate in its benefits. So it cannot easily be claimed that a penal sanction which was regarded as barely supportable half a century ago in the circumstances of the time remains indispensable today.[58]

On the right, however, there were complaints that the draft Code was too lenient. It gave too much credence to spurious claims of diminished responsibility in capital cases and, most regrettably, it failed to bring back the lash.[59]

[54] Ibid. 2: *Vorwärts*, 21 Nov. 1909.

[55] Klaus Saul, 'Der Staat und die "Mächte des Umsturzes". Ein Beitrag zu den Methoden antisozialistischer Repression und Agitation vom Scheitern des Sozialistengesetzes bis zur Jahrhundertwende', *Archiv für Sozialgeschichte*, 12 (1972), 293–350.

[56] BA Potsdam 61 Re 1/1768, 2: *Vorwärts*, 21 Nov. 1909; Martin Kitchen, *The German Officer Corps 1890–1914* (Oxford, 1968), 115–86.   [57] BA Potsdam 61 Re 1/1768, 33: *Vorwärts*, 29 Dec. 1909.

[58] Ibid. 25: *Freisinnige Zeitung*, 25 Nov. 1909.   [59] Ibid. 37: *Deutsche Tageszeitung*, 24 Dec. 1909.

Moreover, the new paragraph on sentencing for murder removed the mandatory death penalty and introduced a discretionary sentence of life imprisonment. 'We have such a rich crop of horrible murder cases,' said a Hessian legal official, 'that one could not say that the rising level of education of the people, as one often hears argued, has rendered such harsh measures superfluous.'[60] Whatever the views of the Reichstag had been on the subject of the death penalty in 1870, commented the *Kreuzzeitung*, 'Public opinion has undergone a remarkable transformation in the intervening forty years.'[61] This was an accurate enough observation, as we have seen. Yet the draft Criminal Code still removed the death sentence from aggravated manslaughter, and lowered the sentence for the manslaughter of senior relatives (*Totschlag Verwandten aufsteigender Linie*). This, the conservative paper thought, was to be regretted.[62]

The criminal law commission of the Reich Justice Office completed its task of drafting a new Criminal Law Code, after nearly three hundred sessions, the last of them chaired by the conservative academic lawyer Professor Wilhelm Kahl, in November 1913.[63] The final draft made few concessions to the criticisms levelled at the commission's preliminary proposals on capital punishment in 1909. When the commission sat in 1911 to consider the clauses relating to capital offences, it agreed to retain the death penalty for the four offences listed in the preliminary draft, with the addition of offences covered by the Explosive Substances Law of 1884 and the Slave Robbery Law of 1895. It reported:

No objections have been raised from any side to the principle of retaining the death penalty. . . . Now as before, the decisive argument is that it is indispensable for the time being. In the dominant concept of justice, there are crimes which demand the complete elimination of the perpetrator as expiation; the death penalty, in which the majesty of the state achieves its most powerful expression, is the appropriate means.[64]

The commission recognized, however, that the mandatory death sentence for murder reduced the likelihood of conviction. 'It is undeniable', they conceded some months later, 'that the jurors' deliberations are influenced among other things by the fact that the death sentence is the ineluctable consequence of a guilty verdict.' To counter this tendency, it proposed to write a sentence of life imprisonment into the Code as an alternative, to be decided on by the judge, instead of the decision being left exclusively to the monarch's power of commutation. 'Because a plea of guilty for murder will no longer have the inevitable

---

[60] BA Potsdam 61 Re 1/1768, 49: *Deutsche Tageszeitung*, 15 Oct. 1910.

[61] Ibid. 81: *Kreuz-Zeitung*, 1 Mar. 1910.

[62] Ibid. 109: *Norddeutsche Allgemeine Zeitung*, 9 June 1910.

[63] Ibid.1/1770, 181; note of 22 Nov. 1913.

[64] Ibid. Reichsamt des Inneren 8426: Protokolle der Kommission für die Reform des Strafgesetzbuches, Bl. 55, 6. Sitzung, 24 Nov. 1911.

consequence of a death sentence, the jurors will find it easier to come to a conclusion which corresponds better to the results of the trial.' The preliminary draft proposed that a sentence of death could only be passed if the jury had rejected a plea of mitigating circumstances. Some members of the commission, to be sure, believed

that the jurors, namely in so far as they oppose capital punishment in principle, would be open to the temptation of finding mitigating circumstances merely in order to avoid a death sentence. This is all the more dangerous because of the fact that the grounds on which mitigating circumstances can be found are not precisely delineated by the law. If we stick to the preliminary draft, then it is to be feared that the result in practice will be the abolition of the death penalty.

This point of view was not accepted by the majority. The commission finally agreed on a clause allowing life imprisonment only where there were mitigating circumstances, largely on the grounds that the decision of life or death should rest with the jury, not the judge, and that the power to commute a death sentence so arrived at belonged, not to the judge, but to the sovereign.[65] Clearly the majority of its members still had faith in the retentionist convictions of the people who were likely to be called up for jury service.

These decisions were indicative of official thinking about capital punishment in the last peacetime years of Wilhelmine Germany. They underlined once more the political dimension of the issue. The death penalty had been retained in the Criminal Code voted through by the Reichstag in 1870 in the interests of national unity. It had been reintroduced in practice in 1878 as a means of preserving the political order in the face of a supposed socialist conspiracy to overthrow it. It had been extended in 1884 because the threat of international anarchist terrorism was perceived to demand a response. And it was reformulated in the draft Criminal Code of 1913 in the belief that one of its primary purposes was to protect the sovereign, and that the power of clemency remained a crucial attribute of hereditary monarchy. The death penalty was explicitly retained as an expression of the 'majesty of the state'. Beyond this, it was as a retribution rather than a deterrent that it was demanded by what the commission saw as the dominant legal opinion of the day. Such views were likely to meet with strong condemnation from the opponents of capital punishment when the draft was finally presented to the Reichstag as a bill. The way finally seemed open for a fresh attack on the principle of capital punishment by way of abolitionist amendments in the legislature.

But this never took place: such was the complexity of the draft, so extensive was the debate which it had aroused, and so difficult did it prove after the

[65] Ibid. 8429, Bl. 007–020, 11–12: 141. Sitzung, 12 June 1912.

elections of 1912 to put together a workable government majority in the Reichstag, that Chancellor Bethmann Hollweg failed to find a place for it in his legislative programme in the few months that elapsed between the completion of the draft in November and the end of the parliamentary session a few months later. By the time the Reichstag reconvened, it was too late. Other things were on its mind in August 1914, and the outbreak of war postponed the debate on the draft Criminal Code indefinitely. Yet if there was no chance of the death penalty being abolished in Wilhelmine Germany, then at least there was a possibility that its incidence might be reduced. For opinion among those who were responsible for administering it—the legal profession—became increasingly divided as time went on. At the biennial Lawyers' Congress held in Danzig in 1910, legal experts debated the death penalty at length during a discussion of the draft Criminal Code. Led by Wilhelm Kahl, the retentionists held the field; in the criminal law section of the Congress, their views prevailed by a majority of fifty votes to twenty-four. Undismayed by this setback, the abolitionists returned to the fray in 1912. This time there were 1,800 lawyers present at the Congress, which was held in Vienna, 317 of them taking part in the debate in the criminal law section.[66] Among the papers presented to the Congress was a 200-page submission by Moritz Liepmann, which went through the moral, legal, philosophical, and above all statistical arguments in favour of abolition in impressive detail. It quickly became one of the classic abolitionist texts.[67] The discussion of Liepmann's submission revealed widespread disquiet among lawyers and judicial officials about the practice and principle of capital punishment. One lawyer declared: 'A death sentence is an irreparable sentence. It makes it impossible to correct unavoidable judicial errors.'[68] Another, Dr Warhanek, declared that the death penalty had 'simply lived out its course. . . . It goes against all our feelings that a defenceless individual, however despicable he may be, should be executed by a servant of the state [*applause and unrest*].'[69] The jurists debated once again the time-worn arguments about deterrence, popular opinion, irrevocability, and expiation. Particularly effective points were made against the commonly held view that capital punishment was needed to deal with the outrages committed by anarchists—a view that had been instrumental in securing the rehabilitation of the death penalty in the 1880s. 'Anarchist', as a senior law officer, Max Jacobsohn, from Berlin, wryly observed, was a word that caused usually objective men to leave the paths of reason. The threat of anarchist outrages was still in the

[66] Düsing, *Abschaffung*, 111–18.

[67] Moritz Liepmann, 'Ist die Todesstrafe im künftigen deutschen und österreichischen Strafgesetzbuch beizubehalten?', *Verhandlungen des 31. deutschen Juristentages* (Berlin, 1912), ii. 572–765.

[68] BA Potsdam 61 Re 1/1770, 19–20: *Berliner Volkszeitung*, 3 Sept. 1912: 'Gegen die Todesstrafe. Von Rechtsanwalt Blasse, Berlin.'

[69] Ibid., Auswärtiges Amt IIIa Nr. 51, Bd. 10, Bl. 99: *Vossische Zeitung*, 6 Sept. 1912.

public mind at this time, especially because of the continuing campaign of assassination of government ministers by the populist movement in Russia. But the death penalty, as one speaker in the debate pointed out, could easily be counter-productive in such cases: 'We know from a series of anarchist murderers that the idea of ending one's life on the scaffold as a martyr for an "idea" does not have a deterrent effect on these men's brains but rather inspires them and spurs them on!'[70] Despite a substantial abolitionist presence at the Congress, the motion to support abolition was lost in the criminal law division by one vote— 159 votes to 158—and in the plenary session by 470 votes to 424. As the leading spokesman for the retentionists, Wilhelm Kahl, declared, it would be wrong to jeopardize the Criminal Code as a whole by insisting on abolition when it was clearly unacceptable to the government. The death penalty remained a necessary instrument of deterrence at least for the time being.[71] It was wrong, as Kahl said on another occasion, to listen to 'sentimentalities, which only think of the criminal's pain, but disregard that of the victim and ignore the horror of the crime'.[72]

However, despite this, the narrowness of the vote showed that many lawyers were deeply concerned about the extent to which capital punishment was employed in Wilhelmine Germany. Of course the Congress included ordinary practising lawyers and professors of law as well as judges and prosecutors, and so was not entirely representative of opinion in the legal apparatus of the state. Nevertheless, there is some evidence that lawyers at every level, as well as police officers and (as the criminal law commission pointed out) jurors became increasingly reluctant to prosecute and convict people for murder the more likely it seemed that the death sentence attached to this crime would actually be carried out. In the period 1882–6, for example, some 47 per cent of reported deaths from homicide (murder and manslaughter, in other words) in Prussia resulted in convictions for homicide, and 29 per cent of these convictions resulted in the death sentence. However, only 12 per cent of death sentences were actually carried out, the rest being commuted to life imprisonment on the orders of Wilhelm I in his capacity as King of Prussia. As soon as Wilhelm II began to sign more death warrants, however, these figures began to experience a dramatic change. In the years 1890–4, some 54 per cent of death sentences passed in Prussian courts were actually carried out, and by the period 1901–5 the proportion had climbed to 71 per cent. Everyone concerned with a homicide offence

[70] Ibid. 61 Re 1/1770, 19–20: *Berliner Volkszeitung*, 3 Sept. 1912: 'Gegen die Todesstrafe. Von Rechtsanwalt Blasse, Berlin'; ibid. Auswärtiges Amt IIIa Nr. 51, Bd. 10, Bl. 95: *Vossische Zeitung*, 25 Aug. 1912; ibid., Bl. 98: *Frankfurter Zeitung*, 6 Sept. 1912.

[71] Ibid. 61 Re 1/1770, 27: *Deutsche Tageszeitung*, 18 Oct. 1912.

[72] Ibid. 1/1768, 149: *Deutsche Tageszeitung*, 29 Sept. 1910. See also W. Höpfner, 'Todesstrafe und Abschreckungsgedanke', *Zeitschrift für die gesamte Strafrechtswissenschaft*, 33 (1913), 142–76.

could therefore be absolutely certain that a death sentence was more likely than not to end in the condemned offender being executed. The result was that police, prosecutors, judges, courts, and juries became more reluctant to press for homicide convictions, and the proportion of reported deaths from homicide resulting in convictions for murder or manslaughter fell to 35 per cent in 1890–4 and 21 per cent in 1901–5. A similar decline took place in the proportion of homicide convictions leading to death sentences, which fell to 20 per cent in 1890–4 and 16 in 1901–5. The biggest drop in all of these figures came between 1890 and 1891, or in other words as soon as it had become clear that Wilhelm II intended to refuse clemency to a far higher proportion of capital offenders than either of his predecessors had. Between these two years, the proportion of reported homicide deaths leading to homicide convictions fell dramatically from 47 per cent to 27 per cent, and the proportion of homicide convictions leading to death sentences similarly fell sharply from 30 per cent to 20 per cent.[73]

Without a systematic examination of police and court records, which would take many years even if the archival material could be located in sufficient quantity, it is obviously impossible to say with any certainty why these changes occurred. But it is a reasonable supposition, in the light of the views expressed in the criminal law commission and the Lawyers' Congress, that from 1891 onwards, at the latest, police and prosecutors were more careful about charging offenders with murder or manslaughter rather than with some lesser offence, and courts were more careful about passing death sentences on offenders convicted of homicide. They did not want the responsibility of sending someone to the block unless they were absolutely convinced of the person's guilt, and without a strong belief that such an offender deserved to be executed. This does not mean, of course, that the police and the courts were becoming more critical of the death penalty in principle, but it does mean that they were becoming much more reluctant to apply it in practice once they knew that the room for manœuvre by way of the clemency procedure had become much more limited than it had been in the days of Wilhelm I. A police inspector, an investigating judge, a state prosecutor, a jury, or a trial judge could be fairly sure in the 1880s that only the most clear-cut and (according to the generally agreed values of the day) heinous cases of murder or aggravated manslaughter would lead to execution, and that these would be the exception rather than the rule. In the 1890s and 1900s the reverse was true: almost every conviction for these offences would lead to execution if a death sentence was passed, and so the responsibility of deciding which cases were the most clear-cut and most severe was assumed lower down the chain

---

[73] See the Statistical Appendix, below.

of prosecution, by the police, the prosecutors, and the courts, instead of the Ministry of Justice and the King.

None of this was very welcome to enthusiasts for the death penalty, of course. Indeed, the very existence of the royal clemency itself was coming under attack from the radical right before the First World War, as advocates of an even harsher penal policy began to argue that the monarch was going against the intention of the law (which was to punish murder with death) if he used his right of commutation in any but the most exceptional circumstances.[74] Here was an example of the way in which the 'national opposition' which was emerging in this period was beginning to attack the Wilhelmine system of government from the right, urging the creation of a dictatorship and the launching of a far more aggressive foreign policy than even Wilhelm II was willing to entertain. From this point of view, the state apparatus of Wilhelmine Germany appeared as weak and vacillating rather than authoritarian and undemocratic.[75] Nevertheless, it would be quite wrong to suppose in view of all this that the judicial apparatus in Wilhelmine Germany was becoming more liberal. Judges, prosecutors, and legal officials were loyal servants of the existing political system, and especially in their administration of political justice, in which Social Democrats were regularly and ruthlessly pursued for a whole range of petty offences mainly as a form of political persecution, they automatically identified the Wilhelmine Reich and its institutions with the interests of the German nation and the social order. Imperial Germany was a 'legal state' (*Rechtsstaat*), and the criminal law operated, as we have seen, according to set rules and principles which offered the citizen a range of significant rights, such as legal representation, due process, appeal, and so on. But it was not a state subject to the rule of law. On the contrary, in German parlance, *Rechtsstaat* simply meant that the state agreed voluntarily to implement its purposes by legal means. The distinction might seem a fine one, perhaps even pedantic. But it was crucial. For what the state gave, the state could take away. The legal profession got used to the idea that what was legal was defined by the state, so if the state's interests demanded it, the definition could change. The notion of the law as something independent of and above the state, by which the citizen could obtain redress against the state, was foreign to German legal thinking. This meant that the law could easily be bent to political purposes, and was another source of the politicization of the debate on penal policy in the Wilhelmine period. More ominously, perhaps, the identification by judges and

---

[74] GStA Berlin Rep. 84a/7784, Bl. 294: *Deutsche Tageszeitung*, 19 Aug. 1908.

[75] See Geoff Eley, *Reshaping the German Right: Radical Nationalism and Political Change after Bismarck* (London, 1980), 19–40; and David Blackbourn, *Populists and Patricians: Essays in Modern German History* (London, 1987), 217–45.

prosecutors of the German state with the Wilhelmine system was to make it difficult for them in the longer run to adapt their thinking to a democratic political order when it came, or to cease thinking of socialists and Marxists as anything other than enemies of the state, even when, as they did for substantial periods after 1918, they formed the legitimate, elected government.[76]

d. The Sternickel Trial

A number of central issues in the discourse on capital punishment in late Wilhelmine Germany were dramatized in 1913 by a sensational murder case tried in Frankfurt an der Oder. The principal accused, August Sternickel, was a journeyman miller, born in Silesia on 11 May 1866. He had numerous convictions, and was wanted by the police from 1905 onwards for robbery, murder, and arson. He evaded the police's attention by using a variety of aliases, but by 1908 they were catching up with him, and he was being forced at times to live rough and support himself by begging and petty theft. When the heat was off, he was able to earn a living by labouring.[77] He obtained a job as a farm-hand in Ortwig, near Frankfurt an der Oder, and seems to have worked there for a couple of years, undisturbed by the law, before relations with his employer deteriorated and he faced the prospect of dismissal. In January 1913 Sternickel walked into a lodging-house in Müncheberg and announced he was looking for labourers. Looking 'very fine', and every inch the gentleman, he was taken for a landowner, and three young men agreed to accompany him to the farm at Ortwig. They were Georg Kersten, aged 20, his brother Willi, aged 17, and Franz Schliewenz, and they learned on the way that the 'work' for which Sternickel wanted them was a robbery. Sternickel intended, or so he told the young men, to tie up the farmer and his wife and lock them in the cellar, while the Kersten brothers kept watch over the couple's two adolescent daughters. Then they would ransack the place for valuables. Sternickel and his three companions arrived at the farm according to plan. When they broke in, the farmer resisted, and Sternickel threw him onto the floor. 'What!', said Sternickel to his protesting employer: 'You've annoyed me for long enough, you'll see what will happen!' While his three accomplices held the man down, Sternickel strangled him with a piece of string. As they fell upon the serving-maid and Sternickel began to strangle her too, the others objected; but he threatened them with a revolver, so they held the woman down until she was dead, then went with him into the house, where Sternickel dealt with the farmer's

---

[76] For a reasoned defence of legal positivism and the *Rechtsstaat*, see Thomas Nipperdey, *Deutsche Geschichte 1866–1918*, i. *Arbeitswelt und Bürgergeist* (Munich, 1990), 655–65, and ii. *Machtstaat vor der Demokratie* (Munich, 1992), 182–201.

[77] StA Bremen 4, 14/1. VII. F. 16, pp. 20, 29: *Extra-Beilage zum Deutschen Fahndungsblatt*, 2693 (30 Jan. 1908) and 3122 (28 June 1909).

wife in the same manner, probably killing her with a hammer-blow to the head. Only the intervention of his three accomplices stopped him from murdering the couple's two young daughters as well. After combing the place for money, jewellery, and clothing, they locked the children in the house and took their parents' bodies to a barn, which they set alight. Sternickel remained on the spot so as not to arouse suspicion, but when he later fled, he was arrested. His three accomplices returned to Berlin, where their smart new clothing soon made their acquaintances suspect that they had been up to no good. An innkeeper with whom they had pawned their old clothes found some papers in them which suggested they had been near the scene of the murder in Ortwig recently reported in the press. He alerted the police, and the accomplices, Georg and Willi Kersten and Franz Schliewenz, were arrested and charged with the murder as well.

The four men's trial, held in March 1913, was extensively reported in the press. Its revelations about the Berlin underworld fascinated respectable society, which pruriently devoured the testimony of witnesses such as Elizabeth Klehmer, a Berlin prostitute known as 'Lardycheeks', a close associate of Schliewenz and the Kersten brothers. Sternickel himself struck the pose of the bold robber. He refused 'with a contemptuous smile' to reveal where he had buried the seven thousand marks he had stolen from the miller with whose murder in 1905 he had also been charged. He created what the papers called a 'sensational incident', as he admitted not only that he had a mistress in every place where he worked, but also that 'I'm married, but my wife doesn't know that my life has taken this course.' He aroused further 'movement' in the courtroom by refusing to reveal the identity of his wife, who was evidently living under another name. While Schliewenz and the Kersten brothers rendered lachrymose confessions implicating each other and their ringleader in the crime, Sternickel disputed the details of the prosecution case vigorously and insisted pointedly that he had 'never betrayed other people'. He took his triple death sentence 'without batting an eyelid', while the other defendants 'collapsed, stunned at the announcement of the sentence'. Franz Schliewenz and Georg Kersten were each given two death sentences, while Georg's brother Willi escaped with fifteen years' imprisonment because he was under 18.[78] Trials had become very much a form of public entertainment by the late nineteenth and early twentieth centuries. They were reported blow-by-blow in the press, and a visit to the public gallery in particularly sensational trials was a popular and fashionable amusement among the middle classes. On the last day of the Sternickel trial in 1913, more chairs had to be brought into the courtroom to cope with the extra demand for places, while 'a crowd of people numbering many hundreds has gathered at the nearest

[78] Ibid.: *Bremer Nachrichten*, 15 Mar. 1913; *Weser-Zeitung*, 15 Mar. 1913; *Weser-Zeitung*, 17 Mar. 1913.

available street corner.'[79] Reporting the Sternickel trial in March 1913, one conservative newspaper noted with disapproval the intrusion of the female sex into this part of the public sphere:

Once more, the *female sex*, and especially its members from so-called better circles, constituted a major part of the audience. Do these ladies have any idea of how much they are demeaning themselves and their sex by forcing themselves into notorious trials such as this, in which things have to be mentioned which offend and violate every tender female feeling?!

Admission to the public gallery, argued the paper, should be restricted to men only.[80] Here was another part of the public sphere where acts of violence and brutality were revealed which respectable opinion thought it unseemly for ladies to know about. The comment was a clear echo of similar objections raised to the presence of women at public executions many decades before.

Trials and sentences in Wilhelmine Germany were also becoming part of a public sphere in which decisions of the authorities were being contested. The sensation caused by the Sternickel affair, coming as it did at a time when the movement for the abolition of capital punishment was gathering strength, ensured that the debate did not die down when the sentences were passed. While Sternickel refused to ask for his sentence to be commuted, the lawyers acting for the other two condemned men immediately submitted appeals for the exercise of the royal clemency. They were supported by Hans Hyan (1868–1944), a concerned radical-liberal journalist. Hyan's campaign established him almost overnight as one of the most prominent figures among a new generation of opponents of the death penalty.[81] It concentrated on the Kersten family, with whom the journalist rapidly established close relations. Hans Kersten, the father, was a construction worker in Berlin. On a visit to Hyan, he admitted that he had been unable to control his two boys. They were, he said, 'Berlin street urchins'.[82] Hyan wrote numerous letters and articles in the liberal and left-wing press, and thanks to his contacts with the family was able to use personal documents and correspondence in his campaign to win over public opinion and thus put pressure on the Ministry of Justice and the Prussian King. In June, for instance, he quoted at length from a letter written by Georg Kersten to his mother after sentence had been passed:

Dear mother, is there no chance of rescuing me any more? I haven't killed anyone! Please write to me and tell me whether I can see you both again! Willi is in the cell across the corridor, just down from mine. It is his birthday on Sunday, but I am not allowed to see

[79] StA Bremen 4, 14/1. VII. F. 16: *Weser-Zeitung*, 17 Mar. 1913.
[80] BA Potsdam 61 Re 1/1770, 97: *Deutsche Tageszeitung*, 28 Mar. 1913.
[81] For some of Hyan's verses on capital punishment, see Riha (ed.), *Moritatenbuch*, 427–8 and 438–9.
[82] BA Potsdam 61 Re 1/1770, 114–15: *Berliner Tageblatt*, 30 May 1913.

FIG. 26. *Hans Hyan (1868–1944)*. A journalist and leading campaigner against capital punishment at the time of the Sternickel affair, 1913, and throughout the Weimar Republic, Hyan pioneered the use of emotional appeals based on individual cases as a way of influencing people against the death penalty.

him! Dear parents, if only I had just listened to you and had never left you, none of this would ever have happened! Dear parents, is there really no more prospect of help for me, do I have to die so young, does nobody have any pity for me?[83]

[83] Ibid.: *Leipziger Volkszeitung*, 16 June 1913.

The young man's desperate plea from the death cell to his parents, his obvious remorse, his almost infantile regression; all these directed a new, more emotional appeal to the liberal reading public when they were presented in this way by an abolitionist campaigner such as Hyan. The *Berliner Tageblatt* reported receiving a flood of readers' letters supporting the campaign for clemency.[84]

More powerful still was a letter sent to Hyan, possibly at his request, by Klara Kersten, the mother of the condemned youth. Her three girls, she said, were all well-behaved, and her oldest son, aged 21, was not in trouble. But Georg and Willi were a different matter.

They weren't bad, my two boys! They were so good when they were children! . . . My husband is a labourer, he doesn't earn much, and he has often been without any work at all. So I had to work as well, went washing and charring. I was often away from home the whole day and my children were left on their own. . . . We were always poor, so we couldn't afford to have the boys educated. But they were good all the same, as long as they worked in the factory, up to two years ago, when they went to work for the transport business. Then they met fine friends who persuaded them to go away from Berlin. Then they were without work again, and I told them off so much that they didn't feel at all comfortable. Oh if only they hadn't met that awful man, doing such a deed would never have occurred to them. I have done what I could. . . . Oh, I don't know what more to say! My poor Georg! Help me please! I won't be able to survive it![85]

The appeal of the letter, as it was cited by Hyan, was directed at a number of targets, from the conservative cult of motherhood to the liberal and socialist sympathy with the poor. But supporters of the death penalty found this to be 'inappropriate sentimentality' and accused Hyan of suffering from a 'morbid state of mind'. The offenders were in this view no more than 'inhuman beasts', and common sense demanded 'a corresponding expiation' of the murder they had committed.[86] The *National-Zeitung*, organ of the National Liberals, was particularly strong in its condemnation. Hyan's articles in the press, it declared,

are such a challenge to the healthy feelings of right and wrong which the overwhelming majority of the German populace, numbering not thousands but millions, possesses, and in comparison to which the tiny clique of 'sensitive people' does not count at all, that it seems necessary to speak out against this repulsive campaign on behalf of coarse murdering villains in the press. It is really going off the rails to try to arouse popular sympathy for murderers who managed to pluck up their courage to kill three unsuspecting people one after another in a cowardly and treacherous manner, and who were callous enough to smoke cigarettes while they were doing so. It is the three unfortunate victims and their surviving relatives who deserve sympathy, not their bestial slaughterers.[87]

[84] BA Potsdam 61 Re 1/1770, 114–15: *Berliner Tageblatt*, 30 May 1913.
[85] Ibid. 117: *Berliner Volkszeitung*, 14 June 1913.   [86] Ibid. 130: *Schlesische Volkszeitung*, 31 July 1913.
[87] Ibid. 118: *National-Zeitung*, 21 June 1913.

Hyan's attempt to try to take advantage of the coincidental fact that the three men's execution was scheduled for more or less the same time as King Wilhelm II's silver jubilee was similarly spurned by the paper. The King, the *National-Zeitung* opined loftily, would pay more attention to 'the feelings for justice of the overwhelming majority of the people'. Such sentiments made it clear how far mainstream National Liberal opinion, which this newspaper represented, had come since the radical days of 1870, when the party had been the main force behind abolitionism. Severely depleted in numbers and electoral support, it was taking the populist road, appealing to what it considered to be the opinion of the masses in support of a position that was now not so very different from that of the conservatives. Only a few decades before, when it still believed in an essentially élitist concept of representative parliamentary government, it would have spurned such demagogy.

Sternickel was executed on 30 July 1913, in Frankfurt an der Oder.[88] As he entered the prison courtyard, he is said to have addressed those present with a few words, and concluded: 'I would like to thank you once again for coming along, and hope it gives you the greatest pleasure.'[89] Schliewenz and the Kersten brothers were not reprieved under the royal amnesty,[90] but in July 1913 they were granted clemency in a separate action. Hyan's campaign had triumphed in the end. Of course, ironically, it would have been better from the point of view of demonstrating the injustice of capital punishment had Kersten been executed. Moreover, there was no doubt at all about his involvement in the crime. A real case of wrongful execution would be needed before a campaign of this sort, centred on a single individual, could stand much chance of making a real impact on a general level. Nevertheless, the Sternickel affair was instructive in a number of ways. First of all, it pointed to the continuing public fascination with violence and murder. This was undiminished since the days of the penny-dreadful and the street ballad. Yet this public fascination was taking on new forms. Accounts of 'sensational' murder cases and trials such as this now filled the columns of the newspapers as never before. In the 1920s, indeed, they became the subject of films shown in the new medium of mass entertainment, the cinema. What was changing was not the public's attitude to murder and execution, but the nature of the public sphere through which it was expressed. This suggests a second point of interest. The public dramatization of individual trials such as that of Sternickel, and of the fate hanging over individual offenders such as Georg Kersten, was becoming more elaborate during the Wilhelmine period, and this

[88] StA Bremen 4, 14/1, VII. F. 16: *Bremer Nachrichten*, 31 July 1913.
[89] Quoted in Oppelt, *Unehrlichkeit*, 151.
[90] BA Potsdam 61 Re 1/1527, Bl. 55: *Vossische Zeitung*, 16 June 1913.

was bound to have an effect on the way in which the issue of capital punishment was debated. As we have seen, abolitionists tried a new tactic in 1913: arguing by means of a public campaign for the injustice of the execution of a particular individual. Before long, they would move on to using individual cases as a basis for arguing the injustice of capital punishment *tout court*. On the other hand, as the right-wing press reaction to Sternickel showed, it was also becoming possible to use an individual case of an allegedly particularly brutal murderer to campaign for the retention of the death penalty as well. In both these ways, the Sternickel affair foreshadowed the debates of the 1920s and early 1930s, which would centre on individual offenders as much as on general principles.

Sternickel's crime, and even more, perhaps, the background and upbringing of his two accomplices, the 'Berlin street urchins', also highlighted for conservative commentators the supposed dangers of big-city life. They gave a dramatic support to the anti-urbanism which characterized so much of the radical right during these years. The working-class milieu from which these offenders came illustrated in turn what the right thought of as the morally degenerate social effects of proletarian irreligion. The Social Democrats did their best to counter the Catholic and conservative argument that crime was a product of urbanism, irreligion, and the decline of church attendance by pointing to the higher murder rates in rural areas, where church attendance was higher:

Statistics have proved that the strictly Catholic areas of Germany, in which the clergy hold untrammelled sway and the populace is completely under clerical influence, provide the most convictions for murder, manslaughter and grievous bodily harm, more even than the great cities, in which criminals sought by the police naturally seek to find a hiding place.

Thus in Silesia, for example, there were over twice as many convictions for grievous bodily harm as there were in Brandenburg in 1911, although its population was less than 30 per cent higher.[91] The general statistical point was irrefutable. But few on the right listened. The argument was another example of the politicization which was beginning to overtake the debate on the death penalty in these years, and which was to reach fresh heights, or depths, under the Weimar Republic. Murder and execution, as so often, dramatized and symbolized much wider issues than the rights and wrongs of crime and punishment. In the last years of peace, indeed, the homicide rate, which had fallen throughout the nineteenth century in Prussia and stabilized during the 1890s, began to rise sharply, until the absolute number of deaths by homicide in 1914, at 1,459, was more than double that of eight years earlier, in 1906, when the recorded number

---

[91] BA Potsdam 61 Re 1/1770, 139: *Vorwärts*, 11 Sept. 1913; Johnson, *Urbanization and Crime*, 145–81.

of homicides had been 696. A climate of violence was gathering at home as well as abroad.[92]

e. Wilhelmine Apocalypse

The case of Georg Kersten showed that a working-class youth, part of a class which was causing widespread social anxiety in Germany at this time, could require a major public campaign before obtaining a reprieve from a death sentence, even if he had not struck a single blow and indeed had done his feeble best to restrain the murderer whose accomplice he was. The social considerations at work in the application of the death penalty were graphically illustrated by another sensational case which occurred just a few months later. In the early hours of the morning of 4 September 1913, Ernst Wagner, a 39-year-old Württemberg schoolmaster, stabbed his wife and four children to death while they slept, then betook himself to the village of Mühlhausen, just outside Stuttgart, where he proceeded to set light to all the houses and barns, one after another, waiting outside as the inhabitants, woken from their sleep by the flames, began to emerge. Aiming at them with his Mauser revolver, he shot them one by one, through the heart. By the time the villagers overcame and disarmed him, he had killed ten of them, wounded many others, and even dispatched a few of the village cattle. Badly beaten, he was rescued by the police and taken to hospital, where his arm, seriously mangled in the struggle with the villagers, had to be amputated. Faced with his interrogators, he asked politely to be tried and executed as quickly as possible. His appearance mystified the authorities as much as his crime shocked the public. 'One expected to find', wrote the investigating magistrate, 'a 39-year old serious criminal, but one encounters instead a man who looks about 55, bowed down with sorrow, polite, shy, almost childish in his demeanour.' His colleagues at the school where he taught all testified that he had been a quiet, kindly, reliable, and popular teacher who had never given the slightest indication that he was inclined to violence, let alone to mass murder. The shocking events of 4 September seemed a complete mystery to everyone.

As the investigations into the background to this dreadful crime progressed, it became clear that Wagner had long been suffering from acute paranoia. Over the years, he had been writing a voluminous diary, and with the help of this self-analysis, the psychiatrists traced the origins of his deed back to the day in 1901 when, on the way home from the inn at Mühlhausen, in a drunken state, he had committed a sexual act with an animal in a field. Guilt at this act, which no one ever knew about until the discovery of his diary, led both to self-loathing and to

---

[92] Johnson, 'Roots of Crime', 375–6.

an ever-growing paranoid conviction that the villagers of Mühlhausen were mocking him because of it. Over the years, this conviction grew into a desire for revenge for the imagined slights from which he suffered at their hands. In fact, he was a respected and popular figure among the villagers, who never had the remotest idea how he really felt about them. But Wagner was unable to recognize any of this. Shortly after the incident in the field, he got the innkeeper's daughter pregnant, and he was forced to marry her when the child was born. His growing family he regarded with more than distaste; a widely-read man, he was a convinced eugenicist, and believed that the lower classes—amongst whom he counted himself—should not reproduce. He thought himself hereditarily tainted, and considered his children a danger to the race. His wife, he claimed, had to be killed to spare her the suffering of losing her children. His diaries made it plain that he had been planning his deed for up to five years previously, practising his marksmanship in the woods and reconnoitring the houses he had marked down for destruction. Far from regretting his deed, he felt no remorse at all, and only wished he had had the chance to cause even more mayhem before his apprehension.

When the psychiatrist Professor Robert Gaupp saw him on 11 November, he recognized immediately 'that this was no coarse or brutal criminal but a mentally ill person who committed his terrible deeds as the victim of a terrible delusion'. Gaupp diagnosed paranoia and certified Wagner unfit to plead. The schoolteacher's insanity became all the more obvious with the discovery not only of his diary but also of his vast, unpublished output of dramas, poetry, and other writing. Wagner suffered from literary megalomania as well as from paranoia, a diagnosis later confirmed by witnesses who said that when he had been drunk he had sometimes claimed to be 'a second Schiller'. The other psychiatrists concurred with Gaupp's analysis, and Wagner was sent straight to the asylum in the Winnetal, where he spent the rest of his days pouring out fresh literary offerings and waging a tireless campaign against the poet and dramatist Franz Werfel, whose entire output, he claimed, was a plagiarism of his own. The decision to spare him was a triumph for the psychiatrists. Public opinion was outraged. As Gaupp wrote later,

The anger of the masses, who were disappointed at this outcome of the affair, refused to die away. The Württemberg Justice Ministry felt compelled to publish lengthy extracts from my report in the official gazette. An eminent jurist stated in public that he did not think that §51 of the Criminal Code should retain its decisive and unconditional significance in this case, and that an execution was necessary in order to placate popular feelings. I myself was widely and often inaccurately attacked in the newspapers and also had to experience various kinds of anonymous abuse, most typically an unsigned postcard whose entire text consisted of the words: 'Ass, psychiatric.'

Even as late as 1932, when Gaupp took his patient out of the asylum to parade him before a conference of psychiatrists, the rumour that the murderer was about to be released caused a storm of protest in the press. With the coming of the Third Reich, Wagner saw himself justified. His arch-enemy, Franz Werfel, was a Jew, and he found in Hitler's anti-Semitism a confirmation of all his fears about his hated rival. He described his murderous deeds as 'practical racial hygiene' and considered that the Third Reich was following in his footsteps. In the last few years before his death in 1938, he was proud to describe himself as 'the first National Socialist in Winnetal'.[93]

But for all his later enthusiasm for the Nazi cause, Ernst Wagner was in the end a thoroughly Wilhelmine murderer. A photograph of him taken in 1909 shows him as the very model of Imperial German respectability and self-control, complete with pince-nez, wing-collar, and a moustache turned up at the ends in imitation of the Kaiser. Born into humble circumstances, he was a parvenu in the established world of the Wilhelmine middle classes, and never forgot it. From an early age he was acutely socially conscious and desperately anxious to maintain appearances. Even before his fateful descent into paranoia in 1901, he had lived in a permanent state of anxiety about the possibility of someone discovering the sexual drives which he concealed beneath the outward show of respectable self-repression. He was led by the medical doctrines of the day into a state of obsessive guilt about his habit of masturbating, a practice which he could not give up, but could not come to terms with either. He was also highly susceptible to dubious scientific theories and riddled with fears of eugenic and Darwinian vulnerability. Above all, he was consumed with neurotic feelings of fear and loathing for imaginary enemies whom he eventually called down upon himself by committing an unprovoked act of aggression towards them. His outwardly calm and comfortable life descended into a paroxysm of mass slaughter from which he never recovered. In many ways, his fate can be seen as emblematic for that of Wilhelmine Germany as a whole.

Wagner's life, much to his chagrin, was saved by four things. First of all, he was saved by his class. What Gaupp meant by describing him as 'no coarse or brutal criminal' was basically that he was an educated man, not a worker, not a peasant, not a farm labourer, not poor, uneducated, or badly-spoken with no manners. He had to be a victim rather than a perpetrator. Wilhelmine society was a class society before it was anything else. Secondly, he was saved by the power of psychiatry, which was at its height in that scientifically-oriented age. Every offender the psychiatrists could save from the gallows increased their

[93] Robert Gaupp, 'Krankheit und Tod des paranoischen Massenmörders Hauptlehrer Wagner. Eine Epikrise', *Zeitschrift für die gesamte Neurologie und Psychiatrie*, 163 (1938), 48–80; see also Robert Gaupp, *Zur Psychologie des Massenmords: Hauptlehrer Wagner von Degerloch* (Berlin, 1914).

F IG. 27. *Wilhelmine apocalypse.* The schoolteacher and paranoid mass murderer Ernst Wagner (1874–1938), photographed in 1909. Wagner was certified unfit to stand trial by the psychiatrists, reflecting both their influence in the courts at this time, and their prejudices in favour of an educated middle-class offender.

power and their prestige *vis-à-vis* the law enforcement agencies and the judiciary, and increased the importance of the asylum over that of the prison in Germany's penal system. Since 1851, when the definition of unfitness to stand trial had been written into the Prussian Criminal Code in largely medical terms, the profession's influence in the courts had been growing. By the Wilhelmine period it had become normal to consult forensic psychiatrists in almost every serious criminal case. To be sure, this development never went unchallenged. Already in 1908, for example, the radical right was criticizing what it saw as the tendency of psychiatrists 'to excuse everything' and alleged that the influence of forensic psychiatrists was being abused and exploited by unscrupulous criminals. Murder, one right-wing paper robustly declared, was a crime of such grossness that diminished responsibility was no reason for not proceeding to an execution anyway.[94] A biological, hereditarian view of criminality could only endorse this position. But although it had gained in influence by 1914, this was not yet dominant. Madness was still a reason for certifying offenders unfit to stand trial; it had not yet become a reason for their biological elimination. During the pre-war period, forensic psychiatrists were probably at the height of their influence, and consequently were still able to save middle-class murderers such as Ernst Wagner from the block.

Thirdly, they were enabled to do this by the peculiar thrust of Paragraph 51 in the Reich Criminal Code of 1871, which required doctors to certify that 'free disposal of the perpetrator over his own will was ruled out at the time of the deed' if they wished the court to make a declaration of unfitness. This tended to favour offenders who seemed (at least outwardly) to be normal human beings and who committed their crime in an uncharacteristic moment of madness. Wagner fitted this bill precisely. Had he clearly been a mentally unbalanced individual with numerous previous convictions, acquittal would have proved much more difficult. Finally, Wagner was also saved by the authoritarianism of Imperial Germany. Public opinion, articulated through the media, had become important during the Wilhelmine era, but when it really mattered, it still had to give way to the massive authority of the state. Immured in a carapace of protective laws, the state and the legal system made short shrift of any newspaper editor who ventured too far in his criticism of the existing order. Whatever journalists might say, the authorities had no qualms about ignoring them in a matter of this kind once a decision had been reached. Things would be very different under the Weimar Republic. Meanwhile, however, as Gaupp noted: 'The upset over the teacher's terrible deed among the populace lasted long after, until the Wagner case gradually slipped from the forefront of the public mind with the beginning of the World War.'[95] It was an incomparably greater mass slaughter that began in 1914. Few troubled, or even knew, about the fate of a handful of individual capital offenders within Germany.

Surprisingly, perhaps, the First World War made very little difference to the implementation of the death penalty, at least while it was going on. Despite the

---

[94] GStA Berlin Rep. 84a/7784, Bl. 294: *Deutsche Tageszeitung*, 19 Aug. 1908.
[95] Gaupp, 'Hauptlehrer Wagner', 68.

mass drafting of men onto the battle-front, many millions who were either too young or too old to be conscripted, or who were engaged in jobs and trades deemed to be vital to the war effort, remained at home. Domestic life did not cease, and since the majority of murders continued to be domestic, people did not cease to commit capital offences. If there were on average twenty-eight death sentences passed by Prussian criminal courts during each of the last full years of peace, then there were twenty-five passed in each of the five wartime years. Nor did Wilhelm II become any more lenient, sanctioning on average nineteen executions annually during the last five full years of peace, and fifteen a year during the war. The slight drop in these figures was not particularly significant, and it is fair to regard the practice of capital punishment during the war as continuing the pattern of the pre-war years with very little alteration. Even in military justice, with millions of men mobilized, there were only 150 death sentences passed in the German armed forces during the entire war, and only forty-eight of them were actually carried out, mainly for deserting the colours in the face of the enemy, going over to the enemy, or murder of one kind and another.[96] Far more serious were the mass executions carried out by German troops on civilians in occupied Belgium and northern France. German soldiers became used to treating enemy civilians with considerable harshness during this period.[97] In more than four years of continuous warfare, over two million Germans were killed and many more left crippled and wounded. On the home front, privation, misery, malnutrition, and disease took an increasing toll. The continuous glorification of organized violence was coupled with a steady intensification of political commitment on all sides, as the sacrifices mounted and people demanded greater rewards at the end of the process so as to make them worth while. On the right, the military, large parts of the government, and, increasingly, ultra-nationalist and annexationist pressure groups wanted nothing less than complete German domination over Europe, buttressed with huge territorial gains both on the Continent and overseas. On the left, as opposition to the war gathered strength, demands began to be raised for major constitutional change, for democratization, even for a socialist revolution. Beneath the smooth surface of national unity, a process of political polarization and radicalization was taking place on all sides. And after four years in which the nation had enthusiastically used guns and weapons of all descriptions to try to force its will on other countries, political groupings in Germany, particularly at the extremes of right

[96] Erich Otto Volkmann, 'Soziale Heeresmissstände als Mitursache des deutschen Zusammenbruchs im Jahre 1918', in *Untersuchungsausschuss des Reichstages über die Ursachen des deutschen Zusammenbruchs*, 4th ser., 11/2 (1924), 61–3.

[97] Alan Kramer, '"Greueltaten". Zum Problem der deutschen Kriegsverbrechen in Belgien und Frankreich 1914', in Gerhard Hirschfeld and Gerd Krumeich (eds.), *'Keiner fühlt sich hier mehr als Mensch...' Erlebnis und Wirkung des Ersten Weltkriegs* (Stuttgart, 1993), 85–114.

and left, were more than willing to turn these weapons on each other. When military defeat eventually came in 1918, it took almost everyone in Germany by surprise. Almost to the end, the military leadership under Hindenburg and Ludendorff had led them to believe that victory was only just around the corner, a conviction strengthened by the defeat of Russia and the winning of enormous territorial gains in the treaty signed with the new Bolshevik regime under Lenin and Trotsky at Brest-Litovsk early in 1918. But the entry of the Americans into the war sealed Germany's fate. The generals told the government to sue for peace. In the ensuing uproar, revolution broke out all over Germany, the Kaiser was forced to abdicate, and on 9 November 1918 the Social Democrats declared a Republic. Two days later, an Armistice brought the war to an end. The German Empire founded by Bismarck had collapsed in ruins, amidst bitterness and recrimination on all sides.

The legacy of that Empire for the history of state violence in Germany was a significant one. It had seen the re-establishment of capital punishment as an integral and accepted part of penal policy, and furnished it with new scientific and political justifications which went a long way towards re-establishing its legitimacy after a long period in which it had been keenly contested. It had witnessed the beginnings of a process of the privatization and concealment of executions by those whose task it was to administer them. It had experienced the transformation of the public fascination with murder and retribution into new forms, with the shift of the public sphere from a person-to-person basis into the medium of the printed word. The experience of state violence was becoming vicarious. Even for those who administered it, the idea was gaining ground that it would be better not to see or hear the killing of capital offenders directly. It was important that the re-establishment of the death penalty coincided with the emergence of hereditarian views of criminality which portrayed the capital offender as a damaged, inferior human being to be eliminated from the human race. Such views were undoubtedly stronger, more influential, more widely held, and more dogmatically interpreted in Germany than in Britain, where Lombroso's ideas were weakly translated into a rather vague form of welfarism. The notion of criminals as 'human wreckage' gained currency in Britain too, but it inspired a dismantling of the harsh, punitive prison regime with which the mid-Victorians had sought to break and remould the offender's character, and replaced it with a milder one which was far less punitive in nature. This in turn reflected the growing sense of security in British society, as crime rates declined and anxieties about social disorder and the 'criminal classes' faded. Penal theorists and prison reformers noted that criminals were becoming more 'civilized' as well as fewer in number, and harsh measures no longer seemed necessary to deal with them. Capital and corporal punishment declined in incidence, in a kind of social pacification whose other aspects included the emergence of powerful movements for the prevention of cruelty to children and animals, the regulation of violent sports, and other 'civilizing' impulses. These, too, were less strong in Germany, where the practice of duelling, for example, abolished in Britain in the mid-nineteenth century, continued virtually unabated up to the First World War.[98]

Yet the death penalty was never seriously challenged in Britain, and although its application was drastically reduced with the ending of the 'bloody code' in the 1830s, it continued to be applied far more frequently than in Germany throughout the rest of the nineteenth century and beyond. Even before the abolition of public executions in 1868, the movement for the abolition of executions altogether was never very strong. And afterwards, there was no serious threat to the legitimacy of capital punishment for almost a century. The same could be said of France, despite the retention of public executions down to 1939. In Germany, by contrast, the death penalty became a symbol for rival concepts of the state. This was not possible in Britain, where the Victorian state enjoyed a high degree of legitimacy, or France, where capital punishment had been employed by monarchists, Bonapartists, and republicans alike. But in Germany it became a highly politicized issue, and this made it vulnerable to the campaigns of abolitionists, as became evident both in 1848 and in 1870. The atmosphere of hostility to executions in this mid-century period doubtless affected the German princes and monarchs whose personal interventions did so much to restrict their frequency at this time. Retaining its political charge, capital punishment was reinstated in 1878 and widened in application thereafter for reasons that were largely political. Correspondingly, the rise of abolitionism in the Wilhelmine period was also closely tied to broader political considerations. The small band of radical-liberal abolitionists espoused it in a belief that a scientifically based morality would enable society to overcome all forms of violent conflict, above all, wars. The mass movement of the German Social Democrats adopted an abolitionist stance partly in a belief that they had an historic mission to fulfil the promises of 1848, partly from a conviction that the death penalty was the instrument of a reactionary, authoritarian state which would no longer be required after the revolution. In 1918, the revolution came. We turn now to see whether the Social Democrats managed to keep their promises on this issue.

[98] Wiener, *Reconstructing*; David Garland, *Punishment and Welfare: A History of Penal Strategies* (Aldershot, 1985); V. A. C. Gatrell, 'The Decline of Theft and Violence in Victorian and Edwardian England', in Gatrell *et al.* (eds.), *Crime*, 238–370.

Part IV

11

A New Beginning?

a. *Capital Punishment in the November Revolution*

The overthrow of the Kaiser and the other German monarchs in the Revolution of 1918 did not usher in a period of smooth transition to the new republican order. On the right, radicalized defenders of the old regime mustered themselves, while on the left, revolutionary groups also mobilized in the hope of achieving a thorough transformation of the German social order. In November 1918 and the following months, the prime aim of Friedrich Ebert and the other moderate Social Democrats who led the provisional revolutionary council was to get a grip on the country and manage a smooth transition to a peacetime economy, a stable society, and a parliamentary democracy. The events of the Bolshevik Revolution of 1917 in Russia, and the ensuing Red Terror in 1918–19, in which thousands were brutally murdered by Lenin's secret police, the Cheka, were very much present in the minds of Ebert and his colleagues as they embarked upon this process. In January 1919 'Spartakists', as the adherents of the newly founded Communist Party of Germany were known, attempted to seize power in major cities such as Berlin and Munich from the hands of the central government. The government in Berlin decided to put them down. But instead of enlisting a new republican armed force to do this, Ebert and his lieutenant Gustav Noske turned to former officers of Wilhelm II's army and the volunteer 'Free Corps' which they had recruited, in order to fight 'Bolshevism' in the Baltic states. Legitimated by Noske's command that anyone opposing the government troops with arms would be shot, the Free Corps unleashed an orgy of violence which left over a thousand dead by the end of March. Most prominent among these were the Spartakist leaders Karl Liebknecht and Rosa Luxemburg. Like many others, they were not armed when they were arrested, and were killed in cold blood by vengeful Free Corps troops. Regular military units engaged in putting down the revolutionaries also issued orders on their own authority, providing for the shooting of anyone found concealing arms in their home. There was evidence that people had been killed simply for having Spartakist literature in their possession. This 'White Terror', along with the political violence from the left that sparked it, created a lasting legacy of bitterness for the Weimar Republic, and left attitudes to crime and punishment politicized in the extreme.[1]

A particular role in this development was played by events in Munich. Since the 1918 Revolution, Bavaria had been led by the left-wing intellectual Kurt Eisner, a proponent of workers' councils. Defeated in the first elections held under the new regime, Eisner was about to resign when he was suddenly assassinated, on 21 February 1919. While the workers' councils responded to this outrage by setting up their own government in Munich, the elected, constitutional government of Bavaria, now led by the Social Democrat Hoffmann, withdrew to Bamberg in the north to prepare a counter-attack. On 14 April the Communists took over Munich and established a 'Red Army' and a communist police force, the 'Red Guard'. With heavily armed Free Corps units about to enter the city and re-establish the authority of the Hoffmann government, the 'Red Guard' arrested ten hostages. Six of them were members of the 'Thule Society', a far-right-wing organization allied to the Free Corps. As the news of the first killings committed by the advancing Free Corps arrived in the school where the hostages were being held, the atmosphere turned nasty and there were calls for them to be tried by a revolutionary tribunal and shot in reprisal. Unjustly accused of offences such as looting, or even the murder of Rosa Luxemburg, the ten hostages, selected not least for their aristocratic names—one of them was the Bavarian magnate the Prince of Thurn und Taxis, another was the Countess Hella von Westarp—were hastily tried and shot.[2] The shooting of the hostages provided the Free Corps with the excuse for the bloodbath that followed. 'Pardon will not be granted,' declared one of the Free Corps leaders, and another added: 'Better to put a few more innocent people up against the wall than let even a single guilty person go.' The official death toll of the 'White Terror' that reigned in Munich in the first few days of May was eventually put at 557, but unofficial estimates, such as that of Professor Emil Julius Gumbel (1891–1966), who published a series of studies of political murder in the Weimar years, put it at over a thousand. Many of them were gunned down in cold blood or arrested on suspicion and 'shot while trying to escape'. In numerous cases there was clear evidence that they had been beaten up first—most notoriously in the case of the anarchist Gustav Landauer, arrested as a former member of the Council government. There was no legal justification for these killings, and criminal proceedings were set in motion against a number of the Free Corps troops suspected of them.

[1] H. and E. Hannover, *Politische Justiz 1918–1933* (Frankfurt am Main, 1966), 31–52.
[2] Ibid. 68–71.

They revealed among other things the fact that a good number of those killed had had no connection with the revolutionary regime at all, but had merely been arrested and shot after being denounced as 'Spartakists'. These included twenty-one Catholic journeymen beaten to death or shot on 6 May 1919. Their murder, which was too much even for the 'White' leadership, led to the only successful prosecutions of Free Corps members, though for manslaughter rather than murder, to be undertaken as a result of these events.[3]

In Munich, the leading Communist Eugen Leviné was condemned to death by a drumhead court martial and executed on 6 June 1919. Many other revolutionaries were sentenced to substantial terms of imprisonment.[4] On 19 September 1919 the men accused of murdering the Munich hostages went on trial. The event was turned by the prosecution into a demonstration of the firmly held right-wing belief that revolutionaries were criminals. Of the sixteen men in the dock, four had been cashiered from the army for psychological reasons; seven had been born illegitimate; half of them had previous convictions for offences ranging from theft to living off immoral earnings, and almost all of them had enlisted in the Red Guard because they were unemployed and needed the money. The prosecuting counsel ended his final plea with a demand for the death penalty for ten of the accused, on grounds including the allegation that some of them were 'mentally inferior'. 'The blood of the innocent cries out for expiation!' he shouted. 'An eye for an eye, a tooth for a tooth!' Such behaviour also indicated the startling deterioration of judicial and legal standards which had taken place since the war and the Revolution. Only one of the defendants actually admitted having taken part in the murders, and in the case of some the evidence was less than convincing. Three were indeed acquitted; but eight were sentenced to fifteen years' penitentiary as accessories to murder, while six received the death penalty. In a further trial, two more death sentences were handed down.[5] Such events, unimaginable before the First World War, were clearly straining the judicial system of the new Republic to breaking-point even before any decisions had been taken on the constitution under which it was going to operate. Capital punishment, far from having been abolished by the November Revolution, was being applied on an even greater scale than before, as an instrument of political justice in the civil conflicts that raged across Germany in the months following the abdication of the Kaiser. The legal justification for many of these death sentences was paper-thin. Military justice exercised by unofficial 'Free Corps' was

---

[3] Ibid. 60. See also Emil Julius Gumbel, *Zwei Jahre Mord* (Berlin, 1921), *Vier Jahre politischer Mord* (Berlin, 1922), *Verräter verfallen der Feme* (Berlin, 1929), *Lasst Köpfe rollen* (Berlin, 1932), and his final summary, *Vom Fememord zur Reichskanzlei* (Heidelberg, 1962). Gumbel was forced to emigrate in 1933 and later took up a post at Columbia University, New York.

[4] Hannover, *Politische Justiz*, 53–68.   [5] Ibid. 69–75.

applied with the minimum of ceremony and without due process. Revolutionary justice did not shirk threatening the death penalty either. Not only did the revolutionary government in Munich, as we have seen, execute people largely on grounds of their social origin, but other revolutionary organs also made free with the threat of execution as well. The workers' council in the town of Salzwedel in November 1918 even declared the hoarding of food to be punishable by death.[6] Such incidents were used by the Social Democrats to argue, as they did in June 1919, that the institution of workers' councils always led to 'mass death sentences' and to state terrorism, as in Russia, and that only a parliamentary system could guarantee the rule of law.[7]

In this atmosphere of widespread political violence and the large-scale, often barely legal application of the death penalty by extremists, there were widespread demands by moderates for the abolition of the death penalty. A respected left-liberal newspaper, the *Berliner Tageblatt*, called for capital punishment to be removed from the Criminal Code as a signal of the 'renewal of spirit' which it considered necessary for the firm establishment of a stable new political order. Capital punishment, it declared, should be abolished as a means of overcoming the violence that had recently swept across the country.[8] That war bred violence at home was no new argument;[9] but the cataclysm of 1914–18 was unprecedented. An article in the *Welt am Montag* agreed:

The death penalty is objectionable not only because of the few criminals whom it affects but also because of the way in which it releases terrible instincts in people who otherwise consider themselves to be law-abiding citizens and are also regarded as such. . . . All the murderers put together do not possess as much evil-mindedeness and common inquisitiveness as the pack of hangmen and onlookers who attend executions.[10]

These arguments did not go unanswered by the supporters of the death penalty. The President of the Reich Military Court declared in April 1919 that the continued use of the death penalty was necessary 'to maintain public safety':

The brutalization of large parts of our people has spread in such a regrettable manner, and expresses itself in such repulsive crimes, that the community and the safety of the public are being endangered in a way that gives the greatest cause for concern. In my opinion these facts do not need any special proof. Such a situation must be countered by every available means, and in doing so, a punishment of such proven deterrent effect as the death penalty cannot be dispensed with.[11]

---

[6] BA Potsdam RJM 5665, Bl. 81: *Berliner Lokalanzeiger*, 3 Nov. 1918. See also ibid., Bl. 91: Präsident Reichsmilitärgericht to RJM, 24 Apr. 1919.

[7] BA Potsdam 61 Re 1/1771: *Sozialistische Korrespondenz für In- und Ausland* (Berlin), 11 June 1919.

[8] Ibid.: *Berliner Tageblatt*, 11 June 1919.

[9] Wilhelm Starke, *Verbrechen und Verbrecher in Preussen 1854–1878. Eine kulturgeschichtliche Studie* (Berlin, 1884), 152.

[10] BA Potsdam 61 Re 1/1771: *Welt am Montag*, 21 July 1919.

[11] BA Potsdam RJM 5665, Bl. 91: Präsident Reichsmilitärgericht to RJM (via Reichswehrministerium), 24 Apr. 1919.

The movement to abolish capital punishment, declared the party newsletter of the Nationalists, the radical right-wing successors of the Conservatives, in July 1919, was a socialist trick to increase social chaos and revolutionary disorder. The death penalty was, indeed, the newsletter trumpeted, 'the last corrective for a people sunk in sin and shame':

Here and there people still go 'collecting' with a pistol in their hand, here and there 'dispossession' is still carried out by means of the hand-grenade, and time and again, prisons are broken open and their inmates unleashed upon peaceful citizens. Kid gloves are no use at such a time. Only white terror can bring order. If the death penalty is abolished, criminality will no longer know any bounds.[12]

There was good reason for the writer to be concerned. For as the National Assembly forgathered at Weimar to debate and vote on a constitution for the new republic, it became clear that, despite the blood with which their hands were stained, both moderate and left-wing Social Democrats were going to make a determined attempt to secure the abolition of the death penalty. Such a ploy had a venerable history, going as far back as the 1848 Revolution, of which the Social Democrats in many ways considered themselves the political heirs. Then the right to life had been anchored in the Basic Rights of the German People and in the Frankfurt Parliament's draft Constitution. Now the moment seemed right for the vote of 1848 to be repeated.

b. The Weimar National Assembly

It was not until 17 June 1919, when it had already been sitting for three and a half months, that the Constitutional Committee set up to prepare a document for submission to the National Assembly came to discuss the possibility of including the abolition of the death penalty. The motion, put by the Social Democrats, was evidently a last-minute decision, poorly prepared and poorly defended. It was defeated by a clear majority.[13] On 16 July 1919 the matter came before the full chamber. The Social Democrats moved the insertion into the Weimar constitution of a new Article 113a. It declared simply: 'The death penalty is abolished.' The motion was put by Dr Hugo Sinzheimer (1875–1945), a Social Democratic lawyer. He told his listeners that the precedent of 1848 demonstrated the legitimacy of including a similar provision in the constitution of the Weimar Republic. To a large extent, indeed, the grounds for abolishing the death penalty in 1919 were the same as they had been seventy years before:

[12] BA Potsdam 61 Re 1/1771, Bl. 11: *Korrespondenz der Deutschnationalen Volkspartei*, 18 and 22 July 1919. The word 'collecting' (*Hamstern*) referred to the widespread theft of coal, corn, and other essentials durng the period of shortages and rapid inflation which had begun during the war and was still continuing in 1919.
[13] Düsing, *Abschaffung*, 135–8.

In our opinion, the abolition of the death penalty is the promulgation of a truly and genuinely democratic spirit. Democracy does not just consist in the creation of a democratic constitution, it consists above all in the fact that the noble features of the spirit of reconciliation and humanity are stamped upon all the legislation that emerges from such a democracy. For this reason we demand *the abolition of the death penalty, especially at this time, when we are about to complete the creation of democracy.*

As in 1848, so in 1919, abolishing capital punishment, he said, would have an improving effect on popular morality. There were tendencies in society and politics, he said darkly, 'that are inclined to regard human life as unworthy of respect because of the experience of the war'. The abolition of capital punishment, he concluded, to applause from the Social Democratic benches, 'will help free us from the blood-curse which the war and its effects have laid upon us'.[14] Sinzheimer's plea for abolition as an act of moral leadership by the state was reminiscent of 1848. Nevertheless, the situation in 1919 was different in a number of important respects from what it had been seventy years before. In 1848 there were serious doubts as to whether the constitution and the Basic Rights would actually come into effect. The individual states still retained their powers intact. The need for the national parliament to give a moral lead was thus felt all the more keenly. Moreover, as the deputies in the Frankfurt Parliament realized only too well, any vote they took would still have to be ratified by each of the states if it was to have any practical importance. Germany in 1919 was a much more tightly knit political entity than it had been in 1870 or 1848. Half a century of creeping centralization under Bismarck and Kaiser Wilhelm II had reduced the autonomy of the individual states dramatically. Despite its travails, the revolutionary government in 1919 had achieved far greater security of tenure than its predecessor in 1848–9. To be sure, this was not to last. But at the time of the Weimar National Assembly, the Social Democratic government, led by Friedrich Ebert, seemed to have overcome the opposition of the revolutionary left, and the Weimar politicians felt a good deal more sanguine about the eventual fate of their deliberations than their predecessors of 1848 had been able to do. The greater centralization of power in 1919 made a difference in other respects too. In 1848, the constitution and the Basic Rights had been virtually the only documents in which fundamental principles for the conduct of affairs were laid down for the whole of Germany (even if what Germany meant in strict geographical terms was far from clear). This applied in particular to the Criminal Code. There was no national criminal law system in existence in 1848, nor did there seem to the deputies of the Frankfurt Parliament to be much chance of creating one in the immediate future. It was legitimate, therefore, to use the constitution and

[14] *Stenographische Berichte über die Verhandlungen der deutschen konstituierenden Nationalversammlung zu Weimar*, vol. 6, cols. 3861–3.

the Basic Rights to indicate to the individual states the principles which they would be expected to follow when they revised their own criminal laws in due course.

In 1919, however, Germany had been in possession of a national Criminal Code for nearly half a century. It seemed obvious, therefore, that one of the first acts of the Weimar Republic would be to replace the existing Reich Criminal Code, which was ultimately based on the Prussian code of 1851, with a more modern, more democratic set of laws more suited to the new political circumstances. This was all the more likely since the revision of the Code had already been extensively prepared and debated in the years from 1906 onwards, and had only been cut short by the outbreak of the First World War. A draft was ready and waiting to be passed, subject to the amendments necessitated by the advent of a new political order. All in all, therefore, the arguments for including matters of detail such as the abolition of the death penalty in the constitution seemed much weaker in the Weimar National Assembly in 1919 than they had done in the Frankfurt Parliament in 1848. This point was made by speaker after speaker in the debates of July 1919. Hugo Preuss, the left-liberal legal expert who was the main architect of the Weimar constitution, put it with particular clarity. In doing so, he demonstrated that, in contrast to the circumstances of 1848, many of those who argued against including abolition in the constitution were not retentionists merely using this argument as a delaying tactic, but were genuinely convinced that the exclusion of abolition from this particular document would actually make very little difference in the end. Referring to Sinzheimer's opening speech, Preuss confessed

that my opinion, coinciding completely with that of the previous speaker, is that the *abolition* of the death penalty follows consequentially from the whole spiritual, political, and social process in which we are engaged today, and that it will undoubtedly take place. But as the discussion of this question in the Constitutional Committee has already shown, the majority opinion is that *this point should not and cannot be taken out of the context of the general reshaping of criminal law which is likely to occur.*

The preparatory work for the new Criminal Code, he added, had already been completed before the war, and this, he implied, would greatly accelerate the process of revision, even if the new situation did make certain amendments necessary. Among these, thought Preuss, was indeed the abolition of the death penalty, which he was sure would be achieved as soon as the new Criminal Code came into effect.[15] Other left-liberals echoed these points. Conrad Haussmann, for the Democrats, said the whole parliamentary delegation of the party had decided to reject all additions to the draft constitution, 'in order not to weigh

[15] Ibid., col. 3863.

down the ship of the constitution even more heavily than it is already'. He was himself, he confessed, 'a convinced adherent of the *abolition of the death penalty*'. But abolition belonged to the imminent revision of the Criminal Code, not to the Weimar constitution.[16]

The defection of the Democrats, who represented what was left of the long-established liberal tradition of opposition to capital punishment now that the National Liberals, regrouping themselves under the name of the German People's Party, had drifted to the right on this, as on other issues, must have instilled in the sponsors of the abolitionist motion grave doubts as to their prospects of success. Certainly they did not press their cause very hard. The debate was a surprisingly brief one, with only eight speakers taking part, and none of them holding the floor for very long. Just how much the bitter experiences of war, revolution, and counter-revolution had raised the political temperature in Germany soon became clear, as the arguments put forward for retention or abolition revealed themselves to be more partisan, more emotional, more controversial, and more concerned to score points off rival political groupings than they had ever been before. Even the most traditional kinds of critique or defence of capital punishment were given a new twist by the advent of parliamentary democracy in a post-war, post-revolutionary situation, and put with a new passion and vehemence. The 1919 debate, for example, accorded more importance to public opinion than previous discussions of the subject in the Bismarckian and Wilhelmine periods had felt it necessary to do. Professor Wilhelm Kahl, speaking for the People's Party, asserted 'that right across the population there is a feeling that the death penalty is a means of punishment that cannot be dispensed with'.[17] Conrad Haussmann, too, opined that in troubled and turbulent times such as their own the mass of the people probably considered capital punishment a necessity. To abolish it immediately would be regarded by the population at large 'not as expressing their legislative will . . . but as disregarding their own feelings'. If the constitution were to have any force or validity, it had to have a popular consensus behind it. To include in it such a controversial and probably unpopular measure as the abolition of capital punishment would thus seriously compromise its political viability.[18] Similarly, the German Nationalists, who formed the main political force on the right, and thoroughly disapproved of the new constitution, argued that 'the *general, natural* feeling of the people has always expressed itself in favour of the death penalty'. Such an appeal to democracy suggested that the old Conservatives and newer, extremist groups on the far right who made up the newly founded German Nationalist People's

---

[16] *Stenographische Berichte über die Verhandlungen der deutschen konstituierenden Nationalversammlung zu Weimar*, vol. 6, cols. 3869–70.

[17] Ibid., col. 3866.   [18] Ibid., col. 3870.

Party were far more willing to engage in populist demagoguery than their predecessors had been. The assertion that 'popular feeling' demanded the retention of capital punishment seemed indeed to outweigh almost all other considerations in the mind of Dr Költzsch, the spokesman of the Nationalist Party in the Weimar debate.[19]

With the advent of universal adult suffrage and parliamentary democracy, abolitionists were confronted in a more acute form than ever with the problem of justifying what was widely admitted to be a minority point of view. Hugo Sinzheimer, speaking for the Social Democrats, attempted to deal with it by claiming 'that those who want to keep the death penalty today . . . only make up small, narrow sections of the population'. There was no evidence, he said, that the abolition of the death penalty had been followed by outbreaks of lynching in the states in which it had occurred. The people had not taken the law into their own hands. In any case, if it should in fact prove to be the case that most people favoured capital punishment, Sinzheimer had another argument up his sleeve— indeed, the only possible one under the circumstances. He declared

that, if brutal instincts which desire the murderer's head are still alive, and want to go on living, in the people, then it is our task to make sure these instincts are countered through legislation. [Quite right!—*Social Democrats*] The state does not have to follow all the public's instincts including its erroneous and brutal instincts, and for this reason we do not believe that there is any basis to the objection that the public mood would not accept the abolition of the death penalty.[20]

Thus Sinzheimer, with the approval of his party, returned to the argument, familiar from the debates of 1848 and 1870, that the abolition of the death penalty was justified as an expression of the state's role as the moral educator of the people. Put this way, of course, a similar argument could also be used for retention. The jurist Wilhelm Kahl, for the People's Party, objected strongly to his own views on the topic being described as 'erroneous and brutal instincts'. He recognized the honourable motives of the abolitionists. '*But*', he told them, '*you must also take account of the other part of the population's feeling for justice* [Quite right! *on the right*], a feeling which still regards the death penalty as valuable and necessary.'[21] Pressing home this point, Dr Düringer, speaking for the Nationalists, claimed that, far from the death penalty being an outmoded survival of a barbarous medieval past, it was supported by 'men whose general political position is very moderate'. The violence of the post-war period demanded that the death penalty be exercised.[22] His party colleague Dr Költzsch took this argument further and urged retention because 'it is necessary to contain the beast

[19] Ibid., col. 3871.   [20] Ibid., col. 3862.
[21] Ibid., col. 3867.   [22] Ibid., col. 3864.

in man'.[23] Thus from this point of view retention too could be presented as an educational act, though working through deterrence rather than example.

Whilst a line such as this seemed to regard human beings as full of wild instincts that needed curbing by threats and punishments, the line taken by the abolitionists was based on the view that, as one of them said, 'Man is good!' It followed from this that 'legislation must aim to utilize the good and loving elements in human nature in the fight against crime'.[24] Toni Pfülf, one of the women deputies from the Social Democratic Party, claimed that the question was one of humanity rather than justice. She raised her voice on behalf of abolition 'not on some pedantic, judicial grounds, but from pure humanity and from pure pity for the people whom society has made the way they are'.[25] This laid speakers such as Pfülf open to one of the favourite labels of the retentionists, sentimental humanitarianism (*Humanitätsduselei*). Adalbert Düringer, for the Nationalists, spoke for many on his side when he declared roundly: 'This question cannot be solved by sentimentality.' Sinzheimer therefore went to some pains to argue that 'a humane law is much more help than hindrance to the combating of crime'. After all, as Oskar Cohn, speaking for the left-wing, anti-war breakaway party, the Independent Social Democrats, pointed out,

experience, particularly in the last months, in which there has been a huge increase in capital crimes, has shown that *the real aim of the death penalty, deterrence,* is pointless. Not regard for this heaviest of penalties, but quite other factors can and must provide the internal and external impetus for a defence against serious crime.

It was natural enough that capital crimes had increased after a war such as the one the country had just been through; but at the same time this showed that the death penalty was no deterrent to crimes of this sort. Cohn therefore followed the original speaker for the motion in arguing that the question was 'whether we want to emerge from the madness of the war or not, and we have to use the first opportunity we get to show it'. Abolition, he said, was a necessary step towards 'the moral rebirth of a whole people'.[26]

This view of the significance of the First World War and the ensuing revolution was not shared by the right. For German conservatives, the overthrow of the Kaiser and the establishment of the Weimar Republic marked not the moral rebirth of the nation but its moral collapse. This argument was put most clearly by Dr Költzsch, in a tirade that reduced the Assembly to a state of total uproar. While the Social Democrats and the Independents argued that it was the war that had destroyed morality and order and brought murder into everyday

---

[23] *Stenographische Berichte über die Verhandlungen der deutschen konstituierenden Nationalversammlung zu Weimar,* vol. 6, col. 3872.

[24] Ibid., col. 3863.   [25] Ibid., col. 3871.   [26] Ibid., cols. 3868–9.

life, the Nationalists and their allies put the blame fairly and squarely on the
Revolution:

Alas!—the first thing the Revolution did was to open the prisons and let loose serious
criminals upon mankind. Alas!—the Revolution treated human life cruelly. [*Angry shouts
from the Independent Social Democrats*: the war!] . . . *You only have to remember Munich
and the murder of the hostages* [*major uproar and furious shouts from the Independent Social
Democrats—the Speaker rings his bell*].

The Speaker of the Assembly did his best to calm the rage of the left, but made
no attempt to prevent Költzsch from continuing his diatribe. The Revolution,
Költzsch went on, had opened the floodgates of disorder. The mayhem could
only be stopped by rigorous application of the death penalty. Capital punishment was 'the last remaining thing which is still keeping brutality . . . and even
in my view bestiality in the people and in individuals in check'. Raising his voice
above the din, he continued:

And the Revolution—that cannot be disputed—confused [*furious shouts from the Social
Democrats and Independent Social Democrats*: the war!] many minds and spirits [*uproar
and shouting*], and put robbery and theft, murder and manslaughter on the agenda
[*renewed shouts*].—It is so! The matter is terribly serious. Listen to me calmly! [*agreement
on the right. . . . Furious disagreement and continuing noisy shouting from the Social Democrats and the Independent Social Democrats—the Speaker's bell*].
SPEAKER. I appeal for order! [*the uproar continues*].

The debate ended in total chaos, in a series of personal statements from
speakers who considered themselves to have been insulted during the proceedings. The contrast with the dignified and collegial proceedings of 1848,
or even the measured and serious tone of the discussions of 1870, could not
have been more acute. The bitterness and hatred between left and right,
between Nationalists and Social Democrats, were palpable. In such an inflamed
atmosphere, the chances of the motion getting a reasonable hearing were
minimal.[27]

On the other hand the prospects of the motion being formally approved by the
Assembly did not seem so bad. The moderate left had done well in the post-
revolutionary elections of 1919, when many voters thought they were better
placed to ward off the danger of Communism than were the parties further to the
right. The Social Democrats and their wartime offshoot the Independents, both
firmly committed to abolishing capital punishment, had 185 seats, against the 161
held by the parties committed to retaining the death penalty, namely the Catholic Centre, the Nationalists, the People's Party, and the various minuscule
splinter-groups of the far right. The position of the left-liberal Democrats was
crucial. On a full turn-out of all members of the Assembly, the seventy-five

[27] Ibid., col. 3872.

deputies who sat for the Democrats could swing the vote either way. But these deputies were deeply divided on the subject. Some were convinced abolitionists, while many others were more inclined to support the retentionists, at least in the socially and politically disturbed atmosphere of 1919. Party discipline had never been particularly good on the liberal benches. On the face of it, the motion to abolish capital punishment was doomed by the decision of the party leadership that the Democrats should vote against it on the grounds that the issue belonged more properly to the forthcoming revision of the Criminal Code. But given the unpredictability of the left-liberal deputies, and the excited atmosphere of the debate, nobody could be really certain.

The vote, when it came, was a surprise on a number of counts. The motion to include the abolition of the death penalty in the constitution of the Weimar Republic was lost by 153 votes to 128, with two abstentions. These figures were unexpectedly low. Over a third of the Social Democratic deputies absented themselves. Only 105 deputies voted, all for abolition. The Independents did rather better in mustering their forces, but over a quarter of their members still failed to turn up, leaving only seventeen to cast their votes for abolition. On the retentionist side, the Catholic Centre and the Nationalists both managed to persuade roughly three-quarters of their deputies to cast their votes, making sixty-five and thirty-one votes against abolition respectively. The People's Party mustered some fourteen votes against abolition. If the two Social Democratic parties had been better organized, therefore, the vote might easily have gone the other way. It may well be that many Social Democrats viewed the prospects of getting abolition into the new Criminal Code with such confidence that they regarded its inclusion in the constitution as secondary. Some might have been swayed by the argument that it did not really belong there, and stayed away to avoid the choice of having to cast their vote against their party or casting it against their conscience. Others may have absented themselves because they actually supported the death penalty. It is easy to imagine, for example, that a right-wing Social Democrat such as Gustav Noske, the 'bloodhound of the Revolution', responsible for the violent suppression of a number of revolutionary outbreaks, would have found it difficult to vote for a guarantee of the right to life being written into the constitution.[28] Nevertheless, whatever the reasons, the Social Democrats' lack of party discipline proved in the end to be the crucial factor in the failure of the motion. This was not least because of the chaotic and confused behaviour of the Democrats. Forty Democrats voted against abolition, but no less than 40 per cent of their deputies failed to appear for the crucial vote, most of them probably abolitionists. And among those who did turn up, four

---

[28] Wolfram Wette, *Gustav Noske: eine politische Biographie* (Düsseldorf, 1987).

broke ranks, one (Ernst Remers) to abstain and three (Christian Koch, Otto Nuschke, and Ludwig Quidde) to vote against the party whip, for abolition. Clearly these deputies were not convinced by the party leadership's argument that abolition was best left until later. In fact, it soon became apparent that the party line was a compromise designed to bridge over a yawning gulf between abolitionists and retentionists within the party. Not only the right-wing liberals in the People's Party, but now also, increasingly, the left-wing liberals in the Democrats, were breaking with liberal tradition and voting with the conservatives over the kind of human rights issue that had counted among their most strongly held principles in 1870. Certainly, there were still a number of politicians on the liberal left who considered the abolition of capital punishment a cause worth fighting for. More and more, however, they tended to be those who, like Quidde, were associated with pacifism, a cause which most liberals, as good German nationalists, found completely unacceptable. The internal disunity of the party was to play a role in subsequent attempts to abolish the death penalty. It was the joker in the otherwise predictable parliamentary pack.[29]

c. The Social Democrats and the Death Penalty 1919–1927

For the moment, the abolitionist cause was lost, or at least deferred. On 30 July left-liberal and socialist deputies salved their consciences by passing a motion that the government should speedily prepare a new Criminal Code 'with the aim of removing the death penalty'.[30] How soon this would happen was far from clear. A draft Criminal Code already existed, of course: it had been worked out over a period of some eight years prior to the First World War. But this product of Wilhelmine judicial thinking was unlikely to be acceptable to the Social Democrats. A new draft was therefore needed. The Revolution had not done anything to remove or redeploy the Wilhelmine civil service, so the same official who had been central to the drafting of the new Criminal Code from 1909 to 1913, Curt Joël, was made responsible for producing further drafts, in 1919 and 1920. In September 1922 there was also a joint German–Austrian draft. But it was not until this point that the drafts actually included the abolition of the death penalty. The problem was that all Weimar cabinets had to be put together from a number of different political parties, and these always included the Catholic

[29] Details of the vote in *Stenographische Berichte über die Verhandlungen der deutschen konstituierenden Nationalversammlung zu Weimar*, vol. 6, col. 3872. For the left-liberals in the Weimar Republic, see most recently Larry Eugene Jones, *German Liberalism and the Dissolution of the Weimar Party System 1918–1933* (Chapel Hill, NC, 1988); and idem and Konrad Jarausch (eds.), *In Search of a Liberal Germany: Studies in the History of German Liberalism from 1789 to the Present* (Oxford, 1990).

[30] *Stenographische Berichte über die Verhandlungen der deutschen konstituierenden Nationalversammlung zu Weimar*, 70. Sitzung, 30 July 1919, cols. 2124–5.

Centre, which continued to be strongly in favour of the death penalty. Such coalitions were invariably short-lived, and whether or not the Minister of Justice ordered the civil servants to dispense with capital punishment in the draft Criminal Code depended largely on the Minister's party allegiance and personal convictions. The 1922 draft was compiled on the orders of the only Social Democrat to hold the office of Justice Minister, Gustav Radbruch, an academic lawyer who was strongly opposed to the death penalty and so it excised it, although not from the emergency provisions available to the Reich President under Article 48 of the constitution. A further draft, produced under a different minister in 1924–5, reinstated it, though unlike the 1919 draft it now limited capital punishment to murder.[31]

The 1920 elections registered a sharp swing to the right. The Social Democrats and the other parties which supported abolition suffered heavy losses, while the parties of the right, such as the Nationalists, scored substantial gains. A majority for the abolition of capital punishment was unlikely to be found in the Reichstag unless the left won back everything it had lost in 1920 and more. The next elections, in 1924, registered little change in this respect. Cabinets were predominantly right-of-centre in composition and gave a high priority neither to the reform of the criminal law, which was effectively shelved in 1924, nor to the abolition of the death penalty. The measure about which abolitionists had been so optimistic in the National Assembly seemed to be receding ever further into the distance. Moreover, virtually every party in the Weimar Republic compromised on the principle of capital punishment, and contained individual politicians who were quite prepared to support it in particular instances. The history of these compromises began with the Social Democrats, whose lack of enthusiasm for abolition in the vote of July 1919 was only the first in a long series of retreats from the idea of abolishing the death penalty. Social Democratic thought placed the primary responsibility for crime on the shoulders of capitalist society.[32] The party was firmly committed to an ameliorative concept of punishment and to the abolition of the death penalty. Capital punishment, it argued, was bound 'to brutalize the attitudes of the broad masses of the population to policies on crime'. Abolishing it would have a civilizing, educative effect upon the masses.[33] In pursuit of these ideals, the Social Democrats included abolition in the new party programme voted through at the Görlitz Congress in 1921 and again in its successor issued at the Heidelberg Congress in 1925.[34]

---

[31] BA Potsdam 61 Re 1/1771, Bl. 165: *Deutsche Zeitung*, 21 Jan. 1925; ibid., Bl. 184: *Frankfurter Zeitung*, 13 Mar. 1925; UB Heidelberg Heid. Hs. 3716 I.D. 52: *Fränkische Tagespost*, 25 Sept. 1922 (1. Beilage). See also Düsing, *Abschaffung*, 149–54, 156–8.

[32] BA Potsdam RT 848, Bl. 122: Reichstag, 32. Ausschuss, 21. Sitzung, 27 Oct. 1927: deputy Saenger, 7.

[33] Ibid., RJM 6097, Bl. 3: *Vorwärts*, 31 May 1925.   [34] Düsing, *Abschaffung*, 145–7, 162–3.

Nevertheless, it was far less easy for the Social Democrats to mount a consistent and principled opposition to the death penalty under Weimar than it had been under the Kaiserreich, when the judicial and penal system could simply be portrayed as an instrument of bourgeois rule. Now they had acquired a degree of responsibility for its administration themselves. This was particularly the case in Prussia, where they dominated the government, in which, under the federal system, the power of confirming or commuting death sentences still lay. Working with institutions inherited from the Kaiser's days proved no easier here than in other spheres. Some Social Democrats like Albert Grzesinski, chief of police in Berlin and Prussian Minister of the Interior in 1926–30, or Karl Zörgiebel, his successor in the police job, were opposed to capital punishment,[35] but the long-time Minister of Justice in the Social Democrat-dominated Prussian coalition government, Hermann Schmidt, a Catholic Centre Party politician, went on record in 1927 in favour of retention.[36] And Grzesinski's predecessor and successor as Prussian Minister of the Interior, the Social Democrat Carl Severing (1875–1952) declared in 1927:

Without betraying any official secrets, I can say that I supported clemency in all cases in which the condemned appeared to be not only criminals but also victims, under the influence of the war and its consequences, because of their milieu and because they were led astray. Still, there were death sentences, passed on notorious antisocial elements, for which it would have been unjust and unfair to have granted a reprieve, in view of the persons who were threatened in times of political instability with summary courts martial and death sentences to be carried out immediately.[37]

The principle of comparison which Severing enunciated here reflected a long-established Social Democratic view that the law was unequally and unfairly applied to different sectors of the population, as well as an equally long-standing fear and contempt of the 'dangerous classes' on the part of organized labour. Using the shooting of prisoners by army units and Free Corps during the revolutionary upheavals of the Republic's early years as a justification for continuing to execute people later on seemed to be a rather paradoxical way of going about things for a member of the party ostensibly most committed to the abolition of capital punishment. If Social Democratic government ministers put forward arguments such as this, it seemed unlikely that the abolition of capital punishment would be achieved in the immediate future, if at all. It was not surprising that they were heavily criticized for failing to call a halt to the execution of capital offenders. Such men, said the liberal

[35] BA Potsdam RJM 6097, Bl. 22: *Berliner Tageblatt*, 22 Jan. 1927. See also BA Potsdam 61 Re 1/1772, 101: Albert Grzesinski, 'Fort mit der Todesstrafe!', *Berliner Morgenpost*, 14 May 1928.
[36] Ibid., RJM 6097, Bl. 74: *Kölnische Zeitung*, 30 June 1927.
[37] Ibid., Bl. 29: *Berliner Tageblatt*, 26 Jan. 1927.

Vossische Zeitung, were worse than the arch-conservative Kaiser Wilhelm I in this respect.[38]

The Social Democratic Reich President, Friedrich Ebert, sanctioned the use of the death penalty by military courts against those whom he regarded as violent revolutionaries earlier in the Weimar Republic, above all in the early spring of 1920. In the March of that year, unwilling to return to normal civilian life, the Free Corps under General von Lüttwitz marched on Berlin. The government, headed by the Social Democrat Gustav Bauer, fled, while the Free Corps installed a reactionary and monarchist regime in the capital city, led by the former civil servant Wolfgang Kapp. The putsch was quickly put down by a general strike, endorsed by the Bauer government, but its leaders were allowed to flee; only one was eventually tried and condemned to a brief confinement in a fortress, while the judges counted his 'selfless patriotism' as a mitigating cirumstance, and all the others, including many regular troops, who had supported Kapp were amnestied on 4 August. Before his inglorious withdrawal, Kapp had incidentally managed to issue a decree making the organization of strikes punishable by death.[39] It was as futile as all his other proclamations, but it did indicate the willingness of the far right, once more, to use capital punishment as an instrument of policy in an emergency. Meanwhile, in the heavy-industrial region of the Ruhr, the workers striking against the Kapp putsch had organized themselves into a 'Red Army', which managed to neutralize the military units that came out in support of the new government in Berlin. After the defeat of the putsch, however, the same army units were sent back into the area to restore order and force the 'Red Army' to disband. Here, too, there were numerous shootings by drumhead courts martial, many without even the pretence of legal proceedings. As in Munich the previous year, hundreds of workers were killed merely on suspicion of being Communists; many were beaten to death or had their throats slit by the vengeful troops. On 19 March 1920, two days after Kapp's flight, Reich President Ebert legitimated many of these proceedings with a decree issued under the notorious Article 48 of the Weimar constitution, which gave the President virtually dictatorial powers in times of emergency. The decree not only allowed the establishment of extraordinary military courts to assist in the 'combating of the disturbances' but also proclaimed that 'the sentence can only be death'. The accused were not to be allowed a defence lawyer and there was to be no appeal. More seriously still, the decree was given retrospective effect back to 13 March, the first day of the putsch. This was a breathtaking breach of the fundamental legal principle—*nulla poena sine lege*—that punishments cannot be applied to

[38] BA Potsdam RJM 6097, Bl. 194: *Die Rote Fahne*, 15 Jan. 1928; ibid., Bl. 191: *Der Tag*, 13 Jan. 1928; ibid., Bl. 11: *Vossische Zeitung*, 18 Apr. 1928.

[39] Hannover, *Politische Justiz*, 76–7.

offences committed before they are made legal, because, had they applied at the time of those offences, their deterrent effect might have prevented the offences from being committed. So the decree proved an ominous precedent for the future. For the moment, as critics subsequently complained, it amounted to little more than an 'empowerment of counter-revolutionary troops to shoot defenceless prisoners at will'.[40] And this is precisely what happened. Such was the confusion of the situation that it remained unclear precisely how many people were executed under its terms. The Army Ministry's reported total of twenty-four executions carried out in 1920 'by drumhead courts martial held by troop units' was without doubt a massive underestimate. These courts were abolished on 25 March, leaving the extraordinary military courts to deal with the remaining cases.[41] According to a Communist Reichstag deputy, at least two hundred people were summarily shot under the retrospective protection of Ebert's decree, many by the very same troops that had supported the putsch and now obviously welcomed any chance to vent their fury on the 'Communists'.[42]

Not all of these sentences were carried out before the decree came into effect. As the troubles died down, the proceedings of the army courts became a little more regular, and appeals for clemency began to be transmitted to Reich President Ebert. They did not meet with the sympathetic hearing one might have expected from a member of a party which had been formally committed to the abolition of capital punishment for the previous thirty years. In 1920 Ebert refused to commute a number of death sentences passed by military courts on members of the 'Red Army' in the Ruhr. A typical case was that of Josef Biesemann, a worker condemned to death by an extraordinary military court in Essen on 13 April 1920 for 'robbery with extortion' and other offences which would not have earned him the death penalty under the existing Reich Criminal Code. Biesemann was executed by firing-squad after his appeal for a reprieve had been turned down by the Reich President. Similarly, Christian Kopp, another worker, was condemned for attempted murder and serious theft by three civilian judges sitting on an extraordinary military court in Wesel on 17 April 1920. Kopp admitted having shot a prisoner, Lieutenant Weber, in Lippe Castle, near Wesel, on 28 March, but there was no evidence that he had actually killed him; instead, Weber had probably died later, when his throat had been slit by another member of the 'Red Army'. Kopp also admitted having returned to plunder the corpse.

---

[40] Quoted ibid. 89.
[41] BA Potsdam RJM 5665, Bl. 154: Reichswehrministerium to RJM, 26 July 1922; ibid., Bl. 156: Nachweisung über die durch Standgerichte von Truppenteilen verhängten Todesstrafen (Reichswehrministerium, 1920); ibid., Bl. 137 (notes); Erhard Lucas, *Märzrevolution 1920*, iii. *Die Niederlage* (Frankfurt am Main, 1979), 397–401; see also BA Potsdam 61 Re 1/1768, 1/2: *Die Freiheit*, 29 Apr. 1920, and Hannover, *Politische Justiz*, 89.
[42] *Stenographische Berichte über die Verhandlungen des deutschen Reichstags*, Bd. 344, col. 393, 2 July 1920.

Serious though these crimes were, they too would not have earned Kopp the death sentence in normal times. But his sentence was still confirmed by Ebert, and he was shortly afterwards shot by the army.

Critics ascribed Ebert's refusal to commute death sentences to his 'megalo-mania'. They compared it unfavourably to the line taken by Kaiser Wilhelm I, who for many years had refused to confirm any death sentences at all. For decades, they pointed out, Ebert had subscribed to Point 8 of the Erfurt Pro-gramme, which had demanded the abolition of capital punishment. Now he seemed to have abandoned all his principles. 'In earlier times,' complained an Independent deputy in 1920, 'there were even princes who never confirmed a death sentence.'[43] They poured scorn on the Social Democrats' claim that Ebert was bound by his office and that he could no longer be expected to carry out the policy of a particular political party.[44] Several local branches of Ebert's party passed resolutions criticizing him for these decisions. His defenders within the party maintained on the other hand that 'if Ebert has confirmed death sentences, they were not death sentences against revolutionary fighters but death sentences against criminals'. 'According to your ideology,' exclaimed a Communist deputy in the Prussian parliament, turning to the Social Democrats as he did so, 'all political fighters are criminals!' But of course the fact was that the power to confirm or commute death sentences passed on common criminals lay not with Ebert but with the governments of the federated states, so it was only in extraordinary situations that Ebert was called upon to exercise it, and inevitable therefore that he exercised it only in relation to political offences tried by summary process established under emergency decrees which he himself had issued.[45] Ebert's stance was supported by the Bavarian Justice Minister, Ernst Müller-Meiningen, a member of the Democratic Party, who spoke on behalf of the Hoffmann Government in Bavaria, in March 1920 in the following terms:

In normal times, the question of abolishing the death penalty may be one for discussion. In times of the complete disintegration of our state and social order, at a time when crime is increasing terribly, and in which the most serious crimes are being committed with frighteningly greater frequency, to abolish the death penalty would be to take a risk of the most dangerous kind in penal policy. That is also the view of the Reich government, and in particular of Reich President Ebert. On the basis of Art. 48 of the Reich constitution, he has extended the death penalty in the Ruhr and other areas to crimes other than murder. . . . In the present time, when the holder of the highest office in the Reich has ordered the extension of the death penalty in this manner, a motion to abolish the death penalty can only have the significance of a demonstration.[46]

[43]   *Stenographische Berichte über die Verhandlungen des deutschen Reichstags*, 1. Wahlperiode, 1920, cols. 379–86, 29 July 1920 (deputy Vogtherr).
[44]   BA Potsdam 61 Re 1/1768: *Die Freiheit*, 28 May 1920.
[45]   *Stenographische Berichte über die Verhandlungen des Preussischen Abgeordnetenhauses*, 31. Sitzung, 30 June 1921, col. 2053 (deputy Karz).
[46]   BA Potsdam, RJA 5665, Bl. 140: *Münchener Neueste Nachrichten*, 26 Apr. 1920.

The President's position on the death penalty was thus far more than a mere personal idiosyncrasy, or a consequence of his belief that he had to maintain a degree of political neutrality as Reich President: it reflected a substantial body of opinion in the Social Democratic Party at this time.

That the Social Democrats were more than prepared to use capital punishment in defence of their position during the early years of the Weimar Republic was illustrated by their behaviour when Foreign Minister Walther Rathenau was assassinated by the far-right-wing terrorist 'Organisation Consul' on 24 June 1922, following a bitter press and political campaign against him for his policy of 'fulfilling' the terms of the Versailles Treaty. The next day, Ebert issued a decree 'For the Protection of the Republic', which was confirmed by a law steered through the Reichstag by the Justice Minister, Gustav Radbruch, on 21 July 1922. The decree contained provisions directed against violent attacks on the 'republican form of state' in Germany. The first clause, clearly inspired by the Rathenau murder, applied the death penalty to anyone who 'participated in a conspiracy or arrangement which includes the aim of removing members of a republican government of the Reich or of a province through death'. It also threatened execution to anyone who knowingly supplied such an organization with funds. The law passed on 21 July watered these provisions down somewhat, applying the death penalty only in cases where the organization in question actually committed or attempted to commit a murder. But this still constituted a substantial extension of the death penalty. The Law also set up a special 'State Court' (*Staatsgerichtshof*) to try such cases. To try and get round the ultra-conservatism of the judiciary, six out of the nine members of the court were to be appointed by the President. They did not have to be professional judges. The court meted out tough custodial sentences to those involved in the conspiracy, though the assassins themselves did not reach trial: they had been cornered by the police and died in the subsequent shoot-out, one by his own hand. An attempt on the life of the Social Democratic politician Philipp Scheidemann also brought stiff sentences from the court. Apart from these two trials, however, the court did not prove to be of any great use against the assassination squads of the far right. The judiciary soon got control over the six places reserved for laymen on the bench, and after the arch-conservative Field Marshal Paul von Hindenburg was elected Reich President following Ebert's death in 1925, the conservative character of the court was even more strongly assured.[47] The great majority of cases which were brought before the ordinary criminal courts against right-wing defendants under the Law for the Protection of the Republic were dismissed or reversed on appeal.[48] Only three offenders were sentenced to death under the Law, for

[47] Hannover, *Politische Justiz*, 125–34.
[48] See the judgments reprinted in Ilse Stauff, *Justiz im Dritten Reich. Eine Dokumentation*, 2nd edn. (Frankfurt am Main, 1978), 13–22.

participating in a conspiracy to kill a member of the government, in 1925. The Law lapsed on 22 July 1929, and its replacement, voted through on 25 March 1930, no longer contained the death penalty.[49]

The introduction on the initiative of the Social Democrats of a law handing out the death penalty for political murder fatally compromised their stance on the issue of capital punishment in general. The Social Democrats protested in defence of their action that while the death penalty continued to exist, there was no reason why it should not be used in defence of the Republic.[50] But this was a feeble excuse, given the fact that they had been committed to its abolition for decades and continued to be so according to their party programme. Right-wing critics compared the severity of this law polemically to the mildness of Bismarck's Anti-Socialist Law of 1878–90. At least, they said, no new capital offences had been created by the latter. But this argument, too, was somewhat disingenuous. For high treason, the attempted or actual assassination of the Kaiser or one of the princes, had of course been a capital crime according to the Criminal Code of 1871, and the Social Democrats were doing no more than adapting it to the new circumstances of a republican regime by introducing the law of 1922. Ministers had merely been the Kaiser's servants before 1918, but now they were the people's servants; they were still entitled to the full protection of the law. In this context, the comparison with the Anti-Socialist Law was completely irrelevant, since the latter had not been concerned with treason, but merely with the suppression of an organization and the banning of its publications.[51] But the Communists pointed out, not entirely unfairly, that while the Social Democratic Party 'is opposed to the death penalty as a normal penal measure',

> in times of disturbances, of the so-called inner disintegration of the structure of the state, exceptional courts are set up once a state of emergency has been declared, and on every occasion, these courts are given powers to hand out death sentences for a whole series of offences which do not otherwise carry this sentence.[52]

The Social Democrats' behaviour, and in particular their approval of the application of capital punishment by emergency decrees, administered through special courts packed with hand-picked judges, stored up a dangerous precedent for the future; indeed, the Nazis were to build on it when they came to power in 1933.

---

[49] Düsing, *Abschaffung*, 154–6.

[50] Ernst Rudolf Huber, *Deutsche Verfassungsgeschichte seit 1789*, vi. *Die Weimarer Reichsverfassung* (Stuttgart, 1969), 674; BA Potsdam RT 948, Bl. 125: Reichstag, 32. Ausschuss, 21. Sitzung, 27 Oct. 1927 (deputy Rosenfeld). See also Gotthard Jasper, *Der Schutz der Republik* (Tübingen, 1962).

[51] BA Potsdam RT 848, Bl. 132: Reichstag, 32. Ausschuss, 23. Sitzung, 7: deputy Lohmann (DNVP).

[52] GStA Berlin Rep. 84a/7786, Bl. 196–210: Preussisches Abgeordnetenhaus, cols. 4599–4600 (deputy Obuch).

d. Capital Punishment and Party Politics

Of all the political parties in the Weimar Republic apart from the Social Democrats, it was the Communists who were most vociferous in their opposition to capital punishment. The Communist Party's sharp criticism of the Social Democrats' contradictory stance on the issue reflected the fact that this new and, from the collapse of the Independent Social Democrats in 1922 onwards, mass working-class party regarded itself as the most sincere proponent of the abolition of capital punishment under Weimar. Its deputies were active in bringing abolitionist motions before legislative assemblies at every level throughout the 1920s. In some ways they took up the unambiguously abolitionist legacy of the German labour movement before 1914. But they were hampered from the outset by the need to defend the use of the death penalty in the Soviet Union. For German Communists, Russia was the only country that had undergone a true proletarian revolution, so defending it against its bourgeois detractors came before anything else. The awkward fact that the Russian regime made free use of the death penalty posed very real problems for the German Communist Party, which in the 1920s had to try bridge the gap between its roots in the German labour movement and its allegiance to the new doctrines of Bolshevism. Unlike their German counterparts, the Russian socialists had never included the abolition of capital punishment in their party programme. From 1918 onwards the Soviet regime was responsible, through its feared political police, the Cheka, for the summary execution of tens of thousands of Lenin's opponents on all sides of the political arena. Such attitudes were quite foreign to the traditions of the German labour movement, and reflected the Bolsheviks' indebtedness to the traditions of Russian populism, with its long history of murder and assassination, going back to the killing of Tsar Alexander II and beyond. Even official statistics showed that revolutionary tribunals sentenced nearly 7,000 people to death in the Soviet Union in 1920. Long before the revolution, Lenin had dismissed the campaign to abolish capital punishment as 'an inadmissible weakness, a pacifist illusion'. 'A revolutionary who does not want to play the hypocrite,' he said in 1918, 'cannot dispense with the death penalty. There has not been a single revolution, or era of civil war, without executions.'[53] In the course of the next three years, he demonstrated his own lack of hypocrisy with a vengeance.

The Communists' understanding of the law and the penal system amounted in practice to little more than the vulgar-Marxist concept of a means by which one social class cemented and perpetuated its rule against another. In 1920, one Communist deputy tried to explain this position as follows: 'The fact that Soviet Russia has secured itself in its struggle for survival by applying the death penalty

[53] George Leggett, *The Cheka: Lenin's Political Police* (Oxford, 1981), 62–3, 182–5, 468.

is a historic right of the proletarian state, while it is a historic wrong for a collapsing capitalist society to create such security measures.'[54] This was a line that laid the Communists wide open to attacks from other parties for maintaining a double standard in the matter of capital punishment. When a Communist deputy attempted to deal with this problem during a debate on the subject in 1928, he soon ran into trouble:

It is claimed that the Soviet Union still recognizes capital punishment in the context of its Criminal Code. But the Soviet Union does not recognize the concept of punishment at all. The Soviet Union is a state in which the ruling class is just a different one from the ruling class in Germany. It cannot refuse to defend itself. As long as the bourgeoisie of the world carries on the struggle against the Soviet Union, the methods of class struggle must fit those of the methods of this assault. So one must not confuse the death penalty in the Soviet Union with the death penalty in Germany. [*Laughter. Shout from the Social Democrats*: What nonsense!][55]

As the Social Democratic spokesman in the debate not unfairly complained, 'The reasons which the Communist speaker gives for the retention of the death penalty in Russia are exactly the same as those which the German Nationalists give for its retention in Germany, the ideas of deterrence and retribution.'[56] He had a point. 'The self-defence of the proletarian state against the counter-revolution', declared another Communist deputy in 1927, citing Lenin, 'is thus an urgent moral duty, because it is carried out in the interest of the overwhelming majority of the people against a tiny minority.' But the 'interests' of the majority and the moral duty that they implied were of course to be decided 'objectively' by the Bolshevik regime itself, even if the majority thought 'subjectively' that their real interests might lie elsewhere. Aware of the weakness of these arguments, the German Communists also tried to claim that the executions which had taken place in Russia were merely a transitional phenomenon. Capital punishment, they assured people, would be abolished once the class enemy had been defeated and socialism had been achieved. In the light of what was to come later, this was a very dubious excuse. Transitional, 'emergency' states, in which quasi- or semi-legal executions were carried out in the name of a higher political necessity, acquired in the first half of the twentieth century an unfortunate habit of prolonging themselves indefinitely until they became permanent dictatorships. The claim made by one Communist deputy in 1927 that 'anyway Russia is already on the way to reducing the death penalty'[57] was an almost exact reversal

[54] BA Potsdam RT 848, Bl. 131: Reichstag, 32. Ausschuss, 23. Sitzung, 2 Nov. 1927, 1–5 (deputy Rädel). For the German Communist Party during the Weimar Republic, see Hermann Weber, *Die Wandlung des deutschen Kommunismus. Die Stalinisierung der KPD in der Weimarer Republik* (Studienausgabe; Frankfurt am Main, 1969).

[55] GStA Berlin Rep. 84a/7792: *Frankfurter Zeitung*, 25 Oct. 1928.

[56] BA Potsdam RT 848, Bl. 122: Reichstag, 32. Ausschuss, 21. Sitzung, 27 Oct. 1927, 7 (deputy Saenger).

[57] Ibid., Bl. 131: Reichstag, 32. Ausschuss, 23. Sitzung, 2 Nov. 1927, 1–5.

of the truth. If the mid-1920s did indeed see a certain relaxation of the 'red terror' in Russia after the ending of the Civil War, it was not to last for long. Soon the regime of Stalin, who had consolidated his hold on power well before the end of the decade, would be sending Soviet citizens to their deaths not in tens or even hundreds of thousands, but in millions.

Time was to show that when it came to practical politics, as opposed to rhetoric, the German Communists were a good deal less committed to abolition than they seemed to be. The same was true of the Democrats, who represented the tradition of left-wing liberalism in the Weimar Republic. The party leadership and executive committee were against capital punishment, but the majority of active party members and conference delegates were not.[58] As the Democrats' behaviour in the National Assembly showed, the issue was a divisive one in the party, so divisive indeed that no party whip was imposed during votes on the topic, and individual Democrats were left to vote with their conscience.[59] The Social Democrats accused the party of betraying the liberal abolitionist tradition of 1848 and 1870.[60] But retentionists within the Democrats' Reichstag delegation such as Alfred Brodauf insisted that there had never been a unified liberal stance on the subject.[61] And even the most determined abolitionists in their ranks were not prepared to dispense with the death penalty as a weapon in the arsenal of the Republic's emergency legislation. Erich Koch-Weser, for example, who did more than anyone to further the cause of abolition during the 1920s, declared:

In times of extraordinary peril, the state cannot refuse to use the death penalty; no state in the world has completely abandoned the death penalty for such cases of the self-defence of the state in an emergency. At such times, prison sentences are useless because it is uncertain whether the state which is under attack will be in a position to carry the sentence out.[62]

Implicit in such a statement was not only an approval of Reich President Ebert's application of the death penalty during the revolutionary upheavals of the early 1920s, but also a dangerous concession to the power of emergency legislation as a whole, as was to become painfully evident in the spring of 1933, when the Nazis erected their dictatorial regime on the basis of emergency decrees. In the mean time however, the views of the Democrats became steadily less relevant as their representation in the Reichstag declined with each successive election. By 1930 there were only a handful left, and they had ceased to be in a position to have any influence on the course of events.

[58] Ibid., RJM 6097, Bl. 155: *Tägliche Rundschau*, 5 Dec. 1927.
[59] Ibid., Bl. 75: *Berliner Tageblatt*, 22 Oct. 1927; ibid. Auswärtiges Amt IIIa Nr. 51, Bd. 11, Bl. 110: Antrag Nr. 11 (Reichstag, IV. Wahlperiode 1928, Antrag der DDP-Fraktion zur Abschaffung der Todesstrafe).
[60] Ibid., RJM 6097, Bl. 98: *Vorwärts*, 1 Nov. 1927.
[61] Ibid., Bl. 143: *Kölnisches Tageblatt*, 22 Nov. 1927.
[62] Ibid., Auswärtiges Amt IIIa Nr. 51, Bd. 11, Bl. 114: *Vossische Zeitung*, 18 Oct. 1928.

One party of which this was certainly not true was the Catholic Centre, which largely succeeded in holding its own against the rising appeal of Nazism right to the end of the Weimar Republic. With the Democrats and the Socialists, it was one of the three parties of the so-called Weimar Coalition, which, unlike their various rivals, provided the Republic almost to the end with solid and unwavering support. The Centre Party, which participated in every coalition government at the Reich level from June 1919 to June 1932, and whose influence has often been underestimated by historians, was strongly in favour of capital punishment. Capital punishment was regarded by Centre Party deputies as a necessary act of retributive justice. If self-defence in an emergency was admitted as a legitimate plea brought by an individual faced with a murder charge, then state and society had to recognize that the same principle applied to themselves.[63] More than most, however, the Centre Party and its spokesmen placed the emphasis on execution as a 'just expiation' for the crime of murder:[64]

The Centre Party rejects the principles of revenge and ruthless retribution, just as it rejects a bias in favour of the views of the man in the street and the mood of the people. The proponents of the idea of just expiation are not prepared to give this standpoint up. Exaggerated humanity towards murderers always means inhumanity towards their victims and indeed towards the whole of society.[65]

Similar views were held by the Centre's ally, the Bavarian People's Party, whose spokesman declared that the 'idea of guilt and expiation' was powerfully rooted in popular feeling. 'One must not let the notion of expiation and retribution disappear entirely from view in considering this question.'[66] Criminality, as the Bavarian People's Party deputy Erich Emminger argued, was so widespread that strong deterrents were necessary to reduce it. Abolishing the death penalty was too risky an experiment.[67] Not everyone in the Centre Party's Reichstag delegation agreed with this stance, and at one point the party was even described as 'split'.[68] It was certainly true that isolated Centre Party politicians could be found supporting the idea of abolition.[69] But the vast majority were against it and cast their votes in this sense whenever the topic came up in the legislature.

The same was true of the People's Party, heirs to the old National Liberals of Imperial times. Long before the war, they had lost the commitment to abolition

[63] GStA Berlin Rep. 84a/7792: *Germania*, 19 Oct. 1928.
[64] Ibid.: *8-Uhr Abendblatt*, 25 Apr. 1929; *Frankfurter Zeitung*, 24 Apr. 1929; *Welt am Montag*, 22 Oct. 1928.
[65] BA Potsdam Auswärtiges Amt IIIa Nr. 51, Bd. 11, Bl. 115: *Vossische Zeitung*, 19 Oct. 1928.
[66] Ibid. RT 849, Bl. 51–2: Reichstag, 21. Ausschuss, 8. Sitzung, 18 Oct. 1928, 86–7 (deputy Emminger).
[67] GStA Berlin Rep. 84a/7792: *Deutsche Allgemeine Zeitung*, 19 Oct. 1928.
[68] BA Potsdam RJA 6095, Bl. 198: Staatssekretär in der Reichskanzlei to Reichskanzler, 19 Nov. 1928.
[69] See e.g. GLA Karlsruhe 234/6611: *Augsburger Postzeitung*, 15 Mar. 1929. Heinrich Krone, a liberal Catholic Reichstag deputy, wrote against the death penalty in the Catholic newspaper *Germania*, 3 Nov. 1927 (BA Potsdam 61 Re 1/1772, 82).

that had been such a powerful force in the 1860s and 1870s, and by the Weimar Republic they were retentionist almost without exception. Their Honorary Chairman, Wilhelm Kahl (1849–1932), was also their chief legal expert, and a long-time supporter of capital punishment. 'The original right of the state to take human life for its highest purpose, the security of human society,' he said, 'cannot possibly be disputed.'[70] Kahl was a thoughtful and flexible politician, and he was to play a highly ambivalent role in the history of abolition in the Weimar Republic. Many of his colleagues in the People's Party were far more committed in their retentionist views. One, for example, roundly condemned the abolitionists as suffering from the 'sickness of the age', being soft on criminals.[71] Like the Democrats, the People's Party was a force of declining importance, and in the last years of the Republic it lost almost all its seats in the Reichstag. Nevertheless, its stance on the issue was one of a number of indicators that the middle-class parties and their voters—most of whom eventually defected to the National Socialists— had shifted their views decisively in favour of capital punishment since the war and the Revolution, if not before.

More significant than the People's Party as proponents of capital punishment were the Nationalists, the main party of the right for most of the decade until they too suffered a precipitous decline under the electoral onslaught of the Nazis. Forming an uneasy coalition of fairly traditional conservatives with elements of the radical right, the Nationalists put forward a variety of justifications for the death penalty in the debates of the Weimar years. Most Nationalist defenders of the death penalty placed their emphasis on the need to protect society, the principle of deterrence, and similar points.[72] As one of their most prominent representatives, Oskar Hergt, Reich Justice Minister from 1 February 1927 to 29 June 1928, declared, the death penalty owed its principal justification to 'the idea of expiation, of righteous retribution'.[73] The threat of execution was needed to deter bandits and sex murderers. The possibility of miscarriages of justice was remote.[74] But the Nationalists too had their problems with capital punishment. For it was from circles close to them that the notorious death squads of the early Weimar Republic emanated, and they were more than a little inclined to protest if one of the assassins of politicians such as Walther Rathenau, of men whose association with the Treaty of Versailles made them in the eyes of the Nationalists no better than traitors, was convicted and sentenced to death for his crime.

---

[70] GStA Berlin Rep. 84a/7792: *Deutsche Zeitung*, 19 Oct. 1928.

[71] Ibid.: *8-Uhr Abendblatt*, 26 Apr. 1929 (Reichstag deputy Wunderlich).

[72] For the deterrence argument, see GLA Karlsruhe 234/6611: 'Der Staat und der Mörder', *Münchner Neueste Nachrichten*, 30 Nov. 1928.

[73] BA Potsdam RT 848, Bl. 119–21: Reichstag, 32. Ausschuss, 21. Sitzung, 27 Oct. 1927, 1–5.

[74] Ibid. 61 Re 1/1772, 78: Amtsgerichtsrat Dr Herfurth, in *Deutsche Tageszeitung*, 26 Oct. 1927; ibid. 90: *Deutsche Zeitung*, 14 Dec. 1927.

As a Social Democratic spokesman pointed out in a debate on the death penalty in 1925,

The behaviour of the German Nationalists is bizarre. When the nationalist assassins were convicted, they claimed there was evidence of a terrible miscarriage of justice, that these erroneous verdicts emanated from a mass psychosis which was prevalent at the time, and that the sentences must not be carried out. *Where the right is involved, it treads the political stage as the most radical opponent of the death penalty. But things are different today, when the nationalist assassins have been granted an amnesty. The Nationalists are demonstrating the same inner dishonesty as have the Communists, who also want to play the part of opponents of capital punishment here.*[75]

The same could be said with even more force, as we shall see in a later chapter, for the National Socialists.

Given the views of the various political parties on these issues, it was not surprising that the constellation of political forces that dominated the legislatures of the Weimar Republic after the election of 1920 made it virtually certain that the death penalty would not be abolished by majority vote. Nevertheless, numerous attempts were made to achieve this aim during the following years. On 1 July 1921 the Prussian Chamber of Deputies defeated a Social Democratic motion 'that the death penalty is abolished' by 172 votes to 137 with one abstention.[76] Abolitionist motions were regularly put before the Chamber, often in the form of amendments to the budget for the Ministry of Justice. Such motions were defeated, for example, on 7 July 1926 and again on 6 March 1928 (when the voting was 188 in favour of capital punishment to 150 against).[77] A further debate took place in 1929, when the Social Democrats declared abolition to be 'a necessary consequence of the democratic principle. . . . No dictatorship can do without it'.[78] This notion too was lost, as was another one put during a debate on the judicial budget on 17 February 1931.[79] Not all such attempts failed. A motion to abolish the death penalty was passed by the Chamber of Deputies in Hesse in 1927, by 23 votes to 22. The small number of votes cast, however, and the narrow margin, both indicated that this was only 'a chance majority . . . because a large proportion of the bourgeois deputies were out of the chamber at the time'.[80] A majority was also reported for abolition in the Saxon Chamber of Deputies in the same year.[81] But normally, and when it counted, it was clear that abolitionist

---

[75] GStA Berlin Rep. 84a/7792: *Vorwärts*, 25 Oct. 1925.

[76] Ibid. 7785: Preussischer Landtag, col. 2100.

[77] Ibid. 7792: *Vorwärts*, 7 Mar. 1928.

[78] Ibid. 7786, Bl. 213: PJM Aufzeichnung für die Pressekonferenz (18 June 1929).

[79] Ibid., Bl. 196–210 (Preussischer Landtag, cols. 4570–72, 4599–600, 4713), and Bl. 253 (Preussischer Landtag, col. 18307).

[80] BA Potsdam Auswärtiges Amt IIIa Nr. 51, Bd. 11, Bl. 98: *Hannoversche Kurier*, 30 Sept. 1927; GLA Karlsruhe 234/6611: *Frankfurter Nachrichten*, 30 Sept. 1927.

[81] BA Potsdam RJM 6097, Bl. 150: *Vorwärts*, 1 Dec. 1927.

majorities could not be found in any of the legislatures.[82] It was not within the power of any state parliament, even the Prussian one, to abrogate part of the nation-wide law for its own territory alone. Votes taken in these legislatures were thus of purely symbolic importance. Since the death penalty was enshrined in the Criminal Code of 1871, which continued to apply to the whole of Germany throughout the period of the Weimar Republic, it could in practice only be abolished by amending the Code itself, which in turn could only be done by the Reichstag. Nevertheless, a series of substantial majority votes against capital punishment in the Prussian Chamber of Deputies would have made it virtually impossible for the cabinet to continue sanctioning executions. And even the chance majority of one for an abolitionist motion put before the Hessian Parliament by the Social Democrats in 1927 led to the state government systematically commuting all death sentences into life imprisonment thereafter, as the motion had demanded.[83] Moreover, such votes were also important as a form of propaganda, and kept the issue continually under the public eye.

The main running in the movement for the abolition of the death penalty in the Weimar Republic was made by the German League for Human Rights, which had originated as a cross-party pacifist organization, the New Fatherland League, during the war. Its leading figures were pacifists somewhere to the left of left-liberalism and somewhere to the right of the Communists. It was a natural extension of the protest against the loss of human life during the war to protest against its loss in peacetime and, as we have seen, many of the most active abolitionists had come from this milieu in the Wilhelmine period as well. Many of the League's leading personalities were writers and journalists. It was one of their favourite tactics to extract statements supporting their cause from well-known figures in the cultural and artistic scene. Among those whose views were solicited in this way were the artists Ernst Barlach, Käthe Kollwitz, and Heinrich Zille, the conductors Otto Klemperer and Bruno Walter, the writers Bertolt Brecht, Max Brod, Alfred Döblin, Lion Feuchtwanger, Oskar Maria Graf, Emil Ludwig, Heinrich Mann, Thomas Mann, Arnold Zweig, and Stefan Zweig, the theologian Martin Buber, the theatre director Max Reinhardt, and the dramatist Carl Sternheim, all of whom signed a petition to the Reichstag urging the abolition of the death penalty in 1929.[84] Döblin, the novelist, best known for his modernist masterpiece *Berlin Alexanderplatz*, a work in which crime and crimi-

---

[82] GStA Berlin Rep. 84a/7792: *Welt am Montag*, 22 Nov. 1928; *Welt am Abend*, 22 Oct. 1928; *Der Tag*, 24 Oct. 1928.

[83] BA Potsdam Auswärtiges Amt IIIa Nr. 51, Bd. 11, Bl. 100: *Deutsche Allgemeine Zeitung*, 30 Sept. 1927; ibid. 61 Re 1/1772, 68: *Hannoverscher Courier*, 30 Sept. 1927.

[84] Ibid., RJM 6097, Bl. 14–15: *Vossische Zeitung*, 7 Oct. 1926, *Frankfurter Zeitung*, 8 Oct. 1926; Bl. 29: *Berliner Tageblatt*, 18 Feb. 1927; ibid., 6098, Bl. 62: *Vorwärts*, 23 Apr. 1929; Bl. 10: *Vossische Zeitung*, 10 Mar. 1926.

F I G. 28. *Members of the League for Human Rights.* This organization led the fight for the abolition of the death penalty under the Weimar Republic. From left to right: Kurt Grossmann, the League's Secretary, and a prominent figure in the campaign to clear the name of Josef Jakubowski, the Polish labourer who the League believed had been wrongly executed in 1926; Rudolf Olden, a tireless campaigner against capital punishment and author of a pamphlet on the Jakubowski affair; Carl von Ossietzky, the brilliant radical journalist, later imprisoned by the Nazis; and two of the League's lawyers, Alfred Apfel and Dr Rosenfeld.

nals played a prominent part, wrote in 1927 that the death penalty 'is an insult and shows a pathetic view of death; with death', he declared, 'one is not punished as one is with blows or imprisonment'.[85] Gustav Wyneken, a leading light of the independent, middle-class youth movement during this period, was also in favour of abolition, despite his ambivalent position on other issues.[86] The cartoonist Theodor Thomas Heine wrote ironically of claims that capital punishment caused no pain to those who suffered it: 'A painless death is such a beautiful thing that it will never be a punishment. On the contrary, I can think of it as the highest form of reward, perhaps granted to civil servants, and state prosecutors too, as a substitute for an honour.' The radical writers Kurt Hiller, Richard

[85] BA Potsdam Auswärtiges Amt IIIa Nr. 51, Bl. 29: *Berliner Tageblatt*, 18 Feb. 1927.
[86] Ibid., Bl. 212: Gustav Wyneken, 'Der Fall Hein und die Todesstrafe', *Berliner Tageblatt*, 17 Feb. 1928; see also Walter Laqueur, *Young Germany: A History of the German Youth Movement*, 2nd edn. (New Brunswick, 1984), 53–64.

Huelsenbeck, and Ernst Toller were also opponents, as was the novelist Hermann Hesse.[87] The most prominent cultural figure to come out explicitly against capital punishment was Thomas Mann, already a novelist of international renown. In 1926 he wrote in response to an enquiry about his position on the question:

Whatever the status of the death penalty as an idea, the practicalities of its execution attach to it something so undeniably disgusting, dishonouring, and barbaric that I am convinced that every argument that is advanced in an abstract-philosophical manner in its favour is thereby nullified. I have never attended the atavistic ceremony, at which indeed even prayers are said, but I know that at that moment not only would my stomach nerves give way, but I would feel the sight and impression of it as an indelible stain on my life.

Perhaps aware of the limited use these rather self-centred sentences would be to the campaign against capital punishment, he added that in his view the desire to execute people was basically a fascist desire.[88]

The League for Human Rights also had connections with the left-wing jurists who were gathered around the journal *Die Justiz*, including Gustav Radbruch and Hugo Sinzheimer. The journal's petition to the Reichstag to abolish capital punishment in 1928 was signed by 24 professors, 269 lawyers, and 131 judges and other civil servants. The signatories included well-known pacifists such as Hellmuth von Gerlach and Walther Schücking, criminologists such as Gustav Aschaffenburg and Hans von Hentig, and also organizations such as the Republican Lawyers' Association.[89] Its campaign against the death penalty was also backed by the extreme left wing of the liberal, middle-class feminist movement, led by women such as Anita Augspurg and Lida Gustava Heymann, who had close ties to the pacifists. There was a widespread belief among feminists of all political hues that women had a civilizing and pacifying mission to perform in the inter-war years. On a number of occasions the International Women's League for Peace and Freedom, founded as a feminist-pacifist group during the war, petitioned for the abolition of the death penalty and held public meetings to back up the demand.[90] The League for the Protection of Motherhood and Sexual Reform, a feminist organization devoted to pursuing the improvement of the race through mainly 'positive' eugenic measures such as sex education, contraception, and equal rights for unmarried mothers, was also opposed to the

[87] E. M. Mungenast, *Der Mörder und der Staat. Die Todesstrafe im Urteil hervorragender Zeitgenossen* (Stuttgart, 1928), 65–86.

[88] BA Potsdam RJM 6097, Bl. 10: *Vossische Zeitung*, 10 Nov. 1926, citing Thomas Mann, 'Die Todesstrafe' from the *Literarische Welt*. See also GStA Berlin Rep. 84a/7792: *Die Welt am Abend*, 28 July 1928.

[89] Düsing, *Abschaffung*, 164–6.

[90] BA Potsdam RJA 6095 Bl. 102: Internationale Frauenliga für Frieden und Freiheit to RJM, 8 Nov. 1927 (also referring to earlier occasions); GLA Karlsruhe 234/6611: *Volkszeitung Heidelberg*, 10 Dec. 1928. See more generally Richard J. Evans, *The Feminist Movement in Germany 1894–1933* (London, 1976).

death penalty. Its leader, Helene Stöcker, was prominent, too, in the peace movement.[91] The young Democratic deputy Marie-Elisabeth Lüders, another liberal feminist, spoke in favour of abolition in 1927, and the leading 'moderate' feminist, Gertrud Bäumer, a Reichstag deputy for the Democrats, signed an abolitionist motion put forward by her party in 1928.[92] One female Centre Party deputy, Hedwig Dransfeld, voted against her party for the inclusion of abolition in the Weimar constitution in 1919.[93] But women in politics did not make common cause to combat the death penalty, despite their declared belief in the need for a cross-party women's campaign to spread a 'motherly' influence across society. By the later years of the Republic, many leading figures in the main-stream feminist movement were associated with political parties further to the right, such as the People's Party and the Nationalists, and it is likely therefore that their stance on the issue of capital punishment would have been, to say the least, rather more equivocal than before.[94]

Indeed, the redoubtable Paula Müller-Otfried, who sat in the Reichstag for the German Nationalists and led the German-Evangelical Women's League, a deeply conservative organization which represented women in the numerous organiz-ations belonging to the Protestant Church, was a vociferous supporter of capital punishment whenever the issue came up.[95] This earned her vehement criticism from the Social Democrats, who considered such views incompatible with what they saw as women's essentially pacific and non-violent character. Müller-Otfried outraged them even further by demanding the right for women to be executed as well as men, on the grounds that women who committed murder had thereby demonstrated a complete lack of feminine qualities. 'If a woman shakes off her womanliness to such an extent that she destroys the life of her fellow humans, then she must not receive any special treatment just because she is a woman,' she said.[96] Ironically the term 'special treatment', which she used here to mean the avoidance of the death penalty, was to come to mean the exact opposite in the discourse of National Socialism a few years later. Whatever the terminology she employed, however, it was clear that Müller-Otfried was de-manding that women should be killed, and this in itself was enough for the Social Democrats to turn her argument against her and claim that she too was denying her womanhood. 'She has even', exclaimed Julius Moses, a leading Social Demo-

[91] GStA Berlin Rep. 84a/7792: *Berliner Volkszeitung*, 4 February 1928. See also Christl Wickert, *Helene Stöcker 1869–1943. Frauenrechtlerin, Pazifistin, Sozialreformerin* (Bonn, 1991).

[92] BA Potsdam Auswärtiges Amt IIIa Nr. 51, Bd. 11, Bl. 110: Antrag Nr. 11 (RT, 4. Wahlperiode, 1928); ibid., RT 848: Reichstag, 32. Ausschuss, 22. Sitzung, 28 Oct. 1927, 4.

[93] *Stenographische Berichte über die Verhandlungen der konstituierenden deutschen Nationalversammlung zu Weimar, 1919*, vol. 6, col. 3872.

[94] See Evans, *The Feminist Movement*, ch. 8.

[95] GStA Berlin Rep. 84a/7792: *Der Tag*, 24 Apr. 1928; *Volkswacht für Schlesien*, 3 Nov. 1928.

[96] BA Potsdam RT 849, Bl. 76: Reichstag, 21. Ausschuss, 9. Sitzung, 23 Apr. 1928, 14.

cratic doctor in the Reichstag in 1927, 'very clearly demanded equality for the female sex with the male with reference to being beheaded. That a woman of all people should support the retention of the death penalty in this manner is completely incomprehensible to me.'[97]

Müller-Otfried's support for capital punishment reflected the views of most people who were actively religious during the Weimar Republic. As we have seen, both the Catholic and Protestant Churches had traditionally been supporters of the death penalty, and their views were reflected in the retentionist attitudes of the political parties that were closest to them—the Centre Party and the German Nationalists. Individual clergymen frequently declared themselves in favour of the death penalty.[98] They were fond of repeating the biblical doctrine of an eye for an eye. 'The authorities', remarked a theological writer in 1927, 'do not bear the sword of office in vain; they are there to avenge the victims of those who commit evil.'[99] The Catholic padre in the Mannheim gaol complained in 1925 about the 'extremely over-sensitive and tender-nerved society' of the day. His view was that, 'to use Kant's words, only sophistry and the twisting of the law, the cult of sensitivity and affected humanity, are present in the movement against the death penalty'. Executions were necessary, he wrote, 'namely because they honour and preserve the feeling for authority in the people'. They satisfied the need for retribution, which was deeply rooted in popular instinct. They constituted a 'lightning-conductor for the danger of a loss of authority'. 'The authorities, in my opinion . . . could never do without the death penalty; it is the *ultima ratio* of state authority.' Life imprisonment only made the malefactor tougher and less contrite: 'Indeed, the lifers are mostly the biggest trouble and the greatest nuisance in the prison, often far from sensibly filled with gratitude for the preservation of their life, but demanding all the privileges provided for those with limited sentences, rough, dulled, bitter, and angry people.' Far better, he thought, that they should have been executed right away.[100] Similarly, 'a theologian' fulminated in November 1928 in the Bavarian press against the 'vogue for humanity, sentimentality, and false pity' which he thought were being shown towards the 'dehumanized rascals and beasts' who murdered their fellow humans.[101] As in the nineteenth century, so in the twentieth, little or no support for the abolition of capital punishment could be expected from the established German churches.

[97] Ibid., RT 848, Bl. 132, p. 8: Reichstag, 32. Ausschuss, 23. Sitzung, 2 Nov. 1927.

[98] GLA Karlsruhe, 234/6610: Auszug aus dem Tagebuch des evangelischen Strafanstaltsoberpfarres Ebbecke in Bruchsal, 7 Feb. 1924.

[99] BA Potsdam RJM 6097, Bl. 125: *Fränkischer Kurier*, 7 Nov. 1927.

[100] GLA Karlsruhe, 234/6610: Auszug aus dem Jahresbericht des katholischen Anstaltsgeistlichen am Landesgefängnis Mannheim für 1924/25, 13 July 1925.

[101] Ibid. 6611: *Bayerische Staatszeitung*, 22 Nov. 1928.

Right across the range of political opinion, almost every party, group, and institution in the Weimar Republic was compromised on the issue of capital punishment. With the possible exception of the League for Human Rights and its allies in the ultra-liberal milieu of the pacifist and feminist movements, all of them were prepared to allow the death sentence under some circumstances, and the commitment of parties such as the Communists and the Social Democrats to abolition often seemed more rhetorical than real. When faced with political violence on a scale that seemed to threaten the very existence of the state, even the most committed abolitionists caved in and reached for the axe and the guillotine as the favoured means of rescuing the situation. This registered their own insecurity as much as it reflected the depths which political conflict had already reached well before the slide into authoritarianism and dictatorship in the Republic's final years.

e. *The Restoration of Normality*

Whether or not capital punishment was actually applied depended to a large extent on the personal views of the individuals who administered the right of clemency. Under the Weimar Republic, this right rested with the Reich President where capital cases were decided under his emergency decree powers, while in cases that came before the Reich Supreme Court it was effectively the Reich Justice Minister who took the crucial decision. For ordinary cases tried under the Reich Criminal Code, the government of the federated state where the trial was held inherited the power of clemency from the prince or monarch after the latter had been deposed in the Revolution. How these powers were exercised depended largely on the chance composition of Weimar coalition governments at national and state level. In particular, if the Minister of Justice was a convinced abolitionist, he could use his position to implement a systematic policy of reprieve. Towards the end of 1921, for example, when the Social Democratic academic and legal expert Gustav Radbruch took over the Reich Justice Ministry, in the coalition government led by Josef Wirth, he ordered six death sentences meted out to the brothers Gerhard and Werner Fleischer, two smugglers on the German–Dutch border who had committed a series of robberies with murder, to be commuted to life imprisonment. The conservative press immediately accused him of trying to abolish capital punishment unilaterally. 'Do we still have a death penalty?' asked the *Niederrheinische Volkszeitung* rhetorically in the headline to its report;[102] and the *Essener Volkszeitung* went even further: state prosecutors and the court had been in favour of execution, it reported, but the men's parents had

---

[102]   UB Heidelberg Heid. Hs. 3616 I.D. 14: *Niederrheinische Volkszeitung*, 8 Nov. 1921.

managed to exert pressure on the Minister. The exercise of mercy had run counter to popular opinion:

All classes of the population regard this act of clemency with incomprehension. . . . The consistent exercise of the process of reprieve which has been applied in the cases of the two murderous robbers, the Fleischers, must basically be equivalent to the practical abolition of the death penalty. . . . It is a pity the heads of these triple murderers and robbers have been spared the executioner's axe. Understandably, a wave of outrage is passing through the Ruhr coalfield.[103]

The Bavarian government launched a series of personal attacks on him, accusing him among other things of contacts with the Munich Revolution of 1918–19.[104] Radbruch was not deflected from his purpose. But, like other Reich Justice Ministers, he did not stay in office very long. Some Social Democratic state presidents, like Wilhelm Blos in Württemberg, categorically refused to sign any death warrants despite strong recommendations from officials in the Justice Ministry.[105] Here too, however, office was dependent on political circumstances and tenure was often short-lived. By March 1921 there was a new State President in Württemberg, and Eugen Bolz, the Centre Party Minister of Justice, was putting him under heavy pressure to resume executions, declaring that: 'In view of the frequent incidence of murders, it would no longer be responsible not to carry out the death sentence.' The new President agreed: 'No one can fail to recognize that the people's conscience demands that executions be carried out.'[106] Similarly, when in June 1919 the trade unions in Karlsruhe demanded the abolition of the death penalty, the Baden cabinet declared itself in agreement, and guaranteed not to approve any executions while it was in office.[107] Before long, however, a change of government had taken place here too, and executions started up once again.

The conservative bureaucrats who still ran the Prussian Ministry of Justice and its counterparts in the rest of Germany continued to favour the implementation of the death penalty. One official pointed out in 1920 that Germany was going through a 'time of terrifying growth in the number of serious crimes that bring with them a common endangerment of the life and safety of all members of the nation'. The Prussian Ministry of Justice argued consistently that there were always going to be cases where 'a reprieve cannot be responsible and would not

[103] Ibid. 13: *Essener Volkszeitung*, 6 Nov. 1921.

[104] Ibid. 34: *Vorwärts*, 23 Nov. 1921; ibid. 38: *Fränkischer Kurier*, 26 Nov. 1921; ibid. 44a: Philipp Loewenfeld, 'Notreformen unserer Rechtspflege', *Sozialistische Monatshefte*, 1 Jan. 1922, 27–31.

[105] GLA Karlsruhe 234/6610: Württembergisches Justizministerium to Badisches Justizministerium, 30 Dec. 1920.

[106] HStA Stuttgart E 130b Bü 886: Auszug aus dem Protokoll der Sitzung des Staatsministeriums Stuttgart, 15 Mar. 1921.

[107] GLA Karlsruhe 234/6610: Auszug aus der Niederschrift über die Sitzung des Staatsministeriums v. 5. July 1919.

be understood by the great majority of the people in the light of the exceptional seriousness of the deed and the generally dangerous nature of the murderer'.[108] Prussian judicial bureaucrats tried to use Ebert's policy as an argument for increasing the proportion of death sentences actually carried out in the federated states, and reducing the number of commutations to life imprisonment. A typical instance of their attitude to the new situation in which they found themselves after many years of working under the Imperial system could be seen in a case which came before them in 1920, which, they argued, 'has aroused great and widespread anger because of its violence and cruelty'. Referring to the question of whether the offender in the case should be executed or not, they declared:

When reaching the decision which now has to be made, it will not be possible to leave out of consideration the fact that in the new decrees of the Reich President—for example, of 10 April and 5 May 1920 (Reich Legislation, pp. 558, 887)—the death penalty is laid down for acts to which it does not apply according to the general criminal law. It is hard to reconcile the practice of commuting without exception death sentences passed under the general criminal law with the seriousness of such provisions. In addition, the Reich President has not made use of his right of clemency in several cases of death sentences passed by extraordinary courts martial, but had allowed justice to take its course—as did the Bavarian government in earlier cases.

In these circumstances, they therefore argued, it would be wrong to confirm death sentences only in cases connected with 'internal political conflicts'. Ordinary murderers should be punished according to the law as well.[109]

The vast majority of judges and prosecutors were similarly anxious to continue executing people. 'If a people of millions wants to live,' as a judge remarked in passing sentence on a murderer in 1926, 'individuals have to die, when they endanger the life of others.'[110] The judges of the Weimar Republic were not specially appointed but had already begun their careers under the Wilhelmine Empire. Articles 102–4 of the constitution guaranteed their independence and made it impossible for them to be dismissed. The democratic principle of the independence of the judiciary triumphed in the Weimar Assembly over doubts about the political position of the vast majority of German judges.[111] These men were overwhelmingly from the prosperous educated bourgeoisie. They had undergone a lengthy and expensive training and been carefully selected under Wilhelm II for their political reliability. Many of them had delivered numerous judgments against Social Democratic 'subversives' before the First World War.

[108] GStA Berlin Rep. 84a/7786: Preussischer Landtag, 278. Sitzung, cols. 19520–1, 5 May 1927, Drucksache Nr. 4544: Grosse Anfrage Nr. 165 (Pieck und Genossen).
[109] Ibid. 7785, Bl. 166: PJM to all Bundesstaats-Ministerpräsidenten, 14 June 1920.
[110] BA Potsdam RJM 6097, Bl. 18: *Frankfurter Zeitung*, 5 Nov. 1926.
[111] Hannover, *Politische Justiz*, 22–3; Hans Engelhard (ed.), *Im Namen des deutschen Volkes. Justiz und Nationalsozialismus* (Cologne, 1989), 18–19.

Lay assessors were also overwhelmingly drawn from men of the upper and upper middle classes. Women and workers, though eligible for office, were extremely rare.[112] Judges meted out harsh punishments to left-wing political offenders, while showing exceptional leniency to those on the right, with whose views the great majority of them strongly sympathized. Emil Gumbel calculated in 1921 that since 9 November 1918 there had been 314 political murders committed by right-wing forces, which had led to a total sentence of 31 years and 3 months of imprisonment plus life *Festungshaft*, incarceration in a fortress under relatively comfortable conditions, for those convicted. By contrast, the thirteen political murders committed by left-wing forces had earned 176 years and 10 months of imprisonment in regular penitentiaries and no fewer than eight death sentences.[113] The right-wing bias of political justice in this period was notorious, and did much to undermine the Republic's legitimacy in the eyes of the public by encouraging right-wing radicals to try and overthrow it.

Capital punishment in the violent opening phase of the Weimar Republic was thus to a larger than usual extent an instrument of political justice, often meted out by extraordinary courts or military tribunals. This was particularly the case in Bavaria, where the right-wing regime's quest for revenge against the revolutionaries of 1918–19 continued well after the situation had become stable. Essential in this quest were the People's Courts, set up by the revolutionary Eisner regime on 16 November 1918 to deal with cases of looting, murder, manslaughter, and burglary. On 12 July 1919, now under the aegis of those who had put down the Munich Soviet and sought a legal form for the continuation of the 'White Terror', their competence was extended to all forms of treason. There was no appeal, and retrials were not possible. Such emergency courts were made illegal by Article 105 of the Weimar constitution, but continued to operate in Bavaria. The kind of extraordinary justice they meted out was well illustrated by a disturbing complaint received in Munich in February 1921 from Alois Hammerle, a miller in the village of St Mang, in Bavaria:

Death sentences have already been carried out on two occasions on my land (a small wooded area), once in September 1920 and a second time on 2 February 1921. On neither occasion was I asked whether I would be prepared to make the place available. The place is situated roughly 300 metres away from my house. On the second occasion (2 February 1921) about 100 people had turned up for the execution, and watched the whole event.

[112] Hannover, *Politische Justiz*, 29–30. See also Ralph Angermund, *Deutsche Richterschaft 1919–1945* (Frankfurt am Main, 1990), 19–44, and more generally Konrad Jarausch, *The Unfree Professions: German Lawyers, Teachers and Engineers, 1900–1950* (New York, 1990).

[113] See Ernst Fraenkel and Hugo Sinzheimer, *Die Justiz in der Weimarer Republik. Eine Chronik* (Neuwied, 1968); Ernst Fraenkel, *Zur Soziologie der Klassenjustiz* (Darmstadt, 1968); Eike von Repkow and Robert W. Kempner, *Justiz-Dämmerung* (Berlin, 1932); Max Hirschberg, *Das Fehlurteil im Strafprozess* (Frankfurt am Main, 1962).

FIG. 29. *Political justice in the Weimar Republic.* The cartoonist Willibald Krain shows the blindfolded, confused, and rather sickly-looking figure of justice aiming directly for the red mouse on the wall, while the real criminals, the brownshirt, the capitalist, and the soldier, watch on from behind. The caption above it read: 'We shall proceed without respect of person'. The judiciary in the Weimar years was notoriously biased against socialists and communists and in favour of the Republic's nationalist opponents.

Apparently they had heard about it from the carter who had had to fetch the condemned men from the station at Heising, or they had been alerted to it by the military. No preparations were made for the shooting itself. The corpses lay from 4 to 6 o'clock in the clearing and were frightful to behold, since the top of one's skull had been blown away and the brains had splashed onto the other. There was nothing to cover them with. At 6 o'clock two coffins were brought along, but they proved to be too small. The corpses had to be forcibly stuffed into the coffins. In the course of the afternoon people kept coming to have a look at the corpses. Parts of the brains and bits of the skull could still be seen on the ground eight days afterwards. One of my sons found a loaded rifle in the clearing as well. My smaller children, who have to go to school or to church early in the morning, when it is still dark, are frightened to go near the clearing. Nor does my wife, nor my neighbour's wife, dare to pass through the clearing at night. Therefore I am requesting that no more shootings take place on my land in future, especially because more suitable places, for example the shooting-range, are certainly available.[114]

Clearly the line between this kind of summary execution and the open 'White Terror' of the spring of 1919 was a very thin one. These events illustrated the

114 HStA Munich MInn 71559: Hammerle to Justizministerium, Abschrift Kempten, 16 Feb. 1921.

depths to which extraordinary and summary justice could sink in the deeply divided world of Weimar Germany. It was only after Hammerle's intervention that the situation was brought under some kind of control. The military were withdrawn from such duties, and executions were placed once more in the hands of the civil authorities.[115] The Bavarian People's Courts were finally wound up on 1 April 1924, as the result of an agreement with the Reich government which enabled Hitler, who had been arrested after the failure of his 'beer-hall putsch' in 1923, to be tried in Bavaria, where he was likely to be treated leniently, rather than before the court set up in Leipzig under the provisions of the Law for the Protection of the Republic, where his chances were less good.[116] Nevertheless, like so much that happened in 1923, these events provided a dress-rehearsal for the cataclysm that was to overtake the Weimar Republic ten years later.

Amidst all these upheavals, the number of executions was roughly comparable to that of the Wilhelmine period. The most widely accepted official estimates give a figure of 89 condemnations and 10 executions in Germany in 1919, 113 condemnations and 36 executions in 1920, and 149 condemnations and 28 executions in 1921. After falling to 77 condemnations and 15 executions in 1922, the number rose again to 112 condemnations and 23 executions the following year. The annual average from 1919 through 1923 stood at 23. This was far higher than almost anyone had expected during the debates in the Weimar National Assembly in 1919. By far the most active use of the death penalty, as one might expect, was in Bavaria, where the authorities reported in December 1920 that there had been 19 condemnations and 10 executions in 1919, 28 condemnations and 10 executions in 1920, and 21 condemnations and 11 executions in 1921.[117] The Prussian Ministry of Justice reported no executions at all in 1919, 7 in 1920, and 7 again in 1921. Given the fact that Prussia contained more than half the territory of the entire Weimar Republic, and Bavaria only a relatively small part of the south-east, this contrast was striking, especially when compared to the situation in the Wilhelmine period, when the vast majority of executions had taken place in Prussia. While the restraining influence of the Social Democratic politicians on their coalition partners explains the low figures in Prussia under the Weimar regime, the high figures in Bavaria were a consequence of the continuing operation of the White Terror under a series of increasingly right-wing governments. From the overthrow of the revolution at the end of April 1919

[115] Ibid.: Befehlshaber Wehrkreiskommando VII, Bayerische 7. Division, to Bayerischen Minister des Innern, 20 Apr. 1921; Reichswehrminister Gessler to Wehrkreiskommando VII, 28 June 1921; circular of Innenministerium and Justizministerium Bayern, 22 July 1921.

[116] Stauff, *Justiz*, 24–6.

[117] GLA Karlsruhe 234/6610: Bayerisches Justizministerium to Badisches Justizministerium, 31 Dec. 1920.

to the Hitler putsch in November 1923, Bavaria offered unrivalled opportunities for right-wing radicalism, in government as well as on the streets, and the bitterness caused by the revolutionary events of 1919 found a continued outlet in political executions well into 1921, as we have seen.[118]

However, even in the early 1920s, political crimes were beginning to feature less prominently in the capital punishment statistics. The normalization process can be observed in a decline in executions for robbery with murder (*Raubmord*). The boundary between armed robbery and political violence was, to be sure, sometimes hard to draw. In the aftermath of the Revolution, murder for gain was unusually common. One of the most notorious cases was that of Otto Perleberg, who deliberately derailed a train near the Prussian town of Schneidemühl on 20 January 1919 in order to plunder the passengers. Eighteen people died in the crash, and over 300 were injured, many of them seriously. Perleberg was refused clemency by the Prussian government and executed on 7 August 1920.[119] But sometimes robbery had a political motive. During this period, extreme leftists such as Karl Plättner conducted a campaign of 'expropriation of the expropriators', and organized a series of bank robberies and attacks on post offices and other 'bourgeois institutions' as a form of 'propaganda of the deed'. Plättner and his gang were arrested in 1921, as was another far-left bandit leader, Max Hölz, who had committed a series of rather similar crimes. In many ways they resembled the Baader–Meinhof group of the 1970s, in their combination of vague political extremism and ruthless criminal activity.[120] But the term *Raubmord* was in fact frequently used—for example in the cases of the 'Red Army' insurgents in the Ruhr in 1920—to lend political violence a non-political, essentially criminal appearance, especially where prosecutions resulted from the revolutionary upheavals of the immediate post-war period. According to the Bavarian authorities, there were seven condemnations to death for this offence in 1919 (and eight for the alleged murder of hostages at the time of the Munich Soviet), eleven in 1920 and ten in 1922. In 1923, however, when the post-war inflation turned to hyperinflation, money lost its value, and theft of goods reached epidemic proportions, there were only four condemnations in Bavaria for *Raubmord*. In 1924 there were five, in 1925 another five, then the figures sank to one in 1926, two in 1927, one in 1928, and none in 1929.[121] The decline also reflected the gradual

---

[118] GLA Karlsruhe 234/6610: Übersicht über die in den Jahren 1910 bis 1930 rechtskräftig gewordenen Verurteilungen zum Tode. See also the Statistical Appendix, below.

[119] GStA Berlin Rep. 84a, 7785, Bl. 200: PJM notes, 8 Dec. 1920.

[120] Hans Manfred Bock, *Geschichte des linken Radikalismus in Deutschland* (Frankfurt am Main, 1976), 114–15, 303.

[121] HStA Munich MJu 12575: *Berliner Tageblatt*, 12 May 1929, and 'Statistik der Todesurteile 1918 mit 1925'. See also Joseph Hollweck, *Die Todesstrafe im Neuen Reich* (Jur. Diss., Erlangen, 1935), 9–10.

normalization of political conditions and was repeated in other federated states in the Republic.[122]

As governments and politicians became less nervous about the threat of violent political upheaval, the death penalty was used less frequently to symbolize their determination to keep a firm grip on state power. The pressure to prosecute and convict for murder became less severe. Above all, cabinets and Ministers of Justice became more willing to exercise the prerogative of mercy once the days of political emergency seemed to be over. Of course, even in the politically troubled early years of the Republic, according to the Bavarian Ministry of Justice, the majority of murders were of the ordinary, non-political sort. The largest category of condemnations to death from 1919 to 1925 was for the murder of victims closely related to the offender, including twenty-seven spouses, fifteen lovers, nine children, two stepfathers, two fathers, two brothers-in-law, two uncles, one grown-up son, and one mother-in-law. Even in three of the cases involving robbery with murder the victim was a relative of the offender.[123] This pattern of homicide, with the victim known to the offender, is normal in modern Europe, and was normal in the Weimar Republic too. Out of 217 offenders condemned to death in Saxony between 1855 and 1927, for example, all of them for murder, 116 had committed 'crimes of passion', and 80 murder with robbery. The Weimar years did not bring any significant change in this respect.[124] Yet the restoration of something like political and social normality at the beginning of 1924 was to some extent deceptive. The great inflation was over, but it had been succeeded by savage retrenchment. Mass unemployment was soon an inescapable part of the Weimar scene. Political violence, revolution, and terror had declined sharply, but the problems of securing stable coalition government were as intractable as ever. Moreover, it was clear that the judicial and penal practice of the Wihelmine period had survived the upheavals of the previous years virtually unscathed. Capital punishment was being practised on a scale comparable to that of previous decades, even if it had fallen back from the high levels of the early 1920s. Contrary to expectations, it seemed to be built in to the everyday administration of justice once more. How it operated, and what happened to it during the atmosphere of relative stability and optimism that characterized Weimar's middle years, from 1924 to 1929, is the subject of the next chapter.

[122] BA Potsdam RJA 5665, Bl. 126–37, gives generally lower figures for condemnations, but this reflects a different method of calculation (mainly because executions in any one year resulting from condemnations the previous year are not reassigned to the year of condemnation).

[123] HStA Munich MJu 12575: *Berliner Tageblatt*, 12 May 1929, and 'Statistik der Todesurteile 1918 mit 1925'.

[124] GStA Berlin Rep. 84a/7792: *Welt am Abend*, 12 Jan. 1925.

12

'The Death Penalty Practically Abolished!'

a. Criminal Biology and Serial Murder

In 1922 a young man by the name of Florian Huber was sentenced to death in
Landshut in 1922 for breaking into an isolated farmhouse, murdering the farmer
and his wife, plundering the building's contents, and setting fire to it afterwards.
The report submitted by the Bavarian Ministry of Justice recommending the
denial of clemency emphasized, as recommendations for execution had done
since the 1880s, the public interest which the case had aroused. But in the
Weimar Republic it was more legitimate than it had been before to cite public
demand for execution as a reason for not granting a reprieve. There had been, said
the report, 'tremendous anger' in the public against Huber, and violent scenes
had taken place outside the court-house at his trial. 'Embitterment against the
perpetrator is boundless, and the people are generally of the opinion that there
must be no clemency in the case of such a disgusting and bestial murder.' What
was really novel, however, was the tone set by the report's description of Huber's
appearance and personality:

Huber, although in other respects he cannot be proven to be hereditarily damaged,
demonstrated some physical evidence of degeneration: the structure of his physiognomy
is asymmetrical to the extent that the right eye is situated markedly lower than the left;
he has a tendency towards full-throatedness, his earlobes are elongated, and above all he
has been a stutterer since his youth.

In the nineteenth century, incorrigibility had been demonstrated by inward signs
such as lack of remorse and cold-bloodedness; now the signs had moved to the
outside of the body. The authoritative *Handbook of Forensic Psychiatry*, first
published in 1901, noted that in looking for signs of physical degeneration in
offenders, 'for a long time particular emphasis was placed on abnormal formations of the ears'.[1] Before Huber could be condemned beyond doubt on the

[1] Hoche (ed.), *Handbuch der gerichtlichen Psychiatrie*, 414.

basis of the shape of his earlobes, however, it had to be demonstrated that he was responsible for his actions. Here, too, outward signs were telling. He had, the report was forced to concede, a 'somewhat stupid grin'. And during his military service he had been regarded as 'mildly subnormal'. But this was, it suggested, deceptive. Huber only *presented himself* as subnormal. Witnesses came forward to testify that he was not subnormal at all. On the contrary, he was generally considered to be a 'work-shy, shifty person . . . with whom people wanted little to do'. This, once more, was the language of the nineteenth century. It enabled officialdom to slip at will from scientific into moral categories, especially when it was taking the views of the public into account. Public opinion conveniently rejected the idea that he was incapable of standing trial, and the Bavarian Ministry of Justice in this reactionary period was not going to rush to the experts to prove it wrong.

There was another problem to contend with before Huber's condemnation could be confirmed, and that was the fact that he had been wounded during the war. His wounds, indeed, had earned the young man the Iron Cross (second class), a pension of 58 marks 15 pfennigs a month (worth next to nothing by 1922 because of the massive post-war inflation), and a spell of eighteen months in hospital. However, the report concluded, the injuries had not been so serious as to have rendered Huber incapable of answering for his own actions. He had, after all, only been wounded in the left arm, the right leg, both lungs, and the head. Far more important was the fact that he had run away from home to join the gypsies before the war and had been convicted for begging several times by the age of 14. After his discharge, unemployed, and, like many war invalids, probably unemployable, he wandered around Bavaria, hawking, begging, and sometimes stealing, trying to make himself a living. Some months after the murder had been committed, he was arrested for another crime, and under interrogation his activities in Landshut came to light. Whether or not in the circumstances he was guilty seems in fact as open a question as whether or not he was mentally disturbed. A classic example of the social outcast, faced not only with unrelenting popular hostility but also a growing official tendency to stigmatize the 'antisocial' (*Asozialen*), the beggar, the vagrant and the tramp, as unworthy to live in human society, as physically and morally degenerate, Huber did not stand a chance. He was refused clemency by the Bavarian government and executed, like other capital offenders in Bavaria at this time, by a military firing-squad, shortly after 7 a.m. on 8 February 1922.[2]

Medical, eugenic, and psychiatric language and concepts were clearly playing a more important role than before in the assessment of crime and criminals. They

[2] HStA Munich MInn 18016: Staatsanwalt Landshut to Justizministerium, 28 Jan. 1922; ibid.: 'Zu Nr. 6023', 2 Feb. 1922; ibid.: Staatsanwalt Landshut to Justizministerium, 8 Feb. 1922.

were moving from the fringes to the centre of the discourse on crime and punishment. Officials in the Prussian Ministry of Justice used similar language to that of their Bavarian counterparts in the 1920s. One Hermann Schulz, for example, who had a string of convictions for offences against property and people, was found guilty of murdering 'two conscientious servants of the state, both heads of families', when they had tried to arrest him in 1920 in Deutsch-Eylau for stealing a cow. Local opinion, the officials observed in the manner that was now becoming customary, was outraged and demanded Schulz's death. In the Ministry's view, he was 'vermin, who does not deserve any clemency, and from whom human society must be protected for ever'. The use of the word vermin or pest (*Schädling*) was new in this context. Borrowed from the science of zoology, it indicated how the metaphor of the *Volkskörper*, the 'people's body', was entering official discourse on the execution of capital offenders, along with its attendant conceptualization of deviants and criminals as hostile parasites and dangerous, alien micro-organisms that the body had to eliminate if it was to be healthy.[3] As we have seen, a modified version of the hereditarian view of criminality associated with the Italian theorist Lombroso emerged just as the science of criminology was being created in Germany. From the beginning, criminology was strongly biological in character, more so than in most other countries. Criminological science sought the biological roots of criminal behaviour, reducing the criminal to a phenomenon, an object, to be 'scientifically' observed. In pursuit of this objective, the first Criminal Biological Information Centre (*Kriminalbiologische Sammelstelle*) was founded in Bavaria in 1923, dedicated to the collection of data about offenders with a view to developing a picture of their 'criminal disposition', their family history, and any physical traits different groups of offenders might have in common.

It was hardly an accident that the first of these institutions was founded in the German state which was most enthusiastic about the use of the death penalty at this time, and most firmly in the hands of the far right. The head of the Bavarian data-collection centre, Dr. Viernstein, pointed to the political context when he declared on its foundation that its activities

signify a turning-away from the biased environmental theory which reached its high point in the materialistic-economic system of Karl Marx, to a biological point of view which starts from the indissoluble connection of the individual with the inheritance of his forefathers, for which the milieu only provides the release.[4]

Criminal biology, explicitly conceived as a counter to Marxist theories of crime, dominated the field of criminology in this period, pushing even non-Marxist

---

[3] GStA Berlin Rep. 84a/7785, Bl. 200–1: Justizministerium notes of 8 Dec. 1920. See also ibid. 7792: *Deutsche Zeitung*, 1 May 1930.
[4] Quoted in Edmund Mezger, *Kriminalpolitik auf kriminologischer Grundlage* (Stuttgart, 1934), 113.

versions of the social theory of crime out to the margins, and converting even liberals and Social Democrats to its ideas. In the heated political atmosphere of the 1920s, this meant that it became increasingly politicized. The realization of such theories in the early Weimar Republic was most feasible in a state such as Bavaria, which gave free rein to all kinds of splinter-groups and voluntary associations of the far right in the reaction against the Munich Soviet of 1919. Nevertheless, where Bavaria led, other states followed, and soon there were criminal biology centres in Württemberg, Thuringia, and, crucially, Prussia too. All of them began assiduously compiling registers of offenders and their families in order to isolate the 'clans' which criminologists believed were responsible for the majority of crimes in the German population.[5]

A leading criminologist of the day, Gustav Aschaffenburg, thought that at least half of all penitentiary inmates were incorrigible, probably on hereditary grounds. The vast majority of criminals, he said, came from 'inferior material'. Almost inevitably, they had 'physically and spiritually inferior children' who would simply repeat the cycle of crime. It was time, he declared, to prevent them breeding. Criminals must recognize 'that society defends its own with every means at its disposal'.[6] Aschaffenburg in practice did not think the death penalty was either justifiable or necessary. But in the view of others, society's self-defence included not only the sterilization of the 'inferior' but also, as a leading forensic psychiatrist, Alfred Hoche, argued in 1920, their physical extermination. Writing together with a respected lawyer, Karl Binding, Hoche argued for what he called 'permission for the destruction of life unworthy of life', by which he meant the terminally ill, 'incurable idiots', and the congenitally mentally defective. Maintaining such people cost the state a great deal of money which it could scarcely afford. Already, indeed, though Hoche did not mention this, thousands of mental patients had been deliberately starved to death in Germany during the First World War, partly in order to free beds for the war wounded, partly because the exigencies of the war economy had deprived the asylums of the funds to feed them properly. All this indicated an increased willingness to dispense with what Hoche called 'ballast existences', encouraged by the cheapening of human life in the mass slaughter of the war.[7] Already before the war, as we saw in Chapter 9, it was becoming increasingly widely accepted in the welfare, penal, and medical worlds that a large part of criminality was inherited, and eugenic arguments had begun to be used to justify capital punishment. Many of those who championed

---

[5] Schmuhl, *Rassenhygiene*, 31, 94.

[6] Dieter Dölling, 'Kriminologie im "Dritten Reich"', in Ralf Dreier and Wolfgang Sellert (eds.), *Recht und Justiz im 'Dritten Reich'* (Frankfurt am Main, 1989), 194–235, here 222.

[7] Karl Binding, Alfred Hoche, *Die Freigabe der Vernichtung Lebensunwerten Lebens, Ihr Mass und Ihr Form* (Leipzig, 1920), esp. 54–7; Burleigh, *Death and Deliverance*, 11–24. Hoche had made his reputation as a research scientist with electrical experiments on the spinal cords of decapitated criminals.

sterilization did not take the further step of advocating involuntary euthanasia.[8] But increasingly as the Weimar Republic wore on, that step began to seem ominously small. Even lawyers were now becoming accustomed to arguing 'that the higher development of human society demands the extermination of the criminal'.[9] The argument that capital punishment was a deterrent began to lose its significance, 'because of the murderer's special psychology', as one legal expert put it. Murderers were so degenerate that nothing was likely to deter them from committing their foul deeds.[10] Clearly, though not everyone who took this position drew the same consequences from it, this argument could be used to justify capital punishment as a simple form of biological extermination. And it made another consideration irrelevant too—the plea of insanity. For if the death penalty was necessary principally in order to protect society now and in future generations from murderers, then a plea of diminished responsibility was no plea at all; it simply reflected an outmoded, moralistic way of looking at crime.[11] Capital punishment, its proponents were beginning to claim. 'is no medieval retribution. It is liberating, brief, and painless, and therefore humane towards the offender.' And it was 'protective and safeguarding' for society.[12]

The tendency to apply biological and hereditarian principles to the discussion of the criminal personality posed obvious problems for the role of forensic psychiatrists. Psychiatry had become an accepted feature of criminal jurisprudence in Germany well before the end of the nineteenth century.[13] In many ways, indeed, the medical profession, and above all its psychiatric branch, had replaced the clergy in defining for society what was normal and what was not. Psychiatrists were particularly called upon to testify when the defence attempted to obtain an acquittal on the basis of Paragraph 51 of the Criminal Code. Yet by the 1920s the limits which were set to the psychiatrist's freedom of action in testifying were becoming tighter. A notorious example of this was the case of Fritz Haarmann, whose murder of nearly thirty victims over a period from 1918 to 1924 became the subject of a verse still sung in Germany today:

> Wait, just wait a little longer
> And then he'll come along to you:
> Haarmann with his little chopper:
> And he'll make mincemeat out of you![14]

[8] See e.g. Max Flesch, *Gehirn und Veranlagung des Verbrechers. Beiträge zur Aufhebung der Todesstrafe und zur Einführung eines Verwahrungsgesetzes* (Berlin, 1929).

[9] GStA Berlin Rep. 84a/7792; *Kölnische Zeitung*, 26 Nov. 1928.

[10] Ibid.: *Deutsche Allgemeine Zeitung*, 10 Nov. 1929.

[11] BA Potsdam RT 848, Bl. 130: Reichstag, 32. Ausschuss, 23. Sitzung, 2 Nov. 1927, Dr Levy (SPD).

[12] GStA Berlin Rep. 84a/7792: *Deutsche Allgemeine Zeitung*, 10 Dec. 1929.

[13] E. Frey, *Ich beantrage Freispruch. Aus den Erinnerungen des Strafverteidigers Prof. Dr. Gerhard Frey* (Hamburg, 1959).

[14] Rainer Marwedel, 'Von Schlachthöfen und Schlachtfeldern', Introduction to Theodor Lessing, *Haarmann. Die Geschichte eines Werwolfs. Und andere Kriminalreportagen*, ed. Rainer Marwedel (Frankfurt

Haarmann, however, was highly discriminating in his choice of victims. A homosexual, he enticed adolescent boys to his room in a tumbledown part of the town of Hanover, had sex with them, and, as he reached a climax, bit through their jugular vein and killed them. Afterwards he hacked the bodies to pieces and disposed of them in the River Leine, behind the house in which he lived.

Haarmann had an extensive criminal record, and had served several prison sentences, including a five-year stretch from 1913 to the end of the war for burglary. None of this, however, attracted the attention of the police. For, despite attempts to suppress this information, it emerged during his trial that he had been working for them throughout the period during which the murders had been committed. With his extensive contacts in the world of petty crime, Haarmann was a regular police informer who turned over a substantial number of thieves to the authorities, and even at one point founded his own private detective agency. To his neighbours, indeed, he was known as 'Mr Detective'. The years from 1918 to 1924 were the longest period he had spent out of prison since his youth. It was only police protection that had enabled him to commit the long series of horrific murders to which he now confessed. And it was only his status as an informal police agent that gave him free access at night to the railway station and enabled him to pick up young men there under the guise of checking their papers. These allegations were strenuously denied by the Hanover police, whose chief declared in the local press:

The accusation that the police encouraged Haarmann's crimes by intervening too late is absolutely senseless! It must be remembered that these terrible events have taken place in the oldest and most overcrowded part of the town in a quarter in which the most degenerate part of the working class has its dwelling-place. Everyone involved, including most of the unhappy victims, is more or less delinquent and morally inferior—almost all of them have tense relations with the police and regard the police as the common enemy!

Not surprisingly, the inhabitants of the quarter in which Haarmann lived protested in their turn at being described in this way. Seventy-eight of them put their names to a public demand for the retraction of the police statement, which they considered 'is designed to lower the standing of the inhabitants of the Old City'. They were, they said, 'of the opinion that the police shares a high degree of responsibility because of its complete failure in these events'.[15]

am Main, 1989), 7–27, here 7. The verse was an adaptation of a hit song by Walter Koll: 'Wait, just wait a little while | And happiness will come to you'. 'Liver-sausage' was sometimes used instead of 'mincemeat' (Frey, *Ich beantrage*, 60). The song also circulated in political versions later on ('Wait, just wait and then you'll see | And Brüning will impose on you | An emergency decree | And make mincemeat out of you'; see DVA Gr.II).

[15] Quoted in Friedhelm Werremeier, *Haarmann, Nachruf auf einen Werwolf. Die Geschichte des Massenmörders Friedrich Haarmann, seiner Opfer und seiner Jäger* (Cologne, 1992), 112. For an account by Haarmann's defence lawyer, see Frey, *Ich beantrage*, 58–82.

During the trial, the police, the prosecution, and the bench conspired to suppress these facts as far as they were able. The parents of Haarmann's victims protested, and demanded that the responsible police officers be disciplined. The principal critic of the police's behaviour, the radical philosopher and psychologist Theodor Lessing, who taught at Hanover University, was censured by his academic superiors and excluded from the courtroom. Lessing subsequently wrote a remarkable study of Haarmann and his trial, a work which surely deserves to rank as one of the classics of German criminal literature. The book, as well as Lessing's connections with left-wing circles and his consistent criticism of right-wing politicians such as Hindenburg, eventually forced him to leave Germany for Marienbad, where he was murdered by Nazis in August 1933. Meanwhile, Lessing's reporting on the Haarmann trial undoubtedly cast a strongly critical light on the incompetence and corruption of Hanover's police force.[16] But Haarmann was not only known to the police, he also had an extensive psychiatric record by the time he came to trial in 1924. At one time or another in his life, Haarmann had been diagnosed as suffering from a variety of psychiatric disorders, including epilepsy, neurasthenia, 'mental illness', 'youthful madness', and 'idiocy'. As early as 1897, after his arrest for a series of sexual assaults on children, the police had classified him as a 'commonly dangerous lunatic' and confined him by court order to a mental hospital, from which he had escaped after seven months, fleeing to Switzerland to avoid rearrest. Astoundingly, this episode seems to have been forgotten by the authorities later on.[17] In 1902 he had been invalided out of the army on psychiatric grounds, and after his own father had reported him to the police the following year as a danger to society, he had been subjected to another psychiatric examination. It had concluded that Haarmann was immoral, 'but not in any real sense "mentally ill"'.[18] In 1919 he had been submitted to yet another psychiatric examination because he had pleaded unfit to stand trial, and had once more been declared responsible for his actions. In 1922 another psychiatrist found him highly 'idiotic'. Not only was this lengthy psychiatric record repeatedly disregarded by the police during their investigation of the long series of murders that troubled the town of Hanover in the post-war years, it was also dismissed by the psychiatric expert witnesses at his trial, who portrayed Haarmann's behaviour during these previous examinations as consisting of 'hysterical simulation' mounted in order to achieve a specific end such as being invalided out of the army, or obtaining a higher military pension.[19]

One of these expert witnesses was the doctor who had previously declared Haarmann to be sane in 1919, while the other was a police doctor in Hanover.

[16] Rainer Marwedel, *Theodor Lessing 1872–1933. Eine Biographie* (Frankfurt am Main, 1987). See also Lessing, *Haarmann*, 69–72, 76–7, and Werremeier, *Haarmann*, 145.
[17] Lessing, *Haarmann*, 62–5.   [18] Ibid. 67–8.   [19] Ibid. 79–80.

Neither of them could thus be said to have been truly independent.[20] The third and principal expert psychiatric witness, Professor Schultze, a psychiatrist from Göttingen University, examined Haarmann from 18 August to 25 September 1924. He concluded that the accused man's statements about his sexuality had been 'too contradictory' to draw any sound conclusions from them. 'An organic brain disease', he said, was 'to be ruled out'. When he asked the legal authorities whether the trial could be postponed, the prosecutor's office sent him a telegram insisting that this could not be allowed 'in consideration of popular feeling'—a phrase which made it more than clear what he was expected to say when he took the witness stand in the courtroom. As a colleague remarked, any psychiatrist called to testify in the Haarmann case could 'under all circumstances be glad if he can hand him over for punishment, if he can only in some way reconcile this with his psychiatric conscience'. Given this pressure, therefore, it is not surprising that Schultze reached the conclusion that Haarmann, although 'a pathological personality', did not fall under the terms of Paragraph 51. He was 'abnormal and inferior' but not 'unfit to stand trial'.[21] The language used—'inferior', for example—already suggested that Haarmann's life was dispensable. In the Weimar Republic, psychiatric experts in murder cases such as this were more likely than before to bow to the dictates of 'public opinion' and certify the accused man sane. Conservative judges and prosecutors pressed them to certify murderers fit to plead, while the increasingly biologistic language of the experts pushed the authorities in the direction of execution rather than reprieve.

Haarmann was a man clearly driven by forces beyond his control. As his autopsy revealed, he suffered from a physical deformation of the brain. But the restrictive terms of Paragraph 51, which specified momentary madness at the time of committing the crime, allowed the psychiatrists to certify him sane; it was only people who committed murder on a single occasion, like Bruno Gehrt, who murdered two women in a sudden fit of violence, who were likely to be declared unfit to stand trial.[22] Serial killers were by the very fact that they had repeated their crimes difficult to fit into the paragraph's terms. This was by no means unwelcome to Haarmann. He had a lifelong terror of mental institutions, probably as a result of the period he spent in one early in his life. 'Chop my head off,' he told the judges at his trial, 'but don't put me in the madhouse again.'[23] He was sentenced to death on 19 December 1924. The Prussian cabinet confirmed the sentence on 4 April 1925, and Haarmann was guillotined by Carl Gröpler in Hanover prison in the presence of some forty officials and witnesses on 15 April

---

[20] Ibid. 173.   [21] Ibid. 15–16, 115; Werremeier, Haarmann, 124.
[22] Frey, Ich beantrage, 385–405.
[23] Lessing, Haarmann, 65. Parts of Haarmann's brain were fused to the inside of his skull.

F I G. 30. *The trial of Fritz Haarmann, 1924.* An illicit photograph, taken in the Hanover courtroom. Haarmann, who was to be convicted of a series of sexually motivated murders of young boys, is sitting on the right, directly underneath a blackboard plan of the building in which he lived. He was executed on 15 April 1925. The obsessive coverage of such cases by the popular press in the 1920s constituted a powerful influence in favour of the retention of the death penalty.

1925. His brain was taken away for medical examination, and his head was put in a jar of formaldehyde and deposited in the Institute of Forensic Medicine at Göttingen University, where it remains to this day.[24] Haarmann was only one of a number of serial sex-killers who aroused widespread debate during the 1920s. *Lustmord* had been known in Imperial times, but it undoubtedly occurred more frequently, and on a larger scale, under Weimar. Not long after Haarmann's crimes came to light, police in Münsterberg arrested the even more frightening figure of Karl Denke. In December 1924 they discovered the remains of 30 victims in his house and garden shed, as well as various memorabilia including a pair of braces made out of human skin. The 58-year-old Denke confessed to having started his murderous career as long ago as 1903, and to having eaten the flesh of his victims and sold it in the local community under the label of goat-meat.[25] Two similar figures were Friedrich Schumann, condemned to death in

[24] Lessing, *Haarmann,* 304–5.
[25] Kriminaldirektor Polke, 'Der Massenmörder Denke und der Fall Trautmann. Ein Justizirrtum', *Archiv für Kriminologie,* 95 (1934), 8–30; and Magnus Hirschfeld, *Sittengeschichte der Nachkriegszeit* (Leipzig, 1931), ii. 246–9.

Berlin in 1920 for 25 murders, and Bruno Luedke, who in 1928 began a career of necrophiliac serial killing which ended only in 1943, after he had murdered at least 54 women and possibly many more.[26] Even more extraordinary was the place occupied by sex-killings in Weimar culture. Freed from the constraints of Wilhelmine censorship,[27] writers, artists, film directors and playwrights began to depict sexual crimes in a way that had previously been done only in the literary underworld, and never with such power or sophistication.[28] Painters such as Georg Grosz and Otto Dix seemed obsessed with the subject of the violent sexual murder of women, and sex-killers featured centrally in novels such as Alfred Döblin's *Berlin Alexanderplatz* and films such as *The Cabinet of Dr. Caligari*.[29] The proliferation of such cases aided those who argued that there were some human beings who were so bestial, depraved, and degenerate that society had a duty to kill them. The frequent depiction of gruesome murders in Weimar culture also helped convince conservatives and reactionaries, who hated everything that *avant-garde* art stood for, that crime was being celebrated instead of combated in the new democracy.[30] The physical elimination of criminals in the name of society no longer seemed difficult to imagine. The ending of 'life unworthy of life', as the medical scientists Binding and Hoche put it, was openly discussed, and the forcible sterilization of institutionalized patients was actually carried out. In this overheated atmosphere, it became possible to contemplate murder on a scale hitherto barely even dreamt of.

Yet it is important not to succumb to the myth of the Weimar' Republic's 'decadence', a myth essentially put about by the Nazis and their sympathizers and repeated unthinkingly by writers and film-makers ever since. In many ways, the new cultural prominence of serial killers was an aspect of the modernity which Weimar was so adept at rehearsing. It was no more excessive or widespread than the celebration of such figures common in the USA and other 'advanced' Western countries in the late twentieth century. Moreover, all of this was still quite remote from the world of official policy-making. Here, forcible sterilization and the 'euthanasia' of the chronically handicapped and mentally retarded or disturbed was not approved, and the prominence of violence in Weimar culture

---

[26] BA Potsdam RJM 6097, Bl. 187: *Die Welt am Abend*, 12 Jan. 1928; also Bl. 196: *Vorwärts*, 18 Jan. 1928; Frey, *Ich beantrage*, 16–59.

[27] See Rudolf Schenda, *Die Lesestoffe der kleinen Leute* (Munich, 1976), 78–104.

[28] Beth Irwin Lewis, 'Lustmord: Inside the Windows of the Metropolis', in Charles W. Haxthausen and Heidrun Suhr (eds.), *Berlin: Culture and Metropolis* (Minneapolis, 1990), 111–40.

[29] Maria Tatar, *Lustmord. Sexual Murder in the Weimar Republic* (Princeton, 1995). See also Albrecht Wetzel, *Über Massenmörder. Ein Beitrag zu den persönlichen Verbrechensursachen und zu den Methoden ihrer Erforschung* (Berlin, 1920).

[30] See Birgit Kreutzahler, *Das Bild des Verbrechers in Romanen der Weimarer Republik. Eine Untersuchung vor dem Hintergrund anderer gesellschaftlicher Verbrecherbilder und gesellschaftlicher Grundzüge der Weimarer Republik* (Frankfurt am Main, 1987), esp. 44–5.

was earnestly debated and acted as a spur to a renewed tightening of censorship regulations. Many criminal psychologists blamed the wave of serial killing on 'the extensive newspaper reporting of murders, the terrible murder stories in the penny-dreadfuls, whose title-pages try to affect the imagination and feelings of the browser and the reader in the most grotesque manner'.[31] Penal policy, including capital punishment, was one of many areas in which, after the initial turmoil of the revolutionary years, the practice of Weimar institutions was largely dictated by the precedent of Wilhelmine days. The primary conflict here was between those who wished to see tradition continue, and the liberal and Social Democratic reformers who wanted to see it ended in the name of humanitarian penal reform. The popular fascination with capital crime and capital punishment and its celebration in art, drama, cinema, and the novel was a new and significant element in this conflict over penal policy, but it was only one element among many, as we shall now see.

b. Executions and the Public Sphere 1922–1928

Executions under the Weimar Republic were carried out in much the same way as they had been under the Wilhelmine Empire. The only alteration in practice took place after the Prussian Minister of Justice Hermann Schmidt, who belonged to the Catholic Centre Party, attended a beheading in Magdeburg prison in September 1927. Schmidt reported that he had been repelled by 'the peculiar costume which the executioner wears: frock-coat and white waistcoat. It has a strange effect,' he confessed, 'when the executioner throws off his frock-coat in order to strike the decisive blow, and his brilliant-white torso stands out against the black of the rest of his clothing.'[32] The bourgeois dress introduced by executioner Krautz in Bismarckian times seemed anachronistic as well as inappropriate in the 1920s. The Minister immediately ordered the costume to be changed. In October 1927 the executioner agreed 'at future executions to wear a tunic made of black fabric with black buttons and closed at the neck and wrists, instead of the frock-coat'.[33] Otherwise, things continued much as before, with the guillotine used in the south and west of Germany, in Hanover, the Rhineland, and Saxony, and the hand-held axe in the 'old' provinces of Prussia. Theoretically, the sword was still operative in a few places such as Lippe, Mecklenburg, Saxe-Anhalt, and Reuss, but no examples of its use in the twentieth century, or indeed even in the Imperial period, have come to light. In Baden,

[31] Erich Wülffen, *Kriminalpsychologie. Psychologie des Täters* (Berlin, 1925), 428.
[32] BA Potsdam RJM 6097, Bl. 149: *Vossische Zeitung*, 29 Oct. 1927.
[33] GStA Berlin Rep. 84a/4595, Bl. 59: Oberstaatsanwalt Magdeburg to Justizministerium, 4 Oct. 1927.

the execution ceremony was still inaugurated by the breaking of a wand of office.[34] Executions ordered by military or extraordinary courts, as in the Ruhr in 1920 or Bavaria up to 1922, were carried out by firing-squad.

There was, of course, some discussion, as there had been before the war, of other methods of execution than the ones currently in use. In 1924 one writer recommended the use of poison to execute convicted murderers, arguing that this would be more humane than the methods currently in use, such as the axe and the guillotine, or under discussion, such as the gas chamber and the electric chair.[35] In 1926 the governor of the gaol at Freiburg, in Baden, welcomed the execution which had taken place in the prison in October 1924—the first for almost twenty years—but added:

What I found fundamentally repellent in the execution was the endless preparation and the large number of people who had been admitted to the melancholy act; further, the behaviour of the offender, whose limbs were paralysed by the fear of death, and who literally had to be dragged to the scaffold and strapped to the block with a good deal of effort. I could not help considering whether an execution within prison walls still justified all this fuss, whether in the age of chemicals and electricity this bloody medieval drama could not finally be replaced by a simpler and quicker method of killing.[36]

But majority opinion among jurists still favoured decapitation. As the state prosecutor in the south German town of Ulm, Dr Eiwert, remarked in 1927:

A method of death other than decapitation is really hardly thinkable: we will not easily return to the medieval and dishonouring rope, and shooting, which for obvious practical reasons is prescribed by military law, is as unreliable a method of killing as is death by electrocution, which is so popular in America. In any case, our legal instincts demand the act of execution to be carried out in a certain atmosphere of ceremony, which could not always be provided in the case of electrocution or poison.[37]

While the new methods represented a simple means of removing the criminal and nothing more, traditionalists such as Eiwert thus continued to regard the ritual aspects of capital punishment as essential.

Yet even conservatives were in many cases convinced that the guillotine was the most humane way of administering the fatal blow. In other parts of Europe, it had continued to make progress, replacing the axe in Denmark in 1922, for instance.[38] Eiwert reported that he had 'recently had to accompany a poor sinner

[34] Ibid. 7792: *Kölnische Volkszeitung*, 20 June 1932.
[35] BA Potsdam RJM 5665, Bl. 179: *Berliner Morgenpost*, 24 Nov. 1924.
[36] GLA Karlsruhe 234/6610: Auszug aus dem Jahresbericht des Anstaltsdirektors des Landesgefängnisses Freiburg 1924/25.
[37] BA Potsdam RJM 6097, Bl. 39: Staatsanwalt Dr. Eiwert, 'Der Vollzug der Todesstrafe', *Kölnische Zeitung*, 22 May, 1927.
[38] GStA Berlin Rep. 84a/7785, Bl. 282: *Vossische Zeitung*, 27 July 1922.

to the scaffold', and he was convinced that the guillotine had helped keep the man calm:

The condemned man entered the prison courtyard, in which the guillotine had been set up, quietly and calmly. Nor had he shown any sign of emotion when I had been obliged to tell him in his cell a few days before that his appeal for clemency had been rejected and that the sixth morning hour of the following Saturday would be his last. On the contrary, I had the impression that this news was welcome to him, as a release from the painful condition of long waiting and worry in which he had been living. The letters he now wrote to his wife and his brother also breathed the calm assurance that everything would pass off well, and that his coming death would be a just expiation for his deed. Did this calmness not originate in the certainty that decapitation by guillotine was so quick and sure a means of death that one could no longer speak of any sensation of pain or the torture of death? The doctors at least claim so. The reading-out of the gist of the sentence, and the pastor's prayer, lasted a few minutes; but it was after a few seconds, however, in which the executioner and his assistants swiftly strapped the condemned man onto the board, turned it over, and placed the head in the guillotine, that the head fell into the basket which had been placed under it in readiness, severed from the torso by the sharp and heavy blade as it rushed down onto the neck. The cutting-off of the head, the severing of the central spinal nerve, takes place with such lightning speed, that there really is no time for the transmission of any sensation of pain to the brain.[39]

Unaccountably, however, many offenders still failed to find the guillotine reassuring. In 1927, for example, the Polish worker Felix Dymbowski was so terrified of it that he repeatedly asked the prison warders for a revolver or a rope with which to kill himself. As the Hanoverian state prosecutor reported:

Shortly before the execution, he tried to anaesthetize himself in the cell by banging his head against the table and hitting his head with his handcuffs. By doing this, he caused a minor injury to his forehead. In the last minutes before the execution, the condemned man's legs failed him, so that he had to be carried to the execution yard by two strong prison warders.[40]

In the end, of course, no method of execution was able to reassure the condemned. Prosecutors simply rationalized their retention of the methods to which they were used. In north-east Germany it was the hand-held axe that still counted as the quickest and safest means of execution. Dr Eiwert was reflecting current practice in the part of Germany in which he worked when he spoke out in favour of the guillotine. The debate testified once more to the hold of tradition on penal practice in this area.[41]

Meanwhile, executions were kept public by the press, who reported on them with a greater wealth of sensational detail than ever. Special attention was still

---

[39] BA Potsdam 61 Re 1/1772, 34: *Deutsche Tageszeitung*, 28 May 1927.

[40] HStA Hanover Hann. 173a Nr. 442, Bl. 68: Oberstaatsawalt Hanover to PJM, 9 July 1927.

[41] For the introduction of the guillotine in Hanover, Bavaria, Baden, and other German states in the nineteenth century, see above, Ch. 7c and 8d.

paid to the 'hangman's meal' ('cutlet or beefsteak, wine or beer, cigars or cigarettes').[42] Every minute of the criminal's last hours was described. The *BZ am Montag*, in printing what it claimed to be an eyewitness report of the last hours of the serial killer Böttcher before his execution in January 1928, even included an account of the condemned man's dreams. Other papers carried similar stories, full of dramatic descriptions of the last-minute telephone calls made by Böttcher's lawyers to the Justice Ministry in pursuit of a stay of execution, and replete with condemnations of the proceedings which cannot but have appeared hypocritical in the light of the extra circulation which the papers hoped to gain by publishing such stories about them.[43] In 1922, a newspaper account of the last hours of the child-murderer Reusch, in Ravensburg prison, described the last visit of the man's relatives, the smoking of his last cigar, and every last detail of the execution itself, down to the very sounds it made: 'A gurgling noise, a brief splashing of blood, and the act was over.'[44] The year 1927 saw a new variant of this sensationalist, exploitative literature, with the publication of a diary written by an offender in the condemned cell; only at the very end was it revealed that he had been reprieved; the selling-point was obviously the expectation that he had not.[45] The kind of reporting which had so concerned Bismarck in the 1880s was sober indeed compared to this kind of thing; worried judicial authorities in the Weimar Republic actually cited Bismarck's initiative in expressing their disapproval, thus unconsciously demonstrating once more their sense of institutional continuity with the Imperial regime.[46] The democratization of the public sphere in the Weimar Republic brought a new degree of importance to the representation of executions as a ritual of death, while at the same time opening the way to the unscrupulous manufacture and manipulation of 'public opinion' by those who wanted capital punishment retained or even extended in scope.

Sensationalism of this sort attracted solemn condemnations from the more serious newspapers. Such reports, argued the liberal *Frankfurter Zeitung*, 'really serve to awaken evil desires and pleasure in cruelty'.[47] The serial killer Peter Kürten even told the judge and jury at his trial: 'It is through the sensational reports of certain trashy papers that I have become the man you see before you today.'[48] Officialdom, too, viewed such reporting with grave disapproval. In 1921 a meeting of top-ranking state prosecutors in the Justice Ministry in Berlin

[42] GStA Berlin Rep. 84a/4595, Bl. 20a: *8-Uhr Abendblatt*, 26 June 1925.

[43] BA Potsdam RJM 6097, Bl. 187–92: *Die Welt am Abend*, 12 Jan. 1928; *BZ am Montag*, 13 Jan. 1928; *Berliner Tageblatt*, 13 Jan. 1928; *Der Tag*, 13 Jan. 1928; *Die Welt am Abend*, 13 Jan. 1928.

[44] HStA Stuttgart E130b Bü 886: *Süddeutsche Sonntagszeitung*, 23 July 1922.

[45] Erich Zessler-Vitalis (ed.), *Das Tagebuch eines Mörders vom Todesurteil bis vor der Hinrichtung!* (Berlin, 1927).

[46] HStA Stuttgart E130b Bü 886; Generalstaatsanwaltschaft to Justizministerium, 4 Aug. 1922.

[47] BA Potsdam RJM 6097, Bl. 15: *Frankfurter Zeitung*, 8 Oct. 1926.

[48] Ibid., RJM 6099, Bl. 5: *Die Welt am Abend*, 23 Apr. 1931.

recommended a more careful selection of the twelve witnesses required by law to be present at executions, 'since it is to be suspected that inaccurate reports of executions in the newspapers are often caused by the fact that the persons commanded to attend the execution from the local community representation have themselves provided inaccurate reports of what went on.'[49] The Württemberg Ministry of Justice complained in 1922 about 'sensational reports' of executions 'which in no way did justice to the solemnity of so gloomy an act', and recommended a system of entry cards for the gentlemen of the press:

When issuing entry cards, the newspapers which come into consideration for this privilege should be asked by the state prosecution service to avoid any sensationalism—for example, details of what the offender has eaten on the night before his execution, etc.— in their reporting. . . . At the same time, I would like to recommend the Justice Ministry to see if reports about the last actions of the offender, e.g. taking leave of his relatives, last wishes for food, etc., which may well mainly come from the prison staff and then find their way into the press, cannot be stopped.[50]

The Baden Ministry of Justice protested in 1924 about the 'sensational presentation' of executions in the newspapers, and reporters were officially warned that they would not be admitted unless they promised to write sober and responsible stories.[51] The Bavarian Justice Minister, Franz Gürtner, complained in 1925: 'The purpose of excluding the public from the execution of the death penalty will be to some extent frustrated if the press, as happened recently, reports the process of execution in a more or less sensational presentation.' Fresh restrictions were ordered on the admittance of journalists to executions, and those who were allowed in were now required to promise in advance to stick to a brief account of the basic facts.[52]

Keeping executions confidential remained a constant preoccupation of the authorities. In 1921 local officials in Memmingen complained that it was impossible to maintain confidentiality in respect of a forthcoming execution in the town because people could see into the prison yard from nearby houses and observe the preparations taking place. As a result, large crowds were gathering outside the prison every morning, in anticipation of the fatal event.[53] Ministry of Justice officials in Munich agonized over how best to transport the guillotine when they took it by train to such a town. Was the equipment to be conveyed as passenger luggage or rail freight? Where would it be kept?[54] Despite all these

---

[49] HStA Düsseldorf Rep. 145/326, Bl. 43: Generalstaatsanwalt Cologne, 'Auszug aus den Aufzeichnungen über die Besprechungen der Generalstaatsanwälte im Justizministerium am 10. Juni 1921'.

[50] HStA Stuttgart E130b Bü 886: Staatspräsident to Justizministerium, 25 July 1922 (draft).

[51] GLA Karlsruhe 234/6610: Justizminister to Staatsanwaltschaften, 10 Nov. 1924, and Erste Staatsanwalt Karlsruhe to Justizminister, 20 Nov. 1924.

[52] HStA Munich, MJu 13144: Gürtner to Oberstaatsanwälte, 20 Mar. 1925.

[53] Ibid.: Staatsanwalt Memmingen to Oberstaatsanwalt Augsburg, 20 Oct. 1921.

[54] Ibid.: correspondence of Justice Ministry, 1920–1.

anxieties, the practice of issuing entry cards to 'responsible' members of the public continued unchecked. In Hanover executions were usually attended by about twenty such spectators, who 'mainly belonged to the category of civil servants'.[55] In Cologne exceptionally large numbers of spectators were reported attending executions in consequence of the fact that different authorities were issuing entry cards without reference to one another.[56] In Württemberg it was still common in the early 1920s for up to fifty people to be admitted to an execution in addition to those whose presence was required by law.[57] In 1926, after nearly 200 had been reported attending on one occasion,[58] the Justice Ministry finally felt moved to express its doubts: 'The wider one draws the circle of people to be admitted,' it observed, 'the greater will be the danger that the solemnity of the execution process will be adversely affected.'[59]

A traditionalist like Dr Eiwert, who believed in the importance of retaining the ceremonial aspects of capital punishment, was particularly keen to prevent this:

The ceremonial nature of the act of execution demands, however, the greatest possible limitation of the number of spectators. The execution of a death sentence must not become a nerve-tingling sensation. We even owe it to the condemned mass murderer to protect him from the greedy eyes of a gawking crowd when he steps onto the scaffold.[60]

Entry cards continued to be issued, however, and no legislative initiative was undertaken to stop the practice. It was also impossible to keep crowds from gathering outside a prison once it was clear from the rejection of a clemency plea that an execution was about to take place.[61] The press could not be stopped from reporting the last night of the condemned person, the final preparations, the meal, the visit of the priest and the relatives, and the final act. They continued to do so in a way that showed how far the popular interpretation of the execution ceremony had survived the transition of the public sphere from the ritual of face-to-face encounters to the dramatic clichés of the printed word. Indeed, prescient commentators foresaw the day when it would be given new life through the emergence of electronics. Commenting on a detailed description of one execution, a newspaper correspondent mused:

A film cameraman was not among the cardholders according to the report. Otherwise, the crowd outside the prison, having got up just as early as the spectators within, and really having the same right to view the drama or 'act' as they did, could at least have had the comfort of knowing they could watch it being replayed on film.[62]

[55] HStA Hanover Hann. 173a Nr. 442, Bl. 67: Oberstaatsanwalt Hanover to PMJ, 9 July 1927.
[56] HStA Düsseldorf Rep. 145/326, Bl. 63; Generalstaatsanwalt 'Abschrift aus II 90 K 1/24/17', 28 Mar. 1925.
[57] HStA Stuttgart E130b Bü 886; *Amtsblatt* (Tettnang), 17 July 1922.
[58] Ibid.: *Schwäbische Merkur*, 12 Aug. 1926.
[59] GStA Berlin Rep. 84a/7786, Bl. 49: Württembergisches Justizministerium to PJM, 23 Sept. 1926.
[60] BA Potsdam 61 Re 1/1772, 34: *Deutsche Tageszeitung*, 28 May 1927.
[61] HStA Stuttgart E130b Bü 886: *Amtsblatt* (Tettnang), 17 July 1922.
[62] Ibid.: *Süddeutsche Sonntagszeitung*, 23 July 1922.

It was only too bad, he concluded sarcastically, that in the age of the silent film, the viewers would have to miss the sound-effects of the falling blade and the spurting blood which were so graphically described in press reports of the event.

c. *The Crisis of the German Executioner*

The increased openness about public and private violence which characterized the culture of the Weimar Republic was also reflected in the way in which executioners were better known than ever. Of course, their identity had never been a secret, and a man such as Julius Krautz had even attained a considerable degree of notoriety. But the sensation-hungry mass press of the Weimar era offered new opportunities to such men to earn a little extra money to supplement what seemed under the circumstances of the time to be a fast-diminishing income from their main field of activity. For the 1920s brought hard times for executioners. To begin with, it was widely expected that the death penalty would be abolished altogether. Then the actual number of beheadings declined after the initial revolutionary period. And the numerous executions of the turbulent post-war years were mostly military, or quasi-military, and therefore carried out by firing-squad. From various points of view, therefore, the position of the state-appointed official executioners was subject to a number of uncertainties. In a conservative state such as Bavaria, their position was fairly assured. Franz Reichhart, whose appointment dated back to 1894, was still in office in 1920.[63] A pious Catholic, he salved his conscience by paying for a mass to be said for each of his victims. In 1924, aged 70, he retired and was succeeded by his nephew Johann, another knacker, who sought relief from the stress of his new part-time employment by running evening classes in ballroom dancing.[64] In Baden the two rival executioners of the Imperial period, Karl Burckhardt (born 1872) and Karl Müller (born 1882), were still comparatively young, and both had survived extended periods of military service during the war. Both resumed their functions in the new Republic. Müller was also appointed executioner for Hesse.[65] Similarly, in Württemberg the sitting executioner Siller also secured a renewal of his contract.[66]

In Prussia, however, it was far from certain whether the new republican regime would agree to re-employ the executioners whose activities the liberal and Social Democratic press had so sharply criticized during the Imperial period. Moreover, the executioners themselves were presenting difficulties, as usual. Carl Gröpler,

[63] HStA Munich MJu 13144; Erster Staatsanwalt Memmingen to Justizministerium, 7 July 1920.

[64] Berthold, *Vollstreckt*, 22–6.

[65] GLA Karlsruhe 234/6773: Badisches Justizministerium to Hessisches Justizministerium, 29 Aug. 1921.

[66] HStA Stuttgart E130b Bü 886: *Amtsblatt* (Tettnang), 17 July 1922.

Prussia's, and Germany's, best-known executioner, had already asked for a substantial rise in pay on 19 November 1917; as his request had been denied,[67] and mounting inflation was causing his costs to rise very rapidly even during the war, he handed in his notice in 1918 and went back to his laundry business in Magdeburg. Requested to carry out an execution by the state prosecutor in Celle in the summer of 1920, he refused unless he was paid ten times his previous fee, which the authorities refused to do, despite the galloping inflation that had taken a grip on Germany after the wartime years.[68] This left as the sole executioner for the Prussian state Lorenz Schwietz's former assistant Paul Späte. Born in 1875, Späte was a former butcher and slaughterman, now owner of a bar. He had carried out a number of executions under Schwietz's supervision during the war, but, left with little to do in the early Weimar years, he too handed in his resignation in 1920.[69] However, at this point 'normal', non-military executions were just being resumed, so in 1921 the Ministry of Justice reappointed Späte as official executioner for the whole of Prussia at a salary of 5,000 marks. In 1923, he also carried out executions in Saxony during the illness of the regular executioner there. One such was of the mass murderer Friedrich Schumann, condemned to death six times and found guilty of thirty-four offences, in Plötzensee in 1921.[70] Galloping inflation soon rendered his salary nugatory once more, and the rapid decline in the number of executions left Späte with very little to do.[71] So fast was inflation moving, indeed, that the authorities were finding it difficult to pay him at all by the middle of 1923.[72] By September 1923 he was reduced to asking for his travel costs to be paid in advance.[73] By 5 November 1923, at the height of the hyperinflation, he was complaining bitterly to the Prussian Minister of Justice that he was 'not in a position to buy myself anything, however small'.[74]

Growing political controversy over capital punishment during the Weimar Republic was reflected in the personal difficulties which executioners and former executioners began to experience. They had, of course, always been social

[67] HStA Düsseldorf Rep. 126/81: Prussian Justice Ministry to Oberstaatsanwalt Düsseldorf, 11 Dec. 1917.

[68] GStA Berlin Rep. 84a/9397, Bl. 183; Gröpler to PJM, 14 Aug. 1920.

[69] Ibid., Bl. 94: Oberstaatsanwalt Berlin to PJM, 18 Aug. 1916; also Bl. 109, 118, 134, 162.

[70] GLA Karlsruhe 234/6610: Ausschnitt aus Nr. 147 der *Volksstimme* vom 5. Juni 1921.

[71] GStA Berlin Rep. 84a/9397, Bl. 197: Saxon Minister of Justice to PJM, 10 Apr. 1923; ibid., Bl. 245: Generalstaatsanwalt Berlin to PJM, 24 Apr. 1923. In Baden and Hessen the fee per execution was raised to 700 marks in Sept. 1921 (GLA Karlsruhe 234/6773: Generalstaatsanwalt Darmstadt to Badisches Justizministerium, 16 Sept. 1921). By Jan. 1922 this had increased to 1,000 marks (ibid.: Müller and Burckhardt to Badisches Justizministerium, 25 Jan. 1922), by Sept. 1922 to 3,000 (GLA Karlsruhe, 234/10178, Justizministerium to Landeshauptkasse, 25 Sept. 1922). See also Späte's list of charges in StA Bremen 4, 89/1. 236: Todesurteil Friedrich Engel.

[72] HStA Düsseldorf Rep. 126/81: Späte to Oberstaatsanwälte Düsseldorf and Gleiwitz, 26 July 1923 (copy).

[73] Ibid.: Generalstaatsanwalt Düsseldorf, 21 Sept. 1923: Betrifft: Beschwerdesache Späte.

[74] Ibid.: Späte to PJM, 5 Nov. 1923 (copy).

pariahs. The experience of executioner Johann Reichhart's children, who complained about being mocked and bullied at school because of their father's trade, was probably nothing very new.[75] Yet in many ways the ostracism to which they were subjected had weakened over the years, and it was common by the Weimar period for them to engage in fairly respectable trades such as owning a bar, running a laundry, or teaching ballroom dancing. In other respects, however, their situation seemed to get worse. This was a result not only of the new political atmosphere and the falling number of jobs to do, but also of the reluctance of the new regime to help them in the way that, for example, even a difficult character such as Alwin Engelhardt had been assisted by the Prussian Ministry of Justice before the war. A new climate of hostility made itself felt. In 1922 the Baden executioner Karl Müller, whose main living had long been earned as a locksmith, felt obliged to hand in his resignation, because, as the state prosecutor reported,

Müller is at present employed by the firm of Brown and Boveri in Mannheim. After the last execution he performed, his workmates confronted him, called him 'murderer' and harassed him in other ways. Recently such acts have been repeated, and his workmates have threatened that, if he carries out the execution of Leonhard Siefert, they will go on strike and shut down the works until he has been dismissed. Under these circumstances, Müller considers that resigning his office has to take priority over losing his job and over the threat to his life and health.

At most, he said, he was prepared to function in an extreme emergency, if there was nobody else available; but the execution would have to be held before work on a Monday morning, so that he could make the necessary preparations at the weekend, and it was, of course, vital 'that his name is not mentioned in the press'. Müller's situation made it clear why it was difficult for anyone who did not have a small business of his own, like an inn or a laundry, or who did not already work for the police or legal authorities in some other capacity, to act as executioner at a time when trade unionism and worker solidarity were strong. Karl Burckhardt, whom Müller proposed as the sole executioner for Baden, was in a position to continue with his job as the owner of a small farm and knacker's yard. The petty bourgeoisie made the best executioners.

As tradition-bound as they had been before 1918, however, the officials of the Baden Ministry of Justice rejected Burckhardt's approach and appointed one Konrad Widder as Müller's successor. Widder was a court bailiff in Mannheim, and was recommended by the state prosecutor because he 'has already assisted in autopsies for years, and I am told that he carried out execution duties in the East during the war'.[76] But guillotining offenders in prisons in Germany proved to be

---

[75] Berthold, *Vollstreckt*, 60.

[76] GLA Karlsruhe 234/6773: Oberstaatsanwalt Heidelberg to Generalstaatsanwalt Karlsruhe, 24 July 1922.

a far more difficult task than shooting soldiers in Russia. Already on 20 November 1923 it was reported from Bruchsal: 'The executioner, bailiff Widder from Mannheim, who acted as chief executioner, and the deputy assistant executioner, police sergeant Betz from the same town, behaved with a marked lack of dignity. Both of them got so drunk the night before the execution that this aroused the most unwelcome attention.'[77] The executioners were thereupon banned from entering local inns and bars on the day before an execution.[78] Betz was sacked, and although Widder got off with a reprimand, he fell ill shortly afterwards and was forced to resign.[79] The Baden Ministry of Justice received no fewer than thirteen unsolicited applications for the job (none of them with any political content), including one from Karl Burckhardt's 47-year-old brother and assistant Wilhelm. But it played safe, and reappointed the former executioner Karl Müller, who had by now apparently overcome the difficulties with his colleagues that had caused him to leave his job.[80]

The problems experienced by Müller were far outweighed by those faced by executioners who were too old to carry out their job any more. Some of them took to supplying stories of their handiwork to the press to help make ends meet. Executioner Siller, in Württemberg, for example, was living on a small pension and the meagre takings of a small dairy shop when he allowed a newspaper reporter to interview him in his retirement in 1926, doubtless for a fee. In his late seventies, he looked, the reporter commented, like a respectable citizen. 'He regards himself as a servant of justice.' Already running a knacker's yard in Gablenberg by 1880, he had been asked by the then Württemberg executioner Schwarz to assist him and had succeeded him in 1888. But he was too discreet to allow the sensational aspects of his story to get far beyond the headline. Virtually all his fifty-four victims had gone to the block without incident, the old man said.[81] Siller was well off in comparison to others. In 1922 the former Prussian state executioner Lorenz Schwietz had been provided with a regular pension from the Ministry of Justice but, in the rampant inflation of the time, it soon lost its value. Schwietz was too old to run the knacker's yard he owned, and he was unable to find anyone to help him after the death of his son Richard during the war.[82] To try and make ends meet, he started giving paid lectures about his former career as an executioner, and prepared a 'diary', full of sensational stories

[77] Ibid.: Zuchthausdirektion Bruchsal to Badisches Justizministerium, 20 Nov. 1923.
[78] Ibid.: Justizministerium 'Vermerk', 8 Dec. 1923.
[79] Ibid.: Justizministerium, 'Die Scharfrichter betr.', 21 Feb. 1924, and Innenministerium to Polizeidirektion Mannheim, 18 Mar. 1924.
[80] Ibid.: Karl Müller, Annahmeerklärung, 13 Mar. 1924. The thirteen applications follow in the same file.
[81] HStA Stuttgart E130b Bü 886: 'Memoiren eines Scharfrichters', Stuttgarter Neues Tageblatt, 14 Aug. 1926.
[82] GStA Berlin Rep. 84a/9397, Bl. 213: PJM notes, 3 July 1922.

and gruesome details, to sell to the press. But his new literary career met with little success. When the 'diary' was serialized in a mass-circulation newspaper, the *8-Uhr Abendblatt,* it soon became clear that many of the details in it were made up, or at the very least heavily embellished, and eyewitnesses of a number of executions at which he had officiated came forward to denounce them as falsifications.[83] Depressed by his failure to make ends meet, and by the death of his wife in 1923, Schwietz shot himself in May 1925.[84] A similar fate befell his former assistant and successor Paul Späte, whose wife also died, in January 1924, leaving him a 'broken man' and driving him to suicide shortly thereafter.[85] The comforts of a regular home life were evidently crucial to the emotional stability of executioners, unlike that of other types of professional killer such as regular soldiers or the members of paramilitary squads. Another of Schwietz's assistants, Joseph Kurzer, who had worked with the former executioner since 1900, was appointed to the post, despite being in his mid-sixties; he quickly fell ill and died in 1927.[86] This high death rate among the executioners did not go unnoticed by the popular press, who speculated extensively upon the nervous strain and guilt that may have lain behind it.[87]

These events left the Prussian Ministry of Justice in something of a quandary. There was nobody suitable among Schwietz's former assistants, and the retired Alwin Engelhardt was clearly considered to be morally discredited and too unscrupulous to employ. So the bureaucrats at the Ministry swallowed their pride and approached the grasping Carl Gröpler once more. At 56 years of age, Gröpler was still physically fit, and the only sign of advancing age was the fact that he was by now completely bald. Conscious of the strength of his position, he raised a series of predictably exorbitant financial demands which the officials at the Ministry took some time to negotiate down to what they considered to be an acceptable level. In April 1924 Gröpler finally signed a new contract. It gave him a monopoly over all executions carried out in Prussia, and in practice through the whole of north Germany. Now that the inflation was over, and the Rentenmark had brought about a general stabilization of the currency, it became possible once again to pay the executioner a fixed salary. Gröpler was careful to specify that it should be paid in gold. The Ministry agreed to give him a regular retainer of 136 gold marks a month, plus a fee of 60 gold marks for himself and 50 for each of his assistants each time they carried out an

[83] GStA Berlin Rep. 4595, Bl. 20a, 58b, 64c–f; R. Degen, *Das Tagebuch des Scharfrichters Schwietz aus Breslau über seine 123 Hinrichtungen* (Breslau, 1924). Most 'diaries' and 'memoirs' of executioners are unreliable, either almost complete fabrications, like the Sanson family memoirs, or ghost-written by journalists on the basis of interviews, like the oft-quoted but extremely fanciful 'memoirs' of the Austrian executioner Josef Lang, written in fact by Oskar Schalk (*Scharfrichter Josef Lang's Erinnerungen,* hg. v. Oskar Schalk (Leipzig and Vienna, 1920)).

[84] GStA Berlin Rep. 84a/4594, Bl. 294: *Vossische Zeitung,* 7 May 1925.

[85] Ibid., Bl. 275: *Berliner Morgenpost,* 5 Feb. 1924.

[86] Ibid., Bl. 204: Generalstaatsanwalt Berlin to PJM, 10 July 1927.   [87] Ibid. 4595, Bl. 47.

execution.[88] By December he was back at work again, carrying out a beheading in Erfurt.[89] So few were the executions that he was asked to perform, however, that he was complaining by 1930 that he was paid less than an unemployed man. Incensed at what he regarded as the perpetual miserliness of the Prussian Justice Ministry, he gave vent to his resentment in a lengthy series of interviews to a popular newspaper in October 1930. The Ministry, he said, had always been reluctant to reward him adequately for his labours. They had been tight-fisted under the Kaiser, and they were still tight-fisted under the Republic.[90] Alarmed at this adverse publicity, the Ministry instructed Gröpler to maintain a discreet silence about his terms of employment in future.[91]

Such publicity did much to reinforce the mystique surrounding the executioner at this time. Newspapers displayed a strong fascination for the statistical dimensions of the subject, and recounted with a due sense of awe that Gröpler had beheaded 144 offenders, Schwietz 123, Späte 45, Reindel 210, and so on.[92] Whether such impressive statistics could ever be compiled again, however, seemed to be increasingly doubtful as the 1920s wore on. For from a relatively high level during the crisis years of the early Weimar Republic in 1918–23 and their judicial aftermath in 1924, capital punishment now began to undergo a sharp decline: 123 death sentences were passed in Germany in 1922, 77 in 1923, and 112 in 1924, but in 1925 the figure fell to 95, in 1926 to 89, in 1927 to 64, and in 1928 to 40. Moreover, the proportion of these sentences actually carried out also fell. In the last two decades of the Imperial period, roughly 60 per cent of death sentences ended in execution. In the first five years of the Weimar Republic (1919–23), the rate averaged just over 20 per cent. From 20.5 per cent in 1924, however, it fell to 16.8 per cent in 1925, 15.7 per cent in 1926, and 9.4 per cent in 1927. Thus, according to the best available estimates, 25 persons were executed in Germany in 1922, 15 in 1923, 23 in 1924, 16 in 1925, 14 in 1926, and 6 in 1927. Of course, these global statistics concealed substantial variations in practice between the different federated states. In the early years the Bavarians, for example, always executed a higher than average proportion of capital offenders (50 per cent in 1919, 47 per cent in 1920, 52 per cent in 1921, 74 per cent in 1922, 71 per cent in 1923, 74 per cent in 1924, 62 per cent in 1925). But they too began to behave with greater circumspection in the second half of the 1920s, executing only 20 per cent of those condemned in 1926 and 40 per cent in 1927. In Prussia the proportion was always below 10 per cent (except in 1925, when it rose to 14 per cent), and it was the absolute decline in condemnations (from 71 in 1925 to 54 in 1926, 43 in

[88] Ibid. 4594, Bl. 277: PJM notes, 15 Feb. 1924; ibid., Bl. 284: PJM notes 1 Mar. 1924; and ibid., Bl. 323: Generalstaatsanwalt Naumburg to PJM, 23 Apr. 1924.

[89] Ibid. 7785, Bl. 378–9: Bericht des Oberstaatsanwalts Erfurt, 22 Dec. 1924.

[90] Ibid. 4594: *Neue Berliner Zeitung (12-Uhr-Blatt)*, 18–28 Oct. 1928.

[91] Ibid., Bl. 109: PJM to Gröpler, Nov. 1930.

[92] Ibid. 4594, Bl. 275: *Berliner Morgenpost*, 5 Feb. 1924.

1927, and 27 in 1928) that was most striking.[93] By the middle years of the Weimar Republic, there seemed no doubt in statistical terms, therefore, that capital punishment was on the way out all over Germany.

d. The Jakubowski Case 1923–1928

The decline in the number of executions contributed to the fact that the issue of capital punishment in the Weimar Republic was more affected by individual cases than at any time before or since. This was partly because of the way the media worked—by personalizing and dramatizing general issues through human-interest stories—and partly because of the way abolitionists and retentionists followed this trend and sought to influence public opinion by using individual cases themselves, as they had already begun to do in the Sternickel affair, before the First World War. The League for Human Rights campaigned, for example, for the commutation of the death sentence on an infanticidal mother in 1927.[94] More dramatic was the case of the mechanic Otto Götz, condemned to death at the beginning of 1919 for poisoning his fiancée in a disastrously misconceived attempt to abort the foetus of their illegitimate child. His sentence was commuted and he spent the next ten years in prison. In February 1929, however, as the result of renewed consideration of the case, his conviction was set aside. He was now found guilty merely of contravening the abortion law, and was released immediately. Abolitionists rushed to point out what the implications would have been had the death sentence passed on him in 1919 actually been carried out, as it well might have been had he been convicted a few months earlier, while Kaiser Wilhelm II was still on the throne. However, retentionists retorted with some justification that Götz had after all been reprieved. What then was all the fuss about? they asked.[95] Another case that seemed ripe for exploitation by the abolitionists was that of Joseph Mauretz, condemned to death in 1924 for shooting his father. Mauretz's sentence was commuted to life imprisonment because of his youth. But in 1932 the case was reopened. The authorities now accepted that Mauretz's father had committed suicide, and ordered the young man's release. Once more the spectre of a wrongful execution

---

[93] HStA Munich MJu 12575, *Berliner Tageblatt*, 12 May 1929, and 'Statistik der Todesurteite 1918 mit 1925'; BA Postdam RJM 5665, Bl. 261–3; also GStA Berlin Rep. 84a/7785, Bl. 178–9, 210, 276, 290, 337; and ibid. 7786, Bl. 24, 28, 67–9. Military courts continued to pass death sentences under the Weimar Republic: 16 in 1919, 6 in 1920, 3 in 1921, and 2 in 1923. But none of these was carried out. These were different from the judicial or quasi-judicial executions operated by the army in the revolutionary disturbances of 1919–20. The Reichswehr and the Reich Ministry of Defence insisted strongly on the need to retain the death penalty in military justice. See BA Potsdam RJM 5665, Bl. 91: Reichswehrministerium to PJM, 24 Apr. 1919; and GStA Berlin Rep. 84a/7786, Bl. 1–3. More generally, see the Statistical Appendix, below, for full time-series and a discussion of the sources.

[94] BA Potsdam RJM 6097 Bl. 86: *Berliner Morgenpost*, 28 Jan. 1927.

[95] Ibid., Bl. 45, 50: *Berliner Tageblatt*, 26 Feb. 1929, *Die Rote Fahne*, 5 Mar. 1929.

was raised. Once more, however, the abolitionists had to admit that none had actually taken place.[96] The plain fact was that a real case of judicial murder was needed if the tactic of centring the abolitionist campaign on a single individual was to stand any chance of success. In 1928 events seemed to play into the abolitionists' hands with the discovery of what seemed to be a clear case of wrongful execution, not for a political crime, but for common murder, earlier in the decade. The man at the centre of the affair, Osip or Josef Jakubowski, soon became a household name. Thanks to the League for Human Rights,[97] his execution for murder in 1926 achieved the status of a *cause célèbre* that occupied the attention of the police, the courts, and the politicians for years and played a crucial role in the fortunes of the death penalty during the middle and later years of the Weimar Republic. It also cast a lurid light on many aspects of the administration of justice and policing, politics, welfare, and society under the Weimar Republic. And it was particularly revealing of the continued poverty and social backwardness of rural society in large parts of the north German plain, even in the 1920s. For all these reasons, but above all because of its effects on the capital punishment issue under Weimar, it repays particularly close attention.

Born in 1895 near Vilna, the son of a poor peasant in Russian Poland, Josef Jakubowski had been called up to the Tsar's army shortly before the outbreak of war and captured by the Germans in September 1915. From October 1915 to July 1917 he had worked in a factory near the north German city of Lübeck, not far from the Baltic coast. After a spell in hospital, he had settled in the nearby heathland village of Palingen, in Ratzeburg, an exclave of Mecklenburg-Strelitz, not far from Lübeck, in October 1917. He had stayed in the village after the war, successfully resisting attempts to repatriate him to the newly independent Republic of Poland.[98] For Josef Jakubowski had found not only a new job but also a new home and a new family. He began living with a young German woman, Ida Nogens, who bore two illegitimate children, Ewald (1921) and Anni (1923), both of whom Jakubowski acknowledged legally as his own. Ida was hard-working, and the two managed to get by, even if they were still very poor. But in 1923 things began to go wrong. First of all, Ida Nogens fell ill, then on 15 May 1923 she died of pneumonia. Jakubowski was left with the task of supporting the two young children, for whom an official guardian was appointed. He turned in

[96] Ibid. RJM 6098, Bl. 214: *Berliner Tageszeitung*, 27 May 1932. See also Friedrich Wendel, 'Sind Gerichte unfehlbar? Unschuldig zum Tode verurteilt und hingerichtet', *Neue Preussische Kreuzzeitung*, 4 Apr. 1928, in GLA Karlsruhe 234/6611. The article suggested that a man had been wrongly executed in Giessen in 1906, despite consistent denial, for a crime for which a German living in Holland confessed on his death-bed ten years later.

[97] See Richard A. Cohen, 'The German League for Human Rights in the Weimar Republic' (Ph.D. thesis, State University of New York at Buffalo, 1989).

[98] LHA Schwerin S 357: Schlussbericht betr. Voruntersuchung gegen August Nogens und Genossen (Fall Jakubowski), Kriminalrat Gennat 14 Nov. 1928, 39–55.

this situation to Ida's mother Elizabeth Nogens, with whom he and the children lived. But here too there were difficulties. The local pastor described the 45-year-old Elizabeth Nogens as presenting 'a picture of boundless depravity. Even externally she was extraordinarily dirty, both in her clothing and her person, as in respect of her whole running of the household, her children etc. . . . She brought children into the world the identity of whose father she herself may not have been clear about.'[99] There were eight of these children in all, and five of them, the youngest of whom were both under 4 years of age, plus Jakubowski's two children, lived with Elizabeth Nogens in one half of a lonely house on the edge of the heath. Four more people, the petty criminal Paul Kreutzfeldt and his wife, his sister Lene, and her fiancé the farm labourer Heinrich Blöcker, rented the other half of the squalid dwelling. So dire were their circumstances that Elizabeth Nogens's husband had drowned himself in despair in the River Trave in January 1923. There were rumours in the village that Elizabeth Nogens had had sexual relations with a number of other men, and with her older sons as well. She was known to be 'mad on men', and to be intent on remarrying, which she eventually did in 1927.[100] The family was extremely poor and lived mainly off benefits, and at times also from begging.[101] The prospects for the two small children for whom Jakubowski was now responsible were therefore not good, to say the least.

On 10 November 1924 the local gendarme, *Oberlandjäger* Dibbert, put in an official report to the effect that Jakubowski's son Ewald Nogens was missing.[102] On 22 November the child's corpse was found in a rabbit-hole on the Palingen heath. The autopsy noted that Ewald had been strangled with a rope. The next day, proceedings were initiated against Jakubowski and Fritz Nogens, Elizabeth's 15-year-old son, for murder, but Nogens was quickly released and the accusation of murder was now levelled at Jakubowski alone. Soon a mountain of incriminating evidence had been piled up against him. Jakubowski had a clear motive for getting his child out of the way, since the maintenance payments for the two children were proving a substantial burden. He had been summoned to appear before a Guardianship Court on 10 November in order for the payments to be

[99] LHA Schwerin S 354, 21: Vernehmung Pastor Buhre, 2 Aug. 1928 (copy).

[100] Ibid. S 357: Schlussbericht betr. Voruntersuchung gegen August Nogens und Genossen (Fall Jakubowski), Kriminalrat Gennat, 14 Nov. 1928, 4–6. See also the outline of the case in Hans von Hentig, 'Zur Psychologie der Beschuldigung. Eine kriminalwissenschaftliche Bemerkung zum Nogens-Prozess', *Die Justiz,* 5 (1929), 24–38.

[101] LHA Schwerin S 357: Schlussbericht betr. Voruntersuchung gegen August Nogens und Genossen (Fall Jakubowski), Kriminalrat Gennat, 14 Nov. 1928, 36–8.

[102] Dibbert ('Libbert') is the central character in Theo Harych's novel (later filmed) *Im Namen des Volkes? Der Fall Jakubowski* (East Berlin, 1959). The novel features the real characters in the story, and is based on information and documentation supplied by the League for Human Rights, by Jakubowski's lawyer, and by inhabitants of Palingen. It includes lengthy extracts from the trial transcript, from political speeches on the affair, and from correspondence. But, as will become clear, its depiction of the case is not always accurate.

enforced, and indeed increased from a third to a half of his monthly income. The fact that the murder had been committed the previous day seemed too great a coincidence to ignore. Moreover, the children stood in the way of Jakubowski's plans to remarry. The witness August Nogens, aged 19, said Jakubowski had offered him a bicycle in May 1924 to get rid of Anni, his other illegitimate child. Various other statements were also recorded in which the Pole had said similar things to different people over the period following Ida's death.[103] Brought to trial, Jakubowski had little to say in his defence. The prosecution described him as 'a cunning, immoral, and unscrupulous person'.[104] The lawyer provided him by the court, Otto Koch, pleaded for his acquittal on a number of grounds. He would not have been able to kill the child and conceal its body between the two moments when he was seen by witnesses, before and after the murder. He could have escaped the burden of maintenance payments for the children by returning to Poland. He was not cunning, 'but good-natured to the point of stupidity, primitive and honest'. However, the evidence against Jakubowski seemed overwhelming. The court found him guilty of premeditated murder and condemned him to death on 26 March 1925.[105]

In prison awaiting execution, Jakubowski now came forward with new information, incriminating the two men who lived in the other half of the Nogens's heathside house, Heinrich Blöcker and Paul Kreutzfeldt. The latter, he said, had arranged the murder in order to pave the way for Jakubowski's marriage to his sister Lene. But both Kreutzfeldt and Blöcker denied having had anything to do with Ewald's disappearance and, when he came to consider the question in July 1925, the state prosecutor concuded that the evidence was insufficient to warrant their arrest.[106] A further application for a retrial was turned down by the Supreme State Court in Rostock on 10 December 1925. There only remained the hope of an act of clemency by the Mecklenburg-Strelitz government. The responsible official in the Mecklenburg-Strelitz Ministry of Justice, Dr Pagel, did indeed recommend mercy, on the grounds that there was no confession and that the evidence, though convincing, was less than overwhelmingly so.[107] The Minister of Justice, Roderich Hustädt (1878–1958), was a member of the Democratic Party, and his fellow deputies were said to favour clemency. However, several factors influenced him against accepting Pagel's recommendation. First, the Nationalists, to whom both State Prosecutor Müller, who had prepared the charges and put them before the court, and the trial judge, Court President Buchka, belonged,

[103] LHA Schwerin S 353: Bericht über den Fall Jakubowski. Berichterstatter: Regierungsrat Steuding, 1–16, 3, 67–8. See also ibid., S 357: Schlussbericht betr. Voruntersuchung gegen August Nogens und Genossen (Fall Jakubowski), Kriminalrat Gennat, 14 Nov. 1928, 4–6.

[104] Ibid., S 369: Anklage gegen den Arbeiter Josef Jakubowski, 12 Jan. 1925, 11.

[105] Ibid.: Urteil Schwurgericht Neustrelitz, 26 Mar. 1925.

[106] Ibid., S 357: Schlussbericht betr. Voruntersuchung gegen August Nogens und Genossen (Fall Jakubowski), Kriminalrat Gennat, 14 Nov. 1928, 49–56, 116–17.

[107] Ibid., S 364: Zeugenvernehmung Conradi, 4 Apr. 1930.

wanted Jakubowski executed. This would be a signal to the electorate of their commitment to the death penalty and to the maintenance of morality, law, and order. Second, the Democrats depended on the votes of their Nationalist coalition partners for their continuation in office, and Hustädt was unwilling to offend them. Thirdly, Jakubowski, after all, was only a Pole, and this would neither be the first nor the last occasion in which racial prejudice against Poles had been a factor in bringing a man to the block in Germany; indeed, the first two men to be executed in Württemberg after the war, Josef Orlowski and Franz Monkosa, guillotined in 1921, had also been prisoners of war, and had settled in the countryside as farm labourers before committing the crimes that brought them to the block,[108] while a man executed in the province of Hanover at the very end of the war, Johann Chmiel, was also a Russian Pole.[109] Such executions seem to have been particularly common at this time.[110] Finally, Jakubowski himself, instead of confessing and demonstrating contrition in prison, persisted in maintaining his innocence and campaigning for a retrial. This paradoxically made the exercise of clemency more difficult. The Minister of Justice consulted the three trial judges once more. One of them was prepared to support the Minister if he decided to reprieve the Pole. The other two judges were not. Pagel's recommendation was therefore turned down and the death sentence confirmed on 2 February 1926.[111] Jakubowski was executed by Carl Gröpler on 15 February. This happened just as the Presidential elections that brought Field-Marshal von Hindenburg into office as Germany's head of state were reaching a climax.[112] The event therefore went largely unnoticed in the press.

For Jakubowski, this was the end. But for the 'Jakubowski case' it was only the beginning. Jakubowski's defence lawyer Otto Koch was not prepared to let the matter rest.[113] He passed on his doubts about the verdict to a Communist deputy in the Mecklenburg-Strelitz legislature, Rudolf Hartmann, who visited the village of Palingen, where the murder had taken place, and interviewed some of the participants, including August Nogens.[114] On 25 March 1926 Hartmann brought

[108] HStA Stuttgart E130b Bü 866: *Schwäbische Tagwacht*, 19 Mar. 1921, *Württembergische Zeitung*, 23 Mar. 1921.

[109] HStA Hanover Hann. 173a Nr. 440: *Zweites Blatt der Deutschen Volkszeitung*, 1 Nov. 1918.

[110] Ibid., Nr. 442, Bl. 67, for the execution of another Pole, Felix Dymbowski, in Hanover in 1927.

[111] Harych, *Im Namen*, 9, 169, 176–7, 191–3.

[112] LHA Schwerin S 357: Schlussbericht betr. Voruntersuchung gegen August Nogens und Genossen (Fall Jakubowski), Kriminalrat Gennat, 14 Nov. 1928, 4–6.

[113] Harych, *Im Namen*, portrays the gendarme Dibbert ('Libbert'), who conducted the initial investigation, as the main force behind the campaign for Jakubowski's rehabilitation: he had discovered fresh evidence which was rejected by the state prosecutor, Müller. There is no evidence to support any of this in the papers relating to the case, and the most likely explanation is that the character of the gendarme was employed as a useful narrative device by the author and fictionalized in the process. The extracts from 'Libbert's journal' at the end of the book (pp. 241–7) are largely, if not wholly, made up.

[114] LHA Schwerin S 371, 57.

a motion before the Chamber of Deputies censuring the conduct of the Justice Ministry in the case:

I will not say that people are claiming that my information rests on empty rumours that are circulating at present, alleging for example that our Ministers wanted to demonstrate through this case that for once they were masters over life and death. That would be effrontery. It has also been claimed that if Jakubowski had not been a foreigner, he would not have been executed. I am not going to go into that either. I have also heard that he was treated very harshly during the investigation, and repeatedly called 'filth' and 'crook' by the investigating judge. He is also said to have been threatened: Whether you confess or not, Jakubowski, that's all the same, you'll lose your head anyway.[115]

None of this was proven, he admitted rhetorically. The point, he said, was that Jakubowski was innocent. In a lengthy and circumstantially detailed speech, Hartmann alleged that the jurors in the trial, some of whom he had interviewed, had been influenced by directions from the bench, or had thought that Jakubowski knew more than he was letting on, or were afraid of the responsibility of releasing him in case he returned to Palingen and killed his daughter as well as his son. Yet the Pole, he said, was known to have been kind to his children and to have spent money on them. There were rough and brutal people enough in Palingen, but he had not been one of them. It was, said Hartmann, a 'nest of rats'. The case had not been proven beyond all doubt. The government had been irresponsible in refusing clemency to Jakubowski. Poverty and misery in Palingen had caused immorality and desperation. For this the government and the capitalist system were responsible.[116] Hartmann was supported by the Social Democrats, who argued that, where no confession was forthcoming, the state should exercise mercy. Jakubowski's execution was the first in Mecklenburg-Strelitz for decades, and for that reason alone should not have happened. Mecklenburg's Justice Minister Hustädt rejected all these points, noting that Jakubowski's own attempts to obtain a retrial had all been turned down, and claiming that the decision to go ahead with the execution had only been made after full consideration of the material and on the advice of an official from the Ministry who had been present at the trial. The motion was defeated in the Mecklenburg-Strelitz Chamber of Deputies by thirteen votes to ten.[117]

Following this, a radical Social Democrat from the area, Arthur Becker, approached the League for Human Rights. He was supported by the local Catholic priest, who affirmed his belief in Jakubowski's innocence. On 3 February 1927 the League's Secretary Kurt Grossmann argued the case for

[115] Ibid., S 358: *Landtag von Mecklenburg-Strelitz, 47. Sitzung,* 25. März 1926, col. 2022. Also summarized in Harych, *Im Namen,* 193–5.

[116] LHA Schwerin S 358: *Landtag von Mecklenburg-Strelitz, 47. Sitzung,* 25. März 1926, cols. 2023–8. Hartmann was later imprisoned and murdered by the Nazis.

[117] Ibid., cols. 2028–9.

Jakubowski in the Berlin press,[118] but failed to move the Mecklenburg-Strelitz government to a response. So now the abolitionist campaigners Rudolf Olden and Josef Bornstein set to work to investigate the case for the League. They published their conclusions early in 1928. In their view, Jakubowski was entirely innocent of the murder of Ewald Nogens. The likely culprit, they thought, following a suggestion which Jakubowski himself made to his defence lawyer,[119] was Ida Nogens's mentally retarded brother Hannes. The family had deliberately incriminated Jakubowski in order to protect him from the law. The hostility of a small and remote village community to an outsider, and the racial prejudice of the police, judicial, political, and administrative authorities in Mecklenburg against a Polish immigrant, did the rest. Here was a major case of wrongful execution. The campaign to clear Jakubowski's name turned into a public onslaught on the death penalty, waged unrelentingly by the League for Human Rights throughout from this point on.[120] The newspapers sent their own 'special correspondents' to Palingen to interview the inhabitants, and backed up the campaign with details of the evidence supporting Jakubowski's case. A fresh round of newspaper stories alleging Jakubowski's innocence appeared.[121] The physicist Albert Einstein, the novelist Heinrich Mann, the diarist Count Harry Kessler, the radical journalist Carl von Ossietzky, the pacifist Hellmuth von Gerlach, and many other prominent personalities affirmed their support for Jakubowski.[122] In the radical magazine *Die Weltbühne*, Kurt Tucholsky penned a bitter poem on the case, imagining the spirit of Germany rising up at the injustice done to Jakubowski and demanding the execution of the German judicial system.[123] On 14 March 1929 a play, based on the subject and written over the previous few months by Eleonore Kalkowska, opened in the Dortmund City Theatre. Entitled *Josef*, it showed the Nogens brothers carefully plotting the murder of young Ewald, and framing the innocent and trusting Josef for the crime. Kalkowska portrayed the judicial authorities in Mecklenburg as blood-thirsty racists determined to secure an execution. All this was very two-dimensional, little more than agitprop, and was greeted on the opening night with whistles and catcalls. The press condemned the play as a tendentious distortion

[118] BA Potsdam RJM 6097, Bl. 26: *BZ am Montag*, 3 Feb. 1927; Kurt Grossmann, *Ossietzky. Ein deutscher Patriot* (Frankfurt am Main, 1968), 149–51.

[119] LHA Schwerin S 371, 85.

[120] Rudolf Olden and Josef Bornstein, *Der Justizmord an Jakubowski* (Berlin, 1928). See also Kurt Grossmann, *13 Jahre 'republikanische Justiz'* (Berlin, 1931). Rudolf Olden was a lawyer who acted during the 1920s as legal correspondent of the *Berliner Tageblatt* and the *Weltbühne*. He was on the committee of the League for Human Rights. After the Nazi seizure of power he emigrated to England. He drowned when a ship carrying him to Canada was torpedoed during the war. See Hannover, *Politische Justiz*, 29.

[121] LHA Schwerin S 360: *Kieler Neueste Nachrichten*, 7 Jan. 1928, and *Schleswig-Holsteinische Volks-Zeitung*, 5 Jan. 1928.

[122] Grossmann, *Ossietzky*, 155.   [123] Tucholsky, *Gesammelte Werke*, iii. 1270.

of the real course of events which failed to rise above the particular circumstances to take a broader view of the social and political context. Bourgeois commentators found the depiction of incest and murder scandalous, and campaigned to have the theatre's director sacked. *Josef* failed to convince even left-wing critics, and was no more successful when it was performed in Berlin. Nevertheless, its appearance testified to the importance now attached to the case in left-wing circles, and undoubtedly helped give it further publicity.[124]

With the appointment in December 1927 of a new caretaker government, in which the Social Democrat Kurt von Reibnitz was responsible for the Justice Ministry, the chances of reopening the case began to look better.[125] The League approached the new government and received a positive response. Their campaign was thus meeting with some success. State prosecutor Müller, a cantankerous, elderly lawyer steeped in the values of the Wilhelmine period, who had brought the case against Jakubowski in 1925, attempted to head off the campaign with a statement to the press that there was 'complete evidential proof of the accused man's guilt'.[126] But events were playing into the campaigners' hands.[127] On 28 March 1928, having considered the League's request, Reibnitz asked the newly appointed state chief of police, Steuding, to study the files and submit a report on the case, assisted by the criminologist Hans von Hentig. Both men conducted a series of tests and investigations of their own as well as reading all the relevant documentation.[128] Such was the significance attached to the case on the left that the Communist Party in Mecklenburg-Strelitz even agreed not to support any vote of no confidence against the Reibnitz government in order to allow the investigation to continue; its votes would have meant success for the right-wing forces who were mobilizing against the campaign for the posthumous clearing of Jakubowski's name.[129]

Steuding's report, 363 pages long, was a devastating indictment of the original investigation, trial, and verdict. It was clear, wrote Steuding,

that, from the very beginning, the investigators were convinced that Jakubowski was the murderer, and that they ruled all other considerations out. Since the failure to clear up contradictions in the evidence at the start robbed Jakubowski of the chance to defend

---

[124] Eleonore Kalkowska, *Josef. Zeittragödie in 22 Bildern* (Berlin, 1928); Norbert Jaron, *Das demokratische Zeittheater der späten 20er Jahre. Untersucht am Beispiel der Stücke gegen die Todesstrafe. Eine Rezeptionsanalyse* (Frankfurt am Main, 1981), 209–54, 294–5.

[125] The Mecklenburg-Strelitz government consisted of three ministers, each of whom was reponsible for a variety of 'Departments'; for simplicity's sake the Justice Department of the Interior Ministry is referred to as the Justice Ministry.

[126] LHA Schwerin S 364: Kurt Grossmann, 'Jakubowski', *Mecklenburgische Volks-Zeitung*, 19 May 1928.

[127] Harych, *Im Namen*, 237–8.

[128] See Hentig's account in LHA Schwerin S 370: Vernehmung des Zeugen Dr. Hans von Hentig am 5. Juni 1929.

[129] Grossmann, *Ossietzky*, 151–2.

himself, his arrest must have aroused the general impression that he alone was the perpetrator. This caused the local people to be psychologically biased against him—that is an absolutely natural consequence.[130]

In this climate of suspicion against Jakubowski, numerous questions had been left unasked. Important details would now have to be obtained by interviewing people a long time after the original crime had been committed. Memories could not be relied upon. People had had time to concoct plausible-sounding alibis.[131] The behaviour of August Nogens seemed to Steuding and Hentig to have been particularly suspicious. Despite his claim to have been in the nearby village of Lankow on the day of the murder, an independent witness, the cigar-maker Stoltenberg, reported having seen him on 9 November near Palingen. His behaviour had been 'most peculiar', and he had made a 'most distracted impression', standing silently staring into the distance. Not only August Nogens but also Heinrich Blöcker fell under Steuding's suspicion, because he could not account for his own movements at the time of the murder. Furthermore, the discovery of Paul Kreutzfeldt's notebook at the scene of the crime should not have been disregarded: 'An object belonging to a particular person, found near the scene of the crime', Steuding opined, 'is always a suspicious sign, the more so since—as in this case—its owner was one of the inhabitants of the cottage.'[132] The prison warders in Strelitz reported that Jakubowski did not seem to be the unscrupulous individual that the court had held him to be. There were reports from the village that he was fond of children and popular with them. He was hard-working, unlike Blöcker, Kreutzfeldt, and the Nogens family. And he had not tried to escape his responsibilities by leaving the village, observed Steuding, adding: 'This behaviour is all the more remarkable in a Pole, since I know from my own experience that Poles often make poor husbands and fathers, because they abandon their families when their poverty gets too great and set up with another, younger girl.'[133] Citing the latest views of the forensic psychiatrists, Steuding portrayed Jakubowski as a man of limited intellect and education whose knowledge of German was poor and whose evidence was in places contradictory, inexact, or just plain wrong, because he had misunderstood, or been misunderstood by, his interlocutors, and because in his confusion and desperation he may well have told lies in the hope that this would save his head. Even though he knew he was innocent, he would not have trusted the authorities to recognize the truth for what it was. 'Poles, like all Slavic peoples, are generally of a fatalistic nature, and this expresses itself with additional force when they are dealing with a higher power, with the authorities.'[134]

[130] LHA Schwerin S 353: Bericht über den Fall Jakubowski. Berichterstatter: Regierungsrat Steuding, 17, 68.
[131] Ibid. 20, 35, 40.   [132] Ibid. 41–8, 93, 97–9.
[133] Ibid. 69–76, 127–8, 144, 159.   [134] Ibid. 77–85.

Hannes Nogens, at whom the League for Human Rights had pointed the finger, was no longer available for interview. He had been admitted to hospital on 24 July 1925 and died there of tuberculosis on 13 October 1926. But he was universally recognized as a completely harmless idiot, and would not have been capable of executing such a crime. On 6 May Steuding interviewed August Nogens. Under very heavy pressure from his interrogators, August Nogens said that Paul Kreutzfeldt had been the murderer and had told him to incriminate Jakubowski at the trial. 'At the time I was only 19 years old and was afraid of Kreutzfeldt. I kept quiet because I was afraid, and I lied during the investigation because I was afraid, and I gave false evidence to the court because I was afraid.' He pleaded for mercy, and protested that he had never imagined Jakubowski would be executed.[135] This was enough for the Mecklenburg police chief. On 7 May he issued warrants for the arrest of Kreutzfeldt, Blöcker, and August and Fritz Nogens for perjury. Kreutzfeldt admitted nothing. Heinrich Blöcker, how-ever, said that August Nogens was the guilty party, as Fritz Nogens had told him on more than one occasion.[136]

August Nogens was reinterrogated on 8 May. 'I will now tell you', he began, 'what I've kept quiet about up to now:'

I saw Blöcker hanging the child, he had thrown a rope over a branch; the child was still on the ground, it was standing with the rope around its neck beneath the tree. Whether or not the child had already been strangled I don't know. Blöcker pulled the child up about three metres high with the rope. How he got the rope over the branch I didn't see; I don't think the child was kicking any more.

Remaining unobserved, he had returned to the village, where he pedalled past his brother Fritz, and away. 'I had a really funny feeling.' He had not tried to stop Blöcker because he was afraid of him. Later on, his brother Fritz had told him that Blöcker was the murderer and added that he should mind his own business. Confronted with this fresh testimony later the same day, Blöcker stood by his earlier story and continued to insist that August Nogens was the murderer.[137] Steuding did not believe August Nogens's testimony. The man had changed his story too often, each time evidently on tactical grounds, as he realized the previous version was untenable. In the course of doing so, he admitted having been in the village on 9 November and also having been dressed in a military greatcoat that did not belong to him, presumably in order to disguise himself. This was extremely suspicious. Steuding concluded 'that Jakubowski cannot have committed the murder of Ewald Nogens'.[138] Instead, there had been a conspiracy to murder the young boy. Witnesses had testified that Elizabeth Nogens had

[135] Ibid. 168–76.   [136] Ibid. 181–3.
[137] Ibid. 187–93. For the original transcripts, see LHA Schwerin S 358.
[138] LHA Schwerin S 353, 283.

FIG. 31. *The Jakubowski case.* August Nogens at the scene of the crime, with a policeman enacting the strangulation of Ewald Nogens, in a reconstruction staged by Superintendent Gennat, 1928. The Nogens brothers were prime suspects in the reopened case of Josef Jakubowski, who had been convicted of murdering his illegitimate son Ewald in 1924, and in 1926 had gone to the block after what campaigners against the death penalty claimed had been a serious miscarriage of justice.

declared her intention of making sure that 'the Russian' would be found guilty of the murder, 'because people won't believe him as much as her, a grandmother, since he's a Russian'. She seemed to know too many details of the day in question, despite having been away from the village. Was she too involved?[139]

So far, police chief Steuding's investigations had taken place behind closed doors. The arrest of Kreutzfeldt, Blöcker, and the Nogens brothers on 7 May and Steuding's public announcement on 9 May 1928, made after consulting Reibnitz, that Jakubowski was not guilty, created an enormous sensation. 'Innocent Man Executed', screamed the banner headlines in the newspapers, 'Murdered by the State'. 'New Development in the Jakubowski Case—Result of Careful Investigation: The Suspected Murderers Arrested.'[140] The League for Human Rights was jubilant. Outraged citizens bombarded the Mecklenburg authorities with

[139] LHA Schwerin S 353, 194–210, 363.
[140] Ibid., S 359: *Berliner Morgenpost*, 10 May 1928; *Das kleine Blatt* (Vienna), 17 May 1928.

Fɪɢ. 32. *The Jakubowski case.* August Nogens holding the bike which he used to cycle to Lankow to establish his alibi immediately after the murder of Ewald Nogens in Palingen, Mecklenburg-Strelitz, in 1924. Another police photograph taken during the reconstruction of the crime staged by Superintendent Gennat, head of the Berlin murder squad, at Palingen in 1928.

letters and postcards and demanded the dismissal of state prosecutor Müller, who had brought the original case against Jakubowski and continued to insist in 1928 that the Pole was guilty. Müller, said one correspondent, was himself no better than a 'judicial murderer'. Another, anonymous letter sent to state prosecutor Müller in person asked:

What do you think you should do in the case of the poor innocent victim of justice Jakubowski? There must be expiation. Off with the heads of these stupid, conspiratorial, diseased & incompetent German judges, this state prosecutor. To the gallows with this miserable worm, this boil on the German people's body. These self-deceiving fools, who think they know something of the law and yet are unaware of even the most elementary principles of humanity. Off with the heads of these lawyers involved in this affair, they should be lynched. If I was there I would really give them something to think about, these disgusting murderers.[141]

---

[141] Ibid., dated 21 May 1928. The file contains a selection of these postcards and letters.

One correspondent sent in a newspaper report on the case with the word 'class justice' scrawled at the top and a marginal comment against the name of state prosecutor Müller: 'lazytop—must hang himself.'[142]

Müller, wrote another anonymous correspondent on a postcard, was a 'conscienceless murderer' who had demonstrated complete 'stupidity and lack of intelligence': 'Preparations are being made in certain quarters to shoot a bullet into your head to pay you back for this murderous deed.'[143] The most dramatic of these postcards sent to Müller after Steuding's announcement—undoubtedly written by an individual with a powerful imagination—read:

All the papers say you have earned people's hatred by letting the innocent Jakubowski be hanged. Incompetence, obstinacy and arbitrariness have united in you to create the mad illusion that a state prosecutor is a god. But like so many of your colleagues you are a privileged criminal, the first to bend the truth and the law and to plunge people into misery, too cowardly to admit that you have done any wrong. May Jakubowski's blood, the blood of an innocent man wrongly condemned, come upon you and your family! A curse upon the party and the class justice that is undermining the state and the welfare of the people!

In the Jakubowski murder case we demand the fullest expiation, otherwise we are resolved to carry out the sentence ourselves!

The League of Avengers.[144]

These protests hardly breathed the true spirit of principled opposition to capital punishment. Nevertheless, when taken alongside the press reports that appeared on the case in the first few months of 1928, they suggested that there was a considerable body of opinion that now believed the execution of Jakubowski to have been a mistake.

This became a factor in the campaign waged by the League for Human Rights and its allies to get the death penalty abolished. Never had there seemed to be so clear a case of the wrongful execution of a common offender. The opponents of capital punishment exploited this factor in the spring and summer of 1928 for all it was worth. It was above all the Jakubowski case that so many opponents of capital punishment were thinking of when they mentioned miscarriages of justice as a major reason for the stance they took on the issue. By bringing the issue of capital punishment into the limelight once again in the spring and early summer of 1928, it thus set the scene for the legislative moves that were about to follow. The revelation of an apparent miscarriage of justice, backed up by the fresh round of arrests and prosecutions, constituted a powerful argument in favour of abolition. A major public debate was in progress, fuelled by the

---

[142] LHA Schwerin S 359: *Berliner Morgenpost*, 10 May 1928 (pencilled marginalia).
[143] Ibid.: postcard attached to paper sheet dated 15 May 1928.
[144] Ibid. (undated card postmarked Cologne-Osnabrück).

performance of a whole series of abolitionist plays such as Alfred Wolfenstein's *The Night before the Axe* and Leonhard Frank's *The Cause*.[145] The papers were full of articles on the issue. The tide seemed to be turning at last. All that was needed now was for the Reich government to take the initiative and throw its weight behind the abolitionist cause.

e. The Suspension of Executions 1928–1929

In 1927, the long-promised revision of the Criminal Code was at last under way, after the political instability of the previous years had put paid to the attempts made with the drafts of 1919 and 1922.[146] The Reichstag had set up a Criminal Law Committee in order to go over the draft clause by clause. If the Reich government made it known that it wished the clause providing the death penalty to be removed, the Committee, which was made up of deputies appointed in proportion to the strength of their respective parties in the main chamber, was bound to listen. However, much depended on the views of the Reich Minister of Justice. Over the years some, like Gustav Radbruch, had been convinced abolitionists. Others were not. The incumbent when the new draft was put forward was Oskar Hergt, a strong defender of the death penalty. Hergt dismissed the abolitionist campaign as a political fad. 'Demonstrations against the death penalty', he declared, 'can be explained at least in part by the fact that some parts of the population are possessed of a real mania for every kind of innovation.'[147] Such novelties were clearly not going to be in favour while he was in charge of the Justice Ministry. In October 1927 he urged the Criminal Law Committee of the Reichstag not to delete the death penalty from the draft Criminal Code. It was necessary, he delared, in order to deter the criminal violence produced by

the brutalization . . . which the war brought in its train . . . the deterioration of the economic situation, the uprooting of many people's lives, the immigration of elements foreign to our land, the general disintegration of concepts of the law, an extraordinarily reduced estimation of the value of life . . . the present-day need for sensation, a need that sometimes causes even the commonest criminal to appear as a hero.[148]

The Committee duly proceeded to vote along the lines suggested by the Minister. Its composition, of course, reflected the strength of the parties in the 1924 Reichstag election, so the abolitionist parties, the Social Democrats, Communists, and Democrats, were in a minority. Hampered by a split in the

[145] See Jaron, *Zeittheater*, for a full account.
[146] For the details of the various drafts and their respective fates, see Schmidt, *Einführung in die Geschichte der deutschen Strafrechtspflege*, 394–408.
[147] BA Potsdam RT 848: Reichstag, 32. Ausschuss, 21. Sitzung, 27 Oct. 1927, Bl. 121 (p. 6).
[148] Ibid. (p. 5).

Democratic group, the opponents of capital punishment mustered only eleven votes out of twenty-eight.[149] The retention of the death penalty was supported by five votes from the Nationalists, three from the People's Party, four from the Catholic Centre, two from the small Business Party, one from the Bavarian People's Party, and one dissenter from the Democrats, the judge Alfred Brodauf, who wanted to retain capital punishment as a deterrent.[150] In the spring of 1928, therefore, abolition by the means suggested by the vote taken at the end of the debate on the subject in the National Assembly still seemed far away.

However, on 20 May 1928 the country went to the polls again. The resulting disposition of parties was more favourable to the abolitionists than before. The Social Democratic daily, *Vorwärts*, remarked optimistically

The newly elected Reichstag possesses a secure majority against the death penalty. As far as human prediction can tell, the promulgation of the completed reform of the criminal law will include the abolition of the death penalty. The fight against capital punishment in Germany is nearing its end. So even at this moment it is necessary to demand that no more death sentences are carried out.[151]

This demand was far from unrealistic in the circumstances. The elections led to the formation of a Grand Coalition government under the Social Democrat Hermann Müller. The new government's legislative programme, announced on 3 July, explicitly included the abolition of capital punishment as one of its aims.[152] For by this time the Social Democrats had convinced themselves that the course of action they had taken earlier in the decade had, to say the least, been rather unwise. The notorious Article 48 of the Weimar constitution, which gave the President wide-ranging emergency powers, along the lines pioneered by Ebert in his extension of the death penalty against the Red Army, was now more than likely to be directed by Hindenburg, or those who had his ear, against the Social Democrats themselves. Thus in October 1928 a leading party member, Otto Landsberg, announced that the Social Democrats wanted Article 48 restricted by banning its use to create new capital offences. 'Especial consideration must be given to the protection of human life at a time of unrest and political excitement.'[153] The party's second thoughts about its earlier attitude to the death penalty indicated a new seriousness about its abolition, and a greater determination than before to achieve it.

The man responsible for penal policy in the new Grand Coalition government was the Democrat Erich Koch-Weser, who was appointed Reich Minister of

---

[149] BA Potsdam RJM 6097, Bl. 16: *BZ am Montag*, 3 Feb. 1927.
[150] Ibid. 61 Re 1/7792, 83: *Vorwärts*, 3 Nov. 1927; ibid. 119: Alfred Brodauf, 'Die Unentbehrlichkeit der Todesstrafe', *Hamburger Fremdenblatt*, 24 Jan. 1928.
[151] Ibid. 105: *Vorwärts*, 1 July 1928.   [152] Ibid., RJM 6095, Bl. 12.
[153] GStA Berlin Rep. 84a/7786: *Vorwärts*, 24 Oct. 1928.

Justice. Koch-Weser was a committed opponent of the death penalty for murder, and on 13 June 1928 he won the backing of his party for a bill to abolish capital punishment. The bill only applied to the Criminal Code, but on the following day Hermann Müller, soon to become Reich Chancellor, put forward another bill abolishing the death penalty in military law and emergency decrees as well.[154] Koch-Weser therefore had Müller's backing when he resolved to press on as quickly as possible with the completion of the new Criminal Code, and to force the Criminal Law Committee of the Reichstag to reconsider its previous vote on the issue.[155] The representation of the Social Democrats and Communists on the Committee had been strengthened as a result of the 1928 election, and that of the retentionist forces and the vacillating Democrats weakened. In addition, these events fell right into the middle of the sensation caused by the reopening of the Jakubowski case. So the prospects for the Code passing into law, complete with the replacement of death by imprisonment as the punishment for murder, seemed to be good. On 3 July Müller declared that it was his government's intention to abolish capital punishment. Until then, he urged all the federated states not to proceed with any executions.[156] A week later, on 10 July 1928, backed by Müller, Koch-Weser issued a circular to all governments in the federated states advising them not to carry out any executions until the new Criminal Code had been voted into effect by the Reichstag, an event which he confidently expected to occur during the lifetime of the government of which he was a member.[157] Predictably enough, Koch-Weser's circular was condemned by the right-wing press as 'an outrage', a 'protection for murderers', and a breach of the Weimar Constitution.[158] But Koch-Weser was unmoved. Conservative ministries in some of the states took strong exception to the circular as well. The Bavarian Minister of Justice, Franz Gürtner, put heavy pressure on Koch-Weser to agree exceptionally to the execution of the double murderer Hein early in 1929, 'the more so', he wrote, 'since popular opinion is virtually demanding Hein's execution'. Hein's lawyer Victor Fraenkel was desperate enough to go straight to the Reich Justice Ministry on being told by the Bavarian authorities that they were unwilling to grant his client a reprieve. Koch-Weser made a point of insisting on the commutation of the sentence, and on 10 March 1929 Gürtner and the Bavarian cabinet gave in, and Hein was spared.[159] The Baden Minister of

[154] Düsing, *Abschaffung*, 171–2.   [155] GStA Berlin Rep. 84a/7786: *Deutsche Zeitung*, 19 Oct. 1928.
[156] Düsing, *Abschaffung*, 172.
[157] BA Potsdam RJM 6095, Bl. 12: Anlage zum Sprechzettel, report of statement by Reichskanzler Müller in the Reichstag on 3 July 1928, and circular of the RJM, 10 July 1928. Another copy of the circular of 10 July can be found in GLA Karlsruhe 234/6610.
[158] BA Potsdam RJM 6095, Bl. 184: *Hamburger Nachrichten*, 28 Sept. 1928.
[159] Ibid., Bl. 243: 'Vermerkt am 4. März 1929'; ibid., Bl. 246: Fraenkel to RJM, 6 Mar. 1929; ibid., Bl. 248: Haniel to RJM (Abdruck), 11 Mar. 1929; see also ibid. 6098, Bl. 53: *Berliner Volkszeitung*, 10 Mar. 1929.

Justice also regretted what he saw as the inevitable abolition of capital punishment after the elections, but saw it as unavoidable.[160]

In Württemberg, the Justice Ministry was put under pressure by 'public opinion' too, by the son of a murdered woman, who wrote to the State President in 1928 to protest against the commutation of the death sentence passed on the murderer, Karl Mayer:

Mr State President, were you aware of the implications of your action, and can you answer with your conscience before God for the fact that you have reprieved such a bestial, degraded man, a previously convicted robber and murderer, and that you have thereby opened the gates to further murderous deeds? Did you not think of your own mother, or of the family of the murdered woman, who are still bowed with grief even today, who have been robbed of their home by this terrible crime? Is it not a mockery of justice that such a monster, who destroyed a noble human life, should still be allowed to live among humans? The feelings of the general public revolt against the idea of keeping such an inferior subject, a robber and murderer, alive at the cost of the state.[161]

However much the government in the conservative south German state might have wished to sign the death warrant for Mayer, it felt unable to do so in the face of the Koch-Weser circular. Although it was argued on the right that the circular was an infringement of their judicial sovereignty,[162] the states realized that to disobey it would lead to a crisis in relations with the Reich. In the circumstances of gathering economic gloom in the summer and autumn of 1928, this was something which they could well do without. So they followed Koch-Weser's instructions. In 1928, therefore, there were no executions anywhere in Germany, despite the fact that some forty offenders had been condemned to death. And the following year, 1929, out of thirty-eight death sentences, not a single one was actually carried out.[163] 'The death penalty practically abolished!' declared the Social Democratic daily paper *Vorwärts* already on 4 July 1928,[164] and the reality of this *de facto* abolition of capital punishment soon dawned on the retentionists as well. 'There is no capital punishment any more', complained a Nationalist publication in December 1928, before going on to supply its readers with a list of the murderers it thought should be executed all the same.[165] The law still laid down death as the punishment for murder, complained Koch-Weser's critics, yet it was now being disregarded on the orders of the Reich government. 'Such a unilateral action', one newspaper alleged in February 1929, 'has nothing or very

[160] GLA Karlsruhe 234/6610: Auszug aus dem amtlichen Bericht über die 37. Sitzung des Badischen Landtags vom 20. Juni 1928, Justizminister Dr. Trunk.

[161] Quoted in ibid. 6611: 'Um die Todesstrafe. Von Landgerichtsdirektor Dr. A. Hanemann, MdR', *Breisgauer Zeitung*, 5 Oct. 1929.

[162] Ibid.: *Germania*, 2 Oct. 1928.   [163] HStA Munich MJu 12575: *Berliner Tageblatt*, 12 May 1929.

[164] BA Potsdam RJM 6097, Bl. 238: *Vorwärts*, 4 July 1928.

[165] GStA Berlin Rep. 84a/7792: *Der Montag*, 10 Dec. 1928.

FIG. 33. *Erich Koch-Weser (1875–1944).* As Reich Justice Minister in 1928–9, Koch-Weser, a convinced opponent of capital punishment, ordered a moratorium on executions until the abolition of the death penalty had been secured in the proposed Criminal Code.

little to do . . . with a serious fight against the death penalty.'[166] The fact that capital punishment had effectively ceased to be applied would make it difficult to resume executions at any point in the future because of the patent unfairness to

[166] Ibid.: *Bremer Nachrichten,* 14 Feb. 1929.

the individual offenders concerned. Thus the pressure was now increased on the legislature to turn a *de facto* situation into a *de jure* provision and vote for the formal, legal abolition of the death sentence as a provision of the new Criminal Code.

There was a further factor in favour of abolition which seemed calculated to win favour on all sides. This was the fact that, as Wilhelm Kahl noted: 'The death penalty has been abolished in Austria. A German dualism will be hard to bear in the long run.'[167] It was already common to argue against the death penalty by alleging 'that its retention in the new draft of the German Criminal Code makes a *union* in this area with our German compatriots in Austria infinitely more difficult to achieve'.[168] In 1918 the collapse of the Habsburg Empire, the creation of an independent Czechoslovakia, Yugoslavia, and Hungary, and the secession of other areas to Poland and Romania had left the German-speaking community, some six million strong, in the rump of Austria around Vienna and in the Alpine provinces, eager to merge with the new German Republic. The idea had been welcomed in Germany itself. The left was as keen on the project as the nationalist right was. The Austrian Socialists thought that joining in with the more industrialized and advanced neighbour to the north would hasten the day when socialism came to their part of the world, while the German Social Democrats favoured the incorporation of 'German-Austria' in deference to their long-held 'Greater German' view of the nationality question. Only the intervention of the victorious western Allies had forced German-Austria to establish itself as an independent state. But throughout the inter-war period it remained a state that few people in Austria itself really wanted. Plagued by economic crises, political conflict, and mounting violence, it never really seemed viable to the people who lived in it. Throughout the 1920s, therefore, hopes of a merger with Germany were kept alive by close and frequent contacts at all levels between the two countries. In the words of the leading conservative statesman of the period in Austria, Ignaz Seipel, they formed 'one nation, two states'.[169] It was one of the few issues on which practically all the different political parties in the two countries were able to agree.[170]

As in many other areas, so in the field of legal reform, efforts were thus made to ensure that Austria and Germany did not drift too far apart. A joint legal commission was set up to bring about a harmonization of the two legal systems, and in 1928 the German Jurists' Annual Conference met in Vienna. The abol-

---

[167] GStA Berlin Rep. 84a/7792: *Germania*, 19 Oct. 1928 (Rosenfeld) and *Deutsche Zeitung*, 19 July 1928 (Kahl).

[168] Ibid.: *Frankfurter Zeitung*, 24 Jan. 1928 and *Neue Preussische Zeitung*, 17 Jan. 1928.

[169] See Karl R. Stadler, *Austria* (London, 1971), 106–34.

[170] See also Liselotte Jelowik, *Zur Geschichte der Strafrechtsreform in der Weimarer Republik* (Martin-Luther-Universität Halle-Wittenberg, Wiss. Beiträge 1983/13, B17; Halle an der Saale, 1983), 21.

ition of the death penalty in the Austrian Republic provided a golden opportunity for abolitionists in Germany to portray its abolition in the Weimar Republic as a patriotic act. Nationalism, which had demanded the insertion of capital punishment in the Criminal Code 1870, now seemed to demand its removal. Erich Koch-Weser made a point of the need to achieve a unity of practice between the two nations in his speech advocating abolition to the Criminal Law Committee of the Reichstag in October 1928.[171] The Austrian question also helped sway the divided loyalties of Wilhelm Kahl, the Committee's Chairman, in the direction of abolition.[172] In Britain and France, where suspicions of Germany's intentions towards Austria ran deep, the press even regarded the systematic commutation of death sentences in the Weimar Republic from 1928 onwards as evidence of the desire for union.[173] 'The whole question of union with Austria, the famous "Anschluss"', commented the *Observer* in May 1931, at a time when the subject was the focus of intense international debate because of the Allies' imposition of a veto on a proposed Customs Union between the two countries, lay 'behind the scenes to-day of so many political activities in Germany.' The paper went on to claim that it was 'likely to stand or fall' on the issue of capital punishment. This was surely something of an exaggeration. But it showed the seriousness with which the question was taken by international as well as national opinion.[174] On the right, of course, hardline retentionists suggested that the problem would best be dealt with by the Austrians deciding to reintroduce capital punishment rather than by the Germans deciding to abolish it.[175] This was not a view that won much support. It was generally recognized that the chances of the Austrians changing their minds were slim. The issue of compatibility between the two penal systems became another pressure acting in favour of abolition.

A new cabinet committed to abolishing the death penalty; a Reich Minister of Justice who had ordered a nation-wide suspension of executions; a widely felt need to bring German penal practice into line with that of Austria, where capital punishment no longer existed; a major scandal over a wrongful execution; and a probable majority for abolition in the legislature: such were the hopeful circumstances in which the Criminal Law Committee of the Reichstag reconvened on 17 October 1928. The first session was addressed by the Minister himself. The time had now come, Koch-Weser told the Committee's members, for capital punishment to be finally abolished. All other forms of bodily punishment

---

[171] BA Potsdam Auswärtiges Amt IIIa Nr. 51, Bd. 11, Bl. 114: *Vossische Zeitung*, 18 Oct. 1928.
[172] Ibid., Bl. 115: *Vossische Zeitung*, 19 Oct. 1928.   [173] Ibid., Bl. 177: *L'Œuvre*, 29 Apr. 1931.
[174] Ibid., Bl. 178: *Observer*, 10 May 1931.
[175] Ibid., RT 848, Bl. 122, p. 7 (Reichstag, 32. Ausschuss, 21. Sitzung, 27 Oct. 1927); see also ibid., Bl. 83: *Berliner Börsen-Zeitung*, 27 Oct. 1927.

had disappeared over the course of the years, and execution was the only one remaining. It was now applied, in contrast to the past, to only a handful of offences. Evidently thinking of the Jakubowski case,[176] he went on:

The pronouncement of a death sentence on an innocent man, which cannot be ruled out even in the best trial procedure and with the best judges, must be regarded as a terrible tragedy, because it can never in any way be made good again, and indeed on every occasion such a mistaken verdict deals a serious and almost irreparable blow to the people's trust in the law

Like other abolitionists before him, Koch-Weser thought that society was becoming more civilized, and that executions belonged to an essentially backward and barbaric past. No doubt recalling the arguments put forward in the National Assembly at Weimar in 1919 about the effects of the war on standards of behaviour, Koch-Weser declared now

that the manner in which our people has found its way back to morality and a consciousness of the State after the horrors of the war, the confusion of the revolution and the emergencies of the inflation, is as incomparable as one could have hoped. This justifies the expectation that our people will develop its moral consciousness to ever greater heights.

Abolition, he thought, was not only justified by this general improvement in morals, but would also give a further boost to the 'victory of the more noble forces' in society.[177]

There was a whole world, however, between noble sentiments such as these and the basic political horse-trading that had to take place in the Criminal Law Committee of the Reichstag in order to get abolition through. As in the debates of 1870, the clauses on the death penalty were by far the most controversial in the draft, and threatened to hold up the progress of the entire Code. The Chairman of the Committee, Professor Wilhelm Kahl, of the People's Party, previously a champion of the death penalty, decided to sacrifice his principles in order to get the legislation through. A respected senior member of the legal profession, nearly 80 years old, he had also been involved in an earlier attempt to reform the Criminal Code before the First World War. He had a particular commitment, therefore, to the success of the draft under discussion in 1928. So he agreed to drop his opposition to abolition. However, this was on strict conditions. As he told the Committee: 'The offender who has been condemned to life imprisonment has to a certain extent a licence to commit more murders. He cannot be condemned to any extra punishment even if he murders his warder, the padre, or some visitor. This is a weakness of the abolition of the death penalty.' So he insisted that, if capital punishment were to be abolished, convicted murderers

176 GLA Karlsruhe 234/6611: *Berliner Tageblatt*, 10 Oct. 1928.
177 BA Potsdam Auswärtiges Amt IIIa Nr. 51, Bd. 11, Bl. 114: *Vossische Zeitung*, 18 Oct. 1928.

would never be allowed to return to society. Life should mean life. And to prevent any further crimes being committed by such offenders, they should be perpetually imprisoned under a particularly strict and harsh regime which allowed them no possibility of misbehaving.[178] These somewhat Beccarian conditions, of course, were open to the objection that they assisted rather than prevented the convicted murderer in the perpetration of further crimes. Since they were already subject to the harshest possible punishment under the law, such prisoners would be able to commit further crimes—for example, the murder of a prison warder—with impunity. If on the other hand the principle of remission were accepted, and an offender released on parole, then further punishment would become possible for additional crimes, and the deterrent effect of punishment would be retained. The same point held good for Kahl's demand that murderers should be imprisoned under a specially tight security regime. If such a regime were relaxed on good behaviour, then it once more became possible to treat them more harshly should they offend again. Underlying Kahl's conditions was the typical retentionist view that once a murderer, always a murderer; reform and improvement were impossible, and if prisoners had killed on one occasion, it was likely that they would kill on others, irrespective of the specificities of their original offence. Normally this was a justification for capital punishment, and it is easy to see how Kahl was attempting to turn life imprisonment into a kind of 'living death' that would reassure people who thought of murderers the way he did. But these assumptions were not acceptable to the majority of abolitionists. It quickly became apparent that the proposals with which Kahl was attempting to satisfy them were not acceptable either.

After two days of debate, the Committee took a series of votes on the issue on 1 November. First, the Communists, supported by the Social Democrats, put forward a motion for the deletion of the words 'death penalty' from the Criminal Code. Supported by Kahl's vote from the chair, and by the Democrats, and aided by the abstention of the retentionists, the motion was carried. So far, therefore, Kahl's tactics for dealing with the problem seemed to have been accepted by all sides. Next, however, his own motion for the amendment of Clause 33 of the Code was put to the vote. It was supported by the Social Democrats but defeated by a combination of the retentionists, who objected to the proposal that murder could only be punishable by imprisonment, and the Communists, who viewed the condition of a special security regime for imprisoned murderers as too tough. In effect, therefore, the Committee had failed to vote for the replacement of the existing clause which laid down the death penalty for murder, with a new clause which did not. In accordance with the procedure outlined by Kahl at the

[178] Ibid., Bl. 115: *Vossische Zeitung*, 19 Oct. 1928.

FIG. 34. *Voting in the Criminal Law Committee of the Reichstag.* Taken early in 1930, this photograph shows one of many votes held in the Committee under the chairmanship of Professor Wilhelm Kahl (1851–1932), the bearded figure at the far end of the table. Kahl was the criminal law expert of the German People's Party and had been a leading defender of capital punishment during the debates at the Lawyers' Congress in 1912. Despite being pressed to complete its work by Reich Justice Minister Erich Koch-Weser, the Committee failed to agree on either the abolition or retention of capital punishment in the planned Criminal Code. The woman on the right is the German Democratic Party deputy and prominent feminist, Marie-Eisabeth Lüders.

beginning, therefore, the vote to remove the words 'death penalty' from the Code was taken again. This time, Kahl, anxious to obtain a result, switched sides and voted with the retentionists. But the result was a dead heat. The Nationalists, People's Party, Catholic Centre, and Bavarian People's Party mustered a total of fourteen votes, as did the Communists, Social Democrats, and Democrats. The rules did not provide for a casting vote from the chair. What they did say was that a motion had to have a simple majority to get through. So this motion, too, was rejected. Finally the Committee voted on the whole of the existing, unamended Clause 33 of the Code, which provided the death penalty for murder. This met with the same fate, with a vote of fourteen to fourteen. The result of all this was that no decision had really been taken. The political forces on the Committee, in a classic example of Weimar politics, simply cancelled each other out. Small wonder that the newspapers carried headlines such as 'Has the death penalty been dropped? Confusion in the Criminal Law Committee.'[179]

The confusion was not to be removed easily. Rather than keep going over the same ground, with no likelihood of a different result, the Committee now moved on to other business. Time would, it no doubt considered, bring the solution to the deadlock, especially if—as in 1870—the rest of the Code was agreed and only the resolution of the capital punishment question stood in the way of its completion. With a Justice Minister determined to force abolition through, and executions already effectively abolished all over Germany, the prospects still seemed good despite this initial setback. The voting, after all, had been as close as it could possibly be, and the pressures to resolve the issue on the Committee all seemed to be running in the direction of abolition. As so often, capital punishment and its abolition had become a potent political symbol, this time of the democratic hopes and aspirations of the stable, middle years of the Weimar Republic, when things seemed at last to be going the Republic's way. All that was needed to complete the revision of the Criminal Code and to give a formal, legal foundation to the ending of executions, was time. But by the end of 1928 time was running out.

[179] GStA Berlin Rep. 84a/7792: *Volkswacht für Schlesien*, 3 Nov. 1928; ibid.: *Vorwärts*, 1 Nov. 1928; ibid.: *Deutsche Allgemeine Zeitung*, 1 Nov. 1928; BA Potsdam RJM 6098, Bl. 7: *Die Rote Fahne*, 1 Nov. 1928; ibid., Bl. 8: *8-Uhr Abendblatt*, 1 Nov. 1928.

13

'Murderers Amongst Us'

a. The Failure of Criminal Law Reform 1929–1930

On 11 April 1929 the prospects for abolition, which had seemed so bright in the second half of the previous year, were suddenly darkened by the enforced resignation of Erich Koch-Weser as Reich Justice Minister. There was no scandal or political disagreement with the Reich Chancellor; it was simply a matter of coalition arithmetic. Given the existence of half a dozen well-established major political parties, and the system of election by strict proportional representation, every government in the Weimar Republic was of necessity a coalition government. Chancellors therefore had to look continually to the balance of forces within their cabinets if they were to keep all their coalition partners happy. Occasionally, a minor adjustment was needed to prevent the coalition from breaking up. Some ministries, such as Labour or Foreign Affairs, were more or less monopolized by a single party or even a single individual through a whole string of coalition governments. But not the Ministry of Justice. On the contrary, it served under the Weimar Republic as a means of restoring the balance of parties in a coalition cabinet when it seemed to have become upset. Koch-Weser was the eleventh occupant of the office in as many years, and the Democrats, to whom he belonged, were the fifth political party to have supplied the incumbent since 1920. Small wonder that it proved difficult to develop a consistent or long-term judicial policy at the Reich level. The disadvantages of this situation were revealed afresh as the continuation of Müller's Grand Coalition came in early April 1929 to require that the Justice Ministry be passed over from the Democrats to the Catholic Centre Party, which had not previously been fully integrated into the cabinet. Koch-Weser was thus forced to resign his office for the greater political good of the coalition.[1]

---

[1] Heinrich August Winkler, *Der Schein der Normalität. Arbeiter und Arbeiterbewegung in der Weimarer Republik*, ii (Berlin and Bonn, 1985), 583; Anton Golecki (ed.), *Akten der Reichskanzlei: Kabinett Müller II*, i. 524–45; BA Koblenz Nachlass Koch-Weser 99, Bl. 27: *Stuttgarter Neues Tageblatt*, 12 Apr. 1929.

Commentators generally agreed that Koch-Weser had done more than anyone to press ahead with the drafting of the new Criminal Code and in particular with the search for a politically acceptable way of abolishing the death penalty.[2] His successor, the Centre Party politician Theodor von Guérard, was a political animal of a very different colouring. His party had traditionally been in favour of capital punishment, and at this time, towards the end of the 1920s, it was moving to the right on a variety of issues. Guérard was no exception to these generalizations. He was well known as a convinced supporter of the death penalty.[3] No sooner had he taken up office than he made it clear that he thought Jakubowski had been guilty and his execution justified. It was his firm conviction, he said, 'that in practice there have been no cases of the execution of a mistaken death sentence in Germany'.[4] This tough stance on the case that more than any other divided abolitionists from retentionists under the Weimar Republic was a clear signal that Guérard had no intention of pursuing the same line as his predecessor. Addressing the Criminal Law Committee of the Reichstag at the end of April 1929, he declared: 'Capital punishment is a just punishment, because it contains expiation.' State and society were entitled to 'emergency self-defence' in stormy times.[5] Like many Centre Party politicians, Guérard believed above all in the retributive function of capital punishment. He declared: 'Its execution expiates in the most obvious way the dreadful deeds for which in my opinion it is the only punishment that can be considered in future.'[6] Not surprisingly, therefore, he immediately withdrew the circular in which his predecessor had instructed the federated states not to execute any more offenders. More than this, on 25 April 1929, Guérard obtained an explicit endorsement of the death penalty from the Reich cabinet. Capital punishment, he told his Social Democratic and other colleagues, was demanded by the people. Not for the first time on this particular issue, Hermann Müller and his fellow abolitionists swallowed their principles in the interests of short-term political expediency. If the Centre Party demanded a commitment to the death penalty as the price of loyalty, then that was what they would get. Bigger issues, after all, were at stake.[7] Suddenly the abolition of capital punishment seemed a good deal less likely than it had done at the end of 1928.[8]

[2] BA Potsdam RJM 6098: *Berliner Tageblatt*, 26 Apr. 1929; Ibid. 61 Re 1/1773, 183: *Berliner Tageblatt*, 26 Apr. 1929.

[3] Ibid., RJM 6098, Bl. 66: *Berliner Volkszeitung*, 25 Apr. 1929.

[4] Ibid. Auswärtiges Amt IIIa Nr. 51, Bd. II, Bl. 123: *Berliner Tageblatt*, 25 Apr. 1929; GLA Karlsruhe 234/6611: *Vorwärts*, 26 Apr. 1929.

[5] GStA Berlin Rep. 84a/7792: *8-Uhr Abendblatt*, 25 Apr. 1929.

[6] BA Potsdam Auswärtiges Amt IIIa Nr. 51, Bl. 123: *Berliner Tageblatt*, 25 Apr. 1929.

[7] GStA Berlin Rep. 84a/7786: RJM notes, 25 Apr. 1929.

[8] BA Potsdam RJM 6098, Bl. 86: *Vossische Zeitung*, 4 May 1929.

Under these altered circumstances the Criminal Law Committee of the Reichstag returned once more to consider the clauses on capital offences in the draft Criminal Code. Its chairman, Wilhelm Kahl, made one last effort to achieve a compromise. Realizing that the whole piece of legislation would be threatened if he failed to bring about a speedy resolution of the impasse over the death penalty, Kahl softened the conditions under which he was prepared to accept abolition, in the hope that this would win the Communists over.[9] But in a series of votes taken in late April and early May 1929 the Committee still rejected his motion for amending the clause relating to murder so that imprisonment would be the statutory punishment, this time by sixteen votes to twelve. In the middle of a 'revolutionary' phase, and not least under pressure from Moscow, the Communists were determined not to enter into any compromises or agreements which might lend the Weimar Republic and its 'bourgeois' institutions the slightest degree of legitimacy. So they sabotaged the Committee's proceedings by persisting in the argument that the punishment proposed by Kahl, even in its reduced form, was too harsh. A Centre Party motion to restore the death penalty for repeated or mass murder or parricide was also lost, by fourteen votes to fourteen. Finally the original, unamended Clause 33, laying down capital punishment for murder, did not get through either, with the votes again fourteen on each side. The result was that, once more, no decision had been reached. 'Evidently', observed a liberal daily newspaper, the *Frankfurter Zeitung,* 'an unlucky star is shining down upon the Criminal Law Committee of the Reichstag's votes on capital punishment.'[10]

For a while it seemed possible that the situation might be rescued through a deal struck between the Centre Party and the other coalition members behind the scenes. There were reports that the Catholic politicians were prepared to give way to the abolitionists on the issue of capital punishment in return for a commitment on the government's part to introduce tougher legal sanctions against divorce.[11] But these discussions came to nothing. The Social Democratic Chancellor Hermann Müller and his colleagues were rumoured at least to have secured the Centre Party's agreement that Guérard's declarations would have no immediate practical effect, and indeed he did not actively seek to encourage executions while the Criminal Code was still under discussion. Accordingly, none actually took place during his tenure of office at the Justice Ministry.[12] But it was equally clear that Guérard was not particularly interested in pushing the

[9] BA Potsdam RJM 6098, Bl. 35: *Berliner Tageblatt,* 5 Jan. 1929.
[10] Ibid. 61 Re 1/1773, 186: *Vossische Zeitung,* 4 May 1929; GStA Berlin Rep. 84a/7792: *Frankfurter Zeitung,* 3 May 1929; ibid.: *Kölnische Zeitung,* 3 May 1929; ibid.: *8-Uhr Abendblatt,* 26 Apr. 1929; ibid.: *Vorwärts,* 5 May 1929.
[11] BA Potsdam RJM 6098, Bl. 86: *Vossische Zeitung,* 4 May 1929; ibid., Bl. 87: *Frankfurter Zeitung,* 7 May 1929.
[12] Ibid. 61 Re 1/1773, 186: *Vossische Zeitung,* 4 May 1929.

new Criminal Code through the legislative process. Without the drive of the Justice Minister behind it, the Criminal Law Committee slowed down. Before long, the government had much weightier matters to occupy its attention. A cataclysmic stock market crash in New York inaugurated a world-wide economic crisis that quickly plunged Germany into social and political turmoil as bankruptcies and closures swept the country and millions were thrown out of work. Under these pressures, the task of getting a large and diverse coalition of political parties to agree on a policy to meet the emergency proved too much, and the Müller cabinet broke asunder at the end of March 1930.

The aged President of the Weimar Republic, Field Marshal von Hindenburg, now appointed a 'cabinet of experts' under the conservative, monarchist Centre Party politician Heinrich Brüning. Guérard was replaced by a new Reich Justice Minister, Viktor Bredt, who represented the small, right-wing Business Party. Bredt was a supporter of the death penalty, and declared officially that state governments were in no way bound by the Koch-Weser circular of two years before.[13] But in September 1930 Bredt too resigned, along with his party, from the government. For the moment, the ministry was run by its senior civil servant, the State Secretary, Curt Joël, who eventually took over as Minister in 1931. He too was against the abolition of capital punishment.[14] The Reich government was now essentially non-party. It was considerably weakened by its lack of support in the Reichstag, above all after the elections of September 1930, which brought over a hundred National Socialists into the legislature and soon reduced it to a state of impotence. No majorities could be found for anything any more. By 1931 the Reichstag was meeting less frequently and breaking up in disorder when it did so; in 1932 it hardly sat at all. The government ruled by decree, through the emergency powers wielded by the President. But it was unable to do anything positive any more. The Weimar Republic was politically paralysed.

b. The End of the Jakubowski Case 1928–1932

These setbacks for the abolitionist cause were compounded by a series of fresh twists and turns in the complex investigations surrounding the execution of Josef Jakubowski. Following on his arrest of August and Fritz Nogens and their mother Elizabeth, in May 1928, Mecklenburg-Strelitz's chief of police Steuding had accused the Mecklenburg state prosecutor of creating 'the threat of a cover-up' in the case.[15] His bitter rival, State Prosecutor Müller, had repeatedly de-

---

[13] GLA Karlsruhe 234/6611: *Vorwärts*, 10 June 1930.
[14] Heinrich August Winkler, *Der Weg in die Katastrophe. Arbeiter und Arbeiterbewegung in der Weimarer Republik*, iii (Berlin and Bonn, 1986), 262.
[15] LHA Schwerin S 358, 201.

clared his belief in Jakubowski's guilt. According to Jakubowski's supporters, Müller had been doing his best to undermine Steuding's investigation from the start.[16] On 14 May he interviewed August Nogens, who now withdrew the admissions he had made to Steuding. Emboldened by this coup, Müller now ordered the release of all the suspects, and although Fritz Nogens, whom Steuding had not been able to interrogate, was arrested in Bremen on 16 May, he refused to admit anything and was also released.[17] The situation seemed to have reached an impasse, and it was difficult to see how it could be resolved while Mecklenburg's state prosecutor and chief of police were working so openly against each other. On 22 May 1928, therefore, the government brought the rival investigations to a halt.[18] To try and resolve the differences between the prosecution service and the police, it commissioned a fresh report from a legal expert nominated by the Reich Minister of Justice. Since the pre-election Reich government was still in power at this moment, and the Nationalist Reich Justice Minister Oskar Hergt had not yet been replaced by the abolitionist Democrat Erich Koch-Weser, it was not surprising that the expert the Minister nominated was a conservative, who would be more likely than not to come out in favour of Jakubowski's guilt.[19] This was the former Saxon Minister of Justice and recently ousted Minister-President Wilhelm Bünger. On 11 July 1928, after the elections, he submitted a confidential 44-page report. Steuding, he said, had been right to suspect August Nogens, but August's mother Elizabeth had probably been involved too. A letter she had written after Ewald's disappearance certainly seemed to give an exaggerated impression of the emotional effect it would have had on her, and therefore had to be treated with some suspicion. The petty criminal Paul Kreutzfeldt, who lived in the other half of the house inhabited by the Nogenses, was a known man of violence and was party to the conspiracy too, since he wanted Jakubowski to marry his sister. His influence on the labourer Heinrich Blöcker and the Nogens brothers was considerable. Bünger's conclusion was that Jakubowski had indeed been guilty of the murder of Ewald Nogens, but that all these other people had been involved in the crime in one capacity or another as well.[20]

[16] Harych, *Im Namen*, 236–40. Here, as in some other places, Harych reorganizes the facts and reshuffles the dates, not only in the interests of a more dramatic narrative, but also, it must be said, in the interests of the case for Jakubowski. For the correct sequence of events, see the protocol of the dispute between State Prosecutor Müller and League for Human Rights' lawyer Brandt in LHA Schwerin S 370: Beeidigung der Zeugen Landgerichtspräsident von Buchka, Staatsminister a. D. Dr. Hustaedt und Oberstaatsanwalt Dr. Müller (n.d.).

[17] LHA Schwerin S 371, 60.

[18] Ibid., S 357: Schlussbericht betr. Voruntersuchung gegen August Nogens und Genossen (Fall Jakubowski), Kriminalrat Gennat, 14 Nov. 1928, 39–55.

[19] Harych, *Im Namen*, 242.

[20] LHA Schwerin S 439: Gutachten des sächsischen Staats- und Justizministers a. D. Dr. h.c. Bünger über den Fall Jakubowski.

Bünger's report was enough for the Mecklenburg-Strelitz Ministry of Justice to institute full proceedings against all the suspects. But rather than rely on his own police or prosecution service, which had not been able to come up with any satisfactory conclusions to date, Minister Kurt von Reibnitz followed another of Bünger's recommendations and went straight to the top, to the best detective available in Germany: the head of the murder squad in Berlin, Ernst Gennat.[21] Gennat was a well-known personality in the Weimar Republic. Immensely fat (he weighed 270 pounds by this time), with a fatal weakness for cream cakes, he was involved in a number of the most famous murder cases of the day.[22] He was a known supporter of the death penalty. But it would be unfair to see in his appointment on 20 July 1928 a mere attempt to reassert the original verdict; the fact that it was now conceded that Jakubowski had not done his deed alone was in itself an indictment of the sloppy investigation and prosecution that had brought him to the block. Assisted by two other Berlin detectives, Gennat spent four months in Mecklenburg, working full-time on the case. His investigation was a model of the new professionalism of Germany's, and especially Berlin's, police techniques in the Weimar period: thorough, careful, and extremely sophisticated.[23] His report, submitted on 14 November 1928, in a typewritten document extending to over 300 pages and accompanied by three stout files of evidence, left no stone unturned. And a good number of nasty new things were to be seen crawling out from underneath.

It was clear, wrote Gennat, that since the various arrests and investigations had been widely reported in the press, the witnesses were expecting to be interrogated again and knew what was at stake. 'All the participants found themselves to some extent in the position of actors waiting for the cue to utter their no doubt well-prepared statements.'[24] Gennat and his team made them wait, therefore, while they re-examined all the evidence relating to the case so far, collected new material,[25] and subjected all the other witnesses to intensive re-interrogation. Only then, towards the end of August, did they question the principal suspects once more. Fritz Nogens was interviewed on 27 and 28 August, but persistently denied all the allegations brought against him.[26] On the 29th, it was the turn of August Nogens. He too began by stubbornly refusing to admit anything, contrary to his previous record of concocting one contradictory story after another. Clearly this time, as Gennat had suspected, the Nogenses had agreed in advance on the tactic of silence. But confronted, in many hours of patient questioning,

---

[21] Ibid., S 371, 60.   [22] Frey, *Ich beantrage*, 56, 440.

[23] Richard Bessel, 'Policing, Professionalisation and Politics in Weimar Germany', in Clive Emsley and Barbara Weinberger (eds.), *Policing Western Europe: Professionalism and Public Order, 1850–1940* (London, 1991); Hsi-Huey Liang, *The Berlin Police in the Weimar Republic* (Berkeley, 1970); Johannes Buder, *Die Reorganisation der preussischen Polizei 1918–1933* (Frankfurt am Main, 1986).

[24] LHA Schwerin S 357, 16.   [25] Ibid., S 371, 62–71.   [26] Ibid., S 355, 51–65.

with the evidence, and with new statements obtained from other witnesses, August Nogens suddenly suffered a dramatic collapse. As the stenographic report of the interrogation noted:

August Nogens shrinks back into himself ever more—his head droops down onto his chest—of his own accord he puts out the pipe which he has been allowed. He is now asked to make a renewed statement about the points which have just been touched upon in the record. August Nogens declares hereupon—instead of answering, August Nogens props his head up on both his hands—lays his head, supported by his hands, on the edge of the table, sobbing bitterly, whimpering and moaning. He then fell back into himself more and more. When an attempt was made to set him back on the chair in an upright position, he finally fell over onto the floor, and stayed there, lying on his face. He whimpered the whole time and screamed out loud. It did not seem to be an attack of cramp or some similar condition, but rather a physical collapse brought on by severe emotional distress. After the moaning and whimpering had finally stopped, an attempt was made to put Nogens back on the chair—he struck out about him with his hands and feet, so that the decision was taken to put him in fetters. However, he finally quietened down, straightened out his clothing, and soon reached again for his pipe of tobacco.[27]

As Gennat subsequently noted, this collapse signified the 'birth-pangs of the approaching confession'.[28] Fully fifty minutes passed before August recovered and began to tell the truth at last.

Over several more sessions the true story was gradually wheedled out; not by threats or promises, still less by physical intimidation, but rather by ceaseless, patient, and endlessly wearying, detailed questioning. In a case such as this, subjected as it was to the full glare of national publicity and the alert attention of organizations such as the Communist Party and the League for Human Rights, which would have been only too pleased to have had an excuse for criticizing the Berlin police force and heaping further opprobrium upon the organs of justice in Mecklenburg, Gennat and his team could not afford the merest suspicion of irregularity. Warned expressly by the interrogator, therefore, 'to tell the truth without qualifications and not to do anything such as he had once done before with Blöcker, like making a false accusation against Jakubowski',[29] August Nogens now gave a detailed account of the murder. After cycling to Palingen, he had brought the child out of the house to Jakubowski, waiting on the heath.

Question: And then?
Answer: Then Josef said to me 'I must press the air out of him.' I replied that I couldn't do this—he had to do it himself. Then he knelt down with the child and I turned away.
Question: What happened after that?
Answer: After that, he gave him back to me. Then I took him to Fritz and went away on my bike.
Question: Where was Fritz, and how did you know where he was?

[27] LHA Schwerin S 357, 82.   [28] Ibid., S 357, 182.   [29] Ibid., S 355, Bl. 253–4.

Answer: Josef had told me he was by the fir-trees. So I went there with the child, Fritz was there too. Then I gave him the child to take away.

Question: Where was he to take it?

Answer: I didn't say anything to Fritz about that—Josef had told me Fritz knew what to do.[30]

The military greatcoat which August had borrowed was a device to conceal the child's body as he carried it into the wood.[31] Fritz Nogens, called back on 30 August for a further session and confronted with his brother's confession, now confirmed this story. It had been Jakubowski who had conceived the idea of killing Ewald. He had planned the child's murder in considerable detail and offered to reward the brothers with a bicycle and new clothes if they took part. Aged only 15 and 19 at the time, and living in circumstances of dire poverty and degradation, they had agreed.

On 5 September 1928 Gennat and his team met the investigating judge, the Vice-President of the Berlin Police, and the Mecklenburg Justice Minister von Reibnitz, and brought them up to date with the investigation. This was the breakthrough the Mecklenburg government had been waiting for. Their political exploitation of these new revelations was palpable. A press release was issued, reporting triumphantly that their investigations 'leave no room for doubt about the fact that Ewald Nogens was murdered by the subsequently executed Joseph Jakubowski'.[32] Not surprisingly, this failed to convince Jakubowski's former defence lawyer Otto Koch. He issued a statement of his own, declaring that his belief in his client's innocence remained unaffected by the new investigation. Fritz Nogens, he now maintained, was the guilty party. 'Who in all the world', he asked rhetorically, 'is going to believe these fairy-stories told by that sly Fritz Nogens, these gross and brazen lies about Jakubowski being the murderer? . . . The sequence of events which Fritz Nogens has described is not that of Jakubowski's deed but his own.'[33] The press release, issued little more than a month before the Criminal Law Committee of the Reichstag met to debate the removal of the death penalty from the new Criminal Code, began to throw serious doubt on the case for Jakubowski none the less. It may well have influenced the views of some of the members. Meanwhile Gennat's interrogations continued. Fritz and August confirmed their confessions and added new details. On 16 September 1928, told that it would be the final interrogation session, their mother Elizabeth broke down weeping and confessed her involvement. Jakubowski had arranged for her to be away from the village during the

[30] Ibid., S 356, Bl. 20.   [31] Ibid., S 357, 172–9.

[32] Ibid., S 355, Bl. 199a–b: Veröffentlichung einer amtlichen Notiz über das bisherige Ergebnis der Voruntersuchung gegen August Nogens und Genossen.

[33] Ibid., S 356, Bl. 1: *Schönberger Tageblatt*, 15 Sept. 1928.

murder, but she had discussed the crime with him in advance and had been told about it afterwards.[34] Gennat had all three Nogenses repeat their confessions and got them to write their life-histories in prison, where they once more freely admitted to their involvement.[35] He took August and Fritz back to Palingen separately to repeat their confessons and re-enact the crime on the spot.[36] Frau Nogens (now remarried as Kähler) was recorded telling her new husband the truth, in front of prison officers. Gennat thought it unlikely that these confessions represented any kind of 'fall-back' position planned for the eventuality that the original, obviously agreed denials had to be abandoned. He was convinced that they represented the truth.[37]

How could Gennat account for the earlier, contradictory statements made by Jakubowski and the three Nogenses? And what of Kreutzfeldt and Blöcker, the two Palingen labourers whom almost all of the other suspects had at one time or another blamed for the murder? The Berlin detective concluded that a good deal of Jakubowski's testimony had been false. As the Pole's situation after the trial had begun to look serious, he had started blaming Kreutzfeldt and Blöcker. This was because he had not wanted to implicate any of the Nogenses in case they provided further details incriminating him.[38] But neither Kreutzfeldt nor Blöcker had an adequate motive for killing Ewald. Kreutzfeldt also had a cast-iron alibi—he had independent witnesses to testify that he had been out of the village, a long way away, on the day of the murder—while Blöcker's statements since the reopening of the case had been consistent and were evidently truthful.[39] August Nogens's later attempt to incriminate the two men had been made on the basis of his discovery while he was in prison of the attempt made by Jakubowski to fasten the blame on them, and could be disregarded.[40] Jakubowski, it seemed, was guilty after all. Even Steuding had had to admit that he had had by far the most obvious motive for killing young Ewald.[41] Athough he had fallen behind in his maintenance payments, there was some evidence to suggest that Jakubowski had done this in order to force the Guardianship Court to intervene and place the children in foster-care. But his citation before the court for the readjustment of his payments must have made it clear to him that this tactic was not working. Even at their original rate, the payments cannot have been a light matter for a poor labourer, and they were to have been increased very substantially on 10

[34] LHA Schwerin S 357, 168–72.

[35] Ibid., S 355, Bl. 106–7: Lebenslauf Fritz Nogens (eignhändig); ibid., S 356, Bl. 46–9: Lebenslauf Frau Kähler (verw. Nogens) (eigenhändig) and Lebenslauf August Nogens (eigenhändig).

[36] Ibid., Bl. 30: Lichtbilder aufgenommen anlässlich des Lokaltermins in Palingen am 16. 9. 1928.

[37] Ibid., S 357, 180–96; ibid., S 371, 71–2; also ibid., S 362: Urteil Nogens u. a., 17 June 1929, 21.

[38] Ibid., S 357, 218–38.   [39] Ibid. 241–50, 254–5; see also ibid., S 371 (Anklage), 76–8.

[40] Ibid., S 357, 251.   [41] Ibid., S 353, 359.

November.[42] Jakubowski's various marriage projects had run into difficulties because it was repeatedly made clear to him that his two children were a serious deterrent to any prospective wife.[43] It now emerged, moreover, that Ewald had not been Jakubowski's son at all; according to Elizabeth Nogens and to conversations reported by other witnesses, the boy was Ida Nogens's child by another man.[44] Jakobowski had officially acknowledged his fatherhood of Ewald only because this had been a condition of his marrying Ida and had helped him stay in Germany, thereby avoiding a return to the even more miserable poverty he faced in Poland.[45] Gennat was struck by the strong motives shared by Frau Nogens and Jakubowski: 'No fewer than eight children—including four aged between 18 months and $3\frac{1}{2}$—and on top of that, an idiot as well—populated Frau Nogens's dwelling. Low income—intention to marry on the part of both Frau Nogens and Jakubowski. . . .'[46] No one else had such powerful or compelling reasons for doing away with Ewald.

As soon as Ida Nogens, a hard-working woman who played her part in supporting her children, Ewald and Anni, was dead—so Gennat concluded—Jakubowski and Frau Nogens had begun a lengthy and increasingly desperate series of attempts to place them in foster-care.[47] When all these had failed, Jakubowski had offered material rewards to the Nogens brothers to help him murder one or other of the two children.[48] There was firm evidence that he had discussed poisoning Anni to get her out of the way before she fell ill in the autumn of 1924.[49] With Anni not expected to live, Jakubowski's attention had turned to Ewald. Here Gennat pointed out that it was impossible for Fritz and August to have carried out the murder on their own, on their mother's orders, since a third person was needed to make sure that the other children were not around to witness the crime, and various pieces of testimony pointed to the fact that this had been Jakubowski, since only he had actually been present in the vicinity the whole time on the day of the murder. Neither August nor Fritz had incriminated Jakubowski in his confession as a means of exculpating himself; they had already admitted their part in the murder, so there seemed no reason for

[42] See also the conclusion of the court in 1931 (ibid., S 365: Beschluss Landgericht-Strafkammer Neustrelitz, 18 Dec. 1931, 4–5).

[43] Ibid., S 371 (Anklage), 15–17, 81–3.

[44] Ibid. 3–4. The portrayal of Ida in Harych, *Im Namen*, as an innocent virgin raped by the local kulak is purely imaginary, since more than one male witness admitted to having had sexual intercourse with her, and there was considerable dispute as to who actually was the father of Ewald Nogens.

[45] LHA Schwerin S 357, 58.

[46] Ibid. 83. See also the detailed enumeration of evidence in ibid., S 371, 13–21.

[47] Ibid. 21–6, detailing approaches made to thirteen different people.

[48] Ibid., S 357, 84–116; LHA Schwerin S 371, 26–9.

[49] For Anni's illness, see ibid., S 362: Urteil Nogens u. a., 44. For the crucial 'poisoning conversation', see ibid., S 365: Beschluss Oberlandesgericht-Strafsenat Rostock, 31 Mar. 1932, 3.

mentioning Jakubowski unless it was simply the truth.[50] With Elizabeth Nogens's knowledge, Jakubowski had bribed August to kill the child and Fritz to dispose of the body. By dividing the task in this way, neither Fritz nor Jakubowski would have been absent from the village for long enough to cause comment, and August, having cycled over to Palingen in secret on a day on which everyone thought he was elsewhere, would have had time to return to Lankow to establish an alibi. Gennat thought it was likely that August had strangled the child with the belt from August's greatcoat. He considered Jakubowski to have been too weak a man, personally too kind to children, to have done the deed himself. Moreover, in his petitions and statements after the sentence, Jakubowski had always insisted he was innocent because he could not be condemned for a crime which he had not 'carried out'. As he had said to a prison warder shortly before his execution, he had only been the 'look-out' and was therefore not guilty of murder; a concept of guilt common among criminals and evidently shared by the Nogenses themselves.[51] August had got Ewald out of the house and, contrary to his confession, had, as planned, killed the child himself. The evidence for this lay both in August's cynical boast to the Communist deputy Hartmann that he regarded the notorious child-murderer Tiedemann as his role-model, and in reports of various conversations with his brother Fritz. After killing the child, August had carried the body to the wood under his greatcoat and given it to the waiting Fritz, who had then disposed of it. Satisfied that this was the truth, the Mecklenburg authorities brought the Nogenses to trial in the spring of 1929.

Things now looked very bad indeed for the supporters of Jakubowski.[52] The League for Human Rights, on behalf of Jakubowski's parents in Poland, who had been visited by the League's Secretary Kurt Grossmann, tried to rescue the situation by bringing a private prosecution against the Nogenses for having slandered Jakubowski's memory by accusing him of murder. As the League's lawyer Arthur Brandt told the judges and assessors at the Nogens trial:

What gives this trial its unique character, what is arousing the public interest to an unusual degree, what is causing everyone with a sense of justice to hold his breath, is above all the fact that the person whose guilt or innocence we are here attempting to establish has long since been dead, that the death sentence was carried out on him on the basis of circumstantial evidence, which everyone who possesses the merest spark of a feeling for justice is convinced is untenable.[53]

---

[50] LHA Schwerin S 357: Ermittlungssache gegen August Nogens und Genossen wegen Mordes, Schlussbericht des Kriminalrats Gennat, 268–72.

[51] Ibid., S 370: Gutachten des Sachverständigen Aschaffenburg, 11.

[52] Ibid., S 371: Nebenakten in der Strafsache gegen Nogens und Genossen wegen Mord, I: Handakten der Staatsanwaltschaft, Bd. 6, 1929 (Anklage).

[53] Ibid., S 370: Prozess Nogens in Neustrelitz: Plaidoyer des Vertreters der Nebenkläger Rechtsanwalt Dr Brandt, 1.

'The accused have two murders on their conscience', he went on, turning to the Nogenses: 'because they killed Jakubowski as well.'[54] Brandt was able to call the former Mecklenburg Justice Minister and the judges and prosecutors from Jakubowski's trial to the witness stand. Justice Minister Hustädt in particular, he said dramatically, had the Pole's blood on his hands after having refused him clemency. Hustädt and his colleague state prosecutor Müller for their part accused Steuding and the League for Human Rights of dragging their names through the mud for low political motives.[55] Hustädt added, in an involuntary confession of the anti-Slav prejudice that ran through the case, that it was not in the interests of the German Reich to complain of the unjust execution of a single Russian when so many German soldiers had died in Russia during the First World War.[56] It was shameful, said Brandt in his turn, that Müller had misused his office to obstruct the investigation of the case.[57] The motives of the League for Human Rights, which he represented along with Jakubowski's parents, were not political: 'What I feel is that the question of whether or not an innocent man has been executed is not a political matter; it is a question that concerns every decent person in the entire world.'[58] Alongside the detailed examination of the evidence, as this furious row revealed, much larger issues were clearly at stake.

On 17 June 1929, at the end of an elaborate trial, in which 125 witnesses and four medical experts were called upon to testify, the judges and lay assessors accepted the bulk of the prosecution's case against the Nogenses. But they also temporized on the key issue before them, the guilt or innocence of Jakubowski. It was not possible to say who had actually killed Ewald Nogens, nor could it be proven beyond doubt whose idea it was. No one could even know with any certainty why he had been killed. Indeed, the court concluded that the new evidence 'admits of some doubt, though in view of the incriminating evidence not a great deal of doubt, as to the guilt of Jakubowski in the opinion of the court'.[59] The court merely concluded that the murder had been planned and carried out by a number of people and that the three Nogenses were among them. All three of them, certified the expert psychiatric witness Professor Gustav Aschaffenburg, though at one and the same time 'primitive people' and accomplished liars, were fully responsible for their actions. August Nogens had been diagnosed as suffering from syphilis, but this had not affected his brain.[60] He was condemned to death for the murder of his nephew Ewald. His mother Elizabeth received six years' penitentiary for assisting in the crime and for perjuring herself. Fritz Nogens was sentenced to four years and one month in

[54] Ibid. 2.   [55] Ibid. 6.

[56] Ibid. 11. Jakubowski, though a Pole, had been a Russian subject during the war.   [57] Ibid. 9.

[58] Ibid. 10.   [59] Ibid., S 362: Urteil Nogens u. a., 43–4.

[60] Ibid., S 370: Gutachten des Sachverständigen Aschaffenburg (7 June 1929).

prison for perjury and assisting in a murder, and Heinrich Blöcker to one year and six months for perjury. Their eight months on remand were counted against these sentences, and Fritz was to be released after a year and five months on good conduct, against a further suspended sentence of five years.[61] Yet the case was far from over at this point. The Nogenses withdrew their confessions, though August reinstated his before finally retracting it again. This was obviously tactical; the original confessions have every appearance of having been sincere.[62] Having failed to exculpate themselves by this means, the three Nogenses then appealed against their convictions for murder and assisting in murder, and the case went to the German Supreme Court, which considered it on 23 December 1929. Here they had more luck. The Supreme Court found that the court in Neustrelitz had reached a self-contradictory and therefore faulty judgment. It had been necessary for it to decide on the guilt or innocence of Jakubowski in order to reach a legally defensible verdict on the guilt or innocence of the Nogenses and it had failed to do this. So the Supreme Court quashed the verdicts and referred the case back for a retrial.[63] The argument was a reasonable one in law. The Neustrelitz court had indeed contradicted itself. Politically, however, the Supreme Court's decision amounted to an open invitation to the Mecklenburg court to reaffirm Jakubowski's guilt. On 14 April 1930 the Neustrelitz court, this time with a different bench of judges and lay assessors, reached its decision after hearing the pleas and considering a small amount of fresh evidence. Jakubowski, it decided, had planned and carried out the murder and been present when Ewald Nogens was killed, though the actual strangling was probably carried out by August Nogens. The sentences were all upheld, and the subsequent appeals rejected by the Supreme Court on 19 September 1930 after Arthur Brandt's appeal on behalf of Jakubowski had also been thrown out.[64]

This proved to be more or less the end of the affair. August refused to appeal for clemency on the grounds that this would imply an admission of guilt. But the exasperated state prosecutor, while declaring that he had no doubts that August had been the actual murderer, and remarking in passing that he was also an 'almost pathological liar', accepted his lawyer's plea for mercy on the grounds that it was necessary to keep August in gaol for as long as it took for him to tell

[61] LHA Schwerin, S 372: Nebenakten in der Strafsache gegen Nogens und Genossen wegen Mord. II. Strafvollstreckung an den Arbeiter August Nogens, Bd. 20. 1929–31. Harych, *Im Namen*, 244–6, alters the dates and rearranges the facts, but gives the sentences correctly.

[62] LHA Schwerin S 363: Fritz Nogens, letter to his lawyer of 28 Dec. 1912 (copy); ibid., S 357, 180–96; ibid., S 371, 71–2; ibid., S 362: Urteil Nogens u. a., 17 June 1929, 21, ibid., S 363: police Vermerk, 3 Mar. 1930.

[63] GStA Berlin Rep. 84a/7792: *Vossische Zeitung*, 24 Dec. 1929; LHA Schwerin S 363: Reichsgericht Urteil, 23 Dec. 1929.

[64] Ibid., S 364: Urteil und Gründe 14 Apr. 1930, esp. 35–40; Reichsgericht Beschluss 22 Aug. 1930 and Urtei 1 19 Sept. 1930.

the complete truth about the affair. His sentence was commuted to life imprisonment on 24 October.[65] He remained in the penitentiary until a general review of prisoners was carried out during the war. Ascertaining that he had been convicted in 1925 of sexual intercourse with a minor (his sister), as well as of murdering another child (his nephew Ewald), the Reich Ministry of Justice decided that he was irredeemably and hereditarily antisocial. 'His father was a drinker and hanged himself. The oldest brother Wilhelm was a criminal with numerous convictions. The mother and sister were morally depraved. Any respect for morality, justice, and law must be lacking in August Nogens.' He was transferred to the concentration camp in Neuengamme on 23 June 1943, where he doubtless perished.[66] August's mother Elizabeth continued to protest her innocence and to throw the blame on Blöcker and Kreutzfeldt, as well as on Jakubowski.[67] She did not complete her prison sentence, however, for she died of jaundice on 5 November 1932, before she had served out her time.[68] Fritz Nogens was released from prison on the completion of his sentence on 17 June 1931. Ten days later, he changed his name to escape the notoriety attaching to the Nogenses by this time.[69] On 16 June 1936 he wrote to the authorities. His suspended sentence had come to an end, he said, and he enclosed certificates of good conduct from the local authorities in the village where he now lived. He did not, he said, want enquiries into his conduct from the authorities in Neustrelitz because this would lead to 'the withdrawal of the trust which our parish has shown in me, and this would put my family life at risk. I am', he added proudly, 'parish representative of the German Labour Front.'[70]

Kurt Grossmann, the Secretary of the League for Human Rights, continued to maintain that the Nogens family had organized and carried out the murder and put the blame on Jakubowski, in whose innocence he firmly continued to believe.[71] The League's lawyer Arthur Brandt continued to pursue the project of a separate retrial for Jakubowski through 1931, arguing once more that Paul Kreutzfeldt had been the originator of the murder plan. His application was rejected on 18 December 1931, however, as was his appeal against this decision on

---

[65] Ibid. S 372: Nebenakten in der Strafsache gegen Nogens und Genossen wegen Mord. II. Strafvollstreckung an den Arbeiter August Nogens. Bd. 20. 1929–31; ibid., S 364: Rechtsanwalt Müller to Innenministerium, Abteilung für die Justiz, 17 Oct. 1930, and Oberstaatsanwalt Neustrelitz to Innenministerium, Abteilung für die Justiz, 20 Oct. 1930.

[66] Ibid., S 364: notes of 11 Dec. 1942, and 25 June 1943.

[67] Ibid., S 364: Vernehmung Elizabeth Nogens, 25 June 1931.

[68] Ibid., S 364: Direktor Landeesstrafanstalt Strelitz-Alt to Oberstaatsanwalt Neustrelitz 9 Nov. 1932.

[69] Ibid.: Namensverleihung (copy), 16 July 1931.

[70] Ibid., S 373: Nebenakten in der Strafsache gegen Nogens und Genossen wegen Mord. II. Strafvollstreckung gegen Fritz Nogens, Bd. 21, 1929–36.

[71] Ibid., S 356, Bl. 73: Grossmann to Gennat, 10 Oct. 1928 (copy). See also Grossmann, *Ossietzky*, 154–5.

29 March 1932.[72] Whatever the facts were, the Jakubowski case had now become a litmus test for attitudes to capital punishment in Germany. The League for Human Rights, the Communist Party, and the abolitionist movement in general were no more likely to be persuaded of Jakubowski's guilt than their opponents were of his innocence, no matter how much fresh evidence came to light. To the partisans of Jakubowski, the case seemed to symbolize the dominance of conservative, racist values in the Weimar judicial system, the closing of the Establishment's ranks when it was accused of a miscarriage of justice, and the backwardness of feudal or semi-feudal communities in the north German countryside. To their opponents, the abolitionists seemed to be deliberately undermining the rule of law in an attempt to overthrow the existing social and legal order. The Jakubowski issue remained controversial even after the Second World War, as the publication of Theo Harych's book and the subsequent film about the case showed. Now, however, after the opening of the files, the historian is better placed to attempt a dispassionate judgement.

Was Jakubowski wrongly executed? The question cannot be answered without qualification. For opponents of the death penalty, all executions are wrongful executions. For its supporters, all executions, for murder at least, if not for other crimes, are rightful executions. Nevertheless, the very full evidence collected by Ernst Gennat, and recently made available to historians by the Mecklenburg state archives, strongly suggests that Jakubowski was guilty, along with the Nogens brothers and their mother, of Ewald Nogens's murder. Under the German Criminal Code in effect at the time, the sentence of death was therefore legally justified.[73] Jakubowski's surviving letters to his lawyer from prison, outlining his case for a retrial, show him to have been an intelligent man with a good command of detail, quite capable of such a deed, and also, incidentally, with a reasonable though rather ungrammatical knowledge of German.[74] Yet supporters of his cause were right to take exception to the fact that clemency had not been granted by the Mecklenburg government. Jakubowski's trial and execution came at a time when capital punishment was rapidly on the decline. In other parts of Germany, only serial killers and mass murderers were being executed in 1926. The penal practice of the later 1920s dictated that a commonplace murder would not have been punished by death, especially not where the murderer had been

[72] LHA Schwerin S 365: Brandt to Landgericht Neustrelitz, 1 Dec. 1931; Landgericht-Strafkammer Beschluss, 18 Dec. 1931; ibid.: Beschluss Oberlandesgericht Strafsenat Rostock, 29 Mar. 1932.

[73] Ibid., S 362: Urteil Nogens u. a., 41.

[74] Ibid., S 361: copies of Jakubowski's letters to Koch, Aug. 1925–Jan. 1926. The conclusion, reached in a later court case, that Jakubowski's German was weak, is difficult to sustain. The letters do not seem to have been written with anybody's help. See ibid., S 365: Landgericht-Strafkammer Beschluss, 18 Dec. 1931, 3. For evidence of Jakubowski's ability to follow the proceedings at his trial, and the concessions made to him in view of the fact that German was not his first language, see ibid., S 370: Vernehmung des Zeugen Amtsgerichtsrat Dr. Horn am 3. Juni 1929, 4.

convicted in the absence of a confession, on the basis of evidence that seemed less than overwhelmingly convincing and which, as it turned out later, only covered a small part of a much more complex truth. Had the involvement of the Nogenses been known at the time of Jakubowski's trial and condemnation, it is probable that he would have been reprieved, since, although he planned and organized the murder, it was unclear who struck the fatal blow, and in any case the Mecklenburg authorities would have hesitated before executing both him and August Nogens together, and they could not have treated them unequally. In 1930 the Mecklenburg authorities had no hesitation in granting clemency to August Nogens. It was only the particular political circumstances of Mecklenburg in 1925–6, under a government dominated by the Nationalists, that denied Jakubowski the reprieve that his lawyers and supporters so confidently expected. That, and the fact that he was Polish. Political and racial factors were always prominent among the reasons why particular offenders were executed at various junctures in modern German history. It was Jakubowski's misfortune that they operated against him in 1926. It was the retentionists' misfortune that the gross errors committed in his prosecution and trial came to light in 1928. And it was the abolitionists' misfortune that his guilt was reaffirmed so convincingly in the conviction of his accomplices in 1929–30. For by the end of the Jakubowski trials the political atmosphere had changed once more, and politicians and jurists were able to use the final verdicts in the case to assert that, since Jakubowski had not been unjustly executed after all, the German judicial system had yet to be shown to have sent an offender to the block by mistake. Thus the turnaround in the Jakubowski case proved the harbinger of a general political swing back in favour of capital punishment towards the end of Weimar, as we shall now see.

c. An Execution in Württemberg

The changed political circumstances of 1930 made it easier for those federated states which had been prevented from carrying out executions by Koch-Weser to resume their work. While the reform of the Criminal Code still seemed a possibility, which is to say for most of 1929, they hesitated. But by 1930 it was clear that the attempt to redraft the Code had failed. Conservative state governments now felt able to go ahead with the reintroduction of capital punishment. The first state to break ranks was Württemberg. At this time, the south German state was governed by a centre-right coalition goverment in which the Nationalists played a leading role.[75] The State President (or head of the state government),

Eugen Bolz, was a Catholic Centre politician who had previously served as Württemberg's Justice Minister and Minister of the Interior. The cabinet was clearly strongly in favour of the death penalty and urged Bolz to take a tough line in the case of Julius Zell, from Zweifelsberg, a 25-year-old peasant farmer convicted of parricide. Zell had lived alone with his 65-year-old father and shot him in the back, without warning or provocation, because he thought the old man would not accept his taking a wife to live in the family home.[76] Every single legal instance, up to the Reich Supreme Court, rejected Zell's appeals against the death sentence, while all the official submissions in the clemency procedure recommended the rejection of Zell's plea for mercy. Nevertheless, the political pressures on the State President to grant a reprieve were considerable. It was in the teeth of considerable national disapproval that he went ahead and denied it to the condemned man.

There seems little doubt that Bolz wanted to assert his independence from the Reich government, and that the issue of capital punishment offered a good symbolic opportunity for doing this. On the other hand, there is little doubt either that he was a man of sincere convictions who believed in what he was doing. During the Third Reich, indeed, he gravitated towards the conservative-nationalist resistance movement and was eventually executed on 23 January 1945, having agreed to serve in the government planned by Carl Goerdeler for the aftermath of the Bomb Plot against Hitler in July 1944.[77] On 16 June 1930 he sanctioned Zell's execution. Parricide evidently still counted as an offence of an exceptionally heinous nature, and the Württemberg government saw no grounds for a reprieve. In an official declaration, it later said it had noted the Koch-Weser circular and discussed whether or not to commute the sentence on this ground. The circular, complained the leading Nationalist in the cabinet, was 'totally wrong'.[78] The Württemberg cabinet declared:

In principle it is necessary to insist on the fact that death is still the legal penalty for murder, and that before the legislator has decided on its retention or abolition, no one has the right to demand of those who have the power of clemency that they should refrain from carrying out the legal punishment even though the person and deed of the condemned offer no grounds for granting a reprieve.[79]

The Criminal Law Committee of the Reichstag formally requested the Reich government to intervene and prevent the execution. Bolz's action was wrong, it

[76] BA Potsdam RJM 6098, Bl. 138: *Berliner Tageblatt*, 21 June 1930.

[77] Joachim Köhler, *Christentum und Politik. Dokumente des Widerstands. Zum 40. Jahrestag der Hinrichtung des Zentrumspolitikers und Staatspräsidenten Eugen Bolz am 23. Januar 1945* (Sigmaringen, 1985).

[78] HStA Stuttgart E130b Bü 153: Auszug aus der Niederschrift über die Sitzung des Staatsministeriums am Montag, den 16. Juni 1930, Vormittags 9 Uhr.

[79] GLA Karlsruhe 234/6611: *Deutsches Volksblatt* (Stuttgart), 15 July 1930.

said, because the death penalty might soon be abolished with the reform of the Criminal Code. The Württemberg government knew, of course, that such a reform was now extremely unlikely. Ever optimistic, all the same, the Criminal Law Committee of the Reichstag voted by fifteen votes to ten to ask the Reich government to intervene to prevent any more executions taking place in this way.[80] Viktor Bredt, the Reich Minister of Justice at this time, added his voice to the chorus, asking for a stay of execution while at the same time making it clear that he no longer felt bound by Koch-Weser's declaration of two years before.[81] The newspapers headlined the story excitedly with slogans such as 'Reichstag against Württemberg'.[82] But the Württemberg cabinet predictably insisted that the Reich had no right to interfere 'in the exercise of the right of clemency by the responsible agencies in the federated states'.[83] A last-minute petitioning campaign by the Democrats, the Social Democrats, the German Peace Society, the Women's International League for Peace and Freedom, and other abolitionist associations had no effect.[84] Zell was guillotined in the prison yard at Ravensburg on 21 June 1930, the first person to suffer capital punishment in Germany for more than two years.[85]

Zell's execution aroused widespread protests, not least because one newspaper report depicted him being dragged to the guillotine 'more dead than alive' (although according to the Württemberg government he was 'calm and resolute').[86] A large crowd gathered outside the prison on the morning of the execution.[87] An eyewitness report sold to a local news agency described the condemned man's last night and final meal in the usual detail, but noted only that he was rather pale as he knelt down to pray, kissed the crucifix, and gave himself up to the executioner.[88] Bolz was slated in the liberal and socialist press for his particularist zeal in going ahead with an execution in Württemberg while the issue of capital punishment was still undecided at the Reich level.[89] The

[80] BA Potsdam RJM 6098, Bl. 140: *Vorwärts*, 21 June 1930; ibid., Bl. 148: *Frankfurter Zeitung*, 22 June 1930; GLA Karlsruhe 234/6611: *Vorwärts*, 20 June 1930.

[81] HStA Stuttgart E130b Bü 153: Bredt to Württ. Staatsministerium, telegram, 20 June 1930; ibid., Bü 886: *Berliner Tageblatt*, 21 June 1930.

[82] Ibid.: *Vorwärts*, 21 June 1930.

[83] Ibid., Bü 153: notes for the press, Staatsministerium 28 July 1930; and *Berliner Büro für die Zentrumspresse*, 21 June 1930.

[84] Telegrams (copies) in HStA Stuttgart E130b Bü 153.

[85] Ibid.: 'Verschiedenes—Vom Oberland, 23. Juni' (press clipping, no source given).

[86] BA Potsdam RJM 6098, Bl. 152: *Die Welt am Abend*, 23 June 1930; GLA Karlsruhe 234/6611: *Deutsches Volksblatt* (Stuttgart) 15 July 1930; HStA Stuttgart E130b Bü 153: Pressestelle des Staatsministeriums, notes of 25 July 1930.

[87] HStA Stuttgart E130b Bü 153: typed and handwritten notes 'Zu Nr. 4780', 21 June 1930.

[88] Ibid.: *Süddeutsches Correspondenz-Bureau; württembergische Landeskorrespondenz*, 1461, Ravensburg, 22/6.

[89] Ibid.: *Deutsches Volksblatt*, 23 June 1930, reporting comments in the *Schwäbische Tagwacht* and *Frankfurter Zeitung*.

critics accused him of sacrificing Zell to 'a demonstration against the Reichstag'.[90] It did not say much for the idea of legal unity across the nation if murderers were punished by death in Württemberg but not elsewhere.[91] Even the Centre Party's news agency in Berlin regretted the fact that the case 'shows us how little we are one people'. It went on:

The Criminal Law Committee and the Reich Minister of Justice ask Württemberg's Head of State to prevent the execution. It goes ahead all the same because the State President in Stuttgart takes a different view. Was the execution of the murderer Zell such an urgent matter that it could not in God's name have been postponed for a few days longer? Would it not have been an idea, in view of the intervention of the Reich and of several political parties, at least to have made such a controversial act, upon which a human life depended, and which has shocked the German people most deeply, the subject of discussion between Stuttgart and Berlin? At this point the uncomprehending public is simply confronted with the execution of a fateful order of state, with which certainly only a minority will sympathize. Simple political calculation should have stopped the Württemberg government from going ahead with its high-handed action.[92]

Public opinion, if gauged by press reaction, was indeed uncomprehending in the face of the action of the Württemberg authorities.[93] Partly for this reason, therefore, Zell's execution had no immediate further effect. It was widely recognized as an isolated incident with no wider implications for the fate of capital punishment in the Reich as a whole. Controversy over Zell's execution, and above all over the clash it signified between Berlin and the federated states, perhaps also helped dissuade other state governments from repeating the experiment tried in Württemberg. It was certainly difficult for them to sanction executions unless they could argue, along the lines used by Bismarck to support the reintroduction of capital punishment in Prussia in 1878 and subsequently, that the crime concerned was so exceptional that it fell completely outside the normal range of capital offences for which clemency was by now being routinely granted. Zell thus remained the only one out of forty-six people condemned to death in Germany in 1930 to be executed.[94] All the others had their sentences commuted to life imprisonment.

[90] HStA Stuttgart E130b Bü 866: *Berliner Tageblatt*, 21 June 1930.

[91] GLA Karlsruhe 234/6611: *Frankfurter Zeitung*, 21 June 1930; ibid.: *Vossische Zeitung*, 22 June 1930; HStA Stuttgart E130b Bü 886: *Württemberger Zeitung*, 21 June 1930.

[92] Ibid., Bü 153: *Berliner Büro für die Zentrumspresse*, 21 June 1930.

[93] Ibid., Bü 886, for a sample of opinion; see HStA Munich MA 101130 for more extracts from the press.

[94] The number was 43 according to the *Statistisches Jahrbuch für das deutsche Reich 1933*, 535. For the figure of 46, see BA Potsdam RJM 5665, Bl. 274: RJM to Oberstaatsanwalt Moencke, Leipzig, 10 Sept. 1932.

d. The 'Düsseldorf Vampire'

Zell's crime, though serious, had not been of a nature to arouse any particular interest among the media for its own sake. Part of the reason for the widespread disapproval of his execution was the fact that he did not seem to be more deserving of death than did any of the other forty-five murderers condemned in Germany that year. It needed a really exceptional murder case for the climate to change. Just such a case arose at the beginning of 1931 with the arrest of Peter Kürten, the 'Düsseldorf vampire', for nine murders and seven attempted murders, all committed in Düsseldorf and the surrounding area in the same year, 1929, under circumstances so gruesome as to cause a nation-wide sensation.[95] Kürten had eventually been arrested after being recognized by a woman whom he had raped, but neglected to murder. On his arrest, he is said to have exclaimed to the police: 'What a pity that I've been arrested just at this point! The really amazing part was still to come! I'd planned to kill two people a day!'[96] Well before his arrest, there had been a growing public outcry in Düsseldorf about the rising number of unsolved murders in the town; the Communist Party had begun a campaign against what it saw as the inactivity of the local police force in the matter; a reward of 10,000 marks had been offered to anyone giving information leading to the culprit's arrest; the great Berlin detective Ernst Gennat had been dispatched to Düsseldorf to help clear the matter up;[97] and even the thriller writer Edgar Wallace had offered his advice to the local police.[98] Following on extensive speculation about the nature of the murders, fuelled by mocking letters to the press written by Kürten himself, the arrest of the culprit had unleashed a pack of voracious newshounds onto the unprepared flock of legal officials in the Rhineland city. The media build-up to Kürten's trial was enormous, with background features of several pages appearing in the newspapers day after day in the weeks before it began. So massive was the public interest, so much difficulty did the police and the judicial authorities experience in satisfying it within the normal parameters of crime and court reporting, daily press conferences, and official briefings, that relations between the press and the authorities quickly deteriorated, when enterprising reporters tracked down key witnesses and sub-

[95] Ibid., RJM 6099, Bl. 4: Walter Kiaulehn, article in *BZ am Montag*, 23 Apr. 1931.

[96] HStA Düsseldorf Rep. 17/714: *Mittag*, 16 May [i.e. April] 1931; ibid. 715: *Oberhessische Zeitung*, 17 Apr. 1931.

[97] Ibid. 719: Niederschrift uber die am 2. Dezember 1929, Nachmittags 5 Uhr, stattgefundene Besprechung (Abschrift, Düsseldorf, den 3. 12. 1929); ibid.: Polizeipräsident Düsseldorf, 25 Nov. 1929, betr. Grosse Anfrage der kommunistischen Abgeordneten des Preussischen Landtages. See also ibid. 538, Bl. 20: Gennat Aktenvermerk, 7 Nov. 1929, and the numerous letters of advice from Gennat to the local police in the same file.

[98] Ibid. 538 Bl. 189: *Extrablatt* (Berlin), n.d.

jected them to lengthy interviews—even, in some cases, before the police had had a chance to talk to them properly.[99] As soon as they could, therefore, the police and the courts moved to get the situation under control.

The judicial administration in Düsseldorf was concerned that the sexual details in the case would be 'catastrophic' for 'young people still in the course of growing up' if they were fully reported in the press, and held consultations with media representatives to ensure both that the reporters admitted to the courtroom confined themselves to 'restrained reporting' and that the 'worst excesses' of the 'big-city press' would be quickly dealt with by the appropriate authorities elsewhere.[100] As a result of attending a conference called by the court press office before the trial opened, the 'responsible press' agreed up to a point, carrying lengthy articles by specialists reassuring their readers that no harm would be done to young people by their reporting of the case.[101] During the trial, it emerged that the police and judicial authorities had their own, particular ideas about how 'responsibility' should be interpreted: for the first occasion on which the judge threatened to close the proceedings to the press was when the accused man began a bitter and detailed denunciation of the treatment he had received at the hands of the Prussian prison service during his youth.[102] On other occasions, the public and a good part of the press were excluded and those present warned not to make the more lurid sexual details of the evidence public. This did not stop some papers from reporting at least some of them, especially after Wolff's news agency broke the agreement with the authorities and transmitted them to newspapers all over the country.[103] But much of the evidence was indeed left out of the press reports, particularly the precise physical descriptions supplied by the pathologists' reports and the medical evidence of the wounds suffered by the victims. The authorities pronounced themselves satisfied with the press's behaviour during the trial, and praised the editorial interventions that had reduced the purpler passages penned by newspaper reporters in the courtroom to a level of grey uniformity on the page. Worried about possible censorship measures being introduced after massive official criticism of its behaviour in one or two earlier major cases, the press had censored itself. The trial itself had been conducted quietly and with dignity, with no major clashes between prosecution and defence. And nobody had had any sympathy at all with the defendant.[104]

[99] HStA Düsseldorf Rep. 17/720: Bericht über 'Kürtenprozess und Presse' (Justizpressestelle Düsseldorf 1931), Bl. 5.

[100] StA Bremen 4, 89/1.9: Justizpressestelle Düsseldorf to Leiter der Justizpressestellen im Reich, 19 Mar. 1931.

[101] HStA Düsseldorf Rep. 17/727: 'Für Hochschule und Jugend. Der Fall Kürten: Ein Sensationsprozess in Sicht', *Frankfurter Zeitung*, 13 Apr. 1931.

[102] Ibid. 712: *Die Freiheit*, 13 Apr. 1931.

[103] Ibid. 720: Bericht über 'Kürtenprozess und Presse' (Justizpressestelle Düsseldorf 1931), Bl. 57.

[104] Ibid., Bl. 65–72.

Nevertheless, newspapers that acted 'responsibly', by reporting that 'the method with which he tortured his victims to death was so repulsive and horrific that it is impossible to recount',[105] titillated their readers almost as much as they would have done by actually providing descriptions in sober factual detail. It was already apparent before the proceedings began that Kürten's trial would be one of the media events of the year. It lasted for a total of eleven days and was held in a specially equipped courtroom, with three hundred witnesses summoned to the box, and a special telephone exchange installed for reporters to phone their stories direct to their editors, wherever they might be. The trial was in itself, as one newspaper noted, a 'huge demonstration' in favour of the death penalty.[106] Long before it began, the newspapers were unanimous in declaring Kürten guilty.[107] Crowds gathered outside the court and lined the streets along which the accused man was driven to and from the prison; and press reports made it clear that their overwhelming view was that Kürten should be quickly dispatched.[108] Touts queued outside the court-house every night in order to be sure of obtaining entry cards to sell for the following day's proceedings.[109] Reporters appeared from abroad and offered to buy translations of the relevant police documents for substantial sums of money.[110] The press carried verbatim accounts of the proceedings every day, complete with photographs and line drawings of the various figures in the trial and comments by observers. Banner headlines drew the public's attention to the latest 'sensational development' or 'dramatic incident' in the trial. For over a week, Germany's newspapers were dominated by the story: a public drama of crime and retribution was unfolding in the mass media.

Kürten himself was centre-stage throughout. The fascination of the press with his appearance and his personality seemingly knew no bounds. As the proceedings began, one reporter complained

that the mass murderer is disappointing to look at. His face is round and rosy. Hardly a wrinkle or a furrow. No trace of pleasure and none of suffering. This 47-year-old had no difficulty in making himself look ten years younger to his lady-friends when the brass band at the parish fair struck up for the *danse macabre*.[111]

Another newspaper noted 'how little of this man stands written in his face'. The reporter thought 'that this man would in no way stand out in a group of petty-bourgeois'.[112] Married to an unsuspecting wife, and employed for years in a regular job, Kürten was outwardly a paragon of respectability despite his long

[105] Ibid. 713: *Hamburger Echo*, 15 Apr. 1931. [106] BA Potsdam RJM 6099, Bl. 78.
[107] HStA Düsseldorf Rep. 17/727, Bl. 5: *Kölnische Zeitung*, 7 Jan. 1931.
[108] Ibid. 712, Bl. 1: *Kölner Tageblatt*, 13 Apr. 1931.
[109] Ibid. 717: *Kölnische Volkszeitung*, 21 Apr. 1931.
[110] Ibid. 720: Bericht über 'Kürtenprozess und Presse' (Justizpressestelle Düsseldorf 1931), Bl. 5.
[111] Ibid. 727, Bl. 7: *Hamburger Anzeiger*, 14 Apr. 1931.
[112] Ibid., Bl. 9: *Frankfurter Zeitung*, 25 Apr. 1931.

record of criminal convictions.[113] All the same, the disappointment of the media at his harmless appearance was artificial, a literary conceit. The theme of the mass murderer in the innocent guise of the petty-bourgeois ran through much of the trial reporting. Not all the newspapers were happy with the attention given to these points. As one critical voice complained, bemoaning the effect the publicity given to Kürten would have on the young:

> The reports are once more composed at epic length, with corresponding embellishments. In the centre: the 'hero', Kürten. At the outset it is reported that he appears clean-shaven before the judges' bench, that he has an upright figure that betrays no hint of the rigours of his imprisonment on remand, that his hair is well-groomed, that even the hair-oil which many other mortals are forced to do without in these hard times does not appear to be lacking. Externally, therefore, quite the gentleman![114]

Conventional though his appearance might have been, in every other respect Kürten more than met the media's desire for sensational material. He described his crimes in minute and lurid detail, winning the mock-reluctant praise of a grateful press for his astonishing feats of exact memory.[115] More than any previous trial, even that of Fritz Haarmann or the Nogenses, the Kürten case grabbed the nation's attention and focused it on the issue of capital punishment in the most dramatic possible way.

One of ten children born into a poor working-class family, Peter Kürten, a 47-year-old journeyman mason, had begun his life of crime at a tender age. During the trial he claimed to have drowned two of his playmates in a river when he was only 8 years old. Well before the First World War, he became a professional burglar, specializing in robberies of pubs and bars, for which he was convicted dozens of times and spent a total of over twenty-two years in prison. It was while he was engaged in such a crime that he committed his first generally acknowledged murder, in 1913, when, for no obvious reason, he strangled then stabbed an 11-year-old girl he found asleep in one of the bedrooms in an inn that he was robbing.[116] He soon began to attack women and young girls, and occasionally men too, more frequently. From 1913, he spent a good deal of time in prison, and in the early and mid-1920s he seems to have lived a quieter life, got married (to a woman a few years older than himself), found two regular mistresses, and obtained a regular job. From 1926, when domestic violence ended his relationship with his two mistresses, he began to find sexual release through watching the fear and panic of the victims of a series of acts of arson which he committed up to early 1929, twenty-seven in all, according to the court.[117] On emerging from an

---

[113] HStA Düsseldorf Rep. 17/716: *Solinger Tageblatt*, 18 Apr. 1931.
[114] Ibid. 714: *Schlesische Landeszeitung*, 15 Apr. 1931.
[115] Ibid. 727, Bl. 8: *Kölnische Zeitung*, 14 Apr. 1931.
[116] Ibid. 712, Bl. 1: *Kölner Tageblatt*, 13 Apr. 1931.   [117] Ibid. 700, Bl. 25–6.

eight-month prison sentence in October 1928, he entered on the last, most radical phase of his criminal career. 'I hoped to get from this', he confessed, 'a sadistic release of tension, which indeed then happened.'[118] He would deliberately make the acquaintance of his victims and befriend them, sometimes going to a good deal of trouble to strike up a relationship. Then, as 'the excitement' began to overcome him, as he said, he stabbed them. What he wanted, he confessed, was only to see blood; whether his victims lived or died was a matter of secondary importance, and some of them, indeed, did survive the experience. Once he hit a major artery and the blood began to spurt, Kürten put his lips to the wound and drank it as it pulsed out. Only then, finally, could he achieve the orgasmic release which he sought.[119]

Kürten, soon dubbed 'the Düsseldorf vampire' in popular parlance, was generally believed to have been completely indiscriminate in his choice of victims; all he wanted was to see blood, and taste it,[120] and it scarcely mattered whose it was:

Kürten explains . . . that, driven by his disposition, he very frequently wandered about in lonely parts without any particular plan, looking for any victim that might come along. Sometimes his condition was such that he also attacked animals in order to kill them, just as he did not mind at all whether his victims were men or women, old or young people, or even children.[121]

In fact, only two of his victims, Rudolf Scheer and Heinrich Kornblum (who survived), were male, although he most probably committed other acts of violence against men, without the cases ever coming to court. It was only when he was desperate for blood that he attacked animals, as in the incident of November 1929, when he cut the throat of a swan in Düsseldorf's town park to quench his blood-thirst.[122] In general, Kürten undoubtedly preferred girls, mainly domestic servants, occasionally prostitutes.[123] He commonly had sexual intercourse with his victims, some of them as young as 5 years of age, and in some cases inflicted deep wounds not only in their throat and body, but also in their sexual organs; many of them died from loss of blood rather than from internal damage.[124] Kürten also set light to the corpses of some of his victims, again getting sexual gratification from the act.[125] Few of these details were reported in the press. Kürten himself claimed early in the trial that the murders he

---

[118] Ibid. 712, Bl. 3: *Düsseldorfer Stadt-Anzeiger*, 14 Apr. 1931.
[119] Ibid. 713: *Hamburgischer Correspondent*, 15 Apr. 1931; ibid. 700, Bl. 44.
[120] Ibid. 713: *Neue Arbeiterzeitung* (Hanover), 16 Apr. 1931.
[121] Ibid. 712, Bl. 10: *Vereinigte Zeitungen 'Der Niederrhein'*, 14 Apr. 1931.
[122] Ibid. 717: *Solinger Tageblatt*, 21 Apr. 1931; ibid. 700, Bl. 18; ibid. 728, Bl. 95.
[123] Ibid. 712, Bl. 10: *Vereinigte Zeitungen 'Der Niederrhein'*, 14 Apr. 1931; ibid. 700, Bl. 89.
[124] Ibid. 714: *Mittag*, 15 May [i.e. April] 1931; ibid. 700, Bl. 85–7.
[125] Ibid. 712, Bl. 1: *Kölner Tageblatt*, 13 Apr. 1931.

committed were his revenge on society for the cruelty he had experienced in prison.[126] But he contradicted this argument by also admitting that he had courted solitary confinement and incarceration in the dark in order to be able to indulge in his private sadistic fantasies more effectively. In the face of overwhelming evidence that the attacks had been of a sexual nature, he was forced to change his story, and blamed his sadistic sexuality on the bad influences to which he had been exposed in his youth. These included, he said, 'penny dreadfuls, and visits to the chamber of horrors in a wax museum', reading about Jack the Ripper, receiving beatings from his father, and participating from the age of 5 in acts of cruelty to animals carried out by an uncle, who was state knacker and dog-catcher in Mülheim and slaughtered dogs in his own home.[127] These confessions, whether or not they were true, fuelled the Weimar debate on censorship, which reached new heights in the immediate aftermath of the trial, with the release of Fritz Lang's celebrated film *M*.[128]

When Lang's film was first shown in May 1931, its appearance was greeted in the press, in the light of the Kürten case, as a plea 'for capital punishment'.[129] One of the earliest of the talkies, *M* was originally going to be called *Mörder unter uns* (*Murderers amongst Us*). Set in Berlin, the film was scripted before Kürten's arrest, and was based on the general phenomenon of the serial killer rather than on the Kürten case as such.[130] The film begins with the disappearance of Elsie, a young child, whose body is subsequently discovered, the victim of a brutal sex attack. As other murders take place, it becomes clear that a serial killer is at large. The city is plunged into a state of terror, suspicion is everywhere, and the police mount a massive manhunt for the murderer. So pervasive does the police presence become that the Berlin underworld is seriously disrupted in its everyday pursuit of normal crime. The organized criminals of the Berlin mafia, the notorious *Ringvereine*, decide to catch the murderer themselves. The two manhunts move in parallel, the police identifying the suspect as a former inmate of a lunatic asylum, and the underworld gang tracking him down to his lair with the aid of a blind beggar. The murderer, played by Peter Lorre, is dragged off to a disused factory and put through a mock trial in which the criminals act as prosecuting authority, judge, and jury, while providing the accused with an obviously crooked lawyer as his defender. Despite the lawyer's surprisingly eloquent pleading, they find the accused guilty and sentence him to death. As they rush towards him for the kill, the police burst in, arrest him, and take him off for a proper trial.

---

[126] HStA Düsseldorf Rep. 17/712, Bl. 3: *Düsseldorfer Stadt-Anzeiger*, 14 Apr. 1931.

[127] Ibid. 713: *Hamburger Echo*, 15 Apr. 1931.

[128] BA Potsdam RJM 6099, Bl. 50: *Vorwärts*, 13 May 1931. Roswitha Kaever and Elisabeth Lenk, *Leben und Wirken des Peter Kürten, genannt der Vampir von Düsseldorf* (Munich, 1974), prints the trial documents.   [129] GStA Berlin Rep. 84/7794: *8-Uhr Abendblatt*, 12 May 1931.

[130] Fritz Lang, *M: Protokoll* (Cinemathek, 3; Hamburg, 1983), 123–7.

M was packed with bold and daring images and sound effects: moving, comic, suspenseful, and intellectually challenging in turn. Its release during the Kürten case immediately made it the object of fierce political controversy. Many commentators took its final scene as a plea for Kürten to be executed; and the arguments which convinced the court of criminals on the cinema screen that he did not deserve to live were taken as arguments for capital punishment in reality.[131] Abolitionists were therefore quick to condemn the 'scandalous film "M" by Fritz Lang, which is designed to excite the sadistic urges of the viewers'.[132] It was condemned not least because the Kürten case had already sparked a lively debate about the possible corruption of the cinema, popular literature, and other branches of the entertainment media by the sensational reporting of the trial in the newspapers. Lang himself always denied that he had made the film in support of the death penalty, and indeed *M* shows many different sides of the argument. Throughout the proceedings, the film makes it clear that his murderer is in the grip of irrational forces far beyond his control. 'The spectres are always pursuing me', he shrieks at his underworld judges, '—unless I do it. And afterwards, standing before a poster, I read what I have done. Have I done this? But I don't know anything about it. I loathe it—I must—loathe it—must—I can't go on . . .'[133] As played by Peter Lorre, the murderer is a weak, pathetic, almost childish creature who is not responsible for his own actions. The underworld judges themselves are, it is made clear, not without a good deal of blood on their own hands. Yet it is difficult to see how the film could in the circumstances of the time have been taken as anything other than a powerful plea for Kürten to be executed. The murderer's crime, in killing innocent young children and destroying the family lives of the honest poor, is portrayed as being different in kind and degree from that of the mafia bosses, who at least (it is implied) choose responsible adults as their victims. And among the assembled people who shout down the defence attorney and demand the murderer's execution, the loudest and most passionate voices are those of the mothers of the victims, not criminals but ordinary, decent working-class women whom he has robbed of what little happiness they formerly possessed. Like so many of those who supported the death penalty under the Weimar Republic, *M* gave the last word to the people. It was their opinion that was decisive in weighing the scales of justice in favour of death.

One of the most telling arguments in the film is the fact that the murderer was previously released from a lunatic asylum as cured of his derangement. Surely, reason his accusers, this is exactly what will happen again if he is allowed to plead

[131] For a brief analysis of Lang's film in its contemporary context, see Siegfried Kracauer, *From Caligari to Hitler: A Psychological History of the German Film* (Princeton, 1947), 219–22.

[132] BA Potsdam 61 Re 1/1773, 60: *Berliner Tageblatt*, 13 May 1931.

[133] Kracauer, *From Caligari*, 221. The account in Tatar, *Lustmord*, 153–72, is unconvincing.

insanity. A few years in the asylum, then if he behaves himself, or falls under the terms of an amnesty, he will be released to wreak havoc upon the city and its children once again. In taking this line, which is accepted by the assembled underworld crowd, the film was countering the most powerful point made by the abolitionists against Kürten's execution, namely that he was insane and therefore not responsible for his actions. As in the Haarmann case, the suggestion that the offender was 'degenerate' implied to many that there would be no further point in keeping him alive:

That a degenerate person of such a format must never enter society again, that there must never even be the faintest possibility of this occurring, is an imperative demand of the whole human community. In comparison to this, debates about how a man could develop into a murderer like this are of only secondary importance.[134]

The three expert witnesses called to testify on Kürten's mental state all agreed that he was not mentally ill. There were no signs of epilepsy or brain damage. One expert considered that his sadism was learned rather than inherited and noted that there was no history of mental illness in his family. The drunkenness and violence of his father, who had been convicted in 1897 of incest with his eldest daughter, were taken by another medical report as evidence that Kürten's 'psychopathic tendency ... which to a degree has been passed on to Kürten by inheritance through a chain of ancestors'.[135] But all the expert witnesses agreed that Kürten was an intelligent man who could legitimately be held responsible for his actions. He had gone for lengthy periods without committing any murders, and had kept his violent impulses to a large extent in check in a number of his sexual relationships with women. He had begun his career of vampirism only at a fairly advanced age, and with the express intention of gaining a more intense sexual satisfaction than he had obtained through his arson campaign, or through his affairs. The fact that in a number of cases he had broken off his attack on a victim and fled when disturbed in the act showed that he had his wits about him and was fully conscious of what he was doing. He might be a 'psychopath', suffering from 'callousness and emotional impoverishment, ruthless egotism, a desire for revenge, a pronounced tendency to cruelty, and a high degree of moral and ethical inferiority', but he was not insane. It was clear, the psychiatrists concluded, that Peter Kürten 'cannot have been acting under an irresistible compulsion'.[136] After all, he was not an otherwise normal person whose balance of mind had been suddenly disturbed at the moment of the offence. This was

---

[134] HStA Düsseldorf Rep. 17/714: *Mittag*, 15 May [i.e. April] 1931.
[135] Ibid. 718: *Düsseldorfer Stadt-Anzeiger*, 21 Apr. 1931. See also ibid. 700, Bl. 5–7.
[136] Ibid., Bl. 156–7; ibid. 731 Bl. 244–70; ibid. 730, Bl. 236–93; ibid. 728, Bl. 250–80.

enough to ensure that he qualified as fit to stand trial under the rather narrow terms of Paragraph 51 of the Criminal Code.[137]

Kürten's defence lawyer Alex Wehner entered a passionate plea at the end of the trial for the jury to put aside all thought of 'an eye for an eye, a tooth for a tooth'. 'Do not let him be expelled from human society as a beast; *even he, after all, wears a human countenance.*' But the jurors, perhaps, like the press, convinced that the human countenance which Kürten displayed to the world was an illusory one, refused to accept that he deserved sympathy on the grounds that he was a creature of a fate he could not control.[138] They agreed instead with the Düsseldorf state prosecutor's view: 'In the main proceedings, Kürten did not give the impression of being a penitent and remorseful human being; on the contrary, he gave the impression of a great play-actor.'[139] He was cool, collected, and intelligent in giving his evidence. He was responsible for what he did. The best way to describe him was as a genuine sadist. Moreover, although he claimed that he had not intended to kill his victims, the sexual excitement he obtained from revisiting the corpses of some of those he had killed, his complete lack of remorse at their death, and the obvious pleasure which he gained from the sensation caused by the murders in the public, suggested rather the opposite. 'Anyone', as the final judgment observed, 'who, like the accused, cuts the throat of Christine Klein with a pocket-knife and uses the knife four times for this purpose, intends to kill.'[140] On 22 April he was sentenced to death on nine counts of murder, and to fifteen years' imprisonment on seven counts of attempted murder.[141] There was little doubt that he was guilty of many further attacks; more than the same number again are listed in the official documents, though they were allowed to rest on file and never came to trial.[142]

But was Kürten really sane? From puberty onwards he was clearly only able to achieve sexual fulfilment by murder and violence. A few attempts at non-violent sexual relations did not lead to orgasm. Moreover, a Kafkaesque incident in prison in 1911, when Kürten believed he had been turned into a silkworm, covered his cell window with his mattress, crawled under his table and wrapped himself in silk, remaining there until he was discovered by a warder, did indicate a serious disturbance of mind.[143] But he does not seem to have been schizophrenic, he did not hear voices telling him to kill, and his pursuit of violence, both in fantasy and in reality, was deliberately undertaken for the purpose of achieving sexual gratification.[144] Whatever the origin of his sexual perversion—

---

[137] Ibid. 717: *Solinger Tageblatt*, 21 Apr. 1931; ibid. 700, Bl. 149, 159–60.   [138] Ibid. 705, Bl. 45–6.
[139] Ibid.: Generalstaatsanwaltschaft Begnadigungtsgutachten ER 838/29, 10 June 1931.
[140] Ibid. 700, Bl. 161.   [141] Ibid., Bl. 1–4, 150–1.   [142] Ibid., *passim*.
[143] Ibid., Bl. 14. See also the stenographic report of Kürten's lengthy and detailed responses to the psychiatrist's questioning, in ibid. 732, Bl. 60–245, and Kaever and Lenk, *Leben und Wirken*.
[144] He only once claimed to have heard voices, at the grave of one of his victims: see ibid. 730, Bl. 226.

and it seems legitimate to call it such—its expression in acts of murder and vampirism was conscious, planned, and calculated. In terms of Paragraph 51 of the Criminal Code, he probably was reponsible for his actions in the end. Whether the paragraph's formulation itself was adequate to deal with the question of diminished responsibility was, of course, another matter altogether. On his request, Kürten's defence lawyer quickly submitted a plea for clemency on grounds of diminished responsibility, demanding that the condemned man be put through a course of psychoanalysis to determine the merits of his case.[145] But the state prosecutor did not find it difficult to counter this. Psychoanalysis, he noted, was still a controversial and relatively untried science, and in any case Kürten's responsibility for his actions had been attested by no fewer than three respectable scientific experts. There was no possibility of an error of justice having been committed. Kürten had confessed all his crimes, and made it clear that he had put a good deal of planning and forethought into them. He lived in secure circumstances in the later 1920s, and could not claim that social or economic desperation had turned his mind. He had killed for pure pleasure, and shown no mercy to his victims, not even to the small children he numbered among them. 'Kürten', he concluded, 'is thoroughly undeserving . . . of a reprieve; that is demonstrated by his total moral depravity, as well as by the extraordinary seriousness and frequency of his crimes.' If he was spared, he might at some time in the future be released, and might offend again. There was no evidence that prison would do him any good. Indeed, over the previous years it had actually made him worse, since, as the judgment reported, he found chains and fetters sexually arousing and worked himself up to orgasm by imagining acts of violence, murder, and 'mass catastrophes' such as 'blowing up bridges and poisoning the population's water supply with bacilli'. Finally, the prosecutor pointed out that 'the public mood, as far as it is represented in the press', was calling loudly 'for a just balance in which the punishment really corresponds to the crime, and for a sure and lasting liberation of society from this member who is unworthy to be called a human being'.[146]

The prosecutor's assumption that public opinion could fairly be gauged by the fulminations of the popular press suggested how powerful the mass media were now becoming, and gave some indication as to the importance they had attained in the administration of justice under the Weimar Republic. Just as significant was his reference to public demands for the elimination of an individual who was unworthy of belonging to the human race. Such terminology already adum-

---

[145] Ibid. 705, Bl. 3–4: Wehner to Oberstaatsanwaltschaft Düsseldorf, 22 May 1931.
[146] Ibid., Bl. 48–54: Begnadigungsgutachten 15 K 1/31, 3 June 1931; ibid. 700, Bl. 11, 14. Kürten himself declared that little would be achieved by his execution: 'It's doubtful whether they'll wash off the blood I've spilled. It's just an act of revenge demanded by the people.' (Kaever and Lenk, *Leben und Wirken*, 345).

brated the language of Nazism. Nevertheless, public opinion was less than unanimous in favour of Kürten's execution. Opposition came particularly from the movement for the abolition of capital punishment, which realized that the political context made this case—unlike that of Julius Zell in Württemberg the previous year—of vital importance for the future of the death penalty. In a public meeting held by the League for Human Rights on 12 May 1931, the Social Democratic legal expert and former Reich Justice Minister Gustav Radbruch, long a leading figure in the campaign against capital punishment, condemned the 'instincts of revenge' which he now considered dominant in the popular discourse on the Kürten case.[147] 'Why', he asked, 'has the abolition of the death penalty become the symbol of the whole criminal law reform?' He provided the answer himself:

The punishment which stands at the top of the penal system determines the character of the whole criminal law. If the penal system culminates in the death penalty, all its punishments share something of its reek of blood, of its spirit of retribution and revenge. The spirit of a new, social criminal law can only assert itself if the ghost of capital punishment is exorcized. We are not fighting for Kürten, but against the death penalty. *We demand that the death penalty is not carried out against Kürten, because after Kürten's head falls, many others will follow in future,* including less dangerous and less guilty ones— and also, in view of the danger of a faulty conviction, a danger which can never be wholly excluded from the realms of possibility, innocent ones.

The only reason for the general clamour for Kürten's execution, he declared, was 'the desire for retribution'.[148] The meeting duly voted to press the Prussian government for clemency. But even in the League for Human Rights opinion was divided. Although some eminent jurists, such as Eberhard Schmidt, gave their support to the motion, others did not. The meeting as a whole was described in the press as 'stormy', which suggests strongly that even in abolition-ist circles the case was seen by some as exceptional. Nor could those who believed Kürten was insane be accused of taking a soft line. The Social Democratic eugenicist Alfred Grotjahn, for example, while pleading for Kürten's life on grounds of diminished responsibility, also argued that Kürten and similar 'psychopaths' should be compulsorily castrated.[149]

But in the fevered political circumstances of 1931, when public opinion was polarized between right and left, and the middle classes had already largely deserted Liberalism and Nationalism for the National Socialists, it was difficult for such voices to be heard. The press, too, had moved substantially to the right

[147] BA Potsdam RJM 6099, Bl. 50: *Vorwärts*, 15 May 1931.

[148] Ibid. 61 Re 1/1773: *Berliner Tageblatt*, 13 May 1931.

[149] Ibid. RJM 6099, Bl. 42; *Berliner Tageblatt*, 5 May 1931; ibid., Bl. 30: *Montag Morgen*, 27 Apr. 1931; see also HStA Düsseldorf Rep. 17/727, Bl. 12: *Berliner Tageblatt*, 6 May 1931.

since the middle years of the Republic.[150] Popular opinion, articulated through
the media, made it effectively impossible to reach a verdict of diminished
responsibility in the Kürten case. Any notion that Kürten was unfit to stand trial
was swiftly dismissed.[151] Such an argument, declared conservatives, amounted to
'sympathy with a sadist'. Soon, they complained, almost any crime would be
ascribed to 'any kind of sexual defect' and the perpetrator declared not responsible for his own actions.[152] During the trial itself, numerous articles in the press
put the case for Kürten's execution. He suffered from 'sadistic degeneration',
opined one report.[153] 'He is the very embodiment of evil', noted another commentator during the trial:

After the first day of the court proceedings, in which the mass murderer dominated the
scene with great skill, the psychiatrists, when asked for their opinion, simply shrugged
their shoulders. The Peter Kürten case had nothing to do with their science any more.
The protection of Paragraph 51, mental confusion at the moment when the deed was
committed, could naturally not be extended to him. One does not, after thirty-nine
years—and that is the length of the vampire's criminal career, from his eighth year to his
forty-seventh—suddenly become mentally confused precisely at the moment of the
crime. Beyond establishing this necessary fact, those psychiatrists present at the trial
wanted nothing more to do with the case. Their science is the study of people's mental
constitution, of their spiritual state, of human desires. But: mind, spirit, indeed, desires
that were in any way human? This beast committed evil acts not for advantage or pleasure
but just for the sake of evil itself. It is a paradox that no science or study can illuminate.[154]

The message was clear: human psychiatry stopped where a criminal was an evil,
subhuman 'beast'.

Press reports of the trial regularly carried headlines such as 'Sadist and Murderer without Restraint'.[155] The language in which the progress of the trial itself
was reported amounted to an implicit plea for execution, with the 'weeping
parents' and fainting female victims on the witness stand contrasting sharply with
the calm and collected central figure in the dock, the human victims with the
inhuman and degenerate murderer.[156] A number of citizens wrote to the judicial
authorities in Düsseldorf demanding Kürten's execution and requesting to be
admitted when it took place.[157] By contrast, the handful of people who wrote in
support of clemency mostly seemed to be mentally unbalanced or religiously
obsessed.[158] Kürten himself did his own cause no good when he admitted to his

[150] Modris Eksteins, The Limits of Reason: The German Democratic Press and the Collapse of Weimar
Democracy (Oxford, 1975).
[151] BA Potsdam RJM 6099, Bl. 45: Welt am Montag, 11 May 1931; ibid., Bl. 92: 8-Uhr Abendblatt, 2 May
1931.
[152] Ibid. 61 Re 1/1773, 58: Deutsche Tageszeitung, 24 Apr. 1931.
[153] HStA Düsseldorf Rep. 17/713: Neue Arbeiterzeitung (Hanover), 16 Apr. 1931.
[154] Ibid. 727, Bl. 7: Hamburger Anzeiger, 14 Apr. 1931.
[155] Ibid. 714: Mittag, 15 May [i.e. April] 1931.   [156] Ibid. 715: Freie Presse (Elbing), 17 Apr. 1931.
[157] Ibid. 707 and 708, passim.   [158] Ibid. 706, passim.

gaolers that he accepted his sentence because he thought that the Social Democratic ministers in the Prussian government would never agree to its being carried out.[159] Even his own relatives joined the chorus of voices clamouring for his death.[160] On 20 June the court official responsible for making recommendations for clemency to the Prussian Ministry of Justice in Berlin submitted a lengthy report which left the issue in no doubt: Kürten had to be killed.[161]

The overwhelming pressure for Kürten's execution reflected among other things the growing public criticism of the abolition of capital punishment in the last years of the Weimar Republic. Attacks on abolitionists as 'idealists and fantasists', or alternatively revolutionaries 'who follow doctrines hostile to the state', became increasingly common.[162] 'In every middle-class family—in trains—in pubs—everywhere, there is a tremendous storm blowing up against the abolition of the death penalty,' wrote an irate Bavarian, Herr K., from Landshut, to the Reich Ministry of Justice on 14 June 1929. Abolitionists, he declared, were suffering from 'mawkish sentimentality'.[163] Commenting on the Kürten case in the press in April 1931, Hans Krobath wrote:

Sentimentality in the application of the criminal law, basing itself on claims that are completely unsubstantiated, has already wrought enough havoc. When human life counts for less and less, it is precisely the time when the deterrent function of punishment must come to the fore. . . . Many an innocent life would be saved if everyone who contemplated a murder had to reckon with the certainty of the death penalty if he carried it out.[164]

Whether Kürten himself would have been deterred, the author did not say. Nevertheless, his argument was characteristic of the new, tough tone taken by many commentators on penal policy. The far right considered it almost unpatriotic to argue that the German judicial system could make a mistake (except, of course, where its own representatives in the paramilitary and terrorist organizations that flourished under the Weimar Republic were concerned). Retentionists emphasized their belief that, despite the furore created by the Jakubowski case, judicial errors in Germany were in fact unknown.[165] As one newspaper, attacking the campaign for Jakubowski's posthumous rehabilitation, argued:

[159] Ibid. 705, Bl. 9: Strafanstaltsdirektor Düsseldorf-Derendorf to Beauftragter für Gnadensachen beim Landgericht Düsseldorf, 19 June 1931.

[160] Ibid., Bl. 73: Nachtrag to letter of Polizeipräsident Düsseldorf to Beauftragter für Gnadensachen, 19 June 1931. Their letters are printed in Kaever and Lenk, *Leben und Wirken*.

[161] Ibid., bound copy of report from Beauftragter für Gnadensachen to PJM, 20 June 1931 (pages unnumbered).

[162] GStA Berlin Rep. 84a, 7792: *Kölnische Zeitung*, 26 Nov. 1928.

[163] BA Potsdam RJA 6095: K. to RJM, 14 June 1929.

[164] BA Potsdam 61 Re 1/1773, 56: Hans Krobath, 'Mordseuche und Todesstrafe' (typescript, Allgemeine Zeitungsdienst, 15 Apr. 1931).

[165] GStA Berlin Rep. 84a/7792: *Hannoverscher Kurier*, 26 Mar. 1929; *Bremer Nachrichten*, 14 Feb. 1929.

Germany has always had grounds for pride in the reliability of its administration of the law. Anyone who has had the opportunity to draw comparisons with the situation in other countries knows that, as does anyone who has studied the judgment of experts abroad. But it also corresponds to the German people's moral right of self-preservation that it should refuse to tolerate the machinations of people whose heart only bleeds for the criminal, not for the decent people whom he threatens. Such people are sowing confusion about the law, engaging in clandestine revolutionary activity, and have a personal need to stir things up.[166]

The ex-worker and former trade unionist turned apostle of the far right, August Winnig, was quoted in 1929 as arguing that the effective abolition of the death penalty was a characteristic sign of the chronic weakness of the Weimar Republic. 'At the end of the road stands the complete self-abnegation of the state as the guarantor of a penal power founded in morality.'[167]

That public opinion was so overwhelmingly against clemency for Kürten was a strong indication of the change in atmosphere that was taking place in the last years of the Weimar Republic, as all the bourgeois parties moved rightwards in an attempt to stem the haemorrhage of their supporters to the National Socialists. Wilhelm Kahl, the Chairman of the Criminal Law Committee of the Reichstag, who had once been prepared to compromise on the issue, declared that failure to execute Kürten would unleash such a wave of protest that the abolition of the death penalty would thereby be rendered impossible for the forseeable future.[168] The paradox seemed implausible, if not disingenuous. The Catholic Centre Party and all political groupings right of the Social Democrats demanded execution. 'In Germany, in view of the Kürten case, we are witnessing an outcry in favour of capital punishment,' conceded the liberal *Frankfurter Zeitung*: 'It would be foolish to deny that this is popular at the moment.'[169] The Reichstag elected in 1930, commented Hans Krobath, was very unlikely to agree to the abolition of capital punishment. It was time for the Prussian government to abandon its policy of automatic commutation.[170] Further to the right still, others attacked the notions of retribution and deterrence in the new language of eugenic cleansing that had become so widespread in discussions of penal policy by this time:

We do not want to punish Kürten because of the deeds he committed, we want to exterminate him, to kill him in the quickest possible way. The problem of the Kürten trial is not to render him harmless because he is a pest, a plague of the people and of mankind.

[166] GStA Berlin Rep. 84a/7792: *Deutsche Allgemeine Zeitung*, 15 May 1928.

[167] Quoted in GLA Karlsruhe 234/6611: 'Um die Todesstrafe. Von Landgerichtsdirektor Dr. A. Hanemann, MdR', *Breisgauer Zeitung*, 10 Oct. 1929.

[168] Ibid. 60: *Vorwärts*, 13 May 1931.

[169] HStA Düsseldorf Rep. 17/727, Bl. 9: *Frankfurter Zeitung*, 25 Apr. 1931.

[170] Ibid. 716: *Mittag*, 18/19 Apr. 1931 (Hans Krobath, 'Mordseuche und Todesstrafe: Notwendige Bemerkungen zum Mordprozess Kürten').

The problem of the Kürten trial is not that of a human soul, or of the milieu from which it has emerged, nor is it of the kind of punishment which he should suffer—the terrible example which the mass murderer Peter Kürten gives to an attentive world shows the end-point of the racial decline of a family, points up the terrible route taken by degeneration.

The sterilization of the 'born criminal', the writer thought, was the logical consequence of these lessons from the Kürten trial.[171] The case had turned into a referendum on the death penalty, and the vote was for its immediate reinstatement.

e. The Restoration of Capital Punishment 1931–1932

The responsibility for confirming or commuting Kürten's sentence lay with the Social Democrat-dominated minority government of Prussia. With some reason, the press thought 'that a refusal to carry out the death sentence on Kürten would very quickly be the subject of political exploitation against the Prussian government'.[172] On the other hand, as Rudolf Olden pointed out: 'The refusal of a so-called act of clemency would mean in practice nothing other than the reintroduction of the death penalty, because it has in reality already been abolished.'[173] It was widely recognized that much more was at stake than Kürten's head. Up to now, the Prussian government had stuck by Koch-Weser's principles and refused to confirm any death sentences in view of the possible abolition of capital punishment in the new Criminal Code.[174] The Social Democratic press was solidly against the execution. The party's official daily paper, *Vorwärts*, spoke for the party as a whole when it asked agonizingly:

Must the State, just because a sport of nature brings out a Peter Kürten once every ten years, put up another man to carry out for money, as a business, and in the name of the authorities, exactly the same kind of deliberate killing to which the State attaches the severest of punishments because it is the most reprehensible of all crimes?[175]

But the Social Democratic ministers in the Prussian cabinet were under immense public pressure to agree to Kürten's execution. Already in deep political trouble on other fronts, the Prussian cabinet devoted a special sitting on 30 June 1931 to the case. Opinion was divided. The Ministry of Justice was still held by Hermann Schmidt, a representative of the Catholic Centre party. Ironically, although his party supported the death penalty, Schmidt himself had been converted to abolition after attending an execution in person.[176] Although he was unwilling to sanction any executions until the completion of the new Criminal Code, his party put strong pressure on him to change his mind. The Catholic press was reported as warning him: 'There is only one way to protect the human race from future acts of cruelty of a Kürten, and that is to carry out the death sentence.' By April 1931 he seems to have come round.[177] After a good deal of agonizing, and despite Schmidt's reported reversion to his original opposition to the execution, the cabinet decided to reject the appeal for clemency. It was clear that the Social Democratic ministers were mainly responsible. Otto Braun, the Minister-President, at least according to his memoirs, was not one of those who voted to cut Kürten's head off: 'As an opponent of the death penalty on principle,' he said, 'I never voted in favour of an execution, but nor could I persuade myself to assert my authority in the cabinet in a few special cases—horrible mass murders—so in these instances I let the majority decide.'[178]

Probably at Braun's prompting, the cabinet agreed to say nothing about the reasons for its decision.[179] Indeed, the whole matter was kept as secret as possible. Even communication by telegram was to be avoided for fear of leaks, and most of the arrangements for Kürten's execution were made by telephone. The Justice Ministry in Berlin instructed the state prosecutor in Düsseldorf to prevent any word of the event getting out in advance:

Particular attention is to be given to keeping all preparations for the execution *secret*, and above all, care is to be taken to adhere to the relevant regulations concerning admission to the execution, and only to grant it, apart from those persons listed in §454 of the Criminal Procedure Regulations (New Series), to a few persons, and only to those who can be guaranteed not to be contemplating relaying to the press details of the execution calculated to gratify the public's need for sensation.[180]

So secret were the proceedings that only sixteen entry cards were issued and the press were banned altogether from the execution.[181]

Perhaps because their representatives were not allowed to be present, the newspapers vied with one another for the most sensational headlines and stories of the execution: 'Scenes of Horror at the Scaffold'; 'Kürten's Head Falls under the Guillotine: First Confession, then the Hangman's Axe'; 'Dragged to the

---

[176] GStA Berlin Rep. 84a/7786, Bl. 196–210: *Verhandlungen des Preussischen Landtages*, cols. 4570–2, 4669; ibid. 7792: *Berliner Morgenpost*, 6 Mar. 1929.

[177] BA Potsdam 61 Re 1/1773, 59: *Deutsche Tageszeitung*, 25 Apr. 1931; ibid. 61: *Vorwärts*, 3 July 1931.

[178] Ibid., RJM 6099, Bl. 77: *Welt am Abend*, 2 July 1931; ibid., Bl. 89: Abschrift zu RK 7007, Sitzung des Preussischen Staatsministeriums am 30. Juni 1931; Otto Braun, *Von Weimar zu Hitler*, 2nd edn. (Hildesheim, 1979), 321.

[179] BA Potsdam 61 Re 1/1773, 63: *Berliner Tageblatt*, 3 July 1931.

[180] HStA Düsseldorf Rep. 17/544, Bl. 3: PJM to Generalstaatsanwalt Düsseldorf, 30 June 1931.

[181] Ibid., Bl. 30–1: Oberstaatsanwalt Düsseldorf to PJM, 3 July 1931, and attached copy of entry card.

Guillotine—Beheaded in Three Minutes'. There were diagrams of the prison in Cologne with arrows pointing to the site of the guillotine, descriptions of 'The Last Night', and dramatic depictions of Kürten's 'Nervous and Frightened Condition'. In fact, according to the state prosecutor in Düsseldorf, Kürten spent the night before his execution writing to his surviving victims and the relatives of those he had killed, drinking one and a half bottles of wine, eating a schnitzel with fried potatoes and salad, making his confession, and taking communion. 'His comments', noted the prosecutor, 'showed that he now felt genuine contrition and wanted to expiate his crimes through his death.' Against the background of the tolling bell, Kürten was led into the prison yard at 6.02 a.m. After a brief word with the clergy, he heard the sentence confirmed, was handed over to executioner Gröpler's assistants, and quickly fastened to the guillotine. It was all over in ninety seconds.[182] His corpse was immediately passed over to a medical team from Berlin University's Anatomical Institute for experimentation, which was carried out in a neighbouring room.[183]

Kürten's case was clearly regarded by the Social Democrats as an exception. But, as one newspaper prophesied, 'the "exception" will soon become the rule'.[184] Everyone was clear about the implications of the event. 'Capital punishment has been reintroduced,' wrote Rudolf Olden: 'The republic's achievements are being sacrificed one by one by the republicans themselves.' And indeed other executions now followed. On 1 May 1931 another offender, Tetzner, was executed in Regensburg.[185] Two more beheadings took place in Thuringia the same year (making a total of four executions out of forty-nine condemnations in 1931 in Germany as a whole). Two more followed in Württemberg and one in Baden in 1932, making three executions in all out of fifty-two condemnations in the year.[186] None of these offenders was an 'exceptional' criminal in the sense of Kürten or Haarmann. In 1932 the Reich Minister of Justice Curt Joël, formerly the top civil servant in the Ministry, noted that the executions of Zell, Tetzner, and Kürten, together with the two carried out in Thuringia, made it clear that the federated

---

[182] BA Potsdam RJM 6099, Bl. 65–77: *Deutsche Zeitung*, 2 July 1931; *Berliner Nachtausgabe*, 2 July 1931; *Deutsche Tageszeitung*, 2 July 1931; *Berliner Volkszeitung*, 2 July 1931; *8-Uhr Abendblatt*, 2 July 1931; *Welt am Abend*, 2 July 1931; HStA Düsseldorf Rep. 17/727, Bl. 17: *Hamburger Anzeiger*, 2 July 1931, and following clippings to Bl. 26.

[183] Ibid. 544, Bl. 25–9: Oberstaatsanwalt Düsseldorf to PJM, 3 July 1931.

[184] BA Potsdam RJM 6099, Bl. 36: *Welt am Abend*, 20 Apr. 1931.

[185] GLA Karlsruhe 234/6611: *Frankfurter Zeitung*, 30 Apr. 1931.

[186] BA Potsdam RJM 5665, Bl. 274: RJM to Oberstaatsanwalt Dr Moericke, Leipzig, 10 Sept. 1932; ibid. 5666, Bl. 159: RJM to Landgerichtsrat Dr Stock, 7 Dec. 1933; see also the figures in HStA Munich M Ju 12575. The figures in the *Statistisches Jahrbuch für das deutsche Reich* are 49 condemnations and 4 executions for 1931 (1931, p. 546), and 52 condemnations and 3 executions for 1932 (1932, p. 534). The published figures appear to be the most accurate. The two executions in Thuringia were carried out by Gröpler in Gera on 25 Sept. 1931. The bodies were taken for anatomy at Jena University (GStA Berlin Rep. 84a/6447: *Berliner Tageblatt*, 24 Sept. 1931, and *BZ am Mittag*, 25 Sept. 1931).

FIG. 35. *Peter Kürten (1884–1931), the 'Düsseldorf vampire'.* A police photograph from 1930, showing the man whose execution for a series of brutal sex killings paved the way for the reintroduction of capital punishment towards the end of the Weimar Republic.

states no longer regarded Koch-Weser's circular as relevant. 'At the time when that circular was sent out,' declared Joël, 'one could reckon on the completion of the criminal law reform within a foreseeable time. This prospect is with us no longer.'[187] The Criminal Law Committee of the Reichstag had by now abandoned its work. When it met for the last time, on 12 January 1932, it was boycotted by the far right. The National Socialists, taking the Nationalists and the small Business Party with them, had declared the retention of the death penalty to be a fundamental principle on which there could be no debate. The Democrats, now renamed the State Party and reduced to only a handful of deputies at the election, were paralysed, and refused to commit themselves. The aged Chairman of the Committee, Wilhelm Kahl, now in his eighties, changed his mind once again, and said he was no longer willing to compromise with the Social Democrats and other abolitionists:

Homicide offences have increased, indeed at times and in places have become a downright method used by the political parties in the struggle against one another. Above all, the number of murder cases of a particularly horrible kind has grown to such an extent that some federated states, including Prussia, whose judicial chief belongs among the most outspoken opponents of the death penalty, have not been able to follow the Reich government's advice, but have had to decide to carry out death sentences themselves. These events have heightened the present mood against the abolition of this punishment. Is the legislator permitted to ignore this?[188]

But Kahl's views in any case were now purely academic. The Committee did not manage to get any further with its business. Kahl died soon afterwards, a

---

[187] BA Potsdam RJM 6095: Zum Sprechzettel Nr. 94 (n.d.), Bl. 5.
[188] Ibid. 61 Re 1/1773, 70: *Vossische Zeitung*, 27 Jan. 1932; ibid. 71: *Reichs-und Staatsanzeiger*, 27 Jan. 1932.

disappointed man. The total paralysis of the legislature meant that even if the Committee had agreed a draft, there would have been no chance of getting it passed into law. So it gave up.[189]

The execution of Peter Kürten thus marked a decisive turning-point in the history of capital punishment in the Weimar Republic. The case itself had been largely free of political overtones. To be sure, revelation that Kürten had once belonged to the Social Democratic Party's paramilitary wing, the 'Reich Banner', as well as to the works council of a factory in which he had been employed in the mid-1920s, and had been politically active enough to have been sent as a delegate to a regional conference of the Social Democrats in Erfurt, caused predictable glee on the political right, who saw it as 'striking proof of our allegations that the subhuman dregs of society are to be found in the Marxist associations'.[190] His brief political career had been confined, however, to a relatively quiet period in the 1920s, when he had got married, had a steady job, and kept his violent impulses largely, though not wholly, under control.[191] It was of no more significance in the history of his crimes than was the fact that some of them had been committed with a large pair of scissors decorated with metal reliefs of ex-Kaiser Wilhelm II and his wife.[192] The Communist Party focused on Kürten's victims, whose fate, claimed its daily paper, Die Rote Fahne ('The Red Flag'), showed 'how little the bourgeois State protects the safety of people who belong to the proletarian class'. In point of fact, Kürten's victims had included quite a number of non-proletarians. But the Communists were only capable of putting one interpretation on the case, no matter how much misrepresentation this involved; their comment showed how far the left, as well as the right, would go in the heated atmosphere of Weimar's dying years to make political capital out of issues of law and order.[193] In the end, it was difficult to interpret the case plausibly in any sense other than that of Kürten's own individual transgression.

The change in atmosphere that had taken place by the early 1930s was indicated by the failure of either the press or the abolitionists to make anything very much of the fact that another man, Hans Strausberg, had been wrongly arrested for five of the murders committed by Kürten and sent to an asylum for the dangerously insane. Had Strausberg been even superficially normal, the outcome for him could have been a very different one.[194] But scarcely anyone wanted to know. The mood of the times, troubled by massive political violence on the streets, and unsettled by a deep anxiety at government paralysis in the face

[189] Ibid., RJM 6098, Bl. 201: Germania, 27 Jan. 1932; ibid., Bl. 203: Die Welt am Abend, 27 Jan. 1932.
[190] HStA Düsseldorf Rep. 17/717: Preussische Zeitung, 20 Apr. 1931.   [191] Ibid. 700, Bl. 21–2.
[192] Ibid., Bl. 33.   [193] BA Potsdam RJM 6099, Bl. 4: Die Rote Fahne, 24 Apr. 1931.
[194] HStA Düsseldorf Rep. 17/538: Aufstellung der Morde und Ueberfälle in Düsseldorf seit Februar 1929 (26 Nov. 1929).

of economic collapse, mass unemployment, and political stalemate, demanded a symbolic assertion of public order and state decisiveness. The execution of Kürten provided an ideal opportunity. It signalled the fact that the abolition of capital punishment was no longer on the political agenda. The attempt to write it into the new Criminal Code had foundered, along with the Criminal Code itself, in the legislative chaos of the early 1930s. The Reich Justice Ministry was now in the hands of men who were strong supporters of the death penalty. The abolitionist movement, with the failure of the attempt to rehabilitate Jakubowski, was on the retreat. In Berlin, government had taken an authoritarian turn. National Socialism was on the march. Yet the wholesale resumption of executions was still by no means a foregone conclusion in 1931–2. The legal power to grant or refuse a reprieve to capital offenders still lay with the individual state governments. Here the picture was far from clear. Above all, in Prussia, the Social Democrats continued to dominate, and there was every sign that they intended to regard the Kürten case as a singular exception rather than a general precedent. In the early 1930s, as the Social Democrats turned to the left, their opposition to capital punishment, if anything, grew stronger. The execution of Kürten, ironically, only legitimated the resumption of executions in other parts of Germany. As in so many other areas, therefore, Prussia, the bulwark of Weimar democracy, seemed to be holding out against the general trend. Its Minister-President Otto Braun, indeed, considered this one of the reasons for the growing unpopularity of the Republic among the voters: 'Large parts of the people felt their primitive sense of justice, which was still overwhelmingly governed by feelings of revenge and expiation, affronted by this, and turned away from the democratic regime.'[195] It was not just popular opinion that was alienated. In 1932 conservative and reactionary forces in politics and the army began to mobilize against the Social Democratic cabinet in Prussia, the last obstacle to the replacement of the Weimar Republic by an authoritarian regime. And, as we shall now see, one of the major targets of their attack was the continuing reluctance of the Prussian government to implement the death penalty.[196]

[195] Braun, *Von Weimar*, 321.   [196] Heinrich Kühle, *Staat und Todesstrafe* (Münster, 1934).

Part V

14

'Healthy Popular Feeling'

a. Uncertainty on Death Row, 1932–1933

By the beginning of 1932 it was widely expected that the minority Prussian cabinet led by the Social Democrat Otto Braun, assailed on all sides and weakened by the electoral success of the National Socialists, would be replaced by a conservative government willing to implement the death penalty. So, in a classic example of the way in which conservative civil servants managed to undermine, or disregard, the authority of left-of-centre governments in the Weimar Republic, officials in the Ministry of Justice began refusing to forward clemency cases to the Prussian cabinet.[1] This left a number of prisoners on death row in a state of considerable uncertainty about their eventual fate, a situation which few officials in the judicial bureaucracy found very satisfactory.[2] The situation became even more confused when the new, ultra-conservative Reich Chancellor Franz von Papen, who had succeeded Brüning at the head of another 'non-party' government, unilaterally sacked the Braun cabinet on 20 July 1932. The police chief of Berlin was dismissed. Police powers were given to the army. This amounted to nothing less than a military-backed *coup d'état*, carried out against the last, if rather wobbly, bastion of Weimar democracy. The way was clear for the creation of some kind of authoritarian system or dictatorship without the danger of objections from the rulers of Germany's largest federated state.[3] The reactionary intentions of the coup were symbolically signalled, as so often in such cases, by a decree on capital punishment. On 5 October 1932 Papen, acting as Reich Commissioner in charge of Prussia, ordered that the guillotine, that un-Prussian symbol of French revolutionary justice, should no longer be

---

[1] GStA Berlin Rep. 84a/7792: *Neue Berliner Zeitung*, 23 Nov. 1932, and *12-Uhr Abendblatt*, 23 Nov. 1932.

[2] For earlier complaints, see HStA Hanover Hann. 173a Nr. 437, Bl. 160–5, correspondence of Oberstaatsanwaltschaft Celle from 27 Nov. 1924 to 29 Mar. 1926.

[3] Hagen Schulze, *Otto Braun, oder Preussens demokratische Sendung. Eine Biographie* (Frankfurt am Main, 1977), 745–86.

employed for executions in the province of Hanover, where it had been introduced in the mid-nineteenth century, or in the Cologne court district, where it had been in use since the Napoleonic occupation. Henceforth, beheadings were to be carried out in a manner which conservatives regarded as quintessentally Prussian: by the hand-held axe.[4]

Perhaps no other single decree signalled more clearly the reactionary and restorationist thrust of Papen's coup. Prussian values, Prussian customs, and Prussian traditions were to be reinstated in place of what the conservatives regarded as the alien rule of Social Democracy. The French Revolution was to be rolled back and its historical consquences annulled. In the mean time, faced with the probability of a hopeless fight against the army if they took to the streets, the Social Democrats challenged the 'Papen coup' in the courts. Whilst the legal situation remained unresolved, the question of who possessed the sovereign power of clemency traditionally vested in the head of state also remained undecided. Did Papen, as Reich Commissioner, have the right to confirm or commute death sentences? Or did it still lie with Braun? What if the Reich Commissioner allowed some criminals to be executed and then the Supreme Court ruled that he had no legal power to do so? The punctilious bureaucrats of the Prussian Ministry of Justice decided that this was not a risk worth taking. So they continued to sit on all the capital sentences that came onto their desks in 1932, waiting for a decision by the courts that would allow them to recommend the exercise or denial of mercy to the properly constituted and legally recognized sovereign authority.[5] As a result of this undetermined politico-legal conflict, offenders convicted of capital crimes began to accumulate in Prussia's gaols from the beginning of 1932. Papen's government grew increasingly aware of the problems to which this was giving rise, but repeatedly failed to do anything about them, preferring to await a ruling on the location of sovereignty in Prussia by the Supreme Court. When it came, on 25 October 1932, the ruling completely failed to clarify the situation; Otto Braun, indeed, felt enabled to contest Papen's right to wield the power of clemency and to demand it back for his ousted cabinet. His bid was unsuccessful. Nevertheless, the Prussian Ministry of Justice continued to find its hands tied in the matter.

In December 1932, doubtless at the Ministry's prompting, State Secretary

---

[4] See the summary of decrees on this subject in PRO/FO 945, no. 318: 'Carrying-Out of Death Sentences in Germany' (British Special Legal Research Unit, memorandum of 14 Mar. 1947), para. 3. For examples of official reports by the state prosecutor on the use of the hand-axe in Hanoverian executions after this date, see HStA Hanover Hann. 173a Nr. 442, Bl. 89 (30 June 1933), Bl. 213 (13 Sept. 1934). For the introduction of the guillotine in Hanover and elsewhere in the 19th c., see above, ch. 7*c* and 8*d*.

[5] Ernst Rudolf Huber, *Deutsche Verfassungsgeschichte seit 1789*, vii. *Ausbau, Schutz und Untergang der Weimarer Republik* (Stuttgart, 1984), 1015 (for the coup), 1120–35 (for the legal proceedings), and 1192–7 (for the continuing dispute).

Hölscher reported: 'The present situation is unbearable for the Justice Ministry.' There were now seventeen prisoners on death row in Prussia's gaols awaiting a decision on their fate, he said.[6] But nothing could be done about the matter, in view of the legal battles still being fought between Braun, and his Prussian cabinet, the Reich Commissioners under Papen, and the lawyers acting for the condemned men, about who had the power of sovereignty. As State Secretary Hölscher wrote in January 1933:

For the condemned, the uncertainty about their fate means a particular spiritual torture, which must in the long run have a deleterious effect upon their condition. Consideration for the condemned therefore means that the period for which they have to wait for a decision must be kept as short as possible. This obvious requirement of humanity cannot be followed in the present situation. For in view of the public position taken by the Prussian cabinet with regard to the exercise of the right of clemency, the Reich Commissioners must have some doubts about taking a decision of the kind in question, in which the life or death of those concerned is at stake, as long as their responsibility for taking it remains in dispute. It would not be a tenable situation if, for example, after the Commissioners had decided in a particular case not to make use of their right of reprieve, the Prussian cabinet was telephoned by the condemned with the request to make a decision in the opposite sense, and at the same time the public was stirred up by propagandistic claims about a 'judicial murder'.[7]

This memorandum made it clear that political as much as legal considerations were behind the reluctance to come to a decision on any of the individual cases in question. More ominously, it also revealed, between the lines, that both the bureaucrats in Berlin, and the reactionary politicians they were advising, assumed that such a decision, when it came, would be more likely to be for the implementation of a death sentence than against it.

Meanwhile, the *de facto* reintroduction of capital punishment since 1930 had been formally endorsed by an emergency decree on political violence, issued by Papen in his capacity as Reich Commissioner in Prussia on 9 August 1932. Clashes between gangs of Nazi brownshirts, bands of Communist 'Red Front-Fighters', Nationalist 'Steel Helmets', Social Democratic 'Reich Banner', and other armed paramilitary groups were causing mounting casualties and deaths despite the efforts of the police to control them. Already in the summer of 1931 the indefatigable statistician of political violence, Professor Emil Julius Gumbel, calculated that out of sixty-three political murders committed since 1924, no fewer than thirty-eight had occurred during the previous eighteen

---

[6] Anton Golecki (ed.), *Akten der Reichskanzlei: Weimarer Republik: Das Kabinett von Schleicher 3. Dezember 1932 bis 30. Januar 1933* (Boppard, 1986), 137, 181 n. 7. See also Schulze, *Otto Braun*, 773–6, and Braun, *Von Weimar*, 436–9.

[7] Golecki (ed.), *Akten . . . Das Kabinett von Schleicher*, 80–2. The Prussian cabinet (*Staatsministerium*) referred to was of course the ousted Braun cabinet.

months.[8] The level of violence continued to escalate throughout 1932, and was exacerbated by Papen's ban on political rallies, imposed from 29 July, which left political extremists with few legal outlets for their dynamism. Papen's emergency decree of 9 August made the killing of a person in a political fight, motivated by anger or hatred, punishable by death. It was, of course, arguable that such cases were already covered by Paragraph 211 of the Criminal Code, the murder paragraph. However, in the circumstances of 1932, the Chancellor thought it necessary to signal his determination to impose the death penalty by issuing a special decree. Papen made it clear that its basic thrust was against the Communists, whom he blamed for the violence, rather than the National Socialists, to whom he was broadly sympathetic.[9] But two hours after the decree came into force, in the small hours of 10 August 1932, a group of drunken brownshirts, armed with a rubber truncheon, pistols, and broken-off billiard cues, entered a farmhouse in the Upper Silesian village of Potempa and attacked one of the inhabitants, the agricultural labourer Konrad Pietzuch, a Pole well known as a sympathizer with the Communist Party. After hitting him in the face with a billiard cue, beating him mercilessly for a lengthy period, and kicking him repeatedly as he lay on the floor, the brownshirts finished him off with a revolver. This was only one of many such incidents at this time, and it was caused as much by local, personal rivalries as by racial and political antagonisms. But the fact that it fell under the terms of Papen's decree of 9 August gave it national significance. Brought to trial in Beuthen, the brownshirts were accused of political manslaughter under the terms of the decree, and on 22 August five of them were found guilty and sentenced to death. The National Socialists immediately protested, and there were violent physical attacks on Jewish businesses and liberal and left-wing newspaper premises in the town. Hitler condemned the passing of 'this monstrous blood-judgment', while Hermann Göring telegraphed the condemned men to express his 'limitless embitterment and outrage at the terroristic sentence which has been passed on you'. Both promised their solidarity and support in the fight to overturn the verdict.[10]

Meanwhile, Reich President von Hindenburg was considering bringing the Nazis, who had formed by far the largest party in the Reichstag since the elections of July 1932, into the cabinet, in order to give the Papen government a degree of popular legitimacy, which it had so far entirely lacked. 'I have not', he told Hitler on 13 August, 'had any doubts about your patriotism. But I shall

[8] Gumbel, *Lasst Köpfe*, 6. See also Christian Jansen, *Emil Julius Gumbel. Portrait eines Zivilisten* (Heidelberg, 1991).

[9] See Papen's speech, quoted in Hannover, *Politische Justiz*, 298.

[10] For the verdict, and public reactions to it, see Paul Kluke, 'Der Fall Potempa', *Vierteljahreshefte für Zeitgeschichte*, 5 (1957), 279–97. See Richard Bessel, 'The Potempa Murder', *Central European History*, 10 (1977), 241–54, for further details of the case.

intervene very toughly against acts of terrorism and violence', he added, 'such as have regrettably been committed by members of the SA-divisions' (i.e. brownshirts). Hitler rejected the offer on the grounds that he was unwilling to enter any government except as its head. In his public account of the negotiations, he made the Potempa verdict the reason:

Comrades in the German people! Anyone amongst you who has any feeling for the struggle for the honour and freedom of the nation will understand why I am refusing to join this government. Herr Papen's justice will perhaps eventually condemn thousands of National Socialists to death. Did anyone think they could put my name as well to this blindly aggressive action, this challenge to the entire people? The gentlemen are mistaken! Herr von Papen, I know your bloodstained 'objectivity' now! I want victory for a nationalistic Germany, and extermination for its Marxist destroyers and corrupters. I am not suited to be the hangman of the German people!

And he promised that the struggle against 'the Beuthen verdict' would continue.[11] 'In the National Socialist Reich', he added on 7 September, 'five German men will never be condemned because of a Pole.'[12]

While the Nazis cynically tried to turn a squalid act of murder into a heroic act of nationalist self-defence, the liberal press was caught in a classic dilemma. Should they endorse the Potempa verdict and thus abandon their opposition to the death penalty? Or should they stick to their principles and risk playing into Hitler's hands? The venerable *Frankfurter Zeitung* chose the latter course, and declared on 23 August that it would be wrong to execute the five men. Similarly, the Social Democrats' daily paper, *Vorwärts*, commented:

The Potempa murder was a mean and shameful deed. Nevertheless, the thought that five men must lose their lives for it is shocking. These five are not the most guilty parties in this affair! The most guilty ones are those people who have been encouraging political murder in Germany for years. From the murder of Erzberger and Rathenau to the assassination attempts of recent times, the footprints of these politicians are dripping with blood. They are demanding clemency for the people whom they have taught the art of murder, but in the same breath they are screaming for the wheel and the gallows, for the axe and the block, for those who are daring to oppose a new religion of humanitarianism to their blood-curdling fantasies. . . . We Social Democrats are not looking for an alliance with the hangman when we fight the good fight.[13]

Hitler's open support of the murderers, declared the *Frankfurter Zeitung*, demonstrated that it was time 'to stop giving credence to the eternal bawling about the "legal intentions" of the National Socialists (which would really be equivalent to a recognition of the inviolability of the law)'. Hitler, said the liberal daily, had 'torn the mask from his face'.[14]

---

[11] Hannover, *Politische Justiz*, 308–9. [12] Ibid. 310. [13] Quoted ibid. 307.
[14] Quoted ibid. 309. For the *Frankfurter Zeitung*, see Eksteins, *Limits*, and, more generally, Oron J. Hale, *The Captive Press in the Third Reich* (Princeton, 1964).

Despite this row, Chancellor von Papen had not given up the idea of co-opting the Nazis into his government. If the death sentences passed on the Potempa murderers were an obstacle, that could easily be dealt with. President Hindenburg was in favour of commuting their sentences to life imprisonment. But the matter lay within the competence of the Prussian government. On 2 September, under the chairmanship of Papen as Reich Commissioner, it decided—despite the dubious legality of its position and the disputed status of the power of clemency—to reprieve the killers on the grounds 'that, at the time of the offence, the condemned men had not taken any cognizance of the Reich President's decree of 9 August against political terror and the severe penal sanctions contained therein'. The five brownshirts were thus the only capital offenders in Prussia whose death sentences were commuted in 1932. All the others awaited a decision on the locus of sovereignty in Prussia well into the following year. By the time it was reached, the Potempa murderers were free again, released from prison under an amnesty issued on 23 March 1933 for political offences committed by 'champions of the national revival'.[15] The Chancellor of the government that issued the amnesty was Adolf Hitler, appointed to the post by President Hindenburg on 30 January 1933, with Papen as his deputy, hoping, in vain as it quickly turned out, to keep him in check.[16]

b. The Reichstag Fire and the Lex van der Lubbe

As the serried ranks of torch-bearing brownshirts paraded through the streets on the night of his appointment as Reich Chancellor, Hitler knew that the real 'seizure of power' was still to come. For the majority of his cabinet colleagues were not Nazis at all, but conservatives such as Papen. These men regarded Hitler as a political amateur and thought they had manœuvred him into providing them with no more than passive mass support in their bid to restore an authoritarian regime rather like the one that had gone under with the abdication of the Kaiser in 1918. They soon found out how wrong they were. At first, although Nazi violence against Communists and Social Democrats escalated as the brownshirts were given effective immunity by enrolment as auxiliary policemen, Hitler seems to have had little concrete idea of how to convert his position as head of yet another Weimar coalition into the one-party dictatorship that was his aim. Then, unexpectedly, on the night of 27–8 February 1933, he was presented with a golden opportunity. A young Dutch anarchist, Marinus van der Lubbe,

---

[15] Hannover, *Politische Justiz*, 310; see also Karl-Heinz Minuth (ed.), *Akten der Reichskanzlei: Weimarer Republik: Das Kabinett von Papen 1. Juni bis 3. Dezember 1932* (Boppard, 1989), 146, 491–5.

[16] For a convenient summary of these events, see Martin Broszat, *Hitler and the Collapse of Weimar Germany* (Oxford, 1987).

decided on a dramatic protest against the recently appointed Nazi–conservative coalition government, and against the failure of the German Social Democrats and Communists to rise up in arms to overthrow it. On the evening of 27 February 1933 he made his way to the Reichstag, armed with a bagful of firelighters, matches, and flammable material. Once inside, he raced through the building, setting light to the curtains and the dry wooden benches and fittings in the restaurant and the chamber of deputies. Soon the whole building was in flames. By the early morning it was gutted.[17]

This famous crime symbolized for many, not least for the Nazis themselves, the kind of disorder and chaos for which the Weimar Republic was so despised. Hitler, Göring, and Goebbels quickly pinned the blame on a Communist conspiracy. They portrayed it as the first act in the planned left-wing uprising which the Nazis so much feared. Hitler obtained from the aged President Hindenburg a far-reaching decree 'for the protection of people and state', which suspended basic civil rights and provided the legal, or pseudo-legal, justification for the mass arrests of Communists, Social Democrats, and trade unionists that immediately followed. Thousands of Hitler's opponents were placed in 'protective custody', beaten up, tortured, and physically abused. Many were killed. The labour movement was crushed.[18] Shortly afterwards, a general election was held in which Hitler was able, thanks to the suppression of the Communists and the help of his conservative allies, to win a parliamentary majority. He used it to pass an 'Enabling Act' giving him virtually unlimited power to bypass the parliament and override the constitution. By the early summer, all remaining civil liberties had been suspended, all political parties except the Nazis banned, and virtually the whole of the public sphere and organizational life in Germany brought under total Nazi control.[19]

The wave of letters, telegrams, and petitions that flooded in to the Reich Ministry of Justice immediately after the Reichstag fire testified to the success scored by the Nazi propaganda machine in portraying it as a Communist revolutionary plot. Over two hundred telegrams from all over Germany demanded that the 'subhumans who wanted to destroy the Reichstag building in its

---

[17] Horst Karasek, *Der Brandstifter. Lehr- und Wanderjahre des Maurergesellen Marinus van der Lubbe, der 1933 auszog, den Reichstag anzuzünden* (Berlin, 1980); and Fritz Tobias, *The Reichstag Fire* (London, 1963). For the controversy over attempts by the Communists and others to prove that the fire was deliberately started by the Nazis, see Karl-Heinz Janssen, 'Geschichte aus der Dunkelkammer. Kabalen um den Reichstagsbrand. Eine unvermeidliche Enthüllung', *Die Zeit*, 38–41 (Sept.–Oct. 1979), and Uwe Backes *et al.*, *Reichstagsbrand: Aufklärung einer historischen Legende* (Munich, 1986).

[18] Martin Broszat, 'The Concentration Camps 1933–45', in Helmut Krausnick (ed.), *Anatomy of the SS State* (London, 1968), 397–504, here 400–30. More generally, see Lothar Gruchmann, *Justiz im Dritten Reich 1933–1940. Anpassung und Unterwerfung in der Ära Gürtner* (Munich, 1988), 535–44.

[19] Karl Dietrich Bracher, *Stufen der Machtergreifung*, vol. i of idem, Wolfgang Sauer, and Gerhard Schulz, *Die nationalsozialistische Machtergreifung. Studien zur Errichtung der totalitären Herrschaftssystems in Deutschland 1933/34* (Opladen, 1960).

entirety',[20] the 'red ruffians',[21] the 'Reichstag criminals and the Marxists who are pulling their strings' should be shot or hanged.[22] Many of these messages were obviously from local party or brownshirt organizations, sent in the attempt to put pressure on a judicial administration that everyone knew to be still largely in the hands of conservative jurists appointed during the Imperial period. They spoke a general language of hatred and contempt against the 'red rabble'.[23] 'Only the complete extermination of the pack of red criminals', wrote Georg S. from Königsberg on 2 March, 'will guarantee political renewal.'[24] The ironmonger Hermann K., writing the same day from Krefeld, demanded the 'elimination of the murderous Communist plague'.[25] Another petition declared on 3 March:

The straight-thinking part of the population of Tann, without distinction of political or ideological position, is outraged and filled with repugnance by the criminal attack on the Reichstag building and the demonic exterminatory plans of the infernal instincts which would have turned our Fatherland into a blood-soaked ruin. With passionate fervour we expect in the most definite way possible that the Reichstag assassin and all the spiritual originators of this criminal action will be condemned to death ruthlessly and without delay as a warning to the victims of their seductive power.[26]

The half-panicky, half-vengeful language of many telegrams was unrestrained in its blood-lust. 'We demand the head of the arsonist of the Reichstag building—Several citizens.'[27] 'The population of the Mosel wants the Reichstag perpetrator and his accomplices to be put up against a wall.'[28] 'String up the Reichstag assassin—Women of Nuremberg.'[29] 'Demonstration of assembled national comrades demands the strangulation of the arsonist of the Reichstag in front of the Reichstag building—NSDAP Winzig.'[30] The authors of one petition even attempted to set it in verse: 'The bullet is a soldier's end, for this man it's much too kind, he is a traitor, use your bullet later. Give van der Lubbe a rope, give the people freedom and hope', wrote the 'nationalists of Southern Franconia', from the town of Weitlingen.[31]

It is obviously difficult to gauge how much of this torrent of hatred was channelled and directed by the Nazi media. The language of extermination was doubtless borrowed partly from the Nazi press, and the demands to hang van der Lubbe 'and his accomplices' clearly took their cue from the Nazi leadership. But

[20] BA Potsdam RJM 5666, Bl. 14: Einwohner von Guntershausen to RJM, 4 Mar. 1933.
[21] Ibid., Bl. 92: Robert E., Stralsund, to RJM, 3 Mar. 1933.
[22] Ibid., Bl. 47: Stadtrat H., Rostock, to RJM, 4 Mar. 1933.
[23] Ibid., Bl. 104: O., Königsberg, to RJM, 2 Mar. 1933.
[24] Ibid., Bl. 103.   [25] Ibid., Bl. 89.
[26] Ibid., Bl. 15.   [27] Ibid., Bl. 30 (Frankenberg, 6 Mar. 1933).
[28] Ibid., Bl. 33 (5 Mar. 1933).   [29] Ibid., Bl. 2 (4 Mar. 1933).
[30] Ibid., Bl. 130 (3 Mar. 1933).
[31] Ibid., Bl. 197 (4 Mar. 1933). The original German verse did not scan either.

however much it was encouraged by the fury and panic of Hitler, Göring, and Goebbels on 27–8 February, the surge of demands for van der Lubbe to be killed also had its own sources in the revolutionary impatience of much of the party rank and file, an impatience that at times was so violent that Hitler and the Nazi leadership made public attempts to rein it in.[32] 'Fear unrest because Reichstag assassin not yet punished', telegraphed the mayor of Bad Bramstedt, in Holstein, on 3 March;[33] and he was echoed by Albert H., of Bogenthin, Kolberg, on the Baltic coast, the next day: 'Population is upset that the Reichstag assassin is not yet hanging from the gallows.'[34] 'Among the working people there is bitterness and disappointment about . . . the failure to condemn the Reichstag arsonist', as another submission put it;[35] and there were numerous telegrams expressing 'amazement' at the fact that 'the Reichstag arsonist has not been shot yet'.[36] All this was a characteristic example of the revolutionary populist-dema-gogic dialectic that propelled Hitler's Chancellorship of a conservative-domi-nated coalition government in early February 1933 into a one-party dictatorship by the end of June.

It was striking that so many of the petitions and telegrams urged that the arsonist should be shot or decapitated. Evidently hanging did not occur to many Germans. Yet Hitler, determined on sending van der Lubbe to an ignominious death, had declared that the arsonist would be hanged.[37] In doing so he was perhaps forgetting the fact that, while hanging was the prescribed method of execution in his native Austria, it had not been used in Germany since the eighteenth century, and was not provided for in any law code or statute book. Moreover, since the middle of the nineteenth century, arson had not been punishable by death anyway. Confronted with the obvious legal difficulty of putting his threat into action, Hitler was forced to seek expert advice. On 4 March 1933 he sent a formal request to three conservative professors of law, who were known to be sympathetic to the Nazi cause, for an opinion on the matter. They replied that van der Lubbe could possibly be convicted of the capital offence of high treason if it could be proved that he had set fire to the Reichstag in order to overthrow the state. A special law, however, would be needed if a

[32] Timothy W. Mason, *Sozialpolitik im Dritten Reich. Arbeiterklasse und Volksgemeinschaft* (Opladen, 1977), 82–8.
[33] BA Potsdam RJM 5666, Bl. 164.
[34] Ibid., Bl. 175.
[35] Ibid., Bl. 215, 6 Mar.
[36] Ibid., Bl. 28, 6 Mar. For the debate, see Gruchmann, *Justiz*, 822–9.
[37] Hitler frequently declared that 'traitors' of various kinds would be hanged (see Eberhard Jäckel (ed.), *Hitler. Sämtliche Aufzeichnungen 1905–1924* (Stuttgart, 1980), 371, for an example from 1921; see also BA Potsdam RJM 5666, Bl. 28: Karl Köhler to RJM, 30 Mar. 1933). Indeed, on the night of the fire, Hitler declared that all the Communist deputies in the Reichstag would be hanged (Tobias, *Reichstag Fire*, 112).

special court were to be set up to try him. Otherwise the case would have to go through the normal judicial process. Another special law would be required if hanging were to be used as a punishment. Moreover, there was a more serious problem to be dealt with. Professors Oether, Nagler, and von Weber pointed out that it was against all legal principle to pass a law applying a penalty retrospectively to a crime that had not carried it at the time when it had been committed. If the death penalty had been in force at the time of his offence, then van der Lubbe might have been deterred from his actions, and he might never have committed the crime in the first place. In any case, the professors added, a retrospective application of the death penalty was sure to attract widespread public criticism.[38]

The conservative bureaucrats in the Reich Justice Ministry reinforced this opinion. They advised that a retrospective application of the decree was likely to lead to a 'confusion of the general consciousness of right and wrong'.[39] Nevertheless, the Nazi leadership and its allies in the cabinet decided to go ahead anyway, not least in view of the pressure to do so that was being exerted from the Nazi rank and file. On 29 March 1933 the government, acting through Hindenburg, applied the death penalty provisions of the Reichstag fire decree of 28 February 1933 retrospectively to offences committed since 31 January 1933, Hitler's first full day in office. These included treason, poisoning, arson, conspiracy to kill the President or any member of the government, encouragement of any attempt to do so, armed insurgency, and the taking of political hostages. The decree, soon known as the Lex van der Lubbe, allowed the death penalty to be executed by hanging for any of these offences.[40] Just as Hitler's legal advisers had predicted, this came in for a good deal of criticism. The *Frankfurter Zeitung*, once one of Germany's great liberal dailies, and still not entirely subservient to Goebbels's orchestration of the press, recognized that the decree was an attempt to apply retrospective justification to Hitler's incautious promise that van der Lubbe would be hanged. It condemned the law's breach of the legal principle *nulla poena sine lege*, no punishment without a law. This was an innovation of profound importance for the future. Now nobody could be sure what the punishment for their offence would be by the time they came to trial.[41]

Yet the matter was not as clear-cut as the paper maintained. Hardly anyone under the Weimar Republic, not even the most persistent advocates of abolition, had been prepared to abandon the principle of capital punishment for politically

[38] BA Potsdam RJM 5666, Bl. 7–9: Anlage I—Gutachten; also Anlage II—Aufzeichnung zur Frage der Bestrafung der Täter, die am 27. Februar 1933 das Reichstagsgebäude in Brand gesetzt haben.

[39] Ibid., Bl. 16.

[40] GStA Berlin Rep. 84a/7792: *BZ am Mittag*, 1 Apr. 1933, and *Frankfurter Zeitung*, 2 Apr. 1933.

[41] HStA Munich MJu 13144: *Frankfurter Zeitung*, 2 Apr. 1933. See also GStA Berlin Rep. 84a/7786, Bl. 321: *Deutsche Allgemeine Zeitung*, 23 May 1933.

motivated murder, treason, and other offences in times of emergency, when the
state was under threat. The Social Democrats had included it in the Law for the
Protection of the Republic and made it applicable to the attempted murder of
government ministers; Reich President Ebert had extended it by decree to a
further range of offences and made it retrospective; Reich Justice Minister Koch-
Weser, the most effective opponent of the death penalty under Weimar, had
explicitly foreseen its retention under emergency legislation even while proposing
its deletion from the Criminal Code; the Communists had defended it as an
emergency weapon of self-defence by the Soviet regime in Russia; the Nationalists and the far right, who were committed to the retention, indeed the extension,
of the death penalty in criminal law anyway, had applauded its summary use
against revolutionary workers in Munich in 1919 and 'Red Army' units in the
Ruhr in 1920. There had thus been almost universal consensus on the retention
of capital punishment as a measure of self-defence by the state in time of
emergency. The Nazis built on this consensus in the permanent state of emergency on which the legislation of the Third Reich largely rested. These similarities to legislation already enacted under the Weimar Republic helped dull the
minds of conservatives and other sympathizers with the new regime to the fact
that it was engaged in a fundamental subversion of the principles of justice, a
subversion which in due course would go far beyond anything they had so far
envisaged or were initially prepared to support.[42]

In the mean time, determined to pin the blame for the fire on a Communist
conspiracy, the Nazis and the police arrested the head of the Western European
office of the Communist International in Berlin, the Bulgarian Georgi Dimitrov,
and a number of his party comrades, and brought them to trial, along with van
der Lubbe, before the fourth criminal senate or division of the Supreme Court in
Leipzig in September. The presiding judge was none other than Dr Wilhelm
Bünger, the People's Party lawyer and politician from Saxony who had produced
such a hostile report on Jakubowski for the Mecklenburg-Strelitz government
some years previously. Prejudiced though he was, Bünger was not a man to ride
roughshod over questions of legality and proof in the interests of political
expediency. Indeed, in his re-examination of the evidence in the Jakubowski case,
he had been the first person to come close to the likely truth. And hard though
the Nazis tried, they could bring no evidence forward to show that any of the
accused apart from van der Lubbe had been directly involved in the burning of
the Reichstag. Dimitrov defended himself with ingenuity and skill, delivering
in the process a good deal of Communist rhetoric and doing what he could to pin
the blame for the fire on the Nazis. Bünger and his fellow judges concluded that

[42] For the legal implications of the Reichstag fire decree, see Gruchmann, *Justiz*, 535–44.

the Communist Party had indeed deliberately planned the fire as the signal for a revolutionary uprising, and thus retrospectively justified the measures taken by Hitler and his government in its immediate aftermath. They did not doubt van der Lubbe's guilt, and sentenced him to death in accordance with the Lex van der Lubbe, the Nazi decree promulgated earlier in the year in order to make this possible. But Dimitrov and the others were acquitted. The evidence of their guilt, said the court, was insufficient, and the true conspirators still had to be found.[43] The Nazis trumpeted the verdict in public as proof 'that the new Germany, whose national revolution has been carried out with remarkable discipline, is sticking to the law'.[44] The trial had been the subject of an international campaign on Dimitrov's behalf, orchestrated from Moscow,[45] and the regime was clearly concerned to counter its effects on public opinion outside Germany. Privately, however, Hitler and the leading Nazis were furious. The legal system had failed to support them. They could not even fulfil Hitler's promise that van der Lubbe would be hanged. In May 1933 executioner Gröpler had reported that he was certainly in a position to hang people, if that was what was required.[46] But executions ordered by the Supreme Court were customarily carried out by the guillotine, and this is what, on 10 January 1934, happened to van der Lubbe. Already by this time, the Nazi leadership was making sure that, whatever the result of the Reichstag fire trial, the Dutchman did not have to suffer this fate alone.

c. National Socialism and Capital Punishment

Like many others on the far right, including a large number of Nationalists, the Nazis regarded penal policy not as the outcome of moral principles or rational considerations, but as an expression of racial character. Paula Müller-Otfried, the anti-Semitic Nationalist Reichstag deputy and women's leader, said in 1929: 'Simple, natural, primitive-thinking people, namely in the so-called working population, are demanding the retention of the death penalty, while people whose nature is troubled with problems, people who question everything, are demanding its abolition.'[47] 'Primitive' here was a word with positive rather than negative connotations. 'Homage' was paid to 'healthy popular feeling, that

[43] H. Bernhard *et al.* (eds.), *Der Reichstagsbrandprozess und Georgi Dimitroff: Dokumente* (2 vols.; Berlin, 1982–9), and Georgi Dimitroff, *Reichstagsbrandprozess. Dokumente, Briefe und Aufzeichnungen* (Berlin, 1946). Until the fall of the Communist regime in East Germany in 1989, a large part of the Supreme Court building in Leipzig was given over to a museum celebrating Dimitrov's life and work and his role in the Reichstag fire trial.

[44] Alfons Sack, *Der Reichstagsbrandprozess* (Berlin, 1934).

[45] Anon. (ed.), *Braunbuch über Reichstagsbrand und Hitlerterror* (Basel, 1933).

[46] GStA Berlin Rep. 84a/7786, Bl. 349–51.

[47] Ibid.: *Bremer Nachrichten*, 14 Feb. 1929.

demands the severest expiation for the severest guilt', as a right-wing jurist put it in 1927.[48] 'In these matters', one retentionist writer opined in 1931, 'the people has a far surer judgement, and a far healthier instinct than politicians, men of letters, and theoreticians, who will always find in every murderer something to serve as an excuse for his deeds, no matter how much of a monster he might be.'[49] Such anti-intellectualism had long been common on the populist wing of the far right. What was new was the racial connotation. 'Healthy popular feeling' became a synonym for public opinion, reconceptualizing it in biological terms. The demand for executions, as one right-wing lawyer put it in 1928, came 'from the general need of the people for retribution, which is connected with the instinct for self-preservation'.[50] Thus the principles of revenge and retribution were transformed from relics of a barbaric past into immutable principles of biological self-defence in the struggle between the races for the survival of the fittest. A whole literature had indeed grown up, in which legal ethnologists traced back the death penalty and the ceremonies connected with its implementation to the Germanic tribes in the days of Arminius and his defeat of the Roman legions in the Teutoburg forest. The death penalty was an expression of the Germanic racial soul's desire for justice in the face of its perversion by Marxists and Jews. Its exercise would be a demonstration of the determination of the 'Aryan' race to defend itself and recover from the weakness of the Weimar years.[51]

As far as the Nazis were concerned, indeed, the abolitionist movement of the Weimar years was a wicked conspiracy led by a clique of Jewish lawyers.[52] As early as 1920, Hitler himself had condemned the abolition of the death penalty as a trick advocated by the Jewish race 'for its own security'.[53] 'The Jewish-Marxist press, so-called doctors, psychologists, and defenders of human rights' had deliberately undermined the security of the German race by encouraging softness towards crime, he said. 'Marxism had made its baleful influence felt in the German judicial system in that humanitarianism was misused and blindly applied to penal policy.'[54] Looking back on the penal policy of the Weimar Republic in the late summer of 1933, Roland Freisler, defence lawyer for Nazis in numerous criminal trials, and, after the seizure of power, State Secretary in the Prussian Justice Ministry, considered that the various theories which had informed it, from deterrence to improvement, had all reflected the excessive individualism of the period:

[48] BA Potsdam RJM 6097, Bl. 79: Amtsgerichtsrat Dr Herfurth, in *Deutsche Tageszeitung*, 26 Oct. 1927.
[49] Ibid. 61 Re 1/1773, 56: Hans Krobath, 'Mordseuche und Todesstrafe' (typescript, Allgemeine Zeitungsdienst, 15 Apr. 1931).
[50] GStA Berlin Rep. 84a/7792: *Kölnische Zeitung*, 26 Nov. 1928 (Rechtsanwalt Klesisch).
[51] See the discussion of this literature in the Introduction to the present book.
[52] BA Potsdam RJM 5667, Bl. 17: *Deutsche Zeitung*, 9 May 1933.
[53] Jäckel (ed.), *Hitler*, 275.   [54] GStA Berlin Rep. 84a/7792: *Vorwärts*, 29 May 1929.

In the period of individualism, it was inevitable that people's attention was fascinated by the individual in every policy or consideration that was undertaken, in this case towards the criminal. To win back his 'personality', through love, understanding, goodness, to shower murderers, burglars, and rapists with good deeds and lead them upwards, that was in the end the meaning of penal policy.

The result, he claimed, had been a massive crime wave. Those sentenced to prison had had it very easy, with lots to eat and plenty of leisure. They would now have to work extremely hard, he promised, to cancel out their offences. 'Everyone must expiate the evil he does.' For murder, the only possible expiation was death.[55]

In 1930, therefore, the Nazis demanded a plebiscite on the issue of the death penalty, alleging:

We know for certain that the broad mass of the German people, who have still preserved a clear and healthy attitude in all basic questions despite all the poison spread about by the Jews in these matters, has made our views, National Socialist views, their own, and with their natural instincts condemn those sex killers, those beasts who murder and rob, to death, instead of excusing them with 'repressed emotional complexes'.[56]

This was, to be sure, mere polemic. The Nazis took no practical steps in the direction of a plebiscite. Nevertheless, the party argued from the outset that capital punishment was primarily an act of racial self-defence. What the interests of the race were, of course, would be defined by the Nazis themselves. In his early speeches in Munich, Hitler had not been slow to demand the death penalty for a whole variety of offenders, from white slavers and revolutionary leaders to 'all profiteers and black marketeers', whose execution was also demanded in the Nazi Party Programme of 1921. All these groups of offenders Hitler explicitly branded as Jewish, and on 2 February 1922, speaking before an evidently excited and enthusiastic party audience in Munich, he said: 'Every Jew who is caught with a blonde girl should be . . . ['strung up!'] . . . I don't want to say, strung up, but there should be a court to condemn these Jews [*applause*].'[57] The statement, and the excited atmosphere in which it was made, testified not only to the Nazis' indelible racism and murderous anti-Semitism, but also to the sexual prurience which often accompanied these ideological impulses. The demand for the death penalty for sexual relations between Germans and Jews was subsequently repeated by the Nazi ideologue Alfred Rosenberg in his *Myth of the Twentieth Century*.[58] And in his autobiographical and progammatic book *Mein Kampf*

[55] BA Potsdam 61 Re 1/1773, 83: Zeitungsdienst (Berliner Dienst), 7 Aug. 1933: Roland Freisler, 'Gedanken zum Strafvollzug'. See also Roland Freisler, *Nationalsozialistisches Recht und Rechtsdenken* (Berlin, 1938), 43.

[56] BA Potsdam 61 Re 1/1773: *Der National-Sozialist*, 14 Mar. 1930.

[57] Jäckel (ed.), *Hitler*, 115, 132, 166, 198, 252, 455, 565.

[58] Alfred Rosenberg, *Der Mythus des 20. Jahrhunderts*, 38th edn. (Munich, 1934), 580.

('My Struggle'), published in two volumes in 1925–6, Hitler called for the death penalty for everyone who had been involved in the November Revolution of 1918, which he regarded (in defiance of the facts) as having been responsible for Germany's defeat in the First World War, declaring 'that petty thieves should not be hanged so that big ones can run around freely, but some time a National Socialist Court must condemn and execute some ten thousands of the organizing and therefore responsible criminals of the November treachery and everything connected with it'.[59] The Potempa case had also indicated that the Nazis thought that Germans should never be executed for killing Poles. The death penalty in the Third Reich, declared the party's daily newspaper, the *Völkischer Beobachter*, in 1931, two years before the Nazi seizure of power, would be applied not just to murderers but to 'murderers of the people' as well. 'Those who destroy the race, or betray the armed forces, are far worse in the consequences of their deeds than is the individual murderer.' Such enemies of the race as pacifist propagandists were included in the category of 'murderers of the people', and the newspaper promised that the National Socialist state, when it was established, would get rid of them without delay.[60]

Nazi propaganda in the Weimar Republic repeatedly portrayed Social Democrats and Communists as murderers, in order to create a climate in which the killing of left-wing paramilitaries, politicians, and trade unionists by the brownshirts could be justified in terms of self-defence.[61] Writ large, this also involved the presentation of Nazi political violence in terms of self-defence by 'the nation'. Verdicts were regarded by the Nazis quite explicitly as political, and they sharply attacked the 'objectivity' of the judges, who failed to distinguish between violence against patriotic National Socialists and violence against revolutionary 'Jewish Bolsheviks'. 'One person is not the same as another,' as the *Völkscher Beobachter* declared, 'nor is one deed the same as another.' On 11 August 1932 the Nazi paper, ironically in view of subsequent events, condemned the Papen government's decree on political murder as weak and ineffective, assuming, before the Potempa case came to light, that it was directed against the left. Street fighting, declared the paper, was entirely the fault of Communist and 'Marxist'—or, in other words, Social Democratic—revolutionaries. A National Socialist government, it promised, would stop it 'by the immediate arrest and condemnation of all Communist and Social Democratic party officials, the concentrated smoking-out of the murder-quarters and the *accommodation* of

[59] Adolf Hitler, *Mein Kampf* (Munich, 1942), 610.
[60] BA Potsdam 61 Re 1/1773: *Völkischer Beobachter*, 4 July 1931.
[61] Hannover, *Politische Justiz*, 275–6. Also, Friedrich Karl Kaul, *Geschichte des Reichsgerichts*, iv. *1933–1945* (East Berlin, 1971). For the origins of Nazi criminal legal thought, see Erhard-Josef Lüken, *Der Nationalsozialismus und das materielle Strafrecht* (Ph.D. diss., Göttingen, 1988).

Paragraphen gegen Freiheitskämpfer

Unser das Recht — euer die Justiz!

F IG. 36. *The Nazi view of Weimar justice.* 'Justice is ours, the law is yours!' Note the 'Jewish' features of the figure standing behind the judge who is holding up the lawbook. The cartoon makes clear both the Nazis' contempt for the letter of the law and their conviction that the judicial system was run by a Jewish conspiracy. The brawny, threatening presence of the brownshirt on the left, fist clenched at the ready, already suggests the way in which the Nazis were to bully and intimidate the legal profession once they were in power. The title reads: 'Paragraphs against Freedom-fighters'.

suspects and intellectual instigators in *concentration camps*.[62] Such a threat indicated the determination of the Nazis to use the law as a weapon in the political struggle. It was not to be taken lightly. The death penalty was to apply not just to murderers, but to anyone who flouted the will of the nation as the Nazis defined it. Taking his cue from Hitler's early speeches, Joseph Goebbels, Gauleiter of Berlin and later Propaganda Minister under the Third Reich, told the Reichstag in 1929: 'We National Socialists won't leave any room for doubt: we are no supporters of political murder; on the contrary, our view is that in Germany the time will one day come when those who have plunged the German

[62] Quoted in Hannover, *Politische Justiz*, 301–6.

people into the deepest disaster will be strung up legally.'[63] A clear echo of earlier demands by Hitler for the most ignominious means of execution to be applied to the Nazis' most committed opponents, this was no mere rhetoric. But too many of the Nazis' opponents thought it was. In 1928 the Nazi deputies in the Reichstag put forward a motion demanding the death penalty for any German who attempted 'to cripple or destroy the will of the German people to political and cultural self-assertion'. Such a line of argument adumbrated the distinction that would be drawn so sharply in the Third Reich between racial 'comrades' (*Volksgenossen*) and 'community aliens' (*Gemeinschaftsfremde*). It resolved the apparent self-contradiction of those Nationalists who had campaigned for the retention of the death penalty in general while sharply criticizing the idea of applying it to the assassins of Weimar politicians like Walther Rathenau in particular. Such men were not criminals in this view because they were acting to defend the Germanic race against its enemies.

'Anyone who illegally destroys a human life', declared the Nazi daily paper in July 1931, 'will thereby become liable to destruction himself, unless his deed was justified in a higher interest, that is, the interest of the nation.'[64] As another article in the same paper proclaimed in 1929, 'In a National Socialist State, not just murder, but also equally *every capital crime against the interests of the nation* must have as its consequence the death of the culprit.' In redefining the death penalty as a weapon in the struggle for political regeneration and racial supremacy, the Nazis took the opportunity to deliver a few sideswipes at the conservative and Nationalist right as well as attacking what they saw as the 'sentimental humanitarianism' of the liberal and Marxist left. Impatiently sweeping away the religious trappings of the conventional right-wing demand for death as a 'just expiation' for murder, the Nazis presented capital punishment purely in terms of biological extermination:

The concept of punishment as expiation can have no justification any more in the nationalistic state. . . . The conscious nationalist is more honest here. What serves him as the foundation of his legal system is not pharisaic hypocrisy, but the *law of might*, which incorporates itself in the ties which bind his own people together in blood and war. For this reason, there can be no 'punishment', no 'expiation' in the nationalistic state either, concepts with which the feeble type of mentality of the respectable bourgeois is accustomed to maintain itself. There is no such thing as justice or law in itself. Anything which has asserted itself as 'law' in the struggle for power must be protected, for the sake of the victorious power itself as well. . . . *Criminals are not punished, only rendered harmless.*

[63] *Stenographische Berichte über die Verhandlungen des deutschen Reichstags*, 25 June 1929 (quoted in Hannover, *Politische Justiz*, 277).

[64] Quoted in Hans-Ludwig Schreiber, 'Die Strafgesetzgebung im "Dritten Reich"', in Dreier and Sellert (eds.), *Recht und Justiz*, 151–79, here 156.

'Rendering harmless', a phrase used by criminologists since the turn of the century to mean anything from imprisonment to sterilization, acquired a new, unequivocally murderous meaning here. Thus in answer to the question posed in the title of his article, 'Punishment or Extermination?', the author, Ludwig Binz, came down explicitly on the side of the latter.[65] The death penalty was to be transformed from an instrument of penal policy into a tool of racial and political engineering. Capital punishment was not merely a matter of retribution but also of eugenic policy. It was necessary to protect society against habitual criminals, whether they had murdered or not.[66] 'Punishment', wrote the Nazi ideologue Alfred Rosenberg in 1935, 'is . . . simply the weeding-out of alien types and beings foreign to our species.'[67] As such, it could even be presented as more humane than its application under Weimar. As the Nazis' daily paper declared in 1931:

There is nothing more hypocritical than the cheap self-satisfaction which the ordinary middle-class man expresses at the execution of a murderer. . . . For us, the murderer is *a tragic child of fate*, often the product of the depraved blood of whole generations, from which irresponsible governments have neglected to provide us with eugenic protection.

There was only one way to deal with such individuals, the newspaper concluded: they must be 'destroyed'.[68]

Such ideas drew heavily on the rhetoric of racial hygiene and 'negative eugenics' which had become so widespread in penal and criminological discourse during the Weimar years, simplified it, politicized it to an unprecedented degree, and carried it further than almost anyone had so far imagined it could or should be taken. The function of the death penalty in weeding out criminals from the chain of heredity, and thus strengthening the German race, had already been pointed out by Social Darwinists like Ernst Haeckel before the First World War. As we saw in Chapter 12, the search for the biological roots of criminality did not necessarily lead in every instance to the conclusion that hereditary criminals should be sterilized or eliminated, as in the case of Hans von Hentig, who was simultaneously an adherent of the biological view of criminality and an opponent

---

[65] BA Koblenz R22/1314, Bl. 20: Ludwig Binz, 'Strafe oder Vernichtung?', *Völkischer Beobachter*, 5 Jan. 1929.

[66] GStA Berlin Rep. 84a/7792, Bl. 196–210: *Stenographische Berichte über die Verhandlungen des Preussischen Landtags*, 6 Mar. 1929, col. 4787. See also ibid., Bl. 253: *Stenographische Berichte über die Verhandlungen des Preussischen Landtags*, 27 Feb. 1931, col. 18307.

[67] Quoted in Werner Johe, *Die gleichgeschaltete Justiz. Organisation des Rechtswesens und Politisierung der Rechtsprechung 1933–1945 dargestellt am Beispiel des Oberlandesgerichtsbezirks Hamburg* (Frankfurt am Main, 1967), 39. See also Diemut Majer, *Grundlagen des nationalsozialistischen Rechtssystems* (Stuttgart, 1987), esp. 117–200. For the Nazi equation of law and racial morality, see Klaus Anderbrügge, *Völkisches Rechtsdenken. Zur Rechtslehre in der Zeit des Nationalsozialismus* (Berlin, 1978), 136–46.

[68] GStA Berlin Rep. 84a/7792: *Das freie Wort*, 12 July 1931 (quoting *Völkischer Beobachter*).

of the death penalty; indeed, Hentig, who thought that criminal 'clans' were dying out with the advance of civilization, was dismissed from his post in 1933 for protesting against the dehumanization of criminology and the implementation of compulsory sterilization for such people under the Third Reich.[69] Nor was the great Italian pioneer of the biological approach to criminology, Cesare Lombroso, often quoted directly by Nazi criminologists, because he was Jewish. But on the whole the 'criminal-biological' orthodoxy, like other areas of mainstream science and scholarship, adapted itself easily to the new ideological conditions of the Third Reich.[70] Despite the fact that it seemed on the face of it to reduce the influence of specialist medical knowledge in identifying candidates for imprisonment, sterilization, and, ultimately, death, the Nazi inclusion of political deviants, pacifists, and Communists in the category of the biologically unfit drew little comment from the criminologists, most of whom held strongly right-wing political views. Even Hans von Hentig, after all, had followed Lombroso in thinking that revolutionaries were biologically degenerate.[71] And, while continuing to reject Lombroso's argument that criminals were 'born' as 'atavistic' human types, textbook writers such as Edmund Mezger still insisted on the importance of heredity as a predisposing factor, of varying but in principle measurable influence in the making of the 'criminal personality'. Scientifically based data collection by the Criminal Biological Information Centres, established in Bavaria and elsewhere under the Weimar Republic, would identify the 'hereditarily damaged' and distinguish the habitual criminal from the casual offender. Already in 1933, the criminologist Edmund Mezger drew the consequence from this. The aim of penal policy, he wrote, was 'the elimination from the national community of elements which damage the people and the race'.[72] That this would be done not only by a policy of compulsory sterilization but also by the reinstatement of the death penalty and its extension to new kinds of offences was clear from the very beginning.

d. *Legal Reform and the Death Penalty 1933–1939*

Almost as soon as they came to power, the Nazis began applying the death penalty to new offences in conformity with this ideology. The emergency decree

---

[69] Marlis Dürkop, 'Zur Funktion der Kriminologie im Nationalsozialismus', in Udo Reifner and Bernd-Rüdeger Sonnen (eds.), *Strafjustiz und Polizei im Dritten Reich* (Frankfurt am Main, 1984), 97–120, here 101. Hentig returned after 1945 to become one of the founders of criminology in West Germany. Gustav Aschaffenburg, who was Jewish, was also forced to emigrate in 1933.

[70] e.g. Robert Ritter, *Ein Menschenschlag. Erbärztliche Untersuchungen über die—durch 10 Geschlechterfolgen erforschten—Nachkommen von Vagabunden, Jaunern und Räubern* (Leipzig, 1937); or Ferdinand von Neureiter, *Kriminalbiologie* (Berlin, 1940). See Joachim S. Hohmann, *Robert Ritter und die Erben der Kriminalbiologie* (Frankfurt am Main, 1991).

[71] Hentig, *Über den Zusammenhang.*   [72] Mezger, *Kriminalpolitik*, 18–25.

of 28 February 1933 prescribed it for anyone undertaking armed rebellion, causing a death in the process of opposing the government, or inciting someone to do so. On 21 March 1933 another decree extended it to those convicted of committing or threatening an offence against a person or property with the aim of causing public panic.[73] On 4 April 1933 capital punishment was made applicable to a range of offences covered by the Explosive Substances Law of 1884 and the paragraphs of the Criminal Code dealing with the deliberate damaging of railway lines, arson, flooding, and other acts of sabotage. On 13 October 1933 the attempted or planned assassination of any judge, civil servant, policeman, soldier, brownshirt, SS man or Nazi Party official was made punishable by death, if the assassination had been for political reasons or because the real or prospective victim had been singled out on account of his official duties. On 24 April 1934 capital punishment was extended to anyone found guilty of planning to alter the constitution or detach any part of Germany from the Reich by force or threat of force, planning an act of high treason in these senses by distributing leaflets, suborning or subverting the army or police, or acting in a conspiracy to commit the offence. This effectively made the printing and distribution of Communist propaganda, which was still being carried out by the underground resistance movement, punishable by death.[74] On 20 December 1934 the death penalty was also applied to anyone convicted of uttering a particularly 'hateful' statement, claim, or even joke about a leading person in the state or the party. The stream of such measures continued unabated, and on more than one occasion indeed repeated the breach of the principle of *nulla poena sine lege* first undertaken in the Lex van der Lubbe. On 22 June 1938, for example, Hitler personally ordered a new law to be passed during the trial of two brothers accused of highway robberies committed against vehicles being driven on his proud new motorways, the *Autobahnen*, making this type of offence punishable by death, and extending it backwards to cover the date at which the two brothers' crime had been committed.[75]

With this murderous new spirit breathing through the criminal law, the Nazi regime took up once more the preparation of a revised Criminal Code to replace the existing one originally voted by the Reichstag in 1870–1. There had already been numerous drafts under Wilhelm II and during the Weimar Republic, but none had ever reached the statute book. The job of preparing a new, Nazi draft was given to a commission of experts rather than, as previously, to a committee of the Reichstag. The commission was chaired by Reich Justice Minister

[73] Hollweck, *Todesstrafe*, 18–20.

[74] Eduard Kohlrausch (ed.), *Deutsche Strafgesetze vom 19. Dezember 1932 bis 12. Juni 1934* (Berlin, 1934).

[75] Gruchmann, *Justiz*, 897–8. For a useful collection of documents relating to National Socialist criminal law, see Martin Hirsch *et al.* (eds.), *Recht, Verwaltung und Justiz im Nationalsozialismus* (Cologne, 1984), 421–556.

Gürtner. The experts included Professors Georg Dahm, Wenzel Count von Gleispach, Eduard Kohlrausch, Edmund Mezger, and Johannes Nagler, joined later by Friedrich Schaffstein and Hans von Dohnanyi. All of them were legal specialists sympathetic to the Nazi point of view. Although he had resigned as Rector of Berlin University in May 1933, so as not to have to implement Nazi policies, Kohlrausch still produced amended versions of his edition of the Reich Criminal Code, incorporating Nazi laws, all the way up to 1944. He was a Kantian retributionist. Gleispach was an Austrian Nazi, former Rector of Vienna University, who had moved to Berlin in December 1933 to become Professor of Law.[76] Nagler had for many years been a champion of the retributive theory of punishment and an opponent of 'rationalism' in penal policy. He had already been consulted by Hitler during the preparations of the Lex van der Lubbe.[77] Mezger, Professor of Criminal Law at Munich University, was a criminologist who supported, as we have seen, the systematic compilation of a 'criminal-biological' register of offenders, such as had already been instituted under the Weimar Republic.[78] Apart from the Nazi jurists Roland Freisler and Otto-Georg Thierack, however, there were no active party members on the commission, and indeed Dohnanyi subsequently gravitated towards the resistance to Hitler and was executed in April 1945.[79] Nevertheless, there could be no doubt that the members of the commission shared a basic consensus about the nature of their task. As Mezger declared in the preface to his textbook on criminology, written in October 1933:

The massive political and spiritual revolution of the German freedom movement has put the life of the German state on a new political footing. The new total state is constructing itself on the two basic concepts of people and race. . . . The German criminal law reform of the past years did not reach a conclusion; it failed because of the inner divisions and contradictions of warring schools of thought. The new criminal law will start from two leading principles, not (as hitherto) as a compromise, but as a synthesis: the principle of the individual's responsibility to his people, and the principle of the racial improvement of the people as a whole.[80]

By agreeing to sit on the unelected commission set up by the Nazis, all the participants implicitly or explicitly subscribed to this view of its principal aims, even if they thought that they might be able to modify their implementation in matters of detail.

[76] Eduard Rabofsky and Gerhard Oberkofler, *Verborgene Wurzeln der NS-Justiz. Strafrechtliche Rüstung für Zwei Weltkriege* (Vienna, 1985), 130–70.

[77] Johannes Nagler, *Die Strafe. Eine juristisch-empirische Untersuchung* (Leipzig, 1918), i. 557–734.

[78] Dürkop, 'Zur Funktion', 99. Mezger continued to champion this idea after 1945, and republished the textbook he first issued in the Third Reich, merely omitting the sections dealing with 'Jewish criminality' (ibid. 97–100).

[79] Schreiber, 'Die Strafgesetzgebung', 151–79, here 153–5.

[80] Mezger, *Kriminalpolitik*, p. v.

After no fewer than a hundred sittings, the commission completed its work in 1936. The draft which it produced declared 'healthy popular feeling' to be the basis of criminal law. The purpose of the law was to protect the racial community. Morality and law were to be united. The commission had no hesitation in prescribing the death penalty for a wide range of offences. The objections which had been raised to it under Weimar no longer counted. And the issue of legal unity with Austria, which had played such a notable part in the debates on the death penalty in the 1920s, was resolved in June 1934 by the swift reintroduction of capital punishment by the clerico-fascist dictatorship that had seized power in Austria under Engelbert Dollfuss earlier in the year.[81] In any case, it would by this time have made no difference even if the Austrians had not resumed executions. Hitler regarded the Austrian Republic as German, and in March 1938 he invaded it and incorporated it into the Third Reich, subjecting it immediately to all the laws and decrees which he had introduced since 1933. Factors such as these undoubtedly made the commission's work easier than that of its predecessor in the Weimar Republic. Yet the draft Criminal Code of 1936 was not a success.[82] The Nazi Party's own legal experts declared it unsatisfactory, and it was withdrawn. As we have seen, numerous decrees and orders had been passed from the beginning of the Third Reich, creating an increasing number of additional offences and so altering the criminal law by themselves. These amendments and additions to the criminal law were one of the reasons why the reform took so long to complete, as the commission struggled to incorporate them in the draft, while fresh amendments were being decreed to the existing Code all the time without consulting it. The draft of 1936, indeed, was out of date almost before the ink was dry.

By 1939, when the commission issued a second draft, the progressive radicalization of the regime was overtaking the reform of the Criminal Code once more. Some German legal historians have argued that the draft reflected a desire on the part of the commission to uphold the principles of justice and legality in the face of the arbitrariness of the Third Reich. Certainly, its ideas turned out in the end to fall far short of what the Nazis wanted. Retaining the principle of a written set of legal provisions which had to be adhered to by all connected with the administration of criminal justice, was a principle which Nazi arbitrariness would always seek to circumvent. Gürtner and other conservatives hoped that the Third Reich would give them the opportunity to create a firm, consistent, and ideologically clear basis for criminal law reform. But the commission compromised with the dictatorship's undermining of fundamental principles of

---

[81] BA Potsdam Auswärtiges Amt IIIa Nr. 151 Bd. II, Bl. 203: Gesandtschaft Wien (Prinz zu Erbach) to AA, 28 June 1934.

[82] For a detailed account of the drafting, see Gruchmann, *Justiz*, 822–924.

justice all along the line. All the same, although the basis on which the commission worked was thoroughly Nazi, the very idea of a set of judicial rules by which the criminal law had to operate had become by 1939 a brake upon the freedom of action of the Nazi dictatorship. Although the draft Code made it clear that the Führer's word was law and could therefore override its provisions at any time, the pedantic precision with which the legal experts on the commission had framed the individual clauses of the draft had by now become an irritation. Interrupted by the war, the Code was never put into effect. The work of the criminal law commission had been a monstrous irrelevancy.[83]

While they were busily promulgating all these new capital laws and decrees, the Nazis were still confronted with the fact that the vast majority of judges and legal officials, as the Reichstag fire trial showed, were wedded to traditional, conservative maxims of legal administration and judicial practice. Very few of them had been active Nazi Party members before 1933. Educated and trained under the old, authoritarian Empire, and hostile to the Weimar Republic's democratic institutions, most judges, state prosecutors, and jurists welcomed, with or without reservations, what they saw as the restoration of order and authority under the Third Reich. Typical was the distinguished lawyer Erwin Bumke, born in 1874 and a judge from 1903 to 1907. A member of the Criminal Code commission of the Reich Justice Ministry before the war, Bumke had also spent the period from 1920 to 1929 as a senior official in the Reich Justice Ministry working on the new reform of the Criminal Code. When it ran into political difficulties in 1929, he became President of the Reich Supreme Court. He continued in this position under the Nazis, although he did not join the party until 1937. In 1945, he committed suicide rather than suffer the indignity of being brought to trial by the Allies.[84] Bumke was representative for the collaborationist majority of the legal profession at all levels. Another conservative jurist of this type was the Reich Minister of Justice, Franz Gürtner. Born in 1881, he had been a state prosecutor and judge in Munich before the First World War and had served as Bavarian Minister of Justice at various periods since 1922. On 1 June 1932 Papen had nominated him as Reich Minister of Justice and Gürtner continued to serve in this capacity without a break until his death in January 1941,

[83] Schreiber, 'Die Strafgesetzgebung', 163–6. For the full text of the various drafts and deliberations, see Jürgen Regge and Werner Schubert (eds.), *Quellen zur Reform des Straf- und Strafprozessrechts, II. Abteilung: NS-Zeit (1933–1939)—Strafgesetzbuch,* i. *Entwürfe eines Strafgesetzbuchs;* ii. *Protokolle der Strafrechtskommission des Reichsjustizministeriums* (2 vols.; Berlin, 1988–9), and Franz Gürtner (ed.), *Das kommende deutsche Strafrecht. Bericht über die Arbeit der amtlichen Strafrechtskommission* (2 vols., Berlin, 1935–6). For the renewed, and equally unsuccessful, attempt at a codification in 1944, see Gerhard Werle, *Justiz-Strafrecht und politische Verbrechensbekämpfung im Dritten Reich* (Berlin, 1989), 661–78. For a detailed account of the reform's fate, see Gruchmann, *Justiz,* 753–821.

[84] Dieter Kolbe, *Reichsgerichtspräsident Dr. Erwin Bumke: Studien zum Niedergang des Reichsgerichts und der deutschen Rechtspflege* (Karlsruhe, 1975).

one of a number of Hitler's conservative coalition cabinet partners who went along with every radicalizing step in Nazi policy, however reluctantly. To some extent, and according to his own estimation, Gürtner hoped that, by remaining in post, he would be able to stave off the worst excesses of Nazi contempt for the law. At best, however, this involved a degree of self-deception with which it is hard to credit an experienced politician such as he was. As Lothar Gruchmann has pointed out in his monumental study of Gürtner's tenure of the Ministry of Justice, he was also a Nationalist who agreed with many of the things the Nazis were trying to do. His sense of duty and patriotism prevented him from leaving his post, no matter how deep the humiliations to which the Nazis subjected him. As a result, he allowed himself to be implicated in the undermining of many of the legal principles to which he was ostensibly committed. As Gruchmann has put it, he went through a process of 'adaptation and subordination' which left the judicial system in tatters by the time of his death in 1941.[85]

All over the country, state-employed judges, prosecutors, and legal officials followed suit, and stayed on. Only those who happened to be of Jewish descent, such as the long-serving State Secretary in the Reich Justice Ministry, Curt Joël, were forced to resign. If, like Joël, who was classified as a 'full Jew', they had powerful friends and patrons, they could continue to live in Germany under the new regime; Joël himself died in Berlin on 14 April 1945.[86] But such cases were very rare. Jewish lawyers and judges were stopped from practising by Nazi demonstrations in their courts, then dismissed by a law passed on 7 April 1933. Only a few old-established legal officials and ex-soldiers were enabled to continue for a while. The small number of liberal and left-wing lawyers also were summarily sacked or prevented from working.[87] In all, a mere 586 out of some 45,000 judges, state prosecutors, and judicial officials in Prussia were dismissed or transferred to other duties as a result of the Nazi seizure of power in 1933.[88] All the rest stayed. The conservative judicial establishment that had done so much to undermine the legitimacy of the Weimar Republic thus remained more or less intact under the Third Reich. Some critical jurists have argued subsequently that judges accommodated to the Nazi period because the tradition of legal positivism had robbed them of the intellectual means of justifying their opposition to the state. Others have suggested instead that the legal profession co-operated en-

[85] Gruchmann, *Justiz,* 9–83.

[86] Engelhard (ed.), *Im Namen,* 13–16. See also Horst Göppinger, *Die Verfolgung der Juristen jüdischer Abstammung durch den Nationalsozialismus* (Villingen, 1963), and Klaus-Detlev Godau-Schüttke, *Rechtsverwalter des Reiches. Staatssekretär Dr. Curt Joël* (Frankfurt am Main, 1981).

[87] Engelhard (ed.), *Im Namen,* 72–82.

[88] Ibid. 272. See also Lothar Gruchmann, 'Die Überleitung der Justizverwaltung auf das Reich 1933–1935', in Anon. (ed.), *Vom Reichsjustizamt zum Bundesministerium der Justiz. Festschrift zum hundertjährigen Gründungstag des Reichsjustizamts* (Cologne, 1977).

thusiastically with the Third Reich because its ideology and its aims were close to the Nazis'.[89] Both these arguments have a good deal of truth in them. Yet the judicial establishment's collaboration with the regime was always somewhat uneasy. Overwhelmingly nationalist, right-wing, and sympathetic to the Nazi cause, German judges and prosecutors were nevertheless sticklers for legal principles, and determined to defend their own autonomy against encroachments from rival agencies like Himmler's SS, which by 1936 had effectively taken over the running of the police, including the feared Secret State Police (Gestapo) in the whole of Germany. The ambivalence of their position was a source of constant conflict with the regime.[90]

What the legal profession was up against in the attempt to defend its values and its status was made clear as never before on the so-called 'Night of the Long Knives' on 30 June–1 July 1934, when the regime indulged in another orgy of extra-legal bloodletting. In the late spring of 1934, Hitler was facing threats to his supremacy from disillusioned conservative collaborators around Deputy Chancellor von Papen on the one hand, and the revolutionary leadership of the paramilitary brownshirts, now some three million strong, around Ernst Röhm, on the other. The regular army was alarmed at the brownshirts' demands to replace it with a 'brown militia', and was pressing Hitler to do something to stop it. Among the public at large, there was widespread discontent at the failure of the Third Reich to bring about a significant improvement in the economic situation or reduce the rate of unemployment. Confronted with mounting challenges to his authority, Hitler struck out in both directions, and sent armed bands of blackshirted stormtroopers belonging to the SS, his personal bodyguard, into action against his opponents. By 2 July they had shot a total of eighty-nine people, ranging from Röhm himself, who was murdered in Dachau concentration camp, to Papen's adviser Herbert von Bose, leader of the conservative opposition within the regime, who was machine-gunned in Papen's office. Other victims included the former Reich Chancellor Kurt von Schleicher and his wife, killed in their home by a Gestapo squad, and a number of senior brownshirts such as the Breslau Chief of Police Edmund Heines, shot by firing-squad in Stadelheim prison. Hitler also took the opportunity to murder a number of individuals against whom he had a personal grudge, such as the Bavarian politician Gustav von Kahr.

None of these murders was preceded by any kind of judicial proceedings, not even by a mockery of a trial. Yet Minister of Justice Franz Gürtner defended them retrospectively as acts of 'self-defence' taken by the state in an emergency

[89] Udo Reifner, 'Justiz und Faschismus. Ansätze einer Theorie der Vergangenheitsbewältigung der Justiz', in Reifner and Sonnen (eds.), Strafjustiz, 9–40.
[90] Gruchmann, Justiz, 124–289.

(*Staatsnotwehr*): a classic defence of capital punishment now applied to state-sponsored murder. Attempts by some local judicial authorities to bring the apparatus of justice to bear on the most brutal of the murders were cut short by Hitler's intervention, eventually supported by Gürtner himself. Perhaps Gürtner thought that by giving in on this point he would be able to commit the Nazi leadership to maintaining the legal system in future. But the tolerance of murder on this scale by the judicial élite, up to and including its highest representatives, testified to a frightening inability to deal with concepts like due process and the rule of law, or to recognize when they were being violated. It is difficult to avoid the conclusion that jurists were affected by the long-held doctrines of legal positivism and accepted the murders mainly because they were sanctioned by the state. The tradition of the *Rechtsstaat*, a state which ruled through the law rather than being ruled by it, revealed here its most fatal weakness, for it left the legal profession intellectually impotent in a situation in which the state redefined the law in terms of its leader's 'world-historical mission'. Beyond this, the equanimity with which these events were accepted by German élites in a wider sense showed once more the degree to which they had come to tolerate political violence carried out in their name since 1918. As a result, from this point onwards, the judicial establishment was seriously weakened in its ability to resist the formal illegalities committed by the regime and its agents.[91]

Despite this revealing incident, the judiciary none the less did its best to resist attempts by the brownshirts and the SS to exercise a direct influence on cases that came before the regular courts in the early years of the Third Reich. It was characteristic of the way the regime was established that there were simultaneously uncoordinated attacks on the courts by brownshirt radicals 'from below', and attempts to codify and regulate them by devising new sets of bureaucratic rules imposed 'from above'. All this was backed up by a constant barrage of criticism fired off against the judges by the Nazi leadership. The judges' task, declared the Nazis, was not to apply the letter of the law, but 'to seek with a watchful eye and deep empathetic sensitivity that which the racial community and its state recognizes as just and condemns as unjust—and to apply the result with a clear vision for the exigencies of the individual case'.[92] The Nazi leadership took the view that the judges were not fulfilling this function properly. Hitler's deputy, Rudolf Hess, complained 'that even today some officials in the

[91] Norbert Frei, *National Socialist Rule in Germany: The Führer State 1933–1945* (London, 1993), 3–27, provides a useful summary of these events. For the attitude of the Justice Ministry, see Gruchmann, *Justiz*, 433–80. Otto Gritschneider, '*Der Führer hat Sie zum Tode verurteilt . . .'. Hitlers 'Röhm-Putsch'-Morde vor Gericht* (Munich, 1993), provides details of attempts to bring the surviving perpetrators to justice after 1945.

[92] Roland Freisler, 'Richter und Gesetz', in Hans-Heinrich Lammers and Hans Pfundtner (eds.), *Grundlagen, Aufbau und Wirtschaftsordnung des Nationalsozialistischen Staates* (Berlin, 1936), i. 2. 17, 12.

administration of justice have very little understanding for the basic views and beliefs of National Socialism, and that judgments are pronounced which in their absolutely un-National Socialist tendency arouse general surprise and displeasure'. The pressure to hand out harsher sentences, including the death penalty, was growing, and Hess's complaints were repeated by Martin Bormann, an increasingly influential official on Rudolf Hess's staff, the following September. At the same time, Himmler's deputy, Reinhard Heydrich, circularized police officials in Prussia ordering them to compile details of cases where the courts in their view had been too lenient:

I am repeatedly beset by complaints that enemies of the state are not treated with the necessary severity, or punished as their actions would lead one to expect. In some cases the prosecution has apparently been abandoned without sufficient grounds. In others, the sentence has been too low according to the normal popular feeling. Acquittals have also taken place, it seems, although the public was definitely anticipating and hoping for a sentence to be passed.[93]

The Gestapo, of course, defined what 'normal popular feeling' was themselves. Nevertheless, even putting pressure on the courts in this way was not enough.

In order to speed up the implementation of its policies on crime and punishment, the Nazi regime set up a new system of Special Courts by a decree of 21 March 1933. This innovation built on plans already briefly put into action by the Papen government the previous year, and took as its model the People's Courts set up in the troubled early years of the Weimar Republic. Initially there was to be one for every High Court District. Their competence covered offences against the 'Reichstag fire' decree of 28 February and the Decree for Countering Malicious Attacks on the Government of the National Uprising of 21 March 1933. They were, in other words, political courts. But they were staffed in the main by ordinary judges, and prosecutors whose training and experience had taken place in the Weimar Republic and the Wilhelmine period. Many of them continued to function in the regular courts as well.[94] The institutional edifice of the Special Courts was crowned by the People's Court (*Volksgerichtshof*), set up on 24 April 1934 to compete with the Reich Supreme Court, which had shown itself unreliable in the Reichstag Fire Trial. Established to deal with treason cases, the People's Court was much more a Nazi court, its judges picked for their political reliability. In the early years of its existence, it specialized in trials of Communist Party resistance groups. It was given equal status with the Reich Supreme Court

[93] Engelhard (ed.), *Im Namen*, 251.
[94] Hans Wrobel (ed.), *Strafjustiz im totalen Krieg. Aus den Akten des Sondergerichts Bremen 1940 bis 1945*, i (Bremen, 1991), 21. See also Angermund, *Deutsche Richterschaft*, 133–9, and Peter Hüttenberger, 'Heimtückefälle vor dem Sondergericht München 1933–1939', in Martin Broszat and Elke Fröhlich (eds.), *Bayern in der NS-Zeit. Herrschaft und Gesellschaft im Konflikt* (Munich, 1979), iv. 435–526.

in 1936, following the appointment of Otto-Georg Thierack as its President. The official dress of the judges was determined by Hitler in June 1936. It consisted of a red robe; the traditional colour of the 'blood court' two hundred years before, though few were probably aware of the distant symbolic echo by this time.[95] From now on, the People's Court became much more openly political, and departed increasingly from accepted judicial norms, although it remained the case up to 1941 that fewer than 5 per cent of the cases that came before it ended with the death sentence.[96]

Very quickly, therefore, the Nazis established two parallel sets of criminal and penal justice administration. First, there was the existing, formal judicial apparatus, taken over largely intact from the Weimar years. The Nazis added a substantial number of new capital offences, and put growing ideological pressure on career judges and prosecutors to pass tougher sentences, including the death penalty, and to bend the law in doing so. The legal apparatus, with varying degrees of enthusiasm, complied. Yet, despite a growing harshness on the part of the judicial system, it never satisfied the Nazis. Alongside it, therefore, they established the network of the Special Courts, headed by the People's Court. These too were staffed largely by established, career lawyers, but they operated under much looser rules as a kind of special, rapid judicial system aimed at the quick disposal of political offenders. As explicitly political courts, they were much more ideological in their operation than existing judicial structures were. Even this, however, was not enough, and the Gestapo and SS apparatus increasingly operated an independent system of its own, killing the perceived 'enemies of the Reich' in wholly extra-judicial actions such as the 'Night of the Long Knives', and imprisoning them in concentration camps without even the semblance of a trial. Increasingly, as time went on, this third, informal penal system began to impinge on the other two. While state prosecutors gained a great increase in power over proceedings in the courtroom, as the Nazi state gradually reduced the freedom of manœuvre for the defence, they simultaneously lost it in the world outside, as they were forced to cede more power to the summary 'justice' of the Gestapo and the SS.[97] Thus every compromise that the judges, lawyers, and Ministry of Justice officials made with the security apparatus in the belief that firm guidelines were better than none at all, or in the hope that yielding a little would preserve the judicial system basically intact, simply weakened their own position still further.

[95] Günther Wieland, *Das war der Volksgerichtshof. Ermittlungen—Fakten—Dokumente* (Pfaffenweiler, 1989), 12–24, 39–41.

[96] Hinrich Rüping, 'Die Strafgesetzgebung im "Dritten Reich"', in Dreier and Sellert (eds.), *Recht und Justiz*, 180–93, here 189–90.

[97] Diemut Majer, 'Zum Verhältnis von Staatsanwaltschaft und Polizei im Nationalsozialismus', in Reifner and Sonnen (eds.), *Strafjustiz*, 121–60.

e. The Expansion of Capital Punishment 1933–1939

At the Nuremberg Party Rally on 9 September 1934, the Reich Commissioner for Justice, Hans Frank, proudly proclaimed:

Through the strength of our actions against criminals in the widest sense, above all through the ruthless carrying-out of the death penalty, through the introduction of the Special Courts, and the introduction of the People's Court, for the protection of people and state, we have achieved a disciplining of all the inferior elements which is guaranteeing the security of the decent part of the German people in the highest degree.[98]

Even before the establishment of the one-party state, the Third Reich turned its attention to the resumption of executions after the hiatus of the later years of the Weimar Republic. In February 1933, the first month of Hitler's Chancellorship, there were twenty-nine offenders on death row in Prussia's gaols. They had been waiting for many months for a decision on whether or not they would be granted clemency. One of them had been in the condemned cell for fourteen months. These were long times by German standards.[99] Formally speaking, the right of clemency in these cases rested with the Prussian head of state, but the legality of Papen's dismissal of the Prussian cabinet in July 1932 was still being contested in the courts, and the condemned men's lawyers were busily exploiting this confused constitutional situation with a lengthy series of lawsuits.[100] The press had already complained that these were 'untenable circumstances' which 'are unbearable for a cultured society. This indeterminate period of reprieve', fulminated one newspaper on 30 January 1933, 'must come to an end as soon as possible—whichever way the decision turns out.'[101] As late as 8 March 1933 the cabinet had failed to come to a decision on the matter, still preferring to await a decision on the constitutional position by the Supreme Court.[102]

When Hermann Göring, sweeping aside the constitutional niceties, became Prussian Minister-President under the Hitler regime, and thus—with dubious legal justification—assumed the prerogative of mercy in Prussia, he felt obliged to point out on 5 May 1933

that in all the cases which are now before me, it is extraordinarily difficult to allow justice to take its course after the condemned, as a result of the uncertainty under which they have already been labouring, some of them for an extraordinarily long time, have in any case had to undergo spiritual martyrdom.

---

[98] Quoted in Wieland, *Volksgerichtshof*, 37.
[99] BA Potsdam RJM 6098, Bl. 6: *Kölnische Zeitung*, 17 Feb. 1933.
[100] GStA Berlin Rep. 84a/7792: *Welt am Abend*, 1 Dec. 1932.
[101] HStA Düsseldorf Rep. 145/326, Bl. 87: *Kölner Tageblatt*, 30 Jan. 1933.
[102] Karl-Heinz Minuth (ed.), *Akten der Reichskanzlei: die Regierung Hitler 1933–1938*, i. *1933/34*, (Boppard, 1983), 173–4 n. 5.

Göring, a man not generally known for his sensitivity to human suffering, indeed went on to grant reprieves to a number of these prisoners, precisely on this ground; a telling contrast to the equanimity with which other judicial authorities, in other places and at other times, have regarded the confinement of condemned prisoners on death row not for months, but for years, while awaiting a final decision on whether they should live or die.[103] But those who were not spared by Göring were consigned quickly to the block. One of them, Ernst Reins, convicted in December 1931 of murdering a postman in Berlin, was executed just four days after Göring penned his memorandum. Between Reins's conviction, which had aroused a good deal of public comment at the time, and his decapitation by executioner Gröpler on 9 May 1933 in the Plötzensee prison in Berlin, there had elapsed a period of more than sixteen months.[104] A similar delay took place in the case of another convicted murderer, Kabelitz, executed along with Reins on the same day. The Nazis blamed all this on the ineffectiveness of the Weimar Republic. Decisions on such matters, they promised, would be implemented more swiftly under the Third Reich:

In questions of life and death we shall eliminate the chance factors which already confounded the seriousness of such decisions even before the lack of clarity about the circumstances of Prussia made the fate of the condemned into the subject of an agonizing period in which the files were put away into the cabinet without anything being done.[105]

Measures to speed things up were already in train by the end of May.[106] Just how swift the new procedures would be was soon to become abundantly clear.

Apart from the prisoners on Prussia's death rows, there were other capital offenders waiting for a decision on clemency appeals in Germany's gaols when the Nazis took power. Goebbels's propaganda media left the public in no doubt as to what their fate was likely to be. The debate on the death penalty, the Nazi press announced in March 1933, was over. 'Master Gröpler', as one newspaper reported with satisfaction, 'has work to do again.'[107] Gröpler's first victim under the new regime was in fact not Ernst Reins, but the 24-year-old carpenter Albert Kluge, who had killed his pregnant mistress in August 1932, assisted by his brother. Kluge was executed in Zwickau, in Saxony, at six in the morning on 12 April 1933, the first person to suffer this fate in the state since 1918. The press, already effectively bullied into submission by the Nazis, and in most cases supplied with editors and staff fully in sympathy with the new regime, greeted

---

[103] GStA Berlin Rep. 84a/7787, Bl. 28–61; ibid. 7786, Bl. 320 (Göring memo, 5 May 1933).

[104] BA Potsdam RJM 5667, Bl. 14: *Berliner Tageblatt*, 9 May 1933.

[105] Ibid., Bl. 15: *Berliner Börsen-Courier*, 9 May 1933; see also HStA Düsseldorf Rep. 145/326, Bl. 92: PJM circular, 24 May 1933.

[106] HStA Hanover Hann. 173a/437, Bl. 182: PJM circular to Kammergerichtspräsidenten, Staatsanwälte, etc., 24 May 1933.

[107] BA Potsdam RJM 5667, Bl. 10: *Montag Morgen*, 18 Mar. 1933.

the event as the beginning of a new era in the administration of justice. In doing so, journalists were already using Nazi language that was unmistakable in its vulgar, intimidatory, murderous triumphalism:

The execution in Zwickau demonstrates that the new government has dispensed with the practice followed by governments since 1918, of never carrying out the death penalty. The belief of those gentlemen, the murderers, who cold-bloodedly did away with their fellow men, that they would not be treated according to the maxim 'an eye for an eye, a tooth for a tooth', and that they would not be putting their own precious lives at risk, is thereby fundamentally destroyed. A sharp draught is blowing through Saxon justice once more. Those young men who take a pleasure in murder will hopefully realize this and consider that they will have no right to be treated any differently from the way in which they themselves have treated their fellow men. In the last analysis the state is not here to feed a murderous rabble until they are called away by a natural death. Above all in the case of murder, false sentimentality is out of place.[108]

All the moral and intellectual issues that had troubled both sides in the debate on capital punishment for so many decades were crudely brushed aside. 'The days of softness, of false and mawkish sentimentality', trumpeted another newspaper a month later, when the press was even more firmly under Nazi control, 'are over.'[109] The execution of murderers, if not yet of other kinds of offenders against the interests of the race, would now become the norm.

After the execution of Kluge on 12 April, there were three more executions on 9 May (Reins and Kabelitz in Plötzensee, and a third in Werder, Bavaria), two on 13 June, one on 23 June, another on 30 June, and three more on 1 July. These were all cases resulting from condemnations for murder under the Weimar Republic; the gap between sentencing and execution was over a year in most of them. So far, therefore, the rate of execution under the new regime was not much greater than it had been under the last Kaiser. Up to this point, the Nazis had made little impact on the administration of justice, and the reins of power were still held by senior judicial officials who had begun their careers under Wilhelm II. But in the late summer of 1933 the Nazis began to take a firmer grip on affairs, as the judicial apparatus now began to process the cases of individuals which the new regime itself had condemned. The pace of executions began to increase: 15 in August 1933, 8 in September, 5 in October, 12 in November, and 3 more in December, making a total of 56 altogether according to the records of the Reich Ministry of Justice. In addition, another 11 executions took place in 1933 as a result of condemnations by the new Special Courts, bringing the overall total to 67.[110] Official mortality statistics giving 'execution' as the cause of death showed that there were 64 executions in 1933, 79 in 1934 (not including those killed in the

---

[108] Ibid., Bl. 9: *Leipziger Neueste Nachrichten*, 13 Apr. 1933.
[109] Ibid., Bl. 16: *Deutsche Zeitung*, 9 May 1933.
[110] Ibid. RJM 5670, Bl. 186. The number condemned by the regular courts was 58 not 56, according to the Ministry of Justice's letter to Dr Stock, 7 Dec. 1933, ibid., RJM 5666, Bl. 51.

'Rohm putsch'), 94 in 1935, 68 in 1936, 106 in 1937, 117 in 1938, and 219 in 1939. By 1936, well over 90 per cent of all death sentences were being carried out, and since the Nazis did not publish all the political death sentences arrived at by the courts in the following three years, the mortality figures actually showed an excess of executions over death sentences—123 per cent in 1937, 138 per cent in 1938, and 158 per cent in 1939. The free rein, indeed encouragement, now given to police, prosecutors, judges, and courts to level the highest charge for homicide—murder—and to reach the harshest verdict, must have been a major factor in increasing the murder rate (that is, the number of condemnations for murder per 200,000 population over the age of responsibility) from roughly 0.18 in the last five years of Weimar (1928–32) to 0.38 in the first five years of the Third Reich including January 1933.[111]

Those beheaded now included the political opponents of the regime. The first occasion on which a formal judicial execution was carried out on political rather than ordinary criminal grounds appears to have been on 1 August 1933, when the Communists Bruno Tesch, Heinrich Lütgens, Walter Möller, and Karl Wolff went to the block for their supposed part in the events of 'Bloody Sunday' in Altona in 1932. On this occasion, Nazi brownshirts had been marching through a working-class area in the Prussian municipality of Altona, next to Hamburg, when they had been fired on by Communist snipers positioned at a crossroads. Although a couple of the brownshirts had been killed, the other sixteen dead had been innocent bystanders, or inhabitants of the area going about their everyday business or even sitting in their homes. All of them had been shot by the Prussian police, who had panicked and fired wildly in all directions when they thought they had heard shots ringing out.[112] The police—most of whom continued in their jobs under the Third Reich—immediately tried to cover their tracks by manipulating and fabricating evidence so as to pin the blame on the Communists. Already well before the Nazi seizure of power, a number of Communists had been arrested on the basis of these trumped-up charges. At the end of May 1933 they were brought to trial for allegedly planning an armed uprising. There had, of course, been no planned 'uprising'. Lütgens, condemned to death for

---

[111] Düsing, *Abschaffung*, 210–11.

[112] Heinrich Breloer and Horst Königstein, *Blutgeld. Materialien zu einer deutschen Geschichte* (Cologne, 1982), reprinting many original documents. See also Anthony McElligott, 'Das Altonaer Sondergericht und der Prozess vom Blutsonntag' (Vortrag zum 60. Gedenktag des 'Altonaer Blutsonntags' im Rahmen der Veranstaltung des Stadtteilarchivs Ottensen, der Bezirksversammlung und der Kulturbehörde, Hamburg-Altona, 3 June 1992), and Wolfgang Kopitzsch, 'Der "Altonaer Blutsonntag"', in Arno Herzig et al. (eds.), *Arbeiter im Hamburg, Unterschichten, Arbeiter und Arbeiterbewegung seit dem ausgehenden 18. Jahrhundert* (Hamburg, 1983), 509–16. Kopitzsch is the son of one of the officers in command of the police in Altona during the disturbances, and aspects of his account are unreliable. For a full examination of the evidence, see Léon Schirmann, *Altonaer Blutsonntag 17. Juli 1932: Dichtungen und Wahrheit* (Hamburg, 1994).

supposedly organizing it, was plainly a scapegoat. The other three, Möller, Wolff, and Tesch, were condemned to death for conspiracy to murder. Thus the Nazis and the police collaborated in the manufacture of the myth of Communist insurrectionism, a myth which played a vital part in the regime's justification of the dictatorial powers which it seized in the early months of 1933.[113]

The four condemned men were described by the prison authorities and the police, who were asked for their advice on clemency, as fanatical Bolsheviks who felt no remorse for what they had done. They were 'incorrigible'. The state prosecutor in Kiel, who was responsible for cases brought before the Special Court in Altona, wrote to the Prussian Minister-President, Hermann Göring, advising him not to grant them a reprieve:

The self-preservation of the German people and state imperiously demands the extermination of this enemy by every possible means. . . . The fight against Communism, which has been half-hearted up to now, and therefore unsuccessful . . . compels us to take the sharpest possible measures. From these alone and no others can we expect the elimination of this most embittered and dangerous enemy of the nation. Leniency would certainly not be appreciated by a large proportion of the adherents of Bolshevism, it would be regarded as a sign of weakness. . . . Carrying out the sentences will bring the whole seriousness of their situation graphically before the eyes of people of Communist inclinations; it will be a lasting warning for them and have a deterrent effect.[114]

The four men were executed not because they were guilty—none of them had been convicted of actually murdering the two dead brownshirts or anyone else— but because they offered a blood-sacrifice to vengeful Nazis and a symbol of the regime's political determination. In his prison diary, the young Bruno Tesch— barely 20 years of age—recorded his campaign to prove his innocence, and in his last letters to his parents bequeathed to them the task of vindication. It was not until November 1992 that the verdicts were at last posthumously annulled by a German court.[115]

Scapegoats for other political clashes that had taken place in the final years of the Weimar Republic soon followed Bruno Tesch and his comrades to the block. 'Six Communist Murderers Executed', blared the headline in the *Völkischer Beobachter* on 1 December 1933: 'Expiation for the Cologne Communist Blood-Deed'. By January 1934 the Social Democratic Party in the Saarland, which remained legal because this particular part of Germany stayed outside the Reich under a League of Nations mandate until 1935, was calculating that twenty-four

---

[113] See the account of the forthcoming second volume of Schirmann's study in Wolfgang Zank, 'Blutsonntag in Altona', *Die Zeit*, 30 (17 July 1992), 62.

[114] Quoted in McElligott, 'Altonaer Sondergericht', 20–1.

[115] Extracts from Tesch's diary and letters in Breloer and Königstein, *Blutgeld*, 50–71. See also Franz Ahrens, *Bruno Tesch. Das Sterben eines Hamburger Arbeiterjungen* (Hamburg, 1946), and Zank, 'Blutsonntag'.

political executions had already taken place in the Third Reich. Political death sentences were now outrunning death sentences for ordinary crimes. In the first full year of Hitler's Chancellorship, sixty-seven were passed on political offenders against forty-seven on common murderers. Among the political offenders were a number of women. The first woman to be executed since the Kaiser's time was Emma Thieme, who went to the block on 26 August 1933, followed by Christina Liess on 12 September, and a third Communist woman on 7 November. Even the conservative bureaucrats in the Reich Justice Ministry, who raised no overt objections to any of this, were disturbed enough to note in the margin of their carefully compiled statistics that one of the condemned men executed at this time, Walter Schefranzki, who was beheaded on 28 September 1933, was only 19 years of age.[116] The Nazi campaign of violence and hatred towards the Communists even led them in 1934 to compel forty Communists sentenced in a second mass trial of those allegedly involved in the events of 'Bloody Sunday' in Altona in 1932, the 'red marines', to witness the execution by hand-axe of four of their comrades in the courtyard of the Fuhlsbüttel gaol in Hamburg, while a large number of brownshirts and SS men as well as the fathers and brothers of brownshirts who had died in the street violence of the previous years looked on. One of his comrades recalled the scene as the first of the victims, Johnny Dettmer, was brought out of his cell and confronted by a pastor.

'Go to Hell', said Dettmer to him in a loud voice. Then cries could be heard from many cell windows. 'Good morning, Johnny!'—'Long live the Revolution!'—'Down with Hitler!' Cries of rage and cries of horror. As the hangman's assistant tried to grab Johnny, our comrade resisted with hands and feet. He struggled silently and with all his strength.[117]

The ritual did not impress the other victims either. 'What a performance!' exclaimed another of the 'red marines', Hermann Fischer, as he went to the block. The executions thus turned into a demonstration of Communist solidarity instead of Nazi power; and if the Nazis had thought to achieve a deterrent effect by this measure, they were to be disappointed. Nevertheless, the primary thrust of the Nazis' political justice, against Communists who were either engaged in resistance or who had incurred their wrath through their actions before the seizure of power, was more than plain. The lead was taken by the People's Court. It handed down 4 death sentences in 1934, all of which were carried out. In 1935, it passed 9, and all except one of the condemned were executed. The following

[116] BA Potsdam RJM 5667, Bl. 58: *Völkischer Beobachter*, 1 Dec. 1933; ibid., Bl. 63: *Deutsche Freiheit* (Saarbrücken), 23 Jan. 1934; ibid., Bl. 129–31: Notizen. Of the 114 condemned, some were reprieved, and a substantial number executed after the end of Jan. 1934.

[117] Jan Valtin [i.e. Richard Krebs], *Tagebuch der Hölle* (Berlin, 1958). For an English version, see idem, *Out of the Night* (London, 1941), esp. 518–20.

year saw its activities continuing at roughly the same level, with 10 death sentences and 10 executions. In 1937 the number of condemnations jumped to 37, resulting in 28 executions. In 1938 it fell slightly, to 17 condemnations and 16 executions.[118] The rise and fall of these statistics mirrored the trajectory of Communist resistance and its repression. The executions of 1938 marked the effective ending of organized Communist activities on a wide scale. The party had been ruthlessly suppressed by the Gestapo.

The political use of capital punishment did not escape the attention of public opinion abroad. Exiles from Nazi Germany and their sympathizers began a series of campaigns to stop the killing. In November 1935 a number of leading Scandinavian intellectuals petitioned Hitler to prevent the execution of Communist resisters Albert Kayser and Rudolf Klaus, who had been condemned to death for treason. The protests of people such as Gunnar and Alva Myrdal, Per Lagerkvist, and Vilhelm Moberg may have had some effect in securing clemency for Kayser, a former Reichstag deputy for the Communist Party. Klaus—'one of the most dangerous companions of the terrorist Max Hölz'—was executed on 17 December 1935.[119] In 1938 these campaigns drew a sharp denunciation from Himmler's deputy Reinhard Heydrich, who condemned them in terms that made clear the depth of his ideological commitment to Nazism:

With true Jewish mendacity and hypocrisy, every means is being used to arouse the sympathy of 'world public opinion' for the 'poor victims of Nazi terror'. The Jewish-Bolshevik apostles of the smear do not care in reality about improving the situation of the 'victims of Nazi justice' whom they characterize as martyrs. The one thing that matters to these troublemakers is to contribute whatever they can, at any price, to the general stirring-up of the people.

Heydrich suggested that this was demonstrated by the fact that such campaigns concentrated exclusively on cases still awaiting a final decision, because these were more likely to attract public attention than cases in which the offender concerned had already been executed. In this latter case, he implied, they seldom bothered to do anything. Heydrich complained that the 'protest letters we have received already fill volumes here. Reading through and processing these innumerable letters, leaflets, etc. takes up the energies of many officials who are urgently needed for work on more important matters.' Furthermore, he said, 'delegations are bothering offices and branches of the party, and then when they get home they publish mendacious reports.' His suggested remedy was characteristic. The period that elapsed between sentencing and execution should, he

[118] Wieland, *Volksgerichtshof*, 45.
[119] BA Potsdam Auswärtiges Amt IIIa Nr. 51, Bd. 11, Bl. 218 (Petition—Übersetzung); Bl. 220: 'Deutsche Nachrichtenbüro Nr. 1902 von 17. Dezember 1935'.

argued, be reduced so as to allow less time for such clemency campaigns to be mounted and pursued.[120]

Yet shortening this interval was difficult. Part of the problem lay in the centralization of judicial administration that had taken place under the Third Reich. In the early years of the new regime, once the federated states and provinces had been brought firmly under Nazi control, the prerogative of mercy was exercised by the Reich Commissioner appointed by Hitler to replace the former democratically elected state governments. In February 1935, however, Hitler arrogated this prerogative exclusively to himself, as an essential part of the apparatus of sovereignty which was now attached to the position of the Führer in the aftermath of President von Hindenburg's death the previous year. Judicial officials on the spot were now required to act as a clemency commission and send their recommendations to Hitler via the Reich Ministry of Justice.[121] To protect Hitler's public image as a personally kindly man, the Ministry subsequently ordered that 'in the notices designed for publication in the daily newspapers about the carrying-out of death sentences it must not be mentioned that the Führer and Reich Chancellor has not availed himself of his right of reprieve'. In fact, Hitler can hardly have spent more than a few moments examining the relevant papers, given the large numbers of death sentences now being passed, and given the extreme reluctance he showed to grant anybody a reprieve—a reluctance that was doubtless soon reflected in the practice of the Ministry and the clemency commission as well. All the same, despite encouragement from the Ministry to the local officials to get their recommendations in more quickly,[122] these procedures inevitably made for substantial delays. Inquiries initiated at the Ministry of Justice in response to Heydrich's initiative in 1938 revealed that an average time of two months and six days separated the pronouncement of a death sentence by the court and the completion at the Ministry of a report containing the details and suggesting a provisional recommendation for or against a reprieve. A further three months and four days then passed while the report was being perused by officials at the Ministry before being forwarded to Hitler's office with a firm recommendation one way or the other. Several more weeks then went by until Hitler returned his decision, and, if it was negative (as it usually was), more time passed before the execution was finally carried out. The longest total delay between sentencing and beheading up to the late winter of 1937–8 was ten months and twenty-six days, not far short of the kind of interval which had so

[120] BA Koblenz R22/4086, Bl. 3: Heydrich to RJM (Ministerialdirektor Dr Stademann), 2 Mar. 1938.
[121] Ibid., Bl. 8: Besprechung mit den Vertretern der Landesjustizverwaltungen, 14. Dezember 1934, 6; ibid., Bl: 42: RJM to Generalstaatsanwälte and Oberlandesgerichtspräsidenten, 25 Feb. 1935.
[122] BA Koblenz R22/1314, Bl. 41: RJM to Oberlandesgerichtspräsidenten, 25 Feb. 1935 (referring to the Gnadenordnung of 6 Feb. 1935).

aroused Göring's unexpected sympathy in 1933. Even the average stood at about six months. So the Ministry agreed with Heydrich that the process should be speeded up.[123] A foretaste of what was to come was provided in March 1939 by the arrest and condemnation of a man who had held up and robbed four cars on the open road on 23 February 1939 outside Berlin. Arthur Gose, who had just turned 19 on 13 February, was condemned on 27 February and executed on 1 March. 'It always costs a head!' trumpeted the *Völkischer Beobachter*: 'No mercy for car bandits. Highway robbers fall to the executioner in National Socialist Germany. . . . Only extermination helps!' Less than a week had passed between Gose's crime and his execution.[124]

Thus by the eve of the Second World War the Nazis had made substantial dents in the integrity of the judicial and penal system in Germany. Capital punishment had been extended to a wide range of new offences under the emergency legislation on which the fragile legal legitimacy of the Third Reich rested. The murders and assaults committed by the Nazis in the 'seizure of power', during the 'Night of the Long Knives' and under the cover of the concentration camps, had gone effectively unpunished, protected by the pseudo-legal fiction of the Führer's charismatic authority. This fiction was accepted by lawyers, judges, and prosecutors, however reluctantly, and was not seriously challenged by the legal officials of the Reich Ministry of Justice. Executions had resumed, and then been increased to numbers unknown in Germany since the early modern period. In the process, Hitler had arrogated the sovereign power of clemency to himself. Capital punishment was used not merely as an instrument of penal policy, against murderers, but also as a political weapon in the struggle against Communist resistance. Theorists who argued that crime was racially determined, and that the racially inferior should be compulsorily sterilized or even physically exterminated, were coming into their own. Even representatives of the churches, traditional proponents of capital punishment, approved of the Nazis' use of 'the death penalty' as 'a deed of "positive Christianity"', as one of them put it.[125] There were signs even before the war began that the operation of the death penalty was becoming increasingly arbitrary. The authority of the judicial system, and of the written law on which it depended, over capital punishment was being eroded by the growth of Special Courts acting on political grounds, and by the unilateral decisions of the Gestapo and the SS, above all in concentration camps, to carry out executions without the formal sanction of a court verdict. Increasingly, penal policies were being directed at the person of the

---

[123] Ibid. 4086, Bl. 8–17 (notes). The Reich Ministry superseded provincial Ministries from 1934.

[124] BA Potsdam 61 Re 1/1773, 77: *Völkischer Beobachter*, 3 Mar. 1939.

[125] Gerhard K. Schmidt, *Christentum und Todesstrafe* (Weimar, 1938), 141. For the continued support of the Church of England for hanging during this period, see Potter, *Hanging*, chs. 10–12.

offender—at the 'habitual criminal', the 'antisocial element', the 'stranger to the racial community'—rather than at the offence itself. The regime showed every sign of wanting to speed up the process of execution and to divest it of its traditional, ritual accoutrements, to turn it into a mere act of biological extermination. In the process, as we shall now see, capital punishment itself began to undergo a series of changes more dramatic than any that had taken place since the abolition of open-air executions nearly a century before.

15

The Third Reich and its Executioners

a. Changing the Method of Execution 1933–1936

When the Nazis came to power in 1933, a widespread debate began in judicial circles on which method of execution would be most appropriate in view of the new principles of penal policy being enacted in the Third Reich. At this time traditional methods of execution were still widespread in Germany. The hand-held axe was still used in most of Germany, including Prussia, while the guillotine was employed in Bavaria, Württemberg, Baden, Saxony, Thuringia, Bremen, Oldenburg, and Hesse.[1] The axe was frequently condemned abroad as barbaric, and was felt by some influential figures to be something of a propaganda gift to foreign enemies of the Third Reich, even though it had been widely used under the Weimar Republic. Ernst ('Putzi') Hanfstaengl, one of Hitler's intimates, whom the Führer put in charge of dealing with the foreign press, complained in 1935 that the decapitation of two women by an executioner dressed in top hat, frock-coat, and white gloves, and wielding a hand-held axe, 'has had a damaging effect on the reputation of German culture in the rest of the world, and it will be difficult to restore this reputation in the foreseeable future. It has also led to a renewed, considerable loss of sympathy for Germany abroad.'[2] But the traditionalists in the Reich Ministry of Justice continued to defend the use of the axe in the face of such criticism. In January 1935 they replied in the following terms to sensational accounts in the foreign press which had depicted the German executioner swinging a long-handled axe over his shoulder with an alarming disregard for where it landed:

Execution with the axe cannot be described as an impractical or cruel way of carrying out a death sentence. We are dealing not with a normal 'chopper' but with a specially made execution axe. Because of its unusual weight, it has such a powerful cutting force that it

---

[1] BA Koblenz R22/1314, Bl. 47: Bericht, 25 Mar. 1935.
[2] Ibid., Bl. 86: Ernst Hanfstaengl to RJM, 20 June 1935.

is absolutely unnecessary to 'swing' it. The weight of this instrument of execution also helps achieve a particularly accurate blow.

The axe, they added, was a very quick means of execution, since almost no preparation was needed. There had only been one mistake in recent years, and the responsible executioner had been dismissed. 'After all this, there can be no question of execution with the so-called hand-axe being in any way particularly terrible or causing particular torment to the c[on]d[emned].'[3] The most experienced executioners, such as Carl Gröpler, when consulted on the matter, were of the same opinion.[4]

The criminal law commission devoted considerable time to examining possible methods of execution in 1934–5.[5] Georg Dahm, one of its more traditionalist members, supported the hand-held axe because, as he said: 'The death penalty expresses the superiority of the state, the dignity of the community. This consideration demands a dignified form of execution.' There were reasons for retaining the axe that appealed to Nazi ideology as well. Roland Freisler declared: 'In Germany it is the hand-axe that has become most customary. I do not think one should alter too much in this respect.'[6] 'Beheading by muscle-power', he added on another occasion, 'has something real, manly, natural about it.' This was the first time that manliness, that core Nazi value, had been used as a justification for beheading people with an axe. 'The guillotine', Freisler thought in contrast, 'also has the appearance of something dead, soulless, impersonal.'[7] The jurist Eduard Kohlrausch, by contrast, preferred the firing-squad. 'There is something manly about it, and it demonstrates a certain final respect for the conviction that the perpetrator felt compelled to follow.' This clearly recognized that the majority of offenders executed in the Third Reich were politically motivated rather than criminally inclined. Seen from a political angle, however, the 'manliness' of an execution method was an argument for discarding it rather than employing it.[8] It gave too much recognition to the human dignity of the offender. Thus many considered that punishment in the National Socialist state should be replaced by the simple destruction of enemies of the community. To such people, the axe, even the guillotine and the firing-squad, and the ceremonial aspects of execution, appeared outdated, over-ritualized, and above all unnecessary.

[3] BA Koblenz R22/1314, Bl. 35–36: RJM to Deutscher Schutzbund, Volksdeutscher Arbeitskreis e. V., 14 Jan. 1933.
[4] Ibid., Bl. 112: Erster Staatsanwalt Altenburg to RJM, 7 Nov. 1935; ibid. 1323, Bl. 57: Vermerk, 17 Nov. 1935.
[5] See Regge and Schubert (eds.), *Quellen*, ii, pt. 1, 139–40, 152, 168, 171, 174, 211–12, 418–30, 448.
[6] BA Koblenz R22/1314, Bl. 14–15: Protokoll der 17. Sitzung, 1 Mar. 1934.
[7] Ibid., Bl. 18: Protokoll der 68. Sitzung, 7 May 1935.
[8] Ibid., Bl. 14: Protokoll der 17. Sitzung, 1 Mar. 1934.

FIG. 37. *Roland Freisler (1893–1945).* A leading Nazi defence lawyer under the Weimar Republic, Freisler quickly made his influence felt in the shaping of judicial policy after 1933. As State Secretary in the Ministry of Justice, he was instrumental in bringing about an extension of capital punishment after the Nazi seizure of power, in speeding up the processes of condemnation and execution, and in persuading Hitler to introduce a standard method of execution in 1936. As President of the People's Court from 1942 to 1945, Freisler bullied defendants mercilessly and condemned many of them to death.

The ideal way, some thought, would be to offer the condemned a poisoned chalice with which they could administer their own death in the privacy of a prison cell, as in Roman times. Traditionally, the prison authorities had taken elaborate precautions to avoid condemned prisoners escaping the ritual of the block by committing suicide in their cell.[9] Now, however, this was what precisely what was being suggested. Typically totalitarian, this idea required the citizen's voluntary and enthusiastic affirmation of the state's policy, in this case for his or her own destruction. Advocating the use of the chalice as early as 1929, Ludwig Binz, writing in the Nazi daily paper, had insisted:

Extermination it has to be, for the purposes of deterrence and the reliable protection of society. If the option of suicide is rejected, the murderer or offender against the nation must be killed by chemical means within a further deadline. If some kinds of professionals lose their jobs through this simplification of the execution procedure, and the popular desire for sensation is no longer satisfied, then so much the better. Above all, this method has the advantage that the sympathy which people have with the fate of murderers these days, and which to some extent is justified, will no longer have any ground, and the arguments against killing will no longer have a basis.[10]

Even Freisler was impressed by this argument. 'Perhaps there is a high moral value in it', he conceded in 1934. Kohlrausch agreed: 'There are no technical objections here.' Indeed, virtually all the Commission's members accepted that the poisoned chalice would be a good way of ridding the racial community of criminals.[11] The prison doctor Georg K., from Magdeburg, after having witnessed what he called 'a bloody and pretty coarse pantomine' of a decapitation with the axe in 1934, also favoured poison.[12] The application of the death penalty as a general prevention of racial degeneration, the Nazi daily newspaper, the *Völkischer Beobachter*, had already declared in 1931,

is also effective without the undignified and unnecessary fuss with the hangman, top-hatted witnesses, and deathly pale state prosecutors. . . . The hellish torments of the condemned in the face of the minutely prescribed execution procedure do not constitute an equivalent to his deed but are useless and revolting, without aim or purpose. Anyone who has been condemned to death must be accorded the right to kill *himself* within a determined period. . . . If suicide is refused after the condemnation has achieved the force of law, the desired result is to be obtained by chemical means.[13]

But self-administered poison ran into objections from the churches. 'The state', they complained, 'would be committing incitement to suicide.'[14] In the eyes of Catholics in particular, suicide was a far worse crime than execution with the hand-held axe, no matter who the victim was. For the condemned offender, even for the executioner, there was always the hope of repentance, purgatory, and eventual forgiveness. For the suicide, however, there could be nothing but eternal

[9] See e.g. the lengthy correspondence from the year 1904 in HStA Düsseldorf Rep. 145/325, Bl. 125–50.

[10] BA Koblenz R22/1314, Bl. 20: Ludwig Binz, 'Strafe oder Vernichtung?'

[11] Ibid., Bl. 14: Protokoll der 17. Sitzung, 1 Mar. 1934.

[12] Ibid., Bl. 28: Handschriftl. Brief Dr. Georg K. to Strafrechtsausschuss, 7 Nov. 1934.

[13] BA Potsdam 61 Re 1/1773: *Völkischer Beobachter*, 4 July 1931.

[14] BA Koblenz R22/1314, Bl. 18–19 (Protokoll der 68. Sitzung der Strafrechtskommission, 7 May 1935).

damnation. Anxious in the early years of power not to offend the Catholic Church, whose qualified backing it had obtained through a Concordat with Rome, the Nazi leadership reluctantly abandoned the idea of the poisoned chalice as politically inadvisable.

So the search continued for a method of execution that would not involve the direct application of physical force by one individual human being on another. In December 1933 the German Foreign Ministry asked its ambassador in Washington to send details of recent executions by gassing in the state of Colorado, where the method had been introduced the previous March. The Embassy enclosed a substantial package of information and reported positively. 'Unconsciousness after a few seconds, death confirmed after three minutes. No sign of death-struggle, distortion, or pain, and thus spiritual suffering of relatives reduced.'[15] In 1934 the senior state prosecutor in Berlin, noting that the aim of capital punishment was the 'extermination of the lawbreaker as a threat to the race', urged that 'coarseness' and 'indignity' should be avoided in carrying out this task. 'Germans of healthy sensibility', he thought, found the axe 'repellent' and 'out of harmony with German attitudes'. He too urged the use of poison gas, or possibly poison injections.[16] And Richard E., an ordinary citizen, writing personally to Hitler in 1938, actually offered to construct a gas chamber for executions. Decapitation, he argued, bore too close a resemblance to Jewish methods of slaughtering and was therefore not 'Aryan' enough for use in the Third Reich.[17] But these suggestions were not taken up by the Ministry of Justice either. They were not only expensive and cumbersome, but they also departed too radically from tradition in an area where tradition was strong, reinforced even against the dogmas of the Nazis by the power of historical mystique. Mention of gassing as a method—periodically discussed in official circles in Germany, as we have seen in earlier chapters, since before the turn of the century—inevitably conjures up the grim vision of what was to come during the war. The methods debated in the Ministry were still intended to be applied to individuals. The gas chambers built in Colorado, and subsequently elswhere in the USA, were each designed for one person, not for hundreds. Nevertheless, the idea of gassing did not go away. It was to be put into effect shortly after the outbreak of the war.

Future developments were also foreshadowed in various letters that came in to the Ministry of Justice from members of the general public urging the use of condemned prisoners for medical experimentation. 'What use does the fact of a

[15] Ibid. Auswärtiges Amt IIIa Nr. 51, Nr. 11, Bl. 190: AA to Botschaft Washington, 5 Nov. 1933, and reply (telegram) 9 Dec. 1933. See also ibid. RJM 5666, Bl. 57–60.

[16] GStA Berlin Rep. 84a/7789, Bl. 28-67: Generalstaatsanwalt Berlin to PJM, 13 Mar. 1924.

[17] BA Koblenz R22/1315, Bl. 56: Richard E. to Hitler, 12 Apr. 1938.

chopped-off head have for the people?' asked Robert R., from Bochum, in 1935; and he answered the question himself: '—None, apart from the satisfaction of the desire for revenge, even if this has become an unconscious desire nowadays.' Using criminals for medical tests would be far more beneficial. 'The criminal himself would rather live as a sick person than be buried in the earth with his skull chopped off.'[18] Such apparently charitable intentions were far removed from what another correspondent, Marie D., of Frankfurt am Main, had in mind. Writing to the Minister of Justice as 'a simple racial comrade', she asked:

Why are violent criminals sent to their death by a brief act of execution? Why does the expiation of a sex murder, of a murder for gain, or of a pest who damages the fatherland and the people, only last seconds? And how much suffering have they caused their unhappy victims and their victims' relatives? Why can one not use these dehumanized creatures for the purposes of vivisection? Please, as a judge and helper of mankind, understand my train of thought. All the means of modern medicine can be tried out on criminals, from ordinary injections to the necessary amputations demanded by experiments, according to the seriousness of the crime. How many people would be deterred from committing a grievous bloody crime if the law prescribed, let us say, five years' vivisection. The crime rate would go down at one blow, for criminals are mostly too cowardly to stand pain in their own body. . . . Many sick people could be helped in this way, especially the mutilated: through an operation they could get back a nose, a missing piece of bone, or even their eyesight.[19]

The fact that medical experimentation was carried out not long afterwards in the concentration camps does not imply, of course, that Marie D.'s letter had any influence; the Ministry of Justice had no formal connection with the administration of camps such as Auschwitz. Nor was medical science yet up to the kind of transplant operations which Frau D. suggested. During the peacetime years at least, the human bodies on which medical experimentation was practised were generally already dead.[20]

None the less, medical schools and research institutes soon began to realize that the increased number of executions under the Third Reich could provide an important source of fresh corpses for anatomizing and experimentation. In 1935 the Anatomical Institute of Breslau University asked for executions normally held in Oppeln to be carried out in Breslau instead, so that the bodies which they obtained from them could be as fresh as possible. The Ministry, on this occasion,

[18] BA Koblenz R22/1314, Bl. 62: Robert R. to Göring, 28 June 1935.
[19] Ibid. 1316, Bl. 61: Marie D. to RJM, 26 Feb. 1941.
[20] See Robert Jay Lifton, *The Nazi Doctors: A Study of the Psychology of Evil* (London, 1986), 269–302, 337–84, for experimentation during the war, and, more generally, Robert Proctor, *Racial Hygiene: Medicine under the Nazis* (Cambridge, Mass., 1988).

refused.[21] Three years later, however, it had become evident that some anatomical institutes depended quite heavily on this source of human bodies for experimentation. 'It would be an unsustainable loss for the Würzburg Anatomical Institute', declared its director in May 1938, 'if it had to do without the corpses of executed people in future.'[22] And in February 1941 the doctors in the Women's Hospital in Posen claimed that their research into infertility would benefit greatly if they were supplied with 'fresh testicular material from the criminals who come to Posen for execution'.[23] The dependence of medical research on the repressive apparatus of the Third Reich was obviously growing. But it was still a very big step from requests such as these to the kind of experimentation on living subjects carried out in the concentration camps. A suggestion such as that of Marie D., that execution should be replaced by vivisection as a punishment for 'racial pests', clearly fell into the category of the pathological. But it is doubtful whether its author would have had the nerve to write it without the encouragement provided by the pathological context of the Third Reich.

Similar encouragement was given by the advent of the Nazi dictatorship to the inventors who periodically filled the files of the Ministry of Justice with their plans for new, mechanized means of killing malefactors. It was obvious that this should happen in 1933, as one such enthusiast, a dentist from Berlin-Steglitz, put it in his submission of plans for a new execution machine devised by himself, 'since the death penalty has come into its own again under the National Socialist government'.[24] Another inventor, Artur Georg R., writing from Chemnitz in August 1933, offered the authorities a motorized gallows, in view of the fact that executions were clearly taking place all over the country and the equipment for carrying them out would seem to be in short supply. The advantage 'of my (for the time being only theoretically constructed) machine-gallows', he wrote, was that: 'as an automobile, it can be taken everywhere quickly.'[25] Since the device did not actually exist, however, his suggestion met with a frosty reception from the cautious bureaucrats of the Ministry. Another enthusiastic supporter of the new regime, Ulrich R., from Nuremberg, wrote to Hitler on 6 May 1933 urging him 'for once to put the terror of a public execution in front of the German people's eyes'. He took the opportunity to suggest that the Führer's achievement in uniting all the geographical regions and social classes of Germany into a newly

[21] BA Koblenz R22/1314, Bl. 16: Anatomisches Insitut der Universität Breslau to Preussischer Ministerpräsident, 6 Nov. 1935; reply of Reich Justice Ministry, 4 Dec. 1935.

[22] Ibid. 1315, Bl. 99: Director of Würzburg Anatomical Institute to Generalstaatsanwalt Munich, 28 May 1938.

[23] Ibid. 1316, Bl. 28: Reichsstatthalter Drendel (Generalstaatsanwalt) Posen to RJM, 8 Feb. 1941.

[24] GStA Berlin Rep. 84a/7786, Bl. 338: Eingabe to RJM, 27 Aug. 1933.

[25] BA Potsdam RJM 5666, Bl. 41: Artur Georg R. to PJM, 3 Aug. 1933.

forged national community should find a symbolic expression in a standardization of the method of execution across the whole of the Third Reich:

> While executions in Prussia still take place with the block and the axe, this happens in
> Bavaria and the Rhineland with the guillotine. If the first method must be described as
> medieval and unworthy of the structure of the German people as it now is, then the
> further employment of the guillotine is impossible for patriotic reasons, for this gift from
> the first Napoleon is too reminiscent of our former dependence on France, and cannot be
> reconciled with the freedom of the German spirit.[26]

The association of the guillotine with Revolution and Terror had thus, it seems,
finally lapsed, at least in one man's mind; but in its place came an equally
negative association, with the national enemy, France. Rather than the guillotine,
or the axe, which some Nazis—though not Roland Freisler—considered barbaric, Ulrich R. suggested a German machine, built and operated by a German,
and, as it happened, he himself had been constructing one 'in months of labour'
in preparation for just such an eventuality. Nevertheless, the Ministry was not
convinced, and the suggestion, like all the others which reached it, was filed away
and never acted upon.

Submissions like these were neither eccentric, nor, in contrast to the bloodthirstiness of Frau D., pathological. They were fully in line with mainstream
Nazi thinking on the subject of capital punishment. The standardization of
execution methods was given very serious consideration for precisely the reasons
that the inventor Ulrich R. suggested. This was a centralizing regime, one that
did away for the first time with the federal structures which had provided the
bedrock of German constitutionality for so long, and replaced them with forms
of administration which were intended to express the unity of the race. Pressures
were mounting for the introduction of a unified practice across the whole
Reich.[27] The criminal law commission therefore registered one of its few positive
achievements, if it can be called that, when it finally recommended that the
guillotine should be employed as the standard method of execution throughout
Germany. It was Kohlrausch who persuaded the other members that this was the
best course to take. He opined: 'the mechanical axe is the most appropriate
method of execution according to our sense of culture today. The mechanical
axe', he added, carefully avoiding the French word 'guillotine', 'was not first
invented in the French Revolution but was already being used in Germany in the
fourteenth and fifteenth centuries.'[28] Other members agreed that this was the
best compromise between traditional and modern methods, provided that, as

[26] HStA Munich MJu 13144: Ulrich R. to Hitler, 6 May 1933. Also in GStA Berlin Rep. 84a/7786, Bl.
329 and BA Potsdam RJM 5666, Bl. 36.
[27] BA Koblenz R22/1314, Bl. 50: 'Vertraulich! Reichsjustizministerium: Betr. Vollzug der Todesstrafe,
9. April 1935.'
[28] Ibid., Bl. 14: Protokoll der 17. Sitzung, 1 Mar. 1934.

Freisler commented, 'we avoid the impression that we have found it necessary at this, of all times, to adopt an extremely ugly and historically not exactly celebrated institution of the French Revolution'.[29] Although nobody said so, a mechanical form of execution also had the advantage of requiring little physical exertion, unlike the hand-held axe, so it made it easier to carry out a large number of executions on a single occasion without tiring out the executioner. The final decision on the matter was left to Hitler himself. He eventually opted for the guillotine on 14 October 1936.[30]

b. Capital Punishment and the Divided Public Sphere

In putting Hitler's decision into effect, the Justice Ministry officials initially argued that 'the popular demand for expiation requires the execution to take place as near as possible to the scene of the crime. . . . Execution in close proximity to the scene of the crime has a greater deterrent effect.'[31] So they considered using mobile guillotines which would be driven to their place of operation in official vans. But the number of executions ordered by the judicial authorities of the Third Reich, even in 1935–6, was so great that it made more sense in the end to erect permanent guillotines on selected sites. Once this decision had been taken, in December 1936, the Ministry undertook a census of all the existing guillotines in the Third Reich.[32] The results were not encouraging. In Baden the wooden framework of the guillotine, out of use for some years, had already been found to be rotting and riddled with woodworm, and had had to be repaired.[33] In Hamburg, where the hand-axe had been in use since the end of the French occupation in 1814, the guillotine was kept in the prison museum and was also discovered on inspection to be 'infested with woodworm'.[34] In Weimar the executioner described the guillotine as shaky.[35] In Stuttgart the guillotine still in use was the same one that had been set up in 1853, when it had replaced the sword,[36] as was also the case in Zweibrücken.[37] The problems that could occur with a machine that was 'too old' were revealed when Professor Schreiber, Director of the Anatomical Institute at Frankfurt University, reported that while

[29] Ibid., Bl. 18: Protokoll der 68. Situng, 7 May 1935.

[30] Ibid., Bl. 179: Reichsjustizminister Gürtner, note of 14 Oct. 1936.

[31] Ibid., Bl. 58: Vermerk über die auf das Rundschreiben vom 9. April 1935 (IIIa 18477/35) eingegangenen Äusserungen, 8 June 1935.

[32] Ibid., Bl. 205: RJM circular, 28 Dec. 1936.

[33] GLA Karlsruhe 234/10178: Direktor der Strafanstalten Bruchsal to Bad. Justizministerium, 21 Apr. 1934.

[34] BA Koblenz R22/1314: Präsident der hamburgischen Vollzugsanstalten to Generalstaatsanwalt des Hanseatischen Oberlandesgerichts, 22 Mar. 1937.

[35] Ibid., Bl. 427: Reichhardt report of 6 Feb. 1937.

[36] Ibid., Bl. 426: Generalstaatsanwalt Stuttgart to RJM, 19 Jan. 1937.

[37] Ibid. 1315, Bl. 319: Generalstaatsanwalt Zweibrücken to RJM, 20 June 1939.

a blow with the hand-axe left the surface of the wound on the severed neck smooth and clean, the Frankfurt guillotine left a rough impression, with the skin 'in tatters'. Schreiber suggested 'that this mechanical axe severed the head from the body less through the sharpness of its cutting action than through the crushing weight of its blow'.[38] In view of these negative reports, the Ministry concluded that new machines would have to be constructed. Finding a manufacturer did not prove easy. There had been no new demand for guillotines since the middle of the nineteenth century, when they had first been introduced in a number of German states. The bureaucrats checked through the files to see if the firms that had supplied them eighty or more years before were still in a position to build them now. They did indeed manage to track down one such enterprise, J. Mannhardt & Co. in Munich, which had last built a guillotine in 1859. But although the firm was still in business, it reported that it no longer had the facilities or expertise to supply the Ministry's needs.[39] In the end, the bureaucrats had to order the new machines from anyone they could find. They were not cheap. Alex D., a master cabinet-maker from Cologne, for example, sent in an estimate of 844 Reichsmarks.[40] Nevertheless, guillotines were now refurbished or constructed all over Germany to cope with the new demand.

In implementing Hitler's decision to replace the axe with the guillotine, the Reich Ministry of Justice went to extraordinary lengths to ensure that the innovation did not compromise the aura of secrecy which now surrounded the execution process. 'With the mechanical axe', Freisler had commented during the discussions of 1934, 'it is also more difficult to keep the execution secret, especially if the machine has to be transported.'[41] Some officials suggested 'execution . . . in a town where the executioner lives, so as to avoid the public attention connected with the executioner's arrival'.[42] Others put forward the suggestion that executions should be held not in the major urban centre of each court district but 'at a remoter site' in order to keep them from attracting the attention of the general public.[43] Considerable disapproval was aroused in the Ministry when it was learned that executioner Johann Reichhart and his assistants, after carrying out a beheading in Weimar, had 'breakfasted in the Lion right opposite the entrance to the court-house immediately after the execution, which attracted people's attention and has aroused comment'.[44] Confronted with his

[38] BA Koblenz R22/315, Bl. 53: Generalstaatsanwalt Frankfurt am Main to RJM, 29 Oct. 1940.

[39] Ibid. 1314, Bl. 216: Oberstaatsanwalt München, betr. Hinrichtung mittels Fallbeils, 13 Mar. 1937.

[40] Ibid., Bl. 267: Alex D. to RJM, 19 Mar. 1937.

[41] Ibid.: Protokoll der 17. Sitzung am 1. März 1934.

[42] Ibid., Bl. 58: Vermerk über die auf das Rundschreiben vom 9. April 1935 (IIIa 18477/35) eingegangenen Äusserungen, 8 June 1935.

[43] HStA Düsseldorf Rep. 126/82, Bl. 33: Oberstaatsanwalt to Generalstaatanwalt Düsseldorf, 23 Apr. 1935.

[44] BA Koblenz R22/1314, Bl. 410–11: Erster Staatsanwalt Weimar to Oberstaatsanwalt Weimar, 10 and 19 Aug. 1937.

misdemeanour, Reichhart promised not to repeat his offence,[45] rather late in the day, since two years had already passed since judicial officials in Munich had discussed imposing on the executioner a 'ban on visiting inns in the city'. The Ministry in Berlin suggested that, if the executioners had to stay overnight in a town before an execution, they should be accommodated in the prison rather than an inn.[46] Only in this way could their arrival be kept from the knowledge of the general public.

The authorities also turned their attention to the traditional practice of tolling a special bell during an execution. The Ministry of Justice had already considered abolishing it in June 1935, though it had not immediately acted on the proposal.[47] In February 1936 it was agreed that the prison authorities at Plötzensee in Berlin could stop using the bell because it could be heard, despite everything, in the nearby houses outside the prison compound.[48] A year later the director of the Hanover prison was being questioned about the possibility of the bell being heard within the prison. 'Neither the blow of the falling axe', he assured the state prosecutor in Celle, 'nor the tolling of the bell, whose clapper is muffled in cloth so as to dampen the sound, can be heard by the inmates of the institution.'[49] The bell continued to be used with baffles, so that it could scarcely be heard at all, until February 1939, when it was at last dispensed with altogether.[50] A further step in the direction of concealing executions from the inmates of the prisons where they were held was taken when the Ministry suggested that prison exercise yards should no longer be used for this purpose. They had the disadvantage that the guillotine was always having to be erected and dismantled in full view of the offenders in the surrounding cells. Instead, governors of gaols should undertake the 'erection of a special roofed execution space, with a firmly built-in execution machine'.[51] It was in this spirit that the governor of Plötzensee moved executions in 1937 from the yard to the storeroom, which was specially cleared for this purpose.[52] These measures, of course, were unlikely to have been effective in concealing executions from the well-established clandestine communications networks that functioned among the prisoners. But they did testify to the new vigour with which the penal administration was now

---

[45] Ibid., Bl. 425: Oberstaatsanwalt München 1 to Generalstaatsanwalt beim Oberlandeesgericht München, 6 Nov. 1937; ibid., Bl. 427: second letter of same date.

[46] Ibid., Bl. 60: Vermerk, 8 June 1935.

[47] Ibid., Bl. 58: Vermerk über die auf das Rundschreiben vom 9. April 1935 (IIIa 18477/35) eingegangenen Äusserungen, 8 June 1935.

[48] Ibid., Bl. 144: RJM to Generalstaatsanwalt beim Kammergericht, 11 February 1936.

[49] Ibid., Bl. 303: Strafanstaltsoberdirektor Hannover to Generalstaatsanwalt Celle, 13 Apr. 1937.

[50] Ibid. 5019, Bl. 3: RJM to Reichsgerichtspräsident and others, 19 Feb. 1939; see also Glenzdorf and Treichel, *Henker*, 135–6.

[51] BA Koblenz R22/1314, Bl. 58: Vermerk über die auf das Rundschreiben vom 9. April 1935 (IIIa 18477/35) eingegangenen Äusserungen, 8 June 1935.

[52] Ibid., Bl. 247: Vermerk, 22 Feb. 1937. See also Victor von Gostomski and Walter Loch, *Der Tod von Plötzensee: Erinnerungen, Ereignisse, Dokumente 1942–1944* (Frankfurt am Main, 1993), p. 14.

driving on the quest for secrecy and anonymity in the execution of the enemies of the Third Reich.

The sensational newspaper reporting of executions which had been such a cause of concern from Bismarck's initiative of 1886 onwards, and had reached such heights—or depths—in the Weimar Republic, also became a thing of the past. Goebbels lost no time in bringing the press to heel in 1933, and it was clear that he, too, considered that elaborate descriptions of the last hours of condemned criminal and political offenders tended to evoke sympathy, even sometimes admiration, rather than more appropriate feelings in those who read them. From now on, they vanished from the press entirely. Similar thought was given to the publicity generated by the traditional red posters put up around a town to announce that an execution had taken place. In December 1933 Goebbels ordered that these posters should no longer give the profession of the executed offender. They should simply refer instead to the crime which had led to the condemnation: not 'plumber', for example, but 'murderer', 'knifer' or 'murderous arsonist'.[53] At the same time, Goebbels changed the colour of the posters from the previous pale and pinkish red to a garish, almost fluorescent scarlet, as a way of lending them added emphasis.[54] Secrecy was concentrated on the run-up to an execution. In 1935 the Ministry began to worry about the possibility of the news of an execution getting out in advance of the event through the people whose task it was to produce these posters. It urged a 'careful selection of the workshops in which the announcements are printed'. And it went on to advocate the 'construction of the coffin inside the prison' for much the same reason. Indeed, it declared itself generally in favour of the 'rescinding of older regulations which stand in the way of the maintenance of secrecy', such as the 'publication of a report of the act of execution in the official bulletin'.[55]

The Nazi authorities also took steps to restrict still further the number of people attending a beheading. No entry cards were issued under the Third Reich. The semi-public execution of the 'red marines' in 1934 was a solitary exception. Moreover, the Nazis condemned the compulsory attendance of twelve witnesses as an 'excrescence of liberalistic concepts of the state'. In the Third Reich, they said, the people trusted the state, and their presence was an insult to its new position as the true representative of the whole German race. Hitler in any case did not believe in what he subsequently called 'the whole swindle of jurymen', which contradicted so flagrantly the 'leadership principle' that was so central to

[53] GStA Berlin Rep. 84a/8313, Bl. 43: Memo of 28 Dec. 1933, in response to a request to this effect from Goebbels. See also GLA Karlsruhe 240/1266: Badisches Justizministerium to Staatsanwaltschaften, 9 Mar. 1934.

[54] See the examples in HStA Hanover Hann. 173a Nr. 442, Bl. 145 and 215.

[55] BA Koblenz R22/1314, Bl. 60: Vermerk, 8 June 1935.

the Nazi world-view. So on 21 March 1934 the practice of summoning twelve witnesses to attend every execution was abolished.[56] Even after these steps had been taken, the Ministry of Justice was still concerned to prevent the 'attendance of further persons at the act of execution'.[57] In February 1939 it confirmed that the only people allowed to be present were the executioner and his three assistants, a doctor, a clergyman (who could say a prayer if so desired), a member of the state prosecutor's office, the prison governor, and the offender.[58] The idea tried out in Weimar in June 1938, when a dozen or so young policemen were brought in to witness an execution as part of their training, does not seem to have been repeated.[59]

It is possible to interpret this increasing concern with secrecy under the Third Reich as an aspect of the privatization of death, as the work of both Ariès and Elias, in their different ways, would seem to suggest.[60] Certainly, not least under the pressures of the Nazi regime itself, many ordinary Germans were trying to retreat into a private sphere of their own, away from the imperatives of totalitarian political mobilization ordained by the masters of the Third Reich. But this was not what the regime wanted. On the contrary, it sought to abolish private life altogether, in pursuit of a goal of the complete ideological penetration of everyday life. The socialization and education of children was taken out of the family and given increasingly to organizations such as the Hitler Youth and the League of German Girls; the organization of leisure pursuits, culture, tourism, and the like was undertaken by the 'Strength through Joy' programme; films, radio, books, magazines, newspapers, all were made to a greater or lesser extent to serve the propaganda purposes of the Third Reich.[61] So all-encompassing was the regime's ambition to destroy the concept of privacy that Robert Ley, leader of the Labour Front, once boasted: 'The only person in Germany who still leads a private life is someone who is sleeping.'[62] Moreover, Elias saw the growth of a private sphere, for all its negative side-effects in terms of prudery, embarrassment, and shame, essentially in positive terms: for him, it was a key aspect of the civilizing process. Correspondingly, its reversal under the Nazi regime was an important element in the reversal of the civilizing process which that regime represented. And the growing politicization of German society under the Weimar Republic, and even before, can equally be seen as evidence for the

---

[56] GStA Berlin Rep. 84a/7787, Bl. 131–4: order of 21 Mar. 1934. For Hitler's views, see Henry Pickler (ed.), *Hitlers Tischgespräche im Führerhauptquartier* (Stuttgart, 1976), 158 (29 Mar. 1942).

[57] BA Koblenz R22/1314, Bl. 60: Vermerk, 8 June 1935.

[58] Ibid. 1315, Bl. 218: RJM to Oberlandesgerichtspräsidenten, 19 Feb. 1939, para. 32.

[59] Ibid.: Oberstaatsanwalt Weimar to RJM, 11 June 1938.

[60] See Evans, 'Öffentlichkeit und Autorität', for this point of view.

[61] George L. Mosse, *Nazi Culture: Intellectual, Cultural and Social Life in the Third Reich* (New York, 1966).

[62] Quoted in Charlotte Beradt, *Das dritte Reich des Traums* (Munich, 1966), 5.

origins of this development. To be sure, this is not quite the sense in which Elias intended his arguments to be taken. Nevertheless, the ideological penetration and extension of the public sphere in the Third Reich did represent an obvious way in which German society in the 1930s diverged from its counterparts in Britain, France, and the United States.

Yet, in some ways, this is still taking rather too narrow a view of what was going on. For the Nazis not only regimented the public sphere, they also divided it. They created a 'racial community' of 'healthy' Germans who, increasingly, were the only people who could speak in public, take part in politics, pursue a professional activity, enter a university, and so on. This was the 'public' from whom the various rules and regulations introduced under the Third Reich were designed to keep the facts of capital punishment secret. For executions belonged to a different and separate set of public spheres—those of people who were 'foreign to the community'—above all, Jews, but also gypsies, criminals, the mentally and physically handicapped, prostitutes, homosexuals, Jehovah's Witnesses, active Communists, and other victims or opponents of the regime. These people were consigned to a life which was increasingly, and deliberately, cut off from all contact with that of the majority 'racial community'. And yet this life remained in its own terms public. The Jewish community, for example, continued to have its own institutions and, when it was shipped off to ghettos during the war, its own means of generating public activity within the confines allowed it. And each one of the network of concentration camps, which covered Germany and was extended beyond it from 1939 onwards, also constituted a kind of public sphere in its own right. Here, too, hundreds of thousands of people lived, worked, and died together, under a set of checks and controls more rigorous by far than those which had penetrated the majority community. In these various worlds of Nazi Germany's outcasts, the SS and the Gestapo enjoyed a degree of power they had not yet attained in the majority community of the 'racially pure'.

The measures undertaken to conceal executions from the 'general public' are best understood not as a process of privatization but on the contrary as part of a much wider mapping-out of the boundary between the differing public spheres of the 'racial community' and the 'community aliens'. The ordinary citizens of the Third Reich were to know nothing of what went on in these other spheres. All that was necessary was to make clear the threat that they would be consigned to this outer darkness should they transgress; should they fail to contribute the work demanded of them; should they fail to show the required enthusiasm for the regime; should they engage in any kind of dissent or opposition, whether overt or covert. All that the right-thinking, racially valuable German needed to know was that deviants, Communists and other enemies of the race were being 'dealt with'; and those who were in fact executed by the Gestapo or the SS without trial were generally killed in conditions of the greatest secrecy as far as the general public of the 'racial community' was concerned, their death recorded as resulting from suicide or disease, or the consequence of being 'shot while trying to escape'.[63] For some members of the majority community, this doubtless afforded the dubious gratification of vicarious retribution, as far as their imaginations would take them, rather in the way that the conservative middle classes in modern countries like Britain or the United States demand tougher measures against criminals without necessarily wanting to know in detail what these actually involve. But for most people the secrecy in which these subterranean public spheres were shrouded enabled them to continue with their lives without troubling their consciences overmuch about what went on in them.[64]

c. The Volunteer Executioners

As we have seen, the Third Reich released impulses of hatred and destruction which had already been present, though still to some extent held in check, under the Weimar Republic. By making discrimination, physical violence, and assaults upon the bodily integrity and physical existence of racial, religious, political, sexual, and other minorities not only possible but actually a central part of state policy, the Nazis encouraged many people to realize and act out destructive drives which in normal circumstances would have remained repressed. We have already seen something of this in popular responses to the Reichstag fire and suggestions from the public for novel methods of execution. Even more striking, perhaps, was a sudden flood of offers from members of the public to take on the job of executioner. 'Let me, honoured Mr Minister-President, become an executioner in the new state,' wrote Robert H., from Wesermünde, in 1935: 'I am not driven to do this by sensation or other lusts but merely by the recognition: this is the unshakeable, correct course which our honoured leader Adolf Hitler has taken.'[65] 'Politely ask for information about vacancies for the position of executioner', wrote Paul K., a stormtrooper in the SS: 'to exterminate completely those people who have lost their right to exist in our fatherland, that is my aim, which I seek and want to achieve.'[66] The brownshirt Walter Z., from Berlin-Friedenau, referring to the killing of the man whose life was mythologized in the Nazi Party anthem, told the authorities that in his view, 'it is a matter of honour

---

[63] Gruchmann, *Justiz*, 675–6.

[64] For an interesting discussion of the ways in which people's consciences were dulled under the Third Reich, see David Bankier, *The Germans and the Final Solution: Public Opinion under Nazism* (Cambridge, 1992).

[65] BA Koblenz R22/1327, Bl. 19–20: Robert H. to Göring, 20 Feb. 1935.

[66] Ibid., Bl. 18: Paul K. to RJM, 13 Aug. 1936.

for me to fulfil the promise we gave to our comrade Horst Wessel, and to execute his two murderers who are still alive. So I am requesting appointment as executioner.'[67] Over a hundred such applications arrived at the Ministry of Justice in Berlin from the beginning of 1934, when the need for extra executioners had begun to be apparent, to the end of 1937. They continued to flow into the files of the Ministry of Justice right through the war, making a total of approximately 350 altogether from the beginning of the Third Reich to the end. The Ministry quickly ordered a pro forma reply to be duplicated and sent to all these people: 'The executioner's posts are occupied at this time. New appointments are not to be expected. Applications will not be held in reserve.'[68]

Most volunteers for employment as executioner were not brownshirts, stormtroopers, or even active Nazis, but poor and unemployed men who were simply in need of money. Many gave the desperate economic situation as their principal reason for applying. Only a handful had obvious personal motives, like the Rhinelander Josef S., who told the Justice Ministry:

Offer myself to you as executioner. For years an inner voice has been telling me to take up this profession, as if Providence has destined me for it. I am fully and completely conscious of my duty and responsibility as such. With the thought of completely eradicating all criminals and racial pests through which the German people and its life are endangered, I am courteously asking you to give ear to my request. In 1931/32 I myself was the victim of conscienceless race-pests, for which I had to spend four months in prison. I cannot find words to tell you of my attitude towards criminals.[69]

But if applicants did have personal or psychological resentments and grudges such as these, most managed successfully to conceal them. Nor were the volunteers—with rare exceptions, such as Carl D., who was discovered to have a previous conviction for shooting a man dead in a political argument[70]—obviously violent or pathological by nature. On the contrary, they were overwhelmingly men whose work experience led them to believe that they would remain unmoved by the act of beheading someone: prison warders, policemen and court bailiffs, for example, many of whom had become inured to violence, had an occupational indifference to the suffering of offenders, or had witnessed executions themselves. Gravediggers were also prominent among the applicants, hardened as they were to the sight of dead human bodies; and above all there were large numbers of butchers and slaughterhousemen, the twentieth-century equivalent of the knackers of old. During the war, not a few of the volunteers

[67] BA Koblenz R22/1327, Bl. 32: Walter Z. to RJM, 15 Jan. 1935. See also Imre Lazar, *Der Fall Horst Wessel* (Stuttgart and Zurich, 1980).
[68] BA Koblenz R22/1327, Bl. 139.
[69] Ibid. 1328, Bl. 98: Josef S. to RJM, 29 Mar. 1939.
[70] Ibid. 1329, Bl. 21: Carl D. to RJM, 18 Oct. 1941.

were veterans who had been invalided out of the army. Financial motives are likely to have been strong here too.

With the outbreak of war, the applications began to breathe an increasingly violent spirit of hatred and revenge. 'It is not a desire for sensation', wrote the gravedigger Albert S., from Sondershausen, on 26 September 1939, after offering his services as guillotine operative to the Reich Justice Ministry, 'but my feelings, that drive me to help exterminate such creatures that are endangering the life and property of peaceful people or the peace of the land with criminal intent.'[71] Words such as 'creatures' soon appeared mild in comparison to the language of other applications of this sort. By 1940, too, such sentiments were being directed increasingly against political offenders, and applicants were treating the post of executioner as a political one. Thus Kurt F. of Leipzig wrote to Göring in 1940 in the following terms:

I come to you today with a rare request. I am 28 years old, master butcher by trade. I joined the party as an 18-year-old. But my mission in life, my Führer, is to serve you and my fatherland, and I feel called to do this, and in fact as executioner. For those types who betray our dearly beloved Führer and fatherland do not deserve any mercy. I ask you, Herr General-Field-Marshal, to appoint me to such a post. Heil Hitler!![72]

Here it was the contemplation of traitors and resisters that prompted the young butcher to write. More articulate, but equally typical of these wartime applications, was a letter from Hans N., a 52-year-old party member from Heidenau near Dresden, who wrote on 22 March 1941:

The war that has been forced on our fatherland makes it the duty of every German to dedicate all his powers to helping and serving the fatherland. Unfortunately there are still so many who do the opposite, and thus damage the German military effort and with it the whole German people. That is proven by the many sentences which are passed almost daily by the courts, indeed by the many death sentences which are pronounced and executed. I now wish to co-operate in the wiping-out of criminality, and offer myself if needed and if I am suited for the office of a German executioner to the Reich Justice Ministry.[73]

None of these applications was ever given serious consideration by the Ministry, not even that of Karl F., from Offenbach, who described himself as descending from 'an old family of executioners'.[74]

Although such petitions remained confidential, and never left the files of the Reich Ministry of Justice, the possibility of desperate or politically motivated individuals offering their services to the new Reich was not lost on contempor-

---

[71] Ibid. 1328, Bl. 143: Albert S. to RJM, 26 Sept. 1939.
[72] Ibid., Bl. 187: Kurt F. to Göring. 20 Feb. 1940.
[73] Ibid., Bl. 268: Hans N. to RJM, 22 Mar. 1941.
[74] Ibid., Bl. 152: Karl F. to RJM, 3 Dec. 1939.

aries. There was even a novel devoted to the subject—Arnold Zweig's *Das Beil von Wandsbek* ('The Axe of Wandsbek'). This is the story, written in exile and published in 1943, of a butcher, living in the Hamburg area, who is forced by circumstances into becoming an executioner for the Third Reich. Down on his luck, with his business brought to the edge of ruin by the Depression and by competition from the big department stores, Albert Teetjen writes to an old army comrade who has gained a position of influence in the new regime, to see if he can do anything to rescue the situation. His friend needs someone who can decapitate four Communists, condemned to death for their supposed part in the 'Bloody Sunday' incident in Altona in 1932, with a hand-held axe, in the temporary absence of the regular executioner. He persuades the authorities to offer Teetjen two thousand Marks to do the job. Although the butcher wears a mask while carrying out the execution and does his best to keep the whole thing a secret, word of his identity gradually gets around, the community ostracizes him, he loses his customers, and he eventually commits suicide with his wife in remorse and despair.

The novel is a brilliant exposure of the psychology of complicity, and a powerful portrayal of the roots of resistance. In the course of the narrative, the axe itself becomes a symbol of power that takes on an existence of its own, independent of any resemblance to historical reality, and the group of resisters whose story is told in parallel to that of the butcher-executioner plans, unsuccessfully as it turns out, to use it against Hitler himself. Zweig's artistic device of putting a volunteer executioner at the centre of his novel is triumphantly justified, as Teetjen comes to stand as a metaphor of so many millions more in the Third Reich who became executioners in ways less brutal and direct.[75] But it is historically inaccurate. It was, to be sure, based on a report in a German newspaper published in Prague on 18 April 1937, which claimed that a butcher called Fock, living in Altona, had shot himself because the local people had ostracized him as a result of learning that he had carried out the execution of Bruno Tesch and his comrades. Subsequent researches revealed that a butcher with a similar name had indeed killed himself at about this time. But other butchers in the area, questioned long after the event, strenuously denied that Fock would have been capable of carrying out an execution, and insisted that the rumour that he had done it was based on a misunderstanding. Another witness later reported having seen executioner Gröpler on the train on his way into the city the day before the execution took place. More than six decades later, it is no longer possible completely to disentangle truth from rumour, reality from

[75] Arnold Zweig, *Das Beil von Wandsbek*, 2nd edn. (Berlin and Weimar, 1962). The novel first appeared in Hebrew in 1943; the German version was not published until 1948. It was filmed in 1951.

supposition. But there is no evidence in the official papers that Gröpler was otherwise engaged on 1 August 1933, or that anyone apart from the official executioner was employed on the occasion.[76] The reality was, as the Ministry never tired of telling volunteers for the job under the Third Reich, that the posts of executioner were all filled. And they were filled, as before, from the ranks of the existing executioners and their assistants.

d. Apogee of a Profession

The leading executioner in Germany at the time of the Nazi seizure of power was the Magdeburg laundry-owner Carl Gröpler. He had been in office for more than a quarter of a century and had carried out executions in Prussia, Mecklenburg, Oldenburg, Brunswick, and the Hanseatic cities.[77] Gröpler's laundry had long since gone out of business, and he was in practice entirely dependent on his income from his activities as executioner.[78] He had been seriously underemployed in the last years of the Weimar Republic, and so welcomed the coming of the Third Reich, which granted him a renewal of his contract on 19 February 1933.[79] In addition to his annual retainer of 1,500 Reichsmarks from the Prussian state, he was also due by contract 50 marks per execution in Prussia and 450 or 500 marks per execution in the other states, where he was not paid an annual retainer. He thus gained considerably by the rapidly accelerating number of executions which he was ordered to carry out from the middle of 1933 onwards. Predictably, Gröpler was not slow to demonstrate his enthusiasm for the new regime. He started giving the Nazi salute at executions and punctuating his activities with loud cries of 'Heil Hitler!' The Ministry officials were not amused. While they had 'no objection' to the fact that Gröpler greeted the officiating state prosecutor in this manner on entering and leaving the execution room, they were less happy about other aspects of his new-found political zeal. 'It can be questionable', they commented, 'whether every action, e.g. of his readiness to begin, of the completion of the execution etc., should also be reported with raised arm or even the phrase "Heil Hitler!"' Gröpler was accordingly admonished to restrain his enthusiasm and cease these practices. His cries of 'Heil Hitler!' seemed perhaps to bring the Führer's name in rather too personal and direct a manner into the act of decapitation, instead of presenting the proceedings as an essentially

[76] Breloer and Königstein, *Blutgeld*, 6–10.
[77] BA Koblenz R22/1323, Bl. 66: 'Übersicht über die zur Zeit amtierenden Scharfrichter'.
[78] Ibid., Bl. 152, Bl. 160: 'Vermerk: Neue Verträge mit den Scharfrichtern'; and ibid., Bl. 184: RJM to Reichsfinanzministerium, Apr. 1937 (draft).
[79] HStA Düsseldorf Rep. 126/82: PJM to Generalstaatsanwälte, 10 Mar. 1933.

impersonal process of the physical elimination of an offender in the name of the race.[80]

Anxious that executions should appear modern, the authorities also took exception to Gröpler's habit of wearing a white shirt and waistcoat and a frock-coat while performing his duties. Under the contract of employment which he had signed in 1928, Gröpler had agreed to wear a black tunic closed at the wrists and neck and fastened with black buttons, because the then Prussian Minister of Justice had found the frock-coat, and the act of removing it in order to strike the fatal blow, overly theatrical. But as soon as the Nazis came to power and began to require him to carry out double or multiple executions, Gröpler reverted to the frock-coat. The bureaucrats at the Reich Ministry of Justice, who now ran the execution service nationwide, regarded this as 'anachronistic',[81] and called him in for an interview on 17 June 1935 at the Ministry building in Berlin to answer for his actions. As the official record of the conversation noted,

He explained that, when the tunic was introduced, it prevented him from striking an accurate blow because it did not give him enough freedom of movement. Moreover, it often happened that his under-arm was splattered with blood during an execution, and if he had to carry out another execution immediately afterwards, he had to do it in the bloodstained tunic, which was hardly conducive to the dignity which should be maintained during such an act. Currently he put on his frock-coat between individual executions, thus covering up the bloodstains on the shirtsleeve.

The Ministry accepted this explanation, and he was allowed to continue wearing the traditional dress to which he had reverted on the fall of the Weimar Republic.[82] However, Gröpler's reign as chief executioner was now coming to an end. Born in 1868, and thus 65 years of age at the time of the Nazi seizure of power, he was still evidently more than capable of wielding his axe accurately and efficiently despite the physical demands of the greater number of executions he now had to perform. The hand-axe, he assured the bureaucrats at the Justice Ministry at his interview with them in 1935, was quicker and more secret than the guillotine. Unlike the latter, it could be concealed from the offender. It should continue to be employed. And indeed he continued to use it, delegating the fatal blow to one of his assistants in cases where he considered the level of skill required was no more than average. But in November 1936 the official who dealt with the executioners began to notice that Gröpler's performance 'has lately been falling off a bit'.[83] Well over retirement age, he was now finally

[80] GStA Berlin Rep. 84a/4594, Bl. 44, 47, 51 (notes of RJM); BA Koblenz R22/1314, Bl. 400: RJM to Oberstaatsanwalt Breslau, 15 Oct. 1937; HStA Düsseldorf Rep. 126/82: PJM (Crohne) to Gröpler, 14 Apr. 1934.

[81] BA Koblenz R22/1323. Bl. 55: Generalstaatsanwalt Naumburg to RJM, 12 June 1935.

[82] Ibid., Bl. 57: Vermerk, 24 June 1935.

[83] BA Koblenz R22/1323, Bl. 152: 'Vermerk: Neue Verträge mit den Scharfrichtern, 16. November 1936'.

relieved of his duties and left with his annual retainer of 1,500 marks as a pension. Since this was far below the average wage, and he was otherwise 'penniless', the Ministry evidently feared that he would repeat his protests of previous years.[84] When they discovered that he had received a lucrative offer from New York Radio for his life story, the bureaucrats forced him to give an undertaking that he would not accept it.[85] After this, he finally disappeared from the official record.

Gröpler was of course by no means the only executioner active in Germany, even under the Weimar Republic. Since before the First World War, the northern half of Germany had been divided into two parts for the purpose of executions, and Gröpler had only had charge of the larger, north-eastern section. The other part had been in the charge of the Schwietzes, father and son, and had passed on to their assistants, one of whom, Fritz Reichelt, had taken it over in 1927. Reichelt had only ever attended two executions in his entire career, and had apparently never once wielded the fatal blow himself.[86] He signed a fresh contract with the Prussian Justice Ministry on 9 May 1933.[87] But it soon became clear that he was not up to the job. In October 1933 he took two blows to sever the head of one of his victims. He was immediately dismissed. Reichelt protested to the Prussian Interior Minister, Hermann Göring, that the mistake had occurred because his assistant had failed to position the head correctly on the block. But Göring, once more showing unusual squeamishness in the matter of capital punishment, refused his request for re-employment.[88] Protesting that he had carried out six other executions without incident (whether with the axe or the guillotine he did not say), Reichelt now commenced a campaign to get his job back. 'I am father of a family, and of pure Aryan stock, SA man, my two sons are also SA and SS men, wife and daughter branch leaders of the Women's Organization', he protested in another letter, written a whole year after his dismissal: 'I believe I have a right to an explanation as to the reason why I have been deprived of a living by having my contract revoked.'[89] Reichelt even threatened to make a personal call on Hitler. 'I have', he wrote, 'full trust in my Führer.'[90] But his appeals fell on deaf ears.[91] He was still writing in asking for his job back as late as August 1942, with continuing lack of success.[92]

Reichelt's dismissal presented the authorities with a dilemma. They were

[84] Ibid., Bl. 184: RJM to Reichsfinanzministerium, Apr. 1937 (draft).
[85] Ibid., Bl. 218: Gröpler to Oberstaatsanwalt Naumburg, 26 Aug. 1937.
[86] GStA Berlin Rep. 84a/4595, Bl. 191: RJM to Oberstaatsanwälte.
[87] HStA Düsseldorf Rep. 126/82: PJM to Generalstaatsanwälte, 28 May 1933.
[88] GStA Berlin Rep. 84a/4595, Bl. 191: Reichelt to Göring, 5 Jan. 1934 and reply.
[89] BA Koblenz R22/1323, Bl. 11: Reichelt to PJM, 26 Oct. 1934.
[90] Ibid. 1328, Bl. 183: Reichelt to RJM, 13 Feb. 1940.
[91] Ibid., Bl. 184: Reichelt to RJM, Aug. 1942.
[92] Ibid. 1329, Bl. 68: Reichelt to RJM, 15 Aug. 1942.

unwilling on principle to accede to any of the numerous requests from ordinary citizens for employment as executioner. Since Reichelt's inexperience had been at the root of his problems, they needed to appoint someone of proven ability with the axe. But the long period in the late 1920s and early 1930s during which there had been virtually no executions at all in Prussia and the other German states meant that such a person was not to be found among the ranks of the assistants of the existing executioners. And Carl Gröpler and his team were already fully occupied in their part of the Reich. At this point, salvation came from an unexpected quarter. Hearing of Reichelt's dismissal, the former executioner Alwin Engelhardt now wrote in to the Justice Ministry asking for his old job back.[93] Engelhardt had himself been sacked from his post nearly thirty years before. He was indeed Carl Gröpler's predecessor and had trained him in his craft. His enforced retirement had been on grounds not of technical incompetence but financial irresponsibility. The former assistant of executioner Friedrich Reindel, he had also married Reindel's daughter and thus joined a long-established dynasty of executioners.[94] Born on 17 May 1875, he was, as the state prosecutor in Dessau described him in August 1933, a 'strong, stocky man with a fresh appearance, calm and disciplined'.[95] He seemed the ideal solution to the Ministry's problems, and the officials quickly re-engaged him. It was not long before they began to wish that they had not.

Engelhardt was allotted Saxony (including Anhalt) and Thuringia as his area of operations, and by early 1934 had carried out four executions, all with the guillotine, all of them, as the state prosecutor in Dessau reported, satisfactory. They included the Reichstag arsonist Marinus van der Lubbe, condemned to death by the Supreme Court in Leipzig and executed on 10 January 1934.[96] But the financial problems which had dogged Engelhardt during his earlier period of employment had not gone away. Nor, it seems, had the excessive addiction to drink which, according to Carl Gröpler, had caused them.[97] Engelhardt was not given an annual retainer, but was paid 350 Reichsmarks per execution (reduced to 150 in the case of additional executions held on the same day). Out of this money he had to find all his expenses and pay the fees of his three assistants.[98] Even in the circumstances of the Third Reich, when executions were taking place with ever-increasing frequency, this fell a long way short of the income he needed

[93] GStA Berlin Rep. 84a/4595, Bl. 188–90: Engelhardt to PJM, 1933 (various dates).

[94] Ibid., Bl. 191: Sächsisches Justizministerium to PJM, 30 Dec. 1933; Thüringisches Justizministerium to PJM, 3 Jan. 1934.

[95] BA Koblenz R22/1322, Bl. 42: Generalstaatsanwalt Naumburg to RJM 23 Mar. 1935 (Anlage).

[96] Glenzdorf and Treichel, *Henker*, 148.

[97] GStA Berlin Rep. 84a/4595, Bl. 99–108: *Neue Berliner Zeitung*, 18–28 Oct. 1930 (interview with Carl Gröpler).

[98] BA Koblenz R22/1323, Bl. 66: 'Übersicht über die zur Zeit amtierenden Scharfrichter'.

to stave off his creditors. Since 1910 he had been the owner of a knacker's yard found for him by the Prussian Ministry of Justice. By September 1934 he had accumulated unsecured personal debts of 7,954 marks 39 pfennigs and was also experiencing problems in meeting the repayments on the mortgage of 22,503 marks he owed on the yard.[99] It was small wonder, therefore, that he tried to secure the succession to Gröpler when the latter retired from his post as chief executioner in Prussia.[100] Meanwhile, it became apparent that Engelhardt's creditors were beginning to claim rights over his future income from executions. The feeling that this was improper had been the reason for his original dismissal by the Prussian Ministry of Justice back in 1906. Such was the Third Reich's need for executioners that he was retained in office despite this fact. But worse was to come. In March 1935 the police barred him from carrying on as a knacker because he had been discovered selling meat from his yard that was clearly unfit for human consumption. Engelhardt was forced to sign on for welfare relief, and found the experience unpleasant. He complained that 'he had recently been obliged to hear people around him say as he was collecting his welfare benefit: "He hasn't hacked off anyone's head for a long time!"'[101] In June 1935 the Reich Post Office obtained a court order on his property to enable it to recover the 106 marks 35 pfennigs he owed them in telephone bills unpaid since the beginning of January 1933.[102]

Under these circumstances, Engelhardt, who was still working as an executioner, took the desperate step of writing to Hitler in person for financial support. 'I am a long-time, faithful supporter of the movement', he wrote to the Führer on 18 September 1935, 'and it was only because I was always too poor to pay the subscription that I was not able to become a member, but I went to every meeting and already fought in the difficult years of struggle'.[103] Of his five children, he wrote proudly, one had been a brownshirt since 1931. But, he complained to Hitler: 'I have a very high esteem for my office, though this is not widely shared among the people, and therefore I must regard it as an exceedingly gross humiliation, that as executioner I am temporarily obliged to draw a weekly welfare benefit of RM 8.' The letter, like all such petitions, was passed on to the Reich Ministry of Justice, who chose discreetly to ignore it.[104] Not content with writing to Hitler, in April 1936 Engelhardt also tried to reach the Reich Justice Minister, Franz Gürtner personally, by writing to Gürtner's wife at their home address.[105] The shock of receiving a letter from a state executioner evidently upset

---

[99] Ibid., Bl. 94: Vermerk, 28 May 1936.
[100] Ibid., Bl. 13: Engelhardt to RJM, 15 Nov. 1934.
[101] Ibid., Bl. 92–3: Engelhardt to RJM, June 1935.
[102] Ibid., Bl. 75: Reichspostdirektion to RJM, 11 June 1935.
[103] 'Years of struggle', i.e. before 1933.   [104] Ibid., Bl. 79–80: Engelhardt to Hitler, 18 Oct. 1935.
[105] Ibid., Bl. 86: Engelhardt to Frau Gürtner, 16 Apr. 1935.

Frau Gürtner, for her outraged husband now set in motion a full-scale investigation into Engelhardt's affairs. On 28 April 1936 his officials reported that, while
Engelhardt was without doubt a highly competent executioner, the files gave
them a poor impression of his personal qualities, and they recommended his
summary dismissal to avoid further embarrassment. He had in any case, they
pointed out, reached the age of 60, which could be regarded as an appropriate
moment for an executioner to retire.[106] So Engelhardt was informed that his
services would no longer be required. Predictably, he entered an immediate
protest against his sacking, and embarked on a determined campaign of letter-
writing in an effort to get the Ministry to change its mind.[107] By December 1937
he was threatening to exhibit his equipment for money, despite being paid an
annual pension of 600 marks,[108] and he rejected a request from the alarmed
officials at the Ministry to undertake that he would not do anything to publicize
his experiences as an executioner.[109] This prompted the Ministry to place the
matter in the hands of the Gestapo, Himmler's feared secret political police.[110]
They confiscated Engelhardt's equipment and placed him under surveillance to
make sure he would not talk.[111] The former executioner protested that it was
'unbelievable that I am being treated in this way'. He demanded compensation
of between 30,000 and 50,000 Reichsmarks, which he said was the price his
equipment could command on the open market.[112] The Gestapo estimated its
value more modestly at 50 marks, a thousand times less, but offered him 400 just
to keep him quiet. Engelhardt rejected this offer, demanding a monthly increase
in his pension of between 125 and 150 marks instead.[113] By now he had fallen
seriously ill, and his handwriting was so shaky that it was clear he was in no state
to wield the axe again, or even to pull the lever on a guillotine.[114] 'The negotiations with E.', complained the Gestapo in January 1938, 'are turning out to
be very difficult because of his very pronounced sense of honour, and also
because of his heart condition.'[115] Through all this, Engelhardt was becoming
steadily more embittered. 'We are now in the Third Reich', he wrote in December 1938, 'and no longer in the system-time, in which only clichés and empty
words were valued, but in the NSDAP, where we are getting to see deeds.'[116] He

106 BA Koblenz R22/1323, Bl. 94: Vermerk, 28 Apr. 1936.
107 Ibid., Bl. 91: Engelhardt to Crohne, 10 June 1936.
108 Ibid., Bl. 112–13: Engelhardt to RJM, 5 Dec. 1937.
109 Ibid., Bl. 110: RJM to Engelhardt, 24 Nov. 1937.
110 Ibid., Bl. 116: Amtsgericht Schmölln to RJM, 3 Dec. 1937.
111 Ibid., Bl. 118: Generalstaatsanwalt Jena to RJM, 21 Jan. 1938.
112 Ibid., Bl. 126: Engelhardt to RJM, 23 Feb. 1938.
113 Ibid., Bl. 118: Generalstaatsanwalt Jena to RJM, 21 Jan. 1938; ibid., Bl. 126: Engelhardt to RJM, 23
Feb. 1938; and ibid., Bl. 113: Engelhardt to RJM, 5 Dec. 1937.
114 Ibid., Bl. 134: Engelhardt to Wiedemann, 14 Aug. 1938.
115 Ibid., Bl. 118: Generalstaatsanwalt Jena to RJM, 21 Jan. 1938.
116 Ibid. 1324, Bl. 20: Engelhardt to Seyss-Inquart, 11 Dec. 1938. The 'system-time' (*Systemzeit*) was the
Nazi designation for the Weimar Republic.

was still living off his monthly pension of 50 marks from the Ministry of Justice at this time. He eventually succumbed to his heart complaint in October 1940, another example of an executioner who died an unhappy man.[117]

In the reorganization of the execution service that was undertaken by the Reich Justice Ministry in 1936, the southern part of Germany was given to Johann Reichhart, an experienced executioner who belonged to an established Bavarian dynasty of hangmen. Born in 1893, the year before his father Franz became chief Bavarian executioner, he had assisted the older man a number of times in the early Weimar Republic before taking over himself in 1924. Even in Bavaria, however, there had been so few beheadings between 1924 and 1933 that Reichhart had taken up residence in Holland for most of this period.[118] Not long after moving back to Munich, he got into trouble when it was discovered that his assistant since 1924, Hermann Donderer, had been making some money on the side by operating the guillotine exhibited in Valentin's Panoptikum, a wax museum with the usual 'Chamber of Horrors', in Munich. The state prosecutor visited the exhibition in November 1934 and primly ordered the tableau, which showed the execution of Kürten, to be closed and the guillotine removed.[119] The owner, Karl Valentin, admitted that the idea of setting up the scene had been his. 'The old deceased executioner Herr Reichhart', he said, 'was our vet. He used to relate the course of every execution to my parents.'[120] These admissions did not improve his position. Donderer was sacked, and Reichhart replaced him in the execution team with his own younger brother Georg.[121] Furious at being deprived of this source of income, Donderer blamed the Munich executioner for his misfortune and sent in one of those comprehensive denunciations that were such characteristic expressions of everyday tensions and petty quarrels of this kind under the Third Reich. It was Reichhart who was to blame in his view for the closure of the Panoptikum display:

During my work there Herr Reichhart came along for a visit with his current mistress— he is married with four children—saw the guillotine and told the Senior State Prosecutor right away. Reichhart used to be one of the biggest Communists. . . . In 1919 during the workers' council period he once sought refuge with my fiancée, who refused, after he had already spent several days hidden in a beer-barrel in the Hacker Beer Cellar.[122]

The malicious intent behind such claims was transparent. But denunciations were always investigated in the Third Reich, no matter how tainted the motives

[117] Ibid., Bl. 69: Generalstaatsanwalt Jena to RJM, 6 Nov. 1940.
[118] Ibid., Bl. 147: Reichhardt to RJM, 31 Jan. 1944.
[119] Ibid., Bl. 51: Oberstaatsanwalt Munich to RJM, 22 Nov. 1934.
[120] Ibid., Bl. 21: Valentin deposition, 29 Jan. 1935. Knackers traditionally acted as vets, though by this time entirely unofficially. Karl Valentin was a well-known cabaret artiste.
[121] Ibid., Bl. 36: Oberstaatsanwalt beim Landgericht München I to Generalstaatsanwalt beim Oberlandesgericht München, 12 Mar. 1935.
[122] Ibid., Bl. 19: Donderer to RJM, 18 Feb. 1935.

behind them.[123] So Reichhart was summoned by his employers in the judicial administration in Munich for an interview.

Questioned by the state prosecutor on 18 March 1935, Reichhart strenuously denied all the allegations that had been levelled at him. He had never been a Communist. He did not have a mistress. He had not taken refuge in a beer-barrel during the Revolution. Moreover, as the authorities agreed, he bore the sole responsibility of employing his assistants and could dismiss them at any time if he so wished.[124] Given the sensitivity which the authorities, even under the Third Reich, habitually showed towards the involvement of the official executioners in any public exhibitions or newspaper stories, Reichhart had done no more than safeguard his own position by denouncing the tableau at the Panoptikum. In December he was duly rewarded with the confirmation of his position as the executioner responsible for the southern half of Germany, in a further reorganization of duties now undertaken by the Justice Ministry in Berlin.[125] He was granted an annual salary of 3,000 marks. From this sum he also had to find the expenses and fees for his long-time assistant Josef Nikl, and his brother Georg Reichhart, who had taken over from the disgraced Donderer. Each of the three men also received a fee of 60 marks for each beheading. Given the substantial rate of executions by this time, this must have amounted to quite a respectable income; one to which the executioner clearly attached a good deal of importance. The officiating prosecutor complained of Johann Reichhart after an execution in Weimar in 1937 that 'for the executioner the key thing seemed to be to get his money and to get away as quickly as possible. Right after the execution was over, he came up to me with a big bill, which he wanted to be paid into his bank account.'[126]

By this time, Carl Gröpler's responsibilities had been taken over by the man who had been acting as his assistant since January 1934. This was Ernst Reindel, grandson of the former executioner Wilhelm Reindel, and a relation by marriage of Gröpler's colleague and teacher Alwin Engelhardt.[127] Reindel had been standing in for Gröpler on a regular basis, delivering the fatal blow himself at every third beheading, since March 1935.[128] From the end of 1936 he replaced him

[123] Robert Gellately, *The Gestapo and German Society: Enforcing Racial Policy 1933–1945* (Oxford, 1990). For the Donderer affair, see also Gerould, *Guillotine*, pp. 239–43.

[124] BA Koblenz R22/1323, Bl. 35: Generalstaatsanwalt beim Oberlandesgericht München to RJM, 18 Mar. 1935.

[125] Ibid., Bl. 66: Übersicht über die zur Zeit amtierenden Scharfrichter; ibid., Bl. 230: Richtlinien für Scharfrichter.

[126] Ibid. 1314, Bl. 10–22: Erster Staatsanwalt Weimar to Oberstaatsanwalt Weimar, 10 and 19 Aug. 1937 (copies).

[127] GStA Berlin Rep. 84a/4595, Bl. 191: RJM to Oberstaatsanwälte, 6 Jan. 1934.

[128] BA Koblenz R22/1323, Bl. 30: RJM to Generalstaatsanwalt Naumburg, 11 Mar. 1935; HStA Düsseldorf Rep. 126/82, Bl. 26: RJM to Generalstaatsanwälte, 24 June 1935.

entirely, and also took on his former assistants, except for one—Herbert Engler, who had been arrested and sentenced to eighteen months' imprisonment the previous year for embezzlement and bribery of officials, though probably not in connection with his duties as deputy executioner.[129] The establishment of the German executioners was completed by Friedrich Hehr, who had started as assistant to the executioner for Baden, Württemberg, and Hesse, Karl Burckhardt, in 1925, and took over in 1935 for an annual retainer of 400 marks plus 50 marks per execution.[130] In 1937, at 57 years of age, Hehr was described as 'physically and mentally so hale that he is most certainly capable of performing the tasks of the executioner'. In carrying out beheadings, he was, wrote the state prosecutor in Stuttgart, 'very skilled'.[131] However, on attending one of Hehr's executions in 1937, the state prosecutor in Schneidemühl reported that although he had been undeniably proficient with the guillotine, 'it was none the less noticeable that he cried "Attention!" before he released the blade on the execution machine'. 'I do not think that is right', noted Freisler primly in his reply, and Hehr was ordered to stop.[132] Moreover, the Justice Ministry also forced him to sack one of his assistants, Karl Werner, because he not only had a previous conviction for theft and criminal damage, but was also described by the Stuttgart state prosecutor as 'politically unreliable'.[133] Hehr's professional milieu was obviously suspiciously close to the underworld. However, once these problems had been sorted out, he was officially appointed as the Third Reich's third executioner, alongside Ernst Reindel and Johann Reichhart. It was striking how much continuity these appointments exhibited with past tradition. Not only did Reindel come from an old-established dynasty of executioners, but Reichhart and his brother Georg were also carrying on a family business, even if one of rather more recent origin. Moreover, both Georg Reichhart and Ernst Reindel were owners of knacker's yards, just as Alwin Engelhardt and so many of their predecessors had been. Hehr's mentor and predecessor, the Baden-Württemberg executioner Karl Burckhardt, had also been a tanner by trade.[134] These connections both reflected and perpetuated what Johann Reichhart called 'the continuing and probably always insuperable ostracization of his trade'.[135] Among the

[129] BA Koblenz R22/1323, Bl. 60–1: Oberstaatsanwalt Altenstein to RJM, 15 July and 6 Sept. 1935.

[130] Ibid. 1322, Bl. 21: Generalstaatsanwalt Darmstadt to RJM, 21 Mar. 1935; ibid., Bl. 23: Zahlungsanweisung, 4 Jan. 1935; ibid., Bl. 18: Württembergisches Justizministerium to Staatsanwälte und Oberlandesgerichte, 5 Mar. 1934 (the note on Bl. 166 seems to be in error).

[131] Ibid. 1323, Bl. 193: Generalstaatsanwalt Stuttgart to RJM, 8 Apr. 1937.

[132] Ibid. 1314, Bl. 402: Oberstaatsanwalt Schneidemühl to RJM, 28 Sept. 1937 and reply, 5 Oct. 1937.

[133] Ibid. 1323, Bl. 199: Generalstaatsanwalt Stuttgart to RJM, 15 June 1937.

[134] Ibid. 1322, Bl. 29: Oberstaatsanwalt for Landgericht Munich I to RJM, 18 Mar. 1935; ibid. 1323, Bl. 30: RJM to Generalstaatsanwalt Naumburg, 11 Mar. 1935.

[135] Ibid. 1314, Bl. 145: Oberstaatsanwalt Munich to Generalstaatsanwalt beim Oberlandesgericht München, 6 Dec. 1935 (copy).

assistants of the three chief executioners were two mortuary workers, a master smith, two commercial travellers, a haulier, a pensioner, and a nurse, as well as Georg Reichhart the knacker. The mixture of traditional trades which would have prepared those engaged in them for dealing with beheadings, and trades which appeared to be unrelated to these, had become more pronounced.[136] Nevertheless, the influence of tradition was strong here too.

In previous decades, executioners, despite the brutalizing effects of their background and experience in the knacking trade, had often succumbed to the nervous strain which they clearly experienced as a result of beheading their fellow humans. One after another, they took to the bottle, became involved in brawls and scandals of various kinds, and went into a querulous retirement which in a striking number of cases was cut short by suicide. A cool, unmovable figure such as Carl Gröpler was the exception rather than the rule. In the Third Reich, this situation changed. Men like Reichhart, Reindel, and Hehr and their assistants showed few such signs of stress. Paradoxically, this may have been the result of the greatly increased numbers of executions which they carried out, which reduced the exceptionality of each occasion and made killing into a routine. Also, the abandonment of the hand-axe after 1936 freed them from worries about the accuracy of their blow and reduced the degree of personal responsibility which they had to shoulder for the rapid and smooth carrying-out of a beheading. Beyond this, however, they were now operating in a fundamentally new context. For almost a century, executioners had been unique figures in German society, the only individuals charged by the state to kill its own citizens. The long-running debate on capital punishment, with the various periods in which it virtually ceased to be carried out, had rendered their position marginal, and it was clear to them that they were doing something of which a great many Germans strongly disapproved. Officialdom treated them with disdain and distaste. From 1933 onwards, all this changed. Violence and murder against the regime's opponents was now tolerated by the state and encouraged by Goebbels's propaganda machine. Nazi newspapers blared forth the message that criminals and traitors deserved to be killed, and advertised the fact that the regime fully intended to carry this threat into reality. All around the regular executioners, brownshirts and SS men, Gestapo agents and others were executing people as well, beating them up and killing them on the streets, above all in 1933 and 1938, but at other times too, shooting them because they were supposedly trying to escape, or torturing and killing them in the prisons and concentration camps of Hitler's Third Reich. The Nazis created a climate of violence in which, as we have seen, ordinary citizens as well as brownshirts and party members felt moved

---

[136] BA Koblenz R22/1323, Bl. 251: Oberstaatsanwalt Hanover to RJM, 4 Dec. 1937.

to write in to the government either offering their services as executioners or demanding the public hanging, shooting, or beheading of enemies of the Reich like Marinus van der Lubbe. Small wonder, therefore, that the officially appointed state executioners seemed to feel a new pride and confidence in their work and ceased to suffer from the psychological disorders which had so often plagued them in the past.

Like other servants of the established German state, executioners saw themselves in the course of the 1930s being gradually confronted with rivals operating within a parallel set of institutions established by the party and its ancillary organizations such as the SS. From almost the very beginning, the regular prisons bequeathed to the Third Reich from the Weimar and Imperial periods proved inadequate to hold the large numbers of people arrested by the brownshirts and other 'auxiliary police' as 'enemies of the people'. The rapid overcrowding of the prisons during the 'seizure of power' in the spring of 1933, and the anxiety of the state penal and judicial systems to rid themselves of the responsibility for prisoners who had not been condemned by any court of law, led to the hasty erection of concentration camps, where many of the Nazis' opponents were moved in late March and April 1933. Here and in numerous other 'private' prisons and cellars set up by the brownshirts and SS, over 30,000 Communists, Social Democrats, liberals, Jews, and others were incarcerated for varying periods of time, maltreated, or put to death. The few attempts made by the judicial authorities to follow up cases of murder within the camps did not get very far: those who were arrested were amnestied on 21 March, when a decree issued by Hitler gave the camps and those who ran them virtual immunity from prosecution. It remained in force until the end of the Third Reich. The thousands of people who were arrested and placed in 'protective custody' in concentration camps such as Dachau in the spring of 1933 were sent there without any court proceedings, despite the attempts of the Reich Ministry of Justice to get such arrests subjected to formal judicial process. Hitler, indeed, expressly forbade the involvement of lawyers in such cases.[137] Arrests of this kind continued throughout the Third Reich. Physical maltreatment of prisoners in concentration camps was the norm, and murders and executions were far from uncommon. The concentration camps were a kind of 'no-go area' for the law. When the legal authorities did, exceptionally, arrest, try, and condemn camp personnel for the torture of prisoners at the Hohenstein concentration camp in Saxony in 1935, Hitler personally intervened to grant the guilty men a free pardon, and the state prosecutor who had led the case against the men was forced to resign. In any case, these men were

---

[137] Engelhard (ed.), *Im Namen*, 251; Broszat, 'Concentration Camps'; Gruchmann, *Justiz*, 525–7. For a regional study, see idem, 'Die bayerische Justiz im politischen Machtkampf 1933/34. Ihr Scheitern bei der Strafverfolgung von Mordfällen in Dachau', in Broszat and Fröhlich (eds.), *Bayern*, ii. 415–28.

brownshirts; prosecution of the SS, who had taken over the running of most camps by this time, was out of the question.[138] Further attempts to intervene were quickly squashed. The most that could happen to a camp officer charged by the state prosecution service with the murder of inmates was dismissal, and even this was extremely rare. The Reich Justice Ministry made strenuous efforts to ensure that the courts paid due regard to the 'need to protect the racial community' in sentencing offenders, in order to keep at least a semblance of control over proceedings and ensure that matters were not taken out of its hands altogether. But in doing so, of course, it was giving in to the very pressures which it was ostensibly trying to resist.[139]

In the early concentration camps, such as Dachau, disobedience or incitement to mutiny were punishable by death. Sentences were imposed on prisoners by a 'court' headed by the camp commandant. A number of inmates were also beaten to death or killed with a shot in the head at close range, without any prior decision having been taken in the camp management. Jews were particularly liable to such treatment, which was officially recorded as 'suicide' or 'shot while trying to escape'. Partly as a result of the scandal aroused by such incidents, and the legal difficulties to which they led, Himmler ordered Theodor Eicke to take over as commandant of Dachau in June 1933. Born in 1892, he had been a member of the SS since 1930, and with him, the SS effectively assumed control of the camps. Eicke systematized and regularized the running of Dachau, and the rules which he drew up became the basis for the management of all subsequent concentration and extermination camps after he became Inspector-General of Concentration camps on 4 July 1934. He added political incitement and the spread of 'atrocity propaganda' to the list of capital offences, and specified execution by hanging or shooting. Escape attempts were punishable by immediate execution.[140] Executions were to be carried out by camp guards, not by specially detailed or trained executioners. During peacetime, however, these regulations were not used because of the threat of prosecution by the judicial authorities. Even if such prosecutions were unlikely to result in the imprisonment of the culprits, they were none the less seriously embarrassing for the SS and the Nazi leadership, and both Eicke himself and the Gestapo, separately, ordered camp commandants to refrain from imposing the death penalty from 1936 onwards. In contrast to the first eighteen months or so of Nazi rule, therefore, there were relatively few deliberate killings of prisoners in the concen-

---

[138] *Nazi Conspiracy and Aggression* (Office of the United States Chief of Counsel for Prosecution of Axis Criminality, 5 vols.; Washington, 1946), i. 228; and Broszat, 'Concentration Camps', 422–4.

[139] Engelhard (ed.), *Im Namen*, 280–1, 287–8; Broszat, 'Concentration Camps', 430, and Gruchmann, *Justiz*, 320–432, 632–57.

[140] Günther Kinnel, 'Das Konzentrationslager Dachau. Eine Studie zu den Nationalsozialistischen Gewaltverbrechen', in Broszat and Fröhlich (eds.), *Bayern*, ii. 349–413, here 353–62.

tration camps from 1935 to the outbreak of war in September 1939. All the same, the concentration camps represented an area in which capital punishment could be administered effectively without the intervention of the regular judicial apparatus. This applied not only to political prisoners, but to other categories of offender as well. The task of the police, explained Reich Leader of the SS and Chief of German Police Heinrich Himmler in 1937, was 'to render harmless all evil-intentioned opponents and enemies of the National Socialist State'. SS and Gestapo complaints about the 'leniency' of the courts were, as we have seen, frequent, and increased after the centralization of the police apparatus under Himmler and his Reich Security Head Office in 1936. But the Gestapo was not always content with passing on its views on 'lenient' sentencing of offenders dealt with in the regular courts to the Reich Justice Ministry.[141] As such prisoners were released, the Gestapo frequently rearrested them and placed them in 'protective custody' in concentration camps. The Reich Justice Ministry was simply forced to agree to such actions.[142] Justice Minister Gürtner even ensured that the state prosecutors' offices kept the Gestapo informed of the dates of release of political offenders from gaol, so that they could be taken into 'protective custody' and put in a concentration camp if so desired.[143]

e. 'Antisocial Elements'

Such measures were by no means confined simply to political offenders. In 1933 the Law for the Prevention of Hereditarily Diseased Offspring, which permitted compulsory sterilization on eugenic grounds, was extended to the 'socially feeble-minded' such as beggars, vagrants, and tramps. A Law against Dangerous Habitual Criminals, passed on 24 November 1933, allowed the indefinite internment in state prisons of offenders with two or more criminal convictions to their name. It still required a legal decision to be taken before such offenders could be permanently imprisoned. By the beginning of 1935, however, the police were consigning such people to the concentration camps without reference to the judicial authorities.[144] Criminal-biological investigation of such offenders could lead to sterilization or castration. Psychiatrists did their bit, consigning outpatients whom they regarded as 'antisocial alcoholics', 'parasites', or 'work-shy psychopaths' to the concentration camps as well.[145] On 23 February 1937

---

[141] Angermund, *Richterschaft*, 158–9.   [142] Ibid. 159.

[143] Engelhard (ed.), *Im Namen*, 261; Werle, *Justiz-Strafrecht*; Karl-Leo Terhorst, *Polizeiliche planmässige Überwachung und polizeiliche Vorbeugungshaft im Dritten Reich* (Heidelberg, 1985); Gruchmann, *Justiz*, 658–74, 719–45.

[144] Broszat, 'Concentration Camps', 448. See also Joachim Hellmer, *Der Gewohnheitsverbrecher und die Sicherungsverwahrung 1934–1945* (Berlin, 1961).

[145] Burleigh, *Death and Deliverance*, 62–3.

Himmler ordered the incarceration in concentration camps of some two thousand 'generally dangerous offenders against the morality laws and professional and habitual criminals who are without a job'; they were arrested on 9 March. Later the same year, the Reich and Prussian Ministries of the Interior defined 'antisocial elements' as people whose behaviour, though not necessarily criminal in strictly legal terms, none the less showed that they were not willing to fit in to the 'national community'. These included not only tramps, vagrants, and beggars but also gypsies, prostitutes, pimps, alcoholics, and the carriers of sexually transmitted diseases. Traffic offenders, 'grumblers', and 'hooligans' were added to the list. Offenders with more than one conviction for crimes of violence were also targeted. Labour exchanges provided the names of the 'work-shy' or the long-term unemployed. Mere suspicion constituted sufficient grounds for 'preventive' arrest. Following on these measures, the police carried out massive raids in March and June 1938 on doss-houses, night shelters, gypsy camps, and the haunts and dwellings of people with long criminal records. The raids also picked up substantial numbers of Jews. All of these people were partly intended to provide slave labour for the newly founded industrial enterprises of the SS. But their primary purpose was to remove them from the public sphere of the 'racial community'. During the year, the concentration camp population grew as a result from 24,000 to 60,000.[146]

In the summer of 1938 a special camp was built at Flossenbürg, in Bavaria, to cater for 'habitual criminals' and 'antisocial elements' from all over the Reich. It formed part of an economic enterprise of the SS, the German Ore- and Stoneworks, and was devoted to quarrying granite for the megalomaniac building schemes of Hitler and his personal architect Albert Speer. By the end of 1938 some 1,500 prisoners had been delivered to the camp from Dachau, Sachsenhausen, and Buchenwald, having originally been arrested in the course of the great police sweeps of February 1937 and March and June 1938. Most of them were petty criminals rather than dangerously violent people. Sexual offenders— mostly convicted of crimes against minors—were given the option of castration and release, but most of the rest were kept in the camp well into the war. Conditions were severe, the labour in the quarry was hard, rations were poor, and disease common. The economic function of the camp, however, prevented it from being used as a place of execution during peacetime, though the rules devised in Dachau applied and attempted escapees could be shot. What the erection of Flossenbürg indicated was rather the way in which the SS and Gestapo were now arresting and incarcerating common criminals without any

[146] Burleigh and Wippermann, *Racial State*, 167–73; Schmuhl, *Rassenhygiene*, 170–1; Jeremy Noakes, 'Social Outcasts in the Third Reich', in Richard Bessel (ed.), *Life in the Third Reich* (Oxford, 1987), 183–96; Broszat, 'Concentration Camps', 448–59.

interference from the law, a development which potentially allowed an expansion of all types of punishment, including the death penalty, by the police apparatus, beyond the confines of the judicial system.[147] Similar steps were also taken with respect to the gypsies, indicating once more how closely the Nazis linked the questions of race and criminality. The Sinti and Roma, as they are more properly called, were traditionally independent nomads, whose way of life had long caused them to be regarded by the German authorities as 'work-shy' and 'criminal'. It did not fit in at all well with the Third Reich's emphasis on order, regimentation, and work. By the late 1930s, with the armaments boom creating a serious labour shortage in the economy, people who did not participate in the conventional labour market were coming to be regarded by the Nazis as little better than traitors to the national cause. In this sense, the Sinti and Roma belonged to the category of 'antisocial elements', such as vagrants and tramps, which the regime was determined to dispense with. In 1936, Dr Robert Ritter, a specialist in 'criminal biology', set up a research centre, supported by Himmler's Reich Security Head Office, dedicated to identifying Germany's gypsy population as a preliminary to taking it out of circulation. By the outbreak of the war, it was well on the way to doing so. The SS and police campaign against 'gypsy criminality' culminated in a conference held in Berlin on 21 September 1939, which ordered the deportation of large numbers of Sinti and Roma from Germany. In December 1942 their persecution became a systematic extermination, and other countries in the Nazi empire, too, were combed for gypsies, up to half a million of whom ended in the gas chambers of Auschwitz.[148]

Some historians have argued that the Sinti and Roma were deported and killed as a measure of eugenic crime prevention,[149] while others have condemned this view as 'misleading and justificatory', 'prejudiced', and even 'racist', and have sought instead to portray the persecution and extermination of the gypsies as motivated purely by racial considerations.[150] The opposition, however, is a false

---

[147] Toni Siegert, 'Das Konzentrationslager Flossenbürg, gegründet für sogenannte Asoziale und Kriminelle', in Broszat and Fröhlich (eds.), *Bayern*, ii. 429–93.

[148] Burleigh and Wippermann, *Racial State*, 113–35; Rudko Kauczinki, 'Hamburg soll "zigeunerfrei" werden', in Angelika Ebbinghaus *et al.*, *Heilen und Vernichten im Mustergau Hamburg. Bevölkerungspolitik im Dritten Reich* (Hamburg, 1984, 45–65); Wolfgang Wippermann, *Das Leben in Frankfurt zur NS-Zeit*, ii. *Die nationalsozialistische Zigeunerverfolgung* (Frankfurt am Main, 1988); Michael Zimmermann, *Verfolgt, vertrieben, vernichtet. Die nationalsozialistische Vernichtungspolitik gegen Sinti und Roma* (Essen, 1989); Ulrich König, *Sinti und Roma unterm Nationalsozialismus* (Berlin, 1989).

[149] Hans-Joachim Döring, 'Die Motive der Zigeunerdeportation von Mai 1940', *Vierteljahreshefte für Zeitgeschichte*, 7 (1959), 418–28; idem, *Zigeuner im nationalsozialistischen Staat* (Hamburg, 1964); Hermann Arnold, *Zigeuner, Herkunft und Leben im deutschen Sprachgebiet* (Olten, 1965).

[150] Burleigh and Wippermann, *Racial State*, 365; Matthias Winter, 'Kontinuitäten in der deutschen Zigeunerforschung und Zigeunerpolitik', in *Beiträge zur nationalsozialistischen Gesundheits- und Sozialpolitik*, vi (Berlin, 1988), 135–52. In Arnold's case, these remarks are justified: see Joachim S. Hohmann, 'Die Forschungen des "Zigeunerexperte" Hermann Arnold', *1999: Zeitschrift für Sozialgeschichte des 20. und 21. Jahrhunderts*, 10 (1995) 3, 35–49.

one. It is not necessary to accept the premiss of Nazi and pre-Nazi 'criminal biology' 'that middling and especially petty criminality is significantly higher among gypsies—and in particular gypsy half-breeds—than among the settled, non-gypsy population',[151] to recognize that penal and racial policies were intertwined in this case. The fact that Sinti and Roma showed up proportionately more often in the statistics of petty crime reflected the disproportionate attention paid to them by law-enforcement agencies and the harsh atttitude taken towards them by judges and juries as much as, perhaps even more than, it expressed the exigencies of their existence on the margins of society. The offences of which they were so frequently accused often derived from the intrusion of traffic, trespass, education, and other, similar laws into their nomadic way of life. Yet the assumption of 'gypsy criminality' was fundamental to Nazi policy towards the Sinti and Roma. The basic decrees on the arrest and deportation of the gypsies from Germany were published, for example, in a collection entitled 'Crime Prevention'.[152] As Burleigh and Wippermann themselves concede, the 'problem' of 'antisocial elements' was solved by the Nazis 'in line with racial criteria'.[153] In this sense at least, the gypsies were a special case of a more generally applicable rule. Nazi 'criminal biologists' like Robert Ritter considered the Sinti and Roma, especially the 90 per cent of them who were said to be of 'mixed blood', to be hereditarily inclined to criminality. Should they further intermarry with 'Aryans', the spread of criminal tendencies among the population at large would be unavoidable. The persecution and extermination of the Sinti and Roma was thus intimately connected with Nazi criminal policy in general; and indeed, the gypsies in the camps were not given their own special insignia, but shared those of the 'antisocial elements'.

'Habitual criminals' and 'antisocial elements' formed two special groups among the inmates of concentration camps, with their own specially coloured cloth triangles—respectively, green and black—sewn onto the camp uniforms, to identify them and distinguish them from pink-triangled homosexuals, red-triangled 'politicals', yellow-triangled Jews, and the rest. Unlike these latter groups, however, they have not been intensively studied by historians, and it is easy to see why. Other victims of the Nazis can be portrayed as innocent, but not the criminals. Many of them had indeed been convicted of serious offences. The camp commandants often used them to intimidate the other inmates, and there were many examples of the brutal and corrupt behaviour of a number of them when given positions of responsibility in the camps. Nevertheless, the 'antisocial elements' should not be neglected. The processes by which they were arrested

[151] Döring, 'Die Motive', 418.
[152] Ibid. 419 n. 3.
[153] Burleigh and Wippermann, *Racial State*, 181.

and delivered into the camps, with or without a formal conviction, inevitably netted many individuals who by no stretch of the imagination could be regarded as hardened criminals. There are also many instances of 'criminals' behaving kindly towards political prisoners in their charge, and showing a good deal of moral courage in trying to save Poles and others from execution during the war.[154] Moreover, whatever their moral standing, and however horrific their abuse of power within the camp system, it remains the fact that most of them were incarcerated, and in the end exterminated, with little or no due process, and without the opportunity to defend themselves in a court of law. Punishment, up to and including the death penalty, in effect, was being extended to wider and wider circles of the deviant population with a decreasing amount of formal legal justification. From arresting, brutally mishandling, and sometimes killing their political opponents at the beginning of the Third Reich, the Nazis had extended their reach to encompass the extra-judicial incarceration of virtually all those whom they defined as 'outsiders' to the racial community by the eve of the Second World War. This was part of a process in which the SS and police apparatus took away an increasing amount of power and competence from the regular judicial system and the Special Courts. 'Antisocial elements' became in this way pawns in the power games played between the Reich Security Head Office and the Reich Ministry of Justice, between Himmler and Gürtner and his successors. These were to reach new heights during the war.

War was what Nazism existed for. Right from the very beginning, it had made no secret of its militarism, its belief in conflict, and its determination to avenge the defeat of 1918. Nazi racial ambitions could only be realized in and through a general European war. As early as 1933, Hitler had confided in his associates his intention of unfolding a secret campaign to kill the mentally and physically handicapped and allegedly incurably ill inmates of hospital and other institutions.[155] That year, the Prussian Ministry of Justice, under Nazi prompting, had declared that such killings should not be subject to criminal proceedings. But it had run into strong opposition both from the churches and from the judicial establishment. Hitler had decided, as he said privately in 1935, that it would be easier to carry out such a campaign of involuntary euthanasia under cover of war, when police controls over society were tighter, and the churches would be less inclined to voice open opposition. During the 1930s the SS argued in favour of killing the mentally ill and disabled on a number of occasions, without, however, being able to put its ideas into effect. In August 1939 the criminal justice commission was persuaded to agree on the legalization of 'help in dying' for the chronically or terminally ill, and the 'destruction of

---

[154] Siegert, 'Konzentrationslager Flossenbürg', 454–60.
[155] Burleigh, *Death and Deliverance*, 37–8.

life unworthy of life'.[156] Although the way had thus been smoothed for the killing of the chronically handicapped, Hitler considered the formal publication of a law along these lines inexpedient. Instead, he issued a 'confidential order' in October 1939, backdated to 1 September, which authorized the setting up of a team by members of one of his own offices, backed by medical specialists, to carry out these schemes. Based at Tiergartenstrasse 4 in Berlin, it initiated a programme of extermination, through starvation, injection, and mass gassing, which killed perhaps as many as 200,000 people by the end of the war. The specialists of 'Action T4', as it was known, were transferred to the east to set up the gassing facilities at Auschwitz and elsewhere which would implement mass murder on an even greater scale, in the so-called 'Final Solution of the Jewish Question'.[157] Hitler's written 'euthanasia' order dated 1 September 1939 was used as an authority to override objections from local police and legal authorities, especially in the districts where the killings took place. In effect, therefore, asylums and similar institutions were now taken outside the law, and attempts by the Reich Ministry of Justice to obtain a formal legal ruling on the question of 'euthanasia' came to nothing.[158] These people, and the many thousands more starved to death or injected with fatal doses of drugs in the so-called wild euthanasia actions which continued after the formal abrogation of the programme in August 1941, had not been condemned by any court. Their names were selected in hasty, arbitrary, and often grossly negligent meetings of the doctors who ran the programme, on the basis not of a personal examination of the proposed victims, but merely of a cursory perusal of their files.[159]

'Action T4' encompassed many different kinds of people, men, women, and children. Among them were individuals who had been charged with rape, child abuse, homosexuality, crimes of violence, and even political offences, and had been found unfit to plead by the courts. There was a special category of the criminally insane on the forms used by doctors for recommending death. Many of those consigned to the gas chambers in this way were guilty of no more than a few petty thefts. A good number were alcoholics.[160] To underline this extension of the extermination programme beyond the seriously mentally and physically handicapped, Heinrich Wilhelm Krenz and Siegfried Koller pleaded openly for the 'special treatment' of a supposed 1,600,000 'persons incapable of belonging

[156] Schmuhl, *Rassenhygiene*, 293–7.

[157] Burleigh, *Death and Deliverance*, esp. 93–100, is now the best account of these events and their origins. For the SS, see ibid. 44.

[158] Ibid. 299–304.

[159] Burleigh, *Death and Deliverance, passim*; Götz Aly *et al.* (eds.), *Reform und Gewissen. 'Euthanasie' im Dienst des Fortschritts* (Berlin, 1985); idem *et al.* (eds.), *Aussonderung und Tod. Die klinische Hinrichtung der Unbrauchbaren* (Berlin, 1985); and idem and Karl Heinz Roth, *Die restlose Erfassung. Volkszählen, Identifizieren, Aussondern im Nationalsozialismus* (Berlin, 1984).

[160] Burleigh, *Death and Deliverance*, 220–30.

to the community' in Germany in the early years of the war.[161] A further programme, 'Action 14f13', addressed itself to these people. '14f' was the numerical code for the office of the inspectorate of concentration camps, and 13 referred to the 'special treatment' of sick prisoners—one of a long list of numbers standing in the official documents for causes of death in the camps (2 was suicide, 3 was 'shot while trying to escape', and so on). The programme began in the spring of 1941 and involved T4 doctors selecting sick prisoners for gassing in one of the asylums used for the 'euthanasia' campaign since 1939. It was supposed to be confined to the mentally ill from April 1941 onwards, but this category provided the basis for including 'antisocial psychopaths', who were identified by 'criminal biologists' from amongst the petty criminals, prostitutes, vagrants, beggars, and tramps held in the camps. Over 8,000 victims were gassed at Hartheim under this programme before the end of the war, and at least 1,000 more in the two other gassing centres by 1942.[162] Racial prejudice played a key role in guiding the doctor's hand to the space on the form for recommending death, and many of those killed were Jewish, marked down as 'parasites' or identified as behaving with 'insolence and laziness' in the camps.[163] After the end of the official T4 action in August 1941, other means were found to deal with these unfortunates, principally chemical injections or starvation. Asylums were deliberately underheated, increasing the likelihood of premature death from the malnourished inmates. Clearly, the Nazi authorities were now moving towards a policy of exterminating the 'criminal' as well as the handicapped or the terminally ill in the German population.[164]

This process was made explicit by a series of new decrees issued at the beginning of the war. On 1 September 1939 it was made easier for the Special Courts to try ordinary criminal offences, thus extending their remit beyond the political cases on which they had hitherto concentrated. On 3 September 1939 Hitler empowered the Security Police to 'liquidate' persons found to be causing 'demoralization' (*Zersetzung*) in the armed forces, or engaging in Communist propaganda, hoarding, or sabotage. Such offenders were to be sent to concentration camps and, subject to the personal approval of Himmler, executed. The Gestapo was to issue 'protective custody' warrants to forestall the intervention of the courts. A large number of arrests immediately followed, including some of

---

[161] Heinrich Wilhelm Krenz and Siegfried Koller, *Die Gemeinschaftsunfähigen* (3 vols., Giessen, 1939-41).

[162] Noakes and Pridham (eds.), *Nazism*, 1045-6; Walter Grode, *Die 'Sonderbehandlung 14f13' in den Konzentrationslagern des Dritten Reiches. Ein Beitrag zur Dynamik faschistischer Vernichtungspolitik* (Frankfurt am Main, 1987); Stanislaw Klodzinski, 'Die "Aktion 14f13". Der Transport von 575 Häftlingen von Auschwitz in das "Sanatorium Dresden"', in Götz Aly (ed.), *Aktion T-4, 1939-1945* (Berlin, 1987), 136-46.

[163] Burleigh, *Death and Deliverance*, 226.

[164] Schmuhl, *Rassenhygiene*, 226-7.

people who were already serving sentences for criminal offences in the regular prisons. In Sachsenhausen a worker who had refused to carry out air-raid protection duties at an aircraft factory was shot on Himmler's personal orders on the very first night of the war. From then on, such executions took place frequently. The normal method was shooting, and it was applied not only to political offenders but also to common criminals whose court sentences in Himmler's view had been too lenient.[165] Thus the concentration camps were now formally turned into places of execution, in addition to their other functions. This was a development of far-reaching importance for the future. On hearing of it, Reich Justice Minister Franz Gürtner complained to Hitler about this bypassing of the judicial system and asked for the situation to be regularized. But on 3 October 1939 Hitler informed him that it was his will that such actions should be taken, because the courts had failed to adapt their sentencing practice to wartime desiderata. Following this declaration, the SS and police authorities set in motion a fresh wave of arrests of political suspects, 'psychopaths', the 'work-shy', and others.[166] All these measures, from the 'euthanasia' campaign and the gypsy deportations to the SS and police imprisonment of 'habitual criminals' and 'antisocial elements' undertaken in September 1939, belonged together. They signalled a shift of gear in the Nazi penal and racial policy. The war which the Nazis had brought about provided them with the opportunity to begin a wide-ranging programme of 'racial hygiene', which was soon to become one of mass racial extermination.

[165] Rudolf Höss, *Commandant of Auschwitz* (London, 1961), 83, 90–1, 94–5, 99.
[166] Broszat, 'Concentration Camps', 464–8; Gruchmann, *Justiz*, 675–89.

16

From Execution to Extermination

a. Capital Punishment and the Judiciary 1939–1942

On the outbreak of war in September 1939, Roland Freisler, writing on behalf of the Reich Minister of Justice, warned state prosecutors and judges that they would have to become even tougher than before:

Germany is engaged in a fight for honour and justice. More than ever, the model of devotion to duty for every German today is the German soldier. Anyone who, instead of modelling themselves on him, sins against the people, has no place in our community. Not to apply the most extreme severity to such pests would be a betrayal of the fighting German soldier![1]

A series of decrees gave concrete form to this principle. Many of them involved the application of the death penalty. Up to the outbreak of war in 1939, it has been calculated, the Third Reich had sentenced some 664 people to death and executed about the same number.[2] This was already a huge increase on the performance of previous regimes in modern German history. But now the death penalty was extended even further. The war provided the occasion for its application to a wide variety of new offences. On 1 September 1939, for instance, the premeditated spreading of 'news, broadcast by foreign radio, which is designed to undermine the resistance of the German people' was made punishable by death in especially serious cases.[3] Similarly, anyone convicted of 'publicly' attempting to 'subvert or cripple the will of the German or of an allied people to military self-assertion' was also made subject to the death penalty. The term 'publicly' was soon given an extremely wide interpretation by the courts.[4] The Decree against

---

[1] Quoted in Engelhard (ed.), *Im Namen*, 287.
[2] From 1933 to 1938 inclusive 528 were executed, although many of those executed in 1933 had been condemned during the Weimar years. In 1937, 1938, and 1939, increasing numbers were executed without having been condemned; the execution figures are taken from mortality statistics giving cause of death. See Düsing, *Abschaffung*, 210–11, and the Statistical Appendix, below.
[3] Wrobel (ed.), *Strafjustiz*, 46.
[4] Quoted in Engelhard (ed.), *Im Namen*, 211; for sample judgments, see ibid. 211–13.

Racial Pests (*Verordnung gegen Volksschädlinge*) of 5 September 1939 added still further to this massive extension of the death penalty.[5] Death was now applicable to any crime against property or persons committed 'by exploiting the measures taken for defence against the threat of air raids', to arson, and to other 'crimes posing a danger to the public' if they were held to 'damage the strength of the German people to resist'. Any other crimes which exploited the 'exceptional circumstances' caused by the war could also lead to execution, if 'healthy popular feeling' demanded the death penalty 'because of the particular reprehensibility of the crime'. In occupied (or 'liberated') territories, any civilian caught looting would be hanged.

On 5 December a new 'decree against violent criminals' made the death penalty mandatory in cases of the use or threatened use of guns in committing a robbery, a rape, or any other serious crime of violence, or in resisting arrest.[6] By the beginning of the 1940s there were over forty offences punishable by death according to the laws of the Third Reich.[7] Moreover, the Reich Criminal Code itself was now amended to apply the death penalty to anyone convicted of providing a 'contribution' to the enemy or causing a 'disadvantage' to Germany or its allies (Para. 91b). The murder paragraph (Para. 211 of the Reich Criminal Code of 1871) was amended to bring it into line with Nazi ideology, and now read: 'The murderer will be punished by death. A murderer is someone who maliciously or cruelly, or by means which pose a common threat, kills a person out of pleasure in murdering, to satisfy the sexual urge, from greed, or from other base motives, or to facilitate or conceal another criminal action.' A sentence of life imprisonment was now only allowed for murder 'in special, exceptional cases'. In February 1941 the Criminal Code was further amended to make serious 'habitual criminals' and 'sex criminals' liable to the death penalty.[8] On 4 September 1941 the death penalty was applied to all offenders in these two categories 'if the protection of the racial community or the need for a just expiation demand it'.[9] The direction of penal policy away from the crime and towards the criminal was signalled by tiny linguistic changes in the Code such as these; it was no longer murder, or a sexual offence, or recidivism, which was in focus, but 'the murderer', 'the sexual offender', or 'the habitual criminal'. In the course of further amendments to the criminal law, the death penalty was applied to serious cases of hoarding or destruction of important raw materials or products.[10] On 5 May 1944 another decree made it possible for any crime whatsoever to be punishable by death if 'healthy popular feeling' considered the sentence provided

---

[5] Wrobel (ed.), *Strafjustiz*, 46.   [6] Ibid. 47.

[7] Engelhard (ed.), *Im Namen*, 149–50. See also Schreiber, 'Die Strafgesetzgebung', 172.

[8] BA Potsdam 61 Re 1/1773, 865: *Völkischer Beobachter*, 19 Feb. 1941.

[9] Wrobel (ed.), *Strafjustiz*, 47.   [10] Ibid. 49.

for in law to be insufficient.[11] Not only was the law amended so as to extend the death penalty until it was potentially applicable to almost anything, but the regime also intensified its efforts to reshape the judiciary into servants of Nazi politics. On 24 October 1939 judges were warned by the Ministry that 'peacetime criteria' were no longer appropriate when deciding upon sentences. They were put under renewed pressure to pass maximum sentences. Some, though not very many, proved reluctant to do so. The majority complied.

Hitler had a long-standing belief that the judicial system 'does not grasp the current danger, which consists in the fact that the criminal underworld opens up for itself a kind of breaking-and-entering point, in order to stream into society when the time seems to it to have come'. The only way to ward off this danger, he said privately on 8 February 1942, was by using the death penalty. Too many burglars and thieves were sent to prison, where they were 'fed at the cost of the racial community' and lived 'a wonderful life'. 'After ten years of penitentiary', Hitler declared, 'a man is in any case lost to the racial community. . . . Such a fellow must either be put in a concentration camp or killed.' Recently, he added for good measure, 'the latter is the more important, for the sake of deterrence.'[12] Hitler thought that due process was completely unnecessary in such cases. 'But one must always let the punishment follow immediately after the crime, if the thing is to work, thus for example condemning criminals who have committed their offence during the black-out right after their offence and shooting them straight away.'[13] Such views were recorded with relative frequency by Hitler's entourage in the spring of 1942, and suggest that the problem of wartime criminality was preoccupying him more than usually at this time. Repeatedly, Hitler came back to the need to protect the soldiers at the front, and the dire consequences which he thought this had had in the First World War. It was necessary, he declared on 15 April, to be 'swift and brutal' in wartime penal policy. In justifying this statement, Hitler argued characteristically by analogy from the natural world. After watching a film on wild horses, he remarked to his cronies:

It's just like it is among the wild horses, and among every community of living things that wants to assert itself in the world. If the bell-wether is missing, the herd atomizes itself, and everything comes to an end. It is for this reason that for example apes trample outsiders to death as community aliens. And what holds good for apes, must hold good for humans to an even greater extent. Bismarck was quite right when he said that human society would abandon itself if it abandoned the death penalty as the absolute form of defence against the community alien, just because of possible miscarriages of justice; what

[11] Schreiber, 'Strafgesetzgebung', 171.
[12] Pickler (ed.), *Tischgespräche*, 103–4; also in Werner Jochmann (ed.), *Adolf Hitler: Monologe im Führer-Hauptquartier 1941–1944. Die Aufzeichnungen Heinrich Heims* (Hamburg, 1980), 271–2.
[13] Pickler (ed.), *Tischgespräche*, 280 (10 May 1942).

would the individual come to, what would the community come to, if we got tired of taking decisions just because we were afraid of making mistakes?[14]

Whether Bismarck had in fact made any such statement must be doubted. Nevertheless, the claim showed that Hitler was thinking of the death penalty in the widest possible terms. 'How', he asked in May 1942,

does one want to try to prevent offences like handbag-thefts, the rape of women, and— when front doors are open, cellars have been exposed by air raids, and so on—break-ins of all kinds, during the war, and in the black-out, without using the most barbaric means: one must therefore keep the death penalty as the absolute punishment in all these cases, no matter whether the offender is 60 or 17 years of age.

If this did not happen, he said, criminality would be unstoppable.[15] Yet judges were always finding excuses not to pass the death penalty. 'I always have to get angry about the administration of justice', he complained again on 16 November 1941: 'Our Reich would already have been exposed to disintegration by the judicial system we have today if I had not created a corrective in the form of the state's self-help.'[16]

In March 1942 one particular case was to have further-reaching consequences for the judiciary. A man who had beaten and abused his wife until she had died had been sentenced to five years' penitentiary by a court in Oldenburg. On reading the newspaper report of the sentence, Hitler phoned up the Justice Ministry and complained about it 'in the greatest passion' to State Secretary Schlegelberger.[17] Not content with this, Hitler referred to the case on 26 April 1942 in one of his now increasingly rare, and therefore widely broadcast, speeches in the Reichstag. He expected, he said,

the German judicial system to understand that the nation is not there for its own sake, but that it is there for the nation's sake [*vigorous assent*]; that means that the world, of which Germany is also a part, must not fall apart in order for a formal system of law to survive, but that Germany must survive, no matter how much the formal pronouncements of the law may contradict it. Just to mention one example: I don't have any sympathy for the fact that a criminal who married in 1937 and then maltreated his wife so long that she eventually became mentally ill and then died as a result of the last assault, is condemned to five years' penitentiary at a moment when ten-thousands of law-abiding German men have to die in order to protect their wives and children. [*Assent*] From now on I am going to intervene in these cases and relieve of their office judges who are obviously failing to recognize the requirements of the day. [*Applause*][18]

Up to this point, even the Third Reich had not dared to make a formal breach of the principle that judges were independent and could not be dismissed. The

---

[14] Pickler (ed.), *Tischgespräche*, 302 (15 Apr. 1942).   [15] Ibid. 331 (22 May 1942).
[16] Jochmann (ed.), *Monologe*, 60 (14–15 Sept. 1941), and 142 (16 Nov. 1941).
[17] Quoted in Engelhard (ed.), *Im Namen*, 294.
[18] Quoted ibid. 293; see also Stauff. *Justiz*, 95–100.

judiciary for its part had made, willingly or otherwise, innumerable concessions to the drive of the regime to turn the administration of justice into an engine of racial and eugenic extermination. Not surprisingly, therefore, the judges were said to be deeply depressed following this speech. It had, reported the security police at the end of April, 'had something like a shock effect'.[19] The President of the Hanseatic High Court, Curt Rothenberger, drew the conclusion on 11 May 1942 that 'a radical National Socialist reform of the judicial system' was necessary.[20] As a result of Hitler's tirade, sentencing policy now became harsher than ever. Rothenberger introduced a regular system of examining cases, both before and after the verdict was passed, 'in which there is a possibility of a certain contradiction between formal law and the immediate feelings of the people or the National Socialist point of view'.[21] Yet, characteristically, the fact that the pressure on judges was only exercised by way of a mixture of general exhortation and intervention in specific, individual cases meant that no uniform policy on sentencing was ever developed. An increasing arbitrariness in the meting out of death sentences was the inevitable result.

What all this meant, of course, was a rapid increase in the number of death sentences passed by the courts. For all the growth of capital punishment under the Third Reich in peacetime, the outbreak of war marked a major caesura in this respect. Within the 1937 boundaries of Germany, death sentences had increased in number from 96 in 1937 to 173 in 1939, 306 in 1940, and 533 in 1941. In the spring of 1942, however, they suddenly leaped from roughly 60 a month, the rate they had been running at in the last months of 1941, to 96 in March, 129 in April, 149 in May, and 233 in June. Altogether in 1942 there were 1,592 and in the first half of 1943 alone, 1,119. Within the Reich overall, including Austria and the parts of Poland and Czechoslovakia and other territories annexed by 'Greater Germany' from 1938 to 1940, the figures were even more startling. The official statistics issued by the Third Reich itself counted 16,500 death sentences passed by the courts within the changing boundaries of Germany from 1933 to 1944. Roughly 12,000 of them were actually carried out. Well over 11,000 of these executions took place during the war. In addition there were up to 20,000 death sentences passed by military courts during the war as well.[22] In 1941 the courts of the Greater German Reich handed down 1,292 death sentences; in 1942, 4,457;

[19] Engelhard (ed.), *Im Namen*, 296. For the reaction, see also Broszart, 'Zur Perversion der Strafjustiz im Dritten Reich', *Vierteljahreshefte für Zeitgeschichte*, 5 (1958), 390–443, here, 420–36.
[20] Quoted in Wrobel (ed.), *Strafjustiz*, 24.
[21] Johe, *Justiz*, 180–2; Stauff, *Justiz*, 102–6. For Rothenberger's career, see Klaus Bästlein, 'Vom hanseatischen Richtertum zum nationalsozialistischen Justizverbrechen. Zur Person und Tätigkeit Curt Rothenbergers 1896–1959', in idem *et al.* (eds.), '*Für Führer, Volk und Vaterland . . .*'. *Hamburger Justiz im Nationalsozialismus* (Hamburg, 1992), 74–145.
[22] Engelhard (ed.), *Im Namen*, 206.

and in 1943, 5,336. In 1944, the number fell to 4,264, partly as a result of the call-up to the front of young, fanatically Nazi judges on the Special Courts and their replacement by an older generation of judges, many of whom did not belong to the Nazi Party, and partly, as we shall see, as a result of the transfer of jurisdiction of Poles, Russians, and other 'alien races' to the Gestapo and the SS. But this was still a very substantial number none the less. The total of 297 death sentences passed in the final months of the Third Reich, on a drastically reduced and ever-shrinking territorial basis, in 1945, suggests no real diminution in this respect. In total, therefore, the courts of the Third Reich meted out an estimated total of 16,560 death sentences, of which 664 were passed in 1933–9 and 15,896 during the war.[23]

A prominent role was played in this growth of capital punishment by the Special Courts, which were charged with trying the majority of cases brought under wartime capital legislation. Freisler declared on 24 October 1942: 'The Special Courts must always remember that they are to a degree the armoured division of legal administration.' At the head of them stood the People's Court. The expansion of its activities during the war can be measured not least in terms of the huge increase in the number of death sentences which it handed down, especially from 1942 onwards. In 1937 it had sentenced a mere 32 people to death; in 1938, 17; in 1939, 36; and in 1940, 53. With the invasion of Russia and the conquest of territory in the east, the number of death sentences meted out by the People's Court doubled in 1941, to 102. But in 1942 it increased tenfold, to 1,192, and it went on increasing, reaching 1,662 in 1943 and 2,097 in 1944, before falling under the impact of military defeat and territorial losses to a total of 52 in the last few months of the Third Reich, in 1945. In all, some 5,243 death sentences were passed by the People's Court over the whole period of its existence. At a lower level, too, the Special Courts were pursuing the same path. In particular, they began to implement with untrammelled ferocity the capital decrees passed during the war against looting from bomb-damaged buildings and other crimes against property. Out of the 52 death sentences passed by the Special Courts in Dortmund, Essen, and Bielefeld in 1941, for example, 32 were for crimes against property, as were 20 out of 45 passed in the first six months of 1943. In the High Court District of Hamm, 32 out of the 52 death sentences passed by the Special Courts in 1941 were for property offences. In 1943, in the whole of the Greater German Reich, roughly a quarter of the 5,336 death sentences passed were for crimes against property. While 1,745 of them were for treason, only 250 were for murder, attempted murder, and crimes of violence; 236 were for crimes against

    [23] Angermund, *Richterschaft*, 212–15. For the basis on which these figures were calculated, see Düsing, *Abschaffung*, 212–21. For the monthly figures, see BA Koblenz RA22/4066, Bl. 275: 'Todesurteile überhaupt', and the Statistical Appendix, below.

the war economy, 114 for morality offences, 108 for defeatism, 33 for arson, and 11 for listening to foreign radio stations.[24]

Capital punishment during these years was thus aimed increasingly, among other things, at terrorizing the population into maintaining discipline on the home front. It formed the civilian counterpart to the increasingly widespread use of the death penalty in the German army against deserters, mutineers, and other military offenders, up to 20,000 of whom were condemned by German military courts during the war. As early as January 1940 the growing use of capital punishment against civilian offenders was giving rise to reports that many people, including even Nazi party officials, were showing 'a certain concern about the excessive numbers of death sentences'.[25] Reaction from the populace at large was mixed, however. In February 1940 Himmler's Security Service reported that the current 'toughness towards criminals who exploit the war for their deeds is meeting with tremendous approval' among the population at large.[26] In June 1942 there were reports of popular demands for the death penalty to be applied to offenders convicted of stealing field post.[27] On the other hand, Maximilian Wagner, from the Austrian town of Graz, wrote to the government in 1940 complaining:

The death sentences which are so casually pronounced and carried out in criminal cases constitute a serious burden on our Reich government. The double and triple death sentences passed on a single offender will necessarily become even more serious in future. There is no doubt that the abolition of death penalties will cost the Reich more money and trouble than their execution [i.e. by the cost of life imprisonment]. There is thus an urgent necessity not for the removal of those who have strayed from the path, but for their healing. Such are the eternal values which will build us a long and secure future.[28]

No record exists of any reply. Such open protests were in any case extremely rare. Despite the reports of popular support for the death penalty for a wide range of crimes, people became increasingly reluctant to report looting to the authorities in view of the death sentence that would almost invariably follow a conviction. Opinions expressed on the general principle of capital punishment were often no guide to people's behaviour in practice when it came to dealing with individual cases.[29] The courts' particular severity towards looting reflected the growing

[24] Angermund, *Richterschaft*, 209–15.
[25] Ibid. 215; Manfred Messerschmidt and Fritz Wüllner, *Die Wehrmachtjustiz im Dienste des Nationalsozialismus. Zerstörung einer Legende* (Baden-Baden, 1987), and Fritz Wüllner, *Die NS-Militärjustiz und das Elend der Geschichtsschreibung* (Baden-Baden, 1991).
[26] Heinz Boberach (ed.), *Meldungen aus dem Reich. Die geheimen Lageberichte des Sicherheitsdienstes der SS 1938–1945* (Herrsching, 1984), iii. 735–6.
[27] Ibid., x. 3847–8.
[28] BA Koblenz R22/1315, Bl. 315: Wagner to Präsidium des Ministeriums für Kultur in Berlin, 21 May 1940.
[29] Angermund, *Richterschaft*, 210.

impossibility of catching any but a tiny minority of those responsible, given the mounting chaos in Germany's cities under the impact of devastating mass bombing by the Allies. The authorities were increasingly plagued by the anxiety that this would lead to a total collapse of law and order and were using the death penalty as an exemplary form of deterrence.

b. 'Cleansing the Racial Body'

The expansion of capital punishment and its gradual merging into a general system of extermination of 'enemies of the German racial community' during the war did not represent the outcome of anonymous processes of radicalization pushed on from below. More than anything else, they resulted from the personal interventions of Hitler himself. The outbreak of war in September 1939 freed Hitler to let loose many of the murderous impulses which peacetime conditions had forced him hitherto to keep in check. In the earlier part of the war, he would spend some of the evening reading the crime stories in the Nazi party newspaper, the *Völkischer Beobachter*. These were frequently critical of what the newspaper saw as the persistent leniency of German judges. Reading reports of offenders condemned to varying lengths of imprisonment, Hitler would often comment angrily to his companions that the guilty party should have been shot. Acting on the newspaper report, he would tell Himmler or some other senior SS official present in the room to transmit a 'Führer command' by telephone to the Gestapo wherever the trial had been held, ordering the offenders in question to be liquidated. On the basis of this purely verbal legitimation, the secret police officers would then go to the prison where the offenders were being held, take them away, and kill them, despite the fact the courts had not sentenced them to death and despite the fact that no formal legal justification existed for such an act. There could be no better illustration of the extra-legal, charismatic nature of Hitler's dictatorship, nor of the personally murderous instincts of Hitler himself. The party journalists may wittingly or unwittingly have sparked the Führer's intervention, and their attitude may have reflected the views of local party activists in the areas where these criminal cases took place. But, given Hitler's previous record on such issues, there could be little doubt that in doing so they were 'working towards the Führer', or in other words taking a line which they felt to be broadly in accord with his own.[30]

A characteristic example of this procedure was the case of Paul Latacz and Erwin Jakobs, two common criminals who had been arrested trying to rob a bank in Berlin on 30 September 1939. On 13 October they were each sentenced to ten

[30] See Ian Kershaw, '"Working towards the Führer": Reflections on the Nature of the Hitler Dictatorship', *Contemporary European History*, 2 (1993), 103–18.

years' penitentiary by the Special Court in the capital. The next day, however, at eight o'clock in the evening, Himmler put through a telephone call from the Reich Chancellery saying that Hitler wanted them both shot. 'Himmler gave the following further information: the Führer had read of a case in Munich in which a sentence of one year's penitentiary had also been passed for a robbery carried out during the black-out. This culprit must be shot too.' Two days later, on 16 October, the paper duly reported that Latacz and Jakobs had been shot while resisting their transfer from the police cell to the penitentiary. The story appeared to be less than plausible to many readers. Among them was Reich Justice Minister Franz Gürtner, who wrote to Himmler pointing out:

In the case of the shooting of Latacz, who before he was taken away was lying in the prison hospital swathed in traction bandages, which the general public was aware of because it had been informed by press reports the previous day that the main trial had taken place in the remand prison hospital, the public knew that the physical condition of the condemned man hardly allowed him to resist.

This was only one of a number of such cases to take place in the early months of the war. The third offender mentioned in Himmler's phone call was also shot. A fourth, Max Gross, who had been condemned to six months' imprisonment in Munich on 5 January 1940 for a violent sexual assault on a 3-year-old boy, was shot by order of the Führer on 20 January following a telephone call to the local Gestapo from Hitler's adjutant. Another offender, Viktor Meyer, who had been condemned to twelve years' penitentiary in Berlin on 19 January 1940 for robbery with violence was shot the next day following much the same sequence of events.[31]

Hitler's office was not the only quarter from which such criticism of the judiciary emanated during the war years. In May 1941, for example, Himmler's deputy Reinhard Heydrich circularized the SS and police as follows:

The sentences which the courts pass, particularly on violent offenders, do not correspond for many different reasons to healthy popular feeling. I therefore order the following: In all cases in which the court, instead of passing the expected and also necessary death sentence, merely hands down imprisonment for life or for a fixed term, I want to be informed immediately by express letter. . . . I draw your attention explicitly to the fact that no third party must be told anything at all about this order.[32]

Such offenders were then brought to the attention of the Reich Justice Ministry, which frequently quashed the sentences and replaced them with more severe ones.[33] As this suggested, the Ministry of Justice was not so much concerned with the harshness of sentencing as with the open disregard for the decisions of

---

[31] BA Koblenz R22/5019, Bl. 183–90: Gürtner, Vermerkung am 14. Oktober 1939; *Völkischer Beobachter*, 16 Oct. 1939; RJM to Himmler, 30 Nov. 1939; Broszat, 'Zur Perversion'.

[32] Quoted in Engelhard (ed.), *Im Namen*, 252.

[33] Angermund, *Richterschaft*, 183.

the courts shown by the SS and Gestapo, even if it was on Hitler's express command. The Ministry's main aim was to maintain the forms of legality even at a time when, had its officials paused to think, these had become little more than an empty shell. On 25 October 1939, for instance, perhaps prompted by Hitler's action earlier in the month, Friedrich von Eberstein, a senior SS officer in Munich, complained: 'In various cases which have come before the Special Court, the state prosecution service has not had the legal means to require for the punishment of the crime in question the expiation which healthy popular feeling would have demanded in consideration of the present wartime conditions.' If, he wrote, turning his conditional conjectures about popular feeling into definite assumptions, 'the relevant legal provisions do not allow the death penalty which the people demands', then it was necessary for the execution to be approved before the trial, so that the offender could presumably be 'shot while trying to escape' after a custodial sentence had been passed. Such a barefaced attempt to circumvent the law was too much even for the numbed consciences of the Ministry of Justice officials, and Eberstein's request was rejected.[34]

At the same time, the SS and police were also independently carrying out executions without reference to the courts. On 15 September the police shot Paul Müller in Halle for alleged sabotage. On the same day August Diekmann, a Jehovah's Witness in Dinslaken, was shot for refusing to serve in the armed forces. And on 6 November Horst Schmidt, in Kassel, a con-man who had pretended to be a U-boat captain, was killed by the police while in their custody. All these cases were without any sanction by the courts, and indeed only came to light through newspaper reports.[35] A list of such cases compiled by the Reich Ministry of Justice counted nine individuals executed in this way from 6 September 1939 to 20 January 1940. They included a Jew, accused by the police of sexual offences against a 'German' girl and shot on 6 November 1939. Often the offences were minor, such as refusal to work in a 'factory which is important for the war'. Clearly the SS and police apparatus was now bypassing the legal system not only when it came to imprisonment in concentration camps, but also when it came to the administration of the death penalty. Objections to such actions by the judiciary did not imply much more than a concern to maintain their own area of competence. Even while they were stating their disapproval of police executions, for example, the Hamburg judges, led by Curt Rothenberger, agreed that the 'eradication' of 'antisocial elements' was necessary in view of the racially hereditary nature of deviance.[36]

[34] BA Koblenz R22/5020, Bl. 0: Eberstein to Generalstaatsanwalt Nuremberg, 25 Oct. 1939; RJM to Generalstaatsanwalt Nuremberg, 25 Oct. 1939. Eberstein was also a judge on the People's Court.

[35] For a documentation and commentary on these and other cases discussed in this section, see Martin Broszat, 'Zur Perversion'.

[36] Quoted in Angermund, Richterschaft, 194.

The conservative Reich Minister of Justice Franz Gürtner was deeply concerned about these developments. In January 1940 Gürtner sent a personal, handwritten letter to Pastor Traub, a right-wing journalist and former member of the Nationalist Party, who had complained about the abuse of the death penalty during the war, justifying his actions, and pointing out that capital punishment had already been extensively applied to murderers before the war. 'Believe me, dear Dr Traub,' he added, 'the administration of the criminal law, at least as far as serious criminality is concerned, is at the moment the most difficult part of my official duties.'[37] While he might justify the situation to outsiders, however, Gürtner continued in private to be dissatisfied with the circumvention of the judicial system. In his efforts to secure a regularization of the matter, Gürtner was able to cite more than one such instance where he believed the newspaper report that served as the basis for Hitler's execution order to be factually incorrect. The Trampe case was a good example:

Trampe stole jewellery and clothing from the dwelling of a soldier friend of his and pawned them for 200 RM. The soldier's wife and her husband later reached an agreement with Trampe on the loss caused to them. Trampe defended himself by saying that he had acted out of desperation, intended to redeem the stolen things later, and had reckoned from the outset with the forgiveness of the couple from whom he had robbed the goods because of their friendship towards him and because of his desperate situation. The court believed him and condemned him to six years' penitentiary. The press reported that his defence was a lie and that the court had refused to believe it. Trampe was shot on 27 September 1940 on the Führer's orders.

Altogether, from the beginning of the war to the end of January 1940, Gürtner reckoned that some eighteen offenders had been 'extra-judicially shot' on Hitler's personal orders or simply on the initiative of the Gestapo itself.

In eleven of these cases, Gürtner went on, the press had subsequently reported that the victims had been shot while resisting the police or while trying to escape. 'This explanation', the Minister solemnly declared, 'was, as far as is known here, false in virtually every case, and nobody believes it. I think this kind of publication', he went on, 'is extremely dubious and leads to the oddest suspicions and deductions.' With extraordinary cynicism—or was it naïveté?—Gürtner concluded:

Given the very high number of death sentences which are pronounced and carried out every month, it is of no decisive importance whether the one or the other case leads to a death sentence or to a lengthy term of imprisonment; it appears to me to be more important that the people's belief in justice and the law has to be maintained at this time.

The best way to ensure this, he declared, was for the 'Führer command' in each

[37] BA Koblenz NL Traub Bd. 9 (NL 59/9): Gürtner to Traub, 6 Jan. 1940.

individual case to be put in writing, 'and with the signature of the person who has to take responsibility for the correctness of the command and its transmission'.[38] Gürtner did not dispute the fundamental legality of Hitler's death sentences. He recognized the 'Führer', after all, as the supreme source of law in the Third Reich.[39] Gürtner's main objective was to keep the operation of capital punishment as far as possible under the control, or at least within the purview, of the Ministry of Justice. Even in this modest aim, however, he does not seem to have succeeded. Ministry of Justice officials recorded a total of fourteen cases in 1939 in which offenders had been shot 'without court proceedings or following sentences other than death'. Another thirty-three cases were noted in 1940, twenty-two in 1941, and twenty-eight more in 1942, up to the end of July.[40] And these were certainly underestimates. In February and March 1942, in one Berlin court district alone, thirteen offenders sentenced to terms of imprisonment are known to have been executed by the Gestapo because Himmler's office considered their sentences too lenient.[41]

All this indicated a continuing dissatisfaction on the part of the Nazis with the German judiciary. As we have seen, this came to a head in March 1942, with Hitler's open criticism of judges before the Reichstag. In launching such attacks, he was taking advantage of the weakness of the Reich Justice Ministry after the death of its long-serving head Franz Gürtner in January 1941. Gürtner's office was temporarily handed over to Franz Schlegelberger, a career civil servant in the Ministry. In these circumstances, the Ministry proved extremely vulnerable to criticism and attack. It had already proved insufficiently willing to go down the exterminatory road Hitler wanted the judicial system to take, and it was now more than ever unable to defend itself effectively against his increasingly vehement criticisms. On 20 August 1942 Schlegelberger was finally dismissed as lacking in National Socialist conviction, and the Nazi lawyer Otto-Georg Thierack, previously President of the People's Court, was appointed Reich Minister of Justice in his place.[42] Born in Saxony in 1889, Thierack had served in the First World War and become a state prosecutor in 1926. He joined the Nazi Party in August 1932, was nominated Justice Minister in Saxony on 12 May 1933, and brought the judicial apparatus there under Nazi control. In 1936 he became President of the People's Court. Thierack was a committed Nazi ideologue. Under him, the Justice Ministry would be sure to fall in line.[43] To assist Thierack, the Nazi judge Curt Rothenberger was appointed sole State Secretary

[38] BA Koblenz NL Traub Bd. 9. R22/5020, Bl. 240–1: Gürtner, note, Feb. 1940.
[39] Werle, *Justiz-Strafrecht*, 577–602, discusses the legal aspects of these procedures.
[40] BA Koblenz R22/5020, Bl. 242–71: note.
[41] Angermund, *Richterschaft*, 183.
[42] For documentation of the 'judicial crisis' of 1942, see Hirsch *et al.* (eds.), *Recht*, 507–19.
[43] Engelhard (ed.), *Im Namen*, 267.

FIG. 38. *The crisis of the judicial system in 1942.* Hitler shakes hands with Curt Rothenberger at his headquarters in the Ukraine on 20 August 1942, just before the decisive lunchtime meeting held to mark the appointment of Otto-Georg Thierack (looking on, facing camera) as Reich Minister of Justice. Thierack's appointment initiated a vast expansion of capital punishment which continued unabated until the end of the war. In this policy he had the full support of Rothenberger, whose appointment as State Secretary was a reward for the zeal he had shown as a Nazi judge in Hamburg over the previous few years.

to run the Ministry as its top civil servant; another guarantee of ideological conformity. Finally, Roland Freisler, the hardline Nazi who had been State Secretary in the Ministry since the seizure of power, was appointed to head the People's Court. Born in 1893, Freisler had been active in far-right politics since his return from the war in 1920, and had joined the Nazi Party in 1925. A Nazi fanatic, he had tried to push on the Nazification of the judicial system from the very beginning, and, as we have seen, had frequently issued admonitions to the judiciary to act in a more 'National Socialist' manner. As President of the People's Court, he was to become notorious through his conduct of the trials of the conservative resisters who tried to blow up Hitler in July 1944. Meanwhile, his appointment on 20 August 1942, along with that of Thierack, marked the effective ending of the Justice Ministry's role, such as it was, in protecting the judicial system from complete Nazification.[44]

[44] See Helmut Ortner, *Der Hinrichter. Roland Freisler—Mörder im Dienste Hitlers* (Vienna, 1993).

At the lunchtime meeting held on 20 August 1942 to mark the occasion of the new appointments, Hitler told Thierack and Rothenberger, not for the first time, that the punishments meted out to the courts were in his view completely inadequate.[45] Crime was continuing despite the fact that the country was at war. One example, he said, was the fact 'that many women are too afraid to go home from the factory at night in case something happens to them. It's monstrous: the husband is fighting on the battle-front, and his wife doesn't dare go home!' The prevalence of theft and other crimes in Berlin demanded much tougher measures. But, said Hitler, these had not been taken by the courts. For example, a man who had recently killed a chicken belonging to his neighbour, when it had wandered into his garden, had only been given three months' imprisonment. This was far too lenient a sentence. The judicial authorities should make it clear to the nation 'that the state is resolved to put down with the most barbaric means possible any attempt at disruption, and in doing so, one must always take into consideration the necessary disregard which we must have for the life of bad elements who pose a common threat to us all'. In the nineteenth century punishments had previously been criticized because they were thought of as barbaric; now they were praised for the same reason. Extreme harshness, as Hitler explained to his listeners, was necessary not only as a means of deterrence, but also as an instrument of eugenic policy:

Every war leads to a negative selection. The positive elements die in masses. The choice of the most dangerous military service is already a selection: the really brave ones become airmen, or join the U-boats. And even in these services there is always the call: who wants to volunteer? And it's always the best men who then get killed. All this time, the absolute ne'er-do-well is cared for lovingly in body and spirit. Anyone who ever enters a prison knows with absolute certainty that nothing more is going to happen to him. If you can imagine this going on for another three or four years, then you can see a gradual shift in the balance of the nation taking place: an over-exploitation on the one side; absolute conservation on the other!

In order to re-establish the balance, Hitler declared, the 'negative' elements in the population had to be killed in much larger numbers. This was a view he had held for some time. Now the moment had come to put it into effect.[46]

Echoing the contempt for the masses which he had once expressed in those famous passages of his book *Mein Kampf* in which he had described how easily they could be manipulated by orators and agitators such as himself, or by revolutionaries of the sort he imagined had brought about Germany's downfall at the end of the First World War, Hitler continued:

[45] BA Koblenz, R22/4720: copy, 20 Aug. 1942.
[46] See also similar remarks in Pickler (ed.), *Tischgespräche*, 332 (22 May 1942) and Jochmann (ed.), *Monologe*, 125–6 (5 Nov. 1941).

The broad mass of people is neither good nor evil. It possesses neither the courage nor the villainy for really good or really bad deeds. The extremes determine the result. If I decimate the good, while conserving the bad, then what happened in 1918, when five or six hundred ruffians raped the nation, will happen again.

Even here, therefore, the 'legacy of 1918' was present in Nazi thought; the pervasive fear that the regime could suffer in the Second World War the kind of 'stab in the back' from the kind of discontent on the Home Front that Hitler thought had undermined the German war effort in the First.[47] Criminality, political opposition, and racial degeneracy were all merged into one in Hitler's mind, as they had been in so much of the criminological discourse of the far right since the days of Weimar. Warming to his theme, the Führer now drew the practical consequences from these arguments for the administration of justice in the courts. 'Imprisonment is no punishment any longer these days', he declared; least of all at a time when millions of German troops were enduring terrible conditions on the Eastern Front. Only the death penalty would have any effect:

One mustn't under any circumstances fall victim to any kind of sentimentality in wartime . . . on the contrary, one must be hard in the extreme. It doesn't matter how much damage a traitor causes. These are certain crimes of attitude which expel a person from the racial community. Simply from the point of view of a final deterrent, it must be made impossible in this state for a traitor to get away with his life.

It was the task of the judicial system to implement this policy.

The contempt for the letter of the law, indeed for the principle of justice, which had long been evident in Hitler's arbitrary ordering of individual executions, was now made explicit and systematic. Hitler concluded his monologue by outlining the role which he thought the judiciary now had to play:

The judge is the bearer of racial self-preservation. . . . Justice is not an end in itself. It serves the maintenance of human social order, an organism to which we owe culture and progress. Every means is justified if it serves this purpose. Any means which does not do justice to it is wrong. . . . One must extirpate the idea that the judge is there to speak the law even if the world falls apart as a consequence. That is pure madness. It has to be the other way round: maintaining the security of the human social order is the primary task.

In effect, therefore, he was ordering the judiciary to disregard the law and act purely in accordance with the instincts of the race—what the Nazis termed the 'healthy popular feeling'. It no longer mattered what punishment was officially laid down for a particular crime in the Criminal Code. What mattered was harshness and ruthlessness in eliminating 'enemies of the race' The principle of

[47] Mason, *Sozialpolitik*, 15–41.

nulla poena sine lege, first breached in the van der Lubbe case in 1933, no longer existed in the Third Reich at all.[48] With the appointment of Thierack, the moment had arrived for a wholesale reorganization of judicial and penal policy that would finally allow free rein for the exterminism of Hitler and the leading Nazis. To enable this to happen, the lunchtime meeting of 20 August was immediately followed by a decree issued by Hitler ordering the new Reich Minister of Justice 'to build up a National Socialist administration of justice . . . on the basis of my instructions and guidelines' and allowing him to depart from the existing law in doing so. Thierack was named Supreme Reich Judge and, as such, given Hitler's authority to override any judicial decisions he wanted to.[49]

As the new Minister of Justice, Thierack took immediate steps to implement Hitler's views. The specific cases that had aroused the Führer's wrath were dealt with and the sentences revised.[50] Armed with his new powers, Thierack set up a system of so-called Judges' Letters at the beginning of September 1942. From 1 October onwards, the Ministry of Justice sent out regular circulars to judges giving brief summaries of problematical cases, above all those in which party or SS authorities had criticized the 'leniency' of the sentence, and issuing them with instructions on how similar cases were to be handled in future (mostly, though not always, more harshly). Within the Ministry of Justice, Rothenberger now outlined the future basis of judicial policy in the Third Reich. It would be based on the principles enunciated by Hitler at the meeting of 20 August.

For violent offenders and dangerous habitual criminals, the death penalty alone comes into consideration if it is demanded by the need for the protection of the racial community or the demand for a just atonement. The criminal law is thus accorded the task of serving the selection, cleansing, and maintenance of the health of our people. In the course of fulfilling this task, it does not matter whether the individual offences which the criminal has committed are particularly serious in themselves. It is enough that the criminal has shown himself in his whole personality to be a danger to the community through his persistent violation of the law. So the courts must apply the death penalty ruthlessly to actions which damage the people, such as rapes or handbag-thefts deliberately committed during the black-out. Those who steal suitcases on the railways, or field-post parcels and other postal items, must be treated with the utmost severity.

Thus the punishment no longer fitted the crime. Instead, it was completely uncoupled from it and attached instead to the racial status of the offender. The

[48] BA Koblenz, R22/4720: copy, 20 Aug. 1942. See Lothar Gruchmann (ed.), 'Hitler über die Justiz. Das Tischgespräch vom 20. August 1942', *Vierteljahreshefte für Zeitgeschichte*, 12 (1964), 86–101, reporting the monologue; also Jochmann (ed.), *Monologe*, 347–54.

[49] Engelhard (ed.), *Im Namen*, 268.

[50] BA Koblenz R22/4720: Thierack to Bormann, 3 Nov. 1942.

death penalty was applied as an instrument of racial policy, as Nazi thinking on this subject had foreshadowed even before the seizure of power.[51]

In addition, the Reich Justice Ministry also sought to regulate what it called the 'correction of insufficient judicial sentences through special treatment by the police'. On 18 September 1942, at Martin Bormann's suggestion, Himmler, Thierack, and Rothenberger met to draw up a set of rules. 'In principle', they agreed, 'the Führer's time will no longer be taken up with these things at all.' Instead, the decision on overriding sentences would be devolved onto the Reich Justice Minister, to whom Himmler would now report cases where he considered verdicts had been excessively lenient. Bormann agreed to divert all appeals for Hitler's clemency in the same way.[52] In return for the agreement of Bormann and Himmler to regularize the process of appeals for clemency against capital sentences and pass them to the Reich Justice Ministry, Thierack agreed to the

handover of antisocial elements from state prisons to the Reich Leader of the SS for extermination through work. . . . Persons in preventive custody will be delivered without exception, Czechs or Germans with sentences of more than eight years on the recommendation of the Reich Minister of Justice. The most evil antisocial elements among the latter will be handed over first.

The sentences reached on offenders of these categories by the courts were thus rendered effectively meaningless.[53] As Thierack told a meeting of top judges on 29 September, these measures were necessary in order to avoid the emotional strain that would be imposed on them by the duty to pass a death sentence on every 'racial alien' who came before them. The judges accepted the decision; some of them, indeed, welcomed it.[54]

These changes further hastened the process whereby common criminals were subjected to mass extermination instead of being tried and sentenced according to the Criminal Code. They represented a far-reaching transfer of power from the judicial and penal system to the police and SS. And they were acted on immediately. Already in the first half of 1942, 377 out of 1,617 people condemned to death in German courts had been 'habitual offenders' to whom the death penalty had been applicable since the Criminal Code Amendment Law of 4

---

[51] BA Koblenz R22/4720: Rothenberger, 'Die Rechtspflege als Rückgrat von Staat und Volk' (also in R22/4722). See also 'Stellungnahme des Reichsministers der Justiz', in Heinz Boberach (ed.), *Richterbriefe. Dokumente zur Beeinflussung der deutschen Rechtsprechung 1942–1944* (Boppard, 1975), pp. xi–xxv.

[52] Quoted in Engelhard (ed.), *Im Namen*, 269. See Diemut Majer, 'Justiz und Polizei im "Dritten Reich,"' in Dreier and Sellert (eds.), *Recht und Justiz*, 136–50.

[53] Quoted in Engelhard (ed.), *Im Namen*, 269. For the general background to these developments, see P. Wagner, 'Das Gesetz über die Behandlung Gemeinschaftsfremder: die Kriminalpolizei und die "Vernichtung des Verbrechertums"', in Götz Aly *et al.* (eds.), *Feinderklärung und Prävention. Kriminalbiologie. Zigeunerforschung und Asozialenpolitik* (Berlin, 1988), 75–100.

[54] Angermund, *Richterschaft*, 187.

September 1941.[55] Now these people were taken out of the judicial process more and more. In the course of the following year, the prisons of the Reich were systematically combed for offenders of this sort, and many thousands were delivered to the SS to be killed in the labour camps. By 1 April 1943, some 12,658 criminals, 'antisocial elements' and others had been removed from common prisons and penitentiaries to the camps. By this date 5,935 of them, or 47 per cent, had already died, indicating that the phrase 'extermination by work' meant what it said. Among the victims, as we saw in Chapter 13, was August Nogens, one of the central figures in the Jakubowski case. Like the others, he was given rations insufficient to sustain him in the heavy physical labour to which he was put, and if he did not die of disease or malnutrition he was, like many others, probably finished off by a phenol injection when he was no longer able to work.[56] As part of this general reform, on the other hand, the SS and party leadership now ordered local branches and agencies to stop the direct interference in the judicial process which they had begun to exercise once more after Hitler's public criticism of the judiciary for what he saw as its leniency the previous April. From now on, lenient judges were to be dealt with centrally.[57] All of this represented a substantial loss of power from the Justice Ministry to the growing empire of the SS, however much it may have satisfied the judicial bureaucracy by regularizing a situation which had previously seemed to be growing more arbitrary by the day.

Reich Justice Minister Thierack went to some lengths to justify to the German judiciary the transition from execution to extermination. In April 1943 he told them that 'protection of the racial community through the continued organic exclusion of the incorrigible antisocial criminal is a requirement of the self-preservation of our people and thus a requirement of justice'. From the beginning, the Nazis had declared that 'justice' was to be defined primarily in such terms. Now they were at last giving this doctrine its full practical implementation. 'What sense', asked Thierack,

would there be in our doing no more than trying to protect German blood from a pestiferous racial mixing, attempting to prevent hereditarily diseased offspring, and seeking to bring about a progressive improvement in the people's health through a careful health screening of prospective married couples, if we did not at the same time use every means to ensure that this healthy building-up of our people was not destroyed by the attacks of degenerate criminals who do not benefit the community but only damage it? We must not merely look to the future in the implementation of selection, cleansing, and health measures, but we also as far as possible have to make good the mistakes of the past.

---

[55] Boberach (ed.), *Richterbriefe*, 56.

[56] Hermann Kaienburg, '*Vernichtung durch Arbeit*'. *Der Fall Neuengamme. Die Wirtschaftsbestrebungen der SS und ihre Auswirkungnen auf die Existenzbedingungen der KZ-Gefangenen* (Bonn, 1990), 13 n. 3.

[57] Angermund, *Richterschaft*, 255–6.

Thus the killing by the state of the 'incorrigible antisocial criminal' became a co-ordinated policy. Recidivists were to be eliminated because they had shown by their repeated crimes that they were 'a common danger to the community'.[58] But this policy also covered other kinds of common criminals. As Thierack wrote to the judges on 1 June 1943, punishment

in our time has to carry out the popular-hygienic task of continually cleansing the body of the race by the ruthless elimination of criminals unworthy of life. However, the type and degree of sentence is also to be set for the other areas of criminality as well above all according to the principle of protecting the community. What stands out in the foreground as a determining factor in this is not the legal rights of the individual but the life of our ever onward-and-upward-striving people, for that is the highest legal right of the nation. It is on this that sentencing, as one of the means which serves the community in the protection of its will to life, must be based. If the purpose of sentencing lies in the protection of the racial community, then the measure of a just sentence must be the protective requirements of the community at the time, since these are what sentencing is meant to further and maintain. These protective requirements demand that the life and freedom of the lawbreaker must be exterminated according to the degree to which his offence and his personality have assaulted or injured the community.[59]

As the Nazis had insisted from the outset, individual rights were irrelevant. What mattered was the interest of the community, which was defined, of course, by the Nazis themselves.

This view was widely shared by the senior Nazi judges and implemented in courts across the Third Reich. Already in September 1941 a standard legal commentary noted that the protection of the community required the death penalty where 'degenerate criminal personalities' were concerned, and boasted that the Nazis were returning here to the ideas of 'ancient Germanic criminal law', which used the death penalty 'to expunge as energetically as possible anything that did not belong to the race'.[60] Roland Freisler passed sentence 'as a National Socialist', as he wrote in July 1943, picking up Thierack's phrases, and made it his purpose to follow National Socialist precepts in his activities as a judge: 'As far as the fight against serious criminals and antisocial elements is concerned, sentencing . . . in our time must fulfil the popular-hygienic purpose of continually cleansing the body of the race through the ruthless extirpation of criminals unworthy of life.' Despite his concessions of September 1942, however, Thierack resisted attempts by the SS to obtain complete jurisdiction over 'German' defendants. The public, he said, would be far more impressed by the 'extermination' of 'racial pests' 'through the forms of justice' than by a silent

---

[58] Boberach (ed.), *Richterbriefe*, 55–8 (Richterbrief 4).

[59] Ibid. 132. Paragraphing dissolved.

[60] Stauff, *Justiz*, 51, quoting Hans Pfundtner and Reinhard Neubert, *Das neue deutsche Reichsrecht* (Berlin, 1941). See also the Introduction section *a*, above.

elimination by the Gestapo without any judicial window-dressing at all. The People's Court, he assured Ernst Kaltenbrunner, who succeeded Reinhard Heydrich on the latter's assassination by Czech partisans in 1942, would have no difficulty in dealing quickly with such people, or in ordering their execution by hanging, as the SS demanded.[61] Here too, however, the judicial system was enmeshing itself in the machinery of exterminism. Indeed, the Gestapo some-times criticized excessive harshness on the part of the courts as well as what it saw as excessive leniency. Where criminals were regarded as incorrigible, antisocial, and racially dispensable, they were of course to be eliminated; but, where there was hope of returning them to the racial community, a death sentence would be inappropriate in the Gestapo's view. In the struggle of the judicial system to retain a degree of competence over 'malicious' offenders, some judges outdid even the Gestapo in their zeal to consign the guilty to the guillotine or the gallows. In the process, the differences between judicial process and police 'special treatment' all but disappeared.[62]

As Thierack's admonitions suggested, ordinary criminals continued to come before the regular courts all through this period. But the growing pressure to exterminate them inevitably had its effects. Gradually, the customary rules and rituals of judicial condemnation and execution began to be eroded. Psychiatric advice was still taken in capital cases, for example, but it now more than ever acted to confirm the prosecution's wish for a capital sentence. Defendants like the 18-year-old habitual petty thief Karl F., tried before a Special Court in Cologne in 1941, might be certified by a forensic psychiatrist as 'mildly mentally defective' and 'morally and mentally still immature', but in the same breath the expert witness could underline the fact that the offender was 'completely morally depraved' and that he was 'without doubt to be regarded from a criminal point of view as absolutely equivalent to a person over 18 years of age even with respect to the crimes which he committed before he reached the age of 18'. The decisive point, as the court reported, was that the psychiatrist concluded that 'any hope that he could be improved by however tough a custodial sentence, and thereby reintegrated into human society as a useful member of it once more, must be abandoned here!' The justification for killing this offender was thus in essence little different from the justification for killing the chronically handicapped who were the subject of the so-called euthanasia action.[63] By the February 1944, a law had been drafted which provided for a comprehensive policy of surveillance, imprisonment, and extermination for 'community aliens'. The law's definition of a 'community alien' was so vague that it amounted in practice to a *carte blanche*

---

[61] Quoted in Angermund, *Richterschaft*, 188.
[62] Ibid. 200.
[63] Quoted in Engelhard (ed.), *Im Namen*, 219–20.

to the police to terrorize anyone who deviated in any way from the norms which the Nazis were now setting.

A community alien is: (1) anyone who by his personality and way of life, and in particular through unusual deficiencies in understanding and character, shows himself unable to satisfy the minimal demands of the racial community by his own efforts; (2) anyone who (*a*) from work-shyness or frivolity leads a useless, spendthrift, or disorderly life and thereby endangers or burdens the general public, or (*b*) from a tendency or inclination to begging or vagrancy, to idleness or theft, fraud, and deception, or other minor criminal offences, or from a tendency to disorderliness while drunk, grossly violates his duty to sustain the racial community; or (*c*) persistently disturbs the general peace through irritability or pleasure in quarrelling; or (3) anyone whose personality and way of life make it clear that their natural tendency is to commit serious crimes (criminals who are hostile to the community, criminals by inclination).[64]

The leading legal adviser on the law, Professor Edmund Mezger, who had sat on the Criminal Law Commission in the 1930s, prepared a draft preamble which summed up mature Nazi thinking on the topic. It also gave the lie to claims that the Commission's members had been conservatives anxious to preserve the rule of law in the face of Nazi ideology. The document breathed the most unrestrained spirit of Nazi exterminism. 'The experience of decades', wrote Mezger, 'teaches us that criminals are recruited from inferior clans of people':

The individual members of such clans always gravitate towards members of similar bad dynasties and through this ensure that their inferiority is not only passed on from generation to generation but also frequently degenerates into criminality. These people are mostly neither willing nor able to fit themselves into the racial community. They lead a life that is foreign to the idea of the community, they have no feeling for community, and they are often incapable of joining the community or even pose a threat to it, so at any rate are alien to the community.

They included 'failures' who were too weak to contribute to the community, the 'work-shy', the 'immoral', and 'the group who are criminals'.[65] The law was never promulgated, partly because of divisions within the regime over the enormous powers it gave Himmler's police apparatus, partly because Goebbels thought it would make a bad propaganda impression abroad, partly because the regime simply ran out of time; but Mezger's preamble indicated how completely by this time capital punishment had become indistinguishable from racial and eugenic extermination in the eyes of the Nazis.

---

[64] For this law, and a discussion of its background, see Detlev J. K. Peukert, 'Arbeitslager und Jugend-KZ: die "Behandlung Gemeinschaftsfremder" im Dritten Reich', in idem and Jürgen Reulecke (eds.), *Die Reihen fast geschlossen. Beiträge zur Geschichte des Alltags unterm Nationalsozialismus* (Wuppertal, 1981), 413–34, here 416.

[65] Quoted in Norbert Frei, *Der Führerstaat. Nationalsozialistische Herrschaft 1933 bis 1945* (Munich, 1987), 202–8.

c. Towards Assembly-Line Execution

The massive increase in capital punishment during the war soon created problems in its administration. By November 1941 executions were being held so frequently, and in such numbers, that officials were beginning to complain that they were having to get up at four in the morning in order to arrive at the prison at dawn not on the odd occasion, but regularly, almost every day. Could the time of executions, they enquired, not be moved to the early evening instead, so that they could attend them at the end of the working day and go straight home to dinner afterwards? At the Plötzensee prison in Berlin, the regulation prescribing that executions had to take place by 7.15 a.m. at the latest was exacerbating the situation still further. Air raids and air-raid warnings, which obliged everyone to take shelter until the all-clear was sounded, were causing massive disruption. Not infrequently, executions had to be postponed for a full 24 hours because prison officials and executioners were cooped up in an air-raid shelter at a time when they should have been making the necessary prepara-tions.[66] The Reich Ministry of Justice agreed. From now on, it decreed, execu-tions could take place in the evening as well as at dawn.[67] This change in procedure soon proved quite inadequate in the face of the continuing growth in the numbers of people condemned to death and awaiting execution. By January 1942 the state prosecutor in Dresden was desperately informing the Reich Justice Ministry that

The number of condemned prisoners in the remand prison Dresden I is climbing steadily. In mid-October 1941 it was 21, mid-November 34. At the moment it is 59. . . . The large number of these prisoners, who must be treated and supervised in a most particular manner, is imposing a burden on the prison that is no longer bearable. The institution is no longer able to provide secure accommodation and an orderly implementation of sentences. There are not enough suitable cells. These prisoners can only be allowed to move about in the open to a limited extent, which under some circumstances can lead to a diminution of their ability to withstand the conditions of imprisonment. The current shortage of trained warders is such that even with a corresponding increase in the number of auxiliary warders the rules of imprisonment can no longer be followed properly. I only add in passing the observation that the large number of prisoners condemned to death places a strong spiritual strain on the officers and on the governing body of the prison, who are obliged to attend executions at frequent intervals.[68]

But the masters of the Third Reich were not inclined to sympathize with the human weakness of officials worried about the stressfulness of having to attend

---

[66] BA Koblenz R22/1316, Bl. 203: Vorstand der Gefängnisse in Munich to Generalstaatsanwalt Munich, 17 Nov. 1941; see also ibid., Bl. 228: President of the Volksgerichtshof to RJM, 30 Jan. 1940.

[67] Ibid., Bl. 11: Vermerk, 15 Nov. 1941.

[68] Ibid. 1317, Bl. 152: Generalstaatsanwalt Dresden to RJM, 13 Jan. 1942.

too many executions. By December the same year, his protest evidently disregarded, the same official was reporting that the number of condemned offenders in his gaol had now almost doubled again, and stood at 102. They included 75 prisoners from Prague who, he suggested, should be executed somewhere else, such as Leipzig.[69] At the same time, the state prosecutor in Berlin issued a complaint about conditions at the Plötzensee gaol, where there were now no fewer than 216 offenders waiting to be executed, and his colleague in Königsberg wrote in similar terms about the prison there, which housed 112 offenders in condemned cells in May 1942.[70] Conditions must have been the same in many other major gaols by the middle of 1942.

The Justice Ministry reacted not by trying to reduce the number of death sentences, which it was in no position to do even had it wanted to, nor by transferring prisoners to concentration camps, which would have meant surrendering some of its competence to the SS, but by ordering a speeding-up of the execution procedure so that the numbers of capital offenders in the prisons could be reduced by processing their cases more rapidly. In 1940 judicial officials had raised serious objections when they had discovered that 'lightning executions' had been taking place in Munich, only an hour after the condemned person had been informed of the rejection of clemency. Their grounds for doing so had not been humanitarian but bureaucratic: there was not enough time, they had protested, for the necessary paperwork to be completed.[71] By 1 September 1942, however, these objections were being discarded, as the Reich Justice Ministry found it necessary to order a series of measures aimed at the 'Simplification and Acceleration of the Procedure after the Promulgation of a Death Sentence'. The period allowed between the reading out of the rejection of clemency to the accused and the moment of execution (traditionally three days) was now fixed at eight hours. The formal announcement of the sentence and its confirmation at the beginning of the execution ceremony was abolished. And the ringing of the prison bell during executions was finally dispensed with altogether. Executions could now take place at any time, though where possible they should be carried out at night. Capital punishment was from now on to be administered swiftly, silently, and under cover of darkness.[72]

This was not the only way in which procedures were speeded up as the war went on. Hardline Nazis had long been uneasy about the Christian aspects of the

[69] Ibid., Bl. 159: Generalstaatsanwalt Dresden to RJM, 22 Dec. 1942.

[70] Ibid., Bl. 141: Generalstaatsanwalt Berlin to RJM, 23 Oct. 1942; ibid., Bl. 235: RJM to Generalstaatsanwalt Königsberg, 5 Sept. 1942.

[71] Ibid. 1316, Bl. 220: Oberstaatsanwalt at the Landgericht Munich I to RJM (Ministerialrat Altmeyer), 11 Jan. 1940.

[72] Ibid., Bl. 45: RJM to Oberlandesgerichtspräsidenten and others, 1 Sept. 1942, and notes on 'Vereinfachung und Beschleunigung des Verfahrens nach Erlass eines Todesurteils'.

execution ritual but, during peacetime at least, prison pastors and priests had spent a good deal of time and effort in preparing their charges for death, and in trying to convert the atheistical Communists who numbered so many among them.[73] Here was part of the traditional execution ritual that had seemingly survived all the criticism launched against it from the Enlightenment onwards. Now it, too, came under attack. In January 1941 the Reich Security Head Office wrote to the Reich Justice Ministry complaining about the fact that a crucifix was customarily hung on the wall during executions. The condemned person was, it noted, often seen to gaze on it throughout the preliminaries. In Plötzensee, indeed, the execution 'in my experience takes place so quickly that the last conscious sight glimpsed by the condemned is the crucifix, which presents the picture of a martyr's death'.[74] This was objectionable to such Nazi ideologues on more than one count. It implied to offenders a parallel between their fate and that of Christ, and fortified opponents of the regime in their belief that they were not 'enemies of the people' but sufferers in a greater cause. Moreover, as we have seen, the Nazis wanted capital punishment to be a mere elimination of the politically and racially unsound, and felt that the ceremonial aspects of executions were inappropriate, especially if they had resonances such as these. Christianity itself was seen by many of the most fanatical Nazis, above all in the SS, as an alien, 'Jewish' importation which should be replaced in the long run by a truly 'Germanic' folk religion based on practices such as sun-worship. The matter was a sensitive one, because the influence of the Christian churches remained important. So Hitler himself was consulted. However much he might have sympathized with the Reich Security Head Office's complaint, he knew that previous attempts to remove crucifixes from official institutions had caused a good deal of anger among the Christian community, even in one case leading to mass demonstrations for their restitution.[75] So he declared that he did not want to risk causing a conflict between church and state while the war was in progress, and ordered that the crucifixes should remain.[76]

The increasing number of executions was also placing a growing burden on the prison clergy, as Karl Alt, the Protestant city pastor in Munich, complained in March 1942. Writing to the state prosecutor in Munich, he noted:

The Catholic prison padre in Munich, Karl Kinle, who passed on in December 1941, also frequently complained about the physically and spiritually gruelling job of being on permanent call in the poor sinners' cells. Even on his death-bed he complained movingly

---

[73] See the extracts from a prison chaplain's journal in Breloer and Königstein, *Blutgeld*, 96–9.
[74] BA Koblenz R22/1317, Bl. 181: Reichssicherheitshauptamt to Joël, 25 Jan. 1941.
[75] Jeremy Noakes, 'The Oldenburg Crucifix Struggle of November 1936: A Case Study of Opposition in the Third Reich', in Peter Stachura (ed.), *The Shaping of the Nazi State* (London, 1978), 210–33.
[76] BA Koblenz R22/1317, Bl. 182: Vermerk.

to the undersigned about it, and made it responsible for his serious illness and total exhaustion.[77]

Nothing was done to respond to this complaint, and no extra clergy were engaged. Indeed, as the pressures mounted, so the authorities began to consider limiting the role of the clergy at executions, not so much to relieve them from the pressure, but more in order to speed the process of execution up still further. In October 1942 they were given the opportunity to act by an incident in Mecklenburg, when Philipp Kroll, a Catholic priest, was dismissed as prison chaplain because of speaking out in a critical manner during the brief address he gave after an execution. The Ministry of Justice ordered: 'Pastors will not be summoned to attend executions in future. If a prisoner wishes to speak with a pastor, this has to be done in his cell beforehand.'[78] This was not what the Protestant clergy in Munich had been asking for, and they objected to the order, calling the Ministry's attention to the fact that all fifty Protestant offenders executed in the city in the course of 1942 had asked for pastoral care.[79] But now the prayer and sermon went, along with the presence of the clergy. Another long-established part of the execution ritual had been abolished, and the number of people present reduced still further.

Eventually, the numbers of prisoners being executed began to get in the way of the ministrations of religion even in the period before the executions were carried out. On Christmas Eve 1944 Cardinal Bertram, the Chairman of the Fulda Bishops' Conference, wrote to the Reich Ministry of Justice to complain. 'For months', he told the Ministry,

I have been receiving from several people confidential reports of the prevention of the spiritual care of inmates who have been condemned to death, a prevention namely through the fact that a number of executions is fixed for a single day and the time between announcing them and carrying them out is too short.

Prisoners, he protested, now often had only perhaps two hours to make their peace with God between hearing the news that their sentence had been confirmed and being led out of their cell to the guillotine. The cardinal considered that about an hour was needed for proper religious observances to be carried out—prayer, confession, communion, the last rites—in such circumstances. But the time available was mostly used up by the prisoner in making a will, writing last letters to loved ones, and so on, so that in practice only the most hurried and

---

[77] Ibid. 1316, Bl. 259–63: Alt to Generalstaatsanwalt Munich, 28 Mar. 1942, and Karl Alt, *Todeskandidaten* (Munich, 1946).

[78] BA Koblenz R22/1317, Bl. 53: RJM (Thierack) to Bormann, 10 Oct. 1942; see also ibid., Bl. 54: RJM to Generalstaatsanwälte, 15 Oct. 1942.

[79] Ibid., Bl. 104: Evangelisch-Lutherischer Kirchenrat München to RJM, 28 Nov. 1942; ibid., Bl. 106: reply, 13 Jan. 1943.

superficial devotional acts were possible. Delicately alluding, perhaps, to the increasing hostility towards Christianity of powerful forces within the police and judicial administration system, such as the SS, whose power was growing considerably at this time, Bertram brought his complaint to a head in a clear rejection of the way in which the condemned were now being treated:

Even if the prison authorities do not share the Christian, in particular the Catholic, view of Godly confession and life after death, it is still inhumanly hard to deny the malefactor his single last consolation, to make the priest's task a torment for his conscience, and to deny the relatives the comfort of knowing that the executed person left this life reconciled with God.[80]

December 1944 was rather late, perhaps, for the Catholic hierarchy to be complaining about the regime's inhumanity. The Justice Ministry replied on 13 January 1945 that it was unable to go into the matter further because of 'wartime conditions'.[81]

These were not the only steps taken to speed up the process of execution and lighten the ever-increasing burden imposed on judicial officials and others by the rapid growth of capital punishment during the war. It had long been a requirement of the law, for instance, for prison authorities to ask the relatives of the condemned if they wanted the corpse for burial after the execution. Only if they indicated their lack of interest was it made free for anatomical use, or buried in the prison graveyard. Despite growing pressure from the anatomical institutes of German universities, who needed fresh corpses for dissection, especially now that the demands of military medicine meant that they were teaching more students, the Justice Ministry had maintained the relatives' right to the corpse for fear of offending religious and other popular sensibilities. In November 1942, however, the Ministry of Justice ruled that 'enquiries will not be made in future of the relatives of an offender condemned to death, as to whether they wish to receive the corpse after the sentence has been carried out'. Only if the relatives put in a special request on their own initiative was the body to be handed over. To do this, they would have to know the time and place of execution well in advance, which was becoming increasingly difficult as the whole execution process was speeded up during the war. Not surprisingly, the authorities could report by March 1943 that 'the universities' needs are more than met by the corpses of the executed'.[82] By the autumn of 1943, indeed, universities were complaining that 'the massive deliveries of corpses of executed offenders during the last months has led to a complete overcrowding of our storage facilities', and were starting to

[80] BA Koblenz R22/1317. 1318, Bl. 255: Bertram to RJM, 24 Dec. 1944.

[81] Ibid. Bl. 255: RJM to Bertram, 13 Jan. 1945.

[82] Ibid. 1478, Bl. 54: Reichsminister des Innern to Reichsminister für Wissenschaft, Erziehung und Volksbildung, 10 Mar. 1943.

refuse to take any more.[83] Their demands for more corpses had evidently been all too successful. But the real reasons for the ending of the relatives' automatic right to the corpses of executed offenders were administrative, not medical. The authorities simply wanted to be rid of the time-consuming business of having to go through verbal and written negotiations with the relatives. Well before the end of the war, therefore, it had become standard practice for the bodies of executed offenders to be delivered to the anatomists, without any consultation with the families, who were now effectively deprived of their former rights of reclamation.[84] And, the Ministry added: 'The corpses of executed Poles and Jews will not be released for burial by the relatives.' Even their dead bodies were treated differently from those of 'Aryans'.[85]

Up to this point, the members of a court responsible for dealing with objections to an execution, and with petitions by the condemned for their case to be reopened, had been obliged to make themselves available for consultation during the final twelve hours before the execution was scheduled to take place. In some cases, this meant being physically present in the town where the prisoner was being held. The District Court President in Stettin, however, pointed out towards the end of March 1943 that this was extremely inconvenient for busy officials such as himself:

At a time when millions of honourable racial comrades have to put their life at risk and hundreds of thousands are losing it, without being able to prevent or delay their fate by presenting petitions to the authorities, there should be no objection to forbidding serious criminals from writing petitions which are meant to postpone their execution at the last minute—for really, that is all they are doing.[86]

The Ministry agreed that the prison authorities and the state prosecutor in charge of the execution should decide for themselves in future whether there were grounds for a postponement.[87] Any thought that the offenders in question might actually be innocent, or unjustly sentenced, had obviously long since vanished from the minds of such men, who had by now come to see them as vermin to be rubbed out without ceremony or consideration. None of this was sufficient to keep pace with the rapidly increasing number of beheadings. In August 1943 Hitler himself noted that there were over 900 prisoners in condemned cells in the Reich. Many of them had been in custody for over two months. This was not long by the standards of ten years previously. But Hitler was not troubled by the humanitarian aspects of the lengthy wait between sentencing and execution.

[83] Ibid: Generalstaatsanwalt Innsbruck to RJM, 7 June 1943; Director of Anatomical Institute of Jena University to Staatsanwaltschaft Magdeburg, 21 Sept. 1943.
[84] Engelhard (ed.), *Im Namen*, 244.
[85] BA Koblenz R22/13177, Bl. 84: RJM to Oberstaatsanwälte and others, 26 Dec. 1942.
[86] Ibid., Bl. 194–7: Oberlandesgerichtspräsident Stettin to RJM, 29 Mar. 1943.
[87] Ibid., Bl. 198: RJM to Volksgerichtshofpräsident and others, 15 Apr. 1943.

What concerned him was the fact that this was creating an extensive backlog of offenders on death row. As he pointed out to Thierack: 'People condemned to death constitute a danger during enemy air raids, especially in big cities.' If the prison where they were housed should happen to be bombed, there was a chance that they might escape. So Thierack wrote to the Nazi Party boss in Vienna on 31 October 1943:

In order to minimize their number in the prisons as far as possible, it is necessary to speed up the decision-making process on the carrying-out of death sentences. For the duration of the current high danger of severe air raids, the Führer has therefore empowered me to omit the procedure of requesting the views of other administrative authorities on the question of clemency in all cases where there is no doubt, and to give immediate orders for the execution of death sentences on my own responsibility.

Already in mid-August Hitler had ordered the Reich Ministry of Justice to speed up the throughput of condemned offenders so that this situation could be quickly remedied.[88]

Meanwhile the Ministry had already taken steps on its own initiative to reduce the backlog of capital offenders in Berlin. In early September 1943 after an air raid had destroyed part of the Plötzensee gaol, including the guillotine, and forced the prison authorities to accommodate the inmates in extremely cramped conditions in the parts of the prison that had escaped damage, the Justice Ministry ordered that 194 prisoners on death row in Plötzensee should be immediately dispatched in order to reduce the numbers awaiting execution. The message and the list of names of prisoners to be killed were telephoned through to the governor, and the executioner began to hang the prisoners, many of whom were Czechs or Poles, in batches of eight, on the night of 7–8 September. After seventy-eight of them had been killed in this manner, it was discovered that the wrong files had been taken out of the prison office in the rush to do the Führer's bidding, and six of the wrong prisoners had been executed. The Ministry of Justice launched a massive inquiry into what had gone wrong. Characteristically, it was just as concerned about the fact that six prisoners who were on the official list had not been executed as about the fact that six prisoners who were not on the list had. Fresh orders were issued for the six who had momentarily escaped their fate to be hanged as well. Meanwhile the executioner, his request for a 24-hour break to recover from the strain having been refused, continued his work, killing 142 prisoners on the night of 7–8 September and the rest the next day. More were killed on 13 September, bringing the month's total up to 258. Nobody was disciplined for a clerical error that had consigned six of the wrong men to the gallows. Nobody apart from the prison chaplain seemed to be repelled by the fact

[88] BA Koblenz R22/13177, Bl. 64: Lammers to Thierack, 17 Aug. 1943, and Thierack to Dr Jury, 31 Oct. 1943.

FIG. 39. *The guillotine in Plötzensee.* Stationed in an outhouse of the Plötzensee prison in Berlin, the guillotine was used for the execution of hundreds of offenders both before and during the war. Note the board, front left, onto which the prisoner was strapped, with a hole for the chin, before being moved horizontally into position. Behind the guillotine, above the windows, can be seen the beam (with iron hooks) from which prisoners were suspended in primitive mass hangings. Among those dispatched in this way were 142 prisoners killed in the single night of 7–8 September 1943. The picture shows the building used in the later stages of the war, after an earlier one had been destroyed in a bombing raid, along with the original guillotine.

that the corpses were lying about in the open, in the rain, in very hot weather, for days until they could be taken off in a break between air raids to the local Anatomical Institute, where no doubt they would arrive in a state in which they were virtually useless for dissection. And nobody was concerned by the fact hanging was the method used to kill them. These were, after all, in their overwhelming majority racially 'inferior' prisoners, so it did not really matter how they were killed.[89]

Hanging now began to be used more widely in the prisons of the Third Reich, mainly because it was a quicker, cheaper, simpler, and less messy method of execution than the guillotine. In October 1942 the Nazi boss of Pomerania

[89] Ibid. 5019, Bl. 90–1: Westphal, memo, 8 Sept. 1943: ibid., Bl. 114–17: Generalstaatsanwalt at the Landgericht Berlin to RJM (Dr Altmeyer), 17 Sept. 1943, and subsequent correspondence to Bl. 129. These numbers differ slightly from those given in Gostomski and Loch, *Tod*, 23–33, which also contains reports by surviving prisoners.

wrote to Bormann asking him 'to ensure that death sentences against looters are carried out by simple means such as hanging etc., so that manpower and material is not unnecessarily wasted by using the elaborate procedure of execution with the mechanical axe'.[90] Whether or not Bormann or the Ministry of Justice did anything about it, hangings were certainly in use by the end of 1942 as a punishment for treason, probably because they were considered a particularly dishonouring form of execution. In December 1942 a number of prisoners were hanged in Frankfurt am Main.[91] So widespread had hangings become by the end of 1943 that the director of the Institute for Forensic Medicine in Danzig wrote about the matter to the state prosecutor in Posen:

Dear state prosecutor, I have heard that in the Warthegau executions are carried out by the rope. The appearance of someone dying by hanging is especially interesting to forensic medicine. The rapid loss of consciousness, convulsions, and their duration, are of high practical importance for the answering of questions in court by expert medical witnesses. I would like to make a cinematographic recording of what happens at a hanging and use it for education and training purposes.[92]

The Ministry of Justice refused permission.[93] The only execution which was filmed was that of the eight prominent participants in the bomb plot of 20 July 1944, whose death in Plötzensee was recorded on camera and shown to a triumphant Hitler and his entourage shortly afterwards.[94]

Not only was hanging now more or less normal in German prisons, but in November 1942 Hitler also ordered the Ministry of Justice to make it possible for condemned prisoners to be shot by a police or army firing-squad instead of going through what he regarded as the lengthy and elaborate procedure of decapitation by the guillotine. The introduction of new methods in the search for faster executions did not mean, however, that the guillotine was being completely superseded.[95] On the contrary, a new machine came into operation in Graz in August 1943, to relieve the pressure on Vienna, where the number of condemned prisoners had reached a total of 145 by the early

[90] BA Koblenz R22/13177, Bl. 190: Gauleiter Schwede-Coburg to Bormann, 23 Oct. 1942.

[91] Ibid., Bl. 107: Oberstaatsanwalt Frankfurt am Main to RJM, 11 Jan. 1943; ibid.: Vermerk, 12 Dec. 1942.

[92] Ibid. 1318, Bl. 41: Director of Institute for Forensic Medicine, Danzig, to Oberstaatsanwalt Posen, 26 Jan. 1944.

[93] Ibid., Bl. 41: RJM to Generalstaatsanwalt Posen, 26 Jan. 1944.

[94] Peter Hoffmann, *The History of the German Resistance 1933–1945* (London, 1977), 528–9, 721 n. 42; Albert Speer, *Inside the Third Reich* (London, 1971), 531. As we have seen, the execution arrangements in the outhouse at Plötzensee were not set up specially for the participants in the bomb plot, but had already been in place since the destruction of the original outhouse in September 1943.

[95] BA Koblenz R22/1317, Bl. 218: Lammers to Himmler, 27 Nov. 1942 and ibid., Bl. 219–22: Vollzug der Todesstrafe durch Erschiessen, 5 Jan. 1943. Hoffmann (relying on Gerhard Ritter) is in error when he states that hanging was generally replaced by the guillotine in 1942, used again from 1944, then superseded once more in the last two months of the war (Hoffmann, *History*, 527–8).

summer;[96] and seven new machines were ordered by the Ministry, five from Karl Krause's machine factory in Berlin and two from the Francke-Werke in Bremen, at the same time. In order to keep the true nature of the orders from being revealed to the wrong people, the correspondence between the Ministry and the manufacturers, in a euphemistic manner that was characteristic of the Nazis when dealing with such subjects, referred to guillotines as 'special knives' (*Spezialmesser*) or 'F-implements' (*F-Geräte*, 'F' standing for *Fallbeil*, the German for guillotine, a French term which the Nazis, as we have seen, were careful to avoid).[97] At the same time, hangings continued to be carried out on a wide scale. Thus a variety of methods was now being used. On the whole, though doubtless there were exceptions, the guillotine was employed in regular executions for German offenders, while hanging was used for non-Germans. The guillotine was used for criminal offences, while hanging was sometimes, though not always, employed in treason cases—most notoriously, after the bomb plot of 1944, when the plotters were hanged in Plötzensee with specially thin rope, so that they could be sure to die by a specially slow form of strangulation.[98] The method of the 'drop', in which a trapdoor opened to a plunge the length of which was calculated according to the offender's weight, dislocating the neck when it reached the end of the rope, was unknown in Germany. Strangulation, the 'Austrian method', used on Hitler's explicit instructions, was in fact normal.[99] The youthful resisters Hans and Sophie Scholl were guillotined, probably because, as propagandists, they were regarded as less dangerous and less 'dishonourable' than the highly placed generals, officials, and former collaborators with the regime who had tried to blow up Hitler. When there were few prisoners to be executed, the guillotine was often employed; when there were mass executions to be carried out, the rope was generally preferred. The physically cramped conditions of state prisons in Germany do not seem to have permitted Hitler's order for firing-squads to be put into effect.

Meanwhile, the process of execution was being speeded up still further. The administration of the death penalty was degenerating into assembly-line killing, almost entirely without ceremony, ever closer in practice to the much larger-scale killings that had been in progress on the Eastern Front and in the extermination camps since 1941. As the state prosecutor in Hanover pointed out in June 1944, in a request to be excused from attending such occasions: 'If executions in earlier

[96] BA Koblenz R22/1317, Bl. 280: RJM to Volksgerichtshofpräsident and others, 4 Aug. 1943; ibid., Bl. 298: Verzeichnis der am 31. 5. 43 einsitzenden rechtskräftig zum Tode verurteilten Vollstreckungshäftlinge, U-Haftanstalt Wien I.

[97] Ibid. 1318, Bl. 33: Karl Krause to RJM Zentralbeschaffungsstelle, 8 Oct. 1943; ibid., Bl. 36: RJM to Franke-Werke, 27 Oct. 1943.

[98] Hoffmann, *History*, 528.

[99] Hans Halter, 'An der Richtstätte kein Hilter-Gruss', *Der Spiegel*, 33/8 (19 Feb. 1979), 100–1.

times took place with a special ceremoniousness, this was justified by the fact that death sentences had rarity value. This reason no longer applies.'[100] Although condemned offenders frequently asked for clemency, their pleas were seldom heard. No one troubled any more to send papers advising on such matters. 'Since the reasons for the sentence are not known here,' wrote the prison director of a female Jehovah's Witness, convicted of pacifist activities, who had written on 22 November 1943 asking for her death sentence to be commuted, 'I am not inclined to give the request my positive support.' She was executed on 9 June 1944.[101] In November 1944, not least because of increasing communication difficulties, the practice of submitting recommendations for or against mercy to Hitler in person was finally abandoned, except in 'especially important and dubious cases' and in cases of women 'from the occupied or formerly occupied Western territories'.[102] Whether these and other measures had much influence in the reduction of the number of condemned prisoners in death cells in the Reich from a total of over 900 in August 1943, to 687 a year later must be doubted. The Ministry still considered this too many, and Thierack wrote to the People's Court, the worst offender in his eyes, on 1 September 1944 reminding it once more that 'death sentences must be carried out without delay in an effective system of the administration of criminal law'.[103] The fact was, however, that the decline was largely due to the shrinking size of the Reich as the Allied armies advanced, and to the declining importance of the legal operation of capital punishment in the system of extermination as a whole.

d. The Executioners in Wartime

The vastly increased number of executions carried out during the war brought the executioners of the Third Reich a substantial increase in their earnings, with their regular salary of 3,000 Reichsmarks a year augmented by a fee of 60 marks per execution for themselves and each of their assistants.[104] Increasingly, the relatives of the executed person were required to pay the executioner's fee and the prison administrative costs, which seldom came to less than 500 marks.[105] Nevertheless, this does not seem to have affected the executioners' takings. Pressure of business, as well as increased income, was reflected in a request sent

---

[100] BA Koblenz R22/1318, Bl. 125: Auszug aus dem Lagebericht des Generalstaatsanwaltes Hanover, 9 June 1944.

[101] Engelhard (ed.), *Im Namen*, 237–9.

[102] BA Koblenz R22/1318, Bl. 214: Thierack to Meissner, 11 Nov. 1944; ibid., Bl. 288: Meissner to Thierack, 15 Dec. 1944.

[103] Ibid., Bl. 84: Thierack to Volksgerichtshofpräsident, 1 Sept. 1944.

[104] Ibid. 1315, Bl. 276–8: RM to Oberlandesgerichtspräsidenten etc., 19 Feb. 1939, Anlage 1: Richtlinien für Scharfrichter, § 7, Abs. 7.

[105] Engelhard (ed.), *Im Namen*, 240.

in September 1941 by the executioner Johann Reichhart to the Reich Ministry of Transport asking for exemption from the speed limit on Germany's roads. The need to travel rapidly from one place of execution to another, he wrote, had obliged him to buy a 2.5 litre Fiat Ardita Sport limousine, which he wanted to be allowed to drive at 100 kilometres an hour—very fast by the average standards of the day. He admitted that in practice the obligations of his office had already caused him to exceed the legal maximum speed on the roads on more than one occasion. The Ministry refused his request.[106] Evidently the nervous strain of driving at what he considered to be unreasonably slow speeds forced Reichhart to return to rail travel, for a few months later he and his assistants obtained a special pass which required the guard to find them seats if the train on which they were travelling happened to be overcrowded. In this way, Reichhart seems to have been able to continue with his duties right up to the end of the war.[107]

The second of the three-man team of executioners in office since 1937, Ernst Reindel, was not so fortunate. Reindel was a member of Germany's longest-standing dynasty of hangmen, and his links with the past were strengthened by the fact that he was also, like his predecessors in the nineteenth century and earlier, a professional knacker. But tradition and continuity did not save him from financial embarrassment. The income which the executioners received was taxed.[108] The problem was, as the state prosecutor in Naumburg explained on 6 December 1943, that Reindel did not really find it worth while to keep both professions going at the same time:

Because he is most probably the only executioner who has a regular civilian trade as well as his official duties, his earnings as executioner are, looked at purely in monetary terms, mostly taken away in tax. In view of the ever-increasing demands on Reindel as executioner, and the neglect of his other business (knacker's yard) which this is causing, Reindel does not regard the remaining profit accruing to him as sufficient recompense for his difficult office.[109]

Reindel had therefore decided to submit his resignation. The Justice Ministry did not attempt to persuade him to stay on. The Third Reich had made it impossible for the traditional combination of the two trades to continue. The Ministry now began the difficult search for a suitable successor. Normally, the candidate would have been sought from among the retiring executioner's assistants. But it quickly became clear that none of Reindel's men was really fit to take the job on. One of

[106] BA Koblenz R22/1324, Bl. 123, 126: Reichhart to RJM, 24 Sept. 1941; RJM to Reichhart, 10 Nov. 1941.

[107] Ibid., Bl. 146: Oberstaatsanwalt Munich, Bestätigung of 26 Mar. 1942; Oberstaatsanwalt Munich to RJM, 3 Jan. 1944.

[108] Ibid. 1316, Bl. 272: RJM to Oberlandesgerichtspräsidenten and others, 21 May 1942.

[109] Ibid. 1324, Bl. 316: Generalstaatsanwalt Naumburg to RJM, 6 Oct. 1943.

them was '65 years old', a second was 'clumsy', a third was 'very deaf', and a fourth was described as '68 years old, shaky, used-up'. That this situation had been allowed to develop spoke volumes about the reluctance of judicial administrators to interfere with the executioners in the normal course of their business. It also said a great deal about the reluctance of the executioners themselves to change their team once it had been brought together. Until a suitable successor was found, therefore, Reindel was temporarily replaced by Friedrich Hehr, the third of the principal executioners appointed in the general reorganization of 1937.

Hehr continued to function throughout the war and soon came to be recognized as the most important of the executioners in terms of finding and training fresh candidates for the job. His team became little short of a school for executioners. For the sharp increase in the number of executions quickly necessitated a corresponding increase in the number of men hired to carry them out. In 1940 a fourth executioner was added to the list: Gottlob Bordt, one of Hehr's assistants. As a Ministry official noted, Bordt was 'completely occupied by his duties in Posen'. Up to 1942, therefore, there was a fourfold geographical division of responsibility, with Reichhart working in south Germany, Reindel in central Germany and Berlin, Hehr in western and northern Germany, Königsberg, Breslau, and Kattowitz, and Bordt in Posen.[110] Later in the same year, a fifth man, Karl Henschke, an assistant of Bordt, was hired, and two more were added to the list in 1943: August Köster, another of Hehr's assistants, and Alois Weiss, who had hitherto belonged to Reichhart's team. By the end of 1943 the Ministry of Justice had added Willi Röttger, Johann Mühl, and Fritz Witzka to its list. By the spring of 1944 the number of 'executioners' districts' stood at nine.[111] A final addition was made in 1944—Alfred Roselieb, another of Hehr's assistants, replacing Reindel—so that there were now ten principal executioners, with a total of thirty-eight assistants working for them.[112] These ten teams were responsible for all the hangings and guillotinings carried out by judicial order in German prisons. Shootings and other killings in the camps remained the province of the SS, and were not their concern.

Perhaps in order to portray himself as a respectable professional who continued to do his legal duty while all around him the Third Reich descended into a chaos of murder and mayhem, Reichhart subsequently complained that the new executioners were not professionals, but 'party and SS people, who had often put themselves forward merely out of greed and pleasure in killing'.[113] This claim

[110] BA Koblenz R22/1324. 1317, Bl. 25: Westphal (RJM) Vermerk 25 Apr. 1942.

[111] Ibid. 1318, Bl. 91: Vermerk.

[112] Ibid., Bl. 1–7: Liste der Scharfrichter und der Gehilfen (Stand: Ende 1943).

[113] Erich Helmensdorfer, '"Ich tät's nie wieder". Scharfrichter Reichart ist gegen die Todesstrafe', *Die Zeit*, 30 Oct. 1964.

was untrue. Virtually all of the new men came, like Reichhart himself, from the milieu of the professional executioner. And only two of all the executioners active in the Third Reich were actually members of the Nazi Party or one of its affiliated institutions: Josef Nikl, who joined the party in 1937, and—ironically—Johann Reichhart himself, a member since 1 May the same year.[114] But the addition of so many new people, a number of whom had been exposed to only the briefest of training sessions, inevitably led to mistakes in the preparation and execution of beheadings. In March 1940 the guillotine blade 'remained stuck' at the top during an execution in Plötzensee,[115] and a similar incident occurred during the war in Vienna. The condemned man, recalled executioner Reichhart later, 'kept on stammering loudly: "This is a higher justice, I'm innocent!"' But Reichhart fixed the faulty machine and the second time he was successful.[116] The incident cost him four weeks' sick leave, which he spent at home in a state of nervous prostration. In October 1943 the blade jammed half-way down its run at an execution in Breslau.[117] It was also unsurprising that there were complaints about 'the overloading of the execution centre in Plötzensee prison because of war conditions'.[118] In 1941 Hehr's assistant Ludwig Overbeck, who had only been working with the execution team for a year, shifted his grip at the wrong moment while holding the head of the condemned man in place, and had his left thumb sliced off by the falling blade. The wound turned septic, and Overbeck's left arm was amputated. Even this failed to save him, and he died a few weeks later from blood poisoning.[119]

Such incidents dramatized for the authorities the stresses under which the regular system of execution was now labouring. With so many executions now undertaken every day, executioners were bound to feel the strain. Reichhart himself subsequently claimed to have executed a total of no fewer than 2,805 offenders, including 71 in 1939, 163 in 1940, 221 in 1941, 764 in 1942, and as many as 876 in 1943. He continued to keep up this pace in the last months of the war, with 730 executions in 1944 and 51 even in 1945. In the three years from 1942 to 1944, in other words, Reichhart was executing an average of over two people every day, including Sundays and holidays such as Easter or Christmas Day; in fact, of course, given the number of prisons he had to attend, and the backlog of capital cases with which he had to deal, on many days he must have operated the guillotine dozens if not scores of times. The same held good for most of his

[114] Berlin Document Center: Josef Nikl, Johann Reichhart.
[115] BA Koblenz R22 1315, Bl. 396: Generalstaatsanwalt Berlin to RJM, 8 Mar. 1940.
[116] Helmensdorfer, '"Ich tät's"'.
[117] BA Koblenz R22/1324, Bl. 310: Köster, 28 Oct. 1943.
[118] Ibid. 1315, Bl. 352: RJM to Generalstaatsanwalt Berlin, 11 Feb. 1940.
[119] Ibid. 1324, Bl. 108: Oberstaatsanwalt Hanover to RJM, 31 Jan. 1941 and 4 Mar. 1941; ibid., Bl. 118: Oberstaatsanwalt Hanover to RJM, 27 Mar. 1941.

colleagues; the executioner's assistant Klein, for example, was involved in no fewer than 931 executions in the year from April 1944 to March 1945 alone.[120] The strain which this ceaseless blood-letting must have imposed was augmented during 1943 and 1944 by the growing problems which executioners were encountering in travelling round a country which was being subjected to almost continuous heavy bombing raids. So the Ministry of Justice decided that it would be a good idea to use prisoners to operate the guillotines as well as, or even instead of, the existing team of ten regularly employed executioners. The prisoners would be selected from among those condemned to death but granted clemency. But when the Ministry canvassed opinion among the state prosecutors and prison governors, it ran into a barrage of criticism. The terms in which they objected to the idea were more revealing of the continuities that persisted in this area than of the changes that had taken place under the Third Reich. One prison governor declared flatly: 'I believe that it is incompatible with the character of an execution as a highly important sovereign act of state to have the office of executioner exercised by convicted prisoners, and particularly by convicted prisoners found to have merited the death penalty.' It would, he said, pose a threat to good order in the prison. 'There is no doubt that those prisoners who carry out the duties of executioner or executioner's assistant will be *ostracized* by their fellow prisoners. That means that they will have to reckon with mockery and contempt, and probably physical assault as well.' The traditional requirement of coolness and cold-bloodedness would also, thought the governor, be difficult to meet among the inmates of a gaol. Those who volunteered to carry out executions were likely to be sadists, which was not likely to enhance the solemn character of the execution either. And, he added finally: 'The educative effect which imprisonment aims at will be reduced by such an activity, the more so because it is (naturally only *de facto*) the same kind of activity as the criminal activities of the prisoners in question.'[121] Such a position indicated among other things how tenaciously the traditional view of penal policy was still held by judicial conservatives, and how far they had blinded themselves to what was really going on in Germany's gaols in the Second World War.

The state prosecutor in Naumburg, after discussing the matter with the prison authorities in Halle, agreed that the prisoners who acted as executioners would be 'ostracized'. It would be difficult, he said, to find prisoners with a large enough 'degree of energetic will and active powers of decision' to undertake the job, because prisoners were by definition 'inferior'. Moreover, the number of pris-

---

[120] Düsing, *Abschaffung*, 216–18.
[121] BA Koblenz R22/1318, Bl. 240: Dr E. to Ministerialrat Dr Westphal, 31 Oct. 1944; ibid., Bl. 241: RJM to Generalstaatsanwalt at the Kammergericht and Generalstaatsanwalt Naumburg, 6 Nov. 1944.

oners whose death sentences had been commuted to life imprisonment was now very small. Indeed, very few capital offenders had been granted clemency since the inauguration of the Third Reich in 1933 and, of those who had, many had subsequently been taken off by the SS or Gestapo to a concentration camp and killed there. This meant that the majority of 'lifers' had originally been sentenced under the Weimar Republic or even in the Kaiser's day, and they were now therefore mostly too old to do the job. Younger prisoners would therefore have to be used. But they were in turn more likely to get 'blood-lust' from carrying out a beheading, thought the Naumburg prosecutor. The execution of young women, for example—and thirty-two of them had been decapitated in Halle since the erection of a guillotine in the prison there on 24 November 1942, roughly two years before—could easily lead to sexual arousal in the young male prisoners who, it was being proposed, would carry it out, and thus provide an 'occasion for dirty and lecherous jokes and lead to a spiritual pollution and brutalization of the institution'. The prisoners ordered to operate the guillotine would tell other inmates of their experiences, and such stories would arouse the whole gaol to a fever-pitch of vicarious sexual sadism:

The execution of a death sentence has an inherent dignity and ceremoniousness which has deeply impressed me no matter how often I have attended executions. This effect is all the greater in the general public because, thanks to the strict regulations enjoining secrecy on the participants, the details of the execution are shrouded in a certain shadowy mysteriousness. On this rests the deterrent effect of capital punishment. But it would be divested of this effect to a certain extent if—and this would be unavoidable—it became public knowledge that executions were no longer carried out by the mysterious and anonymous person of the executioner with his assistants, but by inmates of the penitentiary.[122]

Such mystification revealed another side of the Third Reich—its irrationalism and anti-intellectualism. Considerations such as these were almost the exact opposite of those which had informed the advice of Savigny a century or so before on the introduction of 'intramural' executions. The obsessive harping of the prosecutor on the sexual aspects of execution perhaps also said more in the end about his own unconscious than about the topic which was ostensibly under discussion, the employment of prisoners as executioners.

Faced with this barrage of criticism, the Ministry gave in, and the official executioners kept their jobs. But by this time the administration of justice was already beginning to crumble under the strain of military defeat. In August 1944 the execution facilities in Hamburg were damaged in a bombing raid, and death

---

[122] Ibid., Bl. 242–4: Generalstaatsanwalt Naumburg to RJM, 20 Nov. 1944; cf. also Generalstaatsanwalt Berlin to RJM, 4 Dec. 1944.

sentences were from now on carried out by firing-squad in the Neuengamme concentration camp just outside the city.[123] A similar change was also proposed for Celle, Kiel, and Rostock.[124] Executions were being taken over, in effect, by the SS. They had already had a presence at normal executions since the beginning of 1943, when it was agreed that a police officer should report back on each occasion to Himmler's SS Security Service.[125] By this time, too, it was not uncommon for the Gestapo to arrive at the end of a regular execution with an unnamed prisoner whom the executioner would have to kill as well, with no questions asked. These so-called N-cases—'N' standing for 'Nameless'—remained completely unknown, even to the officiating state prosecutors; their remains were removed by the Gestapo afterwards, so that no trace was left.[126] But now the SS and Gestapo were becoming more than a presence, as executions were subsumed into the general processes of extermination administered by Himmler's organization. This process was accelerated by the advance of the Allied armies, which made it necessary to begin moving 400 condemned prisoners away from Breslau, Dresden, Munich, Vienna, Königsberg, Stuttgart, and Hamburg to concentration camps in October 1944.[127] At the very end of the war, when the executioners were no longer able to reach the prisons where they were supposed to carry out their job, even their legally approved duties were taken over by others, as in the guillotining of 28 prisoners on 20 April 1945 in the Brandenburg penitentiary, which was carried out by prison officers.[128] The regular executioners for their part always remained servants of the state rather than the party, and owed their allegiance to the judicial system rather than to the apparatus of extermination. But, as the war progressed, these distinctions, as we shall now see, became progressively more devoid of meaning and content. Even if the thousands killed by the official execution teams were only a fraction of the millions killed by the Nazi regime as a whole, they still belonged increasingly in the overall context of mass murder and extermination.

e. Capital Punishment and Racial Extermination 1939–1945

The racism at the core of Nazi penal policy can nowhere be better documented than in the differential treatment meted out to offenders of German and non-German descent during the war. The conquest of a large part of Poland in

[123] BA Koblenz R22/1318, Bl. 240: Generalstaatsanwalt at the Hanseatisches Oberlandesgericht to RJM, 8 Aug. 1944.

[124] Ibid., Bl. 139: Vermerk, 5 Aug. 1944.

[125] Ibid. 1317, Bl. 60: Reichssicherheitshauptamt to RJM 14 Oct. 1942; ibid., Bl. 163: Kriminalrat Dobiat to Oberstaatsanwalt at the Landgericht Munich, 15 Mar. 1943.

[126] Helmensdorfer, ' "Ich tät's" '.

[127] BA Koblenz R22/1317, Bl. 287: Vermerk, 20 Oct. 1944.

[128] Wieland, *Volksgerichtshof*, 98.

September 1939 brought the Nazi government the problem of whether or not to extend German criminal law to the occupied population, as had been done in Austria and Czechoslovakia. Initially, it followed the Czech model; but in November 1940 it was decided to implement a special Criminal Code against Poles, in which offences would be more widely and vaguely defined and punishments far more draconian than they were under existing German law. This came into effect later in the year. A decree issued on 4 December 1941 gave the occupying civil administration blanket powers to apply the death penalty to Poles and Jews 'even in cases for which the law does not foresee the death penalty . . . if the deed was committed from particularly base motives or is particularly heinous for other reasons'. This new provision was expressly extended to 'juvenile serious offenders' or in other words Poles and Jews between the ages of 14 and 18, as well as to adults. And the decree applied not only to Poles and Jews whose offences were committed in the occupied territories, but also to those who had been resident there on 1 September 1939 but committed their crimes within the German Reich. This meant in the first place slave labourers, hundreds of thousands of whom were already in the process of being deported from their homes in Poland and western Russia to work in industry and agriculture in the 'Greater German Reich'.[129] The SS and Gestapo had already been executing Polish and other 'racially alien' forced labourers in Germany, unsanctioned by any authority except their own, long before they acquired the formal power to do so. These executions began in the late summer of 1940 and took place with increasing frequency thereafter.[130] On 25 March 1941 the president of the High Court in Hamm, Westphalia, wrote to the Reich Minister of Justice to report the following incident:

A few days ago the Gestapo hanged a 19-year-old Pole in the so-called Schwerter Forest, near Dortmund, because he had indecently assaulted a German girl. The execution was carried out by two Poles on a gallows which they brought along with them. 300 Poles were forced to watch. The public footpath on which the hanging took place was sealed off during the action. The state police unit for the District of Arnsberg in Dortmund-Hörde has confirmed to the President of the District Court in Dortmund on the latter's request for information that the execution took place.

[129] Wrobel (ed.), *Strafjustiz*, 48. See also Ulrich Herbert, *Fremdarbeiter. Politik und Praxis des 'Ausländer-Einsatzes' in der Kriegswirtschaft des Dritten Reiches* (Bonn, 1985), esp. 116–17, Diemut Majer, *'Fremdvölkische' im Dritten Reich. Ein Beitrag zur nationalsozialistischen Rechtssetzung und Rechtspraxis in Verwaltung und Justiz unter besonderer Berücksichtigung der eingegliederten Ostgebiete und des General-gouvernements* (Boppard, 1981), and Hirsch *et al.* (eds.), *Recht*, 488–500.

[130] Gruchmann, *Justiz*, 689–94. See also Hinrich Rüping, *Staatsanwaltschaft und Provinzialjustizver-waltung im Dritten Reich. Aus den Akten der Staatsanwaltschaft bei dem Oberlandesgericht Celle als höhere Reichsjustizbehörde* (Hannoversche Beiträge zur rechtswissenschaftlichen Grundlagenforschung, Baden-Baden, 1990), 124–6.

'The people are very upset by this "lynch justice",' he reported.[131] The decree of 4 December 1941 regularized this situation and made sure that in future such executions would take place not in the open, but in the secrecy of the concentration camps. It was followed some months later by further measures.

On 18 September 1942, at the meeting which handed over control of 'incorrigible antisocial elements' to the SS, the Reich Ministry of Justice agreed with Himmler 'that with regard to the aims envisaged by the leadership of the state of clearing up the Eastern Question, in future Jews, Poles, gypsies, Russians, and Ukrainians will no longer be condemned by the regular courts for common criminal matters but will be dealt with by the Reich Leader of the SS'. Only Polish citizens classified as 'German' on the basis of their supposed racial background were exempt. Thus formal court procedures, even those as summary as the Special Courts', were now reserved in the occupied eastern territories for ethnic Germans only.[132] These measures were followed up by a further memorandum from Thierack to Bormann, written after consultation with Himmler, on 13 October, 1942:

With a view to freeing the German racial body from Poles, Russians, Jews, and gypsies, and with a view to liberating the eastern territories which have come into the Reich as a settlement area for the German race, I propose to hand over the prosecution of Poles, Jews, Russians, and gypsies to the Reich Leader of the SS. I take as my starting-point the recognition that the judicial system can only contribute in small measure to the extermination of members of these races. Doubtless the courts are passing very severe sentences on such persons, but that is not enough to contribute substantially to the implementation of the above-mentioned ideas. Nor does it make any sense to conserve such persons for years on end in German prisons and penitentiaries, not even when, as happens to a large extent at the moment, their labour-power is used for war purposes. On the contrary, I believe that substantially better results can be obtained by delivering such persons to the police, who can then implement their measures without reference to the legal facts of the criminal cases concerned.[133]

On 5 November Himmler reported that Hitler had given the plan his approval, and ordered all police units in Germany to 'deal with' 'racial aliens' themselves. In the case of Germans who came before the courts, he explained, the law paid close attention to the motives and personality of the offender when considering a sentence. But this would be wrong in the case of non-Germans living within the Reich (i.e. slave labourers):

The personal motives of the offender must be completely disregarded in cases of offences committed by members of alien races. All that matters is that their offences have endangered the German racial order and that steps therefore have to be taken to prevent

---

[131] Engelhard (ed.), *Im Namen*, 256–7.
[132] Ibid. 269.   [133] Ibid. 14.

further endangerment. In other words, an offence committed by a member of an alien race is not to be treated according to the principle of a judicial expiation, but above all according to the point of view of policing and defending against a threat. From this it follows that the administration of criminal law against persons alien to the race must be passed from the hands of the judicial system into the hands of the police.[134]

This policy was resisted by the authorities in the eastern territories, who now faced the loss of their control over non-German workers to the SS, and a lengthy debate ensued before it was definitively ordered on 30 June 1943 that all offences committed by Poles and Russians, wherever they were, lay within the competence of the Gestapo.[135] A few judges registered their doubts about this procedure, but the majority went along with it.[136] From now on, therefore, the Gestapo and SS were regularly executing foreign forced labourers, often for extremely minor offences, all over Germany, without any involvement of the local authorities or the courts at all.

Even in the regular judicial system of the Reich, the differential standards which the law now required to be applied to offences committed by Germans and others meant that, in the first half of 1942, 530 out of 1,146 death sentences passed by German courts were passed against Poles. These included 10 for sexual intercourse with German women, 47 for 'moral offences', 33 for black marketeering and other economic offences, 2 for listening to foreign radio broadcasts, and 14 for 'acts of insubordination by servants to German masters'.[137] Out of 3,363 death sentences passed by German courts in 1942, 1,556 were passed against Germans and non-Germans living within the 1914 boundaries of Germany, while 1,857 were against Poles and Jews in the occupied eastern territories and against inhabitants of the Protectorate of Bohemia and Moravia. All in all, 55 per cent of all those condemned to death by the courts in this year were non-German, although non-Germans made up only a minority of the population of Hitler's Central European empire. In the following year, however, as the judicial system handed jurisdiction over these non-German groups to the Gestapo and the SS, they accounted for only 894 out of a total of 5,536 death sentences—a figure which, therefore, represented a further huge increase in the number of ethnic Germans executed.[138] The missing persons had been transferred to concentration camps for execution; in some instances they were sent on to a gassing centre such as Hartheim. Mass arrests of Poles following the invasion of September 1939 had already led to the creation of special camps to house them early in 1940. These included the former military barracks at Auschwitz, where the IG Farben company soon set up a chemical works using forced Polish labour.

---

[134] Ibid. 15.   [135] Angermund, *Richterschaft*, 189–90.
[136] Ibid. 191.   [137] Engelhard (ed.), *Im Namen*, 228.
[138] Angermund, *Richterschaft*, 216–18.

The forced-labour system expanded from this point on, and increasing numbers of foreign workers were sent to the camps. By August 1943 there were 224,000 inmates in the camps; by August 1944, over half a million; by January 1945, over 700,000. The network encompassed twenty major centres and 165 subsidiary labour camps by the spring of 1944, organized by a special economic department of the SS, established two years previously. This meant that concentration camps were losing their primary function as places of punishment. They began to be distinguished between killing and execution centres on the one hand and labour camps operating as part of the SS's economic empire on the other. This distinction was not always clear-cut, however. Camps such as Dachau, Buchenwald, and Sachsenhausen were used for the mass killing of Soviet prisoners of war, death rates in the labour camps grew, and forced labour was considered increasingly expendable. SS doctors had orders to kill weak or sickly workers by injection. Food rations were too low to sustain people engaged in hard manual labour.[139] Flossenbürg was used with particular frequency as an execution centre, perhaps because of its relative remoteness from major centres of population. From April 1944 until shortly before the camp was liberated by Allied troops, executions took place almost daily in the walled-off courtyard which was used for the purpose. In total they numbered around 1,500, and in the last weeks of the camp's existence up to ninety people were killed every day. Many of them were foreign slave labourers sent in by the police for killing and approved for execution by the Reich Security Head Office. Others included Allied prisoners of war, especially if they were suspected of espionage or acting in liaison with resistance movements; 193 members of the Czech resistance were executed in the camp in February 1945. Such executions in the camps, as usual, were held under conditions of strict secrecy.[140]

In Auschwitz an enclosed courtyard between two of the blocks was used for such executions and, whenever an execution was due to take place, the ordinary inmates were ordered to their quarters and not allowed to come out until the whole procedure was over, including the disposal of the bodies. The people to be executed were forced to strip naked, taken into the execution yard, placed against a black-painted wall, and shot with a pistol. After shooting, the bodies were taken to the crematorium. This assembly-line killing was very similar to the mass shootings carried out by SS death squads in the wake of the German army on the Eastern Front; in its anonymity and lack of ceremony, it was far removed from traditional kinds of capital punishment. Such executions were regularly carried out on Polish intellectuals and professionals, and on Poles singled out for revenge killings in areas where partisans were active. Forty such victims were shot in this

[139] Broszat, 'Concentration Camps', 498–504.
[140] Siegert, 'Konzentrationslager Flossenbürg', 477–8.

way on 22 November 1940, 168 on 27 May 1942, and another fifty-six on 18 August 1942. Auschwitz also served as an execution centre for the Gestapo summary court in Katowice (Kattowitz), which met in Block 11 of the camp, next to the execution yard. In six court sessions held between 2 September 1943 and 30 October 1944, 556 Poles (out of a total of 580 accused) were condemned to death and immediately taken off to be shot. Other victims included political commissars of the Red Army, some 300 of whom were shot in the yard in July 1941, shortly after the German invasion of the Soviet Union, and 'partisans', who were regularly executed in mainly small groups, often including women and children.[141] A similar function was performed by other camps in or near occupied territory, such as the concentration camp of Natzweiler, in Alsace. Here Red Army commissars, Poles, and French hostages or partisans were brought in great secrecy to be shot.[142] In the Reich, camps such as Dachau served as execution centres for Russian prisoners of war, above all in 1941–2. Thirty-one Soviet officers were shot there on 22 February 1944, and another ninety on 4 September, executed by the SS in the high-walled courtyard of the prison crematorium. Although these shootings were supposed to be by firing-squad, according to rules laid down by Himmler, in practice they were increasingly carried out by shots to the back of the neck, and camp inmates were frequently used to perform them.[143] As in Auschwitz, these executions took place in secret.

The total numbers of non-Germans killed by these various methods were staggering. If pistol-shots, firing-squads, injections, and hangings accounted for hundreds of thousands, then starvation and epidemics brought on through deliberate overcrowding and neglect accounted for millions. Up to four million Soviet prisoners of war were killed by these means; shootings were carried out mainly against those suspected of being political commissars, while the majority were simply starved to death or died through disease and neglect. Even more, however, it was the Jews who were subject to the mass extermination practised by the SS and the German army. The story of the 'Final Solution' has been told too often, and too well, by too many historians for it to be necessary to repeat it here. In scale and scope it puts the history of formal capital punishment even in the Third Reich into the shade. But it forms an essential part of the context in which formal processes of execution were stripped of their ceremony and reduced to assembly-line extermination. Already in the summer of 1941, death squads organized by the SS Security Service were shooting thousands of Jews in occupied

[141] Franciszek Piper, 'Ausrottung', in Danuta Czech *et al.*, *Auschwitz. Geschichte und Wirklichkeit des Vernichtungslagers* (Reinbek, 1980), 92–142, here 112–15.
[142] Wolfgang Kirsten, *Das Konzentrationslager als Institution totalen Terrors: Das Beispiel des KL Natzweiler* (Pfaffenweiler, 1992), 8–13.
[143] Kinnel, "Konzentrationslager Dachau', 406.

Eastern Europe. By October the mass killings were being systematized and co-ordinated, and extermination camps were constructed at Belzec, Chelmno, Sobibor, Treblinka, and Auschwitz-Birkenau, with large-scale gas chambers to which, in the course of the next three and a half years, and above all from the spring of 1942 to the late summer of 1943, Jews from all over Europe, including Germany itself, were delivered for killing. Altogether up to six million Jews were deliberately murdered in the process, whether by shooting, gassing, or deliberately induced starvation and disease in the ghettos to which many of them were confined as an interim measure from 1939 onwards. The killing of Slavs and Jews by the Third Reich cannot be explained in terms of ridding the Nazis' European empire of 'social ballast'.[144] Nazi anti-Semitism in particular had a separate history from that of eugenics and 'criminal biology', though at various points it had become intertwined, above all after 1933. The history of capital punishment, even under the Nazis, cannot be used to explain the 'Final Solution'. But there were undoubtedly connections, some of which we will return to in the Conclusion to this book. What is important to note here, however, is the fact that the radicalization of capital punishment within Germany itself, above all from 1942 to the end of the war, took place in a situation in which the police and security apparatus headed by Himmler, the Nazi leadership more generally, and Hitler in particular, were engaged in mass extermination on an unprecedented scale, of people whom they regarded as racially inferior, a threat to the future of the German race, and a danger to the Third Reich's prospects of winning the war.[145] When millions were being killed, the execution of thousands could be made to appear as a kind of normality, as it undoubtedly did to the officials who organized it in the Ministry of Justice.

If these processes of mass extermination were carried out with as much secrecy as the Third Reich could devise, even within the ordinary concentration camps to which people were taken for shooting, then the same did not hold good for the killing of camp inmates involved in escape attempts, who were often executed in public, almost invariably by hanging, in front of all the assembled prisoners.[146] The rules for this procedure, laid down by Himmler on 6 January 1943, required the hanging to be undertaken by a prisoner, who was to receive the princely payment of three cigarettes for his pains.[147] In Auschwitz, two portable gallows,

[144] For these arguments, see Detlev Peukert, 'Alltag und Barbarei. Zur Normalität des Dritten Reiches', in Dan Diner (ed.), *Ist der Nationalsozialismus Geschichte? Zur Historisierung und Historikerstreit* (Frankfurt am Main, 1987), 51–61; discussion and further references in Richard J. Evans, *Im Schatten Hitlers? Historikerstreit und Vergangenheitsbewältigung in der Bundesrepublik* (revised edn. Frankfurt am Main, 1991), 113–17, 256–7.
[145] The literature on the 'Final Solution' is too vast to cite here, even in a representative fashion. For a useful brief overview see Michael R. Marrus, *The Holocaust in History* (London, 1989).
[146] Kirsten, *Konzentrationslager*, 8–13.   [147] Kinnel, 'Konzentrationslager Dachau', 406.

extremely rudimentary in construction, were used for this purpose. Twelve prisoners were hanged in this way for attempting to escape on 19 July 1943, and another nineteen in a nearby sub-camp on 6 December 1943. The purpose of such executions, which were often accompanied by a verbal warning from the authorities not to emulate the executed men in their attempt to gain freedom, was plainly deterrent. If an escape was successful, other prisoners would sometimes be executed, often by starvation to death in a locked cell, as a 'reprisal'.[148] Until the beginning of November 1944 such killings, at least when they were ordered in camps within the Reich such as Dachau, were supposed to be personally approved by Himmler before they were carried out.[149] Even after this, the rules were only relaxed for non-Germans. The numbers involved were considerable. In Flossenbürg, for example, 117 inmates were executed between June and 18 December 1944 alone, for attempting to escape or for alleged industrial sabotage in the quarry. The fact that only three of them were Germans, however, indicates both the extent to which the forced labourers in the camp were by now mostly Russians, Czechs, and Poles, and the way in which such ethnic groups were more likely to be singled out for execution than German 'criminals' and 'antisocial elements', even in the environment of a forced labour camp.[150]

At the end of the war, the Nazis carried out a wave of revenge killings in the camps. At Natzweiler 141 men and women of the French Resistance were secretly shot on the day before the camp was to be evacuated in the face of the Allied advance.[151] But it was not only foreign nationals who were subject to these executions. Hitler had once told Himmler to kill everybody in the concentration camps should the regime be in danger of being overthrown, 'so that the masses will be robbed of their leadership'.[152] Some such motivation, coupled with revenge, seems to have been behind a wave of executions of German nationals personally ordered by Hitler at the end of the war, when he must have known that defeat was near. Already on 18 August 1944 the SS had shot the former Communist Party leader Ernst Thälmann on Hitler's orders in Buchenwald concentration camp.[153] On 8 April 1945, most probably at his command, a drumhead court martial in Flossenbürg condemned a number of members of the German resistance including Admiral Wilhelm Canaris, Major-General Hans Oster, Judge Karl Sack, Pastor Dietrich Bonhoeffer, and General Friedrich von Rabenau to death. They were hanged the following morning. On 23 April 1945

[148] Piper, 'Ausrottung', 115.
[149] Kinnel, 'Konzentrationslager Dachau', 378.
[150] Siegert, 'Konzentrationslager Flossenbürg', 477.
[151] Kirsten, *Konzentrationslager*, 13.
[152] Jochmann (ed.), *Monologe*, 59 (14–15 Sept. 1941).
[153] Hannes Heer, *Ernst Thälmann in Selbstzeugnissen und Bilddokumenten* (Reinbek, 1975), 129–30.

FIG. 40. *Public hanging of black marketeers in Cologne, 1944.* By this time, the policy of public execution, common in the occupied eastern territories from early in the war, was beginning to be used in Germany itself, especially for foreign slave labourers, such as most of these men were. The gang on the gallows had connections with the youthful 'Edelweiss pirates', who had become notorious for their attacks on members of the Hitler Youth and other agencies of the regime.

a large number of former resisters were taken out of prison in Berlin by the SS and shot in the open.[154] In the final stages of the war the processes of summary and public execution which had become customary in the camps began to be extended to the population in Germany as a whole. The barriers so carefully erected between the public sphere of the master-race and the public spheres of the 'subhuman' slave labourers and camp inmates began to break down under the stress of continued and catastrophic defeat. Germany's cities were in ruins and still subject to almost continuous bombing raids; the Allies were advancing into Germany from east and west; living conditions were becoming extremely difficult; and people were growing desperate. The situation of the seven million foreign labourers working in Germany was particularly problematical. Under

---

[154] Siegert, 'Konzentrationslager Flossenbürg', 479–80; Hoffmann, *History*, 528–32. There is no evidence that the hangings in Flossenbürg were carried out with any greater cruelty than was usual in such cases (ibid. 721 n. 42).

guard, kept on meagre rations, isolated from the German population, and engaged in the dirtiest, most difficult, and most dangerous tasks in the bombed-out cities, the foreign workers increasingly began to take matters into their own hands when they could. Not a few Germans followed them. As law and order began to break down, organized black marketeering and theft started to spread in Germany's major cities. Frequently the gangs were armed; some of them had loose relationships with youth resistance gangs such as the famous 'Edelweiss Pirates' in Cologne.

The Nazis reacted to these developments, which were to reach their height in the chaos which ensued during the early post-war months, with an intensification of terror. In the process, the system of summary execution practised against Poles and other minorities, above all in occupied Eastern Europe, and by the SS against refractory prisoners in the concentration camps, began to be applied to the German population at large. On 25 October 1944 eleven foreign slave labourers were publicly hanged in Cologne at three in the afternoon before a substantial crowd of onlookers. They were said to have committed a series of robberies and to have engaged in armed resistance to the police when found out. Not long afterwards, on 10 November, thirteen Germans were publicly hanged on the same spot for their part, or in some cases alleged part, in the illegal activities of the Steinbrück group, a gang of mostly young, armed thieves who had been operating in the city. The order for these public executions was personally issued by Ernst Kaltenbrunner, head of Himmler's Security Service, and the hangings were carried out by Gestapo officers.[155] Such actions became frequent in the last months of the war. On 15 February 1945 they were legitimated by a decree from Hitler, who ordered summary judicial tribunals to be set up in areas threatened by the Allied invasions, with the power to sentence anyone to death who 'attempts to evade his obligations to the generality, and in particular anyone who does this from cowardice or selfishness'. These were civil, not military courts, and each consisted of a criminal court judge in the chair, a Nazi Party official, and an army, Waffen-SS, or police officer. Executions were to follow immediately, and in public. Such courts passed sentence in a number of German towns near the front line, and increasingly as a result offenders of all kinds were summarily hanged in the streets.[156]

The Third Reich was coming to an end in an orgy of destruction. In Stuttgart the red posters put up on 20 October 1944 proclaiming the creation of the *Volkssturm*, the makeshift home defence army which all adult males from 16 to 60 were supposed to join, reminded people of the red placards used to announce

[155] Bernd-A. Rusinek, *Gesellschaft in der Katastrophe. Terror, Illegalität, Widerstand—Köln 1944/45* (Essen, 1989).

[156] Engelhard (ed.), *Im Namen*, 311.

FIG. 41. *Public hanging in the last days of the Third Reich*. By this time, the policy had been extended to ethnic Germans who were thought to be failing in their duty to resist to the last. The sign around the neck of the two offenders reads: 'I've done a deal with the Bolsheviks'.

executions: 'It's announcing an execution too,' people said, 'namely the execution of the whole German people.'[157] The German people, said Hitler, had proved unworthy of him. They did not deserve to survive.[158] Such a conclusion was the logical end of a penal policy which had increasingly been based on political criteria. Where someone who stole a piece of clothing from a bombed-out building, or a chicken from his neighbour's garden, was not considered worthy of life, what hope was there for the individual who tried to bring the senseless slaughter to an end by surrendering to the Allies instead of fighting on? The judicial and police apparatus of the Third Reich continued to consign people to the gallows right to the end, and in a few cases even beyond it. But any pretence of legal normality had long since disappeared. The continual self-radicalization of the Nazi system had turned to self-destruction. As the Allies marched into Germany's heartland, Hitler, Goebbels, and Himmler killed themselves in a final act of defiance and despair. The ruins which confronted the occupying forces after the surrender were not merely physical. Justice had been trampled on and ground into dust as well. How to reconstruct it was one of the severest challenges facing the Allies as they prepared to take over Germany's government at the end of the war.

[157] Roland Müller, *Stuttgart zur Zeit des Nationalsozialismus* (Stuttgart, 1988), 519.
[158] H. R. Trevor-Roper, *The Last Days of Hitler* (London, 1947; rev. edn., 1972), 96.

Part VI

17

Legacies of Terror

a. Capital Punishment and the Occupying Powers 1945–1951

The four countries whose armies occupied the defeated German Reich in 1945 were all firm adherents of the death penalty. Executions for treason, mutiny, and other military offences were commonplace in Britain, France, the United States, and the Soviet Union during the war. Britain still hanged people for murder; France had only stopped guillotining them in public in 1939; the United States made liberal use of the rope, the gas chamber, and the electric chair; while the Soviet Union had been killing its own citizens in staggering numbers ever since the Revolution of 1917. The movement for the abolition of capital punishment had made little political headway in these countries. To be sure, the excessive use of executions by the German judicial system under the Nazis met with the strong disapproval of the occupying powers; but the justice of which they considered this to be a perversion was emphatically a justice that included the death sentence. 'H[is] M[ajesty's] G[overnment]', wrote Lord Simon, Lord Chancellor in Winston Churchill's wartime cabinet in Britain, on 16 April 1945, shortly before the death of the Axis dictators,

assume that it is beyond question that Hitler and a number of arch-criminals associated with him (including Mussolini) must, so far as they fall into Allied hands, suffer the penalty of death for their conduct leading up to the war and for the wickedness which they have either themselves perpetrated or have authorised in the conduct of the war. It would be manifestly impossible to punish war criminals of a lower grade by a capital sentence pronounced by a Military Court unless the ringleaders are dealt with with equal severity.[1]

As Simon hinted, in preparing for their occupation of Germany, the British and their Allies realized that military courts would be sentencing German soldiers to death for offences such as shooting prisoners of war. As the full scale of Nazi

---

[1] Bradley F. Smith (ed.), *The American Road to Nuremberg: The Documentary Record 1944–1945* (Stanford, Calif., 1982), 155–6, doc. 48.

criminality became clear to them, they also realized that it would be necessary to try Germans for other serious offences as well, ranging from the mass murder of civilians by the SS death squads and concentration camp officers and guards, to the 'euthanasia' campaign of extermination against the handicapped and the judicial abuse of the death penalty itself. Allied nervousness about the possibility of a German resistance movement added a strongly political element to the military's call for capital punishment. All this implied to the civil and military authorities, and not only in Britain, the use of capital punishment for war crimes at every level.

The Allies rejected the idea of summary military executions. The only adequate way to deal with war criminals, they thought, was by full legal trials. No one seriously doubted that these would end in a large number of death sentences.[2] Even if the death penalty were to be abolished in Britain as a result of pressure exerted by abolitionists on the new Labour government elected after the end of the war in 1945, the British military authorities, in commenting on the matter two years later, still took the view that

general circumstances and conditions are so different in this country from those now prevailing in Germany that there would seem to be no valid argument for the British Government to exercise such powers as it possesses to secure the abolition of the death penalty in the British Zone of Germany. Apart from the general argument that drastic, severe steps may be essential to preserve the safety and stability of Military Government, it should also be borne in mind [that] the German prisons are in a bad state of repair, are overcrowded, and are staffed by officials who cannot yet be regarded as fully trained or efficient, and it is not unusual for thirty or forty cases of prison breach to occur in any month. Even a small unnecessary increase in the prison population will occasion difficulties,—especially if it be an increase of persons of whose custody particular supervision may be required. At the present time there may be an average of ten to twenty executions a month. As these executions are in respect of offences, seriously prejudicial to law and order in the zone, or in respect of abominable war crimes, Military Government may be expected to react strongly against any proposal to abolish the death penalty in the zone.[3]

Thus the British occupying forces found themselves repeating some of the arguments which the Nazis had used to justify their extension of the death penalty in 1943–4: executions would reduce overcrowding in the prisons, and dangerous offenders had to be done away with expeditiously because of the danger of escape. A vote to abolish the death penalty did in fact pass the House of Commons in April 1948, and its imminence undoubtedly made the military authorities in Germany nervous earlier in the year. In February 1948 the Director of the Penal Branch of the Legal Division of the British Control Commission noted:

[2] Smith (ed.), *American Road,* 164, 167, 186, 198, 207, 220.
[3] PRO/FO 937/156: Germany—Death Penalty, memo of 7 Dec. 1947, 2.

There is a strong possibility that before long a great deal of attention is likely to be focused on our executions at Hameln, both from the Home press and from German sources as well . . . and there is no doubt that what were once quiet little affairs at Hameln are likely to be linked up in big way with very high policy and much criticism.

He therefore ordered that much closer attention be paid to executions, and that he be kept much better informed about them than before. 'Under no circumstances', he thundered, 'will anyone be executed regarding whom there is any possible doubt or for whom a stay of execution has been issued.'[4] But such precautions were unnecessary in the end. The hereditary House of Lords at Westminster, bastion of conservatism in such matters, overturned the vote passed against the death penalty in the lower chamber, and capital punishment remained on the statute book for the time being.[5]

The first task which the occupation authorities set themselves was the trial of the major war criminals, held at Nuremberg before a panel of judges drawn from all four victorious powers from the autumn of 1945 until the autumn of 1946. After the suicide of Hitler, Goebbels, and Himmler at the end of the war, the principal defendants included Hermann Göring, Alfred Rosenberg, Ernst Kaltenbrunner, and Martin Bormann (who was tried *in absentia* but was in fact dead). The trial was held amid massive publicity and heard a vast quantity of evidence from captured German documents, along with testimony from numerous witnesses, of crimes against peace, crimes against humanity, and violations of the rules of war. It was as much a means of public education in Germany as an instrument of justice in the world community. In the end, most of the principal defendants were sentenced to death, while long prison sentences were passed on Rudolf Hess, Albert Speer, and five others. Three were acquitted, including Franz von Papen, the conservative politician who had done so much to put Hitler in power in 1933.[6] This trial was followed by others. At the end of the 'doctors' trial', held before an American military tribunal between 24 October 1946 and 20 August 1947, seven death sentences were passed for a variety of crimes, including the killing of concentration camp inmates in the course of medical experimentation. The seven condemned men included two of the leading figures of the 'euthanasia' campaign, Viktor Brack and Karl Brandt, who were executed in 1948.[7] Prior to this trial, three others had also been hanged at Bruchsal on 14 March 1946 for their part in the campaign.[8] The trial of concentration camp officers, held during 1947, resulted in one execution, while the case of the SS death

[4] PRO/FO 1060/244: Confidential Draft from the Director, Penal Branch, to Mr. J. C. Piegrome, 27 Feb. 1948. Subject: Executions.

[5] Düsing, *Abschaffung*, 227.

[6] See Telford Taylor, *The Anatomy of the Nuremberg Trials: A Personal Memoir* (London, 1993), and Bradley F. Smith, *Reaching Judgment at Nuremberg* (London, 1977).

[7] Norman E. Tutorow, *War Crimes, War Criminals, and War Crimes Trials: An Annotated Bibliography and Source Book* (Westport, Conn., 1986), 464–5, 469.

[8] Burleigh, *Death and Deliverance*, 270–3.

squads, whose members had shot hundreds of thousands of Jews in occupied
Eastern Europe, led to four executions out of thirteen death sentences passed.[9]
And these sentences were only the tip of an iceberg. Many more offenders from
the Nazi regime were executed as a result of smaller, individual trials. The
Americans were particularly hard on German soldiers and SS men who had killed
American prisoners of war or shot American airmen who had baled out of their
damaged aircraft during hostilities.[10] Altogether 5,133 people were prosecuted for
war crimes in the three western zones, of whom 668 were condemned to death.[11]
The Americans were reckoned to have executed 444 war criminals in their zone
altogether.[12] This was capital punishment on a considerable scale.

Not all those sentenced to death were executed, of course. The Allies instituted
a clemency process which took a good deal of time and effort to work through,
unlike the perfunctory procedures of the Nazis, and opened them up to pressures
of various kinds from individuals and organizations anxious to secure reprieves.
As war criminals accumulated on the death rows of the main prisons used by the
Allies to house them, their presence began to cause problems to the Allied
military administration. American officials reported that the Landsberg prison,
taken over by the US army in October 1946, at one time or another housed some
300 war criminals who had been condemned to death.

Approximately 30 percent of these prisoners were convicted by U.S. Army courts for the
murder or mistreatment of prisoners of war, 60 percent were tried by these courts for
concentration camp and other mass atrocities, and 10 percent were sentenced by the
special tribunals at Nuernberg [*sic*] for such crimes as conspiracy to wage aggressive war
and spoliation and looting of occupied areas, in addition to mass atrocity offenses.[13]

By 24 May 1948, the situation had become very difficult indeed, and the US
commander in Germany, General Lucius D. Clay, noted:

As a result of delays in review, stay of sentence pending possible appeal to the Supreme
Court, et cetera, the death sentences imposed by military courts on Germans charged
with the murder of concentration camp inmates, prisoners of war, et cetera, has accumulated until there are now in excess of five hundred awaiting execution. If and when the
status of appeals to the Supreme Court is finally determined, we will then be confronted
with this mass execution. . . . I find it difficult to adjust my own mental processes to
requiring what looks to be almost a mass execution of more than five hundred persons.
I believe it also gives an appearance of cruelty to the United States even though there is

[9] Tutorow, *War Crimes*, 471–4.
[10] NA Washington 260/C7/D3/7/53/34/7/b.91–6.
[11] Martin Broszat, 'Siegerjustiz oder strafrechtliche "Selbstreinigung"? Aspekte der Vergangenheitsbewältigung der deutschen Justiz während der Besatzungszeit 1945–1949', *Vierteljahreshefte für Zeitgeschichte*, 29 (1981), 477–544.
[12] Glenzdorf and Treichel, *Henker*, 138.
[13] NA Washington 260/D5/7/53/36/2–3/b.138: History of the Administration of German Prisons under
U.S. Military Government, 10 (typescript, undated).

no question in my mind that the crimes committed fully justify the death sentence. Moreover, more than three years have elapsed since these crimes were committed.

Clay therefore proposed that these sentences be commuted to life imprisonment 'in substantial measure'.[14] In fact, Clay's number of five hundred turned out to be an overestimate, but his memo indicated the scale of the problem in the eyes of the American Military Government. Reprieves were duly issued in a number of cases. But many were executed all the same.[15] Clay's reaction when the Pope requested clemency for all the German war criminals without exception was hostile.[16] Capital punishment continued to be used with little doubt or hesitation by the occupying authorities on war criminals right up to the end of the 1940s and even beyond.

War criminals were only the most publicized group of capital offenders in occupied Germany. For apart from laying down the death penalty for war crimes and crimes against humanity, the Allies also prescribed it for a wide range of offences relating to the occupation itself. These included acting in contravention of the terms of surrender imposed by the Allies, falsely pretending to be a member of the Allied armed forces, falsely wearing a uniform of a member of the same, furthering the escape of anyone arrested by the same, assisting any member of the enemy forces to avoid capture, interfering with or concealing the archives of the defeated regime, and wilfully misleading the Allied forces, stealing from them, or deliberately interfering with them in the pursuit of their duty. Attempts to revive the Nazi movement by publishing or circulating printed matter in support of it were also made punishable by death. These draconian provisions were issued at a time when the war was still barely over, and there were widespread fears that fanatical Nazis would try to continue the fight using terrorist or guerrilla tactics in the 'Werewolf' organization and similar secret armed bands. In the early months of the occupation, the nervous British authorities applied the death penalty for these activities, even where there was no obvious political connection. One such case was that of Wilfried H., who at the age of 13 had lost his family in the bombing of Dresden, and had then wandered around on his own, earning money from odd jobs, then gradually becoming involved in the flourishing black market. Obtaining a set of false papers under the occupation, he had emigrated to the USA but he had been caught after three months and sent back to Germany to serve a twelve-month prison sentence for his offence. Three months later he had escaped, and thenceforth lived rough and kept himself alive from a life of crime. Caught stealing an American jeep, he was arrested and tried, but when the guard taking him to prison fell asleep in the back of the car, the boy

[14] Jean Edward Smith (ed.), *The Papers of General Lucius D. Clay: Germany 1945–1949* (Bloomington, Ind., 1974), 658–9.

[15] Ibid. 661.   [16] Ibid. 962.

rifled his bag, found a loaded pistol, shot both guard and driver, and escaped. He did not remain at large for long. Shooting members of the occupying forces was always regarded with the utmost seriousness by the military courts. Arrested again at the end of 1948, Wilfried H. was found guilty and sentenced to death in Munich. He was just 17 years of age.

Petitions for clemency from church organizations urged Wilfried H.'s reprieve upon the American military authorities. In the milder climate of the time, it is probable that they were acceded to.[17] For by 1948–9, fears of Nazi resistance had subsided. Earlier on, the Allied judicial authorities had been far more inclined to see a political connection in cases of this kind. Heinz D., from Minden, for example, was sentenced to death in May 1946 for resisting the occupation through his membership of the Edelweiss Pirates. The British military authorities thought this group was steered by ex-Nazis and aimed 'to rob and beat up DPs particularly Poles', to 'victimise German women who fraternise with Allied troops and DPs' and 'to combat the "Black Market"'. It was only because the execution of one of its members would 'tend to glorify the institution in the eyes of hysterically inclined young Germans and to risk raising an unimportant youth to the status of a martyr—another Horst Wessel perhaps' that Heinz D.'s sentence was commuted to ten years' imprisonment.[18] This political interpretation of what was essentially another criminal band was wide of the mark. Not all such cases ended in commutation. A 20-year-old German, Walter K., was condemned to death on 6 October 1947 for a murder committed when he was only 19, during one of a series of armed robberies which he had carried out in the Ruhr. The Chief Judge for the British Control Commission Supreme Court refused a petition for clemency from his father, commenting:

> The Father attributes his son's criminality to Nazi conditions and the evil influence of others. . . . It is tragically true that the morals of many young Germans have been warped by circumstances of their environment; but that is true of the great majority of criminals at all times and in all countries. Their victims and potential victims are even more entitled to consideration than such young savages are, and the sternest deterrents are unfortunately necessary to discourage crimes of this type.[19]

This was not a 'political' crime but, like the others, it did illustrate the use which the Allied occupying powers in Germany made of the death penalty in their efforts to restore order to the shattered country.

The death penalty was also used against people found to be in unlawful possession of firearms. In deciding on clemency for such offenders, the British

[17] NA Washington 260/D5/7/53/36/4/b.77: Petition of the Catholic Youth of Radolfzell, 15 Feb. 1949, and Bockmann to Kollender, 16 Feb. 1949.

[18] PRO/FO 1060/938: Legal Division Report to the Commander-in-Chief upon the Proceedings of a Military Government Court, 16 May 1946.

[19] Ibid. 941: Chief Judge to Military Governor and Commander-in Chief, 8 Nov. 1947.

military authorities were instructed to grant a reprieve on grounds of 'extreme youth' or 'advanced age'. Possession of weapons which were obviously intended for hunting game, or which were in a state of neglect, or were concealed in places difficult of access to the offender, was not regarded as deserving of death. On the other hand, confirmation of the death sentence was more likely if the weapons were found in the hands of people likely to use them against the Allied authorities. The Control Commission pointed out in addition

> that while those persons who have been found in possession of arms may not appear to be personally of a dangerous type or to be likely to use weapons themselves, they may become consenting parties to the use of them by others, either willingly or under duress, and that the place of concealment may well be known to others in the locality . . . [and] that a presumption of innocence cannot safely be drawn from mere protestations of anti-Nazi views in the absence of reliable evidence of consistent conduct or acts substantiating them, and that for this purpose the usual letters from the local Parson and other Worthies are not in the ordinary way sufficient.[20]

Here too, in August 1945, there were clear worries about the possibility of a Nazi resistance movement. Nevertheless, the spectre of the 'Werewolf' failed to materialize. Nothing was more eloquent of the German people's feeling that they had been liberated as much as defeated than the failure of any resistance movement to emerge, contesting foreign occupation on the model of the French, Greek, and other resistance movements under German occupation during the war. Public opinion in the Allied countries soon recognized this fact.

When 23-year-old Karl Krille, who had been denounced for showing a picture of Hitler in the window of his home near Hanover, accompanied by 'four verses of an inflammatory poem', was sentenced to death on 4 July 1946 for advocating the restarting of the Nazi Party, there was an angry leader in the *Manchester Guardian*, and questions were asked in the House of Commons by abolitionist MPs such as Sydney Silverman. Under the pressure from the media and political opinion, Krille was eventually reprieved.[21] Even such trivial incidents as this were relatively isolated. Since fears of a widespread survival, or resurgence, of Nazism, and of general resistance to the occupation, proved to be groundless, the American Military Government agreed that many of these provisions were 'obsolete' and 'emphasized security to a degree now unnecessary'. Three years into the occupation, Germany had become 'a more normal society in which all police agencies are working together more or less satisfactorily in matters of law enforcement'.[22] In July 1948, therefore, most of these offences were made non-capital,

[20] Ibid. 940: Legal Division 'Notes on Review of Death Sentences in Arms Cases', 11 Aug. 1945.
[21] Ibid. 938/76: memo of 26 July 1946, Hansard, 1 Aug. 1946, *Manchester Guardian*, 2 Aug. 1946, and *Daily Graphic*, 8 Aug. 1946.
[22] NA Washington 260/D5/7/53/36/4/b.79: Schopler memo, 'MG Legislation Now Subject to Amendment or Repeal', 17 Feb. 1948, and Kraus to Rintels, 12 Apr. 1948.

though the death penalty could still be handed down by military courts for espionage, armed attack on or murder of members of the occupation forces, or sabotage of their installation, unauthorized possession of arms, ammunition or explosives, rioting or incitement, or 'communication of information which may be dangerous to the security or property of the occupation forces, or unauthorized possession of such information without properly reporting it, or unauthorized communication by code or cipher'.[23] This accentuation of offences such as writing in code, espionage, or communicating dangerous information, was directed not against ex-Nazis or fanatical opponents of the occupation, but against the Russians and their spreading spy network, for by this time relations between the Western Allies and the Soviets had plunged into the muted hostilities of the Cold War.

Allied military courts also applied the death penalty to ordinary criminal offences which did not involve resistance to the occupying forces, but had been committed by non-Germans, other than members of the occupying forces, against Germans and other civilians living under the occupation. Such offences were far from negligible in nature or extent. Violent crime was rife. Well before the final collapse of the Third Reich, as we saw in Chapter 16, the mounting chaos of Germany's bombed-out cities, the open terrorism of the regime, the growing desperation of Germany's inhabitants, and the dire situation of seven to eight million foreign forced labourers working in terrible conditions on German soil had led to an increase in black marketeering, petty theft, casual looting from ruined buildings, and the emergence of large-scale gangs and criminal or semi-criminal networks in the larger urban centres. With the end of the war, these problems were compounded by the arrival of millions of ethnic Germans fleeing from the Red Army or expelled from the countries it had liberated, and the freeing of hundreds of thousands of starving prisoners from the vast network of concentration camps and their satellites run by the SS as part of its huge economic empire. The collapse of war industries led to mass unemployment. Food supplies were difficult to maintain in Germany's ravaged landscape. Sickness, malnutrition, and disease were rife. In this situation people lived from hand to mouth. A crime wave of massive proportions was the result. Life had been cheapened by the war and above all by the murderous terror exerted by the Nazi regime; it could now be taken for a handful of ration cards or a couple of packets of cigarettes.[24]

---

[23] NA Washington 260/D5/7/53/3614/679.: MG Ordinance no. 1, Revised, Article I, 13 July 1948.
[24] K. S. Bader, *Soziologie der deutschen Nachkriegskriminalität* (Tübingen, 1949). See also Alan Kramer, '"Law-Abiding Germans"? Social Disintegration, Crime and the Reimposition of Order in Post-War Western Germany, 1945–9', in Evans (ed.), *The German Underworld*, 238–61.

Order took a while to restore. As late as 1947, there were still about a million displaced persons living in the Western zones of Germany. Most of them were confined to camps run by the Allies, but many managed to escape surveillance and live rough in the forests. In the confused situation of 1945 through into 1946, some of these formed gangs who engaged in criminal activities in the cities and roamed the countryside in search of food and booty. After years of cruel exploitation by the Germans and subjection to the injustice and lawlessness of the Nazis, many displaced persons considered that they had every right to get their own back, and saw nothing wrong in carrying arms now that they were on the winning side. Arrests, condemnations, and executions for such offences took place every week during the first two years of the occupation. In May 1946, for example, two Ukrainians were condemned for a series of armed raids on farms carried out late the previous year. On 17–18 July 1946 four Poles were executed by firing-squad in Hamburg after being sentenced by a British military court on 29 May for murder, armed robbery, and unlawful possession of firearms.[25] On 22 July 1946, a 22-year-old Polish displaced person, Franzizcek S., was sentenced to death in Munich, in the American zone, for shooting a miller in the course of a raid on his premises carried out together with six or seven companions, also Poles. The man's five years in a concentration camp were not allowed to count as a mitigating circumstance. 'The accused', commented Alvin J. Rockwell, Legal Adviser to the American Military Government, 'was mature enough to realize what he was doing.'[26] On 14 August the 20-year-old Pole Felix M., convicted by a British military court of taking part in a series of raids in which two Germans were killed and a number of others wounded, was also condemned to death. His plea for clemency was rejected. 'The accused is young', remarked the responsible official in the Legal Division of the British Control Commission, 'and, like a large number of his countrymen, has suffered from unfortunate experiences and lack of proper upbringing. I do not consider', he added, 'that these facts are, however, sufficient to justify a reprieve.'[27]

In another, similar case, a 26-year-old Pole was condemned to death by an American military court on 20–21 November 1946 for his part in a raid on a farm near Schwäbisch Hall, in which the farmer had been killed and the accused and his four companions had made off with most of his movable possessions. The Pole admitted other, similar offences. The responsible American officer noted: 'It

[25] PRO/FO 1060/239, 221: Penal Hamburg to Concomb, Unclassified Message, 18 July 1946; ibid. 220: Penal Hamburg to Concomb, 17 July 1946.

[26] NA Washington 260/C7/D5/7/53/36/4/b.150: Rockwell to Deputy Military Governor, OMGUS, n.d. [Feb. 1947].

[27] PRO/FO 1060/939: Legal Division Report to the Commander-in-Chief upon the Proceedings of a Military Government Court, 25 Sept. 1946.

has been the practice of Military Government to sentence to death any participants in gang attacks which had been planned as armed robberies in the course of which, as a result of one factor or another, weapons were used and somebody was killed.'[28] Such attacks were extremely common in the eighteen months following the end of the war. In the British zone, they sometimes attracted the death penalty even when nobody had been killed. In the reviews of the cases carried out by the Legal Division of the British Control Commission and forwarded to the Commander-in-Chief for ratification, clemency was seldom recommended. Only where the evidence was in any doubt, or where there were clear mitigating circumstances, were the condemned allowed a reprieve,[29] as when, in one case of robbery with violence brought before a military court in October 1946, 'the violence was not continued to the extent to which raiding Poles so often press it'.[30] Executions of Polish and other displaced persons had thus become commonplace within a few months of the end of the war. 'Polish Displaced Persons are a menace to public order at the moment', noted the Director of the British Military Government Courts Branch, Charles Gerahty, on 14 September 1945. At this point, they were still given some consideration in view of the fact that Poles were technically 'of Allied nationality'.[31] But this was not to last for long. As the real or imagined danger of German revanchism faded, so the threat from Polish gangs and individuals took on more prominence in the minds of the occupying authorities. On 3 December 1946 the Military Governor of the British zone, Air Marshal Sir Sholto Douglas, complained that 'we are having as you know a tremendous lot of trouble with Polish DPs, who are still indulging in the murder of Germans on quite a large scale. The only way we can put a stop to these murders', he considered, 'is by imposing the maximum penalty, namely the death sentence.' This was inevitably causing problems with the Polish government. But Douglas thought that 'the deterrent will be less effective if the Poles feel that they may escape the death penalty by appealing to the Polish Political Mission'. This was dangerous because 'the Polish Mission might object to a death sentence on a Polish D.P. of their own persuasion, but would probably view with equanimity, or even with sardonic pleasure, the death sentence on a Pole who was not of their political persuasion'. By this time, of course, the government of Poland was under strong Communist influence, a fact clearly at the forefront of Douglas's mind. 'In my view', he concluded, 'the only

---

[28] NA Washington 260/C7/D5/7/53/36/4/b.150: Rockwell to Deputy Military Governor, OMGUS, n.d.

[29] For other examples, see PRO/FO 1060/938 and 939, *passim*.

[30] PRO/FO 1060/939: Legal Division Report to the Commander-in-Chief upon the Proceedings of a Military Government Court, 8 Oct. 1946.

[31] Ibid. 934: Report of the Commander-in-Chief upon the Proceedings of a Military Government Court, 14 Sept. 1945.

possible course is to carry out the law, in the case of crimes committed in the British zone, regardless of the nationality or political views of the offender.'[32] This was particularly necessary in view of the fact that the principal motives of most Poles in committing the crimes for which they had been sentenced to death were 'loot and robbery, in fact general criminal lawlessness in which there are no political motives. In the earlier days of the occupation', he added, 'revenge was a common motive, but such cases are now comparatively rare.'[33]

Douglas's policy of using capital punishment as a deterrent did not stop the depredations of displaced Poles. The President of the General Military Court of Düsseldorf commented in April 1946 that 'in the early days pistols were usually carried but rarely fired, but more recently there has been a far greater readiness to shoot'. Theft was 'no longer a sport but a business run by professional criminals'. Many of these were Poles, he said, and the use of the death penalty as a deterrent was suggested by the fact that 'Poles, as opposed to Germans, do not seem the least impressed by long sentences; they are quite sure that they will either escape or be let out soon'.[34] Another armed band of Poles was active near Göttingen as late as 1947; one of them was executed for murder, but two others escaped from prison.[35] The lists of executions carried out in the British zone in the immediate post-war years are full of Poles, Yugoslavs, and Russians, most of them in their early twenties.[36] Thus many of the offenders executed under the Allied occupation, in the Western zones at least, continued to be drawn from the same non-German national groups that had borne the brunt of capital punishment under the Nazis during the war. Here was another continuity across the period from 1942 to 1948, a continuity of plunder, as former slave labourers became displaced persons, self-help under the Third Reich turned into armed robbery under the Allies, and the death penalty was liberally used by the authorities in both cases. These ironies were not lost on some contemporaries. The American Slav Congress, for example, declared the death sentences imposed on four former Polish slave labourers in Germany in a trial held before a British military court in Paderborn in the autumn of 1945 'profoundly shocking to millions of Slavic Americans. While German war criminals as Goering and von Runstedt feast on Allied food with no action yet to punish them, their victims, our allies, are being tried and given such astounding sentences.'[37] The four men

---

[32] Ibid. 945/320, 3a: Douglas to Sir Gilmour Jenkins, 3 Dec. 1946.

[33] Ibid. 13b: Douglas to Jenkins, 21 Jan. 1947.

[34] Ibid. 1060/937, 86a: Chief, Legal Division, to HQ Mil. Gov., North Rhine Division, 18 Apr. 1946 Review of Death Sentence, Mieczislaw B.

[35] Ibid. 241, 85: Leyk to Barnes, 24 Nov. 1947.

[36] See ibid.: weekly lists of condemned prisoners.

[37] Ibid. 22d: George Pirinski, Executive Secretary, American Slav Congress, to Attlee (telegram, copy), n.d. [Oct. 1945]; capitalization removed and punctuation supplied.

in question had been identified as members of an armed gang of forty-eight Poles who had attacked the village of Fürstenau on 29 July 1945, burning down seven buildings and killing seven Germans in reprisal for the killing of a Pole in a brawl there a few nights before.[38] Their defence lawyer, a Polish officer, had noted that these young men had been forced labourers brought to Germany against their will. 'Some of them were still children and had been nourished with the whip.' As possible motives for their actions, he pointed out that the 'Polish Nation always has been the victim of persecution', and reminded the court that 'Hitler and Himmler were worthy successors to Bismark [*sic*]'. 'Anyone who has lived under the Nazi Regime', he said, 'cannot forget his grievances', and there was indeed not a single Pole who had not suffered at their hands. Was it 'any wonder that the Poles hate the Germans?'[39]

After a good deal of controversy, the death sentences in question were eventually commuted.[40] But actual cases of revenge by Poles on Germans who had maltreated them during the war were comparatively rare.[41] In another case, the petition for clemency, on behalf of a 23-year-old Russian Ukrainian sentenced to death in January 1948 for a series of break-ins during which one of his victims was mortally wounded, emphasized his upbringing as a slave labourer and the miserable circumstances under which he had lived. The British authorities were unmoved. The Chief Judge of the British Control Commission Supreme Court wrote:

The petition is a plea for mercy based upon the unfortunate history of the convicted man, the kind of history which is more or less common to most of these young Polish Displaced Persons who commit violent offences in the British Zone. Unfortunate though these histories are, those who have been influenced by them so frequently commit such brutal and senseless crimes that only the severest sentences can be effective in reducing the incidence of these offences and, possibly, saving other lives. I saw D. in the Dock during the hearing of his appeal, and the impression that he made on me and on my colleagues on the Bench is that he is a rather low type of humanity unlikely to be of value to any respectable community at any time.[42]

A verdict such as this, with its mixture of racial and social prejudice, was all too reminiscent of the judgments reached in similar circumstances by the Nazi authorities just a few years before.

[38] PRO/FO 22d.: Report to the Chief of Staff [British Zone] upon the Proceedings of a Military Government Court, Oct. 1945.

[39] Ibid. 3b: Howard to Comd 307 (P) Mil. Gov. Det., 12 Sept. 1945: Paderborn Summary Case no. 71.

[40] Ibid. 17a: secret cipher message, 9 Oct. 1945.

[41] For one such, see PRO/FO 1060/940: Office of the Supreme Court, Legal Division, to Chief Legal Officer, HQ Military Government, Land Niedersachsen, 12 Feb. 1947: Review of Death Sentence, Mieczislaw S.

[42] Ibid. 941: Chief Judge, Control Commission Supreme Court, to Military Governor, Commander-in-Chief, 26 Feb. 1948.

There was in the end little real comparison between the two situations. The Nazis, after all, had regarded all Poles, not just convicted Polish murderers, as belonging to a 'low type of humanity', and had executed them in such numbers that capital punishment, as we have seen, merged into racial extermination. Racial prejudice, however, undoubtedly was present in the treatment of Polish displaced persons by the Allied authorities, and indeed by the Germans themselves. Superficially, it seemed to all of them that post-war Germany was a violent and dangerous place, and that much of the danger and violence was the fault of the DPs. From 1 May to 15 November 1945, the American occupation authorities in the small north German enclave of Bremen recorded 23 cases of murder or manslaughter, 268 cases of armed robbery (45 of them resulting in the death of the victim), 319 cases of breaking and entering, and 582 cases of livestock theft (half of them of rabbits and chickens), committed by offenders among the 100,000 or so mostly Polish displaced persons under their jurisdiction. Yet this testified more to the general circumstances of the time than to any particular criminal propensity of the former slave labourers, since the crime rates per 100,000 of the German inhabitants of the area for the same offences were almost identical.[43] The flourishing black market of the period, while involving an especially high proportion of displaced persons, still depended heavily on the collaboration of the Germans for its successful functioning. However, German public opinion, backed by German politicians and administrators, regarded violent crime as mainly the work of the Poles and others, who, it was frequently (and without any justification at all) alleged, had been supplied to the Nazi regime as slave workers from the criminal population of their native lands. Hostility between Germans and Poles, a deep-seated historical phenomenon, hardly seemed to have diminished at all after the war.

German views of Polish criminality were to some extent shared by the Allies and reflected in the statistics of violent crime. In August 1945 145 out of 520 offenders tried for murder, possession of firearms, and robbery in the British zone were Poles: in September, 259 out of 576; in October, 221 out of 396.[44] These represented proportions of 28 per cent, 45 per cent, and 56 per cent. In the course of 1945, therefore, Polish involvement in violent crime seemed to be on the increase. This was reflected in the figures for death sentences in this early post-war period. From July to December 1945, 56 Germans and 67 Poles (52% of the total) were sentenced to death. From January to June the figures were 35 Germans and 73 Poles (65%). In the second half of the same year, 33 Germans were

[43] Wolfgang Jacobmeyer, *Vom Zwangsarbeiter zum Heimatlosen Ausländer. Die Displaced Persons in Westdeutschland 1945–1951* (Göttingen, 1985), 46–50.

[44] PRO/FO 1060/396: Deputy Director, Military Government Courts Branch, to Chief, Legal Division: Subject: Death Sentences on Polish Nationals, 28 Nov. 1945.

condemned, and 57 Poles (61%). A sharp decline set in after this. In January–June 1947, 9 Germans and 17 Poles (59%) were sentenced to death, and in the second half of the same year, 7 Germans and 21 Poles (48%). In the first period, 49 death sentences were confirmed and 69 commuted; in the second, the figures were 65 and 41; in the third, 51 and 35; in the fourth, 24 and 2; in the fifth, 29 and 6.[45] Only as the DPs were repatriated did the German public in the Western zones gradually begin to scale down their demands for tough measures and recognize that they had a responsibility towards the former slaves of a regime which they themselves had supported for so long.[46] The proportion of non-Germans among those arrested for murder and attempted murder in the British zone declined from 36.6 per cent in the first quarter of 1947 and 32.7 per cent in the second quarter, to 26.1 per cent in the third and 11. 8 per cent in the fourth. A slight rise followed in 1948, with the figures at 18.3 per cent in the first quarter and 31.9 per cent in the second, before falling again to 13.4 per cent in the third, 19.9 per cent in the fourth, with 18.9 per cent in the first quarter of 1949 and 13.1 per cent in the second.[47]

These figures, particularly at the beginning of the period covered, may well have reflected policing priorities and court decisions as much as, or more than, the realities of the involvement of displaced persons in violent crime. It was not even the case that homicide rates were historically high at this time. While the number of deaths from murder and manslaughter in the area of Germany covered by the post-war British zone of occupation rose from 1.0 per 100,000 population in 1938 to 3.0 in 1946, for example, it fell again to 1.8 in 1947 and 1.1 in 1948. These figures were well within the regular variation of the homicide rate in Prussia from 1886 to 1914, which fluctuated between 1.2 and 3.4 per 100,000 population, and were far below the homicide rate in the United States during the Vietnam War of the late 1960s and early 1970s, which reached no less than 9.3 per 100,000 in 1973.[48] Seen in this perspective, the Allies' obsession with the murderous propensities of displaced persons in the immediate post-war years seems exaggerated. All the same, executions for common offences other than war crimes made up a substantial proportion of the post-war numbers. On 31 July 1948 it was reported that there were thirty-three offenders condemned to death by US Military Government courts still awaiting execution.[49] By 18 December 1948

---

[45] PRO/FO 1060/936 and 941: Death Sentences passed by General Military Government Courts and Control Commission High Court. The missing figures were retrials or quashed convictions. The missing nationals were other nationals.

[46] Jacobmeyer, *Vom Zwangsarbeiter*, 210–18.

[47] Kramer, '"Law-Abiding Germans"?', 248.

[48] Ibid. 253; see also Dane Archer and Rosemary Gartner, 'Violent Acts and Violent Times: A Comparative Approach to Postwar Homicide Rates', *American Sociological Review*, 41 (1976), 937–63.

[49] NA Washington 260/C7/D2/51/b.47, 10, table VII.

some 122 Germans had been executed by Allied courts in the British zone since the establishment of the Allied Control Commission, of whom 47 had been sentenced by Military Government courts for offences committed during the occupation, and 75 by military courts for war crimes.[50] In January 1950, the British Control Commission reckoned that altogether 587 death sentences had been passed by military tribunals, Military Government courts, and Control Commission courts in its zone. Of these, 187 had been commuted, and 398 had been carried out. Two of these convicted capital offenders had been handed over to the authorities of the USSR.[51] Offenders executed by Military Government and Control Commission courts numbered 231, while 155 were reprieved; 166 had been executed by military tribunals, and 26 reprieved.[52]

The Military Government dealt with numerous appeals for clemency by offenders whom Allied courts had sentenced to death for war crimes, and granted them especially where—as in the case of Willi Seifert, condemned in the death-squads (*Einsatzgruppen*) trial in 1948, the case was pressed by the churches.[53] By early 1947, indeed, the churches were putting strong and repeated pressure on the military authorities to reprieve condemned war criminals. This could even involve unannounced visits to the prison authorities on the eve of execution by clerics such as Bishop Hans Lilje, who interceded for the war criminal Hans Körbel on 22 January 1947, claiming that fresh evidence had been discovered.[54] Lilje was joined by a Catholic colleague and a number of Christian Democrats and by local branches of the Communists and Social Democrats in the effort to save Körbel, and the military authorities reported that 'a series of glowing testimonials were submitted regarding the high moral character and integrity of Dr. Körbel signed on behalf of various political associations and religious bodies'. The British military authorities tried to take into account what they called the 'humanistic' aspect of the cases that came before them when reaching a decision on clemency.[55] They considered, however, that Körbel, a doctor, was reponsible for the death by starvation of numerous children in his charge, and proceeded with the execution, though after a slight delay.[56] Nevertheless, by 1948 the eagerness of the Western Allies to prosecute, condemn, and execute Nazi war criminals was diminishing. The new priorities of resisting Communism and fighting the Cold War were casting the crimes and criminals of the Third Reich

[50] PRO/FO 945/318: Parliamentary Question for Oral Answer on Wednesday, 18 Dec. 1946.
[51] Ibid. 1060/243, 114: Legal Adviser's Zonal Office, 30 Jan. 1950: Statistics—Death Sentences and Executions (and preceding correspondence with Bernhard Düsing).
[52] Ibid. 89: Legal Adviser's Zonal Office to Foreign Office German Internal Department, 17 Nov. 1949.
[53] NA Washington 260/C7/D2/51/b.51: Clay to Bishop Lilje, Clay to Bishop Wurm 12 Nov. 1948, and further correspondence.
[54] PRO/FO 1060/240, 65: Notes on Case of War Criminal Hans Körbel.
[55] Ibid. 940: Bishop to Commander-in-Chief, 14 Jan. 1947.
[56] Ibid. 240, 65: Notes on Case of War Criminal Hans Körbel, p. 63: Secret Cipher Message.

into a new light. The inhabitants of the Western zones of Germany had to be given responsibility for their own affairs and encouraged to stand up for 'Western' values against the threat from the East. In these circumstances, the Allies' military courts began to wind down their activities. The task of prosecuting German war criminals was gradually passed over to the Germans themselves, as was the administration of justice in general. By this time, the Allies felt confident that they had put in place a revived and reformed German legal system which would be adequate to this task. It was a legal system which, like those of the Allies themselves, had plenty of room for the continued operation of capital punishment.

b. *German Justice and the Restoration of the Death Penalty*

In hunting down the perpetrators of mass murder under the Nazi regime, the Allied courts did not neglect the legal officials and administrators who had presided over the Justice Ministry during the Third Reich. Hitler's first Reich Justice Minister, Franz Gürtner, had died in 1941; his eventual successor, the fanatical Nazi Otto-Georg Thierack, committed suicide while in British custody on 22 November 1946. The President of the Reich Supreme Court, Erwin Bumke, took his own life when he realized Germany was defeated. Roland Freisler, the most notorious of the judges in charge of the People's Court, had been killed in an air raid shortly before the end of the war. But fourteen other senior judicial figures survived to answer charges of crimes against humanity at the 'judges' trial' in Nuremberg. The most prominent of them was Franz Schlegelberger, State Secretary in the Reich Ministry of Justice from 1932 to 1942, and acting Justice Minister between the death of Gürtner and the appointment of his successor Thierack. Schlegelberger argued in his defence that he had been criticized and threatened with dismissal by Hitler and Himmler. If he had not stayed in post, someone worse would have replaced him. This in itself constituted an admission that the laws they were being asked to administer, as well as the political system under which they worked, were criminal and unjust. The Reich Ministry of Justice, declared the Nuremberg court, had effectively turned itself into an instrument of racial extermination and political terror in order to try and retain what little confidence it enjoyed among the Nazi leadership. In doing so, it had provided a cloak of pseudo-legality for acts of unparalleled criminality. Ten of the accused men were found guilty in the judges' trial on 3 and 4 December 1947. Schlegelberger himself was sentenced to life imprisonment, along with another leading bureaucrat, Herbert Klemm. Three more Ministry officials, Wilhelm von Ammon, Günther Joël, and Wolfgang Mettgenberg, were each sentenced to ten years, while the more junior Josef Alstötter was sentenced to five. Curt Rothenberger, who had left his post as President of the High Court

FIG. 42. *The judges' trial at Nuremberg.* The accused are: first row (left to right): Josef Altstötter, Wilhelm von Ammon, Paul Barnickel, Hermann Cuhorst, Karl Engert, Günther Joël, Herbert Klemm, Ernst Lautz; second row (left to right): Wolfgang Mettgenberg, Günther Nebelung, Rudolf Oeschey, Hans Petersen, Oswald Rothaug, Curt Rothenberger, Franz Schlegelberger. By the early 1950s nearly all of those convicted had been released, and one or two of them were able to resume their careers.

in Hamburg for the position of State Secretary in the Reich Justice Ministry in 1942, received seven years' imprisonment for his crimes. The judgment passed on these men at the Nuremberg trial concluded:

None of the accused is indicted on a charge of murdering or ill-treating any particular person. If this had been so, the indictment would doubtless have named the alleged victims. Common murder and individual cases of cruelty do not constitute the object of the accusation. The accused are charged with such immeasurable crimes that mere individual cases of criminal behaviour appear trivial in comparison. The charge, to put it briefly, is that of conscious participation in a system of cruelty and injustice organized by the government and spread across the whole country, in contravention of the laws of war and of humanity, a system established under the authority of the Ministry of Justice and with the aid of the courts. The murderer's dagger was concealed beneath the judge's robe.

No one but the most fanatical of Nazis could seriously doubt the accuracy of this judgment. Most admitted its justice. In strictly legal terms, the fact that the crimes of which the ten men found guilty at the judges' trial were convicted had not existed during the Third Reich, but had been created with retrospective effect by the Allied Control Commission after the war, breached the principle of *nulla poena sine lege*. Yet what was the alternative, when the law itself, as amended and applied under the Third Reich, had been so manifestly unjust by any normal standards of decency and humanity?[57]

Controversy about the legalities of the Nuremberg trials would continue for many years. Meanwhile, as relations between the Western occupying powers and the Soviet Union deteriorated, the process of denazification was wound down under the pressing need to provide the Western zones with trained and experienced German officials, and many leading Nazi criminals were released back into the community. Already the sentences passed in the judges' trial were more lenient than they might have been a couple of years earlier. All the convicted men were out of gaol by early 1951, apart from Mettgenberg, who had died the previous year, and Oswald Rothaug, who was not released until 1956.[58] Günther Joël was soon able to resume his career and in 1973 was even appointed state prosecutor in Hamm, in Westphalia.[59] When a zealous public prosecutor attempted to arraign Franz Schlegelberger in 1965–8 for his part in ordering the mass murder of the handicapped in 1941, along with nineteen other senior judges and prosecutors from the war years, the former acting Minister of Justice managed to block the prosecution at every stage, and it got nowhere.[60] Not one judge who sat on the Nazi People's Court was ever condemned for his crimes.[61] Many of the details of such cases were released by the Communist authorities in East Berlin, who wished to embarrass the West and demonstrate that the Federal Republic was still 'fascist' in all but name, and this in turn enabled the judiciary to counter-attack, condemning the accusations as nothing more than Communist propaganda.[62] Apart from these prominent figures, many hundreds of judicial servants of the former Nazi

[57] Engelhard (ed.), *Im Namen*, 267, 340–2.

[58] Ibid. 340. See also Jörg Friedrich, *Freispruch für die Nazi-Justiz. Die Urteile gegen NS-Richter seit 1948. Eine Dokumentation* (Reinbek, 1983); idem, *Die kalte Amnestie* (Frankfurt am Main, 1984); Michael Stolleis, 'Rechtsordnung und Justizpolitik 1945–1949', in Norbert Horn (ed.), *Europäisches Rechtsdenken in Geschichte und Gegenwart* (Munich, 1982), and Joachim Wenzlau, *Der Wiederaufbau der Justiz in Nordwestdeutschland 1945 bis 1949* (Königstein in Taunus, 1979).

[59] Angermund, *Richterschaft*, 160 n. 64.

[60] Engelhard (ed.), *Im Namen*, 415–16.

[61] Berhard Jahntz and Volker Kähne, *Der Volksgerichtshof. Darstellung der Ermittlungen der Staatsanwaltschaft bei dem Landegericht Berlin gegen ehemalige Richter und Staatsanwälte am Volksgerichtshof* (Berlin, 1986).

[62] Engelhard (ed.), *Im Namen*, 413–14. See also Bernhard Diestelkamp, 'Die Justiz nach 1945 und ihr Umgang mit der eigenen Vergangenheit', in idem and Michael Stolleis (eds.), *Justizalltag im Dritten Reich* (Frankfurt am Main, 1988), 131–50; Hans Wrobel, *Verurteilt zur Demokratie. Justiz und Justizpolitik in Deutschland 1945–1949* (Heidelberg, 1989); Ingo Müller, *Furchtbare Juristen. Die unbewältigte Vergangenheit unserer Justiz* (Munich, 1987); and Angermund, *Richterschaft*, 7–17.

regime also managed to take up their careers again after the brief hiatus of denazification.

These developments cast something of a pall over the judicial reforms which the Allies had initiated on taking over Germany in 1945. It was clear to them that the German courts would have to start functioning as soon as possible. The Allied forces were in no way equipped to deal with the vast mass of litigation and prosecution that is inevitable in any advanced industrial society. The first step they took was to clear away the detritus of Nazi legislation. Article IV, Paragraph 8, of 'Law Number 1' of the Allied Supreme Command in Germany, signed by the American General Dwight D. Eisenhower, declared the laws brought in by the Nazis null and void and explicitly stated: 'No cruel or excessive punishment is permitted. The death penalty is abolished except for offences which were punishable by death according to a law which was either in force prior to 30 January 1933 or has been promulgated by the Military Government or sanctioned by it.'[63] While the numerous Nazi decrees and amendments to the Criminal Code which invoked the death penalty were repealed at a stroke, capital punishment itself was by no means completely abolished with them. Any idea that a comprehensive new set of laws be introduced had long since been dismissed as 'bunk', 'impractical', and 'puerile' by American legal experts.[64] What Eisenhower's decree achieved was the restoration of the status quo before the Nazi seizure of power, or in other words of the Criminal Code of 1871. The Allies thus had no qualms about restoring the validity and operation of capital punishment in German law in 1945. Technically speaking, the new version of Paragraph 211 introduced by the Nazis was retained, but was overridden by Law No. 1, Article IV, Paragraph 8, so that in effect the death penalty could only be imposed if the offender was guilty under the terms of the old Paragraph 211 of the Reich Criminal Code of 1871.

A detailed list repealing Nazi amendments to the Criminal Code of 1871 was issued at the beginning of 1946. Two laws were explicitly excluded from the general repeal and remained in force. One was a decree of 5 December 1939 against violent criminals, which was only amended to allow a sentence of hard labour if there were mitigating circumstances. The other was Hitler's famous *Autobahn* decree of 22 June 1938, which had not only laid down the death sentence for highway robbery carried out with the use of road blocks even where no loss of life was involved, but made life imprisonment for the offence only permissible 'in special exceptional cases'. Evidently the Allied authorities consid-

[63] Gesetz Nr. I der Militärregierung Deutschlands—Kontrolgebiet des Oberbefehlshabers: Aufhebung des Nationalsozialistischen Rechts. Quoted in Wrobel (ed.), *Strafjustiz*, 53.

[64] See marginal comments on W. Fearnside, 'Suggestion that all Nazi Laws be Repealed', in NA Washington 260/C7/D2/51/b.61.

ered such crimes likely enough in the disordered circumstances of the time for these laws to continue in force. Had the Weimar Republic succeeded in abolishing the death penalty, it is thus still by no means certain that it would have vanished completely from German law in 1945. In any case, since it had not, the death penalty remained for murder. It was an ironic comment on all the various attempts that had been made since the turn of the century to bring a new Criminal Code into being, that the first act of the Allied Military Government after Germany's total defeat in 1945 was to restore to validity a Criminal Code that derived in most of its essentials from a law of almost a century before, the Prussian Criminal Code of 1851.[65]

'Law No. 1' closed all German courts for the time being, despite the resistance of judges and prosecutors, who claimed that 'ordinary' justice needed to continue, and could not understand the Allied conviction that all justice in Nazi Germany was Nazi justice. In the following months, 90 per cent of judges and judicial officials were dismissed from office. 'Proclamation No. 3' of the occupying powers abolished Nazi Special Courts and re-established the regular German courts on the basis of equality before the law and the primacy of due process. Long-retired judges and prosecutors last active in the Weimar years were brought back to staff the revived judicial system. But there were too few of them to make the system work. When the German courts reopened on 4 October 1945, former Nazi jurists were quickly allowed onto the bench, provided they sat alongside non-Nazi colleagues.[66] A year later they were in the majority, except at the very highest levels. By the 1960s, they were being promoted here too, and appointments such as that of the new Federal Prosecutor Wolfgang Fränkel, a former Nazi prosecutor, who had recommended a number of sentences to be increased from imprisonment to death during the Third Reich, were causing growing controversy.[67] With such men on the bench, it was not surprising that people unjustly convicted during the Nazi period generally found it extremely difficult to get their sentences revoked. Indeed, although in the early days of the occupation there had been widespread and 'haphazard' mass releases of prisoners from the ordinary German gaols by Allied troops, the German judicial authorities, once re-established, continued to mount prosecutions for crimes committed between 1933 and 1945.[68] In 1946, for instance, a journalist was

[65] PRO/FO 1060/1077: memo of June 1947: Death Sentences imposed by German Courts; *Zentral-Justizblatt für die Britische Zone*, 1/2 (Aug. 1947), 43; and NA Washington 260/C7/D2/51/b.62: Madsen to Chief Legal Officer, OMG Berlin District, w.e.f. 4 Feb. 1946, re: Repealing of Certain Provisions of the German Criminal Code, Art. III.

[66] NA Washington 260/C7/D2/51/b.61: Military Government Regulations, memo of 15 Feb. 1946.

[67] Engelhard (ed.), *Im Namen*, 346–73. Fränkel was subsequently forced to take early retirement. See also Wolfgang Benz, 'Die Entnazifizierung der Richter', in Diestelkamp and Stolleis (eds.), *Justizalltag*, 112–30.

[68] PRO/FO 1060/114, 304/6: Legal Division memo to Penal Branch, 14 Jan. 1948.

arrested and sentenced to prison for having injured a policeman while escaping into Switzerland during the war after being condemned to death by the Nazis for desertion. Convictions handed down by the courts during the Nazi period, including political convictions against Communists, also counted as previous convictions when the courts came to determine sentences for people who had offended under the new regime.[69]

Moreover, just as the law returned, by and large, to the state in which it had been under Weimar, so too did the judges. Political bias quickly crept into prosecution and sentencing decisions. In December 1946, for example, a court in Freiburg acquitted Heinrich Tillessen of the murder of the republican politician Matthias Erzberger in the Weimar Republic on the grounds that the general amnesty, decreed by Hindenburg on 21 March 1933 for all offenders who had committed criminal acts on behalf of the 'national uprising', was still in force. As an observant official in the Legal Advice Branch of the American Military Government noted: 'Sentences such as the one now delivered by the Freiburg Court started the long list of miscarriages of justice which contributed substantially to the downfall of the Weimar Republic.'[70] In May 1947 two brownshirts who had murdered a Jew in the Nazi pogrom of the 'Night of Broken Glass' on 9 November 1938 were convicted of manslaughter rather than murder, although the prosecution had charged the latter, because a court in Bremen accepted their plea that they had only been following orders. The press were quick to note that two out of the three judges on the bench had themselves been implicated in the Nazi regime, one of them having belonged to the Nazi Party, the other to the brownshirts. An element of self-preservation must surely have swayed their judgment in the case. To make matters worse, the Legal Division of the American Military Government in Bremen, anxious for expert advice on the legal principles of the case, turned to none other than Dr Eduard Kohlrausch, the academic lawyer who had sat on the Criminal Law Committee in the Third Reich and continued to produce his edition of the Criminal Code right up to 1944. Despite this past, Kohlrausch had managed to retain his position at the University of Berlin, largely because he had resigned as Rector in 1933. His advice was hardly likely to have been impartial in the matter.[71]

The Allies had no intention of allowing German courts to pronounce and carry out death sentences without reference to the occupying forces. Technically speaking, as well in real terms, the right of clemency over death sentences pronounced by German courts now lay with the Allied Military Government as

[69] Engelhard (ed.), *Im Namen*, 415–16.
[70] NA Washington 260/C7/D2/51/b.48: Dickman to Rockwell, 11 Dec. 1946.
[71] Ibid. 260/D5/7/53/36/4/b.76/Sl: Johnson to German Courts Branch, Legal Division, OMGUS, 22 Aug. 1947.

FIG. 43. *Rebuilding German justice.* 'Justice will be granted here, where the Nazis broke it to pieces.' Poster issued by the occupying authorities to accompany the reopening of German courts in 1946. Many of the judges presiding over the courts had served on the bench in the Nazi era, and had little hesitation in imposing death sentences once they had the power to do so.

the sovereign power in succession to Hitler under the clemency regulations of 6 February 1935, and the role of the former Reich Ministry of Justice in recommending clemency was now supposed to be played by the Presidents of the Provincial Supreme Courts.[72] In May 1946 the Office of Military Government

[72] BA Koblenz Z21/878, Bl. 12: extract from *Schleswig-Holsteinischer Anzeiger,* 8 (15 Apr. 1946), 100.

for Germany for the US zone ordered that any death sentences passed by German courts had to be referred to it for confirmation. No death sentence passed by a German court could be carried out unless the Military Government gave its express permission.[73] A similar order was issued by the Military Government for the British zone in June.[74] In January 1947, however, the Americans decided that the occupying powers should cede their right of clemency over capital offenders sentenced by German courts to the federated states which had been reconstituted in the mean time, despite the fact that the law of 1935 had not yet been formally abolished.[75] The Justice Minister for Greater Hesse explained the procedure in March 1947:

The power to grant clemency is vested in the Land Government of Greater Hesse under Article 109 of the Constitution of the Land Hesse. The Cabinet exercises its clemency powers only in such cases where the death penalty has been given by a German court. The Minister of Justice is appointed in such cases as referent and one other cabinet minister as coreferent. The two ministers prepare a full report to the cabinet after a study of the record which amounts to almost a re-trial. The points considered in such cases are the motives of the criminal, the fact that [i.e. whether] the judgment of the court is based on a confession or on circumstantial evidence, the personality of the accused, and the circumstances under which the accused was living and the general circumstances of the time.

The same procedure obtained in Württemberg-Baden and other federated states as well.[76] The power of clemency over German nationals sentenced by German courts was thus transferred to the governments of the federated states as soon as their Ministries of Justice were established.[77] Berlin remained under Allied control and was divided into four sectors, and did not have a German sovereign governing body of its own. The German courts in Berlin had been set up to serve the whole city, and were not sectorally based. The power of clemency lay therefore with the four-power *Kommandatura* which still governed the city in 1946.[78] This situation continued for some time afterwards, despite the deteriorating relations between the Soviet sectoral authorities and the rest. With this exception, the power over life and death was back with the German political and judicial systems by the middle of 1947.

[73] NA Washington 260/C7/D2/51/b.61: Military Government Law No. 2, Amendment No. 2— German Courts, 1 July 1946, Article VI/13.
[74] HStA Stuttgart EA4/001 Nr. 502: OMGUS Württemberg-Baden, Legal Division (Myers) to Justizminister, Württemberg-Baden, 11 May 1946; BA Koblenz Z21/894, Bl. 14: *Justizblatt für Aurich, Oldenburg und Osnabrück*, 13 Dec. 1946, 138.
[75] NA Washington 260/C7/D2/51/b.49: James E. Heath, 'Interpretation of Pardoning Power by Minister President'; ibid.: memo by Benjamin Habberton, 27 Jan. 1947, and Dickson to Habberton, 31 Jan. 1947.
[76] Ibid. C7/D5/7/53/36/4/b.151: Urman to President of Clemency Board, 13 Mar. 1947.
[77] PRO/FO 1060/1076, 48: MDJ Control Branch Director to Legal Division, Penal Branch, 27 Nov. 1946. See also the material in PRO/FO 1060/114.
[78] NA Washington 260/C7/D2/51/b.62: memo by Alexander Brown (Acting Chief, Legal Advice Branch, OMGUS), 3 July 1946: Death Sentences in German Courts of Berlin.

The power of clemency was not always used. Not only death sentences, but also executions, occurred as a result of the deliberations of German courts in the three Western zones, and in the Western sectors of Berlin, under the Allied occupation. The first execution to be carried out by order of the German courts took place on 21 August 1946 at Spandau prison in West Berlin. The person executed was a certain Karl K., sentenced for murder, and his execution had been approved by the Allied *Kommandatura* in Berlin.[79] In December 1946 it was reported that there had already been nine executions in the British zone as a result of sentences imposed by German courts.[80] By the end of September 1948, twenty individuals had been condemned to death and refused clemency by the Justice Ministry in Lower Saxony, but half of them had already been pardoned by the Minister-President, and it was reported that in 'Hesse und Hamburg the possessor of the power of clemency is basically inclined to exercise it, but here too there has been no definite commitment to a policy of reprieve.' The conference of Justice Ministers of the federated states agreed as a matter of policy that 'the death penalty will be retained in the law as a just expiation of the most serious crimes. But in this case, it must also be applied in special cases, otherwise it will make no sense to threaten it and it will have no deterrent effect. However, it should only be carried out in rare instances.'[81] German courts were by this stage beginning to take over the prosecution of war crimes as well as ordinary criminal offences. By 31 October 1948 two death sentences had been passed by German courts in North Rhine-Westphalia, one in Lower Saxony, and one in Schleswig-Holstein, for crimes against humanity.[82] It may well be that the reluctance of the politicians to use the death penalty was in part a reflection of this fact; executing the servants of the former regime was not likely to bring them great political applause from the electorate.

German courts and German state governments also authorized the execution of a number of common criminal offenders after the war. On 31 July 1948 it was reported that in the American zone there were sixteen offenders who had been condemned to death by German courts, had been refused clemency, and were awaiting execution.[83] In Berlin Walter R. was executed by order of the District Court, confirmed by the Allied *Kommandatura*, on 6 April 1948; Karl K. on 21 August 1946; Helmut K. on 14 January 1947; two women, Hildegard W. and

[79] PRO/FO 1060/239, 246: Legal Branch (Prisons) HQ Military Government British Troops Berlin to Legal Division (Penal Branch), Zonal Executive Offices, Control Commission Germany (British Element), 26 Aug. 1946; ibid. 241: Military Government British Troops Berlin to Control Commission, Unclassified Message, 21 Aug. 1946.

[80] Ibid. 945/318: Parliamentary Question for Oral Answer on Wednesday, 18 Dec. 1946.

[81] HStA Stuttgart EA4/001 Nr. 582: note 4417, date stamp Justizministerium Stuttgart, 24 Sept. 1948.

[82] PRO/FO 1060/149: Consolidation of Returns of Crimes against Humanity pending with and tried by German Courts: State as at 31 Oct. 1948.

[83] NA Washington 260/C7/D2/51/b.47, 10, table VIIB.

Helene W. on the same day; Johann O. on 20 May 1947; Paul S. on 29 April 1949; and the 24-year-old Berthold W. was executed on 11 May 1949 (for murdering an old woman in East Berlin and stealing her potatoes). All of them were German citizens sentenced to death by German courts.[84] Altogether, one death sentence was passed by a German court in Greater Berlin in 1946, and carried out; in 1947 there were 8 death sentences, of which 4 were carried out; in 1948 the figures were 20 and 2; in 1949, 5 and 2. In all, therefore, German courts in the four sectors of Berlin passed 34 death sentences from 1946 to 1949, of which 9 were carried out. In the federated states of the Western zones, a total of 92 death sentences were passed by German courts from 1945 to 1949, of which 15 were carried out. In North Rhine-Westphalia, 5 death sentences were passed in 1947, 10 in 1948, and 3 in 1949. In Bavaria the figures were 5, 11, and 12. The Catholic south German state thus continued the tradition it had begun in the Weimar Republic of being the federated state with the highest absolute number, as well as the highest proportion relative to the population, of death sentences. In Lower Saxony, 11 death sentences were passed in 1948, and none in any other year. In Hesse the figures were 2 in 1946, 1 in 1947, and 5 in 1948. Württemberg-Baden sentenced 1 offender to death in 1948 and 4 in 1949, the Rhineland-Palatinate 1 in each of the same two years, Hamburg 3 in 1947, 2 in 1948, and 4 in 1949, Baden 1 in 1947 and 3 in 1948, Württemberg-Hohenzollern 6 in 1948, and Bremen 3 in 1949. The only state where no death sentences were passed at all was Schleswig-Holstein. Of these 92 offenders who were sentenced to death by German courts, however, only 15 were actually executed, most of them in the new federated state of North Rhine-Westphalia, where 8 executions took place in 1946 as a result of verdicts passed by German courts, 4 in 1947, and 1 in 1948. One offender was executed in Hamburg in 1947, and 1 in Württemberg-Hohenzollern in 1948.[85]

The restoration of the death penalty in post-war West Germany confronted the authorities with the problem of how it should be carried out. The methods favoured by the occupying powers were all very different—hanging in Britain, guillotining in France, the shot in the back of the head in the Soviet Union, the gas chamber, electric chair, or rope in the United States, and of course the firing-squad in the armies of all four states. To some extent the problem of method was resolved in an *ad hoc* way. As far as the major war criminals condemned at Nuremberg were concerned, the French judge on the court suggested that they should be executed by firing-squad, because this was a more honourable form of

---

[84] PRO/FO 1012/681, 29: Military Government Berlin to Penal Branch, Legal Division, 14 June 1948. See also Kurt Geisler, 'Der Scharfrichter, der eine Räuberbande half', *Berliner Morgenpost*, 11 May 1979.

[85] Düsing, *Abschaffung*, 231–2. Some of the federated states listed were reorganized and renamed during this period or later.

death than hanging. But his American colleague did not agree that an honourable death was appropriate except as a form of 'mitigation', which most of the condemned men did not deserve, while the Russian judge favoured the exclusive use of hanging for all of them. In the end, backed by the British, he got his way.[86] The hangings were carried out by Master-Sergeant John C. Woods, an American executioner of fifteen years' experience, in the prison gymnasium at Nuremberg on 16 October 1946. Two representatives of the press from each of the four Allied powers were admitted, together with two Germans (one of them Wilhelm Hoegner, the Minister-President of Bavaria), and a small number of other officials. Hermann Göring poisoned himself with a cyanide pill the night before his execution was due to take place; his petition to die 'the death of a soldier' in front of a firing-squad had been denied, and, he said, 'executing the *Reichsmarschall* by hanging cannot be countenanced. I cannot permit this', he wrote in a note he left behind him, 'for Germany's sake.' The note indicated the persistence with which he harboured the illusion that he was still or indeed ever had been, the guardian of Germany's 'honour', and that Germans would actually care how he died. The other ten men were hanged in quick succession within a space of two hours, between one and three in the morning. Woods was subsequently criticized, largely on the grounds of the photographs of the condemned men taken after execution, which appeared to show that the drop was too short and the ropes not properly tied, so that they had died of strangulation, and some of them had hit their heads on the gallows platform on the way down. The use of a trapdoor system, with the rope tied around the neck and the length of the drop calculated according to the age, height, and weight of the condemned person so as to cause instant death by dislocation of the neck, was a British invention, and it is possible that Woods did not understand how to use it properly, since it was reported that he had simply used a standard eight-foot drop.[87] At any event, it had never been used in Germany before; under the Third Reich, the thousands who had been hanged had all simply been strung up, usually standing on a stool while the rope was positioned, and dying of asphyxiation when the stool had been kicked away. Death by strangulation was the fate which Göring and the others had approved for the conspirators of 20 July 1944, as well as for countless Polish and other foreign slave labourers, Communists, and ordinary Germans; it is at least possible that in the end they did not have to share it themselves.[88]

This does not mean, of course, that hanging, even when practised by an expert, was necessarily 'humane'. The equipment for carrying out British-style

[86]   Smith, *Reaching Judgment*, 172.
[87]   Albert Pierrepoint, *Executioner: Pierrepoint* (London, 1972), 158.
[88]   Taylor, *Anatomy*, 607–20.

hangings in Germany was elaborate, and included special ropes which had to be obtained from Britain. 'As far as is known', remarked the Legal Division of the Control Commission, 'Messrs. Joh. Edgington are the only firm in the U.K. manufacturing and repairing these ropes and their products have always given satisfaction.'[89] There was only one British-style gallows in Germany, located at the gaol in Hamelin, and the administrative effort and cost of moving capital offenders to it from other prisons in the zone was considerable.[90] Nevertheless, the British did not trust any method of execution except their own. Indeed, they even brought over their official civilian executioner, Albert Pierrepoint, who in his normal life was the landlord of a pub, to carry out executions in their zone of occupation. Pierrepoint later estimated that he had hanged some two hundred war criminals in Germany and Austria, including several multiple executions of up to twenty-seven offenders in a day by the method he had developed in England. German circumstances occasionally dictated some variation from normal procedure. When Pierrepoint carried out a series of thirteen war crimes hangings, involving mainly former officials of the Bergen-Belsen concentration camp, including the commandant and three female guards, at Hamelin prison on 13 December 1945, it was

felt that there would be inordinate delay if the bodies were left hanging for an hour or more which, it is understood, is the customary practice in England. The Assistant Director of Pathology B.A.O.R. who was to be the Medical Officer present at the executions was asked by the Director of Medical Services B.A.O.R. whether he considered that there was any objection to injecting the body immediately after execution with a lethal dose of some chemical substance in order to ensure the body could be taken down without delay. The Assistant Director of Pathology felt that there was no ethical objection to such a course and that an injection of 10cc of chloroform would be appropriate.

This procedure was carried out on the thirteen prisoners executed on that day, though it did not become general policy. At the first of a series of double executions held in Hamelin on 15 May 1946, 'respiratory excursions suddenly started' some seven and a half minutes after execution, and the body was immediately injected with chloroform. A similar case occurred in the third execution in the series. In all cases, however, there were no signs of consciousness or movement.[91] The exact cause of death, therefore, remained, at least in a couple of the cases, uncertain.

Hanging was used not only for war criminals but also for other kinds of

---

[89] PRO/FO 1060/244, 6: Legal Division (Penal Branch) to Director of Maintenance, Zonal Executive Office, 22 Mar. 1948.

[90] Ibid. 945/318, 15a: Draft memo to War Office Under-Secretary of State, n.d. [Mar. 1947].

[91] Ibid.: confidential 'Account of Observations made at Judicial Hangings in B.A.O.R.', undated [Mar. 1947]. See also Pierrepoint, *Executioner*, 145–6.

offenders. At the same time, German law specified beheading as the method of execution for people condemned under the Criminal Code, while the firing-squad was considered normal for those who were sentenced for military offences. In February 1946 the American authorities tried to summarize the situation as follows:

The death penalty imposed by a Military Government Court in a case other than a War Crime will be carried out in the case of a United Nations national by *shooting*. If it is a War Crime it can be either by *shooting* or *hanging*. If the person condemned in any case other than a War Crime is other than a United Nations national and the execution is performed by German authorities, it will be by *beheading*. If it is a War Crime the court can direct that the execution be by *beheading* or *hanging*. If the person is other than a United Nations national and the penalty is carried out by U.S. Military authority it can be by *shooting* or *hanging*, regardless of whether it is a War Crime or not.[92]

Hanging aroused some opposition in Germany. A German evangelical pastor who wrote in complaining that hanging had first been introduced by Hitler and was so frightening that it did not allow the condemned the calm that was necessary to make their peace with God, was told that US military courts were not bound by German law and that the matter was one for them to decide, not for the Germans.[93] In October 1946 the Legal Advice Branch of the US Military Government reported that, since the pre-Nazi provisions of the Criminal Code had been reinstated, the situation now seemed to be that executions commanded by German courts had to be carried out by beheading in an enclosed space in front of witnesses. The method of beheading was up to the federated states to arrange. Before Hitler's order of 1936 making the use of the guillotine standard across the whole Reich, it had been carried out by hand-axe in Prussia and most of north Germany, and the guillotine in the south.[94] But no one thought of reverting to the hand-axe. The British military authorities confirmed that the method used for German nationals sentenced to death by Control Commission courts was beheading by the guillotine. They saw no reason why the practice begun by Hitler in 1936 should be abandoned, and indeed there would be some difficulty in finding executioners competent to carry out beheadings by hand-axe. Given the fact that beheading was the method of execution prescribed by the Criminal Code of 1871, their preference for the guillotine was clear if unenthusiastic. 'This method is expeditious', the Legal Division reported, 'but as carried out by the Germans, has certain aspects of brutality.' Shooting was the method

---

    93 Ibid. 260/C7/D2/51/b.61: Uloth to Kontrollrat, 14 Jan. 1946, and van Buskirk to Uloth, 5 Mar. 1946.
    94 Ibid. 260/C7/D2/51/b.48: Dickman to Rockwell, 4 Oct. 1946.

for Allied nationals sentenced to death by Control Commission courts. Since many remaining DPs were now being naturalized as German citizens, the British proposed in October 1946 that shooting be stopped. They briefly considered adopting the guillotine instead, especially since Pierrepoint could only be brought out from England 'at great expense to the British taxpayer', while 'expert German executioners' were available for operating the three guillotines functioning in the British zone.[95] In the end, however, they decided that hanging should be used. It would, reported the Legal Division, 'seem undesirable that a method which is not regarded as suitable for British nationals sentenced to death should be employed in the case of persons sentenced to death by Military Courts in a zone administered by the British'.[96]

In practice, irrespective of which kind of court passed sentence on them, capital offenders who were German nationals tended to be executed by guillotine: one such, Willi H., was decapitated in this way on 30 August 1946 in Dortmund prison,[97] while the prison director reported three more executions with the guillotine on 12 September.[98] Three Poles were executed by firing-squad in Werl on 23 August 1946.[99] Non-Germans were not guillotined.[100] In 1947, the British once more gave considerable thought to using the guillotine for executing war criminals, on the grounds that it would be cheaper and simpler than constantly having to bring Pierrepoint over from the United Kingdom. On the other hand, the proponents of hanging regarded 'the cost of using, say, Pierrepoint as less important than the relative effects of hanging and beheading on the Germans'. Each method of judicial execution, they argued, had 'its psychological (and largely national) flavour', and the fact that 'from the German point of view beheading is not looked upon as so degrading or dishonourable as hanging' was a useful point to bear in mind when considering the method by which Nazi war criminals were to be killed.[101] As Brigadier Paton-Walsh, a former deputy governor of Wandsworth prison who had been put in charge of executions by the British military authorities, wrote to Sir Alfred Brown, Legal Adviser in the Control Office for Germany and Austria, on 21 March 1947:

[95] PRO/FO 1060/240, 81a–b: Appendix A to memo of Legal Division Chief, 12 Feb. 1947: Disadvantages—Judicial Hanging; Advantages—Decapitation by Guillotine.

[96] Ibid. 128–128a: Legal Division memo on Executions, 3 May 1947.

[97] Ibid. 239, 267a: Director of Investigation Prison Dortmund to Generalstaatsanwalt Hamm, 30 Aug. 1946.

[98] Ibid. 267b–d, Director of Investigation Prison Dortmund to Generalstaatsanwalt Hamm, 12 Sept. 1946. Numerous other guillotinings in Dortmund prison are also reported in this file.

[99] Ibid. 249a: Director of Penitentiary Werl to Generalstaatsanwalt Hamm, 23 Aug. 1946.

[100] Ibid. 945/318, S. 5a: memo of 1 Mar. 1947. In a subsequent minute of 2 Apr. 1947 it was conceded that this point rested on recollection and could have been in error.

[101] Ibid., minute 13: memo of 14 Apr. 1947; ibid. 8c, MacGeagh [Judge Advocate General of the Forces] to Brown [Legal Adviser, Control Office for Germany and Austria], 27 Mar. 1947.

There is no doubt that a judicial hanging as carried out in the British method by a real technician such as Albert Pierrepoint is as humane a method as can be devised—it is both speedy & sure, & loss of consciousness instantaneous . . . Albert Pierrepoint might be termed almost an 'artist' in his sideline activities, but there is no one else in the same street now. With Pierrepoint I have never had a moment's worry, but with others I have always been glad when the operation was completed without any hitch.

Multiple hangings were rather slow, given the need to readjust the rope each time according to the weight of the offender. No more than sixteen double hangings could be carried out in a day. 'With the guillotine', wrote Paton-Walsh in March 1947, 'a good man with trained assistants can carry out executions at 5 minute intervals with complete humanity, and without leaving unpleasant signs for the later victims.' The guillotine would also be cheaper because 'German executioners are paid an annual retaining fee, & a small per capita grant. The cost of each execution is therefore not heavy.' On the other hand, Germans should not be used to carry out executions ordered by British courts, and in any case they might refuse, 'it being remembered that the executions are almost all for war crimes as to the merits of which there will always be much doubt in many men's minds particularly in Germany'. Only if all executions were carried out by guillotine would the official German executioners have no qualms about carrying them out, since 'the executioners are not local men necessarily & do not know much, if anything, about the cases of the men executed unless the man had more than local notoriety'.[102]

The major change in the post-war method of execution came about in the light of a rather different consideration, however. In June 1947 the British military authorities ordered that death sentences imposed by Control Commission courts on United Nations nationals would be carried out in future by hanging instead of firing-squad, on the grounds that the replacement of battle-hardened soldiers by young national servicemen made the continuation of the earlier method inadvisable. 'The Army Commander', it was noted, 'considers that these young soldiers should NOT be called upon to undertake this duty which has always been intensely disliked by soldiers of any age or length of service.'[103] It was feared that they would deliberately fire wide.[104] While the firing-squad was now phased out, the guillotine continued to be used, above all on German citizens under the direction of the German courts and state authorities. Such cases were relatively unusual. On 10 December 1948 the prison directorate in Württemberg-Baden reported that it was proving difficult to find an 'execution

---

[102] PRO/FO 945/318, S. 8b: Paton-Walsh to Brown, 21 Mar. 1947. For Paton-Walsh, see Pierrepoint, *Executioner*, 149–50.

[103] Ibid. 1060/240, 188–9: Deputy Chief of Staff (Execution), Zonal Executive Offices, circular on Execution of Death Sentences, 14 June 1947, and Chief of Staff to Legal Division, 13 June 1947.

[104] Ibid. 945/318, S. 5a: memo of 1 Mar. 1947.

machine' in proper working order to carry them out. The guillotines in Stuttgart and Bruchsal had been destroyed in the war, and investigations had revealed 'that the Bavarian machine, in Straubing, is not intact, and the Hessian one in Frankfurt is built in fast to the floor. South Württemberg does not have an execution machine, and South Baden has hitherto operated one made available to it by the French Military Government.' The government of North Rhine-Westphalia had ordered one from the firm of Fritz and Otto Tiggemann in Hamm, which had previously repaired a guillotine in Dortmund, but they reported difficulties in getting hold of a suitable blade and had not yet finished the order.[105] It was not until March 1949 that they finally tracked down a portable guillotine in good working order which they were able to borrow. It was located in the prison at Regensburg, in northern Bavaria.[106] The guillotine used by the Nazis in Hamburg was in working order, but there was none available in Kiel, and so the German judicial authorities 'charged an expert, who built already a beheading-machine for the Hamm court district, with making a beheading-machine', requisitioning from the British military authorities '600 kg steel for building and 250 kg hard wood' for the purpose.[107] Clearly, it was felt that such a machine, requisitioned for permanent erection in a German prison at considerable expense to the authorities, would be in use for some time to come.

The great majority of the eighty-seven Germans guillotined in the British zone up to November 1949 were condemned by Allied rather than German courts. Nevertheless, executions of German citizens apart from war criminals were carried out under the control of the German penal authorities. The lever was pulled in every case by a German executioner. As always, there was no shortage of men willing to perform this task. Given the requirements of age and experience, and the general aura surrounding the trade of executioner over the centuries, it was not surprising that some of the men chosen were the same men as had been carrying out their trade under the Third Reich. To be sure, a good number of the leading executioners of the Nazi era were no longer available. The most prominent of them, Carl Gröpler, long since retired, was arrested at his home in Magdeburg, in the Soviet zone of occupation, in the autumn of 1945 and imprisoned in Halle. He was not brought to trial, but died in prison on 30 January 1949. Two assistant executioners were also executed at this time, both in the Soviet zone.[108] Others had probably perished in bombing raids or in last-

[105] HStA Stuttgart EA4/001 Nr. 582: Direktor des Gefängniswesens von Württemberg-Baden to Justizminister Stuttgart, 10 Dec. 1948.

[106] Ibid. 18 Mar. 1949.

[107] PRO/FO 1060/239, S. 132a: Generalstaatsanwalt Kiel to HQ Military Government Schleswig-Holstein, 8 Apr. 1946.

[108] Glenzdorf and Treichel, *Henker*, 150–1.

ditch fighting. At least one, Willi Röttger, was unlikely to have been acceptable to the German authorities because of the fact that he had carried out the hanging of the men of the July 1944 bomb plot at Plötzensee. But some of the executioners of the Nazi era were luckier. One such was the long-standing Bavarian executioner Johann Reichhart. Fleeing the invading Allied troops in 1945, he recalled later, he realized all was lost, drove the lorry containing his portable guillotine off the road, into the River Danube, and sank it, making his escape into what he hoped would be obscurity.[109] Reichhart claimed to have executed 3,165 people altogether during the Third Reich, including the students Hans and Sophie Scholl, leaders of the 'White Rose' resistance group, and of course many Communist political prisoners as well,[110] and with this kind of record he could not evade the attention of the Allied authorities for long. He was arrested and interned in a camp in Garmisch-Partenkirchen in 1945.[111] But Reichhart was soon needed for his professional services. On 6 April 1946 the Bavarian Ministry of Justice appointed him official executioner at a salary of 3,000 marks a year plus fees and expenses. Although no executions took place in Bavaria as a result of decisions reached by German courts after the war, there were, of course, many carried out by order of American military courts and, as we have seen, these had to be undertaken by German executioners. Reichhart's availability was therefore seized upon by the German government of the new state. Soon he was also employed by the American military authorities as an executioner, responsible both for guillotining common murderers and for hanging SS men and other war criminals. Just a few short years after he had been executing anti-Nazi resisters by the thousand, he thus found himself dispatching some of those whose policies they had been resisting. Altogether he claimed to have hanged forty-two individual war criminals and others after the war. It came as a considerable shock, therefore, when he was rearrested in May 1947 and interned once more because of his activities under the Third Reich. The ex-Nazis with whom Reichhart was imprisoned learned of the executions he had carried out subsequently, and persecuted him so mercilessly in the camp that he was driven to attempt suicide. In December 1948 he was again interned after being classified as a 'sympathizer' of the Nazis. The fact that he had already been an executioner under the Weimar Republic made it impossible to say he had taken up his duties out of political conviction, however. Released in 1950, he retired to take up innkeeping and dog-breeding in Bavaria.[112] By 1964 he was reported to have changed his mind about

[109]   Berthold, *Vollstreckt*, 8–9.
[110]   Ibid. 16.
[111]   HStA Stuttgart EA4/001 Nr. 582: Hessisches Justizministerium to Bayerisches Justizministerium (copy), 11 July 1947.
[112]   Berthold, *Vollstreckt*, 13–15, 30–1, 60–1. However, Reichhart's memory did not serve him particularly well. There is no independent evidence of the use of a mobile guillotine such as he described. He

capital punishment, and to have decided, rather late in the day, that it was useless and pointless.[113] Reichhart was not the only former Nazi executioner re-employed after the war. After all, if former judges and state prosecutors were being hired in the drive to re-establish the rule of law in Germany, why not former executioners? It was not surprising, therefore, that the leading Nazi executioner of the war years, Friedrich Hehr, from Hanover, was appointed official executioner for the new state of Lower Saxony in 1946, and from late 1947 onwards for Hesse as well.[114] In early 1948 it was agreed that Hehr should be responsible for both the British and the American zones of occupation.[115] Not only was he employed by British military courts after 1945, but they also paid him in accordance with the scale of fees originally drawn up by the Nazis.[116] It was this function indeed which had made him an obvious candidate for the post of chief executioner for Lower Saxony, which was situated in the British zone, in 1946.[117] He too, like most of the other executioners of the Third Reich, escaped prosecution, and died peacefully, in 1952.[118]

Reichhart and Hehr were exceptions. The other executioners of the post-war years were mostly new. In the British zone, Hans M. of Bergisch Gladbach signed a contract in April 1946 with the German legal administration in Düsseldorf, Hamm, and Cologne, agreeing his appointment as public executioner for the court districts in question.[119] In Berlin, the last execution in the British sector, on 11 May 1949, was carried out by Horst S. of Neukölln, assisted by Rudi H. and Gerhard R.[120] On 20 May, 24 June, and 1 July 1947 Clemens D., also living in Neukölln, carried out executions by guillotine in Berlin on the orders of the German courts.[121] Little or no information is available on any of these men. It is

claimed to have executed Otto Ohlendorf; but Ohlendorf was not executed until 1951, after Reichhart's retirement, by Pierrepoint. See Glenzdorf and Treichel, *Henker*, 154–5. Moreover, Reichhart's claim to have been taken out of prison to train Allied troops in hanging techniques is also unlikely; the traditional Austrian hanging technique which he used was extremely crude, and was not regarded by the Allies as 'humane'. Pierrepoint condemned the Austrian method as a form of strangulation, and trained Austrian executioners in the use of his 'drop' method; he, or one of his trainees, is likely to have trained Reichhart as well. See Pierrepoint, *Executioner*, 160.

[113] Helmensdorfer, ' "Ich tät's" '.

[114] HStA Stuttgart EA4/001 Nr. 582: Hessisches Justizministerium to Niedersächsisches Justizministerium and Nordrhein-westfälisches Justizministerium, 8 Dec. 1947 (copy).

[115] Ibid.: Niedersächsisches Justizministerium to Hessisches Justizministerium, 16 Jan. 1948 (copy); Glenzdorf and Treichel, *Henker*, 155.

[116] Rüping, *Staatsanwaltschaft*, 159.

[117] PRO/FO 1060/239, 34: Penal Branch, Legal Division, to Public Relations Branch, 7 Dec. 1945.

[118] Glenzdorf and Treichel, *Henker*, 155.

[119] PRO/FO 1060/239, 167: Legal Division to HQ Military Government North Rhine Region, 29 May 1946.

[120] PRO/FO 1012/681, 31: 'Particulars of the Executioner'.

[121] Ibid. 6a: copy of a letter from Generalstaatsanwalt Neumann to D, 23 June 1947; ibid. 14a: copy of letter from Generalstaatsanwalt Neumann to D, 30 June 1947; ibid. 683: Protocol: execution of Johann O., 20 May 1947 (translation).

probable that they came from the same milieu as the executioners and would-be executioners of the Nazi era: butchers, hospital porters, mortuary assistants, knackers. But this can only be a surmise. Even the figure of the most famous, or notorious, self-confessed executioner of the day, Gustav Völpel is obscure. Völpel claimed, implausibly, to have carried out forty-eight executions in West and East Berlin and in the Soviet zone between 1946 and 1948; in fact, this figure far exceeded the actual number of executions ordered by German courts in the Soviet zone, as we shall see in Chapter 18, and Soviet military tribunals did not use German executioners to do their work. Völpel's other claims were also as dubious as most of those advanced by other executioners in their alleged memoirs. Not only did he say that he used the hand-axe, for which there is no evidence in any of the official records, and pose for the camera in a mask which he purported to use at executions, but for which there is no attestation either in tradition or in any regulations or commentaries; Völpel also made the demonstrably false assertion that he had been the man who executed Berthold W. on 11 May 1949, at a time when he was himself behind bars for another offence.[122] We have seen that this execution was in fact carried out by others. Völpel's notoriety came less from his claim to have been an executioner than from his involvement in the crimes of the so-called Gladow Band, a group of violent and daring robbers led by the 18-year-old Werner Gladow, whose depredations caused widespread alarm and sensation in Berlin in the years 1948–9. Nearly fifty people had to answer for 127 offences, including murder, in the trial, which took place in the Soviet sector in March 1950. Völpel, who had acted as the fence for the gang's stolen property, was sentenced to seven years' imprisonment. It is in truth extremely unlikely that he actually had been an executioner. But he certainly succeeded in wrapping himself in the executioner's traditional aura of mystery as much as anyone ever did, and the mystique he created, along with the self-advertising criminal glamour of the rest of the band, proved potent enough not only to attract the attention of journalists and writers but also to inspire a film.[123]

There was thus little in the history of capital punishment in post-war Germany, either in its administration by the Allies or, crucially, in its resumed use by the German judicial system under the provisions of the Criminal Code of 1871, to suggest that it was likely to be abolished. Everything pointed to a restoration of the traditional German system of criminal law and penal adminis-

---

[122] Geisler, 'Der Scharfrichter'.
[123] Thomas Brasch, *Engel aus Eisen. Beschreibung eines Films* (Frankfurt am Main, 1981), with the screenplay and stills from a film made about Völpel and the Gladow Band, and supporting contemporary newspaper and magazine articles.

tration that had emerged in the Imperial period and continued, although in something of a state of crisis, under Weimar. Most German judges, lawyers, prosecutors, and judicial officials who came to office after the war had been trained in this system and few saw any reason to depart from it. The dominant view was that the Third Reich, even during the war, had not succeeded in destroying German legal tradition, though the most fanatical of the Nazis had certainly tried to undermine it. The legitimacy of this tradition had not been seriously challenged by the events of the Nazi years, least of all amongst the legal profession itself, most of whose members had collaborated willingly in the perversion of justice under the Third Reich and thus had every reason to conceal or deny it to the wider public. From this point of view the reassertion of the Criminal Code of 1871, including its prescription of the death penalty for murder, marked a return to healthy, sound, rational legal practice, and was not lightly to be abandoned. The Allies for their part did nothing to discourage the reintroduction of capital punishment. On the contrary, they gave it an emphatic legitimation by their own example. In the British zone, while German courts passed only thirty-eight death sentences and executed fourteen offenders in the years 1945–9, British courts passed no fewer than 587 and carried out 398. In other words, British courts condemned more than fifteen times as many offenders to death, and executed more than twenty-eight times as many, as German courts did in the same area over the same time-span, a disparity that recalled the even greater difference in enthusiasm for capital punishment that had existed in the two countries in the early nineteenth century. While the British and the other Allies were making strenuous efforts to 're-educate' the Germans for democracy, therefore, the example they gave them in matters of penal policy, and especially in the area of capital punishment, did little to discourage the use of state violence against the citizen. The signs did not seem good for the abolition of capital punishment in Germany after the Second World War.

c. The End of the Death Penalty in the West

Opposition to the death penalty was weak in early post-war Germany. The former peace movement and its ancillary organizations such as the League for Human Rights did not manage a successful relaunch in the Western zones. The major pressure group campaigning against the death penalty in the immediate post-war period was the Society of Friends, the Quakers, reflecting a situation in which the churches possessed greater institutional strength and continuity than most secular pressure groups did. The Quakers circularized central and regional governments and administrations and petitioned constitutional assemblies in favour of the abolition of capital punishment.[124] But this campaign did not meet with a great deal of success. Most of the federated governments were strongly in favour of retention. They were mainly dominated by the new Christian Democratic Union (and in Bavaria by its sister-party the Christian Social Union). The Christian Democrats owed much to the tradition of political Catholicism, which had always been in favour of the death penalty. In Württemberg-Baden, the coalition government, led by the Christian Democrats, was clear that executions should continue. In 1948 it rejected a suggestion by the Quakers that it should automatically grant clemency to murderers sentenced to death. The law still prescribed the death penalty for murder: 'The body charged with exercising the right of clemency cannot be expected to decide once and for all that it is going to grant a reprieve in every case. This would be equivalent in effect to an abolition of capital punishment, which must be reserved for the legislature.'[125] Yet on the first occasion on which it was confronted with the necessity of exercising its powers of clemency, the cabinet of the state of Württemberg-Baden voted unanimously in favour of commutation, on the ground that the condemned man, Otto Luther, had had 'an extraordinarily tough and loveless childhood'. Nevertheless, it added: 'The reprieve does not mean any rejection of capital punishment in principle, but is only a decision taken on the basis of a particularly thorough checking of an individual case.'[126] Other states were equally reluctant to abolish capital punishment. Article 21 of the Hessian constitution of 1 December 1946, for example, allowed the death penalty for 'particularly serious crimes', while Article 47 of the Bavarian constitution, passed the following day, assumed that death sentences would continue to be pronounced, and reserved the power of clemency to the state government. The constitution of the new state of Rhineland-Palatinate, while declaring human life to be inviolable, nevertheless went on in its Article 3 to permit executions for serious offences against the person, as did the Baden constitution passed on 19 May 1947 and the constitution passed in the Hanseatic city-state of Bremen on 21 October the same year.[127] No attempt was made by any deputies in the bodies which drew up these documents to follow the example of the Frankfurt Parliament in 1848 and declare the death penalty unconstitutional. Of course, it was undoubtedly true, as most people realized, that such a decision really belonged to the legislative assembly which, it was assumed, would eventually meet to draw up a national constitution for the whole of Germany. It would certainly be anomalous for one state to

[124] BA Koblenz Z21/806, Bl. 3: Eingaben an alle verfassungsgebenden Versammlungen und die gesetzgebenden Körperschaften in Deutschland betreffend die Abschaffung der Todesstrafe, Berlin, 22 Oct. 1946 (copy).

[125] HStA Stuttgart EA1/922 Nr. 5308: Justizministerium to Staatsministerium, 10 Aug. 1948.

[126] Ibid.: Staatsministerium to Justizministerium, 20 Aug. 1948, and Zeitungsnachricht.

[127] Düsing, *Abschaffung*, 229–30.

abolish the death penalty while others retained it. The Criminal Code of 1871 still applied to the whole of Germany, and there were good reasons for thinking that there would be legal difficulties in abrogating or amending it in a single region. Nevertheless, a vote for abolition in one state would at least have given a signal to others.

A few individuals did speak out against the death penalty after the war. The Social Democratic law professor and former Minister of Justice Gustav Radbruch was perhaps the most prominent. To be sure, Radbruch made an exception in the case of the main war criminals, who had after all, he said, brought about so many deaths themselves in the twelve years of Nazi dictatorship and war. He urged the constitutional abolition of capital punishment after their death, so as to restore to the new Germany that respect for human life which had been so singularly lacking in the old.[128] Radbruch's views were mostly advanced in obscure academic journals, and stood little chance of gaining a public hearing. The criminologist Hans von Hentig, who had seen out the Third Reich and the war in exile, like Radbruch, also argued, once more, against the death penalty as a deterrent, on the grounds that most murderers were so 'inferior' that the threat of capital punishment was unlikely to have the desired effect on them. 'Inferiority', of course, had been the very reason why the Nazis had justified killing so many offenders during the war; but Hentig saw no problem in adhering to this point of view. It was up to the state to lead the way in creating a humane society, he wrote, by abolishing the death penalty.[129] Published in English, Hentig's heavy scholarly tomes stood no chance of having an impact in Germany. Rather similar were the writings of the legal historian Eberhard Schmidt, who in his introduction to the history of German criminal law, a student text, condemned the death penalty as immoral.[130] A number of other legal specialists also suggested that a new spirit of humanity would be well served by abolition. But it was noticeable that very few politically active figures joined them. The demand for an end to executions did not really get as far as the broader public sphere. It did not even get debated in the post-war conferences held to relaunch the Social Democratic Party, although opinion in the old Social Democratic Party in 1919, as we have seen, had been strongly, if not unanimously, in favour of abolition.[131]

---

[128] Gustav Radbruch, 'Ars moriendi. Scharfrichter, Seelsorger, Volk', *Schweizerische Zeitschrift für Strafrecht*, 59 (1945), 460–95; Düsing, *Abschaffung*, 225.

[129] Hans von Hentig, *Crime: Causes and Conditions* (New York, 1947), 327; idem, *The Criminal and his Victim*, 104.

[130] Schmidt, *Einführung* 1st edn. (Göttingen, 1947), 376; see also idem, 'Goethe und das Problem der Todesstrafe', *Schweizerische Zeitschrift für Strafrecht*, 63 (1948), 444–64. This Swiss journal was a major outlet for moderately progressive German jurists after the war.

[131] Düsing, *Abschaffung*, 224–6, 229.

There were a number of reasons why the politicians of 1945–6 did not follow those of 1918-19 in raising the cry for the abolition of capital punishment. In the first place, the shock at the mass slaughter in the First World War could not be repeated a second time, even after the far greater scale of the destruction and loss of life that had taken place in 1939–45 became fully clear. Moreover, in 1918 Germans had been alarmed by the violence and disorder unleashed in the revolutionary and counter-revolutionary struggles in the months following the overthrow of the Kaiser and the princes in Berlin, Munich, and elsewhere. It seemed to the proponents of abolition in the Weimar Assembly that something had to be done to stem the rising tide of civil strife. In 1945–6, however, there was no parallel to this. Certainly there was widespread criminality and violence, as we have seen. But most Germans thought that it was Polish DPs who were largely responsible for this, and they did not mind much if they were executed. There was no question, they thought, of German society in itself getting out of control. The Allied occupation forces were certainly not going to allow any mass outbreak of intercommunal violence, political disorder, murder, or assassination. Thus even criminologists who had supported the abolition of the death penalty under the Weimar Republic could be found arguing after the Second World War that the rise of violent crime now rendered the idea premature.[132] Other former advocates of the death penalty, and some criminologists, such as Franz Exner, also came out once more in favour of capital punishment as an indispensable deterrent to murder.[133] More traditional professions also continued their long-held position in favour of retention. One such was the clergy, above all those members of the profession who worked as prison chaplains. Clearly they thought that the abolition of the death penalty would rob them of the most rewarding part of their work. Sigisbert Greinwald, former prison chaplain in Munich, argued passionately in favour of capital punishment for murder, because by deterring would-be killers it saved their potential victims from the sudden death that robbed them of the opportunity to make their peace with God. The capital offenders to whom he himself had ministered during the Nazi period, by contrast, had all been reconciled with their maker before they went to the guillotine. Greinwald admitted that many executions under the Nazis had been unjust. However, his overall argument showed a disturbing degree of complacency about the administration of the death penalty by the Hitler regime, and about the part which he himself had played in it.[134]

None of this can be said to have amounted to a real public debate. One commentator, indeed, in defending the death penalty as necessary because it

[132] Düsing, *Abschaffung*. 226.
[133] Franz Exner, *Kriminologie* (Berlin, 1949), 104.
[134] Sigisbert Greinwald, *Die Todesstrafe* (Westheim bei Augsburg, 1949), esp. 59–61.

'incorporates the majesty of the law and hence of the community', even referred to the movement to abolish it in the past tense, assuming that it had ceased to exist with the fall of the Weimar Republic.[135] Despite this widespread indifference to the question, there was little doubt that abolitionist sentiment remained widespread on the left of the political spectrum. For all their tergiversations on the subject under Weimar, the majority of Social Democrats were still opposed to the death penalty on principle. The Communists, who had also re-established themselves in the West after 1945, would welcome its abolition in capitalist society. Although there was no major campaign, an opportunity for the abolitionists to put their case before a major constitutional legislature presented itself in the autumn of 1948, and they were not slow to seize it. The growing Cold War between the Soviet Union and the three Western Allies had found its expression in Germany in a widening gap between the Soviet zone of occupation and the rest. In 1948, as the culmination of a process of integration between the American, British, and French zones which had begun many months before, the various states in these zones, with the encouragement of the Western Allies, came together to found a new federal state on German soil. The Federal Republic was in some senses intended to be provisional, built on an acceptance that the division of Germany was inevitable, but only for the time being. It was intended to provide Germans in the Western zones with a democratic state of their own built on democratic principles and capable of withstanding the threat of Communism posed by the East. As preparations began for the framing of the new state's provisional constitution, the moment seemed opportune to many on the left to attempt the abolition of the death penalty by writing in a provision to that effect.

Work on the constitution of the proposed Federal Republic began in earnest when a small Constitutional Convention, consisting of experts appointed by the governments of the federated states, met at the Herrenchiemsee palace in the Bavarian Alps in August 1948. One of its three subcommittees recommended further discussion of the option of including the abolition of the death penalty, especially for political offences, in the new constitution.[136] After further discussion in the plenary session of the Convention on 23 August,[137] the Convention's report noted that no agreement had been reached on the matter.[138] Constitutional experts were clear in 1948, as they had been during the debates on the subject at Weimar nearly thirty years before, that including abolition in the constitution would be difficult. The final draft presented by the expert Constitu-

---

[135] Helmut von Weber, *Grundriss des deutschen Strafrechts* (Bonn, 1946), 20, 136–7.

[136] Peter Bucher (ed.), *Der Parlamentarische Rat 1948–1949. Akten und Protokolle*, ii. *Der Verfassungskonvent auf Herrenchiemsee* (Boppard, 1981), 218.

[137] Ibid. 441–2.   [138] Ibid. 575.

tional Convention to the full Parliamentary Council on 21 September, therefore, still included the explicit recognition that it would be lawful in the new state for the death penalty to be carried out.[139] The Parliamentary Council, which was charged with finalizing the constitution (or Basic Law, as it was called) of the new Federal Republic of Germany, was put together from representatives of the different federated states such as Bavaria, with the addition of five non-voting members from Berlin. The delegates had to be elected members of the legislatures of the federated states, one for each three-quarters of a million inhabitants. This made the Council, with sixty-five voting members, much more representative than the appointed Constitutional Convention, but also smaller than the legislatures which had considered this question of capital punishment in 1918, 1870, and 1848. Nevertheless, it still had a strongly representative, democratic basis of legitimacy. Many of its members had been active in politics under the Weimar Republic. Some of them had indeed taken part in previous debates on the death penalty. The Social Democrat Paul Löbe and the Christian Democrat Helene Weber had both belonged to the Weimar National Assembly, while the Christian Democrat Paul de Chapeaurouge had also been present at the debate on capital punishment held in the Lawyers' Congress of 1912. Altogether there were 27 Christian Democrats and 27 Social Democrats in the Council, with the balance being held by 5 Free Democrats, heirs of Germany's liberal tradition, 2 members of a small, far-right particularist grouping, the German Party, 2 representatives of the moribund Centre Party, and 2 Communists. On past experience, the Social Democrats and the Communists could be expected to be opponents of the death penalty, the Christian Democrats, Centrists, and German Party representatives could be expected to favour retention. This left the Free Democrats holding the balance. The evidence of the liberals' behaviour in the Weimar Republic suggested that they were likely to be divided on the issue at the very least, if not hostile, and could not be relied upon to support a proposal for abolition.[140]

On the face of it, therefore, the prospects for the constitutional removal of the death penalty seemed uncertain, to say the least. The hostility of the conservatives was underlined on 3 November 1948 by the decision of the Christian Democratic delegation to vote for the retention of capital punishment for 'the most serious of crimes', not including political offences.[141] In view of this resolution, the chances of persuading the full Parliamentary Council to include

---

[139] Eberhard Pikart and Wolfram Werner (eds.), *Der Parlamentarische Rat 1948–1949. Akten und Protokolle*, v. *Ausschuss für Grundsatzfragen* (Boppard, 1993), 19.

[140] Düsing, *Abschaffung*, 276–8.

[141] Rainer Salzmann (ed.), *Die CDU/CSU im Parlamentarischen Rat. Sitzungsprotokolle der Unionsfraktion* (Forschungen und Quellen zur Zeitgeschichte, 2; Stuttgart, 1981), 122, 125.

abolition in the Basic Law seemed poor. When the work of drafting the final version of the Basic Law was handed over to the Council's 21-person Main Committee, however, matters took an unexpected turn. A key figure here was the Silesian refugee Hans-Christoph Seebohm, who with his secretary Hans-Joachim von Merkatz represented the right-wing German Party on the Council. Although Seebohm, according to one of the Social Democratic deputies, 'was one of the Chamber's most conservative members',[142] he surprised everybody on 6 December 1948 by bringing in a formal proposal to include the abolition of the death penalty in a new article which would also guarantee the freedom of the individual, protect the citizen's body from interference by the state, ban corporal punishment, and outlaw abortion under all circumstances.[143] On 18 January 1949 Seebohm repeated his proposal during a debate on Clause 2 of the Basic Rights, dealing with the right to life:[144]

We believe that it is necessary to add the phrase 'the death penalty is abolished' because the abolition of capital punishment, which has already occurred in a number of European states, will underline the German people's rejection of any kind of political system based on force and its revulsion at the large number of death sentences carried out in the last few years. . . . If I wish to see the abolition of capital punishment and its replacement by fairly lengthy terms of imprisonment, it is because a custodial sentence should serve to give to a person who has been sentenced to death under the law in force up to this point the opportunity for inner purification and for changing his position. We have seen many examples—I do not need to list them here—in which really fundamental and momentous changes have resulted and taken place. I have always taken this standpoint and represented it in the Lower Saxon cabinet as long as I was a member of it.[145]

Seebohm's formulations made it clear that he was thinking in the first place not of the vast numbers of death sentences carried out under the Nazis, but of the much smaller, though still considerable, number of executions of German war criminals carried out under the Allied occupation. In urging the opportunity for 'inner purification'; he was addressing himself in the first place to former servants of the Third Reich. At this time, the German Party was attempting to broaden its traditional base in the Protestant particularism of the former Kingdom of Hanover by appealing to the ex-Nazi electorate, with public pronouncements in favour of the restoration of national pride, the reintroduction of the black, white, and red flag of the old Empire, and the official recognition of former members of the Waffen-SS as veteran soldiers.[146] Seebohm's intervention was made in

---

[142] Carlo Schmid, *Erinnerungen* (Berne, 1979), 409.
[143] Salzmann (ed.), *CDU/CSU*, 857.
[144] Ibid. 877, 923; Düsing, *Abschaffung*, 279.
[145] *Parlamentarischer Rat: Verhandlungen des Hauptausschusses* (Bonn, 1948/9), 534.
[146] Horst W. Schmollinger, 'Die Deutsche Partei', in Richard Stöss (ed.), *Parteien-Handbuch. Die Parteien der Bundesrepublik Deutschland 1945–1980* (Opladen, 1983), i. 1025–1111, here 1033.

conjunction with others of the same sort, including one in which his party attempted to revive the title of 'German Reich' in place of 'Federal Republic'.[147] Moreover, his plea for the abolition of the death penalty was coupled with a further amendment to the relevant clause of the Basic Rights extending the right to life to the unborn child, in an attempt to link the two issues in a general 'protection of life' which would appeal to his conservative constituency. The German Party's initiative seems to have taken everyone by surprise. It met with a frosty response on all sides. As might have been expected, the Christian Democrats were receptive to the idea of extending the constitutional right to life to embryos, but failed to speak up in favour of including the abolition of capital punishment. Theodor Heuss, for the Free Democrats, thought that the abolition of the death penalty should be left to a revision of the Criminal Code—another example in a long series of liberal equivocations on this subject over a number of decades. Even the Social Democrats on the Main Committee failed to speak out in favour of Seebohm's motion, and one of them actually spoke out against it in much the same tenor as Heuss. Only the Communist Heinz Renner supported it explicitly, pointing out that capital punishment had been abolished in the Soviet Union two years earlier. In a body that contained 8 Social Democrats, the motion was only able to gather 6 votes, while 9 deputies voted against. The amendment to extend the right to life to the unborn child was rejected by a larger majority, 11 votes to 7, which suggests that two deputies must have abstained on the first motion and one switched sides.[148]

The cause was not yet lost, however. With the German Party breaking ranks on the right, the time seemed to at least some of the Social Democrats to be ripe for a determined attempt to push through their long-held desire to abolish the death penalty.[149] As Carlo Schmid argued, the death penalty was a 'barbarity' which only encouraged brutal crimes rather than deterring them. The state merely degraded itself by implementing it. With this stronger backing on the left, Seebohm redirected his appeal towards the crucial votes of the Christian Democrats, revealing more clearly his true motives for bringing forward the motion as he did so. Abolition was necessary, he declared on 10 February 1949, in view of the excessive number of executions 'not only in the period up to 1945, but also in the period since 1945'. It was in order to stop this situation continuing that abolition was so urgent.[150] In making this plea, Seebohm was again thinking above all of the execution of war criminals, to which he and his party were bitterly opposed. Preventing Nazi war criminals from being sentenced to death

[147] *Parlamentarischer Rat: Stenographische Berichte über die Plenarsitzungen* (Bonn, 1948/9), 174.
[148] Ibid. 535; Düsing, *Abschaffung*, 279–80. For the Soviet Union, see p. 806, below.
[149] Schmid, *Erinnerungen*, 375–6.
[150] Düsing, *Abschaffung*, 281.

would certainly help the German Party in its search for voters on the far right. But it also appealed to at least some of the Christian Democrats on the Main Committee. Two of the party's deputies, supported by the spokesman for the liberal Free Democrats, pointed to the precedent of the Weimar constitution and argued for a decision on the matter to be postponed until the promulgation of a new Criminal Code by a legislative assembly directly elected by the people. But another Christian Democrat, Heinrich von Brentano, declared that there was no reason why the Basic Rights should not include the right to life. With the support of one of his colleagues, he suggested that each of the party delegations should make its mind up on the matter before it was debated again.[151] Returning to the matter in a caucus meeting on 22 February 1949, the Christian Democrats were now much more divided on the issue than they had been previously. Among the fifteen members present at the meeting, a clear shift of opinion had taken place against the death penalty. In order to paper over their differences on the issue, they now retreated from their decision of the previous November. 'After a lengthy debate', it was reported:

The majority of the parliamentary delegation does not think it is possible to abolish capital punishment. In order not to unleash a public discussion on the issue, we should seek to arrange with the other parliamentary parties to postpone the debate and let a subsequent government decide, or if this is impossible, to reach a decision along the lines that a future legislature should limit capital punishment to very rare cases.[152]

These exceptional cases, it seems reasonable to infer, would be confined to serial killers like Haarmann or Kürten. The death penalty would not be applied either to war crimes or to political offences.[153] Nevertheless, if it proved impossible, or impolitic, to uncouple war crimes and political offences from common murder, there was clearly now a sizeable minority that favoured getting rid of both. For when it came to the vote in the Main Committee three months later, on 5 May 1949, roughly half the Christian Democrats came down on the side of abolition, giving fifteen votes in favour and only four against.[154] With nearly 80 per cent of the members of the Main Committee favouring the inclusion of abolition in the Basic Law, the chances for success in the plenary session of the Parliamentary Council, which debated the issue the following day, now seemed much improved on what they had been at the beginning of the year.

The strong swing of opinion against capital punishment in the Parliamentary Council over the early months of 1949 was not at all to the liking of a sizeable number of Christian Democrats. One of their number, the Hamburg conservative Paul de Chapeaurouge, swiftly put forward a motion in which—very much

[151] Düsing, *Abschaffung*, 281–2.   [152] Salzmann (ed.), *Die CDU/CSU*, 411.
[153] Ibid. 418.   [154] Düsing, *Abschaffung*, 282–3.

in the manner of retentionists in the Weimar Republic—he tried to exploit a particularly shocking murder case, that of Irmgard Swinka, on trial at the time for poisoning seven women and trying to kill another twelve, to argue that it would be wrong to get rid of capital punishment altogether.[155] Not only was the Council not competent to decide the issue, he declared, but it would also be flying in the face of public opinion if it decided to rob the fledgling republic of its most important protection against serious crime. The matter, he said, had simply not been discussed in enough detail or depth, when one compared the brief debates of the Main Committee with the lengthy deliberations of the Lawyers' Congress which he had attended in 1912. For the abolitionists, the Social Democratic lawyer Friedrich Wilhelm Wagner denied vehemently that the republic required the death penalty for its own protection. Cases such as that of Irmgard Swinka, he said, had occurred despite the fact that the death penalty was still in force, not because it seemed likely to be abolished (which it did not at the time when she committed the crimes of which she was being accused). The Germans had the duty to reach a clear decision against capital punishment, after the way in which it had been so massively applied during the Third Reich. The Communist Heinz Renner added that the experience of Nazi Germany showed just how ineffective the death penalty was as a form of protection for the state. In view of the Nazi past of most present West German judges, he added, it was necessary to remove from them the possibility of sentencing people to death in case they started using it 'as a political weapon against the progressive and democratic forces in the state', by which he meant, of course, Communists like himself.[156] Yet these were not the arguments that counted when it came to the vote. Certainly, the twenty-nine Social Democrats and Communists who had seats in the plenary session of the Council supported them. But they by no means made up the necessary majority, and four out of five of the Free Democrats in the Council remained steadfastly retentionist, marking a further stage in the long retreat of German liberalism from its originally abolitionist position over the preceding century. Surprisingly, perhaps, the two representatives of the small Catholic Centre Party voted for abolition, declaring that the right to give and take life belonged to God, not to the state. But the key lay with the two German Party deputies who voted for abolition, and with the substantial numbers of Christian Democrats who followed them. Chapeaurouge had only been able to gather ten signatories, including his own, for his motion to delete the draft clause on 6 May, so it is reasonable to assume that most of the remaining seventeen Christian Democrats in the Council either voted in favour of abolition or abstained, though it later became apparent that at least one deputy, the former

---

[155] Düsing, *Abschaffung*. 281. Swinka received four death sentences on 7 May 1949.
[156] Ibid. 284–5.

mayor of Cologne Konrad Adenauer, soon to be Federal Chancellor, had cast his vote against abolition in spite of having failed to sign Chapeaurouge's motion. Enough Christian Democrats voted to include abolition, at any rate, to get the motion comfortably passed.[157] Indeed, the majority for what eventually became Article 102 of the Basic Law of the Federal Republic of Germany was sufficiently overwhelming for the retentionist side to accept the decision without demur. Once in the final draft of the constitution, it was neither amended nor voted out, and it passed into law with the other clauses a few days later. A two-thirds majority of the projected Federal Parliament would now be required to remove it.[158] This was a far more serious obstacle to the restoration of the death penalty than would have been posed by the inclusion of abolition in a new Criminal Code voted in by the Federal Parliament, which would only have required a simple majority to reverse. No doubt this had been a consideration in the minds of those retentionists who had argued in favour of a deferral. But now it was too late to do anything about it.

The decision of the Parliamentary Council came as a considerable shock to most observers. Gustav Radbruch, the most persistent of Weimar's former abolitionists, described it as 'a surprise for old opponents of capital punishment and for experts in the criminal law'. He warned that there would soon be an attempt to reverse it. While opinion among lawyers and judges was divided, as it always had been, prison governors and chaplains were generally unhappy about the decision, the former because they feared the increased security risk from larger numbers of inmates serving life imprisonment, the latter because, apart from sharing the long-standing general approval given by the churches to the death penalty, they thought it had a useful deterrent effect.[159] They reflected a wide spectrum of right-wing opinion in arguing that the death penalty should continue to be used for common murder but was generally unjust when applied to war crimes. On 19 May 1949 the Catholic and Protestant prison chaplains at the remand prison in Dortmund wrote to the North Rhine-Westphalian Minister of Justice, pointing out that the last time an execution had been carried out as a result of a death sentence passed by a West German court was on 13 March 1948, in Dortmund itself. 'Since this time,' they complained, 'reprieves have been granted to numerous offenders who have murdered for gain and have killed their victims from the most base of motives and with the greatest degree of cruelty.' Yet no fewer than nine civilian offenders had been sentenced to death by British military courts since March 1948. Six of these had already been executed. They would not, declared the chaplains, have been condemned to death by German

[157] For confirmation of this point, see *Deutscher Bundestag*, 1. Wahlperiode, 232. Sitzung, 2 Oct. 1952, 10617C.

[158] Düsing, *Abschaffung*, 286–7, 295.   [159] Ibid. 288–96.

courts. One of them, Konrad K., for example, was executed on 6 July 1948 merely because the fellow members of his gang said he had used a gun on other occasions. Another, Wilfried B., was executed on 23 July 1948 because he had killed a Russian border guard while fleeing from East Prussia. A third, Paul F., from Silesia, had been guillotined as a war criminal after having been convicted for killing Russian prisoners of war under the Nazis. Such draconian sentences, declared the chaplains, showed the double standards being applied by British and German courts.[160] The continuing saga of war crimes trials and executions was still uppermost in many people's minds, and it was a more than rhetorical question when one conservative newspaper, the *Mainzer Allgemeine Zeitung*, pointedly asked the abolitionists whether they would have stuck to their principles if Heinrich Himmler had come before the courts instead of committing suicide.[161] For the fact was, although they were careful not to say so too explicitly, that it was only the hope of being able to save Nazi criminals from the gallows that had persuaded conservative deputies from the German Party and the Christian Democrats to cast their votes in favour of abolition in sufficient numbers to secure its anchorage in the Basic Law. Had it merely been the question of common homicide that was at issue, the vote would never have been passed. As one of the Christian Democratic deputies remarked during a debate on the issue three years later: 'At that time, when the Basic Law was decided upon . . . we were confronted with the terrible experiences of the Nazi period up to 1945 and—it also has to be said in this connection—the terrible experiences of the period since 1945.'[162]

The promulgation of Article 102, which came into effect with the rest of the Basic Law on 24 May 1949, did not bring about the end of capital punishment at a stroke, not even in West Germany. The death penalty still remained in the Criminal Code as the punishment prescribed for murder, and retentionists quickly began to dispute the competence of the Basic Law to override the Criminal Code in this way. The Weimar Republic's constitution had remained to a large extent a collection of pious hopes, a dead letter so long as they were not followed by specific amendments made to the individual laws which dealt with the concrete situations they purported to cover. The conservative legal profession had done much to undermine the liberal intentions of the constitution in this way. It was not impossible that the same thing might happen with the Basic Law. At this point, there were still cases before German courts where the death sentence was a real possibility. In the case of the coal miner Johann K., from

---

[160] BA Koblenz Z21/894, Bl. 24–25: H. W. Röhrig and E. Jäker to Ministry of Justice, North Rhine-Westphalia, 19 May 1949.

[161] Düsing, *Abschaffung*, 288–96.

[162] *Bundestag*, 1. Wahlperiode, 232. Sitzung, 2 Oct. 1952, 10617B (Dr Weber, CDU).

Gelsenkirchen, for example, sentenced to fourteen years' imprisonment for murder on 5 November 1948, the state prosecutor, continuing a practice that had become commonplace under the Third Reich, appealed to a higher authority for the death sentence to be imposed instead. The Senior state prosecutor in Cologne agreed on 24 May 1949 that death was still the penalty for murder according to Paragraph 211 of the Criminal Code, and the paragraph as far as he was aware was still in force whatever the Basic Law—which came into effect that very day—might prescribe. In addition, Law No. 10 of the Allied Control Commission also laid down the death penalty for murder. But this *démarche* did not get very far. The Basic Law, declared the President of the Central Legal Office of the British zone, was not a 'programmatic document' like the Weimar constitution or the Basic Rights of the German People of 1849, but 'immediately valid law'. Technically speaking, it might be true that this meant there was no legal punishment for murder any more, since the Basic Law had now overridden Paragraph 211 of the Criminal Code without replacing it with anything else. But for once, a lawyer showed a bit of common sense. The proper penalty for murder, he declared, was the next most severe possible sentence after death, namely life imprisonment. The courts were in fact already imposing it. The Cologne state prosecutor's appeal was therefore rendered nugatory. On 14 June the Supreme Court for the British zone ruled that life imprisonment was the correct sentence for Johann K., and subsequent discussions among the state prosecutors in the Western zones confirmed in September that the death penalty was no longer allowable in law.[163]

This argument also disposed of another potential obstacle to the full implementation of Article 102, namely the fact that the federated states had their own constitutions, some of which, like the Hessian constitution of 1 December 1946, explicitly affirmed the legality of capital punishment.[164] The Bavarians, who had opposed the Basic Law because it was too centralist, submitted under protest.[165] Having decided that the Basic Law did not allow the death penalty to be carried out on West German territory at all, German lawyers and politicians were confronted with the fact that the military courts of the occupying powers were

[163] BA Koblenz Z21/806, Bl. 7: Generalstaatsanwalt beim Obersten Gerichtshof für die Britische Zone to Präsident des Zentral-Justizamts für die Britische Zone, 24 May 1949; Ibid., Bl. 11: Präsident des Zentral-Justizamts für die Britische Zone circular to Justice Ministries in the zone, 3 June 1949; ibid., Bl. 16: Generalstaatsanwalt beim Obersten Gerichtshof für die Britische Zone to Präsident des Zentral-Justizamts für die Britische Zone, 14 June 1949; ibid., Bl. 28: Protokoll über die Besprechungen auf der Tagung der Generalstaatsanwälte der Westzonen in Neustadt an der Haardt am 19. und 20. September 1949.

[164] Düsing, *Abschaffung*, 423.

[165] For the general background, see Theodor Eschenburg and Wolfgang Benz, 'Der Weg zum Grundgesetz', in Theodor Eschenburg (ed.), *Jahre der Besatzung 1945–1949* (Geschichte der Bundesrepublik Deutschland, 1; Stuttgart, 1983), 459–514.

still empowered to condemn civil as well as military offenders to death should they so wish. The British Military Government insisted that it considered the death penalty essential, and pointed out that it had not yet been abolished in the United Kingdom.[166] Nevertheless, the German state prosecutors decided to ask the occupying powers to stop passing death sentences, including sentences passed against war criminals, thus incidentally underlining once more the role of such considerations in establishing Article 102 in the first place. The situation was now thoroughly confused. Not only did Allied courts sentence war criminals to death, they also continued to pass death sentences on offenders from Germany and other countries for murders which fell under the aegis of Paragraph 211 of the German Criminal Code. One such offender, a Pole, won an appeal in September 1949 against a death sentence for murder passed by the British High Court after the Basic Law had come into force, on the not unreasonable grounds that he would only have received a custodial sentence had he been condemned by a German court. Similar appeals were successful in the French and American zones. Meanwhile, German judicial officials were ordered by the meeting of senior state prosecutors of the federated states not to co-operate in any more executions that were ordered by military courts. Technically speaking, they might well be guilty of murder under German law should they do so.[167]

The British Control Commission accepted in July 1949 the argument that Germans should not have to assist in carrying out executions.[168] The use of the guillotine was abolished on 17 July 1949 by order of the Military Governor.[169] The last person to be guillotined in an area controlled by the Western Allies was Berthold W., aged 24, who was convicted by a German court in Berlin for murder and sexual crimes and executed, as we have seen, at Lehrterstrasse prison at 6.30 in the morning on 11 May 1949.[170] Henceforth, all executions ordered by the occupying powers in the Western zones were carried out by hanging. The 'staffs who man the guillotine' were dismissed by the governments of the federated states.[171] On 25 November 1949 the Allied High Commission agreed that while the Basic Law did not affect the competence of Allied courts, the High

[166] BA Koblenz Z21/894, Bl. 28: Protokoll über die Besprechung mit Mr. Boulton und Mr. Romberg vom 22. Juni 1949.

[167] Ibid. 806, Bl. 28: Protokoll über die Besprechungen auf der Tagung der Generalstaatsanwälte der Westzonen in Neustadt an der Haardt am 19. und 20. Sept. 1949.

[168] PRO/FO 1060/243, 30: Land Legal Department Hanover to Deputy Legal Adviser, Zonal Office of the Legal Adviser, 7 July 1949.

[169] Ibid. 371/1672: Telegrams from Foreign Office to Wahn, 25 Nov. 1949, Lübbecke to Foreign Office 30 Nov. 1949, and draft parliamentary reply 1 Dec. 1949 to question by Elwyn Jones, MP.

[170] Ibid. 1060/243, S. 7: Telegram from Military Government Berlin to Penal Branch Zonal Office of the legal Adviser Herford, 11 May 1949. Another execution was carried out in the same prison on 29 April (ibid. 5, 29 Apr.).

[171] Ibid. 28: Confidential memo, Inglis to Moller, 6 July 1949.

Commission would ensure that 'persons sentenced by Allied courts pursuant to German laws shall not be sentenced to death', while 'persons sentenced under Allied law may be condemned to death' but only 'in cases clearly affecting the interests of the Occupation and in war crime trials'. The minimum age for execution was now fixed at 18. These decisions were not to be made public to the Germans.[172] The right-wing politicians who had ensured that the abolition of capital punishment was written into the Basic Law had thus failed in their primary objective of stopping executions for war crimes. In June 1950 there were still fifteen people awaiting execution in Landsberg prison after being sentenced to death by the International Military Tribunal, and another fifteen on death row who had been sentenced by other war crimes tribunals. There was also a solitary offender who had been condemned by a military court for the common murder of an Allied national.[173] The last major group of war criminals, including the senior SS officer Otto Ohlendorf, was executed in the prison as late as 1951, two years after the Basic Law came into force. In 1952, however, it was decided that executions would cease once the new 'Contractual Agreement between West Germany and the Western Allies' was promulgated. And by March 1953 the British Foreign Office was insisting in any case that 'judicial hangings should no longer be carried out in Germany', in the light of a 'ruling by the Prime Minister that we should not take advantage of the fact that we were occupying Germany to offend the susceptibilities of the inhabitants'. 'As far as we are concerned,' the Foreign Office stated, 'Northern Army Group can dismantle their gallows.'[174] It was removed from Hamelin prison in 1954 and eventually transferred to Pentonville prison in London early in 1956.[175]

d. The Campaign to Reintroduce Capital Punishment

As Gustav Radbruch had predicted, the fact that capital punishment had been outlawed in the Basic Law did not prevent conservative politicians from trying to reintroduce it. Scarcely a year had passed when, on 24 February 1950, the Bavarian Party, which had not been represented in the Parliamentary Council and which had bitterly opposed the Basic Law in the Bavarian Parliament, put forward a motion for the reintroduction of capital punishment to the Federal Parliament which had been elected the previous year. The Bavarian Party had 17

[172] NA Washington 260/C7/D2/b.46: Allied High Commission Council Decisions requiring Unilateral Implementation—Meeting of 5 Jan. 1950; see also Düsing, *Abschaffung*, 298.

[173] NA Washington 260/C7/D37/53/36/2/b.137: Draft Studies for Inter-Governmental Study Group, 15 June 1950 (H. H. Urman).

[174] PRO/FO 371/109595: Johnston to Hancock, 19 May 1954, and reply, 14 June 1954.

[175] Ibid. 1060/417, 58: Chown (Commander-in Chief, BAOR), to Legal Branch, UK High Commission, 18 Sept. 1954; ibid. 70: Roots (British Embassy, Bonn) to PS I Branch HQ, Northern Army Group, 23 Dec. 1955.

seats in the Federal Parliament. The Christian Democrats had 142, and the predominantly retentionist Free Democrats 53, and there were a number of right-wing splinter-groups which might also be expected to vote for reinstatement. Moreover, a majority of the German Party, who had been responsible for the original motion for abolition, had now swung round in favour of capital punishment once more. Their spokesman argued that the only proper justification for the death penalty was retribution for murder, and that this view was shared by all sectors of the population. So the chances even of a two-thirds majority did not seem entirely hopeless, given the fact that the Social Democrats had 136 seats out of a total of 410, or just short of a third.[176]

The motion came up for debate on 27 March 1950, scarcely a year after the original decision to abolish the death penalty in the Basic Law. Introducing it, Hermann Etzel, of the Bavarian Party, began by reminding the deputies that the debate on the subject had been in progress for almost two centuries, in effect since Beccaria. The arguments for and against, he said, had changed little since the Lawyers' Congress of 1912: 'Murderers do not hesitate to send their poor, innocent victims to their death, coldly and brutally, just because it is the twentieth century.' Etzel called for a more sober, less passionate debate than the one which had led to the inconclusive votes of the Criminal Law Committee of the Reichstag in 1929. He pointed out that no previous German constitution had contained the abolition of the death penalty. He could understand the motives of the Parliamentary Council in voting for it. But in doing so, they had failed to consult the people. The Parliamentary Council was not a democratic assembly: it was composed of representatives of the legislatures in the federated states, and some of these were themselves not democratically elected bodies. It was clear

that the sense of right and wrong of the vast majority of the population does not feel that a custodial sentence, not even one of life imprisonment, constitutes a punishment sufficient to the severity of the crime, that society has the right to defend itself against the bestiality of monsters in human form, against criminals who murder their fathers, mothers, children, who murder often many times for gain, or for sexual motives, and that this right empowers it to exterminate violent criminals by killing them, as expiation, as a deterrent, and for its security, and to prevent a future amnesty or political revolution, which, as history shows, often enlists the most cold-blooded, most ruthless, and most energetic elements from the penitentiaries to help it, from providing the opportunity for new misdeeds or the possibility of further increasing the enormously negative selection of our people caused by two world wars by reproducing itself.

Etzel's speech was remarkable not only for its unconscious use of Nazi language ('exterminate . . . negative selection') but also for its perpetuation of the far-right

[176] Düsing, *Abschaffung*, 301–3; *Bundestag* 1. Wahlperiode, Drucksache Nr. 619.

fantasy of the Weimar years, according to which revolutions were caused by professional criminals. The German people, he said, in a further distortion of the facts, did not understand why German courts could not condemn to death the foreigners who were responsible for the vast majority of murders in Germany. He pointed out that the main opponents of the death penalty, the Social Democrats, had themselves supported it in the Law for the Protection of the Republic which they had introduced in 1922.[177]

Unfortunately for the proponents of reintroduction, the Federal Justice Minister Thomas Dehler, although a Free Democrat, was a strong supporter of abolition. In his response to the motion, he told the deputies that he would shortly be introducing a major reform of the criminal law. That was the proper time and occasion for a debate on the death penalty. An attempt to revise the Basic Law so soon after its promulgation, coupled with such a strong attack on the legitimacy of the body that had passed it, could only be seen as an attack on the Law itself.[178] Speaking for the Social Democrats, Friedrich-Wilhelm Wagner accused the Bavarian Party of acting out of pique because they had been denied a seat on the Council. Amidst furious shouts and objections from the Bavarians, he declared that what they really wanted was to get rid of the Basic Law altogether. In claiming that no German constitution had ever abolished the death penalty, he said, Etzel had forgotten the constitution of 1848–9. Moreover, the Reichstag of the North German Confederation had abolished it in 1870, and only reinstated it after 'an extraordinary intervention by the government'. As a member of the Criminal Law Committee of the Reichstag in 1929, Wagner could also confirm that a majority of members had been in favour of abolition there too. Moving on to the central issue, he pointed out that where the death penalty had been abolished, as in Italy between 1890 and 1925, there had been no noticeable increase in the murder rate as a result. If there were more murders in post-war Germany than before, this was not because there was no more death penalty, but because there was a general increase of criminality of all kinds, caused by the disruptive effects of the war. Irresponsible reporting in the newspapers, together with 'trashy literature', had made things worse. And finally, Nazism had destroyed respect for life and law. 'You can only combat murder', he said, 'by implanting in people a respect for the sanctity of the law ... The crueller the punishments, the crueller the crimes!' Society would be sufficiently protected by putting murderers in gaol. The demand for capital punishment was no more than a primitive demand for revenge and retribution. If the supporters of reintroduction really thought executions would act as a deterrent, why did they not demand that they be carried out in public? It was time that respect for

[177] *Bundestag*, 1. Wahlperiode, 52. Sitzung, 27 Mar. 1950, 1894–5.
[178] Ibid. 1895–6.

life became more general in Germany—a respect which, he said, Etzel seemed to lack, if his use of the word 'exterminate' was anything to go by. Only if states came to respect life within their own boundaries would they desist from venturing to take it elsewhere, through conflict, invasion, and war. The Bavarian Party wanted to bring back executions, but, he asked them, if an executioner came and sat at their table in their local inn, 'would you stay at that table, shake his hand, and drink a glass with him?' Wagner doubted it. The demand for the death penalty might be a popular one, he conceded, but it reflected 'a dark impulse' which people recognized as such by their behaviour in such matters. It was not for the Parliament to give way to it.[179]

Although the Social Democrats and Communists remained solidly in favour of keeping Article 102, and the Bavarian Party and other small splinter-groups of the right solidly against, a number of political groupings in the Parliament were seriously divided on the issue. The particularist German Party, as in the previous year, was split down the middle, a majority arguing for the death penalty as the only just expiation for murder, a minority, represented by Hans-Joachim von Merkatz, declaring that the Federal Republic had to take a stand on behalf of humanitarianism in the face of the 'subversion of our Western spirit' which he believed was taking place.[180] In this view, capital punishment, ironically, now appeared as a Communist policy, a view which the Communist speaker Heinz Renner did nothing to counter when he defended its use by the Soviet Union against Western imperialist agents. Renner reflected post-war hostility between the Communist Party and the Catholic Church by denouncing the long tradition of Catholic support for the death penalty.[181] While the few Communists in the Parliament were solidly abolitionist, the liberal Free Democrats were split, as German liberals had been for many decades. One group of deputies, led as we have seen by Justice Minister Thomas Dehler, supported the retention of Article 102, but another, represented by Fritz Neumayer, came down in favour of its deletion. The retributive instinct might be primitive, admitted Neumayer, but primitive urges could sometimes be a good thing. Like other speakers in the debate, too, he noted that the Western democracies mostly retained the death penalty. Serious crime was on the increase, and a serious deterrent was necessary. Respect for life in society at large demanded not the abolition of capital punishment but its reinstatement as the only way of reducing the murder rate.[182]

It was remarkable indeed how many of the speakers who supported reintroduction rested their case primarily on the idea of retribution. Herwart Miessner, of the neo-Nazi German Reich Party, while conceding, for example, that there

---

[179] *Bundestag*, 1. Wahlperiode, 52. Sitzung, 27 Mar. 1950, 1897–1904.   [180] Ibid. 1909–12.
[181] Ibid. 1915–17.   [182] Ibid. 1912–13.

was some doubt about the deterrent effects of capital punishment, had no doubts at all about the rightness of retribution:

The theory of expiation or retribution . . . is the one that is really rooted in the people. Criminal law, more than any other, has to be close to the people. Ask people of every class—especially the earthiest and most uneducated classes—and above all, ask women! They will support capital punishment in their overwhelming majority, from their natural instincts.[183]

Here was a whole bundle of Nazi arguments, and older ones too: 'healthy popular feeling', the superior legitimacy of instinct, blood, and soil, the closeness of women to earth and nature. But such language cut less ice than it had done before. Crucial to the outcome of the debate was the fact that a number of Christian Democrats thought it unwise for the Basic Law to be disputed at this early stage.[184] Thus ironically, while German unity had been argued by Bismarck as a reason for continuing to use the death penalty, it was now used by men in some ways as conservative as he was to argue for continuing to do without it. In both cases, the broad principle of national unity took precedence over the narrower principle of criminal law. In both cases, the other side was reassured that the proper time to look at the question would be when a new Criminal Code came before the Parliament. While the German Empire was built symbolically on the retention of capital punishment, however, the Federal Republic was built symbolically on its abolition. There could be no more striking illustration of the differences in the spirit animating their foundation, as well as of the circum-stances in which they had come into being. Yet, despite the commitment to democracy shown by the framers of the Basic Law, public opinion was not permitted to weigh the scales of the legislature in favour of reintroducing the death penalty. As the Social Democrat Carlo Schmid remarked, if there had been a referendum on the burning of witches a couple of hundred years before, the bonfires would still be blazing. The Social Democrats, following the example of their predecessors on the abolitionist side in 1870 and 1919, argued that it was the legislature's job to educate the population, not to follow the least humane of its instincts. The damage done to public morality by the Nazis had to be made good. This view was shared not only by a substantial number of Free Democrats but also by Hans-Joachim von Merkatz from the German Party, who had been one of the sponsors of the original motion to abolish the death penalty in the Basic Law. 'A democracy', he said, 'must move forward, and to a certain extent construct authority from above.'[185] It would not help the construction of such authority if they started tinkering about with the Basic Law so soon after it had

[183] Ibid. 1917–18.
[184] Düsing, *Abschaffung*, 306–7.
[185] *Bundestag*, 1. Wahlperiode, 52. Sitzung, 27 Mar. 1950, 1911–12, 1918–19.

been passed. On the left as well as on a significant part of the right, therefore, there was a feeling that, once the constitution had been passed, it should not be tampered with. Since the Bavarian Party's motion failed to win the support of any Communists or Social Democrats, and even found opponents further to the right, among the Free Democrats, the German Party, and the small Union for Ecomonic Reconstruction (which commanded twelve seats in the Federal Parliament), it not only failed to win the two-thirds majority necessary to pass into law, but even fell short of obtaining an absolute majority from the 345 deputies present in the chamber during the debate.[186]

Two years later the supporters of capital punishment tried again. This time the initiative came from the Christian Democrats, whose parliamentary delegation in the Federal Parliament voted on 4 September 1952 to support a motion for the reintroduction of the death penalty. Proponents of capital punishment such as Wilhelm Keil argued that the issue should be put to a free vote, as a matter of individual conscience, and should not be subjected to party discipline, particularly since there had always been individual Social Democrats who had disagreed with their abolitionist party line on this issue.[187] But the Christian Democratic parliamentary delegation was itself divided on the question, so that a free vote would also have been unlikely to have won the majority required for a constitutional change. At this point, the German Party, which had joined the government coalition led by the Christian Democrats, took up the baton and put a motion for the deletion of Article 102 of the Basic Law before the Federal Parliament. Their move provided the occasion for the last great parliamentary debate on the death penalty, on 2 October 1952. Introducing the motion, Hans Ewers, for the German Party, noted that the promised revision of the criminal law had not materialized. In the mean time, a particularly serious murder case in Verden, from where a 'criminal' had sent parcel-bombs to a number of ex-Nazis, had aroused widespread disquiet because it had not been possible to condemn the offender to death. The Protestant Church in Lower Saxony had passed a resolution in favour of capital punishment in general as a result, reflecting a belief in what Ewers described as 'the retributive point of view, which in the end is the only possible justification for capital punishment'. Ewers reflected the far right's anti-Americanism as well as its bid for the ex-Nazi vote when he blamed violent crime in Germany on those 'who are importing American gangsterism onto Central European territory'. This could only be combated by capital punishment.[188] He was backed by Hermann Etzel, who advocated the death penalty not

---

[186] Düsing, *Abschaffung*, 310.

[187] HStA Stuttgart EA 1/106 Bü 1060: Wilhelm Keil, 'Der Pressechef erklärt', *Ludwigsburger Kreiszeitung*, 9 Sept. 1952.

[188] *Deutscher Bundestag*, 1. Wahlperiode, 232. Sitzung, 2 Oct. 1952, 10606–9.

only for murder but also for kidnapping, of which there had been a number of cases carried out by East German agents in West Berlin.[189]

The high point of the debate was a lengthy, detailed, and powerful speech from the Justice Minister Thomas Dehler. Tracing the history of capital punishment since the Middle Ages, Dehler reminded his listeners of the debates that had taken place in 1848, 1870, and 1919, as well as in the Lawyers' Congress of 1912 and the Criminal Law Committee of the Reichstag in 1928–9. Under the Third Reich, some 16,500 death sentences had been passed, and it was not least under the impact of these events that the Parliamentary Council had taken its celebrated vote on Article 102. Not only the German constitution of 1848, but also the constitutions of Italy, Austria, Portugal, Switzerland, Nicaragua, Colombia, Ecuador, and Uruguay had abolished capital punishment. He recalled that one's views on the death penalty depended partly on one's concept of death, as Bismarck had noted in 1870, partly on one's concept of the state. If both were secular rather than religious, as Dehler clearly believed they should be, then the logical consequence was bound to be opposition to capital punishment. Christianity as a whole was inconclusive on the issue: for every quotation supporting capital punishment in the Old Testament, it was possible to find another opposing it in the New. And to the central point made by the restorationists— that the death penalty was favoured by the mass of the people—Dehler gave the classic reply: that parliamentary democracy was a representative system, and that the deputies had to make their own mind up on the issues before them. Public opinion in any case varied under the influence of events: after a particularly terrible murder it was strongly in favour of capital punishment, after a case of wrongful execution, strongly against. To argue for retribution meant putting the state on the same level as the criminals it was condemning. The state was only entitled to use the death penalty in self-defence when it was subjected to 'a great number of attacks which are in the last analysis also directed against the community'. Even here, however, as history showed:

The maintenance of the death penalty for a small number of offences, even for one alone, contains in itself the danger of expansion. If the fundamental decision is for capital punishment, then the decisive threshold has been crossed; in this case, its extension is not a matter of principle any more. Anyone, ladies and gentlemen, who has experienced, as I have, how people in the last world war were taken to the scaffold for a word, one can say, for a gesture, for an attitude, even if scarcely articulated, or for economic behaviour, knows what dangers lie in the possibility of extending the death penalty.

With the death penalty, it was all or nothing, he said.

In terms of necessity and utility there were several arguments against capital punishment, he went on. It did not fit in well with modern penal principles. It

[189] Ibid. 10609–10.

was *qualitatively* different from other punishments, and yet punishments were otherwise graded in *quantitative* terms, according to the severity of the offence. It was an absolute penalty, yet guilt—it was generally admitted—was relative, it was greater or lesser according to the circumstances, and was usually shared with other individuals, with social influences, and other factors besides the responsibility of the individual offender. 'I would experience the death penalty', Dehler said, 'as a foreign body . . . in our penal system, because our age regards the decisive or at least the principal task of penal sanctions as the resocialization, the amelioration, of the human being.' Prison chaplains, he conceded, had reported that condemned people had experienced an 'inner conversion' in the face of imminent execution. But it was quite possible, he said, that this was merely superficial, born of fear or of a desire for a last-minute reprieve. Genuine remorse was much more likely to occur during a long term of imprisonment. As for the claim that capital punishment was deterrent, surely, argued Dehler, the not infrequent demand made by murderers in the dock to be executed showed that few of them were afraid of death—a conclusion confirmed by the fact that no fewer than 153 out of 287 murderers in Berlin between 1926 and 1932 had committed suicide. It was clear enough in any case 'that it is precisely the countries and the times of the toughest penalties that have witnessed the bloodiest and must inhuman crimes'. The murder rate, he pointed out in some detail, was falling in Germany, a fact which demonstrated the irrelevance of the death penalty as a deterrent. Moreover, as the Berlin suicide figures suggested, most murderers committed their deeds in an abnormal state of mind in which they were unlikely to think of the consequences anyway. Far from deterring people, capital punishment awakened the beast in them and made murder more rather than less likely to occur. A murderer threatened with capture by the police was more likely to kill for his freedom if the death penalty threatened his life. The evidence showed that most murderers were people without previous convictions, unlikely to kill again, and conducted themselves well in prison. Capital punishment could only make things worse. Finally, he said, the danger of judicial error could never be ruled out.[190]

Dehler's speech dominated the debate. In comparison, the other contributions were mere footnotes. Friedrich Wilhelm Wagner, the Social Democrats' main spokesman on the issue, added (in an exact repetition of the arguments used by his predecessors in 1919) that the state should lead the people rather than follow; it was vital that it should stick by its declared support for the sanctity of life. The Free Democrats admitted that they were divided on the issue, and limited themselves to putting the arguments for both sides without coming down on

---

[190] *Deutscher Bundestag*, 10610–16.

either. The Communist speaker, Walter Fisch, launched a tirade against West German judges, who (he said) would resume 'the old practice of Freisler's Special Courts' if given half a chance, and denounced the Catholic Church, with whose crusades against heresy in the Middle Ages he compared the desire of some of the government's supporters to punish 'any political opposition against the war-course Adenauer government'.[191] Support for reintroduction had grown among the Christian Democrats since 1950, not least because it was now generally felt that the Basic Law had established its legitimacy firmly enough to be able to withstand amendments on specific points.[192] Moreover, deputies reported being put under pressure by constituents demanding they support the death penalty.[193] Nevertheless, the solid support of the Social Democrats, together with the continuing divisions among the Free Democrats, Christian Democrats, and German Party deputies on the issue was enough to ensure that the motion to delete Article 102 was lost by a substantial majority. The second motion, to restore the death penalty for murder and kidnapping, was lost by a narrower margin, 151 votes to 146 with two abstentions.[194] Neither therefore got any further in the legislative process.

e. Article 102 and the Legacy of the Third Reich

Despite this setback, the proponents of reintroduction did not abandon their quest. Given the obvious difficulties of obtaining a two-thirds majority, it is hard not to feel that the continued public agitation for the return of the death penalty was principally directed to voters outside the Federal Parliament. Politicians on the right were well aware that this was a popular issue. In February 1949 a poll carried out by the Allensbach Institute revealed overwhelming support for retention. Asked whether it should be included in a new Criminal Code, 77 per cent said yes, and only 18 per cent no. Traditional attitudes were reflected in the fact that the only crime which a majority of those questioned thought should definitely be punished by death was murder (73 per cent in favour, 27 per cent against). For all other crimes, opinion was opposed to capital punishment by a substantial majority. The effects of the Nazi period were shown by the fact that among those aged 30 and under the majority in favour of retention was 81 to 15 per cent, while among the 31- to 50-year-olds it was 76 to 19 per cent, among 51- to 65-year-olds 69 to 22 per cent, and among those aged 65 and over, 64 to 26 per cent. Both men (77 to 18 per cent) and women (72 to 21 per cent) were strongly retentionist. The differences between Catholics and Protestants were negligible,

[191] Ibid. 10623–8.   [192] Ibid. 10618B.
[193] Ibid. 10622D.
[194] HStA Stuttgart EA 1/106 Bü 1060: *Offenburger Tageblatt*, 3 Oct. 1952.

though the majorities in favour seem to have been exceptionally strong in those Protestant electoral bastions of Nazism before 1933, Lower Saxony (79 per cent in favour, 18 against) and Schleswig-Holstein (86 per cent in favour, 8 against) and unusually low in the traditional electoral centres of liberalism, Baden (65 per cent in favour, 30 against) and Württemberg (62 per cent in favour, 28 against).[195] The tide of popular opinion continued to flow in favour of the death penalty throughout the 1950s and showed no sign of ebbing: 55 per cent of those asked wanted the return of capital punishment in 1950; 54 per cent ten years later. When asked whether they favoured it for murder without mitigating circumstances, no fewer than 80 per cent said 'yes' in 1950, and 71 per cent ten years later.[196] One 'honourable, reasonable-minded' man who wrote to the Württemberg government in February 1959 surely spoke for many when he said 'I curse Hitler, who has brought untold misery over the human race. But in one area he created order, and it is worth imitating him in this: he made short shrift with violent crime.'[197] Refugee and expellee groups favoured reintroduction as well.[198] With over eleven million ethnic German refugees and expellees from East-Central and Eastern Europe now living in the Federal Republic, mostly deeply conservative and violently hostile to the Communists whom they blamed for the loss of their homes and properties, such opinions were sure of a wide hearing on the right. Among occupational groups the police, despite a few dissenting voices in their ranks,[199] were also in favour, as might be expected.[200] It was undeniable, one officer declared, 'that the death penalty can only be welcomed as an expiation for a murderer whose previous life has been one of professional crime'.[201] Another policeman revealed his inability to rethink the categories common under the Third Reich when he referred to murderers as 'subhumans' who had to be exterminated.[202] Such arguments received backing from Dehler's successor as Federal Justice Minister, the Free Democrat Fritz Neumayer, who argued for reintroduction on the ground 'the more serious a crime is, the more serious the punishment should be. For the administration of

[195] BA Koblenz Z21/806, Bl. 6: *Echo der Woche* (Munich), 25 Feb. 1949.

[196] Karl-Heinz Reuband, 'Sanktionsverlangen im Wandel. Die Einstellung zur Todesstrafe in der Bundesrepublik Deutschland seit 1950', *Kölner Zeitschrift für Soziologie und Sozialpsychologie*, 32 (1980), 535–58, here 542–3.

[197] HStA Stuttgart EA1/922 Nr. 5308: anon. postcards, received 9 Feb. 1959.

[198] BA Koblenz NL Lüders 118: Vorschlag für die Wiedereinführung der Todesstrafe (Verein Politischer Ostflüchtlinge, Berlin-Steglitz, 7 May 1954).

[199] Ibid.: 'Um die Wiedereinführung der Todesstrafe', *ÖTV Presse Fachbeilage 'Polizeidienst'*, Jan. 1955, 19; W. Schnesche, 'Wiedereinführung der Todesstafe? Nein!', *ÖTV Presse Fachbeilage 'Polizeidienst'*, Feb. 1955, 35.

[200] Ibid.: M. Helmecke, 'Todesstrafe ist Notwehr', *ÖTV Presse Fachbeilage 'Polizeidienst'*, Apr. 1955, 98.

[201] Ibid.: A. Knupfer, 'Wiedereinführung der Todesstrafe', *ÖTV Presse Fachbeilage 'Polizeidienst'*, Apr. 1955, 98.

[202] Ibid.: S. Aigner, 'Für und wider die Todesstrafe', *ÖTV Presse Fachbeilage 'Polizeidienst'*, Mar. 1955.

German law in its present practice,' he added, 'I regard capital punishment as indispensable.'[203] Even in the 1950s, German liberals were still divided on this issue, and liberal supporters of the death penalty such as Neumayer were far from unusual. Not only was public opinion broadly in favour of capital punishment during the 1950s, but calls for the reintroduction of the death penalty multiplied when particularly serious individual cases of murder were reported in the mass media. In 1958, the killing of a child in Württemberg gave rise to renewed calls for the reintroduction of capital punishment.[204] A number of deputies tried on 14 January 1958 to amend Article 102 of the Basic Law so as to remove the abolition of the death penalty, while the German Party once more brought in a motion to reintroduce capital punishment (by beheading) for murder, on 14 May 1958.[205] In July 1958 the Minister of the Interior in Adenauer's government, Gerhard Schröder, spoke out in favour of the death penalty for 'traitors' and 'enemies of the state'. But there was a split within the Christian Democratic Party on this issue, with the Catholic politicians reportedly favouring reintroduction and the Protestants on the whole opposing it.[206] Evidently the long tradition of Catholic support for the death penalty still lived on. However, it was no longer strong enough to affect the issue. The new Justice Minister Ewald Bucher was personally opposed to capital punishment, and made it clear during preparations for the Criminal Code that it could not override the Basic Law. In 1963–4 reports that the cabinet had still to make up its mind on the issue encouraged restorationists to attempt to force capital punishment into the new Code.[207] But as on so many previous occasions in German history, the attempt to put through a new Criminal Code came to nothing. The draft produced in 1962 was widely regarded as unacceptably old-fashioned, though not admittedly in its attitude to the death penalty. It emphasized retribution as the primary principle of punishment and proposed the criminalization of homosexuality, adultery, and artificial human insemination. In the more liberal climate of the 1960s, it stood little chance of success, and was superseded from 1969 onwards by a series of piecemeal, largely liberal criminal law reforms.[208]

One of the many considerations that led to this decision was the fact that it was becoming clear that the abolition of capital punishment in the Basic Law had not increased the murder rate. According to official statistics, there had been 163 condemnations for murder in 1933, 319 in 1934, 170 in 1935, 153 in 1936, 179 in

---

[203] Ibid.: *Hamburger Anzeiger*, 29 Jan. 1955.

[204] HStA Stuttgart EA 1/106 Bü 1060: *Frankfurter Allgemeine Zeitung*, 5 Oct. 1962.

[205] *Bundestag*, 3. Wahlperiode, Drucksache Nr. 361, 389, 390, 391.

[206] HStA Stuttgart EA 1/106 Bü 1060: *Frankfurter Allgemeine Zeitung*, 14 July 1958.

[207] *Bundestag*, 4. Wahlperiode, debate of 28 Mar. 1963 (70. Sitzung), 3168 and 3217; ibid., 138. Sitzung (16 Oct. 1964), 6872.

[208] Hinrich Rüping, *Grundriss der Strafrechtsgeschichte* (Munich, 1981), 113–18.

1937, and 125 in 1938. Superficially, therefore, it seemed that the reintroduction and expansion of the death penalty under the Nazis had led to a decline in the number of condemnations, at least in peacetime. However, the figures were not very persuasive, given the fact that political murders carried out by the Nazis in 1933 and 1934, and in the concentration camps subsequently, were not punished, while those allegedly carried out by Communists in the late 1920s and early 1930s were—hence the high number of condemnations in 1934. What was really striking in the light of the debate on the death penalty after the war was that the number of condemnations for murder actually fell after the promulgation of Article 102, from 198 in 1949 to 136 in 1950 to 110 in 1951, 138 in 1952, 145 in 1953, 95 in 1954, and 123 in 1955. The murder rate stood at 0.28 per 100,000 population in the 1930s, and fell to 0.26 in the 1950s.[209] If we take the broader statistical measure of homicide (murder and manslaughter) convictions, we get figures of 757 in 1947, 521 in 1948, 427 in 1949, 410 in 1950, 361 in 1951, 379 in 1952, 308 in 1953, 270 in 1954, 348 in 1955, and 316 in 1956. Of course, in part this reflected the fact that DPs, the source of a substantial proportion of these convictions, were gradually being repatriated in this period. And the decline of the black market and the organized, violent crime that went with it undoubtedly also played a role. Yet the rate of homicide convictions per 100,000 people in Germany above the minimum age of criminal responsibility seems in the longer term to have been relatively unaffected by the vagaries of the implementation of the death penalty. Standing at 0.66 in 1900–14, it rose to 1.07 in 1919–32, fell slightly to 0.96 in 1933–8, and then dropped further to 0.73 in West Germany in 1950–5.[210] In the 1880s, when the death penalty had been the punishment for murder or aggravated manslaughter, and when the number of executions had actually been growing, there had been eight homicide condemnations per million population in Germany, while by the years 1954 to 1962 the figure had declined to six.[211] It was impossible for anyone to argue convincingly from these statistics that capital punishment was an effective deterrent against homicide, or that its abolition in the Basic Law had led to a dramatic rise in the murder rate.[212]

The demand for the reintroduction of capital punishment in the Federal Republic was raised, therefore, on the basis of individual cases rather than global statistics. A particular role here was played by organizations acting on behalf of

[209] Albert Scheffbuch, 'Mörder werden durch Tod nicht abgeschreckt', *Stuttgarter Nachrichten*, 26 July 1958, in HStA Stuttgart EA 1/106 Bü 1060. See also BA Koblenz NL Lüders 118: *ÖTV Presse Fachbeilage 'Polizeidienst'*, Nov. 1952, 345 (giving a figure of 138 for 1950 and 98 for 1951).

[210] HStA Stuttgart EA 1/106 Bü 1060: Günter Kohlmann, 'Im Zweifel gegen die Todesstrafe', *Handelsblatt*, 9/10 Oct. 1964. Another set of figures for homicides and attempted homicides gives 572 in 1947, 483 in 1948, 351 in 1949, 314 in 1950, and 295 in 1951 (BA Koblenz NL Lüders 118: *ÖTV Presse Fachbeilage 'Polizeidienst'*, Nov. 1952, 345).

[211] HStA Stuttgart EA 1/106 Bü 1060: *Die Welt*, 8 Dec. 1964.

[212] See also Düsing, *Abschaffung*, 311–19, and Statistical Appendix, below.

groups of people who considered themselves to be especially vulnerable. In 1962, the murder of a taxi driver led to calls for the reintroduction of the death penalty from the Taxi Drivers' Union.[213] Yet public opinion, at least as it was articulated through the press, was lukewarm on the issue. 'As soon as a horrible crime is committed in Germany, such as the murder of a child or a particularly evil-minded murder for gain, there are crowds of people who demand that the state should no longer refrain from availing itself of the most draconian means to combat criminality', noted the influential liberal-conservative daily, the *Frankfurter Allgemeine*, in October 1962. Yet, the newspaper went on, the death penalty was not a 'miracle weapon in the state's crime-fighting arsenal'. Its deterrent effects were unproven. The decisive point was that a full-scale parliamentary debate on its reintroduction would give the wrong impression abroad, especially since it coincided with the ending of the legal time-limit for the prosecution of war crimes. Foreign opinion would see in the two measures a dangerous backsliding into Germany's old ways. The paper condemned, therefore, what it called 'this dangerous game with the death penalty'.[214] Two years later, in 1964, the murder of the Bonn taxi driver Karl-Heinz Koch unleashed yet another nation-wide debate on capital punishment. Once more, given the public outcry and the evidence of the opinion polls, which showed an increase in support for the death penalty over the previous year, politicians on the right saw a chance of winning popularity by coming out in favour of restoration. The parliamentary delegation of the Christian Democrats approved the bringing in of a motion to remove Clause 102. Rainer Barzel, their parliamentary floor leader in the 1960s, was in favour, as was the party's parliamentary business manager Will Rasner.[215] However, the minority of abolitionists in the governing coalition, which included Federal Chancellor Ludwig Erhard, was strong enough to force Barzel to promise a free vote on the issue.[216] In the end, it was never held, since the chances of getting a two-thirds majority were so small. Demands for a referendum on the issue met with little success, since the destabilizing effects of referendums in the Weimar Republic had caused the framers of the Basic Law to forbid them without exception.[217]

These events showed that support for capital punishment was finally beginning to decline on the right. In 1960, when Federal Justice Minister Fritz Schäfer, speaking to a conference of legal experts in Munich, declared himself in favour of a reintroduction of capital punishment, he was greeted not only with applause

---

[213] HStA Stuttgart EA 1/106 Bü 1060: *Stuttgarter Nachrichten*, 6 Oct. 1962.

[214] Ibid.: Johann Georg Reissmüller, 'Das gefährliche Spiel mit der Todesstrafe', *Frankfurter Allgemeine Zeitung*, 8 Oct. 1962.

[215] HStA Stuttgart EA 1/106 Bü 1060: Ibid.: *Stuttgarter Zeitung*, 6 Oct. 1964.

[216] Ibid.: *Stuttgarter Zeitung*, 7 Oct. 1964; *Die Zeit*, 9 Oct. 1964.

[217] Ibid.: *Stuttgarter Nachrichten*, 10 Oct. 1964 (Letters to the Editor).

but also with hissing from the audience.[218] His successor Richard Jaeger, member of the Christian Social Union and another proponent of the death penalty, was no more successful in winning adherents for his views.[219] When former Federal Chancellor Konrad Adenauer spoke out in public in favour of reintroduction in 1962, he was accused of trying to make capital for the forthcoming election campaign, and his initiative met with a negative response in the youth organization of his party.[220] Nor did the floor leader of the Bavarian sister-party of the Christian Democrats, the Christian Social Union, Richard Stücklen, have much success when he urged the Federal Parliament to consider the introduction of capital punishment for child murderers in 1967. The Federal Justice Ministry was forced to dissociate itself from his views and declare that it had no intention of trying to change the law in this respect.[221] Politicians were becoming aware that majority public support for the death penalty was finally disappearing. Between 1964 and 1971, the percentage of the population favouring capital punishment declined from 52 to 43; by 1972 it had fallen to 33, rising to 45 at the height of the Baader–Meinhof terrorist campaign in 1977, only to fall back once more to 28 by 1980. Even the percentage answering 'yes' to the somewhat loaded question: 'Are you for or against the death penalty for murder where there are no mitigating circumstances?' fell from 80 in 1958 to 65 in 1964, 53 in 1973, and 44 in 1974, following the broader trend in rising again to 61 in 1977, then falling back again. Even among Christian Democratic voters, the percentage favouring the death penalty in general had fallen to 34 by 1980, with 45 per cent against, while among Social Democratic supporters the majority against, at 59 to 23 per cent, was still more decisive. Correspondingly, even conservative politicians now began to realize that it was pointless to try and gain political capital out of the issue. This new trend of public opinion against the death penalty reflected a generational change now in progress in West Germany, culminating in the student revolt of 1968. Younger people were clearly against the death penalty, with those born in the 1940s and educated largely in the post-Nazi period showing much less enthusiasm for it than older age cohorts. During the 1950s, the more educated groups in society tended to support capital punishment to a greater extent than their less educated counterparts, reflecting the long tradition of the identification of the middle and upper classes with conservative and authoritarian values and the equally long tradition of support on the part of manual labourers and their families for the abolitionist Social Democrats. But by the 1970s this relationship

---

[218] HStA Stuttgart EA 1/106 Bü 1060.: *Stuttgarter Nachrichten*, 24 Oct. 1960.
[219] Ibid.: *Stuttgarter Nachrichten*, 3 Nov. 1965.
[220] Ibid.: *Frankfurter Allgemeine*, 5 Oct. 1962; *Stuttgarter Nachrichten*, 6 Oct. 1962.
[221] Ibid.: *Stuttgarter Zeitung*, 7 Sept. 1967; *Stuttgarter Nachrichten*, 8 Sept. 1967.

had been reversed, with support for the death penalty decreasing with the level of general education. This reflected the spread of liberal and left-wing values in the universities and increasingly among high-school teachers on the one hand, and the decay of old labour movement traditions in the fact of the 'levelled-out middle-class society' created by West Germany's post-war 'economic miracle' on the other. By 1980 only 14 per cent of West Germans with university entrance qualifications were in favour of capital punishment, as opposed to 29 per cent of those who had finished their education at the legal school-leaving age. Overall, some 49 per cent of West Germans were now against the death penalty, and only 28 per cent in favour, with 23 per cent unable to decide.[222] Just over a decade later, in 1992, support for capital punishment had fallen to 24 per cent in the former West Germany, with 56 per cent against and 20 per cent undecided.[223]

This dramatic change of public opinion reflected to some extent the effects of anti- or at least non-Nazi education in the 1950s and 1960s, which marked off the younger generations from those who had been taught in the 1930s and early 1940s that killing criminals was a good thing, that life was a struggle for survival, and that enemies of the race deserved to die. Even more than this, however, it was the product of the more open debate which began in West Germany in the second half of the 1960s about the crimes committed by the Nazis. For a quarter of a century after the end of the war, there had been little public discussion about the Third Reich, as West Germans concentrated on reconstruction and did their best to forget the recent past. Following on the Eichmann trial in Jerusalem in 1960 and the Auschwitz trials in Frankfurt am Main in 1964, however, younger West Germans became increasingly eager to learn the facts about Nazi rule. One of the major sources of tension with their elders was the ignorance in which they had been kept up to this point. The massive wave of publications, newspaper and magazine articles, radio and television programmes, public debates, lectures, and courses about the Third Reich that began at this time and reached a climax with the fiftieth anniversary of the Nazi seizure of power in 1983 had little specific to say about the use of capital punishment under the Third Reich. But on a more general level the revelation of the full extent of Nazi exterminism convinced a majority of West Germans that they should not allow even the faintest echo of it to sound in their country. Unlike public opinion in Britain and the United States, therefore, which has remained solidly, even overwhelmingly in favour of

[222] Reuband, 'Sanktionsverlangen'; Elisabeth Noelle-Neumann and Edgar Piel, *Allensbacher Jahrbuch der Demoskopie 1978–1983*, viii (Munich, 1983), 312.

[223] Elisabeth Noelle-Neumann and Renate Köcher, *Allensbacher Jahrbuch der Demoskopie 1984–1992*, ix (Munich, 1993), 607.

the death penalty right up to the present,[224] public opinion in West Germany turned against it in the 1960s and remained opposed thereafter. Yet this was not the end of the story of capital punishment in Germany. For, while the cause of abolitionism was triumphing in the West, a very different story was unfolding in the East, as we shall now see.

[224] Potter, *Hanging*, 255 nn. 24 and 36.

18

'In the Interests of Humanity'

a. Capital Punishment in the Soviet Zone 1945–1950

As far as the administration of the law was concerned, the Soviet zone of occupation was initially established on the same basis as the others, with a Soviet Military Administration controlling Soviet military tribunals which could try German and other civilians, and a revived German judicial system with jurisdiction over Germans alone, run by the five federated states into which the zone was divided. The German population was subject to roughly the same restrictions and regulations as in the West, with the Red Army's primary concern to prevent any resurgence of Nazism. The Soviet military tribunals held a substantial series of war crimes trials, and also operated severe sanctions, including the death penalty, against any Germans who looked like resisting the military occupation, against anyone committing common murder, and above all against Nazi war criminals. All this was roughly comparable to what went on in the West. According to one estimate, Soviet military tribunals passed a total of 436 death sentences on German citizens in the Soviet zone from 1945 to 1952, which—given the size of the population, at around 19 million compared to about 55 million, and given the fact that by no means all of the people condemned were executed, was very similar to the rate of capital sentencing in the Western zones; indeed the rate in the British zone, where 537 death sentences were passed on war criminals and 398 carried out, was if anything slightly higher.[1] Even the estimate, recently supplied from Soviet archives, of 756 death sentences passed by Soviet military tribunals, was by no means significantly higher than comparable figures in the West, and of course includes a substantial number of people condemned for offences other than war crimes.[2] According to confidential information made available in 1994, executions carried out by order of Soviet military tribunals in

[1] Karl Wilhelm Fricke, *Politik und Justiz in der DDR. Zur Geschichte der politischen Verfolgung 1945–1968. Bericht und Dokumentation* (Cologne, 1979), 135–7.
[2] Michael Klonovsky and Jan von Flocken, *Stalins Lager in Deutschland. Dokumentation, Zeugenberichte 1945–1950* (Frankfurt, 1992), 18.

1945 and 1946 included a number for offences such as robbery committed while wearing stolen Red Army uniforms, suggesting that criminal gangs were as common in the Soviet zone at this time as they were in the West. The same source gives the figure of 483 death sentences passed by Soviet military tribunals from 1945 to 1952, or 545 for the entire period of their operation up to 1954. Of these, however, at least 200 are known to have been for offences other than war crimes (mostly espionage, especially after 1949). A total figure of around 300 death sentences passed by Soviet military tribunals on war criminals in the Soviet zone does not seem to be very far from the truth, therefore.

One unexpected reason for this surprisingly low figure was the fact that the death penalty was abolished in the Soviet Union on 26 May 1947 and not reintroduced until 31 January 1950 (and then only for treason and espionage; it was not restored for murder until 1954). It formed part of a wide-ranging series of reforms which also included major increases in labour camp sentences, and reflected Stalin's self-confidence after his victory in the war.[3] The decree of 26 May 1947 stated:

The historic victory of the Soviet people over the enemy has made manifest not only the growing power of the Soviet state, but also the extraordinary commitment of the whole people of the Soviet Union to its Soviet home and to the Soviet government. At the same time, the international situation as it has emerged in the period following the capitulation of Germany and Japan shows that peace has been secured for a long time to come despite all attempts by aggressive elements to provoke a war. In recognition of this situation and of the wishes of the trade unions of manual and white-collar workers and of other influential organizations which represent the views of large parts of society, the Presidium of the Supreme Soviet of the USSR has reached the opinion that there is no longer any compelling reason for the application of the death penalty in peacetime circumstances.[4]

This law did not apply in Germany. But the Soviet Military Administration in Germany publicly declared its extreme reluctance to pass or carry out death sentences from this moment on.[5] In 1947 Soviet military tribunals are known to have passed thirty-five death sentences, at least two of which were carried out (before the abolition of capital punishment), but only nine were passed the following year, and fourteen in 1949, and none of them in either year is known to have resulted in an execution.[6] In their running of the zone, the Russian occupiers were aided by a group of German Communists who had survived from

---

[3] Alexander Solzhenitsyn, *The Gulag Archipelago 1918–1956*, Part II (London, 1974), 439. See also Will Adams, 'Capital Punishment in Soviet Criminal Legislation, 1922–1965', in R. F. Kanet and I. Volgyes (eds.), *On the Road to Communism* (Lawrence, Kan., 1972).

[4] Quoted in Düsing, *Abschaffung*, 273.

[5] *Lausitzer Rundschau*, 7 June 1947, 3.   [6] Confidential information received in 1994.

the days of the Weimar Republic, most of them in exile. Men such as Walter Ulbricht, who had run the Berlin branch of the Communist Party in the early 1930s, or Wilhelm Pieck, a Communist deputy in Weimar and companion in misfortune of Karl Liebknecht and Rosa Luxemburg, whose fate at the hands of the Free Corps he had only narrowly escaped sharing in 1919, were brought into Germany by the Soviet authorities and quickly set to work gathering power behind the scenes. This did not mean, however, that the German Communists, who took over the Social Democratic Party in the Soviet zone by a forced merger in 1946 to form the 'Socialist Unity Party', were complete Soviet stooges. On the contrary, in these early post-war years, they were able to insist, with Moscow's tolerance, that they were building an 'antifascist-democratic transformation' which would set Germany, or at least its Eastern part, on a specifically German road to socialism, which might differ from that taken by the Soviet Union in crucial respects. German political parties such as the Christian Democrats were allowed to function, though within strict ideological limits which set them sharply off from their counterparts in the West. Much was made of a partnership between the Communists and others in local and state governments, even if the Socialist Unity Party did hold the key positions and even if free elections were ended after 1946. German democratic and socialist traditions were to be respected, at least in appearance; and during this period, so too was German law (suitably purged, as in the West, of its Nazi excrescences, of course). The properly democratic administration of the law was assured in the eyes of the Communists by the sacking of all the old judges and legal officials, except for those few who accepted the ideology of the new regime, and the appointment of a whole new judiciary and prosecution service, chosen not for its training and expertise but for its ideological reliablility.

In the immediate post-war years, therefore, the Criminal Code of 1871 still obtained, and murder was punishable by death. Many of the capital cases that came before German courts in the Soviet zone at this time had their counterparts in the West. On 4 November 1946, for example, Alfred O., who had murdered and robbed a black marketeer and two other people towards the end of the previous year, was condemned to death by a German court in Chemnitz. He was refused clemency on 11 July 1947 and guillotined in the yard of the Regional Court in Dresden at 6.14 a.m. on 26 July 1947.[7] His crime reflected a situation of black marketeering and organized violence very similar to that which existed in the Western zones at this time; and it was dealt with by the East German judicial system in a very similar way. Judgments on the whole were made without reference to socialist dogma, and defence appeals against death sentences met on

---

[7] BA Potsdam DP 1 VA 353, Bl. 166–9: judgment and report.

a number of occasions with success.[8] The press in the Soviet zone could also criticize verdicts, as in the case of the murderer and thief Georg S., condemned to death in December 1947 in a judgment which one newspaper considered excessively harsh because it ignored the obvious mental abnormality of the offender.[9] This intervention prompted the Saxon provincial government to commute the man's sentence to life imprisonment in July 1947 after further consideration of the medical evidence.[10] Such a step was not unwelcome to the Soviet military authorities, in view of the fact that the death penalty had only just been abolished back home; but it also showed the relative, if far from unlimited, freedom that existed in the administration and public role of German justice in the Soviet zone at this time.

In 1947, after the abolition of capital punishment in the Soviet Union, the Soviet Military Administration made clear its strong disapproval of a number of aspects of executions as they were administered by the German authorities. In the autumn of 1947 it seems that the shooting in Dreibergen prison of a married couple for murder committed in the course of a robbery was heard by the other prisoners, who then created a major disturbance. Major Jakupow, on behalf of the Soviet Military Administration, summoning German judicial officers, 'disapproved of the procedures there in the strongest terms'. The means by which offenders were executed in the early post-war months varied widely, and included hanging, guillotining, and shooting. The method was not related to the offence or to the offender, but was simply chosen according to what was available in the responsible prison.[11] The German law officers had to agree that shooting was not allowed in German law as a means of execution. If there was no guillotine to hand in the provinces, it was always possible to borrow one from Berlin.[12] In practice this posed considerable difficulties, given the chaotic state of the transport system in post-war East Germany.[13] But the guillotine now established itself as the normal method of execution for offenders condemned by German courts, while death sentences passed by Soviet military courts continued to be carried out by firing-squad. Major Jakupow revealed another continuity between the practice of German courts and states in the Soviet zone and their predecessors in earlier times, when he objected to the practice of taking the

[8] See BA Potsdam DP I VA 353, Bl. 166–9: collection of successful appeal cases.

[9] Ibid. VA 360, Bl. 205: *Die Union* (Dresden), 20 Dec. 1947.

[10] Ibid., Bl. 222: Generalstaatsanwalt im Lande Sachsen to Deutsche Justizverwaltung der Sowjetischen Besatzungszone in Deutschand, 31 July 1947.

[11] BA Potsdam DP I VA 6495, *passim*, esp. cases 011, 013, 018, 019, 26, 30, and 60.

[12] Ibid. VA 353, Bl. 13–14: Bericht über den Vortrag bei Oberstleutnant Jakupow in Berlin-Karlshorst am 18. Nov. 1947; ibid., Bl. 15, record of a meeting between Gentz, Melsheimer, Winkelmann, and others on 21 Nov. 1947.

[13] Ibid. VA 360, Bl. 121–2: Justizministerium Sachsen-Anhalt to Deutsche Justizverwaltung der sowjetischen Besatzungszone in Deutschland, 6 Aug. 1948, and following telegram, 19 Aug. 1948.

executed offender's corpse to the nearest anatomical institute. In response, the German judicial authorities underlined the fact that established German law only allowed this to happen when the relatives of the deceased did not lay any claim of their own on the body. Pressure from Major Jakupow, backed by the Soviet Military Administration, now obliged them to consider discontinuing this practice. However, in January 1948 the anatomical institutes in Berlin pressured for it to be retained irrespective of the wishes of the relatives.[14] The same legal official who had previously defended the use of the guillotine, Gentz, pointed out that this was not desirable:

Such a measure would in my opinion constitute an interference in the personal rights of the relatives. It would have no basis in law. The rights of the state over the person of the condemned cease with his execution. Such an interference cannot be justified on grounds of scientific interest. Such an interest exists in every hospital, but the anatomizing of the body of a deceased person there also requires his relatives' consent. I do not see how this could be regarded as an exceptional measure against someone who has been executed, as a consequence of his offence or a by-product of the sentence. . . . There are numerous countries in which capital punishment has been abolished or is no longer carried out in practice, and science manages there without anatomical investigations of this kind. German science will not be damaged by having to dispense with histological exercises carried out on the corpses of executed offenders, as Sweden, Belgium, and Switzerland have had to do.[15]

In 1947, a total of eleven corpses of executed offenders were delivered to the anatomical institutes in the Soviet zone. In 1948 the total was fifteen. These were insignificant numbers in view of the hundreds of corpses that were actually needed for anatomy teaching.[16] Eventually, in 1950, the dispute was resolved by a compromise: the corpses of those prisoners who had died naturally would be made available to the anatomical institutes provided the relatives did not want them, while the corpses of those who had been executed would not.[17]

Following the incident at Dreibergen, the Soviet administration also took the view that executions should no longer be held within prisons. Gentz underlined this in a circular noting:

The director of a large penal institution which has been selected by the state's Ministry of Justice as an execution site has resigned his post on the grounds that he cannot be expected to establish an educational penal administration in a prison in which the inmates are aware that he is ordering death sentences to be carried out in complete contradiction to the prison's educational task, and in which, therefore, he would lose most of the ability to have an educational effect. Beyond this, carrying out an execution in a prison would

[14] Ibid., and Bl. 21: von Renthe to Justizverwaltung, 27 Jan. 1948.
[15] Ibid., Bl. 31: Gentz to Abteilung III, 16 Feb. 1948.
[16] Ibid. VA 353, Bl. 46: Lanke to Justizverwaltung der Sowjetischen Besatzungszone, Mar. 1949; ibid.: Stoletzky to same, 27 Apr. 1949.
[17] Ibid., Bl. 57: Heinze to Innenministerium, 10 Jan. 1950.

cause such significant and long-lasting unrest among the inmates that attempts to gain a positive influence over them would be seriously interrupted.[18]

Nevertheless, this initiative on the part of the Soviet Military Administration was bypassed as well. German judicial officers in the zone had already reported that no practical alternative existed, and in any case in most prisons, they claimed, executions took place very discreetly. So Gentz's admonitions had little practical effect.[19] The whole incident was revealing not only of the extent to which German penal administration in the zone conformed to non-Communist German precedent and tradition at this time, but also of the limited ability of the Soviet Military Administration to influence it in the direction which it desired.

Despite the abolition of the death penalty in the Soviet Union, therefore, German courts in the Soviet zone continued to condemn offenders to death throughout the later 1940s. According to one rather rough and probably incomplete list drawn up in 1950-1, German courts condemned 4 people to death in 1945, 25 in 1946, 34 in 1947, 23 in 1948, and 32 in 1949. There were 2 executions in 1945, 2 in 1946, 7 in 1947, 16 ir 1948, 2 in 1949, and 7 in 1950. In view of the fact that, as we have seen, eleven corpses of executed offenders were delivered to the anatomists in 1947, the figures for the earlier years are likely to be underestimates. The list does not always give the crime for which the offender had been condemned. However, from what we do have, it seems that of those executed, thirteen were condemned for crimes committed under the Third Reich. They incuded two doctors who had carried out 'euthanasia' killings (Paul Nitsche and Gerhard Göbler), two men described as 'executioners' in the file (in fact assistant executioners), two Gestapo agents, and a number of concentration camp guards and 'Kapos' or criminals put in charge of huts in the camps. One of the men executed, Albert B., had committed the crime of denouncing to the Gestapo someone who had been killed by them as a result. While thirteen of those executed in this period were war criminals, fourteen had been condemned under § 211 of the Criminal Code for murder committed in the zone, and included not only two offenders who had murdered policemen, but also three who had killed in order to conceal a crime, two sex murderers, and one person refused clemency because he had committed a 'double murder out of greed'. All of this was fairly similar to what was going on in the West at this time.[20]

In October 1947 the Soviet Military Administration in Germany also com-

[18] BA Potsdam DP 1 VA 6495, Bl. 36: Gentz to Landesregierungen, 11 Sept. 1948.

[19] Ibid., Bl. 23: Justizministerium Sachsen-Anhalt to Deutsche Justizverwaltung der Sowjetischen Besatzungszone, 17 Feb. 1948.

[20] Ibid. VA 6495, *passim*, esp. cases 011, 013, 018, 019, 26, 30, and 60. See also Gustav Radbruch, *Gesetzliches Recht und Übergesetzliches Recht* (Heidelberg, 1946), 13.

plained 'that sometimes one year and more pass after the sentencing by the court before the sentence is carried out. This must be regarded as an indefensible spiritual burden for those affected.' It was itself responsible for the final judgment on clemency cases, on the same lines as its Western counterparts. The Soviet Military Administration not only ordered therefore that the appeals and clemency process had to be speeded up,[21] but also devolved the power of clemency onto the new provincial governments, in the hope of expediting matters, while however retaining the right to intervene if it saw fit.[22] However, the situation did not improve: most of the executions carried out in 1948, for example, resulted from decisions taken by the courts in 1947 and even in 1946.[23] Where appeals and counter-appeals prolonged a case, and especially where the execution of one offender was postponed in order for him to appear as a witness, the authorities usually commuted the sentence. In the case of Kurt O., who was still under sentence of death in March 1950, more than three years after he had been condemned, the state prosecutor in Halle said that he 'believes that the execution of a death sentence which achieved legal validity three years ago already is in no way defensible'. His opinion was shared in the Justice Ministry in Berlin, and the man's sentence was commuted to life imprisonment. There were other instances of even longer delays between sentence and execution at this time.[24] Here again, the intervention of the Soviet authorities seems to have had little effect. On a larger historical scale, however, this situation was now about to undergo a dramatic change.

With the onset of the Cold War in 1948, Stalin moved to tighten his grip on East-Central Europe in the face of what he took to be the attempts of the United States to seduce its governments with the financial inducements of the Marshall Plan. By attempting to cut off West Berlin from land supplies to the West, a gambit successfully countered from the West by the Berlin airlift, Stalin provoked the division of Germany and the foundation of the Federal Republic out of the three Western zones, paralleled on 7 October 1949 by the creation of the German Democratic Republic out of the Soviet zone. Initially the new Republic left the door open to reunification with the West, a policy which Stalin—with how much sincerity has been hotly disputed—pursued until early in 1952. As a consequence of this, the constitution of the new state was largely modelled on the Weimar constitution of 1919, as in many ways the Basic Law of the Federal

[21] BA Potsdam DP 1. VA 353, Bl. 3: Landesregierung Sachsen-Anhalt circular, 10 Oct. 1947.
[22] Ibid., Bl. 9: Landesregierung Brandenburg, Minister der Justiz, circular, 2 Oct. 1947.
[23] Ibid. VA 6495, *passim*, esp. cases 011, 013, 018, 019, 26, 30, and 60.
[24] Ibid. VA 353, Bl. 300: Fischl to Justizministerium Sachsen-Anhalt; ibid., Bl. 302: Böhme to Justizministerium Berlin, 12 May 1950; ibid. DO 1/32/3710, Bl. 81–180, for another case; BA-SAPM Berlin JIV 2/2/217, Bl. 15: Zum Protokoll Nr. 117, § 16 (24 June 1952); BA Potsdam DO 1/32/39710, Bl. 592.

Republic was. The multi-party system remained. Political groupings such as the East German Christian Democratic Union were forced to join with the other parties in a 'unity list' in rigged elections where there was no choice of candidates. Their leaders were strictly controlled by the Socialist Unity Party's Politburo. They soon came to function largely as 'transmission belts' for the official Communist ideology to groups in the population thought to be hostile or indifferent to it. But they stayed in existence, and were thus a potential source of political pluralism. Above all, the constitution followed its Weimar predecessor in guaranteeing that judges were 'independent in their administration of the law, and subordinate only to the constitution and the law'.[25] Yet, as the division of Germany quickly hardened, it soon became apparent that the constitution was in many ways a dead letter. It was not long before judges were being hand-picked for their political reliability and their verdicts and sentences being determined in advance by the Socialist Unity Party's Politburo and its servants. Walter Ulbricht and the leading German Communists abandoned the compromises of the 'antifascist-democratic transformation' and the 'German road to socialism' and went all-out for the imposition of a rigid Soviet model. The German Democratic Republic was to become a Stalinist state representing the dictatorship of the workers and peasants and aiming to follow the Soviet Union on the road to Communism. The Soviet judicial principles that now became paramount in East Germany had been developed as a tool of the Bolshevik regime in Russia after the Revolution of 1917. In reforming the criminal law in the years after the Revolution, the Soviets had placed increasing emphasis on the threat, or alleged threat, posed to the post-revolutionary social order by the offender. In the Soviet Criminal Code of 1926, even the concept of punishment was replaced by that of measures for the protection of society. This enabled the death penalty, which, as we saw in Chapter 11, was strongly defended by Lenin, to be used against 'class enemies' and 'counter-revolutionaries'. In 1932 it was even extended in the Soviet Union to cover theft from the state and from co-operatives, a measure intended not least to legalize the terror then in progress against peasants who were resisting Stalin's drive for collectivization. The same principles were taken over by the East German regime as a justification for its use of capital punishment.[26] Thus the death penalty, reintroduced for political offences in the Soviet Union in January 1950, was justified in East Germany in a similar manner, principally in terms of the protection of state and society.

[25] For these quotes, and for a general overview of this process, see Karl Wilhelm Fricke, 'Aus "erzieherischen Gründen" wurde die Todesstrafe verhängt. Die Strafjustiz in der DDR war dem SED-Parteiapparat untergeordnet', *Frankfurter Rundschau*, 29 Oct. 1992, 24.

[26] Friedrich-Christian Schroeder, *Das Strafrecht des realen Sozialismus. Eine Einführung am Beispiel der DDR* (Opladen, 1983), 19–23.

The signal for the new direction was clearly given by the Soviet Military Administration. In November and December 1950, a Soviet military court condemned eleven Germans to death by firing-squad for spying for the West. In another trial, held in December, six Germans were condemned to death for having allegedly been sent into the Soviet zone by the Americans, armed with 'radio transmitters of American origin, secret scripts, codes, invisible inks', and other equipment. A number of others were condemned to long sentences of imprisonment on the same counts. They were supposedly directed to carry out acts of sabotage against the Soviet occupying forces. Another group was condemned to death by firing-squad in 1950. It consisted mainly of men who had held relatively senior positions in local or provincial governments. One, for example, was a civil servant in the Thuringian Economics Ministry, while another was a member of the regional government in Weimar. The acts of sabotage which they were supposed to have committed consisted mainly of arson attacks on farms and the sabotage of nationalized industrial enterprises. In reality, this probably meant that they were not co-operating with the East German regime's policies in these areas. A series of Jehovah's Witnesses were also arrested as American spies, in an ironic reminder of the way in which they had been persecuted under the Third Reich. The language used in the judgment delivered at their trial was characteristic of the new style of political justice in the Eastern part of Germany:

In their struggle for world domination, the American imperialists will stop at no crime, however common, will shrink back before no deception. They are making use of hired killers and provocateurs. They are strengthening their espionage, sabotage, and terrorist activities against the Soviet Union, the People's Democracies, and the German Democratic Republic.[27]

In January 1951 the same Soviet military tribunal sentenced three men to death, and several others to long periods of imprisonment, for allegedly supplying military information to the British secret service. It was claimed that photographs, forged documents, plans, and 'espionage information' had been found on them when they were arrested. All had confessed to their alleged crimes, though what they had really done was much less clear. Two further death sentences for similar offences were passed later in the year.[28] All this was a clear indication of the line which the East German regime was now expected to take. In constructing socialism, the German Democratic Republic would be surrounded by enemies, faced with infiltration from the West, open to espionage and sabotage. In the narrow, suspicious minds of Stalin and his

[27] INGASA Nottingham 25/Prozesse 1950–1/2: *Tägliche Rundschau*, 22 Dec. 1950, *Tägliche Rundschau*, 19 Dec. 1950, *Tägliche Rundschau*, 22 Nov. 1950, and *Der Tagesspiegel*, 22 Nov. 1950.
[28] Ibid: *Der Morgen*, 13 Jan. 1951, *Telegraf*, 1 Jan. 1953.

henchmen in East Berlin, any indication of ideological deviation, managerial incompetence, or even unauthorized contacts with the West was clear evidence of subversion inspired by Western intelligence, and had to be treated with the utmost severity.

Parallel with these measures, the Soviet Military Administration handed over its functions in trying and punishing war criminals to the East German regime. Since 1945 the Russians had administered a substantial network of prison camps in the Soviet Zone. Up to 180,000 Germans had been interned under harsh conditions; perhaps a third of them died in the camps, while perhaps as many as 25,000 were deported to the Soviet Union, to remain there well into the 1950s.[29] Internment on this mass scale served the function of enforcing Soviet control and deterring any serious opposition to the policies of the occupying forces; Social Democrats who objected to the enforced merger of their party in the Soviet zone with the Communists in 1946, for example, were as likely to be interned in the camps as were former Nazis.[30] In 1949 over three thousand inmates of the Waldheim prison were handed over to the East Germans for trial; despite four years of imprisonment, they had not so far been found guilty of any offence. The East German authorities saw this as the occasion to demonstrate to their Soviet masters their antifascist will, and their determination to root out any principled opposition to their policies. Ten show trials of senior Nazis, camp commanders, and SS men from Waldheim were held amid a good deal of publicity in the summer of 1950. The proceedings against more than 3,000 other defendants were held behind closed doors. The judges selected to preside over the trial were all members of the ruling Socialist Unity Party. Those who had a 'tendency towards objectivism', or who refused to agree to follow the instructions of the Party on sentencing, were rejected. Even so, the judges who presided over the trial did not go along with every demand raised by the prosecution. The state secretary in the Justice Ministry, Helmut Brandt, attempted to intervene to ensure proper judicial procedure, and also got Otto Nuschke, the leader of the Christian Democratic Party in East Germany, to intervene, though without result. This only led to Brandt's arrest later in the year and his imprisonment as a member of a group of 'conspirators'. He was not released until 1964. The judges were given instructions from the office of Walter Ulbricht, relayed through a political adviser attached to the court. Under pressure from Ulbricht, they passsed thirty-one death sentences. All except one of the condemned men immediately appealed for clemency.[31] The right of reprieve had been exercised by the federated states in the

[29] Klonovsky and Flocken, *Stalins Lager*, 17–19.
[30] Fricke, *Politik und Justiz*, 55.
[31] Wolfgang Eisert, *Die Waldheimer Prozesse. Der stalinistische Terror 1950. Ein dunkles Kapitel der DDR-Justiz* (Munich, 1993), 17–37, 181–2, 56–8, 136–9, 102.

Soviet zone since their post-war formation, subject to the approval of the Soviet Military Administration,[32] but with the creation of the German Democratic Republic it had passed to the President, Wilhelm Pieck, who acted on the recommendation of the Ministry of Justice.[33] In August 1950, however, the Politburo decided to restrict this right to cases where the death penalty had been passed by the Supreme Court. In other cases, the right of clemency was devolved once more onto the federated states.[34] This step was taken principally because Otto Nuschke and the other Christian Democrats in the multi-party national government of the Republic had proposed that the Waldheim trials and verdicts all be quashed and that all the accused be retried in public and according to the law. On Ulbricht's orders the Saxon cabinet met in Dresden on 2 November 1950 to consider all the cases once more, taking into account petitions from the condemned men's families and new material that had come to light in the mean time. The Saxon cabinet granted clemency to five of the condemned men, but refused it to the other twenty-six.[35] Although these men were duly executed, possibly by strangulation, possibly by a shot in the back of the head, it was clear that members of East Germany's coalition governments at national and state level were now objecting to the use of capital punishment on this scale, and for obvious political purposes, and were causing trouble as a result.

b. The Stalinization of East German Justice 1949–1953

These events were profoundly disturbing to the leadership of the German Democratic Republic. They suggested that the path to the creation of a willing and pliant justice system would not necessarily be a smooth one. In September 1950, while the wrangling over the Waldheim sentences was still going on, the Justice Ministry of the German Democratic Republic revealed its ideal of the judicial system as the tool of the 'antifascist-democratic' rule of the working masses, when it declared:

In close co-operation with the security organs, democratic jurists will demonstrate their union with the fate of the working people and mete out hard and rapid punishment to all enemies of our antifascist-democratic order and all saboteurs of the popular elections on 15 October. The lackeys of Western imperialists have chosen crime as their way of working. As criminals they will feel the sharp sword of democratic legality. No freedom for the enemies of democracy![36]

[32] BA Potsdam DP 1 VA 418, Nr. 137/6: Oberstaatsanwalt at the Landgericht Schwerin to Deutsche Justizverwaltung der Sowjetischen Besatzungszone in Deutschland, 2 July 1948.
[33] Ibid. VA 373, Bl. 257: Justizminister der DDR to Herrn Präsidenten der DDR, 15 Oct. 1949.
[34] BA-SAPM Berlin J IV 2/2/105, Bl. 190: Draft: Anordnung des Präsidenten der Deutschen Demokratischen Republik über die Ausübung des Begnadigungsrechtes (22 Aug. 1950).
[35] BA-SAPM Berlin J IV 2/2/116, Bl. 9: Protokoll Nr. 16, § 5 (31 Oct. 1950).
[36] INGASA Nottingham 25/Prozesse 1950–1/1: Der Morgen, 20 Sept. 1950. For the official account, see Hilde Benjamin et al., Zur Geschichte der Rechtspflege der DDR 1945–1949 (Berlin, 1976).

These were no idle threats. In 1950, it was reported, Soviet and East German courts passed a total of 17,012 sentences for 'anti-Communist activity' and 'boycott campaigns against the Soviet Union', totalling over 63,000 years of imprisonment. An additional 17,900 sentences totalling over 24,400 years of imprisonment were passed for 'economic sabotage'.[37] Moreover, the death penalty was also applied, not only against war criminals but also against ex-Nazis who had attracted the particular animosity of the Socialist Unity Party. A massive trial was held in July 1950 of former brownshirts involved in the 'Köpenick blood-week' in June 1933, when some ninety trade unionists, socialists, and Communists had been severely tortured, a number of them with fatal consequences. Six of the men found guilty in 1950 were guillotined in Frankfurt an der Oder on 20 February 1951.[38] These sentences had little to do with the existing criminal justice system, and obviously those jurists who implemented them were effectively ignoring its central precepts at the behest of the East German regime. Yet as late as March 1950 the trial of the Gladow Band in East Berlin took a largely traditional form, which would not have been out of place in the West; and if the circumstances of Berlin were rather special, there is reason to believe that traditional judicial language and procedure were still widely used in the East throughout 1950 and into 1951.[39]

Neither this situation, nor the prospect of further opposition along the lines mounted against its policy during the Waldheim trials, was acceptable to the Politburo of the Socialist Unity Party. In May 1951, the Politburo issued a formal complaint that the judicial system had not yet been brought into line with the new, Soviet-driven style of the regime. 'Right up to the most recent times,' it noted, 'the necessary measures have not been undertaken for a cleansing of the judicial investigation authorities of reactionary and dubious elements and the strengthening of these organs with tried cadres who are capable of work.' There were still too many instances of the 'application of considerate penalties'. Justice Minister Max Fechner, they claimed, had not paid these matters sufficient attention, and the Minister for State Security Zaisser had not troubled to involve himself in the matter as he should have done.[40] Fechner was not one of the central ruling group, but a former Social Democrat. As one of the few survivors of the Social Democratic Party Executive of the Weimar Republic to remain in

[37] INGASA Nottingham 25/Prozesse 1950–1/2: *Telegraf*, 20 Feb. 1951.

[38] BA-SAPM Berlin IV 2/13/434: Vollstreckungsgericht in der Strafsache gegen Plönzke u. A. (Köpenicker Blutwoche). The executioner refused to act because two of the condemned were old schoolfriends of his; eventually he shared the execution with a new appointment. The condemned men, on being told the night before of their impending death, said they had thought they were being sent to a labour camp in Siberia.

[39] Brasch, *Engel aus Eisen*.

[40] BA Potsdam DP 1. 418, Bl. 211–12: Merkblatt 'An Ulbricht u. Zaisser schreiben, 15/5'. See also the Russian version, ibid., Bl. 217–18.

the Soviet zone, he had played a leading role, along with Otto Grotewohl, in bringing about his party comrades' acceptance of the enforced merger with the Communists in 1946. The Justice Ministry had been his reward. But as former Social Democrats were being purged in large numbers lower down the political hierarchy, Fechner found himself coming under increasing pressure from Ulbricht and the ex-Communist leadership as well. He had not been included in the Politburo of the Socialist Unity Party, established in 1949.[41] Fechner responded to the criticism with a speech urging the adoption of Soviet criminal law in place of the German model. Criminal law, he said, was a 'means of class struggle against bourgeois ideology'. It had to avoid being 'objectivistic' and to take the 'social danger' posed by the offender into account.[42] The courts were ordered not to pass lesser sentences than those demanded by the prosecutor.[43] A range of punishments, including death, for offences not covered by the Criminal Code had already been made possible by the constitution of the German Democratic Republic; in particular, the catch-all Article 6, which declared 'boycott campaigns against democratic institutions and organizations, murder campaigns against democratic politicians, expressions of religious, racial, or international hatred, militaristic propaganda, campaigns for war, and all other actions directed against equal rights' to be 'crimes within the meaning of the Criminal Code'.

This constitutional amendment of the existing law was to be extensively used during the following years. For these new offences were vague and ill-defined, and capable of very wide interpretation. 'Boycott campaigns', for example, could be interpreted to mean almost any statement or action which might encourage people to not to co-operate with the state, or indeed with the Socialist Unity Party, which after all was officially regarded as a 'democratic institution'.[44] And all these offences were punishable in severe cases by death. On 16 December 1950 the regime promulgated a Law for the Protection of Peace which made six further offences punishable by death, including propagation of an aggressive war or the participation of Germans in an aggressive military bloc, inciting Germans to take part in military actions 'which serve the oppression of a people', and encouraging the breach of international agreements which assisted 'Germany's development on a democratic and peaceful basis', if such offences were committed 'in the direct service of states, or their institutions or agents . . . which carry out campaigns for war or an aggressive policy towards peaceful peoples'.[45] Again, these provisions were capable of extremely wide and arbitrary interpretation. It was

---

[41] Hermann Weber, *Geschichte der DDR* (Munich, 1985), 76, 183–4.
[42] INGASA Nottingham 25/Prozesse 1950–1/1: *Der Tagesspiegel,* 19 May 1951.
[43] Ibid.: *Telegraf,* 16 Nov. 1956.   [44] Fricke, 'Aus "erzieherischen Gründen"'.
[45] INGASA Nottingham 25/Prozesse 1950–1/2: *B.Z. am Abend,* 18 Dec. 1950.

axiomatic to the East German regime that the Federal Republic was engaged in 'campaigns for war', like all Western imperialist states. Thus even listening to a West German radio station such as RIAS in West Berlin, which the East German authorities defined as an arm of West German intelligence, could be—and was—interpreted as putting oneself in the service of a foreign, warmongering state. Encouraging the breach of international agreements which helped Germany develop in a democratic (i.e. Communist) direction could mean no more than advocating German reunification, which of course would involve the abrogation of East Germany's agreements with the Soviet Union. These provisions now served as the essential basis for the prosecution of all those who opposed the regime's Stalinist course.

On 11 December 1951, probably acting on the prompting of the Russians, the Politburo issued another sharp attack on what it saw as the inadequacies of the administration of justice in East Germany, for which it made 'bad party work in the judicial apparatus' at least partly responsible. It accused judges, prosecutors, and lawyers of a 'lack of ideological consciousness' which 'shows itself particularly strongly in the fact that judges and state prosecutors still frequently use fascistic-imperialistic legal theories and base their judgments on Supreme Court commentaries from the period of fascism'. It is unlikely in practice that judges and prosecutors were using legal documents from the Third Reich, but it is more than likely, given the relatively non-socialist character of the legal system between 1945 and 1949, that they were using lawbooks from an earlier era, and this, with characteristic ideological exaggeration, is what the Politburo was objecting to. For all its biases and faults, the legal system of the Imperial and Weimar periods was not a mere tool in the hands of the government of the day. The Politburo was determined that its successor in the German Democratic Republic should be. In particular, it complained:

Because of the weaknesses under which they still labour in the ideological field, the members of the judicial apparatus are not in a position to combine theory and practice and to reach a correct decision in the obtaining political situation. To some extent they still take the erroneous view, for example, that the judge and the state prosecutor has to be unpolitical and neutral and that only under these circumstances is he in a position to reach an 'objective' verdict. Because of the unsatisfactory ideological standard, they have not yet come to recognize that there is no neutrality of the state and that there are therefore no neutral or unpolitical state servants. They are thus not in a position to recognize that every verdict is a political verdict.[46]

Steps were taken to bring the Justice Ministry and its officials into line with party policy. The party's representation in the Ministry and at all levels of the judicial

[46] BA-SAPM Berlin NL 90/440, Bl. 192–3: Massnahmen zur Verbesserung der Organe der Justiz und ihrer Arbeit in der Deutschen Demokratischen Republik und in Berlin.

system was strengthened and a comprehensive programme of indoctrination set in motion. New, politically committed judges and state prosecutors were appointed, and the prison administration was brought into line by being placed under the administration of the People's Police, the new, 'democratic' policing apparatus brought into being after the war.[47]

These changes were cemented by a Law on the State Prosecution Service passed on 23 May 1952 and a Court Procedure Law passed on 2 October in the same year. These enabled the East German political leadership to control prosecutors and judges and subordinate the judicial system explicitly to the 'construction of socialism'.[48] Ultimately, the Politburo intended to cement its control over the legal system by promulgating a new Criminal Code. The old Criminal Code of 1871 under which the judiciary of the German Democratic Republic had hitherto operated, said the Politburo in an official statement announcing this plan, was capitalist in spirit, even if it had been amended in many respects to bring it into line with the new regime. The proposed new Code, by contrast,

utilizes all the experiences which have been gathered in the application of the laws which have been promulgated since 1945, particularly in the fight against saboteurs, diversants, agents and spies, economic criminals, and offenders against socialist property. It rests on the insights of the progressive legal science of the Soviet Union and on the research of our academic criminal lawyers.

West German law, it added, was a means of arbitrary power exercised by the imperialist bourgeoisie over the working class. The new East German criminal law, by contrast, would be an important means by which a socialist society would come into being.[49] The proposed retention of the death penalty was justified principally with reference to 'the dangerousness of the attacks to which the German Democratic Republic is exposed from the enemies of our state'. Its application to common murder was mentioned only as an afterthought, without any justification.[50] A new Criminal Code, in fact, as things turned out, would be a long time coming. In the mean time, the death penalty, said Otto Grotewohl, the Minister-President and former Social Democrat who was one of the two joint leaders of the Socialist Unity Party, was 'a necessary instrument in the struggle for the maintenance and secure establishment of peace, for the protection of the people's power of the German Democratic Republic, and for the building of

[47] Ibid., Bl. 196–7: Verbesserung der Parteiarbeit; ibid., Bl. 198–210: Massnahmen zur Hebung des ideologischen Niveaus der Mitarbeiter der Justiz.

[48] Fricke, 'Aus "erzieherischen Gründen"'.

[49] BA-SAPM Berlin NL 90/444, Bl. 18: Erklärung des Politbüros zum Entwurf eines neuen Strafgesetzbuches.

[50] Ibid., Bl. 28: Begründung zum Entwurf des Allgemeinen Strafgesetzbuches der Deutschen Demokratischen Republik.

socialism' as well as a 'still-necessary, most severe punishment for rendering the most dangerous enemies of the working people harmless'.[51] Capital crime, it was clear, would now be given a political interpretation, whether it was political in intent or not.

Meanwhile, even under the old Criminal Code, death continued to be treated as the normal penalty for murder, and a sentence of life imprisonment had to be specially justified by the courts.[52] This undoubtedly made it easier for the courts to hand down a death sentence when political circumstances made it desirable in the eyes of the party leadership and security apparatus. Over 90 per cent of the offenders who were convicted of murder every year ended up by receiving sentences of life imprisonment; the other 10 per cent were carefully selected for political reasons.[53] The purpose of the retention of the death penalty was to symbolize the intention of the party leadership to brook no opposition in its drive to Stalinize state and society. As the Supreme Court declared in a judgment of 25 May 1952:

In the present-day situation of continually increasing attacks on our peaceful order, democratic justice cannot do without the application of the strongest means of social self-protection, the death penalty. The protection of our working people from attacks of this kind demands the hardest measures of defence. The accused's crimes are so great that the court must pronounce the death sentence against him.[54]

East German courts repeatedly described the purpose of death sentences as rendering the condemned person 'harmless'.[55] In a similar way, penal policy in the German Democratic Republic was now based on the concept not of the guilt of the individual, but of the danger he or she posed to the new social and political order. The end of the period of the 'democratic-antifascist transformation' in the Soviet zone meant the end of individual peasant holdings and the beginning of their merger into state-run collective farms; the end of toleration for a substantial private sector in the economy; the end of any dreams of a particular 'German way' of socialism. The resistance from peasants and small businessmen, and the accompanying mass emigration to the West, which these moves provoked, was stemmed but by no means halted by the creation of a security zone along the entire East–West German border, reinforced in time with a high fence, watch-towers, minefields, and tripwire gun emplacements. After 1952, anyone wanting to leave East Germany for the West had to make the crossing in Berlin, still under joint four-power control, and fly out from there to freedom. Hundreds of thousands did. Within East Germany itself, the Socialist Unity Party cemented

[51] BA-SAPM Berlin NL 90/444, Bl. 189.
[52] BA Potsdam DP 1 VA 5110, Bl. 5–7: Auswertung der OG-Urteile zum § 322 StGB, 18 Oct. 1965.
[53] Ibid., Bl. 7, § 3B.
[54] Quoted in Wolfgang Schuller, *Geschichte und Struktur des politischen Strafrechts der DDR bis 1968* (Ebelsbach, 1980), 95.
[55] Quoted ibid., see also ibid. 154.

its dominance over the other 'block parties' by a renewed series of purges and arrests. All this created a rising wave of discontent, documented in the files of the Stasi, the Ministry for State Security. Armed with its new controls over the judicial system, the regime proceeded in 1952 to organize a series of major show trials, not of war criminals, but of ordinary citizens, to terrorize and indoctrinate key sectors of the population into submission.

The atmosphere of suspicion in the Soviet bloc in 1952, above all following the spectacular show trial of former deputy Communist Party leader Rudolf Slansky in Czechoslovakia, was so powerful that Ulbricht and the Politburo could not have avoided staging show trials even had they wanted to. The Politburo was involved at every level. In August 1952 it ordered General State Prosecutor Ernst Melsheimer to brief it on important trials before they began.[56] In this way it would be able to keep control over the proceedings and the publicity to which they gave rise. When it decided on a show trial, the regime moved into action to ensure the maximum publicity in the press and radio, with selected people invited to sit in the public gallery to learn the lessons of the trial at first hand. Whatever the actual crimes of the accused, the security apparatus ensured that they were embellished and dramatized for maximum effect. When the federated states were abolished and replaced with much smaller districts, under tighter central control from Berlin, in the course of the centralizing reforms of 1952, the right to reprieve capital offenders reverted to the President of the German Democratic Republic, Wilhelm Pieck. It was wielded behind the scenes by the Politburo.[57] The Justice Ministry continued to pass death sentences through its clemency commission, but the Politburo reserved the right to inspect them, and clemency cases thought to be of political significance were frequently the subject of detailed recommendations passed on to it by the legal division of the Party's Central Committee. These cases were usually considered by the Politburo as the last item of business in its meetings, after more pleasant matters such as holidays and health cures for Politburo members, the wording of slogans for the Party Congress, and the organization of celebrations for various Communist anniversaries. Usually the Politburo simply approved the recommendation before it, though in some cases it intervened actively and referred cases back to the clemency commission.[58] It was not until 11 April 1958 that the Politburo's role in confirming death sentences became known to the West German news media after the defection of an official on Pieck's staff. Clemency, he reported correctly, was almost never granted.[59]

[56] BA-SAPM Berlin J IV 2/2/228, Bl. 4: Beschluss 8/2.
[57] See e.g. ibid., J IV 2/2A/243, Bl. 27: Zum Protokoll Nr. 5/53, § 17 (27 Jan. 1953); ibid., J IV 2/2A/466, Bl. 175: Zum Protokoll Nr. 28/53 § 25 (26 May 1956).
[58] See e.g. ibid., J IV 2/2A/257, Bl. 107: Zum Protokoll Nr. 19/53, § 24 (31 Mar. 1953).
[59] NGASA Nottingham 25, 1958/1: Der Tag, 11 Apr. 1958.

Nevertheless, capital punishment, though ruthlessly employed, was held within bounds. In the eleven show trials held by the Supreme Court from December 1949 up to the end of 1953, only three death sentences were pronounced. One of them, involving Johann Burianek and a number of alleged co-conspirators supposedly working for Western intelligence agencies, provided a copy-book example of a show trial involving errant economic managers. In the proceedings, which were held before the Supreme Court from 22 to 25 May 1952, one of the defending lawyers was struck by the willingness of the accused to confess. He described later how, when he had met his client for a consultation in his prison cell, the latter

got carried away in boundless self-incrimination to the point that he was virtually tearing himself to shreds. I could not confirm any outward signs of ill-treatment; on the contrary, his physical condition could in no way be criticized. All the more astounding, therefore, were his verbal self-lacerations. . . . During the main trial, not only did my client behave in exactly the same way as in his cell the day before, but so too did all the other accused. Beyond this, they admitted things which were neither known to the defence nor noted in the files. The trial itself proceeded in the now familiar way. If one of the accused should stumble in his speech and appear to have lost the thread, all Melsheimer had to do was to give a keyword, like a prompt in the theatre, and the accused continued the undeviating flow of his speech as before.[60]

Burianek confessed to blowing up a bridge, though he was unlikely to have done any such thing. The story had been drummed into him by the Stasi until he had virtually come to believe it himself. The proceedings were broadcast for the maximum publicity. They did not impress listeners in the West. A Western commentator remarked: 'The conduct of the trial, as can be followed from the wireless, hardly differs from the methods used by Freissler [*sic*].'[61] But a better comparison would have been with Stalin's notorious prosecutor Vishinsky, in the great show trials of the Old Bolsheviks in the 1930s. The ritual confessions, learned by rote, which Vishinsky pioneered, were quite foreign to Nazi judicial procedure. Often enough under the Nazis, the offences of resistance to or dissent from the regime which brought people before the courts were real enough, as for example—classically—after the bomb plot of July 1944. In East Germany they were in large part imaginary. The uniformly penitent, self-accusatory, and co-operative behaviour of the defendants in these show trials derived not least from the flood of orchestrated petitions from factories and villages demanding their condemnation, the weeks of lengthy reports in the press proclaiming their guilt, and the atmosphere of grim intimidation and indoctrination in which they had been living for months on end in prison. Harsh and brutal treatment, isolation,

    60 Fricke, *Politik und Justiz,* 276.
    61 INGASA Nottingham 25/Prozesse 1953–4/1: *Deutsche Zeitung,* 6 Jan. 1954.

and frequent interrogations directed them towards the public confession of what the authorities wanted to hear.[62] Unlike in the Third Reich, direct physical violence and brutality, deliberate physical torture, physical beating, and physical humiliation do not seem to have been common. But then the objectives of the two systems were quite different; the Third Reich, faced with real, organized resistance, above all from the Communists, sought to terrorize and ultimately liquidate its opponents, while the German Democratic Republic, from which almost all the people most fiercely opposed to the regime had fled to the West, merely sought to indoctrinate them or intimidate them by example. For those most immediately affected, of course, the results were the same. Johann Burianek's appeal for clemency was turned down by the Politburo on 17 June 1952,[63] and he was executed on 2 August 1952.[64]

A similar kind of brainwashed compliance was observable in the case of the engineer and electrician Kurt König, sentenced to death on 30 June 1953 for boycott campaigning and warmongering allegedly aimed at destroying the democratic institutions of the German Democratic Republic. Given his position in the East German energy supply system, it is likely that he had been guilty either of incompetence or mismanagement, perhaps in conjunction with maintaining contacts with the West. There was no evidence that he had been involved in the military aspects of his trade. König wrote to the President begging for clemency. 'From March 1951 to May 1951', he confessed, 'and from September 1951 up to the day of my arrest on 7 November 1951, I carried out military espionage against the USSR on the territory of the GDR.' It did not do in such documents to question the verdict, or to alter the confession which the authorities had prepared. All he could do was to confess that he had seen the light. Indeed, so as to give his application a chance, König added that he had only recognized the error of his ways thanks to

the practical example of correctness and concern for people given to me by members of the state security organs in these months of imprisonment. This gave the lie to all the criminal slanders which the imperialists have deliberately been spreading. And it told me only too clearly the serious nature of the crimes of which I was guilty. The realization that I had reached out my hand to the Devil and fought against Good has long since become part of my knowledge and conviction. How correctly I have been treated during this 8-month imprisonment—it makes me dreadfully ashamed—although I have surely sinned against every one of these people through my misdeed! Oh—how sincerely I regret my disgrace with all my heart! I have only one wish: that I should be given the opportunity to make recompense.

The degree of contrition and compliance in this document, and its simple-

---

[62] For a good description of this process, see Walter Janka, *Spuren eines Lebens* (Berlin, 1991), 29–406.

[63] BA-SAPM Berlin J IV 2/2/216, Protokoll Nr. 20 (17 June 1952).

[64] BA Potsdam DO 1/32/39710, Bl. 586.

minded use of religious imagery in describing the contrast between socialism and capitalism, must have been music to the Politburo's ears. But Pieck, Ulbricht, and their advisers were deaf to such pleas. König was more useful to them dead than alive. 'Your prisoner today will be your most passionate propagandist tomorrow', promised König. But he was not to have the chance. He was guillotined at 4 in the morning on 3 October 1953.[65]

As was usual in such trials, only the man singled out—usually in an entirely arbitrary manner—as the ringleader was condemned to death. This was the case with König and Burianek. It was also the case with another show trial which began shortly after Burianek's execution. This involved a group which had allegedly been in contact with a human rights organization, the Combat Group against Inhumanity (*Kampfgruppe gegen die Unmenschlichkeit*), which operated from West Berlin and monitored human rights violations in the East. The Politburo and the Stasi were concerned to discredit such groups in the eyes of the East German population by portraying them through such show trials as stooges of Western secret services, engaged in violent campaigns of sabotage and subversion. In this trial the alleged ringleader, Wolfgang Kaiser, was condemned to death for his activities in the organization, while three of his fellow members received lengthy prison sentences. Hilde Benjamin, the presiding judge on the Supreme Court, accused the group of being a cover for a campaign of terrorism organized from Bonn and financed by the American Secret Service. Its aim—so the unlikely story, rehearsed by the prosecutor and repeated in Kaiser's confession, went—was to spread terror in the population and destabilize the state by causing explosions and poisoning cigarettes.[66] A spokesperson for the group in West Berlin declared that Kaiser's confession had been extracted by prolonged torture. They knew it was false.[67] In fact, Kaiser, to use a concept commonly employed at the time, had probably been psychologically brainwashed rather than physically tortured. His confession was widely publicized in the East German media. Despite the fact that nobody had been killed or even injured by the group, which even according to the prepared confessions had only done damage to property, Kaiser was condemned to death for treason under Article 6 of the German Democratic Republic's 1949 constitution. The Politburo rejected his appeal for clemency on 19 August and he was executed by beheading in Dresden on 6 September 1952.[68]

[65] BA Potsdam DO 1/32/39710, Bl. 370–3: König to Pieck, 8 July 1953; ibid., Bl. 400: Auf- und Abgangsbogen. The Auf-und Abgangsbogen was the form used to register the admission and discharge of prisoners from gaol. If they were discharged dead, having been executed, this was recorded on the form too.

[66] INGASA Nottingham 25/Prozesse 1950–1/2: *Tägliche Rundschau*, 10 Aug. 1952.

[67] Ibid.: *Der Tagesspiegel*, 10 Aug. 1952. For an eyewitness report of the use of torture in order to extract a confession, see ibid., Rechtswesen 1953: *Der Tagesspiegel*, 19 July 1953.

[68] BA Potsdam DO 1/32/39710, Bl. 362–4: Wolfgang Kaiser; BA-SAPM Berlin J IV 2/2/227, Nr. 19/1.

The calculated dramaturgy of such trials did not involve the wholesale slaughter of the defendants, but rather a carefully graded set of punishments, fixed according to the type and degree of offence for which the authorities wanted them to be convicted. But show trials before the Supreme Court were only one facet of the instrumentalization of justice for political ends by the regime. Apart from such economic offences, the death penalty was also used ruthlessly against anyone who killed an official representative of the state. On 17 May 1952, for example, the District Court in Mühlhausen sentenced 'the murderers of the antifascist Alfred Sobik, the agents of Western imperialists, Ernst Wilhelm und Johann Muras, to death'. They had beaten him to death at a works meeting of the potash mine at Obergebra on May Day, after a political argument.[69] Together with their workmates, they had spent the evening drinking in the village inn at Obergebra. After singing a number of 'militaristic songs', they began to quarrel. Obviously extremely drunk, Ernst Wilhelm 'yelled: "One people, one Reich, one Führer!" and insulted the working class's red flag in a particularly obscene manner'. As one of the others, the 'antifascist' Alfred Sobik, objected, Muras and Wihelm fell upon him and beat him up. They were dragged away by their workmates, but despite the brevity of the brawl, Sobik fell over and died in a matter of minutes. He had been suffering from a heart complaint. For the two accused, Sobik's weak heart was a misfortune. For the judges, it was an irrelevancy. The key fact was that he had been 'a very active functionary of the SED [Socialist Unity Party]'. His attackers had shown themselves to be fascists at heart and were guilty of 'encouraging murder' under Article 6 of the constitution not through words, but '*through their deeds*'. This was, to say the least, a bold interpretation of the constitutional provision in question. It was hardly likely that the accused men had deliberately killed their victim in order to encourage others to kill officials of the Socialist Unity Party as well. Nevertheless such a crime could not go unpunished in case it made it easier for such attacks to occur in future. In addition, the accused had admitted under interrogation that they listened to RIAS, the American radio station based in West Berlin. Many if not most East Germans probably did this at the time. But this made Muras and Wilhelm in the eyes of the court into agents of what the prosecution portrayed as the station's systematic encouragement of murder and sabotage in the East. Muras's and Wilhelm's execution was approved by the Politburo without debate on 19 August and they were guillotined shortly after 4.30 in the morning on 6 September 1952.[70]

Another typical example of the regime's cynical manipulation of the judicial system can be found in a newspaper report of November 1952 describing the trial

---

[69] INGASA Nottingham 25/Prozesse 1950–1/2: *Tägliche Rundschau*, 19 May 1952.

[70] BA Potsdam DO 1/32/39710, Bl. 334–61: Todesstrafe Muras, Johann; ibid., Bl. 631: Ernst Wilhelm; BA-SAPM Berlin J IV 2/2/224, Nr. 28; ibid., J IV 2/2/227, Nr. 18 (19 Aug. 1952).

in Haldensleben of three people for murdering a staff sergeant in the People's Police. The paper reported that 'the trial aroused massive interest among the inhabitants of Calvörde, where the policeman lived. Along with the working people of the Magdeburg district, they had demanded the harshest punishment for the criminal in innumerable declarations and resolutions.' The inhabitants of the area had in fact most probably been forced to attend, and the petitions, as usual, had all been orchestrated. The alleged ringleader, the 39-year-old butcher Hermann Lindecke, was condemned to death, and his two fellow offenders, Wilhelm Barner and Anneliese Stölting, to life imprisonment. The authorities linked the murder above all to the political situation and the current party line of combating Western 'sabotage'. The court's judgment alleged that the murder had been inspired by Western media attacks on the People's Police, and emphasized that the East German people 'trust the People's Police and regard them as their helper and friend. For this reason, they regard any attack of grubby provocateurs on officers of the People's Police as an attack on themselves and therefore demand the harshest punishment.'[71] Lindecke was guillotined on 24 January 1953, just three months after the end of his widely publicized trial.[72] But the crime in reality had been far from politically motivated and the popular anger had been a propaganda invention. What had happened had been much less dramatic or political. Over a period of time, the murdered policeman had made himself unpopular in some circles in the village of Calvörde by his strict interpretation of the drink laws. In the village inn, one of the men he had particularly offended, Wilhelm Barner, sought towards the end of an evening's drinking to persuade him of the error of his ways. The policeman succeeded in calming him, and Barner agreed to drink a toast with him.

Shortly afterwards, however, he started to sing the 'Horst Wessel Song' loud and clear, as well as the 'Merry Brunswickers'. At this provocation, police officer Panneck declared that drinking time was up. The accused Barner insulted the policeman in the foulest manner. The exact expressions could not be repeated in court because Barner claimed not to be able to remember them. His fellow accused Lindecke immediately joined in the singing of the 'Horst Wessel Song'. He too participated in no lesser degree in the insulting of Panneck. Thus he said to Panneck, 'You red hounds should be put down, there's nothing more to be done with you.' At this infamous slander, the People's Police Officer declared the accused Lindecke and Barner were arrested.

As he went to seek assistance for the arrest, Lindecke pounced on him outside the door of the Black Eagle and hit him repeatedly about the head, so that he fell over. Lindecke continued to hit him in the face until he began to bleed profusely. The men then went home, and the third of the accused, the innkeeper Anneliese

[71] INGASA Nottingham 25/Prozesse 1950–1/2: *Tägliche Rundschau*, 16 Nov. 1952.
[72] BA Potsdam DO 1/32/39710, Bl. 320–33: Hermann Lindeke [*sic*].

Stölting, left the policeman unattended while she washed the glasses. By the time that Panneck was discovered, he had bled to death. The murder was in truth little more than a squalid village brawl, such as might have occurred at any time over the previous few centuries. But by first insulting then threatening and finally murdering a policeman, and by using Nazi language in doing so, the offenders fell foul of Article 6 of the constitution. They had, said the judgment, 'carried out incitement to murder and boycott against our democratic institutions. . . . They thereby revealed themselves as open enemies of our order.' The murder was carried out in order to conceal the political provocation, said the judges. All this was extremely unconvincing. But the verdict showed the determination of the GDR judiciary to pass the harshest possible sentence on anyone who attacked the People's Police, and to give a brutal warning to anyone who was thoughtless enough to sing Nazi ditties in the course of an evening's drinking.[73]

Even more striking in this context was the case of Kurt Lübeck, found guilty on 12 December 1952 by the District Court in Cottbus of having engaged in 'a campaign of boycott against democratic institutions, incitement to murder democratic politicians, and murder of a functionary of the Alfred Scholz Works in combination with the origination and dissemination of rumours prejudicial to peace'. The 42-year-old Lübeck had never had a proper job for the first years of his adult life, during the Depression. He had never managed to get any training for a trade. Like many of the unemployed, he had been active during the Weimar Republic in the Communist Party. During the Third Reich, however, he joined the brownshirts and found work in an open-cast lignite mine. This was a protected job, and he did not fight in the war, except in the improvised home defence units of Hitler's *Landsturm* in January 1945. After the end of the war, as the new regime was establishing itself in the Soviet zone, he joined the People's Police. This enabled him to find a position in the lignite mine again, and soon he was a member of the Communist Party once more. As the court not unfairly remarked, his Communist commitment was 'merely formal', like all the other political commitments he had undertaken. Like many other men at this time, he had a collection of war weapons but, unlike most of them, he fitted a silencer to one of them and did regular shooting practice. In 1951–2, the court alleged, he began to carry out acts of sabotage by causing fires to break out at the end of the shift, but remained unsuspected by the authorities since he had helped to put them out. He had been bought by Western agents. As he turned up to work drunk and began loading the oven wrongly once more, so that it threatened to burst into flames and cause another fire, he was confronted by an overseer with this 'act of sabotage' and reported to the works supervisor.

[73] Ibid., Bl. 323–8: Bezirksgericht Magdeburg, Strafsache gegen Hermann Lindecke, Wilhelm Barner, Anneliese Stölting.

Faced with the prospect of disciplinary action and probably dismissal unless he did something, he tried to explain himself to the overseer, and as the attempt failed, shot him dead. Lübeck denied having met any agent in West Berlin and denied any acts of sabotage. He also denied another accusation, that he had been spreading 'agitational leaflets'; he had certainly found some, he admitted, but he had dumped them in a pond and only shown one to a couple of friends. His defence lawyer pointed out that he kept the weapons for hunting purposes, and that he had several convictions for poaching. There was no evidence to link him with the various fires that had broken out previously in the works, especially since they had not occurred during his shift. For the court, however, everything fitted together too well. Lübeck was not an unskilled, clumsy, drunken labourer fearful of losing his job because of the mistakes he made, and angry at his overseer for having reported him to the supervisor and for having sent him home before the shift was over. He was a fully paid-up Western agent, engaged in a systematic campaign of propaganda, sabotage, and terror. During the Third Reich, he had 'consciously gone over to the class enemy's camp':

The division of Germany which the imperialists accomplished in 1948 emboldened him to renew his fascist activities by building up a store of weapons over the following years and revealing his negative attitude to our order in discussions with progressive comrades. The agitational leaflets found in his possession strengthened his negative attitude, incited him to boycott and murder campaigns, and reached their apogee in the murder of the progressive functionary Dobberstein, a man loved by all. Dobberstein was portrayed by all the witnesses as a calm, collegial, and responsible colleague, whose behaviour expressed the fact that he was a model to everyone in the complete devotion of his powers to the construction of socialism and the maintenance of peace. The murder was therefore an action directed against the forces of peace.

Kurt Lübeck was duly convicted under Article 6 of the constitution, sentenced to death, and executed in Cottbus on 28 February 1953.[74]

Some capital prosecutions were directed at genuine, deliberate criminality, though these did not necessarily involve offences which were punishable by death according to the Criminal Code. Even in the early 1950s, there was still a flourishing black market in East Germany, and after the closing of the border in 1952, a further trade in smuggling people and goods beckoned to those who did not care too much for the law. In April 1953 Hans Leipner was condemned to death for 'boycott campaigning', 'warmongering', propagation of National Socialism, and 'the spreading of tendentious rumours'. His crime, and that of the others in his group, appears to have been the manufacture and distribution of false ration cards. The prosecution alleged that this had been a plot organized by

---

[74] BA Potsdam DO 1/32/39710, Bl. 306–19: Lübeck, Kurt; ibid., Bl. 646–53: Bezirksgericht Cottbus, Urteilsbegründung; ibid., Bl. 654–7: Berufung (18 Dec. 1952).

the American secret service as part of its plan to destroy the economy of the German Democratic Republic. But in fact the sentence was obviously intended to warn and deter other profiteers and small-time crooks of this kind from trying anything similar. They were made scapegoats for the problems of food supply which East Germany was experiencing at this time.[75] Article 6 of the constitution provided the means by which the East German leaders could rid themselves of other embarrassing individuals who had not committed any capital offence according to the Criminal Code. In October 1953, for example, Albrecht Gessler was condemned to death as an agent of the Combat Group against Inhumanity. He had supposedly tried to blow up a factory and destroy railway lines around Magdeburg.[76] In fact, he seems to have been a petty thief who aroused the wrath of the GDR authorities by wearing a Soviet uniform as he carried out armed robberies.[77] A similar, if more serious, case took place on 7 February 1953, when Walter Schönbrodt, born in 1897, was sentenced to death by a court in Halle. A member of a gang of smugglers and black marketeers, he had run into a trap set by police and customs men and had pulled a pistol. In the ensuing struggle, an officer had been killed. 'Sch.,' remarked the Police Minister Michalke not long after his arrest, 'is the epitome of the permanent lawbreaker. In the prison community he is a well-disguised subversive influence.'[78] Schönbrodt, indeed, even claimed to have belonged to the notorious Plättner Band, a group of far-left terrorists active after the First World War.[79] He was executed on 14 October 1953.[80] Killing a policeman in East Germany usually led to execution.

Stanislaw Rucz, a Pole, was executed on 17 October 1953. He had been convicted of murder by the District Court at Chemnitz on 27 January 1953. Rucz and a companion had shot an officer of the People's Police who had caught them trying to enter East Germany illegally.[81] Rucz had been a forced labourer and claimed to have been used as an object of medical experimentation in a number of Nazi concentration camps, including Dachau and Sachsenhausen. He listed the diseases with which he had been injected, including malaria and typhus, and the Polish doctors who had treated him after the war.[82] But none of this saved him from the wrath of the East German regime. The authority of the People's Police had to be maintained at all costs. Ordinary murders were also given a

---

[75] INGASA Nottingham 25/Prozesse 1953–4/1: *Tägliche Rundschau*, 14 Apr. 1953; ibid.: *Neues Deutschland*, 16 Apr. 1953.
[76] Ibid.: *Neue Zeitung*, 4 Oct. 1953.
[77] BA Potsdam DO 1/32/39710, Bl. 642–6: Oberstes Gericht.
[78] Ibid., Bl. 421: Schönbrodt: Michalke 'Beurteilung', 11 Dec. 1952.
[79] Ibid., Bl. 439–40: Berufung (Haenisch), 11 Feb. 1953.
[80] Ibid., Bl. 445: Auf- und Abgangsbogen.
[81] Ibid., Bl. 794, 815–18: Vollzug, Berufung; INGASA Nottingham 25/Prozesse 1953–4/1: *Telegraf*, 3 Feb. 1953.
[82] BA Potsdam DO 1/32/39710, Bl. 840–2: Rucz to Red Cross, Geneva, 11 July 1953.

political interpretation where the perpetrator was an official representative of the state. In such cases, the failure of the accused to co-operate with the regime invariably brought retribution. On 19 March 1952, for example, the District Court in Magdeburg condemned Rudolf Schmidt, a former member of the People's Police, to death for murder. On 20 November 1950, overcome by financial worries, he had hacked his wife to death with an axe, then strangled his two young sons so that they would not be used as witnesses against him. In prison awaiting the outcome of his appeal, he 'slandered and insulted the People's Police on many occasions and expressed himself in a very negative manner with regard to our antifascist democratic order', as the prison authorities reported. He had wrecked his cell and created a stir on numerous occasions. Such behaviour was particularly reprehensible in the case of a former East German policeman, who was supposed to set an example to others. 'He does not demonstrate the least remorse about his crime', the prison authorities added. After the rejection of his appeal on 17 July, almost a year passed before he was guillotined in Magdeburg, on 2 July 1953.[83] It was perhaps difficult to find anything political in the circumstances which had led to Schmidt's trial, but the resentment he expressed in prison at the regime's policies, which he clearly felt had made it impossible for him to support his family, undoubtedly contributed to the decision to execute him.

Executions also continued to take place in East Germany throughout this period for war crimes, but increasingly they occurred only when a crime of this kind could be exploited for the political purposes of the regime, as we have already seen in the Waldheim trials.[84] A Nazi past could make the difference between life imprisonment and execution in capital cases. On 7 July 1952 Siegfried Erbe was sentenced to death for crimes against humanity and for contravening Article 6 of the East German constitution. He confessed to having been sent into the East as an agent charged with carrying out acts of sabotage and espionage, after a career of cruelty and brutality towards foreign slave labourers during the war.[85] He was recommended for clemency, but the Politburo asked for his case to be referred back to the clemency commission in March 1953.[86] The intervention did not produce a favourable outcome for Erbe, who was executed in June 1953.[87] Sometimes these cases were left over from the period before the foundation of the German Democratic Republic. In May 1954, for example, the

---

[83] BA Potsdam DO 1/32/39710: Strafvollzugsamt Magdeburg-Sudenburg, Bl. 541–56: Rudolph [*sic*] Schmidt: Wycisk to Staatsanwalt, 28 Aug. 1952; Urteilsbegründung.

[84] For one example, see ibid., Bl. 491–514: Personalakten der Straf-gefangenen-verwahrten Walk, Johannes.

[85] Ibid., Bl. 452–89, Erbe, Siegfried.

[86] BA-SAPM Berlin J IV 2/2A/257, Bl. 107: Zum Protokoll Nr. 19/53, § 24 (31 Mar. 1953).

[87] Ibid., J IV 2/2/284, Bl. 3: Zum Protokoll Nr. 30/53, § 6 (2 June 1953).

Politburo approved the executions of Horst Spalteholz, Georg Döring, Felix Wittig, and Walter Linzer for war crimes, although it also passed a resolution censuring the conduct of Chief State Prosecutor Melsheimer and several of his colleagues in the affair in causing a delay of five years since the men's condemnation.[88] The head of the Central Committee's Department of State Administration, Anton Plenikowski, who at this time was responsible for advising the party leadership on such matters, told the Politburo: 'The fact that the sentences were passed almost four years ago cannot be a reason for failing to carry them out. Irresponsible delays on the part of the organs of justice must not accrue to the advantage of these fascist criminals. The Justice Minister and the General State Prosecutor refuse a reprieve.'[89]

Such symbolic measures had little effect in stemming the rising tide of discontent that began to flow after the death of Stalin in the spring of 1953. After years of repression and privation, ordinary workers and their families now began to hope for something better. Under pressure from Moscow, the East German leadership adopted a 'New Course' on 9 July, which among other things promised a re-examination of possible excessive sentences passed by the courts in the past three years. But it was too late. Popular anger and disappointment overflowed on 17 June 1953 into a series of mass demonstrations and strikes all over the country. Originating in a demand for lower work norms and better pay, they soon took on a political character, as ex-Social Democrats began to lead the call on the street for free elections and a change of regime. Demanding the release of political prisoners, the strikers stormed the gaols in nine towns and cities across the country, freeing over 1,300 inmates. As the Politburo's grip faltered, the Red Army stepped in, and the uprising was crushed by Soviet tanks in a few hours. Nevertheless, the regime was severely shaken. In the wake of the uprising of 17 June 1953, Western sources estimated that over 6,000 people were arrested. Sixteen people were condemned to death and shot by Soviet military tribunals by the middle of August. One was executed on the orders of an East German court, while a number of death sentences passed by other East German courts were commuted to life imprisonment.[90] Three workers in the copper mines at Eisleben were condemned and shot on 4 July,[91] while two employees of the Sachsenwerk Dresden were shot on 24 June for having blown up a Russian tank the previous day. In Erfurt two policemen, Bähr and Kupse, were shot for refusing to carry out orders, as were three policemen in Berlin, shot on 18 June. Five workers in Magdeburg, alleged to be ringleaders, were also executed, as was the worker

[88] Ibid., J IV 2/2/360, Bl. 6: Zum Protokoll Nr. 4/54, § 13 (11 May 1954).
[89] Ibid., J IV 2/2A/348, Protokoll Nr. 15: Vorlage für das Politbüro, 19 May 1956, 3–5.
[90] INGASA Nottingham 25/Prozesse 1953–4/1: Telegraf, 19 August 1953.
[91] Ibid.: Telegraf, 22 July 1953.

Diener in Jena.[92] In Potsdam the worker Prahst was executed, while in Döbernitz, in the Delitzsch district, the mayor Hartmann, a member of the Socialist Unity Party, who had prevented a policeman from shooting at the demonstrators, was also executed by order of a Soviet military court. All this was summary justice, without any elaborate court proceedings and in the absence of any real attempt at propaganda exploitation. Show trials were out of the question for genuine opponents of the regime.

Nevertheless, the East German authorities did give publicity to a few cases arising from the events of 17 June. They focused especially on the case of Erna Dorn, a former concentration camp guard in Ravensbrück who during the uprising had been sprung from gaol in Leipzig, where she was serving a sentence for war crimes. Attempting to suggest that such people were typical of those involved in the events of 17 June, the courts convicted her of working in the 'provocateurs' general staff.' Erna Dorn does not seem to have done anything special during the uprising, but she was sentenced to death all the same, in order to strengthen the regime's portrayal of the uprising as a fascist plot.[93] She was executed in Halle on 1 October 1953.[94] The gardener Ernst Jennrich, a former Social Democrat, was also executed for his role in the events of 17 June. He had come across 'a crowd of people . . . who were being egged on by a provocateur', and allegedly joined it in order 'to commit terrorist acts' and to bring about the fall of the government. Seizing a weapon from one of the 'provocateurs', he had joined in the attack on the Magdeburg prison and court-house, firing at least one shot. After the Russian tanks had begun restoring order, he had claimed to a policeman to have killed three members of the People's Police. Three policemen had indeed been shot. On 26 August 1953 the district court in Magdeburg found there was no hard evidence to support the view that Jennrich had pulled the trigger and sentenced him only to life imprisonment. The prosecution, however, appealed, and the Supreme Court ordered a retrial, indicating that he should be charged with murder, and that the provision in § 211 of the Criminal Code for life imprisonment instead of death for murder 'in special, exceptional cases' did not apply.[95] Sentenced to death at the retrial on 6 November 1953, Jennrich was executed on 20 March 1954.[96]

During these trials, judges and prosecutors were directed by a special politico-judicial staff assembled in East Berlin. For the next ten years, the judicial system was controlled by 'brigades of instructors' steered by the Justice Ministry, which

[92] INGASA Nottingham 25/Prozesse 1953–4/1: *Der Tag*, 4 July 1953.

[93] Ibid: *Der Tag*, 24 June 1953; Fricke, *Politik und Justiz*, 290.

[94] BA Potsdam DO 1/32/39710, Bl. 515–16: Dorn, Erna.

[95] Ibid., Bl. 637–40: Oberstes Gericht.

[96] Ilse Spittmann and Karl Wilhelm Fricke (eds.), *17. Juni 1953. Arbeiteraufstand in der DDR* (Cologne, 1982), 73.

monitored court proceedings and told the judges what to do.[97] The wave of repression that followed the uprising of 17 June 1953 extended far down the penal scale; prison sentences, dismissals, disciplinings were widespread. The Ministry for State Security was merged into the Interior Ministry and Willi Zaisser, the incumbent Minister on 17 June, and a critic of Ulbricht, was sacked by order of the Politburo and replaced by Ernst Wollweber.[98] The Justice Minister, Max Fechner, a former Social Democrat who was incautious enough to denounce many of the arrests that followed the uprising as illegal, and to insist publicly on the constitutional right of workers to go on strike, was sacked on 16 July. Two years later, on 24 May 1955, he was arrested, put through a secret trial, and imprisoned for eight years as an enemy of the state.[99] He was replaced in 1953 by Hilde Benjamin, a Communist lawyer who had been imprisoned for six years under the Nazis. Since 1949 she had presided over numerous show trials as Vice-President of the Supreme Court. Known popularly as 'the red guillotine', Benjamin was a hardline Stalinist who could be trusted to bring the judicial apparatus to heel.[100] One of the first casualties of Benjamin's term of office was the draft Criminal Code begun earlier in the year. She evidently considered that it made too many compromises with the old criminal law, and withdrew it in order to prepare a much more thoroughgoing revision at a later date. Thus ironically the codification of the criminal law ran into as much trouble, and encountered as many delays, in the German Democratic Republic as it had done in the Imperial or Weimar periods or the Third Reich.

Nevertheless, the East German state had not only succeeded in establishing a fully functioning system of Stalinist justice by 1953, it had also managed, more by luck than by judgement, to defend it in the face of popular opposition, and indeed to use it effectively as a means of political repression when that opposition spilled over into open revolt. Despite the death of Stalin, Ulbricht had not only survived but had actually cemented his grip on party and state. In the politically directed judicial system, capital punishment was ruthlessly used as a real and symbolic means of supporting the 'construction of socialism'. Apart from the period following 17 June 1953, citizens were normally executed not so much for real acts of opposition or rebellion—for those most determinedly opposed to the regime simply voted with their feet and left via Berlin for the West—but as examples, to deter more minor acts of dissidence among those who chose to remain. The conditions under which East Germany had come into existence did not allow the wholesale slaughter of real and potential dissidents such as had

[97] Fricke, 'Aus "erzieherischen Gründen"'.
[98] BA-SAPM J IV 2/2A/291: Protokoll der Sitzung am 18. Juli 1953, Nr. 3.
[99] Weber, *Geschichte*, 245.
[100] Hermann Weber, *DDR. Grundriss der Geschichte 1945–1990* (Hanover, 1991), 261.

taken place in the Soviet Union under Stalin. The legitimacy of the state was too weak, its international situation too precarious, its neighbour in the Federal Republic too attractive and available a haven, to allow such a policy to be adopted. During the 1950s, and indeed subsequently, the German Democratic Republic was continually caught in a dilemma. On the one hand, it needed to win over its own citizens and gain sympathizers in the West, among other things by projecting an image that was positive, progressive, and humane; on the other hand, it wanted to eliminate opposition to its policies by applying penal sanctions harsh enough to persuade its citizens that resistance was not worth the risk. It sought to escape this dilemma by portraying itself as beset by evil-minded, hostile, fascist, and imperialist states, hell-bent on undermining the construction of socialism by any means possible, including subversion, sabotage, and terror. In this way, at least, it followed the example of the Soviet Union from the 1920s. But it softened the impact of state terror by using capital punishment in a highly selective manner. Ever since the nineteenth century, if not before, the death penalty had been used by the state in Germany as a symbolic signal of its political intent. The German Democratic Republic did not deviate from this general pattern. Only the Third Reich, when capital punishment merged into a far wider policy of racial extermination, had been an exception to this rule. What distinguished the East German regime was the calculated and systematic way in which it used the death penalty for political purposes. This was made possible by the almost total control which it established over the judicial system in the early 1950s, achieving a degree of precision in directing criminal prosecutions and trials to which the masters of the Third Reich could only aspire. By the middle of the 1950s, in the wake of the failed workers' uprising, this system of manipulation and control seemed to have been perfected.

c. Espionage, Sabotage, 'Diversion': The Aftermath of 17 June

The power struggle that had begun within the East German Politburo on Stalin's death, and helped create the climate of uncertainty that led to the uprising of 17 June 1953, was ultimately resolved in favour of the Stalinist party leader Walter Ulbricht. East Germany's master, the Soviet Union, was forced to concede that Ulbricht's dismissal, followed by a liberalization of the system, would have been tantamount to a confession that the demonstrators had been right. Ulbricht used the opportunity to tighten his grip still further. This involved a fresh series of show trials, this time with an even stronger emphasis on espionage and sabotage than before. The death penalty was reserved especially for officials within the state and government apparatus who had been in contact with the West. On 9 September 1953, for example, Werner Hoffmann, an official in the East German

Ministry of the Interior, was sentenced to death and four others were given long prison sentences for 'espionage, warmongering, and endangering, peace'.[101] On 30 October 1953 an engineer, Christian Lange-Werner, aged 49, was condemned along with six others by the district court in Cottbus. While the others all received prison sentences, however, Lange-Werner was condemned to death. An aviation specialist and an officer-instructor in the People's Police since August 1952, he was a former Nazi Party member, although he claimed to have joined for purely professional reasons. He was said to have been recruited by an agent called 'Sylvia' in West Berlin to supply information about the People's Police, their strength, structure, and training, and about the engine of a new training aeroplane which he was involved in developing. He and his group were found guilty of serious military espionage. Their appeal was rejected by the Supreme Court on 24 November 1953 and he appears to have been executed in March 1954, though there is no formal record of his death.[102] In 1954 two officers of the military wing of the People's Police, the *kasernierte Volkspolizei*, Werner Schneider and Martin Dölling, were sentenced to death by an officers' court for similar offences.[103] And on 11 March 1955 Heinz-Georg Ebeling was condemned to death under Article 6 of the constitution for betraying Stasi secrets to Western agents.[104]

An employee of the Stasi, Ebeling had been sacked in 1953 for 'lack of vigilance' and had gone to West Berlin, where he was said to have been interrogated by the American Secret Service and to have told them all he knew about his former employers. He had been promised a new life as a political refugee only if he agreed to turn a number of his old colleagues into double agents. How much truth there was in these allegations was anybody's guess. The clemency commission's recommendation was made on 4 March and agreed by the Politburo on 8 March, even before Ebeling had been found guilty by the courts. 'The sentence', added the commission, 'is to be carried out immediately after it has acquired the force of law and a reprieve has been turned down.'[105] It is worth pausing for a moment to consider the implications of this fact. The control of the Politburo over the judicial system was now so complete that it was resolving on the President's rejection of clemency before the offender in question had even been found guilty and condemned. Nothing indicates more graphically the function of the courts as far as the party leadership was concerned. They were not organs of a neutral justice, they were arms of the working-class drive to create a socialist society. Why should the people who considered they were leading that drive

---

[101] BA Potsdam DO 1/32/39710, Bl. 185–201: Hoffmann.
[102] Ibid., Bl. 669–705: Berufung, Urteilsbegründung, Übergabeprotokoll.
[103] INGASA Nottingham 25/Prozesse 1953–4/1: *Der Tag*, 9 Oct. 1954.
[104] BA Potsdam DO 1/32/37910, Bl. 240–5: Strafsache gegen Heinz-Georg Ebeling.
[105] BA-SAPM Berlin J IV 2/2A/412: Vorlage für das Politbüro betr. Strafsache gegen Heinz Ebeling, 4 Mar. 1955 (Rost).

pause, therefore, to contemplate the fact that they might appear to be prejudging a judicial decision that still hung in the balance? There is no indication that any of the members of the Politburo thought there was anything embarrassing about the timing of their vote. If the meeting at which they considered clemency petitions happened to take place before the trial in question was over, so what? They had decided the accused was guilty and deserving of death anyway; and—the crucial point—they had supervised the direction of the prosecution service and the judges in the case from the very start, so that there was no possibility of a surprise verdict or sentence being arrived at.

As this example showed, the regime was particularly hard on serving or retired Stasi employees who came into contact with the West. In June 1955 the Politburo discussed the case of Bruno and Susanne Krüger. Stasi officers, they had fled from Schwerin to the West in August–September 1953 and were said to have betrayed 'all the secrets they knew to the American Secret Service, to the Combat Group against Inhumanity, to the so-called Committee of "Free Jurists", and to Department K 5 of the West Berlin police'. These included the structure and methods of the Stasi, names of officers, details of prisons, current operations, and so on. The Politburo was told that they had tried to turn former colleagues to the service of Western intelligence as well, and had distributed 'inflammatory leaflets' to the East German population. Moreover, they had attempted to force the resignation of a large number of former colleagues by exposing them, with names and addresses, in this literature, and by sending them postcards which made it look as if they were carrying on illegal contacts with the West. In view of this 'unscrupulousness', it was suggested to the Politburo that they be executed without delay. How true all the allegations against them were was uncertain. But the Politburo agreed that they should not be granted clemency.[106] They were guillotined on 14 September 1955, and care was taken to ensure that the execution was formally announced 'to all colleagues in official meetings of the main Divisions, Departments, and local offices' of the Ministry for State Security, to ensure that they all got the message.[107] Stasi chief Ernst Wollweber, in announcing the verdict, told his staff that the Krügers'

treachery was as comprehensive and unrestrained as only degenerate types, acting from the basest and most selfish motives, can commit. They are thereby expelling themselves from the working class and become low and malevolent tools of the enemies of the working class and of its workers' and peasants' state. . . . The tasks with which our institutions are charged require a staff that must remain honest and true to our party and government in every situation. That is the meaning and content of the obligation which

[106] BA-SAPM Berlin. J IV 2/2A/431: ZK 01 Tgb. Nr. 297: Vorlage für das Politbüro. Betrifft: Strafsache gegen Krüger Bruno und Krüger Susanne, 10 June 1955.
[107] BStU ZA: Anweisung VVS 4507/55.

every officer of the State Secretariat for State Security freely takes upon him- or herself and makes effective with a signature. Anyone who violates this obligation has earned the severest of penalties for this offence. . . . Every traitor to our just cause will get his just deserts. He will be caught, just like the KRÜGER couple, however safe he believes his hiding-place may be, and he will never escape his just punishment, for the power of the working class stretches forth across every boundary.

Just to ensure that the lesson was learned, Wollweber even arranged for every Stasi officer to sign a form certifying that he had taken note of the verdict on the Krügers, and the offences which had given rise to it.[108]

This was far from being the only case of its kind at this time. At its meeting on 21 June 1955, for example, the Politburo approved three more death sentences. One of them was against Manfred Hebestreit, another former employee of the Stasi, aged just 20, who had been 'in an operational department' before being demoted 'because of unsuitability' and had thereupon gone to West Berlin and told all he knew to the American Secret Service and had allegedly returned to East Germany as a spy. Klaus Sorgenicht, the head of the legal department of the Central Committee, told the Politburo that Hebestreit had shown 'not the slightest remorse'. 'During his interrogation he was constantly provocative and made his antagonistic attitude clear. In his cell, he incited his fellow prisoners against our workers' and peasants' state.'[109] On 14 March 1955 Paul Köppe was sentenced to death under Article 6 of the constitution, and his wife Edith Köppe received a prison sentence of eight years. Köppe was a long-time Communist, but according to the judgment of the court, he had suffered from alcoholism, and had embezzled money from the State Security Ministry, where he had been employed as a driver. To avoid discovery, he had fled to West Berlin, where it was alleged he had been picked up by the American Secret Service, to whom he had passed on a great deal of important information about the Ministry, its layout, and the people who worked there. He had also been interrogated by French and British intelligence and persuaded by the West German political police to contact his wife in Leipzig and get her to recruit one of his former colleagues in the State Security Ministry as a Western agent. The couple were arrested as Köppe paid his wife an ill-advised visit to make further arrangements for their espionage activities.[110] The clemency commission told the Politburo firmly that he had to be executed:

In view of the unscrupulousness with which K. betrayed all the secrets he knew to imperialist secret services, in view of the fact that he expressed himself willing without further thought to recruit more agents from the Secretariat for State Security in order to

[108] Ibid.: Befehl Nr. 224/55, 5 Aug. 1955.
[109] BA-SAPM Berlin J IV 2/2A/432: Vorlage für das Politbüro, 3 May 1955.
[110] BA Potsdam DO 1/32/37910, Bl. 235–9: Strafsache gegen Paul und Edith Köppe.

weaken the defensive preparedness of our security organs against hostile attacks, the commission suggests after thorough discussion that Köppe should be sentenced to death. The sentence is to be carried out immediately after it acquires the force of law and after the President of the German Democratic Republic has refused a reprieve.[111]

The Politburo confirmed his death sentence on 8 March, once more well in advance of the verdict, indeed almost a week before the offender was found guilty and sentenced to death by the court.[112]

Trials against Stasi operatives were usually kept very quiet. The regime did not want anybody to get the impression that there was disloyalty in the ranks of its security service. But the charge of espionage was also laid against others apart from members of the Stasi. On 23 June 1955 Gerhard Benkowitz, Hans-Dietrich Kogel, and Jan Kubanka were also sentenced to death for this offence. Benkowitz was a schoolteacher, and Hans-Dietrich Kogel an official working for the town council in Weimar. They were convicted of spying on behalf of the Combat Group against Inhumanity, which was accused of planning to blow up bridges and destroy power supplies.[113] Their lack of connection with the Stasi enabled the authorities to mount a major show trial, with the offence of sabotage as its centre-piece. In fact, of course, neither the Group nor the accused had any interest in blowing up bridges in the German Democratic Republic. The Western powers considered the risk of nuclear war too high to indulge in the deliberate invasion of East Germany or in acts of sabotage designed to prepare it. When real Western spies were discovered in sensitive positions in the East German regime, they were likely to be disposed of in conditions of the strictest secrecy. So it was with Elli Barczatis, who had been appointed chief personal secretary to Minister-President Grotewohl on his marriage to her predecessor in April 1950. After three years at the heart of the regime, she left his service and was promoted to an administrative position in June 1953. At some point, however, the Stasi became suspicious and bugged her flat. As a result of what was revealed by this surveillance, she was arrested in March 1955 together with her lover Karl Laurenz. Elli Barczatis disappeared without trace. Not even her family was told where she was. After months of interrogation, she was condemned for espionage in a secret trial held in November, and secretly guillotined, along with Laurenz, in November 1955, in the courtyard of the prison at Frankfurt an der Oder.[114] No details of her crime were ever released. All this suggested strongly

[111] BA-SAPM Berlin J IV 2/2A/412: Vorlage für das Politbüro betr. Strafsache gegen Paul Köppe, 4 Mar. 1955 (Rost).
[112] Ibid.: minutes of meeting of 8 Mar.
[113] BA Potsdam DO 1/32/39710, Bl. 254–7: Strafsache Benkowitz-Kogel; INGASA Nottingham 25/ Prozesse 1955/1: *Telegraf*, 24 June 1955; ibid.: *Berliner Zeitung*, 22 June 1955; ibid.: *Neues Deutschland*, 24 June 1955.
[114] INGASA Nottingham 25/1956/2: *Die Welt*, 15 Mar. 1956.

that, in contrast to the great majority of people convicted for espionage in East Germany, Elli Barczatis really was a Western spy.

Show trials in the German Democratic Republic were thus reserved for people who were not really dangerous. These events were set up under the supervision of the Politburo, and planned down to the last detail. A textbook example of such planning can be found in one of a series of grand show trials of the so-called 'Gehlen Organization', held in early November 1954, of people who had supposedly been working for the West German intelligence service, which was run by General Reinhard Gehlen at the time. The crime of Karl Bandelow and his accomplices, as the Politburo was privately told, was industrial espionage. Bandelow, a senior civil servant in the transport ministry in East Berlin, and Ewald Misera, an employee of the East German railway organization, the *Deutsche Reichsbahn*, also in Berlin, had provided Western intelligence with information on economic planning, resources, the volume and type of goods traffic on the railways, construction work, and so on. Other members of the group were said to have informed Western agents about Soviet troop installations. They were all employed in administrative positions in economic enterprises in the East. The Politburo was told by the Stasi that the information they supplied was also intended for use by the West in case of war—a fiction, but one which both Stasi and Politburo may actually have believed.[115] Having decided on a show trial, the Politburo went to great lengths to extract the maximum publicity from it. On 25 September it considered a lengthy paper from the head of the Central Committee's Department of State Administration, Anton Plenikowski, who had been asked to prepare the spectacle. To get the maximum effect from the case, he said, there were to be separate, linked trials of the various people involved in the conspiracy. The main trial was to be held before the Supreme Court, but it was to be backed up by others, of the secondary figures, in the districts of Magdeburg, Erfurt, and Frankfurt an der Oder. At this point, only prison sentences were 'envisaged'. The document listed them in detail. Every sentence was planned well in advance of the trials. For these were not seen primarily as legal events, as procedures devised in order to determine the guilt or innocence of the accused. As Plenikowski told his colleagues:

The purpose of carrying out these trials in public is to further expose the Gehlen Organization as a gang of war criminals, fascists, and revanchists, who endanger the peace not only of Germany but also of the world. The trials are the logical continuation of the activities through which the organs of state security have begun exposing the espionage activities and the damage caused by the Gehlen Organization but which were insufficiently utilized in the preparation of the general elections. Investigations have shown that agents of the Gehlen Organization have approached all classes of the

---

[115] BA-SAPM J IV 2/2A/377: ZK 01 Tgb. Nr. 531: Vorlage für das Politbüro, 25 Sept. 1954, 1–9.

population with criminal methods in order to win them over or, if they refuse, to put them under pressure.

Since it saw the activities of the 'Gehlen Organization' not least in terms of their effects on public opinion in the East, the Politburo agreed that the trials had to be accompanied by 'a broad campaign of enlightenment', in which the population of the German Democratic Republic had to be made aware of the 'vast scale of the Adenauer Government's betrayal of the national cause' so that it was more vigilant against 'hostile activities' in future. With this aim in mind, the Politburo assigned Erich Mielke, from the Ministry of State Security, to prepare an 'argumentation for speakers and campaigners' about the Gehlen Organization. About 120 people, mostly colleagues of the accused, were forced to attend the trials in the public gallery, and ordered to report back to their workmates every day, just to ram the message home in institutions such as the Transport Ministry and the Railway Directorate that behaviour such as that of Bandelow and Misera should not be repeated. Moreover, the Politburo ordered that the media should also play a central role:

The ADN and the central GDR press will take part in the proceedings. The most important results are to be reported every day and, after the procedings are over, there is to be a report summing them up. The radio will tape the result and will broadcast important excerpts from the trial proceedings. The DEFA is required to film particularly effective parts of the trial for eyewitnesses.[116]

By presenting a group of cowed and penitent defendants, confessing to crimes committed at the behest, and in the pay, of the Gehlen Organization, the regime aimed to frighten their colleagues in the state service, and if at all possible the rest of the citizens of the German Democratic Republic, into avoiding even the tiniest, most apparently innocent contact with Westerners, whether they were agents or not.

For it was not industrial espionage with which Bandelow, Misera, and the others were accused when they came to trial, but, far more seriously, a bombing campaign aimed at the 'mass extermination of the population' and the destruction of the country's economy. Witnesses were brought forward from prison to testify that they belonged to the same organization as the accused. The defendants confirmed the prosecution's allegations in detail under questioning, in rehearsed statements, and confessed to everything. Amidst massive publicity, Bandelow and his alleged accomplice Ewald Misera were condemned to death for these crimes. The condemned men's defence lawyers stood up in court and expressed their emphatic approval of the sentences. Bandelow himself used his

---

[116] BA-SAPM J IV 2/2A/377 ZK 01 Tgb. Nr. 531: Vorlage für das Politbüro, 25 Sept. 1954, 11. The ADN was the official East German news agency; the DEFA the state-owned film company.

final speech to the court to urge all the remaining members of the Gehlen Organization to throw themselves on the mercy of the authorities. Despite this compliant behaviour, there was no hope of clemency. The Politburo had decided that the trial was important enough to justify the death sentence for the two principal defendants, and a reprieve would be out of place. Misera, a Catholic, was even refused access to a priest before his execution. He and Bandelow were guillotined between 4.18 and 4.22 in the morning on 11 November, in Dresden. Five others were condemned to long periods of imprisonment.[117] Another blow had been struck against Western intelligence and its fascist plans for subversion and destruction. And another propaganda lesson had been rammed home to the population of the German Democratic Republic. The fact that the offences for which these men were condemned were not the ones which they had probably committed may or may not have been known to their colleagues. But in a sense this was irrelevant. Those who knew Bandelow and Misera would be aware that industrial espionage could be punishable by death in practice, whatever the Criminal Code might say. Those who did not might well be persuaded that Western intelligence was harmful and destructive in intent, as, from the point of view of the regime, of course, it was.

A similar kind of thinking was most probably behind the great majority of the show trials of this time—and a similar kind of deception and manipulation. In the mid-1950s the East German regime could still think of gaining economic and technological advantages over West Germany, where the 'economic miracle' had only just begun. Industrial espionage was thus seen as especially dangerous because it gave the West the chance of catching up. In January 1956 the use of capital punishment for this purpose was underlined when Max Held and Werner Rudert were condemned to death for espionage, as fascist agents who had supposedly been working for the USA by passing on industrial secrets.[118] Death sentences also continued to be passed for incompetence in the economy. In September 1955 director Nellis of the J. W. Stalin Electrical Works in East Berlin was condemned to death, and three of his functionaries were given long prison sentences. He had tried to flee to the West and with his assistants was convicted of 'faulty planning' which had cost the works 35.7 million marks. Observers remarked 'that the physical state of the two principal defendants appeared to be completely shattered'. The workers at the plant were obliged to hold a meeting to pass a resolution in support of the sentence.[119] These tactics could also be

---

[117] BA Potsdam DO 1/32/39710, Bl. 231–3: Aufnahme- und Abgangsbogen, Vollstreckungsprotokoll; ibid., Bl. 246–9: Vollstreckungsprotokoll; INGASA Nottingham 25/Prozesse 1953–4/1: *Telegraf*, 10 Nov. 1954; ibid., *Tägliche Rundschau*, 2 and 9 Nov. 1954.
[118] INGASA Nottingham 25/Prozesse 1956/2: *Neues Deutschland*, 28 Jan. 1956.
[119] Ibid. 1955/2: Nellis (*Telegraf*, 7 Sept. 1955).

employed at a much humbler level, and as much in relation to culture as to the economy. For instance, in June 1955 Joachim Wiebach was sentenced to death as an agent of RIAS, the radio station of the American Sector of West Berlin. The charges prepared by General State Prosecutor Melsheimer described RIAS as 'a centre of American agents disguised as a radio station'. Wiebach had allegedly been supplying it with sensitive information.[120] This was clearly meant as a warning not only to people who had contacts with the station, but also to anyone who dared to listen to its broadcasts. The draconian punishment was an exemplary act of terror. So too was the death sentence meted out to Wilhelm Wolff, former head of economic management in the People's Own Land Collective of Polssen, in July 1954. This was a time when the regime was beginning to drive full-tilt towards a fully collectivized farm system on the Soviet model, amalgamating the small farms into which it had divided the big Junker estates after the war and effectively dispossessing a large proportion of the small farming population. Wolff was the alleged leader of a 'group of saboteurs' which had purportedly attempted to undermine East German agriculture through acts of sabotage aimed at restoring the rule of the Junkers.[121] These had included spreading epidemics among farm animals, stealing sugar beets, and falsifying his potato returns.[122] Wolff was condemned to death, not for his evident opposition to collectivization (which no doubt never really went as far as causing epidemics) but for crimes against humanity committed during the German occupation of Poland. In recommending a confirmation of his death sentence, Klaus Sorgenicht told the Politburo in March 1955, after Wolff's appeal had been summarily rejected:

The serious crimes which the condemned man committed against the Polish population do not permit the granting of a reprieve. But also the fact that after 1945, although considerable trust had been put in him, Wolff's fascist attitudes have caused him to turn to crime once more, makes it necessary to exclude him from human society.[123]

This was a classic example of how the regime linked fascism with opposition to its own policies; and of how it ordered the execution of carefully chosen individuals in particular areas as propagandistic acts of deterrence to others in the same walk of life.

Another characteristic condemnation along these lines took place in February 1955, when Erich Kutzner, a railway clerk, was sentenced to death for sabotage. Kutzner had supposedly deliberately switched the points at the station in

---

[120] INGASA Nottingham 1955/1: *Neues Deutschland*, 25 June 1955; ibid.: *Tägliche Rundschau*, 28 June 1955.

[121] Ibid. 1953–4/1: *Tägliche Rundschau*, 11 July 1954.

[122] Ibid.: *Neues Deutschland*, 10 July 1954.

[123] BA-SAPM Berlin J IV 2/2A/412: Vorlage für das Politbüro betr. Todesurteil gegen Wilhelm Wolff (Sorgenicht), 1 Mar. 1955. For Sorgenicht, see Jochen Cerny (ed.), *Wer war wer—DDR. Ein biographisches Lexikon* (Berlin, 1992), 429–30.

Fürstenwalde on the night of 23–4 October 1954 in order to cause a crash between a goods train and a passenger train, in which numerous wagons had been wrecked and the driver of the train killed. In the classic manner familiar from such show trials, Kutzner confessed that he had caused the crash in order to wreck a Soviet military train that was due to come into the station a few minutes later and would have ploughed into the wreckage but for a fortunate chance.[124] The likelihood was that he was merely incompetent, or drunk; but other employees in responsible positions in the railway system should, it was evidently thought, be admonished to vigilance by his execution, which duly took place shortly afterwards. Even the most ordinary murder cases could also be given a political twist. On 12 April 1954, for example, Werner Thieme, a 26-year-old farmer in the Dresden area, was sentenced to death for murdering a woman who was carrying his child, because she had refused either to have an abortion or to flee with him to the West. Thieme was already living with another woman and their baby at the time. This was in the end, indeed, a commonplace rural murder such as might have happened anywhere in Germany over the previous centuries. But the condemned man's parents were not optimistic. 'What should we do now?' they asked him on 4 May.[125] After his appeal had been rejected, they wrote to the East German President, Wilhelm Pieck, begging for clemency for their son. They claimed that the pregnant woman had been lying, and that her child had been fathered by another man.

For us, his parents, it is scarcely comprehensible how he could have done such a terrible thing. He was normally such a calm person, who enjoyed his work . . . He was not the man portrayed in the papers. He, ourselves, and our parents and grandparents have never been convicted of any crime before. He had put himself at the disposal of the new era, worked in the Mitschurin circle and joined the voluntary fire brigade. Both organizations are undoubtedly committed to the German Democratic Republic.[126]

The condemned man's fiancée added her pleas to those of his parents.[127] But Pieck and his advisers were unmoved. For the condemned man had been found guilty of contravening Article 6 of the East German constitution. Not only did he have a large collection of weapons at home, left over from the war, he also borrowed the murder weapon from an older man in the village who was found by the police to have a collection of Nazi literature in his house.[128] These rather tenuous political connections were enough to ensure that Werner Thieme was guillotined in Dresden prison on 12 October 1954.[129]

[124] INGASA Nottingham 25/Prozesse 1955/2: Erich Kutzner (*Telegraf*, 17 Feb. 1955).
[125] BA Potsdam DO 1/32/39710, Bl. 284: Oskar and Else Thieme to Werner Thieme, 4 May 1954.
[126] Ibid., Bl. 278: Oskar Thieme to Wilhelm Pieck, 16 May 1954.
[127] Ibid., Bl. 279: Margarete Böhmig to Wilhelm Pieck, 16 May 1954.
[128] Ibid., Bl. 294–9: Oberstes Gericht, Berufungszurückweisung, 18 May 1954.
[129] Ibid., Bl. 259: Aufnahme- und Abgangsbogen Werner Thieme; ibid., Bl. 300: Todesanzeige.

Another example of the Politburo's politicization of common murder cases occurred when, on 8 March 1955, coming to death sentences, as usual, for the last item of the day's business, it rejected the case for clemency for Fritz Rudloff, a senior nurse who had been condemned to death for poisoning four patients of Dr Rahn, one of the physicians in the hospital where he worked. Rudloff, a jealous man, had been told by his mistress Erna Sahlender, a nurse in the same hospital, that Rahn was sexually harassing her, and had decided to get the doctor sacked for incompetence by the rather drastic expedient of killing off his patients. While the General State Prosecutor recommended mercy, Minister of Justice Hilde Benjamin, supported by Ernst Wollweber, head of the Stasi, argued that he should be executed, and the Politburo agreed. Its grounds were, as always, primarily political. As Klaus Sorgenicht noted,

The evidence for the accused's crime is completely convincing. The four people whom Rudloff killed stood in no relationship to him at all; their death was only the means to an end for him, namely the removal of the doctor who stood in his way. He committed this crime against patients with whose care he was entrusted and who had sought out the hospital in the expectation of being healed. Above and beyond these personal and human considerations it is also necessary to consider the damage which Rudloff has caused more generally to the trustworthiness of our state and in particular its health care institutions. In this sense, his crime is also directly aimed against the order of our state.[130]

Thus once more the crucial factor was not the motive for the deed, but the damage it was thought to do to the state and the sociopolitical order in East Germany. Rudloff was executed, in effect, not as a common murderer, but as a responsible state official who had failed in his duty.

Such cases were readily exploited by the propaganda machine of the German Democratic Republic to attack the state of morality in the West and to warn its own citizens against harmful Western influences. Karl-Ernst Hahn and Alfred Rzepio, condemned to death in May 1955 for the attempted murder of a taxi-driver, were said by the East German media to have been corrupted by watching American gangster films and 'crime thrillers'. Their fate was described as 'a warning to all parents and educators'.[131] The harsh sentence was also, in all probability, designed to appeal to popular sentiment in West Germany, where public opinion was strongly in favour of the death penalty, as we have seen, and anti-Americanism still relatively influential on the far right and left. Similarly, the death sentence passed in September 1955 on Gerhard Wich, responsible for a series of robberies in Halle, during which one of his victims had been killed, was

---

[130] BA-SAPM Berlin J IV 2/2A/412: Vorlage für das Politbüro betr. Todesurteil gegen Fritz Rudloff, 1 Mar. 1955 (Sorgenicht).

[131] *Ost-Zeitung*, 27 May 1955, 4.

justified by the East German newspapers on the grounds that Western influences had corrupted him beyond redemption:

He was the epitome of the gangster created by the American way of life in the 'Golden West'. Trashy reading, adventure films, mixing with American soldiers and with criminals in West German prisons have infected Wich to the marrow. The orderly circumstances of our workers' and peasants' state were unable to transform him.[132]

Thus the death penalty was used by the regime for a variety of purposes, many of which seemed entirely traditional: deterrence, warning, education, the enforcement of state policy by judicial terror. Despite all the vagaries of the political situation between 1949 and 1955, there was no sign that it was falling out of use in East Germany. Statistics in this area are inevitably rather murky, nor did the regime publish any, but from information made available in 1994, it is at least possible to arrive at a rough estimate. In 1950 East German courts handed down 31 death sentences in the Waldheim trials and 15 in the Köpenick blood-week trial, as well as two others for more ordinary offences; 28 of these offenders are known to have been executed. In 1951 there were 6 death sentences, one of which is known to have been carried out. The following year saw 7, all executed, and in 1953 there were 14 death sentences and 9 executions. In 1954 there was roughly the same number, with 7 death sentences passed by East German courts, all carried out.

Up to this point, and with the exception of the Waldheim and Köpenick trials, the figures had been relatively low because of the continuing role of Soviet military tribunals in trying certain kinds of offence. In 1950 they were said to have passed no fewer than 128 death sentences, including 69 for espionage; 11 are known to have been carried out. The following year saw the same high rate of condemnations, with 102 death sentences and 2, possibly 6, executions. In 1952, Soviet military tribunals sentenced 93 East Germans to death, almost all of them for espionage: only one of them is known with any certainty to have been executed. In 1953, they passed 75 death sentences, including 21 for involvement in the uprising of 17 June. Of these latter 19 were executed, along with 20 others, making a total of 39. The figures for 1953 appear to be much more reliable than for previous years, perhaps because monitoring by West German agencies was more accurate in view of the attention focused on East Germany at the time of the uprising. If this rate, leaving aside the executions in connection with the uprising, was similar to that of earlier years, it would mean that about a third of the death sentences passed by Soviet military tribunals were carried out, so that the figures of known executions for 1950–2 are almost certainly serious underestimates of the real figures. In 1954, however, the rate plummeted, with only 8

[132] *Freiheit*, 10 Sept. 1955.

death sentences passed and no known executions. This was because the Soviet military tribunals were now passing their jurisdiction over to East German courts. Correspondingly, in 1955 the number of condemnations by East German courts shot up to 29, with 18 known to have been carried out. Of these 3 were for criminal offences, and 3 for war crimes; all the rest may be regarded as political, of the sort previously dealt with by the Soviet tribunals. Clearly, therefore, as 1955 came to an end the East German regime, far from scaling down its use of the death penalty, seemed if anything to have decided to increase it.

d. *Destalinization and its Limits 1956–1961*

On 24 February 1956 the delegates and guests at the Twentieth Congress of the Communist Party of the Soviet Union were unexpectedly summoned to a secret evening session, where they were addressed by Nikita Khrushchev, the man who had emerged from the power struggles after Stalin's death as the undisputed leader of the country and with it the Eastern bloc. They were stunned to hear him denounce his predecessor as a mentally unbalanced megalomaniac responsible for a massive perversion of justice and for the unjust arrest, imprisonment, and death of vast numbers of Soviet citizens. The process of 'destalinization' had begun. It was hastened by broadcasts of a pirated version of the speech from the Western media. Soon expectations of a major relaxation in the regime were rife among ordinary people in the German Democratic Republic. The East German Communist Party leaders, who were present at the Congress, were taken by surprise. Khrushchev's speech put them in a difficult situation. The German Democratic Republic had grown up under Stalin's tutelage and had slavishly subscribed to the 'cult of personality' which Khrushchev now denounced. The Socialist Unity Party's leading figure, Walter Ulbricht, was particularly closely identified with the Stalin cult, and owed virtually everything to Stalin's patronage. Like other Eastern European leaders, he was now in a very vulnerable position. The new developments opened the way for his rivals in the party leadership to replace him. Faced with this threat, Ulbricht began to steer a compromise course. He associated himself with some of Khrushchev's criticisms of Stalin. When one of his major rivals in the Politburo, Karl Schirdewan, implicitly attacked miscarriages of justice and the abuse of power by the Stasi at a Central Committee meeting on 22 March,[133] Ulbricht attempted to take the wind out of his sails by associating himself with the rhetoric of legality. Many people, he told a Stasi meeting in May 1956, had been wrongly arrested. This created a dangerous climate in the country. The Stasi, he insisted, had to

[133] Armin Mitter and Stefan Wolle, *Untergang auf Raten. Unbekannte Kapitel der DDR-Geschichte* (Munich, 1993), 163–240, esp. 198–207.

stop any tendencies to become a state within a state. It had to subordinate itself to the judicial apparatus of the Republic and, above all, it had to place itself under the leadership of the party.[134]

Ulbricht, supported by Otto Grotewohl, conceded on a broader front that there had been miscarriages of justice in the past.[135] The implication that things would have to be different in future was clear to all. Soon, East German lawyers openly complained that defending counsel had been denied their rights at trials and demanded a fairer treatment for the accused.[136] They were reinforced by a special party commission on the administration of justice, which added its voice to the growing chorus of criticism in July.[137] Articles began to appear in the GDR press complaining about the maltreatment of the accused and their denial of defence lawyers until they had confessed.[138] The party's flagship paper, *Neues Deutschland*, launched a personal attack on Justice Minister Benjamin, State Prosecutor Melsheimer, and Stasi chief Wollweber, for applying Marxist principles in a manner that was 'schematic and unbending'.[139] In the course of 1956, some 21,000 prisoners were amnestied and released from prison, as the Socialist Unity Party officially admitted that many of the sentences passed by East German courts in the past few years had been too severe. Among the amnestied prisoners was the former Justice Minister, Max Fechner, who had been gaoled for his failure to condemn the uprising of 1953 in sufficiently rabid terms.[140] Ulbricht, it seemed, had started a process that was threatening to get out of control. But his regime was saved by events elsewhere in Eastern Europe. In Poland and Hungary the old Stalinist leaders were overthrown, and in Budapest a popular uprising was in progress by October 1956. Such radicalism was unacceptable to Khrushchev, and Russian troops and tanks were sent in to crush the rebellion. By the middle of November, after days of fierce fighting, it was over. These events played into the hands of the hardliners in East Berlin. Rising student unrest, a wave of strikes in the factories, demonstrations, and demands for democratic reforms raised the spectre of the Hungarian situation repeating itself in the German Democratic Republic. Under these circumstances, the Soviet regime felt that it could not afford to show any weakness or make any further concessions. Ulbricht was safe.[141] The criticism of the judicial apparatus came to a stop.[142] The hardline Minister of Justice, the 'red guillotine', Hilde

---

[134] Ibid. 241–4.
[135] INGASA Nottingham 25/1956/1: *Der Kurier*, 26 Apr. 1956.
[136] Ibid.: *Der Tagesspiegel*, 19 Dec. 1956.   [137] Ibid.: *Der Kurier*, 10 July 1956.
[138] Ibid.: *Der Kurier*, 2 Sept. 1956 (article by Karl Kleinschmidt).
[139] Ibid.: *Telegraf*, 22 June 1956.
[140] Weber, *Geschichte*, 282. Fechner was readmitted to the Socialist Unity Party in 1958 and died in 1973, aged 81. See Weber, *DDR*, 264. See also Fricke, *Politik und Justiz*, 332–3.
[141] Mitter and Wolle, *Untergang*, 214–72.
[142] Schroeder, *Strafrecht*, 29–32.

Benjamin, now felt able to come out into the open to defend her record. On 17 October 1956, answering questions put to her by Eastern bloc journalists, many of them still sympathetic to the new course in Poland, Hungary, and elsewhere, she underlined her tough stance by insisting: 'We cannot allow ourselves to dispense with the death penalty.' Benjamin flatly denied that there had been any miscarriages of justice in East Germany. She reacted with some hostility to the suggestion that confessions in show trials had been forced out of the accused by torture. She refused to contemplate a posthumous rehabilitation of any of the executed, despite the fact that this was going on elsewhere in the Eastern bloc.[143] On 29 November Ulbricht and the hardliners struck back at their critics, arresting a group of moderate reformers around the Marxist philosopher Wolfgang Harich, and mounting a show trial against them in the spring of 1957, accusing them of conspiracy to overthrow the existing party leadership. Ulbricht also struck against the Politburo member Karl Schirdewan, who had attempted with Khrushchev's backing to push on the process of destalinization, including the removal of Ulbricht, until the Hungarian débâcle put paid to Moscow's support. Among Schirdewan's supporters was the head of the Stasi, Ernst Wollweber, who was forced to resign 'on health grounds' in November 1957. He was replaced by Erich Mielke, who remained in charge of the political police agency for the next thirty years and more. A wave of arrests and purges followed at every level, eliminating liberals and nonconformists from the party and the state. Order was restored in the universities. Hilde Benjamin declared in October 1957 that she intended 'no kind of measures for the liberalization of our criminal law'.[144] From now on, the leadership made it clear that only unconditional obedience to the party line was to be tolerated.[145]

Correspondingly, the regime continued to justify the use of the death penalty above all as a means of defending the political and social order. On 10 December 1960, for instance, Professor Joachim Renneberg told a meeting at the Academy of Law, in Potsdam, that 'capital punishment was in itself alien to the essence of socialist criminal law', but was at the same time 'still necessary in the present period of our struggle against the imperialist-militarist counter-revolution *as an extraordinary penal measure* to combat the most serious crimes against peace, against the power of the workers and peasants, and against the life of the citizens'. His views were underlined by the standard textbook on East German criminal law, which proclaimed:

[143] INGASA 25/1956/1: *Der Tagesspiegel*, 18 Oct. 1956.

[144] Weber, *Geschichte*, 283.

[145] Mitter and Wolle, *Untergang*, 273–94. For documentation on these events, see Dierk Hoffmann, Karl-Heinz Schmidt, and Peter Skyba (eds.), *Die DDR vor dem Mauerbau. Dokumente zur Geschichte des anderen deutschen Staates 1949–1961* (Munich, 1993), esp. 233–90; and Fricke, *Politik und Justiz,* 331–70.

Capital punishment is thus an extraordinary penal measure within our penal system and merely serves to *render harmless* such persons as have committed the most serious crimes against the life of the people and the citizen. *At the same time, it is intended to deter other reactionary forces hostile to our social order from committing such crimes.*

Both statements thus saw the death penalty not as an integral part of the socialist system, but as a regrettable necessity. In doing so, they were conceding that it would be abolished when state and society were secure from the threat of subversion from the agents of imperialism. This was not only a concession that it was difficult to legitimate in itself, but also a response to the persistent public criticism which for some time had been directed against the use of capital punishment in the East by government and media in West Germany, where of course it had been abolished in 1949. The standard legal textbook already quoted managed to blame the persistence of the death penalty in East Germany firmly on the West, in a remarkable piece of casuistic reasoning:

The campaign waged by Western propaganda against the retention and application of the death penalty in the German Democratic Republic will rebound on its originators. For these people themselves are forcing our democratic state to retain this penalty by their systematic organization of criminal attacks on the workers' and soldiers' power and the socialist achievements of the working people.

If the West gave up its subversive activities in the East, therefore, capital punishment would be abolished there.[146] These arguments, of course, completely ignored the fact that the death penalty was still regularly applied to common, non-political murder cases in the German Democratic Republic. Even more they skated over the fact that most of these 'criminal attacks' existed only in the minds of the East German Politburo and its servants. Nevertheless, all this pointed the way to a more circumspect use of death sentences by the leadership than had hitherto been the practice.

Thus the experience of 1956 did in the end lead to a permanent change. The death penalty was no longer used afterwards to the degree that it had been before. Walter Janka and the other supposed members of the alleged Harich conspiracy were sentenced to imprisonment, even though their trial bore all the classic hallmarks of the traditional Stalinist show, complete with confessions written by the Stasi and chants of 'Down with the traitors! Put the criminals in gaol!' from the public gallery. A few years earlier, the shouts would have been for their execution.[147] Even espionage now generally led to the penitentiary rather than the guillotine, unless it was a real case of serious professional spying.[148] Confidential sources made available in 1994 indicate that there were only eight death

[146] *Argumente-Dokumente-Zitate*, 56 (27 Nov. 1964), 1–3.
[147] Walter Janka, *Schwierigkeiten mit der Wahrheit* (Reinbek, 1989), 90–1.
[148] INGASA Nottingham 25, 1957/2: *Neuer Tag*, 22 Nov. 1957 (Grabosch case).

sentences passed in East Germany in 1956, of which one is known to have been carried out. In 1957 there were no death sentences or executions at all. 1958 saw three, including two prisoners who had killed a (reputedly sadistic) prison warder during an attempted gaol break; the murder of a uniformed official, as we have seen, was always treated with special severity. In 1959, one offender was sentenced to death for espionage, but the sentence was subsequently commuted to fifteen years' imprisonment. The following year, two war criminals were executed, along with one renegade member of the Stasi. Thus from the thaw of 1956 through to the end of 1960, only six executions were reported in the German Democratic Republic: a dramatic change from the frequency with which capital punishment had been employed in the first six years of the Republic's existence. On 11 December 1957, indeed, the East German parliament passed a composite set of revisions to the Criminal Code which lowered a number of sentences, and restricted the death penalty to murder and serious arson, and to cases of treason, espionage, sabotage, diversion and the like, where loss of life or damage to property had been caused, or where the German Democratic Republic had been seriously endangered.[149] These amendments were a temporary substitute for the full-scale revision of the Criminal Code which had been shelved in 1953. They led the State Secretary in the Justice Ministry, Dr Töplitz, to declare that 'humanitarianism' had now become the 'basic principle of our criminal law'.[150] But the measures were taken partly to disguise the fact that the reform package also contained new and sharper penal sanctions against people who tried to leave East Germany for the West, as they were doing at this time in their hundreds of thousands. They marked a major step towards the formal assimilation of East German criminal law to the Soviet model.[151] As a whole, the package was by no means as liberal as some of its provisions made it appear. Its primary thrust was directed against political dissent.[152]

All the same, from the point of view of capital punishment, the new laws did mark a distinct and explicit step towards a more liberal penal policy. Of course, there was no question of abolishing the death penalty altogether. In May 1957 the East German lawyers' journal *Neue Justiz* repeated that the death penalty would continue to have the 'function of suppressing the enemies of the working people and its state and social order'.[153] Two members of the committee charged with preparing the amendments declared in 1958:

[149] INGASA Nottingham 25, 1957/2.: Heinrich Löwenthal, 'Einheit von Strafe und Erziehung', *Sonntag*, 22 Dec. 1957. Löwenthal was the Chief Judge on the GDR's Supreme Court. See also ibid.: *Neues Deutschland*, 21 Dec. 1957 ('Strafgesetze mit sozialistischem Inhalt').

[150] Ibid. 1957/1: *Neues Deutschland*, 17 Dec. 1957.

[151] Ibid. 1959/1: *Bild-Zeitung*, 6 June 1959.

[152] Fricke, *Politik und Justiz*, 371–81.

[153] INGASA Nottingham 25, 1957/1: *Telegraf*, 12 Mar. and 16 May 1957.

The death penalty must be retained to a limited extent in future in order to deal with the most serious counter-revolutionary offences which damage the life of the people to the highest degree. This penalty will have to be retained as long as the working people need to defend themselves against the aggressive impulses of the imperialist-fascist robbers, their drive for civil war, and the activities of their innumerable secret agents' organizations, and have the historic task of nipping all such activities in the bud.

The new, more political thrust given by the 1957 reforms to the criminal law was reflected in the fact that common murder would now normally be punished by twenty-five years' imprisonment instead of death. Life sentences would be abolished.[154] In a decision of 1959, the Supreme Court declared that the practice which had obtained in the early 1950s of treating death as the normal penalty for murder, and allowing life imprisonment only in exceptional cases, was a principle 'introduced by Nazi legislation and contradicts socialist law'. Every punishment had to be justified with particular reasons: 'Sentencing to death instead of to life imprisonment requires its special justification from the greater moral-political reprehensibility of the crime in comparison to that of other murder cases.'[155] This principle was generally applied from now on.[156] Moreover, while the court conceded again in 1963 that the death penalty was allowable where the maintenance of peace or the achievements of the working class and the state were endangered, it now threw serious doubt on the necessity of applying it in any cases of common murder at all.[157]

The kind of political function to which the death penalty was now put was revealed by the case of the former East German border police officer Manfred Smolka, who was abducted from West German territory on 22 August 1959 as he approached the border in Franconia with the intention of entering East Germany to get his family out. While Smolka was undergoing interrogation by his former employers, the Stasi staff worked out a plan for his trial for espionage. They concluded: 'The proceedings are suited on educational grounds for sentencing Smolka to death.'[158] Smolka was duly condemned for espionage and treason on 5 May 1960.[159] The description of his offences circulated for educational purposes to the staff of the Ministry for State Security by its chief, Erich Mielke, bore an uncanny resemblance to the depictions of the moral careers of criminals by the balladeers of the late eighteenth century on the occasion of public executions:

[154] Ibid. 1958/1: *Neues Deutschland*, 24 Oct. 1958 ('Die Entwicklung des sozialistischen Strafrechts').
[155] BA Potsdam DP 1 VA 5110, Bl. 3: Auswertung der OG-Urteile zu § 211 StGB, 18 Oct. 1965, § 2.
[156] Ibid., § 2.
[157] Ibid., § 3.
[158] *Frankfurter Allgemeine Zeitung*, 21 May 1991.
[159] Fricke, *Politik und Justiz*, 339; *Der Tagesspiegel*, 5 July 1960.

Although *Smolka* was given every encouragement by his superiors, by the soldiers, and by the members of the party of the working class to overcome his moral weaknesses and character deficiencies, he was arrogant and markedly egoistic in his attitude and so rejected this help. He disregarded not only the directions and commands of his superiors but also the leading role of the party. . . . *Smolka* would not accept any instruction and thereby reached such a deep state of moral and political depravity that in October 1958 he had to be cashiered from the ranks of the German Border Police.

Following his dismissal, Mielke continued, Smolka refused the jobs he was offered and fled to the West, abandoning his family in the process. He then offered his services to the American Secret Service, betrayed numerous official secrets about border emplacements, and began to work for them in organizing 'major provocations on the border, and other crimes against the GDR'. He was eventually arrested on one of his numerous armed incursions into East German territory. Persuaded by threats to his family, who still lived in the East, Smolka confessed to all this, although the truth, as we have seen, was very different. According to one of his fellow prisoners, Smolka's original disenchantment with his service in the border police had been caused by the constant demands of his superiors to shoot attempted escapees on sight. He had been kidnapped; there was no armed incursion. Smolka was executed on 12 July 1960 in Dresden.[160]

In a fashion equally reminiscent of the old ballads, Mielke then proceeded to draw the moral of the story for the benefit of his audience. 'There is no doubt that desertion and treachery to the interests of peace and socialism are the severest of crimes and can only be expiated by the severest of punishments.' Even the concept of expiation was present in his memorandum. After reminding the entire Stasi of their duty to defend the German Democratic Republic against its enemies, Mielke ordered:

1. This order on the crime and punishment of *Smolka* is to be made known to all members of the Ministry for State Security.
2. The contents of this order, together with the 10 commandments of our socialist ethics and morality, are to form the topic of thorough discussion and instruction in service units in order to heighten their vigilance and solidarity and further to strengthen the political-moral unity and team-spirit in our ranks.
3. All colleagues in the Ministry are to be trained to hate treachery, to work as Chekists towards overcoming political-moral weaknesses, and to improve their technical qualifications, so that they will place their whole strength at the service of the successful implementation of the political-operational tasks which are entrusted to them.

Finally, Mielke ordered further measures 'to train all colleagues to become uncompromising fighters against the enemies of peace and socialism'.[161]

[160] Klaus Schmude, *Fallbeil-Erziehung. Der Stasi/SED Mord an Manfred Smolka* (Böblingen, 1992).
[161] BStU ZA Befehl Nr. 357/60, 18 July 1960.

Smolka's fate reflected the extreme nervousness of the East German authorities about the flight of their citizens to the West at this time. Over two million of their subjects had fled to the West since 1949. If they could not trust the border police to do their best to prevent this mass emigration, all would be lost. No wonder that Mielke made an example of him. By the summer of 1961, however, it was clear that nothing short of drastic action could remedy the situation. On 13 August, with the approval of the Soviet Union, Ulbricht's regime constructed a series of improvised barriers between West Berlin and the East, which in the following weeks became the infamous Berlin Wall, constructed under the direction of Ulbricht's protégé Erich Honecker. From now on it was virtually impossible for East Germans to leave their country. Those who attempted to do so by breaking through the wall or the fortified East–West border were shot without compunction. Within the German Democratic Republic itself, this measure was backed up by a new wave of repression, symbolized as so often in German history by an increase in the number of death sentences, of which there were 5 in 1961, 5 in 1962, and 6 in 1963. Only 2 of these were directly connected with the new situation: they involved the murder of a taxi-driver during a flight attempt in 1962, and the killing of a member of the People's Police by the 25-year-old Siegfried Oehlberg the following year during an attempt to steal weapons for an escape. Of the other death sentences passed during these three years of heightened repression, 3 were for war crimes (2 in 1962 and 1 in 1963), while 4 were regarded in the West as political. All 3 of those sentenced in 1960 were executed, 2 of those in 1961, and 1 each in 1962 and 1963.[162]

Not all these cases were quite what they seemed to be. The murder of a taxi-driver and of a uniformed official both fell into an established pattern of capital crime in East Germany, so that the connection with attempts to break through the wall was only secondary. An overtly political angle could be found in 1961 in the case of the 50-year-old arsonist Walter Praedel, from Torgelow, in the district of Bad Freienwalde, who was sentenced to death for 'diversion'. Praedel had set light to two barns on a collective farm. He confessed to objecting to the Berlin Wall, listening to Western radio, and wanting to wreck the collective. What sealed his fate, however, was the fact that he was a former member of the SS who had been condemned by a Soviet military tribunal in 1955 as a 'war criminal', so that the East German propaganda media could publicize his case and link the activities in which he had indulged to fascism and Western influences. No one seems to have been killed as a result of Praedel's activities, but he was sentenced to death none the less.[163] His case was followed in 1962 by that of the 37-year-old arsonist Gottfried Strympe in Dresden for twenty-eight offences of destroying

---

[162] Figures based on information supplied in 1994.
[163] *Der Tagesspiegel*, 29 Dec. 1961; *Neues Deutschland*, 28 Dec. 1961.

property and sixty-six acts of theft. Strympe confessed that he had been encouraged to embark on this career of crime by Western agencies, but the truth seems to have been that he committed these crimes because of his embitterment over the collectivization of East German farms, which had been gathering pace at the end of the 1950s and which, he thought, denied him steady work. Wounded in the war, Strympe had been unable to find a steady job in the countryside or pursue his earlier career as a musician. His campaign of arson and theft was directed against collective farms in the Bautzen disctrict. No loss of life seems to have occurred as a result of his offences. But the authorities decided to make a severe example of Strympe, as of Praedel, as a warning to other opponents of collectivization, which had been one of the major factors behind the mass flight to the West in the late 1950s and was continuing to arouse widespread opposition in the countryside. Once more, capital punishment was used to get across a political message in a particularly drastic way.[164]

Executions for war crimes also continued sporadically into the 1960s, as a means of reinforcing East German propaganda against the Federal Republic in the West. In January 1962, the shepherd Martin Bründel and his father-in-law Christian Kunst were condemned to death in Schwerin for crimes committed in 1945, at the end of the war. Leading Nazis in the village of Müsselmow, they had decided to commit suicide with their families rather than outlive the Third Reich, but after killing their wives and children by drowning them in a nearby lake or beating them to death on the shore, they had lacked the courage to drown themselves and had arranged the corpses so that it looked as if the women and children had been murdered by the Red Army. After the war, alleged the prosecution, they had incited the village to resistance against the new socialist order, but they had been denounced after the building of the Berlin Wall in August 1961. The death sentences were proclaimed as evidence that the GDR took the task of exacting retribution for Nazi crimes seriously, in contrast to the West, where—an East German press campaign was alleging at this time—ex-Nazis occupied high positions in a number of areas, including the judicial system.[165] This, it was hoped, would win over sympathizers among anti-Nazi forces in the West, as well as cementing the loyalty of the population in the East. Virtually from the very beginning, the East German regime portrayed itself as fighting a continuing struggle against 'fascism', represented now by West Germany, in the tradition of the antifascist fighters of the 1930s. The 'fascists' were seeking to undermine the German Democratic Republic and sow havoc and destruction in preparation to a full-scale invasion and takeover. It was this, more than anything else, that justified the continued application of the death penalty and prompted the linking of fascism and crime.

[164] INGASA Nottingham 25, 1962/1: *Neues Deutschland* 3 Feb. 1962.
[165] Ibid. 19 Jan. 1962.

e. The End of the Death Penalty in the East

During the 1960s the East German regime became more secure following the erection of the Wall and the completion of collectivization, and the state not only stabilized but moved forward self-confidently into a future which Ulbricht and the Politburo firmly believed was theirs. In recognition of this increased sense of security, the number of officially registered death sentences declined to a trickle. From 1964 onwards, there was usually only one every year. Few death sentences were now political, in comparison to earlier times. Executions were still carried out on war criminals in the 1960s and early 1970s. In July 1966 Horst Fischer, found guilty earlier in the year of crimes against humanity committed as a doctor in Auschwitz, was executed;[166] in 1968 the same fate befell Kurt Wachholz, a concentration camp guard; and in 1969 and 1971 two members of the SS death squads on the Eastern Front, Josef Blösche and Hans Baumgartner, were executed for war crimes as well.[167] The sentences on these men were passed after well-publicized trials, like most previous sentences passed on such people in the German Democratic Republic; but whereas in the 1950s the East German regime had been attempting to draw a contrast between its own zeal and the West Germans' laxity in this area, the boot was now on the other foot. Following on the establishment of a central agency for the prosecution of war crimes in the Federal Republic in 1958, the 1960s saw for the first time a series of major trials in the West, beginning with the Auschwitz trials of 1964. Soon there could be little doubt that the West Germans were taking the prosecution of war criminals seriously. This obviously began to undermine the East Germans' claim that the Federal Republic was a 'fascist' state, as did the accession of the Social Democrats to power in 1969, led by Willy Brandt and, later on, Helmut Schmidt. The East Germans felt obliged to respond to this new challenge. They could not afford to let it seem as if the running in the struggle to bring Nazi war criminals to book was now being led by the West.

Internally, the state's greater sense of stability was reflected in the end of executions for 'sabotage', 'diversion', and the like. The main focus of capital punishment in the East now shifted to sex murderers. In 1964, for instance, there was only one death sentence, passed on the 27-year-old Siegfried Rogge for raping and murdering a young woman whom he met at a dance in Röblingen. It was significant that the East German press felt the need to justify the court's action to 'all who perhaps find this sentence too harsh': 'Indeed it is very harsh. Our socialist society takes trouble over everyone. It is patient, where patience is appropriate, it educates where education is useful. But it is unsparingly hard where it has to protect its people from elements of an egoistical, brutal, antisocial

[166] Ibid. 1966/2: *Neue Zeitung*, 9 July 1966.
[167] *Berliner Zeitung*, 4 May 1969; information supplied in 1994.

character of the type of Rogge.'[168] Additional reasons for the severity of the sentence lay in the fact that, as another newspaper reported, Rogge had twice deserted the People's Police, of which he had been a member for some time, and visited West Germany on a number of occasions without permission. Once again, a political gloss was being given to an unpolitical crime.[169] Nevertheless, this set a pattern for subsequent court decisions. In 1965 two death sentences were passed, one of them for murder committed in conjunction with rape, the other for murder committed in the course of a robbery.[170] Of the three death sentences passed in 1966, one was for a sexually motivated murder, one for a common murder, one for a war crime.[171] In 1967, two of the three offenders sentenced to death were sex murderers.[172] In each of the following two years, as we have seen, only one offender, a war criminal, was sentenced to death, and the same was the case in 1971. In 1970, the two offenders executed were Heinrich Sameck, who had committed a murder while trying to flee the country, and Hilmer Zwinka, a doctor who had killed his wife and her lover. In the first of these two cases, it was the circumstances which counted; in the latter, most probably the responsible position and status of the offender. During the 1970s the focus on sex offenders became even clearer. It was dramatized in 1972 by the execution of Erwin Hagedorn, a young man who had murdered three children. Hagedorn was only 16 when he killed his first two victims in 1969. Two years later, he murdered an 11-year-old boy, chopped up the corpse, and satisfied his lusts on the remains. He was discovered, condemned to death, and executed on 15 September 1972; his parents' appeal for clemency had gone unanswered.[173] In February 1974 a court in Magdeburg condemned the 20-year-old worker Peter Albrecht to death for murdering his former girlfriend, her current lover, and another woman, a witness to the crime, in an orgy of violence after a day of heavy drinking.[174]

By this time, a new Criminal Code had finally been put in place. It had been promised at various junctures since the early 1950s. It was finally promulgated in 1968. Once more, as so often in the past, a new codification had proved unexpectedly problematical and had taken decades rather than years to complete. The notorious Hilde Benjamin had retired as Minister of Justice on reaching the age of 65 the year before; her long period of office, beginning in the aftermath of the uprising of 1953, had symbolized the continuity of the Stalinist tradition in this area. The Code did not depart significantly from this tradition. Indeed, it had

[168] INGASA Nottingham 25, 1964/2: *Die Freiheit* (Halle), 14 Apr. 1964, 'Kein Platz für Mörder'.
[169] Ibid.: *Der Neue Weg* (Halle), 11/12 Apr. 1964.
[170] *Der Tagesspiegel*, 1 June 1965.
[171] Information supplied in 1994.
[172] *Der Tagesspiegel*, 24 May 1967.
[173] Friedhelm Werremeier, *Der Fall Heckenrose* (Munich, 1975).
[174] BA Potsdam DP 1 VA 5110, BL. 28–43: Urteil gegen Peter Albrecht.

been drawn up under Benjamin's supervision, in a series of eighteen committee meetings held between 1963 and 1967. Adopting as its model the Soviet Criminal Code of 1926, it finally did away with the German Criminal Code of 1871 as the formal basis of the criminal law of the German Democratic Republic. Many of its provisions represented a simple modernization of the law which even West German commentators found timely and appropriate. On the other hand, it also went further than the reform of eleven years previously in giving the state virtually unlimited legal powers to prosecute political dissidents. The new Code retained the death penalty for eleven separate offences. The justification given by the East German authorities was as follows:

In so far as the death penalty serves the security and the reliable protection of our sovereign socialist state, the maintenance of peace and the life of its citizens, it possesses a humanitarian character. To apply it to those offenders who threaten the life of our people and the stability of our nation by committing the most serious crimes is an unconditional requirement of socialist legality.[175]

As amended in 1974 and 1977, the Code applied the death penalty to the planning and execution of wars or serious acts of aggression, and especially serious cases of crimes against humanity, war crimes, high treason, espionage, treasonable breach of loyalty, terror, diversion, sabotage, and murder, where the definition of what was especially serious rested on either the loss of life or the endangering of peace or the security of the German Democratic Republic as a result of the crime. It was also applicable in military law to offences such as desertion, cowardice, mutiny, and looting. The Code thus incorporated previous special laws passed in the early 1950s and now to a large extent replaced the catch-all provisions of Article 6 of the former constitution.[176]

The death penalty was to be executed by shooting in the back of the head, Soviet style, rather than by guillotining, which had been the normal method in East Germany up to this point. As so often in the German past, the change was pregnant with political symbolism: this time, it denoted the final abandonment of German penal tradition and its replacement by the Soviet model.[177] Executions continued to be carried out in a cell converted for the purpose in Leipzig prison in the early 1960s. The prison governor, Hugo Friedrich, was in charge of what the official instructions called the 'realization' of the death sentence, and six or seven others were usually in attendance, including two of his officials, a doctor, and a state prosecutor from the General Prosecutor's office in

---

[175] Quoted in Fricke, *Politik und Justiz*, 522.
[176] Jürgen Rosenthal (ed.), *Strafrechtsreform in der DDR* (Bonn, 1968), contains the full text of the Code.
[177] BA Potsdam DP 1 VA 5110, Bl. 19: Wilamowski to Henning, 2 Jan. 1969. See also Rosenthal (ed.), *Strafrechtsreform*, 40 (*Strafgesetzbuch der DDR*, § 60).

Berlin, usually Kurt Kunze. If a Stasi officer was executed, a Stasi representative was also present. The regulations laid down that the state prosecutor had to inform the offender briefly of the rejection of clemency. The two warders then took him by the arms into the execution chamber, where executioner Lorenz stepped out behind him and killed him with what the regulations described as an 'unexpected shot at close quarters in the back of the head'. Such executions were organized by a small staff in the Ministry of the Interior. In the 1960s they took place at 4 in the morning, but later on the time was moved to an hour more convenient for those officiating: 10 a.m. The corpse was normally taken to the local anatomical institute.[178] In this way, the execution was robbed of all ceremony: there was no formal confession, no priest, not even any advance warning. The elimination of offenders considered a danger to state and society had become a clinical act, deprived of virtually any element of ritual or ceremony.

Within a few years, however, the implementation of the death penalty became more difficult for the East German regime. Capital punishment became the focus of international attention with the execution of five Basque terrorists by the Franco regime in Spain on 27 September 1975. The executions led to world-wide protests and demonstrations, and fifteen European governments recalled their ambassadors from Madrid.[179] The German Democratic Republic joined in the condemnation of the executions, but in doing so laid itself open to the charge of hypocrisy in view of the continuing presence of the death penalty on its own statute book. The criticisms along these lines made by the West German press struck home.[180] The East German government was forced to defend the existence of capital punishment in the German Democratic Republic to a United Nations inquiry sparked by the events in Spain. It repeated the earlier formulation that the death penalty was 'humanitarian' in character, and added: 'At the same time, the implementation of the death penalty documents the lack of prospects for success, and the possible consequences, of criminal assaults on the state and social order of the GDR.'[181] To most observers, such views seemed merely to support the charge of hypocrisy rather than refute it. The justification of capital punishment as a means of defending socialism as the highest form of human community had, as we saw in similar arguments put forward by the Communist Party in the Weimar Republic, a lengthy history that ultimately went back as far as Lenin. That the leading group in the East German regime, after Ulbricht's enforced retirement in 1971 led by Erich Honecker, had all started their political

178 Hans Halter, '"Nahschuss in den Hinterkopf"', *Der Spiegel*, 45/35 (26 Aug. 1991), 84–6.
179 Paul Preston, *Franco: A Biography* (London, 1993), 775–6.
180 *Berliner Morgenpost*, 30 Sept. 1975.
181 BA Potsdam DP 1 VA 5110, Bl. 45: Entwurf zur Beantwortung des von dem Vereinten Nationen übersandten Fragebogen über die Todesstrafe, gerichtet an die Regierungen zur Vorbereitung des Ersten Fünfjahresberichtes 1975.

careers as members of the Communist Party in the 1920s and 1930s was surely no coincidence in this context. Nevertheless, in 1976, partly in response to international and especially West German criticism of East German penal policy, new regulations regarding the exercise of clemency came into force. Its status had been unclear since the death of Wilhelm Pieck in 1960 and the consequent abolition of the office of President. The Presidency had been replaced by a State Council, but in effect the Politburo had continued to take the real decisions. From 1976, the power of clemency lay with the President of the State Council, who happened to be the same person as the General Secretary of the Party and the chairman of the Politburo: Erich Honecker. The practical difference was therefore negligible. But Honecker used this new power to declare a series of amnesties. In 1977, the first full year of its operation, he commuted the prison sentences of eighty-four offenders sentenced to life for murder.[182] Amnesties and reprieves continued into the 1980s and often reflected recommendations passed up from lower authorities to the State Council.

The efforts of the East German authorities to show a humane face towards the West in the later 1970s met with a good deal of scepticism. The popular West German newspaper *Bild-Zeitung* reported in 1977 that offenders, mostly common murderers, had been executed for some years by a mobile guillotine set up inside a large van in the prison yard at Torgau. It was only in 1968 that shooting had been introduced and a regular room in the prison set aside for executions. This sensational report named three men who had been executed, but rested on the testimony of a released prisoner, and was extremely hazy about dates. Nevertheless, it was interesting that the three were all sex murderers: Rolf Albert, aged 20, who had raped and strangled a 12-year-old girl; Rolf Czepernick, aged 30, who had killed an old woman; and Paul Pessler, an alleged 'vampire' from Jena. None of these executions, however, took place after 1975. For from that point onwards, Honecker systematically reprieved common murderers. 'The man is surely sick. EH', was the comment on a file granting clemency to a sex murderer in the later 1970s.[183] All subsequent executions in East Germany were of Stasi officers and members of the security and armed forces who were convicted of spying. Such offenders were treated with extreme severity, for the edification of their fellow officers, at the behest of Erich Mielke, the head of the Stasi, who said to his senior colleagues on one occasion:

We're not immune from having the occasional swine amongst us. If I knew who one of them was today, he wouldn't be alive tomorrow. Short shrift! Because I'm a humanitarian. That's why I think in this way. . . . All that waffle about not executing people,

[182] BA Potsdam DA-5, 4/1140, Bl. 2: Kurzangaben zu dem Gnadenentscheidungen 1977, Bl. 2. See also ibid. 4/1185, Bl. 1–2.
[183] INGASA Nottingham 25, 1977/8/1: *Bild-Zeitung*, 15 Mar. 1977, Haller '"Nahschuss"'.

abolishing the death sentence—all codswallop. Comrades, execute, if necessary without a death sentence too.[184]

Honecker evidently felt unable to cross Mielke on this point. So even at a time when the price of administering the death penalty according to the law had become too high for the German Democratic Republic in international terms, executions continued to be carried out on Stasi and other uniformed officers of whom Mielke wanted to make an example. In 1975 Egon Glombik, a Stasi interrogator, was executed on his orders for allegedly spying for the West Germans. On 5 June 1979 Rear-Admiral Winfried Baumann-Zakrzowski was arrested for alleged spying for a Western agency. He too was condemned to death and executed.[185] Gert Trebeljare and Werner Teske were two more Stasi officers who were shot after being tried for treasonable conduct, respectively on 14 December 1979 and 26 June 1981.[186] Werner Teske had concealed files in a cellar. He admitted being a West German agent, although the West Germans claimed to have no knowledge of him. His trial, like those of the other Stasi officers, was clandestine. No word of it reached the general public. The executions of these offenders also took place in secret, and the death certificates were falsified, usually describing the death of these men as due to natural causes. The execution procedures in the Leipzig gaol were undocumented and any even vaguely relevant papers had to be delivered to Berlin after the event.[187] As far as the public was concerned, the death penalty had ceased to be applied in 1975, and the regime stuck to this story for the rest of its existence.

All this was strong evidence of the international pressure on the German Democratic Republic to abolish capital punishment. It had forced the regime to stop executions for murder in 1975. The execution of Werner Teske in 1981 was the last for any offence. For in that year the East German Foreign Ministry became worried about a proposal which West Germany's Foreign Minister Hans-Dietrich Genscher was putting to the United Nations for a declaration outlawing the death penalty. This would certainly put the East Germans at a moral disadvantage.[188] The Foreign Ministry promised: 'The German Democratic Republic will not be the last state to abolish capital punishment.' It noted that crime had decreased on its territory, and claimed: 'For this reason, death

---

[184] Quoted from a tape recording, in Johannes Beleites *et al.* (eds.), *Stasi Intern. Macht und Banalität. Herausgegeben vom Bürgerkomitee Leipzig*, 2nd edn. (Leipzig, 1991), 213.

[185] Karl Wilhelm Fricke, *Zur Menschen- und Grundrechtssituation politischer Gefangener in der DDR*, 2nd edn. (Cologne, 1988), 29.

[186] Karl Wilhelm Fricke, *MfS Intern. Macht, Strukturen, Auflösung der DDR-Staatssicherheit* (Cologne, 1991), 64.

[187] Halter ' "Nahschuss" '.

[188] BA Potsdam DP 2/2041, Bl. 42: Positionspapier betreffend die Frage der Abschaffung der Todesstrafe, Ministerium für Auswärtige Angelegenheiten, Abteilung Rechts- und Vertragswesen, 17 Sept. 1981.

sentences have neither been pronounced nor carried out in recent years.' In fact, as we have seen, the latest execution had taken place in secret less than three months before this mendacious statement was made. The Foreign Ministry was demonstrating either its ignorance of what went on in Stasi circles, or its confidence in the utter secrecy in which such goings-on were shrouded. Officially, the Foreign Ministry played for time, and reserved its position, while expressing doubts as to whether a United Nations resolution or convention was the right way to go about abolishing capital punishment world-wide. Its problem was, of course, that capital punishment still existed and was being carried out in a number of other socialist states in Eastern Europe, including the Soviet Union.[189] In practice, therefore, the East German delegation was instructed to defend the death penalty as it existed in East German law, if a general attack was mounted which looked like leading to a resolution being put before the General Assembly.[190] As before, it reserved the right to defend the socialist order against foreign, 'fascist' subversion through the use of capital punishment. The examples of Stasi and other uniformed officers of the state who were secretly executed right up to the end of June 1981 bore silent witness to the fact that this was no mere form of words.

Yet the more the party leader Erich Honecker attempted to gain international recognition and respect for his state, the more obvious it became that the death penalty would have to be removed from the Criminal Code. It was not until 1987, however, that the Politburo finally bit the bullet and set up a working party chaired by Honecker's designated successor Egon Krenz to examine the question. The working party recommended abolition. On 14 July 1987 the Politburo approved.[191] The decision was announced with a fanfare of publicity on radio and television by the State Council on 17 July. The declaration of abolition said:

The death penalty in the Criminal Code of the GDR rested on the historic requirement to prosecute to the last consequence war crimes, Nazi crimes, crimes against peace, humanity, and human rights, and the most serious crimes against the sovereignty of the GDR and the life of its citizens. In these respects the death penalty constituted an important contribution to the comprehensive protection of the socialist state and its citizens from the most serious crimes of this kind.

However, it went on, the prosecution and suppression of National Socialism and militarism had been successful, and a socialist society in the GDR had now become stable, so that criminality had continuously declined, and crimes of violence in particular were now extremely rare. 'It thus corresponds to these

---

[189] Ibid., Bl. 50.
[190] Ibid., Bl. 59: Positionspapier: Gesetzgebung und Praxis der gerichtlichen Entscheidungen hinsichtlich des Ausspruches der Todesstrafe.
[191] BA-SAPM Berlin J IV 2/2/2230: Bl. 34–7: Anlage Nr. 3 zum Protokoll Nr. 28 vom 14. 7. 1987.

changes in the character and dimensions of crime as well as to the humanitarian nature of socialist society that no death sentences have been pronounced for years by courts in the GDR.' The Criminal Code contained sufficient provisions to prevent a rise in violent crime. Punishment, it added, was in any case 'not revenge or retribution against criminal offenders' but consisted in the protection of law-abiding citizens, and of the socialist order, against criminality, and the education of the offender to socialist responsibility. By abolishing the death penalty, therefore, the German Democratic Republic claimed that it was advertising the state of social peace which it had achieved, and fulfilling the general human rights policy of the United Nations.[192]

The interpretation put on the announcement by ordinary people in East Germany was very different. They knew that Erich Honecker, the General Secretary of the Socialist Unity Party and Head of State, was about to embark on a long-planned official visit to West Germany, which he regarded as important evidence of the political acceptability and stability of his state in Germany, Europe, and the wider world. The abolition of the death penalty was coupled with a wide-ranging amnesty for prisoners of various kinds, issued to mark the thirty-eighth anniversary of the Republic's foundation in 1949. The prisoners amnestied included a number who had committed political offences or who had been caught trying to leave the country for the West. A secret report by the Stasi surveillance service reported that the two decisions

have been generally welcomed and evaluated as extraordinarily important measures of domestic and foreign policy which were not expected at this point in time or for the reasons given. All the reactions available to us draw a direct connection between the decisions of the State Council and the announcement of the visit to the Federal Republic of Germany of the General Secretary of the Central Committee of the SED and President of the State Council of the GDR, comrade Erich HONECKER. They foreground the argument that the party and state leadership of the GDR wishes to influence the political climate in a positive way in the run-up to the visit, to create a favourable basis for the conduct of the discussions and negotiations, and to remove from the Federal Republic's side the possibility of concentrating on so-called human rights questions and to divert attention from the principal concern of the visit, which is to make a contribution to the securing of peace and disarmament.

Such remarks betrayed a more sober, even cynical interpretation of the measures than the one which appeared in the propaganda accompanying them. Stripped of its jargon, the report suggested that people did indeed regard them as

[192] BA Potsdam DA 5, 4/1655, Bl. 24–6: Beschluss des Staatsrates der Deutschen Demokratischen Republik über die Abschaffung der Todesstrafe im der Deutschen Demokratischen Republik, vom 17. Juli 1987; BA-SAPM Berlin J IV 2/2A/3039: Vorlage für das Politbüro des ZK, 9 July 1987, betr. Abschaffung der Todesstrafe in der Deutschen Demokratischen Republik; another copy in BStU ZA ZAIG 7862.

primarily directed towards the outside world. This perception, as we have seen, was accurate enough. But the professional optimists of the Stasi managed to give this interpretation a positive gloss:

The decisions to abolish capital punishment and to amend and extend the judicial procedure law have been unanimously appreciated and fully accepted, as evidence for the political stability of the GDR, the continual process of perfection of socialist democracy, and the deeply humanitarian character of socialist society. People emphasize the fact that the GDR is the first socialist state to abolish capital punishment. (Individual reports refer to information about executions in the USSR not being a good advertisement for socialism, and the hope is expressed that other socialist states will follow the GDR's example.)[193]

Subsequent reports only served to strengthen these impressions. People were said by the Stasi to have remarked that previous amnesties had only been issued 'on round-number anniversaries of the foundation of the GDR'. 'The GDR', they said, 'is thus making an "advance contribution" to the achievement of a favourable political climate during the visit.'[194]

The amnesty, to be sure, ran into widespread criticism from the anxiety-prone East German population. Security, social stability, and a low crime rate, after all, were some of the major compensations for the lack of material prosperity under which they knew they were labouring in comparison to the West; and the regime was not slow to point out to them that the affluence of the Federal Republic brought with it a whole slate of social problems, from drug abuse to violent crime, that were virtually unknown on their side of the Berlin Wall. People were therefore afraid that the amnesty would release all kind of disorderly elements back into society to disturb their enjoyment of social tranquillity.[195] But if the amnesty did not meet with popular approval, the abolition of capital punishment certainly did. It might not have been quite true to say, as the Stasi report claimed, that everyone agreed that it was 'an expression of the high internal political stability and the humanitarian character of our social order, in comparison to which the capitalist states have nothing of equal value to offer'.[196] But people to whom I spoke during a prolonged stay in East Germany to carry out research for this book in the autumn of 1987 were unable to conceal a sense of satisfaction, even pride, in the abolition of the death penalty. After all, it brought them finally

---

[193] BStU ZA ZAIG 4228, BStU-Zählung 000002–3: Hinweise zu ersten Reaktionen der Bevölkerung der DDR auf den Beschluss des Staatsrates der DDR über eine allgemeine Amnestie aus Anlass des 38. Jahrestages der Gründung der DDR sowie die Beschlüsse zur Abschaffung der Todesstrafe und zur Änderung und Ergänzung des Gerichtsverfassungsgesetzes der DDR, 22 July 1987.

[194] Ibid., BStU-Zählung 000009: Hinweise über Reaktionen der Bevölkerung der DDR auf die Beschlüsse des Staatsrates der DDR vom 17. Juli 1987, 7 Aug. 1987.

[195] Ibid., passim. The bulk of the two reports cited in nn. 193 and 194 above is devoted to listing complaints about the amnesty.

[196] Ibid., BStU-Zählung 000009.

into line with the situation in the West, and if people were still sometimes shot while trying to break through the Wall, at least the citizens of the German Democratic Republic no longer had to hang their heads in shame for belonging to a state which openly prescribed the death penalty for crimes which, it is clear, most of them, like their counterparts in the West, and for much the same reasons, no longer thought it was appropriate.

Whether this really gave ordinary East Germans the sense of superiority which the Stasi hinted they felt in comparison to the Soviet Union, however, may be doubted. For the reforms of the new leader of the Communist Party, Mikhail Gorbachev, appointed two years previously, in 1985, were already beginning to bite, and East Germans were starting to hope that his policies of *glasnost* and *perestroika*, 'openness' and 'restructuring', could be adopted in their country too. Honecker and the Politburo still took the line that the German Democratic Republic was the Eastern bloc's most advanced society, from which the Soviet Union had a lot to learn—a view which Gorbachev himself had appeared to share, at least in his early days of office. This convenient fiction, however, was rapidly turning into fantasy. By 1988, as Gorbachev's reforms in Russia grew more sweeping, popular discontent in the German Democratic Republic began to mount. By the following spring, it was becoming unstoppable. People were no longer prepared to accept rigged elections, they had grown tired of their poor standards of living, and they started to organize openly for emancipatory and democratic reform. When Gorbachev declared that the Soviet Union would no longer interfere in the internal affairs of the other states in the Warsaw Pact, the entire political system of the German Democratic Republic began to crumble. Caught in a pincer movement between thousands fleeing to the West through the newly opened Hungarian border, and mass demonstrations for major reforms at home, the Honecker regime fell; the Berlin Wall was opened; attempts by Egon Krenz, Honecker's successor, to rescue the system came to nothing; and in October 1990, within a year of celebrating the fortieth anniversary of its foundation, free German elections had been held and the German Democratic Republic had been taken over by the West.

During the forty years of its existence, the German Democratic Republic had carried out well over 200 executions as a result of court proceedings, probably more. The bulk of these, as we have seen, had taken place during the early-to-mid 1950s. From 1949 to April 1958, at least 195 death sentences were passed in the GDR, 95 of them for political offences. Not all of them, of course, were put into effect.[197] In 1956, the use of the death penalty by the regime declined as a result of destalinization. Up to 1964, according to one source, 172 executions were carried out by order of the East German courts, 109 of them for political offences.[198] Another estimate gives a figure of at least 90 offenders executed for war crimes, 21 for political offences, and 25 for murder from 1949 to 1964.[199] In practice, as we have seen, the different categories of offence were often hard to distinguish from one another. 'Political' executions could be ordinary cases of murder given a political interpretation by the regime; 'war crimes' were often punished by execution for political reasons, either because the offender had resisted the regime in some way, or because the Politburo felt the need to appear tough towards former Nazis in the light of some particular judicial or political situation in the West. Often, particularly in the case of the show trials of the early 1950s, offenders were singled out as examples to others, and cases of mismanagement, corruption, or lack of co-operation in the economic policies of the regime were given exemplary punishment under Article 6 of the constitution. Death sentences were meted out to selected offenders who had killed a policeman or some other representative of the state, to violent professional criminals, of whom there were very few left after the early 1950s, to Stasi agents, policemen, and other uniformed officers who had failed in their duties or maintained suspicious contacts with the West, and to 'war criminals' who had the misfortune to be caught at times when the regime needed to demonstrate its anti-Nazi credentials. The death penalty was used in some cases to warn people against Western cultural influences of various kinds, from radio programmes and gangster films to detective novels and pulp fiction.

From 1964 onwards, with the stabilization of the East German political and social system after the building of the Berlin Wall and the end of the ensuing period of increased repression, the number of executions seldom exceeded one a year, and a substantial proportion of them was for sex murders which even East Germany's political leaders could not portray as political in character, although in the stultifying atmosphere of petty-bourgeois morality which pervaded the regime, such crimes were evidently regarded as the *ne plus ultra* of moral and social deviance. From 1975 these executions stopped too. After this, capital punishment was only carried out in secret, on renegade or allegedly treacherous Stasi and other uniformed officials; after 1981 these too stopped and there were no more executions at all. In 1987 the death penalty was finally abolished altogether. Over the whole period from 1949 to 1981, there is no doubt that the East German regime made liberal use of the death penalty, but there is also no doubt that its incidence steadily declined from the beginnings of destalinization in 1956 onwards. One reliable source gives a total of 194 executions resulting from death

[198] *Argumente–Dokumente–Zitate*, 56 (27 Nov. 1964), 6.
[199] See the estimates of the West German Federal Justice Ministry in *Bundestag*, 7. Wahlperiode, 192. Sitzung, Bonn, 15 October 1975, 13360.

sentences passed by East German courts from 1949 to 1968. Of these 69 were for political offences (espionage, sabotage and the like), while 75 were for war crimes. The remaining 50 were for common murder.[200] Adding on the executions known to have taken place from 1969 to 1981 gives a final total of 205, including 73 for political offences, 77 for war crimes, and 55 for common murder, all resulting from death sentences passed by East German courts. These figures are of course less than complete, but the actual totals, not including sentences passed by Soviet military tribunals, are unlikely to have been a great deal higher.

The Communist regime in East Germany, as we have seen, used the death penalty for explicitly political purposes. In this, it did not differ in kind from previous regimes in German history, only in degree. For the Socialist Unity Party's system of rule achieved a level of control greater even than that of the Nazis. Here indeed was a Foucauldian dystopia of total surveillance and manipulation. Capital punishment fitted into this system of control in a carefully calculated way, with individuals selected for execution in order to terrorize specific sectors of the population, from recalcitrant farmers to industrial workers, from economic and transportation managers to officers of the State Security. This was not so much a system of terror directed at oppositional elements, who until 1961 had the option of fleeing to the West, and did so in such large numbers that there were scarcely any of them left by then. Rather, it was directed against people who worked for the regime, or had agreed to stay and accept the basic premises of its operation. This applied even to former Nazis, whom the East German leadership had made serious efforts to placate in its early years, even founding a special political party, the National Democratic Party, to represent their interests. The regime did not use capital punishment, as the Nazis had done, to destroy its opponents; from 1949 to 1968 it used the guillotine and, from 1968 to 1981 the pistol, to enforce obedience and loyalty on its supporters. The show trials of capital offenders, and the propagandistic exploitation of their alleged offences, were powerful weapons in the picture which the East German leadership was attempting to construct in the 1950s, and did its best to maintain thereafter, of a small, progressive, and peaceful state beset on all sides by evil-minded Western powers, led by fascists and imperialists, hell-bent on destroying the German Democratic Republic by any means possible, including terrorism, explosions, subversion, and murder. This picture was beamed not at the outside world in general, but at the population of the Republic itself, its tiny band of supporters in the West, its masters in Moscow, and its allies in the rest of the Communist bloc; just as, on a smaller scale, the propagandistic exploitation of

---

[200] Fricke, *Politik und Justiz*, 525.

the secret trial and execution of errant Stasi officers in the late 1970s and early 1980s was aimed not at East Germans at large, who, it was thought, should not be entrusted with such dangerous knowledge, but at the rest of the staff of the Ministry of State Security.

Real opposition, such as it was, could better be quelled by imprisonment, which the regime used freely not only as a deterrent, but also as a means of ridding itself of turbulent subjects, since from the 1960s onwards the West German regime bought out a total of over 30,000 political prisoners for hard currency which was badly needed by the East German economy.[201] And of course, anyone brave—or foolish—enough to try to penetrate the fortified barrier that separated East from West after 1952, or to cross the Berlin Wall once it was erected, in 1961, faced the likelihood of being killed by automatic gun emplacements or land-mines, or being shot by a border guard from one of the watch-towers that covered every inch of the country's frontiers. That several hundred died in this way demonstrated with brutal clarity that the regime was not afraid of killing its own citizens without compunction when it thought it desirable. But formal, ritual, publicly decreed capital punishment was largely a propaganda weapon. It testified to the fact that this was a regime that lived and died by propaganda. When East Germany was seeking integration within the Warsaw Pact in the 1950s and 1960s, the death penalty was seen as useful in propaganda terms, not least as a form of reassurance to the Soviet Union of the regime's total commitment to the Communist cause. When East Germany made its major effort to achieve respectability on the international scene at large, and secure acceptance by the Federal Republic in the West, capital punishment's usefulness declined until it finally became an obstacle to the foreign policy goals of the state leadership, and therefore had to be abolished.

Thus, by several measures, people were unjustly executed in East Germany between 1949 and 1981. They were executed to serve the propaganda purposes of their rulers. They were executed for offences for which the death penalty was not laid down by the Criminal Code, only in the country's undemocratically imposed constitution; they were executed for offences which, in many cases, they had not committed; and they were executed on the basis of forced confessions to invented crimes, in trials whose outcome was determined in advance, after clemency procedures that were little more than a sham, and which were sometimes concluded even before their conviction for the crime with which they had been charged. The judicial system which condemned them was not a dispenser

---

[201] See Ludwig A. Rehlinger, *Freikauf. Die Geschäfte der DDR mit politisch Verfolgten 1963–1989* (Berlin, 1990).

of justice in any real sense of the word. The 'socialist legality' which some apologists for the German Democratic Republic still defended after reunification was a perversion of legality.[202] It was not surprising, therefore, that voices were raised in the early 1990s calling for the East German leadership to be put on trial for its abuse of the death penalty. The state of Saxony, indeed, established a special prosecutor's office to gather information about death sentences passed under the Communist regime with a view to bringing prosecutions for murder. Erich Honecker, the former East German leader, was brought before a court in the newly reunited Germany for having ordered the building of the Wall and therefore sanctioning the deaths of those killed trying to break through it. But such atttempts did not yield any significant results. Honecker was able to evade justice by pleading that he was too sick to stand trial, and emigrated to Chile, where he died in 1994. Erich Mielke, former head of the Stasi, could only be tried, bizarrely, for a murder in which he had allegedly been implicated as a young Communist before the Nazi seizure of power. The other surviving former leaders of the regime languish in obsure retirement, but by and large they have not so far been put in prison.

There were some who argued that this was a disgraceful state of affairs. Just as Germans came to terms with one system of injustice, after 1945, so, it was claimed in the early 1990s, it was time for them to come to terms with another, after 1989.[203] But the crimes of the two systems of Nazism and Stalinism in Germany were very different in nature and scale. The notion that both were similar because both regimes were 'totalitarian' is as untenable as the notion that Hitler's Germany and Mussolini's Italy were similar because both were 'fascist'. Nazi Germany was unique in Europe in the centrality it gave to racism in its organization of politics and society, and in the murderous extremes to which it took that racism during the war. Murderous though the German Democratic Republic was, its victims can be numbered only in hundreds, not in millions. Moreover, while Walter Ulbricht and his henchmen certainly adopted the ideology and style of Stalinism in the early 1950s, Stalin himself was dead before the state they created had been in existence for more than four years, and destalinization, as we have seen, had a real effect on their political and judicial practice from 1956 onwards. Even at the height of its most Stalinist phase, in 1951–3, the German Democratic Republic never so much as contemplated mass murder, extermi-

---

[202] For the views of East German judges themselves after reunification, see Gilbert Furian, *Der Richter und sein Lenker. Politische Justiz in der DDR* (Berlin, 1992).

[203] Christa Hoffmann, *Stunden Null? Vergangenheitsbewältigung in Deutschland 1945 und 1989* (Bonn, 1992); Werner Filmer and Heribert Schwan, *Opfer der Mauer. Die geheimen Protokolle des Todes* (Munich, 1991); Armin Mohler, *Der Nasenring. Die Vergangenheitsbewältigung vor und nach dem Fall der Mauer*, 2nd edn. (Munich, 1991); Heiner Sauer and Hans-Otto Plumeyer, *Der Salzgitterreport. Die zentrale Erfassungsstelle berichtet über Verbrechen im SED-Staat* (Munich, 1991).

nation programmes, or wars of foreign conquest and extermination, as Hitler's Third Reich did from the very beginning. Of course, people like Walter Ulbricht, Erich Mielke, Hilde Benjamin, and Erich Honecker were perfectly capable of mass murder, and the behaviour of those among the leadership who had been in Moscow during the purges left no doubt about their ruthless disregard for human life. But the circumstances of the German Democratic Republic did not allow such a course: this was a weak state, without serious military power, lacking in legitimacy from the beginning, and forced to win its people over by propaganda rather than by open or indiscriminate terror, given the existence of another, much larger state on German soil, to which they could flee without great difficulty up to 1961, and which, backed by NATO, would undoubtedly have posed a real threat to East Germany's existence if at any time after that Ulbricht or Honecker had decided on the large-scale killing of their own citizens. The emigration of nearly three million East Germans up to the building of the Wall took away almost all potential dissidents, and it was not until a new generation came to adulthood, after a quarter of a century of the Wall's existence, that a serious opposition on a large scale finally began to emerge. Under these circumstances, a fully blown Stalinist dictatorship, such as had existed in the Soviet Union, never stood a chance of emerging in the German Democratic Republic.

The Nazi and East German regimes differed in another crucial respect too. The Third Reich emerged on German soil, without foreign interference, and drew on deep-seated German traditions and patterns of thought and behaviour. That is why the established German judicial and penal systems found it so easy to compromise with the Nazi regime and to embark on the slippery slope from willing collaboration with what looked like a restoration of law and order in 1933, to what became mass murder with the stroke of a pen a mere decade later. That is also the reason why denazification was so difficult, and why so few of the judicial servants of the regime were ever sucessfully prosecuted. The East German state, by contrast, was imposed, and, as 17 June 1953 showed, maintained from outside, by the Soviet Union, and it was only when the Soviet Union withdrew its support, in October–November 1989, that it finally fell. The system of justice and repression that it operated from 1950–1 onwards was an alien system, operated by people specially selected and trained in its special principles: it was not an outgrowth of earlier traditions, not even the traditions of the German labour movement, which until the arrival of Communism after the Russian Revolution had always respected the rule of law and believed in the ideal of judicial neutrality, even if it thought it was being flouted by the capitalist society in which it lived. Experience was to show in the early 1990s that the effects of forty years of socialization and indoctrination on the East German population had been greater than anyone expected. But one thing was clear: few of them, if any, were prepared to justify or excuse mass murder, armed aggression, or racial extermination, as so many other Germans had been after 1945. History does not repeat itself: and to equate 'destalinization' in the early 1990s with denazification four and a half decades earlier was to equate two phenomena which had very little in common in the end.[204]

Nevertheless, the legacy of Nazism could be seen in East Germany just as it could be seen in the West. In 1949, liberals and Social Democrats in West Germany felt shame at the mass executions of the Nazi era, and wanted to distance the new Federal Republic from the exterminism of the Third Reich. This combined with anxiety on the right about the continuing application of the death penalty to war criminals who many conservatives thought were none, to bring about the abolition of capital punishment by constitutional fiat. Many years later, the Honecker regime in East Germany, which constantly sought to depict West Germany as the 'fascist' successor to the Hitler dictatorship, felt anxiety at the prospect of the Federal Republic projecting itself on the world stage as the more humane, the more just of the two German states. This led first to the scaling-down, then to the suspension, and finally to the abolition of the death penalty in the East. In the intervening period, East Germany had managed to bypass the historical legacy of Nazism and its symbolic expression in the issue of capital punishment by portraying itself as the quintessence of antifascism, obliged to use the death penalty only as a means of self-defence against the threat from murderous imperialists in the West. It was a tactic that stored up serious trouble for the future, as East Germany's citizens were never forced to confront the legacy of the Third Reich or develop the habit of reflection on where racism and prejudice could lead. But it was also a tactic that became ever less plausible as time went on. In the 1950s the German Democratic Republic could shore up its claim to embody the anti-Nazi tradition in German history by publishing the names and past misdeeds of hundreds of ex-Nazis who had attained prominent positions in West German society and politics. The widespread silence and evasion that characterized attitudes to the Nazi past in the Federal Republic in the first decade or so of its existence gave further credence to East German claims. But as time went on, as ex-Nazis retired or died, and as West Germans began to develop a more open and more honest way of coming to terms with the Hitler period, these claims began to lose credibility. As they did so, the continued presence of the death penalty in the East German Criminal Code began to look more and more like evidence of a failure to recognize how fatally the Nazis' vast

[204] Eberhard Jäckel, 'Die doppelte Vergangenheit', *Der Spiegel*, 35/52 (1991), 39–43. See also the title story in the same issue, '"Kein Verbrechen ohne Schuld"', pp. 30–8.

programme of executions had undermined the legitimacy of capital punishment in any German society that claimed to be truly democratic. In the end, therefore, the abolition of the death penalty owed as much to the legacy of the past in East Germany as it did in the West.

Conclusion

a. Four Centuries of the Death Penalty in Germany

Not only in the German Democratic Republic, but also in earlier German regimes, from the Prussian Absolutism of the eighteenth century through the Revolution of 1848, the Bismarckian Empire, and the Weimar Republic, the death penalty was an instrument of state politics as much as, at times even more than, an aspect of penal policy. Debates about its retention or abolition were always more concerned with the symbolic meanings it had for the state than with its efficacy or otherwise as a means of combating crime. That is why the major attempts at abolition were made at great turning-points in German history: in the liberal Revolution of 1848, at the creation of the German Empire in 1870, at the establishment of the Weimar Republic in 1919, at the founding of the Federal Republic in 1949. Even its formal abolition in East Germany in 1987 was largely a consequence of that state's declining legitimacy in the face of its more successful neighbour to the west, and a harbinger of the collapse that was to follow little over two years later. When parliamentarians debated the death penalty on such occasions, it was almost invariably to dwell upon its consequences for the ethos of the state whose creation was being considered. A heavy burden of symbolic meaning rested upon the enthusiastic abolition of capital punishment by the revolutionaries of 1848 in the name of freedom and humanity, upon the reluctant retention of the death penalty by the liberals of 1870 in the explicit interests of national unity, upon the failure of the Weimar democrats to abolish executions as a gesture of national pacification and reconciliation in 1919, upon the unexpected, soon regretted, but fundamentally irreversible decision to outlaw the ultimate penalty in the Basic Law of 1949. In each case, the legislators ran true to form. The liberals of 1848 were idealistic but impractical, and failed to put their motion into effect in the most important states; the liberals of 1870 were divided, and surrendered their liberalism to their nationalism in sufficient numbers to ensure that Bismarck's Empire began with the authoritarian gesture of retaining the death penalty; the democrats of 1919 failed to take decisive action and were left hoping that something better would turn up in the future; the politicians of 1949 voted for abolition against the better judgment of many of them, and put through a decision that was not widely accepted for another twenty years or more.

Debates about the death penalty took place at other times and in other circumstances, but seldom with as much effect. This was because the other major occasion for considering the principle of capital punishment apart from constitutional change—the passing of a new Criminal Code—was repeatedly beset by technical and political difficulties. In the eighteenth century the Prussian General Law Code took decades to complete and was only passed in 1794, long after the death of its instigator, Friedrich II. Attempts to promulgate a Criminal Code dragged on without result through the 1820s, 1830s, and 1840s and only bore fruit in the panic reaction of 1851 after the failure of the Revolution. The Code of 1871 went through relatively smoothly because it was in essence an extension of its Prussian predecessor of 1851 to the rest of the German Empire—a neat symbol of Prussian dominance in the new nation-state. Attempts to replace it commenced in 1906, were interrupted in 1914 by the First World War, fell apart in the political disintegration of late Weimar, and were outflanked in the 1930s and 1940s by the Nazis' preference for *ad hoc* action over written regulations. The much-heralded issue of a new Criminal Code in the Federal Republic came to nothing with the failure of the draft of 1962, and was replaced instead by a series of piecemeal reforms. Plans to issue a new Code in East Germany in the 1950s fell foul of political developments and were only realized in 1968. Legal reform moved much more slowly than political and constitutional change.

The political significance of the death penalty can be seen even more clearly in the vagaries of its administration. This was above all a consequence of the right of clemency, which survived as a central aspect of sovereignty through all the vicissitudes of modern German history. Every change in the locus of sovereign power was closely followed by the power over life and death, from the mainly hereditary state sovereigns of the eighteenth and nineteenth centuries through the Presidents and federated state cabinets of Weimar to the supra-legal figure of the Führer in the Third Reich, the provincial state governments of West and East in the second half of the 1940s, and the Politburo of the Socialist Unity Party in the German Democratic Republic, acting through the figurehead of the President and subsequently the President of the Council of State. The operation of clemency more than anything else was what turned capital punishment from a penal into a political act. It was intended to demonstrate not only ideological understanding for—or disapproval of—the attitudes thought to lie behind certain types of murder, but also the political stance taken by those in power towards the maintenance of order and hierarchy in society. Capital offenders were reprieved for a variety of reasons, varying from the legal status of their conviction to the personal religious beliefs of the sovereign, but the major criteria for deciding upon execution or commutation at this level were political: above all, the weight attached by the regime in power to the repression of rebellion and dissent, and the judgment reached by that regime on the extent to which the nature of a particular crime required it.

Thus the absolute number of executions followed closely the successive waves of authoritarianism and liberalism or humanitarianism in German history. En-lightened Absolutists such as Friedrich II of Prussia sharply reduced the number of executions; Joseph II of Austria abolished them altogether. The reactionary regimes of the post-Napoleonic era increased them as part of a general repressive package which also included measures such as the Karlsbad decrees. The liberal era of the *Vormärz* saw a reduction, the reaction of the 1850s an increase, the liberal apogee of the 1860 and 1870s a virtual cessation of executions in most of Germany. Bismarck's notorious 're-foundation' of the German Empire on con-servative lines in 1878 was signalled by the renewal of executions, Wilhelm II's pronounced authoritarianism from 1892 onwards by a sharp increase, and the Weimar Republic's slow and fitful progress towards democratic stability by a gradual decline, then a *de facto* abolition in 1928–30. The collapse of Weimar democracy was accompanied by a renewal of executions in 1931–2, the advent of the Third Reich by a major expansion, and the descent of the Nazi regime into mass extermination during the war by an exponential increase until formal capital punishment was effectively swallowed up in the larger machinery of human destruction. The mixture of restoration and liberal democracy in post-war West Germany saw a return to executions on the limited scale of the 1880s, and then their abolition, while the turn of the East German Communists to an authoritarian, Stalinist regime in 1949–50 was bolstered by a sharp, if carefully targeted, increase in executions only scaled down in the wake of destalinization from 1956 onwards. At every juncture, therefore, capital punishment was con-sciously used as an instrument of state power. Its effectiveness, indeed its very meaning as a symbol of sovereignty, depended on its essential arbitrariness. It was not the Criminal Code, not the justice system, which decided on the life or death of a capital offender, but the whim of the sovereign. Up to a point, of course, this was calculated and predictable; but the basis of the calculation often changed virtually without warning, and was never made explicit in law. Indeed, the exercise of clemency could often run counter to the intentions of the law, as in the 1820s, when the careful gradations of capital punishment laid down in the Prussian General Law Code were overturned by the operation of clemency to commute the majority of sentences other than breaking with the wheel. Lawyers were increasingly aware of these facts, and from the middle of the nineteenth century at the latest, prosecutors, investigating judges, juries, and criminal courts in general became increasingly reluctant to pass death sentences when they knew—as in the 1890s, for example—that there was a better than even chance of their being carried out. The judges of Imperial Germany may have been conservative, but they were morally scrupulous.

The problem for all of them was that the death penalty, grounded in politics and sovereignty, had grown increasingly at odds with the penal system as a whole since the Age of the Enlightenment and the abolition of other kinds of overtly public and corporal punishment. The anomaly of executions taking place in the open air while other punishments took place inside prisons was dealt with in the 1850s and 1860s by putting executions inside prisons as well. But the strong feeling for much of the liberal nineteenth century that the primary purpose of penal policy had to be ameliorative rather than retributional put capital punishment in an exposed position. During a crisis that lasted from the 1840s to the 1880s, its demise was constantly expected, and on numerous occasions and in numerous German states it was abolished for significant periods of time. It was only when, in the 1880s and above all the 1890s, that ameliorative doctrines of punishment began to give way to hereditarian views of criminality that the way was open once more for the integration of the death penalty into the general structure of penal policy. Even so, the new doctrines remained contested, and many of their adherents balked at taking them to their logical conclusion and demanding the execution of serious offenders on eugenic grounds. It was only in the conflict-laden atmosphere of Weimar, with its political murders and serial sex killers, that a significant number of people began to take this step, and only in the Third Reich, with a gang of murderous racists at the helm, that they were seriously put into effect.

The political and ideological aspects of capital punishment were paramount in the immediate determination of its enactment, but they did not operate in a social or cultural vacuum. Élite attitudes changed faster than their popular counterparts. The death penalty in popular culture was always a form of retribution; but it was administered not so much by the sovereign or the law, as by God and fate. In the seventeenth and eighteenth centuries, all the evidence suggests that executions were carried out with a good deal of popular consent, which may have increased as they were more confined to various kinds of homicide. Such consent varied in strength, was sometimes conditional, and in some cases merely grudging; yet the shared cultural processing of capital punishment by the community and the élite during this period was a powerful disincentive to its being withheld altogether. It was only in the course of Enlightenment reforms that a serious gap began to open up, much later than in other areas of cultural relations between the élites and the plebeian mass of the people. The authorities tried to enforce a secular understanding of the public execution as an act of abhorrence and deterrence upon the watching crowd, and to undermine the popular interpretation of the scene at the scaffold as an act of physical retribution and spiritual repentance, expiation, and absolution. This policy was largely unsuccessful. Much to the chagrin of judicial bureaucrats, the crowd continued to articulate magico-religious beliefs at executions right up to the moment when they were removed within prison walls and in some cases even beyond. But in other respects the resonances of capital punishment in popular culture changed as popular culture itself altered. Throughout the eighteenth and nineteenth centuries a steady secularization of the popular understanding of capital punishment was in progress, accompanied by a gradual transferral of its appropriation from oral to written culture. The depiction of suffering was pared down, the promise of redemption abandoned, and execution became an act of secular finality rather than a spiritual rite of passage. All the time, there was a notable concentration on the last moments of the condemned. In this respect, the lurid stories of the malefactor's last night delivered by the yellow press of the Weimar Republic were little different from the ritual depictions of death and deliverance offered by the folk-songs and ballads of an earlier era.

Popular tradition was aware from the start that capital punishment was meted out almost exclusively to the poor and the powerless. The extent to which its representation of executions was compensatory and subversive, as in the Schinderhannes ballads or some of the accounts of infanticide, was none the less strictly limited. In the course of the later nineteenth century, however, this recognition was politicized, and the inequality with which homicidal aristocratic duellists and homicidal drunken labourers were treated by the state—the former suffering a brief confinement, the latter going to the block—became part of the folklore of Social Democracy, reflected in rank-and-file opinion as well as in political polemic. The educative effects of social deprivation and political indoctrination created generations of working-class people whose view of capital punishment, at least as an abstract principle, was markedly more negative than that of the élites. At the same time, the radical, modernist culture of the Weimar Republic was both overwhelmingly hostile to the death penalty and fatally fascinated by the crimes which carried it. The paradox was that the cultural representation of serial killing, even in such a complex and many-layered form as Theodor Lessing's depiction of Haarmann, Bertolt Brecht's ballad of 'Mack the Knife', or Fritz Lang's film *M*, was almost bound to fuel demands for retribution by its emphatic foregrounding of the enormity of the crimes in question. The cultural representation of innocence, as in the various poems, essays, and dramas centred on the tragic figure of Jakubowski, had little to offer by way of competition. And the previous stress on the social injustice of execution had given way to something more ambivalent: for whatever the sympathies of the author, it was difficult to represent a figure like Kürten, or the character played by Peter Lorre in *M*, as the victim of social injustice. In Weimar culture, psychological factors often took precedence over social ones in the representation of transgression. Yet social and ethnic inequality runs through the history of capital punishment in Germany like a red thread in a tapestry. The poor were always more likely to be executed than the rich, and in the eighteenth and nineteenth centuries those who killed a social superior—a master, a father, a husband—were much more likely to go to the block than those whose victim was lower down the social scale—an apprentice, a son, a wife. The advent of hereditarian ways of thinking about crime simply reinforced this pattern, as in the reprieve of the schoolteacher Wagner in 1913. And there is also a good deal of evidence to suggest that ethnic differences played a part. Poles in particular were much less likely to be shown mercy than ethnic Germans were even in the early nineteenth century, when only a third of capital offenders in Posen were granted clemency as opposed to four-sevenths in Brandenburg and two-thirds in Westphalia.[1] This situation continued during Bismarck's initial attempts to Germanize Prussian Poland in the 1880s through to the days of Jakubowski and on via the explicit racial discrimination of the Third Reich to the occupying powers' policy towards DPs in the second half of the 1940s. In the history of the death penalty, Poles play the same role in Germany as African-Americans have done in the USA.

The cultural representation of execution included at various times the ambivalent figure of the executioner, and he too formed an essential element in the experience of capital punishment in German history. In the seventeenth and eighteenth centuries, he was an accepted member of a complex social hierarchy based on ascribed and largely hereditary status, part of an entire caste of the 'dishonourable', the German equivalent of Hindu untouchables. The boundaries between honour and dishonour may have been fluctuating and unclear, but they were real all the same. As this social system broke down and was gradually replaced by a class- and gender-based society, the executioner became as much of an anomaly as the punishment which he carried out. The anonymous, red-cloaked agent of divine retribution became the identifiable individual in the frock-coat whose attempts to find bourgeois respectability were belied by his notoriety in popular culture and the evident distaste with which he was handled by the authorities. With the professionalization of the execution business in the hands of Julius Krautz and his successors, the

---

[1] Anon., *Statistik des Preussischen Staats. Versuch einer Darstellung seiner Grundmacht und Kultur, seiner Verfassung, Regierung und Verwaltung im Lichte der Gegenwart* (Berlin, 1845), 285.

hangman took his place in the hierarchy of popular icons as well as the history of petty-bourgeois entrepreneurship. Yet a man who, uniquely, was sanctioned to kill by the state, and on a regular basis, occupied a peculiar and in many ways unstable position. Social ostracism continued and reinforced the executioners' existing tendency to build dynasties. Their hereditary connection with the knacking trade was not broken, not even in the Third Reich, although it was augmented with a supply of executioners from similar occupations which not only gave their exponents a familiarity with blood and guts but also in many cases attracted the continuing obloquy, or at least suspicion, of respectable society: gravediggers, mortuary attendants, horse-butchers, prison warders. Hardened as they were to the sight, sound, and smell of violent and bloody death, executioners were nevertheless seldom able to stand the strain of killing offenders in a society where the very principle of capital punishment was perpetually contested. Constantly worried about their income and position, they succumbed in the majority of cases to drink and got into trouble varying from indebtedness to homicide. Only in the Third Reich did the political atmosphere, with its never-ending public cult of hatred and violence, give them a sense of security.

Up to the decision to carry out all executions by the guillotine in 1936, the executioners themselves had been solidly in favour of traditional methods, notably the hand-held axe. The force of tradition in this area was enormous: even in the 1950s and 1960s, the guillotine continued to be used in East Germany, while it was always proposed as the method of execution by the advocates of reintroduction in the West. Despite occasional signs of interest in novel methods shown by Bismarck, and periodic suggestions for new machines of individual destruction by enterprising inventors, it was in the end the Nazis who proved most fertile and most influential in this area. Even while traditional methods such as the guillotine and the rope (brought in during the war) continued to be used on legally condemned capital offenders, shooting and gassing were being employed to carry out policies of mass extermination in the East. Initially, there had been a strong current of opinion within the Nazi regime in favour of poisoning, which only foundered because of opposition from the Catholic Church. During the war, however, lethal injections were increasingly used as a method of execution in concentration camps. They are now fast becoming the most widespread method of execution in the United States. The inventor and supplier of the machines by which they are administered, as well as of a new generation of electric chairs, Fred Leuchter, has also been active in neo-Nazi circles as the author of a report alleging that no gassings were carried out in Auschwitz, a central text in the literature of 'Holocaust denial'. The idea of using lethal injections was first canvassed in New York in the 1880s, by the commission which eventually recommended the electric chair; it was also considered and rejected by a British Royal Commission after the Second World War. But there is no doubt that it was the Nazis who first used it.[2]

b. Discourses of Cruelty, Critiques of Justice

Connections such as these bring us to the wider issues which this book has been seeking to address: the transformation of the discourse, culture, and experience of capital punishment in Germany over the last four centuries and its relation to the outbreak of human cruelty and destructiveness in Hitler's Third Reich. As we saw in the Introduction and at various points thereafter, many historians, philosophers, and sociologists have tackled these issues, or aspects of them, over the decades. In particular, the classic work of Michel Foucault on the history of punishment has informed much of the research behind this book, provided many of the questions to be answered, and generated numerous insights into the material which has emerged from the archives and libraries. At the same time, as we have seen, a number of Foucault's theses do not stand up to critical scrutiny when confronted with systematic empirical research. To begin with, he grossly overestimated the transgressive potential of the medieval and early modern world. Interrupted only by serious disorder, civil conflict, war, or pestilence, when the state and its law enforcement agencies were seriously disorganized, early modern society, from the village and town community to the civil and military authorities, experienced a general, long-term decline in interpersonal violence and serious crime. Imprisonment was more widespread than Foucault believed it to have been. By the early eighteenth century, the number of public executions, either in England, or in France, or in Germany, which could even superficially be interpreted in terms of the carnivalesque, was minuscule. On the very rare occasions on which the watching crowd did rebel, it was not because of the execution itself, but because something had gone wrong with it. There is no evidence that the people took a delight in displays of physical cruelty and suffering; on the contrary, the major reason for a crowd attacking an executioner was when he caused unnecessary pain to the condemned, beyond what was ritually prescribed, through failing to wield the sword or the axe in an efficient manner.[3] Foucault and his followers overestimated the disorderliness of public executions not least because they treated the long early modern period as a single unity and failed to note that the ceremony of execution broke down at specific,

---

[2] Stephen Trombley, *The Execution Protocol* (London, 1993), 84–8.
[3] The stoning of executioners in post-revolutionary France when the guillotine failed to work properly was not a new phenomenon, as Arasse, *Guillotine*, 124–5, supposes, but a traditional act common in other countries as well, as we have seen.

exceptional times and places, and for specific, exceptional reasons.[4] Foucault knew little in practice of the realities of early modern society, and he seriously underestimated the importance not only of ritual and ceremony, but also, crucially, of religion, formal and informal, magical and ecclesiastical, in shaping and giving meaning to people's lives. At every stage Foucault discounted or seriously underplayed the input of popular notions of justice and retribution into the penal system, and failed to explore the multiple meanings of punishment in the structures of popular culture, consciousness, and experience.[5]

Into this world of structured retributive practices there erupted the disturbing influence of the Enlightenment; but this was not governed, as Foucault and his followers have suggested, merely by a fresh desire for repression and control, masked by a deceptive rhetoric of freedom, justice, and humanitarianism. On the contrary, it was inspired by the ambition of restructuring human behaviour and human society along rational lines, in which the rationality of the individual would be the object and the focus of judicial and penal practice. It meant dispensing with the supernatural and the divine in the ordering of society, and so it constituted an attack on popular judicial custom and belief, on religion, and on cultural identity. But it also meant recognizing and if possible protecting the rights of the rational individual to a fair hearing and, if the verdict was guilty, to a punishment commensurate with the crime and addressed to the thinking capacities of the malefactor. Foucault's apocalyptically gloomy view of the Enlightenment and its consequences altogether failed to acknowledge these achievements. There was no necessary contradiction of the sort which he assumed between the control of deviants and the humane treatment of offenders. As we have seen, in describing the reforms of the Enlightenment as humanitarian, one most bear due regard to the particular concept of humanity which the Enlightenment mobilized in the course of advocating these reforms; a concept which had its restrictive as well as its liberating aspects. Yet the changes that took place in penal practice and ideology at this time must be analysed in the broader context of the gradual establishment of open trial, due process, freedom from arbitrary arrest, the right of the accused to a fair hearing, and the formal equality of all citizens before the law. From the perspective of the twentieth century, which has seen one dictatorship after another dispense with these inconveniences in the interests of untrammelled power, mass murder, torture, violence, and total domination over the body of the citizen, these seem to be rights worth defending.

[4] Farge, *Fragile Lives*, notes the gradual breakdown of authority in late 18th-c. Paris, but fails to relate it to her account of public executions on pp. 183–225, which is largely undifferentiated in temporal terms; Laqueur, 'Crowds', completely fails to account for change over time in the two and a half centuries about which he writes; M. Bée, 'Le Spectacle de l'exécution dans la France de l'ancien régime', *Annales ESC* 4 (1983), 843–73, similarly deploys the concept of a unitary 'old regime'.
[5] David Garland, *Punishment and Modern Society: A Study in Social Theory* (Oxford, 1990), 153–63.

They are not to be dismissed, as Foucault and his disciples have dismissed them, as fig-leaves for the institution of a 'carceral society.'

Foucault has sometimes been accused of regarding any kind of historical theory or interpretation as a form of confining discourse, imposing, as the sociologist Bryan Turner has alleged, 'a false uniformity on events, people and places'. But this is to go much further than Foucault himself did. In arguing that it was time to dismantle 'a comprehensive view' of history which saw 'the past as a patient and continuous development', Foucault was doing little more than tilting against the Marxist-Leninist teleologies favoured by his rival Sartre.[6] He did not really think that discourses were free-floating assemblages of arbitrary signs, or that history was merely a chain of accidents.[7] On the contrary, Foucault followed the *Annales* school in arguing that long-term demographic developments, the growth of life expectancy, and the decline of famine and disease, were behind changing attitudes to the body, and he saw the advent of capitalism and the triumph of the bourgeoisie as crucial constituents of the 'field of transformations' which framed the discursive changes in which he was interested.[8] He was sharply critical of other thinkers who reduced everything to a kind of linguistic determinism, ignoring the real social context within which language is formed. In the thought of Jacques Derrida, for instance, Foucault complained,

discursive traces are reduced to textual traces; events occurring there are elided and kept only as markers for a reading; voices behind the texts are invented so as not to have to analyse the ways in which the subject is implicated in discourses; the original is allocated to what is said and not-said in the text, so as not to put discursive practices back into the field of transformations in which they are carried out.

That Foucault himself paid relatively little attention to this 'field of transformations' merely adds an element of irony to what was a critique devastating in its acuity. Derrida's 'deconstructionism', declared Foucault, was 'minor pedagogy'. It 'teaches the pupil that there is nothing outside the text'. Foucault was quick to see the intellectual narcissism behind this approach. It gave the teacher's voice, he said, 'unlimited sovereignty'.[9] If all the world's a text, if history exists only in texts, and if any text is capable of an almost infinite number of equally valid interpretations, then this gives enormous power and importance to those intellectuals who possess the key to such interpretations. This was not something that Foucault claimed for himself, or wanted anyone else to claim.

[6] Michel Foucault, *Language, Counter-Memory, Practice: Selected Essays and Interviews*, tr. Donald F. Bouchard and Sherry Simon (Ithaca, NY, 1977), 153.

[7] See e.g. Bryan S. Turner, *The Body and Society: Explorations in Social Theory* (Oxford, 1984), 158–74 (followed, in places word-for-word, by Outram, *Body*, 17–21).

[8] Turner, *Body*, 158–74.

[9] Michel Foucault, *Histoire de la folie à l'âge classique* (Paris, 1972), 602, quoted in Eribon, *Foucault*, 121.

Yet in many ways Foucault's theory was crude and arbitrary too, and paid scant regard to the complexities of historical processes. Foucault saw human affairs above all in terms of authority and obedience. 'The tacit social theory of Foucault's *Discipline and Punish*', as Michael Ignatieff has remarked, 'describes all social relations in the language of power, domination and subordination.'[10] Likewise, the historian Lawrence Stone criticized the French philosopher's 'recurrent emphasis on control, domination, and punishment as the only mediating qualities possible in personal and social relationships.' In all his work, Stone alleged, 'we find a denial of the Enlightenment as an advance in human understanding and sensibility, and a causal linkage of it to the sexual fantasies of domination, violation, and torture which obsessed the mind of Sade.'[11] That Foucault also saw any limitations on sexual behaviour as inherently disciplinary and repressive, and argued for the decriminalization of pederasty and rape at this time,[12] was not unconnected with these arguments. For Foucault's book also had its particular, personal agenda. In his brilliant account of the philosopher's life and thought, the American writer James Miller has argued forcefully that Foucault was driven by a desire for what he called 'limit-experiences' of the body, achieved above all through the practice of sado-masochistic sex. It was not until after he had written *Discipline and Punish* that he discovered the most elaborate and extreme forms of sado-masochism in the gay bathhouses and clubs of San Francisco. Nevertheless, he had already found at least intellectual inspiration in the work of the Marquis de Sade, and running through much of his work in the 1970s is a Sado-Nietzschean view of history in which physical cruelty takes on the form of Dionysiac release. It was for this reason that he argued that public executions invested the crowd with a huge latent power, fuelled by the pleasure they gained in watching elaborate acts of torture performed on the malefactor, and expressed not only in the carnivalesque reversal of rules and overturning of authority that so frequently took place on such occasions, but also in the eruption of popular energy in events such as the September massacres. It was for this reason, too, that he argued that a figure such as the peasant Pierre Rivière, who hacked his mother, sister, and brother to death in 1835, then wrote a detailed description of the murders and the events that had led up to them, was a tragic hero whose gratuitous, Sadean act was a 'total contestation' of modern, disciplinary society, whose 'sacrificial and glorious murders' inspired 'a sort of reverence' and whose memoir was 'so strong and so strange that the crime ends up not existing any more'.[13]

[10] Michael Ignatieff, 'Recent Social Histories of Punishment', in Stanley Cohen and Andrew Scull (eds.), *Social Control and the State* (London, 1983), 75–105, here 97.

[11] Lawence Stone, 'An Exchange with Michel Foucault', *New York Review of Books*, 31 Mar. 1983, 42.

[12] James Miller, *The Passion of Michel Foucault* (London, 1993), 250–1, quoting interviews from 1977 and 1979. [13] Quoted in Miller, *Passion*, 225–7.

Sade and Nietzsche, therefore, were prominent among the spiritual mentors of *Discipline and Punish*. Foucault's book owed an immense amount to Nietzsche's thesis, advanced in the *Genealogy of Morals*, that human beings had once been creatures of instinct, and that public punishments had been cruel and fearful in order to burn the threat of retribution into the psyche of the onlooker with such force that it too became instinctual. But cruelty itself, Nietzsche went on, was a basic human instinct, and so public punishment was 'festive', a celebration as well as a curbing of the will to power and an impulse towards turning it inwards onto the self. Nietzsche argued that the moral repressiveness he saw all around him in Imperial Germany, the Victorian crushing of basic human impulses, was crippling society and robbing it of energy. So he called for the release of the Dionysiac impulses in humanity, the restoration of animality to the human condition, and, famously, the creation of the 'superman', whose will to knowledge and power would be untrammelled by any boundaries of law or convention, whose joy in life would be created through, and expressed in, the infliction and suffering of cruelty and pain.[14] Foucault modified this position by adding in the Sadean impulse to Nietzsche's concept of the Dinoysiac at one end of his history, and at the other by conceptualizing the repressiveness that Nietzsche so detested through the idea of panopticism, the total supervision and control, developed and legitimated by the growth of the disciplining and classificatory apparatuses of the medical, psychological, and social sciences, to which he believed the Sadean impulse was so fatally subjected in modern society.[15]

Factors such as this help explain why Foucault's vision of early modern punishment was so distorted. But they are less significant by far than the overall historical context of the time at which *Discipline and Punish* was written. Foucault himself taught us to minimize the importance of the individual author, and to emphasize rather the general discourse within which the individual author was writing. If such a procedure is applied to Foucault's own work of the early to mid-1970s, it quickly becomes clear that his ideas on the history and function of punishment were by no means so idiosyncratic as one might suppose. For it was not so much Nietzsche and de Sade, as Marx and Mao, who were the book's spiritual godfathers and presided over its inception. Despite its neglect of agency and causation, 'there is,' as the writer Michael Ignatieff observed, 'more than a touch of Marxist reductionism in Foucault's treatment of law as a pliable instrument of the ruling class.'[16] The reasons for this lie in the circumstances in which

---

[14] Friedrich Nietzsche, *On the Genealogy of Morals*, tr. Francis Goffing (New York, 1956), ii. §§ 16, 17, 18.

[15] Miller, *Passion*, 216–44.

[16] Ignatieff, 'Recent Social Histories of Punishment', 95. More generally, see Hans Steinert, 'Ist es aber auch wahr, Herr F.?', *Kriminalsoziologische Bibliographie*, 5 (1978), 30–45.

Discipline and Punish was written. Published in 1975, the book emerged from and contributed to a specific historical and intellectual context, not just in France, but also more generally. 'Social control' was one of the key concepts not only of much sociological work on deviance published in the early to mid-1970s but also of a good deal of historical research as well.[17] The powers of the state, exercised through the disciplining 'matrix of the authoritarian society',[18] in which the social order was stabilized by the classification of the population as conformist or deviant, were widely thought to have increased enormously with the Industrial Revolution, as the transition from the face-to-face world of the pre-industrial age to the anonymous, impersonal world of modern society rendered informal community sanctions useless.[19] Sociologists and historians taught that the ruling class under capitalism sustained itself by using the law as an instrument of class control, simultaneously indoctrinating the ruled into a belief that the combating of 'crime' was in their own best interests. This was the intellectual context into which *Discipline and Punish* fell.

Yet the book, as Michelle Perrot has remarked, was also developed out of Foucault's involvement in political struggles during the 1970s.[20] Previously a career academic of seemingly conformist demeanour, Foucault was politicized by the events of 1968, when student revolts in Paris began a chain of events that led to the downfall of General de Gaulle. A key event in this process was his experience of the brutal behaviour of the notorious French riot police, both against the ultra-leftists with whom he was now beginning to associate, and against the students of the radical University of Vincennes, where he was briefly head of the philosophy department in 1968–9. This directed his attention to the repressive apparatus of the state. He soon became involved in a campaign to improve prison conditions for political militants who had been arrested for incitement to violence and other, similar offences, and gravitated towards the Maoist hyper-radicals who were now making the running on the far left in France. At this time, the idea of unofficial tribunals or 'people's courts' was popular on the left. They were set up to try 'cases' ranging from American war crimes in Vietnam to individual cases of alleged brutality and murder by the prison and police authorities in France. But Foucault objected in principle to anything even resembling a court of law. Interviewed by a Maoist publication in February 1972, he argued that the very notion of a neutral judge and jury was 'bourgeois'. It implied, he said,

---

[17] Paul Rock and Mary McIntosh (eds.), *Deviance and Social Control* (London, 1974); Anthony P. Donajgrodzki (ed.), *Social Control in Nineteenth-Century Britain* (London, 1977).

[18] The phrase is taken from Hans-Ulrich Wehler, *Das deutsche Kaiserreich 1871–1918* (Göttingen, 1973).

[19] Howard S. Becker, 'Labelling Theory Reconsidered,' in Rock and McIntosh (eds.), *Deviance*, 41–66, here 60.

[20] Eribon, *Foucault*, 229, 236–7.

that there are categories which are common to the parties present (penal categories such as theft, fraud; moral categories such as honesty and dishonesty) and that the parties to the dispute agree to submit to them. Now, it is all this that the bourgeoisie wants to have believed in relation to justice, to its justice. All these ideas are weapons which the bourgeoisie has put to use in its exercise of power.

The law itself, therefore, any law, was nothing more than an instrument of bourgeois class rule.

Popular justice did not involve any kind of neutral arbiter, it simply involved 'the masses and their enemies'. Foucault's historical ideal in this respect was that of the September massacres of prison inmates in Paris, carried out during the French Revolution in 1792. He wrote:

The September executions were at one and the same time an act of war against internal enemies, a political act against the manipulations of those in power and an act of vengeance against the oppressive classes. Was this not—during a period of violent revolutionary struggle—at least an approximation to an act of popular justice; a response to oppression, strategically effective and politically necessary?

Foucault deplored the attempts made by the more organized revolutionaries in 1792 to intervene in the massacres by setting up tribunals to establish which of the prisoners should be killed. 'Can we not see', he asked. 'the embryonic, albeit fragile form of a state apparatus reappearing here?' The political task in hand could be explained, he said, historically:

In societies such as our own, the judicial apparatus has been an extremely important state apparatus of which the history has always been obscured. . . . There was a particular period when the penal system, of which the function in the Middle Ages had been essentially a fiscal one, became organized around the struggle to stamp out rebellion. Up until this point, the job of putting down popular uprisings had been primarily a military one. From now on it was to become taken on, or rendered unnecessary, by a complex system of courts/police/prison . . . This is why the revolution can only take place via the radical elimination of the judicial apparatus and anything which could reintroduce the penal apparatus, anything which could reintroduce its ideology, and enable this ideology to creep surreptitiously back into popular practices must be banished.[21]

Foucault sometimes protested that his political activities had nothing to do with his philosophical work, but in this case some scepticism is permitted. For these are the very themes that found their way into the heart of his analysis in *Discipline and Punish*. As he himself wrote at the end of the book's introductory chapter, the subject that interested him was not simply the past, nor even 'writing a history of the past in terms of the present', but rather, in view of his involvement in political campaigns at the time, 'writing the history of the present'.[22]

[21] Michel Foucault, *Power/Knowledge: Selected Interviews and Other Writings, 1972–1977*, ed. and tr. Colin Gordon (New York, 1980), 1–32.
[22] Foucault, *Discipline and Punish*, 31.

Foucault did not confine his admiration for popular justice, therefore, to the September massacres, but also put it into practice in his own day. One example of this was his involvement in the case of Pierre Leroy, a well-off, middle-class notary who was alleged to have murdered and mutilated the corpse of a young girl in the village of Bruay-en-Artois in 1972. While Leroy's friends in the local Rotary Club demanded his release, a crowd of villagers stoned his house and demanded that he be castrated. Their cause was taken up by the Parisian Maoists, whose newspaper *la cause du peuple* called for Leroy's lynching in the name of 'people's justice', and one of their leaders, François Ewald, took Foucault to the village to see things for himself. Foucault reportedly returned persuaded of Leroy's guilt—which was in fact never proven—and convinced that the Maoists had succeeded in politicizing the crime. He subsequently became involved in other attempts to build campaigns on individual cases of murder, or alleged murder, particularly where racist motives were held to have been involved.[23] Foucault retained his fascination for, and belief in, popular justice, and it resurfaced in an even more controversial form in a series of articles he wrote on the Iranian revolution in 1978. Seeing the uprising that overthrew the Shah as 'the most mad and most modern form of revolt', he praised the Teheran crowds for forging a genuine collective will which offered the possibility of a 'total transfiguration of this world' through the creation of a new form of 'political spirituality', under an authentic Islamic government which articulated 'the anger and aspirations of the community'. Early the next year, after the Shah had fled and been replaced by a new theocracy in which tens of thousands of Iranians were tortured and killed for no other reason than their Westernized habits and lifestyle, a regime which stoned adulterous women to death and sent homosexuals to the firing-squad, Foucault published another article praising 'the revolutionary experience' and declaring:

Last summer the Iranians said, 'We are ready to die by the thousand in order to get the Shah to go.' Today it is the Ayatollah who says, 'Let Iran bleed so that the revolution may be strong.' There is a strange echo between these phrases which links them to one another. Does the horror of the second condemn the rapture of the first?

This, then, is the milieu of political engagement out of which *Discipline and Punish* emerged, and on which many of its ideas were based.[24]

Foucault's half-Maoist, half-anarchist position in the early to mid-1970s was in no way untypical of the far left at this time. For this was the period when the heady optimism of 1968 was giving way to a grimmer, more despairing mood, in which the powers of authority seemed greater, more pervasive, more immovable

[23] Macey, *Lives*, 298–303.
[24] Ibid. 304–6; Miller, *Passion*, 203–7, 306–4. See also Stephan Breuer, 'Foucaults Theorie der Disziplinargesellschaft. Eine Zwischenbilanz', *Leviathan*, 15 (1987), 319–37.

than they had done in the hopeful atmosphere of the year of student revolts. In other countries too, a significant part of the far left gravitated towards a cult of political violence, as the possibilities of a peaceful transformation of the political system seemed to recede into the distance. In Germany this led to the armed robbery, arson, kidnapping, and terrorist campaigns of the Baader–Meinhof gang, justified by their many intellectual sympathizers in vague but extreme terms as an attack on capitalism and its symbols and a resurrection of the armed proletarian resistance of the early Weimar years.[25] In the USA this was a time when prison revolts were seen by the left as political events and the violent rhetoric of the Black Panthers made them into cult figures among radicals.[26] In Britain the early to mid-1970s saw the radical deviancy theorists of the previous decade abandon the hopes of reform with which they had begun. The old 'new criminologists' of the 1960s had held out the prospect of a liberal social order in which nonconformists would no longer be labelled as criminal, and in which tolerance and permissiveness would flourish.[27] Their successors of the mid- to late 1970s abandoned this optimism and retreated into a crude, economistic Marxism where everything they had fought for now appeared to be no more than a means of shoring up the bourgeois capitalist state and social order.[28]

Yet the hyper-radical moment of the mid-1970s was not to last for long. Foucault's total repudiation of the law, of any law, as merely an instrument of domination—an 'ideological state apparatus', to borrow the phrase of the French structuralist Marxist Louis Althusser, whose influence was at its height in the mid-1970s[29]—was never widely accepted on the left, as his dialogues with the Maoists indicated. As the influence of the feminist movement grew, so the implementation of penal sanctions against rape and the physical and sexual abuse of women and children gained a new legitimacy. By the late 1980s all but a tiny minority on the fringes of the left had also come to accept the murderous, even genocidal potential of unregulated, revolutionary justice as practised by the Parisian crowd in the September massacres of 1792. It had been all too dramati-

[25] Stefan Aust, *The Baader–Meinhof Group: The Inside Story of a Phenomenon* (London, 1985).

[26] For a classic account of the most important of the revolts, see Tom Wicker, *A Time to Die: The Attica Prison Revolt* (London, 1976).

[27] Stanley Cohen (ed.), *Images of Deviance* (Harmondsworth, 1971); Ian Taylor and Laurie Taylor (eds.), *Politics and Deviance* (Harmondsworth, 1973); Stanley Cohen, *Folk Devils and Moral Panics: The Creation of the Mods and Rockers* (London, 1972); and Jock Young, *The Drugtakers* (London, 1971).

[28] See especially Ian Taylor, Paul Walton, and Jock Young (eds.), *Critical Criminology* (London, 1975); Frank Pearce, *Crimes of the Powerful: Marxism, Crime and Deviance* (London, 1976); John Clarke *et al.* (eds.), *Permissiveness and Control: The Fate of the Sixties Legislation* (London, 1980); and Bob Fine *et al.* (eds.), *Capitalism and the Rule of Law: From Deviancy Theory to Marxism* (London, 1979). As late as 1983, work within this paradigm could still be carried out entirely free from Foucault's influence: see e.g. Steven Box, *Power, Crime, and Mystification* (London, 1983).

[29] For E. P. Thompson's self-indulgent but effective polemic against Althusser, see his book *The Poverty of Theory and Other Essays* (London, 1978).

cally illustrated by the Stalinist liquidation of the kulaks in Russia, the excesses of the 'cultural revolution' in China, and the brutal exterminism of the Pol Pot regime in Cambodia. The case against Foucault's hostility to any form of law or tribunal was eloquently put at the time by the great Marxist historian E. P. Thompson, whose studies of law, capitalism, and society in eighteenth-century England, *Whigs and Hunters* and *Albion's Fatal Tree*—the latter written in collaboration with a group of younger colleagues—appeared in 1975, the same year as *Discipline and Punish*. These works represented the perspective of an alternative, radical historiography which sought to unmask the alleged stability and tranquillity of the period as a metaphor for the oppression of the common people by a grasping and corrupt landed capitalist oligarchy. Yet, although the law had been systematically used by this oligarchy to legitimize and cement its domination, Thompson rightly warned against the crude reductionism which saw the law simply as an instrument of control and nothing else. 'For', he wrote, 'there is a very large difference, which twentieth-century experience ought to have made clear even to the most exalted thinker, between arbitrary extra-legal power and the rule of law. . . . People', Thompson observed, 'are not as stupid as some structuralist philosophers suppose them to be':

If the law is evidently partial and unjust, then it will mask nothing, legitimize nothing, contribute nothing to any class's hegemony. The essential precondition for the effectiveness of law, in its function as ideology, is that it shall display an independence from gross manipulation and shall seem to be just. It cannot seem to be so without upholding its own logic and criteria of equity; indeed, on occasion, by actually *being* just. . . . The rhetoric and the rules of a society are something a great deal more than sham. In the same moment they may modify, in profound ways, the behaviour of the powerful, and mystify the powerless. They may disguise the true realities of power, but, at the same time, they may curb that power and check its intrusions. And it is often from within that very rhetoric that a radical critique of the practice of the society is developed.

The rule of law, the elaboration of a set of rules for regulating human conflict, was, Thompson concluded, a 'cultural achievement of universal human significance'. The realities of power meant, to be sure, that it had seldom been wholly realized. Yet without a firm belief in its virtues, the struggle against tyranny would be impossible.

Thompson castigated the ultra-radicals of the 1970s who made no distinction between 'bourgeois' democracy and fascist dictatorship, between the arbitrary exercise of power and the effective rule of law:

We ought to expose the shams and inequities which may be concealed beneath this law. But the rule of law itself, the imposing of effective inhibitions upon power and the defence of the citizen from power's all-intrusive claims, seems to me to be an unqualified human good. To deny or belittle this good is, in this dangerous century when the resources and pretensions of power continue to enlarge, a desperate error of intellectual abstraction. More than this, it is a self-fulfilling error, which encourages us to give up the struggle against bad laws and class-bound procedures, and to disarm ourselves before power.

In warning against such a political error, Thompson was also warning in part against the historical error which treated laws, penal policies, and judicial reforms as nothing more than instruments of control.[30] His critique might almost have been aimed directly at Foucault's book. For if there has been one criticism above all others of the French philosopher's work, it is that it implicitly denies the possibility of resistance to all-pervasive discourses which shape people's behaviour by structuring the language in which they conceive it. Society appears as a clear field, a *tabula rasa* on which the dominant discourse inscribes itself. The *ancien régime* had allowed people their negotiated illegalities. The disciplinary society of the modern world had taken this freedom away. Yet this view sees power too much, as Michael Ignatieff has commented, 'as a strategy, as an instrumentality, never as a social relation between contending social forces . . . Foucault's conception of the disciplinary world view, the *savoir* as he calls it, effectively forecloses on the possibility that the *savoir* itself was a site of contradiction, argument and conflict.'[31] Because he was not a historian, but a philosopher, who was uninterested in problems of agency and causation, and carried out his archival researches in a casual and unsystematic way, Foucault was unaware of, or unwilling to recognize, the contingency of historical outcomes. In the real past world, the disciplinary discourse, as we have seen throughout this book, was multifaceted, fragmented, disputed, contested, mediated by social relations, and never more than partially realized.[32]

Foucault himself came to recognize after 1975 that the political and intellectual position which he took in *Discipline and Punish* and in his other work in the area of penal policy was too close for comfort to what his fellow philosopher Gilles Deleuze called the 'micro-fascism' of the ultra-left, the cult of violence and despair that brought it perilously near to the murderous impulses of the Nazi era. Foucault himself subsequently regretted the political positions he took at this time, and his revolutionary enthusiasm had largely disappeared by the beginning of the 1980s. He later criticized some of his political activities of this period, and eventually abandoned his advocacy of popular justice along revolutionary lines.[33] He repudiated the untrammelled Sadean impulses which he had formerly celebrated as the ultimate 'total contestation' of modern social norms. No longer

[30] E. P. Thompson, *Whigs and Hunters: The Origin of the Black Act* (London, 1975), 258–69; see also Hay *et al.*, *Albion's Fatal Tree*.

[31] Ignatieff, 'Recent Social Histories of Punishment', 86.

[32] For criticisms of Foucault as an historian, see in particular Michelle Perrot (ed.), *L'Impossible Prison. Recherches sur le système pénitentiaire au XIXe siècle* (Paris, 1980).

[33] Macey, *Lives*, 198–304, and Miller, *Passion*, 231–3.

was transgression welcomed in his work as an unqualified good. Instead, in his later thought, he pointed to the link between de Sade's ideal of a 'society of blood' which would embrace savagery, suffering, cruelty, and death, and 'the fascism in us all', the yearning for 'a violent, dictatorial, and even bloody power' which had found its ultimate expression in the 'absolutely murderous state' that Hitler built. In a curious way, therefore, he had come unwittingly to echo Thompson's sombre warning about the self-fulfilling potential of a nihilistic critique of justice, and for much the same political and historical reasons. For the remaining years of his life, he would turn from the advent of the disciplinary society in the nineteenth century to the study of sexuality in the ancient world, in a quest for a Nietzschean state of transcendence not only beyond good and evil, but also beyond death and desire.[34]

c. *Cultural Change and Capital Punishment*

If the views put forward by Foucault at the time of *Discipline and Punish* are in some ways ill-equipped to deliver specific historical explanations, then it is necessary to turn to others for enlightenment. As we saw in the Introduction, a major contribution was made to this subject by Norbert Elias, writing in exile from Hitler's Third Reich, in 1939. Elias developed his concept of the 'civilizing process' in Western Europe in conscious opposition to the Nazi view of Western European decadence. Where the Nazis placed their emphasis on Germany's rejection of Western European values, Elias sought to reinstate them as the basis of a civilized society and to insist on their universal validity. He was writing, essentially, in defence of the traditional liberal idea of progress, in defence of the Enlightenment, against an ideology that rejected these things. A critic of the rabid nationalism espoused by the Nazis, he accepted the historical and cultural validity of the nation-state, but saw it in the end as only a step along the road to his ideal of a world government, a government that would in his view build on the achievements of European civilization over the past five hundred years. Yet, however understandable and defensible it may have been in its original historical context, Elias's Eurocentrism inevitably appears in a very different light today. As more than one critic has pointed out, his use of the term 'civilization' is more than a little unfortunate in its implication that cultures which eat their meals without using knives and forks, expose their nakedness to the gaze of all, or lack

---

[34] Miller, *Passion*, 241–2. Partly under the influence of Foucault's work, more perhaps under the impact of the decay of the legal system in their own country, some American writers have recently revived some of the arguments of the 1970s and suggested that all legal systems are entirely arbitrary. Judges make their decisions, it has been argued, only on *ad hoc* grounds, influenced by the political context they are in. (Stanley Fish, *There's No Such Thing as Free Speech and It's a Good Thing Too* (Oxford, 1994)). This argument, however, is open to the same objections as Foucault's.

the basic feelings of embarrassment and shame at the basic functions of the body, are somehow 'uncivilized' and lagging behind the Europeans in their historical development. To portray the repression of the animal side of human nature as the great achievement of European civilization necessarily implies that non-European indigenous peoples living in stateless societies are somehow closer to the animals, somehow less human. European customs are elevated in this theory into the universal measure of what is good. Thus Elias's theory implicitly justifies racism and imperialism, as they were indeed practised by the liberal states such as Britain and France whose political cultures he so admired when he wrote his book.[35] Quite apart from these disturbing implications of the theory, however, anthropologists have amassed a great deal of data to demonstrate that nudity and emotionality can go together in some societies with peaceful and altruistic behaviour,[36] while the evolutionary content of the theory seems to be confounded by the progressive dismantling of the formal rules of etiquette and the advent of the 'permissive society' in Europe since the 1960s. Moreover, whether what Elias considers to be basic human instincts, such as aggression, anger, genital sexuality, self-preservation, and so on, which were tamed in the course of the civilizing process, really are universal, as he argues on the basis of psychoanalytic theory, or whether they are variable in terms of culture, gender, and history, is more than open to question.[37] Looked at half a century later, therefore, and considered on a global scale, Elias's fundamental cultural and historical equations simply do not seem to work.

Equally problematical is Elias's implicit view of the medieval European as a childish individual, subject to uncontrollable emotion, a creature of pure, unadulterated passion.[38] The aggressiveness of the medieval knight in armour, far from being merely brutish, as Elias sees it, was, as many historians have shown in great detail, highly ritualized. The same goes, in the context of the present work, for the punishments and sanctions which were mobilized against deviants and malefactors. An early modern execution was no outburst of insensate rage on the part of the community, no act of personal or symbolic revenge by the sovereign. In considering the application of Elias's theory to this area of study by his disciple Spierenburg, one inevitably runs up against the problem of linking the theory with the evidence. Spierenburg delivers a careful empirical account of early

---

[35] See the critique by Anton Blok, reported by Nico Wilterdink, 'Die Zivilisationstheorie im Kreuzfeuer der Diskussion. Ein Bericht vom Kongress über Zivilisationsprozesse in Amsterdam', in Peter Gleichmann, Johan Goudsblom, and Hermann Korte (eds.), *Macht und Zivilisation. Materialien zu Norbert Elias' Zivilisationstheorie*, ii (Frankfurt am Main, 1984), 280–304, esp. 287–91.

[36] Hans-Peter Duerr, *Nacktheit und Scham. Der Mythos vom Zivilisationsprozess*, i (Frankfurt am Main, 1988).

[37] Wilterdink, 'Zivilisationstheorie', 296–8.

[38] Spierenburg, *Broken Spell*, passim.

modern punishments, and details their decline and eventual supersession very clearly; he establishes beyond any doubt the long-term nature of the historical change which this represented. These findings have been amply confirmed by the evidence brought forward in the present study. But Spierenburg's linkage of all this to the rise of the modern state, the growth of national self-consciousness, and in broad, general terms the 'civilizing process', as posited by Elias, is no more than conjectural. Spierenburg presents no evidence to support his view that late medieval and early modern punishment was a form of revenge visited upon the malefactor by the injured sovereign. Nor does he take sufficient account of the elements of popular and community justice or of religious ritual in the penal ceremonies of the seventeenth and eighteenth centuries. He exaggerates beyond what is permissible the contrast between the insecurity of the early modern European state and the stability of its nineteenth- and twentieth-century successors: the state in the seventeenth and eighteenth centuries was certainly able to maintain internal order reasonably well during times of peace, while the modern state has equally certainly suffered major waves of crime and violence at times of crisis, such as 1918–23, 1929–33, and 1945–8 in Germany. Finally, Spierenburg provides no evidence at all to demonstrate that objections to public punishment resulted from a process of 'conscience formation' in which the different groups in a given state came to identify more closely with one another, and each individual began to empathize with the sufferings of others. This may be because he does not trouble to describe the actual process of reform in any detail, or provide any information about the reformers and their motives. His research stops before the reforms begin. It may also be because there is in fact no evidence for 'conscience formation' in attitudes to public executions in eighteenth- and nineteenth-century Germany, as we have seen. Capital punishment's relationship with state formation seems to have been positive rather than negative. With the rise of the modern state, the right of execution, of power over life and death, came to be monopolized by the state and treated as an essential aspect of sovereignty. The systematic use of the royal and princely clemency dated from the emergence of Absolutism. By reprieving offenders who had been condemned to death by due process of law, sovereigns demonstrated that they were above it. In practice, of course, their room for manœuvre in dispensing with the law in most areas was fairly limited, and in this sense, the royal clemency was more symbolic than real. Nevertheless, it was tenaciously defended by sovereigns throughout Europe during the eighteenth and nineteenth centuries. It was this, more than anything else—more even than popular support for capital punishment, which was scarcely able to be articulated politically before the advent of democracy—that ensured the survival of capital punishment through its decades of crisis from the 1840s to the 1880s, at a time when it seemed to run counter to the penal principles in which most of the political class had come to believe. Most strikingly of all, the affirmation of capital punishment came to be an integral part of the foundation of the German Empire in 1870–1 and its renewal under conservative auspices in 1878–9.

This raises in turn the question of German exceptionality, a question which was central to the genesis of Elias's own work, though it has largely been neglected in that of his disciples. Was it the case, in the end, that Germany's experience of power, violence, cruelty, terror, and death inflicted by the state upon its citizens differed significantly over the long run from the experience of other European states in this respect? The English traveller John Taylor, with whose description of a German execution this study opened, certainly underlined the drastic nature of German punishments in comparison to those current in his homeland, though he did so partly, of course, in order to titillate his readership by an adroit piece of early modern sensationalism. But were the differences really so great? Englishmen were still having their ears, noses, and hands cut off in public decades after Taylor wrote, they were still put in the stocks or the pillory, publicly whipped, branded, and otherwise bodily maimed and mutilated by the emissaries of the law and the state well into the eighteenth century, and traitors were still hanged before large crowds, cut down while still alive, and publicly disembowelled in England a hundred years and more after Taylor penned his ironic encomia to the mildness of the English hangman. The fact is that, while there were of course national variations in the chronology of penal reform, they cannot be made to add up to a long-term, deep-rooted deviation of Germany from the 'normal path' taken by the rest of Western Europe. The death penalty was no exception in this regard. Corporal punishment lasted far longer in Britain than it did in Germany or France; transportation to penal colonies was the prerogative of countries with large and far-flung colonial empires of a sort that Germany did not acquire until the legitimacy of transportation was under threat. The ameliorative principle was adopted across Europe in the early nineteenth century. State formation did not lead to the permanent abolition of the death penalty in the classic lands of nationalism such as France and Italy.

German exceptionality lay in the early abolition of capital punishment for theft, and the relatively low incidence of executions from the middle of the eighteenth century onwards, up to the end of the Weimar Republic. The penal reforms undertaken in England by Sir Robert Peel, with his abrogation of the 'Bloody Code' and his introduction of a professional police force in the late 1820s, were only following the example set by the Enlightened monarchs of Central Europe a good three-quarters of a century before. None the less, what strikes the observer of this period of European history is the fact that similar changes in penal practice happened virtually everywhere at roughly the same epoch. In almost all major European states, the eighteenth and early nineteenth centuries saw a diminution of public punishment, the abolition of torture, the banishing of the more baroque cruelties from the scene of the scaffold, and the decisive phase in the rise of imprisonment. Everywhere, the middle of the nineteenth century saw the ending of public executions, or at least their restriction to a small number of spectators and the stripping-away of the most elaborate embellishments of public ritual associated with them. Even in France, severe restrictions were placed on the publicity of capital punishment at this time. The contrast which might at first sight appear with France diminishes when it is remembered that the French held executions outside prison gates, with relatively few spectators, from the middle of the nineteenth century onwards, while the Germans admitted scores, sometimes hundreds of spectators to executions for many decades after they began to be held inside prisons. Right across Europe, the same period saw the culmination of a long-heralded crisis in the legitimacy of capital punishment, as liberal penal reformers came to argue that the death penalty was incompatible with the ameliorative principles which had come to govern the philosophy and practice of criminal justice. By international standards, the number of people executed in Prussia and the other German states was relatively low from the middle of the eighteenth century onwards; by comparison with England and Wales, indeed, it was tiny, and remained low even after the ending of the 'Bloody Code' in the later 1820s and 1830s. After a rise in the 1850s, capital punishment almost ceased in Germany in the 1870s, in contrast to its continued operation in many other parts of Western Europe. Even after its effective resumption in the 1880s, it was applied sparingly by international standards, and it virtually ceased to operate once more in the later stages of the Weimar Republic. As far as the history of penal sanctions in general, and the death penalty in particular, are concerned, there is no evidence that the Germans were more inclined to cruelty, brutality, and the infliction of suffering, pain, and death than were other European nations in the eighteenth and nineteenth centuries as a whole.

Elias's arguments about the deficits of the 'civilizing process' in Germany were, to be sure, advanced on a broader front than this. But most of his assertions rest on very little evidence and have been seriously undermined by subsequent research. His idea, for instance, that the German bourgeoisie adopted the habits of the military aristocracy without internalizing their civilized values is mere conjecture; there is a mass of research, mostly carried out in the 1980s, that demonstrates the German bourgeoisie to have had its own value-system, its own culture, and its own well-defined set of attitudes, which were largely shared by the professional, industrial, and financial middle classes elsewhere in Western Europe and indeed assimilated to a very considerable extent by the German aristocracy in the course of the nineteenth century.[39] There is nothing in the history of attitudes to the death penalty in England or France to suggest that capital punishment was 'feudal', 'aristocratic', or 'pre-industrial' and that opposition to it came from 'modern' or 'bourgeois' forces in society, even though that is how the abolitionists in Germany frequently portrayed it. On a more general level, Elias's argument that the Germans 'regressed' to earlier levels of barbarism because the German state had never been stable enough to allow them to internalize the control of aggression once more lacks any real empirical foundation. France, after all, experienced a succession of revolutionary changes of state system, from monarchy to republic and empire twice over, in the course of the nineteenth century. Moreover, there was a strong degree of institutional continuity in areas such as police and penal policy, across the different regimes in Germany. Germany did indeed develop nationhood relatively late, though Elias overdraws the contrast by confusing England with Britain, where national identity was essentially the creation of the era of the French Revolution.[40] But the extent to which nationhood gave, say, the French a feeling of empathy with, and emotional restraint towards, their fellow citizens, must be doubted, as the violent and bloody conflicts which litter modern French history, from the massacre of the Communards in 1871 to the mass slaughter of collaborators with the occupying Germans in 1944–5 would seem to suggest.

Elias's assumption that various human desires and emotions are 'natural' is nowhere more questionable than in his thesis that the Germans desired unity throughout their modern history, and longed for a strong leader who would be able to provide it. The evidence for this, such as it is, consists of selective quotations from a small number of German authors who were in no way representative of the general view, if indeed there was one. This applies equally to all of Elias's generalizations about 'the Germans', such as their alleged lack of political realism and their unwillingness to compromise when the interests of the nation were at stake. There is as little concrete basis for these suppositions as there is for Elias's belief that the Germans were made politically submissive by their long tradition of Absolutist monarchy.[41] Germany from the late nineteenth century was not a politically indifferent and deferential society, but on the contrary highly politicized, with astonishingly high voter participation rates in elections, and a level of political mobilization in the Weimar Republic that has seldom been surpassed in any modern society. Germany's peculiarities lay far more in the depth and complexity of the country's internal divisions—social, regional, religious, generational, gender-based—than in the tenacity of its Ab-

---

[39] Elias, *Studien*, 13; Blackbourn and Evans (eds.), *The German Bourgeoisie*.
[40] Elias, *Studien*, 417–19.
[41] Ibid. 514–15.

solutist tradition, the strength and universality of which has been seriously overestimated by many historians in the past. The trouble with all this is that it differentiates insufficiently between the constituent groups of this deeply divided society—groups which, as we have seen, varied widely in their attitudes to subjects such as capital punishment and the penal system in the late nineteenth and early twentieth centuries, as they differed about so many central aspects of political principle and practice.

Ultimately, Elias gained his notions of German peculiarity from a kind of history of ideas approach which made a handful of writers representative of a whole society. The inadequacies of such an approach have long been apparent.[42] More fundamentally, however, the weakness in Elias's general theory is that it does not satisfactorily link the 'civilizing process', in areas such as social mores and the growth of manners, to the political history, and above all to the phenomena of Nazism and mass murder, which it is trying to explain. There is, unfortunately, nothing to suggest that Nazi anti-Semitism was a regressive outburst of uncontrolled, childish destructiveness; nothing to suggest that the 'civilizing process' in areas such as political and racial violence is continuing or irreversible. We might wish to use the word 'barbarism' to express our moral disapproval of the Third Reich, but as a theoretical concept it will not do, and in any case, taken at any level deeper than the merely rhetorical, it is an insult to barbarians to apply the term to the crimes of Hitler's Germany. Elias's great work, born as a tremendous attempt to achieve a historical and intellectual understanding of the process that led to his own exile from the country in which he was born, and to the death of his mother in Auschwitz, ironically works much better as an exercise in the history of everyday life than as a contribution to the history and prehistory of Nazi exterminism.

The German experience of capital punishment in the nineteenth century differed from that of Britain and France not in terms of culture or civiliization but in terms of politics. Only in Germany did the abolition of the death penalty become identified, above all through the experience of 1848, as a central tenet of political liberalism. Only in Germany did the retention of capital punishment come to serve so powerfully as a symbol of sovereignty, authority, and the rejection of liberal beliefs such as tolerance, participation, and the freedom of the individual. As we have seen, the rise and fall of the execution rate in nineteenth-century Germany mirrored precisely the varying fortunes of liberalism and authoritarianism. No such pattern can be observed in the case of France, despite the frequent changes of regime which took place during the period. From the Restoration through to the liberal 'July Monarchy', the radical Second Republic,

---

[42] See the various essays in Richard J. Evans (ed.), *Society and Politics in Wilhelmine Germany* (London, 1978), for a critique.

the dictatorship of Napoleon III, the 'liberal Empire' of the late 1860s, the conservative Third Republic, and the triumph of radical republicanism after the Dreyfus affair, the alternation of liberal and authoritarian periods of government in French history left no trace in the administration of the death penalty. The fundamental dividing lines of French politics in the nineteenth century and for long afterwards were drawn by the French Revolution of 1789–94. Given the role played by the guillotine in the Revolution, it was scarcely surprising that the left in France was disinclined to fight for the abolition of the death penalty; while, on the other side of the dividing line, adherents of the right stoutly defended its use, as most European conservatives did, to suppress rebellion against legitimate authority.

In Britain, too, governments of the right and the left came and went without any noticeable impact on the administration of capital punishment. In the 1830s there was a widespread consensus between the Conservative leader Sir Robert Peel, whose reforms had begun the abolition of the 'Bloody Code' and the reduction of execution rates to the European norm, and the Whig governments who pushed these reforms through to their conclusion after the extension of the franchise in 1832. The ending of public executions in 1868 was intended not least to confer greater legitimacy on the death penalty and bring it more closely under state control: it emasculated the cause of abolition in England for the best part of a century. In Germany, by contrast, while public executions were abolished for much the same reasons, the close identification of the death penalty with the triumph of reaction in the 1850s—a period which saw execution levels soar far above those being experienced in England at the time—ensured that abolition remained a liberal cause *par excellence.* Correspondingly, the defeat of abolition was the inevitable concomitant of the defeat of liberalism later in the century. In the 1880s, the reintroduction of the death penalty as a normal part of penal policy signalled the triumph of Bismarck's creation of a conservative regime on the domestic front. Executions had become an easy way of demonstrating the state's determination to resist the forces of revolution long before Hödel was sacrificed to Bismarck's desire to advertise his hostility to the Social Democrats; they were increased sharply by Wilhelm II in 1892 as soon as he decided that making friends with the workers had been a mistake. In the Weimar Republic, abolition became a token of democratic reconciliation, and correspondingly, from the very beginning of their regime, the Nazis turned to it almost without thinking as a symbol of their extreme rejection of 'Jewish liberalism' and everything it stood for. By the time this happened, the administration of the death penalty had already become inextricably intertwined with notions of eugenic purification and the elimination of criminality from the chain of heredity. In bringing all this together with a monomaniacal reduction of everything to a question of race, the Nazis had already pre-programmed the exterminism of the Third Reich a decade before they came to power. They implemented it with a ferocity among whose lesser by-products was an expansion of capital punishment far beyond anything experienced elsewhere, even in Fascist Italy, where the reintroduction of the death penalty in 1931 led to a total of precisely eighty-nine executions by the time that Mussolini was ousted from power twelve years later.[43]

One of the most striking peculiarities of German history from the 1840s to the 1940s was the way in which social problems and tensions were diverted upwards into politics.[44] This was particularly true of crime and social disorder. The determination of Enlightenment reformers to remould human nature through a rational and graded system of punishment quickly ran up against the limits of cost and of practicability. All the way through the nineteenth century, parsimonious governments denied the prison administration the funds the reformers wanted to make it effective. Society was cushioned by a long-term decline in violence which, for all the occasional scares and moral panics which affected it, relegated penal policy to a political issue of no more than secondary importance. Under Wilhelm II, however, and no doubt encouraged by his violent rhetoric and his unprecedentedly frequent use of the death penalty, a culture of violence began to emerge, reversing this social process and creating a growing social concern at the sharp rise in the homicide rate which had taken place by the outbreak of the First World War. Dramatized in public trials such as those of Sternickel, Haarmann, and Kürten, this culture of violence increasingly led to calls to violate the bodily integrity of offenders through the use of eugenic intervention and the death penalty. The Nazi movement was a child of this culture, nurtured in the exponential increase in violence represented by the First World War: the control, disciplining, invasion, and ultimately the extermination of the human body. Capital punishment, always more political than penal, served as a central symbol of Nazi intentions and a key component of the terroristic techniques of rule adopted in the Third Reich, until it too became swallowed up in the wider policies of extermination which the peculiarities of its development in Germany over the previous century had ultimately encouraged.

d. *Experiences of Mortality, Harbingers of Destruction*

If neither the 'emergence of a carceral society' nor the deficit of 'the civilizing process' seems in its broad outlines to fit the long and complicated story we have followed in these pages, then perhaps the history of capital punishment in

---

[43] Düsing, *Abschaffung*, 249.
[44] For this argument, see Blackbourn and Eley, *Peculiarities, passim*.

Germany will be better illuminated by the research done by historians such as Philippe Ariès on the history of death. Certainly Ariès, who had a much better knowledge of social history than either Foucault or Elias, pointed in his work to a number of changes in attitudes to death, and the experience of other people's death by the living, which seem to fit in quite well with the long-term historical changes which took place in the administration of the death penalty in Germany over the period covered by this book. The change from the eighteenth-century pattern of dying on the scaffold amidst elaborate rituals, in front of a large crowd, with massive all-round publicity, to the twentieth-century pattern of dying in a courtyard or chamber, with little or no ceremony, virtually alone, and in conditions of considerable secrecy, can be seen as a clear parallel to the broader transition of dying from a public to a private, a collectively celebrated to a lonely and largely hidden act. In so far as the history of capital punishment is part of the history of death, it shares the principal features of this broader transition; and attitudes to capital punishment obviously reflect attitudes to death in a broader sense. The same factors might therefore help account for the changes observable over time in both: above all, the demographic transition, from a society in which life expectancy was low, and death a common, everyday occurrence, to one in which life expectancy is high, and death an uncommon experience. Early modern society was not callous or indifferent to death, but it did require all kinds of psychological assistance in coming to terms with its omnipresence. Ritual enactments and religious ceremonies occupied a central place in this process; and the spectacle of a 'good death' enacted on the scaffold played its part here too. Moreover, in the absence of antibiotics, antisepsis, anaesthetics, and the other devices which modern society has to reduce the burden of physical suffering, most people in the seventeenth and eighteenth centuries suffered for most of the time from bodily ailments, injuries, deformities, sicknesses, and pain of one kind or another. The mental and spiritual adjustments which this caused them to make had a profound effect on their attitudes to the infliction of pain and the violation of bodily boundaries, and permitted the kind of public corporal and capital punishments which later ages came to regard as barbaric.

While early modern and medieval society had thus by necessity evolved many different ways of coming to terms with death, however, it is important not to become nostalgic about them. These attitudes cannot simply be regarded as positive. A well-prepared, calm, and peaceful death of the sort described by Ariès was, after all, only a rarely attained ambition in this society: accidents, interpersonal violence, sudden attacks of illness, unexpected and violent death in many forms were all normal, far more so than in modern society. In relying so much on literary models for his theory, Ariès fell into the trap of taking the ideal for reality. An active fascist in the inter-war years, and a far-right publicist after

1945, he was led to history by the political enthusiasm for a purely imaginary Middle Ages which characterized the *Action Française*, of which he was a member; and if his immersion in the material, and his craftsmanship as an historian, led him far away from these intellectual roots, a strong element of nostalgia nevertheless remained.[45] It is permissible, therefore, to see the early modern attitudes to death revealed in the present book in a more critical light. This was, in the end, a society in which life was relatively cheap, and in which sanctions against physical cruelty, to people and also to animals, were relatively weak. The sufferings of the body caused it to be regarded as relatively unimportant in comparison to the soul. Religious faith held out the prospect of a better life to come, a life which physical pain in some ways made it easier to attain. It was in this context that public executions attained their real significance. For, as the French writer Albert Camus observed,

the supreme punishment has always been, throughout the centuries, a religious penalty. Inflicted in the name of the King, God's representative on earth, or by priests in the name of society considered as a sacred body; it denies, not human solidarity but the guilty man his membership in the divine community, the only thing that can give him life. Life on earth is taken from him, to be sure, but his chance of making amends is left him. The real judgement is not pronounced; it will be in the other world. Only religious values, and especially belief in eternal life, can therefore serve as a basis for the supreme punishment, because, according to their own logic, they keep it from being definitive and irreparable.[46]

Correspondingly, as we have seen, it was only with the beginnings of secularization in the Enlightenment that capital punishment began to be submitted to a critique. It was above all the growing belief that death was final which prompted Enlightened and above all liberal thinkers to feel that capital punishment was indeed irreparable. Once the rationalistic policies of deterrence introduced by Enlightened reforms such as the Prussian General Law Code of 1794 were seen to have failed, there seemed to an increasingly large body of informed opinion to be no logical reason for retaining the death penalty at all.

Secularization, the decline in religious belief and practice, accompanied the rationalization and bureaucratization of punishment and underpinned it in terms of both élite and popular attitudes. It was a far-reaching process in nineteenth-century Germany, marching in pace with rapid industrialization and urbanization. Well before the end of the century, Germany's great cities were described as 'spiritual cemeteries', where the vast mass of people were scarcely even aware of Christianity, let alone inclined to practise it.[47] The Christian

[45] Philippe Ariès, *Un historien du dimanche* (Paris, 1980).
[46] Camus, 'Reflections', 158. See also Bée, 'Spectacle', and Potter, *Hanging*, 160–6.
[47] See Evans, *Rethinking*, ch. 4, for a survey of these developments.

Churches, Catholic and Protestant, and the political groupings most closely associated with them, were the most consistent supporters of capital punishment during this period, and the groups most hostile to them—in particular, the Social Democrats—were the most consistent advocates of abolition. The secularization not only of the working-class but also of the middle-class mind in the second half of the nineteenth century involved placing a higher value on human life than on the redemption of the disembodied soul after death, and underpinned the crisis of capital punishment observable in German society and politics from the 1840s to the 1880s. Popular support for capital punishment, expressed obliquely through the magico-religious practices which depended on it, was not transferred from rural society to the urban working class. The retention of the death penalty by Wilhelm I of Prussia and his grandson Wilhelm II owed something at least to their conception of their own sovereign powers as divinely ordained. While secularist and anticlerical left-liberals and Social Democrats continued to dispute these powers, however, eugenics began to supply a new justification of the death penalty based on secular rationality; one which had made substantial advances among middle-class opinion by 1914, spread still further during the 1920s, and became official government policy with the Nazi seizure of power. Underlying changing attitudes to capital punishment were changing attitudes to death: from the death of the body and release of the soul into eternity, to the final death of the individual, to death as the elimination of a link in the chain of heredity. In this sense, the links posited by Ariès between the rise of individualism and the rise of new attitudes to death are plausible ones. In Germany the attack on individualism launched by Social Darwinists and eugenicists from the 1890s onwards, where the death of the individual body was regarded as justifiable in the interests of the larger entity of the nation or the race, went further than elsewhere and acquired more widespread support. It too can be seen as an aspect of secularization, drawing on the rejection of religion just as much as the movement for the abolition of the death penalty had done in the middle decades of the nineteenth century.

The attack by Enlightenment legislators in the late eighteenth and early nineteenth centuries on the religious aspects of executions, which they saw as frustrating the secular purpose of deterrence through the religious glorification of the malefactor, shattered the early modern synthesis of élite and popular culture which had persisted in the execution ritual even when it had decayed in other areas. The decline of a feudal or neo-feudal 'society of orders' based on hereditarily ascribed status and institutionalized through serfdom, in the guilds, and by the law, formed a second major social process underpinning the changing nature of punishment in late eighteenth- and nineteenth-century Germany. As Foucault hinted obliquely in *Discipline and Punish*, while the growing mastery of humankind over the environment reduced the need for magical and religious modes of thinking to cope with the inexplicable omnipresence of suffering and death, the penetration of capitalism into European society required the implementation of more regular, predictable, and orderly habits of mind and modes of behaviour than had been common under the *ancien régime*. At the same time, the growth of the bureaucratic state arrogated the power of punishment, and especially of capital punishment, that supreme symbol of sovereignty, to central government. Yet these processes had to be achieved by a degree of consent, the freeing of the individual from the straightjacket of feudal society and the construction of mechanisms which would facilitate the growth of civil society: political representation, equality before the law, mobility of labour, a free market in goods, money, and land. All this required new mechanisms of social order and control. Honour, the invisible glue that bound together a society of ascribed social status-groups, became increasingly meaningless in this new situation, and penal sanctions based on the public degradation of the body were phased out as ineffective and unnecessary. These sanctions included many kinds of capital punishment, from breaking with the wheel to burning at the stake and dragging to the scaffold on a wet oxhide. Here was another reason why the death penalty became reduced to the penalty of death, no more and no less; and as such, it became increasingly vulnerable to rationalistic arguments based on new principles of the rights of the individual, above all the right of secular redemption. Self-improvement and moral regeneration had become the objectives of penal policy in liberal opinion by the 1840s, and capital punishment stood out against this background as a startling anomaly which was quickly labelled anachronistic in the ameliorative discourse of the reformers. It only regained its legitimacy when this discourse began to be replaced by the hereditarian and eugenic discourse towards the turn of the century and after.

The shift from a status-based to a class -based society broke down the formal structures of community and crowd and, together with the growing incompetence of executioners as the opportunities for practice diminished with the decline in executions, turned public executions into a threat to public order. And it was fear of disorder, as we have seen, that proved the major impulse for the abolition of public executions in the middle of the nineteenth century. This crucial step did not mean that executions became 'private'. At this point, the vague formulations of Ariès are of little help for, if normal death became confined to the family sphere in the nineteenth century, executions emphatically did not. What was actually happening was an accommodation of capital punishment to changing structures of the *public* sphere,[48] in which the emergence of a new, male-dominated bourgeois public led to increasing attempts at the removal or containment of the inchoate, 'female', emotional 'mob'. In practice, therefore,

---

[48] See, classically, Jürgen Habermas, *Strukturwandel der Öffentlichkeit. Untersuchungen zu einer Kategorie der bürgerlichen Gesellschaft* (Frankfurt am Main, 1968).

putting executions inside prison, but still admitting scores or even hundreds of male spectators, provided they came from the 'respectable' classes of society, simply meant treating them as public events in the sense, say, that parliamentary debates were. It was not long before shifts in popular culture, from the sung or spoken to the written word, began to undermine this development by relocating the popular fascination with executions into the popular press and the penny dreadful, transforming it in the process from a religious to a secular form. A complete control over the public sphere was no more possible here than it was anywhere else; the bourgeois public sphere never went uncontested. The ending of executions 'in the open air' had nothing final about it. By the Weimar Republic, executions and the crimes which led to them had become fodder not only for the mass-circulation press but also for stage and screen. Popular cultural representations of violent death still found a ready audience, as they do indeed today. There are obviously many reasons for this; but the evidence presented in this book suggests that one of the most powerful is simply curiosity about an experience which eventually comes to us all, and which no one who has undergone it can report about: the only experience of living human beings which is necessarily vicarious and voyeuristic.

In the larger public sphere of the politically and ethnically correct, death administered by the Third Reich became ever more secretive, ever more anonymous. A process which began with the speeding-up and standardization of executions in the 1930s ended in the assembly-line killing of the war years, extended to encompass the administration of mass murder as well. That continuities can be observed in this area is not surprising, since the judicial officials in charge of it had mostly been in positions of authority for a long time before the Nazis came to power. The drive for greater secrecy extended previous trends as well as being a response to the immediate situation. Yet the biological elimination of deviants implied a simple operation without ritual or ceremony, and that is what the Nazis eventually got. Whatever the elements of embarrassment and squeamishness in the administration of the death penalty in the nineteenth and early twentieth centuries, most judicial officials and commentators still considered an element of ritual to be central to the proceedings. The Nazi elimination of ritual marked a sharp departure from previous practice in this area. As far as the public sphere of 'racial comrades' in the Third Reich was concerned, the deviants simply disappeared. It was only in the smaller public sphere, or spheres, of the 'community aliens' in the concentration camps that the realities of execution were omnipresent, and that a crude element of ritual survived; only at the very end of the war that public hangings and shootings, now brutally makeshift in character, indicated an extension of this sphere to encompass the disintegrating German society as a whole. In all this, it is crucial to distinguish between the normal administration of capital punishment and the mass extermination programmes administered by the Nazis against criminals, deviants, and racial minorities during the war. The real change here came about in wartime; to a degree, capital punishment under the Nazis up to 1939 represented strong continuities with Weimar, though the Weimar of the post-revolutionary White Terror in 1919–21, not the Weimar of the later years. The departure from normal capital punishment to mass execution and planned extermination derived in large measure from developments which took place outside the history of the death penalty, not within it: in particular, the conflation of racism, negative eugenics, and a radically political dictatorship. Clearly, it could not have taken place in a society where attitudes to the death penalty were still governed mainly by religion, or where executions still took place in public. But since most European societies effectively restricted public participation in executions by this time, this is not really saying very much. No direct lines can be traced from the Enlightenment or the French Revolution to the killing fields of Poland or the gas chambers of Auschwitz. Similarly, the political instrumentalization of capital punishment in the Stalinist regime of the German Democratic Republic owed more to the murderous traditions of the Russian revolutionaries than it did to the humane secularism of German Social Democracy, still less to the principle and practice of socialism itself.

In their different ways, theories such as those of Foucault, Elias, and Ariès all predict 'the end of history', and so too does the idea that capital punishment essentially belongs to a 'barbaric' past which we have now put behind us. Yet while growing numbers of countries have been abolishing it, the death penalty has actually been reintroduced and employed with increasing frequency in others, most notably the United States of America. Who is to say that where America leads, other countries will not follow, as they have done so often before? The most appropriate myth for our own times is that of Sisyphus, who was condemned to roll a huge stone up a mountain, only to find he was unable to stop it rolling back down as soon as he got near the top.[49] The fight against capital punishment may be over—for the time being—in Germany, but it continues, often under difficult circumstances, in other parts of the world. It seems appropriate in conclusion, therefore, to ask whether there are any lessons—positive or negative, encouraging or depressing—to be learned for it from the history surveyed in this book.

e. Reflections on the Death Penalty

The Nazi experience, it seems fair to say, discredited eugenic and Social Darwinist justifications for the death penalty not only in Germany but also

---

[49] Albert Camus, *Le Mythe de Sisyphe. Essai sur l'absurde* (Paris, 1942).

across the world. Fifty years on, they have nowhere recovered their legitimacy. On a wider time-scale, arguments for and against the death penalty in Germany over the last four centuries have revolved much more persistently around two major principles: deterrence and retribution. Of these, the proposition that capital punishment deters people from committing the crimes to which it applies has been widely questioned from the eighteenth century onwards. Already by the early nineteenth century critics were pointing out that rational criminals do not believe they will be caught, while those who murder in the heat of the moment—the vast majority—are in no state to consider the long-term consequences of their actions. This insight seems to me to be essentially correct. When debates began about the statistical evidence for deterrence, in the wake of Mittermaier's work, nobody was able to prove either that the abolition of the death penalty led to an increase in the murder rate, or that its reintroduction led to a decline. This was not least because of the contingent nature of definitions of murder; but even taking the coroner's figures of death by homicide as the yardstick, it is still impossible to prove any clear relationship.[50] Modern statistical studies have demonstrated that widely publicized executions actually lead to a short-term increase in crimes of violence and homicide through their brutalizing effect, much as many critics of public executions in early nineteenth-century Germany feared.[51] On a longer-term basis, the point made by abolitionists on many occasions, that societies with a high execution rate and draconian punishments tend historically to be societies with high levels of homicide and interpersonal violence, seems undeniable. Few people now, indeed, would give much credence to the deterrence factor in arguing for the death penalty, and in retreating from this argument, the proponents of capital punishment have essentially recognized its long-term lack of credibility.

In essence, most defenders of the death penalty in Germany recognized the weakness of the deterrence argument and opted for retribution as the principal justification for beheading murderers instead. This had a venerable biblical and above all philosophical tradition, incorporated in the writings of Immanuel Kant. The classic defence of capital punishment has for centuries been that the only adequate way of paying back murderers is to make them suffer as their victim or victims did: the ultimate crime deserves the ultimate penalty.[52] The

---

[50] Welsh S. White, *The Death Penalty in the Eighties: An Examination of the Modern System of Capital Punishment* (Ann Arbor, 1987), 155; see also the numerous studies summarized in Michael L. Radelet and Margaret Vandiver, *Capital Punishment in America: An Annotated Bibliography* (New York, 1988).

[51] William J. Bowers, 'The Effect of Executions is Brutalization, Not Deterrence', in Kenneth C. Haas and James A. Inciardi (eds.), *Challenging Capital Punishment: Legal and Social Science Approaches* (Newburg Park, Calif., 1988), 49–90. See also William J. Bowers, *Legal Homicide: Death as a Punishment in America 1864–1982* (Chicago, 1984), 383–4.

[52] Sorell, *Moral Theory*, 147.

problem with this argument is that there is no obvious reason why the retributive principle should apply to murder and to no other crime. No one would dream of suggesting that someone who steals a million pounds should be punished solely by being forced to pay it back to the victim, or that someone who runs over a pedestrian in his car and breaks the victim's leg should have his own leg broken in turn. In practice, the retributive principle of punishment does not demand that like is repaid with like, only that there is a graded scale of punishments corresponding to the generally accepted estimation of the severity of the offence; but this does not have to include death as the ultimate penalty: the highest punishment can in principle be set at any level.[53] Moreover, in practical terms, as we have seen time and again in this book, death sentences for murder are carried out for reasons which have little to do with the crime. As the American abolitionist Hugo Adam Bedau has remarked,

The death penalty, today as in the past, symbolizes the ultimate power of the state, and of the government of society, over the individual citizen. . . . Anxiety about war, fear of crime, indignation at being victimized, provoke the authorities to use the power of life and death as a public gesture of strength, confidence, and reassurance.[54]

In such a situation, retribution is bound to be arbitrary. Because not all murderers, let alone offenders convicted of other forms of homicide, are executed, the death penalty never operates as an exact or consistent retribution in practice.[55] Moreover, there is a sense in which no really exact retribution is ever possible for the crime of murder. Capital offenders may be killed, but they are not killed in the same way as they killed their victims. Above all where serial or multiple homicides are concerned, the unique death of the perpetrator can never be an adequate retribution for the many deaths of his victims. How could anyone possibly maintain, for example, that the law of 'an eye for an eye' was being applied in the execution of a mass murderer like Hermann Göring or Otto Ohlendorf? Once it is admitted that the level of retributive punishment is arbitrary, then it becomes clear that human society has the freedom to set it at any level it wishes, and other factors come into play.

Defenders of capital punishment have argued that judicial error is impossible, or so insignificant as to be acceptable provided that it is only caused by human fallibility;[56] but the historical record shows not only that it is possible, but also, crucially, that the translation of the death sentence into the actual execution of

[53] Hugo Adam Bedau, *Death is Different: Studies in the Morality, Law, and Politics of Capital Punishment* (Boston, 1987), 243–4.
[54] Ibid. 246.
[55] Amnesty International, *When the State Kills: The Death Penalty and Human Rights* (London, 1989), for this and other arguments against retributionism.
[56] Sorell, *Moral Theory*, 122.

the offender in question depends strongly on class, age, status, ethnicity, the political circumstances of the time, and the opinions and character of the sovereign power whose right it is to grant clemency. Legal systems in the end are run by human beings, and are subject to political influences; they do not operate in a rigid or automatic way simply according to abstract philosophical principles. Distinguishing capital varieties of homicide from non-capital—for example, murder from manslaughter—involves subjective judgements which are again heavily influenced by extraneous factors, just as are further judgements on whether or not a particular individual is fit to stand trial or deserving of mercy. Translated from principle into practice, capital punishment inevitably takes on a degree of arbitrariness which makes the fate of the individual capital offender dependent on a whole series of chance circumstances.

Many defenders of the death penalty have therefore argued that it should not be a normal punishment but a wholly exceptional sanction wielded only against wholly exceptional crimes:

The question is whether there are not certain acts committed against humanity that are so beyond the pale of normal social intercourse that even considerations of mercy, justice, or forgiveness cannot serve to mitigate the ultimate penalty of death. . . . The use of the death penalty in such limited and extreme cases does not necessarily undermine the overall argument for abolition, but may, on the contrary, give it added emphasis.[57]

Historical experience shows, however, as far as Germany is concerned, that the category of the wholly exceptional is very elastic, and what is beyond the pale of normal social intercourse is susceptible of many different definitions, which change according to political circumstance. Already in 1848 the liberals at Frankfurt compromised themselves fatally by admitting the death penalty in military law, as Prussian and other reactionaries were quick to note; thirty years later, Bismarck reintroduced executions after a ten-year abeyance with the argument that the crime in question—Hödel's—was wholly exceptional, only to expand this category during the 1880s so that, by the time Wilhelm II began to demonstrate his unquenchable thirst for blood, what was regarded as wholly exceptional in the way of homicides was not very different from what had been regarded as more or less normal a couple of decades before. The politicians of Weimar all made similar compromises. The hard truth is that arguments against the death penalty cannot stick if they are made only on the basis of mitigation, for an offender will always be found whose crimes, it can plausibly be argued, admit of none. To concentrate on the innocent prisoner on death row, to prove that someone has been wrongly executed, to argue that a capital offender should not

[57] Leon Shaskolsky Sheleff, *Ultimate Penalties: Capital Punishment, Life Imprisonment, Physical Torture* (Columbus, Ohio, 1987), 216–17.

be killed because he might be persuaded to change his ways, or because he is not responsible for his own actions, or because he has been selected for death on racial or political criteria, may be important in individual cases, and may well help to discredit capital punishment in practice, but it does not destroy it as a principle. To be convincing and effective, the argument for the abolition of the death penalty has to be applied without any exceptions at all, not even for a man such as Peter Kürten: not even, if it had come to it, for a man such as Adolf Hitler.

This does not mean, of course, that opponents of the death penalty have by definition to be pacifists, nor that they are logically compelled to oppose tyrannicide. The point at issue is the state's right to kill its own citizens, not the state's right to kill external enemies, or the people's right to rid themselves of a tyrant. The central reason for opposing capital punishment surely has to be that it demeans and degrades the state and, through it, all of us, its citizens, to use its power to terminate the life of an individual. Defenders of the death penalty argue that it is necessary for the law to retain powers of life and death in order to express its own dignity, and thereby to provide a unifying factor in society: 'Executions, solemnly witnessed and carried out, are not barbaric; on the contrary, they enhance the awesome dignity of the law and of the moral order it serves and protects.'[58] But this argument renders its actual application even more arbitrary. The death penalty becomes, as some of its critics have remarked, 'a punishment in search of a crime'.[59] In a society which values human life, the state, as the Social Democrats argued in Germany at the end of the First World War, should lead by example. Capital punishment does not enhance human dignity, it degrades it, and with it degrades the state in which human society organizes itself. It is a poor moral order which requires repeated acts of arbitrarily applied revenge to keep itself together.[60] The death penalty has never been convincingly shown to have achieved anything. A grave measure such as killing a human being surely requires a very strong justification before it can be undertaken, and no such justification has been advanced beyond reasonable doubt, either in Germany or anywhere else, in the case of capital punishment. A corollary is, of course, that some individuals must be kept in prison at considerable expense, some of them for the rest of their life; yet economy should not be allowed to take precedence over ethics where human life is concerned and, in any case, recent American studies have shown that while the legal and administrative costs of executing a capital offender average out at around $3,200,000, the same offender could be

---

[58] Walter Burns, *For Capital Punishment: Crime and the Morality of the Death Penalty* (New York, 1979), 188.

[59] Franklin E. Zimring and Gordon Hawkins, *Capital Punishment and the American Agenda* (Cambridge, 1986), 77.

[60] Roger E. Schwed, *Abolition and Capital Punishment. The United States' Judicial, Political, and Moral Barometer* (New York, 1983).

kept in prison for the rest of his life—which on average would be about forty years—for no more than $600,000, or less than a fifth of the cost.[61]

Proponents of capital punishment argue that it can now be administered humanely, but in truth there is no clean or easy way of executing someone, just as there is no clean or easy way of dying naturally.[62] States have clung to traditional methods out of ingrained habit, or searched for new ones in the desire to protect those who order, administer, and witness the punishment, rather than those who undergo it; yet even in the case of lethal injection, not to mention the electric chair, mistakes have caused great suffering to the condemned and danger to the executioners on a number of occasions.[63] French legislators used to vote against the ending of public executions on the grounds that it would make them more acceptable if people were not able to witness how they were done; and certainly ignorance of the physical realities of executions seems to make it easier to tolerate, condone, or support them, as it did for the majority of people in Nazi Germany. Proposals to televise real executions have so far not made a great deal of headway in the United States, partly because of the controversy they would arouse. On the other hand, executions in the United States routinely attract widespread public support, including crowds gathered outside the prisons where they are held, cheering on the executioners as the hour approaches. The popular enthusiasm for capital punishment which this indicates has always been one of the main stumbling-blocks for abolitionists. The élitist views of the men of 1848, who argued that they knew what was best for the people, would not be tolerated in a modern democracy. At the same time, however, democracies also have to defend minority rights, especially when the majority wishes to abrogate them.

Balancing out these various factors is far from easy. Yet there is a case for treating convicted criminals as a minority whose rights the legislator has to preserve in the face of majority hostility. Moreover, there is nothing inevitable or correct about the majority support for the death penalty that exists in Britain and the United States. In the United Kingdom, indeed, there is evidence that opinion is at last beginning to move in an abolitionist direction. Ultimately, enthusiasm for capital punishment, along with the incarceration of a high proportion of offenders, reflects a widespread culture of retribution. In America this in turn reflects the steady growth of religious fundamentalism in recent decades, as the practice of capital punishment has spread with the growing influence of the Christian right. The fact that the churches in America are now overwhelmingly abolitionist seems to make very little difference to this process. The death penalty

[61] Information from Michael L. Radelet, lecture at the Institute of Advanced Legal Studies, London, 27 Feb. 1995.
[62] Sherwin B. Nuland, *How We Die* (London, 1994).
[63] Trombley, *Execution Protocol*, 71–83.

is similarly retained in Islamic fundamentalist states such as Iran and Saudi Arabia, and indeed wherever human life, and human values, take second place to religion, or to a totalitarian secular ideology, as in Hitler's Third Reich or the former German Democratic Republic, it is likely, as this book has shown, to be held of little account.

In the United States the recent growth of capital punishment, which was reinstated in 1987 after a fifteen-year gap ordered by the Supreme Court, shows no signs of stopping or even of levelling off. It is closely linked to a popular toleration, even encouragement, of interpersonal violence which is largely foreign to most European countries. In European cultures where capital punishment was abolished in the nineteenth century—Finland (1826), Norway (1875), Denmark (1892), Sweden (1910), the Netherlands (1850), and Belgium (1863), violent death and violent crime rates have been among the lowest in the world throughout the twentieth century.[64] For most of this period, however, Germany was not among these countries. The movement for the abolition of the death penalty failed. A culture of violence was already beginning to develop before the First World War, and permeated Weimar, to reach its nadir under the Third Reich. But cultures can be changed. Germany is a good example of a country where bitter experience has led to a strong distaste for public and private violence. This distaste has found its way into a dramatic shift of majority opinion against the death penalty in the last quarter of the twentieth century. In this respect at least, where Germany leads, other countries can follow. Let us hope that they will.

[64] Jean-Claude Chesnais, *Histoire de la violence en Occident de 1800 à nos jours* (Paris, 1981), 125–6.

STATISTICAL APPENDIX

At various points in this book, figures of death sentences and executions have been quoted for various years or sets of years. The purpose of this Statistical Appendix is to present longer time-series relating to the history of capital punishment in Germany, to provide details of the sources from which they have been gathered, and to correlate and compare them with various other relevant indicators. Such figures were regularly compiled within the Justice Ministries of the various German states from the early nineteenth century onwards, and in some instances even earlier, though they only began to be published much later. They are not without problems. Sometimes different sets exist within the same file, without the differing basis of compilation being explained. The Prussian and Bavarian statistics are reasonably complete, but there are gaps in some of the others, and for many of the smaller German states, where executions were extremely uncommon, no figures exist at all for much of the nineteenth century.

A further problem vitiates the whole enterprise of trying to compare condemnations and executions on an annual basis and to work out the commutation rate year by year. Given the slowness with which communications worked and the length of time it took courts to deal with appeals, Justice Ministries to compile clemency recommendations, and monarchs to make up their minds as to whether a criminal should be executed or not, a period of months often elapsed between a criminal being sentenced to death and the fatal blow being struck. This means that a substantial number of criminals were executed in the calendar year following their condemnation. An offender sentenced to death in November or December would almost never be executed before the following January or February, and the same could be said of many criminals sentenced in October, September, or even August. There is no way of finding out from the statistics how many executions in a given year resulted from condemnations arrived at the previous year. To make matters worse, some officials charged with compiling the statistics seem to have been aware of this problem, and there are indications that for some periods they tried to reassign executions back to the year of condemnation in order to get a truer picture. The confusion is completed by the fact that they failed to indicate whether or not they were adopting this procedure in the files. For some brief periods, the existence of two quite sharply differing sets of figures can probably be traced back to the adoption of these two different procedures. Finally, for Prussia, there is the problem that at some times the figures included the Rhine province, where a different legal system obtained, and at others not. Nevertheless, although they have to be treated with caution, the figures do present some clear patterns over time, as we have already seen at various points in the book.

From 1860 onwards, statistics are available for the German Reich in the territory which it covered from 1871 onwards. The relative sophistication and standardization of statistics in this period enable us to attempt a comparison of capital punishment statistics with the incidence of the crimes for which it was laid down. However, there are problems here too. Contemporaries used the figure of murders per 100,000 population of responsible age, but this would have to be compared with condemnations per 100,000 population to obtain a true comparison. Moreover, murder statistics reflect only the number of guilty verdicts by the courts, which further reflects the decisions made by police, prosecutors, judges, and juries on the offence to be charged and the judgment to be reached. As we have seen, these decisions were strongly influenced by the perception of the likelihood of execution, based on the clemency policy of the monarch and government of the day, so that a falling murder rate could in practice have been above all else the result of a growing reluctance on all sides to initiate legal proceedings which might lead to execution if the monarch—say, Wilhelm II—was clearly following a policy of refusing clemency in all but a small number of cases. On the other hand, the rise in the murder rate under the Third Reich probably indicates a greater willingness to prosecute and convict for capital offences, encouraged by the regime. A better indicator would be the number of homicides as recorded by coroners (see Table 3). The figures provided (with gaps) in Table 1 make clear above all that Bismarck's reintroduction of capital punishment in Prussia in 1878 had far-reaching effects on the rest of the German Empire, where executions sharply increased almost immediately and reached levels in the 1880s not seen for many decades.

Table 1. *Death sentences, executions, and murder rates, German Reich or territory of German Reich, 1860–1940*

Year	Death sentences	Executions	%	Murder rate
1860	62	12	19.5	
1861	72	9	12.5	
1862	63	11	17.5	
1864	60	8	13.3	
1865	52	9	17.3	
1866	50	8	16.0	
1867	69	6	8.7	
1868	82	4	4.9	
1869	77	3	3.9	
1870	42	0	0.0	
1871	51	0	0.0	
1872	63	0	0.0	
1873	70	5	7.1	
1874	75	1	1.3	
1875	92	1	1.1	
1876	87	3	3.4	
1877	89	1	1.1	
1878	109	6	5.5	
1879	103	3	2.9	
1880	82	6	7.3	
1881	70	6	8.6	
1882	85	16	1.8	0.48
1883	90	13	14.4	0.48
1884	69	15	21.7	0.43
1885	59	15	25.4	0.39
1886				0.44

Year	Death sentences	Executions	%	Murder rate
1887				0.40
1888				0.28
1889				0.31
1890	133			0.39
1891	88			0.25
1892	144			0.41
1893	114			0.32
1894	110			0.31
1895	113			0.31
1896	108			0.29
1897	101			0.27
1898	106			0.28
1899	79			0.20
1900	89			0.23
1901	84			0.21
1902	103			0.26
1903	86			0.21
1904	94			0.23
1905	91			0.22
1906	93			0.22
1907	82			0.19
1908	80			0.18
1909	96			0.21
1910	93			0.20
1911	93			0.20
1912	94			0.20
1913	110			0.23
1914	82			0.17
1915	68			?
1916	74			?
1917	71			?
1918	87			?
1919	89	10	11.2	0.35
1920	113	36	31.9	0.44
1921	149	28	18.9	0.50
1922	124	26	20.1	0.42
1923	77	15	19.5	0.29
1924	112	23	20.5	0.41
1925	95	16	16.8	0.39
1926	89	14	15.7	0.35
1927	64	6	9.4	0.25
1928	46	2	4.3	0.18
1929	39	0	0.0	0.14
1930	43	1	2.3	0.18
1931	49	4	8.2	0.19

Table 1. (*cont.*)

Year	Death sentences	Executions	%	Murder rate
1932	52	3	5.8	0.20
1933	78	64	82.0	0.32
1934	102	79	77.4	0.63
1935	98	94	95.9	0.33
1936	76	68	89.5	0.29
1937	86	106	123.2	0.34
1938	85	117	137.6	0.25
1939	139	219	157.5	0.29
1940	250			0.14
1941	1,292			
1942	4,457			
1943	5,336			
1944	4,264			
1945	297			
1946	3	1		
1947	8	4		
1948	20	2		
1949	5	2		

Sources: The source for the figures from 1860 to 1885 is BA Potsdam Reichsjustizamt 5664, Bl. 97; for the capital punishment figures from 1890 and the murder figures from 1882 Düsing, *Abschaffung*, 131–2, 175–6. Düsing, *Abschaffung*, 210–11, bases execution figures for the Third Reich on mortality statistics, giving cause of death; the same source, 217–19, uses figures supplied by Thierack for 1941 and 1943 and estimates 1942 and 1945 using the proportion between executioner Reichhart's reports of his own activities, which are complete for all the war years, and Thierack's, as a basis for estimation. The figures for 1945–9 are for condemnations and executions by order of German courts in the three Western zones and in Greater Berlin (Düsing, *Abschaffung*, 231–2).

The Reich Ministry of Justice also kept a monthly statistical record of death sentences passed in the 'Greater German Reich', or in other words Germany including Austria, and reannexed parts of Poland and France, during the war. These figures do not include death sentences passed by Special Courts in the annexed eastern territories, except that from December 1943 onwards they do include figures from the Protectorate of Bohemia and Moravia. As shown in Table 2 they provide a dramatic indication of the steady expansion of the use of the death penalty in this period, and the sharp increase which took place during the 'judicial crisis' in the spring of 1942, as Hitler publicly attacked the judiciary for what he regarded as its excessive leniency, and demanded that a higher proportion of offenders brought before the courts be sentenced to death.

Table 2. *Death sentences in the Greater German Reich,*
monthly totals, February 1940–August 1944

Month	Death sentences	Month	Death sentences
Feb. 1940	33	Jan. 1943	248
Mar.	28	Feb.	367
Apr.	47	Mar.	471
May	38	Apr.	403
June	43	May	375
July	37	June	314
Aug.	32	July	351
Sept.	36	Aug.	304
Oct.	29	Sept.	710
Nov.	29	Oct.	391
Dec.	57	Nov.	340
		Dec.	164
Jan. 1941	53	Jan. 1944	206
Feb.	43	Feb.	189
Mar.	31	Mar.	238
Apr.	63	Apr.	236
May	68	May	274
June	41	June	281
July	64	July	242
Aug.	35	Aug.	349
Sept.	52		
Oct.	64		
Nov.	60		
Dec.	63		
Jan. 1942	66		
Feb.	90		
Mar.	96		
Apr.	129		
May	149		
June	233		
July	241		

Note: As Chapter 16 indicated, these figures represent a decreasing proportion of those actually executed, since during the war, and especially from September 1942 onwards, certain categories of offender were taken out of the jurisdiction of the courts which supplied them.

Source: BA Koblenz R22/4086, Bl. 274–5: 'Gesamtzahlen der Todesurteile' and 'Todesurteile überhaupt'.

Figures are also available for some of the larger German states. The best-documented is perhaps Prussia. Table 3 provides time-series from 1818 to 1933.

Table 3. *Homicide and its punishment in Prussia, 1818–1918*

Year	Death sentences	Executed	Commuted	Other	Homicide deaths	Homicide convictions
1818	17	9	8	0		
1819	24	8	16	0		
1820	21	13	8	0		
1821	15	14	1	0		
1822	20	5	14	1		
1823	27	10	17	0		
1824	22	12	10	0		
1825	15	4	11	0		
1826	16	5	11	0		
1827	24	7	17	0		
1828	29	12	17	0		
1829	17	5	12	0		
1830	18	4	14	0		
1831	22	9	13	0		
1832	28	2	26	0		
1833	30	2	28	0		
1834	21	2	19	0		
1835	36	7	29	0		
1836	22	4	18	0		
1837	34	4	30	0		
1838	17	7	10	0		
1839	24	8	16	0		
1840	23	5	18	0		
1841	14	2	12	0		
1842	39	8	31	0		
1843	29	5	24	0		
1844	25	10	14	1		
1845	27	7	18	2		
1846	23	6	17	0		
1847	28	7	21	0		
1848	26	1	25	0		
1849	26	7	16	3		
1850	42	15	21	6		
1851	60	20	36	4		
1852	40	25	14	1		
1853	40	30	7	3		
1854	37	28	9	0		
1855	45	28	13	4		
1856	36	26	9	1		
1857	42	14	27	1		
1858	38	4	31	3		
1859	25	4	20	1		

Year	Death sentences	Executed	Commuted	Other	Homicide deaths	Homicide convictions
1860	24	2	21	1		
1861	37	5	30	2		
1862	32	3	28	1		
1863	30	13	17	0		
1864	37	5	30	2		
1865	39	8	29	2		
1866	28	4	24	0		
1867	52	5	46	1		
1868	62	4	58	0		
1869	58	0	58	0		
1870	28	0	28	0		
1871	28	0	28	0		
1872	45	0	45	0		
1873	41	0	41	0	516	
1874	44	0	44	0	556	
1875	64	0	64	0	547	
1876	60	0	60	0	471	
1877	58	0	58	0	543	
1878	67	1	66	0	471	
1879	72	0	72	0	455	
1880	46	1	44	1	470	
1881	55	4	50	1	432	
1882	68	4	64	0	444	199
1883	55	4	47	4	406	185
1884	53	4	49	0	419	162
1885	39	7	32	0	446	173
1886	42	8	34	0	432	166
1887	33	5	28	0	374	153
1888	25	6	19	0	377	112
1889	23	7	15	1	320	130
1890	39	13	25	1	275	130
1891	24	11	13	0	442	121
1892	38	25	13	0	485	174
1893	44	27	16	1	516	180
1894	34	22	11	1	517	156
1895	39	28	11	0	471	?
1896	40	26	13	1	587	?
1897	23	11	10	2	524	150
1898	28	16	11	1	534	126
1899	22	10	12	0	569	128
1900	20	13	7	0	684	139
1901	23	22	1	0	664	122
1902	32	23	8	1	580	154
1903	21	13	8	0	691	152

Table 3. (*cont.*)

Year	Death sentences	Executed	Commuted	Other	Homicide deaths	Homicide convictions
1904	19	14	0	7	708	140
1905	16	8	8	0	697	135
1906	22	14	8	0	696	150
1907	10	13	7	0	788	159
1908	17	9	8	0	?	155
1909	29	20	9	0	?	160
1910	30	23	7	0	800	174
1911	23	15	8	0	?	185
1912	22	15	5	0	804	182
1913	34	22	10	2	889	217
1914	22	13	9	0	1,459	179
1915	18	15	3	0	?	?
1916	26	19	7	0	?	?
1917	27	20	7	0	?	?
1918	16	4	12	3	?	?
1919	45	0				
1920	79	7	72			
1921	103	7	96			
1922	94	9	83			
1923	52	1	51			
1924	73	5	68			
1925	71	10	61			
1926	54	4	50			
1927	43	4	39			
1928	27	0	27			
1929	18	0	18			
1930	22	0	2			
1931	24	1	23			
1932	39	0	39			
1933	65	49	16			

Note: The column 'Other' includes offenders who died, committed suicide, or escaped, after final condemnation but before the King had reached a decision on clemency.

Sources: The figures for 1818–70 were published by the Ministry of Justice in 1870 in a background paper for the debate on capital punishment in the Reichstag (*Ueber die Todesstrafe: Stenographische Berichte über die Verhandlungen des Reichstages des Norddeutschen Bundes. 1. Legislatur-Periode, Session 1870. Anlagen zu den Verhandlungen des Reichstages von Nr. 1–72, Bd. 3, 2: Anlage 2 zu Nr. 5 (Motive des Strafgesetz-Entwurfs für den Norddeutschen Bund*), p. vii). These were taken from manuscript tables in GStA Berlin Rep. 84a/ 8143, Bl. 70–1, 79–80, 96–7, 104–5, 120–3, 126–9, 134–5, 144–5, 152–3, 161–2, 175–6, 195–6, 213–14, 218– 19; and ibid. 8144, Bl. 5, 10–11, 22–3, 26–7, 45–6. The homicide figures were compiled from coroners' reports giving death by cause, in Eric A. Johnson, 'Women as Victims and Criminals: Female Homicide and Criminality in Imperial Germany, 1873–1914', *Criminal Justice History*, 6 (1985), 151–75, here 160, and idem, 'Roots of Crime', 361. The Weimar statistics were drawn from BA Potsdam RJA 5665, Bl. 126–8.

Table 3 shows clearly that the number of convictions for murder and manslaughter was a function not of the number of recorded homicides but of the number of executions. Police, prosecutors, and courts remained extremely reluctant to prosecute and convict for capital offences when it was likely that this would lead to execution, as it was throughout the reign of Wilhelm II. Thus the useful compilations of statistics provided by Düsing, *Abschaffung*, are vitiated by his use of the 'murder rate', or in other words conviction figures, in his attempt to argue on a statistical basis that the death penalty was not a deterrent. It could equally be argued by the proponents of capital punishment in the years 1906–14 that a greater willingness to prosecute and convict for murder would be the most effective response to the growing number of homicides. The fact was, in the end, that capital punishment was more closely related to the political situation than to trends in the crimes which some people argued it was meant to deter. The figures in Table 4, derived from the above, clearly indicate the trends: as capital punishment was reintroduced in the 1880s, and executions as a percentage of death sentences increased, convictions for homicide declined as a proportion of reported deaths from homicide, and death sentences fell as a percentage of homicide convictions.

Table 4. *Homicide and the death penalty in Prussia, 1882–1914*

Year	Convictions for homicide as % of reported deaths from homicide	Death sentences as % of homicide convictions	Executions as % of death sentences
1882	45	34	6
1883	46	30	7
1884	39	33	8
1885	39	23	18
1886	38	25	19
1887	41	22	15
1888	30	22	24
1889	41	18	30
1890	47	30	33
1891	27	20	46
1892	36	22	66
1893	35	24	61
1894	30	22	65
1895	?	?	72
1896	?	?	65
1897	29	15	48
1898	24	52	57
1899	22	17	45
1900	20	14	65
1901	18	19	96
1902	27	21	62
1903	22	14	74
1904	20	14	74
1905	19	12	50

Table 4. (*cont.*)

Year	Convictions for homicide as % of reported deaths from homicide	Death sentences as % of homicide convictions	Executions as % of death sentences
1906	20	15	64
1907	20	13	65
1908	?	11	53
1909	?	18	69
1910	22	17	77
1911	?	12	65
1912	23	12	77
1913	24	16	65
1914	12	12	59

Figures are also available for women executed in Prussia in the 1890s and 1900s: 2 in 1898, 1 in 1899, 2 in 1901, 3 in 1902, 1 in 1903, 1 in 1904, 2 in 1905, 1 in 1907. It can thus be said that under Wilhelm II the execution of women was normal in Prussia, even if it took place only very infrequently. (*Source*: BA Potsdam Reichsjustizamt 5665, Bl. 12: Statistisches Landesamt Berlin to Reichsjustizamt, 31 Aug. 1908.)

Figures are also available for Bavaria. Here some of the same trends can be observed as in Prussia, including a sharp rise in condemnations after the 1848 Revolution, and an increased willingness to use the death penalty during the 1890s. The enthusiasm for capital punishment on the part of government in the early 1920s was a peculiarly Bavarian phenomenon, reflecting the 'White Terror' and counter-revolutionary atmosphere in the state. The time-series in Table 5 run from 1801 to 1932.

Table 5. *Death sentences and executions in Bavaria, 1801–1933*

Year	Death sentences	Executions	Year	Death sentences	Executions
1801	4		1814	8	
1802	6		1815	3	
1803	6		1816	1	
1804	10		1817	6	3
1805	7		1818	9	6
1806	6		1819	6	3
1807	7		1820	8	4
1808	6		1821	6	3
1809	4		1822	5	3
1810	5		1823	10	5
1811	7		1824	6	1
1812	6		1825	6	0
1813	5		1826	9	3

Year	Death sentences	Executions	Year	Death sentences	Executions
1827	7	3	1871	12	0
1828	5	1	1872	5	0
1829	3	1	1873	16	2
1830	4	2	1874	9	0
1831	5	1	1875	17	1
1832	2	1	1876	11	2
1833	5	1	1877	13	0
1834	11	2	1878	13	1
1835	10	2	1879	14	1
1836	10	3	1880	8	0
1837	8	0	1881	14	1
1838	2	0	1882	13	1
1839	2	1	1883	20	3
1840	10	0	1884	13	2
1841	5	1	1885	11	2
1842	2	0	1886	15	3
1843	6	1	1887	16	4
1844	6	1	1888	5	0
1845	4	0	1889	10	1
1846	6	0	1890	10	4
1847	12	2	1891	5	1
1848	14	0	1892	10	2
1849	39	1	1893	5	2
1850	39	5	1894	4	1
1851	3	0	1895	9	3
1852	3	0	1896	9	2
1853	7	2	1897	14	8
1854	14	4	1898	12	5
1855	5	?	1899	9	0
1856	7	?	1900	5	0
1857	5	?	1901	8	6
1858	14	6	1902	5	1
1859	20	5	1903	8	3
1860	9	0	1904	11	4
1861	11	2	1905	6	2
1862	6	0	1906	12	0
1863	14	1	1907	4	0
1864	4	0	1908	6	1
1865	7	0	1909	2	0
1866	12	2	1910	5	1
1867	13	1	1911	5	1
1868	14	0	1912	6	0
1869	9	0	1913	7	1
1870	13	0	1914	6	0

Table 5. *(cont.)*

Year	Death sentences	Executions	Year	Death sentences	Executions
1915	1	6	1924	19	14
1916	0	5	1925	11	8
1917	0	0	1926	10	2
1918	3	2	1927	10	4
1919	22	0	1928	4	0
1920	36	1	1929	8	0
1921	21	0	1930	3	0
1922	19	0	1931	10	1
1923	14	2	1932	3	0

Sources: HStA Munich MJu 12575: Verzeichniss der in Bayern vom Jahre 1858–1872 erfolgten Verurtheilungen wegen Mordes; Statistik der Todesstrafe; Übersichten über die in Bayern rechtskräftig gewordenen Todesurteile. The 19th-c. figures were obtained by adding up the statistics for the various Bavarian provinces. The figures for the early 1850s are drawn from HStA Munich MA 93516: Die Anwendung der Todesstrafe in Bayern, mit statistischen Listen (Findbuch—the original files relating to capital punishment in Bavaria up to 1858 were destroyed in an air raid). The same sources provide figures by sex. One woman was executed in each of the years 1821, 1826, and 1828, two in 1834, one each in 1835, 1836, 1847, and 1851, and none at all thereafter as far as is known.

Another long time-series can be supplied for the Grand Duchy of Baden, in Germany's liberal south-west. Here too the significance of the post-revolutionary 1850s in the history of capital punishment in Germany can be observed, as the death penalty was used as a symbol of the state's determination to restore the social and political order. Just as in Prussia, the liberal 1860s and 1870s saw the death penalty virtually in abeyance. Here, however, it was the eary 1900s which witnessed the greatest reluctance to use the princely power of clemency.

Table 6. *Death sentences and executions in Baden, 1812–1933*

Year	Death sentences	Executions	Year	Death sentences	Executions
1812		1	1821		
1813			1822		
1814			1823		
1815			1824	1	
1816			1825		
1817	1		1826	2	
1818	2		1827	1	
1819	2		1828		
1820			1829	2	

Year	Death sentences	Executions	Year	Death sentences	Executions
1830	1		1874	5	0
1831			1875	0	0
1832	1		1876	1	0
1833			1877	2	0
1834	1		1878	3	0
1835			1879	6	1
1836			1880	1	1
1837	3		1881	2	0
1838	1		1882	0	0
1839			1883	3	0
1840	2	0	1884	1	1
1841	6	0	1885	0	0
1842	2	0	1886	0	0
1843	1	0	1887	0	0
1844	1	1	1888	3	1
1845	0	0	1889	1	1
1846	1	1	1890	1	0
1847	0	0	1891	1	1
1848	5	0	1892	4	1
1849	2	0	1893	2	1
1850	0	0	1894	1	0
1851	1	1	1895	0	0
1852	1	1	1896	1	0
1853	3	2	1897	0	0
1854	3	2	1898	0	0
1855	3	1	1899	4	2
1856	4	2	1900	1	1
1857	0	0	1901	1	1
1858	0	0	1902	1	1
1859	2	0	1903	5	5
1860	4	0	1906	1	0
1861	3	2	1907	2	0
1862	0	0	1908	2	1
1863	3	0	1909	0	0
1864	1	0	1910	0	0
1865	1	0	1911	0	0
1866	0	0	1912	4	0
1867	3	0	1913	4	0
1868	2	0	1914	1	0
1869	3	0	1915	0	0
1870	2	0	1916	0	0
1871	2	0	1917	0	0
1872	3	0	1918	0	0
1873	5	0	1919	2	0

Table 6. (*cont.*)

Year	Death sentences	Executions	Year	Death sentences	Executions
1920	3	1	1927	2	0
1921	3	2	1928	0	0
1922	1	1	1929	2	0
1923	2	1	1930	4	0
1924	2	1	1931	0	0
1925	1	0	1932	3	1
1926	1	0	1933	0	0

Note: The execution of women was extremely rare in Baden, occurring only in the years 1812, 1819, 1832, 1853, and 1856.

Sources: The Weimar figures are taken from BA Potsdam Reichsjustizamt 5665 Bl. 266 ff. The earlier figures are from GLA Karlsruhe 234/66098: Justizministerium Generalia: Strafrechtspflege: die Todesstrafe und deren Vollzug 1848 bis 1889: Vollzogene Todesurtheile aus früheren Jahren (1887); and BA Potsdam Reichsjustizamt 5664, Bl. 133.

A similar time-series was complied for Hesse during the Weimar Republic, using archival sources. Clearly, in a small state, the number of death sentences and executions was also small, and it is much more difficult to discern any clear trends.

Table 7. *Death sentences and executions in Hesse, 1817–1933*

Year	Death sentences	Executions	Year	Death sentences	Executions
1817	1	1	1835	2	2
1818	3	3	1836	2	0
1819	0	0	1837	1	0
1820	0	0	1838	1	0
1821	0	0	1839	0	0
1822	0	0	1840	0	0
1823	0	0	1841	1	1
1824	0	0	1842	3	2
1825	1	1	1843	2	0
1826	1	1	1844	0	0
1827	0	0	1845	3	0
1828	2	2	1846	3	0
1829	4	0	1847	1	0
1830	0	0	1848	2	0
1831	0	0	1849	0	0
1832	1	0	1850	0	0
1833	2	1	1851	0	0
1834	2	1	1852	2	2

Year	Death sentences	Executions	Year	Death sentences	Executions
1853	1	0	1894	1	1
1854	2	1	1895	0	0
1855	0	0	1896	0	0
1856	4	0	1897	0	0
1857	1	0	1898	2	2
1858	1	0	1899	0	0
1859	1	1	1900	1	1
1860	3	0	1901	0	0
1861	2	0	1902	0	0
1862	2	0	1903	1	1
1863	4	0	1904	1	1
1864	0	0	1905	1	0
1865	1	0	1906	1	0
1866	1	0	1907	0	0
1867	2	0	1908	0	0
1868	3	0	1909	1	1
1869	0	0	1910	0	0
1870	0	0	1911	1	1
1871	1	0	1912	0	0
1872	1	0	1913	0	0
1873	1	0	1914	3	1
1874	1	0	1915	0	0
1875	3	0	1916	0	0
1876	1	0	1917	1	1
1877	2	0	1918	0	0
1878	2	0	1919	3	0
1879	0	0	1920	4	2
1880	1	1	1921	2	1
1881	2	1	1922	0	0
1882	0	0	1923	1	1
1883	1	1	1924	2	2
1884	0	0	1925	0	0
1885	1	1	1926	1	0
1886	0	0	1927	0	0
1887	0	0	1928	0	0
1888	1	1	1929	0	0
1889	2	1	1930	0	0
1890	1	0	1931	1	0
1891	2	2	1932	1	0
1892	2	2	1933	1	1
1893	1	0			

Sources: Krämer, *Mord*. For 1930–3, the figures are compiled from BA Potsdam Reichsjustizamt 5665, Bl. 266 ff. See also the compilation in BA Potsdam Reichsjustizamt 5664, Bl. 133.

From the same series of dissertations in which Krämer published his archival investigations towards the end of the 1920s came another thesis by Franz Exner on Saxony, particularly valuable because of the subsequent destruction of the archival record. The figures in Table 8 show once more quite clearly the effects of the resumption of executions inspired by Bismarck in the 1880s after the refusal of King Johann to sign any death warrants during most of the liberal 1860s and 1870s. Also noticeable is the complete cessation of executions during the Weimar Republic; the execution in 1918 took place under the Empire, those in 1933 under the Third Reich.

Table 8. *Death sentences and executions in Saxony, 1855–1933*

Year	Death sentences	Executions	Year	Death sentences	Executions
1855	2	0	1888	2	0
1856	1	0	1889	3	2
1857	1	1	1890	6	3
1858	7	3	1891	1	1
1859	2	1	1892	2	0
1860	1	0	1893	3	1
1861	4	0	1894	1	0
1862	3	1	1895	2	0
1863	3	1	1896	3	1
1864	4	0	1897	4	3
1865	4	0	1898	2	1
1866	3	0	1899	1	0
1867	4	0	1900	3	2
1868	0	0	1901	2	0
1869	0	0	1902	0	0
1870	0	0	1903	1	1
1871	4	0	1904	1	0
1872	1	0	1905	3	2
1873	1	0	1906	1	1
1874	3	0	1907	2	2
1875	2	0	1908	4	1
1876	2	0	1909	3	1
1877	5	0	1910	6	1
1878	2	0	1911	4	2
1879	4	0	1912	0	0
1880	5	0	1913	0	0
1881	6	1	1914	3	1
1882	3	2	1915	0	0
1883	5	3	1916	3	1
1884	0	0	1917	5	4
1885	6	2	1918	5	1
1886	7	2	1919	7	0
1887	3	2	1920	8	0

Year	Death sentences	Executions	Year	Death sentences	Executions
1921	4	0	1928	4	0
1922	6	0	1929	6	0
1923	1	0	1930	8	0
1924	1	0	1931	1	0
1925	4	0	1932	5	0
1926	1	0	1933	5	3
1927	3	0			

Sources: Franz Exner, 'Mord und Todesstrafe in Sachsen 1855–1927', *Monatsschrift für Kriminalpsychologie und Strafrechtsreform*, 20 (1929), 1–17. These figures do not tally with the provisional statistics compiled in BA Potsdam Reichsjustizamt 5665, Bl. 266 ff., though the latter have been used for the figures for 1928–33. There is another, also slightly differing set of figures in BA Potsdam Reichsjustizamt 5664, Bl. 97–9.

In the city-state of Hamburg condemnations and executions were relatively rare, so that it is unnecessary to list every year. Table 9 gives figures for all years in which offenders were condemned to death. It illustrates once more the decline of capital punishment in the 1860s, its resumption towards the end of the 1870s, its institutionalization in the time of Kaiser Wilhelm II, and its effective abolition under Weimar. Noticeable is the infrequency of commutation; the liberal Senate of Hamburg, the sovereign body of the city-state, was extremely sparing in its use of the power of clemency: 18 out of 27 offenders condemned to death were executed in the period 1854–1918, exactly two-thirds.

Table 9. *Death sentences and executions in the Free and Hanseatic City of Hamburg, 1854–1933*

Year	Death sentences	Executions	Year	Death sentences	Executions
1854	1	1	1901	2	0
1859	1	1	1902	1	1
1863	1	1	1903	2	1
1873	1	0	1909	1	1
1876	1	1	1910	1	1
1877	2	1	1911	1	1
1878	2	1	1913	1	1
1882	1	0	1915	1	1
1887	1	0	1916	1	1
1888	1	1	1918	1	0
1889	1	1	1919	10	0
1890	1	1	1920	3	1
1898	2	1	1921	1	1

Table 9. *(cont.)*

Year	Death sentences	Executions	Year	Death sentences	Executions
1922	2	0	1925	1	0
1923	2	0	1926	1	0
1924	1	0	1927	1	0

Note: The date of execution, recorded by calendar year in the documents, has been assimilated back to the year in which the executed offender was condemned.

Source: BA Potsdam Reichsjustizamt 5665, Bl. 99, 137.

Apart from these long time-series, there is a shorter one available for Hanover from 1841, when a new Criminal Code came into effect, up to the Kingdom's conquest by and absorption into Prussia in the war of 1866. It shows a mildly declining trend. For a relatively small state such as Hanover, the overall number of executions seems high.

Table 10. *Death sentences and executions in the Kingdom of Hanover, 1841–1866*

Year	Death sentences	Executions	Year	Death sentences	Executions
1841	5	0	1854	9	2
1842	8	4	1855	7	2
1843	2	1	1856	6	3
1844	6	0	1857	3	2
1845	3	1	1858	4	2
1846	4	2	1859	11	1
1847	4	1	1860	6	2
1848	3	0	1861	6	2
1849	4	2	1862	5	1
1850	5	3	1863	3	1
1851	5	1	1864	10	0
1852	3	0	1865	6	4
1853	8	1	1866	4	0

Source: *Ueber die Todesstrafe*, p. xlii, Anlage E. The source notes that in each of the years 1844, 1850, 1853, and 1854 one condemned offender committed suicide before being executed, while in 1853 and again in 1865 a condemned offender escaped.

Further figures are available for Württemberg. A peculiarity of this particular set of statistics is that each year between 1827 and 1859 inclusive was counted from 1 July to 31 June. To assimilate them to the other figures in this Appendix, they have all been counted forward to the next year: thus '1835', for example, refers in fact to 1 July 1835 to 30 June 1836. From 1860 onwards the Württemberg statisticians counted by the calendar year like everyone else.

Table 11. *Death sentences and executions in Württemberg, 1827–1933*

Year	Death sentences	Executions	Year	Death sentences	Executions
1827	5	4	1870	1	0
1828	3	3	1871	2	0
1829	1	1	1872	1	0
1830	2	2	1873	0	0
1831	0	0	1874	3	0
1832	1	1	1875	4	0
1833	3	2	1876	1	0
1834	0	0	1877	6	0
1835	0	0	1878	6	0
1836	0	0	1879	3	0
1837	0	0	1880	5	1
1838	0	0	1881	2	1
1839	3	2	1882	3	1
1840	2	2	1883	3	0
1841	1	1	1884	1	0
1842	1	0	1885	0	0
1843	4	4	1886	0	0
1844	1	1	1887	1	1
1845	0	0	1888	1	0
1846	0	0	1889	1	0
1847	4	4	1890	5	0
1848	4	0	1891	3	0
1849	2	0	1892	2	0
1850	0	0	1893	2	0
1851	0	0	1894	3	0
1852	0	0	1895	5	2
1853	4	4	1896	3	1
1854	2	1	1897	0	0
1855	2	1	1898	4	1
1856	2	1	1899	1	1
1857	1	1	1900	4	2
1858	3	1	1901	4	1
1859	4	2	1902	1	0
1860	2	2	1903	6	5
1861	1	0	1904	1	0
1862	6	6	1905	1	1
1863	0	0	1906	2	0
1864	3	2	1907	0	0
1865	1	0	1908	2	0
1866	3	2	1909	1	0
1867	1	0	1910	0	0
1868	0	0	1911	2	1
1869	9	0	1912	1	0

Table 11. (*cont.*)

Year	Death sentences	Executions	Year	Death sentences	Executions
1913	3	0	1921	12	7
1914	2	1	1922	6	2
1915	1	0	1923	2	2
1916	2	0	1924	2	1
1917	1	0	1925	2	
1918	0	0	1926	4	
1919	1	0	1927	3	
1920	2	1	1928	1	

Sources: BA Potsdam Reichsjustizamt 5664 Bl. 97–9 and Bl. 130–1.

According to figures prepared in the *Reichsjustizamt*, there were relatively few executions in the other German states. In Saxe-Weimar-Eisenach, there were 2 condemnations and 1 execution in 1860, the same in 1861, 1 condemnation in 1864, 1 in 1870, and 2 in 1871, but no execution between 1861 and 1878, when, following the Prussian example, 2 out of 3 capital offenders were executed. There was another death sentence in 1880, but no more executions until 1883. There was 1 execution in each of the years 1890, 1891, 1908, 1916, and 2 in 1920. Condemnations also occurred, but were not carried out, in 1886, 1887, 1892, 1895, 1914, and 1917, with 3 more in 1919, 4 in 1921, and 4 in 1923. In neighbouring Saxe-Altenburg there was 1 condemnation and 1 execution in 1860, and further condemnations, not carried out, in 1873, 1879 (2), 1880, 1887 (3), 1890, and 1891, before the next execution took place, in 1898. In 1902 there were no fewer than 3 executions in the state, followed by condemnations, not followed through, in 1903, 1918, and 1921. In Saxe-Coburg-Gotha there was 1 condemnation (carried out) in 1868, and others in 1873, 1876, 1884 (carried out), 1885 (3, 2 carried out), 1886, 1895 (carried out), 1910 (carried out), 1911. In Saxe-Anhalt 2 people were executed in 1880 (out of 2 condemned; there were two other condemnations in 1873), while there were condemnations in 1920 (2), 1921, 1923, and 1924. Saxe-Meiningen passed no death sentences between 1860 and 1880, before resuming the use of the death penalty, though not carrying it out, in 1881 (3 condemnations), 1891, 1894, and 1895. The first execution for many decades took place in Saxe-Meiningen in 1896, followed by a condemnation, not executed, in 1916, a second execution in 1917, and another 4 condemnations in 1919.

By contrast, the tiny Thuringian principality of Schwarzburg-Sondershausen seems to have had a particular enthusiasm for the death penalty in the Bismarckian era, passing 1 death sentence (carried out) in 1860, 1 in 1867, 2 in 1876, 1 in 1877, 1 in 1879, and 2 (both carried out) in 1880. Neighbouring Schwarzburg-Rudolstadt condemmned 1 offender to death in 1880 and another in 1899. No more were recorded in either principality after that. Reuss-Greiz sentenced 1 offender to death in 1864, 2 in 1879 (both executed), and 1 in 1882 (executed), while Reuss-Gera passed 1 death sentence in 1868, 1 in 1874 (carried out), 2 in 1882 (both carried out). The two principalities of Reuss combined sentenced 1 offender to death in 1888, 3 in 1889 (1 executed), 1 in 1895 (executed), 1 in 1897 (executed),

2 in 1898 (1 executed), 1 in 1908 (executed), 1 in 1909 (not executed), and 1 in 1911 (executed).

In the Reich province of Alsace-Lorraine, perhaps contrary to what might have been expected, only 1 person was executed during the period in question, though death sentences were passed in 1874, 1875, 1876 (4), 1877, 1878, 1879 (6, 1 carried out), and 1880 (2). In Lippe-Detmold there were condemnations in 1905 and 1924. Elsewhere, in north Germany, there was an execution in Lübeck in 1913 and a condemnation in 1925 and in Bremen there were executions in 1907 and 1921 (with condemnations, not carried out, in 1883, 1888, 1900, and 1923). In backward Mecklenburg-Schwerin there were 5 death sentences and 2 executions in 1863, 1 death sentence in 1876, 1 (carried out) in 1878, and 1 (carried out) in 1885. In neighbouring Mecklenburg-Strelitz 2 offenders were executed in 1882. In the two Grand Duchies combined there was 1 death sentence in 1907, 1 in 1909, 2 in 1913 (1 carried out), 1 in each of the three years 1916–18, 4 in 1919,·7 in 1920, 2 in 1921, and 2 in 1923, none of them carried out. There were further death sentences passed in Mecklenburg-Schwerin in 1925 (no fewer than 6), 1927 (2), and 1928 (2). In Mecklenburg-Strelitz there was 1 death sentence, carried out in 1926 (this was the famous Jakubowski case), 1 in 1929, and 2 in 1930. In Oldenburg 1 offender was executed in 1884 (with 3 sentences having been passed, but not carried out, in 1878), and 2 out of 3 condemned in 1920. In 1929, 1 more death sentence was passed, and another in 1930. Finally, the Duchy of Brunswick sentenced 1 offender to death in 1860, 1 (executed) in 1868, 1 (executed) in 1869, 3 (all executed) in 1873, 3 in 1878, 2 (executed) in 1883, 1 (executed) in 1885, 1 (executed) in 1887, 1 in 1892, 2 in 1894, 1 (executed) in 1896, 1 (executed) in 1901, 1 (executed) in 1902, 2 (1 executed) in 1904, 1 (executed) in 1912, 1 (executed) in 1913, 1 (executed) in 1916, 1 in 1920, 1 in 1923, 4 in 1924, and 1 each in 1926 and 1929 (figures from BA Potsdam Reichsjustizamt 5664, Bl. 99, 137, and 5665 Bl. 266 ff.).

In order to back up the comparisons made at various points in the book, Tables 12 and 13 provide information about France, and England and Wales. In France, according to one estimate, 354 offenders were executed in the last five years of the Restoration, 564 under the July Monarchy, 141 in the Second Republic, 321 under the Second Empire, 107 in the first decade of the Third Republic, and 155 from 1881 to the turn of the century (BA Potsdam Auswärtiges Amt IIIa Nr. 51, Bd. 7, Bl. 99). In general the nineteenth century was marked by a steady downward trend in the figures.

Table 12. *Death sentences and executions in France (five-yearly annual averages) 1826–1921*

Years	Death sentences	Executions	
		Nos.	% of condemnations
1826–30	111	72	65
1831–5	66	31	47
1836–40	39	29	75
1841–5	48	36	74
1846–50	49	32	65
1851–5	56	31	56

Table 12. (*cont.*)

Years	Death sentences	Executions	
		Nos.	% of condemnations
1856–60	43	24	55
1861–5	22	13	58
1866–70	17	9	54
1871–5	29	15	51
1876–80	25	6	25
1881–5	29	5	18
1886–90	30	8	28
1891–5	28	12	39
1896–1900	17	5	30
1901–5	16	2	11
1906–10	33	5	14
1911–15	20	9	45
1916–20	37	9	24

Note: The figures are missing for 1914–18, so the averages are calculated on the basis of the figures for 1911–13 and 1919–20 for the two relevant periods. See Düsing, *Abschaffung*, 242–3.

The French authorities recognized that statistics of murder conviction and sentencing reflected 'a constantly growing progression of jury verdicts allowing mitigating circumstances in order to avoid applying the death penalty'. Between 1873 and 1880, 92 per cent of all defendants found guilty of capital offences by French juries were also found to have committed their crimes under extenuating circumstances. Such circumstances were declared to have existed in 99 per cent of convictions for arson of an inhabited building, 93 per cent of convictions for poisoning, 83 per cent of murder convictions, and 75 per cent of parricide convictions, suggesting that the nature of the offence rather than the cirumstances under which it was committed was the primary focus of juries in making their recommendations (BA Potsdam Auswärtiges Amt IIIa Nr. 51, Bd. 7, Bl. 98: *Chambre de Députés: No. 388: Neuvième Législature, Session Extraordinaire de 1906; Annexe au procès-verbal de la séance du 5 novembre 1907, 3 and 24*).

Table 13. *Annual average death sentences and executions in England and Wales, by decade, 1841–1950*

Years	Death sentences	Executions
1841–50	18	11
1851–60	17	10
1861–70	23	13
1871–80	27	15

Years	Death sentences	Executions
1881–90	28	15
1891–1900	24	10
1901–10	29	16
1911–20	25	13
1921–30	21	13
1931–40	20	8

Source: Düsing, *Abschaffung*, 244.

It is also appropriate to provide here the full statistics which form the basis for the arguments put forward in Chapter 17 about the movement and structure of public opinion on the issue of capital punishment in West Germany after the war. Opinion polls, of course, were not taken regularly before the 1970s, and so data are available only for certain years. Noticeable here is the relative lack of movement in public opinion until the late 1960s, then the shift back in favour of the death penalty in the mid-1970s in reaction to the terrorist campaigns of the Baader–Meinhof group. Even here, however, the effect was more to make people uncertain (see the 'Don't know' column) than to revive positive support for capital punishment.

Table 14. *Attitudes to capital punishment in the Federal Republic of Germany, 1950–1992 (%)*

Year	For	Against	Don't know	Year	For	Against	Don't know
1950	55	30	15	1966			
1951				1967	50	31	19
1952	55	28	17	1968			
1953				1969			
1954				1970			
1955				1971	43	46	11
1956				1972	33	53	14
1957				1973	30	46	24
1958				1974	36	42	22
1959				1975	35	49	16
1960	54	26	20	1976	34	50	16
1961	51	28	21	1977	45	37	18
1962				1978	31	51	18
1963	50	31	19	1979	30	51	19
1964	49	33	18	1980	28	49	23
1965				1992	24	56	20

Sources: Reuband, 'Sanktionsverlangen', 541; Noelle-Neumann and Piel, *Allensbacher Jahrbuch*, viii. 312; and Noelle-Neumann and Köcher, *Allensbacher Jahrbuch*, ix. 607 (figures only for the 'old federated states'; in the 'new' states, previously part of the German Democratic Republic, the figures were 29% in favour, 49% against, and 22% undecided).

The responses in Table 14 are to the simple question: 'Are you for or against the death penalty?' The responses are somewhat different in the case of the more precise question: 'Are you for or against the death penalty for murder where there are no mitigating circumstances?' Here the declining trend in support for the death penalty is observable a good deal earlier, and the reversal in public opinion in the mid- to late 1970s under the impact of the terrorist movement's murders and kidnappings of prominent Germans is much clearer.

Table 15. *Attitudes to capital punishment for murder in the Federal Republic of Germany, 1958–1978* (%)

Year	For	Against	Undecided
1958	80	17	3
1961	71	20	9
1964	65	27	8
1967	69	20	11
1970	68	27	5
1973	53	34	13
1974	44	44	12
1976	57	41	2
1977	61	38	2
1978	58	40	1

Source: Reuband, 'Sanktionsverlangen', 542.

Perhaps the most interesting result to be obtained from a more detailed breakdown of responses is that respondents with a higher level of education were more in favour of capital punishment in the earlier part of the period surveyed, for the reasons discussed in Chapter 17. In Table 16, the respondents are classified according to level of educational attainment, into those who left school after only completing elementary education (*Volksschule*), those who left after a technical secondary education (*Mittelschule*), and those with an academic school-leaving examination giving entitlement to university study (*Abitur*).

Table 16. *Support for capital punishment in the Federal Republic of Germany 1950–1980, by age and educational attainment* (%)

	Below 30	30 to 49	50 and above
1950			
Elementary education	51	56	50
Technical education	59	65	62
Academic education	74	66	68
1960			
Elementary education	46	59	57

	Below 30	30 to 49	50 and above
Technical education	47	58	51
Academic education	50	61	61
1971			
Elementary education	42	45	56
Technical education	27	27	36
Academic education	0	18	32
1980			
Elementary education	20	27	34
Technical education	12	19	37
Academic education	6	14	27

Source: Reuband, 'Sanktionsverlangen', 550.

BIBLIOGRAPHY

A. ARCHIVAL SOURCES

I. NATIONAL ARCHIVES

1. *Bundesarchiv Koblenz*

R22 Reichsjustizministerium

1143   Behandlung der Strafsachen im Allgemeinen 1934–9
1314   Vollzug der Todesstrafe 1934–7
1315   Vollzug der Todesstrafe 1938–40
1316   Vollzug der Todesstrafe 1941–2
1317   Vollzug der Todesstrafe 1942–3
1318   Vollzug der Todesstrafe 1943–5
1320   Vollzug der Todesstrafe in den eingegliederten Ostgebieten 1942–3
1321   Vollzug der Todesstrafe in den eingegliederten Ostgebieten 1943–4
1322   Verwaltungsbestimmungen der Länder über den Vollzug der Todesstrafe und Vereinbarungen der Länder mit den Scharfrichtern
1323   Scharfrichter 1934–9
1324   Scharfrichter 1939–44
1325   Scharfrichter 1944–5
1327   Gesuche um Verwendung als Scharfrichter 1934–7
1328   Gesuche um Verwendung als Scharfrichter 1938–41
1329   Gesuche um Verwendung als Scharfrichter 1941–5
1478   Verwendung von Leichen für anatomische Zwecke
4086   Auslandshetzpropaganda gegen von deutschen Gerichten in Hoch- und Landesverratsverfahren gefällte Urteile 1938
4202   Polizeiliche Sonderbehandlung nicht genügender Justizurteile
4203   Polizeiliche Sonderbehandlung nicht genügender Justizurteile
4720   Rechtspflege im Allgemeinen
4722   Nationalsozialistische Justizreform
5019   Maßnahmen aus Anlaß von Todesurteilen 1936–44
5020   Maßnahmen aus Anlaß von Todesurteilen 1939–44

Z21 Zentraljustizamt für die Britische Zone
806   Abschaffung der Todesstrafe 1947–9
849   Vollzug der Todesstrafen 1946–9
878   Gnadenrecht—Allgemeines 1946–9

Nachlaß Koch-Weser   99   Zeitungsausschnitte betr. Koch-Wesers Rücktritt als Justizminister 1929

Nachlaß Traub   9   Lebenserinnerungen: Unterlagen zum Manuskript Bd. 4: Vereinzelte Aufzeichnungen aus der Zeit von 1923–44

Nachlaß Lüders   118   Strafrecht

940   *Bibliography*

2. *Bundesarchiv Abteilungen Potsdam*

Reichsjustizamt/Reichsjustizministerium
5664   Die Todesstrafe 1886–1908
5665   Die Vollstreckung der Todesstrafe 1908–12
5666   Die Vollstreckung der Todesstrafe 1933–4
5667   Zeitungsausschnitte betr. Todesstrafe
5670   Unterlagen zur Statistik der Todesstrafe
6095   Einschränkung der Todesstrafe und der lebenslänglichen Freiheitsstrafe 1911–29
6096   Einschränkung der Todesstrafe und der lebenslänglichen Freiheitsstrafe 1930–4
6097   Einschränkung der Todesstrafe und der lebenslänglichen Freiheitsstrafe 1925–9
6098   Einschränkung der Todesstrafe und der lebenslänglichen Freiheitsstrafe 1928–33
6099   Sammelheft betr. Massenmörder Peter Kürten

Reichsamt des Innern
8422   Das Strafgesetzbuch 1909–11
8426   Protokolle der Kommission für die Reform des Strafgesetzbuchs 1911
8429   Protokolle der Kommission für die Reform des Strafgesetzbuchs 1912

Reichskanzleramt
631   Der Entwurf eines Strafgesetzbuches für das Gebiet des Norddeutschen Bundes:
         Todesstrafe, Bd. 1: 1868–70
632   Der Entwurf eines Strafgesetzbuches für das Gebiet des Norddeutschen Bundes:
         Todesstrafe, Bd. 2: 1868–70
647   Die Bundeskommission zur Beratung des Norddeutschen Strafgesetzentwurfs.
         Protokolle 1. Lesung 1869
648   Die Bundeskommission zur Beratung des Norddeutschen Strafgesetzentwurfs.
         Protokolle 2. und 3. Lesung sowie die Entwürfe 1. 2. und 3. Lesung, 1869.

Auswärtiges Amt
IIIa Nr. 51   Todesstrafe und Hinrichtung
              Bd. 3   1886–91
              Bd. 4   1891–3
              Bd. 5   1893
              Bd. 6   1894–8
              Bd. 7   1899–1907
              Bd. 8   1908
              Bd. 9   1908–9
              Bd. 10   1910–15
              Bd. 11   1915–36

Reichstag
848   Das allgemeine deutsche Strafgesetzbuch 1927–8
849   Das allgemeine deutsche Strafgesetzbuch 1928–9

61 Re 1   Reichslandbund—Pressearchiv
              1525   Deportation, Zuchthaus und Gefängnis 1902–5
              1527   Deportation, Zuchthaus und Gefängnis 1911–21
              1528   Deportation, Zuchthaus und Gefängnis 1921–43
              1763   Strafprozeß-Novelle 1901–3
              1766   Strafprozeß-Novelle 1907–8
              1768   Strafprozeß-Novelle 1909–10

1769 Strafprozeß-Novelle 1910–12
1770 Strafprozeß-Novelle 1912–14
1771 Strafprozeß-Novelle 1919–25
1772 Strafprozeß-Novelle 1925–9
1773 Strafprozeß-Novelle 1929–36
1774 Strafprozeß-Novelle 1935–44

D A-5 Staatsrat der DDR
 4   934   3. Sitzung am 6. 10. 1972
     1140 Sitzung am 21. 2. 1977—Punkt 7 der Tagesordnung
     1185 Sitzung am 28. 5. 79—Punkt 4
     1199 Sitzung am 9. Juni 1980—Punkt 3 der Tagesordnung
     1635 Originalbeschlüsse—Umlaufverfahren des Staatsrates—VII. Wahl-
           periode

DO 1 Ministerium des Innern der DDR
    32   Strafvollzug
         39710   Entwicklung des Strafvollzuges 1949–57

DP 1 Ministerium der Justiz der DDR
    VA   Verwaltungsarchiv
         353   Rechtsprechung, Revision, Statistik: Mitteilung von Strafsachen
               1946–50
         360   Rechtsprechung, Revision, Statistik: Mitteilung von Strafsachen
               1947–50
         373   Anklageschriften und Urteile in Strafsachen 1947–50
         418   Mitteilung von Strafsachen, bei denen Todesstrafe beantragt ist,
               1946–51
         5110 Todesstrafe 1965–74
         6495 Liste der Todesurteile 1945–8

DP 2 Oberstes Gericht der DDR
    2041 Abschaffung Todesstrafe 1981–7

3. Public Record Office London

FO Foreign Office
    371 Central Department
         109595 Execution of Death Penalty Sentences in Germany 1954
    937 Control Office for Germany and Austria: Legal
         156 Death Penalty 1947
    938 Control Office for Germany and Austria: Private Office Papers
         76 Sentence of Death on Karl Krille for Showing Hitler's Portrait
    945 Control Office for Germany and Austria: General
         318 Death Sentences—Executions
         320 Death Sentences—Notification to Allied Governments
    1012 Control Commission for Germany: Berlin
         673 Execution of Sentences—German Courts
         681 Death Sentences
    1060 Zonal Office of the Legal Adviser

114   Land Ministries of Justice: Prerogative of Mercy
149   Crimes against Humanity: Policy 1948–9
239   Execution of Death Sentences, Policy 1945–6
240   Execution of Death Sentences, Policy 1946–7
241   Execution of Death Sentences, Policy 1947–8
243   Execution of Death Sentences, Policy 1949–50
244   Judicial Hangings—Instructions 1948–50
417   Executions—Revision of Penal Branch Staff Instructions
930   Execution of Death Sentences—Policy
931   Reviews of Death Sentences: Paderborn 1945
934   Reviews of Death Sentences 1945
936   Reviews of Death Sentences 1945–6
937   Reviews of Death Sentences 1946
938   Reviews of Death Sentences 1946
939   Reviews of Death Sentences 1946
940   Reviews of Death Sentences 1945–7
941   Reviews of Death Sentences 1947–8
1076   Death Sentences 1946
1077   Death Sentences 1946–7

4. National Archives Washington, DC

260   United States Occupation Headquarters, World War II: Office of Military Government for Germany (US) (OMGUS)
    C7   Legal Division
        D2   Legal Advice Branch
            7/53/34/1/b.46–62: Legal Files 1944–50

        D3   Administration of Justice Branch
            7/53/34/7/b.91–6   Review Board 1948–51
            7/53/36/2–3/b.137–8   Criminal Cases and War Crimes 1947–50

        D5   Board of Clemency, OMGUS
            7/53/36/4/b.76   General Records and Correspondence Concerning Petitions for Clemency 1946–9
                b.77   Copies of Legal Opinions, 1946–8
                b.79   Correspondence and Memoranda of Anthony F. Bergson 1947–8
                b.150–1   Miscellaneous Records 1947–8

II. STATE ARCHIVES

5. Badisches Generallandesarchiv Karlsruhe

234   Justizministerium Generalia: Strafrechtspflege
    6609   Die Todesstrafe und deren Vollzug, 1848–89
    6610   Die Todesstrafe und deren Vollzug, 1890–1928
    6611   Die Todesstrafe und deren Vollzug, 1927–32
    6772   Der Vollzug der Todesstrafe, in specie die Scharfrichter, 1836–81
    6773   Die Scharfrichter 1884–1933

6774 Der Vollzug der Todesstrafe, hier insbesondere die Fallbeilmaschine betreffend, 1827–1900

10177 Die in Vorschlag kommende Deportation der Verbrecher in einen überseeischen Staat 1815–28

10178 Der Vollzug der Todesstrafe, hier die Fallbeilmaschine 1901–32

240 Oberlandesgericht

1266 Vollzug der Todesstrafe 1836–1934

6. Bayerisches Hauptstaatsarchiv München

GR Generalregistratur

318 Der Criminal-Prozeß in Bayern

324 U.a. Abschaffung der Galgenpredigten

MA Aussenministerium

101130 Die Anwendung der Todesstrafe in Bayern 1919–1930

65666a Die Mitteilung eines Modelles der in Württemberg und im Kgr. Sachsen eingeführten Hinrichtungsmaschine

65677 Artikel in der Presse über die Vollstreckung der Todesstrafe und die Vorgänge bei derselben 1886

MF Finanzministerium

71 Die Gehälter der Scharfrichter und Wasenmeister

21592 Scharfrichter und Wasenmeister des Königreiches 1810–22

MInn Innenministerium

46136 Vollzug der Todesurteile 1850–67

71559 Vollzug der Todesurteile 1869–1924

71567 Reform des Gefängniswesens und Strafvollzugs

71690 Abschaffung der Todesstrafe 1920–33

72777 Scharfrichter-Stellen 1836–1937

MJu Justizministerium

12575 Statistik der Morde und der Todesurteile 1849–1935

13065 Militärische und Polizeiliche Maaßregeln bey Vollstreckung der Todes-Urtheil

13066 Die Einführung des Fallschwertes

13067 Vollzug der Todesstrafe in den Landesteilen r/Rh. 1855–80

13068 Vollzug der Todesstrafe in der Pfalz 1856–65

13144 Gesetz vom 29. März 1933 über Verhängung und Vollzug der Todesstrafe

17962 Haecker, Gottfried, von Dingolfing, und Baeck, Augustin, von der Au, wegen Mordes 1840–77

17965 Hahn, Dominikus, Schullehrer, v. Konzell; Hahn, Egid und Magdalena v. Pfarrleiten, wegen qualificirten Mordes

18016 Huber, Florian, Hausierer von Tölz, wegen Mordes u.a. Todesurteil 1922

18343 Sumner, Joseph, Arbeiter, von Regensburg, wegen Raubmordes 1919

7. Mecklenburgisches Landeshauptarchiv Schwerin

S Staatsanwaltschaft beim Landgericht Neustrelitz

353 Bericht über den Fall Jakubowski. Berichterstatter: Regierungsrat Steuding

354–56   Voruntersuchung: August Nogens und Genossen. Ermittlungen des Krim.-Pol.-Rats Gennat, Berlin (1928)

357–64   Ermittlungssache gegen August Nogens und Genossen wegen Mordes. Schlußbericht des Kriminalrats Gennat.(1927–43)

365   Strafsache gegen Jakubowski

366–71   Strafsache gegen Nogens und Genossen wegen Mord: Handakten der Staatsanwaltschaft 1929–31

372   Nebenakten in der Strafsache gegen Nogens und Genossen wegen Mord. II. Strafvollstreckung an den Arbeiter August Nogens., Bd. 20. 1929–31.

373   Nebenakten in der Strafsache gegen Nogens und Genossen wegen Mord. II. Strafvollstreckung gegen Fritz Nogens, Bd. 21. 1929–1936.

439   Gutachten des sächsischen Staats- und Kustizministers a. D. Dr. h.c. Bünger über den Fall Jakubowski.

8. *Niedersächsisches Hauptstaatsarchiv Hannover*

Hann. 108   Allgemeine Ständeversammlung
6277   Todesstrafe
6784   Todesstrafe

Hann. 173a   Generalstaatsanwaltschaft Celle
436   Die Vollstreckung der Todesstrafe 1853–1901
437   Die Vollstreckung der Todesstrafe 1902–35
438   Verfahren bei Vollstreckung der Todesstrafe 1857–92
439   Verfahren bei Vollstreckung der Todesstrafe 1891–6
440   Verfahren bei Vollstreckung der Todesstrafe 1897–1905
441   Die Vollstreckung von Todesstrafen 1906–20
442   Die Vollstreckung von Todesstrafen 1921–34

9. *Nordrhein-westfälisches Hauptstaatsarchiv Düsseldorf: Zweigarchiv Schloß Kalkum*

Landgericht und Staatsanwaltschaft Düsseldorf
Rep. 17/538   Arbeiter Peter Kürten in Düsseldorf wegen Mordes. Hauptakten Bd. 1: 1929
544   Desgl. Vollstreckungsband, 1931
700   Desgl. Urteil
705   Desgl. Gnadenheft mit Gnadenbericht 1931
706   Desgl. Anträge gegen Vollziehung der Todesstrafe
707   Desgl. Anträge auf Vollziehung der Todesstrafe
708   Desgl. Anträge auf Zulassung zur Hinrichtung
712–18   Desgl. Presseberichte 1931, 1.–7. Verhandlungtag
719   Desgl. Mitteilungen und Nachrichten der Justizpressestelle Düsseldorf 1930
720   Desgl. Justizpressestelle Düsseldorf. Bericht über 'Kürtenprozeß und Presse' 1931
727   Desgl. Gesammelte Zeitungsberichte der Justizpressestelle Hamburg betr. den Mordprozeß Kürten 1931

11. Staatsarchiv der Freien- und Hansestadt Hamburg

Senat
Cl. VII Lit. Mb No. 3
    Vol. 3   Kriminal-Urteile und Executiones
    Vol. 4a Nachricht, wie es bey der Ausführung eines zum Tode verurtheilten
             Delinquenten gehalten, und was für Mannschaft von der Garnison dabey
             commandirt wird 1780–1804
    Vol. 4b Acta wegen Abstellung der bisherigen Gewohnheit: die Missethäter durch
             Prediger zur Gerichtsstädte begleiten zu lassen 1784
    Vol. 7   Acta, die in Kriminal-Fällen bey der Vorführung der Gefangenen und bey
             der Execution von Todes- und andren Peinlichen Urtheilen zu beobach-
             tende Formalitäten betr. 1816
    Vol. 8   Criminal-Urteile und Executiones 1841–5
    Vol. 9   Criminal-Urteile und Executiones 1854: Acta, betr. die Abschaffung der
             Oeffentlichkeit bei den Hinrichtungen,—und die Einführung des
             Fallbeils
    Vol. 10 Kriminalurteile und Executiones 1856: Hinrichtung des Raubmörders Timm

12. Staatsarchiv Weimar

B Rechtspflege
    2199a Die Gebühren der Scharfrichter für Folterung und Hinrichtung
    2402   Die geistliche Begleitung der Verbrecher zum Richtplatz 1824
    2693   Gertraud Catharina Schmidtin pto. Infanticidii 1752–3
    2693   Die Rudolph Börner zu Bürgel zuerkannte und an demselben vollstreckte
            Strafe des Stranges 1758–61
    2387a Die Aufhebung der Tortur 1817–43

Oberappellationsgericht Jena
267   Die Abschaffung der Tortur 1817–24
452   Untersuchungssache wider Adam Landgraf aus Wittenbach wegen Raubmordes
       und gegen Johann Engelhardt aus Boblas wegen Brandstiftung 1825

13. Württembergisches Hauptstaatsarchiv Stuttgart

EA 1/106 Pressestelle des Staatsministeriums
          Bü 1060   Todesstrafe 1952–67

EA 1/922 Staatsministerium
          5308   Todesstrafe 1948–62

EA 4/001 Justizministerium
          502   Vollzug der Todesstrafe 1945–51

E 130b Staatsministerium
          Bü 153   Gnadensachen: Einzelfälle 1925–8, 1930
          Bü 886   Strafvollzug: Vollstreckung der Todesstrafe 1880–1933

III. MUNICIPAL ARCHIVES

14. Staatsarchiv der Freien- und Hansestadt Lübeck

Rep. 49/1 Polizeiamt
        45 Die Vollstreckung der Todesstrafe 1886–1913
    2816 Abdeckerei 1820–98
    2870 Beschwerden von Gefangenen

15. Staatsarchiv München

App. Ger. Appellationsgericht
    5704 Todesurteile, Verkündung und Vollziehung, betr. dann Koepf-Maschine

16. Stadtarchiv Braunschweig

C VIII 102 Die Vollstreckung von Todesurtheilen 1731, 1807

17. Stadtarchiv Erfurt

1–1, XVI Polizei-Sachen
    e. Attentat auf das Leben Sr. Majestät des Königs vom 26ten Juli 1844 sowie am 22. Mai 1850
    i. Öffentliche Exekutionen und dieserhalbige polizeiilige Verfügungen

18. Stadtarchiv Hannover

A 1117 Die Anwendung der Folter 1754
  1173 Hinrichtungsprotokolle 1727—1756—1771
  1198 Vorfälle bei Hinrichtungen, 1745, 1756
  1200 Abnahme hingerichteter Personen vom Galgen und die weitere Verfügung über deren Körper 1707–71
  1209 Die städtischen Scharfrichter (Personalia) Bd. 2, 1818–60
  1212 Die Kurpfuscherei der Nachrichter 1730–85
  1239 Landesherrliche Verordnungen wegen peinlicher Erkenntnisse bei leichteren Diebereien 1745–80

19. Stadtarchiv Leipzig

L XII G 23 Das Hochgericht 1854
L XII G 23b vol. ii Die Reparierung des Hohen Gerichts oder Galgens, incl. des Rabensteins, wie auch der Vorstellung derer zum Tode Verurtheilten in der Rathsstube 1763–1824

IV. LIBRARIES, INSTITUTES, AND FOUNDATIONS

20. Deutsches Volkslied-Archiv, Freiburg im Breisgau

Bl. Gedruckte Blätter
Gr. I Erzählende Lieder
Gr. II Politische Lieder

21.   Geheimes Staatsarchiv Preußischer Kulturbesitz, Berlin-Dahlem

Rep. 84a   Preußisches Justizministerium

4152   Die Bestimmung des Scharfrichters bey Todesstrafen, die beym Inquisitoriat zu Thorn vorfallen
4586–95   Scharfrichter
4598   Die gutachtlichen Berichte der Landes-Justiz-Kollegium über die Verhältnisse der Scharfrichter
4599   Gesuche um Verwendung als Scharfrichter 1925–34
6447   Die Vollstreckung der Todesstrafe in dem Oberlandesgerichtsbezirk Jena
7781   Die Vollstreckung der Todesstrafe 1800–36
7782   Die Vollstreckung der Todesstrafe 1836–51
7783   Die Vollstreckung der Todesstrafe 1851–68
7784   Die Todesstrafe 1870–1909
7785   Die Todesstrafe 1910–25
7786   Die Todesstrafe 1926–33
7787   Die Todesstrafe
7788   Allerhöchstes Handschreiben Sr. Majestät des Königs Wilhelm I. vom 14. April 1870, betreffend Vollstreckung der Todesstrafe
7789   Akten des Kammergerichts betr. die Anfertigung des Richtbeils und des Richtblocks sowie der Instrumente zum Torturiren
7790   Die Beschränkung des Zutritts bei Hinrichtungen 1886–7
7791   Berichte, betr. die Todesstrafe
7792   Äusserungen der Presse über die Todesstrafe
8143   Verzeichnis der jährlich zum Tode verurtheilten Verbrecher 1818–44
8144   Verzeichnis der jährlich zum Tode verurtheilten Verbrecher 1845–58
8145   Verzeichnis der jährlich zum Tode verurtheilten Verbrecher 1858–83
8146   Verzeichnis der jährlich zum Tode verurtheilten Verbrecher 1883–1934
8230   Mord und Totschlag
8231   Verbrechen und Vergehen wider das Leben
8313   Die Warnungsanzeige in Criminal-Untersuchungen
8312   Die Abschaffung des Halseisens, Bock, Ganten, Fiedel und ähnlicher Strafen
9268   Das Hochgericht zu Berlin
9269   Hinrichtungen in Berlin
9270   Die Ermittelung eines geeigneten Hinrichtungs-Platzes 1857–9
9397   Die Vollstreckung der Todesstrafe in der Provinz Hannover durch die Fallschwertmaschine

Rep. 180   Regierung Danzig
5273   Die Ablösung des Abdeckerey-Zwanges der priviligierten Scharfrichtereien

22. *Institute of German, Austrian and Swiss Affairs, University of Nottingham*

British Military Government in Berlin: Archive of Newspaper Cuttings
25 Legal Matters, Trials

Prozesse 1950–1/1–2
1952 Rechtswesen
1953 Rechtswesen
1954 Rechtswesen
Prozesse 1953–4/1   Allgemein
Prozesse 1955/1   Personen, Firmen, Berufe
1956/1   Rechtspflege
1956/2   Wirtschaftliche und Politische Prozesse
1957/1   Zuchthäuser und Zwangsarbeitslager
1957/2   Wirtschaftliche und Politische Prozesse
1958/1   Amnestie, Zuchthäuser, KZ, Zwangsarbeitslager
1959/1   Amnestie, Zuchthäuser, KZ, Zwangsarbeitslager
1962   Richter, Verhaftungen usw.
1964/2   Verbrechen allgemein, Jugendliche
1966/2   Politische Prozesse
1977/8/1   Haftanstalten

23. *Stiftung Archiv der Parteien und Massenorganisationen der DDR im Bundesarchiv, Berlin*

J IV   Sozialistische Einheitspartei Deutschlands
  2   Zentralkomitee
    2   Politbüro: Beschlüsse/Reinschriftenprotokolle
      105   Sitzung am 22. August 1950
      116   Sitzung am 31. Oktober 1950
      216   Sitzung am 17. Juni 1952
      217   Sitzung am 24. Juni 1952
      227   Sitzung am 19. August 1952
      228   Sitzung am 20. August 1952
      284   Sitzung am 2. Juni 1953
      360   Sitzung am 11. Mai 1954
     2230   Sitzung am 14. Juli 1987

    2A   Politbüro: Arbeitsprotokolle
      243   Sitzung am 27. Januar 1953
      257   Sitzung am 31. März 1953
      266   Sitzung am 26. Mai 1953
      291   Sitzung am 18. Juli 1953
      306   Sitzung am 8. September 1953
      348   Sitzung am 11. Mai 1954
      377   Sitzung am 28. September 1954
      412   Sitzung am 8. März 1955
      431   Sitzung am 14. Juni 1955
      432   Sitzung am 21. Juni 1955
     3039   Sitzung am 14. Juli 1987

13   Abteilung Staat und Recht
433–4   Prozesse gegen Saboteure und Agenten in der DDR 1950–1

NL 90   Nachlaß Otto Grotewohl
440   Aus der Tätigkeit des Ministeriums der Justiz der DDR 1950–1
444   Entwurf eines Strafgesetzbuches 1953

24. Universitätsbibliothek Heidelberg

Heid. Hs. 3716   Nachlaß Radbruch
I.D.   Äußerungen über Gustav Radbruch

V. GOVERNMENT AGENCIES

25. Der Bundesbeauftragte für die Unterlagen des Staatssicherheitsdienstes der ehemaligen Deutschen Demokratischen Republik (Zentralarchiv)

Anweisung VVS 4507/55   Bruno und Susanne Krüger, 1955
Befehl Nr. 224/55   Bruno und Susanne Krüger, 1955
Befehl Nr. 357/60   Manfred Smolka, 1960

Zentrale Auswertungs- und Informationsgruppe
ZAIG 4228   Hinweise zu ersten Reaktionen der Bevölkerung der DDR auf den Beschluß . . . zur Abschaffung der Todesstrafe 1987
ZAIG 7862   Abschaffung der Todesstrafe 1987

26. Berlin Document Center

Documentation on executioners 1933–45

B. PRIMARY PRINTED SOURCES

Allgemeines Landrecht für die Preußischen Staaten von 1794 (Textausgabe, mit einer Einführung von Hans Hattenhauer, 2nd edn., Frankfurt am Main, 1994).

ANONYMOUS PUBLICATIONS

Abschiedslied deren berüchtigten dreyen Rauberen Joße Hinrich Low, Hans Jürgen Schrage and Johan Tobia Reichart, am 16ten Decembris 1754 zu Münster in Westphalen durchs Schwerdt vom Leben zum Todt geschieckt (Munich, 1754).
Anreden, gehalten bey der Hinrichtung des unglücklichen Johann Nicolaus G**, nebst einigen Nachrichten über sein Betragen in den drey letzten Tagen seines Lebens und im Tode. Zum Besten der armen Familie des Hingerichteten (Vienna, 1807).
Auch etwas über die Gewohnheit, Missethäter durch Prediger zur Hinrichtung begleiten zu lassen (Hamburg, 1784).
Ausführliche und wahrhaffte Relation von dem de 21. Maji dieses 1726. Jahres in Dresden von einnem GOtt-vergessenen Bösewicht an dem wohlseligen Herrn M. Hahnen grausam verübten Priester-Mord. Nebst unterschiedenen gewissen Particularien, so denen bisherigen unwahren Erzehlungen entgegen gesetzet werden (Dresden, 1726).
Des bekannten Diebes, Mörders und Räubers Lips Tullians, und seiner Complicen Leben und Übelthaten, dabei GOttes sonderbare Schickung erhellet, als vor der Königl. Commission Neun Personen ohne Tortur, ihre begangenen grossen Missethaten gütlich bekannt haben,

ohngeachtet ihre Viere davon zu anderen Zeiten, die Tortur zu 3. und 4. mahlen ausgestanden, und die Wahrheit halsstarriger Weise verhalten. Und von solchen Fünffte am 8. Mart. 1715, durch das Schwerd von Leben zum Tode gestraffet, und ihre Körper auf 5. Räder geflochten worden. Alles aus denen Judicial-Actis mit Fleiß extrahieret, und dem grossen GOtt zu Ehren, denen Frommen zur Betrachtung der Göttlichen Gerechtigkeit und Barmherzigkeit, und den Bösen zur Warnung und Bekehrung ausgefertigt, und öffentlichen Druck gegeben worden (Dresden, 1716).

Beschreibung des Johann Friedrich Starke, aus Weiler, bey Kreuznach gebürtig, welcher wegen vieler begangenen Diebstähle 34 Monate im Amte Callenberg in Arrest gesessen, und am 15ten November 1808 im 29sten Jahre seines Alters, den wohlverdienten Lohn seiner Taten, am Galgen erhielt (no place of publication, 1808).

Die betrübte Mord-Notification, der grausamen und unmenschlichen Mordthaten, so der Tausend-Künstler der Teufel, durch den Mann Hanß Nicolaus Künstler, zeithero gewesener Bauer und Einwohner in Grossen-Rudolstadt, verübet (Erfurt, 1733).

(ed.), *Braunbuch über Reichstagsbrand und Hitlerterror* (Basel, 1933).

Constitutio Criminalis Theresiana (Vienna, 1768).

Curieuses Gespräch im Reiche der Todten, zwischen dem am 21ten Julii dieses 1733ten Jahres, in Hamburg, wegen verübten Diebstahls, gehängten Juden: Susmann Moses, und dem am 10. Augusti H. A. in Altona, wegen begangenen Mords an seiner leiblichen Frauen, hingerichteten Schusters: Samuel Rattge, worinnen beyde einander ihren bösen Lebens-Wandel erzehlen, und bedauern, daß sie in dem Unglauben und Unbußfertigkeit gestorben sind (Hamburg, 1733).

Der Doppelmord von Langwasser vor dem Schwurgericht (Schwiebus: Druck und Verlag von Hermann Reiche, n.d.).

Eine Doppel-Hinrichtung zu Hirschberg in Schlesien zum 17. Februar v. Js. (Schwiebus: Druck und Verlag von Hermann Reiche, 1904).

Drey Schöne Lieder, Das erste: Ich wär nie dahin gegangen, so wär, &c. Welches ein Übelthäter in der Gefangenschafft selbsten aufgesetzt . . . (1756).

Eine erschreckliche und fast unerhörte Mordthat, Welche ein Vater, Christian Langer, an seinem eigenen und einzigen Zehnjährigen Sohne, begangen, Indem er ihn wegen entwendeter zwey Grüschel, mit einem Messer, mit zwey langsam nach einander geschehenen Schnitten, bey grossem Geschrey, den Kopf abgeschnitten, auch wie er hernach in Grunau, eine Viertel-Meile von Schweidnitz, den 30. Apr. 1739. Nach Urthel und Recht In eine Ochsen-Haut eingenehet, mit Pferden zur Gerichtstädte ist geschleiffet wordem, Auch allda Mit dem Rade, vom Leben zum Tode gebracht worden ([Schweidnitz?], 1739).

Eine erschröckliche Mord-Geschichte, So sich zugetragen Anno 1741, den 14ten Tag May zu Ramsen im Legau, Stockacher-Herrschaft, Welcher Bößwicht, Jacob Sigerist, seinen Vetter, Ulrich Graf, und seiner Frau, Anna Sigristin, und die dritte Anna Maria Titelreichin, eines Musicanten Frau, mit Gifft vergeben, und was sich dabey ferner zu getragen, wie der günstige Leser alles ausführlich in diesem Lied sehen wird. (1741).

Erzählung von dem Leben, dem Verbrechen und der Bekehrung des Friedrich Christian Lorenzen, welcher am 19. April 1825 in der Nähe von Hannover enthauptet wurde. Entworfen von den, mit der Todes-Vorbereitung desselben, beauftragt gewesenen Geistlichen (Hanover, 1825).

Der Freundesmörder Stephan Werner von Bleichstetten. Seine Lebensbeschreibung, Flucht, Verurtheilung und Hinrichtung. Nach den öffentlichen Verhandlungen vor dem Schwurgerichte in Tübingen vom 28. Juni bis 2. Juli 1858. Mit einer Abbildung der Guillotine, 2nd edn. (Tübingen, 1858).

Eine grausame Mordthat | welche geschehen Zu unser frauen Hall | drey stunden von brüssel | wie sich ein amt mannß sohn mit einer Reichen Jungfer versprochen | und von der selben mit gifft ver geben | ihm und ihre mutter jämmerlich umß leben gebracht (1736).

Gründliche Nachricht | Von denen | von Einigen | Räubern und Spitzbuben | An dem Pfarrer zu Edderitz | Herrn Alrico Plesken | Und einem Schneider Hansen Lingen und dessen Ehe-Weibe | In Februariu und Martio 1713. | Ausgeübten Diebstahl | gebrauchten entsetzlichen Marter und respective begangenen Mord | (Cöthen, 1714).

In dem königlichen preußischen Amte Ermsleben bey verschiedenen Executionen bislang gehaltene und auch kunftig bey denen daselbst inhafftirten und bereits zum Rade und andern abscheulichen Todes-Straffen verurtheilten 3. Mördern und Räubern, nemlich: Hans Jürgen Jeckeln, Annen Catharinen Kahnen und Eleonoren Julianen Behtgen, wiederum den ( ) Martii 1715 öffentlich zuhegende Hochnoth-peinliche Hals-Gerichte, welches von denen überflüßigen und unnöhtigen solenniteten gesaubert und in eine kurze Ordnung gebracht ist (1715).

Letzter Zuruff der Armen Sünder als Dieselbe den 3. Januarii 1736. den wohl verdienten und gerechten Lohn ihrer greulichen Mord-That, so sie den 23. Dec. 1735 in Berlin an drey Personen verübet, empfiengen (Berlin 1735).

Lied eines armen Sünders, Namens: Kaspar Sailer, von Langenau, evangelischer Religion, 36 Jahr alt, verheuratheten Standes. Welcher wegen vielen verübten Diebstählen von einer hohen Obrigkeit in Ulm den 5 September 1788 zu dem Schwert verurtheilt wurde (Ulm, 1788).

Melcher Hedloffs sonst Schutze-Melcher genannt, von Kautinchen auß Medziborischer Herrschaft bürtig verübete und begangene Mord-Thaten, welche er innerhalb 15. Jahren mehrentheils mit seinen zwey Röhren verrichtet. Auch wie er den 19. Januarii dieses 1654 Jahrs seiner Arbeit nach, den Lohn empfangen (Breslau, 1654).

Der Mord aus Eifersucht und Liebeswuth, ausgeübt von dem Maurergesellen und Landwehrmann Carl Gottfried Mecke aus Mühlhausen an seiner ehemaligen Geliebten Louise Hagemann zu Erfurt (Hamburg, n.d.).

Nachricht von denen Prediger-Mördern, Raubern und Spitzbuben | Welche den 28. Januar. 1713. Nachts zwischen 12. und 1. Uhr Ihren allerseits Beicht-Vater und 22. jährigen Prediger, Herrn Johann Heinrich Meiern | Zu Rehburg (im Ambte Stolzenau) jämmerlich ermordet | Und der Auf Chur-Fürstl. Durchl. zu Braunschweig Lüneburg Gnädigsten Befehl ergangenen Inquisition und darauf den 6. Dec. 1713 erfolgten Inquisition und darauf den 6. Dec. 1713 erfolgten Execution (Frankfurt am Main, 1715).

'Noch eine bedeutende Stimme für die Todesstrafe', *Zeitschrift für die Criminal-Rechts-Pflege in den Preussischen Staaten mit Ausschluss der Rheinprovinzen* (ed. Julius Hitzig), 24 (1829), 405–23.

'Noch etwas über neue Gesetzbücher', *Zeitschrift für die Criminal-Rechts-Pflege in den Preussischen Staaten mit Ausschluss der Rheinprovinzen* (ed. Julius Hitzig), 21 (1828), 223–34.

Siebenfacher Mord, welcher sich am 22sten October 1838 zu Bebering zugetragen und von einem Manne Namens Wilhelm, Heinrich Schmidt verübt worden ist (1840).

Statistik des Preußischen Staats. Versuch einer Darstellung seiner Grundmacht und Kultur, seiner Verfassung, Regierung und Verwaltung im Lichte der Gegenwart (Berlin, 1845).

Traurige Nachricht von einer erschröcklichen Mordthat, welche sich bey Prenzlau von fünf Bärenführern zugetragen; dabey die grosse Hinrichtung, welche den 10. Weinmonat 1751.

gehalten worden, mit mehreren ausführlich zu ersehen seyn wird. Gedruckt nach dem Berlinischen Exemplar (1751).

Über die Gewohnheit, Missethäter durch Prediger zur Hinrichtung begleiten zu lassen (Hamburg, 1784).

Ueber Zulässigkeit und Anwendbarkeit der Todesstrafe. Sendschreiben an den Herrn Obersteuerprocurator Eisenstuck, veranlasst durch dessen Separatvotum bei den Verhandlungen der Deputation der Zweiten Ständischen Kammer zur Prüfung und Berathung des Entwurfs des Criminalgesetzbuchs (Leipzig, 1837).

Umständliche Nachricht von der am 1sten Martii Anno 1720 geschehenen Enthauptung des auf der Festung Königstein gefangen gewesenen und zu zweyen Mahlen auf der Flucht aus den Arrest ergriffenen bekannten Barons von Kettenberg, welcher desselben letzte Klage und Trost-Worte, auch darauf erfolgte Antwort beygefüget sind (1720).

Eine vierfache Hinrichtung, oder: Die Sühne des Gattenmordes (Schwiebus: Druck und Verlag von Hermann Reiche, 1898).

Eine wahrhafftige neue Zeytung, so sich begeben hat au Eschwein, wie allda ein Mörder ist eingebracht worden, welcher 55. Mord mit seiner eygen Hand verbracht hat, biß er endlich von Gott gestrafft vnnd gericht ist worden den 1. tag May in diesem 97. Jahr | im Thon | Kompt her zu mir spricht Gottes Sohn &c (Coburg, 1597).

Wahrhafte Beschreibung und Abbildung eines 32fachen Raubmordes, welcher sich bei Paris den 25. July 1825 zugetragen hat.

Wohlverdientes Todes-Urtheil nebst einer Moral-Rede des Antoni Pittersohn, welcher auf gnädigste Anbefehlung eines churfürstl. hochlöbl. Hof-Raths allhier in München wegen ausgeübten diebischen Verbrechen halber heut den 20. October 1764 durch das Schwerd vom Leben zum Tod hingerichtet worden (Munich, 1764).

Wohlverdientes Todesurtheil nebst einer Moral-Rede der Barbara N., welche auf gnädigste Anbefehlung eines churfürstl. hochlöbl. Hofraths allhier wegen ihren ausgeübten Diebstahl heut den 30ten Junii 1774 auf der inneren Richtstätt mit dem Schwerd vom Leben zum Tode hingerichtet worden (Munich, 1774).

Wohlverdientes Todesurtheil nebst einer Moral-Rede des Jakob N., vulgo kleine Hansel, welche auf gnädigste Anbefehlung eines churfürstl. hochlöbl. Hofraths allhier wegen ihren ausgeübten Diebstahl heut den 30ten Junii 1774 auf der inneren Richtstätt mit dem Schwerd vom Leben zum Tode hingerichtet worden (Munich, 1774).

Wohlverdientes Todesurtheil, nebst einer Moral-Rede des Johann Heinrich N., welcher auf gnädigste Anbefehlung eines churfürstl hochlöbl. Hofraths allhier in München wegen seinen ausgeübt dieb- und räuberischen Verbrechen heut den 13. Oct. 1774 mit dem Strange vom Leben zum Tode hingerichtet worden (Munich, 1774).

Wohlverdientes Todesurtheil, nebst einer Moral-Rede des Johann N., welcher auf gnädigste Anbefehlung eines churfürstl hochlöbl. Hofraths allhier in München wegen seinen ausgeübt dieb- und räuberischen Verbrechen heut den 5. Jan. 1775 mit dem Strange vom Leben zum Tode hingerichtet worden (Munich, 1775).

Wohlverdientes Todesurtheil, nebst einer Moral-Rede des Joseph N., vulgo Krammerseppel, welcher auf gnädigste Anbefehlung eines churfürstl hochlöbl. Hofraths allhier in München wegen seinen ausgeübt dieb- und räuberischen Verbrechen heut den 9. Dec. 1774 mit dem Strange vom Leben zum Tode hingerichtet worden (Munich, 1774).

Wohlverdientes Todesurtheil, nebst einer Moral-Rede des Mathias N., welcher auf gnädigste Anbefehlung eines churfürstl hochlöbl. Hofraths allhier in München wegen seinen ausgeübt dieb- und räuberischen Verbrechen heut den 12. Dec. 1774 auf dem Hochgericht mit dem Strange vom Leben zum Tode hingerichtet worden (Munich, 1774).

Wohlverdientes Todesurtheil, nebst einer Moral-Rede des Michael N., vulgo Berndl, welcher auf gnädigste Anbefehlung eines churfürstl hochlöbl. Hofraths allhier in München wegen seinen ausgeübt dieb- und räuberischen Verbrechen heut den 15. Oct. 1774 auf dem Hochgericht mit dem Strange vom Leben zum Tode hingerichtet worden (Munich, 1774).

Zwey neue merkwürdige Beschreibungen . . . Zum zweyten eine erschröckliche Frevel-That eines verruchten Meuchelmörders, Nahmens Sebastian Krug, gebürtig von Rappolsweiler, wohnhaft zu Hunneweyer, ohnweit Colmar im obern Elsaß, welcher seine Mordthat an einer Dienstmagd verübet hat, indem er sie in einen tieffen Brunnen gestürzet, allwo er vor seine Bosheit zu Colmar den 13. Oct. 1758. durch das Rad die Straffe empfangen ([Colmar?], 1759).

Zwey erschreckliche Mord-Geschichten. Die erste handelt von einem Sohne, aus dem Coburger Lande, welcher seinen Vater und seine Mutter auf die erbärmlichste Art ermordet hat. Die zweyte handelt von einem Hauptmann, welcher seine Frau und Kinder auf eine grausame Weise ermordet hat (Frankfurt am Main, 1798).

Zwey Schöne Newe Geistliche Lieder. Das Erste. Ein schöne Bekantnuß | oder Klaglied, | Welches ein Malefiz Person | Namens Simon Debel selbsten auffgesetzt, | wie in jedem Gesetz der erste Buchstaben andeutet, | auff seinen Namen gemacht worden. Ist hingerichtet worden durch das Schwerd | zu Peggstall in unter Oesterreich | Anno 1657 (Augsburg, 1657).

Argumente–Dokumente–Zitate.

ASCHAFFENBURG, GUSTAV (ed.), *Bericht über den VII. Internationalen Kongreß für Kriminalanthropologie* (Heidelberg, 1912).

——*Das Verbrechen und seine Bekämpfung,* 3rd edn. (Heidelberg, 1923).

BÄRENSPRUNG, SIEGMUND, *Anrede bey der Execution Maria Charlotta Sanels. Die wegen an der verwittweten Teleni zuvor Mischlets den 7. Februarii dieses Jahrs in Neu Angermünde begangenen Mordthat, den 7. Augustii von oben gerädert und aufs Rad geleget worden* (Berlin, 1733).

BECCARIA, CESARE, *Über Verbrechen und Strafen,* tr. from 1766 edn. and ed. Wilhelm Alff (Frankfurt am Main, 1966).

——*An Essay on Crimes and Punishments, translated from the Italian,* 3rd edn. (London, 1770).

BECKER, B., *Actenmäßige Geschichte der Räuberbanden an den beyden Ufern des Rheins* (2 vols.; Cologne, 1804).

BENJAMIN, HILDE, *et al., Zur Geschichte der Rechtspflege der DDR 1945–1949* (Berlin, 1976).

BERADT, CHARLOTTE, *Das dritte Reich des Traums* (Munich, 1966).

BERGER, J. A., *Ueber die Todesstrafe* (Vienna, 1864).

BERNER, ALBERT FRIEDRICH, *Abschaffung der Todesstrafe* (Dresden, 1861).

——*Die Strafgesetzgebung in Deutschland vom Jahre 1751 bis zur Gegenwart* (Leipzig, 1867).

BERNHARD, H., *et al.* (eds.), *Der Reichstagsbrandprozeß und Georgi Dimitroff: Dokumente* (2 vols.; Berlin, 1982–9).

BEYERLE, ANTON, *Ueber die Todesstrafe* (Stuttgart, 1867).

BINDING, KARL, *Grundriß des deutschen Strafrechts,* 8th edn. (Leipzig, 1913).

——and HOCHE, ALFRED, *Die Freigabe der Vernichtung lebensunwerten Lebens. Ihr Maß und ihr Form* (Leipzig, 1920).

BIRKNER, SIEGFRIED (ed.), *Leben und Sterben der Kindsmörderin Susanna Margarethe Brandt* (Frankfurt, 1973).

BLANC, OLIVIER (ed.), *Last Letters: Prisons and Prisoners of the French Revolution 1793–1794* (London, 1987).

BOBERACH, HEINZ (ed.), *Meldungen aus dem Reich. Die geheimen Lageberichte des Sicherheitsdienstes der SS 1938–1945* (Herrsching, 1984).

——(ed.), *Richterbriefe. Dokumente zur Beeinflussung der deutschen Rechtsprechung 1942–1944* (Boppard, 1975).

BRAUNGART, WOLFGANG, *Bänkelsang. Texte—Bilder—Kommentare* (Stuttgart, 1985).

BROSZAT, MARTIN, 'Zur Perversion der Strafjustiz im Dritten Reich', *Vierteljahreshefte für Zeitgeschichte*, 5 (1958), 390–443.

BRUNNEMANN, JOHANN, *Anleitung zu vorsichtiger Anstellung des Inquisitions-Processes* (Halle, 1697).

BUCHER, PETER (ed.), *Der Parlamentarische Rat 1948–1949. Akten und Protokolle*, ii. *Der Verfassungskonvent auf Herrenchiemsee* (Boppard, 1981).

CARRIÈRE, PHILIPP MORIZ, *Wissenschaft und Leben in Beziehung auf die Todesstrafe. Ein philosophisches Votum von Dr. M. Carrière . . . ein strafrechtliches Gutachten von Dr. F. Noellner* (Darmstadt, 1845).

C.D., *Eigentlicher | Wahrhafftiger und Acten-Mässiger Bericht, | Welcher Gestalt | Der Bösewicht | Augustin Pauli | Von 19. Jahren seines Alters | An Zwoen Personen Mord-Thaten verübet, | Darauff offenbar worden, und in Hafft gebracht, peinlich gefraget, und gebührend abgestrafft worden* (no place of publication, 1683).

CHRISTIANSEN, BOJE KARL, *Die Absurdität der sogenannten Todesstrafe* (Kiel, 1867).

DEGEN, R., *Das Tagebuch des Scharfrichters Schwietz aus Breslau über seine 123 Hinrichtungen* (Breslau, 1924).

Deutscher Bundestag, Stenographische Berichte.

DIMITROFF, GEORGI, *Reichstagsbrandprozeß. Dokumente, Briefe und Aufzeichnungen* (Berlin, 1946).

ENGERER, JOHANN HELUNG, *Treue Warnung von GOttes wegen vor Blut-Schulden, und dem dazu verleitenden Ehe-Bruch, bey vollstreckter Execution einer Kindes-Mörderin zu Schwabach* (Schwabach, 1737).

ENGLER, K., *Der Giftmord-Prozess wider die Frau Hofbesitzer Rosalie Schindler geb. Senkspiel zu Heubude bei Danzig wegen vorsätzlicher und überlegter Tödtung ihres Stiefsohnes George Schindler* (Danzig, 1870).

Entwurf des Strafgesetzbuchs für die Preußischen Staaten (Berlin, 1843).

ERK, LUDWIG, and BÖHME, FRANZ W. (eds.), *Deutscher Liederhort*, i. (Leipzig, 1925).

ESCHENMAYER, PROF., *Ueber die Abschaffung der Todesstrafen* (Tübingen, 1831).

EVANS, RICHARD J. (ed.), *Kneipengespräche im Kaiserreich. Die Stimmungsberichte der Hamburger Politischen Polizei 1892–1914* (Reinbek, 1989).

EXNER, FRANZ, *Kriminologie* (Berlin, 1949).

FALK, VICTOR VON [pseud.: i.e. Heinrich Sochaczewsky?] *Der Scharfrichter von Berlin. Roman, nach Acten, Aufzeichnungen u. Mittheilungen des Scharfrichters Jul. Krautz (Berlin)* (6 vols.; Berlin, 1890–1).

F.C.D., *'Kein Schaffot mehr!' Ein Votum gegen die Todesstrafe, zugleich als Anregung zur Bildung eines deutschen Vereins zur Abschaffung der Todesstrafe* (Darmstadt, 1865).

FERRI, ENRICO, *Das Verbrechen als soziale Erscheinung* (Leipzig, 1896).

FEUERBACH, LUDWIG, *Anselm Ritter von Feuerbach's Leben und Wirken, aus seinen ungedruckten Briefen und Tagebüchern, Vorträgen und Denkschriften* (2 vols.; Leipzig, 1832).

FEUERBACH, PAUL ANSELM RITTER VON, *Aktenmäßige Darstellung merkwürdiger Verbrechen* (2 vols.; Giessen, 1828–9).

—— *Merkwürdige Verbrechen* (abr. edn.; Frankfurt am Main, 1981).

FLESCH, MAX, *Gehirn und Veranlagung des Verbrechers. Beiträge zur Aufhebung der Todesstrafe und zur Einführung eines Verwahrungsgesetzes* (Berlin, 1929).

FONTANE, THEODOR, *Meine Kinderjahre. Autobiographischer Roman*, ed. C. Cole (Leipzig, 1955).

FRAENKEL, ERNST, *Zur Soziologie der Klassenjustiz* (repr. Darmstadt, 1968).

—— and SINZHEIMER, HUGO, *Die Justiz in der Weimarer Republik. Eine Chronik* (repr. Neuwied, 1968).

Frankfurter Allgemeine Zeitung.

FREISLER, ROLAND, *Nationalsozialistisches Recht und Rechtsdenken* (Berlin, 1938).

—— 'Richter und Gesetz', in Hans-Heinrich Lammers and Hans Pfundtner (eds.), *Grundlagen, Aufbau und Wirtschaftsordnung des Nationalsozialistischen Staates* (Berlin, 1936), i. 2. 17, p. 12.

FREUDENTHAL, B., 'Eine elektrische Hinrichtung im Staate New-York', *Zeitschrift für die gesamte Strafrechtswissenschaft*, 28 (1908), 61–6.

FREY, GERHARD, *Ich beantrage Freispruch. Aus den Erinnerungen des Strafverteidigers Prof. Dr. Gerhard Frey* (Hamburg, 1959).

GAUPP, ROBERT, 'Krankheit und Tod des paranoischen Massenmörders Hauptlehrer Wagner. Eine Epikrise', *Zeitschrift für die gesamte Neurologie und Psychiatrie*, 163 (1938), 48–80.

—— *Zur Psychologie des Massenmords: Hauptlehrer Wagner von Degerloch* (Berlin, 1914).

GOETHE, JOHANN WOLFGANG VON, 'Maximen und Reflexionen', 110–11, in *Goethes Werke*, Hamburger Ausgabe, ed. Erich Truntz (Hamburg, 1949–55).

GOLECKI, ANTON (ed.), *Akten der Reichskanzlei: Kabinett Müller II* (Boppard, 1987).

—— (ed.), *Akten der Reichskanzlei: Weimarer Republik: Das Kabinett von Schleicher 3. Dezember 1932 bis 30. Januar 1933* (Boppard, 1986).

GREINWALD, SIGISBERT, *Die Todesstrafe* (Westheim bei Augsburg, 1949).

GRIMM, JACOB, and WILHELM, *Deutsches Wörterbuch* (Leipzig, 1885).

GROSSMANN, KURT, *13 Jahre 'republikanische Justiz'* (Berlin, 1931).

GRUCHMANN, LOTHAR (ed.), 'Hitler über die Justiz. Das Tischgespräch vom 20. August 1942', *Vierteljahreshefte für Zeitgeschichte*, 12 (1964), 86–101.

GUMBEL, EMIL JULIUS, *Laßt Köpfe rollen* (Berlin, 1932).

—— *Verräter verfallen der Feme* (Berlin, 1929).

—— *Vier Jahre politischer Mord* (Berlin, 1922).

—— *Vom Fememord zur Reichskanzlei* (Heidelberg, 1962).

—— *Zwei Jahre Mord* (Berlin, 1921).

GÜRTNER, FRANZ (ed.), *Das kommende deutsche Strafrecht. Bericht über die Arbeit der amtlichen Strafrechtskommission* (2 vols.; Berlin, 1935–6).

HALLE, FELIX, *Deutsche Sondergerichtsbarkeit* (Berlin, 1922).

HARSDÖRFFER, GEORG PHILIPP, *Der grosse Schau-Platz jämmerlicher Mord-Geschichte* (Hamburg, 1606; repr. Hildesheim, 1985).

HARTE, FRIEDRICH LEOPOLD, *Die Hirten-Treue Christi, welche er an einem seiner verlorenen Schafe, nemlich an Gertrud Magdalene Bremmelin, einer vorsetzlichen Kindermörderin, erwiesen zum Preise desselben unendlicher Menschenliebe, wie aus zur Warnung und Besserung, beschrieben, nebst seiner auf dem Rabenstein gehaltene Rede* (2nd edn., Wernigeroda, 1745).

HEDRUSIUS, MILETUS, *Neu eröffnete Mord- und Trauer-Bühne | Darauf sich unterschiedliche | Theils gar sehr traurige und Mord-Exempel, als auch der verschlagenen so genannten Spitz-Buben oder Beutelschneider arglistige Räncke und Tücke | und verschiedene Erscheinungen der Geister repraesentiren. Aus denen beglaubtesten und neuesten Scribenten treulich herausgezogen | und männiglichen zur nothwendigen Warnung, als auch Gemüths- Schaff und Ergötzung herausgegeben* (Schwabach, 1708).

HEER, HANNES, *Ernst Thälmann in Selbstzeugnissen und Bilddokumenten* (Reinbek, 1975).

HEGEL, GEORG WILHELM FRIEDRICH, *Grundlinien der Philosophie des Rechts* (Berlin, 1821).

HEINE, HEINRICH, *Deutschland—ein Wintermährchen* (Hamburg, 1844).

HENTIG, HANS VON, *Crime: Causes and Conditions* (New York, 1947).

—— *The Criminal and his Victim: Studies in the Sociobiology of Crime* (New Haven, 1948).

—— *Die Strafe. Ursprung, Zweck, Psychologie* (Berlin, 1932; 2nd edn., 2 vols., Berlin, 1954–5).

—— *Strafrecht und Auslese* (Berlin, 1914).

—— *Ueber den Zusammenhang zwischen den kosmischen, biologischen und sozialen Ursachen der Revolution* (Tübingen, 1920).

—— 'Zur Psychologie der Beschuldigung. Eine kriminalwissenschaftliche Bemerkung zum Nogens-Prozeß', *Die Justiz*, 5 (1929), 24–38.

HERBST, EDUARD, *Zur Frage der Aufhebung der Todesstrafe* (Vienna, 1879).

HERMANN, HEINRICH LUDWIG, *Kurze Geschichte des Criminal-Prozesses wider die Brandstifter Johann Christoph Peter Horst und dessen Geliebte, die unverehelichte Friedericke Louise Christiane Delitz* (Berlin, 1818).

HETZEL, H., *Die Todesstrafe in ihrer kulturgeschichtlichen Entwicklung* (Berlin, 1870).

HIPPOCRATES, vol. ii, ed. and tr. W. H. S. Jones (Cambridge, Mass., 1923): 'The Sacred Disease', pp. 127–84.

HIRSCH, MARTIN, *et al.* (eds.), *Recht, Verwaltung und Justiz im Nationalsozialismus* (Cologne, 1984).

HITLER, ADOLF, *Mein Kampf* (Munich, 1942).

HITZIG, JULIUS, 'Nachwort des Herausgebers', *Zeitschrift für die Criminal-Rechts-Pflege in den Preußischen Staaten mit Ausschluß der Rheinprovinzen* (ed. Julius Hitzig), 45 (1833), 223–8.

HOCHE, ALFRED (ed.), *Handbuch der gerichtlichen Psychiatrie* (Berlin, 1901).

HOLLWECK, JOSEPH, *Die Todesstrafe im neuen Reich* (Jur. Diss., Erlangen, 1935).

HOLLWECK, LUDWIG, ' . . . *Vom Leben zum Tode hingerichtet'. Todesurteile vor 200 Jahren* (Munich, 1980).

HOLTEI, KARL VON, *Vierzig Jahre* (8 vols.; Berlin, 1843–50), i.

HOLTZENDORFF, FRANZ VON, *Das Verbrechen des Mordes und die Todesstrafe* (Berlin, 1875).

HÖPFNER, W., 'Todesstrafe und Abschreckungsgedanke', *Zeitschrift für die gesamte Strafrechtswissenschaft*, 33 (1913), 142–76.

HÖSS, RUDOLF, *Commandant of Auschwitz* (London, 1961).

JÄCKEL, EBERHARD (ed.), *Hitler. Sämtliche Aufzeichnungen 1905–1924* (Stuttgart, 1980).

JANDA, ELSBETH, and NÖTZOLDT, FRITZ (eds.), *Die Moritat vom Bänkelsang oder das Lied der Straße* (Munich, 1959).

JARCKE, CARL ERNST, 'Die Lehre von der Tödtung: Von den durch härtere Bestrafung qualificirten Arten der Tödtung', *Zeitschrift für die Criminal-Rechts-Pflege in den Preußischen Staaten mit Ausschluß der Rheinprovinzen* (ed. Julius Hitzig), 8 (1826), 351–89.

JARON, NORBERT, *Das demokratische Zeittheater der späten 20er Jahre. Untersucht am Beispiel der Stücke gegen die Todesstrafe. Eine Rezeptionsanalyse* (Frankfurt am Main, 1981).

JOCHMANN, WERNER (ed.), *Adolf Hitler: Monologe im Führer-Hauptquartier 1941–1944: Die Aufzeichnungen Heinrich Heims* (Hamburg, 1980).

JOHN, RICHARD EDWARD, *Ueber die Todesstrafe. Ein populärer Vortrag* (Sammlung gemeinverständlicher Vorträge, ed. Rudolf Virchow and Friedrich von Holtzendorff-Vietmansdorff, 36; Berlin, 1867).

KALKOWSKA, ELEONORE, *Josef. Zeittragödie in 22 Bildern* (Berlin, 1928).

KANT, IMMANUEL, *Anthropologie in pragmatischer Hinsicht abgefaßt* (Breslau, 1798).

—— *Metaphysik der Sitten*, Part II, in *Werke*, iv, ed. Wilhelm Weischedel (Frankfurt am Main, 1968).

—— *Metaphysische Anfangsgründe der Rechtslehre*, 2nd edn. (Breslau, 1798).

KEMMLER, GOTTLOB, *Die Berechtigung der Todesstrafe. Mit besonderer Berücksichtigung der Schrift des Prälaten von Mehring, 'Die Frage von der Todesstrafe'* (Tübingen, 1868).

KLONOVSKY, MICHAEL, and FLOCKEN, JAN VON, *Stalins Lager in Deutschland. Dokumentation, Zeugenberichte 1945–1950* (Frankfurt, 1992).

KOHLER J., and SCHEEL, W. (eds.), *Die Carolina und ihre Vorgängerinnen. Text, Erläuterungen, Geschichte* (4 vols.; Halle, 1900–15; repr. Aalen, 1970).

KOHLRAUSCH, EDUARD (ed.), *Deutsche Strafgesetze vom 19. Dezember 1932 bis 12. Juni 1934* (Berlin, 1934).

KRAEPELIN, EMIL, 'Lombrosos Uomo delinquente', *Zeitschrift für die gesamte Strafrechtswissenschaft*, 5 (1885), 669–80.

KRENZ, HEINRICH WILHELM, and KOLLER, SIEGFRIED, *Die Gemeinschaftsunfähigen* (3 vols.; Giessen, 1939–41).

LAMPRECHT, HELMUT (ed.), *Deutschland, Deutschland. Politische Gedichte vom Vormärz bis zur Gegenwart* (Bremen, 1969).

LANG, FRITZ, *M: Protokoll* (Cinemathek, 3; Hamburg, 1983).

LEA, HENRY CHARLES, *Superstition and Force* (Philadelphia, 1866).

LESSING, THEODOR, *Haarmann. Die Geschichte eines Werwolfs. Und andere Kriminalreportagen*, ed. Rainer Marwedel (Frankfurt am Main, 1989).

LICHTENSTÄDT, PROF. DR., 'Ueber Todesstrafe ohne Qual', *Zeitschrift für die Criminal-Rechts-Pflege in den Preußischen Staaten mit Ausschluß der Rheinprovinzen* (ed. Julius Hitzig), 25 (1829), 338–42.

LIEPMANN, MORITZ, 'Ist die Todesstrafe im künftigen deutschen und österreichischen Strafgesetzbuch beizubehalten?', *Verhandlungen des 31. deutschen Juristentages* (Berlin, 1912), ii. 572–765.

LISZT, FRANZ VON, *Strafrechtliche Aufsätze und Vorträge*, i (Berlin, 1905).

LOMBROSO, CESARE, *Crime: Its Causes and Remedies* (London, 1911).

—— *L'Homme criminel* (Paris, 1895).

—— 'Über den Ursprung, das Wesen und die Bestrebungen der neuen anthropologisch-kriminalistischen Schule in Italien', *Zeitschrift für die gesamte Strafrechtswissenschaft*, 1 (1881), 108–29.

—— *Die Ursachen und Bekämpfung des Verbrechens* (Berlin, 1902).

—— *Der Verbrecher in anthropologischer, ärztlicher und juristischer Beziehung* (3 vols.; Hamburg, 1890–6).

MALBLANK, FRIEDRICH (ed.), *Geschichte der Peinlichen Gerichtsordnung Kaiser Karls V.* (Nuremberg, 1763).

MAYER, HANS, *Georg Büchner, Woyzeck. Vollständiger Text und Paralipomena. Dokumentation*, 9th edn. (Frankfurt am Main, 1962).

MEHRING, G. VON, *Die Frage von der Todesstrafe* (Stuttgart, 1867).

MESSERSCHMIDT, HEINRICH, *Ueber die Rechtsmäßigkeit der Todesstrafe durch Enthauptung und über die bis jetzt gebräuchlichen, aber verwerflichen Verfahrungsarten beim Enthaupten; nebst genauer Beschreibung einer unter dem Namen Collumpön neu erfundenen, allen vernünftigen Anforderungen entsprechenden Enthauptungs-Maschine* (Weimar, 1840).

MEZGER, EDMUND, *Kriminalpolitik auf kriminologischer Grundlage* (Stuttgart, 1934).

MINUTH, KARL-HEINZ (ed.), *Akten der Reichskanzlei: die Regierung Hitler 1933–1938*, i. *1933/34* (Boppard, 1983).

—— (ed.), *Akten der Reichskanzlei: Weimarer Republik: Das Kabinett von Papen 1. Juni bis 3. Dezember 1932* (Boppard, 1989).

MITTERMAIER, CARL JOSEPH ANTON, 'Die Todesstrafe nach dem neuesten Stande der Ansichten in England, Nordamerika, Frankreich, Belgien, Dänemark, Schweden, Rußland, Italien und Deutschland über die Abschaffung dieser Strafart', *Archiv des Kriminalrechts*, NS (1840), 442–63, 583–610, and (1841), 1–23, 311–48.

—— *Die Todesstrafe nach den Ergebnissen der wissenschaftlichen Forschungen, der Fortschritte der Gesetzgebung und der Erfahrungen* (Heidelberg, 1862).

MOELLER-JOCHMUS, MAURITIUS, *Ueber die Todesstrafe. Eine principielle Untersuchung* (Leipzig, 1845).

MOSER, JOHANN JAKOB, *Selige letzte Stunden hingerichteter Personen* (Munich, 1761).

MOSSE, GEORGE L., *Nazi Culture: Intellectual, Cultural and Social Life in the Third Reich* (New York, 1966).

MÜLLER-WALDECK, GUNNAR (ed.), *Die tote Braut und andere Moritaten von dem jetzigen Übelstand in der Welt* (Reinbek, 1984).

MUNGENAST, E. M., *Der Mörder und der Staat. Die Todesstrafe im Urteil hervorragender Zeitgenossen* (Stuttgart, 1928).

NAGLER, JOHANNES, *Die Strafe. Eine juristisch-empirische Untersuchung* (Leipzig, 1918), i.

Nazi Conspiracy and Aggression (Office of the United States Chief of Counsel for Prosecution of Axis Criminality, 5 vols.; Washington, 1946).

NEUMANN, WILHELM, *Ueber die Nothwendigkeit der Abschaffung der Todesstrafe* (Berlin, 1848).

NEUNZIG, HANS ADOLF (ed.), *Das illustrierte Moritaten-Lesebuch* (Munich, 1973).

NEUREITER, FERDINAND VON, *Kriminalbiologie* (Berlin, 1940).

Neues Deutschland (Berlin).

NICOLAI, FRIEDRICH, *Beschreibung einer Reise durch Deutschland und die Schweiz im Jahre 1781*, vi (Berlin and Stettin, 1785).

NIETZSCHE, FRIEDRICH, *On the Genealogy of Morals*, tr. Francis Goffing (New York, 1956).

NOAKES, JEREMY, and PRIDHAM, GEOFFREY (eds.), *Nazism: A History in Documents and Eyewitness Accounts 1919–1945* (New York, 1989).

NOERDLINGER, LEOPOLD, *Mord und Todesstrafe nach dem alten Testament. In Briefen von Herrn Dr. Oscar Wächter, Rechtskonsulent in Stuttgart, Abgeordneter des Bezirks Herrenberg; Herrn Prälat von Moser in Stuttgart und dem Herausgeber, Leopold Noerdlinger, Rechtskonsulent in Stuttgart* (Stuttgart, 1865).

NÖGGELER, J. R., *Der Bayrische Hiesel. Wahre unentstellte Geschichte des Matthäus Klostermeier* (Reutlingen, 1807).

OLDEN, RUDOLF, and BORNSTEIN, JOSEF, *Der Justizmord an Jakubowski* (Berlin, 1928).

Parlamentarischer Rat. Stenographische Berichte über die Plenaritzungen (Bonn, 1948/9).

Parlamentarischer Rat. Verhandlungen des Hauptauschusses (Bonn, 1948/9).

PATZKE, JOHANN SAMUEL, *Aufrichtige Nachricht von der Bekehrung und den letzten Stunden einer Kindermörderin, Nahmens Anna Elisabeth Blumin, welche den 1. des Maymonaths 1767. den Rothensee met dem Schwerdte den Lohn ehrer That empfing; aufgesetzt von de beyden Predigern an den Heiligen Geist Wache. Nebst der Rede, die an der Gerichtsstädte gehalten worden* (Magdeburg, 1767).

PETZOLDT, LEANDER, *Die freudlose Muse. Texte, Lieder und Bilder zum historischen Bänkelsang* (Stuttgart, 1978).

PICKLER, HENRY (ed.), *Hitlers Tischgespräche im Führerhauptquartier* (Stuttgart, 1976).

PIERREPOINT, ALBERT, *Executioner: Pierrepoint* (London, 1972).

PIKART, EBERHARD, and WERNER, WOLFRAM (eds.), *Der Parlamentarische Rat 1948–1949. Akten und Protokolle*, v. *Ausschuß für Grundsatzfragen* (Boppard, 1993).

PLINY, *Natural History* (Loeb edition).

POLKE, KRIMINALDIRECTOR, 'Der Massenmörder Denke und der Fall Trautmann. Ein Justizirrtum', *Archiv für Kriminologie*, 95 (1934), 8–30.

RADBRUCH, GUSTAV, *Gesetzliches Recht und Übergesetzliches Recht* (Heidelberg, 1946).

——(ed.), *Die Peinliche Gerichtsordnung Kaiser Karls V. von 1532 (Carolina)*, 4th edn. (Stuttgart, 1975).

REGGE, JÜRGEN, and SCHUBERT, WERNER (eds.), *Quellen zur Reform des Straf- und Strafprozeßrechts, II. Abteilung: NS-Zeit (1933–1939)—Strafgesetzbuch*, i. *Entwürfe eines Strafgesetzbuchs*; ii. *Protokolle der Strafrechtskommission des Reichsjustizministeriums* (2 vols.; Berlin, 1988–9).

REINSBERG-DÜRINGSFELD, OTTO FREIHERR VON, *Das festliche Jahr* (Leipzig, 1863).

REISINGER, JOHANN BAPTIST, *Dominikus Hahn's Lebensbegebnisse, seine Vorbereitung zum Tode und seine Hinrichtung, dargestellt in einer Predigt* (Straubing, 1847).

REPKOW, ELKE VON, and KEMPNER, ROBERT W., *Justiz-Dämmerung* (Berlin, 1932).

RIHA, KARL (ed.), *Das Moritatenbuch* (Frankfurt am Main, 1981).

RITTER, ROBERT, *Ein Menschenschlag. Erbärztliche Untersuchungen über die—durch 10 Geschlechterfolgen erforschten—Nachkommen von Vagabunden, Jaunern und Räubern* (Leipzig, 1937).

ROCKER, Rudolf, *Johann Most. Das Leben eines Rebellen* (Berlin, 1924).

RODERICH, MAX, *Verbrechen und Strafe. Eine Sammlung interessanter Polizei- und Criminal-Rechtsfälle, nach den Acten bearbeitet* (Jena, 1850).

ROSCHER, GUSTAV, *Großstadtpolizei* (Hamburg, 1906).

ROSENBERG, ALFRED, *Der Mythus des 20. Jahrhunderts*, 38th edn. (Munich, 1934).

SACK, ALFONS, *Der Reichstagsbrandprozeß* (Berlin, 1934).

SALZMANN, RAINER (ed.), *Die CDU/CSU im Parlamentarischen Rat. Sitzungsprotokolle der Unionsfraktion* (Forschungen und Quellen zur Zeitgeschichte, 2; Stuttgart, 1981).

SANSON, HENRI, *Tagebücher der Henker von Paris 1685–1847* (2 vols.; Potsdam, 1923).

SCHALK, OSKAR, *Scharfrichter Josef Lang's Erinnerungen*, hg. v. Oskar Schalk (Leipzig and Vienna, 1920).

SCHLATTER, GEORG FRIEDRICH, *Stimmen gegen die Todesstrafe* (Mannheim, 1862).

SCHMID, CARLO, *Erinnerungen* (Berne, 1979).

SCHMIDT, GERHARD K., *Christentum und Todesstrafe* (Weimar, 1938).

SCHMIDT, MAXIMILIAN, *Julius Krautz, Der Scharfrichter von Berlin. Ein Kulturbild aus dem neunzehnten Jahrhundert* (Berlin, 1893).

SCHROEDER, F. C., *Die Carolina. Die Peinliche Gerichtsordnung Kaiser Karls* (Darmstadt, 1986).

SCHÜTZE, GOTTFRIED, *Register über die sämmtlichen zwölf Theile der Sammlung Hamburgischer Gesetze und Verfassungen mit historischer Einleitung*, Part V (Hamburg, 1774).

Simplicissimus. Illustrierte Wochenschrift.

SMITH, JEAN EDWARD (ed.), *The Papers of General Lucius D. Clay: Germany 1945–1949* (Bloomington, Ind., 1974).

SPEER, ALBERT, *Inside the Third Reich* (London, 1971).

STARKE, WILHELM, *Verbrechen und Verbrecher in Preußen 1854–1878. Eine kulturgeschichtliche Studie* (Berlin, 1884).

Statistisches Jahrbuch für das deutsche Reich 1933.

STAUFF, ILSE, *Justiz im Dritten Reich. Eine Dokumentation*, 2nd edn. (Frankfurt am Main, 1978).

STEINHAGEN, J. H., *Ueber Todesstrafen* (Hamburg, 1855).

Stenographische Berichte über die Verhandlungen der deutschen konstituierenden Nationalversammlung zu Weimar.

Stenographische Berichte über die Verhandlungen des Bayerischen Landtags.

Stenographische Berichte über die Verhandlungen des deutschen Reichstags.

Stenographische Berichte über die Verhandlungen des Preußischen Abgeordnetenhauses.

Stenographische Berichte über die Verhandlungen des Reichstags des Norddeutschen Bundes.

STIELER, KASPAR, *Zeitungs Lust und Nutz. Vollständiger Neudruck der Originalausgabe von 1695*, ed. Gert Hahelweide (Bremen, 1969).

STROMEYER, GEORG FRIEDRICH LOUIS, *Erinnerungen eines deutschen Arztes*, 2nd edn. (Hanover, 1875; repr. Berlin, 1977).

Der Tagesspiegel (Berlin).

TAYLOR, JOHN, *Three Weekes, three daies, and three houres Observations and travel, from London to Hamburgh* (London, 1617), repr. in C. Hindley (ed.), *The Old Book Collector's Miscellany*, iii (London, 1873).

TUCHOLSKY, KURT, *Gesammelte Werke*, ed. Mary Gerold-Tucholsky and Fritz J. Raddatz (Reinbek, 1960).

Ueber die Todesstrafe (*Stenographische Berichte über die Verhandlungen des Reichstages des Norddeutschen Bundes. 1. Legislatur-Periode, Session 1870. Anlagen zu den Verhandlungen des Reichstages von Nr. 1–72*).

VALTIN, JAN, *Out of the Night* (London, 1941).

—— [pseud., i.e. Richard Krebs], *Tagebuch der Hölle* (Berlin, 1958).

Verhandlungen der Versammlung zur Vereinbarung der Preußischen Staatsverfassung (3 vols.; Berlin, 1848).

VOELKER, AMBROSIUS, *Ist der menschliche Wille frei? Mit besonderer Rücksicht auf die Frage der Zulässigkeit der Todesstrafe* (Stuttgart, 1880).

VOGET, FRIEDRICH L., *Lebensgeschichte der Giftmörderin Gesche Margarethe Gottfried, geborene Timm* (2 vols.; Bremen, 1831).

VÖLDERNDORFF UND WARADEIN, OTTO FREIHERR VON, *Harmlose Plaudereien* (2 vols.; Munich, 1892–8).

WAGNITZ, HEINRICH, *Historische Nachrichten und Bemerkungen über die merkwürdigsten Zuchthäuser in Deutschland. Nebst einem Anhange über die zweckmäßigste Einrichtung der Gefängnisse und Irrenanstalten* (2 vols.; Halle, 1791).

—— *Ideen und Pläne zur Verbesserung der Policey- u. Criminalanstalten. Dem 19. Jahrhundert zur Vollendung übergeben* (Halle, 1801).

Der wahre Jacob.

WEISSENBRUCH, JOHANN BENJAMIN, *Ausführliche Relation von der famosen Ziegeuner-Diebsmord- und Räuber-Bande, | Welche | Den 14. und 15. Novembr. Ao. 1726 zu Giessen durch Schwerdt, Strang und Rad, respective justificirt worden, Worinnen, Nach praemittirter Historie von dem Ursprung und Sitten derer Zigeuner &c.&c. die vornehmste und schwerste Begangenschafften mit allen Umständen erzehlet, auch was durante Processu sowol ante- als in—& post Torturam vorgenommen worden, enthalten ist, Aus denen weitläufigen Peinlichen Original-Actis in möglichster Kürze zusammen gezogen, Und auf Sr. Hochfürstl. Durchl. zu Hessen-Darmstadt Gnädigste Spezial-Erlaubnuß, Dem Publico zum Besten, in öffentlichen Druck befördert, Durch D. Johann Benjamin Weissenbruch* (Frankfurt am Main, 1727).

WELLMANN, JOHANN CHRISTIAN, *Das von der göttlichen Regierung | An Denen Mord-Brennern, welche in der Nacht zwischen den 19ten und 20sten May 1723. die Lebusische Vorstadt zu Franckfurt an der Oder auf eine so boßhafte, als entsetzliche Arth an 5. Orten angesteckt, | Bewiesene Denck-Mahl | Der | Schweren und zum Theil | Plötzlichen Rache, | Da der Allwissende und | Gerechte GOtt die so tief verborgene Brand-Stiftung wieder iedermänngliches Vermuthen wunderbar entdeckt | und 6. Personen von denen Brand-Stiftern bald nach vollführter That zur Haft | und danechst zur wohlverdieten Straffe bringen lassen: | Aus | Denen weiläufigen Inquisitions-Actis nach der Ordnung des ergangenen Processes zur wahrhaften Nachricht | nebst denen dabey nöthigen Kupffer-Stichen herausgegeben | Von Johann Christian Wellmann* (Frankfurt an der Oder, 1725).

WETZEL, ALBRECHT, *Über Massenmörder. Ein Beitrag zu den persönlichen Verbrechensursachen und zu den Methoden ihrer Erforschung* (Berlin, 1920).

WIGARD, FRANZ (ed.), *Stenographische Berichte über die Verhandlungen der deutschen constituirenden Nationalversammlung zu Frankfurt am Main*, i (Leipzig, 1848).

WROBEL, HANS (ed.), *Strafjustiz im totalen Krieg. Aus den Akten des Sondergerichts Bremen 1940 bis 1945*, i (Bremen, 1991).

WÜLFFEN, ERICH, *Kriminalpsychologie. Psychologie des Täters* (Berlin, 1925).

Zedlers Grosses Vollständiges Universal Lexicon aller Wissenschaften und Künste (Leipzig and Halle, 1745).

ZESSLER-VITALIS, ERICH (ed.), *Das Tagebuch eines Mörders vom Todesurteil bis vor der Hinrichtung!* (Berlin, 1927).

ZWEIG, ARNOLD, *Das Beil von Wandsbek*, 2nd edn. (Berlin and Weimar, 1962).

C. SECONDARY LITERATURE

ABRAMS, LYNN, *Workers' Culture in Imperial Germany: Leisure and Recreation in the Rhineland and Westphalia* (London, 1992).

ADAMS, WILL, 'Capital Punishment in Soviet Criminal Legislation, 1922–1965', in Kanet and Volgyes (eds.), *On the Road to Communism*.

AHRENS, FRANZ, *Bruno Tesch. Das Sterben eines Hamburger Arbeiterjungen* (Hamburg, 1946).

ALFF, WILHELM, 'Zur Einführung in Beccarias Leben und Denken', in Beccaria, *Über Verbrechen und Strafen*.

ALT, KARL, *Todeskandidaten* (Munich, 1946).

ALY, GÖTZ, *et al.* (eds.), *Aussonderung und Tod. Die klinische Hinrichtung der Unbrauchbaren* (Berlin, 1985).

—— *et al.* (eds.), *Feinderklärung und Prävention. Kriminalbiologie, Zigeunerforschung und Asozialenpolitik* (Berlin, 1988).

—— *et al.* (eds.), *Reform und Gewissen. 'Euthanasie' im Dienst des Fortschritts* (Berlin, 1985).

——and ROTH, KARL HEINZ, *Die restlose Erfassung. Volkszählen, Identifizieren, Aussondern im Nationalsozialismus* (Berlin, 1984).

AMIRA, KARL VON, *Die germanischen Todesstrafen. Untersuchungen zur Rechts- und Religionsgeschichte* (Abhandlungen der Bayerischen Akademie der Wissenschaften, Philosophisch-philologisch und historische Klasse, xxxvi. Bd., 3. Abtlg., vorgelegt in der Sitzung am 6. November 1915; Munich, 1922).

Amnesty International, *When the State Kills: The Death Penalty and Human Rights* (London, 1989).

ANDERSON, MARGARET L., and BARKIN, KENNETH D., 'The Myth of the Puttkamer Purge and the Reality of the *Kaiserreich:* Some Reflections on the Historiography of Imperial Germany', *Journal of Modern History,* 54 (1982), 268–84.

ANDERSON, MICHAEL, *Approaches to the History of the Western Family 1500–1914* (London, 1980).

ANDERSON, PERRY, *A Zone of Engagement* (London, 1992).

ANDREWS, RICHARD, 'The Cunning of Imagery: Rhetoric and Ideology in Cesare Beccaria's Treatise "On Crimes and Punishments"', in Campbell and Rollins (eds.), *Begetting Images.*

ANDERBRÜGGE, KLAUS, *Völkisches Rechtsdenken. Zur Rechtslehre in der Zeit des Nationalsozialismus* (Berlin, 1978).

ANGERMUND, RALPH, *Deutsche Richterschaft 1919–1945* (Frankfurt am Main, 1990).

ELSE ANGSTMANN, *Der Henker in der Volksmeinung. Seine Namen und sein Vorkommen in der mündlichen Volksüberlieferung* (Bonn, 1928).

ANON., *Die königlichen Bayerischen Staatsminister der Justiz in der Zeit von 1818 bis 1918. Ihre Herkunft und Werdegang und ihr Wirken* (Munich, 1931).

ANON. (ed.), *Schilder, Bilder, Moritaten. Sonderschau des Museums für Volkskunde im Pergamonmuseum 25. 9. 1987–3. 1. 1988* (exhibition catalogue, Staatliche Museen zu Berlin, 1987).

ANON. (ed.), *Vom Reichsjustizamt zum Bundesministerium der Justiz. Festschrift zum hundertjährigen Gründungstag des Reichsjustizamtes* (Cologne, 1977).

ARASSE, DANIEL, *The Guillotine and the Terror* (London, 1989).

ARCHER, DANE, and GARTNER, ROSEMARY, 'Violent Acts and Violent Times: A Comparative Approach to Postwar Homicide Rates', *American Sociological Review*, 41 (1976), 937–63.

ARIÈS, PHILIPPE, *Un historien du dimanche* (Paris, 1980).

—— *The Hour of our Death* (London, 1981).

ARNOLD, HERMANN, 'Ländliche Grundschicht und Gaunertum. Zur Kritik von Küthers Buch: Räuber und Gauner in Deutschland', *Zeitschrift für Agrargeschichte und Agrarsoziologie*, 25 (1977), 67–76.

—— *Zigeuner. Herkunft und Leben im deutschen Sprachgebiet* (Olten, 1965).

AUST, STEFAN, *The Baader–Meinhof Group: Inside Story of a Phenomenon* (London, 1985).

BÄCHTHOLD-STÄUBLI, H. (ed.), *Handwörterbuch des deutschen Aberglaubens* (10 vols.; Berlin, 1927–42).

BACKES, UWE, *et al.*, *Reichstagsbrand: Aufklärung einer historischen Legende* (Munich, 1986).

BADER, K. S., *Soziologie der deutschen Nachkriegskriminalität* (Tübingen, 1949).

BAKHTIN, MIKHAIL, *Rabelais and his World*, tr. Hélène Iswolsky (Cambridge, Mass., 1968).

BANKIER, DAVID, *The Germans and the Final Solution: Public Opinion under Nazism* (Cambridge, 1992).

BARBER, PAUL, *Vampires, Burial, and Death: Folklore and Reality* (New Haven, 1988).

BARGHEER, ERNST, *Eingeweide. Lebens- und Seelenkräfte der Leibesinneren* (Berlin, 1931).

BÄSTLEIN, KLAUS, 'Vom hanseatischen Richtertum zum nationalsozialistischen Justizverbrechen. Zur Person und Tätigkeit Curt Rothenbergers 1896–1959', in idem *et al.* (eds.), *'Für Führer, Volk und Vaterland ...'. Hamburger Justiz im Nationalsozialismus* (Hamburg, 1992), 74–145.

F. BAUER, *Das Verbrechen und die Gesellschaft* (Munich, 1957).

BECKER, HOWARD S., 'Labelling Theory Reconsidered,' in Rock and McIntosh (eds.), *Deviance*, 41–66.

BEDAU, HUGO ADAM, *Death is Different: Studies in the Morality, Law, and Politics of Capital Punishment* (Boston, 1987).

BÉE, MICHEL, 'Le Spectacle de l'exécution dans la France de l'ancien régime', *Annales ESC* 4 (1983), 843–63.

BEHRINGER, WOLFGANG, *Hexenverfolgung in Bayern. Volksmagie, Glaubenseifer und Staatsräson in der Frühen Neuzeit* (Munich, 1987).

—— 'Mörder, Diebe, Ehebrecher: Verbrechen und Strafen in Kurbayern vom 16. bis 18. Jahrhundert', in Van Dülmen (ed.), *Verbrechen*, 85–132.

BEIER, A. L., CANNADINE, D., and ROSENHEIM, J. M. (eds.), *The First Modern Society: Essays in English History in Honour of Lawrence Stone* (Cambridge, 1989).

BEIER, LUCINDA MCCRAY, 'The Good Death in Seventeenth-Century England', in Houlbrooke (ed.), *Death*, 43–61.

BELEITES, JOHANNES, *et al.* (eds.), *Stasi Intern. Macht und Banalität. Herausgegeben vom Bürgerkomitee Leipzig*, 2nd edn. (Leipzig, 1991).

BENEKE, OTTO, *Von unehrlichen Leuten. Cultur-historische Studien und Geschichten aus vergangenen Tagen deutscher Gewerbe und Dienste, mit besonderer Rücksicht auf Hamburg* (Hamburg, 1865).

BENTON, TED, 'Social Darwinism and Socialist Darwinism in Germany: 1860 to 1900', *Rivista di Filosofia*, 23 (1982), 79–121.

BENZ, WOLFGANG, 'Die Entnazifizierung der Richter', in Diestelkamp and Stolleis (eds.), *Justizalltag*, 112–30.

BERGER, THOMAS, *Die konstante Repression. Zur Geschichte des Strafvollzugs in Preußen nach 1850* (Frankfurt am Main, 1974).

BERGMANN, JÜRGEN, *Das Berliner Handwerk in den Frühphasen der Industrialisierung* (Veröffentlichungen der Historischen Kommission zu Berlin; Berlin, 1973).

BERTHOLD, WILL [i.e. Stefan Amberg], *Vollstreckt. Johann Reichhart, der letzte deutsche Henker* (Munich, 1982).

BESSEL, RICHARD (ed.), *Life in the Third Reich* (Oxford, 1987).

—— 'Policing, Professionalisation and Politics in Weimar Germany', in Clive Emsley and Barbara Weinberger (eds.), *Policing Western Europe: Professionalism and Public Order 1850–1940* (London, 1991).

—— 'The Potempa Murder', *Central European History*, 10 (1977), 241–54.

BETTENHÄUSER, HERMANN, 'Räuber und Gaunerbanden in Hessen. Ein Beitrag zum Versuch einer historischen Kriminologie Hessens', *Zeitschrift des Vereins für hessische Geschichte und Landeskunde*, 75–6 (1964–5).

BIRTSCH, GÜNTHER, 'Revolutionsfurcht in Preußen 1789 bis 1794', in Büsch and Neugebauer-Wölk (eds.), *Preußen*, 87–101.

BLACKBOURN, DAVID, *Marpingen: Apparitions of the Virgin Mary in Bismarckian Germany* (Oxford, 1994).

—— *Populists and Patricians: Essays in Modern German History* (London, 1987).

—— and ELEY, GEOFF, *The Peculiarities of German History: Bourgeois Society and Politics in Nineteenth-Century Germany* (Oxford, 1984).

—— and EVANS, RICHARD J. (eds.), *The German Bourgeoisie: Essays on the Social History of the German Middle Classes from the Late Eighteenth to the Early Twentieth Century* (London, 1991).

BLANNING, T. C. W., *The French Revolutionary Wars in Germany: Occupation and Resistance in the Rhineland, 1792–1802* (Oxford, 1983).

—— *Joseph II* (London, 1994).

BLASIUS, DIRK, *Bürgerliche Gesellschaft und Kriminalität. Zur Sozialgeschichte Preußens im Vormärz* (Göttingen, 1976).

—— 'Gesellschaftsgeschichte und Kriminalität', *Beiträge zur Historischen Sozialkunde*, 1 (1981), 13–19.

—— 'Der Kampf um die Geschworenengerichte im Vormärz', in Wehler (ed.), *Sozialgeschichte Heute*, 148–61.

—— 'Kriminalität als Gegenstand historischer Forschung', *Kriminalsoziologische Bibliographie*, 25 (1979), 1–15.

—— *Kriminalität und Alltag. Zur Konfliktgeschichte des Alltagslebens im 19. Jahrhundert* (Göttingen, 1978).

—— 'Kriminalität und Geschichtswissenschaft. Perspektiven der neueren Forschung', *Historische Zeitschrift*, 233 (1981), 615–27.

—— 'Kriminologie und Geschichtswissenschaft, Bilanz und Perspektiven interdisziplinärer Forschung', *Geschichte und Gesellschaft*, 14 (1988), 136–49.

—— 'Michel Foucaults "denkende" Betrachtung der Geschichte', *Kriminalsoziologische Bibliographie*, 41 (1983), 69–83.

—— 'Recht und Gerechtigkeit im Umbruch von Verfassungs- und Gesellschaftsordnung. Zur Situation der Strafrechtspflege in Preußen im 19. Jahrhundert', *Der Staat*, 21 (1982), 365–90.

BLASIUS, DIRK, *Der verwaltete Wahnsinn. Eine Sozialgeschichte des Irrenhauses* (Frankfurt am Main, 1980).

BLAUERT, ANDREAS, 'Kriminaljustiz und Sittenreform als Krisenmanagement? Das Hochstift Speyer im 16. und 17. Jahrhundert', in Blauert and Schwerhoff (eds.), *Mit den Waffen*, 115–36.

——and SCHWERHOFF, GERD (eds.), *Mit den Waffen der Justiz. Zur Kriminalitätsgeschichte des späten Mittelalters und der Frühen Neuzeit* (Frankfurt am Main, 1993).

BLOCH, MARC, *Les Rois thaumaturges. Essai sur le caractère surnaturel attribué à la puissance royale particulièrement en France et en Angleterre* (Paris, 1961).

BLOK, ANTON, 'Openbare strafvoltrekkingen als rites de passage', *Tijdschrift voor Geschiedenis*, 97 (1984), 347–69.

BLÜMEL, WILLI, *et al.* (eds.), *Verwaltung im Rechtsstaat. Festschrift für Carl Hermann Ule zum 80. Geburtstag am 24. Februar 1987* (Cologne, 1987).

BOCK, HANS MANFRED, *Geschichte des linken Radikalismus in Deutschland* (Frankfurt am Main, 1976).

BOCKELMANN, PAUL, and GALLAS, WILHELM (eds.), *Festschrift für Eberhard Schmidt zum 70. Geburtstag* (Göttingen, 1961).

BÖER, LUDWIG, *Der Scharfrichter von Bruchsal* (Bruchsal, 1972).

BOWERS, WILLIAM J., 'The Effect of Executions is Brutalization, Not Deterrence', in Haas and Inciardi (eds.), *Challenging Capital Punishment*, 49–90.

——*Legal Homicide: Death as a Punishment in America 1864–1982* (Chicago, 1984).

BOX, STEVEN, *Power, Crime, and Mystification* (London, 1983).

BRACHER, KARL DIETRICH, *Stufen der Machtergreifung*, vol. i of idem, Wolfgang Sauer, and Gerhard Schulz, *Die nationalsozialistische Machtergreifung. Studien zur Errichtung der totalitären Herrschaftssystems in Deutschland 1933/34* (Opladen, 1960).

BRANDT, PETER, *Preußen. Zur Sozialgeschichte eines Staates. Eine Darstellung in Quellen* (Reinbek, 1981).

BRASCH, THOMAS, *Engel aus Eisen. Beschreibung eines Films* (Frankfurt am Main, 1981).

BRAUN, OTTO, *Von Weimar zu Hitler*, 2nd edn. (Hildesheim, 1979).

BREDNICH, R. W. (ed.), *Grundriß der Volkskunde* (Munich, 1988).

BREITHAUPT, WILHELM, *Die Strafe des Staupenschlags und ihre Abschaffung im Gemeinen Recht* (Jena, 1938).

BRELOER, HEINRICH, and KÖNIGSTEIN, HORST, *Blutgeld. Materialien zu einer deutschen Geschichte* (Cologne, 1982).

BREUER, STEPHAN, 'Foucaults Theorie der Disziplinargesellschaft. Eine Zwischenbilanz', *Leviathan*, 15 (1987), 319–37.

BREUILLY, JOHN, Review of Blasius, *Bürgerliche Gesellschaft*, in *Social History*, 3 (1978), 99–102.

BROSZAT, MARTIN, 'The Concentration Camps 1933–45', in Helmut Krausnick (ed.), *Anatomy of the SS State* (London, 1968), 397–450.

——*Hitler and the Collapse of Weimar Germany* (Oxford, 1987).

——'Siegerjustiz oder strafrechtliche "Selbstreinigung"? Aspekte der Vergangenheitsbewältigung der deutschen Justiz während der Besatzungszeit 1945–1949', *Vierteljahreshefte für Zeitgeschichte*, 29 (1981), 477–544.

——and FRÖHLICH, ELKE (eds.), *Bayern in der NS-Zeit. Herrschaft und Gesellschaft im Konflikt* (Munich, 1979).

BROWNING, CHRISTOPHER, *Ordinary Men: Reserve Police Battalion 101 and the Final Solution in Poland* (London, 1992).

BRUNNER, OTTO, CONZE, WERNER, and KOSELLECK, REINHART (eds.), *Geschichtliche Grundbegriffe. Historisches Lexikon zur politisch-sozialen Sprache in Deutschland*, ii (Stuttgart, 1975).

BUDER, JOHANNES, *Die Reorganisation der preußischen Polizei 1918–1933* (Frankfurt am Main, 1986).

BURGHARTZ, SUSANNA, 'The Equation of Women and Witches: A Case Study of Witchcraft Trials in Lucern and Lausanne in the Fifteenth and Sixteenth Centuries', in Evans (ed.), *The German Underworld*, 57–74.

——'Weibliche Ehre', in Gisela Bock, Karin Hausen, and Heide Wunder (eds.), *Frauengeschichte—Geschlechtergeschichte* (Frankfurt am Main, 1992), 173–83.

BURKE, PETER, *Popular Culture in Early Modern Europe* (London, 1978), 270–81.

BURLEIGH, MICHAEL, *Death and Deliverance: 'Euthanasia' in Germany c.1900–1945* (Cambridge, 1994).

——and WIPPERMANN, WOLFGANG, *The Racial State: Germany 1933–1945* (Cambridge, 1991).

BURNS, WALTER, *For Capital Punishment: Crime and the Morality of the Death Penalty* (New York, 1979).

BÜSCH, OTTO, and NEUGEBAUER-WÖLK, MONIKA (eds.), *Preußen und die revolutionäre Herausforderung seit 1789* (Berlin, 1991).

CAMPBELL, M. and ROLLINS, M. (eds.), *Begetting Images: Studies in the Art and Science of Symbol Production* (New York, 1989).

CAMUS, ALBERT, *Le Mythe de Sisyphe. Essai sur l'absurde* (Paris, 1942).

——'Reflections on the Guillotine', in idem, *Resistance, Rebellion and Death* (London, 1961), 127–65.

CERNY, JOCHEN (ed.), *Wer war wer—DDR. Ein biographisches Lexikon* (Berlin, 1992).

CHAUNU, PIERRE, *La Mort à Paris: XVIe, XVIIe et XVIIIe siècles* (Paris, 1978).

——'Mourir à Paris (XVIe–XVIIe–XVIIIe siècles)', *Annales ESC*, 31 (1976).

CHEESMAN, CHRISTOPHER THOMAS, *The Shocking Ballad Picture Show: German Popular Literature and Cultural History* (Oxford, 1994).

——'Studies in the History of German Street Balladry in the 18th and 19th Centuries, with a Select Annotated Catalogue of Printed and Manuscript Sources, 1580–1950' (D.Phil. dissertation, Oxford, 1988).

CHESNAIS, JEAN-CLAUDE, *Histoire de la violence en Occident de 1800 à nos jours* (Paris, 1981).

CHICKERING, ROGER, *Imperial Germany and a World without War: The Peace Movement and German Society 1892–1914* (Princeton, 1975).

CLARKE, JOHN, et al. (eds.), *Permissiveness and Control: The Fate of the Sixties Legislation* (London, 1980).

COCKBURN, J. S. (ed.), *Crime in England 1550–1800* (Princeton, 1971).

COHEN, ESTHER, *The Crossroads of Justice: Law and Culture in Late Medieval France* (Leiden, 1993).

——'Symbols of Culpability and the Universal Language of Justice: The Ritual of Public Executions in Late Medieval Europe', *History of European Ideas*, 11 (1989), 407–16.

COHEN, RICHARD A., 'The German League for Human Rights in the Weimar Republic' (Ph.D. thesis, State University of New York at Buffalo, 1989, University Microfilms no. 95131).

COHEN, STANLEY, *Folk Devils and Moral Panics: The Creation of the Mods and Rockers* (London, 1972).

—— (ed.), *Images of Deviance* (Harmondsworth, 1971).

CONRAD, HERMANN, *Die geistigen Grundlagen des Allgemeinen Landrechts für die Preußischen Staaten von 1794* (Cologne, 1958).

CONZE, WERNER (ed.), *Sozialgeschichte der Familie in der Neuzeit Europas* (Stuttgart, 1976).

COOPER, DAVID, *The Lesson of the Scaffold: The Public Execution Controversy in Victorian England* (London, 1974).

CORBIN, ALAIN, *Pesthauch und Blütenduft. Eine Geschichte des Geruchs* (Berlin, 1984).

CROOK, PAUL, *Darwinism, War and History: The debate over the biology of war from the 'Origin of Species' to the First World War* (Cambridge, 1994).

CRAIG, GORDON A., *Germany 1866–1945* (Oxford, 1978).

CZECH, DANUTA, *et al.*, *Auschwitz. Geschichte und Wirklichkeit des Vernichtungslagers* (Reinbek, 1980).

DANKER, UWE, 'Bandits and the State: Robbers and the Authorities in the Holy Roman Empire in the Late Seventeenth and Early Eighteenth Centuries', in Evans (ed.), *The German Underworld*, 75–107.

—— *Räuberbanden im Alten Reich um 1700. Ein Beitrag zur Geschichte von Herrschaft und Kriminalität um 1700* (Frankfurt am Main, 1988).

DAVIS, DAVID BRION, 'The Movement to Abolish Capital Punishment in America 1787–1861', *American Historical Review*, 63 (1957), 23–46.

DAVIS, JOHN A., *Conflict and Control: Law and Order in Nineteenth-Century Italy* (London, 1988).

DEIMLING, GEORG (ed.), *Cesare Beccaria. Die Anfänge moderner Strafrechtspflege in Europa* (Heidelberg, 1989).

DELANEY, JOHN, 'Bourgeois morals/public punishment. England *c.*1750s–1860s' (Ph.D. thesis, Australian National University, 1989).

DIESTELKAMP, BERNHARD, 'Die Justiz nach 1945 und ihr Umgang mit der eigenen Vergangenheit,' in idem and Michael Stolleis (eds.), *Justizalltag im Dritten Reich* (Frankfurt am Main, 1988), 131–50.

DINER, DAN (ed.), *Ist der Nationalsozialismus Geschichte? Zur Historisierung und Historikerstreit* (Frankfurt am Main, 1987).

DINGES, MARTIN, 'Die Ehre als Thema der Stadtgeschichte. Eine Semantik am Übergang vom Ancien Régime zur Moderne', *Zeitschrift für historische Forschung*, 16 (1989), 409–40.

—— 'Frühneuzeitliche Justiz', in Heinz Mohnhaupt and Dieter Simon (eds.), *Vorträge zur Justizforschung*, i. *Geschichte und Theorie* (Frankfurt am Main, 1992), 269–92.

—— 'The Reception of Michel Foucault's Ideas on Social Discipline, Mental Asylums, Hospitals and the Medical Profession in German Historiography', in Colin Jones and Roy Porter (eds.), *Reassessing Foucault: Power, Medicine and the Body* (London, 1993), 181–212.

DÖLLING, DIETER, 'Kriminologie im "Dritten Reich"', in Dreier and Sellert (eds.), *Recht und Justiz*, 194–235.

DONAJGRODZKI, ANTHONY P. (ed.), *Social Control in Nineteenth-Century Britain* (London, 1977).

DÖRING, HANS-JOACHIM, 'Die Motive der Zigeunerdeportation von Mai 1940', *Vierteljahreshefte für Zeitgeschichte*, 7 (1959), 418–28.

—— *Zigeuner im nationalsozialistischen Staat* (Hamburg, 1964).

DÖRNER, KLAUS, *Bürger und Irre. Zur Sozialgeschichte und Wissenschaftssoziologie der Psychiatrie* (Frankfurt am Main, 1969).

DOUGLAS, MARY, *Purity and Danger: An Analysis of Concepts of Pollution and Taboo* (London, 1966).

DREIER, RALF, and SELLERT, WOLFGANG (eds.), *Recht und Justiz im 'Dritten Reich'* (Frankfurt am Main, 1989).

DUERR, HANS-PETER, *Nacktheit und Scham. Der Mythos vom Zivilisationsprozeß*, i (Frankfurt am Main, 1988).

DÜLMEN, RICHARD VAN, (ed.), *Arbeit, Frömmigkeit und Eigensinn* (Frankfurt am Main, 1990).

—— (ed.), *Dynamik der Tradition* (Frankfurt am Main, 1992).

—— *Frauen vor Gericht. Kindsmord in der frühen Neuzeit* (Frankfurt am Main, 1991).

—— (ed.), *Hexenwelten. Magie und Imagination vom 16.–20. Jahrhundert* (Frankfurt am Main, 1987).

—— 'Der infame Mensch. Unehrliche Arbeit und soziale Ausgrenzung in der Frühen Neuzeit', in idem (ed.), *Arbeit*.

—— *Kultur und Alltag in der Frühen Neuzeit*, i. *Das Haus und seine Menschen*; ii. *Dorf und Stadt. 16.–18. Jahrhundert*; iii. *Magie, Religion, Aufklärung* (Munich, 1990–4).

—— *Theater des Schreckens. Gerichtspraxis und Strafrituale in der Frühen Neuzeit* (Munich, 1985).

—— (ed.), *Verbrechen, Strafen und soziale Kontrolle* (Frankfurt am Main, 1990).

DÜRKOP, MARLIS, 'Zur Funktion der Kriminologie im Nationalsozialismus', in Udo Reifner and Bernd-Rüdeger Sonnen (eds.), *Strafjustiz und Polizei im Dritten Reich* (Frankfurt am Main, 1984), 97–120.

DÜSING, BERNHARD, *Die Geschichte der Abschaffung der Todesstrafe in der Bundesrepublik Deutschland unter besonderer Berücksichtigung ihres parlamentarischen Zustandekommens* (Schwenningen/Neckar, 1952).

EBBINGHAUS, ANGELIKA, *et al.*, *Heilen und Vernichten im Mustergau Hamburg. Bevölkerungspolitik im Dritten Reich* (Hamburg, 1984).

EBELING, ALBERT, 'Beiträge zur Geschichte der Freiheitsstrafe', *Zeitschrift für die gesamte Strafrechtswissenschaft*, 18 (1898), 419–94, 608–66.

EDGERTON, S., *Pictures and Punishment: Art and Criminal Prosecution during the Florentine Renaissance* (London, 1985).

EGGLER, WILHELM, *Der Waldstetter Mord und die letzte Hinrichtung in Walddürn (1818)* (offprint from *Alemmania, Zeitschrift für alemannische und fränkische Geschichte, Volkskunde, Kunst und Sprache*; Freiburg im Breisgau, 1916).

EISERT, WOLFGANG, *Die Waldheimer Prozesse. Der stalinistische Terror 1950. Ein dunkles Kapitel der DDR-Justiz* (Munich, 1993).

EKSTEINS, MODRIS, *The Limits of Reason: The German Democratic Press and the Collapse of the Weimar Republic* (Oxford, 1975).

ELEY, GEOFF, *Reshaping the German Right: Radical Nationalism and Political Change after Bismarck* (London, 1980).

ELIAS, NORBERT, *Studien über die Deutschen. Machtkämpfe und Habitusentwicklung im 19. und 20. Jahrhundert* (Frankfurt am Main, 1992).

—— *Über die Einsamkeit der Sterbenden in unseren Tagen* (Frankfurt am Main, 1982).

—— *Über den Prozeß der Zivilisation. Soziogenetische und psychogenetische Untersuchungen*, i. *Wandlungen des Verhaltens in den weltlichen Oberschichten des Abendlandes*; ii. *Wandlungen der Gesellschaft. Entwurf zu einer Theorie der Zivilisation* (Berne, 1969).

ELWENSPOEK, CURT, *Schinderhannes. Der rheinische Rebell* (Stuttgart, 1925).

EMSLEY, CLIVE, and WEINBERGER, BARBARA (eds.), *Policing Western Europe: Professionalism and Public Order 1850–1940* (London, 1991).

ENGELBERG, ERNST, *Bismarck. Das Reich in der Mitte Europas* (Berlin, 1990).

ENGELHARD, HANS (ed.), *Im Namen des deutschen Volkes. Justiz und Nationalsozialismus* (Cologne, 1989).

ERGANG, ROBERT, *The Myth of the All-Destructive Fury of the Thirty Years War* (Pocono Pines, Pa., 1956).

ERIBON, DIDIER, *Michel Foucault* (London, 1992).

ESCHENBURG, THEODOR, and BENZ, WOLFGANG, 'Der Weg zum Grundgesetz', in Theodor Eschenburg (ed.), *Jahre der Besatzung 1945–1949* (Geschichte der Bundesrepublik Deutschland, 1; Stuttgart, 1983), 459–514.

ESMEIN, A., *A History of Continental Criminal Procedure* (Boston, 1913).

EVANS, E. P. *The Criminal Prosecution and Capital Punishment of Animals* (London, 1906).

EVANS, RICHARD J., *Death in Hamburg: Society and Politics in the Cholera Years 1830–1910* (Oxford, 1987).

—— *The Feminist Movement in Germany 1894–1933* (London, 1976).

—— (ed.), *The German Underworld: Essays in the Social History of Crime in Germany from the Sixteenth Century to the Present* (London, 1988).

—— (ed.), *The German Working Class: The Politics of Everyday Life* (London, 1982).

—— *Im Schatten Hitlers? Historikerstreit und Vergangenheitsbewältigung in der Bundesrepublik*, rev. German edn. (Frankfurt am Main, 1991).

—— 'In Search of German Social Darwinism: History and Historiography of a Concept', in Manfred Berg and Geoffrey Cocks (eds.), *Medicine and Modernity: Public Health and Medical Care in Nineteenth- and Twentieth-Century Germany* (New York, forthcoming).

—— 'Öffentlichkeit und Autorität. Zur Geschichte der Hinrichtungen in Deutschland vom Allgemeinen Landrecht bis zum Dritten Reich', in Heinz Reif (ed.), *Räuber, Volk und Obrigkeit*, 185–258.

—— ' "Red Wednesday" in Hamburg: Social Democrats, Police, and Lumpenproletariat in the Suffrage Disturbances of 17 January 1906', in idem, *Rethinking German History*, 248–90.

—— 'Religion and Society in Modern Germany', *European Studies Quarterly*, 12 (1982), 249–88.

—— *Rethinking German History: Nineteenth-Century Germany and the Origins of the Third Reich* (London, 1987).

—— (ed.), *Society and Politics in Wilhelmine Germany* (London, 1978).

—— *Szenen aus der deutschen Unterwelt. Kriminalität und Strafe im 19. Jahrhundert* (Reinbek, 1997).

—— and LEE, W. R. (eds.), *The German Family: Essays on the Social History of the Family in Nineteenth- and Twentieth-Century Germany* (London, 1981).

————(eds.), *The German Peasantry: Conflict and Community in Rural Society from the Eighteenth to the Twentieth Century* (London, 1986).

EXNER, FRANZ, 'Mord and Todesstrafe in Sachsen 1855–1927', *Monatsschrift für Kriminalpsychologie und Strafrechtsreform*, 20 (1929), 1–17.

FABER, KARL-GEORG, 'Historische Kriminologie und kritische Sozialgeschichte: das preußische Beispiel', *Historische Zeitschrift*, 227 (1978), 112–22.

FARGE, ARLETTE, *Fragile Lives: Violence, Power and Solidarity in Eighteenth-Century Paris* (Oxford, 1993).

FASSBINDER, RAINER WERNER, *Bremer Freiheit. Frau Gesche Gottfried. Ein bürgerliches Trauerspiel* (Frankfurt am Main, 1983).

FEEST, JOHANNES, and MARZAHN, CHRISTIAN (eds.), *Criminalia: Bremer Strafjustiz 1810–1850* (Beiträge zur Sozialgeschichte Bremens, 11; Bremen, 1988).

FILMER, WERNER, and SCHWAN, HERIBERT, *Opfer der Mauer. Die geheimen Protokolle des Todes* (Munich, 1991).

FINE, BOB *et al.* (eds.), *Capitalism and the Rule of Law: From Deviancy Theory to Marxism* (London, 1979).

FISH, STANLEY, *There's No Such Thing as Free Speech and It's a Good Thing Too* (Oxford, 1994).

FLECKENSTEIN, MARTIN, *Die Todesstrafe im Werk Carl Joseph Anton Mittermaiers (1787–1867). Zur Entwicklungsgeschichte eines Werkbereichs und seiner Bedeutung für Theorie- und Methodenbildung* (Frankfurt am Main, 1991).

FOUCAULT, MICHEL, *The Archaeology of Knowledge*, tr. A. M. Sheridan Smith (New York, 1972).

——*Discipline and Punish: The Birth of the Prison*, Alan Sheridan (Harmondsworth, 1977).

——*Histoire de la folie à l'âge classique* (Paris, 1972).

——*Language, Counter-Memory, Practice: Selected Essays and Interviews*, tr. Donald F. Bouchard and Sherry Simon (Ithaca, NY, 1977).

——*Power/Knowledge: Selected Interviews and Other Writings, 1972–1977*, ed. and tr. Colin Gordon (New York, 1980).

——*Surveiller et punir: Naissance de la prison* (Paris, 1975).

FRANKE, MANFRED, *Schinderhannes. Das kurze, wilde Leben des Johannes Bückler. Nach alten Documenten neu erzählt* (Düsseldorf, 1984).

FRAUENSTÄDT, P., 'Das Begnadigungsrecht im Mittelalter: Ein Beitrag zur Geschichte des Strafrechts', *Zeitschrift für die gesamte Strafrechtswissenschaft*, 17 (1897), 887–910.

——'Zur Geschichte der Galeerenstrafe in Deutschland', *Zeitschrift für die gesamte Strafrechtswissenschaft*, 16 (1896), 518–46.

FREI, NORBERT, *Der Führerstaat. Nationalsozialistische Herrschaft 1933 bis 1945* (Munich, 1987).

——*National Socialist Rule in Germany: The Führer State 1933–1945* (London, 1993).

FREVERT, UTE, 'Bourgeois Honour: Middle-Class Duellists in Germany from the Late Eighteenth to the Early Twentieth Century', in Blackbourn and Evans (eds.), *The German Bourgeoisie*, 255–92.

——*Frauen-Geschichte. Zwischen bürgerlicher Verbesserung und Neuer Weiblichkeit* (Frankfurt am Main, 1986).

FRICKE, KARL WILHELM, 'Aus "erzieherischen Gründen" wurde die Todesstrafe verhängt. Die Strafjustiz in der DDR war dem SED-Parteiapparat untergeordnet', *Frankfurter Rundschau*, 29 Oct. 1992, 24.

FRICKE, KARL WILHELM, *MfS Intern. Macht, Strukturen, Auflösung der DDR-Staatssicherheit* (Cologne, 1991).

——*Politik und Justiz in der DDR. Zur Geschichte der politischen Verfolgung 1945–1968. Bericht und Dokumentation* (Cologne, 1979).

——*Zur Menschen- und Grundrechtssituation politischer Gefangener in der DDR*, 2nd edn. (Cologne, 1988).

FRIEDRICH, JÖRG, *Freispruch für die Nazi-Justiz. Die Urteile gegen NS-Richter seit 1948. Eine Dokumentation* (Reinbek, 1983).

——*Die kalte Amnestie* (Frankfurt am Main, 1984).

FUNK, ALBRECHT, *Polizei und Rechtsstaat: Die Entwicklung des staatsrechtlichen Gewaltmonopols in Preußen 1848–1918* (Frankfurt am Main, 1986).

FURIAN, GILBERT, *Der Richter und sein Lenker. Politische Justiz in der DDR* (Berlin, 1992).

GARLAND, DAVID, *Punishment and Modern Society: A Study in Social Theory* (Oxford, 1990).

——*Punishment and Welfare: A History of Penal Strategies* (Aldershot, 1985).

GASMAN, DANIEL, *The Scientific Origins of National Socialism: Ernst Haeckel and the Monist League* (New York, 1971).

GATRELL, VICTOR A. C., 'The Decline of Theft and Violence in Victorian and Edwardian England', in Gatrell *et al.* (eds.), *Crime*, 238–370.

——*The Hanging Tree: Execution and the English People 1770–1868* (Oxford, 1994).

GAY, PETER, *The Bourgeois Experience: Victoria to Freud*, iii. *The Cultivation of Hatred* (London, 1994).

GEISLER, KURT, 'Der Scharfrichter, der eine Räuberbande half', *Berliner Morgenpost*, 11 May 1979.

GEISS, IMANUEL and WENDT, BERND-JÜRGEN (eds.), *Deutschland in der Weltpolitik des 19. und 20. Jahrhunderts*, 2nd edn. (Düsseldorf, 1974).

GELLATELY, ROBERT, *The Gestapo and German Society: Enforcing Racial Policy 1933–1945* (Oxford, 1990).

GENNEP, ARNOLD VAN, *The Rites of Passage* (1908; repr. Chicago, 1960).

GEROULD, DANIEL, *Guillotine: Its Legend and Lore* (New York, 1992).

GIMPEL, KLAUS, 'Nachrichten über die Henker (Büttel, Scharfrichter) in Münster', *Westfälische Zeitschrift*, 141 (1991), 151–68.

GINZBURG, CARLO, *Clues, Myths and the Historical Method* (Baltimore, 1989).

——*Ecstasies: Deciphering the Witches' Sabbath* (London, 1990).

GISMONDI, MICHAEL A., 'The Gift of Theory: A Critique of the *histoire des mentalités*', *Social History*, 10 (1985), 211–30.

GITTINGS, CLARE, *Death, Burial and the Individual in Early Modern England* (London, 1984).

GLEICHMANN, PETER, GOUDSBLOM, JOHAN, and KORTE, HERMANN (eds.), *Materialien zu Norbert Elias' Zivilisationstheorie*, i (Frankfurt am Main, 1979).

—— —— —— (eds.), *Macht und Zivilisation. Materialien zu Norbert Elias' Zivilisationstheorie*, ii (Frankfurt am Main, 1984).

GLENZDORF, JOHANN, and TREICHEL, FRITZ, *Henker, Schinder und Arme Sünder* (Bad Münder am Deister, 1970).

GODAU-SCHÜTTKE, KLAUS-DETLEV, *Rechtsverwalter des Reiches. Staatssekretär Dr. Curt Joël* (Frankfurt am Main, 1981).

GÖPPINGER, HORST, *Die Verfolgung der Juristen jüdischer Abstammung durch den Nationalsozialismus* (Villingen, 1963).

GORER, GEOFFREY, *Death, Grief and Mourning in Contemporary Britain* (London, 1965).

GOSTOMSKI, VICTOR VON, and LOCH, WALTER, *Der Tod von Plötzensee: Erinnerungen, Ereignisse, Dokumente 1942–1944* (Frankfurt am Main, 1993).

GOUDSBLOM, JOHAN, 'Aufnahme und Kritik der Arbeiten von Norbert Elias in England, Deutschland, den Niederlanden und Frankreich', in Gleichmann *et al.* (eds.), *Materialien*, 17–100.

GRAEF, GOTTLIEB, 'Hochgericht', *Fränkische Blätter. Monatsschrift für Heimatkunde des badischen Frankenlandes*, 3 (1920), unpaginated.

GRIESINGER, ANDREAS, *Das symbolische Kapital der Ehre. Streikbewegungen und kollektives Bewußtsein deutscher Handwerksgesellen im 18. Jahrhundert* (Frankfurt am Main, 1981).

GRITSCHNEIDER, OTTO, *'Der Führer hat Sie zum Tode verurteilt ...'. Hitlers 'Röhm-Putsch'-Morde vor Gericht* (Munich, 1993).

GRODE, WALTER, *Die 'Sonderbehandlung 14f13' in den Konzentrationslagern des Dritten Reiches. Ein Beitrag zur Dynamik faschistischer Vernichtungspolitik* (Frankfurt am Main, 1987).

GROSSMANN, KURT, *Ossietzky. Ein deutscher Patriot* (Frankfurt am Main, 1968).

GRUCHMANN, LOTHAR, 'Die bayerische Justiz im politischen Machtkampf 1933/34. Ihr Scheitern bei der Strafverfolgung von Mordfällen in Dachau', in Broszat and Fröhlich (eds.), *Bayern*, ii. 415–28.

——*Justiz im Dritten Reich 1933–1940. Anpassung und Unterwerfung in der Ära Gürtner* (Munich, 1988).

——'Die Überleitung der Justizverwaltung auf das Reich 1933–1935', in Anon. (ed.) *Vom Reichsjustizamt zum Bundesministerium der Justiz. Festschrift zum hundertjährigen Gründungstag des Reichsjustizamtes* (Cologne, 1977).

GUNDERMANN, ISELIN, *Allgemeines Landrecht für die Preußischen Staaten 1794* (Mainz, 1994).

HAAS, KENNETH C., and INCIARDI, JAMES A. (eds.), *Challenging Capital Punishment: Legal and Social Science Approaches* (Newburg Park, Calif., 1988).

HABERMAS, JÜRGEN, *Strukturwandel der Öffentlichkeit. Untersuchungen zu einer Kategorie der bürgerlichen Gesellschaft* (Frankfurt am Main, 1968).

HABERMAS, REBEKKA, 'Frauen und Männer im Kampf um Leib, Ökonomie und Recht. Zur Beziehung der Geschlechter im Frankfurt der Frühen Neuzeit', in Van Dülmen (ed.), *Dynamik der Tradition*, pp. 109–36.

HAGEN, WILLIAM, 'The Junkers' Faithless Servants: Peasant Insubordination and the Breakdown of Serfdom in Brandenburg-Prussia, 1763–1811', in Evans and Lee (eds.), *The German Peasantry*, 71–101.

HALE, ORON J., *The Captive Press in the Third Reich* (Princeton, 1964).

HALL, ALEX, 'By Other Means: The Legal Struggle against the SPD in Wilhelmine Germany, 1890–1914', *Historical Journal*, 17 (1974), 365–80.

——*Scandal, Sensation and Social Democracy: The SPD Press and Wilhelmine Germany 1890–1914* (Cambridge, 1977).

HALTER, HANS, 'An der Richtstätte kein Hitler-Gruß', *Der Spiegel*, 33/8 (19 Feb. 1979), 100–1.

——'"Nahschuß in den Hinterkopf"', *Der Spiegel*, 45/35 (26 Aug. 1991), 84–6.

HANNOVER, HEINRICH and ELISABETH, *Politische Justiz 1918–1933* (Frankfurt am Main, 1966).

HARITOS-FATOUROS, MIKA, 'Die Ausbildung des Folterers. Trainingsprogramme der Obristendiktatur in Griechenland', in Jan Philipp Reemtsma (ed.), *Folter. Zur Analyse eines Herrschaftsmittels* (Hamburg, 1991), 73–90.

HARSTER, THEODOR, *Das Strafrecht der Freien Reichsstadt Speyer in Theorie und Praxis* (Breslau, 1900).

HARTL, FRIEDRICH, *Das Wiener Kriminalgericht. Strafrechtspflege vom Zeitalter der Aufklärung bis zur österreichischen Revolution* (Vienna, 1973).

HARTMAN, MARY, *Victorian Murderesses: A True History of Thirteen Respectable French and English Women Accused of Unspeakable Crimes* (New York, 1977).

HARTMANN, RICHARD, *P. J. A. Feuerbachs politische und strafrechtliche Grundanschauungen* (Berlin, 1961).

HARYCH, THEO, *'Im Namen des Volkes? Der Fall Jakubowski* (East Berlin, 1959).

HAUSEN, KARIN, 'Family and Role-Division: The Polarisation of Sexual Stereotypes in the Nineteenth Century—An Aspect of the Dissociation of Work and Family Life', in Evans and Lee (eds.), *The German Family*, 51–83.

HAXTHAUSEN, CHARLES W., and SUHR, HEIDRUN (eds.), *Berlin: Culture and Metropolis* (Minneapolis, 1990).

HAY, DOUGLAS, 'Property, Authority and the Criminal Law', in idem *et al.* (eds.), *Albion's Fatal Tree: Crime and Society in Eighteenth-Century England* (London, 1975), 17–64.

HEIM, WILLI, *Das Henkersmahl* (Erlangen, 1941).

HELBING, FRANZ, and BAUER, MAX, *Die Tortur. Geschichte der Folter im Kriminalverfahren aller Zeiten und Völker* (Berlin, 1925).

HELLMER, JOACHIM, *Der Gewohnheitsverbrecher und die Sicherungsverwahrung 1934–1945* (Berlin, 1961).

HELMENSDORFER, ERICH, ' "Ich tät's nie wieder". Scharfrichter Reichart ist gegen die Todesstrafe', *Die Zeit*, 30 Oct. 1964.

HERBERT, ULRICH, *Fremdarbeiter. Politik und Praxis des 'Ausländer-Einsatzes' in der Kriegswirtschaft des Dritten Reiches* (Bonn, 1985).

HERZIG, ARNO, *Unterschichtenprotest in Deutschland 1790–1870* (Göttingen, 1988).

——— *et al.* (eds.), *Arbeiter im Hamburg. Unterschichten, Arbeiter und Arbeiterbewegung seit dem ausgehenden 19. Jahrhundert* (Hamburg, 1983).

HEUER, J.-U., *Allgemeines Landrecht und Klassenkampf. Die Auseinandersetzungen um die Prinzipien des Allgemeinen Landrechts Ende des 18. Jahrhunderts als Ausdruck der Krise des Feudalsystems in Preußen* (Berlin, 1960).

HINCKELDEY, CHRISTOPH (ed.), *Justiz in alter Zeit* (Rothenburg ob der Tauber, 1984).

HIPPEL, R. VON, *Die Entstehung der modernen Freiheitsstrafe und des Erziehungs-Strafvollzugs* (Jena, 1932).

HIRSCHBERG, MAX, *Das Fehlurteil im Strafprozeß* (Frankfurt am Main, 1962).

HIRSCHFELD, GERHARD, and KRUMEICH, GERD (eds.), *'Keiner fühlt sich hier mehr als Mensch...' Erlebnis und Wirkung des Ersten Weltkriegs* (Stuttgart, 1993).

HIRSCHFELD, MAGNUS, *Illustrierte Sittengeschichte der Nachkriegszeit* (2 vols., Leipzig, 1931).

HOCH, THEODOR, 'Über ehemalige Folter- und Strafwerkzeuge im Museum und ihre ehemalige Anwendung in Lübeck', *Die Heimat*, 14 (1904), 179–85, 202–8.

HOFFMANN, CHRISTA, *Stunden Null? Vergangenheitsbewältigung in Deutschland 1945 und 1989* (Bonn, 1992).

HOFFMANN, DIERK, SCHMIDT, KARL-HEINZ, and SKYBA, PETER (eds.), *Die DDR vor dem Mauerbau. Dokumente zur Geschichte des anderen deutschen Staates 1949–1961* (Munich, 1993).

HOFFMANN, PETER, *The History of the German Resistance 1933–1945* (London, 1977).

HOHMANN, JOACHIM S., *Robert Ritter und die Erben der Kriminalbiologie* (Frankfurt am Main, 1991).

—— 'Die Forschungen des "Zigeunerexperten" Hermann Arnold', *1999: Zeitschrift für Sozialgeschichte des 20. und 21. Jahrhunderts*, 10 (1995) 3, 35–49.

HORN, NORBERT (ed.), *Europäisches Rechtsdenken in Geschichte und Gegenwart* (Munich, 1982).

HOULBROOKE, RALPH (ed.), *Death, Ritual, and Bereavement* (London, 1989).

HSIA, RONALD PO-CHIA, *Social Discipline in the Reformation: Central Europe 1550–1750* (London, 1989).

HUBER, ERNST RUDOLF, *Deutsche Verfassungsgeschichte seit 1789*, iii. *Bismarck und das Reich* (Stuttgart, 1963).

—— *Deutsche Verfassungsgeschichte seit 1789*, iv. *Struktur und Krisen des Kaiserreichs* (Stuttgart, 1969).

—— *Deutsche Verfassungsgeschichte seit 1789*, vi. *Die Weimarer Reichsverfassung* (Stuttgart, 1969).

—— *Deutsche Verfassungsgeschichte seit 1789*, vii. *Ausbau, Schutz und Untergang der Weimarer Republik* (Stuttgart, 1984).

HÜGEL, HANS-OTTO, *Untersuchungsrichter—Diebsfänger—Detektive. Theorie und Geschichte der deutschen Detektiverzählung im 19. Jahrhundert* (Stuttgart, 1978).

HUGHES, ROBERT, *Culture of Complaint: The Fraying of America* (New York, 1993).

HUIZINGA, JOHAN, *The Waning of the Middle Ages: A Study of the Forms of Life, Thought, and Art in France and the Netherlands in the Fourteenth and Fifteenth Centuries* (London, 1924).

HÜTTENBERGER, PETER, 'Heimtückefälle vor dem Sondergericht München 1933–1939', in Broszat and Fröhlich (eds.), *Bayern*, iv. 435–526.

HUTTON, PATRICK, 'The History of Mentalities: The New Map of Cultural History', *History and Theory*, 20 (1981), 237–59.

IGNATIEFF, MICHAEL, *A Just Measure of Pain: The Penitentiary in the Industrial Revolution 1750–1850* (New York, 1978).

—— 'Recent Social Histories of Punishment', in Michael Tonry and Norval Morris (eds.), *Crime and Justice: An Annual Review of Research* (Chicago, 1981), 153–91; also in Stanley Cohen and Andrew Scull (eds.), *Social Control and the State* (London, 1983), 75–105.

IRSIGLER, FRANZ, and LASSOTTA, ARNOLD, *Bettler und Gaukler, Dirnen und Henker. Außenseiter in einer mittelalterlichen Stadt. Köln 1300–1600* (Frankfurt am Main, 1989).

JÄCKEL, EBERHARD, 'Die doppelte Vergangenheit', *Der Spiegel*, 35/52 (1991), 39–43.

JACOBEIT, WOLFGANG, *Bäuerliche Arbeit und Wirtschaft. Ein Beitrag zur Wissenschaftsgeschichte der deutschen Volkskunde* (Berlin, 1965).

—— 'Vom Aufbruch der Volkskunde: Ein Gespräch', in Jeggle *et al.* (eds.), *Volkskultur*, 9–20.

JACOBMEYER, WOLFGANG, *Vom Zwangsarbeiter zum Heimatlosen Ausländer. Die Displaced Persons in Westdeutschland 1945–1951* (Göttingen, 1985).

JAHNTZ, BERNHARD, and KÄHNE, VOLKER, *Der Volksgerichtshof. Darstellung der Ermittlungen der Staatsanwaltschaft bei dem Landegericht Berlin gegen ehemalige Richter und Staatsanwälte am Volksgerichtshof* (Berlin, 1986).

JANKA, WALTER, *Schwierigkeiten mit der Wahrheit* (Reinbek, 1989).

—— *Spuren eines Lebens* (Berlin, 1991).

JANSEN, FRANZ, *Emil Julius Gumbel. Portrait eines Zivilisten* (Heidelberg, 1991).

JANSSEN, KARL-HEINZ, 'Geschichte aus der Dunkelkammer. Kabalen um den Reichstagsbrand. Eine unvermeidliche Enthüllung', *Die Zeit*, 38–41 (Sept.–Oct. 1979).

JARAUSCH, KONRAD H., 'Toward a Social History of Experience: Postmodern Predicaments in Theory and Interdisciplinarity', *Central European History*, 22 (1989), 427–43.

—— *The Unfree Professions: German Lawyers, Teachers and Engineers, 1900–1950* (New York, 1990).

JASPER, GOTTHARD, *Der Schutz der Republik* (Tübingen, 1962).

JASPER, MICHAEL, '"Hats Off!" The Roots of Victorian Public Hangings', in W. B. Thesing (ed.), *Execution and the British Experience* (London, 1990).

JEGGLE, UTZ, et al. (eds.), *Volkskultur in der Moderne: Probleme und Perspektiven empirischer Kulturforschung* (Reinbek, 1986).

JELOWIK, LISELOTTE, *Zur Geschichte der Strafrechtsreform in der Weimarer Republik* (Martin-Luther-Universität Halle-Wittenberg, Wiss. Beiträge 1983/13; Halle an der Saale, 1983).

JOHE, WERNER, *Die gleichgeschaltete Justiz. Organisation des Rechtswesens und Politisierung der Rechtsprechung 1933–1945 dargestellt am Beispiel des Oberlandesgerichtsbezirks Hamburg* (Frankfurt am Main, 1967).

JOHN, MICHAEL, *Politics and the Law in Late Nineteenth-Century Germany: The Origins of the Civil Code* (Oxford, 1989).

JOHNSON, ERIC A., 'The Roots of Crime in Imperial Germany', *Central European History*, 15 (1982), 351–76.

—— 'Women as Victims and Criminals: Female Homicide and Criminality in Imperial Germany, 1873–1914', *Criminal Justice History*, 6 (1985), 151–75.

—— *Urbanization and Crime: Germany 1871–1914* (New York, 1995).

—— and MCHALE, VINCENT E., 'Urbanization, Industrialization, and Crime in Imperial Germany', *Social Science History*, 1 (1976/7), 45–78 and 210–47.

—— and MONKKONEN, ERIC H. (eds.), *Violent Crime in Town and Country since the Middle Ages* (forthcoming).

JOLL, JAMES, *The Anarchists* (London, 1964).

JONES, LARRY EUGENE, *German Liberalism and the Dissolution of the Weimar Party System 1918–1933* (Chapel Hill, NC, 1988).

—— and JARAUSCH, KONRAD (eds.), *In Search of a Liberal Germany: Studies in the History of German Liberalism from 1789 to the Present* (Oxford, 1990).

KAEVER, ROSWITHA, and LENK, ELISABETH, *Leben und Wirken des Peter Kürten, gennant der Vampir von Düsseldorf* (Munich, 1974).

KAIENBURG, HERMANN, *'Vernichting durch Arbeit'. Der Fall Neuengamme. Die Wirtschaftsbestrebungen der SS und ihre Auswirkungnen auf die Existenzbedingungen der KZ-Gefangenen* (Bonn, 1990).

KAMEN, HENRY, *The Iron Century: Social Change in Europe 1550–1660* (London, 1976).

KANET, F. and VOLGYES, I. (eds.), *On the Road to Communism* (Lawrence, Kan. 1972).

KANNER, LEO, 'The Folklore and Cultural History of Epilepsy', *Medical Life*, 37 (1930), 159–215.

KARASEK, HORST, *Der Brandstifter. Lehr- und Wanderjahre des Maurergesellen Marinus van der Lubbe, der 1933 auszog, den Reichstag anzuzünden* (Berlin, 1980).

KASCHUBA, WOLFGANG 'Mythos oder Eigen-Sinn. "Volkskultur" zwischen Volkskunde und Sozialgeschichte', in Jeggle *et al.* (eds.), *Volkskultur*, 469–507.

——'Ritual und Fest. Das Volk auf der Straße. Figurationen und Funktionen populärer Öffentlichkeit zwischen Frühneuzeit und Moderne', in Van Dülmen (ed.), *Dynamik*, 240–67.

KAUFMANN, JOANNE, 'In Search of Obedience: The Critique of Criminal Justice in Late-Eighteenth-Century France', *Proceedings of the Sixth Annual Meeting of the Western Society for French History* (1979).

KAUL, FRIEDRICH KARL, *Geschichte des Reichsgerichts*, iv. *1933–1945* (East Berlin, 1971).

KAUCZINSKI, RUDKO, 'Hamburg soll "zigeunerfrei" werden', in Angelika Ebbinghaus *et al.*, *Heilen und Vernichten im Mustergau Hamburg. Bevölkerungspolitik im Dritten Reich* (Hamburg, 1984), 45–65.

KELLER, ALBRECHT, *Der Scharfrichter in der deutschen Kulturgeschichte* (Bonn and Leipzig, 1921).

KERSHAW, ANTHONY, *History of the Guillotine* (London, 1958).

KERSHAW, IAN, '"Working towards the Führer": Reflections on the Nature of the Hitler Dictatorship', *Contemporary European History*, 2 (1993), 103–18.

KINNEL, GÜNTHER, 'Das Konzentrationslager Dachau. Eine Studie zu den National-sozialistischen Gewaltverbrechen', in Broszat and Fröhlich (eds.), *Bayern* ii. 349–41.

KIPPER, EBERHARD, *Johann Paul Anselm Feuerbach* (Cologne, 1969).

KIRCHHEIMER, OTTO, and RUSCHE, GEORG, *Punishment and Social Structure* (New York, 1939).

KIRSTEN, WOLFGANG, *Das Konzentrationslager als Institution totalen Terrors: Das Beispiel des KL Natzweiler* (Pfaffenweiler, 1992).

KITCHEN, MARTIN, *The German Officer Corps 1890–1914* (Oxford, 1968).

KLEIN, HERBERT, 'Zum Antoni-Honeder Lied von 1790: Wirklichkeitsgestalt einer salzburgisch-bayerischen Moritat', *Sänger- und Musikantenzeitung. Zweimonatsschrift für Volksmusikpflege*, 11/1 (1968), 3–11.

KLODZINSKI, STANISLAW, 'Die "Aktion 14f13". Der Transport von 575 Häftlingen von Auschwitz in das "Sanatorium Dresden"', in Götz Aly (ed.), *Aktion T-4, 1939–1945* (Berlin, 1987), 136–46.

KLUKE, PAUL, 'Der Fall Potempa', *Vierteljahreshefte für Zeitgeschichte*, 5 (1957), 279–96.

KNAPP, HERMANN, *Das alte Nürnberger Kriminalrecht, nach Rats-Urkunden erläutert* (Berlin, 1896).

——*Das Lochgefängnis. Tortur und Richtung in Alt-Nürnberg* (Nuremberg, 1907).

KÖHLER, JOACHIM, *Christentum und Politik. Dokumente des Widerstands. Zum 40. Jahrestag der Hinrichtung des Zentrumspolitikers und Staatspräsidenten Eugen Bolz am 23. Januar 1945* (Sigmaringen, 1985).

KOLBE, DIETER, *Reichsgerichtspräsident Dr. Erwin Bumke: Studien zum Niedergang des Reichsgerichts und der deutschen Rechtspflege* (Karlsruhe, 1975).

KÖNIG, ULRICH, *Sinti und Roma unterm Nationalsozialismus* (Berlin, 1989).

KOPITZSCH, WOLFGANG, 'Der "Altonaer Blutsonntag"', in Herzig *et al.* (eds.), *Arbeiter im Hamburg*, pp. 509–16.

KOSELLECK, REINHART, *Preußen zwischen Reform und Revolution. Allgemeines Landrecht, Verwaltung und soziale Bewegung von 1791 bis 1848*, 2nd edn. (Munich, 1989).

KOSER, REINHOLD, *Geschichte Friedrichs des Grossen*, 5th edn. (4 vols.; Berlin, 1912–14).

KÖSTLIN, K., and SIEVERS, KAI-DETLEV (eds.), *Das Recht der kleinen Leute. Festschrift für Karl-Sigismund Kramer* (Berlin, 1976).

KOURI, E. I., and SCOTT, TOM (eds.), *Politics and Society in Reformation Europe: Essays for Sir Geoffrey Elton on his Sixty-Fifth Birthday* (London, 1987).

KRACAUER, SIEGFRIED, *From Caligari to Hitler: A Psychological History of the German Film* (Princeton, 1947).

KRAMER, ALAN, '"Greueltaten". Zum Problem der deutschen Kriegsverbrechen in Belgien und Frankreich 1914', in Hirschfeld and Krumeich (eds.), *'Keiner fühlt sich hier mehr als Mensch...'*, 85–114.

—— '"Law-Abiding Germans"? Social Disintegration, Crime and the Reimposition of Order in Post-War Western Germany, 1945–9', in Evans (ed.), *The German Underworld*, 238–61.

KRÄMER, KARL, *Mord und Todesstrafe in Hessen 1817–1929* (Jur. Diss., Gießen, 1932); offprint from *Monatsschrift für Kriminalpsychologie und Strafrechtsreform*, 3 (1932).

KRAMER, KARL-SIGISMUND, *Bauern und Bürger im Nachmittelalterlichen Unterfranken. Eine Volkskunde auf Grund archivalischer Quellen* (Veröffentlichungen der Gesellschaft für fränkische Geschichte, IX. 12; Würzburg, 1957).

KRAUSE, THOMAS, *Die Strafrechtspflege im Kurfürstentum und Königreich Hannover vom Ende des 17. Jahrhunderts bis zum ersten Drittel des 19. Jahrhunderts* (Untersuchungen zur deutschen Staats- und Rechtsgeschichte, NS 28; Aalen, 1991).

KRAUSNICK, HELMUT (ed.), *Anatomy of the SS State* (London, 1968).

KREUTZIGER, B., 'Argumente für und wider die Todesstrafe(n). Ein Beitrag zu Beccaria-Rezeption im deutschsprachigen Raum des 18. Jahrhunderts', in Deimling (ed.), *Cesare Beccaria*, 99–125.

KREUTZAHLER, BIRGIT, *Das Bild des Verbrechers in Romanen der Weimarer Republik. Eine Untersuchung vor dem Hintergrund anderer gesellschaftlicher Verbrecherbilder und gesellschaftlicher Grundzüge der Weimarer Republik* (Frankfurt am Main, 1987).

KÜHLE, HEINRICH, *Staat und Todesstrafe* (Münster, 1934).

KUNZE, MICHAEL, *Highroad to the Stake: A Tale of Witchcraft* (Chicago, 1987).

KUNZLE, DAVID, *The Early Comic Strip: Narrative Strips and Picture Stories in the European Broadsheet from c.1450 to 1815* (Berkeley, 1973).

KUSCHBERT, PAUL, *Quellen und Nachrichten über deutsche Scharfrichter-Sippen*, ii (Cologne, 1941).

KÜTHER, CARSTEN, *Räuber und Gauner in Deutschland. Das organisierte Bandenwesen im 18. und 19. Jahrhundert* (Göttingen, 1976).

—— 'Räuber, Volk und Obrigkeit. Zur Wirkungsweise und Funktion staatlicher Strafverfolgung im 18. Jahrhundert', in Reif (ed.), *Räuber*, 17–42.

LABOUVIE, EVA, *Zauberei und Hexenwerk. Ländlicher Hexenglaube in der frühen Neuzeit* (Frankfurt am Main, 1991).

LAMBRECHT, KAREN, '"Jagdhunde des Teufels". Die Verfolgung von Totengräbern im Gefolge frühneuzeitliche Pestwellen', in Blauert and Schwerhoff (eds.), *Mit den Waffen*, 137–57.

LANDAU, PETER, and SCHRÖTER, FRIEDRICH (eds.), *Strafrecht, Strafprozeß und Rezeption: Grundlagen, Entwicklungen und Wirkung der Constitutio Criminalis Carolina* (Frankfurt am Main, 1984).

LANGBEIN, JOHN H., *Torture and the Law of Proof* (Chicago, 1972).

LAQUEUR, THOMAS W., 'Crowds, Carnival and the State in English Executions, 1604–1868', in Beier, *et al.* (eds.), *The First Modern Society*, 305–55.

LAQUEUR, WALTER, *Young Germany: A History of the German Youth Movement*, 2nd edn. (New Brunswick, 1984).

LAURENCE, ANNE, 'Godly Grief: Individual Responses to Death in Seventeenth-Century Britain', in Houlbrooke (ed.), *Death*, 62–76.

LAZAR, IMRE, *Der Fall Horst Wessel* (Stuttgart and Zurich, 1980).

LEACH, EDMUND, *Culture and Communication: The Logic by which Symbols Are Connected* (Cambridge, 1976).

LEANEY, JENNIFER, 'Ashes to Ashes: Cremation and the Celebration of Death in Nineteenth-Century Britain', in Houlbrooke (ed.), *Death*, 118–35.

LEBRUN, FRANÇOIS, *Les hommes et la mort en Anjou aux 17e et 18e siècles: Essai de démographie et de psychologie historiques* (1971; abr. edn. Paris, 1975).

LEDER, KARL BRUNO, *Todesstrafe. Ursprung, Geschichte, Opfer* (Munich, 1986).

LEGGETT, GEORGE, *The Cheka: Lenin's Political Police* (Oxford, 1981).

LE GOFF, JACQUES, 'Les Mentalités: Une histoire ambiguë', in idem and Pierre Nora (eds.), *Faire l'histoire*, iii (Paris, 1974), 76–94.

LENÔTRE, GEORGES, *The Guillotine and its Servants* (London, 1929).

LESSER, WENDY, *Pictures at an Execution. An Inquiry into the Subject of Murder* (Cambridge, Mass., 1994).

LÉVI-STRAUSS, CLAUDE, *Tristes Tropiques* (London, 1973).

LEWANDOWSKI, HORST H., *Die Todesstrafe in der Aufklärung* (Bonn, 1961).

LEWIS, BETH IRWIN, 'Lustmord: Inside the Windows of the Metropolis', in Charles W. Haxthausen and Heidrun Suhr (eds.), *Berlin*.

LEWIS, W. DAVID, *From Newgate to Dannemora: The Rise of the Penitentiary in New York, 1796–1848* (Ithaca, NY, 1965).

LIANG, HSI-HUEY, *The Berlin Police in the Weimar Republic* (Berkeley, 1970).

LIDTKE, VERNON L., *The Alternative Culture: Socialist Labor in Imperial Germany* (New York, 1985).

LIEBERKNECHT, HERBERT, *Das Altpreußische Zuchthauswesen bis zum Ausgang des 18. Jahrhunderts* (Charlottenburg, 1921).

LIFTON, ROBERT JAY, *The Nazi Doctors: A Study of the Psychology of Evil* (London, 1986).

LINDGEN, E., *Die Breslauer Strafrechtspflege unter der Carolina und der Gemeinen Strafrechtswissenschaft bis zum Inkrafttreten der Josephine von 1708* (Breslau, 1939).

LINEBAUGH, PETER, 'The Ordinary of Newgate and his Account', in Cockburn (ed.), *Crime*, 246–69.

—— *The London Hanged: Crime and Civil Society in the Eighteenth Century* (London, 1991).

—— 'The Tyburn Riot against the Surgeons', in Hay *et al.* (eds.), *Albion's Fatal Tree*, 65–118.

LLEWELLYN, NIGEL, *The Art of Death: Visual Culture in the English Death Ritual c.1500–c.1800* (London, 1991).

LUCAS, ERHARD, *Märzrevolution 1920*, iii. *Die Niederlage* (Frankfurt am Main, 1979).

980   Bibliography

Lucht, Friedrich Wilhelm, *Die Strafrechtspflege in Sachsen-Weimar-Eisenach unter Carl August* (Berlin and Leipzig, 1929).

Lüdtke, Alf, *'Gemeinwohl', Polizei und 'Festungspraxis'. Staatliche Gewaltsamkeit und innere Verwaltung in Preußen, 1815–1850* (Göttingen, 1982).

—— 'The Role of State Violence in the Period of Transition to Industrial Capitalism: The Example of Prussia from 1815 to 1848', *Social History*, 4 (1979), 175–221.

Lüken, Erhard-Josef, *Der Nationalsozialismus und das materielle Strafrecht* (Ph.D. diss., Göttingen, 1988).

McCloy, S., *The Humanitarian Movement in Eighteenth-Century France* (Lexington, Ky., 1957).

McElligott, Anthony, 'Das Altonaer Sondergericht und der Prozeß vom Blutsonntag' (Vortrag zum 60. Gedenktag des 'Altonaer Blutsonntags' im Rahmen der Veranstaltung des Stadtteilarchivs Ottensen, der Bezirksversammlung und der Kulturbehörde, Hamburg-Altona, 3 June 1992).

Macey, David, *The Lives of Michel Foucault* (London, 1993).

McGowen, Randall, 'The Body and Punishment', *Journal of Modern History*, 59/4 (1987), 651–79.

—— ' "He Beareth Not the Sword in Vain": Religion and the Criminal Law in Eighteenth-Century England', *Eighteenth-Century Studies*, 2 (1987/8), 192–211.

Mackey, Philip English, *Hanging in the Balance: The Anti-Capital Punishment Movement in New York State 1776–1861* (New York, 1982).

McManners, John, *Death and the Enlightenment: Changing Attitudes to Death among Christians and Unbelievers in Eighteenth-Century France* (Oxford, 1981).

Maestro, Marcello, *Voltaire and Beccaria as Reformers of Criminal Law* (New York, 1942).

Majer, Diemut, *'Fremdvölkische' im Dritten Reich. Ein Beitrag zur nationalsozialistischen Rechtssetzung und Rechtspraxis in Verwaltung und Justiz unter besonderer Berücksichtigung der eingegliederten Ostgebiete und des Generalgouvernements* (Boppard, 1981).

—— *Grundlagen des nationalsozialistischen Rechtssystems* (Stuttgart, 1987).

—— 'Justiz und Polizei im "Dritten Reich"', in Dreier and Sellert (eds.), *Recht und Justiz*, 136–50.

—— 'Zum Verhältnis von Staatsanwaltschaft und Polizei im Nationalsozialismus', in Reifner and Sonnen (eds.), *Strafjustiz*, 121–60.

Marrus, Michael R., *The Holocaust in History* (London, 1989).

Marten, Detlef, 'Friedrich der Große und Montesquieu. Zu den Anfängen des Rechtsstaats im 18. Jahrhundert', in Blümel *et al.* (eds.), *Verwaltung im Rechtsstaat*, 187–208.

Marwedel, Rainer, *Theodor Lessing 1872–1933. Eine Biographie* (Frankfurt am Main, 1987).

Marzahn, Christian, 'Scheußliche Selbstgefälligkeit oder giftmordsüchtige Monomanie? Die Gesche Gottfried im Streit der Professionen', in Feest and Marzahn (eds.), *Criminalia*, 195–244.

Mason, Timothy W., *Sozialpolitik im Dritten Reich. Arbeiterklasse und Volksgemeinschaft* (Opladen, 1977).

Masur, Louis P., *Rites of Execution: Capital Punishment and the Transformation of American Culture, 1776–1865* (New York, 1989).

MATTHIAS, HORST, *Die Entwicklung des Medizinalwesens im Lande Lippe unter besonderer Berücksichtigung des Scharfrichterwesens und seiner Stellung in der Heilbehandlung* (Münster, 1947).

MEDICK, HANS, and SABEAN, DAVID (eds.), *Emotion und materielle Interessen in Familie und Verwandtschaft. Anthropologische und historische Beiträge zur Familienforschung* (Göttingen, 1983).

MEINHARDT, KARL-ERNST, *Das peinliche Strafrecht der Freien Reichsstadt Frankfurt am Main im Spiegel der Strafpraxis des 16. und 17. Jahrhunderts* (Frankfurt am Main, 1957).

MERZBACHER, F., 'Folter', in Hinckeldey (ed.), *Justiz*, 241–8.

MESSERSCHMIDT, MANFRED, and WÜLLNER, FRITZ, *Die Wehrmachtjustiz im Dienste des Nationalsozialismus. Zerstörung einer Legende* (Baden-Baden, 1987).

MEYER, ALBRECHT, *Das Strafrecht der Stadt Danzig von der Carolina bis zur Vereinigung Danzigs mit der preußischen Monarchie* (Danzig, 1935).

MEYER-KALKUS, REINHART, *Wollust und Grausamkeit. Affektenlehre und Affektdarstellung in Lohensteins Dramatik am Beispiel von 'Agrippina'* (Göttingen, 1986).

MIDELFORT, H. C. ERIK, *Witch-Hunting in Southwestern Germany 1562-1684: The Social and Intellectual Foundations* (Berkeley, 1972).

MILLER, JAMES, *The Passion of Michel Foucault* (London, 1993).

MITTENZWEI, INGRID, *Friedrich II. von Preußen: eine Biographie* (Berlin, 1979).

MITTER, ARMIN, and WOLLE, STEFAN, *Untergang auf Raten. Unbekannte Kapitel der DDR-Geschichte* (Munich, 1993).

MITTERAUER, MICHAEL, and SIEDER, REINHARD, *The European Family: Patriarchy to Partnership from the Middle Ages to the Present* (Oxford, 1982).

MOHLER, ARMIN, *Der Nasenring. Die Vergangenheitsbewältigung vor und nach dem Fall der Mauer*, 2nd edn. (Munich, 1991).

MONTER, E. W., 'La Sodomie à l'époque moderne en Suisse romande', *Annales ESC*, 29/4 (1974), 1023–33.

MOSER, HEINZ, *Die Scharfrichter von Tirol. Ein Beitrag zur Geschichte des Strafvollzuges in Tirol von 1497–1787* (Innsbruck, 1982).

MUCHEMBLED, ROBERT, *La Violence en village. Sociabilité et comportements populaires en Artois du XVe et XVIIe siècle* (Paris, 1989).

MUIR, EDWARD, *Civic Ritual in Renaissance Venice* (New York, 1983).

—— and RUGGIERO, GUIDO, *Microhistory and the Lost Peoples of Europe* (Baltimore, 1991).

MÜLLER, INGO, *Furchtbare Juristen. Die unbewältigte Vergangenheit unserer Justiz* (Munich, 1987).

MÜLLER, ROLAND, *Stuttgart zur Zeit des Nationalsozialismus* (Stuttgart, 1988).

NAUECKE, WOLFGANG, 'Über den Einfluß Kants auf Theorie und Praxis des Strafrechts im 19. Jahrhundert', in Jürgen Blühdorn and Joachim Richter (eds.), *Philosophie und Rechtswissenschaft. Zum Problem ihrer Beziehung im 19. Jahrhundert* (Frakfurt am Main, 1988), 91–108.

NIPPERDEY, THOMAS, *Deutsche Geschichte 1866–1918*, i. *Arbeitswelt und Bürgergeist* (Munich, 1990); ii. *Machtstaat vor der Demokratie* (Munich, 1992).

NOAKES, JEREMY, 'The Oldenburg Crucifix Struggle of November 1936: A Case Study of Opposition in the Third Reich', in Stachura (ed.), *The Shaping of the Nazi State*, 210–33.

—— 'Social Outcasts in the Third Reich', in Richard Bessel (ed.), *Life in the Third Reich* (Oxford, 1987), 183–96.

NOELLE-NEUMANN, ELISABETH, and PIEL, EDGAR, *Allensbacher Jahrbuch der Demoskopie 1978–1983*, viii (Munich, 1983).

——and KÖCHER, RENATE, *Allensbacher Jahrbuch der Demoskopie 1984–1992*, ix (Munich, 1993).

NORDHOFF-BEHNE, H., *Gerichtsbarkeit und Strafrechtspflege in der Reichsstadt Schwäbisch-Hall seit dem 15. Jahrhundert* (Schwäbisch-Hall, 1971).

NORMAND, MARCEL, *La Peine de Mort* (Paris, 1980).

NOTESTEIN, WALLACE, *Four Worthies* (London, 1956).

NOWOSADTKO, JUTTA, 'Die Ehre, die Unehre und das Staatsinteresse. Konzepte und Funktionen von "Unehrlichkeit" im historischen Wandel am Beispiel des Kurfürstentums Bayern', *Geschichte in Wissenschaft und Unterricht*, 44 (1993), 362–81.

NULAND, SHERWIN B., *How We Die* (London, 1994).

OERTEL, RICHARD, *Die letzte Hinrichtung in unserer Heimat* (Oelsnitz in Estel, 1939).

OPPELT, WOLFGANG, *Über die Unehrlichkeit des Scharfrichters* (Lengfeld, 1976).

ORTNER, HELMUT, *Der Hinrichter. Roland Freisler—Mörder im Dienste Hitlers* (Vienna, 1993).

OUTRAM, DORINDA, *The Body and the French Revolution: Sex, Class and Political Culture* (London, 1989).

PARKER, GEOFFREY, *Europe in Crisis 1598–1648* (London, 1979).

PAULSON, RONALD, *Representations of Revolution (1789–1820)* (New Haven, 1983).

PEARCE, FRANK, *Crimes of the Powerful: Marxism, Crime and Deviance* (London, 1976).

PERROT, MICHELLE (ed.), *L'Impossible Prison. Recherches sur le système pénitentiaire au XIXe siècle* (Paris, 1980).

PETERS, EDWARD, *Torture* (Oxford, 1985).

PETZOLDT, LEANDER, *Bänkellieder und Moritaten aus drei Jahrhunderten* (Frankfurt am Main, 1982).

——*Bänkelsang. Vom historischen Bänkelsang zum literarischen Chanson* (Stuttgart, 1974).

PETZOLD, RICHARD, *Die Kirchenkompositionen und weltlichen Kantaten Reinhard Keisers (1674–1739)* (Düsseldorf, 1935).

PEUKERT, DETLEV J. K., 'Alltag und Barbarei. Zur Normalität des Dritten Reiches', in Dan Diner (ed.), *Ist der Nationalsozialismus Geschichte? Zur Historisierung und Historikerstreit* (Frankfurt am Main, 1987), 51–61.

——'Arbeitslager und Jugend-KZ: die Behandlung "Gemeinschaftsfremder" im Dritten Reich', in idem and Reulecke (eds.), *Die Reihen fast geschlossen*, 413–34.

——*Grenzen der Sozialdisziplinierung. Aufstieg und Krise der deutschen Jugendfürsorge von 1887 bis 1932* (Cologne, 1986).

——'Die Unordnung der Dinge. Michel Foucault und die deutsche Geschichtswissenschaft', in Franz Ewald and Bernhard Waldenfels (eds.), *Spiele der Wahrheit. Michel Foucaults Denken* (Frankfurt am Main, 1991), 320–33.

——and REULECKE, JÜRGEN (eds.), *Die Reihen fast geschlossen. Beiträge zur Geschichte des Alltages unterm Nationalsozialismus* (Wuppertal, 1981).

PICK, DANIEL, *Faces of Degeneration: A European Disorder c.1848–c.1918* (Cambridge, 1989).

PINSON, ROLAND W. (ed.), *Liebe, Mord und Schicksalschlag. Moritaten, Bänkel-, Gassen- und Küchenlieder aus drei Jahrhunderten* (Bayreuth, 1982).

PIPER, FRANCISZEK, 'Ausrottung', in Czech *et al.*, *Auschwitz*, 92–142.

POHL, HERBERT, *Hexenglaube und Hexenverfolgung im Kurfürstentum Mainz. Ein Beitrag zur Hexenfrage im 16. und beginnenden 17. Jahrhundert* (Wiesbaden, 1988).

PORTER, ROY, 'Death and the Doctors in Georgian England', in Houlbrooke (ed.), *Death*, 77–94.

POTTER, HARRY, *Hanging in Judgment: Religion and the Death Penalty in England from the Bloody Code to Abolition* (London, 1993).

PRESTON, PAUL, *Franco: A Biography* (London, 1993).

PROCTOR, ROBERT, *Racial Hygiene: Medicine under the Nazis* (Cambridge, Mass., 1988).

PROSPERI, A., 'Il sangue e l'anima. Richerche sulle compagnie di giustizia in Italia', *Quaderni Storici*, 51/17 (1982), 959–99.

PUPPI, LIONELLO, *Torment in Art: Pain, Violence and Martryrdom* (New York, 1991).

PUSCHNER, UWE, *Handwerk zwischen Tradition und Wandel. Das Münchener Handwerk an der Wende vom 18. zum 19. Jahrhundert* (Göttingen, 1988).

QUANTER, RUDOLF, *Die Leibes- und Lebensstrafen bei allen Völkern und zu allen Zeiten* (Dresden, 1901).

——*Die Schand- und Ehrenstrafen in der deutschen Rechtspflege* (Dresden, 1901).

RABOFSKY, EDUARD, and OBERKOFER, GERHARD, *Verborgene Wurzeln der NS-Justiz. Strafrechtliche Rüstung für Zwei Weltkriege* (Vienna, 1985).

RADBRUCH, GUSTAV, 'Ars moriendi. Scharfrichter, Seelsorger, Volk', *Schweizerische Zeitschrift für Strafrecht*, 59 (1945), 460–95.

——*Elegantiae juris criminalis. Vierzehn Studien zur Geschichte des Strafrechts* (Basle, 1950).

——*Paul Johann Anselm Feuerbach—Ein Juristenleben* (Vienna, 1957).

RADELET, MICHAEL, and VANDIVER, MARGARET, *Capital Punishment in America: An Annotated Bibliography* (New York, 1988).

RADZINOWICZ, LEON, *A History of English Criminal Law and its Administration* (4 vols.; London, 1948–68).

RATTELMÜLLER, PAUL ERNST, *Matthäus Klostermaier, vulgo der Bayrische Hiasl* (Munich, 1971).

RAUTER, E. A., *Folter in Geschichte und Gegenwart von Nero bis Pinochet*, 2nd edn. (Frankfurt am Main, 1988).

REEMTSMA, JAN PHILIPP (ed.), *Folter. Zur Analyse eines Herrschaftsmittels* (Hamburg, 1992).

REGGE, JÜRGEN, 'Strafrecht und Strafrechtspflege', in Jürgen Ziechmann (ed.) *Panorama*, 365–75.

REHFELDT, BERNHARD, *Todesstrafen und Bekehrungsgeschichte. Zur Rechts- und Religionsgeschichte der germanischen Hinrichtungsbräuche* (Berlin, 1942).

REHLINGER, LUDWIG A., *Freikauf. Die Geschäfte der DDR mit politisch Verfolgten 1963–1989* (Berlin, 1990).

REIF, HEINZ (ed.), *Räuber, Volk und Obrigkeit. Studien zur Geschichte der Kriminalität in Deutschland seit dem 18. Jahrhundert* (Frankfurt am Main, 1984).

REIFNER, UDO, 'Justiz und Faschismus. Ansätze einer Theorie der Vergangenheitsbewältigung der Justiz', in Reifner and Sonnen (eds.), *Strafjustiz*, 9–40.

——and SONNEN, BERND-RÜDEGER (eds.), *Strafjustiz und Polizei im Dritten Reich* (Frankfurt am Main, 1984).

RENGER, WILHELM, 'Hinrichtungen als Volksfeste', *Süddeutsche Monatshefte*, 10/2 (1913), 8–21.

REUBAND, KARL-HEINZ, 'Sanktionsverlagen im Wandel. Die Einstellung zur Todesstrafe in der Bundesrepublik Deutschland seit 1950', *Kölner Zeitschrift für Soziologie und Sozialpsychologie*, 3 (1980), 535–58.

RICHARDSON, RUTH, 'Why Was Death so Big in Victorian Britain?', in Houlbrooke (ed.), *Death*, 105–17.

RITTER, GERHARD A., and TENFELDE, KLAUS, *Arbeiter im Deutschen Kaiserreich 1871 bis 1914* (Bonn, 1992).

ROCK, PAUL, and MCINTOSH, MARY (eds.), *Deviance and Social Control* (London, 1974).

ROECK, BERND, 'Criminal Procedure in the Holy Roman Empire in Early Modern Times', *Bulletin of the International Association for the History of Crime and Criminal Justice*, 18 (Spring 1993), 21–40.

RÖHL, JOHN C. G., *Wilhelm II* (Munich, 1993), i: *Die Jugend des Kaisers 1859–1888*.

ROPER, LYNDAL, *The Holy Household: Women and Morals in Reformation Augsburg* (Oxford, 1989).

—— *Oedipus and the Devil* (London, 1994).

ROSENFELD, ERNST, 'Die letzte Vollstreckung der Feuerstrafe in Preußen zu Berlin am 28. Mai 1813. Auf Grund amtlichen Materials zusammengestellt', *Zeitschrift für die gesamte Strafrechtswissenschaft*, 29 (1909), 810–17.

—— 'Zur Geschichte der ältesten Zuchthäuser', *Zeitschrift für die gesamte Strafrechtwissenschaft*, 26 (1906), 1–18.

ROSENTHAL, JÜRGEN (ed.), *Strafrechtsreform in der DDR* (Bonn, 1968).

ROSSA, KURT, *Todesstrafen. Ihre Wirklichkeit in drei Jahrtausenden* (Bergisch Gladbach, 1979).

ROTH, GUENTHER, *The Social Democrats in Imperial Germany: A Study in Working-Class Isolation and Negative Integration* (Totowa, NJ, 1963).

ROTH, KARL HEINZ, 'Schein-Alternativen im Gesundheitswesen: Alfred Grotjahn (1869–1931)—Integrationsfigur etablierter Sozialmedizin und nationalsozialistischer "Rassenhygiene"', in idem (ed.), *Erfassung zur Vernichtung. Von der Sozialhygiene zum 'Gesetz über Sterbehilfe'* (Berlin, 1984), 31–56.

ROTHMAN, DAVID, *Conscience and Convenience: The Asylum and its Alternatives in Progressive America* (Boston, 1980).

—— *The Discovery of the Asylum* (Boston, 1971).

RUMMEL, WALTER, *Bauern, Herren und Hexen. Studien zur Sozialgeschichte sponheimischer und kurtrierischer Hexenprozesse 1574–1664* (Göttingen, 1991).

—— 'Soziale Dynamik und herrschaftliche Problematik der kurtrierschen Hexenverfolgung. Das Beispiel der Stadt Cochem (1593–1595)', *Geschichte und Gesellschaft*, 16 (1990), 26–55.

—— 'Verletzung von Körper, Ehre und Eigentum. Varianten im Umgang mit Gewalt in Dörfern des 17. Jahrhunderts', in Blauert and Schwerhoff (eds.), *Mit den Waffen*, 86–114.

RÜPING, HINRICH, *Grundriß der Strafrechtsgeschichte* (Munich, 1981).

—— 'Die Strafgesetzgebung im "Dritten Reich"', in Dreier and Sellert (eds.), *Recht und Justiz*, 180–93

—— *Staatsanwaltschaft und Provinzialjustizverwaltung im Dritten Reich. Aus den Akten der Staatsanwaltschaft bei dem Oberlandesgericht Celle als höhere Reichsjustizbehörde* (Hannoversche Beiträge zur rechtswissenschaftlichen Grundlagenforschung; Baden-Baden, 1990).

RUSINEK, BERND-A., *Gesellschaft in der Katastrophe. Terror, Illegalität, Widerstand—Köln 1944/45* (Essen, 1989).

SABEAN, DAVID, *Power in the Blood: Popular Culture and Village Discourse in Early Modern Germany* (New York, 1984).

SANDMANN, JÜRGEN, *Der Bruch mit der humanitären Tradition. Die Biologisierung der Ethik bei Ernst Haeckel und anderen Darwinisten seiner Zeit* (Stuttgart, 1990).

SAUER, HEINER, and PLUMEYER, HANS-OTTO, *Der Salzgitterreport. Die zentrale Erfassungsstelle berichtet über Verbrechen im SED-Staat* (Munich, 1991).

SAUER, PAUL, *Im Namen des Königs. Strafgesetzgebung und Strafvollzug im Königreich Württemberg von 1806 bis 1871* (Stuttgart, 1984).

SAUL, KLAUS, 'Der Staat und die "Mächte des Umsturzes". Ein Beitrag zu den Methoden antisozialistischer Repression und Agitation vom Scheitern des Sozialistengesetzes bis zur Jahrhundertwende', *Archiv für Sozialgeschichte*, 12 (1972), 293–350.

SCHAMA, SIMON, *Citizens: A Chronicle of the French Revolution* (New York, 1989).

SCHÄR, MARKUS, *Seelennöte der Untertanen. Selbstmord, Melancholie und Religion im Alten Zürich 1500–1800* (Zurich, 1985).

SCHENDA, RUDOLF, *Die Lesestoffe der kleinen Leute* (Munich, 1976).

—— *Volk ohne Buch. Studien zur Geschichte der populären Lesestoffe 1770–1910* (Frankfurt am Main, 1970).

SCHEWARDNADSE, MICHAEL, *Die Todesstrafe in Europa. Eine rechtsvergleichende Darstellung mir einer rechtsgeschichtlichen Einleitung* (Munich, 1914).

SCHIEDER, THEODOR, *Friedrich der Grosse: ein Königtum der Widersprüche* (Frankfurt am Main, 1986).

SCHILD, WOLFGANG, *Alte Gerichtsbarkeit. Vom Gottesurteil bis zum Beginn der modernen Rechtsprechung* (Munich, 1980).

—— 'Das Strafrecht als Phänomen der Geistesgeschichte', in Hinckeldey (ed.), *Justiz*, 7–38.

SCHILLING, HEINZ, 'Sündenzucht und frühneuzeitliche Sozialdisziplinierung. Die calvinistische, presbyteriale Kirchenzucht in Emden vom 16. bis 19. Jahrhundert', in G. Schmidt (ed.), *Stände und Gesellschaft*, 265–302.

SCHINDLER, GEORG, *Verbrechen und Strafen im Recht der Stadt Freiburg im Breisgau von der Einführung des Neuen Stadtrechts bis zum Übergang an Baden (1520–1806)* (Freiburg, 1937).

SCHIRMANN, LÉON, *Altonaer Blutsonntag 17. Juli 1932: Dichtungen und Wahrheit* (Hamburg, 1994).

SCHMIDT, EBERHARD, *Einführung in die Geschichte der deutschen Strafrechts* (Göttingen, 1947; 3rd edn. Göttingen, 1965).

—— *Entwicklung und Vollzug der Freiheitsstrafe in Brandenburg-Preußen bis zum Ausgang des 18. Jahrhunderts* (Berlin, 1915).

—— 'Goethe und das Problem der Todesstrafe', *Schweizerische Zeitschrift für Strafrecht*, 63 (1948), 444–64.

—— *Die Kriminalpolitik Preußens unter Friedrich Wilhelm I und Friedrich II* (Berlin, 1914).

SCHMIDT, GEORG (ed.), *Stände und Gesellschaft im Alten Reich* (Wiesbaden, 1989).

SCHMOLLINGER, HORST W., 'Die Deutsche Partei', in Richard Stöss (ed.), *Parteien-Handbuch. Die Parteien der Bundesrepublik Deutschland 1945–1980* (Opladen, 1983), i. 1025–IIII.

SCHMUDE, KLAUS, *Fallbeil-Erziehung. Der Stasi/SED Mord an Manfred Smolka* (Böblingen, 1992).

SCHMUHL, HANS-WALTER, *Rassenhygiene, Nationalsozialismus, Euthanasie: Von der Verhütung zur Vernichtung 'lebensunwerten Lebens' 1890–1945* (Göttingen, 1987).

SCHOLZ, L., *Die Gesche Gottfried. Eine kriminalpsychologische Studie* (Berlin, 1913).

SCHORMANN, GERHARD, *Hexenprozesse in Deutschland* (Göttingen, 1981).

—— *Der Krieg gegen die Hexen. Das Ausrottungsprogramm des Kurfürsten von Köln* (Göttingen, 1991).

SCHREIBER, HANS-LUDWIG, 'Die Strafgesetzgebung im "Dritten Reich"', in Dreier and Sellert (eds.), *Recht und Justiz,* 151–79.

SCHROEDER, FRIEDRICH-CHRISTIAN, *Das Strafrecht des realen Sozialismus. Eine Einführung am Beispiel der DDR* (Opladen, 1983).

SCHÜDDEKOPF, OTTO-ERNST, *Linke Leute von rechts* (Stuttgart, 1960).

SCHUÉ, KARL, 'Das Gnadenbitten in Recht, Sage, Dichtung und Kunst. Ein Beitrag zur Rechts- und Kulturgeschichte', *Zeitschrift des Aachener Geschichtsvereins,* 40 (1918), 143–386.

SCHUHMANN, HELMUT, *Der Scharfrichter. Seine Gestalt—Seine Funktion* (Kempten/ Allgäu, 1964).

SCHULLER, WOLFGANG, *Geschichte und Struktur des politischen Strafrechts der DDR bis 1968* (Ebelsbach, 1980).

SCHULTE, REGINA, 'Feuer im Dorf', in Reif (ed.), *Räuber,* 100–52.

—— 'Infanticide in Rural Bavaria in the Nineteenth Century', in Hans Medick and David Warren Sabean (eds.), *Interest and Emotion: Essays on the Study of Family and Kinship* (Cambridge, 1984), 77–102.

SCHULZE, HAGEN, *Otto Braun, oder Preußens demokratische Sendung. Eine Biographie* (Frankfurt am Main, 1977).

SCHURR, STEPHAN, 'Studien zur Geschichte der Hinrichtung in Bayern im 19. Jahrhundert' (M.A. diss., Ludwig-Maximilians-University, Munich, 1987).

SCHWARZ, MAX, *MdR. Biographisches Handbuch der Reichstage* (Hanover, 1965).

SCHWED, ROGER E., *Abolition and Capital Punishment. The United States' Judicial, Political, and Moral Barometer* (New York, 1983).

SCHWENNIKE, ANDREAS, *Die Entstehung der Einleitung des Preußischen Allgemeinen Landrechts von 1794* (Frankfurt am Main, 1993).

SCHWERHOFF, GERD, 'Devianz in der alteuropäischen Gesellschaft. Umrisse einer historischen Kriminalitätsforschung', *Zeitschrift für historische Forschung,* 19 (1992), 385–414.

—— *Köln im Kreuzverhör. Kriminalität, Herrschaft und Gesellschaft in einer frühneuzeitlichen Stadt* (Bonn, 1991).

—— '"Mach, daß wir nicht in eine Schande geraten!" Frauen in Kölner Kriminalfällen des 16. Jahrhunderts', *Geschichte in Wissenschaft und Unterricht,* 43 (1993), 451–73.

—— 'Verordnete Schande? Spätmittelalterliche und frühneuzeitliche Ehrenstrafen zwischen Rechtsakt und sozialer Sanktion', in Blauert and Schwerhoff (eds.), *Mit den Waffen,* 158–88.

SCOTT, HAMISH M. (ed.), *Enlightened Absolutism: Reforms and Reformers in Later Eighteenth-Century Europe* (London, 1990).

SCRIBNER, BOB, 'The *Mordbrenner* Fear in Sixteenth-Century Germany: Political Paranoia or the Revenge of the Outcast?', in Evans (ed.), *The German Underworld,* 29–56.

—— 'Politics and the Territorial State in Sixteenth-Century Württemberg', in Kouri and Scott (eds.), *Politics and Society*, 103–20.

SEGGELKE, GÜNTHER, *Die Entstehung der Freiheitsstrafe* (Breslau, 1928).

SHAPIRO, BARRY M., *Revolutionary Justice in Paris 1789–1790* (Cambridge, 1993).

SHARPE, JAMES A., *Crime in Seventeenth-Century England: A County Study* (Cambridge, 1983).

—— '"Last Dying Speeches": Religion, Ideology and Public Executions in Seventeenth-Century England', *Past and Present*, 107 (1983), 144–67.

SHELEFF, LEON SHASKOLSKY, *Ultimate Penalties: Capital Punishment, Life Imprisonment, Physical Torture* (Columbus, Ohio, 1987).

SHORTER, EDWARD, *The Making of the Modern Family* (London, 1975).

SIDER, GERALD, 'The Ties that Bind: Culture and Agriculture, Property and Propriety in Village Newfoundland', *Social History*, 5 (1980), 1–39.

SIEGERT, TONI, 'Das Konzentrationslager Flossenbürg, gegründet für sogenannte Asoziale und Kriminelle', in Broszat and Fröhlich (eds.), *Bayern*, ii. 429–93.

SIEMANN, WOLFRAM, *Die deutsche Revolution von 1848/49* (Frankfurt am Main, 1985).

—— '*Deutschlands Ruhe, Sicherheit und Ordnung*'. *Die Anfänge der politischen Polizei 1806–1866* (Tübingen, 1985).

SIEVERS, KAI-DETLEV, 'Prügelstrafe als Zeichen ständischer Ungleichheit', in Köstlin and Sievers (eds.), *Das Recht der kleinen Leute*, 195–206.

SMITH, BRADLEY F., (ed.), *The American Road to Nuremberg: The Documentary Record 1944–1945* (Stanford, Calif., 1982).

—— *Reaching Judgment at Nuremberg* (London, 1977).

SOLZHENITSYN, ALEXANDER, *The Gulag Archipelago 1918–1956*, Part II (London, 1974).

SOMMER, PETER, *Scharfrichter von Bern* (Berne, 1969).

SORELL, TOM, *Moral Theory and Capital Punishment* (Oxford, 1987).

SPENGLER, KARL, *Münchener Historien und Histörchen* (Munich, 1967).

SPIERENBURG, PIETER, *The Broken Spell: A Cultural and Anthropological History of Preindustrial Europe* (London, 1991).

—— 'The Sociogenesis of Confinement and its Development in Early Modern Europe', in idem (ed.), *The Emergence of Carceral Institutions: Prisons, Galleys and Lunatic Asylums 1550–1900* (Rotterdam, 1984), 9–77.

—— *The Spectacle of Suffering. Executions and the Evolution of Repression: From a Preindustrial Metropolis to the European Experience* (Cambridge, 1984).

SPITTMANN, ILSE, and FRICKE, KARL WILHELM (eds.), *17. Juni 1953. Arbeiteraufstand in der DDR* (Cologne, 1982).

STACHURA, PETER (ed.), *The Shaping of the Nazi State* (London, 1978).

STALLYBRASS, PETER, and WHITE, ALLON, *The Politics and Poetics of Transgression* (London, 1986).

STEKL, HANNES, *Österreichs Zucht- und Arbeitshäuser, 1671–1920. Institutionen zwischen Fürsorge und Strafvollzug* (Vienna, 1978).

STEINERT, HANS, 'Ist es aber auch wahr, Herr F.?', *Kriminalsoziologische Bibliographie*, 5 (1978), 30–45.

STOCKDALE, ERIC, *A Study of Bedford Prison 1660–1877* (London, 1977).

STOLLEIS, MICHAEL, 'Rechtsordnung und Justizpolitik 1945–1949', in Horn (ed.), *Europäisches Rechtsdenken*.

STONE, LAWRENCE, 'An Exchange with Michel Foucault', *New York Review of Books*, 31 Mar. 1983, 42.

STONE, LAWRENCE, *The Family, Sex and Marriage in England, 1500–1800* (London, 1975).

STÖSS, RICHARD (ed.), *Parteien-Handbuch. Die Parteien der Bundesrepublik Deutschland 1945–1980* (Opladen, 1983).

STRENG, ADOLF, *Geschichte der Gefängnisverwaltung in Hamburg von 1622 bis 1872* (Hamburg, 1878).

STRUB, BETTINA, *Der Einfluß der Aufklärung auf die Todesstrafe* (Zurich, 1973).

STUART, KATHLEEN, 'The Boundaries of Honor: Dishonorable People in Augsburg, 1510–1800' (Ph.D. diss., Yale University, 1993).

STÜCKRATH, OTTO, 'Der Schinderhannes im deutschen Volksliede', *Mitteilungen des Vereins für Nassauische Altertumskunde und Geschichtsforschung*, 15/1 (1911), 94–8.

—— 'Unedierte Schinderhanneslieder', *Rheinisch-westfälische Zeitschrift für Volkskunde*, 7/3–4 (1961), 149–55.

STURM, FRIEDRICH, *Symbolische Todesstrafen* (Hamburg, 1962).

TALMON, J. L., *The Origins of Totalitarian Democracy* (London, 1952).

TATAR, MARIA, *Lustmord. Sexual Murder in the Weimar Republic* (Princeton, 1995).

TAYLOR, IAN, and TAYLOR, LAURIE (eds.), *Politics and Deviance* (Harmondsworth, 1973).

—— WALTON, PAUL, and YOUNG, JOCK (eds.), *Critical Criminology* (London, 1975).

TAYLOR, TELFORD, *The Anatomy of the Nuremberg Trials: A Personal Memoir* (London, 1993).

TEETERS, NEGLEY D., *The Cradle of the Penitentiary: The Walnut Street Jail at Philadephia* (Philadelphia, 1935).

TEMKIN, OWSEI, *The Falling Sickness: A History of Epilepsy from the Greeks to the Beginnings of Modern Neurology*, 2nd edn. (Baltimore, 1971).

TERHORST, KARL-LEO, *Polizeiliche planmäßige Überwachung und polizeiliche Vorbeugungshaft im Dritten Reich* (Heidelberg, 1985).

THESING, W. B. (ed.), *Execution and the British Experience* (London, 1990).

THEWELEIT, KLAUS, *Male Fantasies* (2 vols.; Oxford, 1989 and 1991).

THIEL, P., 'Vom Schiffsunglück zur Moritat. Entstehungsweise, Verbreitung und Zensur anonymer Literatur', in Anon. (ed.), *Schilder.*

THOMPSON, EDWARD P., *The Poverty of Theory and Other Essays* (London, 1978).

—— *Whigs and Hunters: The Origin of the Black Act* (London, 1975).

TILLY, CHARLES, LOUISE, and RICHARD, *The Rebellious Century 1830–1930* (London, 1975).

TOBIAS, FRITZ, *The Reichstag Fire* (London, 1963).

TREVOR-ROPER, HUGH R., *The Last Days of Hitler* (London, 1947; rev. edn., 1972).

TROMBLEY, STEPHEN, *The Execution Protocol* (London, 1993).

TROTNOW, HELMUT, *Karl Liebknecht. Eine politische Biographie* (Cologne, 1980).

TURNER, BRYAN S., *The Body and Society: Explorations in Social Theory* (Oxford, 1984).

TURNER, VICTOR, *Dramas, Fields and Metaphors: Symbolic Actions in Human Society* (Ithaca, NY, 1975).

TUTOROW, NORMAN E., *War Crimes, War Criminals, and War Crimes Trials: An Annotated Bibliography and Source Book* (Westport, Conn., 1986).

ULBRICHT, OTTO, 'Infanticide in Eighteenth-Century Germany', in Evans (ed.), *The German Underworld*, 108–40.

—— 'Kindsmörderinnen vor Gericht: Verteidigungsstrategien von Frauen in Norddeutschland 1680–1810', in Blauert and Schwerhoff (eds.), *Mit den Waffen*, 54–85.

VALENTIN, VEIT, *Geschichte der deutschen Revolution von 1848–49* (2 vols.; Berlin, 1930–1).

VOLKMANN, ERICH OTTO, 'Soziale Heeresmißstände als Mitursache des deutschen Zusammenbruchs im Jahre 1918', in *Untersuchungsausschuß des Reichstages über die Ursachen des deutschen Zusammenbruchs*, 4th ser., 11/2 (1924).

VOLKMANN, HEINRICH, and BERGMANN, JÜRGEN (eds.), *Sozialer Protest. Studien zu traditioneller Resistenz und kollektiver Gewalt in Deutschland vom Vormärz bis zur Reichsgründung* (Opladen, 1984).

VOVELLE, MICHEL, *Mourir autrefois. Attitudes collectives devant la mort aux XVIIe et XVIIIe siècles* (Paris, 1974).

——*Piété baroque et déchristianisation en Provence au XVIIIe siècle* (Paris, 1978).

WACHENFELD, FRIEDRICH, *Die Begriffe von Mord und Totschlag sowie vorsätzlicher Körperverletzung mit tödlichem Ausgange in der Gesetzgebung seit der Mitte des 18. Jahrhunderts. Ein Beitrag zur vergleichenden Geschichte der Strafgesetzgebung* (Marburg, 1890).

WAGNER, P., 'Das Gesetz über die Behandlung Gemeinschaftsfremder: die Kriminalpolizei und die "Vernichtung des Verbrechertums"', in Aly *et al.* (eds.), *Feinderklärung*.

WAHRIG, GERHARD, *Das Große Deutsche Wörterbuch* (Gütersloh, 1966).

WARNCKE, JOHANNES, 'Die Reparatur des Prangers und des Hochgerichts zu Lübeck im Jahre 1794. Ein Beitrag zur Verrufserklärung seitens der Handwerker', *Die Heimat*, 21 (1911), 278–83.

WEBB, SIDNEY and BEATRICE, *English Prisons under Local Government* (London, 1922).

WEBER, BEATE, *Die Kindsmörderin im deutschen Schrifttum von 1770–1795* (Bonn, 1984).

WEBER, HELMUT VON, 'Calvinismus und Strafrecht', in Bockelmann and Gallas (eds.), *Festschrift*, 39–53.

——*Grimdroß des deutschen Strafrechts* (Bonn, 1946).

WEBER, HERMANN, *Geschichte der DDR* (Munich, 1985).

——*DDR. Grundriß der Geschichte 1945–1990* (Hanover, 1991).

——*Die Wandlung des deutschen Kommunismus. Die Stalinisierung der KPD in der Weimarer Republik* (Studienausgabe; Frankfurt am Main, 1969).

WEHLER, HANS-ULRICH, *Das deutsche Kaiserreich 1871–1918* (Göttingen, 1973).

——'Sozialdarwinismus im expandierenden Industriestaat', in Imanuel Geiss and Bernd-Jürgen Wendt (eds.), *Deutschland in der Weltpolitik des 19. und 20. Jahrhunderts*, 2nd edn. (Düsseldorf, 1974).

——(ed.), *Sozialgeschichte Heute. Festschrift für Hans Rosenberg zum 70. Geburtstag* (Göttingen, 1974).

WEILL, HERMANN, *Frederick the Great and Samuel von Cocceji* (Madison, Wis., 1961).

WEINGART, PETER, KROLL, JÜRGEN, and BAYERTZ, KURT, *Rasse, Blut und Gene. Geschichte der Eugenik und Rassenhygiene in Deutschland* (Frankfurt am Main, 1992).

WEISMANN, R., *Ritual Brotherhood in Renaissance Florence* (New York, 1982).

WEISSER, MICHAEL, *Crime and Punishment in Early Modern Europe* (Hassocks, 1979).

WENZLAU, JOACHIM, *Der Wiederaufbau der Justiz in Nordwestdeutschland 1945 bis 1949* (Königstein in Taunus, 1979).

WERREMEIER, FRIEDHELM, *Der Fall Heckenrose* (Munich, 1975).

——*Haarmann. Nachruf auf einen Werwolf. Die Geschichte des Massenmörders Friedrich Haarmann, seiner Opfer und seiner Jäger* (Cologne, 1992).

WERLE, GERHARD, *Justiz-Strafrecht und politische Verbrechensbekämpfung im Dritten Reich* (Berlin, 1989).

WETTE, WOLFRAM, *Gustav Noske: eine politische Biographie* (Düsseldorf, 1987).

WETTSTEIN, ERICH, *Die Geschichte der Todesstrafe im Kanton Zürich* (Winterthur, 1958).

WETZELL, RICHARD F., 'Criminal Law Reform in Imperial Germany' (Ph.D., Stanford, 1991).

WHALEY, JOACHIM, 'Symbolism for the Survivors: The Disposal of the Dead in Hamburg in the Late Seventeenth and Eighteenth Centuries', in idem (ed.), *Mirrors of Mortality: Studies in the Social History of Death* (London, 1981), 80–105.

WHITE, HAYDEN, *The Content of the Form* (Baltimore, 1987).

WHITE, WELSH S., *The Death Penalty in the Eighties: An Examination of the Modern System of Capital Punishment* (Ann Arbor, 1987).

WHITING, J. R. S., *Prison Reform in Gloucestershire 1775–1820* (London, 1975).

WICKER, TOM, *A Time to Die: The Attica Prison Revolt* (London, 1976).

WICKERT, CHRISTL, *Helene Stöcker 1869–1943. Frauenrechtlerin, Pazifistin, Sozialreformerin* (Bonn, 1991).

WIELAND, GÜNTHER, *Das war der Volksgerichtschof. Ermittlungen—Fakten—Dokumente* (Pfaffenweiler, 1989).

WIENER, MARTIN, *Reconstructing the Criminal: Culture, Law, and Policy in England, 1830–1914* (Cambridge, 1990).

WILBERTZ, GISELA, 'Das Notizbuch des Scharfrichters Johan Christoph Zippel in Stade (1766–82)', *Stader Jahrbuch*, 25 (1975), 62–3.

——*Scharfrichter und Abdecker im Hochstift Osnabück. Untersuchungen zur Sozialgeschichte zweier 'unehrlicher' Berufe im nordwestdeutschen Raum vom 16. bis zum 19. Jahrhundert* (Münster, 1979).

WILF, STEVEN ROBERT, 'Anatomy and Punishment in late Eighteenth-Century New York', *Journal of Social History*, 23 (1989), 507–30.

WILLS, ANTOINETTE, *Crime and Punishment in Revolutionary Paris* (London, 1981).

WILSON, STEPHEN, 'Conflict and its Causes in Southern Corsica 1800–35', *Social History*, 6 (1982), 33–69.

——'Death and the Social Historians: Some Recent Books in French and English,' *Social History*, 5 (1980), 435–51.

——'The Myth of Motherhood a Myth: The Historical View of European Child-Rearing', *Social History*, 9 (1984), 181–98.

WILTERDINK, NICO, 'Die Zivilisationstheorie im Kreuzfeuer der Diskussion. Ein Bericht vom Kongreß über Zivilisationsprozesse in Amsterdam', in Gleichmann *et al.* (eds.), *Macht und Zivilisation*, 280–304.

WINKLER, HEINRICH AUGUST, *Der Schein der Normalität. Arbeiter und Arbeiterbewegung in der Weimarer Republik*, ii (Berlin and Bonn, 1985).

——*Der Weg in die Katastrophe. Arbeiter und Arbeiterbewegung in der Weimarer Republik*, iii (Berlin and Bonn, 1986).

WINTER, MATTHIAS, 'Kontinuitäten in der deutschen Zigeunerforschung und Zigeunerpolitik', in *Beiträge zur nationalsozialistischen Gesundheits- und Sozialpolitik*, vi (Berlin, 1988).

WIPPERMANN, WOLFGANG, *Das Leben in Frankfurt zur NS-Zeit*, ii. *Die nationalsozialistische Zigeunerverfolgung* (Frankfurt am Main, 1988).

WIRTH, INGO, *Exekution: Das Buch vom Hinrichten* (Berlin, 1993).

WIRTZ, RAINER, *'Widersetzlichkeiten, Excesse, Crawalle, Tumulte und Scandale'. Soziale Bewegung und gewalthafter sozialer Protest in Baden 1815–1848* (Frankfurt am Main, 1981).

WITTROCK, CHRISTINE, *Abtreibung und Kindesmord in der neueren deutschen Literatur* (Frankfurt am Main, 1978).

WOSNIK, RICHARD, *Beiträge zur Hamburgischen Kriminalgeschichte* (Hamburg, 1926).

WRIGHT, GORDON, *Between the Guillotine and Liberty: Two Centuries of the Crime Problem in France* (New York, 1982).

WROBEL, HANS, *Verurteilt zur Demokratie. Justiz und Justizpolitik in Deutschland 1945– 1949* (Heidelberg, 1989).

WÜLLNER, FRITZ, *Die NS-Militärjustiz und das Elend der Geschichtsschreibung* (Baden-Baden, 1991).

YOUNG, JOCK, *The Drugtakers* (London, 1971).

ZANK, WOLFGANG, 'Blutsonntag in Altona', *Die Zeit*, 30 (17 July 1992), 62.

ZEHR, HOWARD, *Crime and the Development of Modern Society: Patterns of Criminality in Nineteenth-Century Germany and France* (London, 1976).

ZIECHMANN, JÜRGEN (ed.), *Panorama der friederizianischen Zeit. Friedrich der Große und seine Epoche* (Bremen, 1985).

ZIMMERMANN, MICHAEL, *Verfolgt, vertrieben, vernichtet. Die nationalsozialistische Vernichtungspolitik gegen Sinti und Roma* (Essen, 1989).

ZIMRING, FRANKLIN E., and HAWKINS, GORDON, *Capital Punishment and the American Agenda* (Cambridge, 1986).

ZMARZLIK, HANS-GÜNTER, 'Der Sozialdarwinismus in Deutschland als geschichtliches Problem', *Vierteljahreshefte für Zeitgeschichte*, 11 (1963), 246–73.

ZUNKEL, FRIEDRICH, 'Ehre', in Otto Brunner *et al.* (eds.), *Geschichtliche Grundbegriffe*.

INDEX

Note: There are no entries for 'capital punishment', 'crime', 'death penalty', 'executions', 'Germany', or 'punishment'. For particular aspects of these subjects, consult the relevant entries below.

READ MORE IN PENGUIN

In every corner of the world, on every subject under the sun, Penguin represents quality and variety – the very best in publishing today.

For complete information about books available from Penguin – including Puffins, Penguin Classics and Arkana – and how to order them, write to us at the appropriate address below. Please note that for copyright reasons the selection of books varies from country to country.

In the United Kingdom: Please write to *Dept. EP, Penguin Books Ltd, Bath Road, Harmondsworth, West Drayton, Middlesex UB7 0DA*

In the United States: Please write to *Consumer Sales, Penguin USA, P.O. Box 999, Dept. 17109, Bergenfield, New Jersey 07621-0120*. VISA and MasterCard holders call 1-800-253-6476 to order Penguin titles

In Canada: Please write to *Penguin Books Canada Ltd, 10 Alcorn Avenue, Suite 300, Toronto, Ontario M4V 3B2*

In Australia: Please write to *Penguin Books Australia Ltd, P.O. Box 257, Ringwood, Victoria 3134*

In New Zealand: Please write to *Penguin Books (NZ) Ltd, Private Bag 102902, North Shore Mail Centre, Auckland 10*

In India: Please write to *Penguin Books India Pvt Ltd, 706 Eros Apartments, 56 Nehru Place, New Delhi 110 019*

In the Netherlands: Please write to *Penguin Books Netherlands bv, Postbus 3507, NL-1001 AH Amsterdam*

In Germany: Please write to *Penguin Books Deutschland GmbH, Metzlerstrasse 26, 60594 Frankfurt am Main*

In Spain: Please write to *Penguin Books S. A., Bravo Murillo 19, 1° B, 28015 Madrid*

In Italy: Please write to *Penguin Italia s.r.l., Via Felice Casati 20, I–20124 Milano*

In France: Please write to *Penguin France S. A., 17 rue Lejeune, F–31000 Toulouse*

In Japan: Please write to *Penguin Books Japan, Ishikiribashi Building, 2–5–4, Suido, Bunkyo-ku, Tokyo 112*

In South Africa: Please write to *Longman Penguin Southern Africa (Pty) Ltd, Private Bag X08, Bertsham 2013*

READ MORE IN PENGUIN

POLITICS AND SOCIAL SCIENCES

Accountable to None   Simon Jenkins

'An important book, because it brings together, with an insider's authority and anecdotage, both a narrative of domestic Thatcherism and a polemic against its pretensions ... an indispensable guide to the corruptions of power and language which have sustained the illusion that Thatcherism was an attack on "government"' – *Guardian*

The Feminine Mystique   Betty Friedan

'A brilliantly researched, passionately argued book – a time bomb flung into the Mom-and-Apple-Pie image ... Out of the debris of that shattered ideal, the Women's Liberation Movement was born' – Ann Leslie

The New Untouchables   Nigel Harris

Misrepresented in politics and in the media, immigration is seen as a serious problem by the vast majority of people. In this ground-breaking book, Nigel Harris draws on a mass of evidence to challenge existing assumptions and examines migration as a response to changes in the world economy.

Political Ideas   Edited by David Thomson

From Machiavelli to Marx – a stimulating and informative introduction to the last 500 years of European political thinkers and political thought.

Structural Anthropology Volumes 1–2   Claude Lévi-Strauss

'That the complex ensemble of Lévi-Strauss's achievement ... is one of the most original and intellectually exciting of the present age seems undeniable. No one seriously interested in language or literature, in sociology or psychology, can afford to ignore it' – George Steiner

Invitation to Sociology   Peter L. Berger

Without belittling its scientific procedures Professor Berger stresses the humanistic affinity of sociology with history and philosophy. It is a discipline which encourages a fuller awareness of the human world ... with the purpose of bettering it.

READ MORE IN PENGUIN

POLITICS AND SOCIAL SCIENCES

Conservatism   Ted Honderich

'It offers a powerful critique of the major beliefs of modern conservatism, and shows how much a rigorous philosopher can contribute to understanding the fashionable but deeply ruinous absurdities of his times' – *New Statesman & Society*

Ruling Britannia   Andrew Marr

'This book will be resented by many of Marr's professional colleagues, for he goes where none of us has dared. He lifts his eyes, and ours ... Everyone with a serious interest in how we might be governed should read it' – *Sunday Telegraph*

Bricks of Shame: Britain's Prisons   Vivien Stern

'Her well-researched book presents a chillingly realistic picture of the British sytstem and lucid argument for changes which could and should be made before a degrading and explosive situation deteriorates still further' – *Sunday Times*

Killing Rage: Ending Racism   bell hooks

Addressing race and racism in American society from a black and a feminist standpoint, bell hooks covers a broad spectrum of issues. In the title essay she writes about the 'killing rage' – the intense anger caused by everyday instances of racism – finding in that rage a positive inner strength to create productive change.

'Just like a Girl'   Sue Sharpe
How Girls Learn to be Women

Sue Sharpe's unprecedented research and analysis of the attitudes and hopes of teenage girls from four London schools has become a classic of its kind. This new edition focuses on girls in the nineties – some of whom could even be the daughters of the teenagers she interviewed in the seventies – and represents their views and ideas on education, work, marriage, gender roles, feminism and women's rights.

READ MORE IN PENGUIN

HISTORY

Frauen Alison Owings

Nearly ten years in the making and based on interviews and original research, Alison Owings' remarkable book records the wartime experiences and thoughts of 'ordinary' German women from varying classes and backgrounds.

Byzantium: The Decline and Fall John Julius Norwich

The final volume in the magnificent history of Byzantium. 'As we pass among the spectacularly varied scenes of war, intrigue, theological debate, martial kerfuffle, sacrifice, revenge, blazing ambition and lordly pride, our guide calms our passions with an infinity of curious asides and grace-notes ... Norwich's great trilogy has dispersed none of this magic' – *Independent*

The Anglo-Saxons Edited by James Campbell

'For anyone who wishes to understand the broad sweep of English history, Anglo-Saxon society is an important and fascinating subject. And Campbell's is an important and fascinating book. It is also a finely produced and, at times, a very beautiful book' – *London Review of Books*

Conditions of Liberty Ernest Gellner

'A lucid and brilliant analysis ... he gives excellent reasons for preferring civil society to democracy as the institutional key to modernization ... For Gellner, civil society is a remarkable concept. It is both an inspiring slogan and the reality at the heart of the modern world' – *The Times*

The Habsburgs Andrew Wheatcroft

'Wheatcroft has ... a real feel for the heterogeneous geography of the Habsburg domains – I especially admired his feel for the Spanish Habsburgs. Time and again, he neatly links the monarchs with the specific monuments they constructed for themselves' – *Sunday Telegraph*

READ MORE IN PENGUIN

HISTORY

London: A Social History Roy Porter

'The best and bravest thing he has written. It is important because it makes the whole sweep of London's unique history comprehensible and accessible in a way that no previous writer has ever managed to accomplish. And it is angry because it begins and concludes with a slashing, unanswerable indictment of Thatcherite misrule' – *Independent on Sunday*

Somme Lyn Macdonald

'What the reader will longest remember are the words – heartbroken, blunt, angry – of the men who lived through the bloodbath ... a worthy addition to the literature of the Great War' – *Daily Mail*

Aspects of Aristocracy David Cannadine

'A hugely enjoyable portrait of the upper classes ... It is the perfect history book for the non-historian. Ample in scope but full of human detail, accessible and graceful in its scholarship, witty and opinionated in style' – *Financial Times*

The Penguin History of Greece A. R. Burn

Readable, erudite, enthusiastic and balanced, this one-volume history of Hellas sweeps the reader along from the days of Mycenae and the splendours of Athens to the conquests of Alexander and the final dark decades.

The Laurel and the Ivy Robert Kee

'Parnell continues to haunt the Irish historical imagination a century after his death ... Robert Kee's patient and delicate probing enables him to reconstruct the workings of that elusive mind as persuasively, or at least as plausibly, as seems possible ... This splendid biography, which is as readable as it is rigorous, greatly enhances our understanding of both Parnell, and of the Ireland of his time' – *The Times Literary Supplement*

READ MORE IN PENGUIN

HISTORY

Citizens Simon Schama

The award-winning chronicle of the French Revolution. 'The most marvellous book I have read about the French Revolution in the last fifty years' – Richard Cobb in *The Times*

The Lure of the Sea Alain Corbin

Alain Corbin's wonderful book explores the dramatic change in Western attitude towards the sea and seaside pleasures that occured between 1750 and 1840. 'A compact and brilliant taxonomy of the shifting meanings of the sea and shore' – *New York Review of Books*

The Tyranny of History W. J. F. Jenner

A fifth of the world's population lives within the boundaries of China, a vast empire barely under the control of the repressive ruling Communist regime. Beneath the economic boom China is in a state of crisis that goes far deeper than the problems of its current leaders to a value system that is rooted in the autocratic traditions of China's past.

The English Bible and the Seventeenth-Century Revolution
Christopher Hill

'What caused the English civil war? What brought Charles I to the scaffold?' Answer to both questions: the Bible. To sustain this provocative thesis, Christopher Hill's new book maps English intellectual history from the Reformation to 1660, showing how scripture dominated every department of thought from sexual relations to political theory . . . 'His erudition is staggering' – *Sunday Times*

Fisher's Face Jan Morris

'*Fisher's Face* is funny, touching and informed by wide reading as well as wide travelling' – *New Statesman & Society*. 'A richly beguiling picture of the Victorian Navy, its profound inner security, its glorious assumptions, its extravagant social life and its traditionally eccentric leaders' – *Independent on Sunday*

BY THE SAME AUTHOR

Death in Hamburg

Winner of the 1988 Wolfson Literary Award for History and the William H. Welch Medal of the American Association for the History of Medicine.

The terrible cholera epidemic of 1892 offers a wealth of insights into the inner life of a great European city at the height of the industrial age. Why were nearly 10,000 people in six weeks killed in Hamburg, while most of Europe was left almost unscathed? As Richard J. Evans explains, it was largely because the town was a unique anomaly: a 'free city' within Germany governed by local notables who believed in the 'English' ideals of *laissez-faire*. Their failures to supply clean water, fresh air and pure food played a major role in the catastrophe. Their medical theories, influenced by political and economic interest, only made matters worse. The whole story of 'the cholera years' is tragically revealing of the age's social inequalities and administrative incompetence; it also offers some disquieting parallels with today's attitudes to AIDS.

'This is a tremendous book, the biography of a city which charts the multifarious pathways from bacilli to burgomaster' – Roy Porter in the *London Review of Books*

'*Death in Hamburg* is a marvellous book, splendidly written, full of wit and anecdote, exuding scholarship and wisdom, and also "a jolly good read"' – *New Scientist*

'A brilliantly written work of great analytical penetration, which is based on very extensive reading . . . about the contemporary relevance of this book there can be no question' – Gordon A. Craig in the *New York Review of Books*

'As complete an anatomy of a past epidemic as we are ever likely to have . . . distinguished by the breadth of its scholarship and the sensitivity with which it treats complex, often tragic historical circumstances' – *The Times Literary Supplement*